WISDEN

INDIA ALMANACK
2019 & 2020

EDITED BY SURESH MENON

WISDEN INDIA
ALMANACK

2019 & 2020

7th Edition

John Wisden & Co.

BLOOMSBURY
NEW DELHI • LONDON • OXFORD • NEW YORK • SYDNEY

JOHN WISDEN & CO.
An imprint of Bloomsbury Publishing Plc.
50 Bedford Square, London WC1B 3DP

WISDEN INDIA ALMANACK

Editor **Suresh Menon**
Senior copy editor **Karunya Keshav**
Assistant editors **Abhishek Mukherjee & the late Sidhanta Patnaik**
Lead designer **Ashish Mohanty**
Correspondents **Manoj Narayan, Hemant Brar, Ananya Upendran,
Disha Shetty, Shashank Kishore, Hardik Worah, Shubham Malaviya**

Reader feedback: suresh@wisden.in

www.wisden.com

Published by Bloomsbury Publishing India Pvt Ltd
Vishrut Building, DDA Complex, Building No. 3
Pocket C-6 & 7, Vasant Kunj
New Delhi 110 070

Printed in India by Thomson Press India Ltd.

HB : 978 93 87457 86 7
PB : 978 93 87457 87 4
Leather Bound: 978 93 89351 58 3

A Taste of Wisden India 2019 & 2020

"My amma suddenly just found something she has in common with both
Javagal Srinath and Sachin Tendulkar."
Bharat Sundaresan, Page 24
* * *

Incessant scrutiny, of course, is what keeps cricket's economy afloat —
from the everyday business of putting big cricket to air to the minute
interest in every moment of Virat Kohli's day.
Gideon Haigh, Page 29

***

Being stubborn in one area may be justified; there is no guarantee that the
majority is always right. But in five?
Mike Brearley, Page 32

* * *

Our association began in a shared love of cricket ("certainly greater than
sex," Harold Pinter famously asserted, "although sex isn't too bad either").
Harry Burton, Page 39

* * *

'Don' Rangan, so named for his Bradmanesque deportment on the
cricket field, his arrogant self-belief disproportionate to his cricketing
accomplishments, was master of all he surveyed on the Pithapuram cricket
ground in south Madras in the 1960s.
V Ramnarayan, Page 49

* * *

A bad internet connection, however, is essential for managing separation
anxiety and its close cousin, FOMO, the Fear Of Missing Out.
Rahul Bhattacharya, Page 70

* * *

Buenos Aires is a frenetic yet ethereal city: too European for Latin America,
too Latin American for Europe.
Andreas Campomar, Page 94

What a finish! Martin Guptill put in a dive but Jos Buttler held on to the throw from Jason Roy and took the bails off on the last ball of the Super Over. With England and New Zealand tied again, the hosts claimed the trophy on boundary count. — *Getty Images*

PREFACE

Our seventh edition arrives later than the other six have, to coincide with the start of the season. For long, the Indian cricket season was like god's love: there was no beginning and no end. But things have changed. The new cycle means we have been able to capture the men's World Cup and the women's World T20 as well as the 2019 IPL in this edition.

It is the first which Sidhanta Patnaik, colleague at the *Almanack* since its inception, will not get to see. He succumbed to cancer at 34, after a long battle. When he regained his consciousness after surgery, the first thing he asked for was his laptop to finish some work for this edition. He continued writing and checking contributions from the hospital's intensive care.

"Cricket is my source of energy," he said in the last piece he wrote, one that ended mid-sentence with the word "and..." The symbolism is inescapable.

When he first walked into our office, Sidhanta said international cricket could take care of itself, he was focused on the grassroots — juniors, Under-19 and women's cricket. His book on the history of women's cricket in India, *The Fire Burns Blue* (co-authored with Karunya Keshav) is a seminal work. He was working on a book on the Ranji Trophy even as his strength ebbed away.

Sidhanta probably did more work in and around the intensive care than most people in plush offices in the same period. He felt personally responsible for the game and for *Wisden India Almanack*. As deadline approached, Karunya took over Sidhanta's responsibilities too. She worked from his bedside, from her home, from the Caribbean while reporting the Women's World T20, and from England during the World Cup. She was never off duty.

It has been a privilege to work with such passionate professionals who extend the definition of the term. To them my gratitude, both for this edition and for the important life lessons along the way. Others from the erstwhile wisdenindia.com website chipped in cheerfully: Shamya Dasgupta, R Kaushik, Manoj Narayan, Shashank Kishore, Hemant Brar, Saurabh Somani ... my thanks to all of them, and to Abhishek Mukherjee who has joined the *Almanack* team.

Thanks also to Ashish Mohanty, our designer who, despite having quit the organisation, put in the weeks necessary to see this one through. All of us once sat under the same roof and worked across one another; now we work from different offices, different cities, and even different countries. You can see in this the marvels of modern technology, or the marvels of old-fashioned passion and loyalty.

My thanks to Bloomsbury, our publishers, both in India and the UK.

As always, special thanks to my wife Dimpy.

SURESH MENON
Bangalore, July 2019

CONTENTS

Part 1 – Comment

Part 2 – World Cup

Part 3 – Domestic review

Part 4 – International series

SYMBOLS AND ABBREVIATIONS

*	In full scorecards signifies captain.
*	In short scorecards, records, signify not out.
*	In other places signifies notes.
†	In full scorecards signifies the designated wicketkeeper.
MoM/PoM	In full and short scorecards signifies Man/Player of the Match.
MoS/PoS	In full and short scorecards signifies Man/Player of the Series.
DLS	Signifies where a result has been decided under the Duckworth/Lewis/Stern method for curtailed matches.
VJD	Signifies where a result has been decided under the V Jayadevan method for curtailed matches.
	Matches abandoned or postponed are either because of rain or bad weather, unless otherwise mentioned.
(Numbers besides dismissal)	In full scorecards of first-class and Test matches signifies the batting order of a batsman in the second innings.
Economy Rate	The figure at the end of each bowler's analysis in full scorecards is the economy rate.

All statistics are valid through July 15, 2019.

FIRST-CLASS MATCHES
Men's matches of three or more days' duration are first-class unless otherwise stated. All other matches are not first-class, including one-day and Twenty20 internationals.

SCORECARDS AND RECORDS
Where full scorecards are not provided in this book, they can be found at Cricket Archive (cricketarchive.com), BCCI website (bcci.tv), Wisden (wisdenrecords.com) or ESPNcricinfo (espncricinfo.com).

More records can be found at www.wisdenrecords.com. The online records database is regularly updated and, in many instances, more detailed than in *Wisden India Almanack*.

Cover: *Rohit Sharma playing his signature pull shot;* **Back cover:** *England celebrate lifting the 2019 World Cup (Getty Images)*

PART ONE

Comment

Wisden India Honours

WISDEN INDIA HALL OF FAME

We honour sportspersons in various ways; by naming streets, roundabouts and stadiums after them, by instituting trophies in their memory, by turning them into adjectives ('Bradmansque'), by arguing, generation after generation, over the relative merits of our heroes. The most enduring and dignified method in recent years has been to induct the best into the Hall of Fame. It is the concept – often a virtual 'hall' – that is the honour, not the bricks-and-mortar building.

Lala Amarnath (Page 89)
Gundappa Viswanath (Page 85)

SIX CRICKETERS OF THE YEAR

Wisden's Cricketers of the Year – a tradition dating back to 1899 in the original Almanack – is given a subcontinental flavour in *Wisden India Almanack*. The six cricketers are picked by the editor, the selection based on the players' positive impact on the season under review. It is necessary to highlight the distinction since in recent years, some players who have made an impact have done so for the wrong reasons. Negative impact does not count.

Jasprit Bumrah (page 104)
Smriti Mandhana (page 101)
Mayank Agarwal (page 108)
Fakhar Zaman (page 111)
Dimuth Karunaratne (page 113)
Rashid Khan (page 116)

BEYOND THE BOUNDARY

'Beyond the Boundary' acknowledges the 'person of the year'. Introduced in the 2016 edition of the *Wisden India Almanack*, it recognises contributions of people off the pitch.

Imran Khan (page 120)

WISDEN INDIA BOOK OF THE YEAR

Cricket Country: The Untold History of the First All India Team
by Prashant Kidambi (page 889)

Notes by the Editor

2019 wasn't the greatest World Cup of all time. There were too few really exciting games, hardly any stunning upsets, and virtually no tactical or strategic advances. But it was a proper showpiece, and the final might have seen the finest one-day finish ever. To the victor the spoils, writes Lawrence Booth in his review here, adding charmingly, "And, for once, to the losers too."

The ICC's decision to field only ten teams had come in for much criticism, but it deserves the benefit of the doubt. Just because television prefers it that way doesn't necessarily make it bad. A qualifying tournament ensures that the best teams make the finals, and that is fair. Every team playing every other once is a good format. And we need to look at Virat Kohli's suggestion that the team finishing on top deserves another shot at qualifying for the final, as in the IPL.

Before the tournament, it was possible to make two lists for India. First, the reasons for an Indian success and second, reasons for failure. The first included the sustained form of their top three batsmen, Shikhar Dhawan (later, K L Rahul), Rohit Sharma and Virat Kohli, the firepower of their fast men led by Jasprit Bumrah and enough runs lower down to cover up for a dodgy middle order. If India failed, it would be because of the middle order and the fact that they might have peaked too early in a tournament lasting nearly seven weeks.

India began well, and quickly looked like the top team. Too quickly. The defeat against England didn't lead to much soul-searching; it was dismissed as "one of those things". Did India get overconfident in the semi-final, especially after rain had ended the first day's play with New Zealand on 211 for 5 in the 47th over? In their final two matches, New Zealand showed themselves to be masters of defending the small total, 239 and 241, and became the favourites everywhere (except in England).

The final was a celebration of cricket, revealing the possibilities of the 50-over game, which was thought to be on its death bed.

For long, it wasn't a particularly good match. The Lord's wicket was too slow and the occasion seemed to get to the performers. But the finish changed everything. A tie is exciting enough, but a double tie? The questions will remain, though. How could England have won when New Zealand didn't lose?

Sport is not perfect. Often imperfection is the crack through which we see it at its best. Rules are arbitrary, so it is as valid to say the team with most boundaries wins as it is to say that the team that loses the fewer wickets does so. In the end, the best team took the title.

The argument that England's 'extra run' led to victory assumes that everything else would have remained exactly the same. But one variable can affect others too in real-life situations.

If New Zealand did not deserve to win the World Cup, it was for one reason only. They played a brand of cricket that was a throw-back to the English style of old: overcautious, unadventurous, risk-averse. This, at a time when the format was in danger of being wiped out by T20, and the sport itself was struggling to attract new fans. Something was needed to provide the energy and flair that would revive it, and England delivered that in style. The accent was on attack — whether batting or bowling — and the approach attractive.

World Cup winners set the agenda. Had New Zealand won, it might have been a step back. England winning means that other teams might attempt to play like them, in a positive, sexy style that can only be good for the game.

New Zealand have been the best-behaved team in international cricket, and in Kane Williamson they had a gracious captain with a fine tactical brain. It was difficult not to love him and his team just as it was difficult not to sympathise with the team for the non-defeat that ended all dreams. In the ideal world, the Cup might have been shared.

But sport abhors such fragmentation. Competition demands that there be one winner, and all games have rules for breaking the tie from penalty shootouts to (in the old days) bowl outs and Super Overs. It is not a perfect system, but it is there, and no one had an issue with it before the tournament began.

Before Duckworth-Lewis appeared and fans stopped complaining about results because they didn't understand the rule, ODIs were decided in a variety of ways. We can get too mathematical about the Lord's final, and forget the human drama and the spirit of the players involved. Ben Stokes, for one, deserves better.

The final was unforgettable, even if Williamson might not echo Roger Federer's words after his loss at Wimbledon a few kilometres and a few minutes away: "I shall try to forget."

Back to the future

We have seen the future of one-day cricket. It is remarkably like the past. In its infancy, the game was about positive batsmanship and negative bowling; in its teens it was about keeping wickets in hand in the first part of the innings, then accelerating, and finally hitting out in the 'slog overs'. Bowlers had realised by then that the best way to keep runs down was to take wickets. That was in the 1980s, and that's how it is now.

What does 'retirement' mean?

World Cups are often viewed as finishing posts to international careers. After 2019, Imran Tahir, Shoaib Malik and J P Duminy called it a day, while Chris Gayle, who had said he would do so, changed his mind and expressed a desire (selectors willing) to take on India in the home series next. Which brings us to the question: What does retirement mean? In 2014, Mahendra Singh Dhoni declared in the middle of a Test series in Australia that he was retiring from Test cricket, but not from the shorter formats. Ricky Ponting had gone in the other direction a decade ago, retiring from T20 cricket to extend his run in Test cricket.

It was so much simpler earlier. A player announced his retirement — which meant he would play no more Test or first-class cricket — and disappeared behind the mike in a broadcasting studio. Today, players announce their retirement from international cricket but hope to continue playing in domestic T20 franchise cricket. The dollar-to-effort ratio is in his favour, after all. After much thought, therefore, we decided to drop the 'Farewell' section this edition. Old cricketers never retire, they merely lose their appeal.

Circle of life

Sport can be cruel. Yesterday's champions become today's no-hopers, top teams sink below competitive level. Younger players and fans know only failures, older ones try to convince them of the power of the glory days.

The four teams at the bottom of the World Cup league table were Afghanistan, West Indies, Bangladesh and South Africa. South Africa were the No.1 team not so long ago and West Indies twice world champions. Afghanistan, except against India, have looked somewhat out of their depth, leaving the romantics struggling to find inspiring things to say about them.

Yet in recent years, Afghanistan's has been the story of cricket. A team put together in times of strife in the refugee camps of another country, whose 'home' turf is a third country. The story has been told many times, yet it still surprises many that someone like Mohammed Nabi looks so "cool and calm" in the face of "great pressure" as he did while nearly getting his team over the line.

A bit of perspective here. Nabi has been through worse than a yorker-rich over from Bumrah. His father was kidnapped and held for ransom while his country was in turmoil. At least one cricketer was killed by an American raid. Years ago, Australian all-rounder Keith Miller put things in perspective after the World War when he said, "Pressure? There's no pressure in cricket. Real pressure is when you are flying a Mosquito with a Messerschmitt up your arse!" No doubt Nabi and his mates will have their own definition of 'pressure'. Cricket is unlikely to figure in it.

Both West Indies and South Africa lost key players through injury, but their decline recently has been the other story of cricket. Rebuilding can be a long and troubling process; after this performance, older players are likely to call it a day, and younger players will wonder if they can handle the transition.

The bottom-placed teams can take heart from India's recovery after their disastrous performance in 2007. India bowed out of that World Cup in some disarray, having failed to qualify for the knockout. The picture of the senior players with shocked expressions, some of them weeping openly, made an impact on a disappointed nation. Yet in four years' time the team had been rebuilt and did well enough to win the World Cup. Sometimes defeat can force changes that lead to victory.

No harm no foul

Some years ago, 'Richie Benaud' tweeted, "Indians just don't get conflict of interest." The account was fake, but the sentiment was sound, as evidenced by the uproar it provoked in cyberspace.

"Indians don't relate to conflict of interest," said the social scientist Shiv Viswanathan. "It is a cultural perception. Conflict of interest is not taken seriously, except for raising some curiosity. We would rather maximise interests than agonise over conflict of interest."

Not so long ago, the president of the BCCI owned an IPL team, his son-in-law was an important official in it while the chief national selector was a brand ambassador of the same team. Wearing two or more hats was not only seen as an individual's due, it was accepted as a perk of his stature in the game.

Then came Justice Mukul Mudgal and his clear delineation of "conflict of interest", and Justice Lodha who ruled on how it ought to be handled. BCCI's Rule 38(4) lists 16 posts of which no two may be held simultaneously. Yet, many stars who became officials at state or national level still kept their other jobs including television commentary.

Players argue that cricket pays the bills even after their playing days, as they turn coaches, commentators, technical advisors, expert columnists, administrators and thus remain attached to the game. To deny up and coming players their experience and expertise would be unfair. The argument, therefore, is that a job in one of these spheres should not make them ineligible for a post in the national or state bodies.

The question that needs to be answered (the issue has been sent to the Supreme Court as we go to press) remains: Is there a balancing point? Can the BCCI work out a compromise where a former player's expertise is at its disposal while ensuring that conflict of interest, though technically present, does no harm?

Perhaps it is time to allow former players a role by introducing the phrase "material difference" into the rule on conflict of interest. If it does not make a "material difference", another old sporting rule may be invoked: No harm, no foul.

For 20 balls fewer

In a few months, there will be yet another doorway into cricket. Nearly half a century ago, when cricket was "dying" (as it is apparently doing again today), the one-day international arrived to rescue it. A few years ago, when cricket was "dying" again, T20 arrived. And now, with cricket "dying" once more, The Hundred is here to rescue it.

It is impossible to tell just how many T20 enthusiasts walked through the door to swell the ranks of Test cricket enthusiasts. Or even if the traffic moved in the opposite direction.

In England, thanks to The Hundred, a five-year television deal worth £1.1 billion will see cricket return on terrestrial TV after two decades. Is The Hundred the answer? The scepticism was summed up by the editor of the *Wisden Cricketers' Almanack* who wrote that this is English cricket's Brexit: "an unnecessary gamble that had overshadowed all else, gone over budget and would end in tears" because it "hung over the English game like the sword of Damocles, suspended only by the conviction of a suited few."

Will a fourth format be a better doorway? Will doorways be different in different countries?

Every new format of the game has engendered sceptics. India were the biggest sceptics when the T20 came around, and were reluctant entrants into the inaugural World Cup in that format.

Then they won, and life changed. The IPL was born, a doorway within a doorway, and millions of dollars, fans, words later, it is the one every player hopes to be picked for.

The average fan at an IPL game is a raucous, impatient supporter of cricketers rather than the cricket (the distinction is an important one) and would be thoroughly out of place, even miserable, at a Test match. T20 has shortened history, with memory that goes back only to a few matches; Tests call for a better historic sense. What IPL has done is create a new audience — one that sees in the match an evening of entertainment and banter rather than one that looks to enhance understanding of the well-bowled off-cutter or the perfect cover-drive that does not go for six. The product is everything, the ends justify the means.

If T20 was a marketing solution to a cricketing problem, so is The Hundred. And should 20 balls make such a difference? How much can we take away from the game and still retain its character?

This is the 'heap of sand' paradox. Imagine a heap of sand. You remove one grain. It is obviously still a heap of sand.

Then you remove two, and three and four and two thousand and five hundred thousand and so on. Is it still a heap when there are just ten grains left? Or three? At what point does the heap cease to be a heap? At what stage does cricket cease to be cricket?

Administrators aren't too fussed about ancient Greek paradoxes. Their philosophical quest is much simpler: to discover at what stage lack of money becomes bagsful of it.

Morality and convention

The charm of cricket has always been its illogicality and complexity. Matches last for five days with no result guaranteed. What is legally fair is often ethically unacceptable. What was unacceptable in one generation is commonplace in another. It is a game of nuance and varying shades, making it difficult for those who think in black and white to understand or appreciate.

There are written laws of the game, and then there are the unwritten rules. The latter have greater power and purpose. A bowler over-stepping is no-balled, a player overstepping is blackballed, sometimes by his own team-mates. In an era when international players have been caught cheating on the field, it might seem precious, even pretentious to criticise a bowler for running out a non-striker backing up too much.

Yet, if you don't understand that this is not cricket, then you don't understand what cricket is.

R Ashwin can argue that in their IPL clash, Jos Buttler was attempting to gain an unfair advantage by stepping out before the ball was bowled; he can also claim that the law allows him to run out such a batsman.

True, and true. And since he himself was leading, there was no call for the captain to interfere, as skipper Virender Sehwag did, recalling Sri Lanka's Lahiru Thirimanne when Ashwin ran him out similarly during a one-day international. "If that was soft," Sehwag was quoted as saying then, "that's the way we are."

When Vinoo Mankad did it in Australia, or Kapil Dev in South Africa, they each warned the batsman first. The law does not require this — yet convention does. And sport has to follow both laws and conventions. There was an element of entrapment about Ashwin's move; he checked his bowling action and waited that split second till the batsman moved out before whipping off the bails. If bowlers did that, about 90 per cent of all dismissals would be run out in this 'mankading' fashion. Especially in the white-ball game.

We confuse morality and convention in sport, thus leading to much sound and fury. The philosopher David Papineau distinguished between the two thus: "Morality is universal, independent of authority, and has to do with genuine welfare, while convention varies across societies, depends on decree, and governs matters of no intrinsic importance."

Sport is of no intrinsic importance, and seen in perspective, it is quite meaningless. But it is this artificiality that makes us infuse it with the kind of ethics that we do not expect in other areas of human endeavour. This is our way of giving sport meaning.

There are those who feel — and this includes players past and present — that too much is made of such incidents, and that ethics have no role to play in sport. Thus you wait for the umpire's signal even if you know you have edged the ball to the 'keeper, or claim a catch despite knowing it wasn't a clean one. The justification is that this is done in the team interest. That is a slippery slope. There are a number of things you can do — injuring a rival player for instance — that can be justified thus.

Trying to bluff the umpire might be a legitimate tactic in some sports, but in cricket it is looked down upon. Yet it is now accepted that batsmen are under no obligation to 'walk', and the DRS has taken the moral weight off the catcher's shoulders.

We can avoid some of the ambiguity of the 'mankading' situation if the law lays down that a batsman must be warned once or twice. Yet, what is gained in clarity is lost in sportsmanship. When conventions become law, it suggests a lack of moral strength. Something is done or not done because the law demands it, not because that is the way the game ought to be played. Players must be given the ethical choice so we can see what they are made of.

There are some things you don't do on a cricket field, because that is the nature of the game. The laws of the game tell us what we should do; the spirit tells us what we should aspire to.

Division of labour

Watching Kohli captain India in the white-ball series against Australia, and to a lesser extent in the World Cup, one thing stood out. He was happy to let former captain Dhoni call the shots when India were fielding.

Indian teams in the past have been led in two different ways: captaincy by the individual and captaincy by committee. Now here is a third, captaincy split between the batting captain and fielding captain. Not entirely, of course, but significantly. Kohli often fielded out of range of the wicketkeeper or bowler, relying on Dhoni's rapport with the spinners in particular to see their spells through.

There is nothing inherently right or wrong, good or bad about this so long as the captains are on the same page and the lines of authority are clearly drawn.

Indian captains have often been burdened by the inclusion in the team of former captains. Dhoni himself led teams with Sachin Tendulkar, Rahul Dravid, Sourav Ganguly and Virender Sehwag in them; all had led earlier. In general, however, seniors have expected younger captains to kowtow to them and behaved like visiting mothers-in-law happy to point out mistakes.

As Mike Brearley wrote in his classic on captaincy, a captain has no place to hide. Yet, an arrangement such as the Dhoni-Kohli one might allow Kohli to look at a game from a different perspective and keep himself mentally fresh if there is a long chase to come.

Dhoni's directives to the spinners captured by the stump mic have been both pragmatic and effective. He instructs, explains and then adds, "but it's up to you". It is a wonderful system so long as it is effective, not so wonderful if there is any confusion especially under pressure.

Captaincy is a difficult job, and anything that makes it easier for the individual or the team should be welcomed. Shared captaincy might become a feature of future ODIs.

Leaving little to imagination

Professional sport is seriously competitive; sportsmen and women react when frustrated or feel badly done by. The distance between the performer and the spectator once lent sport a unique charm — and enabled writers like Neville Cardus to invent conversations. The quotes he fabricated were often humorous or imaginative, so the players didn't mind. And then came the stump mic.

There were two unintended consequences: they picked up the chatter around the bat, and they served as a vehicle for free advertisement.

This last was a response by the Australian team during the 'Sandpaper' series in South Africa when the broadcasters refused to turn down the mics, and the players plugged their personal sponsors. The umpires, sponsored by Emirates, were asked, "How good is Qantas?" and Australian beers were fondly mentioned. Australia had done this in 2006 too when they played Bangladesh.

Whether it is more irritating to hear plugs for sponsors or well-articulated four-letter words and banter that wouldn't pass muster in a low-grade movie is difficult to tell. Broadcasters love it; often listeners too, convinced they are being allowed into the sanctum sanctorum. The adage that what happens on the field should be left on the field no longer applies. What happens on the field lands up in our drawing rooms and on the match referee's table. Pakistan captain Sarfraz Ahmed and West Indies bowler Shannon Gabriel were suspended for racist and homophobic comments respectively, thanks to the all-hearing stump mic.

Cricket is once again being asked to play the moral leader, to set an example for those who get away with casual racism or homophobia in everyday life. Perhaps the message will get through to the general public; perhaps it won't, but there is an argument for keeping the mics on full-time to a) discourage bad behaviour and b) punish it so it stays as an example for those watching who either don't know or don't care that certain behaviour crosses a line.

Should cricketers be subject to such intense scrutiny? A day at a cricket match is work for the players, entertainment for the spectators. Players tend to swear on three occasions: at themselves when they make a mistake, to rile an opponent, or in response to an opponent's attempt at riling.

It is convenient to believe that sledging is a modern phenomenon, invented by Ian Chappell. This is ridiculous. Read what Walter Hammond said to Don Bradman when Bradman was given not out when caught at slip, or the South African fast bowler Peter Heine's threat to English batsman Trevor Bailey: "I want to hit you, Bailey, I want to hit you over the heart."

Has the stump microphone improved player behaviour? Players quickly worked out how to say nasty things just out of range. In 2007 when the stump mic was introduced at the World Cup, the intention was to help umpires with their decisions, not compare the vocabulary of the players.

Perhaps players object to the stump mic because they don't want us to know the real truth: that much of the chatter is banal. The best cricket stories don't come to us via the stump microphone, but through imaginative writing, manufactured post-event.

Cultural revolution

The change has been gathering pace, and now it is clear: India are prepared to win looking "ugly", by grinding it out.

It is the triumph of pragmatism over romance, placing winning above the dictates of looking pretty. Attractive, wristy (often risky) batsmanship and flighted, tantalising spin — the clichés about Indian cricket — have made way for practical run-making and sustained fast bowling. It is a cultural revolution, no less.

It was an attitude anathema to Indians through generations of "going down fighting attractively", of showing flair and flash that contributed little to the result. But the oohs and aahs as a batsman played a beautiful cover-drive usually spared him the condemnations when he threw it away in his 20s or 30s.

Those were the days when a fighting draw was all that mattered. The Indian team transited from perennial Test match losers to one capable of drawing matches to one expected to win as the No.1 side in the world. But through it all, one theme dominated: it was important to look good. Flair and flash, flamboyance, even a bit of ostentation was rewarded with greater public acclaim.

Sunil Gavaskar and Rahul Dravid might have been the bedrock of the batting in their respective eras, but even these masters of defensive batsmanship were stylish, they had what the public called "class".

Class was important. So was charm.

It was the same with bowling. The visual attraction and legends built around the great spinners — Bhagwat Chandrasekhar, Bishan Bedi, Erapalli Prasanna and S Venkataraghavan — were millstones around the necks of generations that followed. Every succeeding left-arm spinner was compared to Bedi and lost out in the comparison. For years Indians never forgave Anil Kumble for lacking the poetic vulnerability of Chandrasekhar, for not being an extravagant turner of the ball. World class did not automatically mean India class!

The Melbourne Test in the Australia series seems to have completed the transition. A generation more intent on the "what" and less focused on the "how" describes both the players and the majority of their audience back home.

Cricket and society reflect each other. Flamboyance as a by-product is acceptable, but as the main event will not be forgiven easily if it doesn't lead to victory. K L Rahul's struggle is both technical and historical. Here's an attractive batsman who is out of step with team philosophy.

Whether Cheteshwar Pujara is a product of the new culture or the one who is driving it, he is certainly its finest exemplar. He made centuries in both the Tests India won in Australia, supremely unconcerned about such mundane matters as strike-rates and putting bowlers in their place with dismissive, even arrogant batsmanship. Pujara is the unexpected Test star of the new India — but unexpected only in the eyes of those who haven't been following the trend away from romanticism.

When Kohli first led in Australia four years ago, romance was still king. He led with flair, making two centuries in a Test and throwing everything into a chase that nearly won India the match. "So near and yet so far" — the staple of headlines on the sports pages not so long ago. Kohli became a hero to the generation espousing romance, but a villain to the pragmatists.

Cricket's ego system

The more sensitive of cricket followers sometimes pause to ask the question: what kind of a national team do we want? In Australia, after the ball-tampering row and the ban on their top players, an official inquiry into the culture of the game there examined that very question.

Can you imagine anyone giving much thought to a related question: what kind of administrators do we want?

In recent years, the Board of Control for Cricket in India has gone from being a powerful body led by powerful men to a bunch of seat-grabbers who have little impact on international affairs, and little energy to expend on the game with everything focused on court battles, finding loopholes in the rulings and playing the victim.

The Committee of Administrators set up by the Supreme Court functions in a manner indistinguishable from the body it was meant to reform.

What kind of BCCI do we want? One which is an arrogant, self-serving, politically-influenced, money-making outfit that still does a lot for cricket and cricketers, or one which follows the rules, and generally appears blameless but contributes nothing to the game?

How much are we willing to sacrifice in terms of international image and acceptance, financial jugglery, wastage, personal convenience and ignored rules in return for efficiency? Should it be 30 per cent mess for 70 per cent effectiveness? 40-60? 50-50? How much of a margin is acceptable?

The choice, naturally, should not be that extreme. Surely we can get a top professional who will do his job without bothering about the next election? Yes, but that will mean changing a feudal system built on favour-mongering and largesse-distribution.

It is a long battle, and changing the culture is not an easy task. The BCCI even at its worst was the best sports body in the country, but self-perpetuation was its unspoken motto. In the Indian folk tale, anyone who sat on the throne of Vikramaditya spoke only the truth. Similarly, anyone who sits on the chairs of administrators behaves like BCCI officials.

The cynics might say that the CoA is enjoying the perks of the job too much to want to change. In effect, therefore, the BCCI is an organization without a proper president or secretary, without an effective CEO and overseen by a committee that has issues of its own. Cricket's ecosystem has been overtaken by its ego system.

The thrice-bowled tale

The first international sporting contest between Uruguay and Argentina was in cricket. To commemorate the 150th anniversary of that event, two exhibition matches were held in Buenos Aires. Our intrepid correspondent, Andreas Campomar, who has written a wonderful history of Latin American football, writes here of the sesquicentennial celebration. The story of cricket in Latin America, and India's connection with it is fascinating; as is the fact that he managed to get bowled three times in the same innings….

The rotating cup syndrome

BHARAT SUNDARESAN

"Rotating cup *da*, rotating cup. It's apparently one of those injuries that's common with your cricket*eers* (Tamil for cricketers)," my aunt screamed from her emergency ward bed of the orthopaedic hospital she'd found herself in. Earlier that day, she'd slipped and fallen on the footpath outside her home. Attempts at breaking the fall with her palm had done severe damage to her right shoulder. And the doctor's prognosis, in her words anyway, didn't sound like any bodily issue I'd ever heard a cricketeer suffer from. It sounded more like a kitchen experiment gone wrong. Eventually it took my cousin to clear the air as he announced, "My amma suddenly just found something she shares in common with both Javagal Srinath and Sachin Tendulkar. She's torn her rotator cuff."

Srinath, after all, was the first Indian cricketer of the modern era to introduce us to this vital part of the shoulder made up of muscles and tendons that assist in all kinds of upper-torso motion, not just in bowling fast. This anatomical enlightenment happened in early 1997 when India's then pace spearhead broke down following a hectic and extended stint on the road. He'd bowled over 400 overs during the previous year across Test matches in England, South Africa and at home. The breakdown was inevitable. Srinath was India's only genuine fast bowler in that era. It was a big deal that he was gone for nearly nine months. So much so that a national daily even carried a spoof story on April 1 of that year claiming that the Mysore Express was planning a return to the team as a left-arm spinner.

But the rotator cuff and shoulder injuries remained "fast bowler" problems and therefore rather alien, not something that would worry Indian cricket too often, till Sachin Tendulkar came under the knife in 2006 for a shoulder surgery. It wasn't the exact same issue though.

Like it had been the case and would continue to be so till the end of his career, a Tendulkar injury ended up burgeoning India's medical vocabulary. And by then, the 'tennis elbow' had already become the all-time most popular sports injury in India. 'SLAP lesion' was only the latest entry into the book. It was basically a muscle tear caused by excessive use, a throwing injury more than a batting or

A Tendulkar injury ended up burgeoning India's medical vocabulary. — *Getty Images*

bowling one. After battling with it for a few months, Tendulkar was finally forced to go for surgery, missing five months of cricket in the process.

India always had a strange connection with the Tendulkar anatomy ever since he made his debut and got struck on the face by Waqar Younis as a 16-year-old baby-faced prodigy, whom everyone in the nation wanted to mother. For all the pages he filled up in the record books over 24 years, Tendulkar's career could easily be converted into a medical journal, the time he spent with physios, trainers and doctors.

"Somebody once told me I could write a book on medicine," Tendulkar would say while launching his autobiography a few years ago.

There was hardly a part of his body that didn't give Indian cricket fans heartache at some point or the other during his career. If it wasn't his back, which was a recurring issue and famously flared up during that 1999 Test against Pakistan in Chennai, it was his toes, his fingers, his ankle, his knee, his hamstring, his neck or his abdomen.

He wasn't feeling the pain alone though. His pain somehow became every Indian's pain.

None of his injuries caught on like the dreaded tennis elbow. It was perhaps the closest Tendulkar came to losing his aura as he struggled to cope with the debilitating injury. It harangued him for nearly two years and forced him to seek Dr Andrew Wallace's help, which led to surgery. Wallace would have Tendulkar in his operation theatre a year later for the aforementioned shoulder issue. While wild theories abound over the cause of this injury — from him having used a heavy bat all his life to this being a karmic conspiracy — every Indian had some definitive knowledge of its effects. Understandably, a lot of them started relating to the tennis elbow issue as well. It didn't seem to matter if they hadn't spent three quarters of their life holding a bat and scoring a multitude of runs or if all they'd ever used their hands to carry were a few utensils at home or a briefcase to work.

There was suddenly a surge in tennis elbow diagnoses, and the demographics of those suffering with the problem ranged from housewives to medical representatives to the nocturnal kinds on a heavy liquid diet.

The tennis elbow has remained in vogue ever since, even as Tendulkar recovered and played for another half-a-dozen years. I know of at least three members in my wife's family, all teachers, who have been diagnosed with the problem as recently as last year. Just saying.

The fast bowling revolution in India kind of coincided with the rapid increase in people taking to running as their primary exercise across the country. It came about in the wake of the many high-profile marathons that propped up in all the major cities. Soon enough, the likes of Zaheer Khan, Ashish Nehra and Munaf Patel would break down with injuries to various parts of their legs. And soon enough, there was a sudden rise in household sports injuries around India, particularly to the lower part of the body. People have been pulling up ever since with bad 'hammies' or the odd 'adductor muscle strain' (the groin) from Cubbon Park to Marine Drive. Even the rotator cuff made a return to the mainstream as Zaheer and Munaf suffered and recovered to win India the 2011 World Cup.

It's not of course only in India where cricketers' injuries and in lieu their bodies become topics of national discourse. Michael Clarke's hamstring was discussed as intensely as craft beer and weather forecasts all across Australia in the lead-up to the 2015 World Cup. As was Shane Warne's shoulder in the lead-up to the 1998-99 Ashes, Andrew Flintoff's knees and ankles through his career and every time Shane Watson walked on to a cricket field.

There have been a few bizarre health issues that didn't quite catch on in everyday use or create much of a stir despite them having inflicted two cricketers of superstar reputation. Harbhajan Singh's groin infection that made him miss a Test in South Africa and Shoaib Akhtar's genital warts that ruled him out of the 2009 World T20, which Pakistan incidentally won, are two examples. For that matter, even Lakshmipathy Balaji's osteitis pubis injury — which put him out for many months — where there's pain and inflammation in the pelvic region, didn't get much attention, maybe because it was just too darn difficult to pronounce.

The days of a multi-billion population fretting over one man's body and its vagaries might be over. Somehow despite Virat Kohli's omnipresence as a cricketing megastar in India, neither he nor anyone else will ever come close to the kind of national importance that used to be attached to Tendulkar's fitness. Kohli's neck injury in the lead-up to what was supposed to be his maiden county stint was on the front-pages with one tabloid even managing to get a sneak peek into the hospital reports and claiming it was a 'slipped disc' — which for good reason wasn't the case considering how staid and non-exotic it sounds.

Cricket will continue to remain a source of medical lessons in India, though, especially with fewer rest days and the amount the players play only burgeoning. Rest assured you haven't heard the last of rotator cuffs, or rotating cups.

Bharat Sundaresan's book The Dhoni Touch *was released in 2018.*

Was the day 'very easy', 'easy', 'moderate', 'moderately hard', 'very hard', 'very, very hard', 'extremely hard', 'sub maximal' or 'maximal'? — *Getty Images*

Play and submit

GIDEON HAIGH

Recently I sat down with an Australian cricketer and caught sight on his phone of the Cricket Australia app — his two-way communication with the organisation's team performance department. I had seen these before, but when I expressed interest, he offered, with a tone of good-humoured chagrin, to take me through its functions.

The app, developed by Microsoft, serves as a diary for every player in CA's elite system — conveying details of games, training, travel et al. In the whirl of the ceaseless Australian season, all but a tiny well-organised minority would be lost without it. Its other purpose is as a real-time monitoring system, collecting data on the players' physical and mental states for synthesising at Brisbane's National Cricket Centre. In the jargon, it goes to the cricketer's IPP (Individual Player Profile) of the AMS (Athlete Management System).

The app's dashboard presents eight options accented to playing and training workloads, calibrated to a fine degree. If a player has batted on a certain day, for example, they must account for the elapsed time and balls faced, and whether the activity was 'very easy', 'easy', 'moderate', 'moderately hard', 'very hard', 'very, very hard', 'extremely hard', 'sub maximal' or 'maximal'.

A wellness section solicits information about sleep, soreness, stress and fatigue. 'How do you rate your fatigue?' the app asks with quiet insistence: are you 'always tired', 'more tired than normal', 'normal', 'fresh' or 'very fresh'? Other pages surveyed 'reflections', on training and on games. Did the player have a 'Clear Plan'? Did the player 'Stick to the Plan'? How had they gone 'Creating a Contest'? Did they achieve 'Focus' and 'Execute Skills'? I was struck by one tiny box on this screen: 'Enjoyment'. "Remember that?" I asked. "Not really," he laughed. Underneath was an instruction: 'Submit'. The choice of word could hardly have been more appropriate.

We were talking cricket, so it wasn't quite the moment to chew on French philosophy, but I reckoned Michel Foucault could have mined that app for tens of thousands of words. Foucault's famous study of the prison, *Discipline and Punish*, originated the concepts of surveillance and panopticism by exploring Jeremy Bentham's scheme for a circular penitentiary, designed in such a way that the inmates could never be sure whether they were being observed from a central tower. Foucault saw this as prefiguring modes of surveillance in modern society so internalised that every man became effectively his own overseer, policing himself for fear of punishment.

The concept is almost a bit hoary now in a world of social media's mass voluntary data collection and personalised content creation. Incessant scrutiny, of course, is what keeps cricket's economy afloat — from the everyday business of putting big cricket to air to the minute interest in every moment of Virat Kohli's day. Cricketers have locked themselves in a gilded jail, consenting to supervision by a staggering profusion of technologies, from pitch microphones to infra-red cameras; CCTV even pursues them into stairwells, as David Warner and Quinton de Kock learned in Durban.

But there is expanding an unseen realm of control that presents itself benignly, in the guise of greater efficiency and improved welfare. It is not yet fearfully efficient; it is data being collected mainly because it can be, and not yet that meaningful because there is so little to compare it to. But it is a phenomenon that in cricket is not to be removed, only expanded and refined, edging cricketers along to road to the status of automata, regulated and perhaps even one day selected by machine-learning algorithms. For a generation of cricketers is emerging whose life has been altogether pervaded by technology, who show off their digital ankle bracelets as jewellery, to whom the word 'submit' has no unsavoury connotations.

The CA app also has two self-reporting features related to psychic wellness: players must regularly update their EPQ (Eysenck Personality Questionnaire), an inventory of character traits, and K10 (Kessler Psychological Distress Scale), an index of depression and anxiety. Interested, I asked around other players to see how they related to this. Shoulders were shrugged: one basically filled in whatever it was felt would keep CA off one's back. To them, the exercise felt tokenistic. I was told the story of a female player who failed to fill in her EPQ and K10 for a couple of weeks because she was depressed. All she received was a call admonishing her for delinquency. So she resumed, reporting low levels of mental wellness for the next fortnight. Nobody contacted her. What mattered, clearly, was ticking her boxes.

Early days yet too, I dare say. But what does it prelude? Players as individuals confiding in a distant database rather than their peers? Players turning aside from one another on the assumption that the system will palliate all suffering? Resourceful and resilient teams have always picked up and carried along their vulnerable members. But what is a 'team' in this schema? Simply a temporary vehicle for self-expression, remotely tended by all-seeing, all-knowing superintendents? As one bonded with cricket a lifetime, I often feel incomparably blessed, spoiled for choice, stimulated by the game's growth, excited by my watching opportunities. But what I'm watching also feels less free, less spontaneous, more contrived and constricted. There are giants who rise above it, and in some ways, they are magnified more than ever; the rewards for the mass, too, have happily never been greater. Yet I cannot help a feeling that these developments have come at a cost to the cricketer's dignity, independence and pleasure. They are all just passing one another by, units of production, never at rest.

The cricketer with whom I was chatting was nearer the end of his career than the beginning, but did not regret it. "Cricket's changed so much even in the last five years," he said. "I know it's always changed, but there's become something about it that's so…" As he reached for a suitable sentiment, I interpolated: "Joyless?" He nodded. "That's the word," he said, looking down at his phone. "Joyless."

Gideon Haigh is an Australian sportswriter and prolific author whose latest is the true crime work, A Scandal in Bohemia.

Prickly to change

MIKE BREARLEY

Five of the major issues facing world cricket over the past forty-odd years have been:

1. The advent of ODIs (1971, World Cup 1975)
2. The advent of T20 cricket (2003, World Cup 2007)
3. The introduction of DRS (2008)
4. The experiment of occasional day-night Tests (Australia v New Zealand 2015)
5. The possibility of cricket applying for admission to the Olympics.

On all these issues, India have at first, and in some cases for years, been reluctant, resistant and at times obstructive.

ODI

Until their surprise (and freakish) World Cup victory in 1983, India showed little interest in one-day international cricket. This was epitomised by Sunil Gavaskar's innings in the first-ever World Cup match, against England at Lord's in 1975.

India's premier batsman amassed 36 not out in 60 overs, England having made a then record score of 334. According to the rules for that competition, in the event of two teams tying in the four-team groups, the one with better run-rate would go into the semi-final. So even if, as was suggested as a reason for his (and the rest of the side's) extraordinary performance, India were almost certain to lose whatever approach they adopted, there was no justification for not bothering about the rate of scoring.

India's supporters, especially those in England (no ODIs were televised live in India until the semi-final against England in 1983) made no secret of their frustration. Police were busy keeping protesters off the ground. Gavaskar said afterwards that the pitch was too slow to play shots — though not apparently for England. The team manager, GS Ramchand, at first defended Gavaskar: he had considered the score unobtainable, Ramchand said, and had used

India showed little interest in ODI cricket early on, as epitomised by opener Sunil Gavaskar's 36 not out in the first-ever World Cup match. — *Getty Images*

the opportunity for practice. Two days later, the manager changed his tune; he now said it was the most disgraceful and selfish performance he had ever seen. Gavaskar too had a different story. He spoke of his 'mental agony'; of how he "couldn't force the pace and nor could he get out". Years later, he went further: he was out of form, played a few slogs early on, then got into a defensive rut.

But what is the evidence for India's (rather than Gavaskar's) stance towards ODIs? One small but striking fact is that whereas England played ODIs from 1971, India did not do so until 1974. Their first ODI captain, Ajit Wadekar, years later commented to Suresh Menon: "We saw the one-day game merely as an extension of Test cricket ... We didn't take the game seriously. And we had no idea of tactics." As John Woodcock wrote in *Wisden* (1984), "In the early years of limited-overs cricket no one, themselves included, took India seriously."

Perhaps the transition from India's old style of cricket — with gifted spin-bowlers, defensively-oriented batsmen and incredibly patient crowds — entailed a revolutionary shift in attitude.

T20

When the Benson and Hedges Cup, an early-season, one-day, domestic competition in UK, came to an end in 2002, the England and Wales Cricket Board needed a second limited-overs competition to boost the game's popularity and to make money. The counties voted 11-7 in favour of the radical proposal for a new county competition of 20 overs each side, which began in 2003. It was instantly successful. The first T20 match at Lord's, between Middlesex and Surrey, attracted an almost full house of 27,509 spectators — the highest crowd for a county match there since the immediate post-War era, the halcyon days of Denis Compton and Bill Edrich.

Pakistan (2004), Australia (2005) and West Indies (2006) followed suit; India eventually inaugurated the IPL in 2008.

The first T20 international took place in 2005, between New Zealand and Australia in Auckland, and this too gained instant appeal. India's first match was not until December 1, 2006, against South Africa in Johannesburg.

When in March 2006, a global T20 tournament was first mooted, BCCI secretary Niranjan Shah was quoted in the Indian media as saying: "T20? Why not ten-ten or five-five or one-one?" And he insisted: "India will never play T20."

India were, then, as with ODIs, initially resistant to this new format, and slower than the other main countries to get involved. Since then, of course, they have run the biggest, razzmatazziest *tamasha* of them all, the IPL.

Now, in the light of the new ECB initiative to be called, it seems, 100-ball cricket, T20 seems almost old hat. Like world records for 100m sprinting, how far down will cricket go? (This could be an expression of my resistance — not to the short game in itself, but to the threat its advance poses to Test cricket.)

DRS

India did agree to try out DRS early in its history, the trial taking place in Sri Lanka in 2008. Notoriously, however, India subsequently refused to join all other Test-playing countries. Different arrangements (no reviews) applied to all Tests involving India — though they had to put up with its use in ICC-run World Cups. For most other Test matches, DRS operated. India seem to have reacted strongly to that experience in Sri Lanka: They lost the series 2-1; of their 21 reviews only one was successful, whereas Sri Lanka succeeded in 11 of their 27 reviews. In reality, India's bigger problem lay in not knowing how to play Ajantha Mendis's unorthodox bowling, alongside Muttiah Muralitharan's.

Officially, India's reasons were three: First, the technology was not perfect. Second, the idea of players being allowed to ask for a review contradicts one of cricket's strongest ethical values, namely that one shouldn't question the umpire's decision. Third, as Anil Kumble argued, it is wrong to have differing final decisions, depending on interpretation by the third umpire, when the situations were identical — in which case DRS is not the final word.

My own views on these issues were, and are, that being imperfect is a matter of degree, and it has long been indisputable that the technology means a higher percentage of correct decisions. Moreover, this feature is not only of value in itself, vindicating truth and therefore justice, but also contributes to better behaviour on the field. As to questioning an umpire's decision, the procedure used formalises the process (as in tennis), lessening the amount of querulous and bitter questioning. As to Kumble's point, there is bound to be an element of interpretation in the reading of any situation, including reading what happens on the screen. Of course, one has to tinker with the procedures, and with the check-list of questions that the

India's call: Reluctanty embracing DRS technology. — *Getty Images*

third umpire must ask himself, but this is true of any set of administrative arrangements.

Many suspected there were also other reasons for India's objections. It was suggested that India's top batsmen were the source of opposition, that they feared they would fare worse with DRS. There was some truth in this: In the first place, umpires are in general slightly less willing to give top players out, since mistakes that apply to the best batsmen tend to make a bigger difference to the outcomes of matches, and a greater degree of scrutiny is given to mistakes involving such batsmen. Second, because opposition captains are more likely to risk losing a review on the chance of reversing a decision of not out against, say, Sachin Tendulkar, than they would against more ordinary batsmen, whom they would expect to dismiss sooner rather than later.

Day-night Tests

India refused to agree to Australia's proposal for a day-night Test in Adelaide in 2018. Coach Ravi Shastri has said that India lack practice in it, while their opponents have played four such Tests.

I fear that though this is understandable, it is narrow-minded, short-sighted and selfish. Day-night Tests are, it seems to me, one small but crucial element in a range of possible remedies for the looming crisis for Test cricket: its vulnerability to gradual diminution if not extinction as a result of the inexorable encroachments of domestic T20 tournaments, which have proliferated and thrived like rabbits did in Australia. Restoring and re-establishing Test cricket at its previous place at the pinnacle of cricket will take as serious an effort as it has taken to save the Madagascar kestrel. It's not that Test cricket has reached the nadir that this kestrel reached — only four pairs remained in the wild when conservationists intervened and bred them in captivity. But the cricketing kestrel of the future needs conservation-minded administrators, not short-term market devotees. I admire Cricket Australia for taking the initiative in staging day-night Test matches. In my view, other countries should see the bigger picture, and make it a priority both to cooperate and to follow suit.

The Olympics

In 2012, the ECB and BCCI were opposed to any application for cricket to be included in the Olympics. By 2018, only India stood in the way.

Here the intransigence seems to be both personal, based on some tension between those running the Indian Olympic Association and senior figures in BCCI, and to do with the issue of omnipotence. While other countries are willing to cede ground to the Olympic association, and to comply with Olympic rules on issues such as sponsorship and drug testing, BCCI continue to jib against the loss of total control over all cricket activities.

Why this intransigence?

Being stubborn in one area may be justified; there is no guarantee that the majority is always right. But in five?

In any family, group or team, people learn to function on give and take. Sometimes we adopt courses of action to fit in with the majority. Sometimes we swallow our pride in the interests of cooperation and experimentation. But not, it seems, India. Or not without an extended wrangle. Why not?

There are many reasons for reluctance to embrace change, some of them good. We may fear unthinking change, or change for the sake of change. We may fear being pulled too far out of our comfort zone. We may lack confidence and be uncertain of our resilience when it comes to untried paths. Or we may be bloody-minded.

Might it be that there is a collective feeling in India of having been for so long ruled over, and over-ruled, by emperors running not only the country but the game? Does a long-term grudge underlie the stance of BCCI in having to have things their way, in their refusal to see others' points of view and to make ordinary compromises?

In 2013, I tried as chair of the World Cricket Committee to contact N Srinivasan with the idea of debating the topic of DRS. I was suggesting a conversation with me and with WCC. Instead of replying, he complained to the chair of ECB, Giles Clarke, who wrote to me as follows: "I would be very grateful if you could follow the established ICC protocols regarding communication with other Boards by any entities from a different country. I will give you the background when I see you, but in the interim should you wish to deal with BCCI, please do so through either myself or David Collier." I found this petty.

With regard to ODIs and T20s, it seems that India fully embrace change only once they have had success, as in 1983 (World Cup winners under Kapil Dev) and 2007 (T20 winners under MS Dhoni, the senior players not having participated).

For whatever reasons, India have often behaved arrogantly with the ICC. They seem to pride themselves on getting their own way, with limited regard for the overall good. Sometimes other boards support them, as when England and Australia collaborated with India in 2014 to create a two-tier system within the ICC. Often other countries are against them, but are nervous about opposing the playground bully with the bulging pockets who keeps other countries bankrolled.

Perhaps India is both an emerging young country full of confidence, brashness and energy, combined with some insecurity, and a conservative one, expressing the unconscious thought: What is five minutes against eternity?

It has been a relief to have a more accommodating and thoughtful voice in international cricket discussions in the form of Shashank Manohar, reappointed in 2018 for a second term as ICC's chairman.

In several of these cases, India have in the end come around. But there often seems to be a prickliness and a stickiness that takes a long time to dissipate.

Mike Brearley played 39 Tests for England, from 1976 to 1981, and was captain in 31 of them. His most recent book is On Cricket.

Shared love of cricket: Nobel laureate Harold Pinter (right) with actor Harry Burton.

Coming home to the Gaieties

HARRY BURTON

The past is a mist — or so Harold Pinter wrote in his bleak late comedy *Moonlight*, about marriage, death and football referees. Back in the days when Pinter's beloved Gaieties CC toured the North-East of England, we actually played in a proper mist once at Gateshead Fell. Summer seemed to have evaded Newcastle entirely. Visibility was down to about 20 yards. If the ball was hit off the square, the only way for a fielder to know if it was heading towards him was Pinter's imperious baritone barking his name from slip.

Founded in 1937 by Lupino Lane, the vaudevillian leaseholder of the Gaiety Theatre (long demolished) in The Strand, Gaieties CC plays wandering Sunday cricket around the M25 motorway — or what used to be called the 'home counties'. I first got to know Harold when I joined Gaieties as a 19-year-old. He'd enlisted in 1969. Our association began in a shared love of cricket ("certainly greater than sex," he famously asserted, "although sex isn't too bad either"). With time, that association became a deep friendship lasting 25 years or so.

Peering into the misty past of my early days with Gaieties, I see myself arriving at the City Road ground of the Honourable Artillery Company (HAC). I'm proudly wearing my school First XI blazer, a sartorial eyesore of black and white zebra-stripes. In those days, some Gaieties players thought public schoolboys needed bringing down a peg or two, and they comprehensively mocked my blazer. I decided never to be seen in it again and the following week I gave it to a thrift shop.

It's about 1.30pm, half an hour before we're due to start what is our first match of the season. HAC sits smack on the northern boundary of the City of London.

Next door in Bunhill Fields burial ground is the grave of William Blake. Once through HAC's gates, however, there is a shocking and unexpected sight. Instead of men at catching practice, before me is an incongruous scene of coordinated military preparation. Battle-dressed personnel swarm the forecourt, drilling and checking equipment. Plumes of diesel fumes and the din of roaring engines choke the turbulent air. Armoured vehicles, Land Rovers and tanks occupy the parking spaces usually reserved on Sundays for cricketers, umpires and spectators.

Adjacent to the freshly whitewashed sight-screen, standing terribly still, is Harold Pinter, Gaieties' chairman, aged 52. He is dressed in black, his face a silent rictus of incandescent fury. We had, after all, gathered in innocence to play cricket. Instead we were confronted by the concrete reality of prime minister Margaret Thatcher's messianic mission to re-take the Falkland Islands from General Leopoldo Galtieri. Pinter barely uttered a word all afternoon, seething impotently at the unthinkable juxtaposition of the thing he loved most — cricket — and the thing he detested most — the human love for warfare. Perhaps it brought back the two trials he endured in 1948 for conscientiously objecting to national service. On that occasion (the public record tells us) he informed the court: "No responsible man shall tarnish his soul by joining such a stupid, sorrowful organisation as the army." He was 18.

The entire match was played to a competing soundscape of barked orders, parading boots and throttled vehicles. The din reverberated eerily off the surrounding buildings, drowning out the batsmen's calls and bowlers' cries of 'Howzat!' Powerless to prevent any of it, Harold furiously smoked his black Sobranie, tipping back the contents of his hip flask as he stalked the boundary rope muttering, "Christ!"

No longer trusting of his eyesight, Pinter stopped playing regularly for Gaieties not long after that. Even after his playing career had ended, he liked to describe himself as "a promising batsman". In his day he captained, and fielded at second slip. As a (promising) batsman he always walked to the wicket with the intention of starting cautiously. But, although he could drive powerfully and sometimes hit the ball straight for six (occasionally off the back foot), he never mastered the art of relaxation at the crease and frequently gave his wicket away, a frustrated victim of the classic rush of blood. Indeed, the scorebook never lies, and the one for 1970 tells us that in the first six games he scored 0, 0, 10, 1, 10 and 0.

As a schoolboy, Harold idolised Len Hutton. Like Hutton, he believed that when you get your opponents down you should drive them into the ground. Go for the jugular. Finish them off. When he was out in the middle he rarely spoke to an opponent. It was not in fact in him to give his opponent an inch at any game, be it cricket, tennis, or bridge. On the sacred field of combat banter was sacrilege. After he stopped playing he umpired regularly. I'm not absolutely certain he ever studied the laws, but he took that role very seriously indeed. His concentration was fierce. He demanded silence on the field, and sometimes off the field as well, occasionally at the cost of confused tears from small children. He indulged no back-chat with the bowler, and only infrequently succumbed, quite involuntarily, to the temptation to raise a partisan finger (once, legend has it, when no Gaieties fielder appealed).

Pinter absolutely hated losing. Defeat always resulted in wrathful, impotent rage. One year, after a Harold Pinter XI had managed (against *The Guardian*) to translate certain victory into ignominious disaster, we stood together at the bar waiting to be served. The silence was intimidating. I couldn't handle it. Like an idiot I attempted consolation: "Well, it's only a stupid bloody game." On the bar sat a reddish brick containing non-safety matches for smokers. He very slowly wrapped a vast hand around its rough edges: "If you don't shut up, I'll put this brick through your skull." I shut up.

Like the questionable aroma of unwashed kit in a long-sealed cricket bag, the Gaieties fixture card of the early 1970s gives off an aroma ripe with the poetry of the great municipal era: Southern Railways;

Watneys; Vauxhall Motors; Pearl Assurance; as well as prosaic sub-urban hubs: Camberley; Hook & Southborough; Banstead; Elmers End; Ickenham; Ewell and Ruxley; Edenbridge, and Brondesbury. Like aboriginal songlines, each cricket ground carries a small fragment of Harold's Gaieties myth, eternally sustained in imagination. Skippering at Guy's Hospital, with only seven players arrived and the rest marooned miles short of the ground in terrible traffic, Harold strode into the changing room, a cricketing Captain Ahab sighting the whale: "I've won the toss, and we're fielding!" There was no arguing with him. Fielding at Ashtead, he resigned his captaincy in

A painting of Harold Pinter batting was commissioned by his fellow Gaieties and presented at a club dinner to mark his Nobel Prize.

the middle of the home side's innings after being called a very short word by his vice-captain during a disagreement about a bowling change. In the next match, the new captain (promoted, at Harold's adamantine insistence, from vice) came to his ex-skipper, pleading for advice on a crucial tactical decision: "I haven't the faintest idea."

Once, in the field at Dover, Harold dropped two sitters off consecutive balls, then ran out our best batsman who was, at that point, just a few nurdled singles short of winning the game. But by no means did he always drop his catches. The circumstances of a very special one, pouched in the slips at Stokesley off the bowling of our Bajan quickie, Ossie Gooding, were immortalised three decades later when Harold's friend Alan Wilkinson sent him 22 forensic questions, published with Pinter's acutely authoritative answers as *The Catch* (as a sample, here's Question Three: "How fast was the ball travelling?" Answer: "Quick.").

We still play every year at Sidcup — a singularly un-idyllic ground, but, because of the tramp's lines in *The Caretaker* about needing to reach Sidcup to retrieve his papers, one with authentic Pinteresque resonance. The fixture almost self-destructed a few years before Harold died. The match had been scheduled recklessly close to the start of Sidcup's rugby season. Late in the afternoon, play was subjected to savage mockery by two inebriated streakers erupting like banshees on to the pitch from a raucous rugby club barbecue. Harold's subsequent outrage was only mollified by written assurances from the chairman of Sidcup Rugby Club: "Unfortunately, the two members cannot personally apologise for their actions because they have left the country. But, as President of the Rugby Club, I would like to apologise on their behalfs. Yours, in Sport, Phil West."

It's summer here in London now, and Gaieties are well into their tenth season since the passing of their chairman. After he died (on Christmas Eve, 2008) the club reeled. Samuel Beckett's lines from *The Unnamable* haunted us: *In the silence you don't know, you must go on, I can't go on, I'll go on.* It would be futile to deny that we staggered around the home counties in shock for a couple of summers. But we knew what Harold would have wanted, so somehow we went on. (Harold had his bleak days, but his literary idol was bleaker. Once, while walking to Lord's to watch England play Australia, Beckett's companion remarked: "On a day like this it's good to be alive". Beckett replied: "Well, I wouldn't go as far as that.")

Glancing up from the computer screen I see pinned before me a small photo of a painting of Pinter batting in the nets, commissioned by his fellow Gaieties to express love and gratitude for four decades of devoted service. The picture was presented at a club dinner to mark his Nobel Prize. Harold was completely bowled over, gazing upon the image of his younger self in astonishment, as close to speechless joy as I ever saw him. The next day a note arrived, absolutely typical in its economy and precision: "A wonderful evening. Thank you. Harold." Beneath those terse syllables flows a subterranean torrent of emotion. It was impossible for him to grope about with words to express the intensity of his feeling for the game, for the club. There was always within him, about the things he cared for passionately, such depth and proportion of true sentiment that he sometimes feared it might overwhelm him. He was moved. That was all.

Harold *was* Gaieties. Still is. Always will be. Each year at the conclusion of the last game of the season at Hampstead, in fading light, all players hushed, he spoke these favourite lines from *At Lord's* by Francis Thompson. It's a tradition we maintain in his honour:

> For the field is full of shades as I near a shadowy coast,
> And a ghostly batsman plays to the bowling of a ghost,
> And I look through my tears on a soundless-clapping host
> As the run stealers flicker to and fro, to and fro:
> O my Hornby and my Barlow, long ago.

Harry Burton is an actor and director. He lives in London and plays cricket for Gaieties CC. His Channel 4 documentary Working With Pinter *is published by Illuminations.*

Graduates of the Class of 2014

LUKE ALFRED

Shortly before the 2014 Under-19 World Cup in the UAE, Ray Jennings had a eureka moment. The South African Under-19 coach, no stranger to flights of fancy, decided to "borrow" a cup from the trophy cabinet at Cricket South Africa's Centre of Excellence at the University of Pretoria. The Under-19 squad was camping at the centre before leaving for the UAE, and the members posed for photographs with the mock trophy.

Jennings even had posters made from the shoot. They said, 'One Team, One Goal' in swaggering font and showed the entire squad and support staff smiling beneath the shade of some nearby pine trees. It was as if the cup was already theirs.

Examine the photograph and you can spot what have since become familiar faces. Bang in the middle of the frame is Aiden Markram, captain of that side. Lying down in front of him, with his hand revealingly on the stem of the cup, is Kagiso Rabada.

On Rabada's shoulder, beaming, is Lungi Ngidi. The powerful KwaZulu-Natal fast bowler wasn't to know it then, but fate was loitering in the wings, an injury ruling him out of the tournament. It transpired that his path to the top was littered with more potholes than it was for Markram and Rabada.

Markram was the beneficiary of one of Jennings's famous hunches. He hadn't been chosen to play for his Under-19 provincial team and, quite literally, was whipped off the beach in late 2012 so Jennings could take a look. He was absorbed into national training squads through 2013 and even taken on tour to India (his performance was mediocre) before Jennings dropped a real humdinger: he made him captain. Some in the system simply shook their heads.

Rabada's route to the top was more of a smooth clip along the high-performance superhighway. He and Jennings knocked heads while the Under-19 squad was in India in 2013. By the time they were posing for photographs, Rabada was in Jennings's inner sanctum. He and Markram played important roles in the UAE, both off the field and on.

Few know it, but although Rabada played four years of first X1

One Team One Goal

"One green light at a time... 'until it's done'"

The pipeline: A hastily made poster of the 2014 U19 World Cup squad posing with a mock trophy before they set out for the event.

cricket at the elite St Stithians College in northern Johannesburg, he never took a five-wicket haul. As a youngster, he arrived as a batsman, a Brian Lara wannabee with a booming cover-drive.

As he strengthened and matured, his school coaches concentrated on his bowling. The wildness was harnessed, the no-ball problem brought under control. Over time he developed into a special athlete. There is no hyperbole in saying that when taking 6 for 25 — in a game televised back home — he terrorised Australia in the Under-19 World Cup semi-final.

Five wickets back home at school were rewarded with a tree being planted in the players' name around the St. Stithians first XI oval. Rabada left school without a tree, so when he'd played South Africa into the final, he woke up his old cricket master in the middle of the night, pleading for a tree.

"We're behind you time-wise Kagiso. It's 3am here, buddy," said Wim Jansen, his long-suffering cricket coach.

"Sorry, sir, I'm just phoning about my tree."

"Which tree would that be?"

"To ask if I can have one after my six wickets against Australia?"

Rabada played a substantial part in the South Africans winning the

2014 tournament, but he wasn't the only one. Markram won Player of the Tournament, following his 120 not out against Zimbabwe in the group match, and 66 not out against Pakistan in the final.

As it was, South Africa won by six wickets with nearly eight overs to spare. There was clearly merit in the idea of the squad taking photos of themselves with the trophy beforehand.

Jennings and CSA parted ways upon the team's return to South Africa. He had been told that his contract would come to an end after the tournament, no matter what the result, and the much-maligned gaffer was on his bike. To adapt a phrase from EM Forster's *A Passage to India*, in which Aziz is summonsed to the civil surgeon at an inconvenient hour, he had "considerably paved the way towards obedience" for his young players.

At first, his relationship with Rabada was itchy, but they soon cobbled together an entente that became fond, even respectful. Markram and Ngidi were more conventional and therefore more pliable characters, so easier for the martinet Jennings to understand.

The arrogance — some might say the hauteur — around Rabada was precisely what allowed him to break into the big time first. Markram followed, with a Test debut against Bangladesh, and Ngidi bobbed along in his wake.

Nigidi's 6 for 39 against India in the Second Test at Centurion in January 2018 was a remarkable return for a debutant. He restricted India to a paltry second-innings total of 151. Until he came along with his height and strength, South Africa were by no means certain of victory, particularly after Virat Kohli's masterful 153 in India's first innings.

All three are now part of South Africa's future in a way that wasn't imagined when they headed off to the UAE in February 2014. They have established themselves quickly, a fact partly accounted for by the retirement of Morne Morkel (in the bowlers' case) and AB de Villiers (in Markram's).

All three look set to be with the team for the next ten years.

Their importance to the Proteas' cause was underlined when Australia arrived for a four-Test series in March 2018. Although Markram responded with a hundred, South Africa lost the First Test arm-wrestle at Kingsmead in a fractious affair. David Warner insulted Quinton de Kock and Nathan Lyon churlishly dropped the ball on de Villiers's head after he'd been run out. South Africa boiled on the quick flight down the coast from Durban to Port Elizabeth.

The loss — and the manner thereof — woke the Saffers from their slumber. Rabada was magnificent in the next Test at St. George's Park. His anger was controlled and he bowled quickly and intelligently on a wicket known to encourage the spinners.

Had de Villiers not unfurled a sublime hundred when South Africa batted, Rabada's match-analysis of 11 for 150 would probably have earned more praise than it did.

Markram, quiet in the middle Tests, responded in the Fourth Test at the Wanderers. Attacking and watchful by turn, his big hundred was masterful, the equal of anything ever seen at the ground. With his hundred came a 3-1 victory in the so-called 'Sandpaper Series'.

The World Cup is a competition in which South Africa have proved wildly creative in snatching defeat from the jaws of victory — and so it was this year too. But with South Africa in a period of manageable flux post the retirement of de Villiers, and the likes of Hashim Amla and even Faf du Plessis in doubt for another shot at the Cup, the three members of the Class of 2014 will be hopeful that World Cup victory at junior level holds them in good stead for an uncertain future.

Luke Alfred is a Johannesburg-based sportswriter with nearly two decades of experience.

The perennials

V RAMNARAYAN

I played collegiate cricket in Madras in the 1960s, and first-class cricket after my move to Hyderabad in 1971. I was 28 when I made my Ranji Trophy debut four years later. I had almost given up hope. I had been sure, even perversely proud, that I would never be a first-class cricketer; surely the loss was for cricket, not me! There were Test cricketers and Ranji Trophy players I admired, but I was drawn to those who didn't make it and carried on regardless, putting up their best show in encounters with players and teams way above their level. I was proud to owe allegiance to this unusual breed of overachievers whom the selectors overlooked year after year.

My Presidency College (Madras) spin twin C S Dayakar was one of them. A left-handed all-rounder, he saved his best for our matches against the College of Engineering, Guindy, perhaps one of the strongest college teams in India. Its captain was S Venkataraghavan, who had debuted as India's off-spinner against New Zealand in the 1964-65 season, and he led a side brimming with talent. Dayakar and John Alexander, our stocky, resolute batsman in the Vijay Manjrekar mould, approached these matches with steely determination and fierce pride, invariably scoring big. Dayakar was selected in the Madras University squad that travelled to Dharwad in Karnataka in December 1969 to compete in the Rohinton Baria Trophy, but declined, certain that the other left-arm spinner of the team, Bhargav Mehta, would be preferred in the playing XI. Dayakar was never picked again in representative cricket, but wheeled away gamely for years for the doughty Indian Overseas Bank team in the highly competitive Tamil Nadu Cricket Association league.

Mehta was to turn out to be a very unlucky cricketer, too, despite a magnificent Rohinton Baria final the very next season, in which he bowled Madras to victory over Bombay with 14 wickets. Amazingly, Mehta never played Ranji Trophy cricket, a mystery perhaps only slightly less puzzling than the story of fast bowler Vikram Thambuswami, who took 8 for 37 in the first innings of his only Ranji Trophy appearance for Tamil Nadu versus Andhra.

Two other Madras University players played stellar roles in that season of triumph for their team under the captaincy of R Ravichandran. P R Ramakrishnan was an upright, stylish batsman from Coimbatore, one of the most prolific scorers in university and junior cricket in the 1970s. His partner in a huge lower-order association at the Osmania University ground in Hyderabad was N Bharathan, an orthodox off-spinner with a lovely action, flight and deception. In that game, both Ramakrishnan and Bharathan scored big hundreds, with the spinner also bagging a rich haul of wickets. Both were successful in the TNCA league for many seasons without ever gaining the selectors' nod. Bharathan was one of the finest off-spinners I have seen or played with. With Venkataraghavan and V V Kumar leading the Tamil Nadu attack for a couple of decades, Bharathan stood little chance of playing Ranji cricket. Ravichandran was a consistently successful captain in junior and university cricket, but had to be content with scoring plenty of runs at that level, never progressing beyond it.

I am focusing here not only on those I consider unfairly treated by selectors, but also others who knew they belonged at the purely local level, with no hope or aspiration for higher honours, manfully turning out for their clubs season after season.

'Don' Rangan, so named for his Bradmanesque deportment on the cricket field, his arrogant self-belief disproportionate to his cricketing accomplishments, was master of all he surveyed on the Pithapuram cricket ground in south Madras in the 1960s. He maintained a superb ground and nets out of his own (some say his family's) hard-earned money. Besides offering net practice facilities through the year, Rangan relished inviting strong visiting teams to 'friendly' matches (though they fit the description only nominally as Rangan was arguably the inventor of sledging, and often cheated at the toss, breezily declaring, "We bat," no matter which way the coin fell) and trying to beat them. 'Opening batsman and wicketkeeper' was his official description, but he sometimes called on some unsuspecting junior player to deputise for him behind the stumps so that he could take an absurdly long run-up to bowl his military medium. His crowing at bowling success, often after he bullied the umpire, would have earned him suspension for at least a couple of matches under today's behaviour norms.

Three brothers bowled medium pace for Mylapore Recreation Club in the same period. P R Sundaram, the eldest and tallest of them, bowled at a sharp pace and extracted steep bounce on the matting wickets of the time. Those who faced him in the league could never figure out why he played only one Ranji Trophy game, and that too with less than impressive returns. An entertaining wielder of the long handle, Sundaram was also a good tennis player. Like Rangan, he too had no respect for the big names, and loved to embarrass them — for example, by bowling them with a googly off the first ball of a match or laughing loudly after gaining an umpire's verdict he considered wrong.

There were many club cricketers of the time who entertained with their skill or idiosyncrasies: Gopalapuram CC's leg-spinner Kannan with his 'donkey drops' of legendary altitude; K C Krishnamurthi, whose constant chatter gained him more notoriety than any fame his fastish leg-breaks might have; Alley Sridhar, possibly the ugliest left-handed batsman in history; medium pacer Rajaraghavan, who religiously called a certain TNCA official once every year to inquire of him why he had been left out of the state team; C B Selvakumar, whose six-hitting prowess won him a large fan base, and P N 'Clubby' Clubwala, who once scored 37 not out in a whole day's batting and held the original title of strokeless wonder before the early Navjot Singh Sidhu. These hardy perennials of Madras cricket lent it its unique personality.

Hyderabad, where I moved in 1971, was no different. My State Bank of India captain was a tiny man with a big heart. Abid Zainulabudin was a gutsy middle-order batsman and thinking captain who never played first-class cricket but defied superior teams with his strategic leadership and brave batting. It was said of Kaleem-ul-Haq, a leg-spinner with a nonchalant spring in his step and jaunty, upswept hairstyle, that he kept a careful record of the number of wickets he grabbed in net practice, rarely missing the hundred mark for the season. He reminded me of two spinners of Madras who for years haunted the nets, even though they did not get to play a single match during the period. Left-armer S K Patel eventually did find success on the field of play: he crossed the fifty mark in the 1975-76 season to pass Mumtaz Hussain's record in the Rohinton Baria, while wrist-spinner V Kannan just faded away from the scene after numerous seasons of net bowling. Many spinners through the decades, from C R Mukundan, K Ganapathy, M K Rajamanickam and M K Mohan in the 1950-60s, to M Subramaniam and N Raghavendran of recent decades, have soldiered on unsung.

Overseas tours with the Hyderabad or Deccan Blues I was part of were a wonderful departure from organised domestic cricket, especially for former internationals and local cricketers who might never make it big. Arranged by P R Man Singh, the manager of the 1983 World Cup-winning Indian team and a cricket tragic with the briefest of brief first-class careers, these tours sometimes threw up unexpectedly high-quality performances from both the Blues and our opponents like the Australian Old Collegians or I Zingari, amateur clubs that both hosted visiting teams and toured the subcontinent. While I was witness to many sterling performances by my teammates on these tours, there were occasions when an unknown opponent gave us a fright. Hyderabad Blues nearly lost a match to Singapore Cricket Club in January 1978, when medium pacer Chris Kilbee, an erstwhile teammate of David Gower at school and college level, took the wickets of Ajit Wadekar, M L Jaisimha and Murtuza Ali Baig in quick succession, and then scored a brilliant 91. At 160 for 2, SCC were poised to overtake our modest 190, when Jaisimha desperately turned to opening batsman Kenia Jayantilal's occasional swing and seam. Jayanti obliged with seven wickets, and the Blues narrowly escaped a humiliating defeat. The tongue-lashing some of us received that night from skipper Jaisimha was of epic proportions.

Once, tired of listening to an interminable lecture by a former Test cricketer about his international exploits, I declared I was proud of the intense cricket some of us played, albeit at a less exalted level than his. I am likewise convinced that the cricket many non-first-class cricketers play is no less competitive.

V Ramnarayan (@pnvram) was an off-spinner for Hyderabad and turned to journalism and teaching after a first-class career that brought him 96 wickets from 25 matches.

Collector's drive

GULU EZEKIEL

"Why do people decide to collect, whether it be stamps or butter-flies, horseshoes or 'cricketana'?"

That's the opening line to *The David Frith Archive* (2009), a door-stopper of a book on the finest private cricket collection in the world, compiled by my cricket guru, an inspiration both for my collecting passion and writing career.

It is also the most expensive — and heaviest — book in my collection, numbering close to 1200, which began with Garry Sobers's account of the 1966 tour of England, *King Cricket*, bought in Kolkata in 1971. *The Gillette Book of Cricket and Football* edited by Gordon Ross was gifted to me in 1969; but it's a mix of football and cricket.

Thanks to a combination of luck and perseverance, these two books are still with me after all these years, surviving shifts to eight homes across five cities.

Wracked by doubt over the cost, I was in a dilemma over the Frith book. It was my late mother who pushed me into buying it, and so I became the proud owner of signed copy No.29 of the 75 that were printed. The 16-page introduction, which tries to answer that question in the opening sentence, is alone worth the price.

A visit to Firth's home and museum in Guildford, Surrey, in 1999, the day after the Lord's World Cup final, was truly memorable and, dare I say for a hardcore atheist, even spiritual. I was allowed to wear Duleepsinhji's cap and hold the bats of RE 'Tip' Foster and Archie Jackson. And I got some ideas for the library/museum/art gallery I would set up at home in the years to follow.

What is the reason I collect? Partly, it's in the genes. Parsis are famous/notorious for hoarding — which is collecting by another name. My brother Jawahar, who collects rock music and space memorabilia, and I must have caught the bug from our Parsi mother, who had a taste for books on cooking, poetry, art and cats and much else besides. There is a photo of one of our uncles holding a massive ball of string our grandmother kept adding to till it grew halfway to the ceiling and had to be gently disposed of, despite strong protests from her. And the great-grandmother who lived to 102? She merely collected cats; I believe there were a dozen crawling all over the family mansion at one point.

But why cricket? The answer to that lies in Ian Peebles's quote: "There are no cricketers like those seen through 12-year-old eyes."

I was 12 in 1971, the most magical year in Indian cricket. I had only a passing interest in cricket before that. In our three years in London, Jawahar and I were totally immersed in football, thanks to England winning the 1966 World Cup just down the road from where we lived in Wembley. Cricket, I used to say, was for sissies.

My collection, which began with photos cut from newspapers and magazines, grew to 42 voluminous scrapbooks, with over 30,000 photos from over 100 different publications from around the world. It helped to have pen-friends from England, Australia and New Zealand, who at the end of every season would send me stacks of newspaper cuttings.

That collection ended in 1983 after India won the Prudential World Cup. The boom in cricket in India and my new career as a journalist meant one just could not keep up.

The 1970s and '80s were the golden age for sports and cricket magazines in India, with three weeklies and numerous cricket magazines that came and went. It meant buying two copies of each: one to cut, one to preserve.

Today my collection has grown to over 5000 magazines from every Test-playing country in the world, except the two most recent ones. A full set of *The Cricketer* (UK), founded by Sir Pelham Warner in 1921 — the first 19 years in original binders and originally the possession of John Arlott — is perhaps the only such private set in India.

Collectors like to have targets, it adds to the motivation. Mine is to have in my possession every issue of *Sport and Pastime*, the weekly magazine published by *The Hindu* group from 1947 to 1968. I have 60 copies and am quite aware it is practically impossible to get every issue. Then again, who knows?

Of course, like any youngster, I also sought autographs eagerly. The first was of Dilip Sardesai — the first time I attended a first-class match, Ranji Trophy, Bombay v Maharashtra, 29 January 1972, Brabourne Stadium, and yes, I still have the pass. It helped that sitting next to us was Sardesai's six-year-old son Rajdeep, whom we recognised from the Sardesai family photos published in *Sportsweek* following the 1971 victories. Rajdeep helped us get his dad's auto-

A gentleman in Delhi, whose relative went on both the 1886 and 1888 Parsi tours of England, sold a match-bill for one of the 1888 matches at an auction in England in 2015 for £1105.

56

graph at the lunch break, when Papa Sardesai came by to admonish his son for not eating the sandwiches prepared by the mother.

Initially, collectors tend to grab everything, and I was no different. Eventually, space, house moves, finances, family (not a problem here being a lifelong bachelor) all encourage a discerning approach. In my case, while books, magazines, souvenir booklets, clothing, signed bats and DVDs (action footage, documentaries, feature films) pile up, the focus is now on autographs, specifically Indian Test cricketers. At the time of writing, my collection stands at 244 out of 295 who have played for India.

The author at David Frith's. The 'pimple' glove on the left belonged to Leo O'Brien (who used it in the Bodyline series). The brown glove was Don Bradman's.

I don't claim to have the biggest or best collection of cricket memorabilia in the country. That distinction perhaps belongs to P R Man Singh, the manager of the 1983 World Cup-winning team, whose museum in Secunderabad was inaugurated by Sachin Tendulkar in November 2004.

The world's richest cricket association has had numerous 'museum committees', but nothing concrete has emerged about setting up a museum of Indian cricket. This while every county in England and every state in Australia has its own museum.

In May 2018, Tendulkar laid the foundation stone for an endeavour in Dharamsala at the Himachal Pradesh Cricket Association headquarters, under the guidance of former BCCI president and politician Anurag Thakur, and it appears promising. In the main, however, it is left to individuals like Man Singh, Mumbai-based journalist and author Clayton Murzello, historian and author Boria Majumdar (his Fanattic Sports Museum in Kolkata is dedicated to the history of Indian sport, with an emphasis on cricket) and real estate tycoon Rohan Pate (his Blades of Glory museum in Pune has a number of signed bats) to build and display collections. Cricket writer Mudar Patherya has a small but lovely collection in Kolkata, including one of the holy grails of Indian cricket collecting, a stump from India's inaugural 1932 Test at Lord's. Srikantan Ramamurthy, born in Coimbatore, residing in Adelaide, whose private collection was considered second only to Frith's, sold it all at a grand auction in Melbourne in August 1997 under pressure from both space and family. It included autographs of nearly every Australian Test cricketer from 1877 to 1995, as well as a selection of artefacts given to him by Victor Trumper's family, including a bat, a cap and a mini diary of the 1902 tour of England — it went for A$29,900.

Ranji, Grace, Trumper, Bradman — most collectors can only dream of possessing something that they have used, written or worn. In India, the magical years are 1886 and 1888 (first cricket tours, by the Parsis), 1911 (first 'All India' tour of England), 1932 and, more recently, 1971 and 1983.

A gentleman in Delhi, whose relative went on both the 1886 and 1888 Parsi tours, sold a match-bill for one of the 1888 matches at an auction in England in 2015 for £1105. It announced: 'The Parsees from Bombay, versus the Scarborough Club. This Grand Match will be played on the cricket ground, North Marine Road, this day. Wickets pitched at 12 o'clock.' Despite its age, the flyer was in excellent condition.

Becoming a member in 1996 of the UK-based Cricket Memorabilia Society (CMS, founded in 1987) was a breakthrough for me. With over 400 members from 12 countries, a quarterly newsletter and a website, it has connected me with fellow collectors.

In 2012, to mark the CMS's 25th anniversary, Frith brought out a book (limited to 150 copies, signed by the author and the then CMS president Tom Graveney), *Cricket's Collectors*, featuring the obsessions of select members. I was interviewed as well, with the focus on the splendid 1984 book *Lord's Taverners Fifty Greatest*, which features the greatest post-Second World War cricketers, including four Indians in Vinoo Mankad, Bishan Singh Bedi, Sunil Gavaskar and Kapil Dev. It took me 17 years starting in 1984, but I eventually got all 50 autographed; for those who had passed away, I pasted their autographs.

In 2003, CMS, which publishes and markets its own memorabilia, brought out a set of 50 cards, depicting various forms of cricket collecting. These ranged from the standard — autographs, books and magazines — to the more unusual — handkerchiefs, advertisements and matchbox labels. Of these 50 forms, I can claim to collect 20 and a couple of others not depicted.

Some forms are now history thanks to technological advances — who remembers the phone cards of the early 2000s? Who these days sends letters, that too hand-written? I have a selection, as well as greeting cards (also now largely extinct). Emails I now print out and file — not the same as a letter, of course.

Having read about an Englishman who has a collection of grass from grounds around the world stored in match-boxes, I thought it was a wonderful idea. But due to security restrictions, I could only get my hands on one through a friend and that is from my favourite venue outside India, Queen's Park Oval, Port of Spain, Trinidad. The grass has turned to hay over the years.

In 1998, on Bradman's 90th birthday, a lovely colour pencil sketch appeared in a Delhi newspaper. I got in touch with the artist and commissioned 14 portraits of some of my favourite cricketers, including Bradman, Tendulkar, Dennis Lillee, Shane Warne, Lala Amarnath, Bedi and Anil Kumble. Each of these legends signed three — the original for me, and colour photocopies for the artist and the cricketer himself.

That year, I collected material from the Indian media and sent it to the Bradman Museum in Bowral, New South Wales, along with the portrait, with a request to pass them on to Bradman for signing. He had announced he would not be signing any more autographs after his 90th birthday, but, sure enough, after a couple of months of anxious waiting, they safely arrived in the post.

So, what are the favourite items in my collection? The colour pencil portrait signed by Bradman — 'To Gulu, Best wishes' — is unique and treasured. So is the Lord's Taverners set. Then there is the photo of Warne and Tendulkar on Bradman's birthday, signed by all three. And the bail bent out of shape after a Pakistan batsman was bowled by Kumble during his Perfect Ten Test in Delhi in 1999, which the bowler so kindly signed and gifted to me when I interviewed him the evening of his feat. Last year, I received 39 historic printed scorecards, a couple of them autographed, of matches played in Bombay in the 1940s and 50s — Ranji Trophy, Test matches and Pentangular matches. There is also a collection of original printed scorecards, with some signed, of famous matches played by India in England — Lord's 1932; The Oval '71; Lord's '83, Lord's '86, Lord's 2011.

Gaps in my collection? The missing autographs of the Test cricketers; an India Test cap; loads of *Sport and Pastime* magazines; about 20 per cent of *Sportsweek* (1968 to 1988) and *Sportsworld* (1978 to 1999) magazines; two *Sportsweek* annuals (1970 and 1971), just one picture card (Eknath Solkar) from the 1972 Kwality ice cream set ('Our victorious 18'), and the set of Wimco matchbox labels depicting Indian and West Indian cricketers in 1974. Fellow collectors who may have some of these may please get in touch!

Frith has written that he is often asked what will become of his vast collection after his passing. On my part, I have bequeathed the collection in my will to two sports journalists who are friends and fellow collectors.

But what if I outlive them both?

Gulu Ezekiel (@gulu1959) is a sports journalist, author and collector based in Delhi.

'In every game in which I put up a good show, the only thing constant was adaptability,' says Unmukt Chand. – *Getty Images*

An analysis of stasis

UNMUKT CHAND

If everything went right for everyone, I would have been out there bumping fists with Virat Kohli, planning India's run chase or celebrating a successful one.

Wearing an India cap is a dream we all grew up with. No lucrative IPL contract can ever replace the soul-warming feel of the Indian cap. But there are only 15 players in the Indian team, so it can never go as planned for anyone but those 15. There are a lot of permutations and combinations that eventually take you to the top. Had this happened or had that happened, 'I would be playing for the country', cricketers say — but that's something no one is interested in. So, what does it take to reach the next level?

One thing that is clear to me is that after a certain level, everyone is the same. Our skill sets might vary, techniques might be different and so too the approach, but as they say in Hindi, '*bas* 19-20 *ka hi farak hota hai*'. It's just the slight difference between 19 and 20. A player can't be defined by these aspects. What carries more weight is the mental aptitude to understand the situation, adapt one's game and have that insatiable hunger to perform each time.

But this is something we are rarely taught. Few coaches discuss these aspects with players; instead, the easiest to tinker with is technique — a favourite for any coach and probably the worst for a player. A few failures and the first thing to be tinkered with is technique. It might help to an extent, but the game is not played with just technique; it's about the ability to understand one's game, minimise the chances of getting out and know how to score runs. Street smartness is important.

Till the junior level, if you had better skills than your opponent, you would mostly succeed. If you had better technique, you would be way ahead. Your stature was daunting to the opposition. Just being talked about gave you so much confidence that you started out three paces ahead from the beginning. This changes when you graduate to the next level. Yes, one still talks about the best batsman or the best bowler in the other team, but you know that you can take him down if plans are executed well. In modern-day cricket, there is no difference between a Delhi or a Vidarbha. Vidarbha, in fact, thrashed the multiple champions to win the Ranji Trophy 2017-18.

I too fell into a technical rut. It took me a long time to come out of it. I was in so deep that I had forgotten to see the damn ball and score runs. Imagine an opening batsman saying this!

When I was young, I loved playing shots. I even used to embrace an edge to the boundary. I loved the sight of bowlers and fielders looking at me like I had all the luck — and it did seem that I got lucky almost every time. But the moment I became too serious about my batting, poof! All my gods left me. Opinions and advice started pouring in and suddenly stance became a major concern. The gap between the feet, tapping, crouching, back lift, grip, bat on the ground or in the air, shuffle or no shuffle, so on and so forth. I didn't realise that whatever feels good, helps you see the ball clearly, and gets you into the perfect position to execute a shot is the best stance for you. Simple.

Understand that I am not against technical changes. All I am saying is that there is a thin line between making the required changes and not sinking deeper.

Of course, sometimes the simplest things are the most difficult to do. It requires effort and consistent application to just watch the ball and play without letting your mind go to technique or pre-determining strokes. I've failed many times trying to play orthodox cricket where there is excessive focus on playing in the 'V'; on most such occasions, I have got out. My innings in the Under-19 World Cup final was one where I was least bothered about technique. My whole focus was on winning that match. Hence, I played according to the situation and I applied myself. I remember that in every game in which I put up a good show, the only thing constant was adaptability; I had no idea how my stance was or of any other mundane stuff.

It's about the practice sessions too. Work on your game, but don't let it confuse you. Remember, what's natural to you should never be compromised. That's one of my biggest lessons from recent years.

With growing up and maturity comes too much analysis, which might lead to paralysis. Expectations when not met lead to insecurities, which hamper performance. Each dismissal takes you into a mental spiral, even as you see your fellow cricketers progressing to the next level. Somewhere in their success, you lose yourself. The more you try, the farther it goes away. For me too, my peers were representing the country one after the other and I was just missing the bus. There was a time two years ago when I was leading the India A side; all the players in that team have gone on to play for the national team, except me. That was a rude awakening. But you can't stop.

That was when spirituality became my friend, and a way of life. The mantra is to keep working hard and smart. Don't let comparisons bother you. Focus on yourself. We all have different journeys, but all roads lead to the same place, eventually, so believe in yours. Cricket is a team sport, but it is also a personal battle.

Also, it is important to keep improving, but with the right mental outlook. Backing your strengths a 100 per cent is a quality of top cricketers. But if the focus is on the inevitable weaknesses, rather than the strengths, the negativity affects performance. For instance, my second Ranji Trophy season was a disaster. We played most of our games at the Roshanara Club in Delhi with a heavy green top, where the scores were low, and I struggled. I got out playing drives and back-foot punches, and was told to stop playing these shots. But these were my bread-and-butter strokes. A time had come when I would drive for a four and curse myself for hitting it again. You do

'Close your eyes and remember the first time you held a bat. It was simple then, and it should be simple now.' – *Getty Images*

realise how foolish that sounds, right? How would I ever score runs if I stopped playing shots that, you know, got me runs! But as stupid as it sounds, I was doing it!

Back then, I didn't understand that it was not about not playing a certain shot, but about realising when to play it. Getting out a few times doesn't mean I stop playing a certain way, when that way had got me runs as well. The lesson: Work on your game, but don't restrict yourself.

At the same time, don't be afraid to unlearn. I have often tried to replicate what worked in previous innings in which I scored runs, but it didn't work out the same way. How could it? Playing in the Dhaka Premier League this season, I got a hundred in the first game. I batted well, I was relaxed. We were batting second and it was very hot. After fielding for 50 overs, obviously the body was tired. But I batted with ease, my heartbeat was calm and slow, my mind was clear, and so, the runs flowed. The next game was a day after my birthday and I had slept late the previous night, so when I got in to bat after we won the toss, I was again not feeling energetic. I decided to be calm again, and it worked again: I got another hundred.

Now, I realised a pattern was forming. The next two games I tried to do the same, but I failed in both. Later, I realised my body was not in sync with my mind. We batted first in the third game and I was full of energy, but I deliberately tried to slow myself down, which was unnatural on that particular day. I should have played with the feeling I had at that moment.

Every game is different, every situation is a new one, and every day is a fresh start. How can you be the same yesterday and today? The best players don't restrict themselves to fixed notions — they keep changing. Sometimes patterns do work, but, in the longer run, flexibility defines a player. You have to unlearn and start afresh every day.

The most important thing is to enjoy this game of cricket. Let's control the controllables and stay happy.

In 2018, I was twice been confronted with situations I was never ready for. I was captaining India A, but was dropped from the Delhi squad. Four days later, I didn't get picked for the IPL. This came as a jolt to me as I understood that I had been reduced to a club-level cricketer. When I woke up after a terrible night, I realised that my love for cricket cannot be measured by selection or non-selection. The fear evaporated, and I practised more ardently, as a purity filtered into the way I played. As chance would have it, Delhi lost four games and I was recalled. I played two matches, scored consecutive fifties and earned one match award.

In the second instance, amid unnecessary politics, I was selected for the Vijay Hazare Trophy squad. A day before the first game, I broke my jaw in the nets. I was devastated — I could not afford to miss any more games. With taping and pills, I played the match against UP and scored a century. It was a fantastic feeling!

When you go out to bat, just remember why you first held that bat in the first place. You could have chosen a tennis racquet, a hockey stick, boxing gloves. But no, you chose this bat and ball and you chose it for a reason. Close your eyes and remember the first time you held it. It was simple then, and it should be simple now.

Unmukt Chand led India to the Under-19 World Cup title in 2012.

Ajit Wadekar: 1941-2018

Captain, conqueror

AYAZ MEMON

Encomiums and tributes came in a deluge when Ajit Wadekar passed away on August 15, 2018, aged 77. He had been unwell for a few weeks.

With greater research going into Indian cricket and more data available, a revisionist view of Wadekar's contribution to Indian cricket has emerged, and what had seemed a so-so career, with one major spike, is now being viewed as far more significant than hitherto imagined.

Wadekar's career can be demarcated into three distinct phases: as first-class cricketer, as captain and post-retirement as administrator/selector/coach. In each of these his influence was significant.

Before he played his first Test, in 1966-67 against West Indies, Wadekar marked himself out as among the most exciting batsmen in the country. Weaned on the maidans of Bombay, his cricket reflected the character and mettle of the 'nursery of Indian cricket'. Tall, slim, square-shouldered and sinewy, he was a stylish, aggressive left-hand batsman who lit up local tournaments as well as grounds across India. He was a strong hooker and cutter of pace bowlers, and played whiplash drives on either side of the wicket, thriving on quicksilver reflexes, sound assessment of line and length, and exquisite timing. Against spinners, he was unafraid to use his feet to hit them off their length.

Wadekar's exploits in domestic first-class tournaments and his contests with the great spin quartet of Prasanna, Chandrasekhar, Venkataraghavan and Bedi are part of Indian cricket folklore. His Ranji Trophy record — 4388 runs in 73 matches at 59.29 — highlight his impact in domestic cricket; yet it took him eight years after his first-class debut (1958-59) to earn his Test cap, against Garfield Sobers's West Indies that toured India.

Unlike his domestic performances, Wadekar's Test stats are mod-

Victory in England, 1971: The true import of what Wadekar achieved only grows with time. – *Getty Images*

est: 2113 runs in 37 Tests. He made only one century — the 143 against New Zealand in Wellington — but it was vital in helping India win their first overseas Test series. The seemingly pedestrian Test record can be attributed to the fact that Wadekar played 18 of his 37 Tests overseas. For someone so gifted, it was nevertheless disappointing, but redeemed by his contribution as captain.

In the last couple of decades, Wadekar has acquired near cult status for leading India to historic series wins over West Indies and England in 1970-71. India's record playing overseas remains frustratingly tepid. A few days before Wadekar breathed his last, India lost the Second Test against England at Lord's (the final scoreline was to be 1-4). It only accentuated the fantastic achievement 47 years before.

India have never won two series on the trot outside the sub-continent since. In fact, Wadekar was the first to helm three successive series wins, beating Tony Lewis's MCC in 1972-73 at home. This has compelled fresh attention to what went right for the team and Wadekar's role as captain in that magnificent phase.

Indeed, Wadekar's appointment as captain in 1970 marked a major and controversial inflection point in Indian cricket history. He was not a unanimous choice, with two of four selectors who were present voting for the incumbent, Mansur Ali Khan Pataudi. The fifth, M N Dutta Roy, was absent for reasons that have never been made clear. This put the onus on the chairman of the committee, Vijay Merchant, who used his 'casting vote' to oust Pataudi.

Despite a modest record, Pataudi was a popular and charismatic player and captain. Apart from a personal saga in courage (he played despite losing 95 per cent vision in one eye in a car accident before his international debut), he is credited with uniting a diverse and divided Indian dressing room when he took over. His demotion (he later refused to go to West Indies and England) was greeted with disbelief and scepticism about the new man in charge. As it happened, India beat West Indies 1-0 and, a few months later, England 1-0.

And to think, India had never won a Test, leave aside a series, in either country before. Indeed, the previous tour of the West Indies in 1962 had resulted in a 5-0 whitewash; in England in 1967, the team had been blanked 0-3.

The reception Wadekar and his team got on their return — a motorcade from the airport to Brabourne Stadium, with thousands of fans lining the streets — showed how deeply fans had craved these wins.

It didn't come easily. West Indies, though an aging team then, still boasted of Sobers, Rohan Kanhai, Wesley Hall and Charlie Griffith, supported by the explosive brilliance of young Clive Lloyd. Ray Illingworth and his England team had returned from the Australian summer with the Ashes and were then widely regarded as the world's best side.

Despite these wins (and the one against Lewis's MCC), acknowledgment of Wadekar's leadership was muted. For critics, he remained a 'lucky captain' and when he lost 0-3 in England in 1974, the sceptics got more grist for their mill. But that point of view changed as no other team could match what Wadekar's boys accomplished, even with all the financial riches that came Indian cricket's way, especially in the last three decades. Now, Wadekar's captaincy emerges as vital to India's win as Sunil Gavaskar and Dilip Sardesai with bat in the Caribbean, and B S Chandrasekhar with the ball in England, to complete what is now known as the 'great Indian summer'.

Those who call Wadekar a 'fluke' overlook the fact that before captaining India, he had captained Bombay for two seasons (1968-

69, 69-70), both times winning the Ranji Trophy. Overall, he led his state association 30 times, won 16 matches, never lost, and won the Ranji Trophy four times.

What was also overlooked in the brouhaha over his appointment as captain was that with a post-graduate degree and as professional banker, he was trained for sound and quick analyses of circumstances and people, and used to tackling stressful situations calmly and tactfully.

For instance, against West Indies in the Second Test at Port of Spain in 1970, he unexpectedly threw the ball to Salim Durrani, who had been having an indifferent series till then. Durrani dismissed Lloyd and Sobers off successive deliveries and India's win was sealed. Against England at The Oval, he brought in his main spinner, Bishan Singh Bedi, who obliged with a wicket, but was changed after only one over, much to the confoundment of critics and experts. The skipper turned instead to Chandrasekhar, who led India to a memorable win.

Shrewd manager: Behind the easy-going demeanour was a hardy and canny cricketer. — *Getty Images*

Despite completing a hat-trick of series wins, Wadekar's captaincy — indeed, his Test career — was cut short. The 1974 tour of England was a nightmare, what with internecine power struggle within the team compounding a 0-3 whitewash. Indian fans, always volatile, were outraged. But what cracked Wadekar's resilience was the selectors dropping him from the West Zone team when the new season began. Miffed, he retired from all cricket immediately, aged only 33.

What made Wadekar

tick as captain? Behind the easy-going demeanour was a hardy and canny cricketer, and a shrewd manager of people and situations. This was evident not just in his playing days, but also when he became coach in 1992-93, which forms the third and equally vital phase of his cricketing life.

For the world outside, he was a source of great fun, almost Wodehousean in demeanour with his trawling gait and one-liners that spared none, including himself. The geniality was not affected, but he was no man's fool. He kept an 'open house' for the media, which allowed for a great deal of transparency about players and selections, but also helped Wadekar keep his ear to the ground about the goings on in Indian cricket, never free from diabolical intrigue.

As coach, he shielded young Sachin Tendulkar and Vinod Kambli as much from themselves as others. They were allowed to pull his leg, but he knew when to rein them in. He also protected Mohammed Azharuddin, hugely vulnerable as captain, against the growing ambitions of rivals in the dressing room.

Wadekar lacked the glamour of Pataudi, and the stats and star value of a Gavaskar, Kapil Dev or Tendulkar, but, the true import of what he achieved only grows with time.

Ayaz Memon (@cricketwallah) is a sports journalist and commentator.

70

Cricket: 'It took over your life. Now there is no escape'. – *Getty Images*

Abstinence

RAHUL BHATTACHARYA

There are good reasons to not watch cricket. It is just that acting on these reasons is difficult. Readers of the *Almanack* are only too aware of the nature of the disease. What started as a fever of passion in youth developed into a chronic condition. It took over your life. Now there is no escape.

There is no need to panic. I recently acquired some experience of not watching cricket and I am here to help.

You might tell yourself, innocently, I will not watch cricket. Banish the thought! Cricket has enough in its arsenal to defeat you. Its *brahmastra* is the 'calendar'. Back in your day, people rarely used this word. Back in your day, the thing now called a calendar was not a multiplying, metastasising organism totally at odds with the stability of a calendar. Formats may get shorter and shorter, disappearing towards nothing, but the feat of the calendar is to not follow. The calendar grows bigger and bigger and bigger.

You should recognise early on that except for the utterly disillusioned, nobody willingly renounces watching cricket. If you are reading this publication, you are not one of the utterly disillusioned. You may have grievances and irritations, but you have managed to take everything from Giles Clarke to Gurunath Meiyappan in your stride. For you, choosing not to watch cricket is as inadvisable as a reckless divorce. At the moment of exercising your choice, you may feel the rush of triumph. By the time the bureaucracy of separation takes effect, regret, remorse, self-loathing and desperation will have made a wreck of you. So don't choose to not watch cricket.

The most sensible way to not watch cricket is having it forced on yourself. You will need to find circumstances that are beyond your control. In my case, it was all the fault of a house-move so bungled and prolonged it required a house-move within the house-move. Conceded, arranging a bungled house-move to not watch cricket is more effort than you bargained for. Consider other means to achieving your ends.

When you boil it down, there are two principal conditions for not watching cricket: You must not have access to a television, and you must have limited access to the internet. You could accidentally cause your TV to fall and break. You could, in a blaze of absent-mindedness, snip off your broadband cable and use it to tie up your old newspapers. Televisions nowadays cost as much as cars, and the hold-time at your internet service provider's call centre will be approximately nine weeks, so it is likely you will be stuck with your new circumstances for a while.

If you live in a house of more than one person, there could be domestic consequences arising from your accidents with the television and the internet. Consider escalating the emotional upheaval caused by these. To successfully not watch cricket, there must be enough on your mind to not just occupy but overwhelm you.

Once you have created the conditions for not watching cricket, be prepared for the consequences. Do not think there won't be separation anxiety, for there will. This is where your limited internet connectivity comes in. If your internet connection is world-class, your not watching of cricket cannot succeed. Everything streams, legally, illegally, and you will hunt it down. You will contract malware, spyware, virus, fungi. If you attempt to not watch cricket while in possession of a good internet connection, you are better off trying to watch cricket.

A bad internet connection, however, is essential for managing separation anxiety and its close cousin, FOMO, the Fear Of Missing Out. A bad internet connection can be defined as one that allows you to follow scores, read reports and outrage, look at Fawad Alam and Rohit Sharma memes, and view video clips of extraordinary, controversial and moronic events, which can sometimes magically converge in a single Cameron Bancroft GIF. I suggest you spare no effort is obtaining internet connectivity that is exactly the right shade of bad. If you live in India, perhaps the data on your phone is perfectly calibrated to the task; else consider switching providers. Otherwise fish out that old dongle you purchased a decade ago and never used or threw away. The dongle level of badness is ideal for your purposes.

Remember, it is important to time your not watching cricket right. Do not stop watching cricket, say, in the middle of the World Cup, unless it is 2007. As a rule of thumb, try to ensure that your forced separation from cricket does not coincide with your main team of interest playing in your main format of interest. It so happened that my cricket abstinence fell between two India Test series, and you could find similar favour with your accidents.

You will observe that once you have completed a short period of not watching cricket, a medium period will not feel all that daunting. You will not rush to fix up your accidentally damaged television and internet connection as quickly as you had anticipated. With some amount of self-coaching, you may realise that not watching cricket is a strategy practised by substantial parts of the human world. Bombing out of the 2007 World Cup, the Indian team sought consolation in the phrase, "No one gives a f**k in China." This is China we are talking about. If they run the world and don't give four letters about cricket, there could be something to it.

Since at any time withdrawal symptoms can prove overpowering, consider maintaining cricket alternatives to not watching cricket. I would have recommended playing cricket, but indulging your delusions of grandeur will lead you straight towards watching it. You could read every page of every previous edition of this book, although that could get in the way of your plans for In Search of Lost Time, which you had carefully saved for the period of your life when you were not watching cricket.

I was able to maintain certain cricket habits through my day job of commissioning and editing extremely detailed cricket articles. I do not believe taking up a job in cricket will necessarily help you meet your goal — unless you already have a job in cricket, in which case the excitement will not overwhelm you. So, all things considered, I recommend organising yourself a job in cricket a few years in advance of your forced leave from cricket.

The whole idea is to help you. If you can organise yourself a torrid house move, or accidentally destroy your television and partially damage your internet, during the period your team is not playing your format, while holding down a job in cricket that you have already held for some years, then, with some inspiration from Chinese philosophy, you too, friend, can not watch cricket.

Rahul Bhattacharya is the author of Pundits from Pakistan *and* The Sly Company of People Who Care.

How the fixing probe unfolded

R K RAGHAVAN

The crisis facing cricket today is very different and far more sinister than the 'Bodyline' controversy. Cricket, as it is played at present, does not appear to be the same game played by Sir Don Bradman or what Neville Cardus wrote about … The romanticism associated with the game is perhaps gone forever. Increasingly, in the playing fields around the world, the music of sweetly timed strokes is being replaced by the harsh cacophony of ringing cell phones.

— The Central Bureau of Investigation (2000) in its final report
to Government of India on the match-fixing scam

When I took over as the head of the CBI in January 1999, little did I imagine that my new and prestigious assignment was going to reconnect me with a sport that no longer excited me as much as it did in my youth. I was surprised when I was directed by the then government to probe the manipulation of cricket matches by a few players for money. The alleged scam had caused dismay to cricket lovers. Suddenly, players who had till then been the darlings of millions in India became 'crooks'. Many Indians could not reconcile themselves to this painful transformation of a sport that had given them joy for so long.

It is in this charged atmosphere that the CBI took up the complaint of large-scale irregularities in cricket matches.

Astonished as I was by the turn of events, I initially argued with the government that the alleged misdeeds of a few cricketers did not warrant a CBI enquiry. I was overruled because the government had already told the parliament that it would conduct a enquiry. Since, *prima facie*, no 'public servant' (as defined by the Criminal Procedure Code and Indian Penal Code) was a suspect in the chain of events under probe, I took the decision to be content with a preliminary enquiry (PE), which was short of a criminal investigation, and stood on a par with an administrative action to ferret out facts.

Ravi Sawani, joint director in the CBI (equivalent to an inspector general in the state police), and his team were initially entrusted with the task. If the CBI's ultimate findings passed muster with the outside world, it was due to the focused energies of this dedicated group. They also received support from another top CBI officer, Neeraj Kumar, joint director, who was on deputation to the CBI from the Delhi police and had been tipped off about the scam by one of his contacts.

His contact put Neeraj (who retired as the Delhi police chief and was until recently head of the anti-corruption bureau of the Board of Control for Cricket in India) on to an M K Gupta, who, by his own admission, emerged as the mastermind in the underworld of betting and fixing of international cricket matches.

At a Delhi hotel, M K gave Neeraj a graphic account of the illegal activity. It is not clear why he was keen to confess to his misdeeds. It is possible that he was rattled by the furore in the media and the CBI taking up the investigation, and he figured the long arm of the law would reach him sooner rather than later. He agreed to sing on an informal promise that he would not receive the usual rough police treatment that he had heard about.

M K's admissions and subsequent CBI enquiries revealed beyond doubt that at least four prominent cricketers, Ajay Sharma, Ajay Jadeja, Mohammad Azharuddin and Manoj Prabhakar, benefited from the cash and kind offered by M K and a few other bookies known to him, who operated independently. That the likes of Azharuddin subsequently got something of a reprieve, mainly on technical grounds, is not relevant to my story.

The CBI took over the enquiry in May 2000. Within months, formal and informal questioning of suspects and their associates, as well as assiduous examination of telephone records, unearthed some sensational facts. The CBI subjected the findings to legal scrutiny to decide on further course of action, including the registration of a case under the Indian Penal Code.

The acts of misconduct on the part of the offending cricketers included passing on to bookies information such as the nature of the wicket, the likely team composition and weather conditions. The most galling aspect of the nexus between the underworld and some active cricketers was the ready willingness of a few of them to under-perform. Also agreed upon were the number of runs that a bowler would concede in a match, and the number of times he would bowl a no-ball. Particularly outrageous was the involvement

R K Raghavan was at the helm when the CBI began investigations into irregularities.

of support staff, like the physiotherapist of the Indian team and the curator of the Delhi cricket ground.

Another revelation was the decision of the Delhi Ranji Trophy team to 'throw' a match because a few in the team were desperate to leave for England to play league cricket there. Here there was possibly no dishonest intent to make a quick buck at the cost of the game.

I was also amused when one former India captain met me at home to complain that one of his successors was also guilty of the same misdeeds that the four named had committed, but had not been hauled up by the CBI. I was both shocked and amused. I don't think the distinguished complainant was satisfied when I told him that we did probe his adversary but found nothing against him. This alone highlighted how at the top of the game there was so much animosity.

CBI's legal team specifically looked into whether, by agreeing to perform certain acts on and off the field, the players under the lens influenced the outcome of a game, and thereby committed the offence of 'cheating' as defined in the IPC. The victims here were not only the State, but also the spectators who had paid to buy tickets for the matches with the belief that every player would perform to his optimum ability.

The CBI looked at the contract between the players and the BCCI. The document did not reveal any explicit promise by a cricketer that he would do a certain act and that he could be hauled up if he did not do so. There was no specific code of conduct, breach of which entailed criminal action.

CBI consulted legal luminaries as eminent as Harish Salve, former Solicitor General of India, and Justice M K Mukherjee, formerly of the Supreme Court of India. They weren't convinced that the players in question had committed a crime.

Legal opinion was that the evidence collected by the CBI did not warrant taking the matter to a court of law, and it was far-fetched to say that the paying public had been 'cheated'. There was no misrepresentation to the public or receipt of money or any other 'valuable security' by the players for doing an act prohibited by law, which could have attracted the provisions of the IPC or any other law. Two of the cricketers involved in this scandal were, by a little stretch of the imagination, 'public servants', who could have been charge-sheeted under the IPC, if they had committed illegal acts. But the evidence did not indicate that they were on a cricket field in the discharge of their public duties. Nor did they commit any act that bordered on illegality.

Ultimately, the CBI was content with sending the final report to the BCCI and the sports ministry, for such action as they deemed fit. On public demand, the CBI report was uploaded on the web. This was an unusual decision, but it enhanced the CBI's credibility and transparency.

Looking back, nearly 20 years after the event, I am satisfied that we did a reasonable job, especially because we kept a low profile. We handled the cricketers well. We enjoyed such independence that we could ignore the representation made on behalf of a cricketer whom we indicted and who had married into a well-connected political family. The event showed that the CBI could be trusted to handle an unusual and sensitive enquiry responsibly.

It is unfortunate that credible reports of irregularities committed by young cricketers have again surfaced. Going by experience, we cannot ignore speculation. Any complacence by the BCCI will prove ruinous to a great game.

RK Raghavan is a former CBI Director.

A law for the fix

NANDAN KAMATH

"Integrity is doing the right thing even when no one is watching," goes a popular saying. In sport, it involves doing it when many millions are!

Indian cricket is no stranger to performance integrity issues involving match participants. What began as manipulation of results involving the throwing of entire matches — known broadly as 'match-fixing' — progressively became more sophisticated, involving the manipulation of segments and phases of play and even specific and singular incidents — commonly termed 'session fixing' and 'spot fixing', respectively. This market reform, if it is appropriate to call it that, was driven by increasing surveillance of players and officials, the live broadcast of matches, and the greater sophistication of the formal and informal (read, illegal) betting markets, among other factors. This remains an active, ongoing cat and mouse game, reminiscent of Tom and Jerry (and we know who usually wins there).

Match manipulation sits in plain sight of Indian cricket administrators as well as the country's legislators. It has been seated there for over two decades, perhaps longer. Yet, not a single cricketer or official has been successfully prosecuted (although they have faced punishment).

Ironically, the biggest fallout of a fixing incident has been on the game's administrators at the Board of Control for Cricket in India. The governing body's apparent unwillingness to independently and fairly evaluate the IPL 2013 spot fixing (involving players such as former Indian international S Sreesanth) and illegal betting cases (involving IPL team owners and officials as perpetrators) opened the door for the highest courts of the land to intervene and first appoint the Justice Mudgal committee and, eventually, the Justice Lodha committee, to evaluate these infractions and then suggest appropriate punishment. This ballooned into the most significant judicial intervention in Indian sports administration, with wide-ranging reforms being imposed on the BCCI.

The Supreme Court, espousing the primary interest of the cricket fan in sports governance, took judicial notice of the Lodha committee's unambiguous view that fixing was "neither pardonable nor a matter for regulation" and that the only way to deal with it was to make it a criminal offence punishable by law, with a recommendation to the legislature to make amendments. The Law Commission of India in its Report No.276 on Gambling and Sports Betting Including in Cricket in India made an identical recommendation. Despite wide-ranging consensus in the recommendations of these key bodies, there has been no sign of any such legislative action.

That is not to say that there has been a void of initiatives to criminalise match manipulation in India over the years. The two most recent attempts were the Prevention of Sporting Fraud Bill (2013), which was drafted at the behest of the government of the day, and the National Sports Ethics Commission Bill (2016), which was a private member's bill. Both were responses to public calls for action. That neither Bill has made headway in Parliament suggests the lack of political will and a sense of urgency.

This reality raises several questions. What are the parameters and standards of 'deliberate underperformance' in sport? In a country where betting is illegal, who are the 'victims' of match manipulation and what is their tangible 'loss'? As the Indian cricket economy continues to grow despite legislative inaction, is this really a 'legal' issue or merely a 'fan management' prerogative? Finally, when must laws of the state intervene in matters that can potentially be dealt with by internal codes of sport?

Answering these is a bit like opening the batting on a green-top on a cold, cloudy day. That said, batting in tough conditions is a challenge that many look forward to and it is this attitude that we must carry into the debate on fixing.

Competitive sport is premised on participants playing to win and always doing their best to arrive at the best result. For the longest time, this was seen as self-evident and did not need codification. The 'spirit of sport' matched the expectation of participants, administrators, audiences and other stakeholders like broadcasters and sponsors. As challenges arose and this pact wore rough around its edges, codes of conduct emerged. Governing bodies began drafting into these codes the responsibility of participants to always give their best and not be influenced by external persons and factors in terms of their on-field conduct. Of course, it must be clarified that there are many instances in which it is in a player's or team's strategic self-interest to ease off for a phase of a match, regain energy, allow an opponent to dominate a segment of play, find an easier path in a tournament draw. The term 'match manipulation' does not (and should not) extend to such conduct when undertaken in good faith. However, it does (and should) extend to deliberate underperformance that is based on a prior agreement with a third party for financial or other non-sporting gain.

It is also worth noting that manipulation does not always determine or influence end results of matches. This often leads to normative dissonance in the minds of sports participants: Was anyone really hurt by that minor dalliance?

The search for a victim of match manipulation is a frustrating one. Is it the team-mates, the fans, the governing body, sponsors, broadcasters? It is anyone at all? This is a dead-end that numerous attempts to prosecute match-fixing under existing Indian criminal law have also encountered. In practice, the existing general criminal laws in India are severely limited in their applicability to matters of participant integrity. For example, offences in the nature of 'cheating' require a victim to be 'deceived' in a manner that causes such person "damage or harm in body, mind, reputation or property". Prosecutors have found it difficult, if not impossible, to prove these elements. It is particularly challenging to identify a victim and the damage or harm caused to him or her.

It doesn't help that betting is, thus far, illegal in India and punters cannot be the putative victims — a legal route that has been successfully used in other jurisdictions such as the UK where match manipulation is also not a standalone offence. For example, the spot fixing sting investigation involving Pakistan Test players Salman Butt, Mohammad Asif and Mohammad Amir culminated in the players being found guilty of conspiracy to cheat at gambling and to accept corrupt payments under the country's Gambling Act of 2005.

The legal void in India has led to players such as Sreesanth and the others accused of IPL spot fixing in 2013 being accused of violating laws relating to organised crime (in this case the Maharashtra Control of Organised Crime Act, 1999), on the claim that they have conspired with the underworld to commit an offence. This is more out of compulsion than choice and such claims have received limited judicial sympathy, especially as the bar is high to prove that the accused players were aware of the involvement of the underworld in the specific case.

Mohammad Azharuddin: A big name at the centre of the match-fixing investigation.
– Getty Images

The lack of a clear substantive offence of match manipulation also creates significant limitations in criminal procedure, of investigation and evidence gathering — keys to effectively prosecuting offences. In any case, administrative bodies that police sport within the governing bodies (such as Anti-Corruption Units) do not have legal powers of search and investigation. Those state bodies that do have these powers are often unable to exercise them effectively given the ambiguous status of match manipulation as a nominated criminal offence.

As mentioned earlier, there have been thoughtful attempts to outline the parameters of the crime of match manipulation. The two Bills mentioned earlier have detailed and carefully worded definitions.

The Prevention of Sports Fraud Bill defined 'sporting fraud' to include (i) manipulation of sports results, irrespective of whether the outcome is actually altered or not, or deliberate misapplication of the rules of the sport, in order to obtain any economic/other advantage or benefits, and any acts resulting in the removal or reduction of all or part of the uncertainty normally associated with the results of a sporting event, (ii) the wilful failure to perform to true potential, unless such underperformance can be attributed to strategic or tactical

Who's the victim of match manipulation?: Is it the team-mates, the fans, the governing body, sponsors, broadcasters? – *Getty Images*

reasons, (iii) disclosure of inside information to any person, with the knowledge that such disclosure is likely to result in financial gain or is likely to be used in relation to betting or manipulation, and (iv) the failure to appropriately report information as to the commission of any of the aforesaid offences. The Bill also delineated abetment to sports fraud as a criminal offence, which means that the entire system including bookies and their agents are within the proposed legal net. It proposed in this Bill that the crime of sports fraud be punished with imprisonment of terms that extended to five years and significant fines that could extend to five times the economic benefit derived from the sports fraud.

The National Sports Ethics Commission Bill similarly defined 'match-fixing' to include instances where a sports participant (i) receives money to underperform, (ii) bets in athletic competitions in which he/she plays or influences a decision that naturally undermines the performance, (iii) passes information to a betting syndicate about team composition, probable result or any other insider information regarding the sports, (iv) is given money to prepare a pitch in a way which suits a betting syndicate; and (v) is used by bookies to gain access to Indian and foreign players to influence their performance for a monetary consideration.

Unlike the Prevention of Sports Fraud Bill, this Bill positioned only the player, coach or a member of the sports federation as potential perpetrators, thereby not recognising the abetment and facilitation of such offences by others outside the system as offences. It proposed that the crime of match-fixing be punished with imprisonment of a minimum of ten years and significant fines that could extend to five times the economic benefit derived by the perpetrator from the 'match-fixing'.

The thrust of both Bills is a wide definition of sports fraud and match-fixing as standalone criminal offences. The extent and nature of punishment also suggest deterrence as well as a disgorgement of unjust gains. More importantly, both these Bills are already fully drafted and close to ready for passage by the legislature after appropriate debate. The only remaining ingredient is political will.

*

What is unambiguous is Indian cricket's continued commercial growth. Media rights and sponsorship values continue to grow exponentially, more or less turning a blind eye to issues of participant integrity. This is simply a factor of the continued growth of the cricket audience, in a country that is still far from saturated. For every fan that questions the authenticity of matches and votes with her eyes, there are still a hundred new ones that will readily turn up to watch the game.

It is the size of the still underserved audience that papers over the deep cracks that lie beneath. This also reflects in how the BCCI have handled the match manipulation cases that have come before them. First, it is noteworthy that a majority, if not all, of those who have served 'bans' have been 'caught' by the police or in media 'sting operations' and not by the governing body's Anti-Corruption Unit. Upon being presented with the evidence by investigating authorities, they have been forced to act and invoke disciplinary proceedings. Bans they have imposed have been struck down by courts on ground of natural justice — that the BCCI did not follow due process in its disciplinary proceedings. This judicial intervention on procedural grounds has been publicly presented by players as 'proof of innocence', a rather creative interpretation of 'innocent until proven guilty'. A prime example of such a case is that of former captain Mohammad Azharuddin. That the BCCI chose to not appeal the verdict and effectively rehabilitated players like him back into the system does not present its administrators as taking these matters particularly seriously.

That not a single incident has come to light, at least in recent memory, where the BCCI has itself found and publicised an instance of match manipulation means that these matters, if and when identified, are probably being handled privately at the administrative level and away from the public gaze. This is at a time when there is more technology available than ever before to monitor match manipulation attempts. When everything is going swimmingly on the commercial front, perhaps it is not seen as very wise to add new waves and counter-currents?

In such a scenario, where the governing body appears to be managing the optics rather than addressing the disease, the clamour for a public law to intervene only grows louder. Cricket's administrators may not see it now, or for a few years or even decades, but at some point, Indian cricket's commercial wishing well will start drying up and this will give pause for them to wistfully look back and ponder — if only we had taken the threat of fixing more seriously! This is not dissimilar to the way the legal response to 'insider trading' in the securities markets evolved — from originally being termed as a 'victimless crime' it soon received its deserved recognition as a serious crime threatening the integrity of capital markets.

As Indian cricket (and sport) continues its onward march, its greatest long-term currency will remain public trust and confidence. These take decades to build and require only seconds to destroy. The sacred bond between athlete and fan underlies great sporting ecosystems — shared identities, beliefs and dreams make elite sport the spectacle that it is. A public law criminalising match manipulation is critical to protect this bond and the sense of fair play and confidence in competitive sport in India. Criminalising an act enables the creation of new norms, recognises public trust as an item of value and presents the opportunity to punish and deter those that might pollute the well they drink from. Unfortunately, our current practices, attitudes and laws are just not good enough.

Nandan Kamath (@nandankamath) is the principal lawyer at LawNK, which specialises in sports, technology and media law, and trustee at GoSports Foundation.

WISDEN INDIA ALMANACK HALL OF FAME

Gundappa Viswanath

SURESH MENON

Gundappa Viswanath is the quintessential Indian batsman, all wristy grace and mischief, eastern magic and unattainability. Indians of his generation liked their sporting heroes to be modest, self-effacing men with a touch of nobility about them. In Viswanath, they found the mix that might make him seem today like a character out of fiction. So much talent and so unassertive?

He was the equal of any batsman in the game, a modern-day Trumper whose statistics didn't hint at the enormous joy he brought to spectators everywhere. An average of nearly 42 over 91 Tests suggests a commendable disdain for padding the figures with easy runs when there was no real challenge. India never lost a Test when Viswanath made a century, and he made 14 of them, beginning with his debut 137 against Australia in Kanpur in 1969-70, where, as a 20-year-old, he struck 25 boundaries.

Trinidad, Melbourne, Lord's, Kolkata and Faisalabad all witnessed classic centuries. His unbeaten 97 against a rampaging Andy Roberts in Chennai in 1974-75 must rate as one of the greatest ever innings under 100.

As Tony Cozier wrote: "The sight of any fast bowler repeatedly beating the batsman with sheer speed is always an exciting phenomenon. For him to be confronted by a batsman equally hostile and belligerent is the stuff of which cricket followers' dreams are made. (Viswanath) met force with force in an amazing display."

Viswanath himself preferred the century he made in the previous Test in Kolkata, saying he had to occasionally bat out of character there. In either case, the scores formed the basis of India's victories after trailing 0-2 in the series.

But to discuss Viswanath in terms of runs and averages would be like reducing Michelangelo to the number of brush strokes or square inches per canvas. Viswanath was a throwback to an era in cricket when style was everything, success incidental. Such an era did not exist, of course, despite the claims of romantics, but we like to pretend it did. Sport affords us that luxury.

Viswanath was the sportsman's sportsman, with a character and temperament that brought lustre to the game, which, when he was batting or captaining, exhibited its best facet. He brought out the best behaviour in people too.

In an era when success is merely a set of figures properly arranged, and anything beyond that is seen as unnecessary, a hankering after aesthetic significance may sound strange. For sheer beauty we are yet to see anything to match a late cut or a leg glance or indeed the patented square cut by Viswanath. Often, this was beauty made thrilling by danger, of the prospect of dismissal. He often got his eye in by playing the kind of shots an average batsman never produces in a lifetime. Like a cat, he never made angles to the wind.

Sunil Gavaskar rated Viswanath higher than himself because he had more shots for every delivery. Ranji, the spiritual father of the wristy, stylish Indian batsman, batted as if he had "no bones" — a description that fit Viswanath equally.

GUNDAPPA RANGANATH VISWANATH was born on February 12, 1949 in Bhadravathi, some 250 kilometres north of Bengaluru. He had his baptism in tennis-ball cricket matches in Visvesvarapuram, where he lived as a boy. He played three or four matches a day before the organisers put a stop to cricket's version of simultaneous chess by forcing him to focus on one match. It was at Fort High School in Bengaluru that he was introduced to proper cricket. At 18, he was mature enough to score a double-century on debut for Karnataka against Andhra. It was a stunning message for those in authority, who felt he was too small to play serious cricket.

"I didn't play state schools cricket at all," he once said, "I heard that I was kept out because I was too thin or too small or too ugly. One of the selectors told me later that he was scared I would get hurt and everybody would blame him." That's a typical Viswanath reaction to disappointment: No malice, merely a shrug of his shoulders and self-deprecating humour.

Viswanath soon grew to become Bengaluru's best-known icon, as dependable as the Vidhana Soudha, as approachable as Cubbon Park. He was the magician with the human touch, exhibiting the best the game had to offer through strokeplay touched by the angels.

In a tribute in the 1970s in *The Indian Express*, N S Ramaswami wrote: "Viswanath's spiritual ancestors were the makers of Belur and Halebid. They carved infinitely graceful sculptures; he creates breathtakingly beautiful cricket strokes. Had he lived in the 11th or 12th centuries, he would have been as great a sculptor as any of those who have carved their names in some of the Hoysala temples."

Such tributes tend to embarrass Viswanath, who is a simple man, happiest when among old friends from his club or Ranji playing days.

Viswanath was that rare sportsman — beloved of colleagues and opponents alike. In Mumbai, when he made his second Test century, England's Tony Greig picked him up in his arms and cradled him to the full-throated approval of a packed house. It was in Mumbai some seven years later that Viswanath, now captain of India, recalled England's Bob Taylor after the umpire had given him out. It cost India the match, as Taylor and Ian Botham put on 171 runs, but it earned the team a reputation for playing to a higher set of rules than required by the scorebook. The Indian team was merely reflecting its captain's philosophy of fair-mindedness. How you played the game was important.

Only four of Viswanath's centuries were made abroad, which might explain the reluctance of his critics to speak of him in the same breath as his brother-in-law Gavaskar. "I have seldom been a very consistent performer, whether in a three-Test or a five-Test series. I tended to take chances," Viswanath once admitted of Gavaskar. On the 1971 tour of England, Brian Johnston thought Viswanath was the more complete batsman, but risk-takers are seldom consistent even if they author memorable innings.

By the '82-83 tour of Pakistan, Viswanath's easy going lifestyle had begun to tell on the field of play. He was not yet 34 and remained a fine catcher at slip, but when in the Karachi Test he was bowled by an Imran Khan inswinger which came in like a throw from the covers, the message was clear: his international career was over. Viswanath played on for another four seasons, relying on the adjustments he had made in the latter part of his career. He switched guard to the middle stump and consciously began to play straight. The natural brilliance of his early days had been replaced by a thoughtful compromise.

In the nearly four decades since Viswanath retired, other middle-order batsmen have made more runs for India, played more Tests, been part of more victories. But none have had his unique combination of heart and wrist. He didn't just patently enjoy his game, he communicated it to the spectators. "Vishy", they called him, like he was a dear friend. Which he remains, to everybody who saw him play.

Career statistics

	M	Inns	R	HS	Ave	100/50	Wkt
Tests	91	155	6080	222	41.93	14/35	1
ODIs	25	23	439	75	19.95	0/2	0
First-class	308	486	17970	247	40.93	44/89	15
List A	59	57	1463	108*	27.09	1/9	4

HALL OF FAME: Lala Amarnath — *Getty Images*

HALL OF FAME: Gundappa Viswanath

CRICKETER OF THE YEAR: Jasprit Bumrah — *Getty Images*

CRICKETER OF THE YEAR: Smriti Mandhana — *BCCI*

CRICKETER OF THE YEAR: Mayank Agarwal — *Getty Images*

CRICKETER OF THE YEAR: Fakhar Zaman – *Getty Images*

CRICKETER OF THE YEAR: Dimuth Karunaratne — *Getty Images*

CRICKETER OF THE YEAR: Rashid Khan — *Getty Images*

An emotional Afghanistan joined the group of Test-playing nations when they were hosted by India in Bengaluru for their inaugural Test. India's Salim Durani (below), who until then was believed to be the only Afghanistan-born player in Test cricket, was a guest of honour. — *BCCI*

It was a proud moment for Ireland when they played their maiden Test against Pakistan at Malahide. — *Getty Images*

The Prithvi Shaw-led India Under-19 side, coached by Rahul Dravid, beat Australia to lift the ICC Under-19 World Cup 2018 trophy in New Zealand. – *Getty Images*

Australia Women lifted their fourth Women's World T20 title with a win against England in the final in a packed stadium in Antigua. — ICC

Nobel Prize winner Malala Yousafzai joined the festivities at the World Cup opening party. — *ICC*

Harmanpreet Kaur was out for 51 off 37 balls, with seven still to get off four. Then, a boundary off the last ball took the Supernovas over the line for a thrilling finish to the second Women's T20 Challenge. – *BCCI*

England lifted the World Cup after a final decided by the slightest of margins: they won by boundary count after the teams were tied after regulation time as well as the Super Over. — *Getty Images*

The ten-team World Cup began in England in the summer of 2019 with much fanfare. — ICC

England tried to force a result in the last moments of the Second Test against New Zealand in Christchurch, but the hosts held on for a draw. — *Getty Images*

Alastair Cook signed off with a hundred and got a guard of honour from the Indian team. — *Getty Images*

WISDEN INDIA ALMANACK HALL OF FAME

Lala Amarnath

SHAMYA DASGUPTA

It was Hardik Pandya's third Test, Sri Lanka the opposition, Pallekele the stage. The very image of the modern-day cricketer, brash, cocksure, aggressive, Pandya scored his first Test century, 108 off 96 balls, in 163 minutes.

The 100th run had come off the 86th ball he had faced, in around 150 minutes.

This was in August 2017. Cut back to December 1933, and there was an Indian all-rounder who scored a Test century too. A more historic one — India's first in Tests. That man was Lala Amarnath. Among the bowlers in the opposition was the fabled Hedley Verity. It was the second innings at Bombay Gymkhana. That century came in 117 minutes, historian Anandji Dossa has noted.

Amarnath was nothing like the go-getting player of today. His place on the cricket field was, to a large extent, thanks to the benevolence of the Maharaja of Patiala. That's how things were then. India was not an independent nation yet. The match was against the rulers, England. Subservience, unless one answered to the name of M K Gandhi or S C Bose or of the many outstanding men and women who birthed India, was the norm.

Not on the cricket field that day. Not for Lala Amarnath.

It was the sort of attitude that made him a legend. And got him into trouble so often. It was what made him who he was — 'Lala'. Not Nanik Amarnath Bharadwaj, the name he was born with. But Lala. Just Lala.

*

The 'stormy petrel' of Indian cricket, the 'enfant terrible'. Someone who likes a scrap and often attracts one. An unconventional, somewhat controversial character. Was there more to him, though? How often have we put Lala in these little boxes and left him there?

The problem is that all the literature on him is either pro-Lala or anti-Lala. The man seems to stir up strong feelings. So there is no complete picture of him. For instance, his youngest son Rajinder's

The Making of a Legend, while full of excellent titbits, is so reverential that you begin to wonder.

Of course, there are the tales. Bowling off the wrong foot — he did jump off the wrong foot, videos prove. And more: sent back from England by his captain, the duplicitous Vizzy, for insubordination in 1936; batsman, bowler, captain, hero, saying-it-like-it-is administrator, selector, champion of women's cricket at a time when it was far from fashionable, commentator; a tyrant of a father whose sons had no way out of becoming cricketers; India's first Test centurion, of course.

They fill in some of the gaps, but not enough. And, really, how good a cricketer was he, beyond the highlights of his career?

The few times this reporter met him, Lala was close to leaving for the great pitch up in the sky. He was past his pink years, quiet, affectionate. But that was age, surely? Because Lala's speech, as is legend, was peppered with a liberal dose of expletives, in Punjabi — which Vizzy, among others, was perhaps subjected to — and in English — which Vizzy, among others, was perhaps subjected to as well. Not to say he wasn't affectionate and all that, of course. In fact, every single person who went into his good books has spoken of his big Punjabi heart.

He loved to talk and had a seemingly unending reservoir of stories. He loved the game and thought a lot about it. But he also felt he knew best. Did he? He certainly knew a fair bit, and people as venerated as Sir Don Bradman have vouched for it. Of course, when it came to the stories he told, each of them had him in the lead.

Former cricketers, one of them among the oldest surviving Indian Test cricketers and another who encountered the old man during their days in Delhi cricket, think back to Lala with blinkers on. It's all water under the bridge now, after all.

But poke and prod a bit, and it comes out. "All bluster, he thought he was the boss," says one. "It was his way or the highway," says the other. "He was arrogant and egotistic. A bluffer."

Did he at least have the good of the game, of Indian cricket, at heart? The oldest of the lot says yes, "definitely". The second is positive Lala saw more than the average Joe — or Sharma — did. A third, very senior, cricketer is doubtful.

There is evidence enough that he thought out of the box.

"His handling of the Indian team in Australia in 1947-48 was masterly," wrote Wally Hammond.

Arthur Mailey wrote after the same series, "His knowledge of Australian pitches is superior to Bradman's."

His record on that tour is the stuff of — with due apologies — legend.

A story Rajinder writes about, and the elderly cricketer remembers, is of Lala's con job on umpires. He wouldn't appeal for plumb lbws, shaking his head when his team-mates went up, and once the umpire was convinced that he only appealed when sanguine, up went Lala, even for clear not-outs, usually when the best opposition batsman was in. Out! It worked more than once.

An octogenarian cricket watcher, who was at Eden Gardens when Pakistan visited in 1952 — it was Lala's last Test — firmly uses the words 'cricket sense' to describe his game: "The Pakistani tail-enders were stepping out to [G S] Ramchand, so the captain [Lala] asked Prabir Sen [the wicketkeeper], to come up to the stumps. They had a chat, because Ramchand was pretty quick. But the captain wanted Prabir Sen up. And both batsmen [Mahmood Hussain and Amir Elahi] were dismissed immediately." Hussain was stumped by Sen, while Elahi was caught behind. Off Ramchand.

There are many stories of Lala, the captain, making unorthodox calls. Sometimes, they didn't come off. More often, they did. All of this added to the myth around the man who strutted the playing fields of India like a colossus, and didn't take too many backward steps when abroad either.

He played the journalism and commentary games much the same way.

The lasting image of Lala for the generations that didn't watch him play is of an elderly man, hair coloured black, usually in a suit and tie, sometimes a hat on — impeccable in C&A shirts and Marks & Spencer jackets — and always, absolutely always, with a pipe between his teeth. He didn't take it out while commentating on radio or TV either. Listeners heard him say, pride bursting through every breath, "My shaun Mohinder has played that …" and knew the pipe was in place.

His way. If he wanted the pipe, he'd have it. Rajinder writes that the tobacco came from England too.

Take the story veteran Pakistani journalist Qamar Ahmed is fond of telling, and retelling. The 1982 India tour of Pakistan. Lala, the honorary Pakistani, was on the tour as a journalist for a news agency. He was expected to send daily match reports. Lala, and a match report? It had to be his expert opinion or zilch. It couldn't be zilch, of course.

Lala's employers called back baffled; Lala, equally baffled, and angry, responded with his brand of pleasantries. "I had to write it," laughs Ahmed, then a reporter for a rival news agency. Only the first day. Lala figured it out after that.

*

For this writer, who was just starting out as a journalist when the grand old man passed away in 2000, Lala was an enigma. A man of so many parts that it would take a Sherlock Holmes to put them all together. Even Holmes might end up with more than the sum of the parts.

Everyone who saw him play had paeans to sing about him, but his record shows 878 runs and 45 wickets from 24 Tests. Yes, many years were lost to one reason or another, but still. Then again, 10,426 runs and 463 wickets in first-class cricket — ah, now we are talking.

Why was he so iconic? Why did women throw their gold at him? Why is he thought of as the man who freed Indian cricket from the clutches of the princes and their princely states when his very existence, in the early years, was because the Patiala royal was his patron?

How could he terrorise his sons as well as play such a part in making two of them Test cricketers, one a mighty successful one too? Really, how could he get away with as much as he did and remain an icon?

It's probably best not to go by the stories around him. From the ones who celebrated him or the ones who hated him. Many of them, certainly, are apocryphal, and he made many of them up himself.

He was of a time, after all. And he was a pioneer. A truly great cricketer, who perhaps didn't rack up the numbers many others did, but when he turned it on, boy, did he turn it on! And if India is a great cricketing nation now, well, it is so because it has ridden on the shoulder of giants like Lala.

The bluster — well …

A cricketing wizard then? Definitely. Egotistic? Large-hearted? Upright? Yes, yes, yes. The stormy petrel of Indian cricket? Ha! Yes, that too. Flawed, most certainly. Even the hater, who credits Lala's success to "bluffing his way through", says, "He must have worked incredibly hard to be the player he was." A bit of a genius too, one has to accept. Above all, a character of the sort legends are spun from.

Career statistics

	M	Inns	R	Ave	100/50	Wkt	Ave	5w/10w
Tests	24	40	878	24.38	1/4	45	32.91	2/0
First-class	186	286	10,426	41.37	31/39	463	22.98	19/3

Shamya Dasgupta of ESPNcricinfo is author most recently of Don't Disturb the Dead: The Story of the Ramsay Brothers.

El críquet, the other beautiful game

ANDREAS CAMPOMAR

Latin America, not unlike India, likes to deal in the fantastic. Last year, the Belgrano Athletic Club in Buenos Aires hosted two exhibition matches to commemorate the sesquicentenary of the first international sporting contest between Argentina and Uruguay. The sport in question was neither football nor even rugby, but cricket.

I had been invited to play for the Uruguay President's XI against an Argentina Masters XI, a team that included a number of ex-internationals, in the opening fixture. This was not for my cricketing prowess — my best seasons, if they could be called that, were far behind me — but rather my nationality. I was one of the few Uruguayans who understood the game, having been educated at an English boarding school (that singular place has produced two very different Test captains in Douglas Jardine and the Nawab of Pataudi jnr). The invitation was of course accepted with eagerness, though the reservations came later. Would I make the long journey south only to get out cheaply or, as they say, *hacer un papelón* ('make a fool of myself')? Before leaving London, a friend of mine, who has played the game at the highest level, proposed an alternative scenario: "You could go all the way there and not bat at all … now that would be worse than being out first ball."

Buenos Aires is a frenetic yet ethereal city: too European for Latin America; too Latin American for Europe. It feels like a city built in grief; a charming city of lost glories. The Argentine novelist, Leopoldo Marechal, had one of his protagonists explain it thus: "He who has never heard the River Plate's voice will never understand the sadness of Buenos Aires. It is the sadness of mud begging for a soul." In this leafy barrio (neighbourhood), where mock-Tudor villas coexist with the high-rise apartment buildings, the Belgrano Athletic Club remains an island of sporting tranquillity. The late-Victorian clubhouse — a romantic ideal of tiled floors and wood panelling — gives out on to a large oval sward, on which cricket is played in the summer and rugby in the winter months. It comes as no surprise that the cricket historian, Rowland Bowen, took a colonial line when it came to Argentina: "The game takes on much more the aspect it would have had years ago in Australia, or in any other 'white' colony." Of all the Latin American republics, it was here that the British felt most at home.

Before the match, in a somewhat makeshift ceremony, we are given our Uruguay caps. It is a small gesture but one that seems necessary. That I am turning out for Uruguay, especially against Argentina, might just be of one the most bizarre, but strangely rewarding, experiences of my life. There is no thought of victory or defeat: for once taking part is enough.

In the end, the 186-run total posted by the Argentines was always going to be a daunting proposition for an amateur Uruguay side. When our wickets fall in quick succession, I forget that this is a T20 match and attempt to anchor the innings. In a surreal passage of play I am bowled three times. The first of these is illegal: the Argentine wicketkeeper, hungry for a caught behind or a stumping, has his gloves in front of the stumps. Of course much remonstrating with the umpire ensues: this being a variation of Jorge Luis Borges's '*Queja de todo criollo*' ('Every criollo's [Argentine's] Complaint': distrustful and disillusioned from the outset). Fortunately, the English umpire doesn't hold with this idiosyncratic interpretation of the laws of the game. Ever the misnomer, the 'free hit' becomes a

The game grows: A small but passionate group of people has taken to cricket in Argentina. – *Cricket Argentina/Twitter*

sucker punch and I am bowled yet again. The Argentines stand their ground and make a point of not helping the umpire resurrect the fallen stumps. I am reminded that 'fair play' is a fluid term in the Río de la Plata. This small humiliation within a smaller humiliation plays on my conscience: I know I should no longer be at the crease. After much playing and missing, I am out again — bowled. There is a sense of relief mixed with pride. Perhaps here, on this coarse uneven wicket, the two parts of my heritage — my north and my south — have come finally together. Of course, the Argentines win the game easily, beating us by 94 runs.

The main attraction, between squad players of both national teams, is a closer run affair. Uruguay, who came runners-up in the South American Championship last August, field 11 Indian players — Mukherjee, Hidhayathullah, Ravi, Gokul, Krishnan, Kanikanti, Rajat, Sidhant, Khaleel, Ramsoorya and Karthikeyan — all of whom work for the conglomerate Tata and have permanent residency in the country. The match is hard-fought; the balance of power shifting at various stages of the game. Unfortunately for Uruguay, the young Argentine Lautaro Musiani, who has learned his cricket at Rugby School, scores 62 in an elegant and fluid manner. Together with Alejandro Ferguson, he puts on 58 runs to take Argentina's score to a respectable 167 for 4. After losing two early wickets, Mukherjee (41) and Hidhayathullah (30) put on 55 runs that nearly put Uruguay in sight of victory. A rather swift and needless batting collapse in the face of a dearth of overs bestows the laurels on Argentina. The margin is 35 runs.

The day has not been so much a commemoration as a celebration of a sport that continues to be seen as somewhat exotic even in this part of the world. For most Argentines and Uruguayans cricket tends to be grasped in terms of football. I remember a Uruguayan diplomat explaining the rules of the game to a colleague: 'It's very simple, *che*. All you need to know about *el críquet* is that when the ball hits those three little sticks, it's a goal.'

Cricket had in fact been the first team sport the British brought to Latin America. Wherever the British settled, social and sporting clubs were soon established. This was true of the Crown colonies but also of Britain's 'informal' empire (through economic power rather than imperial rule) in Latin America. In 1827, mine owners and businessmen founded the Mexico Cricket Club in Mexico City. Cricket clubs now sprung up across the continent. From Chile to

Brazil, matches were often played in fantastic circumstances; though this was due to the topography (deadly pitches tended to wound unsuspecting batsmen) as well as the phlegm of the British. Even political events, which usually took the form of internecine wars, would not interfere with play. It was not uncommon for matches to be played whilst fighting ensued in the surrounding areas. In the late 1850s, with Buenos Aires under siege, British players petitioned the besieging commander to allow them safe passage to their ground beyond enemy lines. As one contemporary traveller observed: "It was a very risky proceeding for a few men to spend the day surrounded by such characters as might be expected in the rear of Urquiza's army." These clubs and their sports provided a bulwark against the harshness of day-to-day life in a place that was both alien and disorientating for the British.

It was in Argentina, however, that the British established their largest community outside the empire. Although the Buenos Aires Cricket Club was founded in 1831, it took another 30 years before the game became an organised pastime. In 1868, nine years before the inaugural Test match between England and Australia, the Buenos Aires Cricket Club played the Monte Video Cricket Club (MVCC) in the Uruguayan capital, thus engendering one of the most fiercely fought rivalries in sporting history. Of course the players — '11 B. Ayreans *contra* 18 Montevideans' — were all British.

Whereas Uruguay failed to develop a rich cricketing tradition — the country became a stop-off for any English touring side — Argentina's golden age would come between the wars with three first-class tours of the country. The 1926-27 tour, 14 years after Lord Hawke had first taken an MCC team to the region, included PF Warner and Gubby Allen. The third match of four was an improbable victory with Argentina winning by 29 runs in a low-scoring match. The locals had been aided by the changeable weather: a downpour washed "the marl off the wicket, making the sandy soil underneath crumble" and thereby ruining the pitch. In Herbert Dorning, a spin bowler who played for Belgrano, the country even possessed its own 'WG Grace' figure. In 1923, when in his fifties, the Buenos Aires Standard described Dorning alliteratively as "doughty and determined, deemed dangerous, deadly, deep, deliberately deceptive and damaging, and even more dauntless on a damp day." In a long career, he had taken five or more wickets in an innings 22 times.

After the war, as President Juan Domingo Perón began to nationalise the British-owned railways, cricket became a visible symbol of 'informal' imperialism. When the Buenos Aires Cricket Club's pavilion burned down, it was not thought to be the result of bad luck. The club committee had unwisely turned down Evita's request that its grounds be requisitioned for one of her welfare schemes. For Anglo-Argentine community, whose numbers now started to reduce, it was time to become more *criollo* (creole). Even though the rules and terminology had been translated into Spanish by JW Williams in an 1881 pamphlet *La tranca* (batsman becoming '*bateador*' and bowler '*boleador*'), the game could never quite make that transition. Football, on the other hand, had been recast in the country's own image.

That Borges considered football popular because stupidity also tends to be popular is well documented; though this was most likely an antipathy to the blind obsession with which his fellow Argentines followed the game rather than an aesthetic judgement on his part. What is perhaps less well known is that the Anglophile man of letters extended this prejudice to most other sports. During a recorded interview in 1972, Borges failed to show restraint on the matter. "It's strange that England — which I love so much — provokes so much hatred in the world but that nevertheless one argument that could be used is never used against England: that of having filled the world with stupid sports."

While Borges's argument may have been shrewd, he ultimately failed to grasp just how identity could be fashioned through the crucible of sporting success. Neighbouring Uruguay and Brazil had demonstrated this by winning the World Cup on the international stage. The idea had also not been lost on CLR James, who had argued that cricket had offered West Indians entry "into the comity of nations". Even in India, where cricket has become integral to the nation's psyche, football has played a part in shaping regional identity.

In 1854, 13 years before the first official fixture took place in Latin America, the Gentleman of Barrackpore and a Calcutta team of civilians competed in the Indian subcontinent's first football match. By the end of the 19th century, the game, which had become especially popular in Bengal and Kerala, changed from a British-only, club-based sport to one played by the locals. For Bengalis, who after the Indian Mutiny were racialised as being untrustworthy and inferior, the physical game was used as the conduit for nationalist sentiment and anti-British subversion. In one of his lectures, Swami Vivekananda emphasised its importance: "Be strong ... You will

In different circumstances, perhaps football and not cricket might have become India's sport. – *Dipanker Dutta/ CC-BY dipu87*

be nearer to heaven through football than through the study of the Gita." After Mohun Bagan secured a famous victory over the East Yorkshire Regiment in the 1911 IFA Shield final, the match became mythologised: it was now seen in the context of colonialism rather than the impressive sporting feat it had been. In different circumstances, perhaps football and not cricket might have become India's sport.

After the post-match celebrations, the Uruguayan players hurry to catch the last ferry to Montevideo. Although the journey is a short one, these expat Indians, who have taken on Uruguayan nationality and re-established a game that had all but died out, are still a long way from home. For a region, so used to immigration but not to an Indian diaspora, the sight of these players taking part in this eccentric game still seems foreign. And yet, this is not the first time India's influence has been felt in the Río de la Plata. In 1924, Rabindranath Tagore spent two months in Buenos Aires, where he was a guest of the philanthropist and publisher Victoria Ocampo. The Nobel laureate was not reassured by what he saw: he felt that Latin Americans had not had the time to discover their soul and were still overly dependent on Europe for their ideas. In questioning the continent's relationship with Europe, Tagore helped stimulate that search for an identity. Perhaps with this newfound Indian influence on what PF Warner once called "more than a game" a passion for Latin America's greatest forgotten sport may yet be reawakened.

Andreas Campomar is publisher at Constable and author of Golazo!: A History of Latin American Football.

CRICKETERS OF THE YEAR

Smriti Mandhana

SNEHAL PRADHAN

The teenage years of indulgence were over. Smriti Mandhana was 21 now, past the milestones of civic adulthood, legally allowed to drive, vote and drink. She was four years into her international career, captain of her state team and vice-captain of her country in the shortest format. But where she had trained us to expect luminescence when she was at the crease, in 2017, her bat had gone inexplicably dark when it was needed most, like a lightsaber doused with water. So 2018 began with questions.

Little did she know then that the year would be plentiful to the point of profligacy. She was the standout player of 2018 and added new strings to her bow in 2019.

But when she took guard for the first time in Kimberley in the ODI against South Africa, seven months after she was dismissed for a duck at Lord's in the World Cup final, there were nerves, nay, knives in her stomach. A sound sleeper when on tour, she had spent much of the previous night awake, tossing and turning.

Time heals everything, except scorecards, and Mandhana's previous seven scores were 0, 6, 13, 3, 4, 8, 2, all in the World Cup in England, after scores of 90 and 106 not out in the first two games.

Logically, fear should not have found her. Since that tournament, she had put the miles in her legs, opened up her stance and scored runs under pressure in domestic cricket. In a game against Railways, she had dragged her team to a target of 132, scoring 67 runs. Most of these were made with the required run-rate of more than eight an over. Her shots included a six that hit the first floor of the adjoining clubhouse, itself a good 15 feet from the ground.

Yet, when she faced the first ball from South Africa, her legs felt like liquid lead, and her stomach like a washing machine stuck on spin. Which is why Mandhana rates the 84 off 98 balls she scored that day as one of her favourite knocks.

Since February 2018, that year, SMRITI SHRINIVAS MANDHANA has scored 531 runs in nine ODIs, averaging 66.37 and striking at 91 against the three teams that had joined India in the last four of the World Cup: Australia, England and South Africa. And, in a year where changed fielding restrictions saw run-rates in women's T20Is spike, Mandhana was the only Indian batter to keep pace with the rest of the world.

In T20Is that year, against the same three teams, Mandhana maintained an average of 49 to go with her strike-rate of 155.2. In the women's tri-series featuring Australia and England, played in the heat of Mumbai, those numbers rose to 69.3 and 165 respectively. After helping India beat the odds and reach the semi-final of the World T20 2018, she carried her form into 2019, averaging almost 70 in ODIs and 42 at a strike-rate of 144 in T20Is.

"Unless batsmen go for their shots, the conditions and rules and wicket can't help," she said. "For that you have to get out of the comfort zone of 'I need four or five balls to get set'. That doesn't work in today's T20 cricket."

More than her mindset has changed. I have had the pleasure of watching Mandhana train from close quarters, as we played for the same state. In the years leading up to her India debut, training sessions began not with willow or leather, but chalk and string: Three stumps would be drawn out beside the hanging ball, which would oscillate into the middle of her bat. Then she would move to underarm lobs, then overarm throws, only after which she would enter the nets.

"Earlier, I would do the basics 80 per cent (of the time) and 20 per cent shots," she said. "Back then, I needed basics more."

Back then, balls hit in training only elevated in error. Now, entire hours are devoted to lofting spin. Sessions mirror situations: hitting bouncers between deep fielders, finding the right moment to step out to the quicks. Looking into this mirror, a 16-year-old Mandhana would not recognise these methods. But she would recognise the brand of cricket she played. Even as an 11-year-old, if she saw a ball to hit, Mandhana hit it. All that has changed now is that there are fewer balls she cannot hit.

In the 2018 Indian summer, Mandhana conquered another demon: her home record. Till that point, her ODI average at home was just 22.5 compared to 47.6 away. She had been typecast as an away performer, despite the annual downpour of runs on the domestic circuit. "I had to prove a point to myself that I can score in India," she said.

She failed in only two matches of the ten India played at home. After missing out on a big score in the second and third ODIs against Australia (67 and 52; dominant while at the crease), she made up in the series against England, with scores of 86, 42 and 53 not out. Both half-centuries helped India chase down targets to win the series.

The first of those marked another node. "I have never played so slowly in international cricket," she said after taking 109 balls to make 86 runs that were worth 14 more. That knock came batting second on a sharp turner, with Mithali Raj having been dismissed for a duck, and Harmanpreet Kaur having thrown away a start. But that didn't shade her intent; she hit four sixes in the innings. India's tail converted her runs into a last-gasp win that soothed some of the pain of Lord's, 2017. "The happiness I had after that knock and winning that match, I didn't feel even for the West Indies hundred (during the World Cup)," she said. "There was an inner satisfaction, that I have done something good today."

We speak on the day after she scored 48 off 20 balls in the Kia Super League, becoming the first Indian to play in the tournament. "If I had made a couple of runs more, I would have scored the fastest fifty," she rues. Two games later, in a six-over affair, she equals the record for the fastest T20 fifty in women's cricket, in 18 balls. Two games after that, she brings up her first hundred in the format, smashing 102 off 61. She missed out on playing on Finals Day, but was still Player of the Tournament for her 421 runs from ten innings at a strike-rate of nearly 175 and will return to Storm in 2019.

Despite not being the finished product — she is over-reliant on boundaries and prone to the odd slump in form, like in the Asia Cup — Mandhana's cricketing clay is taking shape, and the contours of future captaincy are evident. She stood in for an injured Harmanpreet in three T20Is against England early in 2019, and although India lost all three, conducted herself impressively. Off the field, she is among the first crop of female cricketers to endorse some of the most recognisable brands in the country. Her social media following burgeons by the day, and corporates are willing to pay tens of lakhs for her time. But her real value can be divined elsewhere: She now offers India the consistency of Mithali and the combustibility of Harmanpreet. No longer are those two the prize scalps when India bat. Mandhana is the wicket everyone wants.

Put a number on that.

Snehal Pradhan (@snehalpradhan) followed her career as a seam bowler for India with one in sports writing and broadcasting.

Jasprit Bumrah

SANDEEP DWIVEDI

To understand Jasprit Bumrah's greatness, revisit the 2019 India v Bangladesh World Cup game and watch how he gets Mustafizur Rahman. It is an unlikely exhibit of his excellence and it throws up a rather obvious question: Who judges a self-respecting pacer by the way he dismisses Bangladesh's No.11, a batting nobody with a single-digit batting average across formats? But then such are times that Bumrah exudes the aura of world cricket's most feared gun-slinger even when he shoots a sitting duck.

First the background of that magical Bumrah ball. Bangladesh were 286 for 9. Mustafizur had to just survive one ball. It is the last ball of the 48th over, and also the last of Bumrah's spell. In case the No.11 holds on, the better batsman at the crease, Mohammad Saifuddin, playing on 51 from 38 balls, would have a shot at scoring the required 29 from 12 balls.

Just a ball back, the No.10, Rubel Hossain, had fallen to Bumrah's fast and full yorker. Now Mustafizur, himself a death overs specialist, knew that he too would get that special "toe-crushing" reception. Not just him, everybody watching the game knew Bumrah would bowl a second yorker.

Mustafizur sits back deep in the crease. His task, at a very rudimentary level, is this: He has to guard the nine-inch-wide stumps from a leather ball of about 3 inches diameter with a piece of wood that is 4.25 inches broad.

His plan is simple, and very workable. Expecting the ball to dart at the base of the stumps, the Bangladesh batsman only needs to bring his bat, raised just below the hip in his stance, down.

Bumrah does exactly what the fans on the terrace, expert on television or even the novice on the couch at home had predicted. He bowls the yorker. Before Mustafizur's bat hits the ground, the ball, like a lithe cat burglar, sneaks on to the stumps. Bumrah is that fast. He can make the ball travel the length of the pitch, snake in late, before the bat can be grounded. Keep replaying that ball endlessly, but it remains a mystery how the ball reached the stumps.

No.11 clean bowled, game over, India in the semi-final.

It's a tragedy that they say India doesn't have a finisher. It's a travesty that they say Indians freeze under pressure. It's just that when it comes to India, most comments are made keeping in mind the batsmen.

Since the Sunil Gavaskar era, through the Sachin Tendulkar phase and now during the ongoing Virat Kohli period, the world has been in awe of the record-breaking Indian batsmen sitting on tall run piles. But at this World Cup, something significant happened. The land of wristy batsmen and sly spinners, threw up a genuine quick. Bumrah stole the thunder from the batsmen and the wrist-spinner and the world stood up and noticed.

With 18 wickets, he was India's highest wicket-taker and most economical express pacer of the World Cup. For former England captain Michael Vaughan, he was "the best in the world by a country mile".

Even retired Pakistan pacers were asking their present-day fast bowlers to learn from Bumrah. There couldn't have been a bigger compliment for an Indian pacer. The hard-to-please neighbours, the seasoned speed merchants, aren't known to endorse or indulge every pacer who clocks in in the high 140s. The India story had changed.

As for the Bumrah story, it began seven years back with an affable New Zealander sitting in the stands watching a domestic T20 game featuring Gujarat, a modest team with unimpressive cricketing history. Bumrah was bowling. He was barely 19, a rookie pacer, who stood out because of his unconventional bowling action and his economy.

John Wright, the Kiwi talent scout for IPL team Mumbai Indians, was on the lookout for bowlers with unorthodox actions. Bumrah caught his eye, he was anything but textbook. Wright's word resulted in the Ahmedabad speedster getting picked by the Mumbai franchise, the break giving him the escape velocity to reach Indian cricket's higher orbit. As for Wright, he ended up confirming an old stereotype: the unsung, industrious, problem-solving Kiwi.

As luck would have it, at Mumbai Indians, Bumrah would meet Lasith Malinga, the Sri Lankan legend with an unconventional action, known for his speed, accuracy, slower ball and the yorker. Bumrah stuck with him like a shadow, he hung on to everything that Malinga told him. The apprentice would soon have all the attributes of his teacher.

IPL success gave him an international breakthrough in 2016 and within a year he was India's No.1 all-format fast bowler. He made his Test debut in 2018, played a big role in Test wins in South Africa and England and the historic maiden Test series triumph in Australia.

Cuttack to Cape Town, Dharamsala to Dubai, Bumrah would have a new set of fangs for every venue and could always be trusted to sting on most days. Bumrah — a mid-sentence spoiler alert for the batsmen-worshipping cricket fans — was the Kohli of Indian bowling. Of course, minus the endorsements and those on-field expressions.

Again, it's his unique bowling action that made him hard to decipher for the batsmen; the pace and variety just added more layers to his bowling. Google 'Bumrah + bowling action', freeze every possible frame, 'rock-and-roll' back and forth like an undecided third umpire on DRS duty and the science behind this success story stares at you.

The hyperextension of Bumrah's shoulder results in his right arm being ramrod straight and his elbow joint somewhat locked, not bending like most bowlers. This means it is left to his loose and ultra-flexible wrist to whip the ball down towards the batsmen. The hyperextension gives the arm that exaggerated backward loading and the subsequent forward cobra sting.

The high release because of the straight right arm and the whippy release gives Bumrah a couple of advantages: he can be skiddy or he can make ball take off at an unnerving pace. He also imparts backspin to the ball that makes batsmen misjudge the length.

The locked elbow, apparently the most difficult joint in the human body to control, massively reduces the margin of error. A little help from darts — a sport that reveres precision and, unlike cricket, leans heavily on scientific research to achieve it — helps to understand Bumrah. Pro dart players keep their shoulders locked, to ensure that the elbow, bent at right angle makes the forearm repeat a measured pendulum movement. Keeping the shoulder jammed turns a variable into constant, reducing the probability of an off-target strike. It's the same principle when it comes to golfers using the belly putter.

This action wasn't the result of scientific study. It was born out of necessity.

After her long day at work, Bumrah's mother Daljeet, a primary school principal, had a couple of rules for her pre-teen cricket-obsessed son Jappi: Stay indoors and don't raise a din when she enjoyed a well-earned siesta. The obedient son couldn't give up on his indoor bowling sessions in the spacious living room. He found a way out: By directing his deliveries at the floor skirting, he muffled the thud. This is where he first realised that advantage of his straight arm action in bowling yorkers. He would keep tweaking it so that he could repeat it endlessly and with become more accurate with the yorkers.

Raised by his mother, after his father died when he was seven, JASPRIT JASBIRSINGH BUMRAH, born on December 6 in Ahmedabad, was, by all accounts, a calm and responsible child. Studying in the school where your mother is the principal doesn't allow the enfant terrible in you to grow anyway.

Daljeet had reservations about her only son pursuing cricket, a career choice with a drop-out rate of over 95 per cent. Little did she know that her son had a one-in-a-million action with potential to revolutionise pace bowling. Eventually, the teacher in her gave in. Someone who advised parents to allow their children to chase their dreams, she couldn't have forced his son to turn his back to his passion.

She wouldn't regret her decision since Bumrah has looked the part every time he has stepped on the big stage. When your first scalps are Virat Kohli in the IPL, Steve Smith in ODIs, David Warner in T20Is and AB de Villiers in Tests, you know quite early that you belong.

Can Bumrah be India's most lethal pacer ever? His biggest strength, his action, also could also be his weakness. Human arms weren't designed to swing wildly like an excavator. There's also the other fear of the very aggressive Indian captain, Kohli, over-using the pacer, who already has had a couple of breakdowns. To be fair, it's tempting to throw the ball to the 145kph-plus pacer who doesn't tire, doesn't slow down and doesn't mind bouncing the batsmen out. Injuries will happen but whenever he is off the field, Bumrah will remain a fast bowler on his captain's speed dial.

Sandeep Dwivedi is sports editor of Indian Express.

Mayank Agarwal

MANUJA VEERAPPA

It was a muggy day in late October 2017. Soon, it turned positively stifling for Mayank Agarwal, the Karnataka batsman. Mayank, 27, had just collected his second duck in the Ranji Trophy league tie against Hyderabad in Shivamogga, Karnataka. As he trudged back to the pavilion, he seemed to drag a giant ball of lead.

"With that double-bagel, I had hit rock bottom," he admits. "I didn't know what would happen next." The fear of failure, a sportsman's worst nightmare, had struck.

Mayank turned to spirituality, something that had held the Bengaluru youngster in good stead when he was down in the dumps previously. His casual demeanour and easy charm masks this facet of his personality. During his time with Royal Challengers Bangalore in 2011, Mayank, just out of his teens, had been gifted Joseph Murphy's book, *The Power of the Subconscious*, by Ramesh Mane, the team's masseur. Not long afterwards, father Anurag, a businessman, introduced him to vipassana meditation.

"These two things brought about a massive change," he says. "The book got me thinking about my approach to life, and vipassana helped me understand life better. I didn't change overnight. The process has been gradual."

The impact, however, was almost instantaneous. In Karnataka's game against Maharashtra in Pune, Mayank was playing for more than his place in the team. Until that game, he had averaged 23.66 in seven Ranji outings. Now he slayed the demons with an awe-inspiring 304, becoming only the third Karnataka batsman after K L Rahul and Karun Nair to score a triple-hundred in Ranji Trophy. For the most part of his 727-minute stay at the crease over two days, he displayed monk-like composure and temperament.

It was the beginning of a remarkable run-fest. Over the Ranji season, he added a staggering 1160 runs, including five centuries and two half-centuries. The 50-over Vijay Hazare Trophy yielded 723 runs, with three centuries and four half-centuries. Another 258 runs, including three half-centuries, came in the Syed Mushtaq Ali Trophy T20 tournament. The tally of 2141 runs in the three premier tournaments of the season put him in a league of his own.

The talent of MAYANK ANURAG AGARWAL, born February 16, 1991, in Bengaluru, first came to the fore when as a teenager he was prolific in inter-school competitions for Bishop Cotton Boys School. It earned him a place in the Karnataka Under-15 team, and potential was converted into numbers in November 2008 when he scored a patient 410-ball 178 for Karnataka against Punjab in the Cooch Behar Under-19 tournament. Another century — 111 against Andhra — and a couple of half-centuries later, he made it to the India Under-19 team to Australia in April 2009. He announced his arrival with a 142-ball 160 against Australia A.

The following year, he was the lone bright spark and the team's highest run-getter in an otherwise disappointing Under-19 World Cup in New Zealand. Once back, he was fast-tracked into the India A side and the Karnataka T20 side, making his state debut against Goa with a 42-ball 52.

Mayank struggled with consistency in his initial years of senior cricket. The youngster, who had been inspired by Sachin Tendulkar, couldn't seal his place in the Karnataka Ranji squad.

When the opportunity finally came in the second half of 2013-14, against Jharkhand in Mysuru, he scored 90 on debut. He went on to play seven more matches that season, scoring 290 runs in which the 20s and 30s came easily, but he stumbled while converting the starts. While his freshman season was a learning curve, the sophomore one was a reality check. Five matches with 217 runs and an average of 27.12 put him out of the playing XI. It was the time when Karnataka cricket was on a roll, and Mayank watched from the sidelines as R Vinay Kumar's men downed Tamil Nadu to defend their title.

Back in the playing XI the following season, he scored his maiden century, 118 against Delhi, in Hubballi. In six matches, he accumulated 456 runs at 45.60. He took to long distance running and changed his diet to cut the flab.

On the batting front, he turned to his long-time coach for answers. For years, Mayank has worked with R Murali, the go-to man for some of the top batsmen in Karnataka when they want to fix flaws in technique. Murali is known to be meticulous to the point of being boring, but Mayank posed an entirely different challenge.

"It took a lot of time for both of us to get out of this 'technique' mindset and focus on skills," Murali, a former Karnataka age-group coach who now runs his own academy, reveals. "I had to make him get rid of his obsession with technique. It was a combination of both of us being obsessed with technique! We had a great relationship before I finally had had enough because it was tiring to see someone score so many runs and come back with complaints about technique. That's when I figured there needed to be a different way of approaching this."

Mayank abandoned the textbook way of playing the sport and instead looked for consistency in the way he played or approached a shot. Boundaries cascaded off his bat, but there was a cautiousness that comes with maturity.

The long hours spent with Rahul Dravid in the India A set-up helped, too. Dravid told him, "You have to manage your mental energy. If you practice hard for three days before the game and constantly think about it before playing a four-day game, mentally you have already played three days of the four-day game."

Mayank set targets, but learnt to say 'so what' when things didn't go his way. The moment he let go of his obsession with goals, he began opening up and his stay at the crease lengthened.

One of Mayank's biggest gains of the 2017-18 season was his ability to stay in the game mentally and physically for hours. That indicated not just an attitudinal shift but also enhanced fitness levels that allowed for freshness of the mind.

He was a part of the India A sides that toured England and New Zealand, and hosted South Africa A and Australia A. The highlight was a 220 against South Africa A on his home turf and before long came a dream India debut as a late replacement for an injured Prithvi Shaw in Australia in December 2018. In Melbourne he struck a stroke-filled 76 to become the top-scoring Indian batsman on Test debut against Australia, surpassing Dattu Phadkar's score of 51, recorded in 1947 at the Sydney Cricket Ground. He finished the successful series with 195 runs in three innings at an impressive average of 65. Called up as a replacement for an injured Vijay Shankar, he was reunited with his Under-19 and state team-mate Rahul at the 2019 World Cup, but didn't feature in a game.

He will hope it's a matter of time. Mayank's is a classic case of the somewhat belated realisation of extraordinary ability, but it is also an example of what can be achieved simply through adapting to shifting goalposts.

Manuja Veerappa (@manujaveerappa) is a sports writer with the Times of India.

Fakhar Zaman

QAMAR AHMED

In only his fourth ODI, against rivals India in the final of the Champions Trophy 2017 in London, Pakistan's Fakhar Zaman was caught off a no-ball on three. As if that was all the invitation he needed, he grasped at the chance to be Pakistan's next big batting hero; and has since flown with it. The maiden hundred at The Oval was the first of four so far in his short ODI career; the third of those hundreds was Pakistan's first double-century.

In just over a year at the highest level, the explosive left-handed batsman has become the quickest to reach 1000 runs in ODIs, needing only 18 innings to get there. No other batsman, including the great Sir Viv Richards, has done it in fewer than 21 innings. The 515 runs he made in Zimbabwe are the most by any batsman in a bilateral series of five matches. He scores at nearly a run-a-ball in ODIs, and at a strike-rate of nearly 140 in the shortest format.

"I am not big on statistics or records," says Fakhar. "My main objective is to entertain and to win matches for Pakistan."

'Fakhar' means pride in Urdu. The country's batting hero was Pakistani's pride of a different kind before he became an international sportsperson.

FAKHAR ZAMAN was born April 10, 1990, in the remote village of Katlang near Mardan in the Khyber Pakhtunkhwa region in the north of the country. As a schoolboy, the rugged mountainside patch of land was his playground. Even back then, among his friends, he was known to hit the ball harder than anyone else. So much so that his brothers refused to let him play cricket, his elder sibling Asif Zaman says.

Fakhar's parents nudged him towards a career as a soldier, a profession in which youngsters of that tribal area excelled. He was packed off to teeming Karachi to join the Pakistan navy as a sailor. Little did he know that would be the beginning of a career path that would see him represent his country at the international level in a sport he loved.

"I used to look at the deeds of great men of the game like Imran Khan, Javed Miandad, Wasim Akram, Waqar Younis, Saeed Anwar,

Inzamam-ul-Haq, Shahid Afridi and all, and always wondered if I could be one of them one day," he says.

While going through the hard grind of training to be a naval commando, he was lucky to come across Nazim Khan, the Naval Academy coach. Nazim had detected his cricket talent and advised him to come off from the force and re-join as a sportsperson; that would allow him to concentrate on his game and aim for the national cap. It isn't a decision he regrets.

In inter-district Under-19 cricket in Karachi, where he was taken under the wings of Azam Khan, an experienced cricket coach and organiser, he excelled with his consistency. Having got a release from the navy, he played for Karachi Electric, among other teams, punishing bowlers with his attacking cricket and entertaining crowds.

His feats ensured he barely remained in obscurity. He did well in the domestic Pakistan Cup in 2016 and later for Lahore Qalandars in the Pakistan Super League. He made his first-class debut in 2013 in a match between Multan and Karachi and crossed fifty seven times in seven matches that season. From then to his T20I debut against West Indies at Port of Spain in March 2017 and ODI debut against South Africa in the Champions Trophy in Birmingham in June 2017, Fakhar remained the blue-eyed boy of Pakistan cricket.

But that Champions Trophy, when Ahmad Shahzad's failure as an opener allowed him to step in, gave him star status. For a side that has too often for their liking failed against the biggest rivals on the biggest stages, the big-match temperament was gold.

Seemingly thriving under pressure, he helped Pakistan bounce back to take the T20I series against New Zealand. And as if to confirm his ability when the spotlight is trained on him, he was scintillating in Zimbabwe. In the T20 tri-series final against Australia, chasing 184 at the Harare Sports Club, he bludgeoned 91 after Pakistan were reduced to 2 for 2.

Centuries against a weakened side say little, but double-centuries make a statement, and that's what he did in the bilateral series that followed. With his unbeaten 210 off 156 balls in the fourth ODI, he became the sixth in the world after Sachin Tendulkar, Virender Sehwag, Rohit Sharma, Chris Gayle and Martin Guptill to get to the milestone. Saeed Anwar's previous best for Pakistan, the 194 against India in Chennai, was left in the shade.

Fakhar credits Micky Arthur, the head coach, and Grant Flower, the batting coach, for his development and helping him find the balance between going big with every shot and playing smart. He may not be the most elegant player, but he does have the reflexes and the hand-eye coordination to compensate for his unorthodox approach.

Tests, he admits, are the "crowning glory", and in his first chance, brought in for his skill in raising the run-rate, showed a cautious stickiness not automatically associated with him. He announced himself in style, with 94 and 66 at Abu Dhabi, helping Pakistan go one-up in the series against Australia.

In 2019, he has been unable to score with a regularity as alarming he had done earlier, but he has hardly looked out of touch. With Fakhar it has almost always been throwing away promising starts, as in the World Cup matches against India and South Africa. The one time he did get going on the England tour, at the Rose Bowl, his 106-ball 138 brought Pakistan to within 12 runs of the English total of 373.

Along with Imam-ul-Haq and Babar Azam, Fakhar has helped form a solid top order for a side that has often struggled to find quality openers. At a time when 'fearless' cricket is what coaches demand and crowds enjoy, his importance at the top of the order in a team that has risen to No. 1 in the shortest format comes as no surprise.

Qamar Ahmed is a former first-class cricketer from Pakistan. As a journalist, he has covered over 400 Tests.

Dimuth Karunaratne

R KAUSHIK

It was a stroke, he was to say later, that he didn't even intend to play. South Africa were all over Sri Lanka on the opening day of the First Test of a two-match series, in Galle in July 2018. Dale Steyn, on his umpteenth comeback and still some way short of his menacing best, was still quite a handful, as someone with 400 Test sticks will always be. Kagiso Rabada and Tabraiz Shamsi, the left-arm wrist-spinner, were doing the damage as South Africa made inroads, but they just couldn't get the left-handed opener out.

It was a special game for Dimuth Karunaratne — his 50th Test. Given the revolving-door policy that successive Sri Lankan selection panels seem to have perfected, that was quite an achievement. As wickets tumbled around him, Karunaratne held firm. Then, Steyn banged in a short ball. "I actually wanted to leave it, but I accidentally hit that one," Karunaratne admitted later, as he hooked the legend out of the park. It was just his seventh six in Test cricket.

FRANK DIMUTH MADUSHANKA KARUNARATNE, born April 21, 1988, in Colombo, does not have as many initials as many other Sri Lankan cricketers. He also does not possess the same flair, but is made of stern stuff. In a world where the value of a batsman is judged by his ability to hit boundaries, Karunaratne is an anachronism whose game is built around circumspection. Sri Lankan fans used to the pyrotechnics of Sanath Jayasuriya and Tillakaratne Dilshan at the top of the order even in red-ball cricket might not feel similar adrenaline surges when Karunaratne is holding court, straight bat, high right elbow and decisive foot movement. But his team-mates, many of whom use the firm foundation he lays to fashion radically outlandish structures, appreciate the solidity he brings to a line-up that otherwise can go from 0 to 100 or the reverse in the blink of an eye.

Karunaratne, soft-spoken, unassuming, ready with a smile, will get into a snarl only to separate the snarling. In a system that frowns on honesty if it is questioned, he is his own man. At the SSC ground in Colombo in August 2017, after making a second-innings 141 in a losing cause against India, he dissected Sri Lanka's inability to sustain intensity for long periods in Test cricket: "We only have eight or ten domestic first-class games in a season," he pointed out. "We have to play more first-class cricket, only then can we find more players who can dominate the game. That's what SLC (Sri Lanka Cricket) have to work on for the players."

The tone wasn't confrontational, the intent wasn't aggressive. He was just stating a fact. Reward for his grounded attitude and his ability to think about the game came in 2019 when, after disastrous twin tours of the Antipodes, Karunaratne was elevated to the Test captaincy. Sri Lanka turned the world order upside down by stunning South Africa 2-0, becoming the first Asian nation to win a Test series there.

When he was arrested in March for driving under the influence, it could all have gone south. "My actions were utterly unbecoming of a Sri Lankan national cricketer," he apologised, and that was good enough for the board. Impressed with his all-round skills, the selectors did not just recall him to the ODI side for the first time since 2015, but also named him captain for the World Cup.

Karunaratne's cricketing ambitions first received a fillip when he joined St Joseph's College as a 15-year-old, on a cricket scholarship. His early schooling had been at Asoka Vidyalaya, not a traditional cricketing nursery. Asoka in those days had classes only till Grade 7, and several teenagers with cricketing aspirations made the move to Ananda College, which has produced illustrious stars such as Arjuna Ranatunga, the Wettimuny brothers Sidath and Sunil, and, more recently, Dinesh Chandimal. Karunaratne, though, took the road less travelled. St Joseph's have a rich cricketing legacy of their own, and he linked up with future stars Angelo Mathews and Thisara Perera, both of whom have also led the national side.

Harsha de Silva, the coach of the Sri Lankan women's team, was the in charge at the college at the time, and identified Karunaratne as one for the future. "You could see that he had the hunger and the game," said de Silva. "He didn't throw it away. He loved spending long hours at the wicket and stacking up big hundreds.

"By 2008, he had graduated to vice-captain. That year, after 36 years, St Joseph's won the big match against St Peter's. He made 120. By then, he had already represented Sri Lanka Under-16 and Under-19 sides. A senior international debut was a formality."

So taken in were the St Joseph's Old Boys at the end of the drought that, marshalled by Chaminda Vaas, they sent off the titlists on an all-paid-for week-long vacation to Australia! That isn't Karunaratne's only visit Down Under. After his maiden Test appearance in Galle in November 2012, when he followed up a duck in the first innings against New Zealand with an unbeaten 60 in the second, he played his next three Tests in Australia, rounding off the series with 85 in the final innings in Sydney in the New Year's Test of 2013. Australia and England remain the only opponents against whom he doesn't have a Test hundred yet.

He soon picked up a reputation as a 'second-innings batsman'. Four of his first six centuries came in either the third or fourth innings of the match, but since making 93 against Pakistan in the first innings of a two-Test series in the UAE in 2017, he has worked towards setting the record straight. In eight subsequent Tests till July 2018, he scored two centuries and as many fifties in his team's first dig.

Karunaratne has made no secret of the fact that he thinks opening the batting in Sri Lanka is more demanding than anywhere else in the world, because you just can't get a fix on what the ball is going to do. Cocking a snook at his own conviction, he carried his bat in the Galle 'six-off-Steyn' Test, his unbeaten 158 just the fourth instance of a Sri Lankan carrying his bat in Test cricket. He batted six hours, kept out 222 deliveries, and contributed 55.05 per cent of his side's runs. For good measure, he made an aggressive 60 in the second innings; Faf du Plessis's 49 in the South African first innings was the next highest score in the entire game. Dilruwan Perera took ten wickets, but there was no doubt who had fashioned Sri Lanka's 278-run win.

De Silva is insistent that Karunaratne has been a "complete batter" for a while now. "Even when he was St Joseph's, he had it all — could play strokes on both sides of the wicket, both against pace and spin, and off the front foot and back. He had an excellent technique, and he was committed to his cricket." Despite his left-handedness, he may not top the elegance stakes. But when it comes to effectiveness and efficiency, he has few equals.

R Kaushik is a senior sports journalist and credited writer on V V S Laxman's autobiography 281 and Beyond.

Rashid Khan

SIDHARTH MONGA

Rashid Khan is probably the most important cricketer in world cricket today.

This statement could do with some explaining.

Cricket remains an incestuous sport in which the three powerhouses keep finding ways to hoard the resources, exposure and, thus, power. Rashid, from Afghanistan, a country that didn't even have a cricket board 20 years ago, is one of the most sought-after players in the most popular format of the sport today. In a sport where egality is only notional, Rashid represents hope.

Rashid tells you that you don't need to be from a certain country or have godfathers in cricket if you are good enough. He is hope that cricket can someday be as popular as football. He is like those African footballers for whose services teams in Europe go to war.

Outside Rashid's own country, five T20 teams in the world have benefited from his presence. For Adelaide Strikers in the Big Bash League in Australia, Rashid takes a wicket every 16.2 runs and goes for 5.93 an over. For Sussex Sharks in the T20 Blast in England, he takes a wicket every 13 balls. When he turns out for Comilla Victorians in the Bangladesh Premier League and Guyana Amazon Warriors in the Caribbean Premier League, Rashid doesn't even concede a run a ball.

These are not freak numbers over one match or one week or over one season. These are career numbers. Rashid's career began in October 2015. Since then nobody has taken more wickets than his 256. Among those who have taken 50 wickets, nobody comes close to his average of 15.86. His economy rate of 6.04 is untouched. Now add batsmen and all-rounders to the mix, and still Rashid has won more match awards than anyone since his debut.

The year 2018 in India was extra special for Rashid. Four times he was the Player of the Match in the Indian Premier League. In every pressure situation, Sunrisers Hyderabad went to him. He conceded runs at 6.73 an over in a tournament where the average economy rate was 8.28. If the tournament had lived up to its name of being a league in the true sense, Sunrisers would be champions: Rashid carried them to the top of the league table. It was in the knockouts that they faltered. In 2019, his wickets column wasn't up to his usual standard, but he improved on his economy: 6.28, the best among bowlers who'd played at least two matches.

For Rashid, the modern pro, there was no cause for pause. He didn't go home after IPL 2018: he flew straight to England and represented World XI in a Hurricane Relief match. Next he flew back to India, up to the foothills of the Himalayas where Afghanistan were hosting Bangladesh in a T20 international series. This happened to be the month of Ramzan. Fasting, flying, fasting, training, he landed a day before the first match, smoked the first ball he faced for six, and then took a wicket first ball — the first of three — and led his side to a whitewash of Bangladesh. Crowds all over India have taken to him, chanting "Raa-shid, Raa-shid" to the tune of "Sa-chin, Sa-chin". During the 2018-19 BBL, he lost his father, but waited till his team had a few days' break to make a quick visit home; he didn't miss a match.

Not only Rashid's numbers and feats, his ways are revolutionary too. He bowls what falls under the general definition of leg-spin, but he is so much more. He has a long run-up, he runs in quicker than any spinner, and thus brings a lot of energy into his delivery. Leg-spin is predominantly wrist-spun, but Rashid will be the first one to admit he uses his fingers more than the wrist. Fingers to turn the ball, fingers to control where he lands it.

Rashid is the ultimate professional. You can imagine he turns up, changes into the gear of whatever team he is playing for, neatly folds his suit, goes out, does his thing, takes a quick shower, wears the suit back and heads over to the new team. His love of the game is pure and free of nationalistic jingoism and ego. He plays the game for the game. He does so without a coach. Almost every cricketer in the world has someone he can go back to when things are not going right. Rashid swings in and swings out of dressing rooms. Most leave him to his own devices, knowing they don't need to tell him anything. He makes sure he is fit and ready for every assignment. He keeps upgrading his game. Just after the World Cup, Afghanistan named him their captain across formats.

Rashid is the future of the sport, and that is not even half of why he is the most important cricketer in the world today.

RASHID KHAN was born in Achin in the Nangarhar province of Afghanistan on September 20, 1998. The refugees settled in Pakistan would begin to return in a few years' time. Afghanistan, due to its unfortunate strategically advantageous location in central Asia, had been ravaged by war. Religious extremism went to new heights in response. A culturally rich country gave up on joy. Then came cricket, along with the returning refugees who had fallen in love with the game in Pakistan. Initial success and the sport's inherent conservatism — full pants, "gentleman's game" — got it the approval of the extremist groups.

Cricket was joy, freedom, escape. Rashid is the face of that hope in Afghanistan today. There have been other cricketing superstars in the country — big-hitting lovable wicketkeeper Mohammad Shahzad, warpaint-wearing fast bowler Hamid Hassan, the solid all-rounder Mohammad Nabi, the long-haired self-styled Shoaib

Akhtar of Afghanistan cricket Shapoor Zadran — but Rashid is the first true global superstar to emerge from Afghanistan.

Rashid is not just any Afghan cricketer. Afghans are not short on confidence at the best of times, but it is an entirely different inspiration for them to see that one of theirs has risen without infrastructure and support systems to become such a good cricketer that other global superstars are in awe of him. Rashid is aware of the responsibility to share what he learns the world over with the kids in Afghanistan — as is Nabi. Younger bowlers like Mujeeb Ur Rahman are sponges for their experience.

During the IPL, something tragic happened back home in Afghanistan. A cricket tournament, played in the night for the benefit of those fasting, a tournament whose stated purpose is to promote peace and harmony, was targeted by terror. A bomb went off in the stands. National cricketer Sadiq Karim was there. Possible future national players were in the stands and on the ground.

The promoter of the tournament, Hedayatullah Zahir, was among those killed. It is not advisable to speak against terror in Afghanistan, but Rashid tweeted, paying respect to his "bro" who died. Karim followed it with a gesture of his own during the next match Rashid played. He got together a few friends, set up a TV on the pitch of the same ground that burnt a couple of days ago, and watched Rashid play from there. Rashid is very much part of the silent Afghan revolution called cricket, even though he spends a lot of time away from the country.

If the cricketing superpowers have their way, Rashid won't spend so much time away from home. A paper submitted by a core group has suggested players' appearances be restricted to only two T20 leagues a year so that they can protect the "primacy of international cricket", which is euphemism for "we are worried our cricketers will no longer sign their lives off to us whether we give them opportunity or not".

In giving a struggling country joy and hope, in carrying the flag of professionalism and globalisation in a closed sport, in being the face of the sport outside the traditional powerhouses, Rashid Khan is a two-fingered salute to lots that is wrong with cricket, and sometimes with the world. There might be no more significant player in this era.

Sidharth Monga is assistant editor at ESPNcricinfo.

BEYOND THE BOUNDARY

Captain's ideals, politician's ambition

RAJDEEP SARDESAI

Of the many stories that circle around the life and times of Imran Khan Niazi, there is one that stays top of the mind. Imran was leading Pakistan against the West Indies in Sharjah in the late 1980s amidst swirling rumours that a few of the Pakistan players had taken money to under-perform. When Imran heard of this, he was fuming: He called a team meeting, locked the door, and issued a stern warning that if he found any player perform below par, they would be sent back home and never play for the country again. He added that he was betting the entire team's match fees on a Pakistan win. Sure enough, the team responded to their captain's diktat and won the match.

That is the Imran Khan the cricket world learnt to admire, a man of raw courage and great skill, whose self-image was defined by an abiding attachment to traditional notions of Pathan honour and pride. Recall how he pushed for neutral umpires at a time when the Pakistan team was seen to be the biggest beneficiary of brazenly partisan umpiring in home conditions. Remember how he once advised Sunil Gavaskar to wear a helmet because he warned that even a single bouncer could be fatal: this advice from one of the most intimidating bowlers of his time and for whom Gavaskar was the Indian 'enemy' number one.

It was, in fact, Imran who implored Gavaskar to extend his career by another year in 1986 when an India-Pakistan series was planned for the following season so that the two could have one final joust at each other. They may have been fierce rivals on the field, but mutual respect was at the heart of the battle.

Imran v Gavaskar in 1982-83 was probably the defining sub-continental cricket battle of my generation: fast bowler at the peak of his powers versus the supreme batting technician. India were thrashed in the series but the individual contest between the two icons was a draw. The other Indian cricket batting maestro, Gundappa Viswanath, whose career ended in that series, would later suggest that he hadn't faced a faster bowler than Imran at the time. And yet, a few years later, as the wear and tear of the cricket treadmill reduced his

A man for a challenge: "I will be prime minister of Pakistan one day, it's not a question of if, but when!" – *Getty Images*

bowling speed, Imran re-invented himself as a solid middle-order batsman. It was the age of the great all-rounders and Imran was an intrinsic part of it. "I think Botham was the best batsman, Hadlee the best bowler, Kapil had the most natural talent and I guess I just made the most of whatever skills I had," he would later tell me rather modestly.

Truth is, Imran loved a challenge, never taking a backward step right through his cricket career. Leading the Pakistani team to punch above their weight, he even took up the ultimate cricket challenge of the 1980s while attempting to defeat the mighty West Indies in the Caribbean. The series ended in a draw at a time when most teams were whitewashed by the Calypso Kings. That he led Pakistan to a World Cup victory in 1992 was a bonus. It made him a national folk hero who could ride the wave of popularity to first build a charitable cancer hospital, and then launch a political career.

I remember interviewing him in 1996 as his cancer hospital was taking off. The World Cup was being held in the sub-continent and we were talking cricket. During the interview break, Imran turned to me, "You know all this cricket stuff is fine, but I'd rather talk about the hospital, that's my life goal now." He had moved determinedly onto a second innings in life as a philanthropist and appeared keen to slowly erase his cricketing persona.

A few years later, we met again; this time, Imran had entered another avatar, now as a politician. The first election for his fledgling party, the Pakistan Tehreek-e-Insaaf, had been a disaster, with almost all the party candidates losing their deposits. "I guess politics isn't like cricket, you can't win by playing with a straight bat," I suggested politely. Imran was typically unfazed: "Don't worry, my friend, I will be prime minister of Pakistan one day, it's not a question of if, but when!"

During the 2011 World Cup, Imran spent nearly a month with us at the *CNN IBN* news network as an expert commentator. He was a terrific cricket analyst, but his mind was clearly on his politics. One

Legacy: The 1992 World Cup win made him a folk hero, who could ride the wave of popularity, to ultimately get into politics. – *Getty Images*

night, the legendary Sir Viv Richards, who was also on our studio panel, ribbed him, "C'mon, Immy, what's all this politics stuff, how are you going to defeat the big guys in Pakistan," laughed Richards. Imran, never to duck a bouncer, shot back, "Look, if I could bounce you out, I can sure bounce out the politicians!"

In 2013, Imran was back in India, this time for a high-profile media summit. He had just achieved his first breakthrough, his party winning the provincial elections in the Khyber Pakhtunkhwa region along the Pak-Afghan border. During the summit, I was in conversation with Imran when a member of the audience pointed out his alleged Taliban connection. For once, the suave Imran seemed to lose his temper. "What do you mean 'Taliban' Khan?" he responded angrily. "If standing up to a war on terror where innocent people are killed in US drone attacks [earns me that reputation], I will keep speaking up."

In 2015, Imran was again in India for a media conclave. This time, a last-minute meeting was fixed for him with Indian prime minister Narendra Modi. "Quite a nice guy, not at all how I imagined him to be," he would later tell us. One noticed a spring in his step when I asked him where he stood now in Pakistan's political stakes. "It's happening, my friend, a *naya* (new) young Pakistan is emerging where the corrupt Sharifs and Bhuttos will be driven out in the next election!" The dream was alive. I smiled weakly, my scepticism barely concealed.

Three years later, Imran has proven every sceptic horribly wrong, winning an election amid growing voter unease with the corruption of the country's traditional political elites. The cynics may claim that he has benefitted from the all-powerful Pakistani army preparing a perfect pitch for him and that the 2018 elections weren't quite the level playing electoral field that Imran had fought for all his cricketing life. Maybe, Imran's overarching ambition to become prime minister of Pakistan has led him to make compromises with religious extremists and the men in uniform to make himself more politically acceptable. Maybe, he is the army's chosen one. Maybe, he won't succeed in cleaning up the mess in Pakistan with the vigour he once showed in the cricket dressing room. Maybe, he is a Jekyll-and-Hyde character as one of his former wives has rather viciously portrayed, someone whose populist rhetoric and adversarial street-fighter image in Pakistan is in marked contrast to his consummate Oxonian charm and macho good looks that once made him cricket's ultimate pin-up boy. Maybe, Imran the idealist cricketer has mutated into an opportunist politician and a liberal cosmopolitanism has been replaced by a more troubling anti-West Islamist visage.

The challenge he faces now though is gargantuan. Captaining a Pakistan cricket team is a walk along the cobbled streets of Oxford when compared with healing a bloodied, terror-stricken country with a faltering economy. Maybe, Imran as prime minister won't be quite as successful as he was as his country's cricket captain. But then again, when you have kept track of the extraordinary journey of the man, you realise you can never count him out. For sheer staying power and a fierce single-mindedness, Imran Khan deserves his chance as the world's first Test cricketer to become prime minister of his country.

Post-script: Soon after Imran's election win in Pakistan, I sent him a warm congratulatory message. His response was markedly less cordial: "Rajdeep, I am very disappointed with the Indian media, how could you back that corrupt Sharif?" I wanted to protest innocence, but realised he was clearly unhappy, a feeling reinforced when he complained in his opening address to the Pakistani people that he had been painted as a "Bollywood villain" in India. Maybe, the hurt at being projected as someone being remote-controlled by the army was a reflection of Imran's rather unique love-hate relationship with India: This is, after all, a much-travelled man who in a rather mellow mood once told me, "I think I have more friends in Mumbai and London than in Pakistan!"

Rajdeep Sardesai (@sardesairajdeep) is an Indian journalist and author. His book Democracy's XI: The Great Story of Indian Cricket *was one of six shortlisted for the 2018 Cricket Society and MCC Book of the Year award.*

The cradle: Flamboyance marks those emerging from the Shivaji Park Gymkhana.
— *Getty Images*

Bombay *gharana*

SHISHIR HATTANGADI

My birthplace was the city of joy, Calcutta, as it was known back then. A charming black and white city in the 1960s, Calcutta was intoxicated by the residual influence of the British Raj. Straight out of Aparna Sen and Jennifer Kendal's *36 Chowringhee Lane* or Sharadindu Bandyopadhyay's *Byomkesh Bakshi* — the Anglo-Indians, the club culture, the tea-drinking elite and the zamindars. Those who experienced that era strongly believe that the cultural inclination of Calcutta back then was unparalleled. The citizens had this sense of cultural superiority too, and coupled with a preponderance to strongly-held opinions — I sense it came from a robust education system — it meant I was told at an early age that I was at the home of cricket.

The neighbours spoke of a British settlement on the banks of the Hooghly in the 1860s where the sport was first played. I wasn't one to take tales as fact, but I can still hear the congregation of well-spoken colony people (in smoke-filled rooms and sipping Darjeeling tea) giving me history lessons on the origins of the East India Company in Plassey, Bengal, making the state the natural home of the sport. There was little I could contest.

Cricket was fast becoming a working-class man's sport. It had sieved down from the elite '*gora*' and '*sahib*' to the '*bhodrolok*' (gentlemen) and on to the working class.

Bombay had this mysticism from where I was. I was told I was in the land of cricket heritage, but the apparent kings of cricket were Maharashtrians, and the kingdom of the game was Bombay. The colony assemblies gave me inspirational stories of the precision of Vijay Merchant, the genius of Vijay Manjrekar, the calm of Ajit Wadekar, the merlin-like abilities of Subhash 'Fergie' Gupte. Cricket had become a mouth-watering journey of stories and anecdotes heard at congregations. The itch to be a Bombay romantic had been sown — and this romanticism had an old-world charm, for it was built independent of the electronic media, solely through the art of story-telling and visualising those stories.

My interest paid off with an eventual migration from the city of joy to the city of dreams.

It soon became apparent that the gradual metamorphosis of the sport I had witnessed in Calcutta, its transfer from elitist circles to the common man, was a thing of the past.

Bombay in the 1970s was a city that stopped to welcome you with two talking points: Rajesh Khanna and cricket. There was little discrimination about who could hold a bat; it seemed like I had moved from a bastion to a *gharana* —a tradition where flair and passion is upheld by the generation that follows. Bombay's cricketing epicentres ranged from the disciplined Matunga Central strip (the fortress of the sombre Madhav 'George' Mantri, VS 'Marshall' Patil, and the rakish and lively Vasu Paranjape of Dadar Union) and the flamboyant and exuberant Shivaji Park Gymkhana, to the privileged gymkhanas of south Bombay that had their own grounds, sightscreens and sit-down lunches and teas. Your induction in the smallest teams comes with a responsibility to represent those who came before.

The legends extended beyond the Test caps. For a young romantic from Calcutta, it was overwhelming to watch 'Baloo' Gupte, Abdul Ismail, Padmakar Shivalkar, Milind Rege and Vijay Hazare practise in the nets from afar.

In an era of no television, no internet, you went to grounds to see

Club culture has prepared Mumbai for continued success in the Ranji Trophy.
– *BCCI*

these names in flesh and blood. The *gharana* had sucked me in —
cricket became my life.

Undoubtedly, the biggest impact on my generation was from the
tours of the West Indies and England in 1971. Bombay at the forefront, with Ajit Wadekar, Dilip Sardesai, Eknath Solkar and Salim
Durani (a product of Bombay club cricket), and of course a debutant who was about to make the world sit up and watch for the next
decade and a half, a certain Sunil Gavaskar. The predictability of
Gavaskar during that series in producing those huge numbers gave
us the ambition of being world beaters. Sardesai was christened the
Renaissance Man, Solkar provided obstinate support and doggedness never before seen, skipper Wadekar presented a combination
of astuteness and luck that was etched in India's cricket legacy like
a happy ending from a picture book. Young Bombay boys eagerly
waited for score sheets that reached a day later.

Bombay cricket was uncomplicated in the late 1970s. If you wanted to play, you found a club. And if you played reasonably well in
the perception of the pundits, the club found you. There were no
beep or yo-yo tests to measure your worth. If you were a batsman
and needed recognition, get the big hundreds. If you were a bowler
and wanted to move up in the cricketing hierarchy, aim for those
five-wicket hauls.

Club culture prepared you for the big stage; at the maidans, you
often rubbed shoulders with the big names without even realising it.

A different time that was — with different yardsticks of assessment. If you waited under a tarpaulin tent on a maidan in the build-up to a game and saw a cricketer walk in with a square Air India pad, a bat and cream flannels, you knew you were playing a seasoned team. If a fast bowler wore hand-stitched buckskin shoes in the Wadala area with trademark 'R' spikes (and there was only one cobbler who crafted them, I am told), you sensed you were facing someone who knew how to use the seam.

The Bombay culture was cultivated at the club level. Matches were keenly contested. There was no concept of rest, recovery and rehabilitation. Club cricket was the lifeline of Bombay weekends. A gateway to fulfil one's dreams. Seniors looked out for talent, and when you heard a 'good shot' or 'well played' from a senior at slip, you believed you belonged.

Amol Muzumdar: A Mumbai stalwart who never played for India. – *Getty Images*

Ravi Shastri and I, in our college days, grew up dreaming of cricket. Ravi and I came from similar backgrounds: family origins in the south, Jesuit schooling, and a common passion to play cricket. His meteoric rise embodied faith in skill and the area between the ears.

For me, exposure at the club level made the transition to the Bombay dressing room seamless. I entered as an opening batsman, and from the start it was clear — icons had already set the precedent — that big scorers held starting spots. The batting template was about numbers, resilience and attrition. See the numbers of the first batch Merchant downwards, and the trio of Vinoo Mankad, Gavaskar and Dilip Vengsarkar who succeeded him, and you know the shoes you must fill.

The expectations were fair: this presidency had given us the opportunity to evolve among the most talented in the country, and allowed us a chance to gain national recognition through domestic events like the Times Shield. Every state had a stable, but Bombay, with its volume of talent, ensured the product was a thoroughbred. Bombay provided a template for the rest.

Generations of cricketers owe gratitude to their seniors, who taught them what playing for this team means. I remember my entry to the dressing room like it was yesterday. Having a Shastri already settled in was comforting. Seniors even gave you equipment and clothing to set the ball rolling. I had Gavaskar's shoes, Mankad's trousers and Sandeep Patil's bat. And the tradition stays: in my last years as a professional cricketer, it was like turning the clock back to see a junior Manjrekar walk in to stay.

1986-87 will always be special for my generation. To watch two boys grow into giants! One will be remembered as the cricket maverick and one as the man who changed the definition of batting — I refer to messers Kambli and Tendulkar.

On November 9, 2017, Bombay played their 500th Ranji match, against Baroda at the Wankhede. It was a mark of the high standards set and the preparedness of the city. This is not so much about the infrastructure and facilities, but the resilience of a Bombay boy to get up at dawn and make his way to the maidan. The message is loud and clear: It's taken me a lot to get here, I have no intention of buckling without a fight.

Because of these standards, an incumbent icon sees a young debutant as an equal. Then camaraderie weaves its magic, heroes become teammates, icons become human.

Cricket has evolved. Other teams have raised their standards. The awe that Bombay commanded has diminished, but the respect for the work ethic of a Bombay cricketer is still apparent, although fading.

The IPL has its own stories to tell. Of heroics and purchase prices. But explore the romantic history of Indian cricket and Bombay stands tall. The only price that dressing room puts is on the wicket. Till that is alive I have no doubt Bombay cricket — now Mumbai cricket — will live!

Shishir Hattangadi (@shishhattangadi) played 60 matches for Mumbai between 1981 and 1992, averaging 43.78.

What it means to be a global sport

MANOJ NARAYAN

Back in 2015, when the ICC announced their decision to limit the 2019 World Cup to just ten teams, there was understandable derision, even among cricket luminaries. Martin Crowe, Sachin Tendulkar and Rahul Dravid all spoke against the idea, and there were petitions online asking for the decision to be reversed.

You can see why it caused as much an uproar as it did: given all the achievements of Associate sides over the years — Ireland and Afghanistan chief among them — and at a time when FIFA and World Rugby are expanding World Cup berths, cricket seemed intent on being more exclusive.

Yet, for all the arguments for and against a ten-team World Cup, one idea that can be contested that the move is indicative of cricket's niche status, that it isn't a global sport. Simply put, the World Cup, however premier an event, is played just once in four years — it's not an accurate parameter to measure the impact cricket has on a global scale.

"I don't think cricket has been very good at educating the broader community about itself," says Tim Cutler, former chief executive of Cricket Hong Kong. "It's something that FIFA does well with its developmental programmes — they ensure their stories get around. Cricket needs to get better at telling its tales, to everyone."

Tales like the inspiring story of Sian Kelly. As part of her language degree requirements at Oxford, the 22-year-old from Solihull, England, went to South America, and did more than her bit to develop women's cricket in the region. She is now coach of the Argentina national women's team.

In fact, it's striking how many of cricket's best stories relate to sections of society that are discriminated against in some way — women, refugees, ethnic minorities, underprivileged children. The sport has helped break down class barriers, integrate refugees in foreign lands, and put countries on the map — isn't that what a global sport is supposed to be?

"Sometimes, people say it's an expat game, played only by those of a certain ethnic background," says Cutler. "But that should be celebrated. Cricket is giving opportunities to often marginalised people in communities and really bringing them together."

That spirit is no more evident than in Germany. During the refugee crisis in 2015, the country's open-door policy allowed almost a million refugees to take shelter in the country. A lot of them were from Afghanistan, and many of them have taken to cricket to help ease the transition. Some now play for the German national cricket team. Such as Izatullah Dawalatzai. The medium-pacer played five ODIs and four T20Is for Afghanistan till 2015, but then left it all behind and moved to Germany to be with his fiancée. In August 2018, he turned out for Germany for the first time.

While Dawalatzai's story is one of love, others in the cricket circle in Germany are less fortunate. "They've come from places which have a lot of problems, a lot of violence, and they emigrated to Germany," says Brian Mantle, the chief executive of the Deutscher Cricket Bund.

"In the last two years, around 280,000 Afghans have come to Germany. They're nearly all male, they're all fairly young, and we help them play cricket, in clubs and leagues. In return, the Afghans then go out and try and get integrated to Germany.

"It's like a circle. You think about how cricket developed — it's an English sport. England took it to India, Pakistan. The Pakistanis introduced it to the Afghans, and now the Afghans are bringing cricket back to the Europeans."

Germany is now, reportedly, one of the fastest growing centres for cricket, with more regular players than the rest of continental Europe combined, apart from the Netherlands.

Another unlikely cricket destination is Brazil. Known for samba football and jogo bonito, it's also carving a niche for itself in cricket, particularly in women's cricket. So much so that in ten years Brazil will "be a force to be reckoned with" in women's cricket, according to Matt Featherstone, Cricket Brasil's development director.

They won the 2018 South American Women's Championship in Bogota in August, comfortably seeing off Chile and Mexico, and more people than ever before have taken up the sport in the country. The highlight of the year for Cricket Brasil was the sanctioning of government funding — "They are going to come in and support it as a federal sport, recognise it and take it to the next level," says Featherstone.

That is huge: it shows that cricket has already progressed to such an extent as to unlock government investment. "Women's cricket has gone through the roof. It's where we're focusing 70 per cent of our attention," says Featherstone. "We see that Brazil could be a potential force in women's cricket quite quickly. Realistically, being a force in men's cricket is a very long-term project. But in women's cricket, it's not such a distant journey."

Unlike in Germany, cricket's function in Brazil isn't to allow expats to settle down (although that is a nice side-effect); it is to help underprivileged Brazilian children break out from the vicious cycle of poverty, via university programmes, onto the path of something that can lead to a better life.

"There's no doubt that the values of cricket are something that has helped us promote the game," Featherstone continues. "We work with underprivileged kids — almost 99 per cent of the kids we work with are from these backgrounds, without the opportunities a lot of people have.

"We found that cricket has been accepted by communities fantastically well. Not only is it a great game, its values of discipline, respect, teamwork serve us well in life, not just on the pitch. We're seeing it making a difference in community development, to those that don't have a good time in life."

The sport's expanding reach is highlighted by the fact that the locals are the ones benefitting from the sport. "It's all very well having the Indians and the English and the Pakistanis saying what a wonderful game it is, but it really makes a difference in the country once you've got Brazilians living, breathing, playing and loving the sport. That's where the difference is made."

There are plenty of stories of similar spirit from across the world. Other sports do this too, of course, but their reach is nothing like cricket's. According to the ICC's global market research, released in June 2018, cricket has "more than one billion fans worldwide", which makes it the second-most popular team sport in the world.

Even accounting for the fact that nearly 90 per cent of those fans are from the sub-continent — a point always raised by those calling it a niche sport — the scale is huge, given the survey's ambit didn't go past the 12 Full Members, China and the United States, and did not take into account major Associate nations.

"India has a population of 1.2 billion. If even some of them take it all over the world, we could one day have a 20-25 big cricket-playing countries in the world," says Mantle.

Across the divide: Bangladesh, Ireland, PNG, Scotland, Netherlands, Uganda, Thailand and UAE at the ICC Women's World T20 Qualifier 2018, reflecting the spread of cricket away from its traditional centres. – *ICC*

Cutler agrees: "Give me another sport that crosses more cultural divide. Look at India and Pakistan — the background of the guys in the Hong Kong team, a lot of them are of Indian and Pakistani heritage, and they're all together. That's the beauty of cricket.

"People calling it an expat sport don't realise there's an opportunity to learn about these people, see what binds them together, the qualities that can cut through countries."

Yet, despite all that it could offer — and this is the nagging thing about cricket — there's something holding it back from realising all this potential. Something that's led to all the talk of it being an exclusive sport in the first place. "It could be so much more," is how Featherstone puts it.

A step towards that end is fairly straightforward, too. If cricket is made an Olympic sport — and 87 per cent in ICC's survey wanted it to be so — almost every cricket-playing country, including the 104 ICC members, stands to gain.

"Countries like Germany, the money they will get from their governments, it would dwarf what we get from the ICC. The Rugby Association of Germany got a million euros in their first year (as an Olympic sport). They built a fantastic performance centre, they got the best coaches, the best facilities," says Mantle, sounding almost envious.

The example of Rugby is cited in Brazil as well. "All Olympic sports in Brazil receive essential central funding. In ten years, Rugby went from 0 to a 100. In fact, the All Blacks are coming here to play the Brazilian team. That's huge, that's massive. It's like Brazil playing India in cricket."

All of which makes you wonder — why all this fuss about the ten-team World Cup? It's not a sign that cricket isn't a global sport — it is, and more than most. It's just that it can be so much more.

Manoj Narayan (@ojerson8) is a sportswriter whose work has appeared in Wisden, the Guardian *and* the Blizzard.

PART TWO

World Cup

Evenly matched: New Zealand had been England's inspiration for their turnaround after the disappointment of 2015. — *Getty Images*

Good guys finish equal

LAWRENCE BOOTH

England, as if we didn't know, do not win World Cups the easy way. In 1966, their footballers needed extra time to beat West Germany. In 2003, their rugby players beat Australia with the last kick of the game, again in extra time. Now, in 2019, their male cricketers, making use of playing regulations few even knew existed, broke their duck in the most dramatic circumstances imaginable.

After 50 overs of the final against New Zealand, the scores were tied at 241 apiece, sending the match into a Super Over — cricket's answer to the penalty shoot-out. Again, the scores were tied, 15-15 (appropriately, since an epic Wimbledon men's singles final had just concluded a few miles southwest of Lord's). But the rubric, known in advance by both dressing-rooms, stated that the teams would now be separated by boundary countback across the whole game: England won 26-17, and so it was Eoin Morgan, not Kane Williamson, who held the trophy aloft on a glorious evening in St John's Wood. It was the culmination of four years' extraordinary work in which Morgan had turned his side from laughing stock into world beaters.

For New Zealand, it was hard to stomach. Williamson, magnanimous to the last, did his best, and the world loved him even more for it. When it soon emerged that Ben Stokes had wrongly been awarded six runs, rather than five, following an overthrow in the final over of England's 50, New Zealand's sense of injustice burned brighter still. "We're gutted," said Williamson. Being named player of the tournament was little consolation.

Few, though, could argue that England had not been the better side overall. After stumbling in the group stage against Sri Lanka and Pakistan, they were up against a north-face-of-the-Eiger route to the trophy: group matches against India and New Zealand, a semi-final against the resurgent Australians, then another meeting with New Zealand. It said plenty for the reserves of self-belief they had built up since the previous World Cup that the challenge inspired them.

Impetus came from their opening partnership, and in particular from Jason Roy. After missing three group games — including Sri Lanka and Australia — because of hamstring trouble, he returned to take on India and put on 160 with Jonny Bairstow, helping England to a total that proved beyond Virat Kohli's men. Against New Zealand in Durham, the pair added 123. In both games, Bairstow made a century, fired up by public criticism from former England captain Michael Vaughan. Then, in a semi-final in which Australia were demolished by eight wickets, the openers began with 124. Their batting was gloriously uninhibited, at least until New Zealand's seamers cramped their style on a grudging Lord's pitch.

England had heroes with the ball, too — not least Jofra Archer, the 24-year-old Barbados-born fast bowler who had qualified for the team only a matter of weeks earlier. He took 20 wickets, regularly hit top-order batsmen on the helmet, and bowled that Super Over as if he were serving a pint down the local. To concede only six runs from its last four balls was a miracle.

New Zealand would have been first-time winners too, and prepared for the low-scoring thriller at Lord's with a low-scoring thriller at Old Trafford against India. Spread across two days because of Manchester rain, the game was all but settled when India, chasing 240, slid to 5 for 3, then 24 for 4, on the second morning. Ravindra Jadeja, mysteriously ignored by the selectors until India's final group game, rallied, but, not for the first time, MS Dhoni scored too slowly and India fell short. After his side had

Fast-tracked into the squad, Jofra Archer was a star. — *Getty Images* topped the group stage, in which Rohit Sharma scored a World Cup-record five centuries, Kohli was stunned. Asked whether future tournaments should adopt an IPL play-off system, allowing the table-toppers two cracks at the final, his eyes lit up. If that was predictable, the failure of the world's greatest one-day batsman to reach three figures even once was not.

Australia, too, had looked imposing during a 45-match group stage. Outclassed by India at The Oval, they grew in confidence, thanks in large part to their opening partnership of captain Aaron Finch and David Warner. Mitchell Starc's left-arm yorkers were often unplayable — his 27 wickets were a World Cup record — and the one that bowled Stokes in Australia's win over England at Lord's was the ball of the tournament. But, like India, they had problems in the middle order. And, unlike India, for whom Jasprit Bumrah was sensational, their back-up bowlers were underwhelming. When Finch and Warner both failed in a raucous semi-final at Edgbaston, not even the skill of Steve Smith could save them.

For a while, an elongated group stage — too long for some tastes, but at least allowing each team their own mini-final against all other nine — faced two problems. Unseasonally wet weather from the second Monday took the number of no-results or abandonments in the first 18 games to four. Any more, and the World Cup risked farce.

The second problem — of predictable results leading to four predictable semi-finalists — was temporarily solved when England failed to chase 233 to beat Sri Lanka at Headingley. At a stroke, the Sri Lankans, as well as Pakistan, Bangladesh and even West Indies and South Africa had a chance of the semi-finals, lending a frisson to almost all the remaining group games.

In the end, the four — largely predictable — semi-finalists were confirmed by England's victory over New Zealand, who thus entered the knockouts after three successive defeats (they also lost to Pakistan and Australia, and along with Afghanistan were the only two not to make a 300-plus total). It was cruel on Pakistan, who were pipped by New Zealand on net run-rate despite winning their final four group games. It came as no surprise when Pakistan's coach, Mickey Arthur, suggested teams level on points should be separated by most wins, then by head-to-head results.

Bangladesh chased 322 to beat West Indies at Taunton, an anomaly in a competition where the pitches grew slower, and the next best successful pursuit was India's 265 for 3 against Sri Lanka at Headingley. But the Bangladeshis were too reliant on the all-round talents of Shakib Al Hasan and the wickets of Mustafizur Rahman. Soon after their exit, they parted company with coach Steve Rhodes.

Sri Lanka peaked against England, but did little besides, while Afghanistan failed to win a game, squandering strong positions against both India and Pakistan. The two biggest disappointments were South Africa, who never recovered their poise after losing their first three matches, and West Indies, who bounced Pakistan out for 105, but thereafter beat only the Afghans.

Yet those narratives had long since faded as Archer, in front of a worldwide audience of many millions, prepared to bowl the final ball of the Super Over to Martin Guptill, with New Zealand needing two. Brilliantly, he produced a yorker outside leg stump, obliging Guptill to drive to deep midwicket. Roy, after an earlier fumble, collected the ball cleanly and threw to the wicket-keeper's end. As if in slow motion, Jos Buttler demolished the stumps before Guptill dived home. To the victors, the spoils. And, for once, to the losers too.

Lawrence Booth (@the_topspin) is editor of the Wisden Cricketers' Almanack *and a cricket writer for* the Daily Mail.

India get the blues

KARUNYA KESHAV

"Don't know about football, but Manchester was blue today," Virat Kohli tweeted after India's win against West Indies at Old Trafford. The background for his smiling face — and indeed for much of the World Cup in England — was a sea of Indian fans in their sky blue jerseys and waving the tri-colour. England supporters at stadiums sang "Cricket's coming home", their version of the infectious optimism that had swept the country last summer when the national football side reached the semi-final of the World Cup in Russia. But, for all practical purposes, the 'home' side at any cricket stadium, even on these foreign shores, were Kohli and his men in blue.

Coming into the tournament, the team, ranked No.2 in the world and having in their midst the highest ranked batsman (Kohli) and bowler (Jasprit Bumrah), as well as the most in-form top order, were in a good place to make their support base of millions very happy. England may have been the tournament favourites, but over the past four years, India's comparative conservatism had worked well for them. Their top three had made an art of starting cautiously before exploding: their 45 hundreds since the last World Cup before this one was the most for any team, and 13 better than England's; their average was 58.8 as against England's 46.2. Their bowlers had also taken more wickets, and their wrist-spinners were two of the three Indians in the top ten for best averages among frontline bowlers.

These numbers were a testimony to their considerable talent and depth. And it made for remarkable consistency, especially in global tournaments, with India in the top four in all the major tournaments since their 2011 World Cup win. Including that tournament, in 26 World Cup matches, they've lost just four. Unfortunately, two of those were semi-final games — and they stumbled in this edition too.

Rather than a reflection on how the team does under pressure, the knock-out losses point to missteps in planning. The confusion around the No.4 role and the lack of a top-order batsman who could bowl a little, meant they were constantly searching for balance. The Vijay Shankar experiment never really got a proper examination, as the all-rounder went home injured. And Shikhar Dhawan's exit with a finger injury threatened to expose their Achilles heel: the middle order. Since the 2015 edition, India's top order had made 51 per cent of their runs; since the 2017 Champions Trophy, the No.4 and 5 averaged 33.85 runs per wicket. Rohit Sharma was imperious in making a record five World Cup hundreds, but test him and K L Rahul with the moving ball early and the opposition could get a look in. This is exactly what New Zealand's excellent seam bowlers did.

Small margins: M S Dhoni allowed Indian fans to hope for a come-from-behind win until his run-out in the penultimate over changed the game. — *Getty Images*

The world's best batsman never got to three figures and M S Dhoni continued to divide opinion. Was he too slow or simply a brilliant calculator of how and when to attack? Martin Guptill's rocket arm to run him out in the penultimate over, when 25 were needed off 10 balls, means we'll never know, and an illustrious career might have ended without a trademark finish in style.

Even Faf du Plessis had predicted an India v England final, but it wasn't to be. Perhaps England v New Zealand was the best thing to happen for the game: a new winner, and a brand of ODI defined by two gentlemen captains without the jingoism that seems to follow subcontinent teams. There were a fair number of India jerseys in the stands at Lord's, but it was England's powder blue that prevailed. And, despite the controversial finish, you couldn't help but smile at what this group of men had pulled off.

Rarely has a men's team in recent times had to carry the burden of inspiring a generation and making a country fall in love with cricket again. But when Lord's rose as one, Trafalgar Square erupted and a thousand pubs around England roared in celebration on a Sunday summer's evening in July, you'd dare to believe that Eoin Morgan and his men, World Cup trophy aloft, champagne popped, had done just that.

During England's biggest summer of cricket, with the men's World Cup to be followed by the Ashes, the most awaited event on TV was *Love Island*, a reality show as bewildering as its title suggests. Cricket hasn't been on free-to-air TV in the UK since 2005, when Freddie and KP went to town on the Aussies and ignited a thousand cricketing passions. Since then, watching the traditionally English sport on the small screen (legally) has proved remarkably difficult and expensive. That Flintoff's incredible over at Edgbaston in that 2005 series is still invoked in ads 14 years later should suggest just how cricket out of sight has been out of mind. That India, Pakistan and Bangladesh fans at the 2019 tournament out-numbered and out-shouted the 'home' fans reiterated just how comprehensively the home of the sport has shifted to the subcontinent.

So, the pressure to leave a legacy with this World Cup was huge, and England turned to their Irish-born captain to help make new memories. That his side delivered, in a mad and beautiful final that just for one day brought cricket to terrestrial TV and screens in parks and bars and homes and city squares, was more than ICC, the ECB or the organisers could have asked for.

The World Cup need look no further than its winners to see what diversity can do. Their captain figured he had the rub of the green; his star leg-spinner told him "Allah was on our side"; his match-winner on the day was born in New Zealand, his talismanic opener in South Africa, the nerveless youngster bowling the Super Over in Barbados. Cricket has many homes, and the door should be open for more.

ICC Men's Cricket World Cup 2019

England beat South Africa by 104 runs

Faf du Plessis caused a stir by tossing the ball to Imran Tahir to get the World Cup to an unexpected start. Tahir responded by having Jonny Bairstow caught behind with his second ball, but that was where South Africa's dominance in the match ended. The other four men in England's top five — Jason Roy, Joe Root, Eoin Morgan and Ben Stokes — all slammed fifties. A score of 311 for 8 was befitting of England's reputation over the past four years. Jofra Archer, fast-tracked into the England side, then lived up to the hype. He hit the grille of the helmet to force Hashim Amla to retire hurt, had Aiden Markram caught at slip, du Plessis hooking and, later in the day, Rassie van der Dussen caught at mid-on. Quinton de Kock and the amazingly consistent van der Dussen — he arrived in England with a career average of 88.25 — added 85 for the third wicket, but it was never going to be enough, not even after Amla returned to make a battle of it.

The Oval, London, May 30: England 311/8 (Ben Stokes 89, Eoin Morgan 57; Lungi Ngidi 3-66, Imran Tahir 2-61) beat **South Africa** 207 in 39.5 overs (Quinton de Kock 68, Rassie van der Dussen 50; Jofra Archer 3-27, B Stokes 2-12) by 104 runs. *PoM:* Ben Stokes.

West Indies beat Pakistan by seven wickets

Of late, Trent Bridge has multiple hosted run fests including the two highest scores in ODI history, but West Indies showed up with the intention of changing that perception. They had two genuinely quick bowlers and three more who bowled at a brisk pace. They stuck to a simple strategy — one that their predecessors had adapted with much success decades ago: bowl short.

The fast bowlers shot out Pakistan for 105, their second-lowest total in World Cup history. Their top order then chased down the target at almost eight an over. The entire thing lasted 35.2 overs. Fakhar Zaman and Babar Azam took Pakistan to 35 for 1 after Imam-ul-Haq fell cheaply. Then Andre Russell began the rout: a bouncer hit Fakhar on the grille and the ball rolled on to the stumps. Oshane Thomas was accurate, and just like Russell, peppered the batsmen with bouncers, pitching one up for variation. Pakistan's only takeaway from the match was Mohammad Amir's excellent bowling: he maintained a steady line to take all three wickets to fall.

Trent Bridge, Nottingham, May 31: Pakistan 105 in 21.4 overs (Oshane Thomas 4-27, Jason Holder 3-42) lost to **West Indies** 108/3 in 13.4 overs (Chris Gayle 50, Nicolas Pooran 34*; Mohammad Amir 3-26) by seven wickets. *PoM:* Oshane Thomas.

New Zealand beat Sri Lanka by ten wickets

Kane Williamson won the toss on a green pitch and Sri Lanka were bowled out for 136 by Lockie Ferguson and Matt Henry in just 29.2 overs. Martin Guptill and Colin Munro made it through comfortably for New Zealand. Kusal Perera smashed four fours soon after Henry got Lahiru Thirimanne off the second ball of the match, but the innings fell apart once Colin de Grandhomme caught him brilliantly at mid-on. Sri Lanka, 46 for 1 after eight overs, ended up losing 5 for 14 in 44 balls. Thisara Perera launched his characteristic onslaught, lofting de Grandhomme and Jimmy Neesham for sixes, but the damage had already been done. Dimuth Karunaratne, appointed captain just before the World Cup, had not played an ODI for over four years before this summer. He stood tall amidst the carnage with a hard-earned unbeaten 52, setting the 12th instance (and second in World Cup cricket) of a batsman carrying his bat in the format.

Cardiff Wales Stadium, June 1: Sri Lanka 136 in 29.2 overs (Dimuth Karunaratne 52*, Kusal Perera 29; Lockie Ferguson 3-22, Matt Henry 3-29) lost to **New Zealand** 137/0 in 16.1 overs (Martin Guptill 73*, Colin Munro 58*) by ten wickets. *PoM:* Matt Henry.

Australia beat Afghanistan by seven wickets

Afghanistan paid the price for their attractive yet counterintuitive cricket. All Australia needed to do was to stay unfazed, bowl accurately. Once that was done, Aaron Finch went after the bowling to smash 66. David Warner curbed his instincts to bat through the innings for 89, celebrating his return to international cricket. It was not an easy task amidst boos (a couple even dressed up as sandpaper boxes), but he stayed put. The Afghan openers tried to swat Mitchell Starc and Pat Cummins away without bothering to move their feet. Neither managed a single run. Rahmat Shah batted sensibly, but Steve Smith, also making his comeback, caught him and spectacularly ran out Mohammad Nabi to reduce them to 77 for 5. With 15 overs to play and just two wickets in hand, Rashid Khan and Mujeeb Ur Rahman threw their bat around to add 39 in just 15 balls. Zampa's figures (8-0-60-3) reflected the Afghan approach more than anything else: breakneck, outrageous, perilous.

County Ground, Bristol, June 1: Afghanistan 207 in 38.2 overs (Najibullah Zadran 51, Rahmat Shah 43; Pat Cummins 3-40, Adam Zampa 3-60) lost to **Australia** 209/3 in 34.5 overs (David Warner 89*, Aaron Finch 66) by seven wickets. *PoM:* David Warner.

Bangladesh beat South Africa by 21 runs

Having already lost Anrich Nortje and Dale Steyn (and for this match, Amla), South Africa now had to do without Ngidi, who hobbled off with a pulled hamstring after sending down four overs. Kagiso Rabada had an off day, catches flew through gaps, fielders spilled catches in a very un-South African fashion. Despite that, they might have got away against a weaker batting line-up, but Bangladesh had both the quality and depth to take advantage. Soumya Sarkar pulled every short-pitched delivery en route a chancy 42. Then Shakib Al Hasan and Mushfiqur Rahim, in their contrasting styles, added 142 for the third wicket — a record partnership for any wicket for Bangladesh in World Cup cricket. Mahmudullah and Mosaddek Hossain continued with the onslaught, helping Bangladesh post 330 for 6, the highest score in their ODI history.

South Africa started well, but unlike Bangladesh, they never got that one big, decisive partnership. While nine of their men reached double figures, du Plessis was the only one to cross fifty.

The Oval, London, June 2: Bangladesh 330/6 (Mushfiqur Rahim 78, Shakib Al Hasan 75; Andile Phehlukwayo 2-52, Imran Tahir 2-57) beat **South Africa** 309/8 (Faf du Plessis 62, Aiden Markram 45; Mustafizur Rahman 3-67, Saifuddin 2-57) by 21 runs. *PoM:* Shakib Al Hasan.

Pakistan beat England by 14 runs

Pakistan were back to being their unpredictable selves. After being blown away by West Indies (their tenth ODI defeat in a row), they took down favourites and top-ranked England. This, less than a month after they were routed 4-0 in the ODIs by the same team. The same batting line-up that had lasted 130 balls against West Indies put up 348 against England. Then the bowlers restricted England to 334, a total England had exceeded four times in as many attempts in the bilateral series mentioned above. Babar, Mohammad Hafeez, and Sarfaraz Ahmed all scored quick fifties after the openers put up 82. The onslaught was only punctuated by a poignant moment, when Asif Ali walked out to bat — a fortnight after he had lost his 19-month-old daughter to cancer.

Joe Root and Jos Buttler responded by slamming the first two hundreds of the World Cup in contrasting styles, adding 130 in 105 balls. England needed 61 in 34 balls when Amir got rid of Buttler to dent England's progress. Wahab Riaz, a surprise recall to the squad, picked up wickets in consecutive balls in the 48th over to as good as seal the match.

All-round legend: Shakib Al Hasan finished the tournament with 606 runs and 11 wickets. — *Getty Images*

Trent Bridge, Nottingham, June 3: Pakistan 348/8 (Mohammad Hafeez 84, Babar Azam 63; Moeen Ali 3-50, Chris Woakes 3-71) beat **England** 334/9 (Joe Root 107, Jos Buttler 103; Wahab Riaz 3-82; Shadab Khan 2-63) by 14 runs. *PoM*: Mohammad Hafeez.

Sri Lanka beat Afghanistan by 34 runs (DLS method)

Afghanistan will rue letting go the opportunity of winning. The proceedings changed course more frequently than the clouds overhead as Sri Lanka's experience saw them through. Perera got Sri Lanka off to a rollicking start, adding 92 with Karunaratne and 52 with Thirimanne. They started by taking 30 runs off the first two overs of the typically economical Hamid Hassan, and marched on. Not for the first time did Kusal Perera evoke memories of Sanath Jayasuriya at the grand stage. He slashed hard, he went over the top, and his powerful forearms ensured that even the mistimed shots cleared the 30-yard circle. Sri Lanka were 144 for 1 when Nabi began the 22nd over. He had Thirimanne playing on to the stumps with the second ball; Kusal Mendis and Angelo Mathews were caught at slip off the fourth and sixth. The middle order collapsed in a heap, and Sri Lanka were 182 for 8 after 33 overs when rain halted play. By then Perera had fallen for 78. Afghanistan were set 187 in 41 overs, but were quickly reduced to 57 for 5 before Naib and Najibullah added 64. They found Lasith Malinga and Nuwan Pradeep's yorkers too hot to handle, though.

Sofia Gardens, Cardiff, June 4: Sri Lanka 201 in 36.5 overs (Kusal Perera 78, Dimuth Karunaratne 30; Mohammad Nabi 4-30, Rashid Khan 2-17) beat **Afghanistan** 152 in 32.4 overs (Najibullah Zadran 43, Hazratullah Zazai 30; Nuwan Pradeep 4-31, Lasith Malinga 3-39) by 34 runs (DLS). *PoM*: Nuwan Pradeep.

India beat South Africa by six wickets

The odd scheduling meant that India's first match was South Africa's third. After a lower-order resurgence took them from 89 for 5 to 227 for 9, South Africa got Shikhar Dhawan and Virat Kohli out of the way early. But Rohit Sharma weathered the storm to see India home with an unbeaten century. Jasprit Bumrah sent back the South African openers by the sixth over. There was some resistance from du Plessis and van der Dussen before the wrist-spinners, who had routed South Africa repeatedly in their den on the 2017-18 tour, were put into action. Yuzvendra Chahal bowled van der Dussen round his legs and du Plessis through the gate, while Kuldeep Yadav had JP Duminy caught and bowled. Rabada and Chris Morris gave the Indians a torrid time with the new ball. There were a few edges and mistimed shots, but the balls ballooned off the bat to land harmlessly. After de Kock flew spectacularly to his right to catch Kohli, Rohit found allies in KL Rahul and MS Dhoni.

Rose Bowl, Southampton, June 5: South Africa 227/9 (Chris Morris 44, Faf du Plessis 38; Yuzvendra Chahal 4-51, Jasprit Bumrah 2-35) lost to **India** 230/4 in 47.3 overs (Rohit Sharma 122*, MS Dhoni 34; Kagiso Rabada 2-39) by six wickets. *PoM*: Rohit Sharma.

New Zealand beat Bangladesh by two wickets

Had Bangladesh pulled off a heist, New Zealand would have had only themselves to blame. They needed 85 in 19 overs with eight wickets in hand when Williamson tried to clear the midwicket boundary off Mehidy Hasan and failed. The middle order caved in, and suddenly New Zealand found they had to chase 27 with three wickets. Fortunately for them, Mitchell Santner kept his cool after Ross Taylor had held the innings together. The New Zealand fast bowlers were not as effective as against Sri Lanka. Once again Soumya Sarkar was off to a fluent start, and once again he threw it away attempting a slog. The top eight Bangladeshi batsmen all reached double figures, but only one, Shakib, went past 30. Wickets at regular intervals meant they did not have enough in the bank for that final onslaught.

The Oval, London, June 5: Bangladesh 244 in 49.2 overs (Shakib Al Hasan 64, Saifuddin 29; Matt Henry 4-47, Trent Boult 2-44) lost to **New Zealand** 248/8 in 47.1 overs (Ross Taylor 82, Kane Williamson 40; Mosaddek Hossain 2-33, Saifuddin 2-41) by two wickets. *PoM:* Ross Taylor.

Australia beat West Indies by 15 runs

West Indies came into the match with a twofold plan: to pepper Australia with bouncers — it had worked against Pakistan at the same venue, after all — and get their famed line-up of big hitters to have a go. It worked for a while. Australia were reduced to 38 for 4 by the eighth over, but the world champions remained unfazed under pressure. Smith held one end up, Alex Carey got a brisk 45, but the real star was Nathan Coulter-Nile, who slammed his List A highest score of 92, off 60 balls. Before the match, the Australians had had a verbal go at Chris Gayle. He came out all guns blazing, was given out twice, got both upturned, hit four fours, and got out to a ball immediately after a no-ball that was not called — all within 17 balls. Like Smith, Shai Hope held one end up as his big-hitting team-mates went for the kill. In the end, though, Mitchell Starc ran through the lower order.

Trent Bridge, Nottingham, June 6: Australia 288 in 49 overs (Nathan Coulter-Nile 92, Steve Smith 73; Carlos Brathwaite 3-67, Andre Russell 2-41) beat **West Indies** 273/9 (Shai Hope 68, Jason Holder 51; Mitchell Starc 5-46, Pat Cummins 2-41) by 15 runs. *PoM:* Nathan Coulter-Nile.

Pakistan v Sri Lanka: Match abandoned

It rained steadily in Bristol, following which the umpires decided that the outfield was too wet for cricket.

Bristol County Ground, June 7: Pakistan v **Sri Lanka**. Match abandoned.

England beat Bangladesh by 106 runs

England turned things around after their defeat against Pakistan, putting up 386 for 6 — their highest score in the World Cup as well as by any team at this venue — and bowling out Bangladesh for 280. Shakib scored a scintillating century against all odds (and Archer) but found little support from his colleagues. England approached the match cautiously, scoring 15 off their first five overs after Bangladesh opened with Shakib. Roy paced his hundred well. Once there, his third fifty took only 28 balls, and included four sixes. Buttler and Morgan joined in the fun as well, and Woakes and Liam Plunkett added 45 in 17 balls to take the total beyond Bangladesh's reach. Archer began in outrageous fashion: he bowled Soumya with a ball so fast that it hit the stumps and crossed the ropes without touching the ground. Barring Shakib, Mushfiqur Rahim was the only one to put up some fight. Whatever chance they had evaporated when Stokes demolished the lower middle order in a quick burst.

Sofia Gardens, Cardiff, June 8: England 386/6 (Jason Roy 153, Jos Buttler 64; Mehidy Hasan 2-67, Saifuddin 2-78) beat **Bangladesh** 280 in 48.5 overs (Shakib Al Hasan 121, Mushfiqur Rahim 44; Ben Stokes 3-23, Jofra Archer 3-29) by 106 runs. *PoM*: Jason Roy.

New Zealand beat Afghanistan by seven wickets

New Zealand kept their unbeaten run going despite Afghanistan's bright start. The day began with Hazratullah Zazai walking out with the intent of filling the shoes of Mohammad Shahzad, who had returned home with an injury. He slammed three fours in the first over, picking out Henry for special treatment. Noor Ali Zadran dropped anchor at the other end. They raced to 65 at a run a ball before Zazai slogged Neesham to deep point. Two balls later Ferguson had Noor caught down the leg side. Then, on either side of a rain break, Afghanistan were bowled out by the variations of Neesham and the pace of Ferguson. Tom Latham held five catches. Hashmatullah Shahidi's 59 made the collapse look more surreal. There was no Mujeeb, while Rashid did not take field after being hit on the helmet by Ferguson and failing two concussion tests. Aftab Alam struck thrice, including the wicket of Guptill with the first ball of the innings, but it turned out to be a no-contest.

County Ground Taunton, June 8: Afghanistan 172 in 44.1 overs (Hashmatullah Shahidi 59, Hazratullah Zazai 34; Jimmy Neesham 5-31, Lockie Ferguson 4-37) lost to **New Zealand** 173/3 in 32.1 overs (Kane Williamson 79*, Ross Taylor 48; Aftab Alam 3-45) by seven wickets. *PoM:* Jimmy Neesham.

India beat Australia by 36 runs

India's top three had been significantly more prolific than any other side's in the two years before the World Cup. They lived up to their reputation, scoring 256 between them at a run a ball. Dhawan played the big innings — a belligerent, dominating 117 — but it came at a cost. He copped a blow on the thumb from Pat Cummins that ruled him out of the tournament. Hardik Pandya launched a brutal onslaught, while Dhoni's six off Starc over square leg left his partner Kohli open-mouthed. The last ten overs fetched 116.

Smith was jeered by a section of the crowd, only for Kohli to step in and insist they changed the boos into cheers. Australia approached the target by keeping wickets in hand for the final onslaught. Finch was run out just when the first-wicket stand was looking ominous, following which Warner got overcautious. With 118 needed off 11 overs, Australia were still in it, but Bhuvneshwar Kumar sealed it by picking up Smith and Marcus Stoinis in three balls. Chahal got Glenn Maxwell four balls later.

The Oval, London, June 9: India 352/5 (Shikhar Dhawan 117, Virat Kohli 82; Marcus Stoinis 2-62) beat **Australia** 316 (Steve Smith 69, David Warner 56; Bhuvneshwar Kumar 3-50, Jasprit Bumrah 3-61) by 36 runs. *PoM*: Shikhar Dhawan.

Shikhar Dhawan: Hundred and out of the tournament. — *Getty Images*

West Indies v South Africa: Match abandoned

It rained in Southampton 45 balls into the match, and play had to be abandoned. Nevertheless, there was enough time for West Indies to put South Africa in under testing conditions, and for Sheldon Cottrell to snare Amla and Markram, following each dismissal by his now-familiar salute.

Rose Bowl, Southampton, June 10: South Africa 29/2 in 7.3 overs (Sheldon Cottrell 2-29) v **West Indies**. No result.

Bangladesh v Sri Lanka: Match abandoned

Sri Lanka now had their second washed-out match and Bangladesh their first. In fact, things were so murky at Bristol that neither side bothered to leave their hotels before noon. Bangladesh coach Steve Rhodes complained about the lack of a reserve day in the tournament.

Bristol County Ground, June 11: Bangladesh v **Sri Lanka.** Match abandoned.

Australia beat Pakistan by 41 runs

Pakistan were back to being Pakistan: they leaked runs, came back strongly, lost an early wicket, recovered, collapsed, recovered again, and collapsed again. Finch and Warner added 146 in 133 balls at the top on a pitch where neither side fielded a specialist spinner. Pakistan's bowling was erratic, the ground fielding sloppy, the throwing abysmal at times, and many catches went down. However, a collapse in the slog overs restricted Australia to 307 after they were 277 for 5 in 42 overs. The damage was done by Amir; two of his first three overs were maidens. Imam dropped anchor at one end in response, allowing Babar and Hafeez to go after the bowling. A collapse left them reeling at 140 for 6, but Sarfaraz stayed put as Hasan Ali and Wahab hit six sixes at the other end. Pakistan brought it down to 44 from 35 before their last three wickets went down for two runs.

County Ground Taunton, June 12: Australia 307 in 49 overs (David Warner 107, Aaron Finch 82; Mohammad Amir 5-30, Shaheen Afridi 2-70) beat **Pakistan** 266 in 45.4 overs (Imam-ul-Haq 53, Mohammad Hafeez 46; Pat Cummins 3-33, Mitchell Starc 2-43) by 41 runs. *PoM*: David Warner.

India v New Zealand: Match abandoned

India and New Zealand arrived at Trent Bridge unbeaten, and a washout meant that both sides stayed unbeaten. The abandonment also meant that 2019 became the first edition of the World Cup where three matches had to be called off without a ball being bowled.

Trent Bridge, Nottingham, June 13: India v **New Zealand.** Match abandoned.

England beat West Indies by eight wickets

This was Root's match. First he claimed two catches off his own bowling and then made his second century of this World Cup to put the result beyond speculation. England, electing to field, were barely challenged as the fast men struck regularly. The danger men Gayle and Russell both fell pulling to square leg on a ground whose size they seemed to have misjudged. What was required was Root-type gap-finding and running. Nicholas Pooran alone among the West Indies batsmen did that consistently. Root then added 95 with Bairstow, opening the batting for the first time after Roy (hamstring) and skipper Morgan (back spasms) went off the field in the first half. The West Indies too had their problems, Russell hobbling off after his second over. Woakes's 40 at one-drop gave England another option at the top.

Rose Bowl, Southampton, June 14: West Indies 212 in 44.4 overs (Nicholas Pooran 63, Shimron Hetmyer 39; Mark Wood 3-18, Jofra Archer 3-30) lost to **England** 213/2 in 33.1 overs (Joe Root 100*, Jonny Bairstow 45; Shannon Gabriel 2-49) by eight wickets. *PoM*: Joe Root

Australia beat Sri Lanka by 87 runs

At 186 for 2 in the 33rd over, Sri Lanka seemed to be in with a chance. Then Karunaratne fell just short of a century, Starc swung into action, and that was that. Australia looked to have everything tied up after skipper Finch's 173-run partnership with Smith for the third wicket in 118 balls. The overcast skies meant that whoever won the toss would have sent the other side in, and so Sri Lanka fielded first. But batting was easier than anticipated, and Finch enjoyed the diet of short-pitched bowling, hitting square of the wicket with power and consistency. Maxwell followed up his unbeaten 46 in 25 balls with a bowling spell that put the brakes on the scoring and then took the catch at gully to end Karunaratne's innings. Sri Lanka lost four wickets in four overs, and looked like a team that was losing its confidence.

The Oval, London, June 15: Australia 334/7 in 50 overs (Aaron Finch 153, Steve Smith 73; Dhananjaya de Silva 2-40, Isuru Udana 2-57) beat **Sri Lanka** 247 in 45.5 overs (Dimuth Karunaratne 97, Kusal Perera 52; Mitchell Starc 4-55, Kane Richardson 3-47) by 87 runs. *PoM*: Aaron Finch

South Africa beat Afghanistan by nine wickets (DLS method)

South Africa's first win in four matches came against a team that began well but were quickly reduced to 77 for 7. Rain drove the players from the ground a couple of times, but at no point did Afghanistan look like they might surprise the higher-ranked team. Ten wickets fell for 86 as Tahir took charge; Rashid's lower-order heroics ensured the 100-mark would be crossed. With South Africa making just 35 in the first ten overs, there was some speculation about what might have been had Afghanistan put more runs on the board. But there were no hiccups as the 104-run opening partnership between de Kock and Amla took the game away.

Sofia Gardens, Cardiff, June 15: Afghanistan 125 in 34.1 overs (Rashid Khan 35, Noor Ali Zadran 32; Imran Tahir 4-29, Chris Morris 3-13) lost to **South Africa** 131/1 in 28.4 overs (Quinton de Kock 68, Hashim Amla 41*) by nine wickets (DLS method). *PoM*: Imran Tahir.

India beat Pakistan by 89 runs (DLS method)

A dominant India made it 7-0 in World Cup encounters. Pakistan struggled to contain Rohit, after fielding first under skies that might open up any time. Kohli would have fielded too, he said, although former captain and now Prime Minister of Pakistan Imran Khan tweeted this advice: bat first. A 136-run opening partnership with Rahul, moved up in place of the injured Dhawan, set the tone. Amir alone commanded some respect, but the Indians

7-0 for India: Pakistan struggled to contain Rohit Sharma as they slipped to another World Cup defeat against India. — *Getty Images*

had decided to let him run through his overs. There was an air of studied calm about the batting, and even as the lower order perished in search of quick runs, it became clear that the top half had done its job well. Such was India's power that when they lost Bhuvneshwar to injury in his third over, Vijay Shankar who replaced him, claimed a wicket with his first ball on World Cup debut. Fakhar and Babar added 104 for the second wicket, but when Kuldeep bowled Babar through the gate with the ball of the tournament so far, the fight fizzled out.

Old Trafford, Manchester, June 16: India 336/5 in 50 overs (Rohit Sharma 140, Virat Kohli 77; Mohammad Amir 3-47) beat **Pakistan** 212/6 in 40 overs (Fakhar Zaman 62, Babar Azam 48; Vijay Shankar 2-22, Kuldeep Yadav 2-32) by 89 runs (DLS method). *PoM*: Rohit Sharma

Bangladesh beat West Indies by seven wickets

Shakib's century and his 189-run stand for the fourth wicket with Liton Das made it all seem inevitable. This was Bangladesh's highest successful chase, and Shakib's second century in a World Cup, during which he crossed 6000 runs in ODIs. It was further proof that a total of 300 runs was not safe or sacred, merely the starting point of a good response. Three fifties in the Windies' innings might have given the team hope, but a tactic so successful against Pakistan did not work here. Against persistent short-pitched bowling, Shakib cut and occasionally hooked, and Liton took 24 in the 38th off Shannon Gabriel, an over which began with three sixes in a row, two of them off bouncers. Such counterattacking exposed the shortage of ideas in the Windies camp. The lack of a spinner told, as did the fitness of Russell.

County Ground Taunton, June 17: West Indies 321/8 in 50 overs (Shai Hope 96, Evin Lewis 70; Mustafizur Rahman 3-59, Saifuddin 3-72) lost to **Bangladesh** 322/3 in 41.3 overs (Shakib Al Hasan 124*, Liton Das 94*) by seven wickets. *PoM*: Shakib Al Hasan

England beat Afghanistan by 150 runs

Morgan's 17 sixes, a world record for most in an ODI innings, and his 148 off just 71 balls were blows few teams could have recovered from. Bairstow and Root too helped themselves, although at a reduced rate. Rashid, the world's leading leg-spinner, went wicketless, conceding 110 runs — 74 in his last four overs — and suddenly a team that had achieved so much in such little time looked like they had wandered into the wrong party where they were getting hit by the fireworks. England made 198 in their last 15 overs, and all considered, Afghanistan did well to bat out their 50 for their highest score in a World Cup. Statisticians had a field day, marking the most sixes by a single team (25), England's highest score in a World Cup, the most expensive bowling figures in a World Cup and the most sixes conceded by a bowler (11). In the 30th over, England were 164 for 1, Bairstow and Root having laid the platform for Morgan with a second-wicket partnership worth 120. At that stage, sobriety and calm still ruled. Then Morgan walked in, hit his eighth ball for a six, and brutality took over.

Old Trafford, Manchester, June 18: England 397/6 in 50 overs (Eoin Morgan 148, Jonny Bairstow 90; Dawlat Zadran 3-85, Gulbadain Naib 3-68) beat **Afghanistan** 247/8 in 50 overs (Hashmatullah Shahidi 76, Rahmat Shah 46; Jofra Archer 3-52, Adil Rashid 3-66) by 150 runs. *PoM*: Eoin Morgan

New Zealand beat South Africa by four wickets

New Zealand had knocked South Africa out of the World Cup twice before, and they might have made it a third time with this win. Williamson's last-over six off Andile Phehlukwayo brought up his century. Replays showed he had been caught behind in his 70s — Tahir, who had caused Williamson to under-edge the ball, was convinced he had his man — but they didn't take the review. After the match, du Plessis said that might not have been a turning point — after all, South Africa had missed catches and run outs with depressing frequency. He also said he had aged five years in the last overs. It was not an easy wicket to bat on, but South Africa's total still seemed short. Williamson's calmness meshed well with de Grandhomme's fury (his 60 came off 47 balls) as they added 91 for the sixth wicket and took the game away from South Africa.

Edgbaston, Birmingham, June 19: South Africa 241/6 in 49 overs (Rassie van der Dussen 67*, Hashim Amla 55; Lockie Ferguson 3-59) lost to **New Zealand** 245/6 in 48.3 overs (Kane Williamson 106*, Colin de Grandhomme 60; Chris Morris 3-49). *PoM*: Kane Williamson.

Australia beat Bangladesh by 48 runs

Despite Mushfiqur's century, the more powerful and bigger one by Warner (166 off 147) carried too much heft. Warner's sixth 150-plus score in ODIs was his second in a World Cup. At 313 for 1, Australia seemed headed for a 400-plus total, but despite 173 off the last 15, the low-scoring overs earlier put paid to those hopes. Maxwell, in his brief innings of 32 off 10, showed quick scoring was possible once a base had been established. It was a lesson Bangladesh took heart from, moving to 144 for 2 in 24 overs. So long as Tamim Iqbal and Shakib were together, there was hope. But Shakib fell at 102 and Tamim at 144 and despite Mushfiqur's century off 97 balls, Bangladesh lost too many wickets to trouble Australia, pushing discussions into the realm of what-ifs. The biggest of them being what if Warner had been caught at point by Sabbir Rahman when slashing Mashrafe Mortaza. Warner was on ten then.

Trent Bridge, Nottingham, June 20: Australia 381/5 in 50 overs (David Warner 166, Usman Khawaja 89; Soumya Sarkar 3-58) beat **Bangladesh** 333/8 in 50 overs (Mushfiqur Rahim 102*, Mahmudullah 69; Marcus Stoinis 2-54, Mitchell Starc 2-55) by 48 runs. *PoM*: David Warner.

Sri Lanka beat England by 20 runs

England's second loss to a team from Asia was more of a shock than the first against Pakistan. After restricting Sri Lanka to 232 and then getting to

He's still got it: Lasith Malinga bowled with nous and consistency to upset tournament favourites England and keep the World Cup alive. — *Getty Images*

170 for 5 themselves, the favourites contrived to let the match slip. Sri Lanka, let down by their batsmen (barring Angelo Mathews and Avishka Fernando, the latter alone playing a modern one-day innings), were redeemed by their bowlers Malinga and part-timer de Silva. Half-centuries by Root and the valiant Stokes were not enough to compensate for the inexplicable rush to hit big sixes that gripped some of the others. Malinga trapped Bairstow for his second first-ball dismissal in the tournament and bowled with old nous and consistency. Karunaratne led well, placing fields that not only ensured catches went straight to his men, but also dictating what the batsmen may not play. Buttler, with a short mid-on in front, tried to play square instead, and was leg before.

Headingley, Leeds, June 21: Sri Lanka 232/9 in 50 overs (Angelo Mathews 85*, Avishka Fernando 49; Mark Wood 3-40, Jofra Archer 3-52) beat **England** 212 in 47 overs (Ben Stokes 82*, Joe Root 57; Lasith Malinga 4-43, Dhananjaya de Silva 3-32). *PoM*: Lasith Malinga.

India beat Afghanistan by 11 runs

Nabi allowed Afghanistan the luxury of a dream in a tournament they were largely outplayed in. Two wickets and a fifty would have won him the match award had he carried Afghanistan over the line chasing a modest India total. But that honour went to Bumrah, who bounced out two batsmen in the 29th over with Afghanistan on 106 for 2. Nabi batted with the air of a man who knew it was only a matter of time, getting to 52 in 55 balls, which included a six off Bumrah high over midwicket. Then came Mohammed Shami, playing his first match of the tournament, to upset all plans. He first had Nabi and continued through to a hat-trick as Afghanistan, needing 12 off five balls, fell tantalisingly short. They had begun well, with Mujeeb getting Rohit with a beauty and the spinners keeping India in check. Kohli alone among the 22 batted with comfort, making 67 off 63 balls. Dhoni struggled to 28 off 52, much to the displeasure of the crowd. Luckily for India, his self-denial did not harm the team.

Rose Bowl, Southampton, June 22: India 224/8 in 50 overs (Virat Kohli 67, Kedar Jadhav 52; Mohammad Nabi 2-33, Gulbadin Naib 2-51) beat **Afghanistan** 213 in 49.5 overs (M Nabi 52, Rahmat Shah 36; Mohammed Shami 4-40, Yuzvendra Chahal 2-36) by 11 runs. *PoM*: Jasprit Bumrah.

New Zealand beat West Indies by five runs

Of the two close finishes on the same day, in this one too fortune failed to favour the brave. West Indies were 164 for 7, then 211 for 8 and 245 for 9, but Carlos Brathwaite (101 off 82 balls) exploded before he fell to Neesham in the 49th over. West Indies needed 33 from the last three, and Brathwaite looked like he might make all 33. Henry was taken for 25, and it was now eight off two overs. With the main bowlers having finished their quota, it was left to Neesham to stem the tide. Off the last ball, he had Brathwaite caught by Boult inches from the boundary and it was over. Chris Gayle was dropped twice in an over, but the medium-pacers reduced West Indies from 142 for 2 to 164 for 7. The finish meant the focus remained on West Indies, but it was Williamson's second century (148 off 154 balls) in the tournament that made all the difference.

Old Trafford, Manchester, June 22: New Zealand 291/8 in 50 overs (Kane Williamson 148, Ross Taylor 69; Sheldon Cottrell 4-56, Carlos Brathwaite 2-58) beat **West Indies** 286 in 49 overs (C Brathwaite 101, Chris Gayle 87; Trent Boult 4-30, Lockie Ferguson 3-59) by five runs. *PoM*: Kane Williamson.

Pakistan beat South Africa by 49 runs

Haris Sohail (89 off 59 balls) came in for Shoaib Malik and showed the rank foolishness of having kept him out so far. Pakistan were 143 for 2 in the 30th over, and more than doubled their score in the next 20 thanks to Sohail, who helped add 91 in the last ten. They kept their hopes alive after a demoralising defeat against India while simultaneously putting paid to South Africa's hopes. There was no choking this time, just poor cricket. "It's a little bit embarrassing," skipper du Plessis was to say after South Africa's fifth defeat in seven matches. "We keep making the same mistakes over and over again." The skipper top scored, but the team looked a beaten side even as it all began to unravel for them. With 15 overs remaining, South Africa needed to score at more than ten an over, and while Pakistan kept dropping catches — by this stage they had turfed more than any other team in the tournament — it didn't seem to matter.

Lord's, London, June 23: Pakistan 308/7 in 50 overs (Haris Sohail 89, Babar Azam 69; Lungi Ngidi 3-64, Imran Tahir 2-41) beat **South Africa** 259/9 in 50 overs (Faf du Plessis 63,

Quinton de Kock 47; Wahab Riaz 3-46, Shadab Khan 3-50) by 49 runs. *PoM*: Haris Sohail.

Bangladesh beat Afghanistan by 62 runs

Shakib became only the third player, after Kapil Dev and Yuvraj Singh, to score a century and claim a five-wicket haul in the same World Cup. His fifth 50-plus score took Bangladesh to safety, while his 5 for 29 were the best bowling figures in a World Cup for his country. Mushfiqur batted with freedom, but it still took a 35 off 24 by Mosaddek to take Bangladesh past 250. Mujeeb's three had kept the scoring rate in check: there were no boundaries in 12 overs after the 24th. Afghanistan's reply was safe rather than spectacular till Shakib entered the picture, picked up Rahmat in his first over and soon had Naib and Nabi in the space of three balls. If there was the slightest doubt about the winners of this match, Shakib's spell ended that.

Rose Bowl, Southampton, June 24: Bangladesh 262/7 in 50 overs (Mushfiqur Rahim 83, Shakib Al Hasan 51; Mujeeb Ur Rahman 3-35, Gulbadin Naib 2-36) beat **Afghanistan** 200 in 47 overs (Samiullah Shinwari 49*, G Naib 47; Shakib 5-29, Mustafizur Rahman 2-32) by 62 runs. *PoM*: Shakib Al Hasan.

Australia beat England by 64 runs

There was little Stokes could do about Starc's inswinging yorker. — *Getty Images*

A clinical, unfussy win showed off Australia's all-round strength. England's third loss while chasing was not a record the favourites wanted. When Jason Behrendorff swung it in to hit James Vince's middle stump second ball, the stage was set. They fell to 26 for 3 and then 53 for 4. When Stokes was sixth out at 177 it was clearly over. Australia's approach paid off handsomely. Their batting will not be remembered for flashy strokeplay, but they knew there was safety in numbers. Finch's 100 suggested batsmen might have to play the waiting game to be successful on this track, but 123 without loss in the 23rd over indicated the early uncertainties might have been overcome. At 173 for 1, a total of 350 was on the cards, but England did well to prise out 6 for 86.

Lord's, London, June 25: Australia 285/7 in 50 overs (Aaron Finch 100, David Warner 53; Chris Woakes 2-46) beat **England** 221 in 44.4 overs (Ben Stokes 89; Jason Behrendorff 5-44, Mitchell Starc 4-43) by 64 runs. *PoM*: Aaron Finch

Pakistan beat New Zealand by six wickets

Pakistan climbed out of so many pits during this match that the final twist, only a second win in five games, seemed well deserved. Inspired by Afridi, they had reduced New Zealand to 83 for 5 in the 27th over when Williamson was out, before de Grandhomme and Neesham put on 132 for the sixth wicket. Then, chasing a modest score, they were 44 for 2 and seemingly out of it before Babar (101 in 127 balls) and Sohail's 126-run partnership for the fourth wicket changed the momentum. Pakistan approached the game with an aggression that had been missing earlier, held their catches and found in two batsmen players with both self-belief and the game. Fans began to notice similarities with their campaign in 1992 when too they had begun poorly. That was the year they won the title.

Edgbaston, Birmingham, June 26: New Zealand 237/6 (Jimmy Neesham 97*, Colin de Grandhomme 64; Shaheen Afridi 3-28) lost to **Pakistan** 241/4 in 49.1 overs (Babar Azam 101*, Haris Sohail 68) by six wickets. *PoM:* Babar Azam.

India beat West Indies by 125 runs

India's batsmen did give their supporters moments of tension, but their bowlers ensured calm as they dismissed West Indies under 150. Earlier, it was the disciplined approach of the West Indies bowlers that had kept India's batsmen in check. Only Hardik Pandya at No.8 had a strike-rate above 100. The innings was held together by Kohli, who again looked like he was batting on a different surface till a ball from Holder stood up and forced a false stroke. The innings threatened to unravel as Dhoni took time to get into his groove. But then he found his touch and added 70 with Pandya in ten overs to help India cross the 250-mark. It didn't seem a lot till West Indies lost Gayle and Hope by 16. Shami's figures of 6.2-0-16-4 held them in a vice-like grip.

Old Trafford, Manchester, June 27: India 268/7 in 50 overs (Virat Kohli 72, MS Dhoni 56*; Kemar Roach 3-36, Jason Holder 2-33) beat **West Indies** 143 in 34.2 overs (Sunil Ambris 31; Mohammed Shami 4-16, Jasprit Bumrah 2-9) by 125 runs. *PoM:* Virat Kohli

South Africa beat Sri Lanka by nine wickets

Dwaine Pretorius's first spell of 7.2-2-8-3 not only put paid to Sri Lanka's ambitions of making a match of it at this venue's inaugural World Cup match, but also knocked them out of the tournament. For South Africa, dominance was mixed with regret for a team that was no longer in running for a semi-final berth. "It feels hollow," skipper du Plessis said. "It's great winning, but it is very, very bittersweet because you know that we've let a lot of people down, and that was never the plan." Sri Lanka got to their 200 only in the 50th over, showing that South Africa's bowlers both choked their runs and claimed wickets. It began with the first ball of the match when Rabada had Karunaratne caught at slip. Amla and du Plessis made light of the target, putting on an unbroken 175 runs for the second wicket.

158 World Cup

Chester-le-Street, Durham, June 28: Sri Lanka 203 in 49.3 overs (Avishka Fernando 30, Kusal Perera 30; Dwaine Pretorius 3-25, Chris Morris 3-46) lost to **South Africa** 206/1 in 37.2 overs (Faf du Plessis 96*, Amla 80*) by nine wickets. *PoM*: Dwaine Pretorius

Pakistan beat Afghanistan by three wickets

Afghanistan ran their powerful Asian neighbours, India and Pakistan, close, coming within two deliveries of knocking Pakistan out of the tournament here. Imad Wasim kept his head and his wicket as Pakistan scraped through their last 11 overs with the rival spinners threatening to take it away from them. In the end, Afghanistan's inexperience told. Pakistan needed 46 in five, but Imad was struggling against the spinners when skipper Naib decided to bowl his medium-pacers and conceded 18 in the 46th over. Imad rode his luck, Wahab hit a boundary and a six, and the two put on a crucial 24 without being separated.

Afghanistan began well — Mujeeb getting Fakhar in the first over — on a track that was slow and helpful to spinners. The political tensions between the two countries spilled over into the match where supporters of either team threw punches at one another.

Headingley, Leeds, June 29: Afghanistan 227/9 in 50 overs (Asghar Afgan 42, Najibullah Zadran 42; Shaheen Afridi 4-47, Wahab Riaz 2-29) lost to **Pakistan** 230/7 in 49.4 overs (Imad Wasim 49*, Babar Azam 45; Mohammad Nabi 2-23, Mujeeb Ur Rahman 2-34, Mohammad Nabi 2-23) by three wickets. *PoM*: Imad Wasim

Australia beat New Zealand by 86 runs

Australia became the first team to qualify for the semi-final, having improved with every game. New Zealand did everything right: dismissed the openers cheaply, kept the rate in check, and finally Trent Boult finished with a hat-trick, the first in an ODI at Lord's. But Australia had that bit more in their arsenal. They recovered from 92 for 5, Usman Khawaja and Carey putting on 107. Starc's five then played them out of the game. Williamson was just settling in when he was caught behind off Starc to make it 97 for 3. New Zealand were in a better position than Australia were at that stage, but steadily lost the advantage. Starc came within three wickets of Glenn McGarth's World Cup record of 26 in a single tournament (2007), but said after the match, overtaking McGrath wouldn't mean much if "we did not win the World Cup".

Lord's, London, June 29: Australia 243/9 in 50 overs (Usman Khawaja 88, Alex Carey 71; Trent Boult 4-51, Jimmy Neesham 2-28) beat **New Zealand** 157 in 43.4 overs (Kane Williamson 40, Ross Taylor 30; Mitchell Starc 5-26, Jason Behrendorff 2-31) by 86 runs. *PoM*: Alex Carey

England beat India by 31 runs

England rediscovered their touch, striking with their by-now familiar power and poise, and bowling with purpose. It was all too much for India who had been unbeaten so far. England's planned early assault was in sharp contrast to India's planned early defence. Bairstow (111 off 109 balls, 10 fours, six sixes) and Roy showed how pleased they were at reuniting at the top by putting on 160 at over seven an over. Stokes at No.5 made 79 off 54 even as Shami claimed five wickets. India made 28 in their first ten overs, with Rohit (102 off 109) struggling to find his timing. This was his third century in the tournament. With Kohli, he put on 138 for the second wicket, but despite some fireworks from Pandya, India were never really in the game. That they finished 31 short with five wickets in hand could be put down to a feeling that chasing was futile. England's fast men were both accurate and displayed specific plans for individual batsmen. India went in with two spinners who between them gave away 132 runs for one wicket.

Edgbaston, Birmingham, June 30: England 337/7 in 50 overs (Jonny Bairstow 111, Ben Stokes 79; Mohammed Shami 5-69) beat **India** 306 (Rohit Sharma 102, Virat Kohli 66; Liam Plunkett 3-55, Chris Woakes 2-58). *PoM*: Jonny Bairstow.

Sri Lanka beat West Indies by 23 runs

This, the first match where neither team had a chance of qualifying, became a platform for displaying individual skills. West Indies' Pooran (118 off 103 balls) matched Sri Lanka's Fernando (104 off 103) in strokeplay but not in impact on the result. Two men under 25 were making centuries in the same match for the first time in the World Cup. It was a remarkable chase, West Indies needing 31 from three overs with Pooran still at the crease. Then, Mathews, who had not bowled since December 2017, came on, to everyone's surprise, and to even greater surprise had Pooran caught behind off his first ball. "We were in control, but it slipped," Pooran said ruefully later. The youngster, anointed 'mini universe boss' by Gayle, could barely hold back his tears.

Chester-le Street, Durham, July 1: Sri Lanka 338/6 in 50 overs (Avishka Fernando 104, Kusal Perera 64; Jason Holder 2-59) beat **West Indies** 315/9 (Nicholas Pooran 118, Fabien Allen 51; Lasith Malinga 3-55) by 23 runs. *PoM*: Avishka Fernando.

India beat Bangladesh by 28 runs

India became the second team after Australia to qualify for the semi-finals while ending Bangladesh's dream here. Rahul and Rohit put on 180. Rohit's fourth century, equalling Kumar Sangakkara's record at the previous World Cup, might have ended too soon for India to put it beyond their opponents in the first half itself. His dismissal for 104 (92 balls), followed by Rahul's threw the middle order into a tizzy. It was left to Rishabh Pant to display the kind of hitting that the opening partnership warranted. Mustafizur Rahman's five put the brakes on the batting and India appeared short by at least 25 or 30 runs. Bangladesh's initial scoring rate seemed to endorse that, but they kept losing wickets. They needed 70 off 41 and then 29 off 14, but didn't have the batsmen. Pandya's three rattled the top half while Bumrah's four tied it up neatly in the end.

Edgbaston, Birmingham, July 2: India 314/9 in 50 overs (Rohit Sharma 104, KL Rahul 77; Mustafizur Rahman 5-59) beat **Bangladesh** 286 in 48 overs (Shakib Al Hasan 66, Saifuddin 51; Jasprit Bumrah 4-55, Hardik Pandya 3-60) by 28 runs. *PoM*: Rohit Sharma

England beat New Zealand by 119 runs

England's first entry into the semi-finals since 1992 was accomplished with a combination of power and diffidence that their next opponents would have noted. The win virtually knocked Pakistan out, while the defeat didn't throw up any roadblocks en route New Zealand's path to the knockout. Bairstow's 106 (99 balls) and his 123-run opening partnership with Roy showed once again how important it has been in this tournament to get off to a good start. At 206 for 2, in the 32nd over, a total of over 350 was on the cards, before middle-order uncertainty saw England lose six wickets for 99. But Williamson's run-out ensured England didn't have to pay. That happened off the first ball of the 16th over, when a Taylor drive deflected off bowler Mark Wood's fingertips to disturb the stumps while Williamson was backing up.

Chester-le-Street, Durham, July 3: England 305/8 in 50 overs (Jonny Bairstow 106, Jason Roy 60; Jimmy Neesham 2-41, Matt Henry 2-54) beat **New Zealand** 186 in 45 overs (Tom Latham 57; Mark Wood 3-34) by 119 runs. *PoM*: Jonny Bairstow.

West Indies beat Afghanistan by 23 runs

Teenager Ikram Alikhil nearly managed to pull it off for Afghanistan single-handedly, but the Asian team had to bow out of the World Cup without a single point despite the many warm memories they provided. With Rahmat, Alikhil added 133 for the second wicket. West Indies had shown earlier how it could be done, taking 111 off the last ten overs. Pooran's half-century following his century in the previous match gave West Indies a view into a possibly exciting future, while Holder's little cameo, 45 off 34, showed what the present was capable of. "I am upset he missed his World Cup century," said Alikhil's captain, Naib. Had that happened, he would have been the first teenager to score a century at the World Cup; he had to rest content with being the third youngest to score fifty.

Headingley, Leeds, July 4: West Indies 311/6 in 50 overs (Shai Hope 77, Ewin Lewis 58, Nicholas Pooran 58; Dawlat Zadran 2-73) beat Afghanistan 288 in 50 overs (Ikram Alikhil 86, Rahmat Shah 62; Carlos Brathwaite 4-63, Kemar Roach 3-37) by 23 runs. *PoM*: Shai Hope.

Pakistan beat Bangladesh by 94 runs

Pakistan's fifth win — their fourth in a row — was just not good enough to get them into the semi-final, leading their supporters to diss the net run-rate system that allowed New Zealand to advance with the same number of wins. Some idea of Pakistan's desperation can be seen from the math required to win after they had made 315: they needed to dismiss Bangladesh for eight runs. Afridi's haul, the best by a Pakistani bowler in the World Cup, ended Bangladesh's dream of a fifth successive ODI win over Pakistan. Imam's

On the honours board: Shaheen Shah Afridi's 6 for 35 were the best bowling figures for Pakistan in a World Cup. — *Getty Images*

century and Babar Azam's near-one and their 157-run partnership for the second wicket drove Pakistan. For Bangladesh, Shakib's fifth half-century (he had two centuries, besides) took him past 600 runs at this World Cup. This was in addition to his 11 wickets.

Lord's, London, July 5: Pakistan 315/9 in 50 overs (Imam-ul-Haq 100, Babar Azam 96; Mustafizur Rahman 5-75, Saifuddin 4-77) beat **Bangladesh** 221 in 44.1 overs (Shakib Al Hasan 64, Liton Das 32; Shaheen Afridi 6-35, Shadab Khan 2-59). *PoM*: Shaheen Afridi.

India beat Sri Lanka by seven wickets

Rohit's fifth century — the most in a single tournament — and his 189-run partnership with Rahul, who made his first, made the chase smoother than it might have been. Rohit's 14 fours and two sixes in 94 balls contrasted with Rahul's effort off 118 balls (11 fours and a six), but the intent was the same and so were the patches of sheer effortlessness the two batsmen brought to their batting. India had already qualified for the semi-final, the only question being whether they finished second or first, and that would depend on the Australia-South Africa match three hours later. A self-belief among their bowlers reduced Sri Lanka to 55 for 4. Mathews made his third ODI century — all against India, and all in losing causes — and added 124 with Thirimanne. Ravindra Jadeja, playing his first match, claimed a wicket in his first over and had a catch dropped off his bowling later, but increasingly, it appeared as if balance and combination didn't matter, India were that good.

Headingley, Leeds, July 6: Sri Lanka 264/7 in 50 overs (Angelo Mathews 113, Lahiru Thirimanne 53; Jasprit Bumrah 3-37) lost to **India** 265/3 in 43.3 overs (KL Rahul 111, Rohit Sharma 103). *PoM*: Rohit Sharma.

South Africa beat Australia by ten runs

South Africa kept their best for the last, having already bowed out of the World Cup. The win was more than a consolation — it showed what might have been. It also pushed Australia to second place in the points table, giving them a semi-final meeting with England, while India moved to the top and a clash against New Zealand. It was a day when 640 runs were scored and the result came only in the penultimate delivery of the match. Du Plessis's 100 (97 balls) and a stand worth 151 for the third wicket with van der Dussen, who began shakily but finished strongly, meant that Australia had to be at their best to win. But the top order, barring Warner (122 in 117 balls) didn't offer much, and at 119 for 4, Australia had their backs against the wall. It wasn't until Carey joined Warner and added 108 for the fifth wicket that Australia began to look in control. The fast bowlers chipped in with the bat, but 18 off the last over was just beyond reach.

Old Trafford, Manchester, July 6: South Africa 325/6 in 50 overs (Faf du Plessis 100, Rassie van der Dussen 95; Nathan Lyon 2-53, Mitchell Starc 2-59) beat **Australia** 315 in 49.5 overs (David Warner 122, Alex Carey 85; Kagiso Rabada 3-56, Andile Phehlukwayo 2-22) by ten runs. *PoM*: Faf du Plessis

1st semi-final: New Zealand beat India by 18 runs

Rain carried the match into the reserve day — New Zealand were 211 for 5 in 46.1 overs then — and the slowness of the pitch made it a battle of wits. India were 5 for 3 by the fourth over of the chase, their top three, who had made two-thirds of the team's runs in the tournament, dismissed. Two terrific

deliveries picked out Rohit (Matt Henry's sharp leg-cutter had to be played) and Kohli (Boult brought one in to trap him leg before after keeping the ball outside off and moving away), and seemed to take the fight out of India.

New Zealand showed how to bat on this track, eschewing fancy for safety, appearing unadventurous while adding to the total. The fast bowlers then took over before left-arm spinner Santner removed the two youngsters in the middle order, Pant and Pandya, after the batsmen decided to get adventurous. It was left to Jadeja, ignored for much of the tournament, to smash a stunning 77 off 59 balls to resurrect the innings in Dhoni's company. Dho-

Matt Henry destroyed the famed Indian top order. — *Getty Images* ni, batting at No.7 and not at No.5 as many had expected, had a strike-rate below 70, but helped Jadeja add 116 for the seventh wicket before a superb pick up and throw from Guptill ended his innings and India's hopes. Jadeja, who had batted with greater fluency and confidence than anyone else in this match, had fallen in the previous over as the pressure mounted. It meant that New Zealand were in the final for the second time in succession while India were stopped in the semi-final as they had been in 2015. Taylor, who top-scored and remained unbeaten overnight, said later, "I woke up at 3 o'clock this morning, wondering how I was going to bat these last 23 balls. I texted my wife at about five saying I still can't go to bed. She said, 'Oh dear.' I had terrible sleep." Kohli rued the "45 minutes of bad cricket" that ended their campaign. He also suggested that the top team should be given another chance, like in the IPL.

Old Trafford, Manchester, July 9-10: New Zealand 239/8 in 50 overs (Ross Taylor 74, Kane Williamson 67; Bhuvneshwar Kumar 3-43) beat India 221 in 49.3 overs (Ravindra Jadeja 77, MS Dhoni 50; Matt Henry 3-37, Mitchell Santner 2-34) by 18 runs. *PoM*: Matt Henry

2nd semi-final: England beat Australia by eight wickets

England's first entry into the final of the World Cup since 1992 meant that the tournament would have new champions for the first time since Sri Lanka were crowned in 1996. England were so dominant and won with such flair that they might have been the West Indies team of the 1970s, which conquered all before them. It took the fast bowlers Woakes and Archer just 16 deliveries to reduce Australia to 14 for 3. Smith and Carey added 103 for the fourth wicket, after the wicketkeeper-batsman was struck on the helmet by Archer. Bat held safely in one hand, Carey swivelled to catch the helmet before it fell on the stumps, while viewers saw a rivulet of blood on his jaw. There was a swagger about the England bowling and a supreme self-confidence that suggested they were always in control. Woakes didn't even complete his ten overs as Australia were shot out in the 49th. Adil Rashid was given a standing ovation as he finished with three wickets: it was as if no one could believe an English leg-spinner could stun the Australians.

The tempo, the ferocity was maintained by the batsmen, Roy and Bairstow posting their fourth successive century partnership. Roy was particularly spectacular, striking five sixes, three in a row off Smith who was given the ball in some desperation. He was unfortunate to be given out caught behind after England had already used up their review. His furious reaction earned him a fine and two demerit points. Root and Morgan kept up the pressure, with Starc, the pre-match danger man, taken for 70 in his nine overs. Seldom has an England ODI team played such electrifying all-round cricket with the kind of arrogance they displayed here. "When England were batting," wrote Vic Marks, "this game had the air of an exhibition match … we'll get them in sixes appeared to be the plan."

Edgbaston, Birmingham, July 11: Australia 223 in 49 overs (Steve Smith 85, Alex Carey

46; Chris Woakes 3-20, Adil Rashid 3-54) lost to **England** 226/2 in 32.1 overs (Jason Roy 85, Joe Root 49*) by eight wickets. *PoM*: Chris Woakes

Final: Match tied. England beat New Zealand on boundary count after the Super Over was tied.

If this wasn't the greatest ODI ever played, it certainly was the greatest World Cup final. Two teams that hadn't won the title before battled out 100 overs and then another two in the tie-breaker to finish dead level. The rule stated that if the game stretched that far, the team that had hit more boundaries would win. England had 24 to New Zealand's 16, and when Buttler broke the stumps to run out Guptill, he also broke the hearts of New Zealand supporters everywhere. Stokes and Buttler — who had added 110 for the fifth wicket in regulation time — took 15 off Boult in the Super Over. In reply, Neesham swung Archer's second legitimate delivery for a six (the first was a wide), and Guptill needed two off the last ball. It was a yorker, Guptill struck to deep midwicket, from where Roy's throw to Buttler heralded the celebrations. Christchurch-born Stokes guided both the innings and the Super Over to get on top of the hero board.

In the 50th over, with England needing 15, Stokes hit Boult for six (third ball), and New Zealand watched in dismay next ball as a throw from Guptill was deflected to the boundary off the bat of a diving Stokes completing his second run. Stokes was granted two plus four runs; later, former umpire Simon Taufel argued that it should have been one plus four, according to the laws of the game. Stokes apologised, but now England needed three from two, but got only two more as Rashid and Wood were run out going for mad second runs to first keep Stokes on strike, and then complete the winning run.

"It was just not meant to be," said Williamson, later named Player of the Tournament.

Williamson read the wicket correctly and chose to bat. New Zealand once again played a game that was safe rather than spectacular, with England's medium-pacers restricting them. Former skipper Brendon McCullum felt that 240 would be a winning score; New Zealand had shown in the semi-final against India how adept they were at defending small totals on sluggish tracks. Woakes and Liam Plunkett claimed wickets regularly. After Williamson fell, it was left to Taylor, but a poor decision did him. No review was available after Guptill had wasted it earlier.

Roy was reprieved first ball by the umpire's call when the DRS was appealed to, but his dismissal in the sixth over suggested a fight was on the cards. Stokes carried the batting on his shoulders and still had enough energy left to come back to bat in the Super Over. Uniquely, Guptill who faced the first ball of the match also faced the last ball in the topsy-turvy climax.

Lord's, London, July 14: New Zealand 241/8 in 50 overs (Henry Nicholls 55, Tom Latham 47; Chris Woakes 3-37, Liam Plunkett 3-42) tied with **England** 241 in 50 overs (Ben Stokes 84*, Jos Buttler 59; Jimmy Neesham 3-43; Lockie Ferguson 3-50). *PoM*: Ben Stokes. *PoS*: Kane Williamson.

The dream continues: Afghanistan bounced back from the brink to win the World Cup qualifier. — *ICC*

ICC Men's Cricket World Cup Qualifier

Afghanistan's great escape

KUDZAYI CHIPIDZA

The last time Zimbabwe hosted a global ICC tournament was in 2003. The World Cup was being held in South Africa, and Zimbabwe won the bid to play all their group matches in Harare and Bulawayo. So, after a 15-year hiatus, with the World Cup qualifiers taking place in the country in March 2018, cricket fans were excited.

The high level of competitiveness from the ten teams in Zimbabwe, the plentiful upsets, the good entertainment value, and the feverish jostling for the two spots that lasted till the last possible day was a cry to the world governing body to increase the number of teams in the World Cup. It was an acrimonious subject that Zimbabwe's Sikander Raza reiterated in an emotional speech while accepting his Player of the Tournament award.

The award was "a painful reminder … for the 15 million dreams that we crushed", Raza said. "When I started playing cricket, I thought it was to unite countries, players of different background coming together to play this beautiful sport. Unfortunately, you'll see that's not going to happen in next year's World Cup. It's certainly quite a tough pill to swallow.

At the end of 34 matches, Afghanistan and West Indies were the lucky ones.

Full Members West Indies, Afghanistan, Zimbabwe and Ireland, by virtue of being ranked ninth or worse by the deadline of September 2017, had to go through the qualifiers to fight for a World Cup place. In some quarters, this was seen as a sign of decline in their game. Others felt that the event was testament to the hard work and the development of cricket in other nations.

Associates Netherlands and Scotland, who were the best two sides in the ICC World Cricket League Championship, along with Hong Kong and Papua New Guinea who were third and fourth, were added to the mix. Nepal and the UAE, who finished as the top two sides in the ICC World Cricket League Division 2, completed the ten-team contingent.

After the round-robin stage, the best three sides from each group qualified for the Super Sixes. The remaining two from each group featured in play-offs. In the Super Six, teams retained points won off other Super Six sides from their group. The top two at the end of the Super Six stage sealed their spots in the World Cup, and played the final for bragging rights.

In Group A, West Indies showed signs of vulnerability, but still managed to win three in a row. Scotland and Zimbabwe were the quickest off the blocks in Group B going unbeaten in their first three matches before playing out an enthralling tie.

Afghanistan, though, got off to a shocking start, losing three games on the trot, including an unexpected defeat to Hong Kong. This was after their skipper, Asghar Stanikzai, had been ruled out for ten days with appendicitis and had to undergo emergency surgery a day before their first warm-up match. On the brink of elimination, having won only against Nepal, they were left clasping at permutations and what-ifs. Their fate boiled down to the last Group B match: had Hong Kong won against Nepal, Afghanistan would have been destined for Kwekwe for the play-offs. But, Sandeep Lamichhane, a 17-year-old rising star, spun Nepal to victory and revived Afghanistan's bid.

Afghanistan, Hong Kong and Nepal all sat on two points at the end of the group stage, but Afghanistan had a superior net run-rate, which catapulted them from last to third in the group. From very nearly accepting their misfortune and heading to Kwekwe, a small mining town in Zimbabwe's midlands, it only got more miraculous for Afghanistan.

As the competition moved to Harare, Zimbabwe and West Indies were the hot favourites to claim the two spots on offer. The hosts, especially, had attracted the nation's attention and gathered unprecedented support. They needed just one win, against either West Indies or the UAE, after beating Ireland. Scotland, too, playing entertaining cricket, were in hot contention, having beaten the UAE; a win against Ireland or West Indies would have sealed their ticket.

After the second round of Super Six matches, it was anyone's game, with five teams of the six having a chance of making it through.

Then Scotland were undone by a combination of no DRS and no reserve days — they had a controversial decision go against them and were five short of the DLS target against West Indies when the rain came. "We don't deserve what's happened to us this tournament," tweeted Matthew Cross.

And, UAE, playing for pride, shattered Zimbabwe hopes.

In all the number crunching and complex calculations, Afghanistan simply won all three of their Super Six matches. They beat West Indies for the second time in the tournament to seal a dramatic comeback and win the tournament.

There were plenty of individual highlights. Mujeeb Ur Rahman, a rising Afghanistan star, befuddled an experienced Chris Gayle to bowl him past his outside edge. When the ball struck Gayle's off stump, no one was quite sure what they had witnessed.

Mohamad Naveed took five wickets to help UAE start well. West Indies' 21-year-old Shimron Hetmyer scored his maiden ODI century. PNG's Tony Ura scored 151 against Ireland only to have it countered by William Porterfield's 111 in the same match. Rashid Khan became officially the youngest man to captain in ODIs, but Calum MacLeod ruined his day making 157.

The minnows held their own, so much so that the term itself lost its meaning. PNG's exceptional fielding was acknowledged by all the teams they came up against.

Kudzayi Chipidza is a cricket writer and broadcaster based in Zimbabwe.

Group A

Harare Sports Club, Harare, March 4: United Arab Emirates 221 in 49.4 overs (Rohan Mustafa 95, Ashfaq Ahmed 50; Norman Vanua 4-39, Alie Nao 2-42) beat **Papua New Guinea** 113 in 25.5 overs (Charles Amini 24, N Vanua 20; Mohammad Naveed 5-28, Imran Haider 2-21) by 56 runs (DLS method). *MoM:* Mohammad Naveed.

Old Hararians Sports Club, Harare, March 4: Ireland 268/7 in 50 overs (Andrew Balbirnie68, Niall O Brien 49; Timm van der Gugten 3-59) beat **Netherlands** 149 in 32.2 overs (T Gugten 33, Scott Edwards 26; Tim Murtagh 3-28, Boyd Rankin 2-19) by 93 runs (DLS method). *MoM:* Andrew Balbirnie.

Harare SC, Harare, March 6: Papua New Guinea 235 in 50 overs (Tony Ura 151, Chad Soper 25; Andy McBrine 3-38, Boyd Rankin 2-41) lost to **Ireland** 237/6 in 49.1 overs (William Porterfield 111, Ed Joyce 53; Assad Vala 2-39) by four wickets. *MoM:* Tony Ura.

Old Hararians SC, Harare, March 6: West Indies 357/4 in 50 overs (Shimron Hetmyer 127, Chris Gayle 123) beat **United Arab Emirates** 297/6 in 50 overs (Rameez Shahzad 112*, Shaiman Anwar 64; Jason Holder 5-53) by 60 runs. *MoM:* Shimron Hetmyer.

Harare SC, Harare, March 8: Netherlands 176 in 46.3 overs (Wesley Barresi 37, Ryan ten Doeschate 34; Muhammad Usman 36*) in 44 overs (Chirag Suri 78*, Muhammad Usman 36*) by six wickets. *MoM:* Rohan Mustafa.

Old Hararians SC, Harare, March 8: Papua New Guinea 200 in 42.4 overs (Assad Vala 57, Tony Ura 37; Carlos Brathwaite 5-27, Nikita Milier 2-25) lost to **West Indies** 201/4 in 43 overs (Jason Holder 99*, Shai Hope 49*) by six wickets. *MoM:* Jason Holder.

Harare SC, Harare, March 10: West Indies 257/8 in 50 overs (Rovman Powell 101, Jason Holder 54; Tim Murtagh 4-41, Andy McBrine 2-45) beat **Ireland** 205 in 46.2 overs (Ed Joyce 63, Kevin O'Brien 38; Kemar Roach 4-27, Kesrick Williams 4-43) by 52 runs. *MoM:* Rovman Powell.

Old Hararians SC, Harare, March 10: Netherlands 216/8 in 50 overs (Sikander Zulfiqar 53*, Roelof van der Merwe 38; Alei Nao 2-28, Mahuru Dai 2-29) beat **Papua New Guinea**

159 in 42.1 overs (Assad Vala 44, Kiplin Doriga 32*; R Merwe 4-46, Fred Klaassen 2-25) by 57 runs. *MoM:* Roelof van der Merwe.

Harare SC, Harare, March 12: West Indies 309/6 in 48 overs (Evin Lewis 84, Marlon Samuels 73*; Paul van Meekeren 2-37, Roelof van der Merwe 2-46) beat **Netherlands** 167/6 in 28.4 overs (Ryan ten Doeschate 67*, Wesley Barresi 64) by 54 runs (DLS method). *MoM:* Evin Lewis.

Old Hararians SC, Harare, March 12: Ireland 313/6 in 44 overs (Paul Stirling 126, William Porterfield 92; Mohammad Naveed 3-84, Imran Haider 2-73) beat **United Arab Emirates** 91 in 29.3 overs (Boyd Rankin 4-15, Simi Singh 3-15) by 226 runs. *MoM:* Paul Stirling.

Group A Points Table

Teams	M	W	L	T	N/R	Pts.	NRR
West Indies	4	4	0	0	0	8	+1.171
Ireland	4	3	1	0	0	6	+1.479
United Arab Emirates	4	2	2	0	0	4	-1.177
Netherlands	4	1	3	0	0	2	-0.709
Papua New Guinea	4	0	4	0	0	0	-0.865

West Indies, Ireland and United Arab Emirates qualified for the play-offs

Group B

Queens SC, Bulawayo, March 4: Zimbabwe 380/6 in 50 overs (Sikandar Raza 123, Brendon Taylor 100; Basant Ragmi 2-69, Sompal Kami 2-82) beat **Nepal** 264/8 in 50 overs (Sharad Vesawkar 52, Aarif Sheikh 50; S Raza 3-48, Brian Vitori 2-46) by 116 runs. *MoM:* Sikandar Raza

Bulawayo Athletic Club, Bulawayo, March 4: Afghanistan 255 in 49.4 overs (Mohammad Nabi 92, Najibullah Zadran 67; Bradley Wheal 3-36, Richie Berrington 3-42) lost to **Scotland** 256/3 in 47.2 overs (Calum MacLeod 157*, R Berrington 67; Mujeeb Ur Rahman 2-47) by seven wickets. *MoM:* Calum MacLeod

Queens SC, Bulawayo, March 6: Zimbabwe 196 in 43 overs (Brendon Taylor 89, Sikandar Raza 60; Rashid Khan 3-38, Mujeeb Ur Rahman 3-49) beat **Afghanistan** 194 in 49.3 overs (Rahmat Shah 69, Mohammad Nabi 51; Blessing Muzarabani 4-47, S Raza 3-40) by two runs. *MoM:* Sikandar Raza

Bulawayo Athletic Club, Bulawayo, March 6: Hong Kong 91 in 38.2 overs (Nizakat Khan 26; Tom Sole 4-15, Alasdair Evans 3-19) lost to **Scotland** 92/6 in 23.3 overs (Kyle Coetzer 41*, George Munsey 22; Ehsan Khan 3-29, Ehsan Nawaz 2-24) by four wickets.

Queens SC, Bulawayo, March 8: Nepal 149 in 47.4 overs (Paras Khadka 63, Basant Regmi 24*; Stu Whittingham 3-35, Safyaan Sharif

Sandeep Lamicchane played a crucial role in Nepal gaining ODI status. – *ICC*

2-21) lost to **Scotland** 153/6 in 41.3 overs (Kyle Coetzer 88*; B Regmi 2-26, Sandeep Lamichhane 2-31) by four wickets. *MoM:* Kyle Coetzer

Bulawayo Athletic Club, Bulawayo, March 8: Hong Kong 241/8 in 50 overs (Anshuman Rath 65, Babar Hayat 31; Mujeeb Ur Rahman 3-26, Mohammad Nabi 3-48) beat **Afghanistan** 195/9 in 46 overs (Dawlat Zadran 40*, M Nabi 38; Ehsan Khan 4-33, Nadeem Ahmed 2-37) by 30 runs (DLS method). *MoM:* Ehsan Khan

Queens SC, Bulawayo, March 10: Zimbabwe 263/9 in 50 overs (Hamilton Masakadza 84, Brendon Taylor 46; Ehsan Nawaz 4-47, Aizaz Khan 2-41) beat **Hong Kong** 174 in 46.5 overs (Anshuman Rath 85; Sikandar Raza 3-30, Kyle Jarvis 2-20) by 89 runs. *MoM:* Hamilton Masakadza

Bulawayo Athletic Club, Bulawayo, March 10: Nepal 194 in 49.5 overs (Paras Khadka 75, Dipendra Singh Airee 32; Mohammad Nabi 4-33, Rashid Khan 3-45) lost to **Afghanistan** 195/4 in 38.4 overs (Najibullah Zadran 52*, Rahmat Shah 46; D Airee 2-25) by six wickets. *MoM:* Mohammad Nabi

Queens SC, Bulawayo, March 12: Hong Kong 153 in 48.2 overs (Nizakat Khan 47, Ehsan Khan 21; Sandeep Lamichhane 3-17, Basant Regmi 2-20) lost to **Nepal** 155/5 in 40.4 overs (Rohit Paudel 48*, Anil Sah 26; Ehsan 2-34, Aizaz Khan 2-40) by five wickets. *MoM:* Rohit Paudel

Bulawayo Athletic Club, Bulawayo, March 12: Zimbabwe 210 in 46.4 overs (Craig Ervine 57, Brendon Taylor 44; Safyaan Sharif 5-33, Michael Leask 4-37) tied with **Scotland** 210 in 49.1 overs (Richie Berrington 47, Kyle Coetzer 39; Graeme Cremer 3-23, Tendai Chisoro 3-42). *MoM:* Safyaan Sharif

Group B points table

Teams	M	W	L	T	N/R	Pts.	NRR
Zimbabwe	4	3	0	1	0	7	+1.035
Scotland	4	3	0	1	0	7	+0.855
Afghanistan	4	1	3	0	0	2	+0.038
Nepal	4	1	3	0	0	2	-0.893
Hong Kong	4	1	3	0	0	2	-1.121

Zimbabwe, Scotland and Afghanistan qualified for the play-offs

Super Sixes

Harare SC, Harare, March 15: West Indies 197/8 in 50 overs (Shai Hope 43, Marlon Samuels 36; Mujeeb Ur Rahman 3-33, Mohammad Nabi 2-43) lost to **Afghanistan** 198/7 in 47.4 overs (Rahmat Shah 68, M Nabi 31; Jason Holder 3-39, Keemo Paul 2-29) by three wickets. *MoM:* Mujeeb Ur Rahman

Queens SC, Bulawayo, March 15: Scotland 322/6 in 50 overs (Matthew Cross 114, Calum MacLeod 78; Rohan Mustafa 4-56) beat **United Arab Emirates** 249 in 47.4 overs (Muhammad Usman 80, Ahmed Raza 50; Chris Sole 4-68, Safyaan Sharif 2-36) by 73 runs. *MoM:* Matthew Cross

Harare SC, Harare, March 16: Zimbabwe 211/9 in 50 overs (Sikandar Raza 69*, Brendon Taylor 25; Tim Murtagh 3-36, Andy McBrine 2-42) beat **Ireland** 104 in 34.2 overs (Paul Stirling 41; Graeme Cremer 3-18, Tendai Chisoro 3-22) by 107 runs. *MoM:* Sikandar Raza

Harare SC, Harare, March 18: Ireland 271/9 in 50 overs (Andrew Balbirnie 105, Niall O'Brien 70; Bradley Wheal 3-43, Safyaan Sharif 2-52) beat **Scotland** 246 in 47.4 overs (Kyle Coetzer 61, Rchie Berrington 44; Boyd Rankin 4-63, Simi Singh 2-33) by 25 runs. *MoM:* Andrew Balbirnie

Inspired: Zimbabwe put on a show for the home crowds, with only a narrow three-run loss in a rain-hit game denying them a World Cup spot. — *Getty Images*

Harare SC, Harare, March 19: Zimbabwe 289 in 50 overs (Brendon Taylor 138, Solomon Mire 45; Jason Holder 4-35, Kemar Roach 3-55) lost to **West Indies** 290/6 in 49 overs (Marlon Samuels 86, Shai Hope 76; Blessing Muzarabani 2-36, Graeme Cremer 2-63) by four wickets. *MoM:* Marlon Samuels

Old Hararians SC, Harare, March 20: United Arab Emirates 177 in 43 overs (Shaiman Anwar 64, Mohammad Naveed 45; Rashid Khan 5-41, Dawlat Zadran 3-45) lost to **Afghanistan** 178/5 in 34.3 overs (Gulbadin Naib 74*, Najibullah Zadran 63*;M Naveed 2-37, Qadeer Ahmed 2-38) by five wickets. *MoM:* Gulbadin Naib

Harare SC, Harare, March 21: West Indies 198 in 48.4 overs (Evin Lewis 66, Marlon Samuels 51; Safyaan Sharif 3-27, Bradley Wheal 3-34) beat **Scotland** 125/5 in 35.2 overs (Richie Berrington 33, George Munsey 32*; Kemar Roach 2-20, Ashley Nurse 2-35) by five runs (DLS method). *MoM:* Safyaan Sharif

Harare SC, Harare, March 22: United Arab Emirates 235/7 in 47.5 overs (Rameez Shahzad 59, Ghulam Shabber 40; Sikandar Raza 3-41, Tendai Chatara 2-49) beat **Zimbabwe** 226/7 in 40 overs (Sean Williams 80, Peter Moor 39; Mohammad Naveed 3-40, Rohan Mustafa 2-56) by three runs (DLS method). *MoM:* Mohammad Naveed

Harare SC, Harare, March 23: Ireland 209/7 in 50 overs (Paul Stirling 55, Kevin O'Brien 41; Rashid Khan 3-40, Dawlat Zadran 2-54) lost to **Afghanistan** 213/5 in 49.1 overs (Mohammad Shahzad 54, Gulbadin Naib 45; Simi Singh 3-30) by five wickets. *MoM:* M Shahzad

Super Sixes points table

Teams	M	W	L	T	N/R	Pts.	NRR
West Indies	5	4	1	0	0	8	+0.472
Afghanistan	5	3	2	0	0	6	+0.302
Zimbabwe	5	2	2	1	0	5	+0.42
Scotland	5	2	2	1	0	5	+0.243

| Ireland | 5 | 2 | 3 | 0 | 0 | 4 | +0.346 |
| United Arab Emirates | 5 | 1 | 4 | 0 | 0 | 2 | -1.95 |

West Indies and Afghanistan qualified for the final

21st match play-off: Netherlands won by 44 runs

Kwekwe SC, Kwekwe, March 15: Netherlands 174 in 48.2 overs (Max O'Dowd 62, Peter Borren 31; Nadeem Ahmed 3-20, Ehsan Khan 2-30) beat **Hong Kong** 130 in 43 overs (Babar Hayat 52, Kinchit Shah 22; Roelof van der Merwe 4-18, Fred Klaassen 2-30) by 44 runs. *MoM:* Max O'Dowd

22nd match play-off: Nepal won by six wickets

Old Hararians SC, Harare, March 15: Papua New Guinea 114 in 27.2 overs (Dipendra Singh Airee 4-14, Sandeep Lamichhane 4-29) lost to **Nepal** 115/4 in 23 overs (D Airee 50*, Aarif Sheikh 26; Norman Vanua 2-25) by six wickets. *MoM:* Dipendra Singh Airee

7th place play-off: Netherlands won by 45 runs

Kwekwe SC, Kwekwe, March 17: Netherlands 189/9 in 50 overs (Bas de Leede 39, Max O'Dowd 28; Sompal Kami 4-24,Lalit Rajbanshi 2-38) beat **Nepal** 144 in 44.4 overs (S Kami 36, Dipendra Singh Airee 25; Roelof van der Merwe 4-20, Pieter Seelaar 2-30) by 45 runs. *MoM:* Roelof van der Merwe

9th place play-off: Papua New Guinea won by 58 runs

Old Hararians SC, Harare, March 17: Papua New Guinea200 in 48.2 overs (Tony Ura 49, Chad Soper 39; Kinchit Shah 4-10, Nadeem Ahmed 2-41) beat **Hong Kong**142 in 35.2 overs (Babar Hayat 37, Anshuman Rath 24; Norman Vanua 4-24, Charles Amini 4-27) by 58 runs. *MoM:* Charles Amini

Final: Afghanistan won by seven wickets

Harare SC, Harare, March 25: West Indies 204 in 46.5 overs (Rovman Powell 44, Shimron Hetmyer 38; Mujeeb Ur Rahman 4-43, Gulbadin Naib 2-28) lost to **Afghanistan**206/3 in 40.4 overs (Mohammad Shahzad 84, Rahmat Shah 51; Chris Gayle 2-38) by seven wickets. *MoM:* Mohammad Shahzad. *MoS:* Sikandar Raza

Winners: Afghanistan

Most runs: Brendan Taylor (Zimbabwe) (457 runs, 7 matches)
Most wickets: Mujeeb Ur Rahman (Afghanistan) (16 wickets, 7 matches)

One day in 1975

IAN CHAPPELL

When it was first proposed, the inaugural men's World Cup in 1975 was viewed by many purely as an interesting experiment. But, following a spine-tingling final in the fast-fading London light between the two best teams in the competition, the World Cup was assured of a prominent place on future cricket calendars.

For Australia, the 1975 World Cup loomed as the ideal warm-up to the four-Test series with England that followed. Australia's build-up to the tournament consisted of a casually organised trip to Canada, where a match was lost at the Toronto Cricket Skating and Curling Club.

We arrived in England on June 1 to discover it had snowed that day in the UK, but from then on, the sun shone brightly on the World Cup. As a final preparation, Australia played an intra-squad practice match at the Bank of England grounds in London. For the team I led, practice was somewhat diluted when Doug Walters, sharing the new ball with Dennis Lillee, took 5 for 32 to totally wreck the innings. Frustrated as wickets continued to fall, I barked: "To hell with it, this it's supposed to be practice. 'Stumpy' [opening batsman Bruce Laird], put the pads on and go back out at the fall of the next wicket." Another wicket promptly fell to Walters and on Laird's return to the crease, the ever-humorous bowler called out, "Excuse me, batsman, haven't I seen you somewhere before."

In the pre-tournament period, all eight teams stayed at the Kensington Close Hotel in London, as the officials took the opportunity to hold a captains' meeting and take publicity shots.

During the London stay, I also attended a clandestine meeting with a group of Indian entrepreneurs who put forward a proposal for a professional cricket troupe. I was invited to this meeting by Indian left-arm spinner Bishan Singh Bedi. Also in attendance were West Indies captain Clive Lloyd and Australian vice-captain Greg Chappell. Nothing eventuated from this meeting, which was one of three similar gatherings I attended before the advent of World Series Cricket in 1977. The other memorable aspect of the teams staying in the same hotel was the ease with which players from different countries mixed. East Africa's Don Pringle, father of future England medium-fast bowler Derek, and Doug Walters discovered an affinity: they shared the 'legal award' for most time spent at the bar.

However, Australia's first match against Pakistan at Headingley abruptly changed our casual approach to the tournament. Following Australia's 73-run victory in the match, I was grilled about the way we played one-day cricket. English journalists kept telling me, "This is a containment game and

'They attack too much': Australia's ODI style came in for criticism. Here, Pakistan's Asif Iqbal is bowled by Dennis Lillee at Headingley. — *Patrick Eagar/ Getty Images*

Australia attack too much." The constant references to our inability to grasp the concept of one-day cricket were aggravating and also added incentive to our semi-final with England.

To reach the semi-final stage, we needed a second win and we duly claimed victory over Sri Lanka at The Oval. Despite an Alan Turner century, a commanding 60-over total of 328 and a victory margin of 52 runs, this wasn't a comfortable win and it certainly wasn't gained without controversy.

Following our productive innings, I suggested that this would be a good time to improve our PR image, which had taken a hit in the UK due to some inflammatory reporting of the 1974-75 Ashes series. Jeff Thomson was on the receiving end of much of the ill-informed reports and my suggestion was we pitch the ball up rather than bowl short.

The feisty Sri Lankans thrived in this atmosphere and eased their way into the seventies with a series of searing front-foot drives.

I tossed the ball to Thommo, advising him of a change of plan. "We've seen these blokes can play off the front-foot," I growled. "Now let's see how they go off the back-foot."

Thommo promptly hit the opener Sunil Wettimuny with his infamous sand- shoe crusher, not once, not twice, but three times on the same toe. One batsman retired hurt and was off to hospital.

The diminutive Duleep Mendis was next in and he played his shots with great freedom. He reached 32 in a hurry before a 'snorter' from Thomson climbed from back-of-a-length and hit him right between the eyes. When I reached Mendis lying on the ground, I was relieved to see his eyes were open and asked, "Are you alright, pal?" Duleep looked up at me and, with a tear rolling down his cheek, replied, "I am going now."

So much for the PR exercise; two retired hurt, both in hospital.

This wasn't the only controversy of the 1975 World Cup. In the opening game at Lord's, India responded to England's 334 for 4 with a sedate 132 for 3 off the full complement of 60 overs. Opening the batting, Sunil Gavaskar remained unconquered on 36. Whenever I laughingly chastise Sunny about his 36 not out off 60 overs, he's quick to respond with a cheeky grin, "No Ian, in a 60-over innings."

Unlike India, Australia reached the semi-final and fittingly we were drawn to play England at Headingley. We made one change for the semi-final, replacing off-spinner Ashley Mallett with all-rounder Gary 'Gus' Gilmour because the ball had a tendency to swing at that venue. Gilmour proceeded to make the ball deviate alarmingly to take 6 for 14 from 12 overs unchanged and scupper England for a paltry 93.

"You bloody beauty," I thought. "We've beaten England and that'll show those journos what we know about playing one-day cricket."

My euphoria was quickly extinguished and at 6 for 39, Australia weren't in much better shape than England. Gilmour to the rescue again: He clobbered five fours in making 28 not out and in partnership with Walters, took us home without any further calamities.

The next day the headline, above a photo of Gilmour, proclaimed: "Gary Glitter". This was a clever reference to the rock singer of that name who was topping the charts at the time.

Australia's win and West Indies' superiority over New Zealand in the other semi-final meant the two best and most attacking sides were scheduled to meet in the final at Lord's. We arrived at Lord's to be greeted by hundreds of Caribbean fans who created a wonderful atmosphere for the final with their colourful dress and musical instruments. They welcomed us warmly with comments like: "It's going to be a great game, maan," but were never boastful.

Lloyd further fuelled their enthusiasm with a powerful century that led to West Indies setting us a stiff target. Every time Australia appeared to be on track for victory Viv Richards produced a stirring piece of fielding that ended in a run-out. Despite four run-outs and still needing 59 to win, the final pair of Lillee and Thomson provided hope. They had reduced the deficit to 20 when Lillee lofted a shot into the covers and Roy Fredericks accepted the chance. That prompted a pitch invasion, but there was one problem: the catch had been taken off a no-ball and Fredericks had shied at the stumps. The ball disappeared into the crowd and that brought out the optimist in Lillee: "Run, run," he called to his partner, "We can get the 20 we need to win the match."

"Don't be bloody stupid," replied the surprisingly conservative Thommo. "One of these blokes could hide the ball in his pocket and run us out."

Ironically, the match ended a few runs later when Thomson became the fifth run-out victim in our innings.

Lloyd was acclaimed by thousands of Caribbean fans who had flocked onto the ground as he received both the Man of the Match award and the

Leader, legend: Clive Lloyd's powerful century in the final fuelled the crowd's enthusiasm. — *Patrick Eagar/ Getty Images*

winners' trophy. Following the presentation, the Australian team made their way down to the West Indies dressing room to congratulate Lloyd and his team on their stirring victory and to reflect on what had been a vastly entertaining spectacle.

However, proceedings didn't end there. Along with Lloyd, Rod Marsh and I — still in our creams — retired to the Tavern Bar by the Grace gates to wind down after what had been an exhausting day. The Tavern bar was heaving with fans, many of them from the Caribbean, and they came over to offer congratulations to their skipper and tell us in very respectful terms how much they enjoyed the game.

Late in the evening we were joined by South African allrounder Mike Procter, who'd been a spectator at the ground. Shortly afterwards, yet another West Indies supporter came over to offer congratulations all-round and then pointed to Procter and asked, "Who he?"

Being aware of the animosity apartheid aroused in the Caribbean, I thought, "Oh no, I hope a nasty incident isn't going to spoil what has been a great day."

Cautiously I made the introduction: "That's Mike Procter." The West Indies fan gushed as he grabbed his hand— "The great South African all-rounder, it's an honour to meet you."

This delightful example of sport breaking down barriers capped off a highly successful day. It had been a wonderfully entertaining game of cricket that helped ensure the future of the World Cup concept.

Ian Chappell captained Australia between 1971 and 1975, and turned to commentary after his playing days.

The rivalry that isn't

AHMER NAQVI

In one sense, asking a Pakistani to explain why their team has lost to India in every single World Cup/World T20 match, including most recently in 2019, is like asking someone to provide a failsafe cure for cancer. In both cases, if we had the answer already, why wouldn't we have done something about it? Trying to explain Pakistan's 27-year losing streak is a process where probability, divinity, fate and any other paradigm doesn't quite work. That being said, there is a way perhaps to try and contextualise this ignominious record.

The narrative around most sports is hardly distinguishable from that around a soap opera. Most observers and analysts project their own feelings around a match, casting heroes and villains and creating narratives that are simple and binary. So, of course, there are people who will try to explain India's dominance over Pakistan as a function of their economies over this period. Others have tried to explain Pakistan's miserable record as a consequence of their ideological positioning vis-a-vis India (you can thank Shashi Tharoor for that hot take).

Unfortunately, one can't quite analyse this one-sided rivalry using these convenient, overarching storylines. A total of 52 Pakistani cricketers had

Grand theatre: Javed Miandad wasn't a fan of Kiran More's appealing in the neighbours' 1992 clash. — *Patrick Eagar/ Getty Images*

played in the 11 white-ball matches between the two sides at the two world events before the latest. No one player has played more than nine of these matches (Shahid Afridi), which is a simple way of suggesting that there isn't any one recurring element in all these matches, save for the fact that Pakistan — almost inevitably — have lost each time.

A better way of looking at this cursed record might be to break the matches down into three periods: the 1990s, the new millennium till 2008, and the time since 2008. But why these dates?

The first set of World Cup defeats from the 1990s have quite a few things in common. Ten Pakistanis played two of the three matches from this time, with Inzamam-ul-Haq and Saleem Malik featuring in all three. Each of these matches saw Pakistan chasing Indian targets, and in each they failed by almost the same margin (43, 39 and 47 runs respectively).

During that decade, Pakistan won 63 per cent of all matches batting first, as against 57 per cent when chasing — not much of a difference. But when it came to facing India, this changed dramatically. Pakistan had a 70 per cent win record when batting first against India, which dropped to 52 per cent when chasing.

A big reason for this was the typical game plan for the '90s side, which preferred batting first and using a bunch of all-rounders to attack in the death overs, long before the phrase was in vogue. This approach put pressure on the team when chasing, as the lower order was expected to catch up to spiralling run-rates. Given that most of these players weren't proper batsmen, they often wilted under the pressure. In both the 1992 and 1996 matches, Pakistan started strong before collapsing, losing 8 for 68 in the first and 5 for 64 in the second.

Pakistan losing the toss and being forced to chase against their arch-rivals was one reason for the three losses. Another reason, which is harder to prove but far more popular, was the spectre of match-fixing that hung over both teams, but particularly Pakistan, during that decade. In 1992, team leaders like Javed Miandad and Imran Khan had relatively spotless careers, while the others were quite new to the game. But the losses in 1996 and 1999 were far more shocking, with captain Wasim Akram's mysterious absence on the eve of the 1996 match instigating parliamentary inquiries and reports.

What made these losses harder to believe was Pakistan's general record during this decade. They won 61 per cent of all ODIs against India in the period, and five out of eight times when they met in tournament finals or knockouts. And while both the 1996 and 1992 teams met India at moments during the tournament where Pakistan were out of sorts, the 1999 version met India as one of the teams of the tournament, and would go on to play the final.

In many ways, the losses of the '90s are the hardest to explain using just stats and logic. It gets easier later on.

The 2003 World Cup match in Centurion was a symbolic changing of the guard. Pakistan's dominance over India, which some marked back to Miandad's tournament-winning last-ball six in Sharjah in 1986, came to

Where in the 2003 World Cup Pakistan's team was full of veterans, India were a young, transformed side. — *Getty Images*

an apparent end here. On one side was a Pakistani team full of veterans from the previous decade, almost all playing their final tournament. Facing them was a revolutionary Indian side led by Sourav Ganguly, which seemed to have completely transformed its mentality. Despite batting first and posting a huge total, Pakistan's fearsome attack was, for once, left toothless as India stormed to victory.

During the first decade of the 2000s, Pakistan's record versus India in ODIs fell to 22-18, and was 19-16 in their favour for matches before 2008. This decade saw the end of the Sharjah tournaments in which the teams often met, meaning they only met in tournament knockouts twice. Pakistan won the Kitply Cup final, but lost the WT20 final in this decade.

A weaker team playing their rapidly improving rivals less often meant that Pakistan's record of losing in the 2003 World Cup, and failing to win either of the WT20 matches in the 2000s was far less surprising than their record in the '90s. While Pakistan retained a winning record against India in this decade, they had lost the aura they once held against their rivals. The 2007 World Cup might have offered a chance for redemption, but both sides fell to shocking upsets and early exits. Both the WT20 matches also would have ended up being one-sided had it not been for Misbah-ul-Haq, who played valiant knocks each time only to see his team fail.

In 2008, the final period of India's domination began due to events that were far out of Pakistan cricket's control. Misbah's failure to clear the boundary in the 2007 WT20 final led to a series of events that culminated in the launch of the IPL. A year later, the horrifying attacks on Mumbai led to the end of cricketing relations between Pakistan and India, and the unofficial ban on Pakistanis in the IPL. A year after that, the shocking attack on the Sri Lankan cricket team in Lahore led to the end of cricket in Pakistan altogether, as the team entered their exile.

In the decade since, Indian cricket has gone from strength to strength, with its board becoming the de facto power centre of the game, its team becoming one of the strongest across all formats, and its T20 league becoming the

Cross-border relations: Sachin Tendulkar starred in India's 2011 semi-final win.
— *Patrick Eagar/ Getty Images*

world's most important laboratory for developing new skills and making new stars. And all this while, Pakistan cricket has struggled to survive. They've played low-profile sides in empty stadia in the UAE, the Pakistan Super League came years after the IPL, and they've had to watch as players looked increasingly out of touch with the modern game.

Except for the 2011 World Cup semi-final in Mohali, Pakistan have been thrashed in each of the five meetings at world events. Indeed, had it not been for the shock result in the 2017 Champions Trophy final, one would have struggled to continue classifying this as a rivalry anymore.

Perhaps more worryingly, there is a clear inferiority complex for Pakistani teams, one that is clearly highlighted by how rarely they meet their rivals as well as how low their status in world cricket has fallen to. While Pakistan have held the Test mace, as well as the Champions Trophy and the WT20 titles since the exile, these achievements have come in the midst of mediocrity and poor results.

In many ways, the chance for Pakistan to beat India now at any world competition feels slimmer than ever. But given how India's unbeaten run has confounded logic, form and much else, perhaps now when the team is at the strongest, it's time for the run to end.

Ahmer Naqvi (@karachikhatmal) is a freelance writer on cricket and pop culture.

A trophy worth the turmoil

YUVRAJ SINGH

With the hopes of a billion people riding on our shoulders we embarked on our 2011 World Cup journey, determined to end a 28-year wait.

I was not in the best shape physically or mentally heading into the tournament. I had had a difficult few months leading up to our first game, against Bangladesh in Dhaka. Injuries had been my constant companions; I had broken my wrist, sustained multiple fractures in my fingers. I was in and out of the team, and so consistency was elusive. I had just one half-century in nine innings before the World Cup and had an ordinary tour of South Africa, our last engagement before the World Cup, though I did pick up a few wickets.

It was in South Africa in January that I began to sense that all was not well with me physically. I battled insomnia; sleep was elusive, and my body was racked with extended bouts of coughing. The night before the second ODI in Johannesburg, there was lot of purple phlegm in my saliva, which rocked me momentarily. Ironically, I made 53 the next day, my only 50-plus score in the series. Mahi (Mahendra Singh Dhoni) and I ran twos off two successive deliveries. By the fourth run, I was not able to breathe properly. After the game, I told the physio about my breathing issues, and he suggested that we get it checked. I convinced him that we should put it off till we returned to India.

Once we came back, the World Cup camp started in Bengaluru, and was a convenient excuse for me to postpone meeting a doctor. I thought if something came up in the scans, it would be tough for me to focus on the game. By now, I was really struggling; my left nostril was hardly working. I knew something wasn't right, but I didn't want my health to jeopardise my World Cup participation. The opportunity was too big to pass up. We had the best possible team after playing together for nearly nine years.

I used to cough up a little blood during games, but it was minimal, so I wasn't too fussed. However, against West Indies in Chennai — it was really hot and humid — I was consistently coughing. There was more blood than usual, and I was silently alarmed.

My team-mates didn't know about this. I was so out of breath that guys like Bhajji (Harbhajan Singh), Zak (Zaheer Khan) and Ashu (Ashish Nehra) would constantly make fun of me. 'How can you get so tired after bowling spin?' they would joke. I would just laugh it off; there was no point getting them all worried during a momentous time in all our lives.

I had been beating myself up over my injuries and needed some reassurance. I had a chat with Sachin (Tendulkar) at the start of the tournament, venting all my frustrations. I told him that I didn't know what to do to get the negativity out of my system. As usual, he had the right words. He told me to play the tournament for somebody special. He also said, "Before a sea storm, the sea goes really quiet." I knew who that 'somebody special' was for whom I must play the tournament. Sachin had done so much for the country, he had played international cricket for more than 20 years by then, and he deserved to win the World Cup more than all of us. So I told myself, 'Let's play this World Cup for Tendulkar, and let's see how it goes.'

We had the confidence right through the tournament that we could go all the way, but strangely enough, it was after our loss to South Africa in Nagpur that we felt we were on the right track. We were 260-odd for 2 after 40 overs but were bowled out for 296 and lost a tight game in the final over by three wickets. Everything started to flare up: the media had a go, people started talking, there was pressure from outside, all because we had lost one match. That's when we sat down and had a chat. We realised that we were generally playing well as a unit, and that we could afford no distractions. Sachin and Gary (Kirsten, the coach) laid down the rules that evening: Don't get swayed by what's happening around you. No television, no newspapers. Every time in and out of crowds, listen to music on our headphones, cut out the white noise, just get into that space where the focus is only on cricket. Try and keep the team environment positive, and stay together as a unit. We had lost just one game out of five, there was no need to panic.

Before the tournament, and during the last couple of games, we were joined by Mike Horn, the great explorer who has made it a habit of turning the impossible into possible. He is a crazy guy, an amazingly unbelievable inspiration. Listening to him, we could feel the motivation course through our system. He narrated his experiences: going to the Amazon, turning his ship around to escape a tsunami, scaling Broad Peak (altitude 8047 metres) without oxygen. He told us, "If I can do all this on my own, imagine what 11 of you together can do." That was it for us, no way were we not going to win the World Cup.

I was largely batting at No. 4 and No. 5, enjoying the challenge of repeatedly taking the team home from tricky situations. I had done that so often in my career under pressure that it was almost second nature. I didn't allow the situation to bog me down; instead, I used it to spur me on. I was doing the same things as earlier, following the same routines. But where in the recent past I had been unable to build on starts, this time, the runs flowed. The 30s became fifties, and one fifty became a hundred. It all came together at the right time, I felt that it was destined to happen.

The strains of a long, emotional campaign caught up with me when we reached Mumbai for the final. I couldn't make it to practice the day before the final, because I didn't wake up on time. I had spent numerous sleepless nights throughout the tournament, and I had serious neck issues. Practice was at 10 am, and when I woke up, I was aghast to see that it was already 11. It wasn't another half-hour before I reached the Wankhede. Generally, if you are late for practice, your mates seize on the opportunity for justified ribbing, and the coach is ready with a bollocking. But nobody said a thing to me, everyone

Emotional campaign: 'It all came together at the right time, I felt that it was destined to happen.' — *Getty Images*

was so geared up for the final that the focus was entirely on practice.

I walked up to Gary and apologised for turning up late, admitting that I had overslept. And that it was the first night during the World Cup that I had actually slept properly. Gary was sweet, he was as concerned about my physical struggles as anyone else. He called the physio over and joked, "Because tomorrow is such a big day, can we give him a sleeping injection tonight?"

One of the talking points of the final was Mahi batting ahead of me, at No.5. Throughout the tournament, he had been playing well but hadn't got a big score because batting at No.6 isn't easy. I was the form batsman, I had already won four match awards, and I was padded up to go at No.5. But (Muttiah) Muralitharan was bowling alongside the other off-spinner (Suraj Randiv), and Gautam (Gambhir) was already in, well settled. At some stage during the Gautam-Virat Kohli partnership, Gary, Sachin and Mahi decided that if Virat got out, a right-hander would go in because two offies were bowling, and it would be prudent to keep the lefty-righty combination going.

Was I disappointed at not batting at No.5? Not at all. I just wanted us to win the game. It was all about the team, not me. Somebody had to get the job done, it didn't matter who that somebody was. When Mahi went out to bat, I hurried to the washroom and threw up. I coughed up a bit of blood, away from everyone's eyes, and got rid of all the nervousness. Temporarily, I forgot all the issues I was facing. This was the moment of truth.

I was happy to be in the middle when Mahi hit the winning runs. I don't have words to describe what I felt. It was like a dream come true. All these years, you have been thinking of winning a World Cup. All the sacrifices you have made, all the ups and downs, everything just flashed before my eyes. It was a very special moment. All this while, we had seen on television all these great teams winning the World Cup. You don't know what they must have felt; suddenly, I knew exactly what emotions must have run through those guys. After 28 years, we had won the World Cup — we had won it for Tendulkar, we had won it for the country.

Yuvraj Singh (@yuvstrong12) was Player of the Tournament in the 2011 World Cup. He was treated for cancer after the tournament.

South Africa's dark mist

NEIL MANTHORP

The world is divided into people who can roll their tongues and move their ears, and those who can't. It's a genetic thing; it's unavoidable. Some genetic disorders are unexpected and unexplained, others are hereditary. Inheritors of mutant genes may choose to live in denial until the disorder presents itself, at which point there may be anger before confrontation and acceptance.

From time to time over the last 15 years, South African cricket fans could have been forgiven for believing that the national team's failure to perform anywhere near their best when the 'pressure' was at its greatest was a congenital condition.

The string of World Cup chokes might still be explained away as coincidental or merely 'bad luck', but not when examined alongside some pitiful displays at the other ICC events, the World T20 and the Champions Trophy, where the failures have been equally, if not more, spineless. It is also the generally solid, often powerful performances in the round-robin stages that throw a harsh but honest light on the knockout matches, of which South Africa have won just two across events.

Pitiful, yes, but 'spineless'? Perhaps there was too much spine being shown. Bob Woolmer's decision to replace the country's spearhead, Allan Donald, with the youngest and least experienced member of the 1996 squad, Paul Adams, on a dry pitch in Karachi for the quarter-final against West Indies would have been hailed as inspired, brave and visionary had Brian Lara not made one of his best ODI centuries.

Lance Klusener, the Player of the Tournament in 1999, showed the same big match temperament he had displayed throughout when smashing Damien Fleming for two fours in the final over to level the scores in the semi-final against Australia three years later. In the company of last man Donald. But it is the run-out for which his countrymen will always remember him. A decade later he said, "I realised ... that I would have to spend the rest of my life saying 'I'm sorry'."

If that moment was a brain fade, then the failure to read the Duckworth/Lewis graph against Sri Lanka in the home World Cup of 2003 represented more of a collective lobotomy. Mark Boucher unwittingly blocked what turned out to be the final delivery of the match, from Muttiah Muralitharan, in heavy drizzle, believing the revised total was to win, not tie the match. The fact that the D/L method had only recently been introduced — and the target was not displayed on the scoreboard — remain incidental details.

In 2007, there was yet another twist to the debacle of the Proteas' World Cup history — although it can again be argued, at a stretch, that it was an

1999 classic: The brain-fade, the run-out, the tie and a lost opportunity.
— *Getty Images*

attempt to be brave and bold, which ended in a feeble collapse to 27 for 5. Having staged a dominant group campaign, South Africa's insecurity complex against Australia manifested itself in dramatic fashion at the start of the semi-final in St Lucia. A manic, completely out-of-character approach by the top order was most clearly illustrated by the usually phlegmatic Jacques Kallis charging down the wicket to Glenn McGrath to hit him over the top, a tactic not unusual a decade later — and for very different players — but unheard of for the great accumulator that Kallis was.

By 2011, South Africa's reputation for vulnerability in knockout matches was firmly entrenched. Yet another strong group-stage showing left them facing New Zealand in a quarter-final in Dhaka. There was nothing wrong with the bowling performance as the Black Caps limped to 221 for 8 on a slow pitch. But the surface had nothing to do with the response. It was almost all played out in the head — or heads of the run-chasing batsmen. An incessant barrage of reminders about their 'history' took its toll, and when twelfth man Kyle Mills initiated a physical confrontation with a young, naive Faf du Plessis during the final drinks break, South Africa's last hope of victory lost his cool and another chapter of the saga was complete.

Du Plessis was at heart of the final episode, also against New Zealand, in the semi-final at Eden Park in 2015. Such had become the obsession with World Cup success that captain AB de Villiers was consumed by it. He was not alone, but he was comfortably its greatest victim. The political intervention in team selection, which resulted in the in-form Kyle Abbott being replaced by the injured Vernon Philander, was far from unprecedented. It had been the norm for a decade and a half. But this time it was different — it felt

2015 heartbreak: A promising campaign ground to a halt in a dramatic last over against New Zealand. — *Getty Images*

like the weight of the world. It was the beginning of the end for de Villiers, who took an 18-month international sabbatical before rousing himself for a final, stunning home Test series victory against India and Australia. But in truth, it was the 'voodoo' that broke him.

The defeats have been discussed and debated many times by many people, but rarely mentioned in any meaningful way by those who matter. Two coaches, Mickey Arthur and Gary Kirsten, are the exceptions. Arthur said in his 2010 autobiography: "I knew there was a problem before the (2007) semi-final. The atmosphere in the team room was different, it was too quiet, tense. In retrospect, I would have addressed it, but I just hoped it was 'normal' before such a big game and they would be alright in the morning. They weren't."

Having reached yet another semi-final in the Champions Trophy of 2013, the stage was perfectly set on a sunny morning against hosts England at a packed Oval. South Africa batted first and produced a withering anti-climax by collapsing to 80 for 8 inside 20 overs. Asked afterwards whether his team had choked, coach Kirsten — the World Cup-winning messiah (with India) who was supposed to change everything — paused for several seconds to consider his answer and the ramifications thereof: "Yes … I think we did. We've got to accept that it's a dark mist which hangs over the team in knockout matches." There. It was said. Admitted. Perhaps it would be a turning point.

It wasn't.

Fresh young players have come into the team over the years and pronounced themselves 'unscarred' by the failures of the past, undaunted and excited by the challenge. Yet many have found themselves overcome by the ghosts of the past at the critical moment. The 'gene' they believed they did not carry reveals itself. In 2019, it was a new story, not involving genes or choking. South Africa stunned Australia in the league. But by then it was too late. The wait has been extended by another four years.

Neil Manthorp (@NeilManthorp) is a cricket columnist and author based in South Africa.

Not arrogant, just better

VIV RICHARDS

West Indies cricket had its first instance of jubilation in 1950, as the team that travelled to England defeated the hosts at Lord's and won the Test series 3-1. Over the next two decades, the captaincy stints of the legendary Frank Worrell and Garfield Sobers did wonders in shifting the dominance of whites in the region's cricket, making it a more inclusive game for the locals.

In 1974, a bespectacled genius named Clive Lloyd took over captaincy from Rohan Kanhai and guided the team to never imagined heights. 'Big C' went on to lead the team to two World Cups. We had a 27-game unbeaten streak in Tests.

Now, the thing to remember is that when the West Indies of the 1970s and 1980s took the field, they were not just recognised as the 'better' team by results alone. The opposition were intimidated. There was a swagger that came from every member of the team knowing that he was part of an undefeatable unit, and everyone played with that attitude. Call it arrogance, but we knew exactly what we were doing. From chewing gum while walking out to face the opposition's best bowler, to those cheeky comments thrown around — we knew how to use these things to gain an upper hand.

Lloyd took control of a team that possessed very high levels of skill. The batsmen were fearless. We felt no one could conquer us. We've all been knocked out for measly scores several times, but when it happened, the thinking was that "the bowler got lucky"; it was never that he was better. He had gotten lucky, and it would not happen again.

And the bowlers — where do I even begin? Those guys were more warriors than bowlers. The 'Whispering Death', Michael Holding, would barely break stride as he ripped through opposition bowling line ups. Joel Garner, Colin Croft, Malcolm Marshall, Andy Roberts and later Curtly Ambrose were all giants among men — in all aspects. Desmond Haynes once summed it up: "We were really good. End of story. The opposition turned up expecting to get beat and we never liked to disappoint them."

It is said of the other all-conquering sides — Australia under Steve Waugh and Ricky Ponting, for example — that they "hunted in packs". They would go after bowlers or batsmen and even fielders not as individuals, but as a group, attacking from all directions. Us? We didn't need that. When we stepped on to a cricket ground, everyone knew who was the boss. Everyone knew who was better. Everyone could tell who was scared. We walked in and walked out winners. Almost every single time.

Like at the 1975 Cricket World Cup. That was the first time that a world tournament was conducted on such a grand scale. One strange memory that

Australians challenge Viv Richards's throw: 'I think I taught them a lesson or two that day.' — *Popperfoto/ Getty Images*

will always remain is Sunny Gavaskar's bizarre, defensive innings against England in the opening game. We brushed aside Pakistan, Australia and Sri Lanka in the group stages before we met New Zealand in the semi-final. They were going well, before Bernard Julien tore through them like drywall. We had a couple of hiccups, but we chased with time to spare.

Next game, Rohan stuck around for a sensible half-century, but that final was Clive's. He single-handedly took us to 291. My biggest contribution in that game was three run-outs! The Australians seemed to want to run every time there was even a slight misfield. Well, I think I taught them a lesson or two that day. And just like that, we were Champions of the World.

From that day forth, we weren't just another team competing on the world stage — we became 'the' team. The team everyone wanted to beat, but just couldn't find a way to; a bench mark. Everyone wanted to be like us. It wasn't just our cricket: cricketers wanted to chew gum, dominate opponents and walk around with a 'Caribbean swagger'.

In 1976, we travelled to England again. What followed was a demolition: we took the five-Test series to retain the Wisden Trophy and the three-match ODI series without a single defeat. I have fond memories of that tour, as I was the highest run-scorer in both formats. Over the next two years, we played Australia at home and away, claiming handsome victories in the Test series, while the ODIs were a tightly contested draw.

So, when teams put up a fight, it felt surreal. In India, against Sunny's team, we moved from Mumbai to Bengaluru to Kolkata having drawn all three games. The Indians, with a newly instilled sense of fight, took the game from us in Chennai, which was followed by draws in Delhi and Kanpur. The feeling of defeat was not one that we were accustomed to.

As a result, we desperately wanted to win the second World Cup. Heading back home without the trophy was not an option.

We won two out of our three group games, with one being abandoned due to inclement weather.

Semi-final time. Gordon Greenidge and Haynes put on a superb partnership, while Clive and I pitched in with handy knocks, setting Pakistan a competitive total. Colin and I made sure that the Pakistan batting did not get a chance to take off. On to the final.

That game will stay with me forever, as I scored 138 and remained not out, meaning we had a strong total. It was time to turn the screws on the English batting. Joel was on fire, taking five to make sure that they never managed any momentum. Yet again, we were world champions.

In 1980, the year after the World Cup win, I took over as captain. What an honour it was! I think I'm the only West Indies captain who never lost a Test series.

The 1983 World Cup final was heart-breaking. Take nothing away from the Indian team — Kapil Dev and his boys were superb on the day. They had an arsenal of good, hard-working seam bowlers who took full advantage of the conditions. We just felt that we could have taken that game by the scruff of the neck but didn't quite manage to do so. As I walked back to the dressing room following my dismissal, I still felt pretty confident and that we had enough firepower to take the game away. That day I also learnt a very important lesson: While competing at the highest level, losing focus and descending into chaos can have a lasting effect on the psyche of a team, no matter how good or bad they are.

The evening before the big game, we were all relaxed. The Indians were the underdogs, and everybody believed it would be a walk in the park for us. I was so at ease that I played the tabla all night long! Ever since then, I've been in love with the instrument.

West Indies cricket today has reached a kind of an impasse. What transpires over the next three to five years could shape the future of cricket in the Caribbean. There have been some excellent cricketers who wore the famous maroon before me and after me — and there will always be. In 2015, the young Jason Holder was handed the captaincy reins. He is a good, tall and attacking fast bowler; he reminds me of some of my team-mates way back then. He still has a lot to learn, but he is an earnest cricketer, who is performing consistently and hasn't let captaincy affect his game. He must be backed to the hilt.

In this current crop of West Indies cricketers, ability is present in abundance. We have supremely talented cricketers, but I still feel that the fitness levels need to be upped. More rigorous fitness training, mastering the basics and improved self-belief can take this group of youngsters a long way.

People always ask me and players of my generation if we are sad, or if we are disappointed, with what has happened to West Indies cricket. It is true, after the glory days of the late 20th century, West Indies haven't conquered the world. All sports teams go through rough patches, the length of which could vary from a couple of months to a decade. It is about coming back stronger every time. Darren Sammy led the team to two World T20 titles, and that experience, that elation of winning and becoming champions must inspire further success.

I will always love cricket, and I will always love the West Indies. My country, my team. I will always believe that West Indies will rise again as a world-beating force. It may take time, but toppling India, Australia, Pakistan and South Africa now is no easy task. Let it take a while, but one day I believe the West Indies team will walk out on to the pitch chewing gum, with a swagger, knowing that they're just plain better.

Viv Richards is one of the greatest batsmen of all time, with a Test average of 50.23 and an ODI strike-rate of 90.2 in 308 international matches.

Rewired bicycle dynamos and headlines

ANDREW FERNANDO

I remember the grimacing uncles outside the corner shop, fingers pressed to their foreheads, as the school van rounded the corner. Inside the van, the semi-final was all us kids had talked about on the hour-long ride from school. Sanath Jayasuriya and Romesh Kaluwitharana were the men, we had decided. They had thrashed India once already in the tournament, so surely they could thrash them again. Sachin Tendulkar? Puh. That fellow can score all the runs he wants, but who can hammer the bowlers like Sanath and Kalu? They will win the match by themselves.

But something was wrong. I could tell by the looks on the uncles' faces. They were the regular crowd — older neighbourhood men, who through the course of the 1996 World Cup had taken to parking themselves outside the corner shop near our house to watch the matches on the 14-inch television screen inside the store. The van stopped outside our gate. My heart now thumping, I scurried out, tearing up the steps, whizzing through the front garden. Maybe Sri Lanka had only lost the toss, I hoped. That's what the uncles were upset about. Just as I was about to disappear through the front door, another commotion. More slapping of hands on furrowed foreheads. An anguished "aiyoo!" A disgusted "chee!" Schoolbag still on my back, water bottle rattling around by my hip, I raced to the television. Sri Lanka 1 for 2. Sanath, gone. Kalu, gone. I gawped, disbelieving. How could this have happened?

If I said I remembered every shot Aravinda de Silva played over the next 40 minutes, I would be lying. But two things remain crystallised in the memory: The way the ball seemed to disappear in the seconds after de Silva had hit it only to reappear as it leapt off the rope to sting the boundary boards; and the way the knot in my stomach eased through the course of his 47-ball 66.

The three days spent in anticipation of the final felt like three months — though that was not necessarily a bad thing. I was a child of wartime, born in the late 1980s, when an armed uprising was gathering in the south of the island even while a brutal sectarian war raged in the north. I can't remember ever feeling proud of my country until after that semi-final. I'm not sure how many others felt the same, but I do recall that Colombo suddenly burst with Sri Lankan flags. They billowed out of the sides of trishaws, fluttered away in verandahs and balconies, and brought dreary school buildings to life. A rare wildflower had suddenly come into a spectacular urban bloom, decking the city out in saffron, green and maroon.

I also remember the joy in almost every conversation. This may not sound especially remarkable, but if all your life you have only known daily death tolls on the news, lamentations on the costs of living, and the overwhelming fear of bomb attacks, seeing the adults around you break into frequent laughter and hearing them gush for hours on end — these things really could not help but put you into a mild euphoria. I remember my father going over each of India's dismissals with a friend, to work out how many Sanath had been involved in (it was six); I remember my mother raving to her aunty — a hardcore cricket fan to this day — how spirited Sri Lanka's fielding was ("Three fellows chasing the same ball. Have you ever seen that? Three!")

On the day of the final, hysteria gave way to a tense hush. Everyone in the city was cloistered around a TV. Much later in life, while working on a feature story in Jaffna, I would learn how people in the north — folks who had borne the war's profound calamity in ways that we in Colombo could barely

Sachin Tendulkar? Puh. That fellow can score all the runs he wants, but who can hammer the bowlers like Sanath and Kalu? — *Getty Images*

imagine — had spent the day of the final. While we were trading nervous glances, they were hard at work, figuring out how they might get a television set to work. Almost the entirety of Jaffna town and many other villages in the peninsula had been displaced by recent fighting. Although they had taken care of the necessities in their makeshift camps — setting up classrooms beneath coconut trees and hospitals in palmyrah groves — luxuries such as watching a game of cricket they had neglected until the World Cup. Eventually, solutions were found. Some repurposed car batteries to provide the electricity required to run a TV. Others rewired bicycle dynamos and took turns pedalling so the crowd could enjoy the action. There are many examples of sport's power to unite, but are there any more powerful?

Back at our living room in Colombo, a rising thrill took grip as de Silva and Arjuna Ranatunga forged the final partnership. There were howls of joy at every boundary, cackles of delight when Ranatunga plonked a Shane Warne full toss for a six over square leg while Tony Greig boomed: "These Sri Lankans are giving the Aussies a real hiding."

The next day in the school van, even the professed cricket haters were ecstatic, though the skyrockets and firecrackers and unbridled elation had enraptured us into the morning hours. We swapped favourite moments, shadow batted Aravinda shots in our seats, whooped over how the Lahori crowd had obviously barracked for a Sri Lanka win, carrying Sri Lanka flags and anti-Australia banners to the ground. (One of those banners, by the way, was perhaps the wittiest ever seen at a cricket ground, though none of us in that van were of an age to appreciate it. "Hair or no hair, Murali's balls are fair", it read. The World Cup final had come only four months after Muttiah Muralitharan's humiliation at the hands of Darrell Hair at the Boxing Day Test.)

At school, no one touched the syllabus for a week. Teachers could not help but yammer to each other, and to us, about the campaign, reliving every key moment, praising every player — even those who didn't make it into the XI all tournament: "That Upul Chandana, so brave, ah! Standing in the outfield when those people were throwing bottles and all." It was as if we had all been in on the hijinks in those few days. As if we had all devised the audacious plan to open with two aggressive batsmen, as if we had been party to the decision to bank on spin, and to specialise in chasing scores. I don't remember much about the World Cup welcome parade, except that I didn't go, and several friends bragged that they had been allowed to, and had even sighted the trophy with their own eyes. I do recall, though, that the World Cup led the evening news for about a week after the victory.

Eventually, of course, reality returned its tentacles to our throats. In July, four months after the final, a devastating bomb killed 64 and injured 400 in our neighbourhood of Dehiwala, the blast ringing through our home. Long before that, frontline death tolls and economic lamentations had again begun to feature in adult conversation. The grimness in the news bulletins had been restored.

But something vital had shifted as well. Life was similar, but not quite the same as before. A ceiling had been raised. Aspirations had been stoked. The nation may not quite have felt back in love with itself, but if little Sri Lanka could beat the world at such a thing, there was cause to hope, and reason to be optimistic again.

Andrew Fernando (@afidelf) is the Sri Lanka correspondent for ESPNcricinfo.

WORLD CUP RECORDS

OVERALL

Winners and runner-ups

Year	Winner	Runner-up	Venue	No. of teams	No. of matches
1975	West Indies	Australia	England	8	15
1979	West Indies	England	England	8	15
1983	India	West Indies	England	8	27
1987	Australia	England	India, Pakistan	8	27
1992	Pakistan	England	Australia, New Zealand	9	39
1996	Sri Lanka	Australia	India, Pakistan, Sri Lanka	12	38
1999	Australia	Pakistan	England, Ireland, Netherlands, Scotland	12	42
2003	Australia	India	Kenya, South Africa, Zimbabwe	14	54
2007	Australia	Sri Lanka	West Indies	16	51
2011	India	Sri Lanka	Bangladesh, India, Pakistan, Sri Lanka	14	49
2015	Australia	New Zealand	Australia, New Zealand	14	49
2019	England	New Zealand	England and Wales	10	48

Overall summary

Year	Most runs	Most wickets	Overall SR	Overall ER	Mat/300-run total
1975	Glenn Turner (NZ), 333	Gary Gilmour (Aus), 11	59.84	3.91	3.8
1979	Gordon Greenidge (WI), 253	Mike Hendrick (Eng), 10	54.52	3.54	-
1983	David Gower (Eng), 384	Roger Binny (Ind), 18	61.99	4.08	6.8
1987	Graham Gooch (Eng), 471	Craig McDermott (Aus), 18	74.48	4.87	27.0
1992	Martin Crowe (NZ), 456	Wasim Akram (Pak), 18	66.47	4.42	19.5
1996	Sachin Tendulkar (Ind), 523	Anil Kumble (Ind), 15	72.15	4.67	7.2
1999	Rahul Dravid (Ind), 461	Geoff Allott (NZ), Shane Warne (Aus), 20	64.85	4.47	14.0
2003	Sachin Tendulkar (Ind), 673	Chaminda Vaas (SL), 23	72.63	4.76	5.8
2007	Matthew Hayden (Aus), 659	Glenn McGrath (Aus), 26	75.87	4.95	3.2
2011	Tillakaratne Dilshan (SL), 500	Shahid Afridi (Pak), Zaheer Khan (Ind), 21	78.39	5.03	2.9
2015	Martin Guptill (NZ), 547	Mitchell Starc (Aus), Trent Boult (NZ), 22	88.97	5.65	1.7
2019	Rohit Sharma (Ind), 648	Mitchell Starc (Aus), 27	88.15	5.49	1.8

Win-loss record of teams that featured in CWC19

Team	Mat	Won	Lost	Tied	NR	Win %
Australia	94	69	23	1	1	74.73
India	84	53	29	1	1	64.46
New Zealand	89	54	33	1	1	61.93
South Africa	64	38	23	2	1	61.90
England	83	48	32	2	1	59.76
Pakistan	79	45	32	0	2	58.44
West Indies	80	43	35	0	2	55.13
Sri Lanka	80	38	39	1	2	49.36
Bangladesh	40	14	25	0	1	35.90
Afghanistan	15	1	14	0	0	6.67

TEAM

Highest totals

Score	For/Against	O	Venue	Year
417/6	Aus v Afg	50	Perth	2015
413/5	Ind v Ber	50	Port of Spain	2007
411/4	SA v Ire	50	Canberra	2015
408/5	SA v WI	50	Sydney	2015
398/5	SL v Ken	50	Kandy	1996

Lowest totals

Score	For/Against	O	Venue	Year
36	Can v SL	18.4	Paarl	2003
45	Can v Eng	40.3	Manchester	1979
45	Nam v Aus	14	Potchefstroom	2003
58	Ban v WI	18.5	Dhaka	2011
68	Sco v WI	31.3	Leicester	1999

Highest match aggregates

Runs	Team 1	Team 2	W	O	Venue	Year
714	Australia	Bangladesh	13	100	Nottingham	2019
688	Australia	Sri Lanka	18	96.2	Sydney	2015
682	England	Pakistan	17	100	Nottingham	2019
676	India	England	18	99.5	Bengaluru	2011
671	Australia	South Africa	16	98	Basseterre	2007

Largest victories (by runs)

Margin	For/Against	Target	Venue	Year
275 runs	Aus v Afg	418	Perth	2015
257 runs	Ind v Ber	414	Port of Spain	2007
257 runs	SA v WI	409	Sydney	2015
256 runs	Aus v Nam	302	Potchefstroom	2003
243 runs	SL v Ber	322	Port of Spain	2007

Largest victories (by wickets)

Margin	For/Against	Target	Venue	Year
10 wickets	Ind v EA	121	Leeds	1975
10 wickets	WI v Zim	172	Birmingham	1983
10 wickets	WI v Pak	221	Melbourne	1992
10 wickets	SA v Ken	141	Potchefstroom	2002
10 wickets	SL v Ban	125	Pietermaritzburg	2003
10 wickets	SA v Ban	109	Bloemfontein	2003
10 wickets	Aus v Ban	105	North Sound	2007
10 wickets	NZ v Ken	70	Chennai	2011
10 wickets	NZ v Zim	163	Ahmedabad	2011
10 wickets	Pak v WI	113	Dhaka	2011
10 wickets	SL v Eng	230	Colombo (RPS)	2011
10 wickets	NZ v SL	137	Cardiff	2019

Smallest victories (by runs)

Margin	For/Against	Target	Venue	Year
1 run	Aus v Ind	271	Chennai	1987
1 run	Aus v Ind	236	Brisbane	1992
2 runs	SL v Eng	236	North Sound	2007
3 runs	NZ v Zim	243	Hyderabad (Deccan)	1987
3 runs	Aus v NZ	200	Indore	1987
3 runs	Zim v Ind	253	Leicester	1999
3 runs	WI v SA	279	Cape Town	2003

Smallest victories (by wickets)

Margin	For/Against	Target	Venue	Year
1 wicket	WI v Pak	267	Birmingham	1975
1 wicket	Pak v WI	217	Lahore	1987
1 wicket	SA v SL	210	Providence	2007

1 wicket	Eng v WI	301	Bridgetown	2007
1 wicket	Afg v Sco	211	Dunedin	2015
1 wicket	NZ v Aus	152	Auckland	2015

Tied matches

Team 1	Team 2	Venue	Year
Australia	South Africa	Birmingham	1999
South Africa	Sri Lanka	Durban	2003
Ireland	Zimbabwe	Jamaica	2007
India	England	Bengaluru	2011
England	New Zealand	Lord's	2019

BATTING

Most runs

R	Player	M	I	NO	Avge	HS	SR	100s/ 50s
2278	Sachin Tendulkar (Ind)	45	44	4	56.95	152	88.98	6/ 15
1743	Ricky Ponting (Aus)	46	42	4	45.86	140*	79.95	5/ 6
1532	Kumar Sangakkara (SL)	37	35	8	56.74	124	86.55	5/ 7
1225	Brian Lara (WI)	34	33	4	42.24	116	86.26	2/ 7
1207	AB de Villiers (SA)	23	22	3	63.52	162*	117.29	4/ 6

Most runs in a single edition

R	Player	Year	M	I	NO	Avge	HS	SR	100s/ 50s
673	Sachin Tendulkar (Ind)	2003	11	11	0	61.18	152	89.25	1/ 6
659	Matthew Hayden (Aus)	2007	11	10	1	73.22	158	101.07	3/ 1
648	Rohit Sharma (Ind)	2019	9	9	1	81.00	140	98.33	5/1
647	David Warner (Aus)	2019	10	10	1	71.88	166	89.36	3/3
606	Shakib Al Hasan (Ban)	2019	8	8	1	86.57	124*	96.03	2/5

Highest individual scores

R (balls)	Player	4s/ 6s	SR	For/Against	Venue	Year
237* (163)	Martin Guptill	24/ 11	145.39	NZ v WI	Wellington	2015
215 (147)	Chris Gayle	10/ 16	146.25	WI v Zim	Canberra	2015
188* (159)	Gary Kirsten	13/ 4	118.23	SA v UAE	Rawalpindi	1996
183 (158)	Sourav Ganguly	17/ 7	115.82	Ind v SL	Taunton	1999
181 (125)	Viv Richards	16/ 7	144.80	WI v SL	Karachi	1987

Most hundreds

100s	Player	M	I	NO	R	Avge	HS
6	Rohit Sharma (Ind)	17	17	2	978	65.20	140
6	Sachin Tendulkar (Ind)	45	44	4	2278	56.95	152
5	Kumar Sangakkara (SL)	37	35	8	1532	56.74	124
5	Ricky Ponting (Aus)	46	42	4	1743	45.86	140*

* David Warner, Sourav Ganguly, AB de Villiers, Mark Waugh, Tillakaratne Dilshan, Mahela Jayawardene hit four centuries each.

Fastest 50s

Balls	Player	For/Against	Venue	Year
18	Brendon McCullum	NZ v Eng	Wellington	2015
20	Brendon McCullum	NZ v Can	Gros Islet	2007
20	Angelo Mathews	SL v Sco	Hobart	2015
21	Mark Boucher	SA v Net	Basseterre	2007
21	Brendon McCullum	NZ v Aus	Auckland	2015
21	Glenn Maxwell	Aus v Afg	Perth	2015

Fastest 100s

Balls	Player	For/Against	Venue	Year
50	Kevin O'Brien	Ire v Eng	Bengaluru	2011
51	Glenn Maxwell	Aus v SL	Sydney	2015
52	AB de Villiers	SA v WI	Sydney	2015
57	Eoin Morgan	Eng v Afg	Manchester	2019
66	Matthew Hayden	Aus v SA	Basseterre	2007

Most sixes

6s	Player	M	I
49	Chris Gayle	23	22
37	AB de Villiers (SA)	26	26
31	Ricky Ponting (AUS)	46	42
29	Brendon McCullum (NZ)	34	27
28	Herschelle Gibbs (SA)	25	23

Most sixes in an innings

6s	Player	R	Balls	For/Against	Venue	Year
17	Eoin Morgan	148	71	Eng v Afg	Manchester	2019
16	Chris Gayle	215	147	WI v Zim	Canberra	2015
11	Martin Guptill	237*	163	NZ v WI	Wellington	2015
9	David Miller	138*	92	SA v Zim	Hamilton	2015

Ricky Ponting, Imran Nazir, Adam Gilchrist, AB de Villiers and Chris Gayle hit eight sixes each.

Highest partnerships (by runs)

R	Players	Wkt	For/Against	Venue	Year
372	Chris Gayle, Marlon Samuels	2nd	WI v Zim	Canberra	2015
318	Sourav Ganguly, Rahul Dravid	2nd	Ind v SL	Taunton	1999
282	Upul Tharanga, Tillakaratne Dilshan	1st	SL v Zim	Pallekele	2011
260	David Warner, Steven Smith	2nd	Aus v Afg	Perth	2015
256*	David Miller, Jean-Paul Duminy	5th	SA v Zim	Hamilton	2015

Highest partnerships (by wickets)

R	Players	Wkt	For/Against	Venue	Year
282	Upul Tharanga, Tillakaratne Dilshan	1st	SL v Zim	Pallekele	2011
372	Chris Gayle, Marlon Samuels	2nd	WI v Zim	Canberra	2015
237*	Rahul Dravid, Sachin Tendulkar	3rd	Ind v Ken	Bristol	1999
204	Michael Clarke, Brad Hodge	4th	Aus v Net	Basseterre	2007
256*	David Miller, Jean-Paul Duminy	5th	SA v Zim	Hamilton	2015
162	Kevin O'Brien, Alex Cusack	6th	Ire v Eng	Bengaluru	2011
117	MS Dhoni & Ravindra Jadeja	7th	Ind v NZ	Manchester	2019
117	Dave Houghton, Iain Butchart	8th	Zim v NZ	Hyderabad (Deccan)	1987
126*	Kapil Dev, Syed Kirmani	9th	Ind v Zim	Tunbridge Wells	1983
71	Andy Roberts, Joel Garner	10th	WI v Ind	Manchester	1983

Most ducks

0s	Player	Mat	Inn	NO	Runs	Avge
5	Nathan Astle (NZ)	22	22	2	403	20.15
5	Ijaz Ahmed (PAK)	29	26	4	516	23.45

Kyle McCallan, Keith Arthurton, Eoin Morgan, AB de Villiers, Kris Srikkanth, Inzamam-ul-Haq and Darren Bravo have four ducks each.

BOWLING
Most wickets

W	Player	M	O	Avge	BB	ER	SR	5I
71	Glenn McGrath (Aus)	39	325.5	18.19	7-15	3.96	27.5	2
68	Muttiah Muralitharan (SL)	40	343.3	19.63	4-19	3.88	30.3	0
56	Lasith Malinga	29	232.2	22.87	6-38	5.51	24.8	1
55	Wasim Akram (Pak)	38	324.3	23.83	5-28	4.04	35.4	1
49	Mitchell Starc	18	156.1	14.81	6-28	4.64	19.1	3
49	Chaminda Vaas (SL)	31	261.4	21.22	6-25	3.97	32.0	1

Most wickets in a single edition

W	Player	Year	M	O	Avge	BB	ER	SR
27	Mitchell Starc (Aus)	2019	10	92.2	18.59	5-26	5.43	20.5
26	Glenn McGrath (Aus)	2007	11	80.5	13.73	3-14	4.41	18.6
23	Chaminda Vaas (SL)	2003	10	88	14.39	6-25	3.76	22.9
23	Muttiah Muralitharan (SL)	2007	10	84.4	15.26	4-19	4.14	22.0
23	Shaun Tait (Aus)	2007	11	84.3	20.30	4-39	5.52	22.0

Best bowling figures in an innings

Figures	Player	For/Against	Venue	Year
7-15	Glenn McGrath	Aus v Nam	Potchefstroom	2003
7-20	Andy Bichel	Aus v Eng	Port Elizabeth	2003
7-33	Tim Southee	NZ v Eng	Wellington	2015
7-51	Winston Davis	WI v Aus	Leeds	1983

* Nine bowlers took a six-wicket haul each in an innings.

Most five-wicket hauls

5I	Player	M	O	W	BB
3	Mitchell Starc (Aus)	18	156.1	49	6-28
2	Gary Gilmour (Aus)	2	24	11	6-14
2	Vasbert Drakes (WI)	6	51.5	16	5-33
2	Mustafizur Rahman	8	72.1	20	5-59
2	Ashantha de Mel (SL)	9	90.2	18	5-32
2	Shahid Afridi (Pak)	27	184	30	5-16
2	Glenn McGrath (Aus)	39	325.5	71	7-15

Hat-tricks

Player	For/Against	Venue	Year
Chetan Sharma	Ind v NZ	Nagpur	1987
Saqlain Mushtaq	Pak v Zim	Kennington	1999
Chaminda Vaas	SL v Ban	Pietermaritzburg	2003
Brett Lee	Aus v Ken	Durban	2003
Lasith Malinga	SL v SA	Providence	2007
Kemar Roach	WI v Net	Delhi	2011
Lasith Malinga	SL v Ken	Colombo	2011
Steven Finn	Eng v Aus	Melbourne	2015
JP Duminy	SA v SL	Sydney	2015
Mohammed Shami	Ind v Afg	Southampton	2019
Trent Boult	NZ v Aus	Lord's	2019

Best economy-rates (qualification – 1000 balls bowled)

ER	Player	Balls	R	W	BB	5I
3.24	Andy Roberts (WI)	1020.1	552	26	3-32	0
3.43	Ian Botham (Eng)	1332	762	30	4-31	0
3.52	Gavin Larsen (NZ)	1020	599	18	3-16	0
3.57	John Traicos (Zim)	1128	673	16	3-35	0
3.60	Shaun Pollock (SA)	1614	970	31	5-36	1

Best economy-rates in an innings (qualification – 30 balls bowled)

ER	Player	O	M	R	W	For/Against	Venue	Year
0.40	Dermot Reeve	5	3	2	1	Eng v Pak	Adelaide	1992
0.50	Bishan Bedi	12	8	6	1	Ind v EA	Leeds	1975
0.62	Mike Hendrick	8	4	5	1	Eng v Can	Manchester	1979
0.62	Andre Botha	8	4	5	2	Ire v Pak	Kingston	2007
0.66	Shaun Pollock	6	3	4	1	SA v Net	Basseterre	2007

Most maidens

Maidens	Player	M	O	R	W	Avge	ER
42	Glenn McGrath (Aus)	39	325.5	1292	71	7-15	18.19
39	Chaminda Vaas (SL)	31	261.4	1040	49	6-25	21.22
38	Richard Hadlee (NZ)	13	146.1	421	22	5-25	19.13
37	Shaun Pollock (SA)	31	269	970	31	5-36	31.29
33	Ian Botham (Eng)	22	222	762	30	4-31	25.40

Most maidens in an innings

Maidens	Player	O	R	W	For/Against	Venue	Year
8	Bishan Bedi	12	6	1	Ind v EA	Leeds	1975
6	Richard Hadlee	12	10	0	NZ v EA	Birmingham	1975
6	John Snow	12	11	4	Eng v EA	Birmingham	1975
6	Bishan Bedi	12	28	1	Ind v NZ	Manchester	1975
6	Gary Gilmour	12	14	6	Aus v Eng	Leeds	1975
6	Mike Hendrick	12	15	4	Eng v Pak	Leeds	1979
6	Aasif Karim	8.2	7	3	Ken v Aus	Durban	2003

Best strike-rates (Qualification – 30 wickets)

SR	Player	O	R	W	BB	5I
18.6	Mohammed Shami (Ind)	96.1	487	31	5-69	1
19.1	Mitchell Starc (Aus)	156.1	726	49	6-28	3
23.5	Brett Lee (Aus)	137.3	629	35	5-42	1
24.0	Shaun Tait (Aus)	136.3	731	34	4-39	0
24.8	Lasith Malinga (SL)	232.2	1281	56	6-38	1

Most runs conceded in an innings

R	Player	O	M	W	ER	For/Against	Venue	Year
110	Rashid Khan	9	0	0	12.22	Afg v Eng	Manchester	2019
105	Martin Snedden	12	1	2	8.75	NZ v Eng	The Oval	1983
104	Jason Holder	10	2	1	10.4	WI v SA	Sydney	2015
101	Dawlat Zadran	10	1	2	10.1	Afg v Aus	Perth	2015
97	Ashantha de Mel	10	0	1	9.7	SL v WI	Karachi	1987

WICKETKEEPING

Most dismissals

Dis	Player	M	Ct	St	Dis/Inn
54	Kumar Sangakkara (SL)	37	41	13	1.500
52	Adam Gilchrist (Aus)	31	45	7	1.677
42	MS Dhoni (Ind)	29	34	8	1.4
32	Brendon McCullum (NZ)	34	30	2	1.280
31	Mark Boucher (SA)	25	31	0	1.240

Most dismissals in a single edition

Dis	Player	M	Ct	St	Dis/Inn	Year
21	Adam Gilchrist (Aus)	10	21	0	2.1	2003
21	Tom Latham (NZ)	10	21	0	2.1	2019
20	Alex Carey (Aus)	10	18	2	2.0	2019
17	Kumar Sangakkara (SL)	10	15	2	1.7	2003
17	Adam Gilchrist (Aus)	11	12	5	1.5	2007

Most dismissals in an innings

Dis	Player	M	Ct	For/Against	Venue	Year
6	Adam Gilchrist	6	0	Aus v Nam	Potchefstroom	2003
6	Sarfraz Ahmed	6	0	Pak v SA	Auckland	2015

Six wicketkeepers managed five dismissals each in an innings.

FIELDING

Most catches

Ct	Player	M	Ct/Inn
28	Ricky Ponting (Aus)	46	0.61
20	Joe Root (Eng)	17	1.18
18	Sanath Jayasuriya (SL)	38	0.47
17	Chris Gayle (WI)	35	0.49

Most catches in a single edition

Ct	Player	M	Ct/Inn	Year
13	Joe Root (Eng)	11	1.18	2019
11	Ricky Ponting (Aus)	11	1.00	2003
10	Faf du Plessis (SA)	9	1.25	2019
9	Rilee Rossouw (SA)	6	1.50	2015
9	Jonny Bairstow (Eng)	11	0.82	2019

Most catches in a match

Ct	Player	For/Against	Venue	Year
4	Mohammad Kaif	Ind v SL	Johannesburg	2003
4	Soumya Sarkar	Ban v Sco	Nelson	2015
4	Umar Akmal	Pak v Ire	Adelaide	2015
4	Chris Woakes	Eng v Pak	Nottingham	2019
4	Jonny Bairstow	Eng v Ban	Cardiff	2019

ALL-ROUND

Best all-round performances (Qualification – 500 runs, 20 wickets, 8 catches)

Player	M	R	Bat Avge	HS	W	Bowl Avge	BB	Ct
Sanath Jayasuriya (SL)	38	1165	34.26	120	27	39.25	3-12	18
Jacques Kallis (SA)	36	1148	45.92	128*	21	43.04	3-26	13
Shakib Al Hasan (Ban)	29	1146	45.84	124*	34	35.94	5-29	8
Steve Waugh (Aus)	33	978	48.90	120*	27	30.14	3-36	14
Kapil Dev (Ind)	26	669	37.16	175*	28	31.85	5-43	12

Best all-round performances in a match (hundred and three wickets)

Player	Bat	Bowl	For/Against	Venue	Year
Tillakaratne Dilshan	144	4-4	SL v Zim	Pallekele	2011
Feiko Kloppenburg	121	4-42	Net v Nam	Bloemfontein	2003
Sanath Jayasuriya	115	3-38	SL v WI	Providence	2007
Aravinda de Silva	107*	3-42	SL v Aus	Lahore	1996

INDIVIDUAL

Most capped players

M	Player	For
46	Ricky Ponting	Aus
45	Sachin Tendulkar	Ind
40	Mahela Jayawardene	SL
40	Muttiah Muralitharan	SL
39	Glenn McGrath	Aus

Javed Miandad and Sachin Tendulkar are the only players to have played in six editions.

Most matches as captain

M	Player	Won	Lost	Tied	NR	Win %
29	Ricky Ponting (Aus)	26	2	0	1	92.85
27	Stephen Fleming (NZ)	16	10	0	1	61.53
23	Mohammad Azharuddin (Ind)	10	12	0	1	45.45
22	Imran Khan (Pak)	14	8	0	0	63.63

* *MS Dhoni, Clive Lloyd, Eoin Morgan, Graeme Smith captained in 17 matches each.*

OFFICIALS

Most matches as on-field umpire

M	Umpire
46	David Shepherd (Eng)
45	Steve Bucknor (WI)
34	Aleem Dar (Pak)
25	Billy Bowden (NZ)
25	Rudi Koertzen (SA)

Most matches as referee

M	Referee
68	Ranjan Madugalle (SL)
36	Chris Broad (Eng)
34	Jeff Crowe (NZ)
24	Roshan Mahanama (SL)
23	David Boon (Aus)
23	Mike Procter (SA)

INDIA AT THE WORLD CUP

OVERALL

Win-loss record in each edition

Year	M	Won	Lost	Tied	NR	Win %	Captain
1975	3	1	2	0	0	33.33	Srinivas Venkataraghavan
1979	3	0	3	0	0	0.00	Srinivas Venkataraghavan
1983	8	6	2	0	0	75.00	Kapil Dev
1987	7	5	2	0	0	71.43	Kapil Dev
1992	8	2	5	0	1	28.57	Mohammad Azharuddin
1996	7	4	3	0	0	57.14	Mohammad Azharuddin
1999	8	4	4	0	0	50.00	Mohammad Azharuddin
2003	11	9	2	0	0	81.82	Sourav Ganguly
2007	3	1	2	0	0	33.33	Rahul Dravid
2011	9	7	1	1	0	83.33	MS Dhoni
2015	8	7	1	0	0	87.50	MS Dhoni
2019	9	7	2	0	0	77.78	Virat Kohli
Overall	84	53	29	1	1	64.46	

Top-performers in each edition

Year	Most runs	Most wickets
1975	Sunil Gavaskar (113)	Syed Abid Ali (6)
1979	Gundappa Viswanath (106)	Mohinder Amarnath (4)
1983	Kapil Dev (303)	Roger Binny (18)
1987	Sunil Gavaskar (300)	Maninder Singh (14)
1992	Mohammad Azharuddin (332)	Manoj Prabhakar (12)
1996	Sachin Tendulkar (523)	Anil Kumble (15)
1999	Rahul Dravid (461)	Javagal Srinath (12)
2003	Sachin Tendulkar (673)	Zaheer Khan (18)
2007	Virender Sehwag (164)	Zaheer Khan (5)
2011	Sachin Tendulkar (482)	Zaheer Khan (21)
2015	Shikhar Dhawan (412)	Umesh Yadav (18)
2019	Rohit Sharma (648)	Jasprit Bumrah (18)

TEAM

Highest totals

Score	O	Against	Venue	Year
413/5	50	Bermuda	Port of Spain	2007
373/6	50	Sri Lanka	Taunton	1999
370/4	50	Bangladesh	Dhaka	2011
352/5	50	Australia	The Oval	2019
338	49.5	England	Bengaluru	2011

Lowest totals

Score	O	Against	Venue	Year
125	41.4	Aus	Centurion	2003
132/3	60	Eng	Lord's	1975
158	37.5	Aus	Nottingham	1983
182	55.5	NZ	Leeds	1979

183	54.4	WI	Lord's	1983

Largest victories (by runs)

Margin	Target	Against	Venue	Year
257 runs	414	Ber	Port of Spain	2007
183 runs	293	SL	Johannesburg	2003
181 runs	312	Nam	Pietermaritzburg	2003
157 runs	374	SL	Taunton	1999
130 runs	308	SA	Melbourne	2015

Largest victories (by wickets)

Margin	Target	Against	Venue	Year
10 wickets	121	EA	Leeds	1975
9 wickets	222	NZ	Nagpur	1987
9 wickets	103	UAE	Perth	2015
8 wickets	136	Zim	Mumbai	1987
8 wickets	260	Ire	Hamilton	2015

Smallest victories (by runs)

Margin	Target	Against	Venue	Year
11 runs	225	Afg	Southampton	2019
16 runs	253	NZ	Bengaluru	1987
29 runs	261	Pak	Mohali	2011
31 runs	267	Zim	Tunbridge Wells	1983
34 runs	263	WI	Manchester	1983

Smallest victories (by wickets)

Margin	Target	Against	Venue	Year
4 wickets	183	WI	Perth	2015
5 wickets	156	Zim	Leicester	1983
5 wickets	174	WI	Gwalior	1996
5 wickets	208	Ire	Bengaluru	2011
5 wickets	190	Net	Delhi	2011
5 wickets	261	Aus	Ahmedabad	2011

Tied matches

Against	Venue	Year
England	Bengaluru	2011

BATTING

Most runs

R	Player	M	I	NO	Avge	HS	SR	100s/ 50s
2278	Sachin Tendulkar	45	44	4	56.95	152	88.98	6/ 15
1030	Virat Kohli	26	26	4	46.81	107	86.70	2/6
1006	Sourav Ganguly	21	21	3	55.88	183	77.50	4/ 3
978	Rohit Sharma	17	17	2	65.20	140	95.97	6/3
860	Rahul Dravid	22	21	7	61.42	145	74.97	2/ 6

Most runs in a single edition

R	Player	Year	M	I	NO	Avge	HS	SR	100s/ 50s
673	Sachin Tendulkar	2003	11	11	0	61.18	152	89.25	1/ 6
648	Rohit Sharma	2019	9	9	1	81.00	140	98.33	5/1
523	Sachin Tendulkar	1996	7	7	1	87.16	137	85.87	2/ 3
482	Sachin Tendulkar	2011	9	9	0	53.55	120	91.98	2/ 2
465	Sourav Ganguly	2003	11	11	3	58.12	112*	82.30	3/ 0

Highest individual scores

R (balls)	Player	4/ 6	SR	Against	Venue	Year
183 (158)	Sourav Ganguly	17/7	115.82	SL	Taunton	1999
175* (138)	Kapil Dev	16/6	126.81	Zim	Tunbridge Wells	1983
175 (140)	Virender Sehwag	14/5	125.00	Ban	Dhaka	2011
152 (151)	Sachin Tendulkar	18/0	100.66	Nam	Pietermaritzburg	2003
145 (129)	Rahul Dravid	17/1	112.4	SL	Taunton	1999

Most hundreds

100s	Player	M	I	NO	R	Avge	HS
6	Rohit Sharma	17	17	2	978	65.20	140
6	Sachin Tendulkar	45	44	4	2278	56.95	152
4	Sourav Ganguly	21	21	3	1006	55.88	183

Fastest 100s

Balls	Player	Against	Venue	Year
72	Kapil Dev	Zim	Tunbridge Wells	1983
81	Virender Sehwag	Ber	Port of Spain	2007
83	Virat Kohli	Ban	Mirpur	2011
84	Sachin Tendulkar	Ken	Bristol	1999
84	Shikhar Dhawan	Ire	Hamilton	2015

Most sixes in an innings

6s	Player	R	Balls	Against	Venue	Year
7	Sourav Ganguly	183	158	SL	Taunton	1999
7	Yuvraj Singh	83	46	Ber	Port of Spain	2007
6	Kapil Dev	175*	138	Zim	Tunbridge Wells	1983

Highest partnerships (by runs)

R	Players	Wkt	Against	Venue	Year
318	Sourav Ganguly, Rahul Dravid	2nd	SL	Taunton	1999
244	Sachin Tendulkar, Sourav Ganguly	2nd	Nam	Pietermaritzburg	2003
237*	Rahul Dravid, Sachin Tendulkar	3rd	Ken	Bristol	1999
203	Virender Sehwag, Virat Kohli	3rd	Ban	Dhaka	2011
202	Sourav Ganguly, Virender Sehwag	2nd	Ber	Port of Spain	2007

Highest partnerships (by wickets)

R	Players	Wkt	Against	Venue	Year
189	KL Rahul, Rohit Sharma	1st	SL	Leeds	2019
318	Sourav Ganguly, Rahul Dravid	2nd	SL	Taunton	1999
237*	Rahul Dravid, Sachin Tendulkar	3rd	Ken	Bristol	1999
142	Navjot Sidhu, Vinod Kambli	4th	Zim	Kanpur	1996
196*	Suresh Raina, MS Dhoni	5th	Zim	Auckland	2015
74*	Yuvraj Singh, Suresh Raina	6th	Aus	Ahmedabad	2011
116	MS Dhoni & Ravindra Jadeja	7th	NZ	Manchester	2019
82*	Kapil Dev, Kiran More	8th	NZ	Bengaluru	1987
126*	Kapil Dev, Syed Kirmani	9th	Zim	Tunbridge Wells	1983
32	Zaheer Khan, Munaf Patel	10th	Ban	Port of Spain	2007

Most ducks

0s	Player	Mat	Inn	NO	Runs	Avge
4	Kris Srikkanth	23	23	1	521	23.68
3	Zaheer Khan	23	11	2	52	5.77
3	Javagal Srinath	34	18	9	85	9.44

BOWLING

Most wickets

W	Player	M	O	Avge	BB	Econ	SR	5I
44	Zaheer Khan	23	198.5	20.22	4-42	4.47	27.1	0
44	Javagal Srinath	34	283.2	27.81	4-30	4.32	38.6	0
31	Mohammed Shami	11	96.1	15.70	5-69	5.06	18.6	1
31	Anil Kumble	18	173.1	22.83	4-32	4.08	33.5	0
28	Kapil Dev	26	237	31.85	5-43	3.76	50.7	1

Most wickets in a single edition

W	Player	Year	M	O	Avge	BB	ER	SR
21	Zaheer Khan	2011	9	81.3	18.76	3-20	4.83	23.2
18	Umesh Yadav	2015	8	64.2	17.83	4-31	4.98	21.4
18	Roger Binny	1983	8	88	18.66	4-29	3.81	29.3
18	Jasprit Bumrah	2019	9	84	20.61	4-55	4.41	28.0
18	Zaheer Khan	2003	11	88.2	20.77	4-42	4.23	29.4

Best bowling figures in an innings

Figures	Player	Against	Venue	Year
6-23	Ashish Nehra	Eng	Durban	2003
5-27	Venkatesh Prasad	Pak	Manchester	1999
5-31	Robin Singh	SL	Taunton	1999
5-31	Yuvraj Singh	Ire	Bengaluru	2011
5-43	Kapil Dev	Aus	Nottingham	1983

Hat-tricks

Player	Against	Venue	Year
Chetan Sharma	NZ	Nagpur	1987
Mohammed Shami	Afg	Southampton	2019

Best economy-rates (qualification – 100 overs bowled)

ER	Player	O	R	W	Avge	BB
3.66	Madan Lal	116.2	426	22	19.36	4-20
3.76	Kapil Dev	237	892	28	31.85	5-43
3.90	Mohinder Amarnath	110.3	431	16	26.93	3-12
4.08	Anil Kumble	173.1	708	31	22.83	4-32
4.20	Harbhajan Singh	192.2	808	20	40.4	3-53

Best economy-rates in an innings (qualification – 30 balls bowled)

ER	Player	O	M	R	W	Against	Venue	Year
0.50	Bishan Bedi	12	8	6	1	EA	Leeds	1975
1.50	Zaheer Khan	9.2	2	14	3	Ken	Durban	2003
1.50	Jasprit Bumrah	6	1	9	2	WI	Manchester	2019
1.57	Javagal Srinath	7	1	11	1	Ken	Durban	2003
1.57	Madan Lal	9.3	2	15	3	EA	Leeds	1975

Most maidens

Maidens	Player	M	O	R	W	Avge	ER
27	Kapil Dev	26	237	892	28	31.85	3.76
21	Javagal Srinath	34	283.2	1224	44	27.81	4.32
17	Bishan Bedi	5	60	148	2	74.00	2.46
12	Zaheer Khan	23	198.5	890	44	20.22	4.47
12	Madan Lal	11	116.2	426	22	19.36	3.66

Most maidens in an innings

Maidens	Player	O	R	W	Against	Venue	Year
8	Bishan Bedi	12	6	1	EA	Leeds	1975
6	Bishan Bedi	12	28	1	NZ	Manchester	1975
5	Syed Abid Ali	12	22	2	EA	Leeds	1975
4	Srinivas Venkataraghavan	12	29	0	EA	Leeds	1975
4	Kapil Dev	11	21	1	WI	Lord's	1983

Best strike-rates (qualification – 15 wickets)

SR	Player	O	R	W	Avge	BB
18.6	Mohammed Shami	96.1	487	31	15.70	5-69
21.4	Umesh Yadav	64.2	321	18	17.83	4-31
27.1	Zaheer Khan	198.5	890	44	20.22	4-42
27.7	Yuvraj Singh	92.3	462	20	23.10	5-31
28.0	Jasprit Bumrah	84	371	18	20.61	4-55

Most runs conceded in an innings

R	Player	O	M	W	ER	Against	Venue	Year
88	Yuzvendra Chahal	10	0	0	8.80	Eng	Birmingham	2019
87	Javagal Srinath	10	0	0	8.70	Aus	Johannesburg	2003
83	Karsan Ghavri	11	1	0	7.54	Eng	Lord's	1975
75	Ravichandran Ashwin	10	0	1	7.50	Zim	Auckland	2015
75	Mohit Sharma	10	0	2	7.50	Aus	Sydney	2015

WICKETKEEPING

Most dismissals

Dis	Player	M	Ct	St	Dis/Inn
42	MS Dhoni	29	34	8	1.45
18	Kiran More	14	12	6	1.4
16	Rahul Dravid	22	15	1	1.3
16	Nayan Mongia	14	12	4	1.1
14	Syed Kirmani	8	12	2	1.8

Most dismissals in a single edition

Dis	Player	M	Ct	St	Dis/Inn	Year
16	Rahul Dravid	11	15	1	1.454	2003
15	MS Dhoni	8	15	0	1.875	2015
14	Syed Kirmani	8	12	2	1.75	1983
11	Kiran More	6	6	5	1.833	1987

Most dismissals in an innings

Dis	Player	M	Ct	Against	Venue	Year
5	Syed Kirmani	5	0	Zim	Leicester	1983
5	Nayan Mongia	4	1	Zim	Leicester	1999
4	Kiran More	2	2	Zim	Mumbai	1987
4	MS Dhoni	4	0	Ban	Melbourne	2015
4	MS Dhoni	3	1	SL	Leeds	2019

FIELDING

Most catches

Ct	Player	M	Ct/Inn
14	Anil Kumble	18	0.777
14	Virat Kohli	26	0.54
12	Kapil Dev	26	0.480
12	Sachin Tendulkar	45	0.272

Most catches in a single edition

Ct	Player	M	Ct/Inn	Year
8	Anil Kumble	7	1.142	1996
8	Umesh Yadav	8	1.000	2015

8	Dinesh Mongia	11	0.727	2003
8	Virender Sehwag	11	0.727	2003
7	Shikhar Dhawan	8	0.875	2015

Most catches in a match

Ct	Player	Against	Venue	Year
4	Mohammad Kaif	SL	Johannesburg	2003
3	Virender Sehwag	Net	Paarl	2003
3	Dinesh Mongia	Nam	Pietermaritzburg	2003
3	Virender Sehwag	Eng	Durban	2011
3	Zaheer Khan	Aus	Ahmedabad	2011
3	Suresh Raina	UAE	Perth	2015
3	Umesh Yadav	Ire	Hamilton	2015

ALL-ROUND

Best all-round performances (qualification – 300 runs, 10 wickets)

Player	M	R	Bat Avge	HS	W	Bowl Avge	BB	Ct
Kapil Dev	26	669	37.16	175*	28	31.85	5-43	12
Yuvraj Singh	23	738	52.71	113	20	23.1	5-31	4
Sourav Ganguly	21	1006	55.88	183	10	30.5	3-22	1

Best all-round performances in a match (fifty and three wickets)

Player	Bat	Bowl	Against	Venue	Year
Mohammad Azharuddin	54*	3-19	Aus	Delhi	1987
Yuvraj Singh	50*	5-31	Ire	Bengaluru	2011

INDIVIDUAL

Most capped players

M	Player
45	Sachin Tendulkar
34	Javagal Srinath
30	Mohammad Azharuddin
29	MS Dhoni
26	Kapil Dev
26	Virat Kohli

Most matches as captain

M	Player	W	L	Tied	NR	Win %
23	Mohammad Azharuddin	10	12	0	1	45.45
17	MS Dhoni	14	2	1	0	85.29
15	Kapil Dev	11	4	0	0	73.33
11	Sourav Ganguly	9	2	0	0	81.82
9	Virat Kohli	9	7	2	0	77.77

*All records are updated till 15 July 2019.

M – Matches, **I** – Innings, **NO** – Not Out, **R** – Runs, **HS** – Highest Score, **Avge** – Average, **O** – Overs, **W** – Wickets, **BB** – Best Bowling, **5I** – Five wickets in an innings, **SR** – Strike-Rate, **ER** – Economy Rate, **Ct** – Catches, **St** – Stumpings, **Dis/Inn** – Dismissal/Innings.

PART THREE

Domestic cricket

How Vidarbha learnt to dream big

GANESH SATISH

When I decided to move out of Karnataka immediately after we won the Ranji Trophy title in the 2013-14 season, several friends and well-wishers urged me not to give up. After all, I had made a century in the seven-wicket win over Maharashtra in the Ranji final, and followed it up with 84 as we crushed Rest of India in the Irani Cup that followed.

I was clear in my thinking. I was 26 at the time; were I giving up, I would have stayed on with Karnataka and gone with the flow. I wanted to challenge myself, so I decided to move to Vidarbha as a professional. To win the most prestigious title in Indian domestic cricket, the Ranji Trophy, with my adopted home makes the move well worth it.

The Ranji title wasn't something I had even considered when I signed up with Vidarbha; the journey in the two seasons gone by has been truly special. We proved emphatically by retaining the title last season that our maiden triumph in 2017-18 was no flash in the pan. Our march to the title the first time might have taken the rest of the country by surprise, but for us, it was natural progression. Before the 2017-18 season, we had made the knock-outs of the Ranji Trophy twice in three years, we had qualified for the second stage of the Vijay Hazare Trophy 50-over tournament in each of the preceding three years.

One of the most decisive factors was the arrival in 2017-18 of Chandra-kant Pandit as our coach. Chandu sir came with the reputation of being a hard taskmaster and a strict disciplinarian — exactly what we needed. Paras Mhambrey had done an outstanding job for three years, honing raw prod-ucts, and Chandu sir built on that while cracking the whip. Even when I had played against Vidarbha, it was obvious that there was no paucity of talent, but the ambitions seemed limited. Chandu sir exploded the air of complacen-cy, making it clear that merely holding on to one's place in the side was no longer an option. He was not happy with 30s and 40s, or just one good spell a day from a bowler. He wanted us to be hungry, to produce big runs and bowl good spells for extended periods. If it meant dropping established players to make his point, he was willing to do so.

Our first exposure to the unforgiving world of Chandu sir came early in his tenure. We were playing a warm-up tournament in Nagpur against a strong Mumbai side, on a slow turner at the old VCA Stadium in Civil Lines. We made 350-plus, which was a good total under the circumstances, and had them 100-odd for five at lunch on the third day. Between lunch and tea, our spinners beat the bat numerous times, found edges that did not carry to the close-in catchers and picked up only one wicket, but walked back to the dressing-room believing we had had an excellent session.

The bowlers were especially upbeat, little realising that Chandu sir was armed with a rocket. "The ball is turning square, you guys are happy with just one wicket in two hours?" he thundered. "I don't want to see the ball beating the bat, I want to see the ball hitting the stumps. Bowl within the line of the stumps and be effective instead of looking menacing and not getting the rewards." Within half an hour after tea, we had bowled Mumbai out.

The other big difference was the consistency in our batting. In previous years, we didn't often fire as a unit. Faiz Fazal, our captain, would get runs in some games, Sanjay Ramaswamy in other matches, myself in a few of them, but we seldom made runs together. The 2017-18 season was a complete change. Faiz, Sanjay and I were among the top ten run-getters in the country, Wasim Jaffer made nearly 600 runs, and the big totals allowed our bowlers to attack oppositions.

The new-found consistency was due to a combination of factors: Chandu sir's exhortations that stoked our desire, and the fact that we had all played together as a unit for three years and were comfortable with each other's games. Wasim *bhai* was a major influence too. I have been working with Rajesh Kamath for a long time; since I was eight or nine, he has been my batting coach and guru. But before the start of last season, I spent 10 days with Wasim *bhai* in Mumbai. That made a big difference to my batting. We worked on my initial movement, on playing the medium pacers. He suggested that I should improve my play when the bowler targets the fourth or fifth-stump region. His tips were to prove invaluable as I finished with 638 runs. Sanjay also benefited from his guidance, much of his wonderful run streak — 775 runs, the third highest in the tournament — stemmed from his interactions with Wasim bhai.

As that season unfolded, we kept reflecting on what Paras sir had drilled into us during his tenure: You don't need big players to win titles, you need a big team, you need a unit. The team that plays together and works together is the team that is successful. Within our group, there was unity, support and belief. Like Gujarat the season before, we displayed great fighting spirit, we played for each other and we were not afraid to follow our dreams.

When I first came in to the Vidarbha set-up, I was a little apprehensive: the food, the language, the weather, everything was alien to me. But the guys put me at ease and helped me settle in quickly. Nagpur is now my second home, I have struck up several close friendships, and I can play my cricket freely.

The biggest name in our team alongside Wasim *bhai* is Umesh Yadav, and when he comes in between international engagements, he blends into the environment seamlessly. He is very humble and down-to-earth. That is crucial; a happy team can do wonders. A team that is happy only when it is winning will not remain a team for very long.

When I was playing for Karnataka, we always carried the burden of external expectations. Even when I broke into the team alongside other young-

Validation of the process: Vidarbha became only the sixth team to defend their Ranji Trophy title. — *BCCI*

sters, it was taken for granted that we would make the knock-outs and fight for the title. There was no escaping the scrutiny, whether it was your first match or your 100th. When we defeated Maharashtra and wrapped our hands around the trophy, it was special for me personally, and for a lot of the guys. But to the rest, it was no big deal because we were representing Karnataka, always one of the favourites. With Vidarbha, I can't put the feeling in words. No one outside of our group saw it coming. It was the first senior trophy in the history of Vidarbha cricket, and to be a part of that was extraordinary. To top it up the following year was a monumental accomplishment.

We were no longer satisfied with mediocrity as we bought into Chandu sir's philosophy whole-heartedly. Our preparations were impeccable: lots of match simulations and open nets, and our bowling provided that X-factor. Lalit Yadav kicked things off at the start of the 2017-18 season and Rajneesh Gurbani finished it off in style with a succession of five-wicket hauls in the knock-out stage. Rajneesh was in the Under-23 squad when I moved to Vidarbha, and was in and out of the Ranji side until the final league match this season, against Himachal Pradesh. He took five in that game, and didn't look back, establishing himself as our strike bowler. He swings it both ways and is very accurate. He owes a lot of that to Subroto Banerjee, our bowling coach. Like Chandu sir, Subbu sir too stressed the importance of bowling straight and hitting the stumps.

Faiz was a calming influence as the skipper, never looking flustered and always open to adapting to situations and conditions. He sought out Wasim bhai or myself for guidance if he felt the need, but he made his own decisions, thoughtfully. He was always accessible to even the youngest players, but when the need arose, he could put his foot down and read the riot act.

I will treasure our semi-final win against Karnataka on the way to our first Ranji title. It is one of the best games I have been a part of. This was as good as the final in 2010, when I played for Karnataka and we lost to Mumbai by six runs in Mysore. Karnataka were in great form and had just smashed Mumbai in the quarters. Everyone expected an easy run to the final for them, but we believed in ourselves. Even when we conceded a 116-run lead, we never felt we were out of the game. We had run Karnataka close previously but had failed to close out games. After having pushed them all these years, to get over the line was something we needed to do. I am glad I contributed by making 81 in the second innings, and then watched Rajneesh swing them out as we edged home by five runs. We were weak-kneed but delirious.

The Vidarbha Cricket Association have made all of us feel comfortable. We have an excellent grassroots system, and the state Under-19 and Under-16 teams have won titles nationally. In the last two years, five players from Vidarbha have played for India Under-19, and a lot of young talent is coming up because of the academies that have taken root in the districts as well. Prashant Vaidya, the VCA vice-president, has been a big influence. Himself a former India cricketer, he knows what the players need so that they can focus only on cricket.

At a function to celebrate our success, our president, Anand Jaiswal, told us that this is the beginning, not the end. He wanted us to dominate domestic cricket for a long time. By retaining the Ranji title, we justified his faith in the team. As an added motivation, we know that if we keep winning, more players will make the next step up and go on to represent the country.

Ganesh Satish has made 5541 runs in 90 first-class games for Vidarbha and Karnataka.

Record calendar, results showcase depth

R KAUSHIK

When the Ranji Trophy went totally neutral in the 2016-17 season, it was met with understandable scepticism. It wasn't difficult to see why the Technical Committee of the Board of Control for Cricket in India, chaired by former India captain Sourav Ganguly, envisioned the prospect. Too many associations were doctoring pitches and taking home advantage to unsavoury heights. While playing to one's strengths is acceptable, the extent to which sides were willing to bend, if not break, the rules necessitated action.

Going neutral, however, seemed a little extreme. Checks should have been placed in the form of strict match officials and clearly defined dos and don'ts, which would then have encouraged fining errant associations and docking points from teams riding on underprepared surfaces. The 'neutral' concept didn't exactly throw up glorious contests. If, say, Delhi were playing Chennai in Surat, what was the incentive for the curator to work hard and produce a sporting deck?

The voices of protest at the annual captains' and coaches' conclave forced a rethink, and the Ranji Trophy reverted to the home-and-away format from the 2017-18 season. Perhaps chastened by the slap on the wrist of the previous season, serial offenders too resisted the temptation to put out Bunsen burners, which somewhat redressed the balance between bat and ball. But, as always given that the Ranji Trophy straddles the winter, there was a marked difference in how matches panned out. While there was atmospheric assistance for the faster bowlers in the northern and the eastern parts, batsmen were more in focus in the south and the west.

Then, for 2018-19, in keeping with the recommendations of the Lodha Committee, the season was expanded to include 37 teams, and there was an obvious rejig of the structure. Across age groups, the BCCI conducted 2024 matches, 916 more than the previous season. According to figures shared by the board, 3444 match days were accommodated in a season window of 254 days. The scale of operation came with its own challenges — the availability of match officials was a particular issue and one round of Cooch Behar and women's one-day knock-out matches were rescheduled because there weren't enough officials. The umpiring came in for scrutiny as well, with teams pushing for use of DRS and a system of evaluation.

On the field, the action in the 2017-18 season began with the Duleep Trophy. While the Technical Committee had endorsed the continuance of the tournament as a day-night, pink-ball experiment, the BCCI initially scrapped it before bowing to huge pressure and reinstating the first-class competition. The rain-ruined three-team event in Lucknow and Kanpur kicked off the season in September with India Red clinching the title. India Blue surged to the title the following season with a commanding innings win over India Red in Dindigul.

Gujarat's heady success in the 2016-17 Ranji Trophy was a shot in the arm for the so-called 'lesser' sides. Where previously they were happy with just being competitive against the big guns, now they started to dream big. It wasn't that in the past they didn't have the skills or the talent; what they lacked was belief and self-confidence. But with the Indian Premier League acting as a leveller and Gujarat setting themselves up as the shining beacon to emulate, a host of the less celebrated teams made their presence felt, none more tellingly than Vidarbha.

Faiz Fazal's team had been consistent across formats for a while. They invariably made it to the knock-out stages in first-class cricket, as well as in the 50-over Vijay Hazare and the 20-over Mushtaq Ali Trophy tournaments, but seldom found themselves in contention at the business end. All that changed once Chandrakant Pandit, the former India wicketkeeper-batsman and celebrated Mumbai coach, came on board. They have since done the Ranji-Irani double in successive seasons. Pandit has the not unfounded reputation of a hard taskmaster and he played true to form, making sure that the Vidarbha boys were not content with merely making it to the knock-outs.

In his quest for excellence, he found an able ally in Fazal, the skipper, as well as professionals Wasim Jaffer and Ganesh Satish, the batting stalwarts who controlled the middle order beautifully. At the top of the tree, Fazal and Sanjay Ramaswamy formed a formidable opening combine, the latter benefitting from spending a week in Mumbai with Jaffer at the start of the season to work on both his game and his mind.

In their first successful campaign, despite the absence of Umesh Yadav, their most potent bowling weapon, for most of the season, Vidarbha discovered match-winners at crucial times, none more impactful than Rajneesh Gurbani. After his comeback to the side towards the end of the league stage, the right-arm swing bowler was unstoppable. He picked up at least one five-wicket haul in each of the last four matches, and his 12 wickets in the semi-final was responsible for Vidarbha putting it past fancied Karnataka despite conceding a potentially decisive 116-run lead on a pacer-friendly track at Eden Gardens.

Riding the wave of confidence and feel-good, Vidarbha routed Delhi by nine wickets in the final with Gurbani adding a further eight wickets to his tally. It wasn't, however, entirely a Gurbani show. His 39 wickets at 17.12 were complemented by 34 for Akshay Wakhare, the off-spinner, and 29 for Aditya Sarwate, the left-arm spinner.

As if to show that their success the previous season was no flash in the pan, Vidarbha charted an even more emphatic path to the title in 2018-19. As Group A table toppers, they crushed first-timers Uttarakhand and Kerala by an innings in the quarters and semis respectively, and brushed aside a feeble challenge from Saurashtra in the final.

Off-spinner Jalaj Saxena played a significant role in Kerala's maiden entry into the quarter-finals with a season-high 44 wickets in 2017-18. The batting honours for the season were emphatically grabbed by Mayank Agarwal, the Karnataka opener. He smashed 1033 runs in November alone, with a triple-hundred and four other centuries, on his way to a season-leading 1160 runs.

The performances of the new teams provided plenty of fuel to the debate on fast-tracking unprepared sides straightaway to first-class cricket. Group D, which included these teams, threw up 2018-19's leading run-scorer in Sikkim's Milind Kumar (1331) and the leading wicket-taker, Bihar's Ashutosh Aman. With 1037 runs, Jaffer showed that age has done little to slow him down, and Dharmendrasinh Jadeja (50 wickets) made sure Saurashtra didn't miss the other left-arm spinning Jadeja, Ravindra.

Vidarbha went on to lift the Irani Cup both times, even if they didn't make many friends by posting 800 for 7 declared against Rest of India the first time around with 40-year-old Jaffer amassing 286. Their second Irani triumph, against the Ajinkya Rahane-led RoI, also came on first-innings lead.

Delhi made up for the disappointment of losing the Ranji final by defeating Rajasthan by 41 runs for the Mushtaq Ali Trophy 2017-18, while Karnataka were unstoppable in the subsequent 50-over Vijay Hazare Trophy that year. Agarwal was again at the forefront: against his 723 runs, the next highest scorer was Andhra's KS Bharat, with 390 runs. Karnataka added the Mushtaq Ali Trophy to their kitty in 2018-19, embarking on a 12-match unbeaten streak and crushing Maharashtra by eight wickets in the final, newcomer Rohan Kadam the standout performer with a season-high 536 runs.

Mumbai had lifted the Hazare Trophy for the third time at the start of the season, holders Karnataka crashing out after finishing seventh of nine teams in their own Bengaluru fortress.

Delhi and Punjab clinched the Under-23 Col CK Nayudu Trophy in the two seasons, reaffirming the vibrancy of Indian domestic cricket and the mechanism of talent-spotting that exists at the grassroots level.

There was a similar trend in the women's structure as well, with Railways' hold on the trophies finally broken. Bengal, one of the pioneers of women's cricket in the country, swept the one-day tournaments across age groups in the most recent season, while Delhi leant on their experienced hands to shake things up in 2017-18. Across the world, T20 is seen as the vehicle for popularising the women's game, with women's Test cricket all but non-existent. The introduction of new Challenger tournaments and the scrapping of the multi-day format confirmed this trend in India as well. Two seasons on the Women's T20 Challenge on the sidelines of the IPL captured imagination; all that remains now is a full-fledged women's IPL.

Duleep Trophy

India Blue dominated the final, piling on 541 runs in the first innings before their spinners shot India Red out cheaply.

Another medal for Faiz

What's a start to the domestic year without format changes and confusion? The BCCI's Sourav Ganguly-led technical committee had suggested four teams for the Duleep Trophy, but only three were finally named for the pink-ball tournament.

All three round-robin day-night matches ended in a draw, with India Red, the defending champions, and India Blue advancing to the final. In the opening game, Rajneesh Gurbani's 7 for 81 ensured India Red secured a lead against Green, who ended up 28 runs short of Red's first-innings total despite B Indrajith's gritty century. Against Blue, Abhinav Mukund's Red settled for a draw despite being just two wickets shy of a win, knowing that three points would be enough for them to progress. In the last drawn encounter, Dhruv Shorey's 93 helped Blue walk away with three points and a final berth as Red suffered a batting collapse triggered by Jaydev Unadkat and Saurabh Kumar.

Blue completely dominated the final, piling on 541 runs in the first innings on the back of Nikhil Gangta's 130. The trio of Saurabh, Swapnil Singh and Deepak Hooda spun a web around Red, bowling them out for 182 and 172 after following on.

Saurabh, a left-arm spinner, led the tournament's bowling charts, while Dhruv Shorey's 293 runs in five innings came at 58.60.

The **previous season**, Priyank Panchal's twin centuries against an India Green attack comprising the likes of Navdeep Saini, Shahbaz Nadeem and Mohammed Siraj helped India Red assert their dominance in the opening clash. Against India Blue, Indrajith took charge with his maiden first-class double-century. While he scored a 280-ball 200, including 20 fours and six sixes, the second-highest score of the innings was the 36 managed by Panchal, even as Karn Sharma backed up his ten wickets in the opening game with another five-wicket haul.

For Blue, G Hanuma Vihari and Deepak Hooda scored centuries, the draw and three points playing a role in taking them to the final after their match against Green was washed out.

	Most runs	**Most wickets**
2017-18	Priyank Panchal (293 runs, 2 matches)	Karn Sharma (15 wickets, 2 matches)
2018-19	Dhruv Shorey (293 runs, 3 matches)	Saurabh Kumar (19 wickets, 3 matches)

2018-19

NPR College Ground, Dindigul, August 17-20: India Red 337 in 132.5 overs (Ashutosh Singh 80, Mihir Hirwani 61; Ankit Rajpoot 4-57, K Vignesh 3-80) and 262/1 dec. in 79 overs (R Sanjay 123*, B Aparajith 101*) drew with **India Green** 309 in 111.3 overs (B Indrajith 109, Sudip Chatterjee 82; Rajneesh Gurbani 7-81). India Red took first-innings lead. *PoM:* Rajneesh Gurbani.

NPR College Ground, Dindigul, August 23-26: India Red 316 in 114.5 overs (Siddhesh Lad 88, R Sanjay 72; Saurabh Kumar 3-75, Akshay Wakhare 3-76) and 255 in 84.3 overs (S Lad 68, Abhinav Mukund 50; Saurabh 4-79, A Wakhare 4-110) drew with **India Blue** 293 in 95.3 overs (Dhruv Shorey 97, Ricky Bhui 41; Parveez Rasool 4-107, Rajneesh Gurbani 2-29) and 128/8 in 47 overs (D Shorey 45, Faiz Fazal 39; Shahbaz Nadeem 5-53, P Rasool 3-59). India Red took first-innings lead. *PoM:* Siddhesh Lad.

NPR College Ground, Dindigul, August 29-September 1: India Blue 340 in 119.1 overs(Dhruv Shorey 93, Faiz Fazal 76; K Vignesh 5-50, Vikas Mishra 3-93) and 117 in 34 overs (D Shorey 40; Aditya Sarwate 5-32, V Mishra 3-36) drew with **India Green** 257 in 88.5 overs (Prashant Chopra 80, Parthiv Patel 80; Saurabh Kumar 5-98, Jaydev Unadkat 4-16) and 20/2 in 6.4 overs (Saurabh 2-11). India Blue took first-innings lead. *PoM:* Dhruv Shorey.

Points table

Teams	M	W	L	D	T	N/R	Pts.	NRR
India Red	2	0	0	2	0	0	6	-0.028
India Blue	2	0	0	2	0	0	4	+0.093
India Green	2	0	0	2	0	0	2	-0.062

India Red and India Blue qualified for the final

Final: India Blue beat India Red by an innings and 187 runs

A remarkable century by Nikhil Gangta and a trial by spin by the trio of Swapnil Singh, Saurabh and Hooda ensured India Blue's big win over India Red. Opting to bat, India Blue overcame an early wobble, thanks to Ricky Bhui and Anmolpreet Singh's 144-run stand that led them to 260 for 5 by the end of the opening day. The next morning, Gangta, coming in at No.7, shepherded the lower order.

Red's reply suffered due to lack of substantial partnerships even as Swapnil picked up five. B Sandeep's 57 at No.3 was the highest score. Following on, there was no change in India Red's fortunes. Both Saurabh and Hooda took five wickets each.

NPR College Ground, Dindigul, September 4-7: India Blue 541 in 167.3 overs (Nikhil Gangta 130, Anmolpreet Singh 96; Parveez Rasool 4-150, Mihir Hirwani 3-190) beat **India Red** 182 in 69.1 overs (B Sandeep 57, Prasidh Krishna 25; Swapnil Singh 5-58, Deepak Hooda 2-18) and 172 in 38.4 overs (Abhinav Mukund 46, Ishan Kishan 30; Saurabh Kumar 5-51, D Hooda 5-56) by an innings and 187 runs. *PoM:* Nikhil Gangta.

Winners: India Blue

2017-18

Ekana International Cricket Stadium, Lucknow, September 7-10: India Red 323 in 110.5 overs (Priyank Panchal 105, Sudip Chatterjee 52; M Vijay 3-46, Karun Nair 2-17) and 307/2 dec in 75 overs (P Panchal, 133*, Dinesh Karthik 100*; Vijay 2-41) beat **India Green** 157 in 49.5 overs (Prashant Chopra 65, K Nair 37; K Gowtham 5-46, Karn Sharma 4-39) and 303 in 89.2 overs (K Nair 120, R Samarth 59; Karn 6-94, Siddarth Kaul 4-46) by 170 runs. *MoM:* Priyank Panchal.

Green Park, Kanpur, September 13-16: India Red 383 in 108.3 overs (Baba Indrajith 200, Priyank Panchal 36; Ankit Rajpoot 3-56, Manoj Tiwary 2-30) and 133/5 in 35 overs (Rishabh Pant 46, B Indrajith 24*) drew with **India Blue** 444 in 114 overs (Deepak Hooda 133, Hanuma Vihari 105; Karn Sharma 5-94, Basil Thampi 2-97). India Blue won on the basis of first innings lead. *MoM:* Baba Indrajith.

Green Park, Kanpur, September 19-22: India Blue 177 in 52 overs (Manoj Tiwary 78, Suresh Raina 40; Parveez Rasool 5-70, Aniket Choudhary 3-18) drew with **India Green** 100/3 in 31.5 overs (Kaushik Gandhi 39, Prashant Chopra 26). No result. *MoM:* Parveez Rasool.

Points table

Teams	M	W	L	D	T	NR	Pts.	NRR
India Red	2	1	0	1	0	0	7	-0.091
India Blue	2	0	0	2	0	0	4	0.228
India Green	2	0	1	1	0	0	1	-0.118

India Red and India Blue qualified for the knock-outs

Final: India Red beat India Blue by 163 runs

Washington Sundar emerged as an all-round talent to keep a keen eye, his brilliant display with bat and ball powering India Red to the title.

The mercurial Prithvi Shaw was unleashed on the India Blue bowers; he scored a 249-ball 154, and put on a 211-run stand with Dinesh Karthik, who scored a fine 155-ball 111 himself. Then, Sundar came in at No.7 to score an 118-ball 88.

Blue hit back through Abhimanyu Easwaran and Jaydev Unadkat, even as Sundar's five gave Red the innings lead. Blue had little less than a day's play to topple the 393-run target, but their hurry played right into Sundar's hands.

Ekana International Cricket Stadium, Lucknow, September 25-28: India Red 483 in 127.2 overs (Prithvi Shaw 154, Dinesh Karthik 111; Bhargav Bhatt 4-154, Akshay Wakhare 3-95) and 208in 67.5 overs (Baba Indrajith 59, Washington Sundar 42; A Wakhare 4-66, B Bhatt 4-77) beat **India Blue** 299 in 67 overs (Abhimanyu Easwaran 127, Jaydev Unadkat 83; W Sundar 5-94, Vijay Gohil 5-121) and 229 in 48 overs (B Bhatt 51, Suresh Raina 45; W Sundar 6-87, V Gohil 3-102) by 163 runs. *MoM:* Washington Sundar.

Winners: India Red

Vijay Hazare Trophy

Young brigade end Mumbai drought

Shreyas Iyer and Prithvi Shaw helped Mumbai end their 12-season drought as they clinched the Vijay Hazare Trophy 2018-19, their first 50-over title since 2006-07 when it was still called the Ranji Trophy One-Day Tournament.

Iyer finished with 373 runs from six innings at an average of 93.25 and a strike rate of 108.43, while Shaw's 356 runs came from five innings at 71.20 and a strike rate of 144.12. As a result, Mumbai remained unbeaten. On their way, they posted 400 for 5 — the highest team total of the season — against Railways.

Only twice in the tournament did they have to sweat for victory: against Punjab in the group stage, when Dhawal Kulkarni and Shardul Thakur stepped up with the ball, and against Delhi in the final, where Aditya Tare and Siddhesh Lad guided a tricky chase to see them through.

The introduction of nine new teams — Arunachal Pradesh, Bihar, Manipur, Meghalaya, Mizoram, Nagaland, Puducherry, Sikkim and Uttarakhand — took the overall match count to 160. However, 19 of those ended without a result due to rain.

Jharkhand's Shahbaz Nadeem broke Rahul Sanghvi's record (8 for 15) for the best bowling figures in List A cricket. Against Rajasthan, Nadeem registered figures of 10-4-10-8, which included a hat-trick. Uttarakhand's Karnveer Kaushal became the first double-centurion in the Vijay Hazare Trophy with his 202 off 135 balls against Sikkim.

Being a Union Territory, the rules were relaxed for Puducherry on who qualifies as a local player. But following the protests from other state associations, the BCCI had to revoke their special allowance after the first game, which reportedly didn't feature any actual local player.

Elsewhere, Jharkhand were declared winners by two runs via the VJD method in a controversial finish against Bengal. Jharkhand needed four from the last over with one wicket in hand when the umpires deemed the light bad enough to stop play; the slow over-rate from both teams had dragged the match, which had started at 9am, to 6pm.

No batsman, however, dominated as Karnataka's Mayank Agarwal did in **2017-18**. After gathering 1160 runs in the Ranji Trophy and 258 in the Syed Mushtaq Ali Trophy, Agarwal accumulated 723 runs at 90.37 with a strike-rate of almost 108 — easily the most in a single edition of the tournament, cruising past Dinesh Karthik's 607 the previous season. His overall tally of 2141 is the most in an Indian domestic season.

That Karnataka, as a result, won their third Vijay Hazare title in five years didn't come as a surprise.

Out of eight innings he batted, Agarwal crossed 80 on seven occasions.

Mumbai's Vijay Hazare Trophy win in 2018-19 was their first 50-over title since 2006-07. — KSCA

The only thing he might rue is that he could convert just three of those into hundreds. The one innings where he was dismissed for 28, against Punjab, was the only game Karnataka lost in the competition.

In their last league game against Railways — a must-win encounter to qualify for quarter-finals — Karnataka showed faith in the young duo of Prasidh Krishna and T Pradeep. The two picked up four wickets each to defend a modest 257 by 16 runs. Krishna emerged as the joint second-highest wicket-taker of the tournament with 17 scalps from eight games which also included a six-for against Assam in a Group A game.

The team's victories, especially in the league stage, were scripted on the strength of their batting. Apart from Agarwal, Nair, R Samarth and KL Rahul hit centuries. Pavan Deshpande too scored 310 runs at an average of more than 50 and a strike-rate over 100.

Among other teams, Andhra came out as a formidable unit under the captain-coach duo of Hanuma Vihari and Sanath Kumar, winning every match till the semi-final where they lost to Saurashtra. Vihari's 118-ball 169 against Mumbai, which included 16 fours and seven sixes, was the highest individual score of the tournament.

Defending champions Tamil Nadu were marred by injuries to key players Abhinav Mukund, B Indrajith and Vijay Shankar. It worsened when M Vijay failed to report for their league game against Mumbai. The opener was subsequently dropped from the squad even though Hrishikesh Kanitkar, their coach, admitted to a communication gap, stating he was aware of Vijay's shoulder injury that had ruled him out of the Mumbai game. R Ashwin, meanwhile, opted out in the middle of the tournament for personal reasons. All this reflected in their performance as they finished fifth in their group.

Unmukt Chand, who suffered a blow to the jaw while training ahead of the tournament, deserves special mention too: He scored a century against Uttar Pradesh in Delhi's first game, played throughout the competition with a broken jaw, and finished as the side's leading run-getter.

	Most runs	Most wickets
2017-18	Mayank Agarwal (Karnataka) (723 runs, 8 matches)	Mohammed Siraj (Hyderabad) (23 wickets, 7 matches)
2018-19	Abhinav Mukund (TN) (560 runs, 9 matches)	Shahbaz Nadeem (Jharkhand) (24 wickets, 9 matches)

2018-19

Elite Group A

KSCA Ground No 2, Alur, September 19: Baroda 238 in 49.5 overs (Krunal Pandya 85, Yusuf Pathan 40; Dhawal Kulkarni 4-39, Vijay Gohil 2-20) lost to **Mumbai** 239/1 in 41.3 overs (Prithvi Shaw 98, Ajinkya Rahane 79*) by nine wickets.

KSCA Ground No 3, Alur, September 19: Goa 266/7 in 50 overs (Amogh Desai 65, Amit Verma 38, Keenan Vaz 38; Samad Fallah 2-42) lost to **Maharashtra** 267/5 in 47.4 overs (Jay Pande 117*, Ruturaj Gaikwad 67; A Desai 2-39) by five wickets.

KSCA Ground, Alur, September 19: Punjab 290/7 in 50 overs (Shubman Gill 115, Yuvraj Singh 48; Rishi Dhawan 3-50) beat **Himachal Pradesh** 255 in 48.3 overs (Prashant Chopra 95, Ankush Bains 56; Siddarth Kaul 4-55, Arshdeep Singh 2-51) by 35 runs.

Just Cricket Academy Ground, Bengaluru, September 20: Vidarbha 254 in 50 overs (Atharwa Taide 57, Faiz Fazal 56; Lukman Meriwala 3-54, Bhargav Bhatt 2-7) lost to **Baroda** 151/2 in 29 overs (Aditya Waghmode 50, Kedar Devdhar 46) by 37 runs (VJD method).

KSCA Ground, Alur, September 20: Railways 187 in 47.5 overs (Karan Sharma 33, Harsh Tyagi 29; Mayank Dagar 4-38, Ayush Jamwal 3-36) lost to **Himachal Pradesh** 170/5 in 41.3 overs (Prashant Chopra 77, Nikhil Gangta 50; Anureet Singh 2-26) by 33 runs (VJD method).

M Chinnaswamy Stadium, Bengaluru, September 20: Maharashtra 245/8 in 50 overs (Ankit Bawne 104*, Rahul Tripathi 70; Abhimanyu Mithun 2-30, Vinay Kumar 2-33) beat **Karnataka** 107/6 in 22.4 overs (Pavan Deshpande 31, CM Gautam 29; Satyajeet Bachhav 2-19) by 57 runs (VJD method).

KSCA Ground No 3, Alur, September 21: Goa 317/5 in 50 overs (Sumiran Amonkar 82, Snehal Kauthankar 67; Ankit Yadav 2-49) beat **Railways** 275 in 47.2 overs (Amit Paunikar 84, Mrunal Devdhar 68; Krishna Das 4-50, Lakshay Garg 3-61) by 42 runs.

M Chinnaswamy Stadium, Bengaluru, September 21: Mumbai 362/5 in 50 overs (Ajinkya Rahane 148, Shreyas Iyer 110) beat **Karnataka** 274 in 45 overs (Mayank Agarwal 66, K Gowtham 38; Shams Mulani 4-71, Tushar Deshpande 2-68) by 88 runs.

KSCA Ground No 2, Alur, September 21: Punjab 278/7 in 50 overs (Gurkeerat Singh 85*, Yuvraj Singh 41; Shrikant Wagh 3-69, Faiz Fazal 2-41) beat **Vidarbha** 137 in 40.5 overs (Ganesh Satish 60, S Wagh 33; Mayank Markande 3-37, Mandeep Singh 2-15) by 141 runs.

KSCA Ground, Alur, September 23: Goa 148 in 45 overs (Darshan Misal 30, Amit Verma 29; Ayush Jamwal 4-25, Mayank Dagar 2-26) lost to **Himachal Pradesh** 152/6 in 32.1 overs (Prashant Chopra 65, Priyanshu Khanduri 47; Amulya Pandrekar 3-44) by four wickets.

Just Cricket Academy Ground, Bengaluru, September 23: Maharashtra 281/5 in 50 overs (Ankit Bawne 100*, Naushad Shaikh 60; Mayank Markande 2-41, Manpreet Gony 2-49) beat

Punjab 187 in 40.3 overs (Shubman Gill 36, Manan Vohra 27; Satyajeet Bachhav 5-54, Shamshuzama Kazi 2-17) by 94 runs.

M Chinnaswamy Stadium, Bengaluru, September 23: Mumbai 400/5 in 50 overs (Shreyas Iyer 144, Prithvi Shaw 129; Anureet Singh 3-73) beat **Railways** 227 in 42.4 overs (Saurabh Wakaskar 48, Prashant Awasthi 41; Shams Mulani 3-26, Dhawal Kulkarni 2-50) by 173 runs.

KSCA Ground No 2, Alur, September 24: Baroda v **Punjab**. Match abandoned without a ball bowled. No toss.

Just Cricket Academy Ground, Bengaluru, September 24: Goa v **Karnataka**. Match abandoned without a ball bowled. No toss.

KSCA Ground No 3, Alur, September 24: Mumbai v **Vidarbha**. Match abandoned without a ball bowled. No toss.

KSCA Ground, Alur, September 26: Vidarbha 297/7 in 50 overs (Atharwa Taide 148*, Faiz Fazal 91; Vinay Galetiya 2-51, Ayush Jamwal 2-52) lost to **Himachal Pradesh** 298/6 in 47.5 overs (Ankush Bains 173*, Priyanshu Khanduri 63; Akshay Wakhare 2-60) by four wickets.

Just Cricket Academy Ground, Bengaluru, September 26: Karnataka 237 in 50 overs (R Samarth 102, Karun Nair 37; Atit Sheth 4-42, Babashafi Pathan 2-38) lost to **Baroda** 230/3 in 43.3 overs (Kedar Devdhar 123, Deepak Hooda 62*) by seven wickets (VJD method).

M Chinnaswamy Stadium, Bengaluru, September 26: Railways 180 in 48.2 overs (Mrunal Devdhar 64, Ashish Yadav 30; Anupam Sanklecha 2-16, Samad Fallah 2-33, Shamshuzama Kazi 2-33) lost to **Maharashtra** 186/3 in 41.2 overs (Ruturaj Gaikwad 84, Jay Pande 38; Avinash Yadav 2-39) by seven wickets.

KSCA Ground, Alur, September 28: Baroda 281/5 in 50 overs (Kedar Devdhar 107, Deepak Hooda 71; Krishna Das 2-67) beat **Goa** 148 in 42.3 overs (Amit Verma 59, Sumiran Amonkar 35; Krunal Pandya 6-41) by 133 runs.

KSCA Ground No 2, Alur, September 28: Maharashtra 278 in 49.5 overs (Ruturaj Gaikwad 114, Rohit Motwani 53; Prashant Chopra 2-20) beat **Himachal Pradesh** 195 in 44.2 overs (Nikhil Gangta 76, Ankush Bains 62; Samad Fallah 3-18, Shamshuzama Kazi 2-42) by 83 runs.

Just Cricket Academy Ground, Bengaluru, September 28: Mumbai 245 in 49 overs (Jay Bista 68, Siddhesh Lad 35; Manpreet Gony 2-28, Mandeep Singh 2-40) beat **Punjab** 202 in 44.3 overs (Shubman Gill 40, Anmolpreet Singh 35; Dhawal Kulkarni 3-18, Shardul Thakur 3-53) by 45 runs.

M Chinnaswamy Stadium, Bengaluru, September 30: Baroda 269/9 in 50 overs (Aditya Waghmode 74, Krunal Pandya 62; Manish Rao 3-30, Manjeet Singh 3-55) beat **Railways** 89 in 24.4 overs (Manish Rao 23; Babashafi Pathan 5-25, Lukman Meriwala 2-14) by 180 runs.

KSCA Ground No 3, Alur, September 30: Himachal Pradesh 269/6 in 50 overs (Prashant Chopra 86, Rishi Dhawan 53*; Shivam Dube 2-41, Tushar Deshpande 2-65) lost to **Mumbai** 270/4 in 44.3 overs (Suryakumar Yadav 123*, Shams Mulani 41*; R Dhawan 2-42) by four wickets.

KSCA Ground No 2, Alur, September 30: Vidarbha 125 in 36.2 overs (Ganesh Satish 50, Atharwa Taide 32; Shreyas Gopal 3-13, K Gowtham 3-34) lost to **Karnataka** 129/4 in 32.3 overs (Kaunian Abbas 35*, Shreyas Gopal 34*; Yash Thakur 3-22) by six wickets.

Just Cricket Academy Ground, Bengaluru, October 2: Goa 186 in 49.5 overs (Suyash Prabhudessai 52, Amit Verma 49; Dhawal Kulkarni 3-32, Shams Mulani 2-31) lost to **Mumbai** 189/3 in 35.3 overs (Akhil Herwadkar 108*, Jay Bista 32; Krishna Das 2-31) by seven wickets.

KSCA Ground, Alur, October 2: Maharashtra 205/8 in 50 overs (Ankit Bawne 62, Ruturaj Gaikwad 32; R Sanjay 2-20, Darshan Nalkande 2-26) lost to **Vidarbha** 206/7 in 49.2 overs (Akshay Wadkar 82*, D Nalkande 53*; Samad Fallah 2-33) by three wickets.

M Chinnaswamy Stadium, Bengaluru, October 2: Punjab 284/6 in 50 overs (Gurkeerat Singh 101, Yuvraj Singh 96; Chandrakant Sakure 3-85) beat **Railways** 210 in 44.3 overs (Saurabh Wakaskar 104, Manish Rao 30; Mayank Markande 3-40, Arshdeep Singh 2-39) by 74 runs.

KSCA Ground No 3, Alur, October 4: Baroda 153 in 41.2 overs (Kedar Devdhar 41, Aditya Waghmode 29; Mayank Dagar 5-27, Ayush Jamwal 2-35) v **Himachal Pradesh** 41/1 in 11.3 overs (Priyanshu Khanduri 33). No result.

KSCA Ground No 2, Alur, October 4: Punjab 359/4 in 50 overs (Anmolpreet Singh 141, Shubman Gill 73) v **Goa** 46/2 in 10 overs (Amogh Desai 30*). No result.

M Chinnaswamy Stadium, Bengaluru, October 4: Karnataka 229/5 in 42.3 overs (Kaunian Abbas 46; Shreyas Gopal 35*; Manjeet Singh 2-30, Manish Rao 2-32) v **Railways**. No result.

M Chinnaswamy Stadium, Bengaluru, October 6: Karnataka 257/8 in 38 overs (R Samarth 98, Manish Pandey 43; Rishi Dhawan 3-57, Prashant Chopra 2-20) beat **Himachal Pradesh** 162 in 25.3 overs (P Chopra 67, Ankush Bains 26; K Gowtham 4-26, T Pradeep 4-35) by 35 runs (VJD method).

Just Cricket Academy Ground, Bengaluru, October 6: Maharashtra v **Mumbai**. Match-abandoned without a ball bowled. No toss.

KSCA Ground, Alur, October 6: Railways 226/8 in 50 overs (Madhur Khatri 58, Saurabh Wakaskar 57; Darshan Nalkande 3-42, Aditya Sarwate 2-27) lost to **Vidarbha** 176/3 in 37 overs (Ganesh Satish 53*, Akshay Wadkar 49*) by seven wickets (VJD method).

KSCA Ground, Alur, October 8: Baroda 206/8 in 50 overs (Yusuf Pathan 64, Krunal Pandya 52; Samad Fallah 3-21, Satyajeet Bachhav 3-39) lost to **Maharashtra** 207/5 in 44.3 overs (Naushad Shaikh 76*, Rohit Motwani 59; Atit Sheth 3-36) by five wickets.

KSCA Ground No 3, Alur, October 8: Vidarbha 218 in 48.2 overs (Faiz Fazal 49, Atharwa Taide 48; Darshan Misal 4-52) beat **Goa** 217/9 in 50 overs (Amit Verma 45, Suyash Prabhudessai 39; Darshan Nalkande 3-37, Akshay Wakhare 3-39) by 1 run.

M Chinnaswamy Stadium, Bengaluru, October 8: Karnataka 296 in 48.2 overs (BR Sharath 70, Manish Pandey 67; Siddarth Kaul 5-41, Barinder Sran 3-48) lost to **Punjab** 297/4 in 48.5 overs (Anmolpreet Singh 138, Shubman Gill 77) by six wickets.

Points table

Teams	M	W	L	T	N/R	Pts	NRR
Mumbai	8	6	0	0	2	28	+1.634
Maharashtra	8	6	1	0	1	26	+1.003
Baroda	8	4	2	0	2	20	+1.141
Punjab	8	4	2	0	2	20	+0.354
Himachal Pradesh	8	3	4	0	1	14	-0.138
Vidarbha	8	3	4	0	1	14	-0.819
Karnataka	8	2	4	0	2	12	-0.175
Goa	8	1	5	0	2	8	-0.935
Railways	8	0	7	0	1	2	-1.719

Mumbai and Maharashtra qualified for the quarter-final

Elite Group B

Palam A Ground, Model Sports Complex, Delhi, September 19: Andhra 190 in 49 overs (B Sumanth 79, DB Ravi Teja 44; S Midhun 3-56, Sandeep Warrier 2-17) beat **Kerala** 183 in 49.1 overs (Sachin Baby 57, Jalaj Saxena 46; Karn Sharma 3-37, Ricky Bhui 2-8) by 7 runs.

Palam B Ground, Model Sports Complex, Delhi, September 19: Madhya Pradesh 231 in 48.2 overs (Rajat Patidar 49, Saransh Jain 45; Mohammed Siraj 3-42, Akash Bhandari 2-35) lost to **Hyderabad** 235/3 in 47.4 overs (Tanmay Agarwal 83, Rohit Rayudu 78; Rameez Khan 2-34) by seven wickets.

Feroz Shah Kotla, Delhi, September 19: Saurashtra 303/9 in 50 overs (Sheldon Jackson 107, Robin Uthappa 97; Shivam Mavi 5-73) beat **Uttar Pradesh** 278 in 49.1 overs (Akshdeep Nath 62, Priyam Garg 38; Jaydev Unadkat 3-42, Dharmendrasinh Jadeja 3-48, Prerak Mankad 3-63) by 25 runs.

Palam A Ground, Model Sports Complex, Delhi, September 20: Odisha 184/9 in 50 overs (Sujit Lenka 55, Abhishek Raut 41; Karn Sharma 3-29, Shoaib Mohammad 2-32) lost to **Andhra** 186/4 in 47.1 overs (Ashwin Hebbar 92*, DB Ravi Teja 53*; Pappu Roy 2-16) by six wickets.

Palam B Ground, Model Sports Complex, Delhi, September 20: Chhattisgarh 268/7 in 50 overs (Harpreet Bhatia 91, Manoj Singh 41; Ishwar Pandey 4-45, Mihir Hirwani 2-62) beat **Madhya Pradesh** 146 in 38.2 overs (Anshul Tripathi 59; Pankaj Rao 3-14, Jatin Saxena 3-29, Shahnawaz Hussain 3-39) by 122 runs.

Feroz Shah Kotla, Delhi, September 20: Saurashtra 237 in 49.3 overs (Sheldon Jackson 62, Cheteshwar Pujara 53; Subodh Bhati 5-24, Lalit Yadav 2-42) lost to **Delhi** 238/5 in 46 overs (Himmat Singh 74*, Gautam Gambhir 62; Jaydev Unadkat 2-36, Kamlesh Makwana 2-41) by five wickets.

Palam B Ground, Model Sports Complex, Delhi, September 21: Uttar Pradesh 250 in 49.2 overs (Upendra Yadav 85, Rinku Singh 58; Jatin Saxena 4-56) lost to **Chhattisgarh** 252/6 in 49.1 overs (Amandeep Khare 78*, Vishal Kushwaha 52) by four wickets.

Feroz Shah Kotla, Delhi, September 21: Hyderabad 205 in 47.4 overs (B Sandeep 51, Mohammed Siraj 36; Manan Sharma 4-42, Navdeep Saini 2-45) lost to **Delhi** 178/4 in 30.4 overs (Nitish Rana 91*, Gautam Gambhir 41; Ravi Kiran 2-24) by six wickets (VJD method).

Palam A Ground, Model Sports Complex, Delhi, September 21: Odisha 117 in 34.4 overs (Subhranshu Senapati 26; Akshay Chandran 4-29, Jalaj Saxena 3-24) lost to **Kerala** 118/4 in 37.3 overs (Sachin Baby 41, Salman Nizar 31*; Pappu Roy 2-25) by six wickets.

Feroz Shah Kotla, Delhi, September 23: Chhattisgarh 138 in 39.5 overs (Amandeep Khare 36*, Avnish Dhaliwal 24; Jalaj Saxena 4-31, Akshay Chandran 3-13) lost to **Kerala** 133/4 in 40 overs (J Saxena 58*, Daryl Ferrario 33) by six wickets (VJD method).

Palam B Ground, Model Sports Complex, Delhi, September 23: Hyderabad 196/9 in 45 overs (B Sandeep 76, K Sumanth 47; Jaydev Unadkat 4-33) lost to **Saurashtra** 110/3 in 18.5 overs (Robin Uthappa 35, Prerak Mankad 27*; Mehdi Hasan 2-13) by seven wickets (VJD method).

Palam A Ground, Model Sports Complex, Delhi, September 23: Uttar Pradesh 95/2 in 15 overs (Upendra Yadav 42, Shivam Chaudhary 30) v **Odisha**. No result.

Palam B Ground, Model Sports Complex, Delhi, September 24: Andhra v Hyderabad. Matchabandoned without a ball bowled. No toss.

Palam A Ground, Model Sports Complex, Delhi, September 24: Delhi v Uttar Pradesh. Matchabandoned without a ball bowled. No toss.

Feroz Shah Kotla, Delhi, September 24: Kerala v Madhya Pradesh. Match abandoned without a ball bowled.

Feroz Shah Kotla, Delhi, September 26: Chhattisgarh 248/8 in 50 overs (Ashutosh Singh 110, Manoj Singh 62; D Sivakumar 2-42, Shoaib Mohammad 2-42) lost to **Andhra** 249/8 in 50 overs (Karn Sharma 55, Ashwin Hebbar 53, DB Ravi Teja 53; Pankaj Rao 2-42, Shivendra Singh 2-52) by two wickets.

Palam B Ground, Model Sports Complex, Delhi, September 26: Odisha 249/4 in 50 overs (Biplab Samantray 63, Subhranshu Senapati 59) beat **Delhi** 240 in 48 overs (Gautam Gambhir 44, Subodh Bhati 42*; Deepak Behera 2-25, Pappu Roy 2-37) by 9 runs.

Palam A Ground, Model Sports Complex, Delhi, September 26: Madhya Pradesh 136 in 45.5 overs (Saransh Jain 32, Anshul Tripathi 24; Jaydev Unadkat 4-23, Dharmendrasinh Jadeja 3-33) lost to **Saurashtra** 137/3 in 40.3 overs (Arpit Vasavada 38*, Cheteshwar Pujara 36*) by seven wickets.

Feroz Shah Kotla, Delhi, September 28: Delhi 392/3 in 50 overs (Gautam Gambhir 151 retd out, Dhruv Shorey 99*) beat **Kerala** 227/8 in 50 overs (VA Jagadeesh 59*, Sanju Samson 47, Sachin Baby 47; Pawan Negi 3-41, Navdeep Saini 2-14) by 165 runs.

Palam A Ground, Model Sports Complex, Delhi, September 28: Uttar Pradesh 130 in 39.1 overs (Suresh Raina 53, Upendra Yadav 22; Mehdi Hasan 5-20, Mohammed Siraj 2-28) lost to **Hyderabad** 134/1 in 35.2 overs (Akshath Reddy 64, Tanmay Agarwal 62*) by nine wickets.

Palam B Ground, Model Sports Complex, Delhi, September 28: Madhya Pradesh 277 in 49.3 overs (Yash Dubey 75, Anshul Tripathi 52; Deepak Behera 3-38, Govinda Poddar 2-47) beat **Odisha** 276/8 in 50 overs (Anurag Sarangi 78, Abhishek Raut 55*; Rameez Khan 4-49, Puneet Datey 3-65) by 1 run.

Palam B Ground, Model Sports Complex, Delhi, September 30: Saurashtra 214/7 in 50 overs (Arpit Vasavada 55, Chirag Jani 40; Girinath Reddy 2-44, Karn Sharma 2-48) lost to **Andhra** 215/4 in 48.3 overs (DB Prasanth Kumar 71, B Sumanth 43*) by six wickets.

Palam A Ground, Model Sports Complex, Delhi, September 30: Hyderabad 222/9 in 50 overs (Rohit Rayudu 75, B Sandeep 44; Pankaj Rao 3-41, Sumit Ruikar 2-41) beat **Chhattisgarh** 121 in 33.3 overs (Ashutosh Singh 38, Jatin Saxena 37; Mehdi Hasan 3-19, PS Sairam 3-28) by 101 runs.

Feroz Shah Kotla, Delhi, September 30: Madhya Pradesh 277/7 in 50 overs (Venkatesh Iyer 83, Yash Dubey 66; Shiva Singh 2-49, Amit Mishra 2-64) lost to **Uttar Pradesh** 280/5 in 49.3 overs (Samarth Singh 70, Akshdeep Nath 51; Saransh Jain 3-29) by five wickets.

Palam B Ground, Model Sports Complex, Delhi, October 2: Chhattisgarh 212 in 49.5 overs (Harpreet Bhatia 43, Ashutosh Singh 38, Shakeeb Ahmed 38; Anurag Sarangi 3-22) beat **Odisha** 164 in 41 overs (Rajesh Dhuper 38, Biplab Samantray 38; Pankaj Rao 3-15, Shivendra Singh 3-31) by 48 runs.

Feroz Shah Kotla, Delhi, October 2: Delhi 314/5 in 50 overs (Himmat Singh 102*, Unmukt Chand 62; Girinath Reddy 2-67) beat **Andhra** 241 in 49.5 overs (DB Prasanth Kumar 54, Ricky Bhui 48; Nitish Rana 2-9, Kulwant Khejroliya 2-29) by 73 runs.

Palam A Ground, Model Sports Complex, Delhi, October 2: Kerala 189/6 in 50 overs (VA Jagadeesh 62, Vishnu Vinod 34*; PS Sairam 2-27, Ravi Kiran 2-32) lost to **Hyderabad** 190/3 in 46.4 overs (Rohit Rayudu 57*, B Sandeep 48*; Jalaj Saxena 2-22) by seven wickets.

Palam A Ground, Model Sports Complex, Delhi, October 4: Delhi 284/8 in 50 overs (Nitish Rana 107, Dhruv Shorey 67; Mihir Hirwani 4-49, Ishwar Pandey 2-49) beat **Madhya Pradesh** 209 in 42.4 overs (Venkatesh Iyer 53, Saransh Jain 47; Lalit Yadav 5-25, Manan Sharma 2-34) by 75 runs.

Palam B Ground, Model Sports Complex, Delhi, October 4: Kerala 228 in 50 overs (VA Jagadeesh 82, Salman Nizar 43; Saurabh Kumar 3-31) beat **Uttar Pradesh** 227 in 49.5 overs (Suresh Raina 66, Samarth Singh 42; Jalaj Saxena 2-31, Vinoop Manoharan 2-38, KC Akshay 2-38) by 1 run.

Feroz Shah Kotla, Delhi, October 4: Odisha 197 in 49.2 overs (Biplab Samantray 62, Abhishek Raut 36; Jaydev Unadkat 3-39, Yuvraj Chudasama 2-20) beat **Saurashtra** 145 in 38.4 overs (Sheldon Jackson 40, Arpit Vasavada 35; Govinda Poddar 3-33, Pappu Roy 2-19) by 52 runs.

Palam B Ground, Model Sports Complex, Delhi, October 6: Uttar Pradesh 330/4 in 50 overs (Akshdeep Nath 119*, Samarth Singh 115*) lost to **Andhra** 331/9 in 49.3 overs (DB Ravi Teja 79*, Ashwin Hebbar 64; A Nath 3-44, Shivam Mavi 2-64) by one wicket.

Palam A Ground, Model Sports Complex, Delhi, October 6: Saurashtra 110 in 34.4 overs (Arpit Vasavada 34; Sumit Ruikar 6-26, Shivendra Singh 2-20) lost to **Chhattisgarh** 111/1 in 24.2 overs (Rishabh Tiwari 56*, Manoj Singh 36*) by nine wickets.

Feroz Shah Kotla, Delhi, October 6: Odisha 247/8 in 50 overs (Govinda Poddar 93, Subhranshu Senapati 41; CV Milind 6-43) lost to **Hyderabad** 250/9 in 49.2 overs (Tanmay Agarwal 76, Akshath Reddy 63; Pappu Roy 3-38, Suryakant Pradhan 2-52) by one wicket.

Palam A Ground, Model Sports Complex, Delhi, October 8: Madhya Pradesh 155 in 41.4

overs (Anand Singh 70, Yash Dubey 25; Shoaib Mohammad 4-16, Hanuma Vihari 3-31) lost to **Andhra** 156/3 in 34.5 overs (Ricky Bhui 56*, B Sumanth 46*; Kumar Kartikeya 3-28) by seven wickets.

Feroz Shah Kotla, Delhi, October 8: Delhi 245/9 in 50 overs (Lakshay Thareja 53, Unmukt Chand 32; Shivendra Singh 2-31, Shakeeb Ahmed 2-40) beat **Chhattisgarh** 201 in 45.1 overs (Ajay Mandal 40, S Ahmed 38; Kulwant Khejroliya 4-27, Lalit Yadav 2-41) by 44 runs.

Palam B Ground, Model Sports Complex, Delhi, October 8: Kerala 316/7 in 50 overs (Sachin Baby 93, Vishnu Vinod 62; Jay Chauhan 3-63, Yuvraj Chudasama 2-67) beat **Saurashtra** 270 in 49.3 overs (Samarth Vyas 91, Chirag Jani 66; Basil Thampi 4-52, KC Akshay 3-69) by 46 runs.

Points table

Teams	M	W	L	T	N/R	Pts	NRR
Delhi	8	6	1	0	1	26	+1.258
Andhra	8	6	1	0	1	26	+0.100
Hyderabad	8	5	2	0	1	22	+0.539
Kerala	8	4	3	0	1	18	-0.165
Chhattisgarh	8	4	4	0	0	16	+0.278
Saurashtra	8	3	5	0	0	12	-0.475
Odisha	8	2	5	0	1	10	-0.181
Uttar Pradesh	8	1	5	0	2	8	-0.378
Madhya Pradesh	8	1	6	0	1	6	-0.984

Delhi, Andhra, and Hyderabad qualified for the quarter-final

Elite Group C

TI Cycles Ground, Murugappa, Chennai, September 19: Assam v Gujarat. Match abandoned without a ball bowled. No toss.

ICL Guru Nanak College Ground, Chennai, September 19: Haryana v Jharkhand. Match abandoned without a ball bowled. No toss.

MA Chidambaram Stadium, Chepauk, Chennai, September 19: Tripura 118 in 38.4 overs (Bikramjit Debnath 21; Diwesh Pathania 3-28, Abhishek Tiwari 2-15) lost to **Services** 108/3 in 25.3 overs (Rahul Singh 48, Rajat Paliwal 24; Rana Datta 2-29) by seven wickets (VJD method).

SSN College of Engineering Ground, Chennai, September 20: Jammu and Kashmir 96 in 23.4 overs (Mohammed Mudhasir 21; Prayas Ray Barman 4-20, Ishan Porel 3-19) lost to **Bengal** 98/4 in 20.4 overs (Shreevats Goswami 22) by six wickets.

TI Cycles Ground, Murugappa, Chennai, September 20: Rajasthan 73 in 28.3 overs (Ankit Lamba 20; Shahbaz Nadeem 8-10, Anukul Roy 2-23) lost to **Jharkhand** 76/3 in 14.3 overs (Anand Singh 22; Mahipal Lomror 2-22) by seven wickets.

MA Chidambaram Stadium, Chepauk, Chennai, September 20: Tamil Nadu 205/8 in 49 overs (Baba Indrajith 58, Vijay Shankar 47; Piyush Chawla 3-38) lost to **Gujarat** 210/6 in 47.1 overs (Priyank Panchal 117*, Parthiv Patel 24; Sai Kishore 2-37) by four wickets.

MA Chidambaram Stadium, Chepauk, Chennai, September 21: Assam 81 in 30.2 overs (Riyan Parag 24; Amit Mishra 6-13, Arun Chaprana 3-4) lost to **Haryana** 83/2 in 11.2 overs (Harshal Patel 37, Shubham Rohilla 31*) by eight wickets.

SSN College of Engineering Ground, Chennai, September 21: Jammu and Kashmir 79

Uttarakhand's Karnveer Kaushal became the first double-centurion in the Vijay Hazare Trophy with his 202 off 135 balls against Sikkim. — *USCA*

in 30 overs (Ahmed Banday 24; Harmeet Singh 5-10, Neelambuj Vats 3-17) lost to **Tripura** 81/6 in 30.5 overs (Nirupam Sen Chowdhary 24) by four wickets.

IIT Chemplast Ground, Chennai, September 21: Tamil Nadu 315/4 in 50 overs (N Jagadeesan 133, Baba Indrajith 76*; Varun Choudhary 3-63) beat **Services** 232 in 46 overs (Nakul Verma 60, Rajat Paliwal 52; Varun Chakravarthy 5-38, Baba Aparajith 3-29) by 83 runs.

MA Chidambaram Stadium, Chepauk, Chennai, September 23: Bengal 272/9 in 50 overs (Manoj Tiwary 67, Anustup Majumdar 48; Rajat Dey 4-48, Rajib Saha 2-34) beat **Tripura** 263/4 in 50 overs (Smit Patel 135*, Nirupam Sen Chowdhary 53; Prayas Ray Barman 2-42, Ashoke Dinda 2-49) by 9 runs.

ICL Guru Nanak College Ground, Chennai, September 23: Jammu and Kashmir 108 in 34.3 overs (Paras Sharma 25; Amit Mishra 3-26, Arun Chaprana 2-9) lost to **Haryana** 112/7 in 36.1 overs (Himanshu Rana 30, Pramod Chandila 29; Auqib Nabi 3-32, Irfan Pathan 2-7) by three wickets.

TI Cycles Ground, Murugappa, Chennai, September 23: Rajasthan 133 in 37.1 overs (Tajinder Dhillon 55; Sai Kishore 5-39, Varun Chakravarthy 3-28) lost to **Tamil Nadu** 134/9 in 34.5 overs (B Anirudh 40, M Mohammed 22*; Rahul Chahar 3-35, Tanveer-ul-Haq 2-26) by one wicket.

MA Chidambaram Stadium, Chepauk, Chennai, September 24: Assam 221/9 in 50 overs (Sibsankar Roy 46, Wasiqur Rahman 43; Shahbaz Nadeem 3-47, Utkarsh Singh 2-29) lost to **Jharkhand** 222/2 in 31 overs (Ishan Kishan 139, Anand Singh 58; Mukhtar Hussain 2-55) by eight wickets.

SSN College of Engineering Ground, Chennai, September 24: Gujarat 212/6 in 50 overs (Rujul Bhatt 62, Priyank Panchal 39; Harmeet Singh 3-28) beat **Tripura** 138/9 in 50 overs (Joydeep Banik 57, Rana Datta 25*; Piyush Chawla 2-10, Roosh Kalaria 2-10) by 74 runs.

TI Cycles Ground, Murugappa, Chennai, September 24: Haryana 257/8 in 50 overs (Chaitanya Bishnoi 88, Pramod Chandila 57; Diwesh Pathania 5-42) lost to **Services** 260/5 in

47.3 overs (Nakul Verma 95, Rahul Singh 61; Rahul Tewatia 2-53) by five wickets.

MA Chidambaram Stadium, Chepauk, Chennai, September 25: Bengal 129 in 38 overs (Abhimanyu Easwaran 34, Anustup Majumdar 33; Varun Choudhary 3-23, Arjun Sharma 3-30) lost to **Services** 130/2 in 22 overs (Rajat Paliwal 58*, Rahul Singh 53*) by eight wickets.

ICL Guru Nanak College Ground, Chennai, September 25: Rajasthan 179/9 in 50 overs (Chandrapal Singh 82, Chetan Bist 44; Hardik Patel 5-22) lost to **Gujarat** 180/2 in 40 overs (Kshitij Patel 89*, Priyank Panchal 84) by eight wickets.

SSN College of Engineering Ground, Chennai, September 25: Jharkhand 307/8 in 50 overs (Ishan Kishan 85, Saurabh Tiwary 54; Varun Chakravarthy 3-61, M Mohammed 2-41) beat **Tamil Nadu** 299 in 49.5 overs (Baba Indrajith 101, Abhinav Mukund 63; Anukul Roy 3-55, Varun Aaron 3-63) by 8 runs.

TI Cycles Ground, Murugappa, Chennai, September 27: Haryana 304 in 49.2 overs (Pramod Chandila 88, Himanshu Rana 44; Tanveer-ul-Haq 3-62, Chandrapal Singh 2-54) beat **Rajasthan** 157 in 46.4 overs (Abhimanyu Lamba 46, Tajinder Dhillon 28; Harshal Patel 3-19, Chaitanya Bishnoi 2-23) by 147 runs.

MA Chidambaram Stadium, Chepauk, Chennai, September 27: Jharkhand 221/8 in 50 overs (Anukul Roy 96*, Virat Singh 33; Waseem Raza 3-51) beat **Jammu and Kashmir** 148 in 42.2 overs (Mohammad Mudhasir 53*, W Raza 20; Shahbaz Nadeem 5-17) by 73 runs.

ICL Guru Nanak College Ground, Chennai, September 27: Tamil Nadu 334/4 in 50 overs (Vijay Shankar 129, Baba Indrajith 92; Amit Sinha 2-28) beat **Assam** 204 in 44.1 overs (Riyan Parag 45, Wasiqur Rahman 43; Varun Chakravarthy 2-40, Baba Aparajith 2-42) by 130 runs.

ICL Guru Nanak College Ground, Chennai, September 28: Assam 150 in 35.5 overs (Riyan Parag 32, Abu Nechim 31*; Pradipta Pramanik 4-27, Kanishk Seth 2-20) lost to **Bengal** 151/5 in 25.4 overs (Vivek Singh 51, Shahbaz Ahmed 23; Mrinmoy Dutta 3-46, Mukhtar Hussain 2-35) by five wickets.

TI Cycles Ground, Murugappa, Chennai, September 28: Gujarat 219/7 in 50 overs (Rujul Bhatt 56, Parthiv Patel 47; Diwesh Pathania 3-36) lost to **Services** 220/1 in 38.1 overs (Ravi Chauhan 106*, Rahul Singh 55*) by nine wickets.

SSN College of Engineering Ground, Chennai, September 28: Tripura 242/7 in 50 overs (Bravish Shetty 107, Bishal Ghosh 76; Rahul Chahar 3-44, Nathu Singh 2-38) beat **Rajasthan** 194 in 45.1 overs (Robin Bist 42, Chandrapal Singh 38; Rajib Saha 3-50, Harmeet Singh 2-48) by 48 runs.

ICL Guru Nanak College Ground, Chennai, September 30: Jammu and Kashmir 123 in 34 overs (Ian Dev Singh 35, Shubham Khajuria 27; Piyush Chawla 3-29, Hardik Patel 2-11) lost to **Gujarat** 127/2 in 21.1 overs (Priyank Panchal 49, Bhargav Merai 43*) by eight wickets.

SSN College of Engineering Ground, Chennai, September 30:Tripura 171 in 45 overs (Bravish Shetty 60, Bishal Ghosh 36; Harshal Patel 3-19, Rahul Tewatia 3-27) lost to **Haryana** 175/7 in 41.2 overs (Chaitanya Bishnoi 55*, H Patel 41; Rajib Saha 3-25, Nirupam Sen Chowdhary 2-6) by three wickets.

MA Chidambaram Stadium, Chepauk, Chennai, September 30: Bengal 239 in 49.4 overs (Abhimanyu Easwaran 72, Manoj Tiwary 47; Vijay Shankar 4-34, M Mohammed 3-54) lost to **Tamil Nadu** 240/4 in 42 overs (Abhinav Mukund 94, N Jagadeesan 55; Prayas Ray Barman 2-35) by six wickets.

MA Chidambaram Stadium, Chepauk, Chennai, October 1: Rajasthan 217/7 in 50 overs (Manender Singh 101, Mahipal Lomror 54; Jitumoni Kalita 2-48) beat **Assam** 161 in 38.4 overs (Amit Sinha 52, Riyan Parag 45; Tanveer-ul-Haq 3-27, Chandrapal Singh 2-12) by 56 runs.

TI Cycles Ground, Murugappa, Chennai, October 1: Bengal 267/8 in 50 overs (Abhimanyu Easwaran 149, Manoj Tiwary 69; Varun Aaron 3-48, Shahbaz Nadeem 2-60) lost to **Jharkhand** 264/9 in 49 overs (Anand Singh 118, Ishan Kishan 56; Writtick Chatterjee 3-46) by 2 runs (VJD method).

ICL Guru Nanak College Ground, Chennai, October 1: Services 322 in 49 overs (Nakul

Sharma 123, Rajat Paliwal 63; Parveez Rasool 5-62, Mohammad Mudhasir 2-57) beat **Jammu and Kashmir** 220 in 42.2 overs (Paras Sharma 93, M Mudhasir 30; Arjun Sharma 4-43, Nitin Tanwar 3-44) by 102 runs.

MA Chidambaram Stadium, Chepauk, Chennai, October 3: Haryana 247/7 in 50 overs (Himanshu Rana 67, Jayant Yadav 47*; Chintan Gaja 3-44) beat **Gujarat** 203 in 46.1 overs (Chirag Gandhi 52, Manprit Juneja 38; J Yadav 3-35, Harshal Patel 2-33) by 44 runs.

SSN College of Engineering Ground, Chennai, October 3: Rajasthan 218/8 in 50 overs (Salman Khan 60, Manender Singh 50; Parveez Rasool 3-36, Waseem Raza 2-23) lost to **Jammu and Kashmir** 179/7 in 35.3 overs (Shubham Khajuria 57, Ian Dev Singh 51; Rahul Chahar 3-37, Tajinder Dhillon 2-9) by three wickets (VJD method).

ICL Guru Nanak College Ground, Chennai, October 3: Tripura 196 in 46.4 overs (Smit Patel 60, Ninad Kadam 31; Athisayaraj Davidson 3-46, Varun Chakravarthy 2-29) lost to **Tamil Nadu** 197/2 in 31.2 overs (Abhinav Mukund 131*, Narayan Jagadeesan 40; Harmeet Singh 2-46) by eight wickets.

ICL Guru Nanak College Ground, Chennai, October 5: Assam v **Services**. Match abandoned without a ball bowled. No toss.

MA Chidambaram Stadium, Chepauk, Chennai, October 5: Bengal 140/9 in 21 overs (Manoj Tiwary 60, Vivek Singh 30; Harshal Patel 2-25, Arun Chaprana 2-28) v **Haryana** 69/6 in 14 overs (Shahbaz Ahmed 2-18). No result.

TI Cycles Ground, Murugappa, Chennai, October 5: Jharkhand v **Tripura**. Match abandoned without a ball bowled. No toss.

ICL Guru Nanak College Ground, Chennai, October 7: Rajasthan 177/9 in 43 overs (Mahipal Lomror 79*, Manender Singh 31; Ishan Porel 4-30, Shahbaz Ahmed 2-25) lost to **Bengal** 181/4 in 37.4 overs (Vivek Singh 65, Manoj Tiwary 56*; Deepak Chahar 2-29) by six wickets.

SSN College of Engineering Ground, Chennai, October 7: Gujarat 107 in 25 overs (Piyush Chawla 41*; Varun Aaron 3-21, Utkarsh Singh 2-17) lost to **Jharkhand** 108/5 in 21.4 overs (Ishan Kishan 64; P Chawla 3-21) by five wickets.

MA Chidambaram Stadium, Chepauk, Chennai, October 7: Tamil Nadu 168 in 39.4 overs (Abhinav Mukund 49, M Vijay 44; Umar Nazir 4-26, Rohit Sharma 2-31) lost to **Jammu and Kashmir** 169/6 in 40.3 overs (Parveez Rasool 71*, Shubham Pundir 30; Varun Chakravarthy 3-34) by four wickets.

TI Cycles Ground, Murugappa, Chennai, October 9: Tripura 209 in 49.1 overs (Bishal Ghosh 100, Smit Patel 33, Udiyan Bose 33; Arup Das 3-25, Abu Nechim 3-35) lost to **Assam** 211/2 in 44.1 overs (Rishav Das 87*, Riyan Parag 82) by eight wickets.

SSN College of Engineering Ground, Chennai, October 9: Services 139 in 41.1 overs (Ravi Chauhan 47, Rajat Paliwal 26; Rahul Chahar 5-29, Rajesh Bishnoi 2-25) lost to **Rajasthan** 140/3 in 43 overs (Manender Singh 83*, Salman Khan 23) by seven wickets.

ICL Guru Nanak College Ground, Chennai, October 9: Haryana 310/5 in 50 overs (Rahul Tewatia 91*, Himanshu Rana 89*; Varun Chakravarthy 2-55, Washington Sundar 2-58) beat **Tamil Nadu** 233/9 in 50 overs (Abhinav Mukund 47, Vijay Shankar 44; R Tewatia 2-27, Jayant Yadav 2-37) by 77 runs.

SSN College of Engineering Ground, Chennai, October 11: Jammu and Kashmir 272/7 in 50 overs (Ahmed Banday 79, Shubham Khajuria 72) beat **Assam** 193 in 48.2 overs (Amit Sinha 81, Abu Nechim 28; Irfan Pathan 3-38, Umar Nazir 3-54) by 79 runs.

MA Chidambaram Stadium, Chepauk, Chennai, October 11: Gujarat 214/9 in 50 overs (Priyank Panchal 50, Rujul Bhatt 38; Pradipta Pramanik 2-36, Mukesh Kumar 2-43) beat **Bengal** 173 in 44.2 overs (Sudip Chatterjee 36, Manoj Tiwary 34; Roosh Kalaria 3-31, R Bhatt 2-22) by 41 runs.

TI Cycles Ground, Murugappa, Chennai, October 11: Jharkhand 290 in 50 overs (Kumar Deobrat 88, Saurabh Tiwary 65; Diwesh Pathania 2-40, Abhishek Tiwari 2-41) beat **Services** 265 in 47.4 overs (Rahul Singh 75, Rajat Paliwal 68; Anukul Roy 4-53, Varun Aaron 4-55) by 25 runs.

Points table

Teams	M	W	L	T	N/R	Pts	NRR
Jharkhand	9	7	0	0	2	32	+1.347
Haryana	9	6	1	0	2	28	+1.661
Services	9	5	3	0	1	22	+0.597
Gujarat	9	5	3	0	1	22	+0.534
Tamil Nadu	9	5	4	0	0	20	+0.767
Bengal	9	4	4	0	1	18	-0.115
Jammu & Kashmir	9	3	6	0	0	12	-0.855
Tripura	9	2	6	0	1	10	-0.580
Rajasthan	9	2	7	0	0	8	-0.971
Assam	9	1	6	0	2	8	-2.005

Jharkhand and Haryana qualified for the quarter-final

Plate group

GS Patel Stadium, Nadiad, September 19: Mizoram 234/8 in 50 overs (Taruwar Kohli 127, Sinan Khadir 35; Myendung Singpho 2-34) lost to **Arunachal Pradesh** 237/6 in 47 overs (Samarth Seth 107, Kshitiz Sharma 61; Lalrempuia 3-43) by four wickets.

Lal Bahadur Shastri Stadium, Anand, September 19: Nagaland 253/8 in 50 overs (Nitesh Lohchab 79, Imliwati Lemtur 45; Samad Quadri 3-35, Keshav Kumar 2-35) lost to **Bihar** 254/2 in 43.4 overs (Babul Kumar 121*, Keshav 76*) by eight wickets.

Moti Bagh Stadium, Vadodara, September 19: Manipur 120 in 37.1 overs (Lakhan Rawat 29, Yashpal Singh 29; Sarag Udheshi 4-20, Sagar Trivedi 3-47) lost to **Puducherry** 121/2 in 25.3 overs (Shashank Singh 63*, D Rohit 30; Bishworjit Konthoujam 2-22) by eight wickets.

Lal Bahadur Shastri Stadium, Anand, September 20: Uttarakhand 160 in 43.2 overs (Vineet Saxena 57, Deepak Dhapola 38; Anunay Singh 3-21, Samar Quadri 3-37) lost to **Bihar** 163/5 in 37.3 overs (Vikash Ranjan 79, Keshav Kumar 33) by five wickets.

Moti Bagh Stadium, Vadodara, September 20: Sikkim 84 in 37.2 overs (Lee Yong Lepcha 29*; Bishworjit Konthoujam 3-9, Akshaykumar Singh 2-10) lost to **Manipur** 85/0 in 19.2 overs (Lakhan Rawat 44*, Prafullomani Singh 30*) by ten wickets.

GS Patel Stadium, Nadiad, September 20: Mizoram 154 in 43.4 overs (Taruwar Kohli 90, Lalnunkima Varte 34; Raj Biswa 2-14, Abhay Negi 2-24) lost to **Meghalaya** 155/2 in 27.3 overs (Punit Bisht 95*, Jason Lamare 41*) by eight wickets.

Moti Bagh Stadium, Vadodara, September 21: Arunachal Pradesh 306/4 in 50 overs (Techi Doria 122, Samarth Seth 89; Bhusan Subba 2-47) beat **Sikkim** 257/7 in 50 overs (Nilesh Lamichaney 123, Faizan Khan 47; Techi Neri 2-36, Akhilesh Sahani 2-44) by 49 runs.

GS Patel Stadium, Nadiad, September 21: Meghalaya 246/6 in 50 overs (Raj Biswa 71, Yogesh Nagar 58*) lost to **Nagaland** 247/3 in 47.3 overs (KB Pawan 113*, Sedezhalie Rupero 50) by seven wickets.

Lal Bahadur Shastri Stadium, Anand, September 21: Uttarakhand 291/7 in 50 overs (Karn Kaushal 101, Vaibhav Bhatt 73; Pankaj Singh 3/69, Angadu Narayanan 2-65) beat **Puducherry** 226 in 45.2 overs (Abhishek Nayar 94, AS Govindaraajan 58; Sunny Rana 4/52, Deepak Dhapola 2-49) by 65 runs.

Lal Bahadur Shastri Stadium, Anand, September 23: Arunachal Pradesh v **Manipur**.

Match abandoned without a ball bowled. No toss.

GS Patel Stadium, Nadiad, September 23: Mizoram v **Puducherry**. Match abandoned without a ball bowled. No toss.

Moti Bagh Stadium, Vadodara, September 23: Sikkim 121 in 49 overs (Ashish Thapa 46, Plazor Tamang 22; Ravi Maurya 2-20, Imliwati Lemtur 2-20) lost to **Nagaland** 122/3 in 26.2 overs (KB Pawan 83*) by seven wickets.

Lal Bahadur Shastri Stadium, Anand, September 24: Meghalaya 317/4 in 50 overs (Punit Bisht 135, Yogesh Nagar 56; Techi Doria 2-49) beat **Arunachal Pradesh** 61 (Abhay Negi 7-16, Lakhan Singh 2-21) by 256 runs.

GS Patel Stadium, Nadiad, September 24: Bihar v **Puducherry**. Match abandoned without a ball bowled. No toss.

Moti Bagh Stadium, Vadodara, September 24: Nagaland 206/9 in 50 overs (Abrar Kazi 75*, Rongsen Jonathan 33; Deepak Dhapola 4-34, Mayank Mishra 2-46) lost to **Uttarakhand** 210/4 in 47 overs (Vaibhav Panwar 63, Saurabh Rawat 60*; Pawan Suyal 2-29, Imliwati Lemtur 2-49) by six wickets.

Moti Bagh Stadium, Vadodara, September 26: Bihar 211/9 in 50 overs (Anshuman Gautam 40, Keshav Kumar 33, Ashutosh Aman 33; Gurinder Singh 2-32, Lakhan Singh 2-36) beat **Meghalaya** 103 in 42.5 overs (Yogesh Nagar 22, Gurinder Singh 22; Samar Quadri 5-22, A Aman 3-15) by 108 runs.

GS Patel Stadium, Nadiad, September 26: Manipur 125 in 37.4 overs (Yashpal Singh 76; Sunny Rana 3-27, Malolan Rangarajan 2-10) lost to **Uttarakhand** 127/1 in 26.2 overs (Vineet Saxena 52*, Arya Sethi 50) by nine wickets.

Lal Bahadur Shastri Stadium, Anand, September 26: Mizoram 252/6 in 50 overs (Taruwar Kohli 113, Sinan Khadir 36; Plazor Tamang 3-62) beat **Sikkim** 210 in 47.3 overs (P Tamang 47, Lee Yong Lepcha 42; S Khadir 4-35, Lalnuntluanga 2-27) by 42 runs.

GS Patel Stadium, Nadiad, September 28: Arunachal Pradesh 145 in 45.3 overs (Akhilesh Sahani 44, Samarth Seth 43; Keshav Kumar 5-23, Ashutosh Aman 3-15) lost to **Bihar** 150/5 in 26 overs (Babul Kumar 57, Vikash Ranjan 26; Myendung Singpho 3-50, Techi Neri 2-30) by five wickets.

Lal Bahadur Shastri Stadium, Anand, September 28: Manipur 279/4 in 50 overs (Yashpal Singh 102, Chingangbam Singh 75; Lalnunkima Varte 2-37) beat **Mizoram** 69 in 29.3 overs (Rex Singh 5-17, Kabrambam Meitei 3-32) by 210 runs.

Moti Bagh Stadium, Vadodara, September 28: Nagaland 202 in 45.3 overs (Rongsen Jonathan 89, KB Pawan 46; Abhishek Nayar 4-40, V Marimuthu 2-29) lost to **Puducherry** 203/8 in 45.1 overs (Paras Dogra 98*, D Rohit 32; Abrar Kazi 2-19, Inakato Zhimoni 2-40) by two wickets.

Lal Bahadur Shastri Stadium, Anand, September 30: Bihar 338/6 in 50 overs (MD Rahmatullah 156*, Babul Kumar 92; Bhusan Subba 2-63, Padam Limboo 2-77) beat **Sikkim** 46 in 31 overs (Keshav Kumar 3-7, Anunay Singh 3-12) by 292 runs.

GS Patel Stadium, Nadiad, September 30: Manipur 144 in 43.3 overs (Yashpal Singh 41, Priyojit Singh 35; Abrar Kazi 2-13, Arun Chauhan 2-15, Hokaito Zhimoni 2-15) lost to **Nagaland** 147/1 in 34.2 overs (Sedezhalie Rupero 52*, KB Pawan 50*) by nine wickets.

Moti Bagh Stadium, Vadodara, September 30: Meghalaya 141 in 41.2 overs (Yogesh Nagar 44, Gurinder Singh 34; Vaibhav Panwar 3-9, Deepak Dhapola 2-18) lost to **Uttarakhand** 143/2 in 31 overs (Vineet Saxena 66*, V Panwar 30*; Gurinder 2-34) by eight wickets.

Lal Bahadur Shastri Stadium, Anand, October 2: Arunachal Pradesh 271/4 in 50 overs (Kshitiz Sharma 109, Akhilesh Sahani 102*; Arun Chauhan 2-56) lost to **Nagaland** 272/4 in 44 overs (KB Pawan 112, Hokaito Zhimoni 72*; Sandeep Thakur 3-52) by six wickets.

Moti Bagh Stadium, Vadodara, October 2: Uttarakhand 321 in 50 overs (Karn Kaushal 118, Saurabh Rawat 61; Taruwar Kohli 6-65) beat **Mizoram** 169 in 48.4 overs (Sinan Khadir 73*, Akhil Rajput 23; Vaibhav Panwar 3-38, Deepak Dhapola 2-11) by 152 runs.

GS Patel Stadium, Nadiad, October 2: Sikkim 89 in 43.2 overs (Fabid Ahmed 5-8, AM Narayanan 3-21) lost to **Puducherry** 92/1 in 15.2 overs (D Rohit 38, Narayanan 35) by nine wickets.

Moti Bagh Stadium, Vadodara, October 4: Arunachal Pradesh 95 in 34.1 overs (Samarth Seth 32, Techi Doria 21; Akshay Jain 5-13, Fabid Ahmed 4-8) lost to **Puducherry** 100/3 in 18.2 overs (Abhishek Nayar 65*, AM Narayanan 26; Techi Neri 2-6) by seven wickets.

GS Patel Stadium, Nadiad, October 4: Manipur 172/8 in 50 overs (Yashpal Singh 134*; Rehan Khan 3-39, Anunay Singh 2-24) lost to **Bihar** 176/2 in 29.1 overs (Babul Kumar 100*, MD Rahmatullah 50*) by eight wickets.

Lal Bahadur Shastri Stadium, Anand, October 4: Meghalaya 315/5 in 50 overs (Punit Bisht 149, Jason Lamare 55) beat **Sikkim** 166/9 in 50 overs (Lee Yong Lepcha 36, Bijay Subba 27; Gurinder Singh 4-20, Dipu Sangma 2-14) by 149 runs.

Moti Bagh Stadium, Vadodara, October 6: Meghalaya 238/5 in 50 overs (Yogesh Nagar 67*, Punit Bisht 58; Jitender 3-29) beat **Manipur** 170 in 45.4 overs (Yashpal Singh 106*; Lakhan Singh 3-24, Mark Ingty 2-23) by 68 runs.

Lal Bahadur Shastri Stadium, Anand, October 6: Mizoram 100 in 42.2 overs (Taruwar Kohli 33; Inakato Zhimoni 3-8, Imliwati Lemtur 3-24) lost to **Nagaland** 102/2 in 12.5 overs (Nitesh Lohchab 49*, Paras Sehrawat 26; S Zorinliana 2-21) by eight wickets.

GS Patel Stadium, Nadiad, October 6: Uttarakhand 366/2 in 50 overs (Karn Kaushal 202, Vineet Saxena 100; Mendup Bhutia 2-82) beat **Sikkim** 167/6 in 50 overs (Lee Yong Lepcha 65, Padam Limboo 51*; Deepak Dhapola 3-19, Vijay Jethi 2-15) by 199 runs.

GS Patel Stadium, Nadiad, October 8: Uttarakhand 264 in 49.2 overs (Saurabh Rawat 67, Malolan Rangarajan 50; Sams Alam 2-39, Sandeep Thakur 2-41) beat **Arunachal Pradesh** 156/9 in 50 overs (Akhilesh Sahani 41, Samarth Seth 27; Rajat Bhatia 3-17, M Rangarajan 2-12) by 108 runs.

Moti Bagh Stadium, Vadodara, October 8: Mizoram 83 in 27.2 overs (Akhil Rajput 43; Keshav Kumar 4-21, Ashutosh Aman 3-2) lost to **Bihar** 87/1 in 15.4 overs (Vikash Ranjan 59*) by nine wickets.

Lal Bahadur Shastri Stadium, Anand, October 8: Puducherry 324/5 in 50 overs (Paras Dogra 136*, D Rohit 55; Mark Ingty 2-75) beat **Meghalaya** 250/5 in 50 overs (Yogesh Nagar 109*, Gurinder Singh 72) by five wickets.

Points table

Teams	M	W	L	T	N/R	Pts	NRR
Bihar	8	7	0	0	1	30	+2.724
Uttarakhand	8	7	1	0	0	28	+1.820
Puducherry	8	5	1	0	2	24	+1.727
Nagaland	8	5	3	0	0	20	+0.909
Meghalaya	8	4	4	0	0	16	+0.791
Manipur	8	2	5	0	1	10	-0.197
Arunachal Pradesh	8	2	5	0	1	10	-1.928
Mizoram	8	1	6	0	1	6	-2.467
Sikkim	8	0	8	0	0	0	-3.182

Bihar qualified for the quarter-final

1st quarter-final: Mumbai beat Bihar by nine wickets

Reinstated into the domestic fold after a gap of 15 years, Bihar did well to advance to the knock-out stage after topping the Plate group. The joy, however, was short-lived as they ran into Mumbai, who handed them a crushing defeat. After Mumbai opted to bowl on a track with some carry, Tushar Deshpande ran through the Bihar top order, reducing them to 34 for 4 by the 12th over. No batsman could cross 20 as Deshpande took five.

Just Cricket Academy Ground, Bengaluru, October 14: Bihar 69 in 28.2 overs (Tushar Deshpande 5-23, Shams Mulani 3-18) lost to **Mumbai** 70/1 in 12.3 overs (Rohit Sharma 33*, Akhil Herwadkar 24) by nine wickets. *PoM:* Tushar Deshpande.

2nd quarter-final: Delhi beat Haryana by five wickets

Kulwant Khejroliya set up the win with a six-wicket haul before Gautam Gambhir's century helped Delhi chase down a modest total with 64 balls to spare. Haryana would have rued their decision to bat first after being reduced to 37 for 3 inside 10 overs. Chaitanya Bishnoi, the opener, and Pramod Chandila raised 140 runs for the fourth wicket, but Khejroliya's hat-trick to dismiss both the set batsmen and Amit Mishra, put paid to Haryana's plans of setting a big target. Khejroliya went on to collect 6 for 31, his best List A figures. Gambhir negated Haryana's bowling threat with an aggressive start despite and raised his century off just 69 balls.

M Chinnaswamy Stadium, Bengaluru, October 14: Haryana 229 in 49.1 overs (Chaitanya Bishnoi 85, Pramod Chandila 59; Kulwant Khejroliya 6-31, Navdeep Saini 3-39) lost to **Delhi** 230/6 in 39.2 overs (Gautam Gambhir 104, Dhruv Shorey 50; Rahul Tewatia 3-32) by five wickets. *PoM:* Kulwant Khejroliya.

3rd quarter-final: Jharkhand beat Maharashtra by eight wickets

Maharashtra's innings, after being put in, began with a top-order wobble before a brief consolidation and an implosion. Jharkhand's pacers, Varun Aaron and Rahul Shukla, made early inroads, reducing Maharashtra to 55 for 3. The rebuilding came through Rohit Motwani and Rahul Tripathi's 76-run stand, but once Tripathi fell, the tail fell to Anukul Roy's wily spin. Roy ended with career-best List A returns of 4 for 32. Jharkhand's reply was twice interrupted by rain. The first halt, in the sixth over, reduced the target to 174 in 47 overs. When rain arrived again after the 27th over, the target was further revised to 127 in 34. Requiring 38 in 42 deliveries on resumption, Shasheem Rathour and Saurabh Tiwary knocked off the runs.

M Chinnaswamy Stadium, Bengaluru, October 15: Maharashtra 181 in 42.2 overs (Rohit Motwani 52, Rahul Tripathi 47; Anukul Roy 4-32, Rahul Shukla 3-35) lost to **Jharkhand** 127/2 in 32.2 overs (Shasheem Rathour 53*, Saurabh Tiwary 29*) by eight wickets (VJD method. *PoM:* Anukul Roy.

4th quarter-final: Hyderabad beat Andhra by 14 runs

Andhra's well-controlled chase was spearheaded by Vihari and Ricky Bhui, but Siraj's match-turning second spell sealed the deal. Put in, Hyderabad rode on B Sandeep's 96. He led a late flourish — they scored 34 in the last four — before falling in the final over. Siraj struck early in Andhra's reply, but half-centuries from Vihari and Bhui kept things steady. Siraj returned for his second spell, breaking the 112-run third-wicket stand and triggering a collapse. Andhra's lower order slipped from 207 for 4 to 259 for 9 for a close loss.

Just Cricket Academy Ground, Bengaluru, October 15: Hyderabad 281/8 in 50 overs (B Sandeep 96, Tanmay Agarwal 31; B Ayyappa 2-38, Girinath Reddy 2-62) beat **Andhra** 267/9 in 50 overs (Hanuma Vihari 95, Ricky Bhui 52; Mohammed Siraj 3-50, Ravi Kiran 2-60) by 14 runs. *PoM:* B Sandeep.

1st semi-final: Mumbai beat Hyderabad by 60 runs (VJD method)

Rohit Rayudu's solid century went in vain as Mumbai marched into the final with their ninth consecutive win. Hyderabad's 246 for 8 was built on Rayudu's unbeaten 132-ball 121. After the early loss of their openers, Rayudu and B Sandeep stitched a vital 50-run stand for the third wicket. Mumbai, though, raced to 155 for 2 inside 25 overs, thanks to half-centuries from Prithvi Shaw and Shreyas Iyer. Shaw played a major part in the 73-run opening stand with Rohit Sharma. Once he fell, Iyer took over the responsibility before heavy downpour ended the contest early.

M Chinnaswamy Stadium, Bengaluru, October 17: Hyderabad 246/8 in 50 overs (Rohit Rayudu 121*, B Sandeep 29; Tushar Deshpande 3-55, Royston Dias 2-43) lost to **Mumbai** 155/2 in 25 overs (Prithvi Shaw 61, Shreyas Iyer 55*; Mehdi Hasan 2-23) by 60 runs (VJD method). *PoM:* Tushar Deshpande.

2nd semi-final: Delhi beat Jharkhand by two wickets

Navdeep Saini's four-wicket haul and Pawan Negi's crucial rearguard helped Delhi edge past Jharkhand in a thrilling low-scoring semi-final. Chasing a modest 200, Delhi were cruising at 123 for 4 before Jharkhand's bowlers triggered a collapse. From 133 for 7, Negi shouldered the responsibility and stitched a 51-run stand for the ninth wicket with Saini to script an incredible turnaround. Earlier, Saini and Khejroliya reduced Jharkhand to 74 for 5. Had it not been for Virat Singh's resilient half-century, Jharkhand could have ended with a lot less. The left-hand batsman put together a seventh-wicket stand worth 55 with Shahbaz Nadeem and a ninth-wicket partnership of 44 with Rahul Shukla.

M Chinnaswamy Stadium, Bengaluru, October 18: Jharkhand 199 in 48.5 overs (Virat Singh 71, Anand Singh 36; Navdeep Saini 4-30, Kulwant Khejroliya 2-31) lost to **Delhi** 200/8 in 49.4 overs (Pawan Negi 39*, Nitish Rana 39; Anand 3-39, Shahbaz Nadeem 2-34) by two wickets. *PoM:* Navdeep Saini.

Final: Mumbai beat Delhi by four wickets

Having sleepwalked their way to wins in the league phase, Mumbai proved their batting might with the lower order stepping up in a tricky chase to claim the 50-over silverware after 11 years. Chasing a modest 178, Mumbai found themselves 40 for 4 after Saini's brilliant opening burst. Siddesh Lad and Aditya Tare, though, responded with a 105-run partnership for the fifth wicket. Earlier, Delhi suffered due to lack of partnerships after being put in. Mumbai's four-pronged pace attack, led by Dhawal Kulkarni, did most of the damage. Delhi were tottering at 100 for 6 inside 30 overs, and it wasn't until Himmat Singh and Negi got together that they showed any fight.

M Chinnaswamy Stadium, Bengaluru, October 20: Delhi 177 in 45.4 overs (Himmat Singh 41, Dhruv Shorey 31; Shivam Dube 3-29, Dhawal Kulkarni 3-30) lost to **Mumbai** 180/6 in 35 overs (Aditya Tare 71, Siddhesh Lad 48; Navdeep Saini 3-53) by four wickets. *PoM:* Aditya Tare.

Winners: Mumbai

2017-18

Group A

Just Cricket Academy Ground, Bengaluru, February 7: Karnataka 312/9 in 50 overs (Mayank Agarwal 109, R Samarth 77; Rishi Arothe 4-59, Atit Sheth 2-54) beat **Baroda** 180/8 in 37 overs (Kedar Devdhar 48, Krunal Pandya 39; K Gowtham 4-42, Shreyas Gopal 3-30) by 85 runs (VJD method.)

KSCA Cricket (2) Ground, Alur, February 7: Railways 212 in 47.4 overs (Arindam Ghosh 48, Anureet Singh 41; Abhishek Raut 3-45, Suryakant Pradhan 2-45) lost to **Odisha** 213/8 in 47 overs (Govinda Poddar 64, Biplab Samantray 38; Manjeet Singh 5-25) by two wickets.

KSCA Cricket Ground, Alur, February 7: Punjab 247/9 in 50 overs (Yuvraj Singh 43, Surkeerat Mann 42; Jayant Yadav 2-31, Harshal Patel 2-55) lost to **Haryana** 251/8 in 49.5 overs (Shubham Rohilla 96, Chaitanya Bishnoi 44; Mayank Markande 2-37, Siddarth Kaul 2-51) by two wickets.

Just Cricket Academy Ground, Bengaluru, February 8: Karnataka 303/6 in 50 overs (Mayank Agarwal 84, R Samarth 70*; Abu Nechim 2-51, Mrinmoy Dutta 2-67) beat **Assam** 192 in 47.2overs (Sibsankar Roy 64, A Nechim 43*; Prasidh Krishna 6-33, Shreyas Gopal 2-35) by 111 runs.

KSCA Cricket (2) Ground, Alur, February 8: Baroda 250/9 in 50 overs (Vishnu Solanki 67, Deepak Hooda 46; Amit Mishra 3-57, Jayant Yadav 2-31) beat **Haryana** 199 in 45overs (Shubham Rohilla 61, Jayant 55; Swapnil Singh 3-42, Lukman Meriwala 2-17) by 51 runs.

KSCA Cricket (3) Ground, Alur, February 8: Punjab 225 in 49.5 overs (Gurkeerat Singh 106*, Abhishek Sharma 23; Deepak Behera 3-19, Suryakant Pradhan 2-58) beat **Odisha** 139 in 41 overs (Shesdeep Patra 26, Arabind Singh 22; Barinder Sran 4-22, Manpreet Gony 3-25) by 86 runs.

KSCA Cricket Ground, Alur, February 10: Railways 161 in 43.1 overs (Avinash Yadav 30, Abhishek Yadav 27; Jitumoni Kalita 3-23, Arup Das 3-41) beat **Assam** 126 in 39.3 overs (Amit Sinha 39, Abu Nechim 26; Amit Mishra 5-21, Ankit Yadav 3-24) by 35 runs.

KSCA Cricket (3) Ground, Alur, February 10: Baroda 167/7 in 21 overs (Vishnu Solanki 77*, Swapnil Singh 33; Siddarth Kaul 3-36, Sandeep Sharma 2-25) beat **Punjab** 142 in 20.5 overs (Yuvraj Singh 51; Swapnil 2-4, Rishi Arothe 2-16) by 25 runs.

KSCA Cricket (2) Ground, Alur, February 10: Haryana v **Karnataka**. Match abandoned.

Just Cricket Academy Ground, Bengaluru, February 11: Assam 136 in 46.1 overs (Romario Sharma 49, Amit Sinha 28; Suryakant Pradhan 2-14, Abhishek Raut 2-33) lost to **Odisha**

137/1 in 25.4 overs (Rajesh Dhuper 70*, Govinda Poddar 50*) by nine wickets.

KSCA Cricket Ground, Alur, February 11: Railways 272/7 in 50 overs (Mrunal Devdhar 68, Saurabh Wakaskar 58; Harshal Patel 3-62, Ashish Hooda 2-39) beat **Haryana** 221 in 45.1 overs (Chaitanya Bishnoi 79, Rohit Sharma 50; Ankit Yadav 4-36, Karan Thakur 2-37) by 51 runs.

KSCA Cricket (2) Ground, Alur, February 11: Punjab 269/3 in 42 overs (Shubman Gill 123*, Mandeep Singh 64; Vinay Kumar 2-40) beat **Karnataka** 265/8 in 42 overs (KL Rahul 107, Pavan Deshpande 53; Siddarth Kaul 3-47, Barinder Sran 2-76) by 4 runs.

KSCA Cricket (3) Ground, Alur, February 13: Punjab 275/9 in 50 overs (Manan Vohra 78, Abhishek Gupta 53; Pritam Das 3-54, Arup Das 2-34) beat **Assam** 206 in 41.4 overs (Riyan Parag 59, Gokul Sharma 41; Mayank Markande 3-39, Sandeep Sharma 2-34) by 69 runs

KSCA Cricket (2) Ground, Alur, February 13: Baroda 357/7 in 50 overs (Deepak Hooda 161, Kedar Devdhar 111; Amit Mishra 3-55, Ankit Yadav 2-80) beat **Railways** 165 in 37 overs (Arindam Ghosh 69*, Anureet Singh 29; Rishi Arothe 2-26, Atit Sheth 2-37) by 192 runs

KSCA Cricket Ground, Alur, February 13: Karnataka 353/6 in 50 overs (Mayank Agarwal 102, Karun Nair 100; Debabrata Pradhan 2-69, Deepak Behera 2-76) beat **Odisha** 220 in 41 overs (Anurag Sarangi 58, Rajesh Dhuper 53; J Suchith 5-34, K Gowtham 2-38) by 133 runs

KSCA Cricket (2) Ground, Alur, February 14: Haryana 323/9 in 50 overs (Rajat Paliwal 76, Shubham Rohilla 74; Mrinmoy Dutta 5-67, Mukhtar Hussain 2-65) beat **Assam** 237/6 in 50 overs (Romario Sharma 97*, Sibsankar Roy 40; Harshal Patel 3-51) by 86 runs

KSCA Cricket (3) Ground, Alur, February 14: Baroda 317/6 in 50 overs (Krunal Pandya 84, Swapnil Singh 56; Abhishek Raut 2-70) beat **Odisha** 260 in 46.4 overs (Biplab Samantray 74, Prayash Singh 51; Atit Sheth 2-19, Lukman Meriwala 2-31) by 57 runs

Just Cricket Academy Ground, Bengaluru, February 14: Punjab 280/8 in 50 overs (Manan Vohra 143, Yuvraj Singh 35; Avinash Yadav 2-44, Anureet Singh 2-49) lost to **Railways** 283/6 in 49.4 overs (Arindam Ghosh 89, Mahesh Rawat 56; Mayank Markande 2-35) by four wickets

KSCA Cricket (3) Ground, Alur, February 16: Baroda 378/7 in 50 overs (Aditya Waghmode 148, Kedar Devdhar 61; Riyan Parag 2-35, Mukhtar Hussain 2-85) beat **Assam** 99 in 30 overs (Parvez Aziz 50, Romario Sharma 22; Swapnil Singh 2-0, Deepak Hooda 2-13) by 279 runs

Just Cricket Academy Ground, Bengaluru, February 16: Haryana 170 in 45.4 overs (Sanjay Dhull 72, Harshal Patel 50; Deepak Behera 6-22, Jayanta Behera 2-26) lost to **Odisha** 172/1 in 31.4 overs (Anurag Sarangi 84*, Santani Mishra 53*) by nine wickets

KSCA Cricket Ground, Alur, February 16: Karnataka 257 in 48.1 overs (Mayank Agarwal 89, Pavan Deshpande 65; Anureet Singh 3-36, Amit Mishra 3-45) beat **Railways** 241 in 47.1 overs (Anureet 59, Ankit Yadav 51; Prasidh Krishna 4-35, T Pradeep 4-48) by 16 runs

Points table

Teams	M	W	L	D	T	N/R	Pts.	NRR
Baroda	6	5	1	0	0	0	20	+2.012
Karnataka	6	4	1	0	0	1	18	+1.489
Punjab	6	3	3	0	0	0	12	+0.473
Odisha	6	3	3	0	0	0	12	-0.224
Railways	6	3	3	0	0	0	12	-0.444
Haryana	6	2	3	0	0	1	10	-0.426
Assam	6	0	6	0	0	0	0	-2.401

Baroda and Karnataka qualified for the knock-outs

Group B

Atal Bihari Vajpayee Stadium, Nadaun, February 5: Bengal 293/9 in 50 overs (Abhimanyu Easwaran 103, Manoj Tiwary 80*; Anupam Sanklecha 2-39, Satyajeet Bachhav 2-48) lost to **Maharashtra** 294/3 in 45.5 overs (Rahul Tripathi 125*, Ruturaj Gaikwad 77) by seven wickets.

Lohnu Cricket Ground, Bilaspur, February 5: Delhi 307/6 in 50 overs (Unmukt Chand 116, Hiten Dalal 57; Katik Tyagi 2-50, Ankit Rajpoot 2-61) beat **Uttar Pradesh** 252 in 45.3overs (Umang Sharma 102, Akshdeep Nath 54; Kulwant Khejroliya 4-34, Pradeep Sangwan 3-28) by 55 runs.

HPCA Stadium, Dharamsala, February 5: Tripura 229/9 in 50 overs (Yashpal Singh 113*, Rajat Dey 47; Vinay Galetiya 3-21, Pankaj Jaiswal 3-36, Rsihi Dhawan 3-58) lost to **Himachal Pradesh** 230/4 in 45.2 overs (Amit Kumar 101*, Sumeet Verma 55; Saurabh Das 2-47) by six wickets.

Atal Bihari Vajpayee Stadium, Nadaun, February 7: Kerala 235/6 in 50 overs (Jalaj Saxena 100*, Sanju Samson 34; Manoj Tiwary 2-23, Sayan Ghosh 2-56) tied with **Bengal** 235/8 in 50 overs (M Tiwary 73*, Writtick Chatterjee 35; Sandeep Warrier 2-38, KC Akshay 2-45).

HPCA Stadium, Dharamsala, February 7: Tripura 298/7 in 50 overs (Bishal Ghosh 84, Yashpal Singh 61; Kulwant Khejroliya 2-51, Pradeep Sangwan 2-81) lost to **Delhi** 300/3 in 39.1 overs (Nitish Rana 94*, Hiten Dalal 76; Udiyan Bose 2-40) by seven wickets.

Lohnu Cricket Ground, Bilaspur, February 7: Maharashtra 343/5 in 50 overs (Ankit Bawne 117*, Naushad Shaikh 69; Saurabh Kumar 2-51, Kartik Tyagi 2-78) beat **Uttar Pradesh** 238 in 44.3 overs (Mohammad Saif 49, Mohsin Khan 34; Shamshuzama Kazi 3-38, Satyajeet Bachhav 2-25) by 105 runs.

Lohnu Cricket Ground, Bilaspur, February 9: Uttar Pradesh 329/4 in 50 overs (Akshdeep Nath 103*, Prashant Gupta 60; Aamir Gani 2-59) beat **Bengal** 322 in 49.4 overs (Vivek Singh 147, Anustup Majumdar 51; Ankit Rajpoot 3-51, Kartik Tyagi 2-61) by 7 runs.

HPCA Stadium, Dharamsala, February 9: Maharashtra 246 in 50 overs (Shamshuzama Kazi 59, Vijay Zol 46; Pradeep Sangwan 5-41, Pawan Negi 3-40) lost to **Delhi** 250/2 in 44.1 overs (Dhruv Shorey 103*, Hiten Dalal 87) by eight wickets.

Atal Bihari Vajpayee Stadium, Nadau, February 9: Kerala 271/7 in 50 overs (Sachin Baby 95, Vishnu Vinod 66; Pankaj Jaiswal 3-51) lost to **Himachal Pradesh** 273/9 in 50 overs (Ankit Kaushik 83*, Nikhil Gangta 62; KC Akshay 4-32, KM Asif 3-65) by one wicket

Atal Bihari Vajpayee Stadium, Nadau, February 11: Delhi 282/8 in 50 overs (Unmukt Chand 90, Nitsh Rana 48; B Amit 4-52, Kanishk Seth 2-57) beat **Bengal** 193 in 41 overs (Abhimanyu Easwaran 67, Anustup Majumdar 31; Kulwant Khejroliya 3-30, Suboth Bhati 3-38) by 89 runs.

Lohnu Cricket Ground, Bilaspur, February 11: Uttar Pradesh 189 in 42.1 overs (Saurabh Kumar 44, Rinku Singh 31; Ayush Jamwal 3-23, Vinay Galetiya 3-28) beat **Himachal Pradesh** 146 in 42.3 overs (Nikhil Gangta 39, Ankit Kaushik 21; Kartik Tyagi 3-29, Saurabh 2-20) by 43 runs.

HPCA Stadium, Dharamsala, February 11: Tripura 231/9 in 50 overs (Manisankar Murasingh 61, Rajat Dey 46; MD Nidheesh 3-29, Abhishek Mohan 2-40) beat **Kerala** 234/6 in 45.1 overs (Rohan Prem 52, Mohammed Azharuddeen 47; Neelambuj Vats 3-49) by four wickets.

Atal Bihari Vajpayee Stadium, Nadaun, February 13: Bengal 249 in 33 overs (Vivek Singh 84, Abhishek Raman 76; Abhijit Chakraborty 7-40) beat **Tripura** 140 in 29 overs (Joydeep Banik 51, Manisankar Murasingh 23; Alok Singh 4-36, Pradipta Pramanik 3-25) by 109 runs

HPCA Stadium, Dharamsala, February 13: Delhi 177 in 39.3 overs (Dhruv Shorey 71, Pradeep Sangwan 25; MD Nidheesh 4-41, Fazil Fanoos 2-27) lost to **Kerala** 178/8 in 35.4 overs (Sachin Baby 52, Sanju Samson 29; Navdeep Saini 4-39, Kulwant Khejroliya 3-27) by two wickets

Lohnu Cricket Ground, Bilaspur, February 13: Himachal Pradesh v Maharashtra.
Match abandoned

Atal Bihari Vajpayee Stadium, Nadaun, February 15: Himachal Pradesh 304/5 in 50 overs (Prashant Chopra 150, Amit Kumar 52; Ishant Sharma 2-39) beat **Delhi** 302 in 49.4 overs (Rishabh Pant 135, Nitish Rana 52; Rishi Dhawan 3-38, Pankaj Jaiswal 2-55) by 2 runs

HPCA Stadium, Dharamsala, February 15: Kerala 261/9 in 50 overs (Rohan Prem 66*, Arun Karthik 54; Mohsin Khan 4-43, Saurabh Kumar 2-55) beat **Uttar Pradesh** 141 in 39.2 overs (Mohammad Saif 31, Upendra Yadav 22; Sandeep Warrier 3-32, KC Akshay 3-32) by 120 runs

Lohnu Cricket Ground, Bilaspur, February 15: Tripura 222/7 in 42 overs (Manisankar Murasingh 55, Smit Patel 38; Satyajeet Bachhav 2-17, Pradeep Dadhe 2-50) lost to **Maharashtra** 223/6 in 41.1 overs (Ruturaj Gaikwad 115, Ankit Bawne 51; Abhijit Sarkar 2-40, Abhijit Chakraborty 2-49) by four wickets

HPCA Stadium, Dharamsala, February 17: Himachal Pradesh 266/8 in 50 overs (Priyanshu Khanduri 74, Pankaj Jaiswal 62*; Alok Singh 4-53) lost to **Bengal** 268/4 in 48 overs (Manoj Tiwary 104*, Abhimanyu Easwaran 90; Ayush Jamwal 2-50) by six wickets

Lohnu Cricket Ground, Bilaspur, February 17: Maharashtra 273/8 in 37 overs (Naushad Shaikh 76, Ankit Bawne 43; Abhishek Mohan 2-54, Sandeep Warrier 2-74) beat **Kerala** 175 in 29.2overs (Sanju Samson 46, Arun Karthik 23; Shrikant Mundhe 5-26, Satyajeet Bachhav 2-46) by 98 runs.

Atal Bihari Vajpayee Stadium, Nadaun, February 17: Uttar Pradesh 357/8 in 50 overs (Rinku Singh 91*, Akshdeep Nath 87; Saurabh Das 2-44, Abhijit Sarkar 2-53) beat **Tripura** 296/9 in 50 overs (Yashpal Singh 110, Joydeep Banik 50; Saurabh Kumar 3-52, Shanu Saini 2-49) by 61 runs.

Points table

Teams	M	W	L	D	T	N/R	Pts.	NRR
Maharashtra	6	4	1	0	0	1	18	+0.878
Delhi	6	4	2	0	0	0	16	+0.727
Kerala	6	3	2	0	1	0	14	+0.288
Himachal Pradesh	6	3	2	0	0	1	14	-0.108
Uttar Pradesh	6	3	3	0	0	0	12	-0.563
Bengal	6	2	3	0	1	0	10	+0.007
Tripura	6	0	6	0	0	0	0	-1.127

Maharashtra and Delhi qualified for the knock-outs

Group C

Sri Sivasubramaniya Nadar College of Engineering Ground, Chennai, February 5: Rajasthan 229/6 in 50 overs (Chetan Bist 82*, Salman Khan 58 rtd.hrt; B Ayyappa 3-57) lost to **Andhra** 235/4 in 45 overs (B Sumanth 71*, Hanuma Vihari 49) by six wickets.

MRF Pachyappas Ground, Chennai, February 5: Tamil Nadu 318/8 in 50 overs (Kaushik Gandhi 127, Vijay Shankar 100; Chintan Gaja 3-61, Rohit Dahiya 2-46) beat **Gujarat** 235 in 45.1 overs (Bhargav Merai 101, Priyank Panchal 42; Aswin Crist 3-44, Washington Sundar 2-35) by 76 runs.

MA Chidambaram Stadium, Chennai, February 5: Mumbai 311/5 in 50 overs (Suryakumar Yadav 134*, Jay Bista 90; Avesh Khan 2-62) beat **Madhya Pradesh** 258 in 46.1 overs

(Anshul Tripathi 67, Puneet Datey 43; Shams Mulani 4-62, Dhrumil Matkar 3-50) by 74 runs.

MRF Pachyappas Ground, Chennai, February 6: Madhya Pradesh 184 in 44.2 overs (Anshul Tripathi 39, Rajat Patidar 34; Girinath Reddy 6-24) lost to **Andhra** 190/4 in 38.5 overs (Hanuma Vihari 61, Ashwin Hebbar 42; Puneet Datey 2-26) by six wickets.

MA Chidambaram Stadium, Chennai, February 6: Tamil Nadu 210 in 48.5 overs (Baba Aparajith 52, M Vijay 51; Darshan Misal 3-42, Srinivas Fadte 3-51) lost to **Goa** 211/6 in 46.2 overs (Swapnil Asnodkar 103, Sagun Kamat 38; R Ashwin 2-30) by four wickets.

Sri Sivasubramaniya Nadar College of Engineering Ground, Chennai, February 6: Mumbai 317/8 in 50 overs (Siddhesh Lad 129, Aditya Tare 51; Ishwar Chaudhary 3-46, Piyush Chawla 2-69) beat **Gujarat** 276 in 47.4 overs (Priyank Panchal 89, Bhargav Merai 64; Royston Dias 4-64, Dhawal Kulkarni 2-29) by 41 runs

MRF Pachyappas Ground, Chennai, February 8: Rajasthan 266/8 in 50 overs (Chandrapal Singh 71*, Aditya Garhwal 40; Amogh Desai 4-41, Darshan Misal 2-43) lost to **Goa** 267/7 in 49.5 overs (D Misal 66*, Suyash Prabhudessai 59; Abhimanyu Lamba 2-50) by three wickets.

TI Cycles Ground, Murugappa, Chennai, February 8: Gujarat 248 in 49.4 overs (Priyank Panchal 65, Rujul Bhatt 56; Anshul Tripathi 4-37, Rameez Khan 2-38) lost to **Madhya Pradesh** 253/6 in 45 overs (Harpreet Singh 76, Rameez 75; Piyush Chawla 3-54, Chintan Gaja 2-47) by four wickets.

Sri Sivasubramaniya Nadar College of Engineering Ground, Chennai, February 8: Tamil Nadu 183 in 49.3 overs (R Ashwin 41, N Jagadeesan 31; Dhawal Kulkarni 3-44, Shubham Ranjane 2-28) lost to **Mumbai** 184/8 in 48.5 overs (S Ranjane 59*, Shivam Dubey 28; Ashwin 3-35, K Vignesh 2-32) by two wickets.

MA Chidambaram Stadium, Chennai, February 9: Goa 188 in 47.4 overs (Snehal Kauthankar 43, Suyash Prabhudessai 38; Girinath Reddy 4-32, Hanuma Vihari 2-18) lost to **Andhra** 191/9 in 49.3 overs (Ricky Bhui 56*, KS Bharat 30; Lakshay Garg 3-32, Vijesh Prabhudessai 3-43) by one wicket

MRF Pachyappas Ground, Chennai, February 9: Tamil Nadu 302/9 in 50 overs (N Jagadeesan 99, Vijay Shankar 84; Ankit Kushwah 3-59, Ishwar Pandey 2-53) lost to **Madhya Pradesh** 303/2 in 46 overs (Rajat Patidar 158, Rameez Khan 78*) by eight wickets

TI Cycles Ground, Murugappa, Chennai, February 9: Mumbai 268/8 in 50 overs (Siddhesh Lad 100, Prithvi Shaw 52; Khaleel Ahmed 4-35, Chandrapal Singh 2-61) lost to **Rajasthan** 272/4 in 47.3 overs (Amitkumar Gautam 149*, Mahipal Lomror 81; Shivam Dubey 2-36) by six wickets

TI Cycles Ground, Murugappa, Chennai, February 11: Andhra 276/6 in 50 overs (KS Bharat 82, B Sumanth 62*; Rahil Shah 2-39) beat **Tamil Nadu** 247 in 48.5 overs (J Kousik 56, Kaushik Gandhi 44; B Ayyappa 2-37, Hanuma Vihari 2-41) by 29 runs.

India Cement Limited Guru Nanak College Ground, Chennai, February 11: Goa 220 in 48.3 overs (Swapnil Asnodkar 85, Amogh Desai 39; Sohraab Dhaliwal 3-33, Anshul Tripathi 3-40) lost to **Madhya Pradesh** 223/2 in 25.4 overs (Rajat Patidar 124*, Naman Ojha 50) by eight wickets

Sri Sivasubramaniya Nadar College of Engineering Ground, Chennai, February 11: Rajasthan 172 in 47.3 overs (Mahipal Lomror 63, Yash Kothari 29; Piyush Chawla 3-44, Santosh Shinde 2-20) lost to **Gujarat** 176/3 in 33.2 overs (Priyank Panchal 55, Bhargav Merai 41*) by seven wickets

TI Cycles Ground, Murugappa, Chennai, February 12: Gujarat 250 in 50 overs (Rujul Bhatt 74, Piyush Chawla 56; Karthik Raman 4-32, Naren Reddy 2-35) lost to **Andhra** 251/1 in 45.2 overs (KS Bharat 106*, Ashwin Hebbar 99) by nine wickets

Sri Sivasubramaniya Nadar College of Engineering Ground, Chennai, February 12: Goa 266/8 in 50 overs (Suyash Prabhudessai 56, Swapnil Asnodkar 56; Dhrumil Matkar 3-49, Shubham Ranjane 2-39) lost to **Mumbai** 267/6 in 46.3 overs (Suryakumar Yadav 71, Aditya Tare 59; Lakshay Garg 3-52) by four wickets

MA Chidambaram Stadium, Chennai, February 12: Madhya Pradesh 241/9 in 50 overs

(Ankit Sharma 65, Harpreet Singh 55; Khaleel Ahmed 3-51, Mahipal Lomror 2-15) lost to **Rajasthan** 245/3 in 47.2 overs (Aditya Garhwal 108, Amitkumar Gautam 62) by seven wickets
TI Cycles Ground, Murugappa, Chennai, February 14: Andhra 344/5 in 50 overs (Hanuma Vihari 169, KS Bharat 105; Royston Dias 3-77, Dhrumil Matkar 2-60) beat **Mumbai** 315/9 in 50 overs (Siddhesh Lad 118, Shivam Dubey 36; Karthik Raman 3-55, S Ashish 2-51) by 29 runs
Sri Sivasubramaniya Nadar College of Engineering Ground, Chennai, February 14: Gujarat 227 in 49.4 overs (Bhargav Merai 93, Santosh Shinde 27; Darshan Misal 3-36, Amogh Desai 2-28) lost to **Goa** 228/9 in 48.3 overs (Sagun Kamat 110*, Snehal Kauthankar 28; Piyush Chawla 3-27, Kathan Patel 3-42) by one wicket
MA Chidambaram Stadium, Chennai, February 14: Rajasthan 141 in 38.2 overs (Chetan Bist 36, Arjit Gupta 27; R Sai Kishore 5-26, J Kousik 2-12) lost to **Tamil Nadu** 143/3 in 23.3 overs (Baba Aparajith 55*, N Jagadessan 39) by seven wickets

Points table

Teams	M	W	L	D	T	N/R	Pts.	NRR
Andhra	6	6	0	0	0	0	24	+0.626
Mumbai	6	4	2	0	0	0	16	+0.324
Madhya Pradesh	6	3	3	0	0	0	12	+0.112
Goa	6	3	3	0	0	0	12	-0.411
Tamil Nadu	6	2	4	0	0	0	8	+0.468
Rajasthan	6	2	4	0	0	0	8	-0.791
Gujarat	6	1	5	0	0	0	4	-0.321

Andhra and Mumbai qualified for the knock-outs
Group D

Gymkhana Ground, Secunderabad, February 5: Saurashtra 286/7 in 50 overs (Sheldon Jackson 106, Cheteshwar Pujara 60; Pankaj Rao 2-46, Shahnawaz Hussain 2-62) beat **Chhattisgarh** 254/9 in 50 overs (Manoj Singh 58, Vishal Kushwah 51; Dharmendrasinh Jadeja 4-41, Shaurya Sanandia 3-53) by 32 runs.
Rajiv Gandhi International Stadium, Hyderabad, February 5: Hyderabad 329/5 in 50 overs (Akshath Reddy 127, K Sumanth 56*; Raushan Raj 2-57) beat **Services** 201 in 40.4 overs (Rahul Singh 64, Hardik Sethi 38; Mohammed Siraj 5-45, Rohit Rayudu 2-11) by 128 runs.
AOC Centre Thapar Stadium, Secunderabad, February 5: Vidarbha 300 in 49 (Jitesh Sharma 79, Sanjay Ramaswamy 77; Rahul Shukla 4-52, Atul Surwar 2-52) beat **Jharkhand** 293/7 in 50 overs (Saurabh Tiwary 65, Kumar Deobrat 60; Yash Thakur 2-45, Rajneesh Gurbani 2-52) by 7 runs.
Gymkhana Ground, Secunderabad, February 6: Services 219 in 44.5 overs (Rahul Singh 91, Nakul Varma 42; Shahnawaz Hussain 6-44, Vishal Kushwah 2-37) lost to **Chhattisgarh** 221/6 in 48.4 overs (Shashank Chandraker 70, Sahban Khan 52*; Arun Bamal 2-26, Diwesh Pathania 2-43) by four wickets.
Rajiv Gandhi International Stadium, Hyderabad, February 6: Hyderabad 333/7 in 50 overs (Rohit Rayudu 126, Akshath Reddy 75; Rahul Shukla 2-69) beat **Jharkhand** 267 in 46.5 overs (Atul Surwar 58*, Ishan Kishan 51; Ravi Kiran 2-41, Mohammed Siraj 2-51) by 66 runs
AOC Centre Thapar Stadium, Secunderabad, February 6: Vidarbha 245 in 48.2 overs (Ganesh Satish 94, Jitesh Sharma 41; Umar Nazir Mir 3-41, Ram Dayal 2-43) beat **Jammu & Kashmir** 172 in 38.4 overs (R Dayal 55, Bandeep Singh 53; Shrikant Wagh 3-26, Umesh

Yadav 2-30) by 73 runs

Rajiv Gandhi International Stadium, Hyderabad, February 8: Vidarbha 350/7 in 50 overs (Faiz Fazal 103, Ravi Jangid 81; Ravi Teja 2-53) beat **Hyderabad** 113 in 34.2 overs (K Sumanth 30, Ambati Rayudu 21; Karn Sharma 3-38, Shrikant Wagh 2-20) by 237 runs

Gymkhana Ground, Secunderabad, February 8: Saurashtra 267/6 in 50 overs (Aarpit Vasavada 85*, Prerak Mankad 67; Waseem Raza 2-45) lost to **Jammu & Kashmir** 269/4 in 49 overs (Parvez Rasool 67*, Ahmed Bandy 65; Kamlesh Makvana 3-36) by six wickets.

AOC Centre Thapar Stadium, Secunderabad, February 8: Services 202/9 in 50 overs (Hardik Sethi 66, Diwesh Pathania 43; Varun Aaron 3-20, Anukul Roy 2-26) lost to **Jharkhand** 203/5 in 30.5 overs (Ishan Kishan 106, Saurabh Tiwary 56*; Vikas Yadav 2-23) by five wickets.

AOC Centre Thapar Stadium, Secunderabad, February 9: Chhattisgarh 251/8 in 50 overs (Shashank Chandraker 59, Vishal Kushwah 48; Ram Dayal 3-35, Umar Nazir Mir 3-55) beat **Jammu & Kashmir** 246 in 49.3 overs (Ahmed Bandy 75, Parvez Rasool 44; Pankaj Rao 3-44, Shivendra Singh 3-46) by 5 runs

Rajiv Gandhi International Stadium, Hyderabad, February 9: Saurashtra 277/7 in 50 overs (Prerak Mankad 62, Samarth Vyas 57; Mohammed Siraj 3-46) lost to **Hyderabad** 278/6 in 49.3 overs (Akshath Reddy 94, Ambati Rayudu 76; Shaurya Sanandia 2-41, Dharmendrasinh Jadeja 2-49) by four wickets

Gymkhana Ground, Secunderabad, February 9: Vidarbha 267/9 in 50 overs (Apoorv Wankhade 73, Karn Sharma 54; Raushan Raj 3-49, Hardik Sethi 2-28) beat **Services** 250/9 in 50 overs (Diwesh Pathania 100*, Soumik Chatterjee 54; Rajneesh Gurbani 2-47, Karn 2-50) by 17 runs

Rajiv Gandhi International Stadium, Hyderabad, February 11: Chhattisgarh 284/8 in 50 overs (Amandeep Khare 65, Vishal Kushwah 61; Shrikant Wagh 3-58, Rajneesh Gurbani 2-43) beat **Vidarbha** 239 in 46.1 overs (Akshay Karnewar 60, Faiz Fazal 53; V Kushwah 4-54, Shahnawaz Hussain 3-41) by 45 runs.

AOC Centre Thapar Stadium, Secunderabad, February 11: Services 296/6 in 50 overs (Nakul Verma 125, Rahul Singh 71; Abhishek Bhat 2-66) lost to **Jammu & Kashmir** 297/5 in 49 overs (Shubham Khajuria 102, Ahmed Bandy 94; Arun Bamal 2-44) by five wickets.

Gymkhana Ground, Secunderabad, February 11: Jharkhand 329/9 in 50 overs (Ishan Kishan 93, Sumit Kumar 64; Chirag Jani 2-59, Shaurya Sanandia 2-59) lost to **Saurashtra** 333/6 in 48.2 overs (Ravindra Jadeja 113*, C Jani 59; Ashish Kumar 2-64) by four wickets

Gymkhana Ground, Secunderabad, February 12: Jharkhand 288/9 in 50 overs (Saurabh Tiwary 107, Kumar Deobrat 51; Pankaj Rao 4-43, Sumit Ruikar 2-67) lost to **Chhattisgarh** 294/3 in 46 overs (Amandeep Khare 76, Shashank Chandraker 61; Varun Aaron 2-51) by seven wickets

Rajiv Gandhi International Stadium, Hyderabad, February 12: Hyderabad 312 in 50 overs (Rohit Rayudu 130, B Sandeep 72; Umar Nazir 5-52) beat **Jammu & Kashmir** 163 in 34.1 overs (Puneet Kumar 43, Shubham Kajuria 35; Akash Bhandari 3-34, Ravi Kiran 2-17) by 149 runs.

AOC Centre Thapar Stadium, Secunderabad, February 12: Services 176 in 48.2 overs (Soumik Chatterjee 52, Hardik Sethi 33; Dharmendrasinh Jadeja 4-26, Jaydev Unadkat 2-23) lost to **Saurashtra** 181/2 in 21.4 overs (Samarth Vyas 114*, Cheteshwar Pujara 45*) by eight wickets

Gymkhana Ground, Secunderabad, February 14: Hyderabad 280/8 in 50 overs (B Sandeep 79, Ambati Rayudu 46; Pankaj Rao 3-52, Shahnawaz Hussain 2-53) beat **Chhattisgarh** 196 in 44.3 overs (Amandeep Khare 71, Sanjeet Desai 47; Mohammed Siraj 5-37, Mehdi Hasan 2-28) by 84 runs

Rajiv Gandhi International Stadium, Hyderabad, February 14: Jharkhand 296/9 in 50 overs (Virat Singh 96, Sumit Kumar 35; Parvez Rasool 3-46, Umar Nazir 3-71) beat **Jammu & Kashmir** 199 in 46 overs (Shubham Pundir 74, Shubham Khajuria 20; Ashish Kumar 3-23,

Vikash Singh 3-37) by 97 runs

AOC Centre Thapar Stadium, Secunderabad, February 14: Vidarbha 159 in 40.5 overs
(Jitesh Sharma 55, Sanjay Ramaswamy 29; Kamlesh Makvana 2-9, Jaydev Unadkat 2-18) lost
to **Saurashtra** 161/2 in 34 overs (Avi Barot 91*, Cheteshwar Pujara 46*) by eight wickets

Points table

Teams	M	W	L	D	T	N/R	Pts.	NRR
Hyderabad	6	5	1	0	0	0	20	+0.646
Saurashtra	6	4	2	0	0	0	16	+1.017
Vidarbha	6	4	2	0	0	0	16	+0.718
Chhattisgarh	6	4	2	0	0	0	16	-0.103
Jharkhand	6	2	4	0	0	0	8	+0.325
Jammu & Kashmir	6	2	4	0	0	0	8	-1.040
Services	6	0	6	0	0	0	0	-1.508

Hyderabad and Saurashtra qualified for the knock-outs

Quarter-finals

Feroz Shah Kotla, Delhi, February 21: Karnataka 347/8 in 50 overs (Mayank Agarwal
140, R Samarth 125; Mohammed Siraj 5-59, Ravi Kiran 2-61) beat **Hyderbad** 244 in 42.5
overs (Ambati Rayudu 64, Ravi Teja 53; Sheyas Gopal 5-31, Stuart Binny 3-45) by 103 runs.
Palam A Stadium, Delhi, February 21: Mumbai 222/9 in 50 overs (Suryakumar Yadav 69,
Shreyas Iyer 35; Pradeep Dadhe 3-57, Prashant Kore 2-34) lost to **Maharashtra** 224/3 in 46.5
overs (Shrikant Mundhe 70, Naushad Shaikh 51*) by seven wickets.
Feroz Shah Kotla, Delhi, February 22: Baroda 247/8 in 50 overs (Soaeb Tai 72*, Krunal
Pandya 61; Chirag Jani 4-35, Prerak Mankad 2-29) lost to **Saurashtra** 251/7 in 48.4 overs (Avi
Barot 82, Aarpit Vasavada 45*; Atit Sheth 3-38) by three wickets.
Palam A Stadium, Delhi, February 22: Delhi 111 in 32.1 overs (Rishabh Pant 38, Dhruv
Shorey 21; D Siva Kumar 4-29, Bhargav Bhatt 3-28) lost to **Andhra** 112/4 in 28.4 overs
(Ashwin Hebbar 38, Ricky Bhui 36) by six wickets.

Karnataka, Maharashtra, Saurashtra, Andhra qualified for semi-finals

1st semi-final: Karnataka beat Maharashtra by nine wickets

A combined effort with the ball, followed by fifties from Agarwal and
Nair helped Karnataka thump Maharashtra. Shrikant Mundhe and Naushad
Shaikh were the only two batsmen from Maharashtra to come up with a decent contribution. K Gowtham was the pick of the bowlers, while Prasidh,
Pradeep T, Stuart Binny and Shreyas Gopal chipped in. Chasing 161, Agarwal stretched his dream season and added 155 runs for the opening wicket
with Nair.

Feroz Shah Kotla, Delhi, February 24: Maharashtra 160 ni 44.3 overs (Shrikant Mundhe
50, Naushad Shaikh 42; K Gowtham 3-26, Prasidh Krishna 2-26) lost to **Karnataka** 164/1 in
30.3 overs (Mayank Agarwal 81, Karun Nair 70*) by nine wickets.

2nd semi-final: Saurashtra beat Andhra by 59 runs

The two Jadejas put an end to Andhra's unbeaten run. Sent in, the Cheteshwar Pujara-led Saurashtra recovered from 69 for 4 to post 255 in 49.1 overs. In response, Andhra wilted against Dharmendrasinh Jadeja. The Saurashtra recovery was because of a 113-run partnership between Ravindra Jadeja and Arpit Vasavada. Prerak Mankad too chipped in with a quick-fire 28-ball 40. Regular wickets never allowed Andhra to settle into a rhythm. S Bharat, Vihari, Bodapati Sumanth and Ravi Teja got starts but none of them could convert it into anything significant.

Feroz Shah Kotla, Delhi, February 25: Saurashtra 255 in 49.1 overs (Arpit Vasavada 58, Ravindra Jadeja 56; Karthik Raman 4-69, D Siva Kumar 2-19) beat **Andhra** 196 in 45.3 overs (DB Ravi Teja 42, B Sumanth 42; Dharmendrasinh Jadeja 4-40, Shaurya Sanandia 2-40) by 59 runs.

Karnataka and Saurashtra qualified for the final

Final: Karnataka beat Saurashtra by 41 runs

Karnataka coasted to their third Vijay Hazare title in five years as Agarwal continued his red-hot form, scoring a 79-ball 90. No Saurashtra batsman apart from captain Pujara managed more than 30.

Although Nair and Rahul were being dismissed for nought after being put in, Agarwal powered through, putting on 136 with R Samarth (48). Pavan Deshpande and Shreyas Gopal (31) also made strong contributions, even as off-spinner Kamlesh Makvana ran through the tail.

Saurashtra's chase never really took off. Avi Barot kept them going after they were reduced to 15/2, and Pujara made a 127-ball 94, but they got little support.

Feroz Shah Kotla, Delhi, February 27: Karnataka 253 in 45.5 overs (Mayank Agarwal 90, Pavan Deshpande 49; Kamlesh Makvana 4-34, Prerak Mankad 2-54) beat **Saurashtra** 212 in 46.3 overs (Cheteshwar Pujara 94, Avi Barot 30; K Gowtham 3-27, Prasidh Krishna 3-37) by 41 runs

Winners: Karnataka

Deodhar Trophy

Fiery Kishan, Gill entertain

In a tournament tweaked to serve as the best talent audition for the World Cup, the Ajinkya Rahane-led India C beat India B by 29 runs to clinch the Deodhar Trophy.

Usually, the competition would also include the winner of the Vijay Hazare Trophy. But with the World Cup just over seven months away, this edition was held between three teams India A, India B and India C to firm up the set of probables likely to travel to England.

In the final at the Feroz Shah Kotla, Rahane and Ishan Kishan scored centuries, as Shreyas Iyer's effort went in vain.

India B's road to the final was orchestrated by Hanuma Vihari, who struck back-to-back half-centuries in the first two matches. In the opening fixture, his unbeaten 87 and the spin duo of Shahbaz Nadeem and Mayank Markande ensured India A — despite fifties from Dinesh Karthik and R Ashwin — were 43 runs short of the 262-run target. In the next one, Vihari shone again, lifting the side from a precarious 90 for 5 to 231 for 9, as India B trumped India A by six wickets.

In the virtual semi-final, Shubman Gill mounted the first successful chase of the tournament, and sealed a berth in the final with his unbeaten 106 off 111. Abhimanyu Easwaran, Anmolpreet Singh and Nitish Rana struck half-centuries for India A after opting to bat, but their efforts were nullified by Gill's ton, and Suryakumar Yadav and Ishan Kishan's half-centuries. Having lost Rahane and Suresh Raina, India were wobbling at 85 for 3, but Gill and Kishan guided the chase with a 121-run stand, while Yadav applied the finishing touches.

The previous **2017-18** season, Karnataka had an all-win record coming into the final. The Iyer-led India B didn't just put an end to that run, they also avenged the six-run loss from the group phase. R Samarth's second century went in a losing cause.

	Most runs	Most wickets
2017-18	R Samarth (Karnataka) (309 runs, 3 matches)	S Gopal (Karnataka) (7 wickets, 3 matches)
2018-19	Shreyas Iyer (India B) (199 runs, 3 matches)	Vijay Shankar (India C) (7 wickets, 3 matches)

2018-19

Feroz Shah Kotla, Delhi, October 23: India B 261/8 in 50 overs (Hanuma Vihari 87*, Manoj Tiwary 52; R Ashwin 2-39) beat **India A** 218 in 46.4 overs (Dinesh Karthik 99, Ashwin 54; Mayank Markande 4-48, Shahbaz Nadeem 3-32) by 43 runs. *PoM:* Shahbaz Nadeem.

Shubman Gill, whose star had grown since the U19 World Cup, starred with a century in the Deodhar Trophy semi-final. — *ICC*

Feroz Shah Kotla, Delhi, October 24: India B 231/9 in 50 overs (Hanuma Vihari 76, Ankush Bains 25; Rajneesh Gurbani 3-38, Pappu Roy 3-45) beat **India C** 201 in 48.2 overs (Suryakumar Yadav 39, Shubman Gill 36; K Gowtham 3-40, Manoj Tiwary 3-44) by 30 runs. *PoM:* Hanuma Vihari.

Feroz Shah Kotla, Delhi, October 25: India A 293/6 in 50 overs (Abhimanyu Easwaran 69, Nitish Rana 68; Vijay Shankar 3-40, Rahul Chahar 2-79) lost to **India C** 296/4 in 47 overs (Shubman Gill 106*, Ishan Kishan 69) by six wickets. *PoM:* Shubman Gill.

Points table

Teams	M	W	L	D	T	N/R	Pts.	NRR
India B	2	2	0	0	0	0	8	+0.730
India C	2	1	1	0	0	0	4	-0.116
India A	2	0	2	0	0	0	0	-0.632

India B and India C qualified for the final

Final: India C beat India B by 29 runs

Opting to bat first in the final at the Feroz Shah Kotla, Rahane and Ishan Kishan scored centuries in a first-wicket partnership of 210. The young Kishan overcame a slow start on a difficult pitch — he was 6 off 31 balls — to cut loose and bring up his hundred in 76 balls. Suryakumar Yadav smashed an 18-ball 39 down the order and the 15 sixes in the innings lifted India C to an imposing 352 for 7. Shreyas Iyer led from the front in the chase, smashing 148 off 114 balls, but the India C pacers struck regularly to bowl India B for 323 in 46.1 overs.

Feroz Shah Kotla, Delhi, October 27: India C 352/7 in 50 overs (Ajinkya Rahane 144*, Ishan Kishan 114; Jaydev Unadkat 3-52, Mayank Markande 2-70) beat **India B** 323 in 46.1 overs (Shreyas Iyer 148, Ruturaj Gaikwad 60; Pappu Roy 3-75, Navdeep Saini 2-47) by 29 runs. *PoM:* Ajinkya Rahane.

2017-18

HPCA Stadium, Dharamsala, March 4: India A 178 in 41.2 overs (Ricky Bhui 78, Prithvi Shaw 28; Dharmendrasinh Jadeja 4-36, Jayant Yadav 2-25) lost to **India B** 175/2 in 26.2 overs (Hanuma Vihari 95*, Abhimanyu Easwaran 43) by eight wickets (VJD Method). *MoM:* Dharmendrasinh Jadeja.

HPCA Stadium, Dharamsala, March 5: Karnataka 296/8 in 50 overs (R Samarth 117, Pavan Deshpande 46; Siddarth Kaul 3-49, Jayant Yadav 2-48) beat **India B** 290/9 in 50 overs (Manoj Tiwary 120, Siddhesh Lad 70; Shreyas Gopal 3-29, Prasidh Krishna 2-45) by 6 runs. *MoM:* R Samarth.

HPCA Stadium, Dharamsala, March 6: Karnataka 339/4 in 50 overs (Pavan Deshpande 95, R Samarth 85; Mohammed Shami 2-96) beat **India A** 274 in 39.5 overs (Unmukt Chand 81, Ishan Kishan 73; K Gowtham 4-52, Ronit More 3-64) by 65 runs. *MoM:* Pavan Deshpande.

Points table

Teams	M	W	L	T	N/R	Pts.	NRR
Karnataka	2	2	0	0	0	8	0.710
India B	2	1	1	0	0	4	1.038
India A	2	0	2	0	0	0	-1.916

Karnataka and India B qualified for the final

Final: India B beat Karnataka by six wickets

R Samarth scored another superb century but it was overshadowed by an imposing batting effort from India B. Karnataka got off to a terrible start when Mayank Agarwal was run out in unfortunate circumstances in the sixth over and Karun Nair, Pavan Deshpande and Stuart Binny fell to pacers. From 64 for 4, Samarth and CM Gautam added 132 runs for the fifth wicket to bring their team back on the path. Chasing a decent total, Ruturaj Gaikwad, Abhimanyu Easwaran, Shreyas Iyer and Manoj Tiwary all made attractive half-centuries. Playing his first match of the tournament, Gaikwad scored freely. The batsmen played out the spinners and went after the quick bowlers. Tiwary fittingly hit Binny for a boundary and sealed the deal.

HPCA Stadium, Dharamsala, March 8: Karnataka 279/8 in 50 overs (R Samarth 107, CM Gautam 76; Khaleel Ahmed 3-49, Umesh Yadav 2-48) lost to **India B** 281/4 in 48.2 overs (Abhimanyu Easwaran 69, Manoj Tiwary 59*; Shreyas Gopal 2-55) by six wickets. *MoM:* R Samarth.

Winner: India B

Ranji Trophy

Vidarbha triumph in expanded field

Elite Group A

Vidarbha

Vidarbha hadn't even reached the semi-finals of the Ranji Trophy in their past 60 attempts. Chandrakant Pandit, the former India wicketkeeper and Mumbai stalwart, changed that: he first masterminded a coup and then ensured they became only the sixth team ever to defend their title.

Pandit's bloody-mindedness and disciplinarian methods with a young and hungry bunch devoid of egos proved the perfect marriage, even as the senior-most players did their bit. Wasim Jaffer, the all-time highest run-getter in the tournament, hit the winning runs in their victory, and then went on to become the first player to accumulate 1000 runs in two Ranji seasons (he had done so for Mumbai a decade ago). Captain Faiz Fazal prevented a collapse in the semis on a tricky pitch while the heroes of the two finals were Rajneesh Gurbani, who gave up a corporate career after a Civil Engineering degree to bowl on flat Nagpur decks, and Aditya Sarwate, the left-arm spinning all-rounder, who took six second-innings wickets and 11 for the match. Sarwate finished the season as the third-highest wicket-taker with a remarkable average of 19.67 in 11 games and pitched in with handy lower-order runs.

Results: Conceded first-innings lead to Karnataka, took first-innings lead against Baroda, beat Chhattisgarh by ten wickets, beat Railways by 118 runs, took first-innings lead against Gujarat, beat Mumbai by an innings and 145 runs, conceded first-innings lead to Saurashtra, beat Uttarakhand by an innings and 115 runs (quarter-final), beat Kerala by an innings and 11 runs (semi-final), beat Saurashtra by 78 runs.

Most runs: Wasim Jaffer (1037 runs, 11 matches)

Most wickets: Aditya Sarwate (55 wickets, 11 matches)

Akshay Wakhare and captain Faiz Fazal with the coveted trophy. — *VCA*

Saurashtra

The previous season, they had started like a super-sonic jet, but sputtered towards the end like an autorickshaw out of gas. This time they began with purpose, but their path to the final wasn't easy. They went into the knock-outs undefeated — although they were lucky to get away without a defeat to Gujarat. But then they had to dig deep to pull off fourth-innings chases after falling behind to Uttar Pradesh in the quarter-final — for a record chase — and Karnataka in the semis.

Sheldon Jackson propped up the batting until the arrival of Cheteshwar Pujara — straight from the airport, bags in tow, after winning the series for India in Australia. Dharmendrasinh Jadeja's left-arm spin made him the highest wicket-taker in the elite groups, while Jaydev Unadkat, leading the team after Jaydev Shah stepped down, found his rhythm. The team put up a spirited fight, but still fell to their third defeat in a row in Ranji finals.

Results: Beat Railways by three wickets, took first-innings lead against Gujrat, conceded first-innings lead to Baroda, beat Karnataka by 87 runs, beat Maharashtra by five wickets, conceded first-innings lead to Mumbai, took first-innings lead against Vidarbha, beat Uttar Pradesh by six wickets (quarter-final), beat Karnataka by five wickets (semi-final), lost to Vidarbha by 78 runs (final).
Most runs: Sheldon Jackson (854 runs, 11 matches)
Most wickets: Dharmendrasinh Jadeja (59 wickets, 11 matches)

Karnataka

Karnataka fans are unlikely to forgive Cheteshwar Pujara anytime soon for not walking despite an edge in the semi-final. Pujara scored an unbeaten hundred to help Saurashtra chase 279 and knock Karnataka out. It was Karnataka's third defeat in the tournament, two of which came against Saurashtra. The defeat was somewhat unexpected, for at that point Karnataka, having won just one of their first five matches, had peaked at the right time by winning three of the next four.

Shreyas Gopal was Karnataka's star of the season, playing all ten matches with returns of 524 runs and 32 wickets. Contributions came from all corners throughout the tournament, though few were as impressive than that valiant spell from R Vinay Kumar in the semi-final. It was a continuation of their good work from the previous season, when under new coaching staff and driven by a prolific Mayank Agarwal, they barely did anything wrong on their way to the semi-final.

Results: Took first-innings lead against Vidarbha, took first-innings lead against Mumbai, beat Maharashtra by seven wickets, lost to Saurashtra by 87 runs, took first-innings lead against Gujarat, beat Railways by 176 runs, beat Chhattisgarh by 198 runs, lost to Baroda by two wickets, beat Rajasthan by six wickets (quarter-final), lost to Saurashtra by five wickets (semi-final).
Most runs: KV Siddharth (728 runs, 10 matches)
Most wickets: Ronit More (37 wickets, 8 matches)

Gujarat

Gujarat had the misfortune of running into all four semi-finalists over the course of nine matches. They conceded a first-innings lead in two of these and lost the other two, including one in the quarter-final that led to their exit.

Their best performance — an innings win — came against Maharashtra, when Priyank Panchal got his customary big innings. Panchal led from the front with four hundreds and five fifties in nine matches, and his 898 runs were the fourth-highest of the tournament. He found support in Manprit Juneja (average 48.41) and Dhruv Raval (44.08).

Gujarat's success, albeit limited, can be attributed to their bowling quintet. Between them, the five men checked all four boxes, of left-arm and right-arm spin and pace. While there was no standout performer, Piyush Chawla, Roosh Kalaria, Chintan Gaja, Arzan Nagwaswalla (who took a hat-trick against Kerala) and Siddharth Desai all claimed between 20 and 27 wickets, and averaged between 25 and 31.

Results: Beat Baroda by nine wickets, took first-innings lead against Chhattisgarh, conceded first-innings lead to Saurashtra, beat Mumbai by nine wickets, conceded first-innings lead to Railways, conceded first-innings lead to Karnataka, conceded first-innings lead to Vidarbha, beat Maharashtra by an innings and 130 runs, lost to Kerala by 113 runs (quarter-final).
Most runs: Priyank Panchal (898 runs, 8 matches)
Most wickets: Roosh Kalaria (27 wickets, 8 matches)

Baroda

Two of Baroda's three wins came late in the season, though they may take heart from the fact that one of them was against eventual semi-finalists Karnataka. Baroda lost eight wickets to chase down 110 that day — an act only made possible by Yusuf Pathan's 30-ball 41. With 465 runs at 51.67 (and a strike-rate of 79, lest we forget), Pathan had an excellent season. The previous season too he had been in good form, but found to be in violation of the BCCI's anti-doping rules, he had been banned for five months.

Despite playing just three matches between them, the Pandya brothers occupied the top two spots in both batting and bowling averages. Aditya Waghmode scored hundreds in each innings against Vidarbha, as did Krunal Pandya against Railways. Solanki, Waghmode and Devdhar all topped the 500-run mark, while Bhargav Bhatt snared 31 wickets.

Results: Lost to Gujarat by nine wickets, took first-innings lead against Maharashtra, conceded first-innings lead to Vidarbha, took first-innings lead against Saurashtra, beat Chhattisgarh by nine wickets, conceded first-innings lead to Mumbai, beat Railways by 164 runs, beat Karnataka by two wickets.
Most runs: Vishnu Solanki (595 runs, 8 matches)
Most wickets: Bhargav Bhatt (31 wickets, 8 matches)

Mumbai

If getting eliminated in the quarter-finals in 2017-18 was disappointing, it was nothing compared to the ignominy Mumbai suffered the next season, winning one match out of eight and coming nowhere close to the knock-out stage. Their only win came against Chhattisgarh, who finished at the bottom of their group. The nadir was the Vidarbha match, where they lost by an innings inside three days.

Things could have been worse but for Shivam Dube, who had impressed on debut in a losing cause in the 2017-18 quarter-final. This time Dube finished with most wickets and second-most runs his side. However, neither his 632 runs nor his 23 wickets featured anywhere close to the top in a season where 14 men topped 800 runs and 18 men took 40 or more wickets.

Shreyas Iyer's prolonged absence and indifferent performances from most others meant that Siddhesh Lad had an extra workload. None of the several spinners they tried out impressed. Despite toiling hard, Tushar Deshpande and Royston Dias were not consistent enough to pose threats.

Results: Took first-innings lead against Railways, conceded first-innings lead to Karnataka, lost to Gujarat by nine wickets, conceded first-innings lead to Maharashtra, took first-innings lead against Baroda, took first-innings lead against Saurashtra, lost to Vidarbha by an innings and 145 runs, beat Chhattisgarh by nine wickets.
Most runs: Siddhesh Lad (652 runs, 7 matches)
Most wickets: Shivam Dube (23 runs, 7 matches)

Railways

The lack of quality batsmen forced Railways to adopt a defensive tactic. Captain-wicketkeeper Mahesh Rawat was not only their highest scorer or led the averages chart: put a 250-run cut-off, and his batting-strike rate of 69 was almost 25 more than anyone else's.

Harsh Tyagi and Avinash Yadav toiled with their accurate left-arm spin throughout the season, sharing 72 inexpensive wickets between them. However, Amit Mishra, their sole frontline seamer, featured in only three matches, as a result of which the attack had an incomplete look to them every time. in fact, they got all 20 wickets only thrice in eight matches.

Their only win came in their last match, where Maharashtra batted a mere 62.3 overs across innings on a rank turner at Karnail Singh Stadium. Avinash took 9 for 109 in the match and Tyagi 6 for 31.

Results: Conceded first-innings lead to Mumbai, Lost to Saurashtra by three wickets, took first-innings lead against Chhattisgarh, took first-innings lead against Gujarat, lost to Vidarbha by 118 runs, lost to Karnataka by 176 runs, lost to Baroda by 164 runs, beat Maharashtra by an innings and 58 runs.
Most runs: Mahesh Rawat (478 runs, 7 matches)
Most wickets: Avinash Yadav (41 wickets, 8 matches)

Maharashtra

In the season where Agarwal belted 1160 runs, Rohit Motwani's 460 runs came a distant No.36 in the run-charts. They didn't have a single bowler in the top 20 wicket-takers either. That trend continued in 2018-19, when

Maharashtra didn't have a single batsman in the top 50. Rahul Tripathi was the only batsman to cross 500 runs — just about. Numbers like those can't challenge top teams. Collapses for 70 and 131 against Railways in a final group game that lasted two days sealed their relegation.

Results: Conceded first-innings lead to Baroda, lost to Karnataka by seven wickets, took first-innings lead against Mumbai, lost to Saurashtra by five wickets, conceded first-innings lead to Chhattisgarh, lost to Gujarat by an innings and 130 runs, lost to Railways by an innings and 58 runs.
Most runs: Rahul Tripathi (504 runs, 8 matches)
Most wickets: Satyajeet Sunil Bachhav (28 wickets, 7 matches)

Chhattisgarh

In a season of four one-sided defeats and four draws, Chhattisgarh's only face-saving performance was the first-innings lead against Maharashtra. Even there they somehow managed to convert a 223-run lead into a probable defeat, where the seventh-wicket pair had to bat over ten overs to save the match. Their performance led to a relegation to Elite Group C.

The performance of season came from new-ball bowler Pankaj Rao, who snared 11 of the 17 Karnataka wickets to fall at M Chinnaswamy stadium, albeit in a losing cause. Rao had another five-wicket haul, against Railways, but none of his teammates managed even one. Captain Harpreet Singh top-scored, but found little support.

The previous season, Amandeep Khare had become the first player from his state to score a double-century.

Results: Conceded first-innings lead to Saurashtra, conceded first-innings lead to Gujarat, conceded first-innings lead Railways, lost to Vidarbha by ten wickets, lost to Baroda by nine wickets, took first-innings lead against Maharashtra, lost to Karnataka by 198 runs, lost to Mumbai by nine wickets.
Most runs: Harpreet Singh (627 runs, 8 matches)
Most wickets: Pankaj Rao (29 wickets, 8 matches)

Elite Group B

Kerala

Their bright, aggressive brand of cricket was among the reasons Dav Whatmore's men were among the popular sides in 2019-20. After their first match was hit by rain, every single of Kerala's remaining matches produced an outright result. Their bowling attack, one of the most potent of the tournament, went flat out in search of wickets, their batsmen scored runs quickly to allow them that time.

They made it to the semi-finals for the first time before capitulating against Umesh Yadav in an almost anticlimactic fashion.

Some of their performances deserve special mention. Bowled out for 63, they conceded a 265-run lead to Madhya Pradesh. But even at 8 for 4, they

Coached by Dav Whatmore, Kerala played an aggressive brand of cricket to reach the semi-final. — *KCA*

decided to counterattack, and eventually put up 453, albeit in vain. They took 67 overs to win after Himachal Pradesh set them 297. And they bowled out Bengal, Delhi and Gujarat under 200 twice in a match.

Sandeep Warrier emerged as the spearhead of the pace trio that also consisted of Basil Thampi and M D Nidheesh, while Sijomon Joseph was excellent with his left-arm spin. With bat, as many as nine men scored 200 or more.

Towering above all was Jalaj Saxena, who, with his stupendous all-round show (551 runs at 39.35, 28 wickets at 21.89), proved yet again how valuable he is for his adopted team.

Results: Drew with Hyderabad (first innings incomplete), beat Andhra by nine wickets, beat Bengal by nine wickets, lost to Madhya Pradesh by five wickets, lost to Tamil Nadu by 151 runs, beat Delhi by an innings and 27 runs, lost to Punjab by 10 wickets, beat Himachal Pradesh by five wickets, beat Gujarat by 113 runs (quarter-final), lost to Vidarbha by an innings and 11 runs (semi-final).
Most runs: Jalaj Saxena (551 runs, 9 matches)
Most wickets: Sandeep Warrier (44 wickets, 10 matches)

Madhya Pradesh

After a slow start, Madhya Pradesh won three consecutive matches, including one against eventual semi-finalists Kerala. A win at this stage would have helped them pip Gujarat and make it to the top eight, but they finished their campaign by losing to Andhra by 307 runs, when six wickets fell for no runs.

Their biggest win, by an innings and 253 runs, came against Hyderabad, who collapsed in the first morning against Avesh Khan. Avesh took 12 for 54 in the match, but the limelight was stolen by 21-year-old debutant Ajay Rohera. Opening the batting, Rohera slammed 267 not out, the world record first-class score on debut, going past Amol Muzumdar.

The batting stars of the season were Rajat Patidar (713 runs at 54.84) and Yash Dubey (455 at 45.50), while Avesh (35 wickets at 16.37) was one of the three bowlers — Kumar Kartikeya and Shubham Sharma were the others — who took over ten wickets while averaging below 20.

Results: Drew against Tamil Nadu (first innings incomplete), conceded first-innings lead to Bengal, took first-innings lead against Punjab, beat Kerala by five wickets, beat Hyderabad by an innings and 253 runs, lost to Delhi by nine wickets, beat Himachal Pradesh by 140 runs, lost to Andhra by 307 runs.
Most runs: Rajat Patidar (713 runs, 8 matches)
Most wickets: Avesh Khan (35 wickets, 7 matches)

Bengal

Bengal beat Tamil Nadu by the narrowest margin of the tournament. Chasing 216 they were reduced to 150 for 7 before Sudip Chatterjee and Pradipta Pramanik pushed them to a one-wicket win. They beat Delhi as well, but that was not enough for them to go through to the next round.

Despite missing two matches, Abhimanyu Easwaran amassed 861 runs, finishing 245 clear of next-placed Manoj Tiwary. Bengal's only defeat, against Kerala, came in Easwaran's absence. Easwaran also controlled the 322-run chase against Delhi, dominating a strong attack with an unbeaten 183. Barring Easwaran and Tiwary, however, everyone averaged below 33.

Ashok Dinda was Bengal's leading wicket-taker for the sixth time in a row and the eighth time in nine seasons. He was the only specialist bowler to play all eight matches, and even at 35, bowled significantly more than his greenhorn team-mates.

Results: Took first-innings lead against Himachal Pradesh, took first-innings lead against Madhya Pradesh, lost to Kerala by nine wickets, beat Tamil Nadu by one wicket, took first-innings lead against Hyderabad, conceded first-innings lead against Andhra, beat Delhi by seven wickets, conceded first-innings lead to Punjab.
Most runs: Abhimanyu Easwaran (861 runs, 6 matches)
Most wickets: Ashok Dinda (28 wickets, 8 matches)

Punjab

Punjab had an odd season, during which they tried out 21 players, thrashed table-toppers (and eventual semi-finalists) Kerala, but faced the ignominy of losing to Himachal Pradesh (their first defeat against them in 21 matches), that too by an innings. In the first innings of that match, at 28 for 7, they were in danger of getting bowled out below 42, their lowest ever score, before they recovered to 84.

Abhimanyu Easwaran kept Bengal in the hunt for the next round, hitting peak form towards the end of the group state.

One man who did not feature in that match was Shubman Gill, who played a mere five matches but finished at the top of the pile with 728 runs, including a colossal 268 against Tamil Nadu. Even Yuvraj Singh's poor form could not offset Gill's incredible amalgamation of panache and appetite for runs.

Unfortunately, their bowling was too reliant on Siddharth Kaul, Mayank Markande and Vinay Choudhary, who shared 67 wickets out of a total of 111, including 32 in their two ten-wicket wins against Delhi and Kerala.

Results: Conceded first-innings lead to Andhra, conceded first-innings lead to Madhya Pradesh, beat Delhi by ten wickets, lost to Himachal Pradesh by an innings and 107 runs, took first-innings lead against Tamil Nadu, conceded first-innings lead to Hyderabad, beat Kerala by 10 wickets, took first-innings lead against Bengal.
Most runs: Shubman Gill (728 runs, 5 matches)
Most wickets: Mayank Markande (29 wickets, 6 matches)

Himachal Pradesh

Himachal Pradesh won thrice and lost thrice in a series of highs and lows. One of their defeats involved a bold declaration, only for Kerala to chase down 299. Nevertheless, they beat Punjab, Andhra and Tamil Nadu (the first two by an innings) in consecutive matches. These were their first three wins against all three sides. To provide perspective of their performance in 2018-19, Himachal Pradesh had previously won only 31 matches in 33 seasons.

The one constant factor in their wins was Ankit Kalsi, who scored 82, 120 and 144 not out in these three matches. He signed off the tournament with 101 and 64 against Kerala, emerging as Himachal Pradesh's star of the season. Rishi Dhawan (519 runs, 18 wickets), Mayank Dagar (284 runs, 24 wickets), Pankaj Jaswal (25 wickets) and Arpit Guleria (24 wickets) all put in commendable performances.

Results: Conceded first-innings lead to Bengal, conceded first-innings lead to Delhi, lost to Hyderabad by 10 wickets, beat Punjab by an innings and 107 runs, beat Andhra by an innings and three runs, beat Tamil Nadu by nine wickets, lost to Madhya Pradesh by 140 runs, lost to Kerala by five wickets.
Most runs: Rishi Dhawan (519 runs, 8 matches)
Most wickets: Pankaj Jaswal (25 wickets, 8 matches)

Andhra

Andhra failed to win a single match — just as in the previous season — before their last, but to be fair, they were placed comfortably at 93 for 1 in pursuit of 203 against Bengal before a flurry of wickets forced them to finish with 170 for 7. On the other hand, they got away against Delhi, who, requiring 88, could only get 41 for 2.

Andhra's only win came in spectacular fashion, where they had to bowl just 52.4 overs to bowl out Madhya Pradesh for 91 and 35. The second-innings score was Madhya Pradesh's lowest ever.

Ricky Bhui and K V Sasikanth were the sole bright spots in Andhra's ordinary campaign. Bhui's 775 runs included four hundreds in eight matches and were more than twice of what any of his team-mates managed, while Sasikanth took 17 wickets in four matches, including a five-wicket haul in each of his last three.

Results: Took first-innings lead against Punjab, lost to Kerala by nine wickets, conceded first-innings lead to Tamil Nadu, conceded first-innings lead to Delhi, lost to Himachal Pradesh by an innings and three runs, took first-innings lead against Bengal, took first-innings lead against Hyderabad, beat Madhya Pradesh by 307 runs.
Most runs: Ricky Bhui (775 runs, 8 matches)
Most wickets: K V Sasikanth (17 wickets, 4 matches), Shoaib Mohammad (17 wickets, 7 matches)

Hyderabad

The runs flowed for Hyderabad, but not the wins, and they were quickly out of contention for the knock-out matches. Captain Akshat Reddy opened with a double-century against Tamil Nadu, his 250 setting up their massive 565 for 8. Only twice were they bowled out for less than 250. However, with India duties keeping Mohammad Siraj away, they couldn't put together a penetrative bowling attack. And when the batsmen struggled in Indore and Rohera made against them the highest first-class score on debut, an unbeaten 267, they found themselves exposed as their campaign quickly faltered without a single win.

Results: Took first-innings lead against Tamil Nadu, took first-innings lead against Delhi, beat Himachal Pradesh by ten wickets, lost to Madhya Pradesh by an innings and 253 runs, conceded first-innings lead to Bengal, took first-innings lead against Punjab, conceded first-innings lead against Andhra.

Most runs: Akshat Reddy (797 runs, 8 matches)

Most wickets: Tanay Thyagarajan (17 wickets, 5 matches)

Tamil Nadu

Tamil Nadu had the misfortune of starting with three rain-affected draws. They lost only four wickets in each of their first two matches but acquired a total of two points; in the third, they got a first-innings lead in a match that barely went past 200 overs.

They lost twice, but managed to stun Kerala, the surprise of the season, by a massive margin. B Indrajith top-scored in that match as well as in the tournament for Tamil Nadu, while Abhinav Mukund finished a close second. Unfortunately, Tamil Nadu lost to Himachal Pradesh despite hundreds from both men.

Rahil Shah finished fourth on the wickets tally; his ten wickets against Bengal in a narrow defeat was Tamil Nadu's performance of the season — even ahead of Mohammed Mohammed's hat-trick against Madhya Pradesh.

Results: Drew against Madhya Pradesh (first innings incomplete), drew against Hyderabad (first innings incomplete), took first-innings lead against Andhra, lost to Bengal by one wicket, beat Kerala by 151 runs, conceded first-innings lead to Punjab, lost to Himachal Pradesh by nine wickets, took first-innings lead against Delhi.

Most runs: B Indrajith (641 runs, 8 matches)

Most wickets: R Sai Kishore (22 wickets, 6 matches)

Delhi

The win against Madhya Pradesh was Delhi's only one of the season. The star of that match was Anuj Rawat, who outscored Madhya Pradesh's first-innings total on his own despite four of Delhi's top six batsmen falling for ducks. To be fair, they should also have beaten Andhra, but time ran out when they, chasing 88, could only manage 41 for 2.

That apart, they lost by massive margins to both Punjab and Kerala. They also had Bengal at 137 for 3 while defending 322 but failed to take another wicket.

Not a single Delhi batsman got 400 runs in the tournament, while Vikas Mishra's 33 wickets were more than what any two other bowlers managed between them. Among the big guns, both Gautam Gambhir — in his last season — and Ishant Sharma shone in their sporadic appearances.

Results: Took first-innings lead against Himachal Pradesh, conceded first-innings lead to Hyderabad, lost to Punjab by ten wickets, took first-innings lead against Andhra, lost to Kerala by an innings and 27 runs, beat Madhya Pradesh by nine wickets, lost to Bengal by seven wickets, conceded first-innings lead to Tamil Nadu.

Most runs: Hiten Dalal (376 runs, 7 matches)

Most wickets: Vikas Mishra (33 wickets, 7 matches)

Elite Group C

Rajasthan

In 2017-18, Rajasthan finished bottom of the group to round off another poor season. So, when the gloom made way for an inspired performance, it came as a happy surprise. Even when they had been struggling, the inclusion of two home-grown players in the Indian squad had offered some consolation: Khaleel Ahmed, the left-arm fast bowler, was fast-tracked on promise, while Deepak Chahar, who has been toiling for close to a decade, was rewarded for his consistent IPL showing. International commitments kept Khaleel away for all but one game this season, but Chahar remained a consistent force for them. He took 41 wickets while Aniket Choudhary and Tanvir-ul-Haq combined for 100 between them, making for a match-winning pace attack.

In fact, Rajasthan won so much of it: seven outright wins in the group stage, twice coming back from behind, before they were halted by Karnataka in the quarter-final.

Results: Beat Jammu and Kashmir by 75 runs, beat services by five wickets, beat Jharkhand by 92 runs, took first-innings lead against Uttar Pradesh, beat Assam by an innings and 43 runs, beat Odisha by 35 runs, took first-innings lead against Haryana, beat Goa by ten wickets, beat Tripura by an innings and 77 runs, lost to Karnataka by six wickets (quarter-final).
Most runs: Robin Bist (741 runs, 10 matches)
Most wickets: Tanvir-ul-Haq (51 wickets, 10 matches)

Uttar Pradesh

Uttar Pradesh went through the league stage unbeaten, winning five and taking the first-innings lead thrice in nine matches. Even in the other match, against table-toppers Rajasthan, they got to 116 for 2 in pursuit of 330. Their victories included massive innings wins against Goa and Tripura and a ten-wicket victory against Odisha — matches that fetched them 21 points apiece.

Uttar Pradesh led Saurashtra in the quarter-final by 177 runs, which meant that they had to defend 372 despite their low second-innings score. Unfortunately, they ran into a top order that turned out to be immovable, and a season's excellent

Rinku SIngh fell a little short of 1000 runs for the season. — *UPCA*

work was lost in a little over a day's play. Rinku Singh fell short of the 1000-run mark by 47 runs, finishing behind only Milind Kumar and Wasim Jaffer. Priyam Garg and Akshdeep Nath both topped the 700-mark as well. Saurabh Kumar's left-arm spin, on the other hand, fetched him 51 wickets: only four men got more in the season.

Results: Beat Goa by an innings and 247 runs, beat Odisha by ten wickets, took first-innings lead against Services, conceded first-innings lead to Rajasthan, beat Jammu and Kashmir by six wickets, conceded first-innings lead to Jharkhand, beat Tripura by an innings and 384 runs, beat Haryana by six wickets, took first-innings lead against Assam, lost to Saurashtra by six wickets (quarter-final).
Most runs: Rinku Singh (953 runs, 10 matches)
Most wickets: Saurabh Kumar (51 wickets, 10 matches)

Jharkhand

Jharkhand impressed, winning five and losing one out of nine matches, but the tally was not enough for them to make it to the top two. Their bowlers, potent throughout the tournament, put up their finest show at Rohtak early in the season, when they sent Haryana packing for 81 and 72 to win on the second afternoon. While there were some outstanding performers, the star was Anukul Roy, who was still in his teens when the season began. He headed the wickets tally with 30 wickets at 22.70 and scored 374 runs at 28.76.

The big guns — Kumar Deobrat, Saurabh Tiwary, Ishank Jaggi, Ishan Kishan — all got runs, as did the unheralded Nazim Siddiqui. In all, seven of their batsmen crossed the 350-run mark. On the other hand, every specialist bowler averaged below 24. Varun Aaron was quick and hostile and Shahbaz Nadeem incisive, and they had little problem in rolling over one side after another.

Results: Took first-innings lead against Assam, beat Haryana by nine wickets, lost to Rajasthan by 92 runs, beat Goa by seven wickets, beat Odisha by two runs, took first-innings lead against Uttar Pradesh, beat Services by 81 runs, took first-innings lead against Tripura, beat Jammu and Kashmir by an innings and 48 runs.
Most runs: Kumar Deobrat (631 runs, 7 matches)
Most wickets: Anukul Roy (30 wickets, 9 matches)

Odisha

If in 2017-18 Odisha had gained a reputation as one of the weakest teams in the competition, they went some way in rectifying that the following season. And where once the missing young talent had raised doubts about the lack of succession planning, they found in 21-year-old Subhranshu Senapati a feisty batsman. The previous season, in hunting down Tamil Nadu's first-innings 530 to take a lead, incredibly without a single centurion, they showed plenty of pluck, and that was on display again when they came within three runs of victory against Jharkhand. Senapati was unbeaten on 157, having added 64 with No.11 Dhiraj Singh in a chase of 260.

Results: Lost to Uttar Pradesh by ten wickets, beat Assam by nine wickets, beat Tripura by five wickets, lost to Jharkhand by two runs, lost to Rajasthan by 35 runs, beat Jammu and Kashmir by eight wickets, conceded first-innings lead to Services, beat Goa by 276 runs.
Most runs: Subhranshu Senapati (617 runs, 9 matches)
Most wickets: Basant Mohanty (44 wickets, 8 matches)

Haryana

Haryana slumped from 51 for 3 to 81 all out on the opening day of the campaign in a match that lasted two days. In their next game, they looked set to squander a 99-run lead when they crumbled to 34 for 7, but No.7 Pramod Chindila's 122 out of a total of 185 set them up for the first of two outright wins in the season. The inconsistency would be a pattern and even the efforts of Yuzvendra Chahal, the India wrist-spinner, who picked up seven wickets against Jammu and Kashmir, could not push them over the qualification line when needed.

Results: Lost to Jharkhand by nine wickets, beat Goa by 143 runs, lost to Assam by an innings and 35 runs, beat Tripura by 55 runs, lost to Jammu and Kashmir by 130 runs, conceded first-innings lead to Rajasthan, lost to Uttar Pradesh by six wickets, beat Services by six wickets.
Most runs: Himanshu Rana (594 runs, 9 matches)
Most wickets: Tinu Kundu (24 wickets, 4 matches)

Assam

Memories of Assam's showing in 2015-16, where they reached the semi-final for the first time, seem a blur. After Sanath Kumar resigned as coach, they went back to a defensive mindset, and this year, they also lost the experience of Krishna Das, who moved to Goa. Against his old team, Das picked up six and was the last wicket to fall in a thrilling seven-run win for Assam.

Inconsistency was their bane, as they never strung two positive results in a row. Gokul Sharma made their only century all tournament. On the plus side, the emergence of Riyan Parag, a prodigious teenager who represented India at the U19 World Cup, bode well for their batting future.

Results: Beat Tripura by 211 runs, lost to Odisha by nine wickets, beat Haryana by an innings and 35 runs, lost to Rajasthan by an innings and 43 runs, beat Goa by seven runs, lost to Jammu and Kashmir by four wickets, conceded first-innings lead to Uttar Pradesh.
Most runs: Gokul Sharma (570 runs, 8 matches)
Most wickets: Mukhtar Hussain (40 wickets, 9 matches)

Jammu and Kashmir

Floods in the state and politicking in the association had kept Jammu and Kashmir out of the Sher-i-Kashmir Stadium since 2015. They marked their return by skittling out Tripura for 124, with skipper Parvez Rasool's five wickets fuelling the slide. That was one of three outright wins for the side, but overall it was a middling season.

Former India all-rounder Irfan Pathan moved from Baroda, his experience translating into 463 runs and 40 wickets. With medium-pacers Umar Nazir (44 wickets) and Mohammad Mudhasir (46) joining the duo of Rasool and Pathan, the quartet was in sync.

Mudhasir made history on the second day of the tournament when he became only the second Ranji player — after Delhi's Shankar Saini against Himachal Pradesh in 1988 — to dismiss four batsmen in as many balls. All four were lbw. But Rasool was the big all-round star, topping both batting and bowling charts.

Results: Lost to Rajasthan by 75 runs, conceded first-innings lead to Goa, beat Tripura by eight wickets, lost to Services by five wickets, lost to Uttar Pradesh by six wickets, beat Haryana by 130 runs, lost to Odisha by eight wickets, beat Assam by four wickets, lost to Jharkhand by an innings and 48 runs.
Most runs: Parvez Rasool (684 runs, 9 matches)
Most wickets: Parvez Rasool (35 wickets, 9 matches)

Services

Despite some solid individual performances, Services did little apart from winning against Jammu and Kashmir and Assam to avoid the ignominy of relegation. Diwesh Pathania, who got 16 wickets from these two wins, finished the season with 40 wickets.

It could have been so much better, had they made the most when they were on top. They secured the first-innings lead in all three matches they lost. They led Rajasthan by 92 and set them 357 in over four sessions but ended up losing instead. Against Jharkhand they led by 74 but lost by 81 runs. And a second-innings score of 79 all out cost them the match against Haryana.

Rajat Paliwal, who had returned to lead Services after spending two seasons with Haryana, did well. Three others topped the 450-mark, but too many players in the side failed to push their average beyond the low- or mid-30s to make an impact.

Results: Conceded first-innings lead to Tripura, lost to Rajasthan by five wickets, conceded first-innings lead to Uttar Pradesh, beat Jammu and Kashmir by five wickets, conceded first-innings lead to Goa, beat Assam by 10 wickets, lost to Jharkhand by 81 runs, took first-innings lead against Odisha, lost to Haryana by six wickets.
Most runs: Rajat Paliwal (652 runs, 9 matches)
Most wickets: Diwesh Pathania (40 wickets, 9 matches)

Tripura

Neelambuj Vats was the top scorer with 11 runs, captain Smit Patel retired hurt and six batsmen made ducks as Tripura were bundled out for a paltry 35 against Rajasthan — worse than their previous record of 42 against Bengal. This surrender in their final game encapsulated a season where they were found severely lacking in their ability to challenge the bigger teams. Their innings defeat to Uttar Pradesh in Lucknow was the second-biggest in the last 65 years of the tournament.

Uttarakhand had a maiden season to remember, earning promotion. — *UCCC*

Results: Took first-innings lead against Services, lost to Assam by 211 runs, lost to Jammu and Kashmir by eight wickets, lost to Odisha by five wickets, lost to Haryana by 55 runs, beat Goa by ten wickets, lost to Uttar Pradesh by and innings and 384 runs, conceded first-innings lead to Jharkhand, lost to Rajasthan by an innings and 77 runs.
Most runs: Pratyush Singh (464 runs, 8 matches)
Most wickets: Manisankar Murasingh (32 wickets, 8 matches)

Goa

Seven defeats (including one by ten wickets to Tripura) in nine matches summed up Goa's tournament. In the other two, they managed a lead only against Jammu and Kashmir but trailed against Services. They ended up getting relegated to the Plate Division.

Having said that, they could have beaten Assam in a humdinger at Barsapara. Chasing 218, Goa were reduced to 78 for 6 before Amit Verma and Lakshay Garg added 101. Unfortunately, while the tail resisted, they did not do enough, and Goa lost by seven runs. Das, the last man to be dismissed in the match, was playing his first season for Goa after being one of the success stories for Assam in the recent past.

Verma topped the runs chart for Goa, while Snehal Kauthankar finished 40 runs behind. However, the fact that none of the two managed to average even 35 in the season and none of the others even hit the 28 mark cuts a sorry story. Barring Das and Garg, no one impressed with ball either.

Results: Lost to Uttar Pradesh by an innings and 247 runs, took first-innings lead against Jammu and Kashmir, lost to Haryana by 143 runs, lost to Jharkhand by seven wickets, conceded first-innings lead to Services, lost to Tripura by 10 wickets, lost to Assam by seven runs, lost to Rajasthan by 10 wickets, lost to Odisha by 276 runs.
Most runs: Amit Verma (549 runs, 9 matches)
Most wickets: Lakshay Garg (37 wickets, 8 matches)

Plate Group

Uttarakhand

As far as debuts go, you can't better Uttarakhand. A lot of their six victories in the league, which secured them a quarter-final berth, came via performances from home-grown talent. They were defeated by eventual champions Vidarbha by an innings in the knock-out, but their work for the season was done. Four batsmen struck double-centuries. Paceman Deepak Dhapola was the standout bowler with 45 wickets at 15.51. By their coach Bhaskar Pillai's own admission, however, the team's spin attack was lacking. The over-reliance on pace meant the players were fatigued at the quarter-finals. It was still a season to be proud of and earned them a promotion.

Results: Beat Bihar by ten wickets, beat Manipur by eight wickets, beat Sikkim by an innings and 178 runs, beat Arunachal Pradesh by an innings and 73 runs, beat Meghalaya by eight wickets, took first-innings lead against Nagaland, drew with Puducherry, beat Mizoram by an innings and 56 runs, lost to Vidarbha by an innings and 115 runs (quarter-final).
Most runs: Rajat Bhatia (700 runs, 8 matches)
Most wickets: Deepak Dhapola (45 wickets, 8 matches)

Bihar

Bihar returned to the Ranji fold after 18 years but a memorable season for Bihar was under the shadow of a few what-ifs: What if the Puducherry match wasn't a washout? What if they hadn't been bundled out for 60 against Uttarakhand in the first round? Bihar's six wins in eight matches was impressive, but still not enough to stop Uttarakhand from topping the table after the final round of games.

In skipper Ashutosh Aman, they had a record-breaker: the left-arm spinner's 68 wickets in eight matches made him the highest wicket-taker in a single Ranji season, eclipsing Bishan Bedi's 64 for Delhi in 1974-75. His century and five-wicket haul against Mizoram in their penultimate game kept their hopes of progressing alive. The professionals led Bihar's charge — apart from Aman, Samar Quadri also impressed, taking ten wickets in that must-win face-off with Mizoram.

Results: Lost to Uttarakhand by ten wickets, no result against Puducherry, beat Sikkim by 395 runs, beat Arunachal Pradesh by an innings and 317 runs, beat Meghalaya by an innings and 71 runs, beat Nagaland by 273 runs, beat Mizoram by an innings and 216 runs, beat Manipur by three wickets.
Most runs: M D Rahmatullah (375 runs, 8 matches)
Most wickets: Ashutosh Aman (68 wickets, 8 matches)

Puducherry

A campaign with a chaotic start to the season finished in third place in the group. Eight of their players were disallowed shortly into the season, due to legalities. Six uncapped cricketers were given last-minute call-ups. And

Pankaj Singh, one of Puducherry's outstation recruits, kept them in the reckoning for a place in the knock-outs. — *CAP*

despite that, they were still one of two unbeaten sides in the group. Had their clashes against Uttarakhand and Bihar — the teams that finished above them — not been affected by rain, they might well have qualified. Professionals such as Abhishek Nayar and Paras Dogra led the team well, the local players rallied around them, and they proved unity can prevail over any uncertainty. A great season.

Results: Took first-innings lead against Meghalaya, no result against Bihar, beat Mizoram by an innings and 238 runs, beat Sikkim by an innings and 159 runs, beat Arunachal Pradesh by 334 runs, drew with Uttarakhand, beat Manipur by ten wickets, conceded first-innings lead against Nagaland.
Most runs: Paras Dogra (729 runs, eight matches)
Most wickets: Pankaj Singh (45 wickets, eight matches)

Meghalaya

Among the teams that finished mid-table, Meghalaya stood out for their inclination to dominate: They posted 826 for 7 declared against Sikkim, the highest team total of the season, with Puneet Bisht scoring a triple-century. They finished fourth, with four wins and a no-result in their eight matches, but from all the sides from the north-east of the country, they were the best. With their professional players doing their bit and a few impressive first-timers — Raj Biswa scored 546 runs in his debut season, while left-arm spinner Aditya Singhania took 24 wickets — Meghalaya have plenty to build on for the next campaign.

Results: Beat Arunachal Pradesh by seven wickets, conceded first-innings lead against

Domestic review

Puducherry, beat Nagaland by six wickets, beat Manipur by nine wickets, lost to Uttarakhand by eight wickets, lost to Bihar by an innings and 71 runs, beat Mizoram by an innings and 324 runs, took the first-innings lead against Sikkim.

Most runs: Puneet Bisht (892 runs, 8 matches)
Most wickets: Gurinder Singh (53 wickets, 8 matches)

Sikkim

Sikkim's was a one-man campaign. Milind Kumar challenged V V S Laxman's mark with his 1331 runs in the season — the second-highest after Laxman's 1415. And he did that from dangerous positions, such as against Manipur, when he rescued them from 15 for 5 to post 372. He also chipped in with 22 wickets and almost single-handedly helped Sikkim finish fifth, with four wins in eight. Swapping the bench in Delhi for Sikkim couldn't have felt better.

Results: Beat Manipur by an innings and 27 runs, beat Nagaland by nine wickets, lost to Uttarakhand by an innings and 178 runs, lost to Bihar by 395 runs, lost to Puducherry by an innings and 159 runs, beat Mizoram by 105 runs, conceded the first-innings lead to Meghalaya, beat Arunachal Pradesh by ten wickets.

Most runs: Milind Kumar (1331 runs, 8 matches)
Most wickets: Ishwar Chaudhary (51 wickets, 8 matches)

Manipur

Batting was a big issue for Manipur. There simply wasn't enough experience in it to handle the tough situations. Having shifted from Tripura for his 17th domestic season, the former Services man, Yashpal Singh, had a lot of heavy lifting to do, and though the bowlers impressed — local boy Bishworjit Konthoujam finished with 30 scalps — the batsmen didn't pull their weight. Yashpal was later quoted as saying, "They were trying but it wasn't happening. Everybody has learnt by watching on TV." Despite that, they managed three victories, and even in defeat against Bihar, they showed fight and were unfortunate to lose by three wickets. Rex Singh, the teenage left-arm pace bowler who took ten wickets in a Cooch Behar game, impressed with his ability to move the ball and earned a call-up to the India U19 squad.

Results: Lost to Sikkim by an innings and 27 runs, lost to Uttarakhand by eight wickets, beat Mizoram by eight wickets, lost to Meghalaya by nine wickets, beat Nagaland by seven wickets, beat Arunachal Pradesh by 112 runs, lost to Puducherry by ten wickets, lost to Bihar by three wickets.
Most runs: Yashpal Singh (860 runs, 8 matches)
Most wickets: Bishworjit Konthoujam (30 wickets, 8 matches)

Nagaland

Nagaland began with a record total: their 530 for 8 against Mizoram was the highest by a team on debut in the Ranji Trophy. But it was tough going thereafter. Abrar Kazi did a lot of the heavy lifting. He ended the campaign with 814 runs and 34 wickets to become both the team's highest scorer and leading wicket-taker. Captain Rongsen Jonathan was also among the runs (809), including successive centuries in the last two matches, but there was no real support for the duo. Tahmeed Rahman's hat-trick against Manipur was the first for the state. Victories against Mizoram and Arunachal Pradesh were a much-needed boost.

Results: Beat Mizoram by an innings and 333 runs, lost to Sikkim by nine wickets, lost to Meghalaya by six wickets, lost to Manipur by seven wickets, conceded the first-innings lead to Uttarakhand, lost to Bihar by 273 runs, beat Arunachal Pradesh by an innings and 120 runs, took the first-innings lead against Puducherry
Most runs: Abrar Kazi (814 runs, 8 matches)
Most wickets: Abrar Kazi (34 wickets, 8 matches)

Arunachal Pradesh

Do Arunachal Pradesh need more professionals? It could certainly help. Kshitiz Sharma and Samarth Seth did a fair bit, but not as much as expected or required of professionals like them. It meant the inexperienced team were one of the two whipping boys in the group. They lost seven of their eight matches, with their three points coming against table-toppers Mizoram. Arunachal's season ended rather quickly. It was still a learning experience, and will look to address fitness and fielding concerns ahead of the next season.

Results: Lost to Meghalaya by seven wickets, took first-innings lead against Mizoram, lost to Uttarakhand by an innings and 73 runs, lost to Bihar by an innings and 317 runs, lost to Puducherry by 334 runs, lost to Manipur by 112 runs, lost to Nagaland by an innings and 120 runs, lost to Sikkim by ten wickets.
Most runs: Kshitiz Sharma (498 runs, 7 matches)
Most wickets: Deendyal Upadhyay (23 wickets, 4 matches)

Mizoram

Much like Arunachal Pradesh, Mizoram too suffered from their star players not getting enough support. Taruwar Kohli scored 826 runs, but apart from Akhil Rajput to an extent, there wasn't nearly enough support with the bat. Of their seven losses, five were innings defeats, meaning the batsmen just couldn't withstand the opposition. The closes they got to a win was against Arunachal Pradesh, when they needed 166 more with eight wickets in hand, only for rain to wash out the final day's play.

Results: Lost to Nagaland by an innings and 333 runs, conceded first-innings lead to Arunachal Pradesh, lost to Manipur by eight wickets, lost to Puducherry by an innings and 238 runs, lost to Sikkim by 105 runs, lost to Meghalaya by an innings and 324 runs, lost to Bihar by an innings and 216 runs, lost to Uttarakhand by an innings and 56 runs.
Most runs: Taruwar Kohli (826 runs, 8 matches)
Most wickets: Sinan Khadir (22 wickets, 7 matches)

Round-wise review

Round 1: Four in four for Mudhasir

Following on 123 behind Maharashtra, defending champions Vidarbha put up 501 for 9 to save the match, with Faiz Fazal and Akshay Wadkar both getting hundreds. Shivam Dube's hundred was not enough to help Mumbai beat Railways, though, while Chhattisgarh resisted a rampant Jaydev Unadkat to keep Saurashtra at bay.

In Group B, Andhra rode on Ricky Bhui's 181 to snatch a nine-run lead from Punjab. Rain restricted Kerala to a solitary point despite their advantage over Hyderabad.

Despite Ishan Kishan's breakneck hundred, the Jharkhand bowlers did not have enough time to have a shot at Assam in Group C. Biplab Samantray helped Odisha save the match against Haryana after they, trailing by 118, were reduced to 99 for 4. Jammu and Kashmir's Mohammad Mudhasir picked up four wickets in four balls, but his effort went in vain against Rajasthan.

The first-round numbers were a sign of things to come from the Plate Group. Milind Kumar's 261 helped Sikkim drown Manipur, while Nagaland's Abrar Kazi got a double-hundred and nine wickets against Mizoram.

Elite Group A

Moti Bagh Stadium, Vadodara, November 1-4: Baroda 290 in 81.2 overs (Yusuf Pathan 69, Deepak Hooda 63; Siddharth Desai 5-109, Piyush Chawla 3-58) and 179 in 72.2 overs (Pinal Shah 71, Y Pathan 28; Roosh Kalaria 6-35, S Desai 3-57) lost to **Gujarat** 302 in 102.1 overs (Rujul Bhatt 76, Samit Gohel 63; Lukman Meriwala 3-50, Atit Sheth 3-53, Bhargav Bhatt 3-75) and 168/1 in 48.2 overs (Priyank Panchal 112*) by nine wickets. *PoM:* Roosh Kalaria.

MCA Stadium, Gahunje, November 1-4: Maharashtra 343 in 105.5 overs (Chirag Khurana 89, Rahul Tripathi 73; Aditya Sarwate 3-51, Lalit Yadav 3-84) drew with **Vidarbha** 120 in 44.5 overs (Wasim Jaffer 27, A Sarwate 25; Satyajeet Bachhav 3-3, Samad Fallah 2-21) and 501/8 in 175 overs (Faiz Fazal 131, Akshay Wadkar 122*; S Bachhav 3-109, S Fallah 2-84). Maharashtra took first-innings lead. *PoM:* Faiz Fazal.

Karnail Singh Stadium, Delhi, November 1-4: Mumbai 411 in 115.2 overs (Shivam Dubey 114, Siddhesh Lad 99; Harsh Tyagi 4-83, Anureet Singh 3-77, Avinash Yadav 3-99) and 321/5 in 102.4 overs (Aditya Tare 100*, S Lad 76) drew with **Railways** 307 in 104.2 overs (Arindam Ghosh 71, Avinash Yadav 48; Tushar Deshpande 6-70). Mumbai took first-innings lead. *PoM:* Tushar Deshpande.

SCA Stadium, Rajkot, November 1-4: Saurashtra 475 in 142.2 overs (Sheldon Jackson 147, Snell Patel 91; Shahnawaz Hussain 4-97, Sahil Gupta 3-63) and 179/5 in 58.2 overs (S Jackson 53*, Harvik Desai 46; S Gupta 4-69) drew with **Chhattisgarh** 355 in 125.2 overs (Sumit Ruikar 67, Harpreet Bhatia 60; Jaydev Unadkat 7-86, Saurya Sanandiya 2-65). Saurashtra took first-innings lead. *PoM:* Jaydev Unadkat.

Elite Group B

Dr YS Rajasekhara Reddy ACA-VDCA Cricket Stadium, Visakhapatnam, November 1-4: Punjab 414 in 156.2 overs (Sanvir Singh 110, Mayank Markande 68*; B Ayyappa 3-78, Karn Sharma 3-115) and 102/2 in 33 overs (Shubman Gill 54*, Anmolpreet Singh 32) drew with **Andhra** 423 in 155.5 overs (Ricky Bhui 181, KS Bharat 76; M Markande 5-129, Siddharth Kaul 2-72). Andhra took first-innings lead. *PoM:* Ricky Bhui.

Atal Bihari Vajpayee Stadium, Amtar, November 1-4: Bengal 380 in 116.1 overs (Manoj Tiwary 55, Anustup Majumdar 52; Pankaj Jaswal 5-81, Prashant Chopra 2-29) and 203/3 in 67 overs (Abhishek Raman 87, Abhimanyu Easwaran 76; P Chopra 2-53) drew with **Himachal Pradesh** 324 in 115 overs (Ankush Bains 86, Sumeet Verma 46; Pradipta Pramanik 4-60, Aamir Gani 2-51). **Bengal** took first-innings lead. *PoM:* Aamir Gani.

St Xavier's College Ground, Thumba, November 1-4: Kerala 495/6 dec. in 164 overs (Sachin Baby 147, VA Jagadeesh 113*; PS Sairam 3-110, Mehdi Hasan 2-135) drew with **Hyderabad** 228/5 in 112 overs (B Sandeep 56*, Himalay Agarwal 48; Akshay Chandran 2-44). *PoM:* VA Jagadeesh.

NPR College Ground, Dindigul, November 1-4:Madhya Pradesh 393 in 157.4 overs (Rajat Patidar 196, Aryaman Birla 51; R Ashwin 4-85, M Mohammed 4-85) drew with **Tamil Nadu** 236/4 in 77.4 overs (Baba Indrajith 103*, Baba Aparajith 31; Avesh Khan 2-49). *PoM:* Rajat Patidar.

Elite Group C

JSCA International Stadium, Ranchi, November 1-4: Jharkhand 344 in 112.1 overs (Anukul Roy 80, Utkarsh Singh 72; Mukhtar Hussain 5-77, Ranjit Mali 2-78) and 230/4 dec. in 42.5 overs (Ishan Kishan 120, Nazim Siddiqui 48) drew with **Assam** 298 in 105.2 overs (Gokul Sharma 92, Sibsankar Roy 70; Ashish Kumar 5-69) and 140/2 in 39 overs (Sibsankar Roy 52*, Gokul Sharma 48*; Anukul Roy 2-55). Jharkhand took first-innings lead. *PoM:* Ashish Kumar.

KIIT Ground, Bhubaneswar, November 1-4: Odisha 324 in 112.2 overs (Anurag Sarangi 114, Shantanu Mishra 71; Tinu Kundu 4-44, Mohit Sharma 2-63) and 267/7 in 99.2 overs (Biplab Samantray 103*, Subhranshu Senapati 45; Jayant Yadav 2-45, Tinu Kundu 2-64) drew with **Haryana** 442 in 128.3 overs (Himanshu Rana 164, Chaitanya Bishnoi 75; Debabrata Pradhan 3-96, Govinda Podder 2-53). Haryana took first-innings lead. *PoM:* Himanshu Rana.

Sawai Mansingh Stadium, Jaipur, November 1-4: Rajasthan 379 in 109.4 overs (Chetan Bist 159, Ashok Menaria 59; Mohammad Mudhasir 5-90, Rohit Sharma 2-69) and 219/4 dec. in 63 overs (Amitkumar Gautam 68, Tajinder Dhillon 49*; Parveez Rasool 2-50) beat **Jammu and Kashmir** 204 in 71.1 overs (Parvez Rasool 47, Shubham Khajuria 40, Paras Sharma 40; Rahul Chahar 5-59, Tanveer-ul-Haq 3-71) and 319 in 97.4 overs (Parvez Rasool 110*, Ahmed Banday 62; Nathu Singh 4-83, Rahul Chahar 4-89) by 75 runs. *PoM:* Chetan Bist.

Maharaja Bir Bikram College Stadium, Agartala, November 1-4: Tripura 360 in 122.3 overs (Bishal Ghosh 201, Smit Patel 38; Diwesh Pathania 4-79, Sachidanand Pandey 3-105) and 232/2 dec. in 61 overs (Udiyan Bose 109, Smit Patel 56*) drew with **Services** 238 in 85 overs (Anshul Gupta 62, Vikas Hathwala 51; Manisankar Murasingh 7-53, Rana Datta 2-27) and 164/6 in 51 overs (Ravi Chauhan 47, Vikas Hathwala 41; M Murasingh 2-35, R Datta 2-37). Tripura took first-innings lead. *PoM:* Bishal Ghosh.

Modi Stadium, Kanpur, November 1-4: Goa 152 in 35.4 overs (Darshan Misal 43, Sagun Kamat 41; Shivam Mavi 4-25, Saurabh Kumar 2-19) and 165 in 77.1 overs (Darshan Misal 51*, Snehal Kauthankar 28; Ankit Rajpoot 5-41, Saurabh Kumar 4-55) lost to **Uttar Pradesh** 564/4 dec. in 161 overs (Akshdeep Nath 194, Mohammad Saif 126, Priyam Garg 117*; Lakshay Garg 2-109) by an innings and 247 runs. *PoM:* Akshdeep Nath.

Plate Group

Jadavpur University Second Campus Ground, Kolkata, November 1-3: Sikkim 372 in 111.2 overs (Milind Kumar 261, Bipul Sharma 45; Shelly Shaurya 4-39, Rex Singh 3-97) beat **Manipur** 79 in 28 overs (Priyojit Singh 30, Yashpal Singh 29; Ishwar Chaudhary 4-37, Bipul 3-17) and 266 in 80.2 overs (Yashpal Singh 132, Lakhan Rawat 70; Bipul Sharma 4-55, Ishwar Chaudhary 3-52) by an innings and 27 runs. *PoM:* Milind Kumar.

Meghalaya Cricket Association Cricket Ground, Shillong, November 1-4: Arunachal Pradesh 166 in 64.3 overs (Samarth Seth 50, Kshitiz Sharma 30; Gurinder Singh 5-50, Lakhan Singh 3-38) and 131 in 55.1 overs (Kshitiz 41, Kamsha Yangfo 40; Gurinder 4-21, Abhay Negi 4-39) lost to **Meghalaya** 141 in 40 overs (Jason Lamare 70, Aditya Singhania 32; Sandeep Thakur 3-19, Licha Tehi 3-31, Subhash Sharma 3-47) and 157/3 in 32 overs (Punit Bisht 66*, Yogesh Nagar 55*; L Tehi 2-30) by seven wickets. *PoM:* Jason Lamare.

Sovima Cricket Stadium, Dimapur, November 1-3: Mizoram 106 in 47.2 overs (Taruwar Kohli 49, Akhil Rajput 28; Abrar Kazi 4-16, Imliwati Lemtur 2-0) and 91 in 41.4 overs (T Kohli 48*; A Kazi 5-13, Rachit Bhatia 2-12) lost to **Nagaland** 530/8 dec. in 117.2 overs (A Kazi 200*, Rongsen Jonathan 72, K Lalhmingmawia 3-90, A Rajput 2-128) by an innings and 333 runs. *PoM:* Abrar Kazi.

Rajiv Gandhi International Cricket Stadium, Dehradun, November 1-4: Bihar 60 in 22.1 overs (Deepak Dhapola 6-13, Dhanraj Sharma 2-21) and 169 in 50.5 overs (Samar Quadri 36, Anunay Singh 35; Sunny Rana 4-51, D Dhapola 3-48) lost to **Uttarakhand** 227 in 71.3 overs (Karn Kaushal 91; Saurabh Rawat 64; Ashutosh Aman 4-34, Samar Quadri 3-77) and 4/0 in 0.1 overs by ten wickets. *PoM:* Deepak Dhapola.

Round 2: 152 and nine wickets for Jalaj Saxena

A late declaration, followed by Ruturaj Gaikwad's fighting hundred, helped Maharashtra keep Baroda at bay in their Group A game. Chhattisgarh responded to Gujarat's twin centurions with two of their own, while Ravindra Jadeja's seven wickets helped Saurashtra beat Railways.

In Group B, Manoj Tiwary's double-hundred enabled Bengal to force Madhya Pradesh to follow on before Aryaman Birla and Shubham Sharma rose to the challenge. Jalaj Saxena got a hundred and took nine wickets to help Kerala rout Andhra.

Varun Aaron and Ajay Yadav sent Haryana packing inside two days in Group C, while Amit Gautam's fourth-innings 178 helped Rajasthan turn a 92-run deficit into a five-wicket win.

Jalaj Saxena was an all-round asset for Kerala. — *KCA*

In the Plate Group, Milind continued his run-scoring ways, making 224 out of 374 and guiding Sikkim to a nine-wicket win. Deepak Dhapola starred for the second time in as many matches for Uttarakhand.

Elite Group A

Moti Bagh Stadium, Vadodara, November 12-15: Baroda 322 in 83.4 overs (Yusuf Pathan 99, Swapnil Singh 79, Satyajeet Bachhav 4-81, Samad Fallah 2-54) and 410/5 dec. in 82.4

overs (Vishnu Solanki 175, Deepak Hooda 96; Akshay Palkar 2-67) drew with **Maharashtra** 268 in 89.2 overs (Naushad Shaikh 65, Chirag Khurana 56; Swapnil Singh 5-78, Atit Sheth 2-42) and 217/2 in 67 overs (Ruturaj Gaikwad 118*, Ankit Bawne 40; Swapnil 2-59). Baroda took first-innings lead. *PoM:* Swapnil Singh.

Sardar Vallabhai Patel Stadium, Valsad, November 12-15: Gujarat 538/7 dec. in 146 overs (Dhruv Raval 116*, Manprit Juneja 107; Vishal Kushwah 3-92) and 167/5 dec. in 52.4 overs (M Juneja 50*, Priyank Panchal 50; Pankaj Rao 2-31, Shivendra Singh 2-54) drew with **Chhattisgarh** 420 in 127.3 overs (V Kushwah 159; Harpreet Bhatia 110; Arzan Nagwaswalla 4-66, Siddharth Desai 2-86). Gujarat took first-innings lead. *PoM:* Vishal Kushwah.

SCA Stadium, Rajkot, November 12-15: Railways 200 in 64 overs (Mahesh Rawat 46, Pratham Singh 45; Ravindra Jadeja 4-58, Kamlesh Makwana 3-55) and 331 in 119.4 overs (Harsh Tyagi 93, Anureet Singh 44; Dharmendrasinh Jadeja 5-95, R Jadeja 3-123) lost to **Saurashtra** 348 in 118.3 overs (R Jadeja 178*, K Makwana 62; H Tyagi 3-78, Avinash Yadav 3-95) and 186/7 in 49 overs (Sheldon Jackson 54, R Jadeja 48*; Avinash 5-88, Madhur Khatri 2-28) by three wickets. *PoM:* Ravindra Jadeja.

VCAStadium, Jamtha, Nagpur, November 12-15: Vidarbha 307 in 102.2 overs (Ganesh Satish 57, Shrikant Wagh 57; J Suchith 4-33, Abhimanyu Mithun 3-53) and 228 in 86.1 overs (G Satish 79, Apoorv Wankhade 51; J Suchith 5-70, Prasidh Krishna 2-58) drew with **Karnataka** 378 in 134 overs (Dega Nischal 113, BR Sharath 103; Aditya Sarwate 5-91, R Sanjay 2-23) and 76-6 in 33 overs (R Samarth 30; A Sarwate 4-24, Lalit Yadav 2-12). Karnatakatook first-innings lead. *PoM:* D Nischal.

Elite Group B

Eden Gardens, Kolkata, November 12-15: Bengal 510/9 dec. in 149.3 overs (Manoj Tiwary 201*, Koushik Ghosh 100; Shubham Sharma 5-59, Kuldeep Sen 2-66) drew with **Madhya Pradesh** 335 in 105.5 overs (Naman Ojha 74, Rajat Patidar 49; Ashok Dinda 4-78, Anustup Majumdar 3-38) and 240/3 in 68.2 overs (Aryaman Birla 103*, Shubham 100*; A Majumdar 2-60). Bengal took first-innings lead. *PoM:* Manoj Tiwary.

Feroz Shah Kotla, Delhi, November 12-15: Delhi 317 in 92.5 overs (Dhruv Shorey 88, Hiten Dalal 79; Pankaj Jaswal 3-56, Mayank Dagar 3-63) and 281/4 dec. in 67 overs (D Shorey 106*, Gautam Gambhir 49; M Dagar 3-70) drew with **Himachal Pradesh** 223 in 64.3 overs (Rishi Dhawan 64, Ekant Sen 46; Varun Sood 4-53, Ishant Sharma 2-40) and 266/5 in 102 overs (Nikhil Gangta 66*, R Dhawan 52*; Ishant 2-42, Vikas Mishra 2-57). Delhi took first-innings lead. *PoM:* Dhruv Shorey.

St Xavier's College Ground, Thumba, November 12-15: Andhra 254 in 99.4 overs (Ricky Bhui 109, Sivacharan Singh 45; KC Akshay 4-64, Basil Thampi 3-50) and 115 in 51.3 overs (R Bhui 32; Jalaj Saxena 8-45) lost to **Kerala** 328 in 119.2 overs (J Saxena 133, Arun Karthik 56; G Manish 3-81, Shoaib Mohammad 3-89) and 43/1 in 13 overs by nine wickets. *PoM:* Jalaj Saxena.

ICC Ground, Tirunelveli, November 12-15: Hyderabad 565/8 dec. in 186 overs (Akshath Reddy 250, B Sandeep 130; M Mohammed 3-102, K Vignesh 2-102) drew with **Tamil Nadu** 409/4 in 154 overs (Abhinav Mukund 178, N Jagadeesan 131*; Chama Milind 2-46). *PoM:* Akshath Reddy.

Elite Group C

GCA Academy Ground, Porvorim, November 12-15: Goa 468/9 dec. in 188 overs (Snehal Kauthankar 130*, Sumiran Amonkar 73; Irfan Pathan 3-69, Umar Nazir 3-109) drew with **Jammu and Kashmir** 271 in 86.5 overs (I Pathan 60, Shubham Khajuria 53; Lakshay Garg 4-87, Amogh Desai 2-23) and 242/5 in 73 overs (Ian Dev Singh 113*, S Khajuria 54; L Garg 2-31). Goa took first-innings lead. *PoM:* Snehal Kauthankar.

Chaudhary Bansi Lal Cricket Stadium, Lahli, November 12-13: Haryana 81 in 41.3 overs (Shubham Rohilla 36, Himanshu Rana 25; Ajay Yadav 4-24, Rahul Shukla 3-24) and 72 in

28 overs (Varun Aaron 6-32, Ajay 3-31) lost to **Jharkhand** 143 in 44.2 overs (Anukul Roy 27, Ishan Kishan 25; Ashish Hooda 5-37, Poonish Mehta 3-24) and 12/1 in 4 overs by nine wickets. *PoM:* Ajay Yadav.

KIIT Ground, Bhubaneswar, November 12-15: Odisha 256 in 68.1 overs (Subhranshu Senapati 87, Sujit Lenka 46; Ankit Rajpoot 3-61, Yash Dayal 3-62) and 221 in 72.3 overs (Sandeep Pattnaik 46, S Senapati 42; Shivam Mavi 5-68, A Rajpoot 4-64) lost to **Uttar Pradesh** 437 in 130.4 overs (Akshdeep Nath 159, Rinku Singh 72; Basant Mohanty 6-62, Rajesh Mohanty 2-69) and 44/0 in 12.5 overs by ten wickets. *PoM:* Akshdeep Nath.

Sawai Mansingh Stadium, Jaipur, November 12-15: Services 228 in 64.5 overs (Anshul Gupta 54, Vikas Hathwala 49; Tanveer-ul-Haq 4-61, Aniket Choudhary 3-59) and 264 in 81.4 overs (Rahul Singh 107, Vikas Yadav 51; Rahul Chahar 3-45, Nathu Singh 3-76) lost to **Rajasthan** 136 in 56.1 overs (Chetan Bist 46, Mahipal Lomror 28; Sachidanand Pandey 5-58, Diwesh Pathania 3-47) and 357/5 in 125.3 overs (Amitkumar Gautam 159, C Bist 78; Nitin Tanwar 3-82) by five wickets. *PoM:* Amitkumar Gautam.

Maharaja Bir Bikram College Stadium, Agartala, November 12-15: Assam 327 in 104.4 overs (Parviz Aziz 88, Rishav Das 70; Abhijit Sarkar 5-107, Harmeet Singh 2-45) and 239/6 dec. in 57 overs (Riyan Parag 80, Sibsankar Roy 39; Harmeet 2-57) beat **Tripura** 139 in 53.3 overs (Pratyush Singh 47, Ninad Kadam 28; Arup Das 5-42, Mukhtar Hussain 4-43) and 216 in 74 overs (Harmeet 33, Bravish Shetty 31; Mukhtar Hussain 5-73, Ranjit Mali 3-52) by 211 runs. *PoM:* Mukhtar Hussain.

Plate Group

District Sports Association Ground, Jorhat, November 12-15: Arunachal Pradesh 220 in 66.2 overs (Akhilesh Sahani 65, Kshitiz Sharma 49; Taruwar Kohli 3-62, Sinan Khadir 3-66) and 331 in 96 overs (Neelam Obi 80, Kamsha Yangfo 58; S Khadir 3-81, G Lalbiakvela 2-42) drew with **Mizoram** 142 in 43.2 overs (Akhil Rajput 57, T Kohli 28; Kshitiz 4-31,Techi Doria 4-26) and 244/2 in 59 overs (A Rajput 124, T Kohli 85*). Arunachal Pradesh took first-innings lead. *PoM:* Techi Doria.

Sovima Cricket Stadium, Dimapur, November 12-14: Nagaland 179 in 52.5 overs (Rongsen Jonathan 86, Tahmeed Rahman 33; Ishwar Chaudhary 4-65, Bipul Sharma 3-46) and 273 in 95 overs (KB Pawan 134, Imliwati Lemtur 61; I Chaudhary 5-70, Bipul 3-67) lost to **Sikkim** 374 in 82.5 overs (Milind Kumar 224, Bipul Sharma 90; Pawan Suyal 7-108, T Rahman 2-62) and 81/1 in 25.4 overs (Nilesh Lamichaney 33*, Faizan Khan 27) by nine wickets. *PoM:* Milind Kumar.

CAP Siechem Ground, Puducherry, November 12-15: Puducherry 389 in 127.3 overs (D Rohit 138, Paras Dogra 101; Gurinder Singh 4-106, Lakhan Singh 2-103) and 129/7 in 47.1 overs (Vikneshwaran Marimuthu 47; Gurinder 5-44, Aditya Singhania 2-10) drew with **Meghalaya** 326 in 112 overs (Yogesh Nagar 141*, Punit Bisht 58; Pankaj Singh 6-39, Akshay Jain 2-83). Puducherrytook first-innings lead. *PoM:* D Rohit.

Abhimanyu Cricket Academy, Dehradun, November 12-14: Manipur 137 in 42 overs (Yashpal Singh 38, Prafullomani Singh 32; Deepak Dhapola 7-50) and 185 in 74.4 overs (Lakhan Rawat 82, Prafullomani Singh 30; D Dhapola 5-46, Sunny Rana 5-50) lost to **Uttarakhand** 228 in 73.1 overs (Rajat Bhatia 61, Vaibhav Panwar 54; Thokchom Singh 4-50, Bishworjit Konthoujam 4-68) and 99/2 in 17.5 overs (Vineet Saxena 32*, Vaibhav Bhatt 27) by eight wickets. *PoM:* Deepak Dhapola.

Round 3: Twin tons for Aditya Waghmode

Aditya Waghmode's twin hundreds saved Baroda's day against Vidarbha, while Karnataka batted again despite a 195-run lead and failed to beat Mumbai in the Group A games.

Akshdeep Nath struck three tons for UP, including a highest score of 194. — *UPCC*

Kerala's pacers helped them down Bengal by nine wickets in Group B.

Rajesh Mohanty's 11 wickets helped Odisha thrash Assam in Group C, while Pramod Chandila helped Haryana recover from 34 for 7 to reach 185 and eventually beat Goa. Rinku Singh, who'd go on to have a special season for Uttar Pradesh, dazzled against Services.

In the Plate Group, Yashpal Singh's 156 not out was the difference between Manipur and Mizoram. Milind's continued heroics — 194 out of 404 across innings and two wickets — could not prevent Sikkim's loss to Uttarakhand. Rinku Singh of Uttar Pradesh dazzled against Services

Elite Group A

Shaheed Veer Narayan Singh International Cricket Stadium, Naya Raipur, November 20-23: Chhattisgarh 300 in 108 overs (Harpreet Bhatia 79, Amandeep Khare 54; Manjeet Singh 4-85, Karan Thakur 4-98) and 219/5 decl. in 58.1 overs (Sanjeet Desai 67, H Bhatia 59*; K Thakur 3-44) drew with **Railways** 330 in 121.5 overs (Mahesh Rawat 110, Pratham Singh 66; Pankaj Rao 5-72, Sumit Ruikar 2-68) and 70/1 in 20 overs (Nitin Bhille 53*). Railways took first-innings lead. *PoM:* Mahesh Rawat.

GS Patel Stadium, Nadiad, November 20-23: Gujarat 324 in 103.5 overs (Roosh Kalaria 91*, Manprit Juneja 66; Chetan Sakariya 5-83, Dharmendrasinh Jadeja 2-87) and 329/4 decl. in 71 overs (Priyank Panchal 141, Bhargav Merai 102*; Prerak Mankad 2-84) drew with **Saurashtra** 349 in 108 overs (Harvik Desai 82, Jaydev Shah 81*; Siddharth Desai 3-93) and 94/5 in 60 overs (H Desai 50, Rujul Bhatt 2-12). Saurashtra took first-innings lead. *PoM:* Jaydev Shah.

KSCA Stadium, Belgaum, November 20-23: Karnataka 400 in 129.4 overs (K V Siddharth 161, Kaunian Abbas 64; Shivam Dubey 7-53, Dhawal Kulkarni 2-54) and 170/5 decl. in 51 overs (KV Siddharth 71*, Stuart Binny 30; D Kulkarni 2-18, Shams Mulani 2-47) drew with **Mumbai** 205 in 85.5 overs (Jay Bista 70, S Mulani 34; Ronit More 5-52, Shreyas Gopal 2-31) and 173/4 in 64 overs (Suryakumar Yadav 53*, Akhil Herwadkar 53; Abhimanyu Mithun

2-22). Karnataka took first-innings lead. *PoM:* K V Siddharth.

VCA Stadium, Nagpur, November 20-23: Vidarbha 529/6 dec. in 164 overs (Wasim Jaffer 153, Faiz Fazal 151, Akshay Wadkar 102*; Lukman Meriwala 2-79, Bhargav Bhatt 2-111) drew with **Baroda** 337 in 121.5 overs (Aditya Waghmode 103, Deepak Hooda 100; Lalit Yadav 3-42, Aditya Sarwate 3-99) and 216/0 in 59.4 overs (A Waghmode 102*, Kedar Devdhar 101*). Vidarbha took first-innings lead. *PoM:* Aditya Waghmode.

Elite Group B

CSR Sharma College Ground, Ongole, November 20-23: Andhra 216 in 89.5 overs (Girinath Reddy 86*, Sai Krishna 58; M Mohammed 4-70, Sai Kishore 3-29, T Natarajan 3-36) and 8/0 in 7 overs drew with **Tamil Nadu** 254 in 112.4 overs (Baba Aparajith 57, Kaushik Gandhi 38; Karthik Raman 3-51, Shoaib Mohammad 2-15). Tamil Nadu took first-innings lead. *PoM:* Girinath Reddy.

Eden Gardens, Kolkata, November 20-22, Bengal 147 in 56.2 overs (Anustup Majumdar 53, Abhishek Raman 40; Basil Thampi 4-57, MD Nidheesh 3-22) and 184 in 56.5 overs (Manoj Tiwary 62, Sudip Chatterjee 39; Sandeep Warrier 5-33, B Thampi 3-59) lost to **Kerala** 291 in 83 overs (Jalaj Saxena 143, VA Jagadeesh 39; Ishan Porel 4-69, Mohammed Shami 3-100) and 44/1 in 11 overs (J Saxena 26*) by nine wickets. *PoM:* Jalaj Saxena.

Rajiv Gandhi International Stadium, Uppal, Hyderabad, November 20-23: Hyderabad 460 in 170.3 overs (Tanmay Agarwal 120, Ravi Teja 115*; Gaurav Kumar 3-50, Kulwant Khejroliya 3-64) and 156/1 in 43 overs (T Agarwal 82, Rohit Rayudu 61*)drew with **Delhi** 339 in 128.1 overs (Hiten Dalal 93, Nitish Rana 82; Tanay Thyagarajan 5-77, Mehdi Hasan 2-63). Hyderabad took first-innings lead. *PoM:* Tanay Thyagarajan.

Holkar Stadium, Indore, November 20-23: Punjab 293 in 84.4 overs (Jiwanjot Singh 124, Gurkeerat Singh 66; Kuldeep Sen 5-62, Avesh Khan 4-77) and 265/9 dec. in 68 overs (Abhishek Sharma 78, Mandeep Singh 65*; Ishwar Pandey 4-59, Avesh 3-85) drew with **Madhya Pradesh** 315 in 124.2 overs (Rajat Patidar 73, Yash Dubey 65*; Mayank Markande 4-70, Sanvir Singh 2-56) and 67/1 in 35 overs (Mohnish Mishra 34*, R Patidar 25*). Madhya Pradeshtook first-innings lead. *PoM:* Kuldeep Sen.

Elite Group C

Barsapara Cricket Stadium, Guwahati, November 20-22: Assam 121 in 51.1 overs (Ranjit Mali 28; Rajesh Mohanty 5-31, Debabrata Pradhan 2-27) and 132 in 50 overs (Sibsankar Roy 56; R Mohanty 6-55, D Pradhan 2-35) lost to **Odisha** 240 in 85.2 overs (Anurag Sarangi 77, Biplab Samantray 61; R Mali 6-80, Mukhtar Hussain 3-75) and 16 for 1 in 3.3 overs by nine wickets. *PoM:* Rajesh Mohanty.

Chaudhary Bansi Lal Cricket Stadium, Lahli, November 20-23:Haryana 276 in 88 overs (Himanshu Rana 86, Nitin Saini 64; Krishna Das 6-75, Lakshay Garg 3-102) and 185 in 70 overs (Pramod Chandila 122*; K Das 5-41, Felix Alemao 2-23) beat **Goa** 177 in 79.1 overs (Sagun Kamat 68, Snehal Kauthankar 25; Poonish Mehta 4-21, Ashish Hooda 3-36) and 141 in 49.3 overs (Suyash Prabhudessai 36; A Hooda 6-54, Harshal Patel 3-40) by 143 runs. *PoM:* Pramod Chandila.

Sher-e-Kashmir Stadium, Srinagar, November 20-23: Tripura 124 in 42 overs (Ninad Kadam 34; Parveez Rasool 5-30, Irfan Pathan 2-17) and 358 in 123.1 overs (Smit Patel 112, Udiyan Bose 67; Waseem Raza 6-78, Umar Nazir 2-52) lost to **Jammu and Kashmir** 442 in 121 overs (Ahmed Banday 136, I Pathan 85; Harmeet Singh 5-91, Abhijit Sarkar 3-80) and 43/2 in 9.3 overs by eight wickets. *PoM:* Ahmed Banday

JSCA International Stadium, Ranchi, November 20-23: Rajasthan100 in 42.2 overs (Rajesh Bishnoi 33; Varun Aaron 5-22, Ajay Yadav 3-35) and 379 in 127.4 overs (Ashok Menaria 125, R Bishnoi 82; Anukul Roy 4-97, Anand Singh 3-17) beat **Jharkhand** 152 in 58.1 overs (Ishank Jaggi 79; Tanveer-ul-Haq 6-42, Rahul Chahar 2-8) and 235 in 81 overs (I

Jaggi 51, Md Nazim 32; R Chahar 5-77, Nathu Singh 2-52) by 92 runs. *PoM:* Ashok Menaria.
Palam A Ground, Model Sports Complex, Delhi, November 20-23: Services 260 in 92.2 overs (Devender Lohchab 75, Nitin Tanwar 39; Shivam Mavi 4-44, Ankit Rajpoot 4-74) and 225/2 in 88 overs (Ravi Chauhan 114*, Navneet Singh 86) drew with **Uttar Pradesh** 535/9 dec. in 159.2 overs (Rinku Singh 163*, Priyam Garg 88; Diwesh Pathania 4-104, Sachidanand Pandey 3-101). Uttar Pradesh took first-innings lead. *PoM:* Rinku Singh.

Plate Group
Meghalaya Cricket Association Cricket Ground, Shillong, November 20-23: Meghalaya 389 in 110.2 overs (Yogesh Nagar 166, Raj Biswa 111; Pawan Suyal 5-96, Jalaluddin 3-33) and 91/4 in 21.4 overs (Punit Bisht 34*, Y Nagar 29; P Suyal 2-18, Tahmeed Rahman 2-41) beat **Nagaland** 106 in 46.3 overs (Gurinder Singh 4-37, Aditya Singhania 3-12, Lakhan Singh 3-23) and 371 in 114.2 overs (Abrar Kazi 164, Sedezhalie Rupero 68; A Singhania 5-52, Dippu Sangma 2-47) by six wickets. *PoM:* Yogesh Nagar.
District Sports Association Ground, Jorhat, November 20-22: Mizoram 219 in 69.1 overs (Taruwar Kohli 100, Akhil Rajput 61; Bishworjit Konthoujam 3-50, Priyojit Singh 2-23) and 116 in 37 overs (Lalhruaizela 28; Thokchom Singh 4-20, Bishworjit Konthoujam 3-27) lost to **Manipur** 319 in 87 overs (Yashpal Singh 156*, Prafullomani Singh 51; K Lalhmingmawia 3-88, Lalnunkima Varte 2-43) and 19/2 in 7.5 overs by eight wickets. *PoM:* Yashpal Singh.
CAP Siechem Ground, Puducherry, November 20-23: Puducherry vs Bihar. Match abandoned without a ball bowled.
KIIT Ground, Bhubaneswar, November 20-23: Uttarakhand 582/9 dec. in 163 overs (Saurabh Rawat 220, Vaibhav Bhatt 152*, Rajat Bhatia 121; Ishwar Chaudhary 4-105, Milind Kumar 2-115) beat **Sikkim** 264 in 96 overs (Milind 133, Nilesh Lamichaney 57; Dhanraj Sharma 3-36, Malolan Rangarajan 3-67) and 140 in 48.5 overs (Milind 61, Ashish Thapa 35; Deepak Dhapola 4-44, M Rangarajan 2-11) by an innings and 178 runs. *PoM:* Saurabh Rawat.

Round 4: Ten and hundred for Parvez Rasool in defeat
In Group A, Karnataka beat Maharashtra riding on a fourth-innings opening stand of 121; Priyank Panchal's rapid 112 not out got Gujarat full points against Mumbai; and Baroda got first-innings lead despite Saurashtra's 521.

Group B contests were mostly one-sided. Delhi never recovered after the Punjab seamers bowled them out for 107, Ravi Kiran's third-innings burst helped Hyderabad thrash Himachal Pradesh, and Madhya Pradesh bowled out Kerala for 63. Only Bengal's one wicket win in a Chepauk cliff-hanger broke the script.

Group C saw two great escapes. Anukul Roy's 127, scored out of 173 during his stay, turned the match for Jharkhand; Subhranshu Senapati and Abhishek Raut lifted Odisha from 79 for 5 to pull off a 215-run chase. Parvez Rasool's century-and-ten-wickets double went in vain, however.

Ashutosh Aman almost did the double in the Plate Group: he scored 89 and took ten wickets in Bihar's big win. Pankaj Singh, meanwhile, took 11 wickets to bowl out Mizoram for 92 and 45.

Elite Group A
Shaheed Veer Narayan Singh International Cricket Stadium, Naya Raipur, November 28-December 1: Chhattisgarh 232 in 109 overs (Manoj Singh 77*, Harpreet Bhatia 63; Aditya Thakare 5-56, Faiz Fazal 2-15) and 143 in 57 overs (Sumit Ruikar 39*, Shakeeb Ahmed 31;

Saurabh Kumar finished with 51 wickets for
Uttar Pradesh. — *UPCA*

Lalit Yadav 7-56, Yash Thakur 2-33) lost to **Vidarbha** 332-6 dec. in 116 overs (F Fazal 146, Akshay Wadkar 144*; S Ruikar 3-46, Omkar Verma 2-90) and 46/0 in 19.2 overs (A Wadkar 25*) by ten wickets. *PoM:* Lalit Yadav.

Srikantadatta Narasimha Raja Wadeyar Ground, Mysore, November 28-December 1: Maharashtra 113 in 39.4 overs (Ruturaj Gaikwad 39, Rohit Motwani 34; J Suchith 4-26, Ronit More 2-16) and 256 in 97 overs (R Gaikwad 89, Naushad Shaikh 73; Shreyas Gopal 4-64, Vinay Kumar 3-41) lost to **Karnataka** 186 in 84.2 overs (Shreyas G 40, Dega Nischal 39; Satyajeet Bachhav 3-43, Samad Fallah 2-35) and 184/3 in 70.2 overs (Devdutt Padikkal 77, D Nischal 61; S Bachhav 2-56) by seven wickets. *PoM:* Shreyas Gopal.

Wankhede Stadium, Mumbai, November 28-December 1: Mumbai 297 in 80.3 overs (Shivam Dube 110, Siddhesh Lad 62; Arzan Nagwaswalla 5-78, Roosh Kalaria 3-80) and 187 in 75.4 overs (Aditya Tare 59, S Dube 55; Chintan Gaja 4-57, R Kalaria 4-59) lost to **Gujarat** 281 in 99.4 overs (Dhruv Raval 99, Rujul Bhatt 41; S Dube 3-50, Dhawal Kulkarni 3-71, Royston Dias 3-74) and 206/1 in 41.5 overs (Priyank Panchal 112*, Kathan Patel 55) by nine wickets. *PoM:* Shivam Dube.

SCA Stadium, Rajkot, November 28-December 1: Saurashtra 521 in 168.2 overs (Jaydev Shah 165, Arpit Vasavada 120; Atit Sheth 3-74, Rishi Arothe 2-84) drew with **Baroda** 533/9 in 167.2 overs (Kedar Devdhar 224, Vishnu Solanki 116; Hardik Rathod 3-98, Dharmendrasinh Jadeja 3-121). Baroda took first-innings lead. *PoM:* Kedar Devdhar.

Elite Group B

Feroz Shah Kotla, Delhi, November 28-December 1: Delhi 107 in 42.5 overs (Kunwar Bidhuri 27; Siddharth Kaul 6-32, Vinay Choudhary 3-34) and 179 in 84.2 overs (Gautam Gambhir 60, Pulkit Narang 31; V Choudhary 4-39, Mayank Markande 3-30) lost to **Punjab** 282 in 91.5 overs (Mandeep Singh 90, Gurkeerat Singh 40; Simarjeet Singh 4-43, Vikas Mishra 4-57) and 8/0 in 2.1 overs by ten wickets. *PoM:* Mandeep Singh.

Rajiv Gandhi International Stadium, Uppal, Hyderabad, November 28-December 1: Himachal Pradesh351 in 126.4 overs (Prashant Chopra 110, Mayank Dagar 61; Tanay Thyagarajan 4-86, Ravi Kiran 3-68) and 97 in 45.2 overs (R Kiran 4-34, T Thyagarajan 3-9) lost to **Hyderabad** 352 in 130.5 overs (Akshath Reddy 99, R Teja 75; Arpit Guleria 3-64, M Dagar 3-70) and 97/0 in 28.2 overs (Tanmay Agarwal 48*, A Reddy 44*) by ten wickets. *PoM:* Ravi Kiran.

St Xavier's College Ground, Thumba, November 28-December 1: Kerala 63 in 35 overs (Avesh Khan 4-8, Kuldeep Sen 3-17) and 455 in 121.1 overs (Vishnu Vinod 193*, Sachin Baby 143; K Sen 3-69, Shubham Sharma 2-9) lost to **Madhya Pradesh** 328 in 120 overs (Naman Ojha 79, Yash Dubey 79, Jalaj Saxena 4-120, Sandeep Warrier 2-28) and 194/5 in 62 overs (Rajat Patidar 77, Shubham 48*; Akshay Chandran 2-57) by five wickets lead. *PoM:* Vishnu Vinod.

MA Chidambaram Stadium, Chepauk, Chennai, November 28-December 1: Tamil Nadu 263 in 106 overs (Baba Aparajith 103, Kaushik Gandhi 51; Ishan Porel 5-48, Pradipta Pramanik 3-82) and 141 in 62.5 overs (N Jagadeesan 38; Writtick Chatterjee 5-22, Aamir Gani 2-41) lost to **Bengal** 189 in 63.5 overs (Abhishek Raman 98; Rahil Shah 5-46, M Mohammed 4-39) and 216/9 in 82.5 overs (A Raman 53, Sudip Chatterjee 40; R Shah 5-68, T Natarajan 2-49) by one wicket. *PoM:* Abhishek Raman.

Elite Group C

Barsapara Cricket Stadium, Guwahati, November 28-30: Assam 310 in 117.3 overs (Gokul Sharma 96, Sibsankar Roy 49; Poonish Mehta 3-51, Jayant Yadav 3-63) beat **Haryana** 97 in 27.2 overs (J Yadav 30; Arup Das 5-52, Ranjit Mali 3-25) and 178 in 52 overs (Chaitanya Bishnoi 78, P Mehta 70*; A Das 4-37, Mukhtar Hussain 4-58) by an innings and 35 runs. *PoM:* Arup Das.

GCA Academy Ground, Porvorim, November 28-December 1: Goa 364 in 140.2 overs (Amit Verma 154, Sumiran Amonkar 95; Ashish Kumar 3-71, Anukul Roy 2-52) and 131 in 48.3 overs (Suyash Prabhudessai 39, Snehal Kauthankar 35; Rahul Prasad 6-45, A Kumar 3-17) lost to **Jharkhand** 390 in 124.5 overs (A Roy 127, Utkarsh Singh 75; Amulya Pandrekar 3-78, Vishamber Kahlon 2-26) and 108/3 in 32.2 overs (Kumar Deobrat 48*, Saurabh Tiwary 29; Vijesh Prabhudessai 2-22) by seven wickets. *PoM:* Anukul Roy.

DRIEMS Ground, Cuttack, November 28-December 1: Tripura 122 in 43 overs (Pratyush Singh 43; Suryakant Pradhan 7-40) and 304 in 91.3 overs (Manisankar Murasingh 75, Bishal Ghosh 48; Basant Mohanty 4-53, Rajesh Mohanty 4-94) lost to **Odisha** 212 in 59.2 overs (Biplab Samantray 89, Subhranshu Senapati 41; Abhijit Sarkar 3-33, M Murasingh 3-37) and 217/5 in 63.2 overs (S Senapati 84*, Abhishek Raut 83*; M Murasingh 4-54) by five wickets. *PoM:* Subhranshu Senapati.

Palam A Ground, Model Sports Complex, Delhi, November 28-December 1: Jammu and Kashmir 95 in 31.5 overs (Shubham Khajuria 44; Arun Bamal 5-13, Diwesh Pathania 4-30) and 261 in 98.5 overs (Parvez Rasool 115, Waseem Raza 30; D Pathania 4-60, A Bamal 3-90) lost to **Services** 252 in 91.4 overs (Anshul Gupta 59, Navneet Singh 58; P Rasool 8-85) and 107/5 in 36.5 overs (Rajat Paliwal 43*; P Rasool 2-18, Mohammad Mudhasir 2-21) by five wickets. *PoM:* Parveez Rasool.

Modi Stadium, Kanpur, November 28-December 1: Rajasthan 311 in 112.4 overs (Robin Bist 96, Amit Gautam 93; Ankit Rajpoot 5-61, Yash Dayal 2-67) and 232 in 98.2 overs (A Gautam 86, R Bist 32; Saurabh Kumar 6-77, A Rajpoot 2-42) drew with **Uttar Pradesh** 214 in 61.5 overs (Upendra Yadav 67, Suresh Raina 33; Aniket Choudhary 5-64, Tanveer-ul-Haq 3-55) and 116/2 in 36 overs (Mohammad Saif 58, Shivam Chaudhary 36). Rajasthan took first-innings lead. *PoM:* Aniket Choudhary.

Plate Group

DN Singha Stadium, Goalpara, November 28-30: Arunachal Pradesh 105 in 46 overs (Kshitiz Sharma 57; Mayank Mishra 4-23, Sunny Rana 3-30) and 292 in 112.3 overs (Kshitiz 118, Samarth Seth 60, Techi Doria 60; M Mishra 4-57, Malolan Rangarajan 4-78) lost to **Uttarakhand** 470/4 dec. in 108.4 overs (Kartik Joshi 208*, Rajat Bhatia 152*) by an innings and 73 runs. *PoM:* Kartik Joshi.

Moin-ul-Haq Stadium, Patna, November 28-30: Bihar 288 in 90.5 overs (Ashutosh Aman 89, Vivek Kumar 72; Ishwar Chaudhary 6-78, Bipul Sharma 3-83) and 296/7 dec. in 81 overs (MD Rahmatullah 66, Utkarsh Bhaskar 59; Milind Kumar 4-63, Lee Yong Lepcha 2-48) beat **Sikkim** 81 in 39.4 overs (A Aman 5-19, Vishal Das 2-14) and 108 in 43.1 overs (Bipul Sharma 32; A Aman 5-22, Samar Quadri 5-32) by 395 runs. *PoM:* Ashutosh Aman.

Jadavpur University Second Campus Ground, Kolkata, November 28-30: Manipur 211 in 64.1 overs (Prafullomani Singh 64, Yashpal Singh 33; Aditya Singhania 4-42, Gurinder Singh 3-52) and 172 in 43 overs (Yashpal 103*; Gurinder 5-46, Abhay Negi 3-34) lost to **Meghalaya** 326 in 87.4 overs (Punit Bisht 92, Raj Biswa 87; Homendro Meitei 3-27, William Singh 3-66) and 58/1 in 11.1 overs (Raj Biswa 44*) by nine wickets. *PoM:* Gurinder Singh.

Cricket Association Puducherry Siechem Ground, Puducherry, November 28-December 1: Mizoram 92 in 54.4 overs (Michael Lalremkima 25; Pankaj Singh 7-21, Fabid Ahmed 2-22) and 45 in 29.3 overs (F Ahmed 4-8, Pankaj 4-15) lost to **Puducherry** 375/8 dec. in 89.1 overs (F Ahmed 103*, Vikneshwaran Marimuthu 102; Sinan Khadir 5-97) by an innings and 238 runs. *PoM:* Fabid Ahmed.

Round 5: Jaydev Shah, Gautam Gambhir bid adieu

It was a round for farewells. Harsh Tyagi's last-day show nearly helped Railways beat Gujarat. Saurashtra scored 79, but Dharmendrasinh Jadeja took 11 wickets to help them trounce Karnataka in Jaydev Shah's last match. Gautam Gambhir's farewell hundred was overshadowed by Ricky Bhui's 187.

With an unbeaten 267, Ajay Rohera set a new world record for the highest individual score on first-class debut as Madhya Pradesh flattened Hyderabad. Mayank Dagar's all-round show helped Himachal Pradesh beat Punjab for the first time in their history.

Saurabh Kumar's 11 wickets trumped Rasool's all-round show as Uttar Pradesh beat Jammu and Kashmir after trailing by 102. Senapati's epic 157 not out went in vain as Odisha lost to Jharkhand by two runs and Ra-

Dharmendrasinh Jadeja took 59 wickets in the season for Saurashtra, including 11 against Karnataka.

jasthan's Aniket Choudhary blew Assam away twice in three days.

Plate Group threw up double-hundreds galore: Manipur rode on Mayank Raghav's to beat Nagaland, Paras Dogra slammed 253 as Puducherry thrashed Sikkim, and Vineet Saxena and Rajat Bhatia's played key roles in Uttarakhand's innings win against Meghalaya.

Elite Group A

Moti Bagh Stadium, Vadodara, December 6-9: Chhattisgarh 129 in 39.4 overs (Harpreet Bhatia 37, Avnish Dhaliwal 35; Swapnil Singh 5-23, Soaeb Tai 3-36) and 283 in 81.3 overs (A Dhaliwal 79, Manoj Singh 61; Lukman Meriwala 3-18, Yusuf Pathan 2-10) lost to **Baroda** 385 in 84.4 overs (Y Pathan 129*, Bhargav Bhatt 67; Omkar Verma 4-84, Vishal Kushwah 2-23) and 31/1 in 3.3 overs (Kedar Devdhar 25*) by nine wickets. *PoM:* Yusuf Pathan.

Sardar Vallabhai Patel Stadium, Valsad, December 6-9: Gujarat 367 in 93.5 overs (Piyush

Chawla 130, Priyank Panchal 69; Amit Mishra 4-93, Avinash Yadav 2-69) and 191/7 in 92 overs (P Panchal 58, Kathan Patel 50; Harsh Tyagi 4-46, Avinash 2-60) drew with **Railways** 547-9 dec. (Mahesh Rawat 119*, Nitin Bhille 116; Hardik Patel 3-134, Chintan Gaja 2-62). Railways took first-innings lead. *PoM:* Nitin Bhille.

MCA Stadium, Gahunje, December 6-9: Maharashtra 352 in 109.4 overs (Swapnil Gugale 101, Jay Pande 74; Akash Parkar 4-56, Shubham Ranjane 2-30) and 254 in 90.1 overs (Rahul Tripathi 76, Chirag Khurana 38; Shivam Dubey 3-25, Shivam Malhotra 3-41) drew with **Mumbai** 273 in 80.5 overs (Siddhesh Lad 93, Aditya Tare 63; Akshay Palkar 4-62, Samad Fallah 3-55) and 135/5 in 47 overs (A Tare 52*, S Ranjane 35; A Palkar 2-23). Maharashtra took first-innings lead. *PoM:* Swapnil Gugale.

SCA Stadium, Rajkot, December 6-8: Saurashtra 316 in 97.1 overs (Jaydev Shah 97, Kamlesh Makwana 46; J Suchith 6-111, Pavan Deshpande 3-88) and 79 in 27.4 overs (P Deshpande 3-5, Shreyas Gopal 3-10, J Suchith 3-29) beat **Karnataka** 217 in 78.1 overs (Karun Nair 63, Dega Nischal 58; Dharmendrasinh Jadeja 7-103, K Makwana 2-58) and 91 in 36.5 overs (K Nair 30, Shreyas 27; K Makwana 5-28, D Jadeja 4-44) by 87 runs. *PoM:* Dharmendrasinh Jadeja.

Elite Group B

Feroz Shah Kotla, Delhi, December 6-9: Andhra 390 in 121 overs (Ricky Bhui 187, G Manish 36; Subodh Bhati 5-48, Vikas Mishra 2-79) and 130 in 59 overs (Shoaib Mohammed 44, R Bhui 27; Shivank Vashisht 5-49, V Mishra 3-15) drew with **Delhi** 433 in 157.4 overs (Gautam Gambhir 112, Dhruv Shorey 98; G Manish 3-129, Shoaib 3-138)and 41/2 in 5 overs (B Ayyappa 2-19). Delhi took first-innings lead. *PoM:* Ricky Bhui.

Holkar Stadium, Indore, December 6-9: Hyderabad 124 in 35.3 overs (Himalay Agarwal 69*; Avesh Khan 7-24) and 185 in 65.5 overs (Rohit Rayudu 72, Mehdi Hasan 25; Avesh 5-30, Shubham Sharma 2-30) lost to **Madhya Pradesh** 562/4 decl. in 140.4 overs (Ajay Rohera 267*, Yash Dubey 139*; Ravi Kiran 2-103) by an innings and 253 runs. *PoM:* Ajay Rohera.

PCA IS Bindra Stadium, Mohali, December 6-9: Himachal Pradesh390 in 145.1 overs (Ankit Kalsi 82, Mayank Dagar 71; Sandeep Sharma 5-101, Sanvir Singh 2-58) beat **Punjab** 84 in 35.1 overs (M Dagar 4-22, Arpit Guleria 2-24) and 199 in 81.5 overs (Abhijeet Garg 48, Shubek Gill 41; Gurvinder Singh 4-44, A Guleria 2-36) by an innings and 107 runs. *PoM:* Mayank Dagar

MA Chidambaram Stadium, Chepauk, Chennai, December 6-9: Tamil Nadu 268 in 98 overs (Shahrukh Khan 92*, Baba Indrajith 87; Sandeep Warrier 5-52, Basil Thampi 4-62) and 252/7 dec. in 70.5 overs (B Indrajith 92, Kaushik Gandhi 59; Sijomon Joseph 4-51, S Warrier 2-53) beat **Kerala** 152 in 76.5 overs (P Rahul 59, S Joseph 29; Rahil Shah 4-32, T Natarajan 3-43) and 217 in 89 overs (Sanju Samson 91, S Joseph 55; T Natarajan 5-41, B Aparajith 2-36) by 151 runs. *PoM:* T Natarajan.

Elite Group C

GCA Academy Ground, Porvorim, December 6-8: Services 184 in 71.3 overs (Ravi Chauhan 75; Vijesh Prabhudessai 5-52, Amulya Pandrekar 3-27) and 332 in 103.4 overs (Rahul Singh 111, Rajat Paliwal 94; Amit Verma 5-39, V Prabhudessai 2-61) drew with **Goa** 259 in 100.2 overs (Darshan Misal 101, Lakshay Garg 50; Diwesh Pathania 5-74, Sachidanand Pandey 4-59) and 67/2 in 54 overs (Akash Sharma 2-20). Goa took first-innings lead. *PoM:* Darshan Misal.

Gandhi Memorial Science College Ground, Jammu, December 6-9: Jammu and Kashmir 290 in 71.4 overs (Irfan Pathan 91, Parveez Rasool 87; Saurabh Kumar 6-90, Yash Dayal 2-47) and 111 in 48 overs (Saurabh 5-28, Y Dayal 4-26) lost to **Uttar Pradesh** 188 in 57.2 overs (Rinku Singh 66, Akshdeep Nath 43; P Rasool 4-47, Mohammad Mudhasir 3-57) and 218/4 in 59.2 overs (Suresh Raina 66*, Rinku 42*; P Rasool 2-63) by six wickets. *PoM:* Saurabh Kumar.

JSCA International Stadium, Ranchi, December 6-9: Jharkhand 172 in 71.1 overs (Ishank Jaggi 34, Kumar Deobrat 29; Basant Mohanty 5-44, Rajesh Mohanty 3-51) and 288 in 94 overs (Saurabh Tiwary 132*, K Deobrat 37; R Mohanty 4-87, Dhiraj Singh 2-52) beat **Odisha** 201 in 55.4 overs (Anurag Sarangi 58, Suryakant Pradhan 54; Anukul Roy 2-35, Rahul Shukla 2-40) and 257 in 101.3 overs (Subhranshu Senapati 157*, A Sarangi 41; A Roy 4-51, R Shukla 2-43) by 2 runs. *PoM:* Subhranshu Senapati.

Sawai Mansingh Stadium, Jaipur, December 6-8: Assam 108 in 28.1 overs (Arup Das 36*, Ranjit Mali 28; Aniket Choudhary 5-38, Nathu Singh 3-33) and 174 in 59.4 overs (Gokul Sharma 77, Kunal Saikia 49; A Choudhary 5-40, Nathu 2-28) lost to **Rajasthan** 325 in 111.2 overs (Mahipal Lomror 133, Salman Khan 71; R Mali 5-62, Jitumoni Kalita 2-50) by an innings and 43 runs. *PoM:* Aniket Choudhary.

Maharaja Bir Bikram College Stadium, Agartala, December 6-9: Haryana 292 in 100.4 overs (Rahul Dagar 114, Chaitanya Bishnoi 82; Ajay Sarkar 5-57, Manisankar Murasingh 4-74) and 119 in 44.2 overs (Himanshu Rana 64; A Sarkar 3-15, Harmeet Singh 3-45) beat **Tripura** 250 in 76.1 overs (Pratyush Singh 76, M Murasingh 44; Harshal Patel 4-49, Poonish Mehta 2-35) and 106 in 32.3 overs (Amit Rana 4-37, Tinu Kundu 3-19) by 55 runs. *PoM:* Rahul Dagar.

Plate Group

Moin-ul-Haq Stadium, Patna, December 6-8: Arunachal Pradesh 84 in 39.5 overs (Techi Doria 33; Ashutosh Aman 4-26, Vivek Kumar 3-26) and 135 in 47.4 overs (Samarth Seth 58, Akhilesh Sahani 25; A Aman 7-14, Samar Quadri 2-31) lost to **Bihar** 536/5 dec. in 112 overs (Indrajit Kumar 222, Babul Kumar 98; Myendung Singpho 2-90) by an innings and 317 runs. *PoM:* Indrajit Kumar.

Sovima Cricket Stadium, Dimapur, December 6-8: Nagaland 126 in 37.3 overs (Paras Sehrawat 27; Priyojit Singh 3-20, Thokchom Singh 3-32, Homendro Meitei 3-46) and 334 in 98.1 overs (KB Pawan 131, Abrar Kazi 90; Yashpal Singh 5-46, H Meitei 2-58) lost to **Manipur** 336 in 91.4 overs (Mayank Raghav 228, Yashpal 35; Tahmeed Rahman 5-108, Pawan Suyal 2-76) and 128/3 in 36.4 overs (Lakhan Rawat 55, Yashpal 35*) by seven wickets. *PoM:* Mayank Raghav.

Krishnagiri Stadium, Wayanad, December 6-9: Puducherry 647/8 dec. in 157 overs (Paras Dogra 253, Fabid Ahmed 99; Dinesh Rai 2-70, Ishwar Chaudhary 2-118) beat **Sikkim** 247 in 72.2 overs (Milind Kumar 96, Bipul Sharma 47; Pankaj Singh 3-21, D Rohit 3-67) and 241 in 75.5 overs (Milind 77*, Ashish Thapa 52; Abhishek Nayar 5-76, Pankaj 3-40) by an innings and 159 runs. *PoM:* Paras Dogra.

Rajiv Gandhi International Cricket Stadium, Dehradun, December 6-9: Meghalaya 311 in 95.5 overs (Punit Bisht 154, Yogesh Nagar 91; Deepak Dhapola 6-52, Sunny Rana 2-73) and 230 in 66.2 overs (Gurinder Singh 104, Y Nagar 57; D Dhapola 5-59, Dhanraj Sharma 3-66) lost to **Uttarakhand** 491/4 dec. in 163 overs (Rajat Bhatia 212*, Vineet Saxena 202*; Dippu Sangma 2-50) and 53/2 in 6.1 overs (Vaibhav Panwar 32*) by eight wickets. *PoM:* Deepak Dhapola.

Round 6: Gill sparkles with double

Chasing 173, Karnataka ran out of time against Gujarat and finished on 107 for 4. Hardik Pandya's all-round show on comeback for Baroda overshadowed Shreyas Iyer's pyrotechnics and Vidarbha's Aditya Sarwate bowled unchanged in the fourth innings to run through the Railways innings with 6 for 43.

Saxena scored 68 and took nine wickets as Kerala thrashed Delhi, and

Shubman Gill scored a sparkling 268 against Tamil Nadu in Group B.

Irfan Pathan's fourth-innings new-ball burst led to a Jammu and Kashmir triumph against Haryana and Rajasthan beat Odisha despite Basant Mohanty's 11/49. Plate Group saw more mismatches: Puducherry bowled out Arunachal Pradesh for 82 and 71, while Aman took 14 for 68 in Bihar's two-day win against Meghalaya and Kazi saved Nagaland from defeat after Uttarakhand got a 350-run lead.

Elite Group A

Lalabhai Contractor Stadium, Surat, December 14-17: Gujarat 216 in 69.4 overs (Priyank Panchal 74, Piyush Chawla 34; Shreyas Gopal 2-21, Prateek Jain 2-28) and 345 in 124.5 overs (Manprit Juneja 98, Rujul Bhatt 91; Ronit More 4-61, K Gowtham 4-80) drew with **Karnataka** 389 in 121 overs (Shreyas 93, Devdutt Padikkal 74; P Chawla 4-99, Arzan Nagwaswalla 3-48, Axar Patel 3-84) and 107/4 in 27 overs (Mayank Agarwal 53, R Samarth 33; Axar 3-45). Karnataka took first-innings lead. *PoM:* Shreyas Gopal.

Hutatma Anant Kanhere Maidan, Golf Club Ground, Nasik, December 14-17: Saurashtra 398 in 136.3 overs (Vishvaraj Jadeja 97, Snell Patel 84; Anupam Sanklecha 6-103, Samad Fallah 3-69) and 120/5 in 34.1 overs (Harvik Desai 44, Arpit Vasavada 28; Chirag Khurana 2-35, Satyajeet Bachhav 2-41) beat **Maharashtra** 247 in 70.2 overs (Kedar Jadhav 99, C Khurana 30, Rahul Tripathi 30; Chetan Sakariya 6-63, Jaydev Unadkat 2-50) and 267 in 75.2 overs (Rohit Motwani 120*, R Tripathi 38; Dharmendrasinh Jadeja 7-55, Hardik Rathod 2-35) by five wickets. *PoM:* Dharmendrasinh Jadeja.

Wankhede Stadium, Mumbai, December 14-17: Mumbai 465 in 92.5 overs (Shreyas Iyer 178, Siddhesh Lad 130; Hardik Pandya 5-81, Bhargav Bhatt 4-76) and 307/7 dec. in 84 overs (Shivam Dubey 76, Shubham Ranjane 64; H Pandya 2-21, Rishi Arothe 2-51) drew with **Baroda** 436 in 146 overs (Vishnu Solanki 133, Aditya Waghmode 114; Royston Dias 4-99, S Ranjane 3-62). Mumbai took first-innings lead. *PoM:* Shreyas Iyer.

Karnail Singh Stadium, Delhi, December 14-17: Vidarbha 331 in 110.3 overs (Akshay Karnewar 94, Faiz Fazal 53; Avinash Yadav 5-78, Madhur Khatri 2-41) and 147 in 50.5 overs (Aditya Sarwate 39, R Sanjay 26; Harsh Tyagi 7-41, A Yadav 3-102) beat **Railways** 236 in 88.5 overs (Pratham Singh 95, Nitin Bhille 37; Akshay Wakhare 5-71, A Sarwate 3-66) and 124 in 32.2 overs (Manjeet Singh 33; A Sarwate 6-43, A Karnewar 2-20) by 118 runs. *PoM:* Aditya Sarwate.

Elite Group B

Atal Bihari Vajpayee Stadium, Amtar, December 14-17: Andhra 173 in 54.3 overs (Sai Krishna 74, G Manish 32; Pankaj Jaswal 5-50, Arpit Guleria 2-43) and 284 in 100.5 overs (CR Gnaneshwar 103, S Krishna 82; Gurvinder Singh 3-62, Mayank Dagar 3-89) lost to **Himachal Pradesh** 460 in 144.4 overs (Ankit Kalsi 120, Rishi Dhawan 76; G Manish 3-102, Shoaib Mohammad 2-99) by an innings and three runs. *PoM:* Pankaj Jaswal.

Rajiv Gandhi International Stadium, Uppal, Hyderabad, December 14-17: Bengal 336 in 120.3 overs (Abhimanyu Easwaran 186, Sudip Chatterjee 32, Anustup Majumdar 32; Ravi Kiran 4-46, Tanay Thyagarajan 2-69) and 49/1 in 14 overs (S Chatterjee 30*) drew with **Hyderabad** 312 in 123.1 overs (Rohit Rayudu 93, Himalay Agarwal 65; Mukesh Kumar 4-54, Ashok Dinda 4-88). Bengal took first-innings lead. *PoM:* Abhimanyu Easwaran.

St Xavier's College Ground, Thumba, December 14-16: Kerala 320 in 95.3 overs (P Rahul 77, Vinoop Manoharan 77; Shivam Sharma 6-98, Akash Sudan 2-42) beat **Delhi** 139 in 66.2 overs (Jonty Sidhu 41, Shivank Vashisht 30*; Jalaj Saxena 6-39, Sijomon Joseph 2-42) and 154 in 41 overs (Shivam 33, Anuj Rawat 31; Sandeep Warrier 3-39, J Saxena 3-49) by an innings and 27 runs. *PoM:* Jalaj Saxena.

Pujara's return revitalised Saurashtra.
— SCA

PCA IS Bindra Stadium, Mohali, December 14-17: Tamil Nadu 215 in 85 overs (Vijay Shankar 71, Baba Aparajith 40; Manpreet Gony 5-55, Baltej Singh 3-45) and 383/6 in 121 overs (Baba Indrajith 93, Abhinav Mukund 74, Dinesh Karthik 74; Yuvraj Singh 2-29, Sandeep Sharma 2-92) drew with Punjab 479 in 118.5 overs (Shubman Gill 268, Mandeep Singh 50; Sai Kishore 6-107). Punjab took first-innings lead. *PoM:* Shubman Gill.

Elite Group C

Chaudhary Bansi Lal Cricket Stadium, Lahli, December 14-16: Jammu and Kashmir 161 in 47.1 overs (Obaid Ahmed 26; Ajit Chahal 3-31, Yuzvendra Chahal 3-50) and 205 in 54.2 overs (Owais Shah 71, Shubham Khajuria 34; Y Chahal 4-37, A Chahal 3-55) beat Haryana 145 in 48.3 overs (Rohit Sharma 41, Himanshu Rana 29; Umar Nazir 5-55, Mohammad Mudhasir 4-50) and 91 in 33.3 overs (Irfan Pathan 5-18, U Nazir 3-29) by 130 runs. *PoM:* Umar Nazir.

KIIT Ground, Bhubaneswar, December 14-16: Rajasthan 135 in 37 overs (Mahipal Lomror 85; Basant Mohanty 6-20, Rajesh Mohanty 3-63) and 148 in 50.2 overs (Amit Gautam 51, Salman Khan 39; B Mohanty 5-29, Dhiraj Singh 2-27) beat Odisha 111 in 57.2 overs (Debasish Samantray 50; Tanveer-ul-Haq 5-14, Aniket Choudhary 5-49) and 137 in 45.2 overs (Suryakant Pradhan 56, Subhranshu Senapati 36; A Choudhary 5-25, Tanveer 3-39) by 35 runs. *PoM:* Basant Mohanty.

Palam A Ground, Model Sports Complex, Delhi, December 14-17: Assam 211 in 98.5 overs (Amit Sinha 56, Gokul Sharma 49; Sachidanand Pandey 5-74, Diwesh Pathania 3-75) and 256 in 86 overs (Swarupam Purkayastha 74, Gokul S 56; D Pathania 5-56, Arun Bamal 2-53) lost to Services 396 in 136.4 overs (Rajat Paliwal 180, Navneet Singh 79; Jitumoni Kalita 3-99, Ranjit Mali 2-60) and 75/0 in 18.1 overs (Nakul Verma 39*, Navneet 31*) by ten wickets. *PoM:* Rajat Paliwal.

Maharaja Bir Bikram College Stadium, Agartala, December 14-17: Tripura 358 in 115.4 overs (Pratyush Singh 110, Rajib Saha 68; Amit Verma 3-87, Lakshay Garg 3-107) and 9/0 in 0.5 overs beat Goa 192 in 89.4 overs (Snehal Kauthankar 79, Suyash Prabhudessai 34; Abhijit Sarkar 4-29, Ajay Sarkar 3-42) and 173 in 62.2 overs (S Prabhudessai 65, Sumiran Amonkar 29; Harmeet Singh 3-46, Manisankar Murasingh 3-55) by ten wickets. *PoM:* Pratyush Singh

Ekana International Cricket Stadium, Lucknow, December 14-17: Jharkhand 354 in 117.1 overs (Shahbaz Nadeem 109, Ishank Jaggi 95; Pratap Singh 6-105, Imtiaz Ahmed 2-81) and 213/5 dec. in 63.3 overs (Kumar Deobrat 78, Ishan Kishan 53; Yash Dayal 3-49) drew with Uttar Pradesh 243 in 66 overs (Suresh Raina 75, Priyam Garg 54; Rahul Shukla 5-65, Varun Aaron 4-59) and 174/1 in 56 overs (P Garg 80*, Mohammad Saif 64*). Jharkhand took first-innings lead. *PoM:* Rahul Shukla.

Plate Group

DN Singha Stadium, Goalpara, December 14-15: Puducherry 136 in 35.5 overs (Fabid Ahmed 41*; Deendayal Upadhyay 4-36, Techi Neri 3-28) and 351 in 76.2 overs (Paras Dogra 139, F Ahmed 88; D Upadhyay 4-63, T Neri 3-76) beat **Arunachal Pradesh** 82 in 35.5 overs (F Ahmed 6-29, Pankaj Singh 3-20) and 71 in 22.2 overs (Pankaj 5-25, D Rohit 4-7) in 22.2 overs by 334 runs. *PoM:* Fabid Ahmed.

Meghalaya Cricket Association Cricket Ground, Shillong, December 14-15: Meghalaya 125 in 52.5 overs (Raj Biswa 56, Abhay Negi 38; Ashutosh Aman 8-51) and 46 in 26.5 overs (Ashutosh Aman 6-17, Samar Quadri 4-24) lost to **Bihar** 242 in 81.3 overs (Babul Kumar 43, Ashutosh Aman 35*; Lakhan Singh 3-30, Gurinder Singh 3-81) by an innings and 71 runs. *PoM:* Ashutosh Aman.

District Sports Association Ground, Jorhat, December 14-17: Sikkim 332 in 89.5 overs (Milind Kumar 139, Bipul Sharma 50; Sinan Khadir 3-74, Akhil Rajput 2-36) and 170 in 49.1 overs (Bipul 65, Ashish Thapa 44; Taruwar Kohli 5-40, S Khadir 3-50) beat **Mizoram** 161 in 57 overs (T Kohli 74, A Rajput 35; Ishwar Chaudhary 5-57, Milind 2-35) and 236 in 74.5 overs (T Kohli 156, Lalhruai Ralte 32; I Chaudhary 6-111, Milind 2-63) by 105 runs. *PoM:* Taruwar Kohli.

Abhimanyu Cricket Academy Ground, Dehradun, December 14-17: Nagaland 207 in 59.4 overs (Rongsen Jonathan 69, KB Pawan 46; Deepak Dhapola 5/49, Sunny Rana 3/43) and 467/7 in 127 overs (Abrar Kazi 157*, Sedezhalie Rupero 85; Mayank Mishra 3-82, Malolan Rangarajan 2-113) drew with **Uttarakhand** 557 in 151.5 overs (Vineet Saxena 185, Vaibhav Panwar 101; A Kazi 3-124, Rachit Bhatia 2-48). Uttarakhand took first-innings lead. *PoM:* Abrar Kazi.

Round 7: Aman picks up another bagful

K Gowtham's 6 for 30 skittled out Railways to give Karnataka a big win. A closely fought contest between Mumbai and Saurashtra ended in a draw as did the games between Chhattisgarh and Maharashtra, and Vidarbha and Gujarat.

Vikas Mishra took 12 for 71 as Delhi routed Madhya Pradesh. Abhinav Mukund and B Indrajith's hundreds went in vain as Himachal beat Tamil Nadu. Gill's 148 gave Hyderabad a scare as Punjab finished on 324 for 8 in pursuit of 338 before running out of time.

In Group C, Odisha beat Jammu and Kashmir despite Rasool's 158. Priyam Garg's 206 gave Uttar Pradesh an innings win against Tripura. Arup Das picked up 6 for 67 as Assam trumped Goa by seven runs and Shahbaz Nadeem's match haul of 10 for 91 scripted Jharkhand's victory over Services.

Meghalaya thumped Mizoram by an innings and 324 runs in Plate Group, while Aman bagged 12 for 96 as Bihar overcame Nagaland.

Elite Group A

Shaheed Veer Narayan Singh International Cricket Stadium, Naya Raipur, December 22-25: Maharashtra 239 in 68.3 overs (Rahul Tripathi 102, Anupam Sanklecha 66; Vishal Kushwah 4-59, Pankaj Rao 3-32) and 397/9 dec. in 99.5 overs (Kedar Jadhav 103, Ankit Bawne 57; Omkar Verma 4-110, P Rao 3-116) drew with **Chhattisgarh** 462 in 140.5 overs (Ajay Mandal 135, Ashutosh Singh 114, Amandeep Khare 108; A Sanklecha 5-89, Samad Fallah 2-69) and 91/6 in 33.3 overs (Avnish Dhaliwal 41; Swapnil Gugale 3-9, S Fallah 2-26). Chhattisgarh took first-innings lead. *PoM:* Ajay Mandal.

KSCA Navale Stadium, Shimoga, December 22-25: Karnataka 214 in 91.4 overs (KV

Siddharth 69, Dega Nischal 52; Karan Thakur 3-43, Avinash Yadav 3-43, Amit Mishra 3-59) and 290/2 dec. in 84 overs (D Nischal 101, KV Siddharth 84*; Harsh Tyagi 2-78) beat **Railways** 143 in 60.2 overs (Manish Rao 52*, Prashant Gupta 35; Ronit More 5-45, Abhimanyu Mithun 2-22) and 185 in 86 overs (Pratham Singh 48, Saurabh Wakaskar 43; K Gowtham 6-30, Shreyas Gopal 2-39) by 176 runs. *PoM:* Dega Nischal.

Wankhede Stadium, Mumbai, December 22-25: Mumbai 394 in 107 overs (Jay Bista 127, Siddhesh Lad 108; Jaydev Unadkat 4-71, Chetan Sakariya 3-86, Dharmendrasinh Jadeja 3-95) and 238/8 dec. in 48 overs (Shreyas Iyer 83, Shubham Ranjane 43; C Sakariya 3-47, D Jadeja 3-102) drew with **Saurashtra** 348 in 119.3 overs (Sheldon Jackson 95, Chirag Jani 85; Shivam Dube 2-34, Royston Dias 2-63) and 266/7 in 71.4 overs (Vishvaraj Jadeja 71, S Jackson 57; Minad Manjrekar 4-39, S Dube 2-50). Mumbai took first-innings lead. *PoM:* Jay Bista.

VCA Stadium, Nagpur, December 22-25: Gujarat 321 in 108.5 overs (Kathan Patel 105, Dhruv Raval 79; Aditya Sarwate 4-71, Lalit Yadav 2-56) and 214/6 in 93 overs (Rujul Bhatt 64*, Manprit Juneja 42, Karan Patel 42; Akshay Karnewar 5-73) drew with **Vidarbha** 485 in 145.5 overs (Wasim Jaffer 126, Akshay Wadkar 88; Siddharth Desai 8-148). Vidarbha took first-innings lead. *PoM:* Wasim Jaffer.

Elite Group B

Dr YS Rajasekhara Reddy ACA-VDCA Cricket Stadium, Visakhapatnam, December 22-25: Bengal 300 in 110.3 overs (Manoj Tiwary 90, Writtick Chatterjee 76; KV Sasikanth 5-55, Y Prithviraj 3-81) and 223/7 dec. in 40.3 overs (Abhimanyu Easwaran 57, Sudip Chatterjee 47; Y Prithviraj 2-49, PD Vijaykumar 2-84) drew with **Andhra** 321 in 119.3 overs (CR Gnaneshwar 66, KS Bharat 61; Mukesh Kumar 4-45, Pradipta Pramanik 3-69) and 170/7 in 28 overs (Prasanth Kumar 90, Sai Krishna 45; Ashok Dinda 3-50, Mukesh 2-43). Andhra took first-innings lead. *PoM:* KV Sasikanth.

Feroz Shah Kotla, Delhi, December 22-25: Madhya Pradesh 132 in 51.2 overs (Anandsingh Bais 35; Vikas Mishra 6-41, Shivam Sharma 3-48) and 157 in 64.3 overs (A Bais 46, Aryaman Birla 32; V Mishra 6-30, Shivam 3-52) lost to **Delhi** 261 in 69.3 overs (Anuj Rawat 134, Shivam 39; Avesh Khan 6-51, Kumar Kartikeya 2-56) and 31/1 in 6.4 overs by nine wickets. *PoM:* Anuj Rawat.

HPCA Stadium, Dharamsala, December 22-25: Tamil Nadu 227 in 78.4 overs (Baba Aparajith 53, Abhishek Tanwar 44; Pankaj Jaiswal 3-45,Prashant Chopra 2-3) and 345 in 118.3 overs (Abhinav Mukund 128, Baba Indrajith 106; Arpit Guleria 3-56, Rishi Dhawan 3-60) lost to **Himachal Pradesh** 463 in 116.2 overs (Ankit Kalsi 144*, Rishi Dhawan 75; T Natarajan 5-122, Sai Kishore 2-62) and 111/1 in 15.3 overs (Ankush Bains 64*, Raghav Dhawan 39) by nine wickets. *PoM:* Rishi Dhawan.

Rajiv Gandhi International Stadium, Uppal, Hyderabad, December 22-25: Hyderabad 317 in 109.3 overs (Himalay Agarwal 79, Akshath Reddy 77; Mayank Markande 6-84, Siddarth Kaul 2-80) and 323/3 dec. in 86 overs (A Reddy 161*, Tanmay Agarwal 54) drew with **Punjab** 303 in 93.5 overs (Gurkeerat Singh 87*, Anmolpreet Singh 85; Ravi Teja 5-57, Mohammed Siraj 3-74) and 324/8 in 57 overs (Shubman Gill 148, Mandeep Singh 41; M Siraj 4-71, Mehdi Hasan 2-84). Hyderabadtook first-innings lead. *PoM:* Ravi Teja.

Elite Group C

Barsapara Cricket Stadium, Guwahati, December 22-25: Assam 175 in 50.2 overs (Biplab Saikia 41, Swarupam Purkayastha 31, Lakshay Garg 5-73, Krishna Das 2-42) and 235 in 84.3 overs (Rishav Das 67, Amit Sinha 52; K Das 4-69, L Garg 2-70) beat **Goa** 193 in 65.5 overs (Snehal Kauthankar 69, Sumiran Amonkar 35; Mukhtar Hussain 3-67, Arup Das 3-72) and 210 in 63.2 overs (Amit Verma 74, L Garg 73; A Das 6-67, M Hussain 3-65) by 7 runs. *PoM:* Arup Das.

Gandhi Memorial Science College Ground, Jammu, December 22-25: Jammu and Kash-

mir 127 in 53.3 overs (Owais Shah 44, Akash Choudhary 27; Suryakant Pradhan 4-27, Basant Mohanty 3-24) and 391 in 134.4 overs (Parveez Rasool 158, Qamran Iqbal 67; B Mohanty 4-59, Govinda Podder 2-69) lost to **Odisha** 323 in 106.3 overs (Abhishek Raut 116*, Debasish Samantray 85; Irfan Pathan 4-52, Umar Nazir 3-49) and 197/2 in 49.1 overs (Shantanu Mishra 78, Subhranshu Senapati 72*) by eight wickets. *PoM:* Abhishek Raut.

JSCA International Stadium, Ranchi, December 22-25: Jharkhand 193 in 66 overs (Ishan Kishan 68, Kumar Deobrat 48; Arun Bamal 4-37, Raushan Raj 2-29) and 343 in 97.2 overs (Utkarsh Singh 114, K Deobrat 53; Rajat Paliwal 3-29, Diwesh Pathania 2-51) beat **Services** 267 in 93.3 overs (R Paliwal 79, Ravi Chauhan 67; Anukul Roy 4-66, Shahbaz Nadeem 3-29) and 188 in 57.4 overs (Rahul Singh 61, Mohit Ahlawat 52; S Nadeem 7-62) by 81 runs. *PoM:* Utkarsh Singh.

Sawai Mansingh Stadium, Jaipur, December 22-25: Haryana 118 in 36.2 overs (Harshal Patel 53*; Aniket Choudhary 5-45, Khaleel Ahmed 3-33) and 462/8 in 146 overs (Chaitanya Bishnoi 94, Himanshu Rana 83; Rahul Chahar 5-151) drew with **Rajasthan** 490/6 dec. in 158 overs (Robin Bist 150*, Mahipal Lomror 106; Yuzvendra Chahal 3-107). **Rajasthan** took first-innings lead. *PoM:* Robin Bist.

Ekana International Cricket Stadium, Lucknow, December 22-24: Uttar Pradesh 552/7 dec. in 149 overs (Priyam Garg 206, Rinku Singh 149, Akshdeep Nath 106; Saurabh Das 4-164, Rana Datta 2-79) beat **Tripura** 108 in 44 overs (Smit Patel 47; Zeeshan Ansari 3-33, Saurabh Kumar 2-9) and 60 in 25 overs (Ankit Rajpoot 6-25, Imtiaz Ahmed 3-30) by an innings and 384 runs. *PoM:* Priyam Garg.

Plate Group

Meghalaya Cricket Association Cricket Ground, Shillong, December 20-21: Mizoram 86 in 28.1 overs (Lalhruai Ralte 40; Gurinder Singh 5-15, Abhay Negi 2-12) and 100 in 38.3 overs (Sinan Khadir 30, Taruwar Kohli 28; Gurinder 6-41, Aditya Singhania 3-31) lost to **Meghalaya** 510 in 95.4 overs (Yogesh Nagar 144, Gurinder 99; S Khadir 4-151, Lalrempuia Marema 3-90) by an innings and 324 runs. *PoM:* Gurinder Singh.

Moin-ul-Haq Stadium, Patna, December 22-25: Bihar 150 in 46.1 overs (Harsh Singh 48*, Indrajit Kumar 25; Rachit Bhatia 6-44, Abrar Kazi 2-40) and 505/8 dec. in 117 overs (Mangal Mahrour 177, MD Rahmatullah 107; A Kazi 5-107, R Bhatia 2-89) beat **Nagaland** 209 in 75.4 overs (Rongsen Jonathan 53, KB Pawan 39; Ashutosh Aman 7-47, Vivek Kumar 2-65) and 173 in 45.5 overs (R Jonathan 100; A Aman 5-49, V Kumar 5-65) by 273 runs. *PoM:* Ashutosh Aman.

ideocon Academy Ground, Kolkata, December 22-25: Manipur 85 in 26 overs (Deendayal Upadhyay 5-38, Licha Tehi 3-36) and 253 in 56 overs (Hrithik Kanojia 91, Yashpal Singh 51; Techi Doria 3-71, L Tehi 3-74) beat **Arunachal Pradesh** 66 in 23.3 overs (Thokchom Singh 5-16, Bishworjit Konthoujam 4-27) and 160 in 37.3 overs (D Upadhyay 52, Kshitiz Sharma 34; Priyojit Singh 3-33, Thokchom 2-37) by 112 runs. *PoM:* Thokchom Singh.

Cricket Association Puducherry Siechem Ground, Puducherry, December 22-25: Puducherry 23/3 in 15 overs (Dhanraj Sharma 2/7) drew with **Uttarakhand**.

Round 8: Jaffer knocks out Mumbai

Mumbai, Hyderabad, Delhi, Tamil Nadu, Andhra, Maharashtra, Railways and Chhattisgarh found out they had no chance of progressing to the next round. Behemoths Mumbai were knocked out by their former player Wasim Jaffer, while Krunal Pandya followed up his 160 with six in the match to end Railways' hopes.

Abhimanyu Easwaran overcame a first-innings deficit, chasing down 322 with an unbeaten 183 to keep Bengal's dream alive and knock Delhi out. Siddarth Kaul and Gill kept Punjab alive in a ten-wicket thrashing of Kerala.

Chasing 153, Jharkhand ran out of time at 144 for 7 and were left furious at Tripura's over-rate. Dropping points would prove expensive. In a match where bowlers called the shots, Saurabh kept Uttar Pradesh on top with a match haul of 14 for 65. Punit Bisht's 343 was the highest individual score of the season as Meghalaya pushed on for 826 for 7 against Sikkim.

Elite Group A

KSCA Ground, Alur, December 30-January 2: Karnataka 418 in 131.4 overs (Dega Nischal 107, KV Siddharth 105; Pankaj Rao 7-82) and 219/7 dec. in 49.3 overs (Manish Pandey 102*, Abhimanyu Mithun 33*; P Rao 4-67) beat **Chhattisgarh** 283 in 89 overs (Harpreet Bhatia 120, Amandeep Khare 45; Ronit More 5-48, A Mithun 4-64) and 156 in 57 overs (Avnish Dhaliwal 61, A Khare 35; R More 4-35, Shreyas Gopal 4-44) by 198 runs. *PoM:* Ronit More.

MCA Stadium, Gahunje, December 30-January 2: Maharashtra 230 in 67.1 overs (Ruturaj Gaikwad 70, Rahul Tripathi 62; Chintan Gaja 5-57, Piyush Chawla 3-39) and 185 in 55.5 overs (Anupam Sanklecha 40*, Naushad Shaikh 40; P Chawla 3-18, C Gaja 3-47) lost to **Gujarat** 545/8 dec. in 130 overs (Priyank Panchal 141, Kathan Patel 107; A Sanklecha 3-80, Chirag Khurana 3-98) by an innings and 130 runs. *PoM:* Chintan Gaja.

Karnail Singh Stadium, Delhi, December 30-January 1: Baroda 313 in 94 overs (Krunal Pandya 160, Mitesh Patel 61; Amit Mishra 5-76, Avinash Yadav 3-52) and 157 in 55 overs (Krunal Pandya 104; A Mishra 7-50, A Yadav 3-70) beat **Railways** 200 in 68.3 overs (Mahesh Rawat 50, Arindam Ghosh 46; K Pandya 4-40, Bhargav Bhatt 3-33) and 106 in 39.4 overs (M Suresh 29*; B Bhatt 5-43, K Pandya 2-19) by 164 runs. *PoM:* Krunal Pandya.

VCA Stadium, Nagpur, December 30-January 1: Vidarbha 511 in 129.4 overs (Wasim Jaffer 178, Atharwa Taide 95; Dhrumil Matkar 5-141, Shardul Thakur 2-89) beat **Mumbai** 252 in 78.5 overs (Jay Bista 64, D Matkar 62*; Akshay Wakhare 5-85, Aditya Sarwate 3-86) and 114 in 34.4 overs (D Matkar 36; A Sarwate 6-48, Akshay Karnewar 2-19) by an innings and 145 runs. *PoM:* Wasim Jaffer.

Elite Group B

Dr PVG Raju ACA Sports Complex, Vizianagaram, December 30-January 2: Hyderabad 271 in 90.3 overs (Himalay Agarwal 59, Akshath Reddy 57; KV Sasikanth 5-64, Y Prithviraj 3-72) and 251/5 in 85 overs (A Reddy 65, H Agarwal 60*; Shoaib Mohammad 2-70) drew with **Andhra** 502/7 dec. in 154 overs (KS Bharat 178*, Ricky Bhui 129; Mehdi Hasan 3-127, Ravi Teja 2-101). Andhra took first-innings lead. *PoM:* KS Bharat.

Eden Gardens, Kolkata, December 30-January 2: Delhi 240 in 83.3 overs (Jonty Sidhu 85, Shivam Sharma 42; Ashok Dinda 4-62, Mukesh Kumar 2-74) and 301 in 96.4 overs (Subodh Bhati 62, Himmat Singh 51; A Dinda 5-88, Pradipta Pramanik 2-45) lost to **Bengal** 220 in 58.4 overs (Sudip Chatterjee 56, Abhimanyu Easwaran 40; S Bhati 3-28, Kulwant Khejroliya 3-87) and 323/3 in 70.2 overs (Abhimanyu 183*, Anustup Majumdar 69*; K Khejroliya 2-68) by seven wickets. *PoM:* Abhimanyu Easwaran.

Holkar Stadium, Indore, December 30-January 1: Madhya Pradesh 265 in 98.3 overs (Shubham Sharma 54*, Rajat Patidar 47; Pankaj Jaswal 4-56, Rishi Dhawan 3-54) and 193 in 58.5 overs (R Patidar 54, Yash Dubey 31; Gurvinder Singh 6-63, Mayank Dagar 2-40) beat**Himachal Pradesh**127 in 55.3 overs (Raghav Dhawan 37, Prashant Chopra 31; Kumar Kartikeya 6-28, Kuldeep Sen 2-34) and 191 in 44.4 overs (P Jaswal 44, Ankush Bains 26, Gurvinder 26; K Kartikeya 3-58, K Sen 2-30) by 140 runs. *PoM:* Kumar Kartikeya.

PCA IS Bindra Stadium, Mohali, December 30-January 2: Kerala 121 in 37 overs (Vishnu Vinod 35; Siddarth Kaul 6-55, Mayank Markande 2-14) and 223 in 73.1 overs (Mohammed

Azharuddeen 112, V Vinod 36; M Markande 4-56, Manpreet Gony 2-20) lost to **Punjab** 217 in 75.2 overs (Mandeep Singh 89, Jiwanjot Singh 69; Sandeep Warrier 5-83, Basil Thampi 2-46) and 131/0 in 27.4 overs (Shubman Gill 69*, Jiwanjot 48*) by ten wickets. *PoM:* Siddarth Kaul.

Elite Group C

Barsapara Cricket Stadium, Guwahati, December 30-January 1: Assam 128 in 36.1 overs (Mrinmoy Datta 35*; Umar Nazir 3-31, Rohit Sharma 3-43) and 245 in 76.2 overs (Rishav Das 95, Swarupam Purkayastha 46; Parveez Rasool 3-30, Irfan Pathan 3-45) lost to **Jammu and Kashmir** 144 in 43.4 overs (Qamran Iqbal 64, I Pathan 35; Mukhtar Hussain 5-39, Arup Das 3-52) and 231/6 in 69.3 overs (Shubham Khajuria 67, P Rasool 67; A Das 3-46, M Dutta 2-59) by four wickets. *PoM:* Parveez Rasool.

GCA Academy Ground, Porvorim, December 30-January 2: Goa 244 in 80 overs (Snehal Kauthankar 48, Amogh Desai 44; Rahul Chahar 4-86, Tanveer-ul-Haq 2-39) and 291 in 69.1 overs (Amit Verma 118, Sagun Kamat 96; R Chahar 5-81, Tanveer 4-87) lost to **Rajasthan** 513/8 dec. in 138 overs (Robin Bist 169*, Mahipal Lomror 89; Lakshay Garg 3-127, A Desai 2-64) and 27/0 in 5 overs by ten wickets. *PoM:* Rahul Chahar.

Chaudhary Bansi Lal Cricket Stadium, Lahli, December 30-31: Haryana 110 in 43 overs (Himanshu Rana 50; Saurabh Kumar 7-33) and 129 in 37.2 overs (Ankit Kumar 51, Jayant Yadav 26; S Kumar 7-32) lost to **Uttar Pradesh** 133 in 37.2 overs (Rinku Singh 43; Ajit Chahal 5-16, Harshal Patel 3-32) and 110/4 in 21.2 overs (Samarth Singh 53*) by six wickets. *PoM:* Saurabh Kumar.

Keenan Stadium, Jamshedpur, December 30-January 2: Tripura 253 in 89.4 overs (Rajib Saha 48*, Udiyan Bose 44; Rahul Shukla 4-38, Ashish Kumar 2-35) and 308 in 108.3 overs (U Bose 91, Biplab Ghosh 61; Utkarsh Singh 3-65, Anukul Roy 2-42) drew with **Jharkhand** 409 in 111.4 overs (Kumar Deobrat 150, Nazim Siddiqui 134; Neelambuj Vats 5-50, Saurabh Das 2-97) and 144/7 in 21.5 overs (K Deobrat 38, Saurabh Tiwary 37; S Das 2-64) Jharkhand took first innings lead. *PoM:* Kumar Deobrat.

Palam A Ground, Model Sports Complex, Delhi, December 30-January 2: Odisha 177 in 86.2 overs (Abhishek Raut 56, Biplab Samantray 41; Arun Bamal 4-61, Sachidanand Pandey 2-25) and 256/5 in 110 overs (Debasish Samantray 102, Anurag Sarangi 46*; A Bamal 2-58) drew with **Services** 417/8 dec. in 141 overs (Vikas Hathwala 115*, Navneet Singh 64; Govinda Podder 2-85, A Raut 2-103). Services took first-innings lead. *PoM:* Vikas Hathwala.

Plate Group

District Sports Association Ground, Jorhat, December 30-January 1: Bihar 440/9 dec. in 102 overs (Ashutosh Aman 111, Vivek Kumar 102; Lalhruai Ralte 5-122) beat **Mizoram** 77 in 35.5 overs (Akhil Rajput 49; Samar Quadri 6-19, Abhijeet Saket 3-26) and 147 in 62.2 overs (Taruwar Kohli 76, A Rajput 30; A Aman 5-28, S Quadri 4-50) by an innings and 216 runs. *PoM:* Ashutosh Aman.

Sovima Cricket Stadium, Dimapur, December 30-January 1: Arunachal Pradesh 135 in 54.3 overs (Song Tacho 31; Pawan Suyal 4-28, Abrar Kazi 3-13) and 122 in 53.5 overs (Techi Doria 33; A Kazi 6-22) lost to **Nagaland** 377/9 dec. in 77.1 overs (Rongsen Jonathan 131, Paras Sehrawat 112; Deendayal Upadhyay 4-84, Licha Tehi 3-80) by an innings and 120 runs. *PoM:* Rongsen Jonathan.

Rural Development Trust Stadium, Anantapur, December 30-31: Manipur 132 in 39.2 overs (Yashpal Singh 50; Pankaj Singh 4-32, Raiphi Gomez 4-58) and 118 in 31.5 overs (Yashpal 52; Pankaj 4-20, D Rohit 3-22) lost to **Puducherry** 238 in 78.2 overs (S Karthik 55, Saiju Titus 42; Thokchom Singh 4-65, Bishworjit Konthoujam 3-48) and 13/0 in 1.1 overs by ten wickets. *PoM:* Pankaj Singh.

KIIT Ground, Bhubaneswar, December 30-January 2: Sikkim 219 in 63 Overs (Milind Kumar 117, Bipul Sharma 27; Gurinder Singh 3-71) and 304/4 in 108 overs (Milind 127*,

Nilesh Lamichaney 70; Gurinder 3-84) drew with **Meghalaya** 826/7 dec. in 171.4 overs (Punit Bisht 343, Raj Biswa 175, Yogesh Nagar 148, Gurinder 101*; Lee Yong Lepcha 2-157, Milind 2-180). Meghalaya took first-innings lead. *PoM:* Punit Bisht

Round 9: Kerala keep up dream run

Karnataka made it through to the next round despite a loss inside two days to Baroda. This was at the cost of Madhya Pradesh, who suffered a double collapse of their own, losing six for zero to be bowled out for 91 and 35 against Andhra. It confirmed a place for Vidarbha as well, against whom a first-innings lead was enough for Saurashtra.

Himachal Pradesh, also in contention, declared on 285 for 8, asking Kerala to get 297 on the final day. But the gamble backfired. Vinoop Manoharan and Sachin Baby made half-centuries, while Sanju Samson struck a brisk 61 not out off 53. Kerala finished level on points with Gujarat and Baroda in the combined A and B table, but it was the first two of those teams that progressed based on quotient. Baroda, despite doing what was asked of them, lost out. A spirited draw denied both Bengal and Punjab a quarter-final berth.

Rajasthan had already sealed their spot from Group C, while it was heart-break for Jharkhand, who lost out to Uttar Pradesh by one point despite an innings thrashing of J&K.

Elite Group A

Moti Bagh Stadium, Vadodara, January 7-8: Karnataka 112 in 31.2 overs (Manish Pandey 43, BR Sharath 30; Lukman Meriwala 3-22, Bhargav Bhatt 3-27) and 220 in 63.4 overs (KV Siddharth 64, M Pandey 50; Deepak Hooda 5-31, B Bhatt 5-116) lost to **Baroda** 223 in 51 overs (Vishnu Solanki 69, D Hooda 51; Shreyas Gopal 4-47, Shubhang Hegde 4-74) and 110/8 in 28.1 overs (Yusuf Pathan 41; Prasidh Krishna 3-14, Shreyas 2-12) by two wickets. *PoM:* Bhargav Bhatt.

Wankhede Stadium, Mumbai, January 7-9:Chhattisgarh 129 in 42.1 overs (Amandeep Khare 48, Ashutosh Singh 30; Tushar Deshpande 5-46, Shardul Thakur 4-32) and 149 in 32.5 overs (Vishal Kushwah 47, A Khare 33; S Thakur 4-47, T Deshpande 4-53) lost to **Mumbai** 188 in 62 overs (Vikrant Auti 43, Suryakumar Yadav 43; Pankaj Rao 3-53, Abhimanyu Chauhan 2-2) and 92/1 in 24.2 overs (Jay Bista 49*, V Auti 34) by nine wickets. *PoM:* Tushar Deshpande.

Karnail Singh Stadium, Delhi, January 7-8: Maharashtra 70 in 23.2 overs (Avinash Yadav 4-38, Harsh Tyagi 2-2) and 131 in 39.1 overs (Satyajeet Bachhav 27; A Yadav 5-71, H Tyagi 4-29) lost to **Railways** 259 in 77.4 overs (Mahesh Rawat 89, Gandhar Bhatwadekar 37; S Bachhav 8-108) by an innings and 58 runs. *PoM:* Mahesh Rawat.

SCA Stadium, Rajkot, January 7-10: Saurashtra 356 in 136.4 overs (Harvik Desai 74, Dharmendrasinh Jadeja 72; Yash Thakur 4-92, Akshay Wakhare 3-57, Suniket Bingewar 3-68) and 218/2 in 73 overs (Vishvaraj Jadeja 105*, Sheldon Jackson 53*) drew with **Vidarbha** 280/9 dec. in 118 overs (Wasim Jaffer 98, Mohit Kale 66; Jaydev Unadkat 6-56). Saurashtra took first-innings lead. *PoM:* Jaydev Unadkat.

Elite Group B

Jadavpur University Second Campus Ground, Kolkata, January 7-10: Bengal 187 in 69.1 overs (Shreevats Goswami 57, Sudip Chatterjee 52; Vinay Choudhary 6-62, Manpreet Gony 2-19) and 432/6 dec. in 130 overs (Abhimanyu Easwaran 201*, Manoj Tiwary 105; Mayank

Markande 3-123) drew with **Punjab** 447 in 131.3 overs (Anmolpreet Singh 126, Shubman Gill 91; Mukesh Kumar 5-114, Pradipta Pramanik 4-108) and 132/5 in 15 overs (M Gony 58, Mandeep Singh 35). Punjab took first-innings lead. *PoM:* Abhimanyu Easwaran.

Atal Bihari Vajpayee Stadium, Amtar, January 7-10: Himachal Pradesh 297 in 96.1 overs (Ankit Kalsi 101, Rishi Dhawan 58; MD Nidheesh 6-88, Sandeep Warrier 2-66) and 285/8 dec. in 52.1 overs (Rishi 85, A Kalsi 64; Sijomon Joseph 4-51, Basil Thampi 2-63) lost to **Kerala** 286 in 87 overs (P Rahul 127, Sanju Samson 50; Arpit Guleria 5-47, Rishi Dhawan 3-68) and 299/5 in 67 overs (Vinoop Manoharan 96, Sachin Baby 92; Gurvinder Singh 2-58) by five wickets. *PoM:* Vinoop Manoharan.

Holkar Stadium, Indore, January 7-9: Andhra 132 in 54.3 overs (Prasanth Kumar 29; Ishwar Pandey 4-43, Gaurav Yadav 3-21, Kumar Kartikeya 3-23) and 301 in 101.1 overs (Karan Shinde 103*, P Kumar 44; I Pandey 3-55, G Yadav 2-26) beat **Madhya Pradesh** 91 in 35.5 overs (Naman Ojha 30; Girinath Reddy 6-29, PD Vijaykumar 2-14) and 35 in 16.5 overs (KV Sasikanth 6-18, PD Vijaykumar 3-17) by 307 runs. *PoM:* Karan Shinde.

MA Chidambaram Stadium, Chepauk, Chennai, January 7-10: Tamil Nadu 432 in 164.4 overs (Abhinav Mukund 134, Baba Indrajith 86; Vikas Mishra 5-142, Shivam Sharma 4-105) and 113/1 dec. in 40 overs (N Jagadeesan 59*, Baba Aparajith 33) drew with **Delhi** 336 in 133.1 overs (Jonty Sidhu 140*, Lalit Yadav 91; Sai Kishore 5-90). Tamil Nadu took first-innings lead. *PoM:* Sai Kishore.

Elite Group C

Chaudhary Bansi Lal Cricket Stadium, Lahli, January 7-9: Services 170 in 59.3 overs (Vikas Hathwala 54, Arun Bamal 30; Tinu Kundu 6-60, Amit Rana 4-55) and 79 in 29.3 overs (Diwesh Pathania 25; T Kundu 5-35, A Rana 4-24) lost to **Haryana** 149 in 57.5 overs (Shubham Rohilla 64; A Bamal 7-42, Rajat Paliwal 2-30) and 104/4 in 24 overs (Ankit Kumar 72*; Navneet Singh 3-22) by six wickets. *PoM:* Ankit Kumar.

Gandhi Memorial Science College Ground, Jammu, January 7-10: Jammu and Kashmir 151 in 45.4 overs (Owais Shah 76; Ajay Yadav 5-16, Anukul Roy 3-27) and 120 in 49.4 overs (Rasikh Salam 40; Shahbaz Nadeem 4-43, A Roy 3-42) lost to **Jharkhand** 319/9 dec. in 91 overs (Saurabh Tiwary 134, Kumar Deobrat 74; Parveez Rasool 4-98, R Salam 3-47) by an innings and 48 runs. *PoM:* Saurabh Tiwary.

Vikas Cricket Ground, Cuttack, January 7-9: Odisha 352 in 111.5 overs (Sandeep Pattnaik 100, Suryakant Pradhan 65; Amogh Desai 3-77, Lakshay Garg 3-87) and 151 in 43.4 overs (Sujit Lenka 39, Debasish Samantray 31; L Garg 5-75, Krishna Das 4-57) beat **Goa** 116 in 39 overs (Sagun Kamat 43; S Pradhan 5-48, Rajesh Mohanty 3-52) and 111 in 29.5 overs (A Desai 28; R Mohanty 5-49, Basant Mohanty 4-21) by 276 runs. *PoM:* Suryakant Pradhan.

Maharaja Bir Bikram College Stadium, Agartala, January 7-8: Tripura 35 in 18.4 overs (Aniket Choudhary 5-11, Tanveer-ul-Haq 3-1) and 106 in 25.3 overs (Harmeet Baddhan 29; Deepak Chahar 5-17, A Choudhary 2-18) lost to **Rajasthan** 218 in 51.3 overs (Tanveer 37, A Choudhary 30*; Manishankar Murasingh 4-75, Neelambuj Vats 2-45) by an innings and 77 runs. *PoM:* Aniket Choudhary.

Modi Stadium, Kanpur, January 7-10: Assam 175 in 53.4 overs (Pallavkumar Das 75, Sarupam Purkayastha 35; Yash Dayal 3-15, Saurabh Kumar 3-25) and 317/4 in 103 overs (Gokul Sharma 100*, S Purkayastha 67; Imtiaz Ahmed 2-73) drew with **Uttar Pradesh** 619 in 177.4 overs (Rinku Singh 149, Upendra Yadav 138; Ranjit Mali 4-127, Gokul 2-82). Uttar Pradesh took first-innings lead. *PoM:* Rinku Singh.

Plate Group

DN Singha Stadium, Goalpara, January 7-9: Arunachal Pradesh 169 in 49.1 overs (Kshitiz Sharma 59, Prateek Kataria 30; Milind Kumar 5-42, Ishwar Chaudhary 3-55) and 109 in 45.3 overs (Kshitiz 31; I Chaudhary 7-51, Bipul Sharma 2-35) lost to **Sikkim** 262 in 95.3 overs

(Lee Yong Lepcha 58*, Milind 51; Deendayal Upadhyay 4-96, Licha Tehi 2-25) and 19/0 in 1.3 overs by ten wickets. *PoM:* Ishwar Chaudhary.

Moin-ul-Haq Stadium, Patna, January 7-9: Manipur 156 in 32 overs (Mayank Raghav 79, Yashpal Singh 26; Samar Quadri 5-49, Ashutosh Aman 4-39) and 238 in 70.4 overs (Yashpal 105, Priyojit Singh 64; A Aman 7-71, S Quadri 3-93) lost to **Bihar** 257 in 63.1 overs (Vivek Kumar 40, Kundan Gupta 38, A Aman 38; Bishworjit Konthoujam 5-74, Priyojit 5-74) and 140/7 in 25.1 overs (Mangal Mahrour 53, Vikash Ranjan 39; B Konthoujam 3-33, M Raghav 2-29) by three wickets. *PoM:* Ashutosh Aman.

Sovima Cricket Stadium, Dimapur, January 7-10: Nagaland 467 in 106.3 overs (Hokaito Zhimomi 177, Rongsen Jonathan 123, Nitesh Lohchab 100; Raiphi Gomez 3-59, Pankaj Singh 3-118) and 222/6 dec. in 61 overs (H Zhimomi 63*, Abrar Kazi 60; Pankaj 3-61, D Rohit 2-45) drew with **Puducherry** 286 in 98.2 overs (Paras Dogra 144, S Karthik 81; A Kazi 4-62, Imliwati Lemtur 3-57) and 208/3 in 67 overs (Vikneshwaran Marimuthu 64, Karthik 55; I Lemtur 2-43). Nagaland took first-innings lead. *PoM:* Hokaito Zhimomi.

Rajiv Gandhi International Cricket Stadium, Dehradun, January 7-9: Uttarakhand 377 in 83.5 overs (Saurabh Rawat 102, Rajat Bhatia 84; Akhil Rajput 2-21, Sailung Zorinliana 2-52) beat **Mizoram** 198 in 75.2 overs (Taruwar Kohli 96*, Lalhruai Ralte 30; Dhanraj Sharma 3-49, Sunny Rana 2-46) and 123 in 59 overs (T Kohli 68*; R Bhatia 4-17, Mayank Mishra 3-29) by an innings and 56 runs. *PoM:* Taruwar Kohli.

Elite Group A and B points table

Teams	M	W	L	T	D	Pts.	Quotient
Vidarbha	8	3	0	0	5	29	1.332
Saurashtra	8	3	0	0	5	29	1.108
Karnataka	8	3	2	0	3	27	1.316
Kerala	8	4	3	0	1	26	1.156
Gujarat	8	3	0	0	5	26	1.289
Baroda	8	3	1	0	4	26	1.057
Madhya Pradesh	8	3	2	0	3	24	1.144
Bengal	8	2	1	0	5	23	1.076
Punjab	8	2	1	0	5	23	1.017
Himachal Pradesh	8	3	3	0	2	22	1.042
Mumbai	8	1	2	0	5	17	0.925
Andhra	8	1	2	0	5	17	0.900
Hyderabad	8	1	1	0	6	17	0.840
Tamil Nadu	8	1	2	0	5	15	1.016
Railways	8	1	4	0	3	14	0.869
Delhi	8	1	3	0	4	14	0.822
Maharashtra	8	0	4	0	4	8	0.700
Chhattisgarh	8	0	4	0	4	6	0.635

**Vidarbha, Saurashtra, Karnataka, Gujarat and Kerala
qualified for the quarter-finals**

Elite Group C points table

Teams	M	W	L	T	D	Pts.	Quotient
Rajasthan	9	7	0	0	2	51	1.539
Uttar Pradesh	9	5	0	0	4	41	1.964
Jharkhand	9	5	1	0	3	40	1.266
Odisha	9	4	3	0	2	26	1.101
Haryana	9	3	4	0	2	22	0.844
Assam	9	3	4	0	2	21	0.847
Jammu & Kashmir	9	3	5	0	1	19	0.826
Services	9	2	3	0	4	19	0.936
Tripura	9	1	6	0	2	11	0.734
Goa	9	0	7	0	2	6	0.639

Rajasthan and Uttar Pradesh qualified for the quarter-final

Plate Group points table

Teams	M	W	L	T	D	Pts.	Quotient
Uttarakhand	8	6	0	0	2	44	2.435
Bihar	8	6	1	0	1	40	2.307
Puducherry	8	4	0	0	4	33	1.859
Meghalaya	8	4	2	0	2	29	1.349
Sikkim	8	4	3	0	1	27	0.757
Manipur	8	3	5	0	0	18	0.845
Nagaland	8	2	4	0	2	18	1.039
Arunachal Pradesh	8	0	7	0	1	3	0.436
Mizoram	8	0	7	0	1	1	0.385

Uttarakhand qualified for the quarter-final

1st quarter-final: Vidarbha won by an innings and 115 runs

As expected, defending champions Vidarbha thrashed Uttrakhand, the qualifying team from Plate Group. Jaffer starred with a double-century, Aditya Sarwate finished with a hundred and a five-wicket haul, and Umesh grabbed nine wickets as Vidarbha wrapped up the game eight overs into the fifth morning.

Opting to bowl, Vidarbha reduced Uttarakhand to 44 for 3 in ten overs. However, debutant Avneesh Sudha and Vaibhav Singh Panwar made them work hard for further wickets. The two brought up half-centuries during a

140-run stand for the fourth wicket, before Sudha and Saurabh Rawat took the side past 200. While Sudha fell to Akshay Wakhare's off-spin nine short of his hundred, Rawat strung together useful partnerships with the lower order and brought up his century. His 108 included 15 fours and two sixes.

In reply, Faiz Fazal fell early, but R Sanjay and Jaffer took their team to 260 for 1 at the end of the second day, with both batsmen reaching their hundreds. The 304-run stand between the two was broken when Sanjay fell to Dhanraj Sharma for 141. Jaffer, though, carried on and brought up his double-century. The veteran batsman struck 26 fours during his knock of 206, off just 296 balls.Wicketkeeper Akshay Wadkar and Sarwate then added 115 for the sixth wicket. Wadkar fell two short of his hundred, but Sarwate wasn't to be denied. He brought up his second first-class hundred and helped the side to a first-innings lead of 274.

Vineet Saxena and Karn Kaushal gave Uttrakhand a 72-run start before Umesh removed Saxena and Vaibhav Bhatt in quick succession. Kaushal and Sudha rebuilt, but it was again Sarwate who hurt them with his left-arm spin. Once Umesh bowled Sudha for 28, it triggered a collapse in which Uttrakhand lost their last seven wickets in seven runs. Both Umesh and Sarwate picked up five wickets each. Rawat, the centurion of the first innings, bagged a 21-ball duck this time around.

All ten wickets in Uttrakhand's second innings fell without any assistance from the fielders — six bowled, three lbw and one caught-and-bowled — with eight of them failing to reach double digits.

VCA Stadium, Jamtha, Nagpur, January 15-19: Uttarakhand 355 in 108.4 overs (Saurabh Rawat 108, Avneesh Sudha 91; Umesh Yadav 4-90, Akshay Wakhare 2-46) and 159 in 65.1 overs (Karan Kaushal 76, Avneesh Sudha 28; Umesh 5-23, Aditya Sarwate 5-55) lost to **Vidarbha** 629 in 184 overs (Wasim Jaffer 206, R Sanjay 141, Aditya Sarwate 102; Dhanraj Sharma 3-101, Mayank Mishra 3-110) by an innings and 115 runs. *PoM:* Umesh Yadav.

2nd quarter-final: Saurashtra won by six wickets

Harvik Desai's maiden first-class century studded Saurashtra's incredible chase of 372 — the highest successful chase in Ranji Trophy history. The previous record was 371, set by Assam against Services in 2008-09.

Desai was not the only architect of Saurashtra's chase: His knock was complemented by the half-centuries from Snell Patel (72), Cheteshwar Pujara (67 not out) and Sheldon Jackson (73 not out).

Batting first, Uttar Pradesh found themselves in trouble as Jaydev Unadkat removed Rahul Rawat and Mohammad Saif for ducks to reduce them to 7 for 2. Dharmendrasinh Jadeja made it 54 for 4, before Rinku joined hands with Priyank Garg (49) to counter-attack his way to his fourth hundred of the tournament. He eventually fell to Kamlesh Makvana's off-spin for 150, off just 181 balls, with the team on 284. Saurabh Kumar (55) and Shivam Mavi (42) added 76 for the eighth wicket to post a strong total. Unadkat picked up the last three wickets for a five-wicket haul.

Saurashtra stuttered in response as Snell and Vishvaraj Jadeja fell to Ankit Rajpoot in successive deliveries. Pujara, after all his exploits in Australia, struggled with timing and was caught off Mavi for 11. When Yash Dayal dismissed Jackson and Arpit Vasavada, the scoreboard read 86 for 5.

Desai dug deep to hold the innings together, adding 65 for the sixth wicket with Prerak Mankak, but Saurashtra were still 177 in arrears. For UP, their seamers — Dayal, Mavi and Rajpoot — shared the wickets.

At 107 for 1, with Rawat and Saif steady, UP were in control. But three quick wickets including Rinku's for a first-ball duck, turned the game. Chetan Sakariya and Unadkat ensured the tail didn't wag.

Despite the fumble, it was a mammoth target, and the onus was on Saurabh, the left-arm spinner, to take UP to victory. Desai and Snell, though, didn't give them a look in with a 132-run start. Desai brought up his hundred on the final morning. Even after he fell, however, there were no stutters. Pujara and Jackson were hardly troubled during their unbeaten 136-run fifth-wicket stand, seeing the side home.

Ekana International Cricket Stadium, Lucknow, January 15-19: Uttar Pradesh 385 in 103.3 overs (Rinku Singh 150, Saurabh Kumar 55; Jaydev Unadkat 5-86, Dharmendrasinh Jadeja 3-111) and 194 in 72.1 overs (Mohammad Saif 48, Rahul Rawat 37; D Jadeja 4-53, Chetan Sakariya 3-38) lost to **Saurashtra** 208 in 66.4 overs (Harvik Desai 84, Prerak Mankad 67; Yash Dayal 4-55, Shivam Mavi 3-40, Ankit Rajpoot 3-71) and 372/4 in 115.1 overs (H Desai 116, Sheldon Jackson 73*) by six wickets. *PoM:* Harvik Desai.

3rd quarter-final: Karnataka won by six wickets

Unbeaten half-centuries from captain Manish Pandey (87) and Karun Nair (61) guided Karnataka in a tricky chase of 184 on the fourth day against Rajasthan. However, the knock that had put them in the ascendency came from the unlikely bat of their former captain, R Vinay Kumar. His 83 not out in the first innings not only rescued the side from 166 for 9, but also helped them gain a crucial 39-run lead.

But before that, Vinay struck with the ball, sending Rajasthan opener Amitkumar Gautam back for 12 after Karnataka opted to bowl. Shreyas Gopal combined with the veteran to reduce Rajasthan to 82 for 4. Mahipal Lomror's patient 50 and an 85-run seventh-wicket stand between Rajesh Bishnoi and Deepak Chahar gave the total some respectability. Bishnoi hit ten fours and two sixes in his 79, while Chahar played the supporting role.

For Karnataka, R Samarth and K Siddharth added 44 for the second wicket after the early loss of D Nischal. But with Tanveer-ul-Haq dismissing Nair and Pandey cheaply, and Rahul Chahar denting the recovery process by accounting for K Gowtham and Shreyas, Karnataka were staring at a first-innings deficit.

Vinay, though, stood firm, adding 97 with Ronit More for the last wicket, with More's contribution only ten. The two not only took Karnataka past Rajasthan's total, but also gave them a morale-boosting lead. The stand was broken when Rahul trapped More lbw for his fifth wicket.

There was elation as Kerala beat Gujarat to enter their maiden Ranji Trophy semi-final. — *KCA*

Rajasthan were again strong at 107 for 1, but slipped to 123 for 4 against the spin of Gowtham and Shreyas. The good work of Robin Bist and Salman Khan to take them to 186 for 4 was undone when they lost three wickets for just one run. While five of their top six crossed 20, none could reach 50.

Karnataka were precarious at 45 for 3 at the end of the third day, which quickly became 56 for 4 when nightwatchman More fell early the next morning. Pandey got a life on 38 when Deepak grassed an easy chance off his brother Rahul's bowling — the team total was 119. But he kept playing his shots and shifted the pressure to the bowling side. Nair played the anchor's role, their association unbroken at 129.

M Chinnaswamy Stadium, Bengaluru, January 15-18: Rajasthan 224 in 77.1 overs (Rajesh Bishnoi 79, Mahipal Lomror 50; Abhimanyu Mithun 3-48, K Gowtham 3-54) and 222 in 67.2 overs (Robin Bist 44, M Lomror 42; Gowtham 4-54, Shreyas Gopal 3-52) lost to **Karnataka** 263 in 87.4 overs (Vinay Kumar 83*, KV Siddharth 52; Rahul Chahar 5-93, Tanveer-ul-Haq 3-50) and 185/4 in 47.5 overs (Manish Pandey 87*, Karun Nair 61*; Aniket Choudhary 2-32) by six wickets. *PoM:* Vinay Kumar.

4th quarter-final: Kerala won by 113 runs

Taking a step further from the previous season, Kerala entered their maiden Ranji Trophy semi-final, beating Gujarat in a low-scoring match at Krishnagiri Stadium in Wayanad. The path to victory was paved by their pacers Sandeep Warrier and Basil Thampi, who each picked up eight wickets.

After Gujarat captain Parthiv Patel inserted the home team in, Kerala gave away a decent start of 52 for 1, slipping to 52 for 4. Chintan Gaja and Arzan Nagwaswalla accounted for three wickets in four balls. It got worse when Nagwaswalla hit Samson on his right ring finger with a lifter. Samson had to retire hurt on 17; scans later revealed he had a fracture. However, Thampi's

37 off just 33 balls, studded with five fours and a six, helped Kerala to 185.

In return, Gujarat fared even worse, conceding a 23-run lead. Parthiv struck five fours and two sixes in his 43 off just 36 balls, but apart from him and No.9 Kalaria (36), no other batsman crossed 20.

Having lost the Kerala openers on 12, Joseph soaked in the pressure: his 148-ball 56 was the only fifty-plus score of the match. Along with Jalaj Saxena, he added 53 for the sixth wicket. Samson came out to bat with a fractured finger at No.11, but he too was out without troubling the scorers.

Chasing down a target of 195 is never easy in the fourth innings. Besides, Gujarat had to post the highest total of the match for victory. They didn't even get close. Thampi sent back both openers in the first six overs and when Parthiv was run out in the next without opening his account, the result seemed decide. Gujarat's whole second innings lasted just 31.3 overs, with nine of their batsmen failing to reach double-figures.

Krishnagiri Stadium, Wayanad, January 15-17: Kerala 185 in 39.3 overs (Basil Thampi 37, P Rahul 26; Chintan Gaja 4-57, Arzan Nagwaswalla 3-50) and 171 in 59 overs (Sijomon Joseph 56, Jalaj Saxena 44*; Roosh Kalaria 3-36, Axar Patel 3-40) beat **Gujarat** 162 in 51.4 overs (Parthiv Patel 43, R Kalaria 36; Sandeep Warrier 4-42, MD Nidheesh 3-38, Basil Thampi 3-61) and 81 in 31.3 overs (Rahul Shah 33*; B Thampi 5-27, S Warrier 4-30) by 113 runs. *PoM:* Basil Thampi.

1st semi-final: Vidarbha won by an innings and 11 runs

This was an emotional campaign for many in the Kerala side, given the state was hit by the worst floods in decades. There was also turmoil within the camp in the off-season. Their journey to the semi-final was against the odds, but that's where the dream ended. Vidarbha, powered by a ruthless Umesh, who ended with career-best match figures of 12 for 79, eased to an innings-and-11-run victory within two days in Wayanad, after Kerala collapsed in the second innings.

Put in, Kerala were bundled out for 106 in just 28.4 overs in the first innings. Umesh was in tremendous form, returning 7 for 48.

A green, pacy surface had helped Kerala in the quarter-final, but with a bowler with the skill and experience of Umesh in the opposition, they couldn't get the same benefit in the semis. "This was perhaps the fastest track I have bowled at ever in India. We don't get tracks like this usually," the pacer said afterwards.

Vishnu Vinod's 50-ball 37 not out was Kerala's highest score, and at the time, it seemed Vidarbha already were in control. With Fazal scoring a 142-ball 75, they managed a lead of 102. But Warrier and Thampi took eight wickets between them, and on the second morning, Vidarbha collapsed for 208 after resuming at 171 for 5.

Kerala remained in control, with Saxena, KB Arun Karthik and Vishnu Vinod taking them to 59 for 1. But Umesh again triggered an implosion — Kerala lost nine wickets in just 12.3 overs — and were bowled out for 91. Just like that, an emotional journey, a commendable one too, came to a quick end.

Krishnagiri Stadium, Wayanad, January 24-25: Kerala 106 in 28.4 overs (Vishnu Vinod 37, Sachin Baby 22, Umesh Yadav 7-48, Rajneesh Gurbani 3-38) and 91 in 24.5 overs (Arun Karthik 36; Umesh Yadav 5-31, Yash Thakur 4-28) lost to **Vidarbha** 208 in 52.4 overs (Faiz Fazal 75, Wasim Jaffer 34; Sandeep Warrier 5-57, Basil Thampi 3-64) by an innings and 11 runs. *PoM:* Umesh Yadav.

2nd semi-final: Saurashtra won by five wickets

This was a riveting semi-final. From Saurashtra's synchronised clapping to pump themselves up, game-changing umpiring mistakes, and patient, defiant centuries, Bengaluru hosted a thriller. Saurashtra secured a five-wicket win to progress to the finals, but Karnataka didn't let up till the last minute.

The decision of umpire Saiyed Khaled to rule Pujara not out for a caught behind appeal on the fourth day was crucial. Replays indicated a noise as bat passed ball, but Pujara was unmoved, as was the umpire. Pujara was on 34 at the time, after Saurashtra were reduced to 24 for 3 in chase of 279. He went on to score an unbeaten 131 and added 214 for the fourth wicket with Jackson (100).

Karnataka only have themselves to blame, though. That they scored 275 in the first innings was thanks to the middle order — Pandey, Shreyas and Srinivas Sharath scored half-centuries — but both the top and lower order collapsed. Unadkat was a handful in the opening session, plucking out the spine of Karnataka's batting. The home team bowlers did well, though, to keep Saurashtra to 236 in response, with Ronit More a bundle out energy during his 6 for 60.

Once again in the second innings, Karnataka's top order didn't quite get going. They were 52 for 3, and that they managed 239 was largely thanks to Shreyas's 61. Vinay Kumar bowled his heart out on the final morning, and it

Although he played just four games, Cheteshwar Pujara played crucial roles as Saurashtra progressed through the knock-outs. — *Special arrangement*

made for an intense, entertaining battle against Pujara. But this was always Saurashtra's game to lose.

M Chinnaswamy Stadium, Bengaluru, January 24-28: Karnataka 275 in 100.3 overs (Shreyas Gopal 87, S Sharath 83*; Jaydev Unadkat 4-56, Kamlesh Makwana 3-74) and 239 in 80 overs (Shreyas 61, Mayank Agarwal 46; Dharmendrasinh Jadeja 5-78, J Unadkat 3-35) lost to **Saurashtra** 236 in 71 overs (Snell Patel 85, Sheldon Jackson 46; Ronit More 6-60, Abhimanyu Mithun 3-46) and 279/5 in 91.4 overs (Cheteshwar Pujara 131*, S Jackson 100; Vinay Kumar 3-75) by five wickets. *PoM:* Cheteshwar Pujara.

Final: Vidarbha won by 78 runs

On the big stage, Sarwate picked up a career-best 11 for 157 and chipped in with 49 crucial second-innings runs to star in Vidarbha's title defence. They became only the sixth team to retain the trophy. The biggest celebration from Sarwate, the left-arm spinner, was reserved for the wicket of Pujara — twice. While in the first innings the India batsman was done in by the turn, in the second, he fell to a straighter one while playing for turn.

Saurashtra had Fazal's men against the wall several times during the match. In the first innings, Vidarbha were struggling at 196 for 7 before the lower order engineered a rescue. In their second hit, they were 75 for 5, with an overall lead of just 80. However, the champions seized the moments.

Vidarbha have a lot to thank their middle and lower order for. With Unadkat and Makvana chipping away, they were unable to build a partnership after choosing to bat. Coming in at 106 for 4, it was up to Wadkar, who combined with Akshay Karnewar for their best period of the game, adding 59 for the seventh wicket. Karnewar then guided the tail, remaining unbeaten as the last three wickets accounted for 116 runs.

While opener Snell held firm on one end in Saurashtra's reply, he too found the support he needed only from the lower order. Once he was the seventh wicket to fall, soon after his hundred, No.10 Unadkat dug in, frustrating the opposition with a last-wicket stand worth 60 with Chetan Sakariya.

Having done the work with the ball, Sarwate found his team asking a fair bit from him with the bat as well. Coming in at 105 for 6, he top-scored, lifting them to 200 before becoming the last man out. That along would have been a worthy match-winning contribution, if he had not returned to upstage himself by running through the Saurashtra line-up in the fourth innings. He sent back Desai and Pujara in the eighth over, and returned to dismiss Vishvaraj Jadeja — the No.3 was the only batsman to cross 20 in the innings — and Unadkat to ensure there would be no lower-order rescue. Fittingly, Sarwate held on to the catch of Dharmendrasinh that sealed it for his team.

VCA Stadium, Jamtha, Nagpur, February 3-7: Vidarbha 312 in 120.2 overs (Akshay Karnewar 73*, Akshay Wadkar 45; Jaydev Unadkat 3-54, Chetan Sakariya 2-44) and 200 in 92.5 overs (Aditya Sarwate 49, Mohit Kale 38; Dharmendrasinh Jadeja 6-96, Kamlesh Makwana 2-51) beat **Saurashtra** 307 in 117 overs (Snell Patel 102, Jaydev Unadkat 46; A Sarwate 5-98, Akshay Wakhare 4-80) and 127 in 58.4 overs (Vishvarajsinh Jadeja 52; A Sarwate 6-59, A Wakhare 3-37) by 78 runs. *PoM:* Aditya Sarwate.

Ranji Trophy 2017-18

Group A

Feroz Shah Kotla, Delhi, October 6-9: Assam 258 in 95 overs (Swarupam Purkayastha 66, Gokul Sharma 51; Ishant Sharma 5-38, Navdeep Saini 2-53) and 255 in 108.4 overs (Sibsankar Roy 87, Wasiqur Rahman 63; Manan Sharma 3-58, Milind Kumar 2-4) drew with **Delhi** 435 in 135.3 overs (Gautam Gambhir 137, Nitish Rana 110; Abu Nechim 7-68, Krishna Das 2-82) and 49/2 in 8 overs (Unmukt Chand 25*; K Das 2-22). Delhi took first-innings lead. *PoM*: Gautam Gambhir.

Ekana International Cricket Stadium, Lucknow, October 6-8: Railways 182 in 76 overs (Ashish Yadav 53*, Nitin Bhille 42; Ankit Rajpoot 3-30, Zeeshan Ansari 3-78) and 161 in 63.3 overs (Arindam Ghosh 57, Vidhyadhar Kamath 30; A Rajpoot 4-34, Z Ansari 3-47) beat **Uttar Pradesh** 250 in 85.5 overs (Akshdeep Nath 75, Shivam Chaudhary 44; Anureet Singh 3-42, Avinash Yadav 3-86) and 72 in 26 overs (Suresh Raina 29, Rinku Singh 23*; Avinash 4-26, Anureet 3-25) by 21 runs. *PoM*: Avinash Yadav.

Gymkhana Ground, Hyderabad, October 6-9: Hyderabad v Maharashtra. Match abandoned.

Karnail Singh Stadium, Delhi, October 14-17: Delhi 447 in 144.5 overs (Manan Sharma 136, Nitish Rana 89; Anureet Singh 4-92, Avinash Yadav 2-96) beat **Railways** 136 in 59.4 overs (Shivakant Shukla 29, Mahesh Rawat 28; Manan 4-50, Ishant Sharma 3-20, Vikas Mishra 3-37) and 206 in 78.5 overs (f/o) (Nitin Bhille 73, Anureet 27; V Mishra 4-37, Manan 3-67) by an innings and 105 runs. *PoM*: Manan Sharma.

Gymkhana Ground, Hyderabad, October 14-17: Hyderabad v Uttar Pradesh . Match abandoned.

Sri Jayachamarajendra College of Engineering Ground, Mysore, October 14-17: Assam145 in 59.1 overs (Gokul Sharma 55, Rishav Das 26; K Gowtham 4-20, Shreyas Gopal 3-43) and 203 in 73.1 overs (Gokul 66, Sibsankar Roy 44; Vinay Kumar 4-31, Gowtham 3-39, Abhimanyu Mithun 3-47) lost to **Karnataka** 469/7 dec in 126.4 overs (Gowtham 149, R Samarth 123; Arup Das 4-113, Swarupam Purkayastha 3-80) by an innings and 121 runs. *PoM*: K Gowtham.

Barsapara Cricket Stadium, Guwahati, October 24-27: Assam 244 in 93.2 overs (Tajinder Singh 43, Dhiraj Goswami 41*; Deepak Bansal 4-61, Amit Mishra 3-56, Anureet Singh 3-81) and 55 in 32.3 overs (Anureet 5-28, D Bansal 2-6) lost to **Railways** 483/7 dec in 138.4 overs (Arindam Ghosh 109, Nitin Bhille 89; D Goswami 2-93)by an innings and 184 runs. *PoM*: Anureet Singh.

Ekana International Cricket Stadium, Lucknow, October 24-27: Mahrashtra 312 in 106.1 overs (Ankit Bawne 119, Ruturaj Gaikwad 63; Saurabh Kumar 7-110, Ankit Rajpoot 3-68) and 282/7 dec in 84 overs (Rahul Tripathi 91, A Bawne 58; Saurabh 4-105, Shivam Chaudhary 2-38) beat **Uttar Pradesh** 271 in 82.2 overs (Eklavya Dwivedi 71, Almas Shaukat 63; Chirag Khurana 6-53) and 292 in 68 overs (Rinku Singh 122*, Akshdeep Nath 79; C Khurana 6-131) by 31 runs. *PoM*: Chirag Khurana.

KSCA Navule Stadium, Shimoga, October 24-27: Karnataka 183 in 62.2 overs (Stuart Binny 61, Karun Nair 23; Mohammed Siraj 4-42, Ravi Kiran 3-36) and 332 in 105.4 overs (K Nair 134, S Binny 72; Mehdi Hasan 5-88, Akash Bhandari 3-64) beat **Hyderabad** 136 in 64.4 overs (K Sumanth 68, A Bhandari 24; Shreyas Gopal 5-17, K Gowtham 3-56) and 320 in 109.4 overs (Bavanka Sandeep 80, Ashish Reddy 57; S Gopal 4-91, K Gowtham 3-92) by 59 runs. *PoM*: Karun Nair.

Karnail Singh Stadium, Delhi, November 1-4: Hyderabad 474/9 dec in 151 overs (Ambati Rayudu 112, Bavanaka Sandeep 82; Manish Rao 3-76, Karan Thakur 3-96) and 23/0 in 5.2 overs beat **Railways** 246 in 94.2 overs (Anureet Singh 60, Shivakant Shukla 48; Ravi Teja 5-49, Mehdi Hasan 2-37) and 250 in 72 overs (f/o) (Manish Rao 85*, Arindam Ghosh 33; M

Rishabh Pant had a sedate start to the season before exploding with a 99 off 110
balls against Maharashtra. — *KCA*

Hasan 4-35, R Teja 2-37) by ten wickets. *PoM*: Ravi Teja.
Palam A Stadium, Delhi, November 1-4: Uttar Pradesh 291 in 89.5 overs (Mohammad
Saif 83, Upendra Yadav 67*; Ishant Sharma 3-38, Navdeep Saini 3-47) and 229 in 67.5 overs
(Akshdeep Nath 110, Rinku Singh 64; N Saini 4-46, Ishant 3-38) lost to **Delhi** 269 in 87
overs (Dhruv Shorey 98*, Gautam Gambhir 86; Saurabh Kumar 4-87, Imtiaz Ahmed 3-33) and
256/6 in 72.1 overs (Nitish Rana 67, Unmukt Chand 49; Ankit Rajpoot 3-61, M Saif 2-20) by
four wickets. *PoM*: Akshdeep Nath.
MCA Stadium, Pune, November 1-4: Maharashtra 245 in 55 overs (Rahul Tripathi 120,
Naushad Shaikh 69; Vinay Kumar 6-59, Pavan Deshpande 2-38) and 247 in 66.2 overs(Ruturaj
Gaikwad 65, R Tripathi 51; Abhimanyu Mithun 5-66, Ronit More 2-25) lost to **Karnataka**
628/5 dec in 176 overs (Mayank Agarwal 304*, R Samarth 129, Karun Nair 116; Chirag Khurana 3-147) by an innings and 136 runs. *PoM*: Mayank Agarwal.
Barsapara Cricket Stadium, Guwahati, November 9-12: Uttar Pradesh 349 in 73.2 overs
(Saurabh Kumar 133, Upendra Yadav 127; Rajjakuddin Ahmed 3-103, Gokul Sharma 2-10)
and 357/6 dec in 86.4 overs (Umang Sharma 148, Mohammad Saif 77; Abu Nechim 2-58)
drew with **Assam** 318 in 108.1 overs (Sibsankar Roy 72, Rishav Das 52; Saurabh 5-54, Ankit
Rajpoot 2-69) and 148/4 in 55 overs (Gokul 62, S Roy 62; Saurabh 3-52). Uttar Pradesh took
first-innings lead. *PoM*: Saurabh Kumar.
MCA Stadium, Pune, November 9-12: Maharashtra 481 in 155.5 overs (Rohit Motwani
189, Ankit Bawane 92; Amit Mishra 4-98, Karan Thakur 4-114) and 186/6 dec in 37 overs
(Naushad Shaikh 40, Rahul Tripathi 30; K Thakur 3-43) drew with **Railways** 381 in 131.2
overs (Pratham Singh 73, Shivkant Shukla 62; Chirag Khurana 2-58, Pradeep Dadhe 2-64)
and 54/1 in 18 overs (Saurabh Wakaskar 23*). Maharashtra took first-innings lead. *PoM*: Rohit
Motwani.
KSCA Cricket (2) Ground, Alur, November 9-12: Karnataka 649 in 172.2 overs (Mayank
Agarwal 176, Stuart Binny 118; Manan Sharma 3-151, Vikas Mishra 3-152) and 235/3 in 63
overs (KL Rahul 92, R Samarth 47) drew with **Delhi**301 in 95 overs (Gautam Gambhir 144,
Dhruv Shorey 64; Abhimanyu Mithun 5-70, S Binny 2-39). Karnataka took first-innings lead.
PoM: Stuart Binny.
Barsapara Cricket Stadium, Guwahati, November 17-20: Hyderabad 326 in 90.5 overs

(B Sandeep 84, Ambati Rayudu 83; Arup Das 5-112, Rahul Singh 3-60) and 144/6 in 39 overs (A Rayudu 52*, K Sumanth 32; A Das 2-21, Riyan Parag 2-41) beat **Assam** 136 in 48.5 overs (Gokul Sharma 39, Rishav Das 28; Mohammad Muddassir 5-36, Ravi Kiran 3-30) and 331 in 109 overs (f/o) (Amit Sinha 122, Rajjakuddin Ahmed 75; Sudeep Tyagi 3-34, R Kiran 3-75) by four wickets. *PoM*: Ambati Rayudu.

Palam A Stadium, Delhi, November 17-20: Delhi 419 in 111.1 overs (Nitish Rana 174, Rishabh Pant 99; Satyajeet Bachhav 4-87, Chirag Khurana 3-106) beat **Maharashtra** 99 in 35 overs (Chirag Khurana 29, Naushad Shaikh 23; Ishant Sharma 3-14, Lalit Yadav 2-10) and 259 in 63.3 overs (f/o) (Rahul Tripathi 106, Rohit Motwani 39; Navdeep Saini 4-57, Vikas Mishra 4-90) by an innings and 61 runs. *PoM*: Nitish Rana.

Green Park, Kanpur, November 17-20: Karnataka 655 in 186.1 overs (Manish Pandey 238, D Nischal 195; Imtiaz Ahmed 6-110, Dhruv Pratap Singh 3-108) and 262/0 in 59 overs (Mayank Agarwal 133*, R Samarth 126*) drew with **Uttar Pradesh** 331 in 84 overs (Umang Sharma 89, Rinku Singh 73; Shreyas Gopal 3-63, Ronit More 2-79). Karnataka took first-innings lead. *PoM*: Manish Pandey.

Rajiv Gandhi International Stadium, Hyderabad, November 25-28: Delhi 415 in 107.4 overs (Himmat Singh 99, Kunal Chandela 64; Ravi Kiran 3-83, Mehdi Hasan 3-103) drew with **Hyderabad** 205 in 74.2 overs (Tanmay Agarwal 63, B Sandeep 26; Vikas Mishra 4-36, Kulwant Khejroliya 4-48) and 442/8 in 155.1 overs (f/o) (Akshath Reddy 107, Rohit Rayudu 103; V Mishra 5-116, Dhruv Shorey 2-47). Delhi took first-innings lead. *PoM*: Vikas Mishra.

Pune Club Ground, Pune, November 25-28: Assam 279 in 66.2 overs (Gokul Sharma 87, Sibsankar Roy 80; Nikit Dhumal 5-94, Pradeep Dadhe 2-58) and 189 in 63.5 overs (Rishav Das 35, Abhishek Thakuri 35; P Dadhe 5-51, N Dhumal 4-48) lost to **Maharashtra** 253 in 68.2 overs (Ruturaj Gaikwad 126, Prayag Bhati 31; Rahul Singh 4-63, Pallavkumar Das 2-60) and 216/3 in 47.4 overs (Naushad Shaikh 108*, Ankit Bawne 52*) by seven wickets. *PoM*: Naushad Shaikh.

Karnail Singh Stadium, Delhi, November 25-28: Karnataka 434 in 111 overs (Mayank Agarwal 173, Manish Pandey 108; Karan Thakur 3-91, Manish Rao 3-96) and 275/4 dec in 71 overs (M Agarwal 134, R Samarth 56; K Thakur 2-68) beat **Railways** 333 in 98.4 overs (Mahesh Rawat 124, Arindam Ghosh 91; Shreyas Gopal 4-102, K Gowtham 3-70) and 167 in 63 overs (Pratham Singh 36, Mrunal Devdhar 24; Gowtham 7-72, S Gopal 2-59) by 209 runs. *PoM*: Mayank Agarwal.

Group A points table

Teams	M	W	L	D	T	A	Pts.	NRR
Karnataka	6	4	0	2	0	0	32	0.479
Delhi	6	3	0	3	0	0	27	0.333
Maharashtra	6	2	2	1	0	1	16	0.084
Hyderabad	6	2	1	1	0	2	16	-0.156
Railways	6	2	3	1	0	0	14	-0.312
Uttar Pradesh	6	0	3	2	0	1	5	0.508
Assam	6	0	4	2	0	0	2	-0.977

Karnataka and Delhi qualified for the knock-outs

Group B

Sawai Mansingh Stadium, Jaipur, October 6-9: Rajasthan 330 in 115.2 overs (Robin Bist 113, Ashik Menaria 69; Mohammed Mudhasir 5-81, Parvez Rasool 3-50) and 246/4 in 68 overs (Rajesh Bishnoi 101*, Mahipal Lomror 65*; Rohit Sharma 2-28) drew with **Jammu & Kashmir** 436/8 dec in 156.5 overs (Ahmed Bandy 102, Parvez Rasool 97; TM Ul-Haq 3-43, Khaleel Ahmed 2-77). Jammu & Kashmir took first-innings lead. *PoM*: Mohammed Mudhasir.

Chaudhary Bansi Lal Cricket Stadium, Lahli, Rohtak, October 6-8: Saurashtra 278 in 90.3 overs (Prerak Mankad 68, Sheldon Jackson 51; Ashish Hooda 6-61, Deepak Punia 2-47) beat **Haryana** 107 in 42.3 overs (Rahul Tewatia 23; Shaurya Sanandia 4-44, Kushang Patel 3-21, Jaydev Unadkat 3-35) and 140 in 43 overs (f/o) (Chaitanya Bishnoi 56, D Punia 34; J Unadkat 3-55, Chirag Jani 2-12) by an innings and 31 runs. *PoM*: Prerak Mankad.

Greenfield International Stadium, Thiruvananthapuram, October 6-8: Jharkhand 202 in 73.2 overs (Ishan Kishan 45, Ashish Kumar 25; Jalaj Saxena 6-50, Sandeep Warrier 2-51) and 89 in 41.3 overs (Saurabh Tiwary 26*; J Saxena 5-27, K Monish 4-42) lost to **Kerala** 259 in 90.3 overs (J Saxena 54*, Mohammed Azharuddeen 51; Sunny Gupta 6-94, Ashish 2-7) and 34/1 in 5 overs (Arun Karthik 27*) by nine wickets. *PoM*: Jalaj Saxena.

SCA Stadium, Rajkot, October 14-16: Saurashtra 624/7 dec in 135 overs (Ravindra Jadeja 201, Sheldon Jackson 181; Waseem Raza 3-164, Parvez Rasool 2-187) beat **Jammu & Kashmir** 156 in 60.5 overs (Shubham Khajuria 41, Puneet Bisht 34*; Dharmendrasinh Jadeja 6-68, R Jadeja 4-40) and 256 in 84.1 overs (f/o) (Ram Dayal 56, P Bisht 55; Vandit Jivrajani 6-79, R Jadeja 3-69) by an innings and 212 runs. *PoM*: Ravindra Jadeja.

Sawai Mansingh Stadium, Jaipur, October 14-17: Rajasthan 423 in 141.5 overs (Tajinder Singh 134, Amitkumar Gautam 107; Sunny Gupta 3-76, Ashish Kumar 3-83) drew with **Jharkhand** 265 in 97.4 overs (Saurabh Tiwary 83, Ishan Kishan 50; Pankaj Singh 4-48, Mahipal Lomror 2-26) and 332/6 in 103.5 overs (f/o) (Ishank Jaggi 103*, Nazim Siddiqui 100; Pankaj 3-53). Rajasthan took first-innings lead. *PoM*: Amitkumar Gautam.

GS Patel Stadium, Nadiad, October 14-17: Kerala 208 in 66.5 overs (Sanju Samson 51, Sachin Baby 49; Piyush Chawla 5-69, Siddharth Desai 3-90) and 203 in 76.3 overs (Arun Karthik 69, S Baby 59; S Desai 6-80, P Chawla 3-66) lost to **Gujarat** 307 in 106.3 overs (Chirag Gandhi 91, Samit Gohel 69; Akshay Chandran 3-52, MD Nidheesh 3-58, Jalaj Saxena 3-95) and 108/6 in 42.3 overs (Priyank Panchal 30, Bhargav Merai 21; J Saxena 2-16, A Chandran 2-37) by four wickets. *PoM*: Siddharth Desai.

JSCA International Stadium Complex, Ranchi, October 24-27: Haryana 208 in 75.4 overs (Chaitanya Bishnoi 61*, Shubham Rohilla 52; Sunny Gupta 4-67, Jaskaran Singh 3-52)and 296 in 113 overs (Rajat Paliwal 93, Rohit Sharma 71; Shahbaz Nadeem 6-93, S Gupta 2-61) lost to **Jharkhand** 425/9 dec in 133.5 overs (Ishank Jaggi 135, Ishan Kishan 83; C Bishnoi 2-43, Ajit Chahal 2-80) and 81/0 in 10.4 overs (I Kishan 46*, Nazim Siddiqui 24*) by ten wickets. *PoM*: Ishank Jaggi.

Lalabhai Contractor Stadium, Surat, October 24-26: Jammu & Kashmir 261 in 77.2 overs (Shubham Khajuria 54, Ahmed Bandy 54; Piyush Chawla 5-92, Hardik Patel 3-57) and 130 in 34.4 overs (Ram Dayal 29, Parvez Rasool 24; Hardik 5-49, P Chawla 4-38) lost to **Gujarat** 455 in 143 overs (Manprit Juneja 131, Chirag Gandhi 86; Manik Gupta 5-143, P Rasool 4-108) by an innings and 64 runs. *PoM*: Manprit Juneja.

St Xavier's College Ground, Thumba, October 24-27: Kerala 335 in 118.3 overs (Rohan Prem 86, Jalaj Saxena 79; Mahipal Lomror 4-51) and 250/4 dec in 50.4 overs (J Saxena 105*, Sanju Samson 72; Tajinder Singh 2-38) beat **Rajasthan** 243 in 82.3 overs (Dishant Yagnik 62, Tajinder 44; J Saxena 8-85) and 211 in 83.4 overs (Robin Bist 70, M Lomror 53; Sijomon Joseph 5-84, J Saxena 2-62) by 131 runs. *PoM*: Jalaj Saxena.

Madhavrao Scindia Cricket Ground, Rajkot, November 1-4: Saurashtra 553/9 dec in 161 overs (Cheteshwar Pujara 204, Chirag Jani 108; Ashish Kumar 3-76, Varun Aaron 3-96) and 59/4 in 14 overs (Ashish 2-20) beat **Jharkhand** 270 in 82.1 overs (Ishank Jaggi 114, Ishan Kishan 59; Vandit Jivrajani 4-33, Jaydev Unadkat 2-34) and 341 in 83 overs (f/o) (Sumit Kumar 108, Nazim Siddiqui 99; Dharmendrasinh Jadeja 4-108, Ravindra Jadeja 2-44) by six wickets. *PoM*: Cheteshwar Pujara.

St Xavier's College Ground, Thiruvananthapuram, November 1-4: Kerala 219 in 76 overs (Sanju Samson 112, Arun Karthik 35; Parvez Rasool 6-70, Mohammed Mudhasir 2-25) and 191 in 65.3 overs (Rohan Prem 58, A Karthik 36; P Rasool 5-70, Aamir Aziz 3-51) beat **Jammu & Kashmir** 173 in 62 overs (Shubham Khajuria 41, Bandeep Singh 39; KC Akshay 4-37, Sijomon Joseph 3-45, Jalaj Saxena 3-57) and 79 in 41.5 overs (Akshay 5-21, MD Nidheesh 2-7) by 158 runs. *PoM*: Sanju Samson.

Sardar Vallabhai Patel Stadium, Valsad, November 1-4: Gujarat 236 in 84.1overs (Bhargav Merai 52, Rujul Bhatt 40; Amit Mishra 4-63, Rajat Paliwal 2-24) and 281/9 dec in 76.5 overs (Priyank Panchal 67, B Merai 66; Sanjay Pahal 4-54, A Mishra 3-73) beat **Haryana** 157 in 64 overs (Rohit Sharma 65*, Himanshu Rana 50; Piyush Chawla 4-48, Siddharth Desai 3-68) and 122 in 44.3 overs (S Pahal 41; P Chawala 5-44, S Desai 5-46) by 238 runs. *PoM*: Siddharth Desai.

Keenan Stadium, Jamshedpur, November 9-12: Jammu & Kashmir 376 in 100.3 overs (Puneet Bisht 115, Shubham Khajuria 101; Varun Aaron 4-54, Sunny Gupta 2-85) and 265/9 dec in 63.5 overs (Parveez Rasool 70, Owais Shad 50; Utkarsh Singh 3-40, Shahbaz Nadeem 3-70) beat **Jharkhand** 292/9 dec in 108 overs (Nazim Siddiqui 70, Anand Singh 68; Aamir Aziz 4-86, Mohammed Mudhasir 3-54) and 243 in 49.4 overs (S Nadeem 53, Ishan Kishan 52; A Aziz 5-63, P Rasool 5-99) by 106 runs. *PoM*: Parveez Rasool.

SCA Stadium, Rajkot, November 9-12: Saurashtra 570 in 161.4 overs (Cheteshwar Pujara 182, Snell Patel 156; Siddharth Desai 4-154, Chintan Gaja 2-77) and 98/1 in 30.1 overs (Robin Uthappa 64*, Sheldon Jackson 21) drew with **Gujarat** 413 in 145.1 overs (Priyank Panchal 145, Rujul Bhatt 107; Jaydev Unadkat 4-83, Dharmendrasinh Jadeja 3-103). Saurashtra took first-innings lead. *PoM*: Cheteshwar Pujara.

Ch Bansi Lal Cricket Stadium, Rohtak, November 9-12: Haryana223 in 79 overs (Harshal Patel 83, Rajat Paliwal 32; Aniket Choudhary 3-37, Pankaj Singh 3-60) and 179/5 dec in 55 overs (Shivam Chauhan 65, R Paliwal 35, A Choudhary 2-30) drew with **Rajasthan** 150 in 52.4 overs (Tajinder Singh 38, Deepak Chahar 27; Ajit Chahal 3-42, Ashish Hooda 2-20) and 59/7 in 39 overs (Mahipal Lomror 20*; A Hooda 3-8, Harshal 3-29). Haryana took first-innings lead. *PoM*: Harshal Patel.

Lalabhai Contractor Stadium, Surat, November 17-20: Rajasthan 153 in 50 overs (Tajinder Singh 45, Rajesh Bishnoi 43*; Chintan Gaja 8-40) and 341 in 107.3 overs (Robin Bist 81, Mahipal Lomror 60; Siddharth Desai 5-129, Piyush Chawla 3-80) lost to **Gujarat** 601/4 dec in 155 overs (Parthiv Patel 173, Priyank Panchal 152, Bhargav Merai 110) by an innings and 107 runs. *PoM*: Chintan Gaja.

Ch Bansi Lal Cricket Stadium, Rohtak, November 17-20: Haryana 184 in 65.4 overs (Amit Mishra 41, Himanshu Rana 35; Ram Dayal 5-57, Mohammed Mudhasir 4-56) and 167 in 86.3overs (Rajat Paliwal 45, Guntashveer Singh 33; R Dayal 6-44, M Mudhasir 2-32) beat **Jammu & Kashmir** 176 in 54.5 overs (Ahmed Bandy 67, Puneet Bisht 35; Ashish Hooda 3-38, Ajit Chahal 3-64) and 157 in 44.1 overs (Owais Shah 52*, Bandeep Singh 44; A Chahal 5-53, A Hooda 2-41) by 18 runs. *PoM*: Ajit Chahal.

Greenfield International Stadium, Thiruvananthapuram, November 17-20: Kerala 225 in 78 overs (Sanju Samson 68, Rohan Prem 29; Dharmendrasinh Jadeja 6-112, Jaydev Unadkat 2-33) and 411/6 dec in 92 overs (S Samson 175, Arun Karthik 81; D Jadeja 4-153, Jay Chauhan 2-126) beat **Saurashtra** 232 in 78.5 overs (Robin Uthappa 86, Snell Patel 49; Sijomon Joseph 4-43, Basil Thampi 3-36) and 95 in 51.3 overs (Sheldon Jackson 24, Snell 20; Jalaj Saxena 4-29, KC Akshay 3-23, S Joseph 3-27) by 309 runs. *PoM*: Sanju Samson.

JSCA International Stadium Complex, Ranchi, November 25-28: Gujarat 411 in 13.5 overs (Rajul Bhatt 145, Manprit Juneja 67; Ashish Kumar 4-118, Shahbaz Nadeem 3-106) and 16/0 in 1.4 overs beat **Jharkhand** 242 in 86.3 overs (Kumar Deobrat 80, Nazim Siddiqui 71; Kamlesh Thakor 3-43, Chintan Gaja 3-49) and 183 in 62 overs (f/o) (K Deobrat 53, Virat Singh 52; Hardik Patel 4-9, C Gaja 3-37) by ten wickets. *PoM*: Rajul Bhatt.

Sawai Mansingh Stadium, Jaipur, November 25-28: Saurashtra 534 in 143.4 overs (Avi Barot 130, Sheldon Jackson 94; Deepak Chahar 3-110, TM Ul-Haq 3-112) drew with **Rajas-**

than 275 in 102.2 overs (Robin Bist 63, Mahipal Lomror 52; Dharmendrasinh Jadeja 3-42, Shaurya Sanandia 3-62, Jaydev Unadkat 3-77) and 394/7 in 101.2 overs (f/o) (Chetan Bist 109, Rajesh Bishnoi 103*, Amitkumar Gautam 100; D Jadeja 5-167). Saurashtra took first-innings lead. *PoM*: Dharmendrasinh Jadeja.

Ch Bansi Lal Cricket Stadium, Rohtak, November 25-28: Haryana 208 in 81.3 overs (Rajat Paliwal 46, Guntashveer Singh 40; Sandeep Warrier 4-50, Basil Thampi 2-39) and 173 in 78.3 overs (Amit Mishra 40, R Paliwal 34; MD Nidheesh 3-27, Jalaj Saxena 3-37) lost to **Kerala** 389 in 129.3 overs (Rohan Prem 93, J Saxena 91; Ajit Chahal 5-90, A Mishra 3-105) by an innings and eight runs. *PoM*: Jalaj Saxena.

Group B points table

Teams	M	W	L	D	T	A	Pts.	NRR
Gujarat	6	5	0	1	0	0	34	0.097
Kerala	6	5	1	0	0	0	31	0.636
Saurashtra	6	3	1	2	0	0	26	0.245
Jammu & Kashmir	6	1	4	1	0	0	9	-0.077
Haryana	6	1	4	1	0	0	9	-0.506
Jharkhand	6	1	4	1	0	0	8	-0.049
Rajasthan	6	0	2	4	0	0	6	-0.294

Gujarat and Kerala qualified for the knock-outs

Group C

Vikas Cricket Ground, Cuttack, October 6-9: Tripura 194/8 dec in 68 overs (Udiyan Bose 104, Yashpal Singh 20; Dhiraj Singh 5-55, Suryakant Pradhan 2-35) drew with **Odisha** 18/1 in 5 overs. No result.

Holkar Cricket Stadium, Indore, October 6-9: Madhya Pradesh 551/8 dec in 164 overs (Shubham Sharma 196, Ankit Sharma 104; Swapnil Singh 3-136, Atit Sheth 2-90) and 73/2 in 16 overs (Harpreet Singh 44*, Rajat Patidar 23*; A Sheth 2-19) beat **Baroda** 302 in 79overs (Yusuf Pathan 111, Irfan Pathan 80; Ishwar Pandey 2-44, Ankit 2-75) and 318 in 76.3 overs (f/o) (Y Pathan 136*, A Sheth 109; I Pandey 5-40, Mihir Hirwani 3-77) by eight wickets. *PoM*: Shubham Sharma.

MA Chidambaram Stadium, Chepauk, Chennai, October 6-9: Tamil Nadu 176 in 85 overs (Baba Aparajith 51, K Vignesh 25*; Bhargav Bhatt 4-52, Prithvi Raj 3-39) and 350/6 dec in 105 overs (B Aparajith 108*, Abhinav Mukund 95; P Raj 3-61, B Bhatt 2-123) drew with **Andhra** 309 in 123.4 overs (B Sumanth 109, Ashwin Hebbar 64; R Ashwin 4-71, K Vignesh 3-73) and 198/7 in 41.4 overs (KS Bharat 64, Ricky Bhui 40; K Vignesh 3-34, Rahil Shah 2-46). Andhra took first-innings lead. *PoM*: B Sumanth.

Reliance Stadium, Vadodara, October 14-17: Baroda 373 in 128 overs (Kedar Devdhar 93, Swapnil Singh 88; Bandaru Ayyappa 4-69, Karthik Raman 2-81) and 195/6 in 71.4 overs (Vishnu Solanki 68, Aditya Waghmode 56; Ashwin Hebbar 2-16 B Ayyappa 2-35) drew with **Andhra** 554 in 149.5 overs (Hanuma Vihari 150, Ricky Bhui 145; Atit Sheth 5-91, Swapnil 2-95). Andhra took first-innings lead. *PoM*: Hanuma Vihari.

Emerald High School Ground, Indore, October 14-17: Madhya Pradesh 409 in 144.3 overs (Naman Ojha 180, Ankit Sharma 67; Akash Parkar 4-70, Royston Dias 2-57) and 145/6 in 59 overs (Ankit 52*, N Ojha 38; Vijay Gohil 2-30, Minad Manjrekar 2-33) drew with **Mumbai** 440 in 141.4 overs (Jay Bista 135, Suryakumar Yadav 91; Shubham Sharma 2-8, Mihir

Hirwani 2-105). Mumbai took first-innings lead. *PoM*: Jay Bista.

MA Chidambaram Stadium, Chepauk, Chennai, October 14-17: Tripura 258 in 96.1 overs (Smit Patel 99, Yashpal Singh 96; K Vignesh 4-41, Washington Sundar 2-40) and 91/3 in 34 overs (Smit 35*; Rahil Shah 2-30) drew with **Tamil Nadu** 357/4 dec in 88 overs (W Sundar 159, B Indrajith 89*; Abhijit Sarkar 2-43). Tamil Nadu took first-innings lead. *PoM*: Washington Sundar.

Dr PVG Raju ACA Sports Complex, Vizianagaram, October 24-27: Andhra 584/5 dec in 166 overs (Hanuma Vihari 302*, Prasanth Kumar 127, Ricky Bhui 100; Suryakant Pradhan 2-106) drew with **Odisha** 391 in 139.3 overs (Govinda Poddar 111, Subhranshu Senapati 91; Bhargav Bhatt 4-77, Dwaraka Ravi Teja 3-34) and 152/7 in 55 overs (f/o) (Biplab Samantray 62*; B Bhatt 4-40). Andhra took first-innings lead. *PoM*: Hanuma Vihari.

Bandra Kurla Complex, Mumbai , October 24-27: Mumbai 374 in 103.1 overs (Prithvi Shaw 123, Shreyas Iyer 57; Vijay Shankar 4-52, R Ashwin 3-78) and 375/3 dec in 95 overs (S Iyer 138, Akhil Herwadkar 132; Rahil Shah 2-86) drew with **Tamil Nadu** 450 in 142 overs (Baba Indrajith 152, Yo Mahesh 103*; Vijay Gohil 4-129, Dhawal Kulkarni 2-50). Tamil Nadu took first-innings lead. *PoM*: B Indrajith, Yo Mahesh.

Maharaja Bir Bikram College Stadium, Agartala, October 24-26: Tripura 205 in 64.2 overs (Bishal Ghosh 65, Gurinder Singh 57; Ishwar Pandey 3-40, Ankit Sharma 3-61) and 103 in 44 overs (Rajesh Banik 29, Udiyan Bose 27; Mihir Hirwani 5-22, Ankit 4-51) lost to **Madhya Pradesh** 260 in 80.1 overs (Rajat Patidar 79, Harpreet Singh 70; Gurinder Singh 4-94, Manisankar Murasingh 3-28) and 52/0 in 14.2 overs (R Patidar 25*, Harpreet 25*) by ten wickets. *PoM*: Harpreet Singh.

Reliance Stadium, Vadodara, November 1-4: Baroda 521 in 152.2 overs (Vishnu Solanki 116, Atit Sheth 95*; Ajoy Sarkar 3-88, Rana Dutta 2-43) and 85/6 in 35 overs (V Solanki 24; Abhijit Sarkar 5-18) drew with **Tripura** 436 in 156.3 overs (Smit Patel 158, Yashpal Singh 90; Rudresh Vaghela 2-62, Sagar Mangalorkar 2-70). Baroda took first-innings lead. *PoM*: Atit Sheth.

Dr PVG Raju ACA Sports Complex, Vizianagaram, November 1-4: Madhya Pradesh 321 in 122.5 overs (Harpreet Singh 88, Shubham Sharma 60; Prithvi Raj 4-56, KV Sasikanth 2-58) and 119 in 51.1 overs (Devendra Bundela 38, Anikt Sharma 25; B Ayyappa 5-34, P Raj 2-21) lost to **Andhra** 376 in 115.2 overs (Hanuma Vihari 77, Ashwin Hebbar 77; Mihir Hirwani 5-82, Ankit 2-67) and 65/2 in 13.1 overs (H Vihari 28*, Prasanth Kumar 23) by an eight wickets. *PoM*: B Ayyappa.

KIIT Stadium, Bhubaneswar, November 1-4: Mumbai 289 in 99.5 overs (Prithvi Shaw 105, Ajinkya Rahane 49; Basant Mohanty 4-51, Biplab Samantray 2-26) and 268/9 dec in 71 overs (Siddhesh Lad 117, P Shaw 46; Suryakant Pradhan 3-106, B Samantray 2-18) beat **Odisha** 145 in 50.5 overs (B Samantray 72*, Shantanu Mishra 36; Vijay Gohil 3-26, Abhishek Nayar 3-27) and 292 in 85.1 overs (Govinda Poddar 87, S Mishra 49; Akash Parkar 3-40, Dhawal Kulkarni 3-74) by 120 runs. *PoM*: Prithvi Shaw.

Maharaja Bir Bikram College Stadium, Agartala, November 9-12: Andhra 402 in 144 overs (Prasanth Kumar 133, Ricky Bhui 74; Abhijit Sarkar 5-68, Rana Dutta 2-115) and 234/4 dec in 46 overs (KS Bharat 50, Ashwin Hebbar 44*; R Dutta 3-43) drew with **Tripura** 315 in 99.4 overs (Manisankar Murasingh 81, Gurinder Singh 81; Bhargav Bhatt 4-93, Bandaru Ayyappa 2-46) and 272/5 in 56 overs (Smit Patel 107*, Udiyan Bose 53; B Bhatt 2-83). Andhra took first-innings lead. *PoM*: Smit Patel.

DRIEMS Ground, Cuttack, November 9-12: Tamil Nadu 530/8 dec in 165 overs (M Vijay 140, Baba Aparajith 109*, Vijay Shankar 100; Suryakant Pradhan 3-75, Biplab Samantray 2-57) drew with **Odisha** 533/9 in 187.1 overs (Rajesh Dhuper 97, Natraj Behera 91; Washington Sundar 4-95, Yo Mahesh 3-60). Odisha took first-innings lead. *PoM*: Rajesh Dhuper.

Wankhede Stadium, Mumbai , November 9-12: Mumbai 171 in 56.2 overs (Aditya Tare 50, Shreyas Iyer 28; Atit Sheth 5-50, Lukman Meriwala 5-52) and 260/7 in 120.4 overs (Siddhesh Lad 71*, Prithvi Shaw 56; Kartik Kakade 2-50, Swapnil Singh 2-55) drew with **Baroda** 575/9 dec in 180 overs (Swapnil 164, Aditya Waghmode 138; Shardul Thakur 3-95, Dhawal Kulkarni 2-79). Baroda took first-innings lead. *PoM*: Swapnil Singh.

Holkar Cricket Stadium, Indore, November 17-20: Madhya Pradesh 264 in 90.1 overs (Ankit Sharma 77, Ankit Dane 63; K Vignesh 4-32, M Mohammed 3-67) and 351/4 dec in 102.5 overs (Harpreet Singh 100*, Rajat Patidar 89; Vignesh 3-42) drew with **Tamil Nadu** 326 in 105.4 overs (Yo Mahesh 103*, Narayan Jagadeesan 101; Puneet Datey 3-55, Ishwar Pandey 3-67) and 79/1 in 25 overs (Abhinav Mukund 32*, Baba Aparajith 30*). Tamil Nadu took first-innings lead.

Reliance Stadium, Vadodara, November 17-20: Baroda 503 in 137.4 overs (Ninad Rathva 115, Vishnu Solanki 109, Kedar Devdhar 104; Basant Mohanty 5-85, Suryakant Pradhan 2-95) and 259/1 in 43.5 overs (Aditya Waghmode 101*, Deepak

Prashant Chopra made 338 in Himachal Pradesh's 729 for 8 declared against Punjab.
— *HPCA*

Hooda 100*) drew with **Odisha** 445 in 166 overs (Subhranshu Senapati 173, Rajesh Dhuper 86; Swapnil Singh 5-50, Vishnu Solanki 2-48). Baroda took first-innings lead. *PoM*: Subhranshu Senapati.

CSR Sharma College Ground, Ongole, November 17-20: Mumbai 332 in 132 overs (Prithvi Shaw 114, Siddhesh Lad 86; B Ayyappa 4-110, KV Sasikanth 3-61) and 279/6 dec in 57 overs (Shreyas Iyer 89, Abhishek Nayar 38*; P Vijaykumar 2-63) drew with **Andhra** 215 in 77 overs (Hanuma Vihari 70, Ricky Bhui 69; Shardul Thakur 5-55, Dhawal Kulkarni 3-44) and 219/5 in 81 overs (KS Bharat 68, R Bhui 55; Karsh Kothari 3-55, S Thakur 2-52). Mumbai took first-innings lead. *PoM*: Prithvi Shaw.

Holkar Cricket Stadium, Indore, November 25-28: Odisha 147 in 52.2 overs (Shantanu Mishra 60, Govinda Poddar 36; Chandrakant Sakure 4-42, Puneet Datey 3-34) and 350 in 138.2 overs (Subhranshu Senapati 125, Rajesh Dhuper 88; Mihir Hirwani 5-97, P Datey 2-48) lost to **Madhya Pradesh** 388 in 115 overs (Rajat Patidar 123, Devendra Bundela 62; G Poddar 7-102, Deepak Behera 2-42) and 111/3 in 37 overs (D Bundela 50*, Harpreet Singh 37*; D Behera 2-31) by seven wickets. *PoM*: Puneet Datey.

Moti Bagh Stadium, Vadodara, November 25-28: Baroda 309 in 98.1 overs (Swapnil Singh 144, Kartik Kakade 42; K Vignesh 3-52, J Kousik 2-28) and 197 in 57.5 overs (Swapnil 49, Atit Sheth 40; M Mohammed 3-22, Vignesh 3-46) beat **Tamil Nadu** 274 in 95.3 overs (B Aparajith 59, B Indrajith 58; Lukman Meriwala 3-37, A Sheth 2-46) and 130 in 65.1 overs (B Aparajith 60, Yo Mahesh 23; Swapnil 4-21, L Meriwala 4-22) by 102 runs. *PoM*: Swapnil Singh.

Wankhede Stadium, Mumbai, November 25-28: Tripura 195 in 60.4 overs (Manisankar Murasingh 43, Yashpal Singh 33; Akash Parkar 5-32, Dhawal Kulkarni 3-67) and 288 in 78 overs (Yashpal 82, Smit Patel 68; D Kulkarni 4-69, Karsh Kothari 4-72) lost to **Mumbai** 421/8 dec in 111 overs (Jay Bista 123, Siddhesh Lad 123; M Murasingh 5-71) and 64/0 in 6.2 overs (Prithvi Shaw 50*) by ten wickets. *PoM*: Jay Bista.

Group C Points Table

Teams	M	W	L	D	T	A	Pts.	NRR
Madhya Pradesh	6	3	1	2	0	0	21	-0.116
Mumbai	6	2	0	4	0	0	21	0.228
Andhra	6	1	0	5	0	0	19	0.326
Baroda	6	1	1	4	0	0	16	0.508
Tamil Nadu	6	0	1	5	0	0	11	-0.112
Odisha	6	0	2	4	0	0	6	-0.648
Tripura	6	0	2	4	0	0	4	-0.426

Madhya Pradesh and Mumbai qualified for the knock-outs

Group D

Palam A Stadium, New Delhi, October 6-9: Bengal 552/9 dec in 137 overs (Sudip Chatterjee 115, Manoj Tiwary 69; Sachidanand Pandey 4-108, Diwesh Pathania 3-100) and 161/5 dec in 22 overs (Abhishek Raman 40, Abhimanyu Easwaran 39; D Pathania 3-71, Suraj Yadav 2-49) drew with **Services** 359 in 111.2 overs (Navneet Singh 121, Ravi Chauhan 53; Aamir Gani 5-109, Anustup Majumdar 2-63) and 212/7 in 77 overs (Vikas Hathwala 64, Navneet 49; Kanishk Seth 2-18, A Majumdar 2-46). Bengal took first-innings lead. *PoM*: Navneet Singh.

Goa Cricket Association Academy Ground, Porvorim, October 6-9: Chhattisgarh 458 in 161.3 overs (Manoj Singh 125, Jatin Saxena 82; Darshan Misal 5-79, Amit Yadav 3-111) drew with **Goa** 282 in 122.1 overs (Sumiran Amonkar 79, Sagun Kamat 47; Sumit Ruikar 5-72, Shahnawaz Hussain 2-43) and 170/7 in 67 overs (f/o) (S Amonkar 53, Saurabh Bandekar 25; S Ruikar 5-29). Chhattisgarh took first-innings lead. *PoM*: Sumit Ruikar.

HPCA Stadium, Dharamsala, October 6-9: Himachal Pradesh 729/8 dec in 148 overs (Prashant Chopra 338, Paras Dogra 99; Sandeep Sharma 4-149, Manpreet Gony 2-145) and 145/6 in 40 overs (P Dogra 45*, Rishi Dhawan 25; M Gony 2-20, Barinder Sran 2-38) drew with **Punjab** 601 in 154.3 overs (Abhishek Gupta 202, Abhishek Sharma 94; Gurvinder Singh 6-162). Himachal Pradesh took first-innings lead. *PoM*: Prashant Chopra.

Shaheed Veer Narayan Singh International Stadium, Raipur, October 14-17: Bengal 529/7 dec in 147.3 overs (Sudip Chatterjee 118, Koushik Ghosh 114; Shubham Singh 4-162) beat **Chhattisgarh** 110 in 39.5 overs (Ashutosh Singh 53, Sumit Ruikar 22; Ashok Dinda 7-21, MohammedShami 2-44) and 259 in 81.4 overs (f/o) (Abhimanyu Chauhan 115, Ashutosh 71; M Shami 6-61, A Dinda 3-26) by an innings and 160 runs. *PoM*: Ashok Dinda.

PCA IS Bindra Stadium, Mohali, October 14-16: Punjab 161 in 42.2 overs (Abhishek Gupta 89, Yuvraj Singh 20; Lalit Yadav 3-47, Siddhesh Neral 3-48) and 227 in 72.1 overs (Manan Vohra 51, Abhishek Sharma 49; Akshay Karnewar 6-47, Akshay Wakhare 4-83) lost to **Vidarbha** 505 in 153.2 overs (Ganesh Satish 164, Sanjay Ramaswamy 161; Abhishek 4-136, Sandeep Sharma 2-61) by an innings and 117 runs. *PoM*: Ganesh Satish.

HPCA Stadium, Dharamsala, October 14-17: Goa 255 in 85.5 overs (Rituraj Singh 55*, Samar Dubhashi 39; Pankaj Jaiswal 4-59, Sumeet Verma 3-33) and 426/2 in 111 overs (Swapnil Asnodkar 167, Sumiran Amonkar 137) drew with **Himachal Pradesh** 625/7 dec in 144 overs (Ankush Bains 143, Nikhil Gangta 127*, Priyanshu Khanduri 117; Saurabh Bandekar 2-140, Felix Alemao 2-145). Himachal Pradesh took first-innings lead. *PoM*: Pankaj Jaiswal.

GCA Academy Ground, Porvorim, October 24-27: Punjab 635 in 148.5 overs (Jiwanjot

Singh 238, Gurkeerat Singh 114, Anmolpreet Singh 113; Shadab Jakati 5-165, Rituraj Singh 2-36) beat **Goa** 246 in 79.4 overs (Amit Yadav 52*, Sagun Kamat 47; Raghu Sharma 4-50, Vinay Choudhary 3-72) and 256 in 88.1 overs (f/o) (Darshan Misal 64*, Rituraj Singh 51; V Choudhary 3-57, Raghu 3-117) by an innings and 133 runs. *PoM*: Jiwanjot Singh.

Palam A Stadium, Delhi, October 24-27: Himachal Pradesh 364 in 116.3 overs (Nikhil Gangta 130, Ankush Bains 68; Vikas Yadav 5-91, Rahul Singh 3-56) and 176/9 dec 54.4overs (Akash Vasisht 44, Rishi Dhawan 40; Diwesh Pathania 3-36, Rahul 3-37) beat **Services** 215 in 76.3 overs (Nitin Tanwar 55, Navneet Singh 49; Gurvinder Singh 4-58, A Vasisht 4-75) and 228 in 78.4 overs (Ravi Chauhan 97, Vikas Hathwala 29; Gurvinder 6-52, A Vasisht 2-77) by 97 runs. *PoM*: Gurvinder Singh.

Navdeep Saini enjoyed another fruitful season. — *KCA*

VCA Stadium, Jamtha, Nagpur, October 24-27: Chhattisgarh 489 in 163.2 overs (Amandeep Khare 210, Ashutosh Singh 113; Umesh Yadav 3-87, Akshay Karnewar 3-99, Karn Sharma 3-139) and 195/9 in 52 overs (Jatin Saxena 75, Mohammad Kaif 27; A Karnewar 3-43, Umesh 3-50) drew with **Vidarbha** 435 in 124.4 overs (Faiz Fazal 125, Karn 52*; Sumit Ruikar 4-98, J Saxena 2-34). Chhattisgarh took first-innings lead. *PoM*: Amandeep Khare.

Eden Gardens, Kolkata, November 1-4: Bengal 419 in 121.3 overs (Abhishek Raman 176, Manoj Tiwari 123; Rishi Dhawan 4-86, Pankaj Jaiswal 3-83) and 65/4 in 15 overs (Wriddhiman Saha 34*; R Dhawan 4-37) drew with **Himachal Pradesh** 206 in 56.2 overs (Sumeet Verma 64, Priyanshu Khanduri 52; Ashok Dinda 5-61, Mohammed Shami 3-94) and 353 in 115 overs (f/o) (P Khanduri 95, Prashant Chopra 81; M Shami 5-109, A Dinda 3-74). Bengal took first-innings lead. *PoM*: Abhishek Raman.

SVNS Stadium, Raipur, November 1-4: Chhattisgarh 238 in73 overs (Vishal Kushwah 76, Jatin Saxena 52; Manpreet Gony 4-41, Vinay Choudhary 3-56) and 297 in 102.4 overs (Ashutosh Singh 119, V Kushwah 45; Sandeep Sharma 4-89, Barinder Sran 3-65) lost to **Punjab** 653/9 dec in 128.1 overs (Anmolpreet Singh 267, Gurkeerat Singh 111; Shourabh Kharwar 3-107, Prateek Sinha 3-121, Sumit Ruikar 3-174) by an innings and 118 runs. *PoM*: Anmolpreet Singh.

VCA Ground, Nagpur, November 1-4: Vidarbha 385 in 124.5 overs (Faiz Fazal 136, Ganesh Satish 78; Nitin Tanwar 2-44, Diwesh Pathania 2-77) and 223/6 dec in 44 overs (Akshay Karnewar 48*, F Fazal 46; Vikas Yadav 2-39, N Tanwar 2-50) beat **Services** 317 in 113 overs (Nakul Verma 71, Rahul Singh 63; Akshay Wakhare 5-87, Karn Sharma 2-62) and 99 in 28.1 oevrs (Rahul 33, Vikas 30*; A Wakhare 5-16, Karn 3-42) by an innings and 192 runs. *PoM*: Akshay Wakhare.

BCA Ground, Kalyani, November 9-12: Vidarbha 499 in 138.4 overs (Sanjay Ramaswamy 182, Faiz Fazal 142; Ishan Porel 4-139, Ashok Dinda 3-116) and 18/0 in 1.3 oversbeat **Bengal** 207 in 81 overs (Manoj Tiwary 50, Koushik Ghosh 50; Akshay Wakhare 3-45, Aditya Sarwate 2-27) and 306 in 101.4 overs (f/o) (Wriddhiman Saha 97, Sudip Chatterjee 82; Lalit Yadav 4-54, A Sarwate 3-59) by ten wickets. *PoM*: Sanjay Ramaswamy.

HPCA Stadium, Dharamsala, November 9-12: Himachal Pradesh 175 in 44.2 overs (Rishi Dhawan 35, Nikhil Gangta 26; Sumit Ruikar 3-20, Pankaj Rao 3-52) and 167 in 49.5 overs (N Gangta 41, Paras Dogra 35; Shahnawaz Hussain 6-53, P Rao 2-43) lost to **Chhattisgarh** 456 in

135.2 overs (Rishabh Tiwari 131, Amandeep Khare 78; Pankaj Jaiswal 3-85, Sidharth Sharma 3-100, Rishi Dhawan 3-127) by an innings and 114 runs. *PoM*: Rishabh Tiwari.

Palam A Stadium, Delhi, November 9-12: Services 263 in 107.2 overs (Vikas Yadav 84, Nakul Verma 64; Amogh Desai 3-18, Heramb Parab 3-37) and 190 in 55.4 overs (Ravi Chauhan 55, N Verma 30; Darshan Misal 7-68) drew with **Goa** 270 in 117.5 overs (Keenan Vaz 70, A Desai 52; Sachidanand Pandey 5-61, Vikas 2-55) and 128/4 in 50 overs (Sagun Kamat 57*, Sumiran Amonkar 22; Diwesh Pathania 3-37). Goa took first-innings lead. *PoM*: Vikas Yadav.

SVNS Stadium, Raipur, November 17-20: Chhattisgarh 130 in 72.2 overs (Manoj Singh 53, Ashutosh Singh 28; Diwesh Pathania 4-45, Vikas Yadav 3-10) and 133 in 55.3 overs (Abhimanyu Chauhan 43, Rishabh Tiwari 35; D Pathania 7-41, Raj Bahadur 3-25) lost to **Services** 272 in 90.5 overs (Vikas Hathwala 76, Rahul Singh 37; Shahnawaz Hussain 5-59, Prateek Sinha 2-39) by an innings and nine runs. *PoM*: Diwesh Pathania.

Gandhi Sports Complex Ground, Amritsar, November 17-19: Punjab 147 in 46overs (Shubman Gill 63; Boddupalli Amit 3-31, Pradipta Pramanik 3-41) and 213 in 56.1 overs (Gurkeerat Singh Mann 57, Anmolpreet Singh 40; Ishan Porel 5-32, B Amit 2-35) lost to **Bengal** 379/9 dec in 116 overs (Abhishek Raman 155, Abhimanyu Easwaran 117; Siddarth Kaul 5-118) by an innings and 19 runs. *PoM*: Abhishek Raman.

GCA Academy Ground, Porvorim, November 17-20: Goa 239 in 93.4 overs (Keenan Vaz 72, Amulya Pandrekar 33; Akshay Wakhare 4-50, Aditya Sarwate 3-54) and 151 in 53.3 overs (Snehal Kauthankar 56, Vedant Naik 28; A Wakhare 5-54, Lalit Yadav 2-16) lost to **Vidarbha** 427/3 dec in 143 overs (Wasim Jaffer 158*, Ganesh Satish 101*) by an innings and 37 runs. *PoM*: Akshay Wakhare.

Gandhi Sports Complex Ground, Amritsar, November 25-28: Punjab 645/6 dec in 138 overs (Anmolpreet Singh 252*, Shubman Gill 129) and 94/5 in 6.1 overs (S Gill 32, Abhishek Gupta 26; Sachidanand Pandey 3-26) drew with **Services** 315 in 71.2 overs (Vikas Yadav 71, Diwesh Pathania 68; Manpreet Gony 5-63, Siddarth Kaul 2-101) and 458 in 105 overs (f/o) (G Rahul Singh 124, Ravi Chauhan 112; S Kaul 3-96, M Gony 2-95). Punjab took first-innings lead. *PoM*: Anmolpreet Singh.

VCA Ground, Nagpur, November 25-28: Himachal Pradesh 353 in 107.3 overs (Rishi Dhawan 71, Akash Vasisht 69; Rajneesh Gurbani 6-113, Aditya Sarwate 2-38) and 323/8 in 96.1 overs (Nikhil Gangta 101*, Sumeet Verma 59; A Sarwate 6-75, R Gurbani 2-74) drew with **Vidarbha** 456 in 134.4 overs (Faiz Fazal 206, Sanjay Ramaswamy 115; R Dhawan 4-96, Akshay Chauhan 2-89). Vidarbha took first-innings lead. *PoM*: Faiz Fazal.

Eden Gardens, Kolkata, November 25-28: Bengal 379 in 99.3 overs (Shreevats Goswami 139, Anustup Majumdar 119; Lakshay Garg 4-89, Amulya Pandrekar 2-50) and 334/5 dec in 80.5 overs (A Majumdar 108*, Writtick Chatterjee 102*; L Garg 3-74, Felix Alemao 2-71) drew with **Goa** 310 in 105 overs (Amogh Desai 103*, Keenam Vaz 60; Ashok Dinda 5-79, Kanishk Seth 3-77) and 86/2 in 26 overs (Snehal Kauthankar 53*, A Desai 22*; A Dinda 2-13). Bengal took first-innings lead. *PoM*: Anustup Majumdar.

Group D points table

Teams	M	W	L	D	T	A	Pts.	NRR
Vidarbha	6	4	0	2	0	0	31	0.358
Bengal	6	2	1	3	0	1	23	0.367
Punjab	6	2	2	2	0	0	18	0.609
Himachal Pradesh	6	1	1	4	0	0	14	0.300
Chhattisgarh	6	1	3	2	0	1	13	-0.514
Services	6	1	2	3	0	0	10	-0.273
Goa	6	0	2	4	0	0	6	-0.700

Quarterfinals

Sawai Mansingh Stadium, Jaipur, December 7-11: Bengal 354 in 111.5 overs (Abhimanyu Easwaran 129, Anustup Majumdar 94; Ishwar Chaudhary 5-87, Chintan Gaja 3-93) and 695/6 in 231 overs (Writtick Chatterjee 216, A Majumdar 132*, A Easwaran 114; I Chaudhary 2-95, Rajul Bhatt 2-175) drew with**Gujarat**224 in 74.5 overs (Bhargav Merai 67, Parthiv Patel 47; Ashok Dinda 3-48, B Amit 3-53, Ishan Porel 3-64). Bengal took first-innings lead. *MoM*: Abhimanyu Easwaran.

Dr Gokaraju Liala Gangaaraju ACA Cricket Ground, Vijayawada, December 7-11: Madhya Pradesh 338 in 124.1 overs (Harpreet Singh 107*, Ankit Dane 59; Manan Sharma 4-46, Vikas Mishra 3-58) and 283 in 105.5 overs (Harpreet 78, Puneet Datey 60; V Mishra 4-59, Vikas Tokas 3-64) lost to **Delhi** 405 in 119.4 overs (Kunal Chandela 81, Dhruv Shorey 78; Mihir Hirwani 5-89, Ishwar Pandey 2-65) and 217/3 in 51.4 overs (Gautam Gambhir 95, K Chandela 57) by seven wickets. *MoM*: Harpreet Singh.

Lalabhai Contractor Stadium, Surat, December 7-11: Vidarbha 246 in 105.3 overs (Akshay Wadkar 53, Aditya Sarwate 36; KC Akshay 5-66, Jalaj Saxena 3-52) and 507/9 dec in 146.4 overs (Faiz Fazal 119, Apoorv Wankhade 107; Akshay 4-118, J Saxena 3-125) beat **Kerala** 176 in 61.5 overs (J Saxena 40, Sanju Samson 32; Rajneesh Gurbani 5-38) and 165 in 52.2 overs (Salman Nizar 64, Mohammed Azharuddeen 28; A Sarwate 6-41, R Gurbani 2-30) by 412 runs. *MoM*: Rajneesh Gurbani.

VCA Stadium, Nagpur, December 7-11: Mumbai 173 in 56 overs (Dhawal Kulkarni 75, Akhil Herwadkar 32; Vinay Kumar 6-34, S Aravind 2-45) and 377 in 114.5 overs (Suryakumar Yadav 108, Shivam Dubey 71; K Gowtham 6-104, Vinay 2-45) lost to **Karnataka** 570 in 136.3 overs (Shreyas Gopal 150*, CM Gautam 79; S Dubey 5-98, Shivam Malhotra 3-97) by an innings and 20 runs. *PoM*: Vinay Kumar.

Bengal, Delhi, Vidarbha and Karnataka qualified for the semi-finals

Semi-finals

1ˢᵗ semi-final: Delhi beat Bengal by an innings and 26 runs

For a match that had all the ingredients of a classic, this turned out to be a one-sided, three-day encounter. Manoj Tiwary, the Bengal captain, had reminded Delhi of what happened when the sides met in a fiery encounter in 2015, when his side took the innings lead. "If they have forgotten that, we will remind them on the field," Tiwary had said. Delhi took that to heart. They brushed Bengal aside with an all-round display, and claimed bragging rights after shooting out Bengal for just 86 in 25 second-innings overs. Afterwards, K P Bhaskar, the Delhi coach, said: "It (Tiwary's comments) was uncalled for. I thought they were probably overconfident."

Setting aside their collapse, Bengal began the well enough. Opting to bat, they lost Easwaran early, but Sudip Chatterjee guided them to 200. It was a position of strength, but they squandered it. The middle order couldn't handle Manan Sharma and Navdeep Saini: Bengal lost their last six wickets for 86 runs. Gautam Gambhir and Kunal Chandela both scored centuries, putting on 232 for the opening wicket. This despite some threatening bowling from Mohammed Shami and Ashok Dinda.

Shami fought back with six wickets to restrict Delhi's lead to 112, but that was more than enough. Through a combination of excellent bowling — both

Saini and Kulwant Khejroliya returned four-fors — and muddled thinking by the batsmen, Bengal were blown away.

MCA Stadium, Pune, December 17-21: Bengal 286 in 94.2 overs (Sudip Chhatterjee 83, Writtick Chatterjee 47; Navdeep Saini 3-55, Manan Sharma 2-37) and 86 in 24.4 overs (S Chatterjee 21; N Saini 4-35, Kulwant Khejroliya 4-40) lost to **Delhi** 398 in 117 overs (Gautam Gambhir 127, Kunal Chandela 113; Mohammed Shami 6-122, B Amit 2-64) by an innings and 26 runs. *PoM*: Navdeep Saini.

2nd semi-final: Vidarbha beat Karnataka by five runs

Karnataka had a stellar campaign, but it was put to an abrupt stop by Vidarbha, a side desperate to make the final. Not to say Karnataka weren't — "The season is successful only if you win the Ranji Trophy," Vinay declared after the five-run loss.

Karnataka, chasing 198, started the final day on the backfoot at 111 for 7, but with Vinay scoring a measured 36, followed by Shreyas Gopal's careful 24 not out and Abhimanyu Mithun's risk-filled 33, Karnataka edged ever closer. It all changed though when Mithun played a loose shot with nine runs needed. Vidarbha sealed their dramatic win, and the scenes of delirium thereafter were something else.

Karnataka, in hindsight, will blame the top order. In both innings, it left the middle and lower order with too much do. After Abhimanyu Mithun's 5 for 45 had helped bowl out Vidarbha for 185, Karnataka managed 301 in response. But that was because of Karun Nair's 287-ball 153, after the top three managed a combined 21.

Vidarbha put up an improved effort in the second innings — Ganesh Satish, the former Karnataka player, scored a 168-ball 81 — but once again, the Karnataka top order struggled, with only Samarth getting into double digits among the top three.

The real hero was Gurbani. He kept picking away at the batsmen and returned 5 for 94 in the first innings followed by a brilliant 7 for 68 in the second. Fittingly, it was he who sealed Vidarbha's win with the last two Karnataka wickets.

Eden Gardens, Kolkata, December 17-21: Vidarbha 185 in 61.4 overs (Aditya Sarwate 47, Wasim Jaffer 39; Abhimanyu Mithun 5-45, Vinay Kumar 2-36) and 313 in 84.1 overs (Ganesh Satish 81, A Sarwate 55; Vinay 3-71, Stuart Binny 3-71) beat **Karnataka** 301 in 100.5 overs (Karun Nair 153, CM Gautam 73; Rajneesh Gurbani 5-94, Umesh Yadav 4-73) and 192 in 59.1 overs (Vinay 36, A Mithun 33; R Gurbani 7-68, Siddesh Neral 2-37) by five runs. *PoM*: Rajneesh Gurbani.

Delhi and Vidarbha qualified for the final

Final: Vidarbha beat Delhi by nine wickets

Vidarbha put up a performance worthy of champions to lift their maiden Ranji Trophy title with a trouncing of Delhi.

Gurbani again was the hero with the ball. The seamer picked up a hat-trick — only the second bowler to do so in a Ranji Trophy final — en route his 6 for 59 in the first innings before Vidarbha's lower order all but batted Delhi out of the game.

Rajneesh Gurbani followed up his 12 wickets in the semi-final with eight in the final. — *Special arrangement*

Put in, Delhi found themselves struggling at 99 for 4. Debutant Aditya Thakare had struck in the very first over of the match. Dhruv Shorey dug his heels in and added 105 with Himmat Singh for the fifth before Himmat fell to Gurbani. Shorey brought up his hundred and took the side to 290 for 6 but Gurbani's hat-trick — he got Vikas Mishra, Saini and Shorey — meant Delhi could manage only 295.

In response, despite half-centuries from Fazal and Wasim Jaffer, Vidarbha too were 246 for 6 at one stage. But wicketkeeper-batsman Wadkar's 133, coupled with Sarwate's 79 and Siddhesh Neral's 74 from Nos.8 and 9 respectively, helped them to a first-innings lead of 252.

From there, it was always going to be an uphill task for Delhi. Although Shorey and Nitish Rana struck half-centuries, Vidarbha spinners Wakhare and Sarwate shared seven wickets. Chasing a mere 29, Jaffer hit a flurry of boundaries to seal the win on the fourth evening.

For new coach Chandrakant Pandit, it was a validation of his methods and vision. "Everybody likes to win the cup," he said. "This win will not only change the team, but in Vidarbha, every 14-year-old and 16-year-old boy will probably stand up and raise his hand that he can also win. That kind of culture I will be happy to achieve in Vidarbha."

Holkar Cricket Stadium, Indore, December 29-31: Delhi 295 in 102.5 overs (Dhruv Shorey 145, Himmat Singh 66; Rajneesh Gurbani 6-59, Aditya Thakare 2-74) and 280 in 76 overs (Nitsh Rana 64, D Shorey 62; Akshay Wakhare 4-95, Aditya Sarwate 3-30) lost to **Vidarbha** 547 in 163.4 overs (Akshay Wadkar 133, A Sarwate 79; Navdeep Saini 5-135, Akash Sudan 2-102) and 32/1 in 5 overs by nine wickets. *PoM*: Rajneesh Gurbani.

Winners: Vidarbha

Inter-state T20 & Syed Mushtaq Ali Trophy

Kadam leads Karnataka to maiden title

The tenth edition of the Syed Mushtaq Ali Trophy lost a bit of sheen due to its scheduling. Over the last three seasons, the tournament was strategically scheduled to serve as an audition for the IPL auctions. That couldn't happen this season. The addition of nine new domestic teams, taking the overall count to 37, and the absence of an IPL Governing Council perhaps made it difficult.

Despite the carrot of a lucrative IPL contract being out of reach, the emergence of a young batting side augured well for Karnataka, who clinched their maiden domestic T20 title under Manish Pandey. With the eight-wicket win over Maharashtra in the final, Karnataka extended their T20 winning streak to 14 matches, the joint-highest for an India-based T20 side along with Kolkata Knight Riders (IPL 2014).

Rohan Kadam, the 24-year-old left-hand batsman who led the batting charts, was central to their successful campaign. While Mayank Agarwal shrugged off a relatively lean tournament with an unbeaten 85 in the final, it was Kadam's blazing 60 at the top that set the tone for the 156-run target. Kadam finished as the highest run-getter with 536 runs in 12 innings at a strike-rate of 129.78, with five fifties and a century.

Both R Vinay Kumar and Abhimanyu Mithun went unsold in the IPL auc-

The emergence of a young batting side augured well for Karnataka, who clinched their maiden domestic T20 title. — *KSCA*

tions, but the workhorses were vital to Karnataka's campaign. They also had V Koushik, the medium pacer, who finished as Karnataka's leading wicket-taker with 17 scalps in 10 matches at an economy of 6.36.

Maharasthra's journey to the final made for a great lesson on teamwork. Rahul Tripathi, who led from the front, Nikhil Naik and Naushad Shaikh, the all-rounder, drove Maharashtra's strong batting display as they won all their four Super League stage matches to top Group A. On the bowling front, Samad Fallah's experience along with Satyajeet Bachhav's left-arm spin kept Maharashtra in the contest throughout.

In the opening round, Cheteshwar Pujara's maiden T20 century wasn't enough to give Saurashtra a win against Railways. Shreyas Iyer's 147 off just 55 balls against Sikkim was the highest total by an Indian batsman in a T20. Mumbai went on to score 258 for 4 in 20 overs before restricting Sikkim to 104. Andhra, meanwhile, trounced Nagaland by 179 runs: the biggest victory margin by runs in a T20 match. Riding on Ricky Bhui's unbeaten 42-ball 108, Andhra amassed 244 for 4 before their bowlers dismissed Nagaland for 65 runs. It was one of a fair few record-breaking mismatches this year.

Largest T20 wins, by runs

Margin	Team	Match details
179	**Andhra**	**v Nagaland, Mulapadu, Feb 2019**
172	Sri Lanka	v Kenya, Johannesburg, Sep 2007
171	Legends	v Kings Leopard, Sharjah, Oct 2018
167	Trinidad and Tobago	v Leeward Islands, North Sound, Jan 2012
159	Prime Bank	v Mohammedan, Sylhet, Dec 2013
159	**Bengal**	**v Mizoram, Cuttack, Feb 2019**
158	Northerns	v Southerns, Harare, Mar 2008
154	**Mumbai**	**v Sikkim, Indore, Feb 2019**
146	Mumbai Indians	v Daredevils, Delhi, May 2017
146	**Karnataka**	**v Arunachal, Cuttack, Feb 2019**

The **previous year**, the BCCI had gone back to the inter-state knock-out format to give domestic players more chances to display their skills ahead of the IPL 2018 mega-auction. The likes of Dhruv Shorey, Deepak Chahar, Khaleel Ahmed and Kulwant Khejroliya did well and were rewarded with bids.

Rishabh Pant emerged as the star for Delhi, who won the title for the first time. The wicketkeeper-batsman smoked a 32-ball ton against Himachal Pradesh and broke Rohit Sharma's record of the fastest T20 century by an Indian: Rohit took 35 balls against Sri Lanka in Indore; Pant's 116 not out came off 38. It made a mockery of Himachal's 145-run target. He also hit four consecutive fifties to finish with 411 runs in 10 games — the same as Kedar Devdhar, who took eight matches.

Shorey, meanwhile, was at his best in the Super League phase; with scores of 28 not out, 74, 84 and 21, he gave them solidity in the middle order.

Delhi's main strength, though, was their bowlers. Khejroliya, skipper Pradeep Sangwan, Suboth Bhati and Pawan Negi performed consistently throughout the tournament. Yes, the association was in a mess, but that didn't distract the players.

Rajasthan didn't have any big names, but they clicked as a unit and beat almost every team on their way to the final. The top two wicket-takers — Deepak and Khaleel — came from Rajasthan. Rajasthan's victories against heavyweights Karnataka and Mumbai were the highlights of their season.

Devdhar emerged as Baroda's lone warrior, registering a century along with Suresh Raina, Pant and Karun Nair (twice). Raina's unbeaten 126 was, for a season, the highest score of the tournament, going past Unmukt Chand's 125. Deepak, V Athisayaraj Davidson and K Vignesh were the only three bowlers to scalp five-wicket hauls.

	Most runs	**Most wickets**
2017-18	Kedar Devdhar (Baroda) (411 runs, 8 matches)	Deepak Chahar (Rajasthan) (19 wickets, 9 matches)
2018-19	Rohan Kadam (Karnataka) (536 runs, 12 matches)	Satyajeet Bachhav (Maharashtra) (20 wickets, 12 matches)

2018-19

Group A

Chukkapalli Pitchaiah Cricket Ground, Mulapadu, February 21: Nagaland 136/6 in 20 overs (KB Pawan 53*, Rongsen Jonathan 31; Parveez Rasool 2-26) lost to **Jammu and Kashmir** 142/1 in 15.5 overs (Abdul Samad 76*, Jatin Wadhwan 62) by nine wickets.

DV Ramana Praneetha Ground, Mulapadu, February 21: Jharkhand 158/4 in 20 overs (Virat Singh 70*, Anand Singh 37; Subodh Bhati 2-33) beat **Delhi** 155/5 in 20 overs (Dhruv Shorey 70, Unmukt Chand 33; Shahbaz Nadeem 2-26, Rahul Shukla 2-35) by 3 runs.

DV Ramana Praneetha Ground, Mulapadu, February 21: Delhi 186/5 in 20 overs (Sachin Baby 75*, Mohammed Azharuddeen 47; Homendro Meitei 2-25) beat **Manipur** 103/7 in 20 overs (Yashpal Singh 40*, Mayank Raghav 32) by 83 runs.

DV Ramana Praneetha Ground, Mulapadu, February 22: Andhra 244/4 in 20 overs (Ricky Bhui 108*, Girinath Reddy 62; Rachit Bhatia 2-44) beat **Nagaland** 65 in 13.1 overs (Rongsen Jonathan 30; KV Sasikanth 3-8, Karn Sharma 3-14, Shaik Ismail 3-25) by 179 runs.

DV Ramana Praneetha Ground, Mulapadu, February 22: Manipur 113/6 in 20 overs (Yashpal Singh 50, Prafullomani Singh 25; Subodh Bhati 3-15) lost to **Delhi** 119 for no loss in 11.4 overs (Hiten Dalal 56*, Unmukt Chand 53*) by ten wickets.

Chukkapalli Pitchaiah Cricket Ground, Mulapadu, February 22: Jammu and Kashmir 168/9 in 20 overs (Jatin Wadhwan 47, Manzoor Dar 39; Rahul Shukla 5-36, Monu Kumar 2-31) lost to **Jharkhand** 170/1 in 16.4 overs (Ishan Kishan 100*, Anand Singh 48) by nine wickets.

DV Ramana Praneetha Ground, Mulapadu, February 24: Kerala 160/6 in 20 overs (Vishnu Vinod 70, Sachin Baby 38; Girinath Reddy 2-18) beat **Andhra** 152 in 19.4 overs (Prasanth Kumar 57; Sandeep Warrier 3-27, MD Nidheesh 2-25) by 8 runs.

Chukkapalli Pitchaiah Cricket Ground, Mulapadu, February 24: Jammu and Kashmir

189/7 in 20 overs (Shubham Pundir 68, Jatin Wadhwan 57; Subodh Bhati 3-26) lost to **Delhi** 191/6 in 19.5 overs (Lalit Yadav 47*, Anuj Rawat 45) by four wickets.

DV Ramana Praneetha Ground, Mulapadu, February 24: Jharkhand 219/1 in 20 overs (Ishan Kishan 113*, Virat Singh 73*) beat **Manipur** 98/9 in 20 overs (Yashpal Singh 40; Utkarsh Singh 3-7, Rahul Shukla 3-14) by 121 runs.

DV Ramana Praneetha Ground, Mulapadu, February 25: Andhra 146/7 in 20 overs (KS Bharat 41, Hanuma Vihari 28; Ramdayal Punia 2-23) lost to **Jammu and Kashmir** 148/5 in 18.3 overs (Shubham Pundir 51, Parveez Rasool 31; B Ayyappa 2-23, Karn Sharma 2-30) by five wickets.

DV Ramana Praneetha Ground, Mulapadu, February 25: Kerala

Andhra enjoyed a record-breaking win against Nagaland, but overall had a middling campaign in Group A. — *ACA*

139/7 in 20 overs (Vinoop Manoharan 38, Sachin Baby 37) lost to **Delhi** 140/3 in 18.1 overs (Nitish Rana 52*, Unmukt Chand 33) by seven wickets.

Chukkapalli Pitchaiah Cricket Ground, Mulapadu, February 25: Nagaland 132/7 in 20 overs (Abrar Kazi 36, Sedezhalie Rupero 26; Priyojit Singh 3-23) lost to **Manipur** 134/0 in 16.4 overs (Mayank Raghav 80*, Prafullomani Singh 51*) by ten wickets.

DV Ramana Praneetha Ground, Mulapadu, February 27: Delhi 175/8 in 20 overs (Unmukt Chand 70, Lalit Yadav 31; B Ayyappa 2-36) beat **Andhra** 143 in 19.3 overs (Ashwin Hebbar 38, Shoaib Mohammad 26*; Subodh Bhati 4-27, Ishant Sharma 2-17) by 32 runs.

DV Ramana Praneetha Ground, Mulapadu, February 27: Kerala 159/7 in 20 overs (Vinoop Manoharan 52, Mohammed Azharuddeen 32; Irfan Pathan 2-32, Parveez Rasool 2-34) beat **Jammu and Kashmir** 65 in 14.2 overs (S Midhun 3-9, V Manoharan 2-10) by 94 runs.

Chukkapalli Pitchaiah Cricket Ground, Mulapadu, February 27: Jharkhand 197/3 in 20 overs (Kumar Deobrat 69*, Ishan Kishan 52) beat **Nagaland** 143/3 in 20 overs (Rongsen Jonathan 47, Sedezhalie Rupero 38) by 54 runs.

DV Ramana Praneetha Ground, Mulapadu, February 28: Andhra 179 in 19.5 overs (Pranith Manyala 43, Ricky Bhui 38; Shahbaz Nadeem 3-26, Varun Aaron 3-49) beat **Jharkhand** 176 in 19.5 overs (Saurabh Tiwary 54, Kumar Deobrat 27; Y Prithviraj 3-28, Girinath Reddy 2-36) by 3 runs.

Chukkapalli Pitchaiah Cricket Ground, Mulapadu, February 28: Manipur 182/6 in 20 overs (Mayank Raghav 103, Yashpal Singh 51; Rasikh Salam 3-38) lost to **Jammu and Kashmir** 184/2 in 17.1 overs (Bandeep Singh 59*, Jatin Wadhwan 59) by eight wickets.

DV Ramana Praneetha Ground, Mulapadu, February 28: Nagaland 103/8 in 20 overs (Rohit Jhanjhariya 49*; MD Nidheesh 3-17, Basil Thampi 2-14) lost to **Kerala** 105/0 in 12.2 overs (Vishnu Vinod 53*, Rohan Kunnummal 51*) by ten wickets.

Chukkapalli Pitchaiah Cricket Ground, Mulapadu, March 2: Andhra 252/4 in 20 overs (Ashwin Hebbar 71, Pranith Manyala 71; Yashpal Singh 3-40) beat **Manipur** 161/5 in 20 overs (Mayank Raghav 65, Priyojit Singh 45; Swaroop Kumar 3-26) by 91 runs.

Chukkapalli Pitchaiah Cricket Ground, Mulapadu, March 2: Nagaland 118 in 19.4 overs

(Aditya 64; Subodh Bhati 4-14, Nitish Rana 2-10) lost to **Delhi** 119/3 in 12.3 overs (Hiten Dalal 81) by seven wickets.

DV Ramana Praneetha Ground, Mulapadu, March 2: Kerala 176/6 in 20 overs (Sachin Baby 36, Rohan Kunnummal 34; Vikash Singh 2-34, Rahul Shukla 2-40) lost to **Jharkhand** 180/5 in 19.1 overs (Anand Singh 72, Saurabh Tiwary 50*; Sandeep Warrier 2-21) by five wickets.

Points table

Team	M	W	L	T	N/R	Pts	NRR
Jharkhand	6	5	1	0	0	20	+1.838
Delhi	6	5	1	0	0	20	+1.604
Kerala	6	4	2	0	0	16	+1.920
Andhra	6	3	3	0	0	12	+1.832
Jammu and Kashmir	6	3	3	0	0	12	-0.410
Manipur	6	1	5	0	0	4	-3.244
Nagaland	6	0	6	0	0	0	-3.876

Jharkhand and Delhi qualified for the Super League

Group B

Lalabhai Contractor Stadium, Surat, February 21: Gujarat 146/8 in 20 overs (Axar Patel 48; Abhay Negi 3-30, Gurinder Singh 2-10) beat **Meghalaya** 133/8 in 20 overs (Punit Bisht 56; Piyush Chawla 3-17, Tejas Patel 2-27) by 13 runs.

CB Patel International Cricket Stadium, Surat, February 21: Rajasthan 181/4 in 20 overs (Mahipal Lomror 78*, Tajinder Dhillon 38*; M Ashwin 2-33) beat **Tamil Nadu** 128 in 19.5 overs (Khaleel Ahmed 3-14, Deepak Chahar 3-30) by 53 runs.

Lalabhai Contractor Stadium, Surat, February 21: Himachal Pradesh 167/8 in 20 overs (Ekant Sen 52; Nitin Sharma 36; Shrikant Wagh 3-32, Yash Thakur 2-32) lost to **Vidarbha** 171/7 in 20 overs (Atharwa Taide 43, Jitesh Sharma 37; Prashant Chopra 2-18) by three wickets.

Lalabhai Contractor Stadium, Surat, February 22: Bihar 103/8 in 20 overs (Babul Kumar 27; Yash Thakur 2-12, Akshay Karnewar 2-17) lost to **Vidarbha** 104/3 in 14.2 overs (Shalabh Shrivastava 49*, Ravi Jangid 27*; Vivek Kumar 2-27) by seven wickets.

CB Patel International Cricket Stadium, Surat, February 22: Himachal Pradesh 207/4 in 20 overs (Ankush Bains 68, Prashant Chopra 53) beat **Meghalaya** 142/6 in 20 overs (Gurinder Singh 49*, Yogesh Nagar 44; Ankit Maini 3-24, Mayank Dagar 2-16) by 65 runs.

Lalabhai Contractor Stadium, Surat, February 22: Rajasthan 143/7 in 20 overs (Manender Singh 48, Robin Bist 46; Tejas Patel 4-26, Hemang Patel 2-10) tied with **Gujarat** 143/7 in 20 overs (Axar Patel 33, Dhruv Raval 25; Khaleel Ahmed 3-19, Aniket Choudhary 2-24). **Super over: Gujarat** 4/1 in 1 over tied with **Rajasthan** 4/2 in 1 over. Gujarat won on boundary count.

CB Patel International Cricket Stadium, Surat, February 24: Bihar 131/9 in 20 overs (MD Rahmatullah 32; M Mohammed 3-21, R Ashwin 3-31) lost to **Tamil Nadu** 132/4 in 18.5 overs (Baba Indrajith 46, Washington Sundar 38*; Ashutosh Aman 2-19) by six wickets.

Lalabhai Contractor Stadium, Surat, February 24: Gujarat 167/5 in 20 overs (Dhruv Raval 71, Priyank Panchal 40) beat **Himachal Pradesh** 97 in 15.1 overs (Prashant Chopra 35; Hemang Patel 3-14, Hardik Patel 3-29) by 70 runs.

Lalabhai Contractor Stadium, Surat, February 24: Rajasthan 137/5 in 20 overs (Mahipal

Lomror 47, Robin Bist 38; Abhay Negi 2-19) beat **Meghalaya** 65 in 16.1 overs (Nathu Singh 3-7, Tanveer-ul-Haq 3-10, Rahul Chahar 3-13) by 72 runs.

Lalabhai Contractor Stadium, Surat, February 25: Bihar 78 in 18.5 overs (Asfahan Khan 25, Gurvinder Singh 2-11, Ankit Maini 2-14) lost to **Himachal Pradesh** 81/1 in 10.3 overs (Ankush Bains 54*) by nine wickets.

Lalabhai Contractor Stadium, Surat, February 25: Tamil Nadu 125/6 in 20 overs (NS Chaturved 34, Washington Sundar 33; Arzan Nagwaswalla 3-11, Piyush Chawla 2-16) beat **Gujarat** 124 in 19.5 overs (Chirag Gandhi 68*; W Sundar 2-10) by 1 run.

CB Patel International Cricket Stadium, Surat, February 25: Vidarbha 117 in 16.5 overs (Jitesh Sharma 49; Khaleel Ahmed 5-18, Nathu Singh 2-11) beat **Rajasthan** 73 in 16.5 overs (Akshay Karnewar 4-7, Ravi Jangid 2-11) by 44 runs.

Lalabhai Contractor Stadium, Surat, February 27: Gujarat 199/4 in 20 overs (Priyank Panchal 78, Piyush Chawla 41*; Vishal Das 2-40) beat **Bihar** 116/7 in 20 overs (Keshav Kumar 61*; Arzan Nagwaswalla 4-15) by 83 runs.

CB Patel International Cricket Stadium, Surat, February 27: Tamil Nadu 138/9 in 20 overs (M Vijay 77; Ankit Maini 3-29, Kanwar Abhinay 2-30) lost to **Himachal Pradesh** 139/3 in 19 overs (Prashant Chopra 68*, Ekant Sen 35; Abhishek Tanwar 2-14) by 7 wickets.

Lalabhai Contractor Stadium, Surat, February 27: Vidarbha 161/6 in 20 overs (Shalabh Shrivastava 56, Rushabh Rathod 38*; Raj Biswa 2-26) beat **Meghalaya** 129/4 in 20 overs (Gurinder Singh 56*; Yash Thakur 2-27) by 32 runs.

CB Patel International Cricket Stadium, Surat, February 28: Meghalaya 124/8 in 20 overs (Gurinder Singh 39*, Abhay Negi 26; Ashutosh Aman 4-15, Prashant Singh 2-16) lost to **Bihar** 126/9 in 19.5 overs (Keshav Kumar 43, Puneet Malik 33) by one wicket.

Lalabhai Contractor Stadium, Surat, February 28: Himachal Pradesh 150/5 in 20 overs (Ankush Bains 55, Rishi Dhawan 38*; Rahul Chahar 2-21) beat **Rajasthan** 141/7 in 20 overs (Chetan Bist 34, Robin Bist 34; Ankit Maini 3-29, Kanwar Abhinay 2-26) by 9 runs.

Lalabhai Contractor Stadium, Surat, February 28: Vidarbha 141/9 in 20 overs (Rushabh Rathod 51, Jitesh Sharma 26; Abhishek Tanwar 3-22, R Ashwin 2-16) lost to **Tamil Nadu** 142/7 in 19.2 overs (M Vijay 74, J Kousik 41*; Shrikant Wagh 2-23) by three wickets.

Lalabhai Contractor Stadium, Surat, March 2: Rajasthan 129/8 in 20 overs (Robin Bist 34, Mahipal Lomror 29; Prashant Singh 3-23, Vivek Kumar 2-29) beat **Bihar** 110/8 in 20 overs (Mangal Mahrour 33; Aniket Choudhary 3-16, Tanveer-ul-Haq 2-12) by 19 runs.

CB Patel International Cricket Stadium, Surat, March 2: Gujarat 121/6 in 20 overs (Priyank Panchal 38, Chirag Gandhi 30; Atharwa Taide 2-16) lost to **Vidarbha** 122/5 in 18.2 overs (Faiz Fazal 39*, Rushabh Rathod 37*; Manish Sharma 2-25) by five wickets.

Lalabhai Contractor Stadium, Surat, March 2: Tamil Nadu 213/2 in 20 overs (M Vijay 107, Washington Sundar 53; Akash Choudhary 2-39) beat **Meghalaya** 121/4 in 20 overs (Gurinder Singh 38*, Punit Bisht 27; M Ashwin 2-16) by 92 runs.

Points table

Team	M	W	L	T	N/R	Pts	NRR
Vidarbha	6	5	1	0	0	20	+1.083
Gujarat	6	4	2	0	0	16	+1.280
Himachal Pradesh	6	4	2	0	0	16	+0.705
Tamil Nadu	6	4	2	0	0	16	+0.397
Rajasthan	6	3	3	0	0	12	+0.758
Bihar	6	1	5	0	0	4	-1.877
Meghalaya	6	0	6	0	0	0	-2.311

Vidarbha and Gujarat qualified for the Super League

Group C

Emerald High School Ground, Indore, February 21: Mumbai 258/4 in 20 overs (Shreyas Iyer 147, Suryakumar Yadav 63; Milind Kumar 2-30) beat **Sikkim** 104/7 in 20 overs (Bipul Sharma 32; Shams Mulani 2-2, Shardul Thakur 2-13) by 154 runs.

Holkar Stadium, Indore, February 21: Saurashtra 188/3 in 20 overs (Cheteshwar Pujara 100*, Robin Uthappa 46) lost to **Railways** 190/5 in 19.4 overs (Mrunal Devdhar 49, Pratham Singh 40; Dharmendrasinh Jadeja 2-27) by five wickets.

Holkar Stadium, Indore, February 21: Madhya Pradesh 199/4 in 20 overs (Parth Sahani 90, Abhishek Bhandari 54*; Manpreet Gony 2-34) beat **Punjab** 165/9 in 20 overs (Mandeep Singh 64, Gurkeerat Singh 46; Ishwar Pandey 3-17, Avesh Khan 2-27) by 34 runs.

Holkar Stadium, Indore, February 22: Sikkim 100/8 in 20 overs (Lakshay Garg 3-14, Darshan Misal 2-19) lost to **Goa** 104/2 in 14 overs (Sagun Kamat 50*) by eight wickets.

Emerald High School Ground, Indore, February 22: Mumbai 155 in 20 overs (Suryakumar Yadav 80, Shreyas Iyer 46; Baltej Singh 3-30, Barinder Sran 3-34) beat **Punjab** 120 in 18.2 overs (Prabhsimran Singh 54; Dhawal Kulkarni 4-22, Shubham Ranjane 2-14) by 35 runs.

Holkar Stadium, Indore, February 22: Madhya Pradesh 138 in 20 overs (Parth Sahani 49, Abhishek Bhandari 30; Chetan Sakariya 4-38, Jaydev Unadkat 3-19) lost to **Saurashtra** 139/4 in 16.5 overs (Cheteshwar Pujara 68, Harvik Desai 56; Ishwar Pandey 2-26) by six wickets.

Holkar Stadium, Indore, February 24: Goa 164/7 in 20 overs (Suyash Prabhudessai 49; Prashant Awasthi 2-14, Krishnakant Upadhyay 2-27) lost to **Railways** 168/2 in 17.3 overs (Mrunal Devdhar 82, Pratham Singh 60*) by eight wickets.

Holkar Stadium, Indore, February 24: Madhya Pradesh 143 in 19.3 overs (Rajat Patidar 47, Venkatesh Iyer 29; Tushar Deshpande 4-28, Dhawal Kulkarni 2-12) lost to **Mumbai** 145/2 in 16 overs (Shreyas Iyer 103*, Suryakumar Yadav 39*) by eight wickets.

Emerald High School Ground, Indore, February 24: Punjab 122 in 20 overs (Yuvraj Singh 34, Gurkeerat Singh 29; Jaydev Unadkat 3-30, Dharmendrasinh Jadeja 2-11) lost to **Saurashtra** 126/2 in 17.4 overs (Robin Uthappa 54, Cheteshwar Pujara 42*) by eight wickets.

Emerald High School Ground, Indore, February 25: Goa 140/4 in 20 overs (Amogh Desai 38, Sagun Kamat 27, Amit Verma 27) lost to **Mumbai** 141/4 in 18.2 overs (Prithvi Shaw 71, Ajinkya Rahane 31) by six wickets.

Shreyas Iyer's 147 against Sikkim is the highest total by an Indian batsman in a T20 game.

Holkar Stadium, Indore, February 25: Madhya Pradesh 159/6 in 20 overs (Naman Ojha 74, Parth Sahani 40; Amit Mishra 3-19, Anureet Singh 3-24) lost to **Railways** 161/5 in 19.4 overs (Pratham Singh 61, Ashish Yadav 32*; Mihir Hirwani 3-20) by five wickets.

Holkar Stadium, Indore, February 25: Sikkim 75 in 18 overs (Milind Kumar 28; Jaydev Unadkat 2-9, Chetan Sakariya 2-16) lost to **Saurashtra** 79/3 in 8.3 overs (Cheteshwar Pujara 39*, Bipul Sharma 3-23) by seven wickets.

Emerald High School Ground, Indore, February 27: Goa 196/3 in 20 overs (Amit Verma 109*, Suyash Prabhudessai 46*; Ishwar Pandey 2-26) lost to **Madhya Pradesh** 197/6 in 19.4 overs (Parth Sahani 68, Naman Ojha 36; Felix Alemao 2-25, Darshan Misal 2-42) by four wickets.

Emerald High School Ground, Indore, February 27: Railways 175/5 in 20 overs (Pratham Singh 89, Mrunal Devdhar 43; Tushar Deshpande 3-44) beat **Mumbai** 118 in 18.1 overs (Suryakumar Yadav 38; Ashish Yadav 4-32, Amit Mishra 2-14) by 57 runs.

Holkar Stadium, Indore, February 27: Sikkim 90/8 in 20 overs (Milind Kumar 37; Baltej Singh 2-13, Krishan Alang 2-17) lost to **Punjab** 95/1 in 10.5 overs (Shubman Gill 70*) by nine wickets.

Emerald High School Ground, Indore, February 28: Punjab 205/7 in 20 overs (Manan Vohra 87; Malliksab Sirur 2-31, Felix Alemao 2-50) beat **Goa** 126 in 18 overs (Amogh Desai 35, Amit Verma 27; Krishan Alang 4-26, Karan Kaila 3-20) by 79 runs.

Holkar Stadium, Indore, February 28: Mumbai 147 in 20 overs (Prithvi Shaw 36, Shreyas Iyer 36; Prerak Mankad 3-27, Jaydev Unadkat 2-28) beat **Saurashtra** 139 in 19.5 overs (Robin Uthappa 57, Arpit Vasavada 36; Shardul Thakur 3-30, Dhawal Kulkarni 2-23) by 8 runs.

Emerald High School Ground, Indore, February 28: Sikkim 109/5 in 20 overs (Milind Kumar 54; Manjeet Singh 2-17, Ashish Yadav 2-24) lost to **Railways** 113/1 in 13.1 overs (Pratham Singh 53*, Prashant Gupta 40*) by nine wickets.

Emerald High School Ground, Indore, March 2: Goa 99 in 17.5 overs (Vaibhav Govekar 32, Keenan Vaz 30; Jay Chauhan 3-16, Arpit Vasavada 2-9) lost to **Saurashtra** 100/5 in 17.2 overs (Sheldon Jackson 36; Darshan Misal 2-25, Amulya Pandrekar 2-29) by five wickets.

Emerald High School Ground, Indore, March 2: Madhya Pradesh 164/8 in 20 overs (Abhishek Bhandari 46, Parth Sahani 36; Ishwar Chaudhary 3-24, Pritam Nirala 2-23) beat **Sikkim** 114 in 20 overs (Kumar Kartikeya 3-10, Mihir Hirwani 3-24) by 50 runs.

Holkar Stadium, Indore, March 2: Railways 149/5 in 20 overs (Prashant Gupta 54, Pratham Singh 28) lost to **Punjab** 153/7 in 19.5 overs (Mandeep Singh 71*, Yuvraj Singh 26; Anureet Singh 3-52, Harsh Tyagi 2-19) by three wickets.

Points table

Team	M	W	L	T	N/R	Pts	NRR
Mumbai	6	5	1	0	0	20	+1.590
Railways	6	5	1	0	0	20	+1.264
Saurashtra	6	4	2	0	0	16	+1.241
Punjab	6	3	3	0	0	12	+0.581
Madhya Pradesh	6	3	3	0	0	12	+0.179
Goa	6	1	5	0	0	4	-0.802
Sikkim	6	0	6	0	0	0	-4.466

Mumbai and Railways qualified for the Super League

Group D

DRIEMS Ground, Cuttack, February 21: Karnataka 169/6 in 20 overs (Manish Pandey 74, KV Siddharth 27; Abu Nechim Ahmed 2-32) beat **Assam** 154/7 in 20 overs (Wasiqur Rahman 62, Rajjakuddin Ahmed 53*; Vinay Kumar 2-22) by 15 runs.

Barabati Stadium, Cuttack, February 21: Bengal 221/4 in 20 overs (Abhimanyu Easwaran 107*, Shreevats Goswami 55; Taruwar Kohli 2-49) beat **Mizoram** 62 in 13 overs (Prayas Ray Barman 4-14, Pradipta Pramanik 3-13) by 159 runs.

Barabati Stadium, Cuttack, February 21: Odisha 137 in 19.4 overs (Subhranshu Senapati 51, Rajesh Mohanty 36; Aishwarya Mourya 3-20, Shakeeb Ahmed 2-22) lost to **Chhattisgarh** 138/0 in 16.1 overs (Rishabh Tiwari 71*, Shashank Chandrakar 57*) by ten wickets.

DRIEMS Ground, Cuttack, February 21: Arunachal Pradesh 106/6 in 20 overs (Kshitiz Sharma 46*, Samarth Seth 25; Sumit Kumar 3-13) lost to **Haryana** 110/2 in 15.1 overs (Chaitanya Bishnoi 60*, Nitin Saini 45*) by eight wickets.

DRIEMS Ground, Cuttack, February 22: Chhattisgarh 215/3 in 20 overs (Rishabh Tiwari 81, Amandeep Khare 61*) beat **Arunachal Pradesh** 118/8 in 20 overs (Samarth Seth 34; Vishal Kushwah 4-16, Pankaj Rao 2-21) by 97 runs.

Barabati Stadium, Cuttack, February 22: Assam 201/4 in 20 overs (Riyan Parag 63*, Rishav Das 56) beat **Mizoram** 70/6 in 20 overs (Jitumoni Kalita 2-8, Abu Nechim Ahmed 2-16) by 131 runs.

DRIEMS Ground, Cuttack, February 22: Bengal 131 in 19.4 overs (Shreevats Goswami 40, Manoj Tiwary 36; Abhimanyu Mithun 3-22, Vinay Kumar 2-18, Manoj Bhandage 2-18) lost to **Karnataka** 134/1 in 15.5 overs (Rohan Kadam 81*, BR Sharath 50) by nine wickets.

Barabati Stadium, Cuttack, February 22: Haryana 141 in 19.5 overs (Himanshu Rana 25; Pappu Roy 3-9, Suryakant Pradhan 3-31) beat **Odisha** 131/5 in 20 overs (Biplab Samantray 48, Arabind Singh 34*; Ajit Chahal 2-27) by 10 runs.

Barabati Stadium, Cuttack, February 24: Karnataka 226/4 in 20 overs (Manish Pandey 111*, BR Sharath 43; Akhilesh Sahani 2-39) **Arunachal Pradesh** 80 in 14.4 overs (Samarth Seth 49; Shreyas Gopal 5-11, V Koushik 2-13)by 146 runs.

DRIEMS Ground, Cuttack, February 24: Chhattisgarh 194/2 in 20 overs (Harpreet Bhatia 92*, Shashank Chandrakar 56) lost to **Assam** 195/5 in 20 overs (Amit Sinha 77*, Sibsankar Roy 52; Pankaj Rao 2-34) by five wickets.

Barabati Stadium, Cuttack, February 24: Haryana 141/8 in 20 overs (Himanshu Rana 60, Rahul Tewatia 30; Ishan Porel 3-28, Ashok Dinda 2-23) lost to **Bengal** 145/7 in 19 overs (Vivek Singh 32, Manoj Tiwary 30; Ashish Hooda 2-22, Amit Mishra 2-23) by three wickets.

DRIEMS Ground, Cuttack, February 24: Mizoram 91 in 19.1 overs (Taruwar Kohli 37; Pappu Roy 3-8, Rajesh Mohanty 2-12) lost to **Odisha** 95/1 in 12.5 overs (Sandeep Pattnaik 54*, Rajesh Dhuper 38*) by nine wickets.

Barabati Stadium, Cuttack, February 25: Assam 162/5 in 20 overs (Sibsankar Roy 83, Riyan Parag 52; Ashok Dinda 4-17) beat **Bengal** 136/9 in 20 overs (Shreevats Goswami 43; Abu Nechim Ahmed 2-25, Mukhtar Hussain 2-32) by 26 runs.

DRIEMS Ground, Cuttack, February 25: Haryana 210/5 in 20 overs (Chaitanya Bishnoi 65*, Rahul Tewatia 59*; Shakeeb Ahmed 2-38) lost to **Chhattisgarh** 211/5 in 20 overs (Rishabh Tiwary 62, Amandeep Khare 60) by five wickets.

DRIEMS Ground, Cuttack, February 25: Karnataka 242/4 in 20 overs (Rohan Kadam 78, Karun Nair 71; Lalhruai Ralte 2-48) beat **Mizoram** 105/6 in 20 overs (Akhil Rajput 41, Taruwar Kohli 36; Shreyas Gopal 4-8) by 137 runs.

Barabati Stadium, Cuttack, February 25: Arunachal Pradesh 75 in 19.4 overs (Techi Doria 26; Debabrata Pradhan 3-10, Biplab Samantray 2-6) lost to **Odisha** 76/2 in 13.1 overs (Abhishek Raut 41*, Sandeep Pattnaik 28*; Akhilesh Sahani 2-21) by eight wickets.

Barabati Stadium, Cuttack, February 27: Bengal 234/6 in 20 overs (Wriddhiman Saha 129, Vivek Singh 49; Akhilesh Sahani 3-36) beat **Arunachal Pradesh** 127/4 in 20 overs (Kshitiz Sharma 54*, Techi Doria 43) by 107 runs.

Barabati Stadium, Cuttack, February 27: Chhattisgarh 171/3 in 20 overs (Harpreet Bhatia 79, Amandeep Khare 43*) lost to **Karnataka** 175/6 in 19.2 overs (Karun Nair 35, Vinay Kumar 34*; Aishwarya Mourya 2-13, Shubham Singh 2-35) by four wickets.

DRIEMS Ground, Cuttack, February 27: Haryana 205/2 in 20 overs (Guntashveer Singh 100*, Sumit Kumar 41; Lalnunkima Varte 2-30) beat **Mizoram** 166/5 in 20 overs (Taruwar Kohli 63, Akhil Rajput 59; Rahul Tewatia 2-18, Ashish Hooda 2-25) by 39 runs.

DRIEMS Ground, Cuttack, February 27: Assam 142/9 in 20 overs (Sibsankar Roy 47, Jitumoni Kalita 31*; Pappu Roy 4-21) lost to **Odisha** 143/3 in 16.5 overs (Biplab Samantray 49, Anurag Sarangi 43*; Abu Nechim Ahmed 2-29) by seven wickets.

DRIEMS Ground, Cuttack, February 28: Mizoram 122/8 in 20 overs (Taruwar Kohli 52; Akhilesh Sahani 4-35, Kshitiz Sharma 2-13) lost to **Arunachal Pradesh** 125/2 in 11.4 overs (Samarth Seth 66*; Sinan Khadir 2-37) by eight wickets.

Barabati Stadium, Cuttack, February 28: Assam 80/9 in 15 overs (Sumit Kumar 4-20, Jayant Yadav 2-10) lost to **Haryana** 81/3 in 8.4 overs (Yashu Sharma 26) by seven wickets.

DRIEMS Ground, Cuttack, February 28: Bengal 188/4 in 20 overs (Abhimanyu Easwaran 59, Manoj Tiwary 42; Shivendra Singh 2-28) beat **Chhattisgarh** 162/9 in 20 overs (Harpreet Bhatia 54, Amandeep Khare 30; Sayan Ghosh 4-32, Ishan Porel 3-25) by 26 runs.

Barabati Stadium, Cuttack, February 28: Karnataka 155/9 in 20 overs (Rohan Kadam 89; Biplab Samantray 2-10, Pappu Roy 2-21) beat **Odisha** 104 in 18.1 overs (Suryakant Pradhan 32; KC Cariappa 4-15, V Koushik 3-8) by 51 runs.

DRIEMS Ground, Cuttack, March 2: Arunachal Pradesh 102 in 18 overs (Samarth Seth 42; Mukhtar Hussain 4-8, Amit Sinha 2-18) lost to **Assam** 104/1 in 6.4 overs (Rishav Das 39, Pallav Das 34*) by nine wickets.

Barabati Stadium, Cuttack, March 2: Chhattisgarh 220/5 in 20 overs (Rishabh Tiwari 85, Harpreet Bhatia 37; Bobby Zothansanga 2-35) beat **Mizoram** 104/5 in 20 overs (Akhil Rajput 40; Pawandeep Singh 2-8, Shakeeb Ahmed 2-15) by 116 runs.

DRIEMS Ground, Cuttack, March 2: Karnataka 138/9 in 20 overs (Rohan Kadam 25, Manish Pandey 25; Amit Mishra 3-26, Arun Chaprana 3-29) beat **Haryana** 124 in 19.1 overs (Sumit Kumar 63; Shreyas Gopal 3-16, Prasidh Krishna 3-25) by 14 runs.

Barabati Stadium, Cuttack, March 2: Odisha 108/9 in 20 overs (Ishan Porel 3-19, Ayan Bhattacharjee 2-13) lost to **Bengal** 111/2 in 12.4 overs (Wriddhiman Saha 52, Abhimanyu Easwaran 33*) by eight wickets.

Points table

Team	M	W	L	T	N/R	Pts	NRR
Karnataka	7	7	0	0	0	28	+2.959
Bengal	7	5	2	0	0	20	+2.259
Chhattisgarh	7	4	3	0	0	16	+1.539
Assam	7	4	3	0	0	16	+1.400
Haryana	7	4	3	0	0	16	+0.881
Orissa	7	3	4	0	0	12	-0.157
Arunachal Pradesh	7	1	6	0	0	4	-3.885
Mizoram	7	0	7	0	0	0	-5.371

Karnataka and Bengal qualified for the Super League

Group E

Palam A Ground, Model Sports Complex, Delhi, February 21: Tripura 100 in 19 overs (Atit Sheth 5-13, Swapnil Singh 2-8) **lost to Baroda** 101/2 in 16.5 overs (Vikram Solanki 32; Tushar Saha 2-29) by 8 wickets.

Palam B Ground, Model Sports Complex, Delhi, February 21: Puducherry 159/6 in 20 overs (Paras Dogra 89, D Rohit 27; Mehdi Hasan 2-29, Mohammed Siraj 2-43) beat **Hyderabad** 156/9 in 20 overs (Akshath Reddy 69*, Tanmay Agarwal 31; Parandaman Thamaraikannan 4-39, Fabid Ahmed 2-23) by 3 runs.

Palam A Ground, Model Sports Complex, Delhi, February 21: Maharashtra 149/5 in 20 overs (Naushad Shaikh 41, Nikhil Naik 41; Bobby Yadav 2-34) beat **Uttar Pradesh** 137 in 19.3 overs (Samarth Singh 93; Satyajeet Bachhav 3-23, Manoj Ingale 2-18) by 12 runs.

Palam B Ground, Model Sports Complex, Delhi, February 21: Services 164/5 in 20 overs (Rajat Paliwal 54*, Nakul Verma 48) lost to **Uttarakhand** 165/7 in 19.5 overs (Karanveer Kaushal 58, Girish Rauturi 49; Vikas Yadav 5-9) by three wickets.

Palam A Ground, Model Sports Complex, Delhi, February 22: Baroda 152/5 in 20 overs (Kedar Devdhar 61, Yusuf Pathan 47*; Sunny Rana 2-27) lost to **Uttarakhand** 153/3 in 19 overs (Vaibhav Panwar 49*, Saurabh Rawat 41) by seven wickets.

Palam B Ground, Model Sports Complex, Delhi, February 22: Hyderabad 139/7 in 20 overs (B Sandeep 33, Ambati Rayudu 29; Ankit Rajpoot 3-31, Akshdeep Nath 2-18) lost to **Uttar Pradesh** 143/4 in 18.3 overs (Suresh Raina 54*, Samarth Singh 36; Ashish Reddy 3-33) by six wickets.

Samarth Singh led the batting charts for Uttar Pradesh, with three fifties and a strike-rate of 121.45. — *UPCA*

Palam A Ground, Model Sports Complex, Delhi, February 22: Puducherry 101/6 in 20 overs (Paras Dogra 32, T Sargunam 29; Divyang Himganekar 4-19) lost to **Maharashtra** 105/2 in 15.4 overs (Ruturaj Gaikwad 55*, Naushad Shaikh 44*; Pankaj Singh 2-18) by eight wickets.

Palam B Ground, Model Sports Complex, Delhi, February 22: Tripura 157/6 in 20 overs (Manisankar Murasingh 52, Ninad Kadam 32*; Diwesh Pathania 2-29) lost to **Services** 158/2 in 16.5 overs (Nakul Verma 73, Ravi Chauhan 62*) by eight wickets.

Palam B Ground, Model Sports Complex, Delhi, February 24: Hyderabad 131/7 in 20 overs (Akshath Reddy 46, B Sandeep 39; Rishi Arothe 4-18, Atit Sheth 2-37) lost to **Baroda** 134/6 in 19.4 overs (Vikram Solanki 40, Swapnil Singh 36*; Chama Milind 2-18, Mehdi Hasan 2-28) by four wickets.

Palam A Ground, Model Sports Complex, Delhi, February 24: Uttarakhand 141/6 in 20 overs (Vijay Sharma 30*, Rajat Bhatia 30; Fabid Ahmed 2-15) beat **Puducherry** 131/9 in 20 overs (Paras Dogra 53, T Sargunam 26; Himanshu Bisht 2-21, Sunny Rana 2-28, Sunny Kashyap 2-28) by 10 runs.

Palam A Ground, Model Sports Com-

plex, Delhi, February 24:** Maharashtra 116/9 in 20 overs (Ankit Bawne 34; Sachidanand Pandey 3-21, Mohit Kumar 2-24) lost to **Services** 119/4 in 19.2 overs (Ravi Chauhan 45*; Satyajeet Bachhav 2-17, Azim Kazi 2-17) by six wickets.

Palam B Ground, Model Sports Complex, Delhi, February 24: Uttar Pradesh 184/4 in 20 overs (Priyam Garg 59*, Rinku Singh 52*; Tushar Saha 2-33) beat **Tripura** 126/8 in 20 overs (Manisankar Murasingh 28, Sanjoy Majumdar 27; Ankit Rajpoot 4-17, Ankit Chaudhary 3-19) by 58 runs.

Palam B Ground, Model Sports Complex, Delhi, February 25: Hyderabad 124/6 in 20 overs (Rohit Rayudu 47*, B Sandeep 25; Vishal Gite 2-30) lost to **Maharashtra** 125/3 in 18 overs (Ruturaj Gaikwad 54, Naushad Shaikh 42*; PS Sairam 2-38) by seven wickets.

Palam B Ground, Model Sports Complex, Delhi, February 25: Uttar Pradesh 179/4 in 20 overs (Priyam Garg 54, Upendra Yadav 36; Vikneshwaran Marimuthu 2-15) beat **Puducherry** 102/6 in 20 overs (Fabid Ahmed 25*, Parandaman Thamaraikannan 25*; Saurabh Kumar 4-14) by 77 runs.

Palam A Ground, Model Sports Complex, Delhi, February 25: Baroda 75 in 18.2 overs (Vikas Yadav 3-15, Mohit Kumar 2-10) lost to **Services** 76/3 in 16.2 overs (Swapnil Singh 2-16) by seven wickets.

Palam A Ground, Model Sports Complex, Delhi, February 25: Uttarakhand 147/5 in 20 overs (Karanveer Kaushal 58, Vaibhav Panwar 46*; Sanjoy Majumdar 2-18) beat **Tripura** 110 in 19 overs (Nirupam Sen Chowdhary 34, Manisankar Murasingh 33; Rohit Dangwal 3-16, Rajat Bhatia 3-29) by 37 runs.

Palam B Ground, Model Sports Complex, Delhi, February 27: Puducherry 126/5 in 20 overs (Paras Dogra 41, Damodaren Rohit 37; Lukman Meriwala 2-22) lost to **Baroda** 128/6 in 19.4 overs (Kedar Devdhar 51; Pankaj Singh 2-21) by four wickets.

Palam A Ground, Model Sports Complex, Delhi, February 27: Tripura 79/9 in 17 overs (Chama Milind 3-11, Mehdi Hasan 2-11, Ravi Teja 2-11) lost to **Hyderabad** 80/2 in 13.3 overs (Tanmay Agarwal 38*) by eight wickets.

Palam B Ground, Model Sports Complex, Delhi, February 27: Uttarakhand 89 in 18.1 overs (Rajat Bhatia 28, Vaibhav Panwar 25; Satyajeet Bachhav 4-18, Vishal Gite 2-11) lost to **Maharashtra** 90/0 in 8.2 overs (Rahul Tripathi 51*, Ruturaj Gaikwad 28*) by ten wickets.

Palam A Ground, Model Sports Complex, Delhi, February 27: Uttar Pradesh 138/5 in 20 overs (Samarth Singh 70, Rinku Singh 56*; Mohit Kumar 2-23) beat **Services** 137/6 in 20 overs (Vikas Hathwala 39*, Rajat Paliwal 30) by 1 run.

Palam B Ground, Model Sports Complex, Delhi, February 28: Baroda 163/7 in 20 overs (Kedar Devdhar 38, Mitesh Patel 29; Azim Kazi 2-33) lost to **Maharashtra** 164/3 in 19.2 overs (Rahul Tripathi 70, Ruturaj Gaikwad 48) by seven wickets.

Palam A Ground, Model Sports Complex, Delhi, February 28: Puducherry 102/9 in 20 overs (Damodaren Rohit 54; Rana Datta 4-20, Manisankar Murasingh 2-12) lost to **Tripura** 105/2 in 17 overs (Udiyan Bose 72*, Pratik Sargade 2-21) by eight wickets.

Palam A Ground, Model Sports Complex, Delhi, February 28: Hyderabad 135/8 in 20 overs (Akshath Reddy 34, Ravi Teja 31*; Rajat Paliwal 2-9, Mohit Kumar 2-31) lost to **Services** 141/6 in 19.4 overs (Vikas Hathwala 61*, Rajat Paliwal 27; Mohammed Siraj 4-20) by four wickets.

Palam B Ground, Model Sports Complex, Delhi, February 28: Uttar Pradesh 209/6 in 20 overs (Samarth Singh 75, Akshdeep Nath 70; Sunny Rana 2-45) beat **Uttarakhand** 91 in 16.3 overs (Saurabh Rawat 30; Saurabh Kumar 5-28, Ankit Chaudhary 3-9) by 118 runs.

Palam A Ground, Model Sports Complex, Delhi, March 2: Baroda 76/2 in 12.1 overs (Kedar Devdhar 28) vs **Uttar Pradesh**. No result.

Palam A Ground, Model Sports Complex, Delhi, March 2: Hyderabad 57/2 in 4.5 overs (Tilak Varma 40*) vs **Uttarakhand**. No result.

Palam B Ground, Model Sports Complex, Delhi, March 2: Maharashtra 50/3 in 4 overs vs **Tripura**. No result.

Palam B Ground, Model Sports Complex, Delhi, March 2: Services 67/2 in 11 overs (Nakul Verma 31, Ravi Chauhan 25; Satish Jangir 2-8) v **Puducherry**. No result.

Points table

Team	M	W	L	T	N/R	Pts	NRR
Uttar Pradesh	7	5	1	0	1	22	+2.154
Maharashtra	7	5	1	0	1	22	+1.249
Services	7	4	2	0	1	18	+0.529
Uttarakhand	7	4	2	0	1	18	-1.287
Baroda	7	3	3	0	1	14	-0.059
Hyderabad	7	1	5	0	1	6	-0.182
Puducherry	7	1	5	0	1	6	-1.238
Tripura	7	1	5	0	1	6	-1.265

Uttar Pradesh and Maharashtra qualified for the Super League

Super League Group A

Emerald High School Ground, Indore, March 8: Jharkhand 148/7 in 20 overs (Anand Singh 45, Ishan Kishan 39) beat **Gujarat** 147/8 in 18 overs (Karan Patel 35, Axar Patel 28; Utkarsh Singh 2-22, Vikash Singh 2-25, Anukul Roy 2-25) by 1 run.

Emerald High School Ground, Indore, March 8: Railways 142/6 in 20 overs (Ashish Yadav 51, Prashant Gupta 39; Sayan Ghosh 2-26) lost to **Bengal** 143/4 in 18.1 overs (Shreevats Goswami 80, Abhimanyu Easwaran 46; Ashish Yadav 2-20) by six wickets.

Emerald High School Ground, Indore, March 9: Bengal 138/7 in 20 overs (Shahbaz Ahmed 60*, Manoj Tiwary 41; Domnic Muthuswami 3-15, Satyajeet Bachhav 2-34) lost to **Maharashtra** 139/3 in 17.1 overs (Rahul Tripathi 60*, Rohit Motwani 36; Akash Deep 2-21) by seven wickets.

Holkar Stadium, Indore, March 9: Railways 135/8 in 20 overs (Pratham Singh 41, Prashant Awasthi 25; Rahul Shukla 2-18) lost to **Jharkhand** 136/5 in 19 overs (Anand Singh 53, Virat Singh 50*; Harsh Tyagi 2-25) by five wickets.

Holkar Stadium, Indore, March 10: Jharkhand 126/9 in 20 overs (Anukul Roy 37*, Virat Singh 27; Writtick Chatterjee 3-12, Shahbaz Ahmed 2-21) lost to **Bengal** 127/2 in 13 overs (Shreevats Goswami 86*, Varun Aaron 2-24) by eight wickets.

Holkar Stadium, Indore, March 10: Gujarat 143/9 in 20 overs (Chirag Gandhi 35, Priyank Panchal 28; Divyang Himganekar 2-23, Domnic Muthuswami 2-42) lost to **Maharashtra** 149/6 in 19.5 overs (Azim Kazi 39*, D Himganekar 35*; Hemang Patel 2-14, Piyush Chawla 2-24) by four wickets.

Emerald High School Ground, Indore, March 11: Railways 110/9 in 20 overs (Harsh Tyagi 32*; Piyush Chawla 3-12) lost to **Gujarat** 112/3 in 14.1 overs (Piyush Tanwar 55*, Parthiv Patel 25) by seven wickets.

Emerald High School Ground, Indore, March 11: Maharashtra 153/4 in 20 overs (Ankit Bawne 64*, Vijay Zol 50; Varun Aaron 2-22) beat **Jharkhand** 139/8 in 20 overs (Vikash Singh 46*; Satyajeet Bachhav 3-17, Samad Fallah 2-41) by 14 runs.

Holkar Stadium, Indore, March 12: Maharashtra 177/5 in 20 overs (Nikhil Naik 95*, Naushad Shaikh 59; Manjeet Singh 2-36) beat **Railways** 156 in 20 overs (Mrunal Devdhar 55, Pratham Singh 29; Samad Fallah 3-37, N Shaikh 2-8) by 21 runs.

Holkar Stadium, Indore, March 12: Gujarat 121 in 19.3 overs (Axar Patel 53, Piyush Tanwar 29; Sayan Ghosh 5-15, Akash Deep 2-29) lost to **Bengal** 125/3 in 18.2 overs (Wriddhiman Saha 53*, Vivek Singh 28*; Jayveer Parmar 2-26) by seven wickets.

Points table

Team	M	W	L	T	N/R	Pts	NRR
Maharashtra	4	4	0	0	0	16	+0.826
Bengal	4	3	1	0	0	12	+0.827
Jharkhand	4	2	2	0	0	8	-0.786
Gujarat	4	1	3	0	0	4	0.262
Railways	4	0	4	0	0	0	-1.175

Maharashtra qualified for the final

Super League Group B

Holkar Stadium, Indore, March 8: **Delhi** 83 in 16.2 overs (Hiten Dalal 42; Umesh Yadav 2-10, Shrikant Wagh 2-12) lost to **Vidarbha** 85/1 in 8.3 overs (Jitesh Sharma 41, Atharwa Taide 32*) by nine wickets.

Holkar Stadium, Indore, March 8: Mumbai 97/9 in 20 overs (Manoj Bhandage 2-11, Vinay Kumar 2-15) lost to **Karnataka** 98/1 in 13.2 overs (Rohan Kadam 62*, BR Sharath 25) by nine wickets.

Holkar Stadium, Indore, March 9: Karnataka 149/6 in 20 overs (Rohan Kadam 35, Mayank Agarwal 33) beat **Uttar Pradesh** 139/8 in 20 overs (Akshdeep Nath 46, Upendra Yadav 42; V Koushik 3-22, J Suchith 2-19) by 10 runs.

Emerald High School Ground, Indore, March 9: **Delhi** 144/7 in 20 overs (Dhruv Shorey 33, Lalit Yadav 33; Tushar Deshpande 4-19) lost to **Mumbai** 148/2 in 19 overs (Shreyas Iyer 53*, Suryakumar Yadav 42*) by eight wickets.

Emerald High School Ground, Indore, March 10: **Delhi** 109/9 in 20 overs (Nitish Rana 37, Lalit Yadav 33; V Koushik 4-19, KC Cariappa 3-15) lost to **Karnataka** 112/2 in 15.3 overs (Mayank Agarwal 43*, Karun Nair 42*) by eight wickets.

Emerald High School Ground, Indore, March 10: Vidarbha 143/7 in 20 overs (Atharwa Taide 41; Ankit Chaudhary 2-28, Mohsin Khan 2-40) beat **Uttar Pradesh** 133/9 in 20 overs (Samarth Singh 39, Upendra Yadav 26; Shrikant Wagh 3-25, Akshay Karnewar 2-29) by 10 runs.

Holkar Stadium, Indore, March 11: Vidarbha 137/8 in 20 overs (Rushabh Rathod 26, Umesh Yadav 26; Tushar Deshpande 3-38, Shardul Thakur 2-21) lost to **Mumbai** 138/4 in 15.4 overs (Jay Bista 73*, Shreyas Iyer 28; Ravi Jangid 2-23, Akshay Wakhare 2-38) by six wickets.

Holkar Stadium, Indore, March 11: Uttar Pradesh 140/6 in 20 overs (Priyam Garg 30, Shubham Chaubey 29; Pawan Negi 3-9, Navdeep Saini 2-23) lost to **Delhi** 142/6 in 19.4 overs (Dhruv Shorey 62*, Pranshu Vijayran 34; Yash Dayal 2-20, Ankit Rajpoot 2-20) by four wickets.

Emerald High School Ground, Indore, March 12: Mumbai 183/7 in 20 overs (Siddhesh Lad 62, Eknath Kerkar 46; Ankit Rajpoot 3-47) beat **Uttar Pradesh** 137 in 19 overs (Shardul Thakur 3-15, S Lad 3-23, Shivam Dube 3-31) by 46 runs.

Emerald High School Ground, Indore, March 12: Vidarbha 138/7 in 20 overs (Apoorv Wankhade 56*, Akshay Karnewar 33; Vinay Kumar 2-27) lost to **Karnataka** 140/4 in 19.2 overs (Manish Pandey 49*, Rohan Kadam 39) by six wickets.

Points table

Team	M	W	L	T	N/R	Pts	NRR
Karnataka	4	4	0	0	0	16	+1.283
Mumbai	4	3	1	0	0	12	+0.544
Vidarbha	4	2	2	0	0	8	+0.756
Delhi	4	1	3	0	0	4	-1.698
Uttar Pradesh	4	0	4	0	0	0	-0.882

Karnataka qualified for the final

Final: Karnataka beat Maharashtra by eight wickets

• Karnataka extend their winning streak to 14 matches to clinch their maiden T20 title. • Chasing 156, the in-form Rohan Kadam, sets the tempo with a destructive half-century in a 92-run second-wicket stand with Agarwal. • Following Kadam's dismissal, Agarwal changes gears. • The seeds of victory are sown early when Maharashtra are kept in check by Abhimanyu Mithun and Vinay Kumar. • Maharashtra are wobbling at 55 for 3 when Naushad Shaikh and Ankit Bawne rally with an 81-run stand. • Mithun returns to break the partnership, but Shaikh takes Maharashtra to a fair total — which isn't enough.

Holkar Stadium, Indore, March 14: Maharashtra 155/4 in 20 overs (Naushad Shaikh 69*, Rahul Tripathi 30; Abhimanyu Mithun 2-24) lost to **Karnataka** 159/2 in 18.3 overs (Mayank Agarwal 85*, Rohan Kadam 60) by eight wickets. *PoM:* Mayank Agarwal.

Winners: Karnataka

2017-18

North Zone

Feroz Shah Kotla, Delhi, January 8: Himachal Pradesh 194/2 in 20 overs (Prashant Chopra 99*, Paras Dogra 47*) tied with **Haryana** 194/8 in 20 overs (Harshal Patel 73, Rahul Tewatia 42; Kanwar Abhinay 2-38). Haryana 2/2 in 0.3 overs lost to Himachal Pradesh 6/0 in 0.3 overs in the one-over eliminator.

Feroz Shah Kotla, Delhi, January 8: Jammu & Kashmir 128 in 20 overs (Ian Dev Singh 47, Ahmed Bandy 20; Diwesh Pathania 3-28, Arun Bamal 2-19) lost to **Services** 130/1 in 16.5 overs (Ravi Chauhan 86*, Nakul Verma 36*) by nine wickets.

Feroz Shah Kotla, Delhi, January 9: Punjab 170/3 in 20 overs (Manan Vohra 74, Yuvraj Singh 50*; Pawan Negi 2-8) beat **Delhi** 168/4 in 20 overs (Gautam Gambhir 66, Rishabh Pant 38) by 2 runs.

Feroz Shah Kotla, Delhi, January 9: Himachal Pradesh 130/9 in 20 overs (Nikhil Gangta 31, Bipul Sharma 28; Parvez Rasool 2-15, Mohammed Mudhasir 2-20) beat **Jammu & Kashmir** 97 in 17.4 overs (Manzoor Dar 36, Pankaj Jaiswal 4-15, Mayank Dagar 2-7) by 33 runs.

Feroz Shah Kotla, Delhi, January 10: Haryana 153/6 in 20 overs (Chaitanya Bishnoi 65, Shubham Rohilla 44; Suboth Bhati 3-25) lost to **Delhi** 154/3 in 17 overs (Dhruv Shorey 59*, Nitish Rana 39) by seven wickets.

Feroz Shah Kotla, Delhi, January 10: Services 140/9 in 20 overs (Amit Pachhara 37, Vikas Hathwala 25; Manpreet Gony 4-18) lost to **Punjab** 141/2 in 19.1 overs (Mandeep Singh 84*, Yuvraj Singh 35*; Diwesh Pathania 2-17) by eight wickets.

Feroz Shah Kotla, Delhi, January 12: Jammu & Kashmir 100/9 in 20 overs (Parveez Rasool 37, Pranav Gupta 22; Pawan Negi 3-27, Navdeep Saini 2-14) lost to **Delhi** 104/2 in 11.3 overs (Rishabh Pant 51, Sarthak Ranjan 31; P Rasool 2-41) by eight wickets.

Feroz Shah Kotla, Delhi, January 12: Punjab 134/9 in 20 overs (Mandeep Singh 30; Amit Mishra 3-23, Rahul Tewatia 2-15) lost to **Haryana** 136/5 in 17.5 overs (R Tewatia 37*, Harshal Patel 31; Barinder Sran 3-19, Harbhajan Singh 2-16) by five wickets.

Feroz Shah Kotla, Delhi, January 13: Himachal Pradesh 119/8 in 20 overs (Rishi Dhawan 27; Diwesh Pathania 3-16, Avishek Sinha 2-12) lost to **Services** 122/5 in 18.5 overs (Nakul Verma 25, Amit Pachhara 23*; Kanwar Abhinay 2-19) by five wickets.

Feroz Shah Kotla, Delhi, January 13: Haryana 116 in 19.2 overs (Harshal Patel 28; Umar Nazir Mir 3-16, Manik Gupta 3-26) lost to **Jammu & Kashmir** 122/6 in 18.4 overs (Jatin Wadhwan 70*, Manzoor Dar 20*; Harshal 2-18, Amit Mishra 2-29) by four wickets.

Feroz Shah Kotla, Delhi, January 14: Himachal Pradesh 144/8 in 20 overs (Nikhil Gangta 40, Prashant Chopra 30; Pradeep Sangwan 2-39) lost to **Delhi** 148/0 in 11.4 overs (Rishabh Pant 116*, Gautam Gambhir 30*) by ten wickets.

Feroz Shah Kotla, Delhi, January 14: Jammu & Kashmir 164/3 in 20 overs (Ian Singh 43*, Manzoor Dar 38*; Harbhajan Singh 2-12) beat **Punjab** 141 in 19 overs (Manan Vohra 53, Gurkeerat Singh 34; Waseem Raza 4-16, Umar Nazir Mir 2-36) by 23 runs.

Feroz Shah Kotla, Delhi, January 15: Services 140/8 in 20 overs (Nakul Sharma 42, Diwesh Pathania 27; Ajit Chahal 3-36, Jayant Yadav 2-13) lost to **Haryana** 141/6 in 19.5 overs (Shivam Chauhan 54, Rahul Tewatia 29; D Pathania 2-27) by four wickets.

Feroz Shah Kotla, Delhi, January 15: Punjab 211/4 in 20 overs (Manan Vohra 74, Mandeep Sigh 46) beat **Himachal Pradesh** 192/5 in 20 overs (Nikhil Gangta 52*, Prashant Chopra 52; Manyank Markande 2-35) by 19 runs.

Feroz Shah Kotla, Delhi, January 16: Delhi 225/8 in 20 overs (Rishabh Pant 64, Nitish Rana 30; Nitin Yadav 3-53, Nitin Tanwar 2-28) beat **Services** 203 in 19.1 overs (Ravi Chauhan 53, Nakul Sharma 53; Kulwant Khejroliya 3-38, Vikas Tokas 2-36) by 22 runs.

Points table

Teams	M	W	L	T	N/R	Pts.	NRR
Delhi	5	4	1	0	0	16	2.267
Punjab	5	3	2	0	0	12	-0.410
Services	5	2	3	0	0	8	0.121
Haryana	5	2	3	0	0	8	-0200
Himachal Pradesh	5	2	3	0	0	8	-0.804
Jammu & Kashmir	5	2	3	0	0	8	-0838

Delhi and Punjab qualified for the Super League

Central Zone

Shaheed Veer Narayan Singh International Stadium, Raipur, January 8: **Rajasthan** 156/5 in 20 overs (Abhimanyu Lamba 62*, Tajinder Singh 51) beat **Madhya Prasdeh** 120 in 19.4 overs (Rajat Patidar 38, Venkatesh Iyer 21; Chandrapal Singh 3-22, Aniket Choudhary 2-16) by 36 runs.

Shaheed Veer Narayan Singh International Stadium, Raipur, January 8: **Vidarbha** 195/7 in 20 overs (Jitesh Sharma 91, Karn Sharma 25; Vishal Kushwah 2-31, Shakeeb Ahmed 2-37) beat **Chhattisgarh** 147/8 in 20 overs (Shakeeb Ahmed 45*, Manoj Singh 35; Akshay Wakhare 2-22, Shrikant Wagh 2-24) by 48 runs.

Shaheed Veer Narayan Singh International Stadium, Raipur, January 9: **Uttar Pradesh** 146/5 in 20 overs (Eklavya Dwivedi 27, Samarth Singh 26; Tajinder Singh 2-16) lost to **Rajasthan** 150/6 in 19.5 overs (Ankit Lamba 45, Aditya Garhwal 37; Amit Mishra 3-33) by four wickets.

Shaheed Veer Narayan Singh International Stadium, Raipur, January 9: **Vidarbha** 163/7 in 20 overs (Faiz Fazal 45, Apoorv Wankhade 36; Amit Mishra 2-29) beat **Railways** 146/9 in 20 overs (Karan Sharma 35, Mahesh Rawat 22; Ravikumar Thakur 3-26, Shrikant Wagh 2-24) by 17 runs.

Shaheed Veer Narayan Singh International Stadium, Raipur, January 10: **Uttar Pradesh** 108/7 in 20 overs (Sarfaraz Khan 20; Ankit Sharma 2-22) lost to **Madhya Pradesh** 110/3 in 17 overs (Rajat Patidar 51*, Venkatesh Iyer 27*) by seven wickets.

Shaheed Veer Narayan Singh International Stadium, Raipur, January 10: **Chhattisgarh** 175/5 in 20 overs (Amandeep Khare 90, Manoj Singh 21; Amit Mishra 2-30) beat **Railways** 150/8 in 20 overs (Mahesh Rawat 61*, Karan Sharma 32; Shakeeb Ahmed 3-27, Ajay Mandal 2-29) by 25 runs.

Shaheed Veer Narayan Singh International Stadium, Raipur, January 12: **Vidarbha** 156/5 in 20 overs (Apoorv Wankhade 43, Ganesh Satish 35) beat **Madhya Pradesh** 149/9 in 20 overs (Sohraab Dhaliwal 45, Anshul Tripathi 39; Ravikumar Thakur 4-29, Shrikant Wagh 2-23) by 7 runs.

Shaheed Veer Narayan Singh International Stadium, Raipur, January 12: **Chhattisgarh** 103 in 17.4 overs (Amandeep Khare 36, Sahil Gupta 27; Khaleel Ahmed 4-12, Tajinder Singh 2-20) lost to **Rajasthan** 104/3 in 17.3 overs (Ankit Lamba 54*, Mahipal Lomror 29*; Sumit Ruikar 2-28) by seven wickets.

Shaheed Veer Narayan Singh International Stadium, Raipur, January 13: **Railways** 132/8 in 20 overs (Mahesh Rawat 35, Ashish Yadav 32; Ankit Rajpoot 3-30, Saurabh Kumar 2-24) lost to **Uttar Pradesh** 134/3 in 18 overs (Shivam Chaudhary 40, Rinku Singh 37; Abhishek Sharma 2-25) by seven wickets.

Shaheed Veer Narayan Singh International Stadium, Raipur, January 13: **Vidarbha** 131/8 in 20 overs (Ganesh Satish 39, Apoorv Wankhade 24; Khaleel Ahmed 2-19, Deepak

Chahar 2-25) lost to **Rajasthan** 132/4 in 18 overs (Ankit Lamba 51*, Aditya Garhwal 26) by six wickets.

Shaheed Veer Narayan Singh International Stadium, Raipur, January 14: Chhattisgarh 150/7 in 20 overs (Amandeep Khare 47, Vishal Kushwah 32; Avesh Khan 3-29) lost to **Madhya Pradesh** 154/5 in 19.3 overs (Naman Ojha 58, Rajat Patidar 30; Vishal Kushwah 2-22, Shivendra Singh 2-22) by five wickets.

Shaheed Veer Narayan Singh International Stadium, Raipur, January 15: Madhya Pradesh 135/7 in 20 overs (Harpreet Singh 50, Sohraab Dhaliwal 31; Amit Mishra 3-17, Anureet Singh 2-18) beat **Railways** 111/6 in 20 overs (Mahesh Rawat 38, Arindam Ghosh 26; Avesh Khan 2-16) by 24 runs.

Shaheed Veer Narayan Singh International Stadium, Raipur, January 15: Uttar Pradesh 137/8 in 20 overs (Shivam Chaudhary 51, Akshdeep Nath 31; Srikant Wagh 3-28, Ravikumar Thakur 3-29) beat **Vidarbha** 131/8 in 20 overs (Apoorv Wankhade 33, Faiz Fazal 32; Amit Mishra 4-10) by 6 runs.

Shaheed Veer Narayan Singh International Stadium, Raipur, January 16: Rajasthan 150/6 in 20 overs (Tajinder Singh 43*, Salman Khan 40; Amit Mishra 2-34) lost to **Railways** 151/6 in 19.3 overs (Chanderpal Saini 41, Mahesh Rawat 37; Aniket Choudhary 2-31) by four wickets.

Shaheed Veer Narayan Singh International Stadium, Raipur, January 16: Chhattisgarh 113/8 in 20 overs (Amandeep Khare 33, Shivendra Singh 27*; Saurabh Kumar 2-16, Amt Mishra 2-19) lost to **Uttar Pradesh** 114/4 in 11.2 overs (Akshdeep Nath 43*, Rinku Singh 33; Shakeeb Ahmed 2-29) by six wickets.

Points table

Teams	M	W	L	T	N/R	Pts.	NRR
Rajasthan	5	4	1	0	0	16	0.716
Uttar Pradesh	5	3	2	0	0	12	0.585
Vidarbha	5	3	2	0	0	12	0.505
Madhya Pradesh	5	3	2	0	0	12	0.112
Railways	5	1	4	0	0	4	-0.790
Chhattisgarh	5	1	4	0	0	4	-1.237

Rajasthan and Uttar Pradesh qualified for the Super League

West Zone

SCA Stadium, Rajkot, January 7: **Baroda** 210/3 in 20 overs (Deepak Hooda 66, Urvil Patel 50; Tushar Deshpande 2-38) beat **Mumbai** 197/8 in 20 overs (Siddhesh Lad 82, Jay Bista 36; Lukman Meriwala 3-29, Atit Sheth 3-31) by 13 runs.

SCA Stadium, Rajkot, January 7: **Gujarat** 151/8 in 20 overs (Chirag Gandhi 61*, Axar Patel 38; Domnic Muthuswami 4-27) lost to **Maharashtra** 155/6 in 19.3 overs (Nikhil Naik 70*, Ruturaj Gaikwad 26; Piyush Chawla 3-27) by four wickets.

SCA Stadium, Rajkot, January 8: **Saurashtra** 142/9 in 20 overs (Prerak Mankad 34; Domnic Muthuswamy 2-27, Shrikant Mundhe 2-27, Jagdish Zope 2-27) beat **Maharashtra** 138/7 in 20 overs (Ruturaj Gaikwad 41, Naushad Shaikh 24; Yuvraj Chudasama 2-26, Shaurya Sanandia 2-37) by 4 runs.

SCA Stadium, Rajkot, January 8: **Gujarat** 167/7 in 20 overs (Dhruv Raval 73, Axar Patel 35; Dhawal Kulkarni 3-32) lost to **Mumbai** 168/5 in 19.2 overs (Jay Bista 50, Suryakumar Yadav 45*; Piyush Chawla 2-29) by five wickets.

SCA Stadium, Rajkot, January 10: Baroda175/7 in 20 overs (Kedar Devdhar 100, Swapnil Singh 44; Piyush Chawla 3-45, Jayveer Parmar 2-37) beat **Gujarat** 139 in 18 overs (Chirag Gandhi 52, Axar Patel 33; Rishi Arothe 3-26, Atit Sheth 2-15) by 36 runs.

SCA Stadium, Rajkot, January 10: Mumbai 130 in 19.3 overs (Aditya Tare 39, Siddhesh Lad 38; Shaurya Sanandia 4-22, Yuvraj Chudasama 2-21) lost to **Saurashtra** 133/2 in 17.2 overs (Robin Uthappa 52, Kishan Parmar 35*; Shardul Thakur 2-23) by eight wickets.

SCA Stadium, Rajkot, January 11: Maharashtra 89 in 15 overs (Rahul Tripathi 21, Vijay Zol 21; Akash Parkar 3-22, Shivam Dubey 2-7) lost to **Mumbai** 92/3 in 9.2 overs (Aditya Tare 42*, Siddhesh Lad 25) by seven wickets.

SCA Stadium, Rajkot, January 11: Saurashtra 131 in 19.5 overs (Jaydev Unadkat 33, Robin Uthappa 29; Atit Sheth 2-18) lost to**Baroda** 132/2 in 16.3 overs (Kedar Devdhar 62*, Deepak Hooda 32*) by eight wickets.

SCA Stadium, Rajkot, January 13: Saurashtra 133 in 19.2 overs (Vishvaraj Jadeja 48, Prerak Mankad 20; Jayveer Parmar 4-17, Piyush Chawla 2-24) lost to **Gujarat**137/2 in 18.1 overs (Priyank Panchal 76, Bhargav Merai 35*; Shaurya Sanandia 2-25) by eight wickets.

SCA Stadium, Rajkot, January 13: Maharashtra 178/6 in 20 overs (Ruturaj Gaikwad 52, Rahul Tripathi 30; Atit Sheth 3-21) lost to **Baroda**179/5 in 18.3 overs (Deepak Hooda 57, Vishnu Solanki 42; Dominc Muthuswami 3-24) by five wickets.

Points table

Teams	M	W	L	T	N/R	Pts.	NRR
Baroda	4	4	0	0	0	16	1.218
Mumbai	4	2	2	0	0	8	0.803
Saurashtra	4	2	2	0	0	8	-0.222
Gujarat	4	1	3	0	0	4	-0.405
Maharashtra	4	1	3	0	0	4	-1.270

Baroda and Mumbai qualified for the Super League

South Zone

Dr YS Rajasekhara Reddy ACA-VDCA Cricket Stadium, Visakhapatnam, January 8: Karnataka 172/4 in 20 overs (Mayank Agarwal 55, Stuart Binny 28*; Darshan Misal 3-27) beat **Goa** 123/8 in 20 overs (Sagun Kamat 28, D Misal 24; Abhimanyu Mithun 2-13, S Aravind 2-22) by 49 runs.

Dr YS Rajasekhara Reddy ACA-VDCA Cricket Stadium, Visakhapatnam, January 8: Andhra 119/7 in 20overs (Ricky bhui 25, Shoaib Md Khan 20; K Vignesh 2-17) lost to **Tamil Nadu** 122/3 in 14.4 overs (Dinesh Karthik 57, Baba Aparajith 28*) by seven wickets.

Dr PVG Raju ACA Sports Complex, Vizianagaram, January 8: Hyderabad 168/5 in 20 overs (Ambati Rayudu 52*, Akshath Reddy 34; Jalaj Saxena 2-28) beat **Kerala** 158/7 in 20 overs (Sachin Baby 79, Vishnu Vinod 22; Ravi Kran 3-28, Mohammed Siraj 2-28) by 10 runs.

Dr YS Rajasekhara Reddy ACA-VDCA Cricket Stadium, Visakhapatnam, January 9: Tamil Nadu 184/4 in 20 overs (Dinesh Karthik 71, N Jagadeesan 35*; Sandeep Warrier 2-23) beat **Kerala** 149/7 in 20 overs (Sachin Baby 51, Salman Nizar 38; K Vignesh 5-25) by 35 runs.

Dr PVG Raju ACA Sports Complex, Vizianagaram, January 9: Karnataka 156/8 in 20 overs (Sturat Binny 47*, Vinay Kumar 25; KV Sasikanth 3-32, D Siva Kumar 2-29) lost to **Andhra** 157/3 in 18.2 overs (Ricky Bhui 46*, Ashwin Hebbar 35) by seven wickets.

Dr YS Rajasekhara Reddy ACA-VDCA Cricket Stadium, Visakhapatnam, January 9: Hyderabad 181/5 in 20 overs (Akshath Reddy 64, Ambati Rayudu 44; Felix Alemao 2-35, Shadab Jakati 2-39) beat **Goa** 162/9 in 20 overs (Sagun Kamat 47, Keenan Vaz 33; Ravi Kiran

4-23, Mehdi Hasan 2-28) by 19 runs.

Dr YS Rajasekhara Reddy ACA-VDCA Cricket Stadium, Visakhapatnam, January 11: **Karnataka** 205/5 in 20 overs (Karun Nair 77, K Gowtham 57; Ravi Kiran 2-33) beat **Hyderabad** 203/9 in 20 overs (Akshath Reddy 70, Tanmay Agarwal 38; Stuart Binny 3-29) by 2 runs.

Dr YS Rajasekhara Reddy ACA-VDCA Cricket Stadium, Visakhapatnam, January 11: **Kerala** 120 in 12 overs (Vinod Kumar 45, Sanju Samson 32; Harishankar Reddy 4-12. B Ayyappa 3-32) lost to **Andhra** 126/4 in 13 overs (Ashwin Hebbar 64, Hanuma Vihari 25; Basil Thampi 2-35) by six wickets.

Dr PVG Raju ACA Sports Complex, Vizianagaram, January 11: Tamil Nadu 155/5 in 20 overs (Dinesh Karthik 56, Sanjay Yadav 28; Amogh Desai 3-22) beat **Goa** 130/7 in 20 overs (Sagun Kamat 41, A Desai 25; Washington Sundar 2-20, Murugan Ashwin 2-22) by 25 runs.

Dr YS Rajasekhara Reddy ACA-VDCA Cricket Stadium, Visakhapatnam, January 12: **Goa** 138/8 in 20 overs (Keenan Vaz 36, Sagun Kamat 24; KM Asif 3-25, Abhishek Mohan 3-30) lost to **Kerala** 140/1 in 15.5 overs (Sanju Samson 65*, Arun Karthik 37*) by nine wickets.

Dr YS Rajasekhara Reddy ACA-VDCA Cricket Stadium, Visakhapatnam, January 12: **Hyderabad** 129/9 in 20 overs (B Sandeep 39, Ambati Rayudu 24; Harishankar Reddy 3-30, B Ayyappa 2-30) lost to **Andhra** 133/4 in 18.2 overs (Ricky Bhui 73*, Dwaraka Teja 46; Mohammed Siraj 3-26) by six wickets.

Dr PVG Raju ACA Sports Complex, Vizianagaram, January 12: Karnataka 179/9 in 20 overs (Karun Nair 111; V Athisayaraj Davidson 5-30, M Ashwin 2-33) beat **Tamil Nadu** 101 in 16.3 overs (Washington Sundar 34, Vijay Shankar 20; Praveen Dubey 4-19, K Gowtham 2-14) by 78 runs.

Dr YS Rajasekhara Reddy ACA-VDCA Cricket Stadium, Visakhapatnam, January 14: **Tamil Nadu** 193/7 in 20 overs (Sanjay Yadav 42, Vijay Shankar 40; Mehdi Hasan 3-40, Mohammed Siraj 2-39) beat **Hyderabad** 177/8 in 20 overs (Tanmay Agarwal 59, Ambati Rayudu 53; Washington Sundar 3-29, V Athisayaraj Davidson 2-24) by 16 runs.

Dr YS Rajasekhara Reddy ACA-VDCA Cricket Stadium, Visakhapatnam, January 14: **Andhra** 201/4 in 20 overs (Ricky Bhui 65, Hanuma Vihari 57) beat **Goa** 183/6 in 20 overs (Swapnil Asnodkar 72, Sagun Kamat 43; Bhargav Bhatt 2-30) by 18 runs.

Dr PVG Raju ACA Sports Complex, Vizianagaram, January 14: Karnataka 181/6 in 20 overs (Mayank Agarwal 86, R Samarth 27; KM Asif 2-34) beat **Kerala** 161 in 19.2 overs (Sanju Samson 71, Vishnu Vinod 46; Praveen Dubey 3-35, Vinay Kumar 2-22) by 20 runs.

Points table

Teams	M	W	L	T	N/R	Pts.	NRR
Karnataka	5	4	1	0	0	16	1.354
Tamil Nadu	5	4	1	0	0	16	0.435
Andhra	5	4	1	0	0	16	0.109
Hyderabad	5	2	3	0	0	8	-0.074
Kerala	5	1	4	0	0	4	-0.375
Goa	5	0	5	0	0	0	-1.499

Karnataka and Tamil Nadu qualified for the Super League

East Zone

JSCA International Stadium Complex, Ranchi, January 8: Tripura 162/5 in 20 overs (Yashpal Singh 56, Smit Patel 42; Abu Nechim 3-20) beat **Assam** 154/8 in 20 overs (Amit Sinha 64, Sibsankar Roy 46; Ajoy Sarkar 3-31) by 8 runs.

JSCA International Stadium Complex, Ranchi, January 8: Odisha 157/5 in 20 overs (Rajesh Dhuper 90, Anurag Sarangi 23; Manoj Tiwary 2-23, Writtick Chatterjee 2-25) lost to **Bengal** 158/3 in 18.4 overs (Shreevats Goswami 79, Vivek Singh 64) by seven wickets.

JSCA International Stadium Complex, Ranchi, January 10: Jharkhand 163/6 in 20 overs (Virat Singh 43, Ishank Jaggi 33; Gurinder Singh 3-21) beat **Tripura** 139/9 in 20 overs (Smit Patel 49, Udiyan Bose 29; Shahbaz Nadeem 2-18, Kaushal Singh 2-21) by 24 runs.

JSCA International Stadium Complex, Ranchi, January 10: Odisha 128/9 in 20 overs (Debasish Samantray 25, Anurag Sarangi 22; Abhu Nechim 2-13, Pritam Das 2-25) beat **Assam** 77 in 17.2 overs (Rishav Das 26; Prayash Singh 3-6, Abhishek Raut 3-14) by 51 runs.

JSCA International Stadium Complex, Ranchi, January 12: Odisha 179/6 in 20 overs (Govinda Poddar 55, Rajesh Dhuper 42; Sanjay Majumder 2-24) beat **Tripura** 107 in 17.2 overs (Gurinder Singh 39, Manisankar Murasingh 23; Suryakant Pradhan 4-24) by 72 runs.

JSCA International Stadium Complex, Ranchi, January 12: Jharkhand 177/9 in 20 overs (Ishank Jaggi 72, Ishan Kishan 49; Manoj Tiwary 2-27, Ashok Dinda 2-41) lost to **Bengal** 179/4 in 19.2 overs (Vivek Singh 63, Shreevats Goswami 58; Kaushal Singh 2-28) by six wickets.

JSCA International Stadium Complex, Ranchi, January 14: Tripura 169/4 in 20 overs (Smit Patel 73, Gurinder Singh 25) lost to **Bengal** 170/1 in 18 overs (Shrevats Goswami 82*, Vivek Singh 71) by nine wickets.

JSCA International Stadium Complex, Ranchi, January 14: Assam 148/6 in 20 overs (Sibsankar Roy 52, Amit Sinha 40; Monu Kumar 3-23) lost to **Jharkhand** 149/2 in 16 overs (Ishank Jaggi 68*, Ishan Kishan 36) by eight wickets.

JSCA International Stadium Complex, Ranchi, January 16: Assam 143/9 in 20 overs (Rishav Das 53, Manoj Tiwary 4-23) lost to **Bengal** 147/4 in 17.1 overs (M Tiwary 63*, Anustup Majumdar 34; Swarupam Purkayastha 2-24) by six wickets.

JSCA International Stadium Complex, Ranchi, January 16: Odisha 123 in 19.4 overs (Govinda Poddar 64; Monu Kumar 4-14, Atul Surwar 2-27) lost to **Jharkhand** 129/2 in 16.4 overs (Ishan Kishan 51, Ishank Jaggi 40*) by eight wickets.

Points table

Teams	M	W	L	T	N/R	Pts.	NRR
Bengal	4	4	0	0	0	16	0.863
Jharkhand	4	3	1	0	0	12	1.080
Odisha	4	2	2	0	0	8	1.085
Tripura	4	1	3	0	0	4	-1.326
Assam	4	0	4	0	0	0	-1.484

Bengal and Jharkhand qualified for the Super League

Syed Mushtaq Ali Trophy Super League Group A

Jadavpur University Campus 2nd Ground, Kolkata, January 21: Karnataka 158/7 in 20 overs (Aniruddha Joshi 40*, CM Gautam 36; Baltej Singh 3-21, Manpreet Gony 2-8) tied with **Punjab** 158/9 in 20 overs (Mandeep Singh 45, Harbhajan Singh 33; S Aravind 4-32, Praveen Dubey 2-12). Punjab 15/0 in 1 over, Karnataka 11/0 in 1 over. Punjab won the one-over eliminator.

Jadavpur University Campus 2nd Ground, Kolkata, January 21: Mumbai 170/5 in 20 overs (Siddhesh Lad 46, Aditya Tare 45; Atul Surwar 2-35) beat **Jharkhand** 157/7 in 20 overs (Virat Singh 81, Saurabh Tiwary 32; Akash Parkar 2-32) by 13 runs.

Jadavpur University Campus 2nd Ground, Kolkata, January 22: Jharkhand 157/5 in 20 overs (Virat Singh 43, Ishan Kishan 39; Aditya Garhwal 2-15, Deepak Chahar 2-35) lost to **Rajasthan** 158/6 in 19.1overs (A Garhwal 43, Salman Khan 34; Varun Aaron 2-24, Jaskaran Singh 2-42) by four wickets.

Jadavpur University Campus 2nd Ground, Kolkata, January 22: Mumbai 198/4 in 20 overs (Shreyas Iyer 79*, Akhil Herwadkar 42; Mayank Markande 2-32) lost to **Punjab** 199/7 in 19.2 overs (Gurkeerat Singh 43, Manan Vohra 42; Shivam Dubey 3-27) by three wickets.

Jadavpur University Campus 2nd Ground, Kolkata, January 23: Rajasthan 160/8 in 20 overs (Ankit Lamba 58, Aditya Garhwal 31; S Aravind 3-25, Vinay Kumar 2-29) beat **Karnataka** 138 in 20 overs (Aniruddha Joshi 73*; Deepak Chahar 5-15, Chandrapal Singh 2-31) by 22 runs.

Eden Gardens, Kolkata, January 23: Punjab 149/7 in 20 overs (Mandeep Singh 48, Abhishek Gupta 31*; Kaushal Singh 3-26, Varun Aaron 2-20) lost to **Jharkhand** 150/6 in 19.3 overs (Ishan Kishan 54, Kaushal 29; Barinder Sran 2-19) by four wickets.

Eden Gardens, Kolkata, January 24: Rajasthan 175/6 in 20 overs (Mahipal Lomror 74, Tajinder Singh 43; Dhawal Kulkarni 3-35) beat **Mumbai** 158/8 in 20 overs (Akhil Herwadkar 68, Suryakumar Yadav 39; Deepak Chahr 3-27, Tajinder Singh 2-21) by 17 runs.

Eden Gardens, Kolkata, January 24: Karnataka 201/4 in 20 overs (Karun Nair 100, Pavan Deshpande 56; Manu Kumar 2-31) beat **Jharkhand** 78 in 14.2 overs (Vikash Singh 25; S Aravind 2-6, Prasidh Krishna 2-29) by 123 runs.

Eden Gardens, Kolkata, January 25: Punjab 129/9 in 20 overs (Harbhajan Singh 32, Sharad Lumba 31; Khaleel Ahmed 3-17, Deepak Chahar 2-9) beat **Rajasthan** 124/8 in 20 overs (Ankit Lamba 47, Mahipal Lomror 21; Barinder Sran 3-23, Manpreet Gony 2-20) by 5 runs.

Eden Gardens, Kolkata, January 25: Mumbai 175/8 in 20 overs (Suryakumar Yadav 59*, Siddhesh Lad 52; Stuart Binny 3-36, Shreyas Gopal 2-22) lost to **Karnataka** 176/3 in 18.4 overs (Mayank Agarwal 77, Pavan Deshpande 48*; Dhawal Kulkarni 2-36) by seven wickets.

Super League A points table

Teams	M	W	L	D	T	A	Pts.	NRR
Rajasthan	4	3	1	0	0	0	12	+0.519
Punjab	4	3	1	0	0	0	12	+0.080
Karnataka	4	2	2	0	0	0	8	+1.418
Mumbai	4	1	3	0	0	0	4	-0.302
Jharkhand	4	1	3	0	0	0	4	-1.747

Rajasthan qualified for the final

Syed Mushtaq Ali Trophy Super League Group B

Eden Gardens, Kolkata, January 21: Tamil Nadu 145/7 in 20 overs (Vijay Shankar 57, Baba Aparajith 45; Kulwant Khejroliya 4-26) lost to **Delhi** 146/2 in 15.2 overs (Rishabh Pant 58, Nitish Rana 34*; Washington Sundar 2-32) by eight wickets.

Eden Gardens, Kolkata, January 21: Baroda 149/9 in 20 overs (Vishnu Solanki 26, Deepak Hooda 22; Sayan Ghosh 3-37, Manoj Tiwary 2-25) beat **Bengal** 132 in 19.5 overs (Shreevats Goswami 58; Krunal Pandya 3-14, Lukman Meriwala 3-26) by 17 runs.

Eden Gardens, Kolkata, January 22: Uttar Pradesh 235/3 in 20 overs (Suresh Raina 126*, Akshdeep Nath 80) beat **Bengal** 160 in 16.1 overs (Shreevats Goswami 57, Sudip Chatterjee 36; Kuldeep Yadav 4-26, Mohsin Khan 3-35) by 75 runs.

Eden Gardens, Kolkata, January 22: Baroda 140/8 in 20 overs (Kedar Devdhar 77, Vishnu

Solanki 21; Suboth Bhati 4-20) lost to **Delhi** 143/8 in 19.1 overs (Dhruv Shorey 74, Pradeep Sangwan 23*; Lukman Meriwala 4-24) by two wickets.

Eden Gardens, Kolkata, January 23: Bengal 170/6 in 20 overs (Sudip Chatterjee 51, Vivek Singh 32; Kulwant Khejroliya 2-25, Pradeep Sangwan 2-27) beat **Delhi** 167/8 in 20 overs (Dhruv Shorey 84, Lalit Yadav 45; Sayan Ghosh 3-24, Kanishk Seth 3-25) by 3 runs.

Eden Gardens, Kolkata, January 23: Uttar Pradesh 162/4 in 20 overs (Suresh Raina 61, Akshdeep Nath 38*; Washington Sundar 2-32) lost to **Tamil Nadu** 163/5 in 19.2 overs (Sanjay Yadav 52, W Sundar 33; Mohsin Khan 2-20, Ankit Rajpoot 2-37) by five wickets.

Jadavpur University Campus 2nd Ground, Kolkata, January 24: Baroda 192/3 in 20 overs (Urvil Patel 96, Deepak Hooda 45; Mohsin Khan 2-38) lost to **Uttar Pradesh**195/3 in 18.4 overs (Umang Sharma 95, Suresh Raina 56) by seven wickets.

Jadavpur University Campus 2nd Ground, Kolkata, January 24: Tamil Nadu 129/9 in 20 overs (Srikkanth Anirudha 37, Vijay Shankar 27; Kanishk Seth 3-26, Aamir Gani 2-16) lost to **Bengal** 134/3 in 16.2 overs (Sudip Chatterjee 51*, Writtick Chatterjee 44) by seven wickets.

Jadavpur University Campus 2nd Ground, Kolkata, January 25: Delhi 140/9 in 20 overs (Rishabh Pant 58, Milind Kumar 32; Mohd Israr 2-12, Mohsin Khan 2-29) beat **Uttar Pradesh** 137 in 20 overs (Rinku Singh 34, Saurabh Kumar 33; Pawan Negi 2-13, Suboth Bhati 2-28) by 3 runs.

Jadavpur University Campus 2nd Ground, Kolkata, January 25: Tamil Nadu 123/7 in 20 overs (Srikkanth Anirudha 32*, N Jagadeesan 28) lost to**Baroda** 125/5 in 17.1 overs (Kedar Devdhar 68, Swapnil Singh 29) by five wickets.

Super League B points table

Teams	M	W	L	D	T	A	Pts.	NRR
Delhi	4	3	1	0	0	0	12	+0.600
Uttar Pradesh	4	2	2	0	0	0	8	+1.011
Baroda	4	2	2	0	0	0	8	+0.234
Bengal	4	2	2	0	0	0	8	-0.692
Tamil Nadu	4	1	3	0	0	0	4	-1.178

Delhi qualified for the final

Final: Delhi beat Rajasthan by 41 runs

• Gautam Gambhir and Rishabh Pant get Delhi off to a brisk start with an opening stand of 41 off 29. • Dhruv Shorey takes over and Delhi are a solid 81 for 2 in 10 overs. • It becomes difficult to score as the ball gets softer, but Unmukt Chand holds the innings together. • Delhi can only manage 32 runs in the last five overs and find it difficult against Khaleel Ahmed. • Rajasthan are 93 for 3 midway through the 13th over, courtesy Aditya Garhwal's breezy fifty. • But a spectacular slide sees them slump to 96 for 7 in 10 deliveries to hand Delhi their maiden title.

Eden Gardens, Kolkata, January 26: Delhi153/6 in 20 overs (Unmukt Chand 53, Gautam Gambhir 27; Khaleel Ahmed 2-23, Rahul Chahar 2-31) beat**Rajasthan**112 in 19.1 overs (Aditya Garhwal 52; Pradeep Sangwan 2-14, Pawan Negi 2-21) by 41 runs. *MoM: Pradeep Sangwan*

Winners: Delhi

Vidarbha posted the highest total in Irani Cup history on the way to defending their title. — *VCA*

Irani Cup

Vidarbha defend a historic double

Vidarbha became only the third team after Bombay and Karnataka to defend both the Ranji Trophy and the Irani Cup. Hanuma Vihari, riding on the confidence of being a Test player, struck three centuries across both editions for Rest of India, but it was Faiz Fazal's men who reaped the benefits of seasons of hard work and combined effort.

The first time around, Vidarbha won the Cup in emphatic fashion, posting an audacious 800 for 7 declared in the first innings. It was the highest total in Irani Cup history — and at a time when the tournament was being shuffled around to accommodate interests of the IPL, this served as a fine reminder of its high place in history.

On a Nagpur pitch that offered something for everyone apart from bowlers, Rest were completely outplayed by the Ranji Trophy champions. Crucially, the toss went Vidarbha's way. They opted to bat, and did so till the fourth morning. Wasim Jaffer top-scored with a relentless 286, even as Ganesh Satish and Apoorv Wankhade added to their century tallies. RoI used as many as eight bowlers, including R Ashwin, Jayant Yadav and Shahbaz Nadeem, but only three wickets fell in the first two days. Then, the in-form Rajneesh Gurbani bowled out RoI for 390. The lead of 410 was enough for Vidarbha to lift the trophy.

In a match of tall totals, Jaffer and Satish's association was especially sticky: they batted together for almost 90 overs, for most of the second day, adding 289 runs for the third wicket. The veteran Mumbaikar was finally dismissed 14 short of what would have been his third first-class-triple century. Wankhede's was the most aggressive of the team's centuries, his second first-class ton growing to 157, with 16 fours and six sixes.

Reduced to 98 for 6, there was little chance for RoI, but Vihari proved a stubborn fighter and Jayant a fine sidekick. They added 216 for the seventh wicket, their resistance a token, but carrying the game to the final morning.

Next season, for their defence of the trophy, Vidarbha were without an injured Jaffer. But in his replacement, 18-year-old Atharva Taide, they found a capable steady hand. Having lost Fazal in the third ball of the fourth innings in a chase of 280, Taide constructed a half-century during a partnership of 116 with RR Sanjay, before the experienced Ganesh took over. Vidarbha were 269 for 5 when the teams decided to shake hands.

In their first hit, all-rounder Akshay Karnewar had earned them the crucial lead with a century from No.8. Wicketkeeper Akshay Wadkar began the rescue from 168 for 5, before the duo fended off the spin of Rahul Chahar to go past RoI's total of 330.

Captain Ajinkya Rahane played an attacking game, declaring on 373 for 3, and giving his team a good chance. But the lack of support for the impressive Vihari in the first innings after being 171 for 1 proved costly. Vidarbha's spin attack offered good support to Gurbani, with left-arm spinner Aditya Sarwate and off-spinner Akshay Wakhare especially effective in running through the middle order.

2018-19

VCA Stadium, Jamtha, Nagpur, February 12-16: Rest of India 330 in 89.4 overs(Hanuma Vihari 114, Mayank Agarwal 95; Akshay Wakhare 3-62, Aditya Sarwate 3-99) and 374/3 dec. in 107 overs (H Vihari 180*, Ajinkya Rahane 87; A Sarwate 2-141) drew with **Vidarbha** 425 in 142.1 overs (Akshay Karnewar 102, Akshay Wadkar 73; Rahul Chahar 4-112, K Gowtham 2-33) and 269/5 in 103.1 overs (Ganesh Satish 87, Atharwa Taide 72; R Chahar 2-116). Vidarbha took first-innings lead. *PoM:* Akshay Karnewar.

2017-18

VCA Stadium, Jamtha, Nagpur, March 14-18: Vidarbha 800/7 dec in 226.3 overs (Wasim Jaffer 286, Apoorv Wankhade 157*, Ganesh Satish 120; Siddarth Kaul 2-91) and 79/0 in 26 overs (Akshay Wadkar 50*, Sanjay Ramaswamy 27*) drew with **Rest of India** 390 in 129.1 overs (Hanuma Vihari 183, Jayant Yadav 96; Rajneesh Gurbani 4-70, Aditya Sarwate 3-97). Vidarbha took first-innings lead. *MoM:* Wasim Jaffer.

Indian Premier League

Consistency pays off for Mumbai

ABHISHEK MUKHERJEE

The 12th edition of the Indian Premier League was probably the most hard-fought of them all, for no team won more than nine of their 14 league matches; neither did any team win fewer than five. Three teams finished on 12 points and two more on 11. Royal Challengers Bangalore, who came last, now hold the record for the best performance by a wooden spoon holder.

Chennai Super Kings had celebrated their return from exile by steamrolling their way to a title triumph in 2018; in 2019, Mumbai Indians kept their streak of lifting the title in alternate seasons intact. What was more, Mumbai beat Chennai by a solitary run in the final, thus repeating their victory margin in 2017. It will, however, be unfair to go by the winning margin in the final: Mumbai were all over Chennai this time, beating them twice in the league and twice more in the Play-offs. It was, thus, a title well earned.

Mumbai were also the most rounded, most consistent of them all. Hardik Pandya (strike rate 191, economy 9.17) was the big star; Jasprit Bumrah and Quinton de Kock led their bowling and batting charts respectively; teenaged Rahul Chahar claimed 13 wickets while conceding 6.55 an over; and Alzarri Joseph arrived with 6 for 12, the best figures in IPL history. Their strength, however, lay in their core, from which someone invariably stood up. The team management backed this core to an extent that six men featured in all 16 matches, Rohit Sharma missed one (to an injury), and two others featured in 12 and 13.

The Chennai spinners bowled out Bangalore for 70 in the tournament opener. Their batsmen then used up 17.4 overs in the chase. This would be a recurring pattern for Chennai throughout the tournament: they would never cross 180 in the tournament, but barring once, neither would they concede more than nine. Five Chennai bowlers went for under 7.50 an over while only one batsman, MS Dhoni, struck at over 125.

A lot of this had to do with the slow Chepauk pitch, which drew flak even from Dhoni (whose mood would turn so sour over an umpiring decision later in the tournament that he would uncharacteristically march on to the ground to have a word with the umpires). Chennai won six of their eight home matches; Mumbai won the other two.

Unfortunately, Chennai may not be able to retain their core for long. Their 'Dad's Army' had won the title in 2018, but two years would have passed since then by the time the next edition commences. They already had 12 tricenarians before the 2019 final, nine of whom were over 35.

This was in stark contrast with Delhi Capitals, who boasted of 11 men under 24, six of whom were under 22. At 24, Shreyas Iyer was the youngest

Andre Russell made a habit out of bailing his team out of hopeless situations, and finished with most sixes and highest strike-rate in the tournament. — *BCCI/Sportzpics*

to lead in the IPL play-offs. If they retain the same unit, they may be the team to beat in two years' time. The change of name from Daredevils to Capitals worked wonders for reasons unknown. Their top order consisted of a plethora of explosive Indian batsmen, which allowed them to pick and choose from an assortment of overseas bowlers and all-rounders. Kagiso Rabada, the pick of the lot, held the Purple Cap till before the finals despite featuring in only 12 matches.

Hyderabad flirted with the top spot thanks to David Warner and Jonny Bairstow's terrific show at the top. Warner finished almost a hundred runs clear of anyone else, while Bairstow held the second spot for a long time, despite leaving early for pre-World Cup preparations. The pair scored a whopping 48 per cent of Hyderabad's runs off the bat and getting 12 of their 16 fifty-plus scores. Unfortunately, this meant that the middle order was not tested. Hyderabad lost all three matches, including the Eliminator, after the duo left.

Kolkata Knight Riders showed up disguised as Andre Russell, whose pyrokinetic batsmanship bailed his team out of one impossibly hopeless situation after another. Russell finished with most runs and most wickets for them; he also hit most sixes and had the highest strike-rate in the tournament and was named MVP. Despite the omnipresent Sunil Narine, the exciting Sandeep Warrier (whose chance came a tad too late), and some delightful batting from Shubman Gill (who was named Emerging Player of the Tournament), it was difficult to look beyond Russell.

R Ashwin, who caused a stir by Mankading Jos Buttler in Kings XI Punjab's first match, was also their star bowler along with Mohammed Shami. Sam Curran sizzled with bat and ball at times, while Chris Gayle and K L Rahul put up a consistent show at the top. Unfortunately, there was little support from the other bowlers — the mysterious Varun Chakravarthy played a solitary match — as Punjab finished sixth after winning just two of their last eight matches.

A mid-season captaincy change from Ajinkya Rahane to Steve Smith saw a change of fortune for Rajasthan Royals, but a wretched start — a solitary win from their first six matches — meant there was too much to catch up. This, despite Shreyas Gopal being one of the best spinners in the tournament, Buttler making merry during his short stint, Jofra Archer providing glimpses of what lay in store at international level, and Sanju Samson impressing with, among other innings, the first hundred of the edition.

For Bangalore, AB de Villiers, Virat Kohli and Yuzvendra Chahal all had their customary successful IPL, while Marcus Stoinis, Parthiv Patel and Pawan Negi impressed at times. Unfortunately, not for the first time, too many things went wrong for them. They lost Nathan Coulter-Nile and his replacement Dale Steyn to injuries; their young talents, Shivam Dube and Prayas Ray Barman, did not live up to expectations; Shimron Hetmyer found form too late; and Lasith Malinga overstepping in the last ball of a close match was not spotted by the umpire. Moeen Ali's brilliance — strike-rate 165, economy 6.76 — failed to pull them out of the doldrums.

Top five draws in 2019 IPL auctions

Player	Sold for (cr)	Base price (cr)	Performance
Varun Chakravarthy (Kings XI Punjab)	8.4	0.2	1 wicket (1 match)
Jaydev Unadkat (Rajasthan Royals)	8.4	1.5	1 run, 10 wickets (11 matches)
Sam CuRR an (Kings XI Punjab)	7.2	2	95 runs, 10 wickets (9 matches)
Colin Ingram (Delhi Capitals)	6.4	2	184 runs (12 matches)
Shivam Dube (Royal Challengers Bangalore)	5	0.2	40 runs, 0 wicket (4 matches)
Mohit Sharma (Chennai Super Kings)	5	0.5	0 run, 1 wicket (1 match)
Carlos Brathwaite (Kolkata Knight Riders)	5	0.75	11 runs, 0 wicket (2 matches)
Axar Patel (Delhi Capitals)	5	1	110 runs, 10 wickets (14 matches)

Top performers for each franchise

Teams	M	W
Mumbai Indians	Quinton de Kock (529 runs, 16 matches)	Jasprit Bumrah (19 wickets, 16 matches)
Chennai Super Kings	MS Dhoni (516 runs, 15 matches)	Imran Tahir (26 wickets, 17 matches)
Delhi Capitals	Shikhar Dhawan (521 runs, 16 matches)	Kagiso Rabada (25 wickets, 12 matches)
Sunrisers Hyderabad	David Warner (692 runs, 12 matches)	Khaleel Ahmed (19 wickets, 9 matches)
Kolkata Knight Riders	Andre Russell (510 runs, 14 matches)	Andre Russell (11 wickets, 14 matches)
Kings XI Punjab	KL Rahul (593 runs, 14 matches)	Mohammed ShaMI (19 wickets, 14 matches)
Rajasthan Royals	Ajinkya Rahane (393 runs, 14 matches)	Shreyas Gopal (20 wickets, 14 matches)
Royal Challengers Bangalore	Virat Kohli (464 runs, 14 matches)	Yuzvendra Chahal (18 wickets, 14 matches)

2019

MA Chidambaram Stadium, Chepauk, Chennai, March 23: RCB 70 in 17.1 overs (Parthiv Patel 29; Imran Tahir 3-9, Harbhajan Singh 3-20) lost to **CSK** 71/3 in 17.4 overs (Ambati Rayudu 28) by seven wickets. *PoM:* Harbhajan Singh.

Eden Gardens, Kolkata, March 24: SRH 181/3 in 20 overs (David Warner 85, Vijay Shankar 40; Andre Russell 2-32) lost to **KKR** 183/4 in 19.4 overs (Nitish Rana 68, A Russell 49*) by six wickets. *PoM:* Andre Russell.

Wankhede Stadium, Mumbai, March 24: DC 213/6 in 20 overs (Rishabh Pant 78*, Colin Ingram 47; Mitchell McClenaghan 3-40) beat **MI** 176 in 19.2 overs (Yuvraj Singh 53, Krunal Pandya 32; Kagiso Rabada 2-23, Ishant Sharma 2-34) by 37 runs. *PoM:* Rishabh Pant.

Sawai Mansingh Stadium, Jaipur, March 25: KXIP 184/4 in 20 overs (Chris Gayle 79, Sarfaraz Khan 46*; Ben Stokes 2-48) beat **RR** 170/9 in 20 overs (Jos Buttler 69, Sanju Samson 30; Mujeeb Ur Rahman 2-31, Ankit Rajpoot 2-33) by 14 runs. *PoM:* Chris Gayle.

Feroz Shah Kotla, Delhi, March 26: DC 147/6 in 20 overs (Shikhar Dhawan 51, Rishabh Pant 25; Dwayne Bravo 3-33) lost to **CSK** 150/4 in 19.4 overs (Shane Watson 44, MS Dhoni 32*; Amit Mishra 2-35) by six wickets. *PoM:* Shane Watson.

Eden Gardens, Kolkata, March 27: KKR 218/4 in 20 overs (Robin Uthappa 67*, Nitish Rana 63) beat **KXIP** 190/4 in 20 overs (David Miller 59*, Mayank Agarwal 58; Andre Russell 2-21) by 28 runs. *PoM:* Andre Russell.

M Chinnaswamy Stadium, Bangalore, March 28: MI 187/8 in 20 overs (Rohit Sharma 48, Suryakumar Yadav 38; Yuzvendra Chahal 4-38, Umesh Yadav 2-26) beat **RCB** 181/5 in 20 overs (AB de Villiers 70*, Virat Kohli 46; Jasprit Bumrah 3-20) by six runs. *PoM:* Jasprit Bumrah.

Rajiv Gandhi International Stadium, Uppal, Hyderabad, March 29: RR 198/2 in 20 overs (Sanju Samson 102*, Ajinkya Rahane 70) lost to **SRH** 201/5 in 19 overs (David Warner 69, Jonny Bairstow 45; Shreyas Gopal 3-27) by five wickets. *PoM:* Rashid Khan.

Punjab Cricket Association IS Bindra Stadium, Mohali, March 30: MI 176/7 in 20 overs (Quinton de Kock 60, Rohit Sharma 32; Murugan Ashwin 2-25, Hardus Viljoen 2-40) lost to **KXIP** 177/2 in 18.4 overs (KL Rahul 71*, Mayank Agarwal 43; Krunal Pandya 2-43) by eight wickets. *PoM:* Mayank Agarwal.

Feroz Shah Kotla, Delhi, March 30: KKR 185/8 in 20 overs (Andre Russell 62, Dinesh Karthik 50; Harshal Patel 2-40) tied with **DC** 185/6 in 20 overs (Prithvi Shaw 99, Shreyas Iyer 43; Kuldeep Yadav 2-41). **Super over: DC** 10/1 in 1 over beat **KKR** 7/1 in 1 over by three runs. *PoM:* Prithvi Shaw.

Rajiv Gandhi International Stadium, Uppal, Hyderabad, March 31: SRH 231/2 in 20 overs (Jonny Bairstow 114, David Warner 100*) beat **RCB** 113 in 19.5 overs (Colin de Grandhomme 37; Mohammad Nabi 4-11, Sandeep Sharma 3-19) by 118 runs. *PoM:* Jonny Bairstow.

MA Chidambaram Stadium, Chepauk, Chennai, March 31: CSK 175/5 in 20 overs (MS Dhoni 75*, Suresh Raina 30; Jofra Archer 2-17) beat **RR** 167/8 in 20 overs (Ben Stokes 46, Rahul Tripathi 39; Deepak Chahar 2-19, Imran Tahir 2-23) by eight runs. *PoM:* MS Dhoni.

Punjab Cricket Association IS Bindra Stadium, Mohali, April 1: KXIP 166/9 in 20 overs (David Miller 43, Sarfaraz Khan 39; Chris Morris 3-30, Sandeep Lamichhane 2-27) beat **DC** 152 in 19.2 overs (Rishabh Pant 39, Colin Ingram 38; Sam Curran 4-11, Mohammed Shami 2-27) by 14 runs. *PoM:* Sam Curran.

Sawai Mansingh Stadium, Jaipur, April 2: RCB 158/4 in 20 overs (Parthiv Patel 67, Marcus Stoinis 31*; Shreyas Gopal 3-12) lost to **RR** 164/3 in 19.5 overs (Jos Buttler 59, Steven Smith 38; Yuzvendra Chahal 2-17) by seven wickets. *PoM:* Shreyas Gopal.

Wankhede Stadium, Mumbai, April 3: MI 170/5 in 20 overs (Suryakumar Yadav 59, Krunal Pandya 42) beat **CSK** 133/8 in 20 overs (Kedar Jadhav 58; Hardik Pandya 3-20, Lasith Malinga 3-34) by 37 runs. *PoM:* Hardik Pandya.

Feroz Shah Kotla, Delhi, April 4: DC 129/8 in 20 overs (Shreyas Iyer 43; Mohammad Nabi 2-21, Bhuvneshwar Kumar 2-27) lost to **SRH** 131/5 in 18.3 overs (Jonny Bairstow 48) by five wickets. *PoM:* Jonny Bairstow.

M Chinnaswamy Stadium, Bangalore, April 5: RCB 205/3 in 20 overs (Virat Kohli 84, AB de Villiers 63) lost to **KKR** 206/5 in 19.1 overs (Andre Russell 48*, Chris Lynn 43; Pawan Negi 2-21, Navdeep Saini 2-34) by five wickets. *PoM:* Andre Russell.

MA Chidambaram Stadium, Chepauk, Chennai, April 6: CSK 160/3 in 20 overs (Faf du Plessis 54, MS Dhoni 37*; R Ashwin 3-23) beat **KXIP** 138/5 in 20 overs (Sarfaraz Khan 67, KL Rahul 55; Harbhajan Singh 2-17, Scott Kuggeleijn 2-37) by 22 runs. *PoM:* Harbhajan Singh.

Rajiv Gandhi International Stadium, Uppal, Hyderabad, April 6: MI 136/7 in 20 overs (Kieron Pollard 46; Siddharth Kaul 2-34) beat **SRH** 96 in 17.4 overs (Alzarri Joseph 6-12, Rahul Chahar 2-21) by 40 runs. *PoM:* Alzarri Joseph.

M Chinnaswamy Stadium, Bangalore, April 7: RCB 149/8 in 20 overs (Virat Kohli 41, Moeen Ali 32; Kagiso Rabada 4-21, Chris Morris 2-28) lost to **DC** 152/6 in 18.5 overs (Shreyas Iyer 68, Prithvi Shaw 28; Navdeep Saini 2-24) by four wickets. *PoM:* Kagiso Rabada.

Sawai Mansingh Stadium, Jaipur, April 7: RR 139/3 in 20 overs (Steve Smith 73*, Jos Buttler 37; Harry Gurney 2-25) lost to **KKR** 140/2 in 13.5 overs (Chris Lynn 50, Sunil Narine 47; Shreyas Gopal 2-35) by eight wickets. *PoM:* Harry Gurney.

Punjab Cricket Association IS Bindra Stadium, Mohali, April 8: SRH 150/4 in 20 overs (David Warner 70*, Vijay Shankar 26) lost to **KXIP** 151/4 in 19.5 overs (KL Rahul 71*, Mayank Agarwal 55; Sandeep Sharma 2-21) by six wickets. *PoM:* KL Rahul.

MA Chidambaram Stadium, Chepauk, Chennai, April 9: KKR 108/9 in 20 overs (Andre Russell 50*; Deepak Chahar 3-20, Harbhajan Singh 2-15) lost to **CSK** 111/3 in 17.2 overs (Faf du Plessis 43*; Sunil Narine 2-24) by seven wickets. *PoM:* Deepak Chahar.

Wankhede Stadium, Mumbai, April 10: KXIP 197/4 in 20 overs (KL Rahul 100*, Chris Gayle 63; Hardik Pandya 2-57) lost to **MI** 198/7 in 20 overs (Kieron Pollard 83; Mohammed Shami 3-21) by three wickets. *PoM:* Kieron Pollard.

Sawai Mansingh Stadium, Jaipur, April 11: RR 151/7 in 20 overs (Ben Stokes 28; Ravindra Jadeja 2-20, Deepak Chahar 2-33) lost to **CSK** 155/6 in 20 overs (MS Dhoni 58, Ambati Rayudu 57; B Stokes 2-39) by four wickets. *PoM:* MS Dhoni.

Eden Gardens, Kolkata, April 12: KKR 178/7 in 20 overs (Shubman Gill 65, Andre Russell 45; Chis Morris 2-58, Kagiso Rabada 2-42) lost to **DC** 180/3 in 18.5 overs (Shikhar Dhawan 97*, Rishabh Pant 46) by seven wickets. *PoM:* Shikhar Dhawan.

Wankhede Stadium, Mumbai, April 13: MI 187/5 in 20 overs (Quinton de Kock 81, Rohit Sharma 47; Jofra Archer 3-39) lost to **RR** 188/6 in 19.3 overs (Jos Buttler 89, Ajinkya Rahane 37; Krunal Pandya 3-34, Jasprit Bumrah 2-23) by four wickets. *PoM:* Jos Buttler.

Punjab Cricket Association IS Bindra Stadium, Mohali, April 13: KXIP 173/4 in 20 overs (Chris Gayle 99*; Yuzvendra Chahal 2-33) lost to **RCB** 174/2 in 19.2 overs (Virat Kohli 67, AB de Villiers 59*) by eight wickets. *PoM:* AB de Villiers.

Eden Gardens, Kolkata, April 14: KKR 161/8 in 20 overs (Chris Lynn 82; Imran Tahir 4-27, Shardul Thakur 2-18) lost to **CSK** 162/5 in 19.4 overs (Suresh Raina 58*, Ravindra Jadeja 31*; Sunil Narine 2-19, Piyush Chawla 2-32) by five wickets. *PoM:* Imran Tahir.

Rajiv Gandhi International Stadium, Uppal, Hyderabad, April 14: DC 155/7 in 20 overs (Shreyas Iyer 45, Colin Munro 40; Khaleel Ahmed 3-30, Bhuvneshwar Kumar 2-33) beat **SRH** 116 in 18.5 overs (David Warner 51, Jonny Bairstow 41; Kagiso Rabada 4-22, Keemo Paul 3-17, Chris Morris 3-22) by 39 runs. *PoM:* Keemo Paul.

Wankhede Stadium, Mumbai, April 15: RCB 171/7 in 20 overs (AB de Villiers 75, Moeen Ali 50; Lasith Malinga 4-31) lost to **MI** 172/5 in 20 overs (Quinton de Kock 40, Hardik Pandya 37*; Moeen Ali 2-18, Yuzvendra Chahal 2-27) by five wickets. *PoM:* Lasith Malinga.

Punjab Cricket Association IS Bindra Stadium, Mohali, April 16: KXIP 182/6 in 20 overs (KL Rahul 52, David Miller 40; Jofra Archer 3-15) beat **RR** 170/7 in 20 overs (Rahul Tripathi 50, Stuart Binny 35*; R Ashwin 2-24, Arshdeep Singh 2-43) by 12 runs. *PoM:* R Ashwin.

Rajiv Gandhi International Stadium, Uppal, Hyderabad, April 17: CSK 132/5 in 20 overs (Faf du Plessis 45, Shane Watson 31; Rashid Khan 2-17) lost to **SRH** 137/4 in 16.5 overs (Jonny Bairstow 61*, David Warner 50; Imran Tahir 2-20) by six wickets. *PoM:* David Warner.

Feroz Shah Kotla, Delhi, April 18: MI 168/5 in 20 overs (Krunal Pandya 37*, Quinton de Kock 35; Kagiso Rabada 2-38) beat **DC** 128/9 in 20 overs (Shikhar Dhawan 35, Axar Patel 26; Rahul Chahar 3-19, Jasprit Bumrah 2-18) by 40 runs. *PoM:* Hardik Pandya.

Eden Gardens, Kolkata, April 19: RCB 213/4 in 20 overs (Virat Kohli 100, Moeen Ali 66) beat **KKR** 203/5 in 20 overs (Nitish Rana 85*, Andre Russell 65; Dale Steyn 2-40) by 10 runs. *PoM:* Virat Kohli.

Sawai Mansingh Stadium, Jaipur, April 20: MI 161/5 in 20 overs (Quinton de Kock 65, Suryakumar Yadav 34; Shreyas Gopal 2-21) lost to **RR** 162/5 in 19.1 overs (Steven Smith 59*, Riyan Parag 43; Rahul Chahar 3-29) by five wickets. *PoM:* Steven Smith.

Feroz Shah Kotla, Delhi, April 20: KXIP 163/7 in 20 overs (Chris Gayle 69, Mandeep Singh 30; Sandeep Lamichhane 3-40, Axar Patel 2-22) lost to **DC** 166/5 in 19.4 overs (Shreyas Iyer 58*, Shikhar Dhawan 56; Hardus Viljoen 2-39) by five wickets. *PoM:* Shreyas Iyer.

Rajiv Gandhi International Stadium, Uppal, Hyderabad, April 21: KKR 159/8 in 20 overs (Chris Lynn 51, Rinku Singh 30; Khaleel Ahmed 3-33, Bhuvneshwar Kumar 2-25) lost to **SRH** 161/1 in 15 overs (Jonny Bairstow 80*, David Warner 67) by nine wickets. *PoM:* Khaleel Ahmed.

M Chinnaswamy Stadium, Bangalore, April 21: RCB 161/7 in 20 overs (Parthiv Patel 53, Moeen Ali 26; Deepak Chahar 2-25, Ravindra Jadeja 2-29) beat **CSK** 160/8 in 20 overs (MS Dhoni 84*, Ambati Rayudu 29; Dale Steyn 2-29, Umesh Yadav 2-47) by one run. *PoM:* Parthiv Patel.

Sawai Mansingh Stadium, Jaipur, April 22: RR 191/6 in 20 overs (Ajinkya Rahane 105*, Steven Smith 50; Kagiso Rabada 2-37) lost to **DC** 193/4 in 19.2 overs (Rishabh Pant 78*, Shikhar Dhawan 54; Shreyas Gopal 2-47) by six wickets. *PoM:* Rishabh Pant.

MA Chidambaram Stadium, Chepauk, Chennai, April 23: SRH 175/3 in 20 overs (Manish Pandey 83*, David Warner 57; Harbhajan Singh 2-39) lost to **CSK** 176/4 in 19.5 overs (Shane Watson 96, Suresh Raina 38) by six wickets. *PoM:* Shane Watson.

M Chinnaswamy Stadium, Bangalore, April 24: RCB 202/4 in 20 overs (AB de Villiers 82*, Marcus Stoinis 46*) beat **KXIP** 185/7 in 20 overs (Nicholas Pooran 46, KL Rahul 42; Umesh Yadav 3-36, Navdeep Saini 2-33) by 17 runs. *PoM:* AB de Villiers.

Eden Gardens, Kolkata, April 25: KKR 175/6 in 20 overs (Dinesh Karthik 97*; Varun Aaron 2-20) lost to **RR** 177/7 in 19.2 overs (Riyan Parag 47, Ajinkya Rahane 34; Piyush Chawla 3-20, Sunil Narine 2-25) by three wickets. *PoM:* Varun Aaron.

MA Chidambaram Stadium, Chepauk, Chennai, April 26: MI 155/4 in 20 overs (Rohit Sharma 67, Evin Lewis 32; Mitchell Santner 2-13) beat **CSK** 109 in 17.4 overs (M Vijay 38; Lasith Malinga 4-37, Krunal Pandya 2-7) by 46 runs. *PoM:* Rohit Sharma.

Sawai Mansingh Stadium, Jaipur, April 27: SRH 160/8 in 20 overs (Manish Pandey 61, David Warner 37; Jaydev Unadkat 2-26, Oshane Thomas 2-28) lost to **RR** 161/3 in 19.1 overs (Sanju Samson 48*, Liam Livingstone 44) by seven wickets. *PoM:* Jaydev Unadkat.

Feroz Shah Kotla, Delhi, April 28: DC 187/5 in 20 overs (Shreyas Iyer 52, Shikhar Dhawan 50; Yuzvendra Chahal 2-41) beat **RCB** 171/7 in 20 overs (Parthiv Patel 39, Marcus Stoinis 32*; Amit Mishra 2-29, Kagiso Rabada 2-31) by 16 runs. *PoM:* Shikhar Dhawan.

Chennai's Deepak Chahar was the third-highest wicket-taker (22), while also sending down the most number of dot balls (190). — *BCCI/Sportzpics*

Eden Gardens, Kolkata, April 28: KKR 232/2 in 20 overs (Andre Russell 80*, Shubman Gill 76) beat **MI** 198/7 in 20 overs (Hardik Pandya 91, Suryakumar Yadav 26; A Russell 2-25, Harry Gurney 2-37) by 34 runs. *PoM: Andre Russell.*

Rajiv Gandhi International Stadium, Uppal, Hyderabad, April 29: SRH 212/6 in 20 overs (David Warner 81, Manish Pandey 36; R Ashwin 2-30, Mohammed Shami 2-36) beat **KXIP** 167/8 in 20 overs (KL Rahul 79, Mayank Agarwal 27; Rashid Khan 3-21, Khaleel Ahmed 3-40) by 45 runs. *PoM:* David Warner.

M Chinnaswamy Stadium, Bangalore, April 30: RCB 62/7 in 5 overs (Virat Kohli 25; Shreyas Gopal 3-12, Oshane Thomas 2-6) vs **RR** 41/1 in 3.2 overs (Sanju Samson 28). No result.

MA Chidambaram Stadium, Chepauk, Chennai, May 1: CSK 179/4 in 20 overs (Suresh Raina 59, MS Dhoni 44*; Jagadeesha Suchith 2-28) beat **DC** 99 in 16.2 overs (Shreyas Iyer 44; Imran Tahir 4-12, Ravindra Jadeja 3-9) by 80 runs. *PoM:* MS Dhoni.

Wankhede Stadium, Mumbai, May 2: MI 162/5 in 20 overs (Quinton de Kock 69*; Khaleel Ahmed 3-42) tied with **SRH** 162/6 in 20 overs (Manish Pandey 71*, Mohammad Nabi 31; Hardik Pandya 2-20, Krunal Pandya 2-22). **Super over: SRH** 8/2 in 0.4 overs lost to **MI** 9 for no loss in 0.3 overs in super over. *PoM:* Jasprit Bumrah.

Punjab Cricket Association IS Bindra Stadium, Mohali, May 3: KXIP 183/6 in 20 overs (Sam Curran 55*, Nicholas Pooran 48; Sandeep Warrier 2-31) lost to **KKR** 185/3 in 18 overs (Shubman Gill 65*, Chris Lynn 46) by seven wickets. *PoM:* Shubman Gill.

Feroz Shah Kotla, Delhi, May 4: RR 115/9 in 20 overs (Riyan Parag 50; Amit Mishra 3-17, Ishant Sharma 3-38) lost to **DC** 121/5 in 16.1 overs (Rishabh Pant 53*; Ish Sodhi 3-26, Shreyas Gopal 2-21) by five wickets. *PoM:* Amit Mishra.

Chinnaswamy Stadium, Bangalore, May 4: SRH 175/7 in 20 overs (Kane Williamson 70*, Martin Guptill 30; Washington Sundar 3-24, Navdeep Saini 2-39) lost to **RCB** 178/6 in 19.2 overs (Shimron Hetmyer 75, Gurkeerat Singh 65; Khaleel Ahmed 3-37, Bhuvneshwar Kumar 2-24) by four wickets. *PoM:* Shimron Hetmyer.

Punjab Cricket Association IS Bindra Stadium, Mohali, May 5: CSK 170/5 in 20 overs (Faf du Plessis 96, Suresh Raina 53; Sam Curran 3-35, Mohammed Shami 2-17) lost to **KXIP** 173/4 in 18 overs (KL Rahul 71, Nicholas Pooran 36; Harbhajan Singh 3-57) by six wickets. *PoM:* KL Rahul.

Wankhede Stadium, Mumbai, May 5: KKR 133/7 in 20 overs (Chris Lynn 41, Robin Uthappa 40; Lasith Malinga 3-35, Hardik Pandya 2-20) lost to **MI** 134/1 in 16.1 overs (Rohit Sharma 55*, Suryakumar Yadav 46*) by nine wickets. *PoM:* Hardik Pandya.

Points table

Teams	M	W	L	T	NR	Pts.	NRR
Mumbai Indians	14	9	5	0	0	18	+0.421
Chennai Super Kings	14	9	5	0	0	18	+0.131
Delhi Capitals	14	9	5	0	0	18	+0.044
Sunrisers Hyderabad	14	6	8	0	0	12	+0.577
Kolkata Knight Riders	14	6	8	0	0	12	+0.028
Kings XI Punjab	14	6	8	0	0	12	-0.251
Rajasthan Royals	14	5	8	0	1	11	-0.449
Royal Challengers Bangalore	14	5	8	0	1	11	-0.607

Mumbai Indians and Chennai Super Kings qualified for Qualifier 1
Delhi Capitals and Sunrisers Hyderabad qualified for Eliminator

Qualifier 1: MI beat CSK by six wickets

• Both sides field an off-spinner, a leg-spinner and a left-arm finger-spinner on a slow Chepauk pitch; all six live up to expectations. • Chennai begin slowly, meandering to 68 for 4 in 13 overs at the second strategic timeout. • A late recovery from Ambati Rayudu and MS Dhoni is not enough to take them beyond 131 for 4. • Mumbai lose both openers by the fourth over with just 21 on the board. • With a 54-ball 71 not out, Suryakumar Yadav ensures there is no further mishap. • Mumbai beat Chennai for the third time in IPL 2019 and for the sixth time in a row at 'fortress' Chepauk.

MA Chidambaram Stadium, Chepauk, Chennai, May 7: Chennai Super Kings 131/4 in 20 overs (Ambati Rayudu 42*, MS Dhoni 37*; Rahul Chahar 2-14) lost to **Mumbai Indians**

Delhi's young brigade of Pant (in pic), Shaw and Iyer played an exciting brand of cricket that took them to the play-offs. — *BCCI/Sportzpics*

132/4 in 18.3 overs (Suryakumar Yadav 71*, Ishan Kishan 28; Imran Tahir 2-33) by six wickets. *PoM:* Suryakumar Yadav.

Eliminator: DC beat SRH by two wickets

• With four sixes in a 19-ball 36, Martin Guptill helps Sunrisers put up 54 for 1 in the Powerplay. • Amit Mishra (4-0-16-1) pegs Hyderabad back before Vijay Shankar and Mohammad Nabi take them to 162 for 8. • Prithvi Shaw (56 in 38) leads the charge for Delhi; they get 55 for 1 in the Powerplay before losing three quick wickets. • Rashid Khan (4-1-15-2) strikes twice but Rishabh Pant (49 in 21) marches on, taking 22 off the 18th over, bowled by Basil Thampi. • Mishra is given out obstructing the field, leaving Delhi to score two in two balls with two wickets in hand. • Keemo Paul hits the penultimate ball off midwicket for four.

Dr YS Rajasekhara Reddy ACA-VDCA Cricket Stadium, Visakhapatnam, May 8: Sunrisers Hyderabad 162/8 in 20 overs (Martin Guptill 36, Manish Pandey 30; Keemo Paul 3-32, Ishant Sharma 2-34) lost to **Delhi Capitals** 165/8 in 19.5 overs (Prithvi Shaw 56, Rishabh Pant 49; Rashid Khan 2-15, Khaleel Ahmed 2-24) by two wickets. *PoM:* Rishabh Pant.

DC qualified for Qualifier 2

Qualifier 2: CSK beat DC by six wickets

• Two early blows prevent Delhi from getting off to a flying start. • Pant begins cautiously but loses partners at the other end. • He is eventually eighth out, failing to clear long-on in the 19th over. • Faf du Plessis and Shane Watson take their time; only 16 come off the first four overs before they explode, taking 65 off the next six. • Du Plessis and Watson both fall for exactly 50 runs apiece. • It's enough for Chennai to ease to the win in the 19th over.

Dr YS Rajasekhara Reddy ACA-VDCA Cricket Stadium, Visakhapatnam, May 10: Delhi Capitals 147/9 in 20 overs (Rishabh Pant 38, Colin Munro 27; Dwayne Bravo 2-19, Ravindra Jadeja 2-23) lost to **Chennai Super Kings** 151/4 in 19 overs (Faf du Plessis 50, Shane Watson 50) by six wickets. *PoM:* Faf du Plessis.

Final: MI beat CSK by one run

Deepak Chahar strangles Mumbai in the Powerplay; they take seven overs to reach 50. • Kieron Pollard's late flourish — a 25-ball unbeaten 41 — takes them to 149 for 8. • With a 59-ball 80, Watson wages a lone battle for Chennai against Jasprit Bumrah (4-0-14-2) and co. • Dhoni is run out controversially — different angles suggest different outcomes — while trying to make the most of an overthrow. • With five to score off three, Watson is run out attempting a second run. • With two to defend off the last ball, Lasith Malinga traps Shardul Thakur leg-before with a slow, straight yorker. • Mumbai win their third IPL, all in alternate years, and their second consecutive final by a one-run margin.

Rajiv Gandhi International Stadium, Uppal, Hyderabad, May 12: Mumbai Indians 149/8 in 20 overs (Kieron Pollard 41*, Quinton de Kock 29; Deepak Chahar 3-26, Imran Tahir 2-23) beat **Chennai Super Kings** 148/7 in 20 overs (Shane Watson 80, Faf du Plessis 26; Jasprit Bumrah 2-14) by one run. *PoM:* Jasprit Bumrah. *PoS (MVP):* Andre Russell.

Winners: Mumbai Indians

2018

Wankhede Stadium, Mumbai, April 7: MI 165/4 in 20 overs (Suryakumar Yadav 43, Hardik Pandya 41*; Shane Watson 2-29) lost to **CSK** 169/9 in 19.5 overs (Dwayne Bravo 68, Kedar Jadhav 24*) by one wicket. *PoM*: Dwayne Bravo.

PCA IS Bindra Stadium, Mohali, April 8: DD 166/7 in 20 overs (Gautam Gambhir 55, Rishabh Pant 28; Mujeeb Ur Rahman 2-28, Mohit Sharma 2-33) lost to **KXIP** 167/4 in 18.5 overs (KL Rahul 51, Karun Nair 50) by six wickets. *PoM*: KL Rahul.

Eden Gardens, Kolkata, April 8: RCB 176/7 in 20 overs (AB de Villiers 44, Brendon McCullum 43; Nitish Rana 2-11, Vinay Kumar 2-30) lost to **KKR** 177/6 in 18.5 overs (Sunil Narine 50, Dinesh Karthik 35*; Chris Woakes 3-36, Umesh Yadav 2-27) by four wickets. *PoM*: Sunil Narine.

Rajiv Gandhi International Stadium, Uppal, Hyderabad, April 9: RR 125/9 in 20 overs (Sanju Samson 49; SiDD arth Kaul 2-17, Shakib Al Hasan 2-23) lost to **SRH** 127/1 in 15.5 overs (Shikhar Dhawan 78*, Kane Williamson 36*) by nine wickets. *PoM*: Shikhar Dhawan.

MA Chidambaram Stadium, Chepauk, Chennai, April 10: KKR 202/6 in 20 overs (Andre Russell 88*, Robin Uthappa 29; Shane Watson 2-39) lost to **CSK** 205/5 in 19.5 overs (Sam Billings 56, S Watson 42; Tom Curran 2-39) by five wickets. *PoM*: Sam Billings.

Sawai Mansingh Stadium, Jaipur, April 11: RR 153/5 in 17.5 overs (Ajinkya Rahane 45, Sanju Samson 37; Shahbaz Nadeem 2-34) beat **DD** 60/4 in 6 overs (Rishabh Pant 20; Ben Laughlin 2-20) by 10 runs (D/L method). *PoM*: Sanju Samson.

Rajiv Gandhi International Stadium, Uppal, Hyderabad, April 12: MI 147/8 in 20 overs (Evin Lewis 29, Kieron Pollard 28; Sandeep Sharma 2-25, Siddarth Kaul 2-29) lost to **SRH** 151/9 in 20 overs (Shikhar Dhawan 45, Deepak Hooda 32*; Mayank Markande 4-23, Mustafizur Rahman 3-24) by one wicket. *PoM*: Rashid Khan.

M Chinnaswamy Stadium, Bengaluru, April 13: KXIP 155 in 19.2 overs (KL Rahul 47, R Ashwin 33; Umesh Yadav 3-23, Washington Sundar 2-22) lost to **RCB** 159/6 in 19.3 overs (AB de Villiers 57, Quinton de Kock 45; Ashwin 2-30) by four wickets. *PoM*: Umesh Yadav.

Wankhede Stadium, Mumbai, April 14: MI 194/7 in 20 overs (Suryakumar Yadav 53, Evin Lewis 48; Daniel Christian 2-35, Rahul Tewatia 2-36) lost to **DD** 195/3 in 20 overs (Jason Roy 91*, Rishabh Pant 47; Krunal Pandya 2-21) by seven wickets. *PoM*: Jason Roy.

Eden Gardens, Kolkata, April 14: KKR 138/8 in 20 overs (Chris Lynn 49, Dinesh Karthik 29; Bhuvneshwar Kumar 3-26, Billy Stanlake 2-21, Shakib Al Hasan 2-21) lost to **SRH** 139/5 in 19 overs (Kane Williamson 50, Shakib 27; Sunil Narine 2-17) by five wickets. *PoM*: Billy Stanlake.

M Chinnaswamy Stadium, Bengaluru, April 15: RR 217/4 in 20 overs (Sanju Samson 92*, Ajinkya Rahane 36; Yuzvendra Chahal 2-22, Chris Woakes 2-47) beat **RCB** 198/6 in 20 overs (Virat Kohli 57, Mandeep Singh 47*; Shreyas Gopal 2-22) by 19 runs. *PoM*: Sanju Samson.

PCA IS Bindra Stadium, Mohali, April 15: KXIP 197/7 in 20 overs (Chris Gayle 63, KL Rahul 37; Shardul Thakur 2-33, Imran Tafir 2-34) beat **CSK** 193/5 in 20 overs (MS Dhoni 79*, Ambati Rayudu 49; Andrew Tye 2-47) by four runs. *PoM*: Chris Gayle.

Eden Gardens, Kolkata, April 16: KKR 200/9 in 20 overs (Nitish Rana 59, Andre Russell 41; Rahul Tewatia 3-18, Trent Boult 2-29) beat **DD** 129 in 14.2 overs (Glenn Maxwell 47, Rishabh Pant 43; Sunil Narine 3-18, Kuldeep Yadav 3-32) by 71 runs. *PoM*: Nitish Rana.

Wankhede Stadium, Mumbai, April 17: MI 213/6 in 20 overs (Rohit Sharma 94, Evin Lewis 65; Umesh Yadav 2-36, Corey Anderson 2-47) beat **RCB** 167/8 in 20 overs (Virat Kohli 92*; Krunal Pandya 3-28, Mitchelll McClenaghan 2-24) by 46 runs. *PoM*: Rohit Sharma.

Sawai Mansingh Stadium, Jaipur, April 18: RR 160/8 in 20 overs (D'Arcy Short 44, Ajinkya Rahane 36; Nitish Rana 2-11, Tom Curran 2-19) lost to **KKR** 163/3 in 18.5 overs (Robin Uthappa 48, Dinesh Karthik 34*; K Gowtham 2-23) by seven wickets. *PoM*: Nitish Rana.

PCA IS Bindra Stadium, Mohali, April 19: KXIP 193/3 in 20 overs (Chris Gayle 104*, Karun Nair 31) beat **SRH** 178/4 in 20 overs (Manish Pandey 57*, Kane Williamson 54; Andrew Tye 2-23, Mohit Sharma 2-51) by 15 runs. *PoM*: Chris Gayle.

MCA Stadium, Pune, April 20: CSK 204/5 in 20 overs (Shane Watson 106, Suresh Raina 46; Shreyas Gopal 3-20, Ben Laughlin 2-38) beat **RR** 140 in 18.3 overs (Ben Stokes 45, Jos Buttler 22; Karn Sharma 2-13, Dwayne Bravo 2-16) by 64 runs. *PoM*: Shane Watson.

Eden Gardens, Kolkata, April 21: KKR 191/7 in 20 overs (Chris Lynn 74, Dinesh Karthik 43; Andrew Tye 2-30, Barinder Sran 2-50) lost to **KXIP** 126/1 in 11.1 overs (Chris Gayle 62*, KL Rahul 60) by nine wickets (D/L method). *PoM*: KL Rahul.

M Chinnaswamy Stadium, Bengaluru, April 21: DD 174/5 in 20 overs (Rishabh Pant 85, Shreyas Iyer 52; Yuzvendra Chahal 2-22) lost to **RCB** 176/4 in 18 overs (AB de Villers 90*, Virat Kohli 30) by six wickets. *PoM*: AB de Villers.

Rajiv Gandhi International Stadium, Uppal, Hyderabad, April 22: CSK 182/3 in 20 overs (Ambati Rayudu 79, Suresh Raina 54*) beat **SRH** 178/6 in 20 overs (Kane Williamson 84, Yusuf Pathan 45; Deepak Chahar 3-15) by four runs. *PoM*: Ambati Rayudu.

Sawai Mansingh Stadium, Jaipur, April 22: MI 167/7 in 20 overs (Suryakumar Yadav 72,

Rashid Khan's 21 wickets came at an economy-rate of 6.73, the best among bowlers who'd played at least ten games. — *BCCI*

Ishan Kishan 58; Jofra Archer 3-22, Dhawal Kulkarni 2-32) lost to **RR** 168/7 in 19.4 overs (Sanju Samson 52, Ben Stokes 40; Hardik Pandya 2-25, Jasprit Bumrah 2-28) by three wickets. *PoM*: Jofra Archer.

Feroz Shah Kotla, Delhi, April 23: KXIP 143/8 in 20 overs (Karun Nair 34, David MI ler 26; Liam Plunkett 3-17, Trent Boult 2-21) beat **DD** 139/8 in 20 overs (Shreyas Iyer 57, Rahul Tewatia 24; Ankit Rajpoot 2-23, Andrew Tye 2-25, Mujeeb Ur Rahman 2-25) by four runs. *PoM*: Ankit Rajpoot.

Wankhede Stadium, Mumbai, April 24: SRH 118 in 18.4 overs (Kane Williamson 29, Yusuf Pathan 29; Mayank Markande 2-15, Hardik Pandya 2-20) beat **MI** 87 in 18.5 overs (Suryakumar Yadav 34, Krunal Pandya 24; Siddarth Kaul 3-23, Basil Thampi 2-4) by 31 runs. *PoM*: Rashid Khan.

M Chinnaswamy Stadium, Bengaluru, April 25: RCB 205/8 in 20 overs (AB de Villiers

68, Quinton de Kock 53; Dwayne Bravo 2-33, Imran Tahir 2-35) lost to **CSK** 207/5 in 19.4 overs (Ambati Rayudu 82, MS Dhoni 70*; Yuzvendra Chahal 2-26) by five wickets. *PoM*: MS Dhoni.

Rajiv Gandhi International Stadium, Uppal, Hyderabad, April 26: SRH 132/6 in 20 overs (Manish Pandey 54, Shakib Al Hasan 28; Ankit Rajpoot 5-14) beat **KXIP** 119 in 19.2 overs (KL Rahul 32, Chris Gayle 23; Rashid Khan 3-19, Basil Thampi 2-14) by 13 runs. *PoM*: Ankit Rajpoot.

Feroz Shah Kotla, Delhi, April 27: DD 219/4 in 20 overs (Shreyas Iyer 93*, Prithvi Shaw 62) beat **KKR** 164/9 in 20 overs (Andre Russell 44, Shubman Gill 37; Glenn Maxwell 2-22, AMI t Mishra 2-23) by 55 runs. *PoM*: Shreyas Iyer.

MCA Stadium, Pune, April 28: CSK 169/5 in 20 overs (Suresh Raina 75*, Ambati Rayudu 46; Mitchell McClenaghan 2-26, Krunal Pandya 2-32) lost to **MI** 170/2 in 19.4 overs (Rohit Sharma 56*, Evin Lewis 47) by eight wickets. *PoM*: Rohit Sharma.

Sawai Mansingh Stadium, Jaipur, April 29: SRH 151/7 in 20 overs (Kane Williamson 63, Alex Hales 45; Jofra Archer 3-26, K Gowtham 2-18) beat **RR** 140/6 in 20 overs (Ajinkya Rahane 65*, Sanju Samson 40; Siddarth Kaul 2-23) by 11 runs. *PoM*: Kane Williamson.

M Chinnaswamy Stadium, Bengaluru, April 29: RCB 175/4 in 20 overs (Virat Kohli 68*, Brendon McCullum 38; Andre Russell 3-31) lost to **KKR** 176/4 in 19.1 overs (Chris Lynn 62*. Robin Uthappa 36; M Ashwin 2-36, Mohammed Siraj 2-40) by six wickets. *PoM*: Chris Lynn.

MCA Stadium, Pune, April 30: CSK 211/4 in 20 overs (Shane Watson 78, MS Dhoni 51*) beat **DD** 198/5 in 20 overs (Rishabh Pant 79, Vijay Shankar 54*; KM Asif 2-43) by 13 runs. *PoM*: Shane Watson.

M Chinnaswamy Stadium, Bengaluru, May 1: RCB 167/7 in 20 overs (Manan Vohra 45, Brendon McCullum 37; Hardik Pandya 3-28) beat **MI** 153/7 in 20 overs (H Pandya 50, Krunal Pandya 23; Tim Southee 2-25, Mohammed Siraj 2-28) by 14 runs. *PoM*: Tim Southee.

Feroz Shah Kotla, Delhi, May 2: DD 196/6 in 20 overs (Rishabh Pant 69, Shreyas Iyer 50; Jaydev Unadkat 3-46) beat **RR** 146/5 in 12 overs (Jos Buttler 67, D'Arcy Short 44; Trent Boult 2-26) by 4 runs (D/L method). *PoM*: Rishabh Pant.

Eden Gardens, Kolkata, May 3: CSK 177/5 in 20 overs (MS Dhoni 43*, Shane Watson 36; Sunil Narine 2-20, Piyush Chawla 2-35) lost to **KKR** 180/4 in 17.4 overs (Shubman Gill 57*, Dinesh Karthik 45*) by six wickets. *PoM*: Sunil Narine.

Holkar Cricket Stadium, Indore, May 4: KXIP 174/6 in 20 overs (Chris Gayle 50, Marcus Stoinis 29*) lost to **MI** 176/4 in 19 overs (Suryakuamr Yadav 57, Krunal Pandya 31*; Mujeeb Ur Rahman 2-37) by six wickets. *PoM*: Suryakuamr Yadav.

MCA Stadium, Pune, May 5: RCB 127/9 in 20 overs (Parthiv Patel 53, Time Southee 36*; Ravindra Jadeja 3-18, Harbhajan Singh 2-22) lost to **CSK** 128/4 in 18 overs (Ambati Rayudu 32, MS Dhoni 31*; Umesh Yadav 2-15) by six wickets. *PoM*: Ravindra Jadeja.

Rajiv Gandhi International Stadium, Uppal, Hyderabad, May 5: DD 163/5 in 20 overs (Prithvi Shaw 65, Shreyas Iyer 44; Rashid Khan 2-23) lost to **SRH** 164/3 in 19.5 overs (Alex Hales 45, Shikhar Dhawan 33; AMI t MI shra 2-19) by seven wickets. *PoM*: Rashid Khan.

Wankhede Stadium, Mumbai, May 6: MI 181/4 in 20 overs (Suryakumar Yadav 59, Evin Lewis 43; Andre Russell 2-12, Sunil Narine 2-35) beat **KKR** 168/6 in 20 overs (Robin Utappa 54, Dinesh Karthik 36*; Hardik Pandya 2-19) by 13 runs. *PoM*: Hardik Pandya.

Holkar Cricket Stadium, Indore, May 6: RR 152/9 in 20 overs (Jos Buttler 51, Sanju Samson 28; Mujeeb Ur Rahman 3-27, Andrew Tye 2-24) lost to **KXIP** 155/4 in 18.4 overs (KL Rahul 84*, Karun Nair 31) by six wickets. *PoM*: Mujeeb Ur Rahman.

Rajiv Gandhi International Stadium, Uppal, Hyderabad, May 7: SRH 146 in 20 overs (Kane Williamson 56, Shakib Al Hasan 35; Mohammed Siraj 3-25, Tim Southee 3-30) beat **RCB** 141/6 in 20 overs (Virat Kohli 39, Colin de Grandhomme 33; Shakib 2-36) by five runs. *PoM*: Kane Williamson.

Sawai Mansingh Stadium, Jaipur, May 8: RR 158/8 in 20 overs (Jos Buttler 82, Sanju Samson 22; Andrew Tye 4-34, Mujeeb Ur Rahman 2-21) beat **KXIP** 143/7 in 20 overs (KL

Rahul 95*; K Gowtham 2-12) by 14 runs. *PoM*: Jos Buttler.

Eden Gardens, Kolkata, May 9: MI 210/6 in 20 overs (Ishan Kishan 62, Suryakumar Yadav 36; Piyush Chawla 3-48) beat **KKR** 108 in 18.1 overs (Chris Lynn21; Nitish Rana 21; Krunal Pandya 2-12, Hardik Pandya 2-16) by 102 runs. *PoM*: Ishan Kishan.

Feroz Shah Kotla, Delhi, May 10: DD 187/5 in 20 overs (Rishabh Pant 128*, Harshal Patel 24; Shakib Al Hasan 2-27) lost to **SRH** 191/1 in 18.5 overs (Shikhar Dhawan 92*, Kane Williamson 83*) by nine wickets. *PoM*: Shikhar Dhawan.

Sawai Mansingh Stadium, Jaipur, May 11: CSK 176/4 in 20 overs (Suresh Raina 52, Shane Watson 39; Jofra Archer 2-42) lost to **RR** 177/6 in 19.5 overs (Jos Buttler 95*, Stuart Binny 22) by four wickets. *PoM*: Jos Buttler.

Holkar Cricket Stadium, Indore, May 12: KKR 245/6 in 20 overs (Sunil Narine 75, Dinesh Karthik 50; Andrew Tye 4-41) beat **KXIP** 214/8 in 20 overs (KL Rahul 66, R Ashwin 45; Andre Russell 3-41, Prasidh Krishna 2-31) by 31 runs. *PoM*: Sunil Narine.

Feroz Shah Kotla, Delhi, May 12: DD 181/4 in 20 overs (Rishabh Pant 61, Abhishek Sharma 46*; Yuzvendra Chahal 2-28) lost to **RCB** 187/5 in 19 overs (AB de Villiers 72*, Virat Kohli 70; Trent Boult 2-40) by five wickets. *PoM*: AB de Villiers.

MCA Stadium, Pune, May 13: SRH 179/4 in 20 overs (Shikhar Dhawan 79, Kane Williamson 51; Shardul Thakur 2-32) lost to **CSK** 180/2 in 19 overs (Ambati Rayudu 100*, Shane Watson 57) by eight wickets. *PoM*: Ambati Rayudu.

Wankhede Stadium, Mumbai, May 13: MI 168/6 in 20 overs (Evin Lewis 60, Suryakumar Yadav 38; Jofra Archer 2-16, Ben Stokes2-26) lost to **RR** 171/3 in 18 overs (Jos Buttler 94*, Ajinkya Rahane 37; Hardik Pandya 2-52) by seven wickets. *PoM*: Jos Buttler.

Holkar Cricket Stadium, Indore, May 14: KXIP 88 in 15.1 overs (Aaron Finch 26, KL Rahul 21; Umesh Yadav 3-23) lost to **RCB** 92/0 in 8.1 overs (Virat Kohli 48*, Parthiv Patel 40*) by ten wickets. *PoM*: Umesh Yadav.

Eden Gardens, Kolkata, May 15: RR 142 in 19 overs (Jos Buttler 39, Rahul Tripathi 27; Kuldeep Yadav 4-20, Andre Russelll 2-13) lost to **KKR** 145/4 in 18 overs (Chris Lynn 45, Dinesh Karthik 41*; Ben Stokes 3-15) by six wickets. *PoM*: Kuldeep Yadav.

Wankhede Stadium, Mumbai, May 16: MI 186/8 in 20 overs (Kieron Pollard 50, Krunal Pandya 32; Andrew Tye 4-16, R Ashwin 2-18) beat **KXIP** 183/5 in 20 overs (KL Rahul 94, Aaron Finch 46; Jasrit Bumrah 3-15, Mitchell McClenaghan 2-37) by three runs. *PoM*: Jasrit Bumrah.

M Chinnaswamy Stadium, Bengaluru, May 17: RCB 218/6 in 20 overs (AB de Villiers 69, Moeen Ali 65; Rashid Khan 3-27, Siddarth Kaul 2-44) beat **SRH** 204/3 in 20 overs (Kane Williamson 81, Manish Pandey 62*) by 14 runs. *PoM*: AB de Villiers.

Feroz Shah Kotla, Delhi, May 18: DD 162/5 in 20 overs (Rishabh Pant 38, Vijay Shankar 36*; Lungi Ngidi 2-14) beat **CSK** 128/6 in 20 overs (Ambati Rayudu 50, Ravindra Jadeja 27*; AMI t Mishra 2-20, Trent Boult 2-20) by 34 runs. *PoM*: Harshal Patel.

Sawai Mansingh Stadium, Jaipur, May 19: RR 164/5 in 20 overs (Rahul Tripathi 80*, Ajinkya Rahane 33; Umesh Yadav 3-25) beat **RCB** 134 in 19.2 overs (AB de Villiers 53, Parthiv Patel 33; Shreyas Gopal 4-16, Ben Laughlin 2-15) by 30 runs. *PoM*: Shreyas Gopal.

Rajiv Gandhi International Stadium, May 19: SRH 172/9 in 20 overs (Shikhar Dhawan 50, Kane Williamson 36; Prasidh Krishna 4-30) lost to **KKR** 173/5 in 19.4 overs (Chris Lynn 55, Robin Uthappa 45; Carlos Brathwaite 2-21, Siddarth Kaul 2-26) by five wickets. *PoM*: Chris Lynn.

Feroz Shah Kotla, Delhi, May 20: DD 174/4 in 20 overs (Rishabh Pant 64, Vijay Shankar 43*) beat **MI** 163 in 19.3 overs (Evin Lewis 48, Ben Cutting 37; Amit Mishra 3-19, Harshal Patel 3-28, Sandeep LaMI chhane 3-36) by 11 runs. *PoM*: Amit Mishra.

MCA Stadium, Pune, May 20: KXIP 153 in 19.4 overs (Karun Nair 54, Manoj Tiwary 35; Lungi Ngidi 4-10, Shardul Thakur 2-33) lost to **CSK** 159/5 in 19.1 overs (Suresh Raina 61*, Deepak Chahar 39; Ankit Rajpoot 2-19, R Ashwin 2-36) by five wickets. *PoM*: Lungi Ngidi.

Points table

Teams	M	W	L	T	N/R	Pts.	NRR
Sunrisers Hyderabad	14	9	5	0	0	18	0.284
Chennai Super Kings	14	9	5	0	0	18	0.253
Kolkata Knight Riders	14	8	6	0	0	16	-0.070
Rajasthan Royals	14	7	7	0	0	14	-0.250
Mumbai Indians	14	6	8	0	0	12	0.317
Royal Challengers Bangalore	14	6	8	0	0	12	0.129
Kings XI Punjab	14	6	8	0	0	12	-0.502
Delhi Daredevils	14	5	9	0	0	10	-0.222

SRH , CSK , KKR , RR qualified for the playoffs

Qualifier 1: CSK beat SRH by two wickets

• Deepak Chahar, Lungi Ngidi and Shardul Thakur pick up a wicket each to leave Hyderabad at 36 for 3 after Chennai opt to field. • Dwayne Bravo picks up two, as Hyderabad slide to a sorry 88 for 6 after 15 overs. • Carlos Brathwaite slams a 29-ball 43 not out to give the innings respectability. • The target didn't look like much, but Bhuvneshwar Kumar and Siddarth Kaul reduce Chennai to 24 for 3 by the fourth over. • Rashid Khan and Sandeep

Faf du Plessis batted through the innings in a high-pressure game to hold Sunrisers Hyderabad off and carry Chennai Super Kings to another final. — *BCCI/Sportspocz*

Sharma pick up two apiece to leave Chennai in a hole at 113 for 8. • Faf du Plessis plays his best innings of the tournament, unbeaten on 67 in 42 balls after opening the innings to take Chennai to victory.

Wankhede Stadium, Mumbai, May 22: SRH 139/7 in 20 overs (Carlos Brathwaite 43*, Kane Williamson 24; Dwayne Bravo 2-25) lost to **CSK** 140/8 in 19.1 overs (Faf du Plessis 67*, Suresh Raina 22; Rashid Khan 2-11, Sandeep Sharma 2-30) by two wickets. *PoM:* Faf du Plessis.

Eliminator: KKR beat RR by 25 runs

• Rajasthan field, and K Gowtham, Shreyas and Archer strike early to reduce Kolkata to 24 for 3. • Dinesh Karthik, the captain, and Shubman Gill put together 55 runs for the fifth wicket. • Karthik's half-century and Russell's frenetic 25-ball 49 not out takes them to a healthy total. • Rajasthan's chase starts well with a 47-run stand between openers Rahane and Rahul Tripathi. • After Tripathi falls to Piyush Chawla, Rahane and Sanju Samson bat sensibly — but slowly — to add another 62 runs. • Heinrich Klaasen scores a run-a-ball 18 not out, but the chase fades away, putting Kolkata in Qualifier 2.

Eden Gardens, Kolkata, May 23: KKR 169/7 in 20 overs (Dinesh Karthik 52, Andre Russell 49*; K Gowtham 2-15, Jofra Archer 2-33) beat **RR** 144/4 in 20 overs (Sanju Samson 50, Ajinkya Rahane 46; Piyush Chawla 2-24) by 25 runs. *PoM*: Andre Russell.

Qualifier 2: SRH beat KKR by 14 runs

• Wriddhiman Saha and Dhawan put together 56 for the first wicket after Kolkata ask Hyderabad to bat first. • Kane Williamson has a rare failure, but Shakib Al Hasan and Deepak Hooda make sure the momentum isn't lost. • The impetus comes from unlikely quarters, as Rashid Khan blitzes away to 34 not out from just ten balls from No.8. • Kolkata start well, the first two wickets putting up 87 runs, with Chris Lynn solid, and Narine and Nitish Rana blazing away. • Rashid and Shakib (1-16) put the brakes on the scoring with a clutch of wickets to leave Kolkata tottering. • Gill does his bit with a responsible 20-ball 30, but doesn't get support from the other end.

Eden Gardens, Kolkata, May 25: SRH 174/7 in 20 overs (Wriddhiman Saha 35, Rashid Khan 34*; Kuldeep Yadav 2-29) beat **KKR** 160/9 in 20 overs (Chris Lynn 48, Shubman Gill 30; Rashid 3-19, Carlos Brathwaite 2-15) by 14 runs. *PoM*: Rashid Khan.

Chennai Super Kings and Sunrisers Hyderabad qualified for the final

Final: CSK beat SRH by eight wickets

• Shreevats Goswami is run out early after Chennai choose to field, but Dhawan and Williamson do well in a 51-run second-wicket stand. • Williamson falls for an innings-high 47 and Shakib for 23, but Hyderabad have reached a strong 133 by then with 4.1 overs left. • Yusuf Pathan slams an unbeaten 45 in 25 balls and Brathwaite 21 in 11 to take Hyderabad to a competitive total. • Chennai start poorly, Shane Watson taking 11 balls to get off the mark and du Plessis falling cheaply in the fourth over. • Watson picks up speed after that and puts together 117 for the second wicket with Suresh Raina, who scores just 32 of those runs. • Watson is at his all-conquering best, smashing 11 fours and eight sixes in a 57-ball 117 not out to rush Chennai to victory with nine balls left.

Wankhede Stadium, Mumbai, May 27: SRH 178/6 in 20 overs (Kane Williamson 47, Yusuf Pathan 45*) lost to **CSK** 181/2 in 18.3 overs (Shane Watson 117*, Suresh Raina 32) by 14 runs. *PoM*: Shane Watson.

Winners: Chennai Super Kings

Atharva Taide put the disappointment of missing out on U19 World Cup selection behind him to lead Vidarbha to the Cooch Behar Trophy title, making a triple-hundred in the final. — *SLC*

Atharva Taide's steady climb to 300

HEMANT BRAR

It's the second half of 2017. Atharva Taide, the 17-year-old left-hand batsman, is practising hard in the Vidarbha Cricket Association nets. The dream is to represent India at the 2018 Under-19 World Cup. More than his dream, it's his father's dream. After all, a successful campaign would put his son on an elevator to the national side.

In October, in the inter-state leg of the Vinoo Mankad 50-over U19 trophy, Taide leads Vidarbha to the top of Central Zone with five wins in as many matches. He himself makes 491 runs, the second-most in the tournament, with two hundred, two fifties and an unbeaten 27.

The next step is the inter-zonal leg. But apart from 52 not out against East Zone, Taide fails to impress. In November, he travels to Malaysia for the U19 Asia Cup. He gets only one game, against Nepal, scoring 13 and taking one wicket with his left-arm spin, as India fail to qualify for the semi-finals.

Then comes the U19 Challenger Trophy, the last chance to impress the selectors before the World Cup. Playing for India Red, Taide kicks off with a 104 against India Blue, but manages only 44 runs in his next three outings to end with 148 runs at an average 37. The Challenger Trophy ends on December 2, and the next day, when the selectors announce the team for the World Cup, Taide's name is not there.

Taide started his cricket in the lanes of Akola. At the age of seven, he joined the Akola Cricket Club. When he turned 11, his father bought an empty space next to their house and set up a bowling machine, lights and nets there. "In the morning, I used to go to school. After school, it was time for the club. And then at night, I practised under lights," Taide recalls those days. "All I did was just play cricket."

When he was 14, he got selected for the VCA academy in Nagpur and slowly but steadily, started climbing the rungs of age-group cricket. Opening the batting for Vidarbha U14 in the Rajsingh Dungarpur Trophy 2013-14, Taide made 75 against Madhya Pradesh in a two-day match. In 2015-16, in the Andhra Cricket Association inter-state U16 quadrangular series, he scored 112 in three innings at an average of 56. Next season, in the Vinoo Mankad zonal league, he tallied 200 runs in five innings, including two half-centuries.

Taide was scoring runs alright, but he was not able to produce those big knocks that would make selectors take notice. During that period, the VCA appointed a new coach, Umesh Patwal, who worked with Taide to take his game to the next level. It was during this time that the seeds of the World Cup dream were sown.

After failing to make it to the World Cup squad, Taide shifted his focus to the Cooch Behar Trophy, the four-day inter-state tournament. He had missed the first two games because of the U19 Asia Cup in Malaysia, but returned to lead Vidarbha to their first-ever title in the tournament.

Taide's 124 against Punjab in the semi-final took his side to the final, where he emulated Yuvraj Singh by scoring a triple-century: a mammoth 320 against Madhya Pradesh. Taide finished the tournament with 669 runs from eight innings at 83.63.

"After that 300, I got a lot of messages that I could have broken Yuvraj's record [of 358 against Bihar in the 1999-00 final]," Taide says. "But I have no regrets. Maybe it was written in the stars that way.

"On the first day of the match, I pulled my quadriceps muscle while sliding. The second day, I was not able to walk. But then I did a lot of icing, took painkillers and after that, I batted for two and a half days. I knew the team needed me. It was the first time Vidarbha were playing the final, and being the captain, I had to bat. I had to do it for my team."

It made up for the hurt of missing the youth World Cup. Taide puts it this way: "If you ask me now if I wanted to be part of the World Cup or score that 300, I would take the 300."

In July 2018, he travelled to Sri Lanka with the U-19 side and scored 113 and 177 in two Youth Tests, reaping high praise from Chaminda Vaas, currently Sri Lanka U19's fast bowling coach. "He [Vaas] came to me after the second Test and said, 'Your balance is very good while batting, you have got good hands and you bat with courage.' That gave me a lot of confidence."

Breaking through India's rigorous domestic set-up isn't easy, and Taide knows it all too well. But he was ready to snap up the opportunity when it came at the senior level. So what if he missed the World Cup – he had other trophies in his sights.

Opening the batting against Baroda in Vijay Hazare Trophy 2018-19, he scored 57 on his List A debut, followed by an unbeaten 148 against Himachal Pradesh two games later. With 311 runs at an average of 51.83 and a strike rate of almost 90, Taide finished as Vidarbha's top run-getter in the tournament.

He then gave a good account of himself in the Ranji Trophy as well, scoring 95 against Mumbai in only his second first-class game. In the Irani Cup, his 72 in the fourth innings was instrumental in ensuring Vidarbha defended their title. In the Syed Mushtaq Ali Trophy, his 205 runs at an average of 22.77 and a strike-rate of 125.76 were the second-most for Vidarbha, while he also picked up five wickets at an economy of 5.53.

Yes, Taide might have missed the elevator, but he is ready to take the steps, one at a time.

Col C K Nayudu Under-23 Trophy

Perfect ten for Sidak Singh

A match-haul of 12 wickets by Harpreet Brar, the left-arm spinner, followed by his crucial 20 with the bat helped Punjab beat Bengal by one wicket in a low-scoring final. In all, Brar picked up 56 wickets from 11 games at an average of 16.41 and was the third-highest wicket-taker of the tournament.

Punjab, who had topped the Elite groups A and B with six wins from eight games, were otherwise clinical in the knock-outs. In the quarter-final, they trounced Uttarakhand, the qualifiers from the Plate group, by an innings and 406 runs. In the semi-final against Gujarat, they came out victorious by an innings and 42 runs.

In the final, Bengal recovered from 2 for 3 to post 191 after opting to bat. That proved enough for a 58-run lead as Punjab were bowled out for 133 against Bengal's spinners Aamir Gani and Shreyan Chakraborty. However, Bengal then themselves crumbled for 76, with Brar wreaking havoc with 7 for 23 to go along with five in the first innings. Chasing 135, Punjab slipped from 124 for 6 to 124 for 9 within the space of five balls but Arshdeep Singh and Ikjot Singh Thind knocked off the remaining runs to take Punjab over the line.

Another left-arm spinner Sidak Singh —the joint-highest wicket-taker of the season with Nagaland's Shubham Singh — registered a perfect ten (10 for 31) in a league game against Manipur.

In the **previous season**, Simarjeet Singh's six-wicket haul followed by wicketkeeper-batsman Anuj Rawat's twin half-centuries helped Delhi to a five-wicket victory over Mumbai in the final. Delhi's dominance in the tournament was based on their bowlers Tejas Baroka and Shivank Vashisth, who ended with 33 and 30 wickets respectively.

Hyderabad and Rajasthan, the two Plate teams to qualify for the last eight, didn't have luck on their side. Hyderabad lost out to Tamil Nadu on a coin toss after only 16.5 overs of play was possible in the match. Mumbai sneaked past Rajasthan on a two-run first-innings lead.

Delhi opted to bowl in the final and Simarjeet's 6 for 73 ensured Mumbai were out for 230 despite a 119-run opening stand. Delhi declared on 260 for 9 in response, thanks to Rawat (83) and Hiten Dalal (67). Siddharth Akre's 63 in the second innings helped Mumbai set Delhi a target of 238. Delhi once again rode on Rawat's 75, with Dinesh Mor and Lalit Yadav finishing the job.

	Most runs	Most wickets
2017-18	Aryaman Birla (MP) (795 runs, 6 matches)	Tajas Baroka (Delhi) (33 wickets, 6 matches)
2018-19	Manan Hingrajia (Gujarat) (872 runs, 10 matches)	Sidak Singh (Puducherry) (63 wickets, 8 matches)

2018-19

Elite Group A

Rajiv Gandhi International Stadium, Hyderabad, November 2-5: Gujarat 214 in 65.1 overs (KB Panchal 55, MA Hingrajia 46; Jayaram Reddy 4-52, Rajamani Prasad 3-36) and 350 in 98.1 overs (Kathan Patel 157, Rahul Shah 81; Abdul Quraishi 3-88, Kartikeya Kak 3-94) beat **Hyderabad** 109 in 39.1 overs (Abhirath Reddy 38; Hemang Patel 5-28, Tejas Patel 2-25) and 85 in 34.4 overs (Shreyas Vala 32; T Patel 5-16, H Patel 3-53) by 370 runs.

KSCA Navale Stadium, Shimoga, November 2-5: Jharkhand 215 in 92.1 overs (Wilfred Beng 79, Aditya Singh 32; Shubhang Hegde 4-69, MB Darshan 2-31) and 332 in 136.1 overs (ARD Bharadwaj 92, Kumar Suraj 87; Devdutt Padikkal 3-39, V Vyshak 2-65) lost to **Karnataka** 324 in 94.4 overs (S Aditya 80, BR Sharath 51; Shubham Singh 5-66, Vivek Tiwari 2-66) and 227/1 in 28.1 overs (BR Sharath 109, D Padikkal 98*) by nine wickets.

Capt. Roop Singh Stadium, Gwalior, November 2-5: Madhya Pradesh 259 in 83.3 overs (Ajay Rohera 76, Ankush Singh 67; Kiran Akash 4-62, S Swaminathan 3-40) and 363/9 dec. in 109.2 overs (Parth Goswami 132, Tejraj Chauhan 44; RS Jaganathsinivas 3-81, Mohanprasath S 2-60) beat **Tamil Nadu** 131 in 38 overs (Kavin Ravi 52, S Swaminathan 25; Pankaj Patel 5-49, Apurv Purohit 2-12) and 264/9 in 80.4 overs (K Mukunth 74*, Hari Nishaanth 51; Kumar Kartikeya 3-63, Ashwin Das 3-84) by 227 runs.

Feroz Shah Kotla Stadium, New Delhi, November 2-5: Baroda 213 in 69 overs (Mohit Mongia 66, Mitesh Patel 57; Shivank Vashisht 5-59, Simarjeet Singh 2-31) and 266 in 83.1 overs (M Mongia 91, KR Patel 45; S Vashisht 5-57, Gourav Kumar 3-45) lost to **Delhi** 500 in 151.2 overs (Jonty Sidhu 144, Yash Sehrawat 137, Lalit Yadav 128; Rishi Arothe 3-81, Ninad Rathva 3-118) by an innings and 21 runs.

GSFC Cricket Ground, Vadodara, November 14-17: Baroda 592/9 dec. in 159.4 overs (Mitesh Patel 268, Shivalik Sharma 169; Mohanprasath S 5-158, Ashwath Mukunthan 3-92) drew with **Tamil Nadu** 371 in 134.4 overs (S Swaminathan 116*, S Lokeshwar 112; Rishi Arothe 7-105, SD Patel 2-84) and 150/8 in 63 overs (S Lokeshwar 70*, M Siddharth 30*; Ninad Rathva 2-23, SD Patel 2-25). **Baroda** took first-innings lead.

Lalbhai Contractor Stadium, Surat, November 14-17: Delhi 351 in 113.1 overs (Jonty Sidhu 152, Manjot Kalra 45; Hemang Patel 3-72, AP Panchal 2-36) and 295/8 in 112 overs (Kunwar Bidhuri 104, Lakshay 101*; Tejas Patel 3-33, YD Kosamia 2-50) drew with **Gujarat** 296 in 111.5 overs (Het Patel 64, MA Hingrajia 56; Shivank Vashisht 7-91). **Delhi** took first-innings lead.

Gymkhana Ground, Hyderabad, November 14-17: Madhya Pradesh 288 in 88.4 overs (Ajay Rohera 66, Rishabh Choubey 54; Yudhvir Singh 4-61, Vinta Satwick 2-36) and 90 in 40.2 overs (Abdul Quraishi 3-14, Jayaram Reddy 2-19) lost to **Hyderabad** 214 in 78 overs (Shreyas Vala 52, Shashidhar Reddy 36; Pankaj Patel 3-41, Rahul Batham 2-24) and 166/6 in 44 overs (Abhirath Reddy 50, Chandan Sahani 32; Kumar Kartikeya 4-37, Rajarshi Srivastava 2-51) by four wickets.

Alur Cricket Stadium, Bangalore, November 14-17: Assam 247 in 80.2 overs (Mujibur Ali 83, Abhishek Thakuri 42; S Aditya 6-36, MB Darshan 2-24) and 201 in 100.4 overs (Biplab Saikia 93, Raj Agarwal 32; Devdutt Padikkal 4-34, Kushal Pramesh 3-33) drew with **Karnataka** 480/7 dec. in 143 overs (Nikin Jose 187, Sujith Gowda 122; R Agarwal 2-47, Roshan Alam 2-65) by an innings and 32 runs.

Nurul Amin Stadium, Nagaon, November 22-25: Assam 171 in 53.4 overs (Biplab Saikia 52, Erik Roy 29; Sonu Singh 5-50, Vinayak Vikram 3-63) and 240 in 77.3 overs (Rajjakuddin Ahmed 64, Prasenjit Sarkar 45; Sonu 4-64, V Vikram 3-42, Shubham Singh 3-49) beat **Jharkhand** 140 in 53.2 overs (Aditya Singh 33, Bhanu Anand 30; Avinav Choudhury 5-43, Raj Agarwal 3-42) and 116 in 44.1 overs (ARD Bharadwaj 33; A Choudhury 3-18, Dharani Rabha 3-32, R Agarwal 3-38) by 155 runs.

Emerald Heights International School Ground, Indore, November 22-25: Baroda 531 in 159.1 overs (JK Singh 130, Shivalik Singh 118; Ashwin Das 3-85, Anubhav Agarwal 3-92) beat **Madhya Pradesh** 250 in 91 overs (Parth Goswami 64, Apurv Purohit 39*; SS Desai 4-44, SD Patel 2-23) and 203 in 56.1 overs (P Goswami 63, Kumar Kartikeya 43; SS Desai 3-42, Rishi Arothe 3-47) by an innings and 78 runs.

Sardar Patel Stadium, Valsad, November 22-25: Karnataka 243 in 91.5 overs (Devdutt Padikkal 91, KL Shrijith 57; AP Panchal 5-50, Tejas Patel 2-44) and 310 in 95.3 overs (KL Shrijith 116, D Padikkal 82; YD Gardharia 4-105, T Patel 2-28) lost to **Gujarat** 329 in 105.5 overs (Rahul Shah 77, Kathan Patel 76; S Aditya 3-34, D Avinash 2-32) and 226/4 in 51.4 overs (K Patel 110, Rahul Shah 40) by six wickets.

ICL Sankar Nagar Ground, Tirunelveli, November 22-25: Hyderabad 282 in 117.2 overs (Shashidhar Reddy 129, Chandan Sahani 59; Mohanprasath S 3-56, S Swaminathan 3-72) and 83/6 in 70.2 overs (S Reddy 37; M Siddharth 3-27, Mohanprasath S 2-13) drew with **Tamil Nadu** 343/9 dec. in 149 overs (S Radhakrishnan 81, S Swaminathan 63; Rajamani Prasad 3-48, Vittal Anurag 2-58). **Tamil Nadu** took first-innings lead.

Satindra Mohan Dev Stadium, Silchar, November 30-December 3: Madhya Pradesh 401 in 149.2 overs (Ajay Rohera 160, Gaurav Patel 86; Dharani Rabha 5-107, Avinav Choudhury 4-157) beat **Assam** 217 in 89 overs (Abhishek Thakuri 53, Rajat Khan 52; Rajarshi Srivastava 3-63, Pankaj Patel 3-72) and 156 in 41.3 overs (Biplab Saikia 70, Nipan Deka 44; R Srivastava 6-76, G Patel 3-30) by an innings and 28 runs.

Railway Stadium, Dhanbad, November 30-December 3: Delhi 501/9 dec. in 157.1 overs (Sahil Malhotra 188, Lakshay 137; Shubham Singh 3-88) and 215/2 dec. in 46 overs (S Malhotra 100*, Jonty Sidhu 50*) drew with **Jharkhand** 378 in 109.5 overs (Vivek Kumar 111, V Vishal 72; Shivank Vashisht 4-81, Tejas Baroka 3-84) and 81/1 in 23 overs (V Kumar 42). **Delhi** took first-innings lead.

Gymkhana Ground, Hyderabad, November 30-December 3: Hyderabad 179 in 65.3 overs (Chandan Sahani 71, Shashidhar Reddy 47; MB Darshan 7-38, S Aditya 2-34) and 381/5 dec. in 119 overs (S Reddy 132, Nithesh Reddy 123; Aditya 5-85) beat **Karnataka** 249 in 82.4 overs (Kishan Bedare 73, Aditya 53; Kartikeya Kak 8-64, Rajamani Prasad 2-55) and 175 in 63.5 overs (Luvnith Sisodia 50; K Kak 7-54, R Prasad 2-73) by 136 runs.

TNCA Academy, Theni, November 30-December 3: Tamil Nadu 329 in 125.4 overs (K Mukunth 88, S Lokeshwar 85; Shivam Arekar 4-47, YD Gardharia 4-82) and 219/9 in 85 overs (Lokeshwar 57, K Mukunth 54; YD Gardharia 6-76, AP Panchal 3-73) drew with **Gujarat** 414 in 135.2 overs (Rahul Shah 132, MA Hingrajia 101; M Siddharth 4-77, Kiran Akash 2-65). **Gujarat** took first-innings lead.

JSCA Oval Ground, Ranchi, December 8-11: Tamil Nadu 249 in 103.2 overs (S Lokeshwar 88, Vishal Vaidhya 48; Vivek Tiwari 5-68, Surwar 2-39) and 182 in 73.1 overs (Aditya Barooah 68, Ashwath Mukunthan 28; Sonu Singh 5-57, Asif Mansoori 2-52) beat **Jharkhand** 190 in 82.2 overs (Kumar Suraj 40, Sonu 31; Mohanprasath 6-47, RS Jaganathsinivas 2-37) and 87 in 29.2 overs (Mohanprasath 4-23, M Siddharth 4-39) by 154 runs.

Gokulbhai Somabhai Patel Stadium, Nadiad, December 8-11: Baroda 212 in 84.1 overs (Kr Patel 92, SS Desai 53; Tejas Patel 3-36, KR Patel 3-48, Shivam Arekar 3-56) and 463/8 in 153.2 overs (Abhimanyu Singh 100*, AA Pathan 94; KB Panchal 3-30, Kshitij Patel 2-52) drew with **Gujarat** 362 in 112.1 overs (YD Gardharia 88, MA Hingrajia 74; Ninad Rathva 3-68, SD Patel 2-93). **Gujarat** took first-innings lead.

Gymkhana Ground, Hyderabad, December 8-11: Assam 118 in 45.3 overs (Sandip Paul Mazumdar 34, Subham Mandal 32; Kartikeya Kak 5-33, Vittal Anurag 3-23) and 191 in 75 overs (Biplab Saikia 53, Rajat Khan 49; V Anurag 3-33, K Kak 3-69) lost to **Hyderabad** 130 in 61.2 overs (Shreyas Vala 48; Dharani Rabha 5-43, Nipan Deka 3-43) and 180/1 in 62.4 overs (Nithesh Reddy 107*, S Vala 34*) by nine wickets.

Maharaja International School, Rewa, December 8-11: Delhi 280 in 72.1 overs (Priyansh Arya 97, Lakshay 50; Pankaj Patel 3-60, Anubhav Agarwal 2-37) and 236 in 74.1 overs (Ayush

Badoni 54, P Arya 53; Shubham Kathiwas 4-61, Rajarshi Srivastava 2-27) lost to **Madhya Pradesh** 461 in 126.5 overs (Atul Kushwaha 88, Parth Goswami 76; A Badoni 3-63, Nikhil Kumar 3-100) and 56/2 in 17 overs by eight wickets.

Sardar Patel Stadium, Valsad, December 16-19: Gujarat 476 in 136.5 overs (Rahul Shah 149, MA Hingrajia 114; Vivek Tiwari 4-116, Sonu Singh 3-87) beat **Jharkhand** 132 in 49 overs (Rahil Khan 66; Tejas Patel 5-39, Jayveer Sinh 2-33) and 154 in 41 overs (Arnav Sinha 66; YD Gardharia 5-57, KR Patel 4-49) by an innings and 190 runs.

GSFC Cricket Ground, Vadodara, December 16-19: Karnataka 211 in 65.4 overs (SS Sateri 44, Luvnith Sisodia 33; Ninad Rathva 8-87) and 426/6 dec. in 143 overs (Nikin Jose 201*, SS Sateri 74; Ninad Rathva 3-137, Abhimanyu Singh 2-32) drew with **Baroda** 307 in 107.3 overs (PS Kohli 99*, Mohit Mongia 63; MB Darshan 3-43, Shubhang Hegde 3-81) and 116/7 in 40 overs (JK Singh 85*; S Hegde 3-33, Kushaal Wadhwani 2-35). **Baroda** took first-innings lead.

NPR College Ground, Dindigul, December 16-19: Assam 128 in 50.5 overs (Subham Mandal 55, Nipan Deka 28; Mohanprasath S 6-53, M Siddharth 3-24) and 172 in 67.1 overs (Mujibur Ali 53, Biplab Saikia 31; Mohanprasath S 5-29, M Siddharth 5-69) lost to **Tamil Nadu** 364 in 117.1 overs (Aditya Barooah 81, S Radhakrishnan 76; Raj Agarwal 5-139, Avinav Choudhury 3-75) by an innings and 64 runs.

Feroz Shah Kotla Stadium, New Delhi, December 16-19: Hyderabad 193 in 65.1 overs (Vittal Anurag 74, Chandan Sahani 46; Tejas Baroka 3-55, Ayush Badoni 2-23, Lalit Yadav 2-23) and 85 in 42.5 overs (Shashidhar Reddy 30; T Baroka 5-11, L Yadav 3-18) lost to **Delhi** 342 in 90.3 overs (A Badoni 86, Manjot Kalra 75; Ashish Srivastava 5-101, Ajay Goud 4-71) by an innings and 64 runs.

Tinsukia District Sports Association Ground, Tinsukia, December 24-27: Assam 213 in 52 overs (Nipan Deka 57*, Mujibur Ali 25; YD Gardharia 6-88) and 139 in 52.2 overs (Rajat Khan 38; Tejas Patel 4-56, YD Gardharia 3-36) beat **Gujarat** 173 in 51 overs (Jayveer Sinh 39, Kshitij Patel 25; Rajjakuddin Ahmed 3-51, Dharani Rabha 3-25) and 81 in 29.4 overs (MA Hingrajia 29; R Ahmed 5-29, Roshan Alam 3-26) by 98 runs.

BSL Cricket Stadium, Bokaro, December 24-27: Jharkhand 403 in 119.4 overs (Arnav Sinha 81, Surwar 66; Rajarshi Srivastava 3-105, Gaurav Patel 2-108) and 81/3 in 14.4 overs (A Sinha 34, Aditya Singh 25*; R Srivastava 2-23) beat **Madhya Pradesh** 247 in 82.1 overs (Parth Goswami 92, Nikhil Mishra 76; Sonu Singh 6-50, Vinayak Vikram 3-79) and 235 in 78 overs (N Mishra 61, Aman Jain 39; Sonu 4-52, Shubham Singh 2-11) by seven wickets.

Alembic Cricket Ground, Vadodara, December 24-27: Baroda 295 in 81.2 overs (Shivalik Sharma 58, Mohit Mongia 55; Rajamani Prasad 4-67, Vittal Anurag 2-47) beat **Hyderabad** 132 in 40.3 overs (Chandan Sahani 61, Syed Askari 43; SD Patel 4-6, Rishi Arothe 3-23) and 82 in 25.3 overs (C Sahani 26; A Sheth 5-23, R Arothe 4-33) by an innings and 81 runs.

Airforce Complex Ground, Palam, New Delhi Services, December 24-27: Delhi 340 in 113.5 overs (Manjot Kalra 105, Kunwar Bidhuri 76; Kushaal Wadhwani 4-45, S Punith 3-70) and 242/5 in 81 overs (Akshay Solanki 56*, Yash Sehrawat 52; S Aditya 2-18, K Wadhwani 2-81) drew with **Karnataka** 378 in 129.2 overs (Manoj Bhandage 102, Sujith Gowda 70; Mohammed Bilal 4-122, Tejas Baroka 3-89). **Karnataka** took first-innings lead.

Nurul Amin Stadium, Nagaon, January 1-4: Assam 110 in 28 overs (Kunwar Bidhuri 5-28, Mohammed Bilal 4-37) and 117 in 44.3 overs (Abhishek Thakuri 38; Tejas Baroka 6-38, Siddhant Bansal 3-25) lost to **Delhi** 159 in 49.5 overs (T Baroka 70, Lakshay 38; Roshan Alam 4-35, Rajjakuddin Ahmed 3-31) and 72/2 in 16.4 overs by eight wickets.

Railway Stadium, Dhanbad, January 1-4: Jharkhand 407 in 118.1 overs (Arnav Sinha 209, Kumar Suraj 97; Ninad Rathva 5-73, Rishi Arothe 3-71) and 417/6 in 94.5 overs (A Sinha 143, Rahil Khan 91; DV Chauhan 3-109, Mohit Mongia 2-64) drew with **Baroda** 677/4 dec. in 141 overs (AA Pathan 355*, PS Kohli 214; Surwar 2-75) **Baroda** took first-innings lead.

MPCA Cricket Ground, Sagar, January 1-4: Gujarat 475 in 136.3 overs (MA Hingrajia 159*, YD Gardharia 80; Rahul Batham 4-89, Gaurav Patel 3-82) and 181/5 in 24.2 overs (KB

Panchal 64, A Patel 32) beat **Madhya Pradesh** 294 in 98.4 overs (Nikhil Mishra 73, R Batham 62*; KR Patel 5-56, AP Panchal 2-71) and 361 in 93.1 overs (Rajarshi Srivastava 66, Parth Goswami 59; YD Gardharia 4-101, KR Patel 2-101) by five wickets.

SDNR Wodeyar Ground, Mysore, January 1-4: Tamil Nadu 94 in 42.2 overs (S Swaminathan 34*, Ajith Kumar 25; MB Darshan 5-22, Manoj Bhandage 4-12) and 259 in 85.2 overs (S Radhakrishnan 96, K Mukunth 34; S Aditya 2-34, Kushaal Wadhwani 2-58) lost to **Karnataka** 125 in 66.2 overs (KL Shrijith 51, Sujith Gowda 31; Mohanprasath 5-21, A Kumar 3-35) and 234/5 in 87.4 overs (Luvnith Sisodia 93, S Gowda 86; M Siddharth 3-47) by five wickets.

Alembic Cricket Ground, Vadodara, January 9-12: Baroda 323 in 83.1 overs (Ninad Rathva 62, AA Pathan 54; Roshan Alam 4-65, Rahul Singh 4-80) and 257 in 57.1 overs (N Rathva 108, SS Desai 41; Rahul 6-100, R Alam 2-85) beat **Assam** 204 in 67.4 overs (Subham Mandal 77, Erik Roy 64; SS Desai 5-29, N Rathva 3-67) and 232 in 59.5 overs (Rajjakuddin Ahmed 105; SS Desai 4-53, SD Patel 2-21) by 144 runs.

Rajiv Gandhi International Stadium, Hyderabad, January 9-12: Jharkhand 152 in 47 overs (Rahil Khan 50, Amardeep Singh 39; Abdul Quraishi 3-30, Kartikeya Kak 3-36, Rajamani Prasad 3-53) and 291 in 86 overs (Surwar 168, Amardeep 38; K Kak 4-84, R Prasad 2-54) lost to **Hyderabad** 388/8 dec. in 123 overs (Tilak Varma 160, Shashidhar Reddy 134; Sonu Singh 4-96, Shubham Singh 2-57) and 60 for no loss in 8.2 overs (Nitesh Reddy 39*) by ten wickets.

KSCA Stadium, Hubli, January 9-12: Madhya Pradesh 273 in 95.2 overs (Siddharth Patidar 65, Rahul Batham 44, Rajarshi Srivastava 44; Manoj Bhandage 5-70, S Aditya 2-58) and 263 in 87.4 overs (Nikhil Mishra 93, Salman Khan 65; M Bhandage 4-47) drew with **Karnataka** 126 in 42.4 overs (Shrijith 33, Nikin Jose 29; Abhay Tipnis 5-13, R Batham 4-31) and 319/7 in 119 overs (KL Shrijith 94, Sujith Gowda 84; Shubham Kathiwas 2-19, Anubhav Agarwal 2-49). **Madhya Pradesh** took first-innings lead.

NPR College Ground, Dindigul, January 9-12: Delhi 197 in 69.2 overs (Manjot Kalra 67, Sarthak Ranjan 53; Trilok Nag 5-26, Ajith Kumar 3-51) and 192 in 62.4 overs (Kunwar Bidhuri 92*, S Ranjan 62; A Kumar 6-60) lost to **Tamil Nadu** 286 in 96 overs (S Swaminathan 93, Kavin Ravi 92; K Bidhuri 6-63, Kuldip Yadav 2-40) and 106/3 in 33.5 overs (K Mukunth 40, Hari Nishaanth 31) by seven wickets.

Points table

Teams	M	W	L	D	T	N/R	Pts	Quotient
Gujarat	8	4	1	3	0	0	32	1.301
Baroda	8	3	1	4	0	0	30	1.296
Delhi	8	3	2	3	0	0	27	1.296
Hyderabad	8	4	3	1	0	0	26	0.908
Karnataka	8	3	2	3	0	0	24	1.161
Tamil Nadu	8	3	2	3	0	0	24	1.008
Madhya Pradesh	8	3	4	1	0	0	22	0.993
Assam	8	2	6	0	0	0	12	0.682
Jharkhand	8	1	5	2	0	0	8	0.633

Gujarat and Baroda qualified for the quarter-finals

Elite Group B

Bengal Cricket Academy Ground, Kalyani, November 2-5: Bengal 75 in 38.5 overs (Agniv Pan 30, Subham Chatterjee 30; Boby Yadav 3-13, Sunil Kumar 3-28) and 372 in 153.3 overs

(Kazi Saifi 77, A Pan 58; Wajid Ali 5-98, Shiva Singh 3-77) lost to **Uttar Pradesh** 476/5 dec. in 146 overs (Rahul Rawat 189, Shubham Chaubey 145; Akash Deep 3-86) by an innings and 29 runs.

Rajkot, November 2-5: Saurashtra 219 in 82.3 overs (Niket Joshi 73, Kevin Jivrajani 43; A Vinaykumar 4-39, Girinath Reddy 3-36, Manish Golamaru 3-61) and 127 in 57.4 overs (Chetan Sakariya 43*; M Golamaru 5-52, A Vinaykumar 3-33) beat **Andhra** 188 in 64 overs (Karan Shinde 61, Achyuta Rao 31; Yuvraj Chudasama 7-63, Pranav Karia 2-32) and 100 in 27.3 overs (Viharsinh Jadeja 4-18, Y Chudasama 3-56) by 58 runs.

Dhruv Pandove Stadium, Patiala, November 2-5: Maharashtra 178 in 53.1 overs (JP Zope 59*; IA Sayed 34; Ikjot Thind 4-41, Nikhil Chaudhary 3-14) and 232 in 79.4 overs (MS Trunkwala 65, Hrishikesh Motkar 51; Akul Pandove 5-67, Jass Inder 2-14) lost to **Punjab** 435 in 138.2 overs (Mansab Gill 102, Harpreet Brar 77; MM Sayyad 4-88, IA Sayed 2-60) by an innings and 25 runs.

Jaipuria Vidyalaya Ground, Jaipur, November 2-5: Rajasthan 209 in 61 overs (Aditya Garhwal 41, SK Sharma 31; Vijay Gohil 3-42, Minad Manjrekar 3-55) and 321 in 99.4 overs (A Garhwal 73, SK Sharma 59; Kruthik Hanagavadi 4-99, Dhrumil Matkar 3-50) lost to **Mumbai** 259 in 74.3 overs (Armaan Jaffer 84, Yashasvi Jaiswal 49; AR Lamba 3-53, Shiva Chauhan 2-58) and 275/5 in 85.2 overs (Hardik Tamore 112*, Siddharth Akre 59; AR Lamba 2-72) by five wickets.

Pune, November 14-17: Bengal 333 in 124.3 overs (Agniv Pan 104, Sudip Gharami 51; SD Warghante 4-56, OK Akhade 3-95) and 220/8 dec. in 74 overs (Kazi Saifi 102*, Subham Chatterjee 30; MG Choudhary 3-61, OK Akhade 2-45) drew with **Maharashtra** 273 in 130.5 overs (Swapnil Fulpagar 74, Yash Kshirsagar 49; Ananta Saha 5-56, Akash Deep 3-75). **Bengal** took first-innings lead.

Jaipuria Vidyalaya Ground, Jaipur, November 14-17: Rajasthan 298 in 99.4 overs (Aditya Garhwal 102, YB Kothari 51; Wajid Ali 6-56, Shivam Chaudhary 2-50) and 457/9 dec. in 132 overs (SK Sharma 125, RM Chapparwal 90; Boby Yadav 3-92, Abhishek Goswami 2-1) drew with **Uttar Pradesh** 331 in 106.1 overs (S Chaudhary 85, Rahul Rawat 68; AA Khan 3-43, VO Jhorar 2-78) **Uttar Pradesh** took first-innings lead.

Anantapur, November 14-17: Andhra 281 in 113.2 overs (Achyuta Rao 97, Maheep Kumar 63; Neelambuj Vats 5-93, RA Dey 3-22) and 332 in 91.2 overs (M Kumar 129, A Rao 65; TR Mandal 6-85, JB Bhattacharjee 3-91) drew with **Tripura** 360 in 98.4 overs (AA Sinha 149, DB Debbarma 59; CHVS Koushik 5-98, Vinod Naidu 4-69) and 42/1 in 25 overs. **Tripura** took first-innings lead.

Wankhede Stadium, Mumbai, November 14-17: Saurashtra 175 in 63.1 overs (Niket Joshi 57, Yuvraj Chudasama 29; Aquib Kureshi 3-33, Dhrumil Matkar 2-19) and 205 in 81.3 overs (N Joshi 57, Vishvarajsinh Jadeja 48; D Matkar 6-48, Minad Manjrekar 2-56) lost to **Mumbai** 610/5 dec. in 139.4 overs (Armaan Jaffer 300*, Rudra Dhanday 166; Chetan Sakariya 2-122) by an innings and 230 runs.

Police Training Academy Ground, Agartala, November 22-25: Rajasthan 154 in 52.4 overs (Sharad Cheeta 31, Aditya Garhwal 28; Neelambuj Vats 3-23, JB Bhattacharjee 2-23) and 444/9 dec. in 121 overs (S Cheeta 112*, AR Lamba 82; JB Bhattacharjee 4-145, TR Mandal 2-71) drew with **Tripura** 231 in 76 overs (DB Debbarma 126*, TR Mandal 33; SK Sharma 5-76, AR Lamba 3-13) and 301/9 in 106 overs (DB Debbarma 67, N Vats 61*; RM Chapparwal 3-60, AR Lamba 2-30). **Tripura** took first-innings lead.

Madhavrao Scindia Cricket Ground, Rajkot, November 22-25: Saurashtra 328 in 111 overs (Kevin Jivrajani 106, Yuvraj Chudasama 57; MG Choudhary 5-62, JP Zope 4-86) and 195 in 79.2 overs (K Jivrajani 48, Tarang Gohel 35; SD Warghante 5-44, JP Zope 3-59) drew with **Maharashtra** 426 in 148.1 overs (PT Kore 135, OK Akhade 94; Y Chudasama 4-122, K Jivrajani 2-47) and 80/6 in 13 overs (K Jivrajani 2-13). **Maharashtra** took first-innings lead.

Mohan Meakins Ground, Ghaziabad, November 22-25: Andhra 507 in 128.3 overs (Maheep Kumar 137, CR Gnaneshwar 119; Trishal Trivedi 5-123) beat **Uttar Pradesh** 106 in 29.4

overs (Abhishek Goswami 26; S Ashish 4-39, M Kumar 3-18, Harishankar Reddy 3-32) and 323 in 82.2 overs (Sandeep Kumar 72, Hannan Rizwan 67; A Vinaykumar 4-103, S Ashish 3-100) by an innings and 78 runs.

Sharad Pawar Cricket Academy BKC, Mumbai, November 22-25: Punjab 345 in 107.3 overs (Nikhil Chaudhary 96, Akul Pandove 62; Kruthik Hanagavadi 5-102, Minad Manjrekar 3-82) and 163 in 45.1 overs (Anmol Malhotra 38, A Pandove 28; K Hanagavadi 5-49, M Manjrekar 4-71) lost to **Mumbai** 136 in 39.3 overs (Siddharth Akre 38, Bhupen Lalwani 36; N Chaudhary 5-20, Arshdeep Singh 3-52) and 377/7 in 126.5 overs (B Lalwani 127, K Hanagavadi 73; Ikjot Thind 4-91) by three wickets.

Police Training Academy Ground, Agartala, November 30-December 3: Bengal 500/8 dec. in 146.3 overs (Saurabh Singh 171, Agniv Pan 120; BB Debnath 2-71, Arjun Debnath 2-104) beat **Tripura** 180 in 64.2 overs (Neelambuj Vats 59; Ananta Saha 4-29, Ritwik Roy Choudhury 2-11) and 81 in 29.4 overs (RN Saha 29; Shreyan Chakraborty 5-26, Akash Pandey 2-12) by an innings and 239 runs.

Jaipuria Vidyalaya Ground, Jaipur, November 30-December 3: Andhra 194 in 67.4 overs (Karan Shinde 64, Kranthi Kumar 36; VO Jhorar 4-40, Shiva Chauhan 3-45) and 371 in 112.1 overs (CR Gnaneshwar 97, Achyuta Rao 92; S Chauhan 3-62, RM Chapparwal 2-31) lost to **Rajasthan** 351 in 105.2 overs (Aditya Garhwal 123, GR Avasthi 84; Charan Sai 4-26, Vinod Naidu 3-77) and 215/6 in 52.5 overs (YB Kothari 105, RN Tomar 45; V Naidu 3-68) by four wickets.

Dhruv Pandove Stadium, Patiala, November 30-December 3: Saurashtra 167 in 60.2 overs (Parth Bhut 60, Vishvarajsinh Jadeja 49; Akul Pandove 5-52, Ikjot Thind 3-33) and 259 in 124.3 overs (V Jadeja 108, Yash Parekh 35; Harpreet Brar 6-70, Arshdeep Singh 3-70) lost to **Punjab** 265 in 96.2 overs (A Pandove 47, Ramandeep Singh 43; P Bhut 5-94, Pranav Karia 4-50) and 162/1 in 50 overs (Himanshu Sharma 70*, Shivam Bhambri 65*) by nine wickets.

Kamla Club Ground, Kanpur, November 30-December 3: Uttar Pradesh 621 in 167.5 overs (Shubham Chaubey 245, Aryan Juyal 121; Tanush Kotian 5-150, Aquib Kureshi 2-98) and 179/3 in 44 overs (Abhishek Goswami 77, Almas Shaukat 73) drew with **Mumbai** 435 in 123.5 overs (Bhupen Lalwani 166, Sairaj Patil 40; Harshvardhan 3-91, Boby Yadav 2-89). **Uttar Pradesh** took first-innings lead.

Eden Gardens, Kolkata, December 8-11: Mumbai 112 in 36.1 overs (Tanush Kotian 39*; Kanishk Seth 5-40, Ananta Saha 3-49) and 168 in 47.2 overs (Yashasvi Jaiswal 75, Sairaj Patil 26; K Seth 5-82, Akash Deep 2-20) lost to **Bengal** 324 in 84.4 overs (Sudip Gharami 66, Shubham Chatterjee 66; Aquib Kureshi 4-90, S Patil 2-44) by an innings and 44 runs.

Deccan Gymkhana Cricket Ground, Pune, December 8-11: Maharashtra 344 in 120.2 overs (Swapnil Fulpagar 83, OK Akhade 77*; Harshvardhan 3-67, Shiva Singh 3-101) and 149 in 54.4 overs (Yash Kshirsagar 52, MM Sayyad 44; Shiva 4-50, Trishal Trivedi 2-45) lost to **Uttar Pradesh** 347 in 91 overs (Nalin Mishra 131, Almas Shaukat 78; SD Warghante 4-46, JP Zope 4-105) and 152/5 in 47.5 overs (Rahul Rawat 70, A Shaukat 41; SD Warghante 2-57) by five wickets.

Madhavrao Scindia Cricket Ground, Rajkot, December 8-11: Rajasthan 274 in 94.5 overs (YB Kothari 71, GR Avasthi 55; Parth Bhut 4-90, Pranav Karia 3-61) and 246 in 69 overs (Aditya Garhwal 59, GR Avasthi 46, Sharad Cheeta 46; Vivek Agath 3-27, Devang Karamta 2-25) beat **Saurashtra** 268 in 85.4 overs (Samarth Vyas 64, Niket Joshi 41; SK Sharma 5-99, VO Jhorar 4-24) and 177 in 68.3 overs (Jyortir Purohit 40, S Vyas 36, Vishvarajsinh Jadeja 36; SK Sharma 5-52, AB Kookma 3-42) by 75 runs.

Dhruv Pandove Stadium, Patiala, December 8-11: Tripura 120 in 39.1 overs (RN Saha 36; Akul Pandove 3-20, Arshdeep Singh 2-23) and 263 in 80.3 overs (Neelambuj Vats 81, AA Sinha 54; Harpreet Brar 5-75, Jass Inder 4-37) lost to **Punjab** 529 in 126.1 overs (Ramandeep Singh 148, Anmol Malhotra 104; RA Dey 3-42, Arjun Debnath 3-105) by an innings and 145 runs.

Dr PVG Raju ACA Sports Complex, Vizianagaram, December 16-19: Andhra 103 in 39.1

overs (Achyuta Rao 31; Ananta Saha 5-34, Kanishk Seth 4-33) and 75 in 27.2 overs (A Saha 6-33, K Seth 2-14) lost to **Bengal** 227/9 dec. in 64.5 overs (Ritwik Roy Chowdhury 74, Saurabh Singh 40; PP Manohar 6-69, Prithvi Raj Yarra 2-44) by an innings and 49 runs.

Bhamashah Park Ground, Meerut, December 16-19: Uttar Pradesh 447 in 110.3 overs (Aryan Juyal 131, Hannan Rizwan 113; Neelambuj Vats 5-84, RA Dey 4-87) and 107/2 in 19.1 overs (Rahul Rawat 54*, H Rizwan 38) beat **Tripura** 207 in 77.5 overs (RA Dey 64, JT Saha 28; Harshvardhan 4-56, Trishal Trivedi 3-33, Shiva Singh 3-62) and 343 in 114.5 overs (RA Dey 89, AA Sinha 83; Sandeep Kumar 5-28, Shiva 3-91) by eight wickets.

Jaipuria Vidyalaya Ground, Jaipur, December 16-19: Rajasthan 114 in 40.4 overs (Ikjot Thind 6-33, Nikhil Chaudhary 2-35) and 119 in 28.4 overs (Aditya Garhwal 36, RM Chapparwal 30; Arshdeep Singh 8-44) lost to **Punjab** 441 in 109.1 overs (Abhinav Sharma 76, Ramandeep Singh 74; SK Sharma 3-80, VO Jhorar 2-81) by an innings and 208 runs.

Sharad Pawar Cricket Academy BKC, Mumbai, December 16-19: Maharashtra 172 in 82 overs (PT Kore 67, Hrishikesh Motkar 29; Minad Manjrekar 5-36, Kruthik Hanagavadi 2-46) and 251/9 in 85.3 overs (MS Patel 53, MM Sayyad 35; Tanush Kotian 4-70, Aquib Kureshi 2-15) lost to **Mumbai** 430 in 116.1 overs (Yashasvi Jaiswal 131, SZ Mulani 65; OK Akhade 3-66, MM Sayyad 2-74) by an innings and seven runs.

Police Training Academy Ground, Agartala, December 24-27: Tripura 225 in 84.1 overs (Neelambuj Vats 64; PP Das 59; Parth Bhut 3-30, Pranav Nandha 2-47) and 219 in 76 overs (RA Dey 57, CK Paul 48; P Bhut 4-27, P Nandha 2-39) lost to **Saurashtra** 317 in 92.5 overs (Kevin Jivrajani 101, P Bhut 76; CK Paul 4-74, Arjun Debnath 2-46) and 133/3 in 28.2 overs (K Jivrajani 64, Jyortir Purohit 26) by seven wickets.

Eden Gardens, Kolkata, December 24-27: Bengal 162 in 50 overs (Ritwik Roy Chowdhury 54, Shreyan Chakraborty 36*; VO Jhorar 6-45, AR Lamba 2-36) and 264 in 74.1 overs (R Roy Chowdhury 78, Subham Chatterjee 46; AR Lamba 6-70, VO Jhorar 3-73) beat **Rajasthan** 152 in 49.2 overs (SK Sharma 30, Aditya Garhwal 28; Ananta Saha 4-54, Akash Deep 3-46, Kanishk Seth 3-51) and 157 in 48.4 overs (GR Avasthi 28, Sharad Cheeta 28; A Saha 5-47, A Deep 2-62) by 117 runs.

MCA Cricket Stadium, Gahunje, Pune, December 24-27: Andhra 287 in 104.5 overs (Ashwin Hebbar 104, G Jayavardhan 91; IA Sayed 6-49, MG Choudhary 3-65) and 322/4 dec. in 87 overs (Maheep Kumar 73, A Hebbar 69; PT Kore 2-59) lost to **Maharashtra** 181 in 56.1 overs (Prem Salvi 42, MS Trunkwala 30; A Vinaykumar 5-35, CHVS Koushik 2-26) and 433/3 in 97 overs (Swapnil Fulpagar 189, MS Patel 156*; PP Manohar 2-93) by seven wickets.

IS Bindra Cricket Stadium, PCA, Mohali, December 24-27: Punjab 168 in 51 overs (Mansab Gill 52, Anmol Malhotra 41, Nikhil Chaudhary 41; Trishal Trivedi 3-18, Wajid Ali 3-56) and 354 in 90.5 overs (N Chaudhary 123, A Malhotra 86*; Boby Yadav 5-87, Shiva Singh 2-36) beat **Uttar Pradesh** 106 in 24.4 overs (Rahul Rawat 54; Ikjot Thind 4-27, Arshdeep Singh 3-40) and 390 in 97.5 overs (R Rawat 115, Aryan Juyal 93; Harpreet Brar 3-78, Arshdeep 3-89) by 26 runs.

Police Training Academy Ground, Agartala, January 1-4: Tripura 92 in 37.5 overs (SS Sutradhar 26; MG Choudhary 5-36, MM Sayyad 3-29) and 288 in 87.5 overs (SS Sutradhar 102, RN Saha 67; MG Choudhary 7-62, MM Sayyad 2-47) lost to **Maharashtra** 264 in 77.3 overs (MS Patel 77, MS Trunkwala 53; TR Mandal 2-23, SS Ghosh 2-32) and 117/2 in 19.3 overs (MS Trunkwala 66, Prem Salvi 31; TR Mandal 2-24) by eight wickets.

Bengal Cricket Academy Ground, Kalyani, January 1-4: Bengal 337 in 106.4 overs (Ritwik Roy Chowdhury 97, Sudip Gharami 58; Akul Pandove 4-74, Arshdeep Singh 2-44) and 300/9 dec. in 87 overs (Subham Chatterjee 110*, Arif Ansari 62; Gurwinder Bhullar 2-27, Nikhil Chaudhary 2-38) beat **Punjab** 205 in 53.3 overs (Himanshu Sharma 68, N Chaudhary 46; Kanishk Seth 5-71, Ananta Saha 4-60) and 185 in 55.3 overs (Ikjot Thind 61, Himanshu 29; RR Chowdhury 5-21, K Seth 2-25) by 247 runs.

Dr YS Rajasekhara Reddy ACA VDCA Cricket Stadium, Visakhapatnam, January 1-4: Mumbai 131 in 42.3 overs (Chinmay Sutar 64; Imandi Raman 8-58, Harishankar Reddy 2-25) and 462/6 dec. in 108 overs (Yashasvi Jaiswal 241*, Armaan Jaffer 147; I Raman 4-120) drew with **Andhra** 321 in 129.1 overs (Karan Shinde 119, Dhruva Reddy 75; Anjdeep Lad 5-64, Kruthik Hanagavadi 2-85) and 230/6 in 60 overs (K Shinde 98, Achyuta Rao 66; K Hanagavadi 2-40). **Andhra** took first-innings lead.

Kamla Club Ground, Kanpur, January 1-4: Saurashtra 166 in 58.1 overs (Niket Joshi 37, Tarang Gohel 37; Trishal Trivedi 4-18, Shiva Singh 3-61) and 204 in 90.3 overs (Kevin Jivrajani 63, Jyortir Purohit 59; Shiva 5-71, Shivam Chaudhary 2-24) lost to **Uttar Pradesh** 395 in 92.1 overs (Sandeep Kumar 118, Mohammad Saif 53; Yuvraj Chudasama 5-142, Parth Bhut 2-94) by an innings and 25 runs.

Madhavrao Scindia Cricket Ground, Rajkot, January 9-12: Bengal 674/9 dec. in 163.1 overs (Kazi Saifi 215, Ritwik Roy Chowdhury 153, Ankur Paul 139; Yuvraj Chudasama 5-149) drew with **Saurashtra** 201 in 82.3 overs (Kevin Jivrajani 85, Jyortir Purohit 41; Shreyan Chakraborty 4-48, Akash Deep 3-52) and 327/3 in 96 overs (J Purohit 105*, Tarang Gohel 77; S Chakraborty 2-139). **Bengal** took first-innings lead.

MCA Cricket Stadium, Gahunje, Pune, January 9-12: Rajasthan 208 in 96.1 overs (YB Kothari 84, Deepak 32; MG Choudhary 5-67, IA Sayed 3-28) and 436/7 in 126.5 overs (Aditya Garhwal 165, YB Kothari 50; MG Choudhary 3-85, OK Akhade 2-104) drew with **Maharashtra** 450 (Yash Kshirsagar 120, MS Patel 108; AR Lamba 7-95, SK Sharma 2-91). **Maharashtra** took first-innings lead.

Rural Development Trust Stadium, Anantapur, January 9-12: Punjab 374 in 115.5 overs (Akul Pandove 111, Kashish Panseja 66; A Vinaykumar 3-73, Imandi Raman 2-76) and 70/1 in 20.3 overs (Anmol Malhotra 35*) beat **Andhra** 182 in 71.5 overs (Charan Sai 38, Maheep Kumar 29; PP Manohar 29; Harpreet Brar 5-43, Ikjot Thind 2-19) and 261 in 62.1 overs (G Jayavardhan 83, PP Manohar 56; H Brar 3-85, I Thind 2-47) by nine wickets.

Sharad Pawar Cricket Academy BKC, Mumbai, January 9-12: Mumbai 517/6 dec. in115 overs (Bhupen Lalwani 167, Hardik Tamore 109; Arjun Debnath 3-78) beat **Tripura** 319 in 70 overs (AA Sinha 148, A Debnath 61; Minad Manjrekar 4-59, Kruthik Hanagavadi 2-56) and 112 in 38.3 overs (SS Sutradhar 64*; Anjdeep Lad 5-28, A Vashishtha 4-7) by an innings and 86 runs.

Points table

Teams	M	W	L	D	T	N/R	Pts	Quotient
Punjab	8	6	2	0	0	0	39	1.453
Bengal	8	5	1	2	0	0	39	1.592
Mumbai	8	5	1	2	0	0	35	1.391
Uttar Pradesh	8	4	2	2	0	0	32	1.291
Maharashtra	8	2	3	3	0	0	19	0.893
Rajasthan	8	2	3	3	0	0	15	0.916
Saurashtra	8	2	4	2	0	0	14	0.682
Andhra	8	1	5	2	0	0	11	0.859
Tripura	8	0	6	2	0	0	6	0.544

Punjab, Bengal, Mumbai, Uttar Pradesh qualified for the quarter-finals

Elite Group C

Ravenshaw University Ground 1, Cuttack, November 2-5: Haryana 269 in 87 overs (Aakash Antil 67, SP Kumar 48*; Ayaskant Sahu 3-30, Ashish Rai 3-54) and 221 in 62.1 overs

(SP Kumar 114, SD Dhull 52; A Sahu 5-55, Krishna Palai 2-41) beat **Odisha** 136 in 72.3 overs (Raghunath Malla 32, Amrit Khatua 31; MS Rathee 4-36, Aman Kumar 3-31) and 66 in 30.5 overs (Debasish Samantray 25; MS Rathee 5-3, AR Rana 3-5) by 288 runs.

BSP Cricket Stadium, Bhilai, November 2-5: Himachal Pradesh 426 in 116 overs (RI Thakur 158, AA Walia 50; Shubham Singh 4-88, AS Saxena 2-83) and 149/6 in 60 overs (Arslan Khan 55, DB Rangi 33; Shubham 4-35) drew with **Chhattisgarh** 506 in 157.5 overs (AG Tiwary 121, Sahban Khan 104; NK Kanwar 4-97, Arpit Guleria 3-121). **Chhattisgarh** took first-innings lead.

East Coast Railway Cricket Stadium, Bhubaneswar RSPB, November 2-5: Railways 329 in 119.3 overs (Rishabh Mishra 92, Sahim Hasan 82; Abid Mushtaq 4-59, Mohammad Tahir 4-70) and 240/8 dec. in 65.5 overs (Dinesh Mor 84, Yuvraj 50*; Sahil Lotra 2-41) drew with **Jammu and Kashmir** 231 in 106 overs (Suryansh Raina 44, Zaid Bhat 40; Mayank Singh 6-56, OJ Jaiswal 2-53) and 186/7 in 64 overs (A Mushtaq 59*, Z Bhat 43; Mohammad Irfan 2-21, OJ Jaiswal 2-70). **Railways** took first-innings lead.

Thalasseri Cricket Stadium, Kannur, November 2-5: Kerala 289 in 136.3 overs (Daryl Ferrario 92, Anand Joseph 58; NS Parande 4-56, PR Rekhade 3-53) and 159/3 dec. in 39 overs (D Ferrario 100*, Subin S 38*; SR Dubey 2-44) beat **Vidarbha** 108 in 58.2 overs (Sijomon Joseph 3-20, Basil NP 3-23) and 311 in 95.2 overs (MR Raut 76, MR Kale 65; Basil NP 4-71, Harikrishnan KN 2-36) by 29 runs.

Bhilai, November 14-17: Vidarbha 225 in 96.5 overs (MR Raut 69, AD Choudhari 66; SK Chadda 4-31, Shubham Singh 2-49) and 344/7 dec. in 116 overs (MR Kale 114*; AM Kumar 79; Ajay Mandal 3-106) drew with **Chhattisgarh** 209 in 73.4 overs (A Mandal 92, AG Tiwary 25, Sahban Khan 25; SR Dubey 4-66, NS Parande 3-45) and 251/6 in 68 overs (AG Tiwary 97, Amandeep Khare 65; AM Deshpande 4-62). **Vidarbha** took first-innings lead.

JR Institute of Cricket Technology, Barwala, November 14-17: Jammu and Kashmir 202 in 102.1 overs (Shabir Ahmed 56, Hishan Saleem 27; SP Kumar 2-16, MS Rathee 2-18) and 106/3 in 41 overs (Suryansh Raina 36, Surya Mahotra 25*; AR Rana 2-37) drew with **Haryana** 348/7 dec. in 86 overs (YR Sharma 124, SP Kumar 64; Sahil Lotra 5-106, Mohammad Tahir 2-71). **Haryana** took first-innings lead.

Sanguem Cricket Ground, Sanguem, November 14-17: Odisha 293 in 101.5 overs (Debasish Samantray 142*, Kshyamsagar Bal 83; Heramb Parab 3-35, Achit Shigwan 2-16) and 306/9 dec. in 106.3 overs (Amrit Khatua 68, D Samantray 54; Dheeraj Y 3-66, Shubham Dessai 2-40) drew with **Goa** 237 in 76.3 overs (Vaibhav Govekar 79, Nihal S 40*; Kartik Biswal 5-37, Rajkrishan Patel 2-45) and 122/3 in 58 overs (Ishaan Gadekar 55*, Deepraj Gaonkar 36*; Ashish Rai 2-29). **Odisha** took first-innings lead.

Dharamsala, November 14-17: Railways 182 in 47.2 overs (Dhrushant Soni 39, Sahim Hasan 30; Arpit Guleria 5-54, AS Jamwal 4-57) and 214 in 58 overs (Avijit Singh 106, Mohammad Irfan 39; A Guleria 4-48, NN Kanwar 3-60) lost to **Himachal Pradesh** 179 in 50.5 overs (NA Sharma 48*, SR Purohit 36; D Soni 5-53, Mayank Singh 2-11) and 219/7 in 55.2 overs (NA Sharma 56*, SR Purohit 40; Himanshu Sangwan 3-87, D Soni 2-68) by three wickets.

BSP Cricket Stadium, Bhilai, November 22-25: Chhattisgarh 157 in 59.1 overs (MSS Hussain 68, Mayank Wadher 36; Basil NP 4-41, Sijomon Joseph 3-30) and 222 in 99.4 overs (Sahban Khan 63, Shubham Singh 53; S Joseph 3-50, Basil NP 3-51) beat **Kerala** 143 in 63 overs (Albin Alias 34, Subin S 30; SK Chadda 5-46, AS Saxena 3-49) and 137 in 47.4 overs (Rohan Kunnummal 100; Ajay Mandal 6-26, Shubham 4-41) by 99 runs.

VCA Kalamana, Nagpur, November 22-25: Vidarbha 415 in 110.2 overs (MR Kale 89, PR Rekhade 72; Saurabh Kanojia 4-47, Kartik Biswal 3-108) beat **Odisha** 228 in 79.4 overs (Debasish Samantray 54, K Biswal 51; Atharva Taide 3-25, SR Dubey 3-31, RK Choudhury 3-60) and 155 in 102.5 overs (Amrit Khatua 55, Biswajit Bhuyan 48; RK Choudhury 4-34, PR Rekhade 3-29) by an innings and 32 runs.

Railway Cricket Ground, Rajkot RSPB, November 22-25: Haryana 168 in 53.3 overs (Aman Kumar 46, SP Kumar 34; Dhrushant Soni 5-42, Himanshu Sangwan 3-48) and 232 in 73.4 overs (Ankit Kumar 68, YR Sharma 39; D Soni 3-65, Mayank Singh 3-68) lost to **Railways** 251 in 99.2 overs (Rishabh Mishra 137, V Dhaka 26; JA Bhambhu 3-28, Aman Kumar 2-50) and 151/3 in 57.5 overs (Sahim Hasan 78*, R Mishra 30; MS Rathee 2-55) by seven wickets.

Govt Gandhi Memorial Science College Ground, Jammu, November 22-25: **Goa** 255 in 84.1 overs (Achit Shigwan 86, Ishaan Gadekar 55; Sunil Kumar 5-76, Abid Mushtaq 3-48) and 300/8 dec. in 104 overs (VG Kahlon 82, VA Naik 74*; S Kumar 3-80, A Mushtaq 2-74) beat **Jammu and Kashmir** 230 in 91.1 overs (Hisham Saleem 54*, Surya Mahotra 41; Dheeraj Y 4-30, Heramb Parab 4-64) and 174 in 55.1 overs (S Mahotra 37, Zaid Bhat 32; Shubham Dessai 5-44, Dheeraj Y 3-19) by 151 runs.

Vikash Ground, Bargarh, November 30-December 3: **Kerala** 290 in 104.5 overs (Salman Nizar 85, Harikrishnan KN 49; Ashish Rai 5-72, Ayaskant Sahu 3-49) and 283/5 dec. in 63 overs (Subin S 63, S Nizar 56; A Rai 4-69) beat **Odisha** 203 in 80.4 overs (Soubhagya Mishra 51, Debasish Samantray 45; Sijomon Joseph 4-43, Vishweshar Suresh 3-42) and 240 in 93.1 overs (S Mishra 81, Kshyamsagar Bal 76; S Joseph 4-42, V Suresh 3-82) by 130 runs.

BSP Cricket Stadium, Bhilai, November 30-December 3: **Railways** 256 in 87.4 overs (Rishabh Mishra 68, Avijit Singh 47; VNS Tripathi 3-59, Shubham Singh 3-60) and 325/4 dec. in 90 overs (Dinesh Mor 100*, Mohammad Irfan 77*) beat **Chhattisgarh** 121 in 40.2 overs (Ajay Mandal 59; Mayank Singh 5-19, Himanshu Sangwan 3-40) and 119 in 42.3 overs (AG Tiwary 47; Mayank Singh 4-47, H Sangwan 4-48) by 341 runs.

Sanguem Cricket Ground, Sanguem, November 30-December 3: **Goa** 164 in 57.4 overs (Shubham Dessai 43, Deepraj Gaonkar 31; DG Nalkande 5-50, NS Parande 2-29) and 102 in 33.2 overs (Nihal S 34*; DG Nalkande 5-42, PR Rekhade 3-28) lost to **Vidarbha** 338 in 105.1 overs (Atharva Taide 85, SV Thubrikar 54; S Dessai 2-40, Achit Sangwan 2-51) by an innings and 72 runs.

Chaudhry Bansi Lal Cricket Stadium, Lahli, November 30-December 3: **Haryana** 98 in 34.1 overs (JH Saroha 29; NA Sharma 6-28, NK Kanwar 3-40) and 160 in 50.4 overs (Ankit Kumar 53, Aman Kumar 29*; NK Kanwar 4-57, AS Jamwal 3-20) lost to **Himachal Pradesh** 225 in 48.5 overs (RI Thakur 47, MA Sharma 47; SP Kumar 5-72, Vipin Kumar 3-66) and 35/1 in 6.4 overs by nine wickets.

Veer Surendra Sai Stadium, Sambalpur, December 8-11: **Railways** 113 in 37.5 overs (Sahim Hasan 30; Ayaskant Sahu 7-48) and 505/7 dec. in 88 overs (S Hasan 175, Dinesh Mor 154*; A Sahu 3-117, Prashant Pandey 2-65) drew with **Odisha** 384 in 143.5 overs (Sandeep Pattanaik 123, Amrit Khatua 109; Dhrushant Soni 3-55, A Ram 3-74) and 95/6 in 41 overs (Soubhagya Mishra 29*, Kartik Biswal 29; Himanshu Sangwan 4-22). **Odisha** took first-innings lead.

Thalasseri Cricket Stadium, Kannur, December 8-11: **Kerala** 187 in 69.1 overs (Daryl Ferrario 58, Salman Nizar 39; Aman Kumar 3-59, MM Boora 2-34) and 248 in 98 overs (Rohan Kunnummal 81, Albin Alias 63; MM Boora 5-44, SP Jain 4-72) lost to **Haryana** 122 in 41.5 overs (Ankit Kumar 25, MS Rathee 25; Sreehari Nair 5-36, Akshay KC 4-61) and 318/6 in 78.4 overs (Ankit Kumar 110, SG Rohilla 105; Vishweshar Suresh 2-41, S Nair 2-123) by four wickets.

Himachal Pradesh Cricket Association Stadium, Dharamsala, December 8-11: **Jammu and Kashmir** 212 in 75.1 overs (Suryansh Raina 51, Sunil Kumar 40*; AA Walia 3-40, AS Jamwal 3-46) and 193 in 61.1 overs (Zaid Bhat 107; RS Thakur 4-26, Jayshodhan Thakur 2-26) lost to **Himachal Pradesh** 551/8 dec. in 104.4 overs (RI Thakur 177, NA Sharma 164; Mohammad Tahir 3-57, Sahil Lotra 3-97) by an innings and 146 runs.

Sanguem Cricket Ground, Sanguem, December 8-11: **Goa** 193 in 60.3 overs (VG Kahlon 72, Nihal S 36; Shubham Singh 3-50, VNS Tripathi 3-73) and 89 in 47.2 overs (VG Kahlon 41*; SK Chadda 4-33, VNS Tripathi 3-21) lost to **Chhattisgarh** 282 in 83.2 overs (Mayank Wadher 92, Amandeep Khare 55; Nihal S 3-47, Heramb Parab 3-84) and 4 for no loss in 0.1 overs by 10 wickets.

BSP Cricket Stadium, Bhilai, December 16-19: Odisha 138/9 in 64.2 overs (Soubhagya Mishra 38, Kshyamsagar Bal 32; Ajay Mandal 3-27, AS Saxena 2-27) v **Chhattisgarh** 73 for no loss in 14 overs (AG Tiwary 35*, Sanjeet Desai 32*). No result.

Govt Gandhi Memorial Science College Ground, Jammu, December 16-19: Jammu and Kashmir 201 in 74.5 overs (Sahil Lotra 76, Shubham Pundir 46; DG Nalkande 3-36, RK Choudhury 3-49) and 195 in 59.1 overs (Suryansh Raina 92; DG Nalkande 6-73) lost to **Vidarbha** 228 in 77.5 overs (SV Thubrikar 72, YV Rathod 44; Jahid Nazir 4-61, Sunil Kumar 2-32) and 172/3 in 49 overs (SV Thubrikar 82*, SK Wath 42; S Lotra 2-52) by seven wickets.

Railway Cricket Ground, Rajkot RSPB, December 16-19: Goa 138 in 37.5 overs (Heramb Parab 27; Himanshu Sangwan 5-75) and 122 in 40.5 overs (Shivam Amonkar 44, Shubham Dessai 29; H Sangwan 5-20, Dhrushant Soni 3-58) lost to **Railways** 522/9 dec. in 110.4 overs (Sahim Hasan 165, Karan Sharma 132, Dinesh Mor 120; VG Kahlon 7-82) by an innings and 262 runs.

Thalasseri Cricket Stadium, Kannur, December 16-19: Kerala 195 in 59.4 overs (Daryl Ferrario 100; AS Jamwal 5-83, NK Kanwar 2-14) and 153 in 53 overs (Vishnu Raj 59, Salman Nizar 25; AS Jamwal 6-57, AA Walia 3-57) lost to **Himachal Pradesh** 235 in 78.2 overs (SG Arora 109, Arslan Khan 27; Anand Joseph 3-22, D Ferrario 2-33) and 114/7 in 33.1 overs (Arslan 51*, RI Thakur 42; Sreehari Nair 4-33, D Ferrario 2-24) by three wickets.

Gandhi Stadium, Balangir, December 24-27: Jammu and Kashmir 634/8 dec. in 160 overs (Suryansh Raina 228, Abhishant Bakshi 158, Shubham Pundir 104; Anshuman Mishra 3-46, Kartik Biswal 2-154) beat **Odisha** 206 in 93.1 overs (Sandeep Pattanaik 100; Abid Mushtaq 5-50, Paras Sharma 2-18) and 243/2 in 87 overs (Soubhagya Mishra 89*, Amrit Khatua 66*). **Jammu and Kashmir** took first-innings lead.

Sanguem Cricket Ground, Sanguem, December 24-27: Goa 140 in 64.3 overs (Shivam Amonkar 45, Deepraj Gaonkar 43; Sijomon Joseph 5-20, Basil NP 4-57) and 162 in 64 overs (D Gaonkar 68, VG Kahlon 40; Anand Joseph 5-17, S Joseph 2-46) lost to **Kerala** 394 in 109.4 overs (Salman Nizar 177, Sreeroop MP 80; Heramb Parab 5-82, Savio Kaalko 2-41) by an innings and 92 runs.

VCA Kalamana, Nagpur, December 24-27: Vidarbha 342 in 108.2 overs (AD Choudhari 118, SK Wath 99; AA Walia 6-79, Jayshodhan Thakur 2-52) and 17 for no loss in 2.3 overs beat **Himachal Pradesh** 122 in 40.4 overs (NA Sharma 38, Arslan Khan 30; PR Rekhade 4-23, RK Choudhury 4-32) and 233 in 55.4 overs (Arslan 85, AS Jamwal 79; RK Choudhury 5-39, PR Rekhade 4-112) by ten wickets.

Chaudhry Bansi Lal Cricket Stadium, Lahli, December 24-27: Haryana 177 in 62.3 overs (JH Saroha 57, SP Kumar 43; AS Saxena 3-22, Sahban Khan 2-14) and 223 in 62.2 overs (JH Saroha 56, SP Kumar 46; AS Saxena 4-43, SK Chadda 3-64) beat **Chhattisgarh** 145 in 57 overs (Sanidhya Hurkat 51; AR Rana 5-32, Vipin Kumar 2-15) and 133 in 35.5 overs (Shubham Singh 31; AR Rana 5-28, SP Kumar 3-18) by 122 runs.

Thalasseri Cricket Stadium, Kannur, January 1-4: Kerala 284 in 84.5 overs (Rohan Kunnummal 131, Salman Nizar 70; Harsh Tyagi 3-46, Dhrushant Soni 3-54) and 292 in 81.5 overs (Daryl Ferrario 88, S Nizar 58; H Tyagi 4-65, Mayank Singh 2-56) lost to **Railways** 497 in 114.5 overs (Karan Sharma 191, Dinesh Mor 94; Basil NP 4-113, Vishweshar Suresh 3-107) and 82/1 in 17.2 overs (Karan 36*, A Ram 33*) by nine wickets.

VCA Kalamana, Nagpur, January 1-4: Vidarbha 266 in 84.2 overs (AD Choudhari 105, Kushal P 59; MS Rathee 4-76, AR Rana 3-74) and 270 in 90.2 overs (SK Wath 100, SV Thubrikar 64; AR Rana 5-73, MS Rathee 2-84) beat **Haryana** 190 in 61.1 overs (SG Rohilla 122; SR Dubey 2-24, RK Choudhury 2-37) and 216 in 42.3 overs (YR Sharma 120*, MM Boora 25; RK Choudhury 5-64, SR Dubey 3-47) by 130 runs.

Himachal Pradesh Cricket Association Stadium, Dharamsala, January 1-4: Himachal Pradesh 528/8 dec. in 95 overs (DB Rangi 150, RI Thakur 130, AA Walia 103*; Heramb Parab 3-119, Savio Kaalko 2-82) drew with **Goa** 368 in 105 overs (Vaibhav Govekar 128, Kashyap Bakle 69; NA Sharma 3-42, AS Jamwal 3-76) and 384/6 in 105 overs (V Govekar 131, VG

Kahlon 101*; Jayshodhan Thakur 2-55). **Himachal Pradesh** took first-innings lead.

Govt Gandhi Memorial Science College Ground, Jammu, January 1-4: Chhattisgarh 120/9 in 31.5 overs (MSS Hussain 39, Shubham Singh 27; Jahid Nazir 4-32, Auqib Nabi 3-25) and 125 in 47 overs (PM Yadav 35, Sanidhya Hurkat 31; Abid Mushtaq 6-38, Sahil Lotra 4-22) lost to **Jammu and Kashmir** 338 in 98.3 overs (Shubham Pundir 119, Paras Sharma 106*; Gagandeep Singh 5-105, AS Saxena 2-34) by an innings and 93 runs.

Country Cricket Stadium Gharota, Jammu, January 9-12: Jammu and Kashmir 161 in 48 overs (Paras Sharma 42, Muneeb Munaf 34; Basil NP 3-52, Sreehari Nair 2-29) and 304/9 dec. in 83.3 overs (Hisham Saleem 54, Paras 54; S Nair 3-79, Vishweshar Suresh 2-65) beat **Kerala** 63 in 25.3 overs (Auqib Nabi 5-36, Sahil Lotra 4-7) and 149 in 49.4 overs (Albin Alias 35, Rohan Kunnummal 31; Irfan Haq 3-41, S Lotra 2-10) by 253 runs.

Railway Cricket Ground, Rajkot RSPB, January 9-12: Vidarbha 250 in 100.1 overs (AD Choudhari 103, AG Agarwal 66; Yuvraj 4-29, Mayank Singh 4-86) and 259 in 90.3 overs (SK Wath 64, MR Raut 44; Harsh Tyagi 3-60, Himanshu Sangwan 2-21) beat **Railways** 238 in 80.1 overs (Dhrushant Soni 69*, A Ram 35; SR Dubey 5-59, NS Parande 2-48) and 137 in 40.1 overs (H Tyagi 43*; PR Rekhade 5-60, RK Choudhury 3-32) by 134 runs.

JR Institute of Cricket Technology, Barwala, January 9-12: Goa 201 in 86.1 overs (Samar Dubhashi 66*, Shubham Dessai 39; MM Boora 5-42, MS Rathee 4-59) and 405 in 112.1 overs (Kashyap Bakle 180*, Deepraj Gaonkar 104; MS Rathee 6-103, MM Boora 2-80) lost to **Haryana** 526/7 dec. in 121.5 overs (SP Kumar 207, YR Sharma 184; D Gaonkar 2-40, Heramb Parab 2-80) and 81 for no loss in 15 overs (VA Bhardwaj 57*) by ten wickets.

Himachal Pradesh Cricket Association Stadium, Dharamsala, January 9-12: Odisha 161 in 53.5 overs (Ayaskant Sahu 38*, Ashish Rai 29; AS Jamwal 6-53, AA Walia 4-68) and 243 in 101 overs (Soubhagya Mishra 68, Kshyamsagar Bal 63; AS Jamwal 3-44, NA Sharma 2-16) lost to **Himachal Pradesh** 324 in 82.1 overs (DB Rangi 106, Walia 42; Kartik Biswal 7-106, Saurabh Kanojia 2-37) and 82/1 in 13.3 overs (Arslan Khan 40*) by nine wickets.

Points table

Teams	M	W	L	D	T	N/R	Pts	Quotient
Vidarbha	8	6	1	1	0	0	42	1.424
Himachal Pradesh	8	5	1	2	0	0	35	1.257
Railways	8	4	2	2	0	0	29	1.515
Haryana	8	4	3	1	0	0	28	1.165
Kerala	8	3	5	0	0	0	19	1.002
Jammu and Kashmir	8	2	3	3	0	0	18	0.915
Chhattisgarh	8	2	3	3	0	0	18	0.861
Goa	8	1	5	2	0	0	8	0.581
Odisha	8	0	4	4	0	0	8	0.595

Vidarbha qualified for the quarter-finals

Plate Group

Jorhat DSA Stadium, Jorhat, November 2-5: Mizoram 150 in 45 overs (Dhanur Sikri 102*; Akash Kumar 4-45, Arbin Singh 3-27) and 83 in 53.1 overs (Hruaizela 29; Kartik Pawar 5-10, M Nafees 3-14) beat **Meghalaya** 93 in 32.2 overs (Pulkit 28*; Dina 8-37, Hruaizela 2-10) and 106 in 40.3 overs (A Kumar 4-29, Dina 3-47) by 34 runs.

Vikash Cricket Ground, Bhubaneshwar, November 2-5: Sikkim 146 in 51.3 overs (Mohammad Saptula 66*; Nadeem 4-21, Nagaho 4-46) and 142 in 42.5 overs (Yogesh 53; Shubham 4-8, Nadeem 4-40) lost to **Nagaland** 634/5 dec. in 114 overs (Vinayak 214, T Valmik 156, Arvind Verma 100*; Akash Luitel 2-146) by an innings and 346 runs.

Energy Stadium Rajbansi Nagar, Patna, November 2-5: Arunachal Pradesh 134 in 41.3 overs (Uvais 41, Techi Sonam 30; Sachin Singh 5-28, Dilip Kumar 2-24) and 44 in 20.2 overs (Sachin 5-3, Prashant Singh 3-12) lost to **Bihar** 362 in 90 overs (S Gani 145, Vibhooti Bhaskar 52; Abhay Raj 3-82) by an innings and 184 runs.

CAP Siechem Ground, Puducherry, November 2-5: Manipur 71 in 39.5 overs (Sidak Singh 10-31) and 146 in 92.1 overs (Al Bashid 35, Bikash Singh 25; Sidak 4-50, Aravind 2-14) lost to **Puducherry** 105 in 44.4 overs (Paras Ratnaparkhe 41; Bikash 4-22, Thomas M 3-25) and 113/3 in 28.5 overs (Ragu 39, P Ratnaparkhe 33*) by seven wickets.

MCA Cricket Ground, Polo Ground, Shillong, November 14-17: Nagaland 173 in 49.3 overs (Arvind Verma 83, T Valmik 28; Arbin Singh 4-54, Akash Kumar 2-41) and 216 in 46.5 overs (Vinayak 108, A Verma 51; A Kumar 7-33, Arbin 3-55) beat **Meghalaya** 178 in 46.1 overs (Surya Rai 36, Rohit Shah 35; Shubham 4-55, Nagaho 2-49) and 154 in 44 overs (Rohit P 31, A Kumar 30*; Shubham 5-43, Nagaho 2-34) by 57 runs.

Vikash Cricket Ground, Bhubaneshwar, November 14-17: Uttarakhand 534/3 dec. in 115.1 overs (Piyush Joshi 224, Aditya Sethi 113, Kamlesh Kanyal 100*; Mohammad Saptula 2-95) beat **Sikkim** 75 in 19 overs (Bikash 30; Agrim Tiwari 8-37, Pradeep Chamoli 2-14) and 135 in 48.5 overs (Dinesh Dhobi 58*; Harjeet Singh 4-38, P Chamoli 2-23) by an innings and 324 runs.

Bengal Cricket Academy Ground, Kalyani, November 14-17: Manipur 385/9 dec. in 133.2 overs (Aryan Sehrawat 100, Nitesh 82; Dika Ralte 5-78, Dina 4-97) beat **Mizoram** 68 in 33.3 overs (VA Yadav 5-11, Bikash Singh 3-12) and 55 in 30.2 overs (VA Yadav 6-14, Nitesh 2-6) by an innings and 262 runs.

Palmyra Cricket Ground, Puducherry, November 14-17: Bihar 171 in 51.4 overs (S Gani 63, Sachin Singh 28; Akash Kargave 4-54, Sidak Singh 3-39) and 135/8 in 52 overs (Sachin Singh 72; Sidak 4-69, Buvan 2-8) drew with **Puducherry** 288 in 88 overs (Paras Ratnaparkhe 159, Ragu 42; Sachin 7-87). **Puducherry** took first-innings lead.

Nagaland Cricket Stadium, Sovima, November 22-25: Manipur 325 in 115.4 overs (Aryan Sehrawat 74, Kishan 56; Arvind Verma 4-47, Shubham 4-79) and 198 in 85 overs (Kishan 55*, Antriksha 43; Nagaho 4-64, A Verma 3-34) lost to **Nagaland** 462 in 145.4 overs (A Verma 220, T Valmik 52; VA Yadav 4-86, Nitesh 2-111) and 62/1 in 12.5 overs (Rio 31, Vinayak 28*) by nine wickets.

Mangaldai Sports Association Stadium, Mangaldai, November 22-25: Arunachal Pradesh 92 in 29.3 overs (Asif Hossain 41; Sidak Singh 6-28, Madhan 2-8) and 151 in 37.3 overs (A Hossain 39, S Nagar 29; Aravind 3-23, Akash Kargave 3-50, Sidak 3-52) lost to **Puducherry** 293 in 79.5 overs (A Kargave 63, Paras Ratnaparkhe 51; Lee Kamra 4-56, S Nagar 3-54) by an innings and 50 runs.

Rajiv Gandhi International Stadium, Dehradun, November 22-25: Uttarakhand 220 in 76.2 overs (Piyush Joshi 53, Pramod Rawat 39; Arbin Singh 3-59, Kartik Pawar 2-26) and 429/8 dec. in 100.4 overs (Saurav Chauhan 116, Vijay Sharma 116; Akash Kumar 3-97, Arbin 2-83) beat **Meghalaya** 140 in 64.2 overs (Rohit Shah 27, Surya Rai 25; Himanshu Bisht 4-35, Agrim Tiwari 2-24, Pradeep Chamoli 2-24) and 95 in 24.4 overs (Tiwari 32; A Tiwari 5-29, H Bisht 2-6) by 414 runs.

Energy Stadium Rajbansi Nagar, Patna, November 22-25: Bihar 516 in 119.1 overs (S Gani 282, Dilip Kumar 66; Dinesh Dhobi 5-129, Mohammad Rhonak 2-109) beat **Sikkim** 123 in 67.4 overs (D Dhobi 50, Mohammad Saptula 28; Vikas Jha 5-18, Sachin Singh 2-46) and 84 in 37 overs (Akash Luitel 37; Shabbir Khan 4-12, V Jha 4-15) by an innings and 309 runs.

MCA Cricket Ground, Polo Ground, Shillong, November 30-December 3: Manipur 126 in 50 overs (Nitesh 63; Kartik Pawar 3-53, Mohammad Nafees 2-5) and 148 in 48.1 overs (Nitesh 51, Karnajit Y 25; K Pawar 3-61, Arbin Singh 2-51) beat **Meghalaya** 102 in 39.1 overs

(Kishan 6-31, Nitesh 2-28) and 163 in 87.3 overs (IF Thabah 29, Akash Kumar 27; Kishan 4-38, Bikash Singh 3-25) by nine runs.

Golaghat DSA Ground, Golaghat, November 30-December 3: Arunachal Pradesh 302 in 64.2 overs (Asif Hossain 134, AV Jaiswal 51; Arvind Verma 6-61) and 261 in 77 overs (A Hossain 88, AV Jaiswal 57; A Verma 5-35, Shubham 4-44) lost to **Nagaland** 224 in 61.2 overs (T Valmik 76, Nagaho 43; S Nagar 4-31, Gaurav Verma 3-41) and 340/4 in 84.2 overs (Rishav 127, Vinayak 116; S Nagar 3-63) by six wickets.

Abhimanyu Cricket Academy, Dehradun, November 30-December 3: Mizoram 197 in 73.2 overs (Bazid Shah 64, Hruaia 37; Kamlesh Kanyal 3-23, Sunil Bisht 3-51) and 169 in 60.2 overs (Parvez 42*, Gaurav Singh 26; Himanshu Bisht 5-47, Pradeep Chamoli 3-48) lost to **Uttarakhand** 433/6 dec. in 103 overs (Ajit Rawat 226, Vijay Sharma 108; A Kumar 4-65, Dhanur Sikri 2-81) by an innings and 67 runs.

Palmyra Cricket Ground, Puducherry, November 30-December 3: Sikkim 86 in 36.1 overs (Akash Kargave 5-21, Aravind 2-13) and 88 in 29.5 overs (Afzar Hussain 25, Dinesh Dhobi 25; Sidak Singh 7-33) lost to **Puducherry** 313/4 dec. in 48 overs (Paras Ratnaparkhe 101*, A Kargave 81; Aamir 2-49) by an innings and 139 runs.

Jalan Outdoor Stadium, Dibrugarh, December 8-11: Sikkim 32 in 22 overs (Dinpuia 4-5, Sumit 3-8, A Kumar 3-13) and 90 in 36.5 overs (Dinpuia 6-27, A Kumar 3-20) lost to **Mizoram** 99 in 31.5 overs (A Kumar 46, Hruaia 25; Mohammad Saptula 4-22, Mohammad Rhonak 4-36) and 26/1 in 7.4 overs by nine wickets.

Mangaldai Sports Association Stadium, Mangaldai, December 8-11: Uttarakhand 199 in 77.4 overs (Pundir 44, Himanshu Bisht 41; S Nagar 5-42, Asif Hossain 2-13) and 290/9 dec. in 89.5 overs (Dinesh Pawar 100*, Ajit Rawat 73; S Nagar 4-65, Ayush 3-61) beat **Arunachal Pradesh** 70 in 32.5 overs (Agrim Tiwari 4-23, H Bisht 2-0) and 148 in 43.1 overs (AV Jaiswal 54, Gaurav Verma 44; H Bisht 5-38, Harjeet Singh 3-29) by 271 runs.

Videocon Ground, Kolkata, December 8-11: Manipur 59 in 25.3 overs (Prashant Singh 4-19, Shabbir Khan 3-19) and 210 in 63.5 overs (Ronald M 79, Kishan 42; Shabbir 4-46, Sachin Singh 4-68) lost to **Bihar** 271 in 59.1 overs (Sachin 164, S Gani 28; Kishan 3-34, Nitesh 3-71) by an innings and two runs.

Palmyra Cricket Ground, Puducherry, December 8-11: Nagaland 180 in 55.5 overs (Vinayak 50, T Valmik 39; Vengat 5-45, Aravind 2-35) and 211 in 55.5 overs (Nagaho 80*, T Valmik 33; Vengat 5-37, Sidak Singh 3-88) lost to **Puducherry** 325 in 71.2 overs (Paras Ratnaparkhe 106, Akash Kargave 90; Shubham 4-64, Rahul Bisht 2-15) and 67/2 in 16.2 overs (Ragu 42*; Shubham 2-14) by eight wickets.

JU Second Campus, Salt Lake, Kolkata, December 16-19: Arunachal Pradesh 158 in 50.5 overs (Netaji Teron 44, Uvais 43; VA Yadav 5-33, Thomas M 2-17) and 165 in 62.3 overs (Gaurav Verma 58, N Teron 28; Thomas M 5-43, Kishan 2-18) lost to **Manipur** 152 in 56.3 overs (Aryan Sehrawat 33, Kishan 27; S Nagar 5-31, G Verma 2-16) and 172/4 in 53.4 overs (Abhishek 100, Al Bashid 29; Ayush 2-23) by six wickets.

Golaghat DSA Ground, Golaghat, December 16-19: Mizoram 173 in 82 overs (Dhanur Sikri 69, Bazid Shah 29; Shubham 5-21) and 68 in 31.1 overs (D Sikri 34; Shubham 6-27, Nagaho 2-11) lost to **Nagaland** 363 in 79.4 overs (Vinayak 124, Arvind Verma 71; Muanzuala 3-76, Rohan 2-53) by an innings and 122 runs.

Energy Stadium Rajbansi Nagar, Patna, December 16-19: Bihar 56 in 26 overs (Agrim Tiwari 3-19, Pundir 2-11) and 197 in 66.1 overs (Anmol Bonny 77, S Gani 40; Pundir 3-25, Harjeet Singh 3-53) lost to **Uttarakhand** 231 in 59.3 overs (Saurav Chauhan 118, Vijay Sharma 50; Shabbir Khan 5-61, Vikas Jha 3-41) and 25 for no loss in 3.1 overs by ten wickets.

Rural Development Trust Stadium, Anantapur, December 16-19: Meghalaya 405 in 174.3 overs (Rohit Shah 200, Akash Kumar 74; Chandra 6-94, Mohammad Rhonak 2-69) beat **Sikkim** 63 in 46.5 overs (A Kumar 3-14, Arbin Singh 2-8, Kartik Pawar 2-8) and 54 in 34 overs (K Pawar 4-10, Arbin 4-11) by an innings and 288 runs.

Jalan Outdoor Stadium, Dibrugarh, December 24-27: Puducherry 232 in 58.1 overs

(Akash Kargave 75, Ragu 53; A Kumar 4-45, Dika Ralte 3-46, Dinpuia 3-61) and 426/7 dec. in 86 overs (Paras Ratnaparkhe 203, Sidak Singh 78; A Kumar 3-105, D Ralte 2-100) beat **Mizoram** 218 in 93.2 overs (Bazid Shah 74, Dhanur Sikri 71; A Kargave 3-55, Sidak 3-60) and 138 in 56.3 overs (D Sikri 37; Sidak 5-47, Aravind 2-19) by 302 runs.

Mangaldai Sports Association Stadium, Mangaldai, December 24-27: Meghalaya 48 in 23.1 overs (S Nagar 6-23, Rajneesh Kumar 2-7) and 255 in 91.4 overs (Rohit P 75, Rohit Shah 46; S Nagar 4-65, AV Jaiswal 2-67) lost to **Arunachal Pradesh** 163 in 35.1 overs (Asif Hossain 49, S Nagar 35; Kartik Pawar 7-26, Arbin Singh 2-57) and 144/5 in 39.2 overs (Gaurav Verma 53, A Hossain 30*; Akash Kumar 2-22, K Pawar 2-45) by 5 wickets.

Golaghat DSA Ground, Golaghat, December 24-27: Nagaland 154 in 44.2 overs (Wahid 38, Vinayak 30; Prashant Singh 5-38, Shabbir Khan 2-43) and 165 in 56.3 overs (Arvind Verma 35; Manmohan 4-52, Sachin Singh 3-29) beat **Bihar** 114 in 33.3 overs (S Gani 27, Anmol Bonny 26; Shubham 8-41) and 149 in 44.1 overs (S Gani 28; Shubham 8-69) by 56 runs.

Rajiv Gandhi International Stadium, Dehradun, December 24-27: Manipur 118 in 47 overs (Nitesh 46, Bikash Singh 36; Sunil Bisht 4-29, Pundir 2-8) and 90 in 35.1 overs (Thomas M 29; Pradeep Chamoli 5-24, Pundir 2-19) lost to **Uttarakhand** 389/9 dec. in 115.5 overs (Ajit Rawat 114, Sagar 84; Thomas M 5-80, Bikash Singh 2-68) by an innings and 181 runs.

MCA Cricket Ground, Polo Ground, Shillong, January 1-4: Puducherry 276 in 62.3 overs (Paras Ratnaparkhe 79, Ragu 63, Akash Kargave 63; Kartik Pawar 8-89) beat **Meghalaya** 68 in 35.5 overs (Aravind 6-15, Sidak Singh 4-29) and 115 in 35 overs (Kishan 26; A Kargave 5-29, Sidak 5-54) by an innings and 93 runs.

Mangaldai Sports Association Stadium, Mangaldai, January 1-4: Arunachal Pradesh 552/9 dec. in 107.1 overs (Asif Hossain 250*, Nabam Josh 87; Mohammad Rhonak 4-133, Chandra 3-150) beat **Sikkim** 42 in 16.1 overs (S Nagar 6-11, Ayush 3-30) and 54 in 26.3 overs (Hitesh Mehra 3-7, S Nagar 3-11) by an innings and 456 runs.

Moin-ul-Haq Stadium, Patna, January 1-4: Mizoram 148 in 51.3 overs (Dhanur Sikri 98, Bazid Shah 25; Sachin Singh 5-28, Shabbir Khan 3-47) and 93 in 55.3 overs (Gaurav Singh 27; Sachin 4-14, Shabbir 4-23) lost to **Bihar** 283 in 105 overs (Satish Kumar 100, Anmol Bonny 68; A Kumar 4-64, Muanzuala 3-43) by an innings and 42 runs.

Abhimanyu Cricket Academy, Dehradun, January 1-4: Uttarakhand 336 in 130.1 overs (Piyush Joshi 85, Dinesh Pawar 55; Shubham 6-143, Nagaho 3-62) and 264/8 dec. in 66 overs (D Pawar 81*, P Joshi 58; Ashirbad 4-58, Wahid 2-18) beat **Nagaland** 176 in 57.4 overs (Arvind Verma 58, Vinayak 28; Pradeep Chamoli 4-60, Sunil Bisht 3-35) and 183 in 65.4 overs (Vimal 50, Samarat 43; P Chamoli 3-37, Agrim Tiwari 3-54) by 241 runs.

Jalan Outdoor Stadium, Dibrugarh, January 9-12: Mizoram 64 in 32 overs (Bazid Shah 45*; Hitesh Mehra 5-18, S Nagar 4-12) and 40 in 25.4 overs (H Mehra 5-23, S Nagar 2-9) lost to **Arunachal Pradesh** 379/6 dec. in 86 overs (Gaurav Verma 102*, AV Jaiswal 67; Dinpuia 3-114) by an innings and 275 runs.

MCA Cricket Ground, Polo Ground, Shillong, January 9-12: Bihar 151 in 42.2 overs (Shabbir Khan 61*; Akash Kumar 7-68, Kartik Pawar 2-15) and 243 in 66.5 overs (Sachin Singh 75, Abhishek Kumar 67*; K Pawar 6-81, A Kumar 2-61) beat **Meghalaya** 100 in 44.1 overs (K Pawar 32*, Kenny 26; Shabbir 3-15, Sachin 3-16) and 103 in 31.2 overs (Rohit P 30; Sachin 3-17, Vikas Jha 3-30) by 191 runs.

Videocon Ground, Kolkata, January 9-12: Manipur 644/7 dec. in 138.5 overs (Aryan Sehrawat 209, Nitesh 174; Mohammad Saptula 4-173) beat **Sikkim** 91 in 34 overs (VA Yadav 5-25, Thomas M 3-36) and 115 in 42.1 overs (Sanjay Chettri 32; Bikash Singh 5-33, VA Yadav 3-40) by an innings and 438 runs.

Palmyra Cricket Ground, Puducherry, January 9-12: Uttarakhand 533 in 144.4 overs (Himanshu Bisht 155, Piyush Joshi 148, Sagar 101; Vengat 2-41, Akash Kargave 2-74) beat **Puducherry** 76 in 20.5 overs (Sidak Singh 44; Pradeep Chamoli 4-14, Agrim Tiwari 3-29) and 193 in 60 overs (Satish Jangir 70, A Kargave 32; H Bisht 4-27, P Chamoli 2-52) by an innings and 264 runs.

Points table

Teams	M	W	L	D	T	N/R	Pts	Quotient
Uttarakhand	8	8	0	0	0	0	53	3.154
Puducherry	8	6	1	1	0	0	42	1.736
Nagaland	8	6	2	0	0	0	38	1.383
Bihar	8	5	2	1	0	0	35	1.602
Manipur	8	4	4	0	0	0	26	1.160
Arunachal Pradesh	8	3	5	0	0	0	20	1.064
Mizoram	8	2	6	0	0	0	12	0.411
Meghalaya	8	1	7	0	0	0	7	0.767
Sikkim	8	0	8	0	0	0	0	0.140

Uttarakhand qualified for the quarter-finals

Quarter-finals

Dhruv Pandove Stadium, Patiala, January 17-20: Uttarakhand 160 in 43 overs (Vijay Sharma 60, Piyush Joshi 30; Ikjot Thind 3-24, Arshdeep Singh 3-30) and 147 in 31 overs (P Joshi 38, Agrim Tiwari 30; Harpreet Brar 5-60, Arshdeep 2-22) lost to **Punjab** 713 in 183.1 overs (Nikhil Chaudhary 169, Mansab Gill 115, Sanvir Singh 112; Sunil Bisht 5-189, Pradeep Chamoli 2-116) by an innings and 406 runs.

Eden Gardens, Kolkata, January 17-20: Bengal 620/7 dec. in 168.3 overs (Abhimanyu Easwaran 167, Sudip Gharami 148; Arpit Guleria 3-112, NA Sharma 2-57) and 164/3 in 42 overs (Ankur Paul 65, Ritwik Roy Chowdhury 50) drew with **Himachal Pradesh** 406 in 126.1 overs (RI Thakur 112, PS Khanduri 85; Akash Deep 4-142, R Roy Chowdhury 3-50). **Bengal** took first-innings lead.

VCA Kalamana, Nagpur, January 17-20: Vidarbha 331 in 105 overs (Atharva Taide 134, MR Raut 62; Aquib Kureshi 5-62, Kruthik Hanagavadi 3-58) and 221 in 65.4 overs (A Taide 70, RK Choudhry 39; SZ Mulani 5-62, Jay Bista 4-59) beat **Mumbai** 154 in 54.3 overs (J Bista 43, Chinmay Sutar 41; RK Choudhury 4-45, PR Rekhade 3-44) and 104 in 35.1 overs (J Bista 34, C Sutar 31; PR Rekhade 6-36, RK Choudhury 2-21) by 294 runs.

Sardar Patel Stadium, Valsad, January 17-20: Gujarat 428 in 128.2 overs (Kshitij Patel 95, YD Gardharia 93; Harshvardhan 3-64, Trishal Trivedi 3-109) and 322/9 in 100 overs (Het Patel 80, YD Gardharia 75; T Trivedi 4-81, Harshvardhan 2-35) drew with **Uttar Pradesh** 377 in 102 overs (Shivam Chowdhury 144, Sandeep Kumar 79; KR Patel 3-57, Jayveer Sinh 3-62, Tejas Patel 3-86). **Gujarat** took first-innings lead.

Semi-finals

Eden Gardens, Kolkata, January 26-29: Vidarbha 351 in 112.4 overs (Atharva Taide 78, SK Wath 69; Ritwik Roy Chowdhury 3-57, Ananta Saha 3-62, Shreyan Chakraborty 3-108) and 111 in 42.1 overs (Manas Sahare 32; A Saha 5-45, S Sarkar 3-12) lost to **Bengal** 348 in 117.5 overs (Agniv Pan 103, Sudip Gharami 61; SR Dubey 6-89, M Sahare 2-42) and 115/2 in 23.1 overs (Abhimanyu Easwaran 52*, S Gharami 44) by eight wickets.

Sardar Patel Stadium, Valsad, January 26-29: Gujarat 165 in 55.3 overs (KB Panchal 54, YD Gardharia 34; Arshdeep Singh 6-52) and 240 in 71.3 overs (MA Hingrajia 87, Rahul Shah 76; Sanvir Singh 2-16, Arshdeep 2-46) lost to **Punjab** 447 in 105 overs (Ramandeep Singh 138, Mansab Gill 97; KR Patel 3-104, KB Panchal 2-31) by an innings and 42 runs.

Final

Dhruv Pandove Stadium, Patiala, February 4-7: Bengal 191 in 54.2 overs (Subham Chatterjee 64, Ritwik Roy Chowdhury 43; Harpreet Brar 5-62, Arshdeep Singh 2-18) and 76 in 26.2 overs (H Brar 7-23) lost to **Punjab** 133 in 48.1 overs (Ramandeep Singh 37, A Pandove 34; Shreyan Chakraborty 4-28, Aamir 4-53) and 137/9 in 30.1 overs (Anmolpreet Singh 32; S Chakraborty 6-56, Aamir 3-70) by one wicket.

Winners: Punjab

2017-18

Elite Group A

TDSA Ground, Tinsukia, October 8-12: Rajasthan 282 in 91.5 overs (Yash Kothari 87, Mohit Sharma 49; Rajjakuddin Ahmed 5-50, Aryaman Panghal 2-44) and 311/7 dec in 89 overs (Mahendra Singh 69, Ajay Singh 55*; Roshan Alam 3-72, R Ahmed 2-42) beat **Assam** 226 in 63.5 overs (Abhishek Thakuri 97, Biplab Saikia 33; Abhimanyu Lamba 4-36, Chandrapratap Singh 2-26) and 140 in 55.2 overs (Mujibur Ali 62, Yasir Ali 26; Aditya Garhwal 4-13, Shubham Sharma 3-32) by 227 runs.

Dhruv Pandove Stadium, Patiala, October 8-12: Punjab 445 in 153 overs (Karan Kaila 108, Prabjot Singh 98; Jashveerkumar Saini 3-78, Raj Choudhury 3-101) beat **Vidarbha** 129 in 56 overs (Sachin Katariya 31, Zorain 28; Arpit Pannu 5-41, K Kaila 3-27) and 306 in 105 overs (f/o) (Vaibhav Chandekar 56, S Katariya 45; K Kaila 7-114, A Pannu 2-79) by an innings and 10 runs.

Pune Cricket Club Ground, Pune, October 8-12: Delhi 288 in 82.1 overs (Hiten Dalal 74, Dinesh Mor 55; Mukesh Choudhary 4-67, Izhaan Sayed 3-48) drew with **Maharashtra** 274 in 63.5 overs (Murtuza Trunkwala 102, Vijay Zol 86; Tejas Baroka 5-60, Sarang 2-60). Delhi won on the basis of first-innings lead.

Dhruv Pandove Stadium, Patiala, October 15-18: Punjab 529 in 143.1 overs (Anmolpreet Singh 202, Sanvir Singh 105; Arjun Sharma 7-175, Mayank Dagar 3-141) beat **Himachal Pradesh** 177 in 76.5 overs (Ravi Thakur 31, Digvijay Rangi 31; Karan Kaila 5-37, Arpit Pannu 2-33) and 261 in 66.2 overs (f/o) (Ekant Sen 50, M Dagar 41; K Kaila 6-73, A Pannu 2-47) by an innings and 91 runs

VCA Stadium, Nagpur, October 15-18: Delhi 389 in 102.2 overs (Lalit Yadav 154, Dinesh Mor 71; Atharva Deshpande 7-109, Raj Choudhury 2-122) beat **Vidarbha** 114 in 35 overs (Siddhesh Wath 36, A Deshpande 30; Shivank Vashisth 5-32, Tejas Baroka 3-50) and 252 in 84.3 overs (f/o) (S Wath 76, Zorain 55; T Baroka 5-113, S Vashisth 4-80) by an innings and 23 runs

Luhnu Cricket ground, Bilaspur, October 26-29: Maharashtra 153 in 53.4 overs (BC Porohit 52; Arjun Sharma 4-45, Sidharth Sharma 3-44, Abhishek Kumar 3-55) and 364 in 102.4 (Prashant Kore 73, Shamshuzama Kazi 65; Digvijay Rangi 4-31, Sidharth 4-61) lost to **Himachal Pradesh** 195 in 70.1 overs (Mani Sharma 47, Ravi Thakur 39; P Kore 2-4, S Kazi 2-27) and 323/5 in 88.5 overs (Ekant Sen 158*, Shubham Arora 54; IA Sayed 2-62) by five wickets.

IS Bindra Cricket Stadium, PCA, Mohali, October 26-29: Delhi 130 in 50.5 overs (Dinesh Mor 48, Lalit Yadav 24; Jagjit Singh 4-48, Sanvir Singh 3-37) and 159/5 in 58 overs (Rajesh Sharma 61*, Lalit 31; Mayank Markande 2-62) drew with **Punjab** 841/9 dec in 246 overs (Abhijeet Garg 310, Sanvir 231; Shivank Vashisth 6-261). Punjab took first-innings lead.

Deccan Gymkhana Cricket Ground, Pune, November 3-6: Maharashtra 399 in 99.3 overs (Jay Pande 130,Shamshuzama Kazi 74; Raj Choudhury 6-106, Sachin Katariya 3-42) and 119/1 in 31.2 (Murtuza Trunkwala 49*, J Pande 39) beat **Vidarbha** 146 in 70.3 overs (Mohit Kale 65, S Katariya 36; Jagdish Zope 5-33, Prashant Kore 4-10) and 368 in 109.4 overs (f/o)

(M Kale 93, VV Palandurkar 71; J Zope 3-132, S Kazi 3-43) by nine wickets.

Luhnu Cricket ground, Bilaspur, November 3-6: Himachal Pradesh 294 in 86 overs (Ravi Thakur 134, Arjun Sharma 37; Lalit Yadav 5-30, Simarjeet Singh 2-72) and 526/5 in 114 overs (Ekant Sen 237*, Mani Sharma 100*; Sarang 2-78, Shivank Vashisth 2-137) drew with **Delhi** 652/6 dec in 129 overs (Yash Sehrawat 225, Hiten Dalal 167, Rajesh Sharma 119; E Sen 2-40, Digvijay Rangi 2-117). Delhi took first-innings lead.

ADCA Ground, Aurangabad, November 11-14: Punjab 216 in 69.1 overs (Nikhil Chaudhary 71, Karan Kaila 51; Shubham Kothari 5-83, Jagdish Zope 2-41) and 330 in 101.4 overs (Akul Pandove 55*, N Chaudhary 52; J Zope 3-60, S Kothari 3-121) beat**Maharashtra** 114 in 43.5 overs (Jay Pande 53; Sanvir Singh 3-17, N Chaudhary 3-33) and 200 in 62.5 overs (Nikhil Naik 76, Hrishikesh Kale 26*; Akul Pandove 5-57, N Chaudhary 2-10) by 232 runs

Luhnu Cricket ground, Bilaspur, November 11-14: Himachal Pradesh 172 in 48.1 overs (Digvijay Rangi 46, Chahat Malhotra 32; Jashveerkumar Saini 7-69, Harsad Chelwani 2-50) and 205 in 53.4 overs (Shubham Arora 53, Ekant Sen 30; YP Dhude 3-41, J Saini 3-77) lost to**Vidarbha** 302 in 111.1 overs (Mohit Kale 64, Vaibhav Chandekar 58; Arjun Sharma 4-81, Abhishek Kumar 3-49) and 76/5 in 22.3 overs (Saurabh Thubrikar 22; Arjun 3-24, C Malhotra 2-25) by five wickets.

Elite Group A points table

Teams	M	W	L	D	T	N/R	Pts.	NRR
Punjab	4	3	0	1	0	0	23	+0.471
Delhi	4	1	0	3	0	0	14	+0.175
Maharashtra	4	1	2	1	0	0	7	+0.395
Himachal Pradesh	4	1	2	1	0	0	7	-0.128
Vidarbha	4	1	3	0	0	0	6	-0.694

Punjab and Delhi qualified for the knock-outs

Elite Group B

Krishnagiri Stadium, Wayanad, October 8-12: Kerala 497 in 140.5 overs (Salman Nizar 105, Daryl Ferrario 86; Karan Patel 3-104, Abhinav Tandel 3-108) drew with **Gujarat** 159 in 53 overs (Karan ~~Patel~~ 27, Kathan Patel 23; Fabid Ahmed 3-21, M Rabin Krishna 3-34) and 315/9 in 166 overs (f/o) (Kathan 87, Rahul Shah 68; KC Akshay 3-46, Sijomon Joseph 2-62). Kerala took first-innings lead.

ICL Sankar Nagar Cricket Ground, Thirunelveli, October 8-12: Mumbai578 in 156.1 overs (Jay Bista 212, Khizar Dafedar 91; Shahrukh Khan 3-88, Sanjay Yadav 3-118) drew with**Tamil Nadu**307 in 111 overs (J Kousik 121, Suresh Lokeshwar 76; J Bista 3-62, K Dafedar 2-28) and 247/3 in 80 overs (f/o) (Shahrukh 102, K Mukunth 71*; Dhrumil Matkar 2-27). Mumbai took first-innings lead.

Sharad Pawar Cricket Academy BKC, Mumbai, October 15-18: Mumbai 351/8 dec in 98 overs (Hardik Tamore 77, Akshay Sardesai 66; Abhinav Tandel 3-52, Sneh Shah 3-79) drew with **Gujarat** 187/2 in 57 overs (Kathan Patel 100*, Rahul Shah 39). No result.

Chaudhry Bansi Lal Cricket Stadium, Lahli, October 15-18: Haryana 96 in 40 overs (Satyam Sharma 32; Anand Joseph 6-28, Fazil Fanoos 2-18) and 172 in 55.3 overs (Anubhav Ahuja 48, Mohit Hooda 31; Fabid Ahmed 5-31, F Fanoos 3-49) beat **Kerala** 153 in 66 overs (Vihnu Raj 41, Rohan Kunnummal 26; Ravi Balhara 6-50, Tinu Kundu 4-21) and 82 in 37.3 overs (Albin Alias 25; T Kundu 5-23, R Balhara 5-44) by 33 runs.

NPR College Ground, Dindigul, October 26-29: Haryana 70 in 35.5 overs (S Mohanprasath

5-13, Ashwath Mukunthan 3-24) and 123 in 66 overs (Vijayant Sahu 56, Mohit Hooda 24; S Swaminathan 7-44, R Sai Kishore 2-25)lost to **Tamil Nadu** 252 in 99.4 overs (Shahrukh Khan 65; Suresh Lokeshwar 48; Saket Aggarwal 4-55, Tinu Kundu 4-67) by an innings and 59 runs.
Krishnagiri Stadium, Wayanad, October 26-29: Kerala 322 in 93.4 overs (Daryl Ferrario 76, Albin Alias 65; Shams Mulani 4-93, Tushar Deshpande 3-56) and 316/4 dec in 103 overs (Salman Nizar 109*, Harikrishnan KN 104*; Minad Manjrekar 3-48) drew with **Mumbai** 353 in 87.4 overs (Jay Bista 128, Akshay Sardesai 96; Harikrishnan 2-12, Fabid Ahmed 2-69) and 17/1 in 2.1 overs. Mumbai took first-innings lead.
Lalbhai Contractor Stadium, Surat, November 3-6: Tamil Nadu 379 in 124.4 overs (Shahrukh Khan 184*, K Mukunth 42; Arzan Nagwaswalla 3-77, Hardik Patel 3-106) and 112/2 in 25.5 overs (Shahrukh 69*, Mukunth 33*) beat **Gujarat** 170 in 62.2 overs (Aditya Patel 77*, A Nagwaswalla 21; Mohan Abhinav 5-28, Shahrukh 3-47) and 320 in 111.4 overs (f/o) (Karan Patel 54, Kathan Patel 45; S Mohanprasath 3-71, M Abhinav 2-43) by eight wickets.
Sharad Pawar Cricket Academy BKC, Mumbai, November 3-6: Mumbai 532/6 dec in 136.1 overs (Akshay Sardesai 250*, Vaidik Murkar 74; Aman Kumar 3-101) beat **Haryana** 226 in 89.4 overs (Mohit Hooda 69, Aakash Antil 63; Salman Khan 4-39, Karsh Kothari 4-46) and 175 in 65.4 overs (f/o) (Vivek Yadav 39, Vijayant Sahu 38; K Kothari 4-51, Shams Mulani 3-39, Salman 3-61) by an innings and 131 runs.
Krishnagiri Stadium, Wayanad, November 11-14: Tamil Nadu 158 in 51 overs (Kavin Ravi 48, Balchander Anirudh 48; Anand Joseph 5-55, Fazil Fanoos 4-62) and 244 in 64.5 overs (Shahrukh Khan 66, M Abhinav 54*; F Fanoos 7-76, A Joseph 2-64) beat **Kerala** 42 in 16.4 overs (Ashwath Mukunthan 5-26, J Kousik 4-10) and 171 in 53.2 overs (Rohan Kunnummal 53, F Fanoos 36; A Mukuthan 3-58, S Mohanprasath 2-22) by 189 runs
Sardar Patel Stadium, Valsad, November 11-14: Gujarat 282 in 86.5 overs (Kathan Patel 132, Mehfuz Patel 59; Aman Kumar 8-59, Mohit Hooda 2-29) and 171 in 55.4 overs (Kshitij Patel 41, Karan Trivedi 36*; Vivek Yadav 5-43, Saket Aggarwal 2-59) beat **Haryana** 276 in 93.5 overs (Aakash Antil 97, M Hooda 70; Arzan Nagwaswalla 3-60, Kavish Panchal 2-33) and 108 in 28.4 overs (Saket 36, Ashish Parmar 25; K Panchal 4-12, A Nagwaswalla 3-34) by 69 runs

Elite Group B points table

Teams	M	W	L	D	T	N/R	Pts.	NRR
Tamil Nadu	4	3	0	1	0	0	20	+0.114
Mumbai	4	1	0	3	0	0	14	+0.847
Gujarat	4	1	1	2	0	0	8	-0.659
Haryana	4	1	3	0	0	0	6	-0.433
Kerala	4	0	2	2	0	0	4	+0.187

Tamil and Mumbai qualified for the knock-outs

Elite Group C

Bengal Cricket Academy Ground, Kalyani, October 8-12: Bengal 123 in 48.3 overs (Saurabh Singh 39; Yuvraj 3-22, Omprakash Jaiswal 2-6) drew with **Railways** 367/8 in 105 overs (Karan Sharma 86, Faiz Ahmad 79; Ishan Porel 5-87). Railways took first-innings lead.
Dr P.V.G. Raju ACA Sports Complex, Vizianagaram, October 8-12: Baroda 288 in 90.4 overs (Dhruv Patel 84*, Mahir Shaikh 52; K Bhimarao 3-51, I Kathik Raman 3-83) and 206/5 in 67 overs (Shlok Desai 100, Akshay Brambhatt 45; Karthik Raman 3-56) drew with **Andhra** 270 in 106.5 overs (Naren Reddy 68, G Jayavardhan 56; Kartik Kakade 4-64, Shoeb Sopariya 2-57). Baroda took first-innings lead.

KSCA Stadium, Hubli, October 15-18: Andhra 172 in 57.2 overs (Manish Golamaru 44*, C R Gnaneshwar 34; Shubhang Hegde 3-50, Prateek Jain 2-28) and 374/9 dec in 101.3 overs (Gnaneshwar 117, Dhruva Reddy 63; S Aditya 5-69, S Hegde 2-123) beat **Karnataka** 271 in 85.3 overs (KN Bharath 80, Vyshak Vijaykumar 40; K Bhimrao 5-76, A Vinaykumar 2-63) and 111 in 58.5 overs (D Nischal 43, Abhinav Manohar 30; Dharma Reddy 3-10, Bhimrao 3-42) by 164 runs

Motibaug Cricket Ground, Vadodara, October 15-18: Bengal 351 in 122.4 overs (Suvankar Bal 95, Kazi Junaid Saifi 52; Dhruv Patel 2-38, Kartik Kakade 2-86) and 88 in 50.4 overs (S Bal 26; Rishi Arothe 5-31, Dev Patel 4-13) lost to **Baroda** 343 in 126.3 overs (Ahmadnoor Pathan 161, Jyotsnil Singh 63; Anurag Tiwari 4-59, Ishan Porel 3-91) and 97/0 in 26.3 overs (A Pathan 56*, Jyotsnil 37*) by ten wickets.

Bengal Cricket Academy Ground, Kalyani, October 26-29: Bengal 407 in 124.5 overs (Ritwik Chowdhury 90, Agniv Pan 84*; Venu Vinukonda 5-124, Naren Reddy 2-52) beat **Andhra** 149 in 57.1 overs (Karan Shinde 28, C R Gnaneshwar 26; Ananta Saha 3-29, Pritam Chakraborty 3-46) and 232 in 62.1 overs (f/o) (Kranthi Kumar 66, I Karthik Raman 55; Aamir Gani 6-78, A Saha 2-30) by an innings and 26 runs.

Alur Cricket Stadium-II, Alur, October 26-29: Railways 234 in 76.2 overs (Faiz Ahmad 50, Ashish Sehrawat 45; KN Bharath 3-50, M Prasidh Krishna 3-52) and 197 in 63.1 overs (F Ahmad 48, Kushal Kakad 38; Prasidh Krishna 3-30, Bharath 3-37) lost to **Karnataka** 547/7 dec in 151 overs (D Nischal 243, KL Shrijith 110; OJ Jaiswal 4-131, K Kakad 2-73) by an innings and 116 runs.

Diesel Mechanical Works Cricket Ground , Patiala, November 3-6: Railways 286 in 117.2 overs (Omprakash Jaiswal 73, Ashish Sehrawat 33; Kartik Kakade 4-80, Shlok Desai 2-13) and 237/3 in 86 overs (A Sehrawat 117, Kaushal Singh 58*; K Kakade 2-23) drew with **Baroda** 302 in 113 overs (Akshay Brambhatt 89, Dhruv Patel 71; Abhishek Sharma 5-118, Kaushal 2-70). Baroda took first-innings lead.

KSCA Stadium, Belgaum, November 3-6: Bengal 497/9 dec in 155.5 overs (Saurabh Singh 187, Agniv Pan 123, Ritwik Chowdhury 109; M Prasidh Krishna 2-63, KL Shrijith 2-65) drew with **Karnataka** 524/5 in 190 overs (Abhishek Reddy 266, Shrijith 131; Anurag Tiwari 3-148, Kazi Saifi 2-49). Karnataka took first-innings lead.

Karnail Singh Stadium, New Delhi, November 11-14: Andhra 195 in 55.2 overs (Karan Shinde 54, Naren Reddy 50; Abhishek Sharma 5-83) and 196 in 51.4 overs (G Jayavardhan 54, Naren 36; Abhishek 6-65) beat **Railways** 175 in 50 overs (Karan Sharma 65, Ashish Singh 37; Manish Golamaru 7-42, A Vinaykumar 2-54) and 100 in 34.5 overs (Ashish Sehrawat 35; Vinay Kumar 7-35, M Golamaru 3-38) by 116 runs.

SDNRW Ground, Mysore, November 11-14: Baroda 85 in 39.1 overs (Pratyush Kumar 20; S Aditya 5-21, Shubhang Hegde 3-18) and 176 in 51 overs (Dhruv Patel 78, Mahir Shaikh 45; M Prasidh Krishna 4-35, KN Bharath 3-29, S Hegde 3-69) lost to **Karnataka** 197 in 62.2 overs (D Nischal 46, B R Sarath 41; Gurjinder Singh Maan 4-48, Shlok Desai 2-9) and 66/1 in 13.2 overs (Abhishek Reddy 40*) by nine wickets.

Elite Group C points table

Teams	M	W	L	D	T	N/R	Pts.	NRR
Karnataka	4	2	1	1	0	0	16	-0.129
Andhra	4	2	1	1	0	0	13	+0.182
Baroda	4	1	1	2	0	0	13	+0.240
Bengal	4	1	1	2	0	0	9	-0.100
Railways	4	0	2	2	0	0	4	-0.252

Karnataka and Andhra qualified for the knock-outs

Plate Group A

Tinsukia District Sports Association Ground, Tinsukia, October 8-12: Rajasthan 282 in 91.5 overs (Yash Kothari 87, Manish Sharma 49; Rajjakuddin Ahmed 5-50, Aryaman Panghal 2-44) and 311/7 decl. in 89 overs (Manender Singh 69 Ajay Singh 55*; Roshan Alam 3-72, Rajjakuddin 2-42) beat **Assam** 226 in 63.5 overs (Abhishek Thakuri 97, Biplab Saikia 33; Abhimanyu Lamba 4-36, Chandrapratap Singh 2-26) and 140 in 55.2 overs (Mujibur Ali 62, Yasir Ali 26; Aditya Garhwal 4-13, Shubham Sharma 3-32) by 227 runs.

SCA Stadium, Rajkot, October 8-12: Tripura 267 in 106.1 overs (Rajat Dey 87, Subhash Ghosh 60; Agnivesh Ayachi 4-59, Chudasama Yuvraj 4-87) and 159 in 69.5 overs (R Dey 56, Shyamskakil Gan 35; Vivek Agath 3-25, C Yuvraj 3-42) lost to **Saurashtra** 222 in 79.4 overs (Vishvarajsinh Jadeja 59, Viharsinh Jadeja 32*; S Ghosh 3-38, Devnarayan Kumar 3-31) and 205/3 in 53.5 overs (Aezaz Kothariya 113, Vishvarajsinh 38*) by seven wickets.

DN Singha Stadium, Goalpara, October 15-18: Tripura 303 in 114 overs (Rajat Dey 76, Samrat Sutradhar 52; Abhilash Gogoi 3-50, Dhrubajyoti Das 2-33) and 104 in 41.3 overs (Neelambuj Vats 40, Mitan Debbarma 20; Rajjakuddin Ahmed 4-25, A Gogoi 2-16) beat **Assam** 135 in 65 overs (Mujibur Ali 29, D Das 23; D K Singha 4-45, N Vats 3-27) and 111 in 62.5 overs (R Ahmed 36, Biplab Saika 24; Tapash Mandal 8-22) by 161 runs.

KL Saini Stadium, Jaipur, October 15-18: Rajasthan 318 in 93 overs (Aditya Garhwal 128, Ajay Singh 54; Auqib Nabi 4-60, Momin Mansoor 2-51) and 427/6 in 120.1 overs (Abhijeet Tomar 171, Chandrapratap Singh 100*; Mohammad Tahir 4-110) drew with **Jammu & Kashmir** 489 in 134.3 overs (Jatin Wadhwan 175, Shubham Pundir 139; Ajay Singh 4-94, Abhimanyu Lamba 2-82). Jammu & Kashmir took first-innings lead.

Railway Cricket Ground, Rajkot, October 15-18: Saurashtra 428 in 135.5 overs (Kevin Jivrajani 172, Parth Chauhan 102; Vaibhav Govekar 5-56, Vedant Naik 3-104) and 59/1 in 12 overs (Samarth Vyas 32*) beat **Goa** 260 in 80 overs (Rajat Shet 105, Prathamesh Gawas 50; Vivek Agath 3-54, Agnivesh Ayachi 2-47) and 225 in 78.4 overs (f/o) (Vishamber Kahlon 86, P Gawas 33; Chudasama Yuvraj 2-33, A Ayachi 2-44) by nine wickets.

DN Singha Stadium, Goalpara, October 26-29: Tripura 335 in 125.4 overs (Shyamshakil Gan 104, Mitan Debbarma 64; Paras Sharma 3-11, Mohammad Tahir 3-58, Sunil Kumar 3-87) and 146 in 39.5 overs (Rajat Dey 65, Arkaprabha Sinha 32; Yatin Sabharwal 6-48, Paras 2-21) beat **Jammu & Kashmir** 285 in 93.3 overs (Jatin Wadhwan 153, Shubham Pundir 46; Debaprasad Singha 4-39, R Dey 2-29) and 92 in 38.5 overs (Paras 27; Tapash Mandal 5-44, Viki Saha 3-32) by 105 runs.

Sanguem Cricket Gound, Sanguem, October 26-29: Goa 292 in 102 overs (Vaibhav Govekar 51, Rajat Shet 41; Shubham Sharma 3-51, Abhimanyu Lamba 2-51) and 215 in 86.2 overs (Prathamesh Gawas 81, Deepraj Gaonkar 44; Shubham 7-42, Khaleel Ahmed 2-23) lost to **Rajasthan** 508/7 dec in 129.1 overs (Abhijeet Tomar 155, Chandrapartap Singh 138; Vedant Naik 5-126) by an innings and 1 run.

Railway Cricket Ground, Rajkot, October 26-29: Saurashtra 436 in 125.2 overs (Kevin Jivrajani 140, Vishvarajsinh Jadeja 61; Abhilash Gogoi 5-81, Rajjakuddin Ahmed 3-85) and 250/7 dec in 75 overs (V Jadeja 93, K Jivrajani 56; Jitumoni Kalita 2-50) drew with **Assam** 359 in 100.2 overs (R Ahmed 133, Mujibur Ali 90; Vivek Agath 4-115, Parth Chauhan 2-14) and 105/3 in 41 overs (Biplab Saikia 54*). Saurashtra took first-innings lead.

DN Singha Stadium, Goalpara, November 3-6: Jammu & Kashmir 144 in 48 overs (Mohammad Bhat 52, Shubham Pundir 34; Rahul Singh 5-40, Rajat Khan 2-17) and 207 in 56 overs (S Pundir 80, Suryansh Raina 28; Rajat 4-48, Mrinmoy Dutta 2-34) lost to **Assam** 206 in 65.2 overs (Abhishek Thakuri 64, Biplab Saikia 40; Yatin Sabharwal 5-78, Momin Mansoor 2-6) and 149/5 in 47.2 overs (Prasenjit Sarkar 56*, Rajjakuddin Ahmed 41; Paras Sharma 2-30, Sunil Kumar 2-46) by five wickets.

Sanguem Cricket Gound, Sanguem, November 3-6: Tripura 240 in 98 overs (Shyamshakil Gan 73, Arkaprabha Sinha 45; Amulya Pandrekar 5-93, Vedant Naik 3-44) and 200 in 73.2 overs (Samrat Sutradhar 54, S Gan 46; A Pandrekar 4-90, Lakshay Garg 2-26) beat **Goa** 209 in 74.2 overs (Vaibhav Govekar 53, Suyash Prabhudessai 33; Tapash Mandal 5-66, Viki Saha 3-50) and 206 in 79.5 overs (Samar Dubhashi 59, S Prabhudessai 40; V Saha 5-69, T Mandal 4-71) by 25 runs.

SMS Stadium, Jaipur, November 3-6: Saurashtra 416 in 116.2 overs (Vishvarajsinh Jadeja 117, Kevin Jivarajani 109; Abhimanyu Lamba 3-83, Arafat Khan 2-76) and 300/7 in 85.4 overs (Samarth Vyas 136, K Jivrajani 60; A Lamba 2-34, Arafat 2-37) drew with **Rajasthan** 515 in 130 overs (Aditya Garhwal 316, Yash Kothari 67; Chetan Sakariya 4-110, K Jivrajani 2-48). Rajasthan took first-innings lead.

Sanguem Cricket Gound, Sanguem, November 11-14: Assam 329 in 111.2 overs (Rajat Khan 103, Prasenjit Sarkar 65; Sachin Burkkam 3-46, Achit Shigwan 3-59) and 227 in 94.1 overs (Biplab Saikia 84, Yasir Ali 30; A Shigwan 4-15, Vishamber Kahlon 3-62) drew with **Goa** 354 in 115.4 overs (Prathamesh Gawas 96, V Kahlon 89; Rahul Singh 5-75, Abhilash Gogoi 2-61) and 48/3 in 17 overs (Rahul 3-14). Goa took first-innings lead.

SMS Stadium, Jaipur, November 11-14: Tripura 123 in 49.5 overs (Viki Saha 26, Shyam-shakil Gan 26; Vikas Jhorar 5-29, Abhimanyu Lamba 2-37) and 119 in 35.3 overs (Devnarayan Kumar 29, Arkaprabha Sinha 26; A Lamba 6-26, Chandrapratap Singh 2-21) lost to **Rajasthan** 616/7 dec in 128 overs (Rajat Chapperwal 306*, Shiva Chauhan 153; Neelambuj Vats 2-103, Devnarayan 2-121) by an innings and 374 runs

Railway Cricket Ground, Rajkot, November 11-14: Saurashtra 588/4 dec in 153.5 overs (Samarth Vyas 322, Niket Joshi 114*; Auqib Nabi 2-62) and 306/7 in 91 overs (Parth Chauhan 60, N Joshi 45; TL Slathia 2-35, Yatin Sabharwal 2-80) drew with **Jammu & Kashmir** 365 in 97.3 overs (Shubham Pundir 85, Surya Mahotra 65; Chudasama Yuvraj 4-103, Karan 3-127). Saurashtra took first-innings lead.

Sanguem Cricket Gound, Sanguem, November 17-20: Goa 398 in 128.5 overs (Vishamber Kahlon 103, Achit Shigwan 89; Momin Mansoor 4-69, Aman Sharma 4-71) and 25/2 in 8 overs (Jatin Wadhwan 2-19) drew with **Jammu & Kashmir** 393 in 96.3 overs (Shubham Pundir 194, Paras Sharma 143; Shubham Desai 4-36, Lakshay Garg 3-86). Goa took first-innings lead.

Plate Group A points table

Teams	M	W	L	D	T	N/R	Pts.	NRR
Rajasthan	5	3	0	2	0	0	24	+0.630
Saurashtra	5	2	0	3	0	0	19	+0.252
Tripura	5	3	2	0	0	0	18	-0.431
Assam	5	1	2	2	0	0	8	-0.341
Goa	5	0	3	2	0	0	6	-0.281
Jammu & Kashmir	5	0	2	3	0	0	5	+0.177

Rajasthan and Saurashtra qualified for plate semi-finals

Plate Group B

BSL Cricket Stadium, Bokaro, October 8-12: Jharkhand 450 in 121.1 overs (Utkarsh Singh 162, Kumar Suraj 100; Shanu Saini 4-138, Harshvardhan 2-57) drew with **Uttar Pradesh** 272/9 in 91 overs (Madhav Kaushik 100, Sandeep Kumar 54; Monu Kumar 6-41). No result.
Gandhi Stadium, Balangir, October 8-12: Odisha 111 in 58 overs (Rajesh Dhuper 36, Devendra Kunwar 21; Ajay Mandal 6-26, Shakeeb Ahmed 2-13) and 272/3 in 84 overs (R Dhuper 123, Debasish Samantray 106*; A Mandal 2-82) drew with **Chhattisgarh** 283/7 dec

in 77.3 overs (Sahban Khan 86, Shakeeb 50; Subham Nayak 2-55, Debabrata Pradhan 2-58). Jharkhand took first-innings lead.

Emerald Heights International School Ground, Indore, October 8-12: Hyderabad277 in 102.5 overs (Abhirath Reddy 56, K Nithesh Reddy 44; Vivek Singh 5-79, Ashwin Das 3-51) and 325/4 dec in 90.3 overs (A Reddy 95, GV Vinith Reddy 83; Vivek 2-75) drew with **Madhya Pradesh** 227 in 89.3 overs (Tejraj Chauhan 104, Chandan Gill 23; Ravi Teja 6-52, Tanay Thyagarajan 2-65) and 274/5 in 68.1 overs (Salman Khan 102*, C Gill 74; T Thyagarajan 2-100). Hyderabad took first-innings lead.

BSL Cricket Stadium, Bokaro, October 15-18: Hyderabad 389 in 120.5 overs (P Rohith Reddy 130, Ravi Teja 78; Monu Kumar 5-57, Pratik Ranjan 3-100) and 166/6 in 85 overs (Chandan Sahani 72*, Tanay Thyagarajan 30; Vinayak Vikram 2-23, Shasheem 2-38) drew with **Jharkhand** 394 in 140.2 overs (Utkarsh Singh 130*, Shasheem 64; T Thyagarajan 5-129, Y Shravan Kumar 2-40). Jharkhand took first-innings lead.

BSP Cricket Stadium, Bhilai, October 15-18: Uttar Pradesh 243 in 86.3 overs (Parth Mishra 55, Hardeep Singh 44; Vishwaranjan Tripathi 3-32, Shakeeb Ahmed 3-61) and 290/8 dec in 109 overs (Himanshu Asnora 120, Madhav Kaushik 43; Shubham Thakur 3-72, Ravi Singh 2-47) drew with **Chhattisgarh** 226 in 73.5 overs (Sahban Khan 61, Rishab Choubey 56; Shanu Saini 4-39, Trishal Trivedi 3-27) and 32/1 in 10 overs (R Choubey 28*). Uttar Pradesh took first-innings lead.

Holkar Stadium, Indore, October 15-18: Odisha 173 in 66 overs (Debasish Samantray 32, Rajesh Dhuper 29; Mohd Arshad Khan 5-38, Venkatesh Iyer 3-39) and 445/8 in 168 overs (Subhransu Senapati 162*, Devendra Kunwar 59; Naman Bhatt 3-90, V Iyer 2-61) drew with **Madhya Pradesh** 399 in 160.4 overs (Aryaman Birla 153, Ajay Rohera 82*; Shubham Nayak 5-114, Ashutosh Das 3-64). Madhya Pradesh took first-innings lead.

Veer Surendra Sai Stadium, Sambalpur, October 26-29: Odisha 227 in 82.4 overs (Amrit Khatua 59, Sarbeswar Mohanty 47; Mohsin Khan 4-47, Trishal Trivedi 3-28) and 368/5 in 138.1 overs (A Khatua 150*, Debasish Samantray 78; Parth Mishra 3-81) drew with **Uttar Pradesh** 460 in 121.1 overs (Abhishek Goswami 189, T Trivedi 63; Pappu Roy 5-105, Debabrata Pradhan 3-91). Uttar Pradesh took first-innings lead.

Rajiv Gandhi International Stadium, Hyderabad, October 26-29: Hyderabad 483 in 201.4 overs (P Rohith Reddy 124*, Tanay Thyagarajan 96; Shubham Thakur 3-119) drew with **Chhattisgarh** 315 in 154.4 overs (Ajay Mandal 63, Sanjeet Desai 56; Ravi Teja 3-80, T Thyagarajan 3-82). Hyderabad took first-innings lead.

Holkar Stadium, Indore, October 26-29: Jharkhand 251 in 94.4 overs (Kumar Suraj 75, Pratyush Singh 48; Kuldeep Sen 5-49, Aryaman Birla 2-13) and 293 in 92.2 overs (Rahil Khan 67, Supriyo Chakraborty 67; Ashwin Das 6-62) lost to **Madhya Pradesh** 507 in 129.5 overs (Vivek Singh 111*, Ajay Rohera 109; Pratyush 3-70, Shubham Singh 2-64) and 40/1 in 9.3 overs (Sagar Solanki 30*) by nine wickets.

Keenan Stadium, Jamshedpur, November 3-6: Jharkhand 319 in 109.3 overs (Utkarsh Singh 114, Virat Singh 43; Sahban Khan 3-42, Vishwaranjan Tripathi 2-48) and 285/6 dec in 60.5 overs (Virat 115, Pratyush 58; Ajay Mandal 4-97) drew with **Chhattisgarh** 306 in 123.1 overs (Sanjeet Desai 97, Anuj Tiwary 47; Pratik Ranjan 5-74, Vinayak Vikram 3-63) and 124/2 in 44 overs (A Tiwary 53, Anupam Toppo 26; Ronit Singh 2-28). Jharkhand took first-innings lead.

Gymkhana Ground, Hyderabad, November 3-6: Hyderabad 428 in 146.5 overs (Tanay Thyagarajan 152, Chandan Sahani 94; Preet Chohan 4-94, Debabrata Pradhan 2-73) beat **Odisha** 174 in 51.2 overs (Satyajit Sabat 46, D Pradhan 27; T Thyagarajan 4-61, P Praneeth Reddy 3-25) and 195 in 64 overs (f/o) (Rajesh Dhuper 123; P Reddy 3-29, T Thyagarajan 3-77) by an innings and 59 runs.

Maharaja International School, Rewa, November 3-6: Madhya Pradesh 395 in 113.4 overs (Aryaman Birla 137, Salman Khan 81; Vineet Panwar 6-60, Harshvardhan 3-74) and 305/4 in 80 overs (Sagar Solanki 121, Venkatesh Iyer 68; Shubham Chaubey 3-36) drew with

Uttar Pradesh 449 in 135.2 overs (Madhav Kaushik 136, Abhishek Goswami 116, Himanshu Asnora 112; A Birla 5-63, Kuldeep Sen 4-77). Uttar Pradseh took first-innings lead.

BSL Cricket Stadium, Bokaro, November 11-14: Odisha 186 in 55.5 overs (Devendra Kunwar 31, Amrit Khatua 30; Ronit Singh 7-42) and 303 in 99.2 overs (Debabrata Pradhan 66, Debasish Samantray 43; Vinayak Vikram 6-89, Shasheem 2-17) lost to **Jharkhand** 426 in 100.5 overs (Virat Singh 121, Kumar Suraj 53; Subham Nayak 5-152, Pappu Roy 2-145) and 67/1 in 7 overs (Shasheem 41, Pratyush Singh 25*) by nine wickets.

Rajiv Gandhi International Stadium, Hyderabad, November 11-14: Uttar Pradesh 234 in 82.1overs (Shubham Chaubey 96, Himanshu Asnora 44; PS Chaitanya Reddy 4-38, Y Shravan Kumar 2-24) and 229 in 63 overs (Madhav Kaushik 70, Sahim Hasan 50; Mir Omer Khan 4-79, Y Shravan 2-21) lost to **Hyderabad** 579 in 176.1 overs (P Rohith Reddy 181*, Tanay Thyagarajan 109, GV Vinith Reddy 107; Vineet Panwar 3-90, Harshwardhan 2-83) by an innings and 116 runs.

MPCA Cricket Ground, Sagar, November 11-14: Madhya Pradesh 469 in 138.2 overs (Aryaman Birla 230, Ashwin Das 50; Ajay Mandal 5-116, Shubham Thakur 3-92) and 181 in 67.3 overs (Ajay Rohera 68, Salman Khan 47; Vishwaranjan Tripathi 5-73, Shakeeb Ahmed 3-29) drew with **Chhattisgarh** 401 in 121.2 overs (Sanjeet Desai 109, S Ahmed 86; A Das 3-76, Sagar Solanki 2-20) and 38/3 in 10 overs. Madhya Pradesh took first-innings lead.

Plate Group B points table

Teams	M	W	L	D	T	N/R	Pts.	NRR
Hyderabad	5	2	0	3	0	0	21	+0.002
Madhya Pradesh	5	1	0	4	0	0	14	+0.472
Jharkhand	5	1	1	3	0	0	13	+0.397
Uttar Pradesh	5	0	1	4	0	0	10	-0.082
Chhattisgarh	5	0	0	5	0	0	7	-0.091
Odisha	5	0	2	3	0	0	3	-0.855

Rajasthan and Saurashtra qualified for plate semi-finals

Semi-finals

Emerald Heights International School Ground, Indore, November 23-26: Rajasthan 212 in 57.5 overs (Shiva Chauhan 55, Abhimanyu Lamba 40; Avesh Khan 4-61, Sagar Solanki 2-9) and 268 in 100.4 overs (Mahendra Singh 86, Aditya Garhwal 61; Venkatesh Iyer 3-48, Avesh 3-70) beat **Madhya Pradesh** 244 in 85.2 overs (S Solanki 77, Salman Khan 37; Khaleel Ahmed 5-98, Vikas Jhorar 2-10) and 210 in 81.1 overs (V Iyer 97, Ajay Rohera 64; K Ahmed 7-69, Shubham Sharma 3-55) by 26 runs.

Gymkhana Ground, Hyderabad, November 23-26: Hyderabad 664 in 181.4 overs (Tanay Thyagarajan 151, P Rohith Reddy 134; Chudasama Yuvraj 5-193, Chetan Sakariya 3-104) and 120/2 in 21.5 overs (Chandan Sahani 57*, K Nithesh Reddy 55) drew with **Saurashtra** 462 in 137.5 overs (Samarth Vyas 88, C Yuvraj 73; Kartikeya Kak 4-93, Y Shravan Kumar 3-47). Hyderabad took first-innings lead.

Rajasthan and Hyderabad qualified for knock-outs

Plate 3rd place play-off: Madhya Pradesh won by first first-innings lead
SCA Stadium, Rajkot, December 8-11: Madhya Pradesh 227 in 99.5 overs (Aryaman Birla 75, Venkatesh Iyer 54*; Chudasama Yuvraj 5-71,Brijesh Lakadiya 3-21) and 534/7 in 152.1

overs (Salman Khan 136, A Birla 118, V Iyer 107; Aezaz Kothariya 3-93) drew with **Saurash-tra** 212 in 80.3 overs (Niket Joshi 89, Yash Parekh 55; Avesh Khan 7-66, Surendra Malviya 2-44). Madhya Pradesh took first-innings lead.

Quarter-finals

Emerald Heights International School Ground, Indore, November 29: Tamil Nadu 38/1 in 16.5 overs (Balchander Anirudh 22) v **Hyderabad.** Tamil Nadu won by spin of coin.

Mumbai, November 29 - December 2: Andhra 160 in 60.1 overs (Ricky Bhui 45, CR Gnaneshwar 34; Tejas Baroka 5-48, Gaurav Kumar 2-21) and 203 in 55.5 overs (G Jayavardhan 48, Naren Reddy 39; Gourav 3-51, T Baroka 3-52) lost to **Delhi** 533 in 160.4 overs (Himmat Singh 148, Jonty Sidhu 109, Lalit Yadav 101; Manish Golamaru 6-222, Ashwin Hebbar 2-32) by an innings and 170 runs.

Mumbai, November 29 - December 2: Mumbai 278 in 88 overs (Hardik Tamore 54, Akhil Herwadkar 48; Khaleel Ahmed 5-90, Chandrapratap Singh 3-30) and 440 in 139.2 overs (Shams Mulani 145, Vaidik Murkar 73; Abhimanyu Lamba 3-86, Aditya Garhwal 3-37) drew with **Rajasthan** 276 in 87.2 overs (Rajat Chapperwal 52, Shiva Chauhan 39; S Mulani 3-40, SS Jadhav 3-54) and 159/0 in 29.5 overs (Abhijeet Tomar 103*, Yash Kothari 52*). Mumbai took first-innings lead.

Patiala, November 29 - December 2: Karnataka 116 in 51 overs (KN Bharath 40; Mayank Markande 4-31, Sanvir Singh 3-22) and 235 in 77.3 overs (D Nishchal 64, Bharath 61; M Markande 5-19, Karan Kaila 2-53) lost to **Punjab** 353 in 114.3 overs (Anmolpreet Singh 132, Sanvir 76; M Prasidh Krishna 3-64, S Aditya 3-61) by an innings and two runs.

Tamil Nadu, Delhi, Mumbai and Punjab qualified for the semi-finals

Semi-finals

Dhruv Pandove Stadium, Patiala, December 8-11: Mumbai 289 in 135.5 overs (Hardik Tamore 67, Shams Mulani 65; Mayank Markande 4-59, Jagjit Singh 3-64) and 74/4 in 53 overs (H Tamore 29, Vaidik Murkar 23; M Markande 3-18) drew with **Punjab** 205 in 84.4 overs (Akul Pandove 44, Abhijeet Garg 38; S Mulani 7-75, Dhrumil Matkar 3-43). Mumbai won on the basis of first-innings lead.

Airforce Complex ground, Palam, New Delhi, December 8-11: Tamil Nadu 229 in 73.1 overs (N Jagadeesan 113, Kavin Ravi 29; Lalit Yadav 3-10, Tejas Baroka 3-89) and 234 in 67.2 overs (Jagadeesan 64, K Vishal Vaidhya 44; T Baroka 6-84, Simarjeet Singh 3-14) lost to **Delhi** 479 in 143.2 overs (Dinesh Mor 152*, Jonty Sidhu 110; M Abhinav 6-115) by an innings and 16 runs.

Mumbai and Delhi qualified for final

Final: Delhi won by five wickets

BKC Ground, Mumbai, December 17-20: Mumbai 230 in 58 overs (Jay Bista 66, Hardik Tamore 53; Simarjeet Singh 6-73, Shivank Vashisth 2-46) and 267 in 91.1 overs (Siddharth Akre 63, Akshay Sardesai 45; Gourav Kumar 4-87, S Vashisth 2-33) lost to **Delhi** 260/9 dec in 64.5 overs (Anuj Rawat 83, Hiten Dalal 67; Sairaj Patil 4-25, Minad Manjrekar 3-58) and 239/5 in 54.5 overs (A Rawat 75, Dinesh Mor 46*; S Patil 2-57) by five wickets.

Winners: Delhi

Under-19 Vinoo Mankad Trophy

Vidarbha take junior honours too

The revamp of the domestic structure meant there was no zonal league or inter-zonal games this time around in the Under-19 Vinoo Mankad Trophy. Instead, 35 teams — slotted under Elite Group A, B, C and Plate Group — contested over 143 games with Vidarbha beating Tamil Nadu by 83 runs in the final to clinch the title.

Batting first, Vidarbha posted 297 for 6 on the back of the centuries from Yash Rathod and Aman Mokhade. The two put together 194 for the third wicket after the side had lost both openers by the end of the 11th over. Captain Yash Kadam's unbeaten 24 off 12 ensured Vidarbha finished strongly.

In response, Tamil Nadu — who had qualified from Elite Group C and were unbeaten in the tournament till then — were bundled out for 214 with Rohit Dattatraya picking up 5 for 37. Each of Tamil Nadu's top six batsmen reached double figures, but none could convert their knocks into something substantial.

Dattatraya's effort in the final helped him eclipse Manipur's Rex Singh as the leading wicket-taker. Rex's 26 wickets came from seven matches, including an astonishing 8 for 3 against Puducherry. In that game, he also picked up four wickets in four balls across two overs.

Piyush Kumar Singh (534) of Bihar and Tilak Varma (507) of Hyderabad breached the 500-run mark. Piyush's 145 against Sikkim was also the highest individual score of the tournament.

Most runs: Piyush Singh (Bihar) (534 runs, 7 matches)
Most wickets: Rohit Dattatraya (Vidarbha) (28 wickets, 11 matches)

Elite Group A

CK Pithawala Ground, Surat, October 5: Gujarat 210/8 in 50 overs (LM Kocher 78, Akash 64; AR Pore 3-39, RS Hangargekar 2-48) lost to **Maharashtra** 214/3 in 48.4 overs (SA Veer 80, SS Nawale 60; Jaymeet Patel 2-41) by seven wickets.

Kholvad Gymkhana Ground, Surat, October 5: Assam 144 in 47.5 overs (Denish Das 40; Suraj Vashisht 4-17, Sagar Solanki 3-20) lost to Madhya Pradesh 150/1 in 31 overs (Rahul Chandrol 83*, S Vashisht 54*) by nine wickets.

Lalbhai Contractor Stadium, Surat, October 5: Karnataka 251 in 49.4 overs (Luvnith Sisodia 81, Prajwal Pavan 66; Karan Lal 3-37, Prabhat Maurya 3-50) beat **Bengal** 243/9 in 50 overs (Ankit Shukla 69, P Maurya 40*; Shubhang Hegde 4-39, Venkatesh M 3-58) by eight wickets.

Kholvad Gymkhana Ground, Surat, October 6: Gujarat 142 in 49.2 overs (Umang 51, Jaymeet Patel 26; Arjun Tendulkar 5-30) lost to **Mumbai** 143/1 in 38 overs (Suved Parkar 67*, Divyaansh 45) by nine wickets.

CK Pithawala Ground, Surat, October 6: Uttar Pradesh 276/8 in 50 overs (Aryan Sharma 94, Harsh Tyagi 75; Akash Sengupta 3-52, Sunil Lachit 3-53) beat Assam 116 in 32.2 overs

(Akhil Kalita 33, Hrishikesh Borah 27; Purnank Tyagi 3-27, Kunal Yadav 3-35) by160 runs.

Lalbhai Contractor Stadium, Surat, October 6: Jharkhand 148 in 45.4 overs (Kumar Kushagra 42, Prem 31; Sai Prajwal Reddy 3-11, Aman Khan 3-34) beat **Karnataka** 104 in 40.1 overs (Manishi 4-10, Sushant Mishra 3-24) by 44 runs.

Kholvad Gymkhana Ground, Surat, October 7: Bengal 114 in 32 overs (Diganta Neogi 29, Abhijeet Bhagat 26; Aakash Sharma 3-23, Arjun Tendulkar 3-28, Atharva Ankolekar 3-32) lost to **Mumbai** 116/3 in 30.3 overs (Divyaansh 56*, Pragnesh Kanpillewar 31*) by seven wickets.

Lalbhai Contractor Stadium, Surat, October 7: Uttar Pradesh 255/6 in 50 overs (Aryan Sharma 68, Sameer Rizvi 38; LG Sonawane 3-33, RS Hangargekar 2-50) beat **Maharashtra** 162 in 39.5 overs (YS Dongre 82, Om Bhosale 26; Shivam Sharma 3-39, Kritagya Singh 3-46) by 93 runs.

CK Pithawala Ground, Surat, October 7: Madhya Pradesh 273/6 in 50 overs (Suraj Vashisht 109, Chanchal Rathore 59; Yuvraj Kumar 2-43, Amit Kumar 2-59) beat **Jharkhand** 99 in 33.5 overs (Yuvraj 31, Sahil Raj 25; Mohammad Baggad 5-21, Rishabh Chouhan 2-8) by 174 runs.

CK Pithawala Ground, Surat, October 9: Madhya Pradesh 266/7 in 50 overs (Irfan Ali 69, Rahul Chandrol 60; Atharva Poojari 2-40) beat **Mumbai** 257 in 46.4 overs (Atharva Ankolekar 70, Suved Parkar 48; Omkar Singh 5-65, Suraj Vashisht 2-20) by nine runs.

Lalbhai Contractor Stadium, Surat, October 9: Gujarat 165 in 50 overs (Sunpreet Bagga 55, Priyesh 27; Karan Lal 3-37, Prabhat Maurya 2-27) lost to **Bengal** 169/6 in 43 overs (Ankit Shukla 50, Ankit 26; SM Prajapati 2-27, Jaymeet Patel 2-28) by four wickets.

Kholvad Gymkhana Ground, Surat, October 9: Karnataka 272 in 50 overs (Prajwal Pavan 78, Venkatesh M 43; SA Veer 3-33, AJ Rodrigues 3-53) beat **Maharashtra** 256 in 49.1 overs (SA Veer 55, SS Nawale 38, AK Kale 38; Venkatesh M 3-49, Santokh Singh 2-27) by 16 runs.

Lalbhai Contractor Stadium, Surat, October 10: Uttar Pradesh 177/9 in 40 overs (Sameer Choudhary 41, Kritagya Singh 36; Tripuresh Singh 3-25, Rishabh Chauhan 3-34) beat **Madhya Pradesh** 160/9 in 40 overs (Sagar Solanki 39, Rahul Chandrol 25, Irfan Ali 25, Lucky Mishra 25; Mohit Jangra 2-27, S Choudhary 2-31) by 17 runs.

Kholvad Gymkhana Ground, Surat, October 10: Jharkhand 177/9 in 43 overs (Shresth Sagar 59, Ankit 32; Arka Sarkar 2-23, Prabhat Maurya 2-31) beat **Bengal** 96 in 31.4 overs (Manishi 3-27, Sahil Raj 2-8) by 81 runs.

CK Pithawala Ground, Surat, October 10: Assam 249/7 in 49 overs (Sourav Saha 82, Hrishikesh Borah 45*; LG Sonawane 2-31, Om Bhosale 2-57) beat **Maharashtra** 248 in 49 overs (O Bhosale 71, HA Kate 55, SA Veer 40; H Borah 4-49, Amlanjyoti Das 2-32) by one run.

Kholvad Gymkhana Ground, Surat, October 12: Jharkhand 171 in 49 overs (Shresth Sagar 35, Kumar Karan 32; Hrishikesh Borah 4-15, Sunil Lachit 2-30) beat **Assam** 94 in 33.1 overs (Denish Das 48; Sushant Mishra 4-22, Manishi 3-14) by 77 runs.

CK Pithawala Ground, Surat, October 12: Mumbai 196/9 in 50 overs (Atharva Ankolekar 69*, Vedant Murkar 41; Venkatesh M 4-30, Devdutt Padikkal 2-26) lost to **Karnataka** 197/6 in 42.1 overs (Shivakumar BU 81, Prajwal Pawan 25; Akshat Jain 2-3, Sagar Chhabria 2-37) by four wickets.

Lalbhai Contractor Stadium, Surat, October 12: Uttar Pradesh 221/6 in 50 overs (Sameer Rizvi 79*, Sameer Choudhary 61; SA Desai 2-27) beat **Gujarat** 166 in 46.2 overs (RD Patel 43, SD Chauhan 32; Purnank Tyagi 3-32, Kritagya Singh 3-39) by 55 runs.

Lalbhai Contractor Stadium, Surat, October 14: Madhya Pradesh 232 in 48.2 overs (Rishabh Chouhan 60, Rahul Chandrol 44; SA Veer 2-25, SS Churi 2-28) lost to **Maharashtra** 233/4 in 46.3 overs (SA Veer 85, Om Bhosale 51; R Chouhan 2-47) by six wickets.

Kholvad Gymkhana Ground, Surat, October 14: Karnataka 250/7 in 50 overs (Shivakumar BU 102, Venkatesh M 46; Jaymeet Patel 3-55) beat **Gujarat** 215 in 48.4 overs (Sunpreet Bagga 49*, Priyesh 48; Venkatesh M 3-44, Shubhang Hegde 2-27) by 35 runs.

CK Pithawala Ground, Surat, October 14: Bengal 213/7 in 50 overs (Shakir Gandhi 54*, Ankit Shukla 40; Rituraj Biswas 3-30, Amlanjyoti Das 2-37) beat **Assam** 84 in 38.5 overs (Akash Sengupta 33*; Kaushik Maity 4-10, Arka Sarkar 3-11) by 129 runs.

CK Pithawala Ground, Surat, October 16: **Jharkhand** 135 in 49.1 overs (Ayush 46; Shivam Sharma 2-12, Purnank Tyagi 2-31) lost to **Uttar Pradesh** 136/6 in 41.5 overs (Dhruv Jurel 57*, Aanjaneya Suryavanshi 31; Sushant Mishra 3-53) by four wickets.

Lalbhai Contractor Stadium, Surat, October 16: **Assam** 99 in 40.4 overs (Denish Das 34, Amlanjyoti Das 29; Arjun Tendulkar 3-14, Divyaansh 2-6) lost to **Mumbai** 102 for no loss in 21.5 overs (Yashasvi Jaiswal 56*, Suved Parkar 41*) by ten wickets.

Kholvad Gymkhana Ground, Surat, October 16: **Gujarat** 148/9 in 50 overs (Jaymeet Patel 37*, LM Kocher 34; Mohammad Baggad 3-16, Suraj Vashisht 2-23) lost to **Madhya Pradesh** 152/4 in 39 overs (Rishabh Chouhan 41*, Irfan Ali 39) by six wickets.

Kholvad Gymkhana Ground, Surat, October 18: **Karnataka** 93 in 32.4 overs (Prajwal Pavan 31; Kritagya Singh 4-19, Shivam Sharma 3-24) lost to **Uttar Pradesh** 97/2 in 29.1 overs (Sameer Rizvi 28*, Kritagya 26*) by eight wickets.

CK Pithawala Ground, Surat, October 18: **Madhya Pradesh** 332/5 in 50 overs (Rahul Chandrol 102, Rishabh Chouhan 72*, Irfan Ali 67; Prabhat Maurya 2-71) beat **Bengal** 268 in 45.5 overs (Shakir Gandhi 65, Sourav Paul 60; Prankesh Rai 4-44, R Chouhan 3-54) by 64 runs.

Lalbhai Contractor Stadium, Surat, October 18: **Maharashtra** 179 in 36.3 overs (AV Kale 81, Om Bhosale 35; Atharva Ankolekar 5-41, Aakash Sharma 3-41) lost to **Mumbai** 180/3 in 44 overs (Yashasvi Jaiswal 51, Divyaansh 42*) by seven wickets.

CK Pithawala Ground, Surat, October 20: **Bengal** 231 in 49.3 overs (Diganta Neogi 88, Prabhat Maurya 31; LG Sonawane 3-28, SS Churi 3-46) beat **Maharashtra** 202 in 45.2 overs (TS Jain 53, SS Nawale 39; Prayas Ray Barman 4-25, P Maurya 3-58) by 29 runs.

Lalbhai Contractor Stadium, Surat, October 20: **Jharkhand** 129 in 46.3 overs (Ankit 40; Atharva Poojari 4-31, Arjun Tendulkar 2-30) lost to **Mumbai** 130/1 in 24.4 overs (Yashasvi Jaiswal 63*, Suved Parkar 32) by nine wickets.

Kholvad Gymkhana Ground, Surat, October 20: **Assam** 140 in 43.2 overs (Sourav Saha 57, Nilotpal Das 27; SM Prajapati 4-29, Jaymeet Patel 3-17, SA Desai 3-20) lost to **Gujarat** 141/4 in 39.4 overs (LM Kocher 61*) by six wickets.

Lalbhai Contractor Stadium, Surat, October 22: **Jharkhand** 196/8 in 50 overs (Shresth Sagar 56*, Sahil Raj 44; SA Desai 2-29, SM Prajapati 2-31) lost to **Gujarat** 197/1 in 45 overs (LM Kocher 75*, Priyesh 69*) by nine wickets.

CK Pithawala Ground, Surat, October 22: **Madhya Pradesh** 243 in 50 overs (Rishabh Chouhan 82*, Shivang Kumar 37; Venkatesh M 3-65, Uttam Gowda 2-42) beat **Karnataka** 182 in 45.1 overs (Shubhang Hegde 39, Devdutt Padikkal 38; Prankesh Rai 3-41, Omkar Singh 2-11) by 61 runs.

Kholvad Gymkhana Ground, Surat, October 22: **Mumbai** 202 in 46.2 overs (Yashasvi Jaiswal 77, Pragnesh Kanpillewar 46; Mohit Jangra 4-39) lost to **Uttar Pradesh** 205/5 in 46.1 overs (Sameer Choudhary 81*, Kritagya Singh 33; Atharva Ankolekar 2-24, Atharva Poojari 2-34) by five wickets.

Lalbhai Contractor Stadium, Surat, October 24: **Assam** 77 in 30 overs (Shubhang Hegde 5-15, Venkatesh M 3-22) lost to **Karnataka** 80/2 in 5.5 overs (Devdutt Padikkal 55*) by eight wickets.

CK Pithawala Ground, Surat, October 24: **Maharashtra** 267/8 in 50 overs (SS Nawale 75, Om Bhosale 35; Manishi 2-45, Amit Kumar 2-49) beat **Jharkhand** 200/6 in 50 overs (Kumar Kushagra 79, Satya Setu 55*) by 67 runs.

Kholvad Gymkhana Ground, Surat, October 24: **Bengal** 231/8 in 50 overs (Diganta Neogi 98, Aishik 34; Mohit Jangra 3-42, Akshay Sain 3-43) beat **Uttar Pradesh** 77 in 35.3 overs (Dhruv Jurel 27; SK Ajharuddin 4-14, Prayas Ray Barman 3-9) by 154 runs.

Points table

Teams	M	W	L	D	T	N/R	Pts	NRR
Uttar Pradesh	8	7	1	0	0	0	28	+0.799
Madhya Pradesh	8	6	2	0	0	0	24	+1.121
Karnataka	8	5	3	0	0	0	20	+0.216
Mumbai	8	5	3	0	0	0	20	+0.864
Bengal	8	4	4	0	0	0	16	+0.295
Maharashtra	8	3	5	0	0	0	12	-0.186
Jharkhand	8	3	5	0	0	0	12	-0.465
Gujarat	8	2	6	0	0	0	8	-0.430
Assam	8	1	7	0	0	0	4	-2.131

Uttar Pradesh and Madhya Pradesh qualified for the quarter-finals

Elite Group B

Vidarbha Cricket Association Stadium, Jamtha, Nagpur, October 5: Chhattisgarh 161 in 48 overs (Ayush Pandey 41, Prabhash Shukla 34; Deepin Chitkara 5-32, Amit Shukla 3-17) lost to **Punjab** 162 for no loss in 35.4 overs (Arjun Azad 93*, Pukhraj Mann 61*) by ten wickets.

VCA Stadium, Civil Lines, Nagpur, October 5: Hyderabad 238/8 in 50 overs (Tilak Varma 77, Varun 76; Satvik 4-48) lost to **Andhra** 244/5 in 48.1 overs (Yara Sandeep 65*, Harsha Vardhan 54; E Sanketh 2-35, Rathan Teja 2-42) by five wickets.

VCA Kalamana, Nagpur, October 5: Haryana 291/7 in 50 overs (Nehal Pajni 80, Sagar Dahiya 78; Vijay 2-73) beat Baroda 157/7 in 50 overs (MR Solanki 45*, Sumedh Marathe 26; AS Sandhu 2-30, Rahul Thakran 2-43) by 134 runs.

Vidarbha Cricket Association Stadium, Jamtha, Nagpur, October 6: Tripura 219/9 in 50 overs (Sankar Paul 60, Sridam Paul 37; RT Taank 4-51, Shashwat Mishra 3-35) beat **Chhattisgarh** 140/7 in 50 overs (Ayush Pandey 39, UM Tiwari 29*; S Paul 3-29, Bikram Das 2-19) by 79 runs.

VCA Stadium, Civil Lines, Nagpur, October 6: Andhra 272 in 49.3 overs (Subramanyam 57, Nithish Reddy 47; Harsh Dubey 3-65, Gulam Ali 2-40) beat **Vidarbha** 154/9 in 50 overs (H Dubey 46*, Dandewar Siddhesh 41; Durgakumar 4-29) by 118 runs.

VCA Kalamana, Nagpur, October 6: Delhi 213/9 in 50 overs (Ekansh Dobal 44, Bharat Sindhwani 34; Yashjeet Balhara 3-39, AS Sandhu 2-44) beat **Haryana** 162 in 38.3 overs (SK Panchal 48, AS Sandhu 34; Anirudh Chowdhary 4-31, Prince Choudhary 2-24) by 51 runs.

Vidarbha Cricket Association Stadium, Jamtha, Nagpur, October 7: Baroda 146 in 41.4 overs (VS Patil 44, P Patidar 32; Parvez Sultan 3-31) lost to **Tripura** 147/3 in 41.2 overs (Bikram Das 63, Arup Datta 37) by seven wickets.

VCA Stadium, Civil Lines, Nagpur, October 7: Vidarbha 156 in 47.5 overs (Yash Kadam 47; Yuvraj Choudhary 2-24, Ketan Mankotia 2-25) beat **Punjab** 97 in 30.3 overs (Arjun Azad 26; Rohit Dattatraya 4-32, Y Kadam 2-11) by 59 runs.

VCA Kalamana, Nagpur, October 7: Delhi 167 in 44 overs (Ekansh Dobal 35, Prashant Bhati 35; E Sanketh 3-36, Rathan Teja 2-17) lost to **Hyderabad** 168/4 in 40.3 overs (Varun 84*, Surya Teja 52) by six wickets.

Vidarbha Cricket Association Stadium, Jamtha, Nagpur, October 9: Tripura 176 in 50 overs (Bikram Das 53, Rajib Hossain 36; Hitesh Yadav 3-21, Rathan Teja 2-25) lost to **Hyderabad** 177/2 in 44 overs (Varun 75*, Tilak Varma 73*) by eight wickets.

VCA Stadium, Civil Lines, Nagpur, October 9: Baroda 183 in 49.1 overs (Lucky Barot 82, MR Solanki 35; RT Taank 2-25, Shashwat Mishra 2-28) lost to **Chhattisgarh** 184/3 in 47.1 overs (Ayush Pandey 85*, AG Rao 53) by seven wickets.

VCA Kalamana, Nagpur, October 9: Punjab 215/9 in 50 overs (Arjun Azad 70, Nehal Wadhera 55; Yashjeet Balhara 2-28, Aman Sahrawat 2-55) beat Haryana 112 in 35.4 overs (Tejpreet Singh 3-21, Deepin Chitkara 2-16) by 103 runs.

VCA Stadium, Civil Lines, Nagpur, October 10: Vidarbha 206/8 in 50 overs (YV Rathod 72, A Mokhade 45; Hitesh Yadav 3-38, G Anikethreddy 3-45) beat Hyderabad 188 in 48.1 overs (Tilak Varma 55, Owais Wahed 36; Tekan 3-27, Harsh Dubey 2-34) by 18 runs.

Vidarbha Cricket Association Stadium, Jamtha, Nagpur, October 10: Delhi 330/8 in 50 overs (Anuj Rawat 120, Priyansh Arya 59; Ashutosh Das 3-51, Harsh Katarmal 2-43) beat **Baroda** 210/6 in 50 overs (KT Marathe 67, VS Patil 51; Hrithik Shokeen 3-47, Mayank Rawat 2-19) by 120 runs.

VCA Kalamana, Nagpur, October 10: Punjab 249/9 in 50 overs (Prabhsimran Singh 118, Deepin Chitkara 30; Nitish Reddy 3-45, Vasu 2-46) beat **Andhra** 210/9 in 50 overs (Dheeraj Kumar 68, Vamsi Krishna 44; Tejpreet Singh 3-29, Sumit Sharma 2-31) by 39 runs.

Vidarbha Cricket Association Stadium, Jamtha, Nagpur, October 12: Andhra 206/8 in 50 overs (Nithish Reddy 40, Prudhvi 34*; Mayank Malhotra 4-37) beat Delhi 202 in 49.2 overs (Vaibhav Kandpal 73, Mayank Rawat 34; Satvik 3-32, Mettela Bhargav 3-46) by four runs.

VCA Stadium, Civil Lines, Nagpur, October 12: Haryana 194 in 50 overs (DA Thakral 95, Nehal Pajni 30; Bikram Das 4-42, Sankar Paul 3-35) beat **Tripura** 41 in 22.3 overs (Manish Baberwal 3-16, Naman Bansal 2-5) by 153 runs.

VCA Kalamana, Nagpur, October 12: Vidarbha 254/6 in 50 overs (Nayan Chavan 112*, Harsh Dubey 68; Parivesh Dhar 3-43, Shashwat Mishra 2-49) beat Chhattisgarh 181/8 in 50 overs (RV Sharma 62, Harsh Sahu 29; Rohit Dattatraya 4-27) by 73 runs.

Vidarbha Cricket Association Stadium, Jamtha, Nagpur, October 14: Hyderabad 257/9 in 50 overs (Tilak Varma 82, Pragnay Reddy 55; Amit Shukla 6-47, Sumit Sharma 3-45) lost to **Punjab** 260/2 in 43.3 overs (Arjun Azad 122*, Prabhsimran Singh 103*) by eight wickets.

VCA Stadium, Civil Lines, Nagpur, October 14: Haryana 203 in 49.5 overs (Aman Sahrawat 49, Sagar Dahiya 39; RT Taank 3-23, Anurag Yadav 3-28) beat **Chhattisgarh** 129 in 38.4 overs (Harsh Sahu 30; A Sahrawat 3-23, Manish Baberwal 2-37) by 74 runs.

VCA Kalamana, Nagpur, October 14: Baroda 201/9 in 50 overs (Kinit Patel 50, A Rangwani 33*; Nithish Reddy 2-41, Mettela Bhargav 2-43) lost to **Andhra** 204/7 in 47.4 overs (N Reddy 76, Harsha Vardhan 39; A Rangwani 2-41) by three wickets.

VCA Stadium, Civil Lines, Nagpur, October 16: Delhi 246/9 in 50 overs (Anuj Rawat 65, Gagan Vats 38, Vaibhav Kandpal 38; Rohit Dattatraya 3-45) beat Vidarbha 128 in 35 overs (YV Rathod 51; Anirudh Chowdhary 2-18, Prashant Bhati 2-20) by 118 runs.

Vidarbha Cricket Association Stadium, Jamtha, Nagpur, October 16: Andhra 341/7 in 50 overs (Dheeraj Kumar 74, Nithish Reddy 69; Sayan Chowdhury 2-54, Chandan Ray 2-66) beat Tripura 178/9 in 50 overs (Bikram Das 36, Arup Datta 27; Subramanyam 4-28, Yara Sandeep 2-11) by 163 runs.

VCA Kalamana, Nagpur, October 16: Hyderabad 222 in 49.5 overs (Tilak Varma 56, Surya Teja 40; Shashwat Mishra 4-43, UM Tiwari 2-42) beat **Chhattisgarh** 171 in 47.4 overs (AG Rao 69*, Kivnoor Singh 27; Mohammad Adnan 3-32, Hitesh Yadav 2-19) by 51 runs.

VCA Stadium, Civil Lines, Nagpur, October 18: Haryana 209/7 in 50 overs (Ayush Negi 68*, DA Thakral 46; Harsh Dubey 3-28) lost to **Vidarbha** 213/4 in 46.3 overs (YV Rathod 113*, A Mokhade 58; Manish Baberwal 2-38) by six wickets.

Vidarbha Cricket Association Stadium, Jamtha, Nagpur, October 18: Baroda 232/9 in 50 overs (Kinit Patel 62, KT Marathe 54; Rathan Teja 3-47, Mohammad Adnan 2-35) lost to **Hyderabad** 234/2 in 44.1 overs (Tilak Varma 103*, Varun 54*) by eight wickets.

VCA Kalamana, Nagpur, October 18: Tripura 77 in 35.5 overs (Amit Shukla 4-15, Ketan Mankotia 3-22) lost to **Punjab** 81/2 in 17.1 overs (Prabhsimran Singh 50*) by eight wickets.

Vidarbha Cricket Association Stadium, Jamtha, Nagpur, October 20: Punjab 303/9 in 50 overs (Arjun Azad 78, Deepin Chitkara 77; Vijay 3-56, Nisarg Patel 2-50) beat **Baroda** 261 in 48.3 overs (Shashwat Rawat 109, Kinit Patel 63; Amit Shukla 3-50, Ketan Mankotia 2-34) by 42 runs.

VCA Stadium, Civil Lines, Nagpur, October 20: Delhi 286/7 in 50 overs (Mayank Rawat 87, Gagan Vats 64; Chandan Ray 3-31, Sankar Paul 2-34) beat **Tripura** 164/8 in 50 overs (Arup Datta 53, S Paul 38; Anirudh Chowdhary 2-21, Hrithik Shokeen 2-22) by 122 runs.

VCA Kalamana, Nagpur, October 20: Chhattisgarh 115 in 37 overs (Ayush Pandey 42, AG Rao 26; Vasu 5-20) lost to **Andhra** 116 for no loss in 22 overs (Vamsi Krishna 60*, Harsh Vardhan 50*) by ten wickets.

Vidarbha Cricket Association Stadium, Jamtha, Nagpur, October 22: Delhi 353/7 in 50 overs (Mayank Rawat 106, Priyansh Arya 100*; AG Rao 2-39) beat **Chhattisgarh** 204/6 in 50 overs (AG Rao 74, RV Sharma 46) by 149 runs.

VCA Stadium, Civil Lines, Nagpur, October 22: Haryana 181/8 in 50 overs (Sagar Dahiya 55, Ayush Negi 40; G Anikethreddy 3-23, Hitesh Yadav 2-34) beat **Hyderabad** 163 in 47.4 overs (Tilak Varma 54, PSV Reddy 34; AS Sandhu 2-16, KP Yadav 2-22) by 18 runs.

VCA Kalamana, Nagpur, October 22: Vidarbha 241/7 in 50 overs (Nayan Chavan 77, Harsh Dubey 42*; Sankar Paul 2-40) beat **Tripura** 177 in 47.3 overs (Sridam Paul 45, Amit Das 28; Tekan 3-29, Rohit Dattatraya 3-42) by 64 runs.

Vidarbha Cricket Association Stadium, Jamtha, Nagpur, October 24: Haryana 173 in 49.4 overs (Sagar Dahiya 50, Nehal Pajni 27; Nithish Reddy 2-22, Vasu 2-24) lost to **Andhra** 176/8 in 46.1 overs (Yara Sandeep 43, Dheeraj Kumar 31; Manish Baberwal 3-27) by two wickets.

VCA Stadium, Civil Lines, Nagpur, October 24: Punjab 225 in 47.3 overs (Nehal Wadhera 68, Yuvraj Choudhary 59; Prashant Bhati 3-40, Mayank Rawat 2-24) lost to **Delhi** 230/7 in 48 overs (Ayush Badoni 89*, Vaibhav Kandpal 36; Sumit Sharma 3-40, Deepin Chitkara 2-26) by three wickets.

VCA Kalamana, Nagpur, October 24: Vidarbha 240/7 in 50 overs (Yash Kadam 49*, Sanket Khedkar 47; Malhar Ghevaria 2-39) beat **Baroda** 221 in 46 overs (KT Marathe 74, Shashwat Rawat 36; Y Kadam 5-46, Harsh Dubey 2-40) by 19 runs.

Points table

Teams	M	W	L	D	T	N/R	Pts	NRR
Andhra	8	7	1	0	0	0	28	1.085
Delhi	8	6	2	0	0	0	24	1.336
Vidarbha	8	6	2	0	0	0	24	0.038
Punjab	8	6	2	0	0	0	24	0.918
Haryana	8	4	4	0	0	0	16	0.484
Hyderabad	8	4	4	0	0	0	16	0.170
Tripura	8	2	6	0	0	0	8	-1.434
Chhattisgarh	8	1	7	0	0	0	4	-1.551
Baroda	8	0	8	0	0	0	0	-1.055

Andhra, Delhi and Vidarbha qualified for the quarter-finals

Elite Group C

Jaipuria Vidyalaya Ground, Jaipur, October 5: Himachal Pradesh 189 in 48.4 overs (Rohit Narang 36, Deepinder Rana 32; Yazh Arun 2-24, Sonu Yadav 2-36) lost to **Tamil Nadu** 191/6 in 48.5 overs (Pradosh Paul 67, Abhishek Selvakumar 36) by four wickets.

SMS Stadium, Jaipur, October 5: Rajasthan 211/9 in 50 overs (SA Ahuja 66, DO Choudhary 52; Akshay Manohar 2-20, Ananthakrishnan J 2-33, Adithya Krishnan 2-33) beat **Kerala** 102 in 38.3 overs (A Manohar 33; RM Bishnoi 5-19, RA Choudhary 3-23) by 109 runs.

KL Saini Stadium, Jaipur, October 5: Saurashtra 204/7 in 50 overs (HS Kotak 54, Siddhant Rana 43; Taizeem Tak 2-28, Govind Sharma 2-29) beat **Jammu and Kashmir** 114 in 34.2 overs (Abdul Samad 25; Rahul Vankani 3-19, Smit Patel 3-30) by 90 runs.

KL Saini Stadium, Jaipur, October 6: Goa 199 in 49 overs (Alam Khan 59, Rahul Mehta 36; Yazh Arun 3-29, Deeban Lingesh 3-30) lost to **Tamil Nadu** 202/3 in 37.5 overs (Nidhish Rajagopal 102*, Sonu Yadav 68*) by seven wickets.

SMS Stadium, Jaipur, October 6: Odisha 165 in 49.1 overs (Swastik Samal 37, Subham Satrujit 28; RA Choudhary 3-25, MJ Suthar 2-15) lost to **Rajasthan** 168/2 in 33.5 overs (DR Gajraj 83*, KG Baniwal 48) by eight wickets.

Jaipuria Vidyalaya Ground, Jaipur, October 6: Saurashtra 178 in 49.4 overs (H Desai 42, HS Kotak 36; Nakson Rahul 3-29, Adithya Krishnan 2-27) lost to **Kerala** 180/7 in 49.2 overs (Vathsal 49, Ashwin Anand 44; Amit Ranjan 2-35, Smit Patel 2-46) by three wickets.

KL Saini Stadium, Jaipur, October 8: Saurashtra 132 in 45 overs (Rishi Patel 36; Swastik Samal 3-13, Shekhar Majhi 2-16) lost to Odisha 133/3 in 32.2 overs (Raghunath Malla 61*, Jyoti Behera 26*) by seven wickets.

SMS Stadium, Jaipur, October 8: Jammu and Kashmir 168 in 50 overs (Qamran Iqbal 55, Govind Sharma 35; Shivam Sharma 3-34, Shourya Garg 2-15) lost to **Himachal Pradesh** 169/3 in 43.4 overs (Vaibhav Sharma 100*, Prashant Tomar 35) by seven wickets.

Jaipuria Vidyalaya Ground, Jaipur, October 8: Rajasthan 263 in 49.3 overs (RM Bishnoi 92, HK Joshi 43; Vrusaj T 4-46, Shubham Tari 2-49) beat **Goa** 135 in 39 overs (Alam Khan 45*; AM Singh 5-16, HD Sharma 3-38) by 128 runs.

Jaipuria Vidyalaya Ground, Jaipur, October 9: Kerala 224/8 in 50 overs (Nikhil T 59, Akshay Manohar 50; Binit Mohanty 2-4) beat **Odisha** 210 in 49.1 overs (Subham Satrujit 96, Swastik Samal 25; A Manohar 3-24, Vathsal 3-45) by 14 runs.

SMS Stadium, Jaipur, October 9: Himachal Pradesh 249/6 in 50 overs (Vaibhav Sharma 120, Harshit Bisht 55; Alam Khan 3-50) beat **Goa** 156/6 in 50 overs (Alam 52, Digesh Raikar 36*; Parikshit Kashyap 2-11) by 93 runs.

KL Saini Stadium, Jaipur, October 9: Jammu and Kashmir 227 in 49.5 overs (Qamran Iqbal 101, Vivrant Sharma 32; Sonu Yadav 5-29, Yazh Arun 3-38) lost to **Tamil Nadu** 228/6 in 48.3 overs (Pradosh Paul 94, Nidhish Rajagopal 58; Taizeem Tak 2-32, Mujtaba Yousuf 2-41) by four wickets.

Jaipuria Vidyalaya Ground, Jaipur, October 11: Jammu and Kashmir 225/7 in 50 overs (Jiyaad Magrey 101, Raghav Sharma 40; Nakson Rahul 4-48, Adithya Krishnan 2-33) beat **Kerala** 189 in 46.4 overs (Aadidev TJ 44, Vathsal 42; Ananthakrishnan J 42; Govind Sharma 4-40, Javid Ahmad 2-28) by 36 runs.

KL Saini Stadium, Jaipur, October 11: Saurashtra 233/8 in 50 overs (H Desai 83, HS Kotak 41; Rahul Mehta 4-36, SA Mishra 3-39) beat **Goa** 148 in 42.2 overs (Gauresh Kambli 43, Krishna Thakur 25; Adityaraj Rathore 3-17, Rahul Vankani 3-43) by 85 runs.

SMS Stadium, Jaipur, October 11: Rajasthan 171 in 48.4 overs (DB Vairagi 41, SA Ahuja 27; Trilok Nag 3-36) lost to **Tamil Nadu** 176/7 in 46 overs (Yazh Arun 41*, Sonu Yadav 37; AM Singh 2-25, RM Bishnoi 2-30) by three wickets.

Jaipuria Vidyalaya Ground, October 13: J&K 221 in 48.5 overs (Kanhaiya Wadhawan 64, Javid Ahmad 27*; Ruthvik Naik 3-60, Krishna Thakur 2-39) beat Goa 181 in 46.5 overs (Alam Khan 63, Gauresh Kambli 53; Abdul Samad 2-18, Taizeem Tak 2-31) by 40 runs.

SMS Stadium, Jaipur, October 13: Saurashtra 205 in 49.5 overs (H Desai 88, Jay Gohil

38; Pradosh Paul 3-29, Yazh Arun 3-51) lost to **Tamil Nadu** 206/3 in 45.1 overs (P Paul 63, Abhishek Selvakumar 48*) by seven wickets.

KL Saini Stadium, Jaipur, October 13: Odisha 238/6 in 50 overs (Aakash Nayak 67*, Subham Satrujit 66; Harsh Jamwal 2-32, Yutish Jamwal 2-46) lost to **Himachal Pradesh** 242/4 in 47.3 overs (Aman Jainwal 90*, Rohit Narang 55*; Nitish Samantray 2-31, Shekhar Majhi 2-53) by six wickets.

SMS Stadium, Jaipur, October 15: Saurashtra 200 in 50 overs (H Desai 104, Rishi Patel 46; RM Bishnoi 4-47, AM Singh 2-50) lost to Rajasthan 201/2 in 42.4 overs (DR Gajraj 101*, SA Ahuja 61*) by eight wickets.

Jaipuria Vidyalaya Ground, Jaipur, October 15: Jammu and Kashmir 276/6 in 50 overs (Qamran Iqbal 107, Jiyaad Magrey 72; Suman Das 3-37) beat Odisha 191 in 39.2 overs (Swastik Samal 122, Nitish Samantray 40; Abdul Samad 5-22, Taizeem Tak 4-20) by 85 runs.

KL Saini Stadium, Jaipur, October 15: Himachal Pradesh 112 in 36.2 overs (Aman Jainwal 35, Prashant Tomar 28; Nakson Rahul 4-31, Akshay Manohar 2-10) lost to **Kerala** 113/3 in 26.4 overs (Vathsal 43*, Nikhil T 39*) by seven wickets.

SMS Stadium, Jaipur, October 17: Himachal Pradesh 185/9 in 50 overs (Vaibhav Sharma 112*; AM Singh 3-38, RM Bishnoi 3-44) lost to **Rajasthan** 188/1 in 44 overs (DR Gajraj 72, HK Joshi 67*) by nine wickets.

Jaipuria Vidyalaya Ground, Jaipur, October 17: Kerala 232/7 in 50 overs (Aadidev TJ 59, Vathsal 51; Trilok Nag 4-33, Sonu Yadav 2-51) lost to **Tamil Nadu** 235/5 in 45.4 overs (Abhishek Selvakumar 66, Sonu 66; Akshay Manohar 2-37, Ajith Jacob 2-51) by five wickets.

L Saini Stadium, Jaipur, October 17: Goa 248 in 49.5 overs (Rahul Mehta 64, Yash Porob 33; Suman Das 2-38, Pritam Jena 2-44, Satyakam Bharadwaj 2-44) lost to **Odisha** 252/4 in 49 overs (Swastik Samal 95, Raghunath Malla 62; Udit Yadav 2-34) by six wickets.

KL Saini Stadium, Jaipur, October 19: Rajasthan 302/6 in 50 overs (SA Ahuja 92, SV Joshi 79*; Taizeem Tak 3-56) beat **Jammu and Kashmir** 169 in 36.2 overs (Qamran Iqbal 54, Jiyaad Magrey 30; RA Choudhary 3-18, DR Gajraj 2-17) by 133 runs.

Jaipuria Vidyalaya Ground, Jaipur, October 19: Himachal Pradesh 238/6 in 50 overs (Rohit Narang 65, Vaibhav Sharma 50; Deep Patel 3-46, Rishi Patel 2-53) lost to **Saurashtra** 241/3 in 46.5 overs (H Desai 139, R Patel 44; Hritik Kalia 2-45) by seven wickets.

Jaipuria Vidyalaya Ground, Jaipur, October 21: Odisha 215 in 47.3 overs (Raghunath Malla 40, Swastik Samal 35; Kishan Kumar 3-28, Sonu Yadav 2-44) lost to **Tamil Nadu** 218/1 in 29.4 overs (Praveen Kumar 116*, Pradosh Paul 83*) by nine wickets.

KL Saini Stadium, Jaipur, October 21: Kerala 242/5 in 50 overs (Ananthakrishnan J 69, Nikhil T 67; SA Mishra 2-54) beat **Goa** 154 in 47.4 overs (Mohit Redkar 65; Akshay Manohar 3-30, Vathsal 2-14) by 88 runs.

Points table

Teams	M	W	L	D	T	N/R	Pts	NRR
Tamil Nadu	7	7	0	0	0	0	28	0.718
Rajasthan	7	6	1	0	0	0	24	1.421
Kerala	7	4	3	0	0	0	16	0.099
Saurashtra	7	3	4	0	0	0	12	0.198
Himachal Pradesh	7	3	4	0	0	0	12	-0.037
Jammu and Kashmir	7	3	4	0	0	0	12	-0.279
Odisha	7	2	5	0	0	0	8	-0.611
Goa	7	0	7	0	0	0	0	-1.446

Tamil Nadu and Rajasthan qualified for the quarter-final

Plate Group

Railway Stadium, Bhubaneshwar, October 5: Manipur 166 in 44.3 overs (Shubham Chauhan 74; Arbaaz Uddin 3-32, Nithishkumar 2-10) beat **Puducherry** 23 in 9.4 overs (Rex Singh 8-3) by 143 runs.

Vikash Cricket Ground, Bhubaneshwar, October 5: Bihar 262/6 in 50 overs (Piyush Singh 101, Akash Raj 36*; Yash Tandon 3-41) beat **Nagaland** 123 in 39.2 overs (Vipul Kapoor 33; A Anand 4-13, Shivam Kumar 2-24) by 139 runs.

KIIT Cricket Stadium, Bhubaneshwar, October 5: Arunachal Pradesh 209 in 50 overs (MD Bilal 110; Nunfela 3-37) beat **Mizoram** 198/7 in 50 overs (Shubham Yadav 68, Lalhriatrenga 51; Govind Mittal 3-32) by 11 runs.

KIIT Cricket Stadium, Bhubaneshwar, October 6: Manipur 233 in 50 overs (Rex Singh 83, Deepak 27; MD Shah 3-41, Arif Ansari 2-24) beat **Sikkim** 57 in 28.3 overs (Anwesh 25; Rex 5-15, Sohail 2-7) by 176 runs.

Railway Stadium, Bhubaneshwar, October 6: Bihar 239/6 in 45 overs (Piyush Singh 74, Harsh Raj 58; Sumit 3-35, Harman 2-37) beat **Uttarakhand** 116 in 33.2 overs (Gaurav Joshi 50; Malay Raj 3-18, Shivam Kumar 3-43) by 123 runs.

Vikash Cricket Ground, Bhubaneshwar, October 6: Mizoram 112 in 37 overs (Debojyoti Chanda 36*, Atul Singh 30; Ashif Khan 3-31, Abhishek 2-16, Swastic 2-10) lost to **Meghalaya** 113/3 in 23.4 overs (Ashif 28*, Raghav Kapur 27*) by seven wickets.

Vikash Cricket Ground, Bhubaneshwar, October 7: Arunachal Pradesh 136 in 38.4 overs (MD Shah 3-25, Anwesh 2-27) beat **Sikkim** 68 in 32.2 overs (Yorjum Sera 6-25, Hardik 2-4) by 68 runs.

KIIT Cricket Stadium, Bhubaneshwar, October 7: Puducherry 94 in 39 overs (Avneesh Sudha 4-13, Sumit 3-18) lost to **Uttarakhand** 97/2 in 19.1 overs (A Sudha 56*) by eight wickets.

Railway Stadium, Bhubaneshwar, October 7: Nagaland 189 in 40 overs (Hem 74, Harsh Keshari 52; Abhishek 6-37, Swastic 3-39) beat **Meghalaya** 159 in 47.1 overs (Raghav Kapur 71, Ashif Khan 47; Chiranjivi 3-22, Yash Tandon 2-21) by 30 runs.

Railway Stadium, Bhubaneshwar, October 9: Nagaland 324/7 in 50 overs (Vipul Kapoor 124, Shamphri 60; MD Shah 2-59, Anwesh 2-62) beat **Sikkim** 107 in 46.1 overs (Anwesh 42; Joshua 2-4, Abhishek 2-10) by 217 runs.

KIIT Cricket Stadium, Bhubaneshwar, October 9: Manipur 230 in 39.1 overs (Hrithik Kanojia 51, Shubham Chauhan 36; Hardik 3-47, Govind Mittal 2-28) beat **Arunachal Pradesh** 96 in 28.1 overs (MD Bilal 26; Sadananda 4-9, Rex Singh 3-23) by 134 runs.

Vikash Cricket Ground, Bhubaneshwar, October 9: Mizoram 170 in 48.4 overs (Lalhriatrenga 51, Shubham Yadav 32; Rajaram S 2-22, Arbaaz Uddin 2-34) beat Puducherry 169 in 44.5 overs (Rishab Belavadi 29, KSS Varma 27; Tluanga 2-20, Dina 2-30, Vanlal Remruata 2-30) by one run.

Railway Stadium, Bhubaneshwar, October 10: Nagaland vs **Uttarakhand**. Match abandoned without toss.

KIIT Cricket Stadium, Bhubaneshwar, October 10: Arunachal Pradesh v **Meghalaya**. Match abandoned without toss.

Vikash Cricket Ground, Bhubaneshwar, October 10: Bihar v **Puducherry**. Match abandoned without toss.

Railway Stadium, Bhubaneshwar, October 12: Bihar v **Meghalaya**. Match abandoned without toss.

KIIT Cricket Stadium, Bhubaneshwar, October 12: Mizoram v **Sikkim**. Match abandoned without toss.

Railway Stadium, Bhubaneshwar, October 12: Manipur v **Uttarakhand**. Match abandoned without toss.

Railway Stadium, Bhubaneshwar, October 14: Nagaland 154 in 41 overs (Hem 38*, Vipul Kapoor 33; KSS Varma 2-6, Nipun Gaikwad 2-23) beat **Puducherry** 41 in 20 overs (Yash Tandon 8-20) by 113 runs.

Vikash Cricket Ground, Bhubaneshwar, October 14: Manipur 187/3 in 36 overs (Shubham Chauhan 80*, Johnson 52) beat **Mizoram** 61 in 22 overs (Shubham Yadav 25; Rex Singh 4-18, Deepak 3-0) by 126 runs.

KIIT Cricket Stadium, Bhubaneshwar, October 14: Bihar 257/3 in 50 overs (Akash Raj 101*, Piyush Singh 77) beat **Arunachal Pradesh** 152 in 42.4 overs (MD Bilal 43, Vishek Kumar 41; A Raj 3-17, Shivam Kumar 3-30) by 105 runs.

Railway Stadium, Bhubaneshwar, October 16: Uttarakhand 255/7 in 50 overs (Gaurav Joshi 82, Samarth 66; Abhishek 3-42) beat **Meghalaya** 139 in 44.5 overs (Hrithik Sharma 50, Anish Charak 34; Harman 2-18, S Juyal 2-28) by 116 runs.

KIIT Cricket Stadium, Bhubaneshwar, October 16: Bihar 354/2 in 50 overs (Piyush Singh 145, Harsh Raj 115*) beat **Sikkim** 77/8 in 50 overs (Anwesh 33; A Anand 5-12) by 277 runs.

Vikash Cricket Ground, Bhubaneshwar, October 16: Manipur 149 in 45.3 overs (Shubham Chauhan 42, Hrithik Kanojia 36; Chiranjivi 4-27, Tohuka 2-20) lost to **Nagaland** 150/5 in 37.5 overs (Chiranjivi 40, Hem 33*; Bidash 2-32, Rex Singh 2-40) by five wickets.

KIIT Cricket Stadium, Bhubaneshwar, October 18: Uttarakhand 387/6 in 50 overs (Avneesh Sudha 129, Arya Sethi 100; Nunfela 3-83, VL Remruata 2-52) beat **Mizoram** 123 in 41.2 overs (Debojyoti Chanda 70*; A Sudha 2-7, Jagmohan Nagarkoti 2-12) by 264 runs.

Railway Stadium, Bhubaneshwar, October 18: Arunachal Pradesh 95 in 43.2 overs (Abhi Singh 35; Hem 5-10, Harsh Keshari 2-9) lost to **Nagaland** 99/2 in 19.3 overs (Shamphri 29, Kanishk 26*) by eight wickets.

Vikash Cricket Ground, Bhubaneshwar, October 18: Puducherry 258/6 in 50 overs (S Sanjay 70, Arbaaz Uddin 67; Adars 2-63) beat **Sikkim** 86 in 41.1 overs (Anwesh 33; A Uddin 5-15, Naveen Siranjeevi 3-11) by 172 runs.

Vikash Cricket Ground, Bhubaneshwar, October 20: Arunachal Pradesh 190/9 in 50 overs (MD Bilal 70, Govind Mittal 54; Arbaaz Uddin 3-46, Nipun Gaikwad 2-21) beat **Puducherry** 160 in 42.4 overs (Logesh 59, N Gaikwad 37; Yorjum Sera 5-34, D Bagra 3-23) by 30 runs.

KIIT Cricket Stadium, Bhubaneshwar, October 20: Meghalaya 288 in 49.5 overs (Hrithik Sharma 109, Raghav Kapur 79; Robin Limboo 4-50, Adars 2-43) beat **Sikkim** 90 in 35 overs (Arif Ansari 25; Abhishek 5-23, Aryan 3-18) by 198 runs.

Railway Stadium, Bhubaneshwar, October 20: Manipur 149 in 48.4 overs (Johnson 30, Hrithik Kanojia 29, Bidash 29; Shivam Kumar 3-26, A Anand 2-22) lost to **Bihar** 153/2 in 36.1 overs (Piyush 63*, Harsh Raj 58) by eight wickets.

KIIT Cricket Stadium, Bhubaneshwar, October 22: Manipur 236/6 in 50 overs (Shubham Chauhan 106*, Hrithik Kanojia 60; Aryan 2-24) beat **Meghalaya** 221/8 in 50 overs (Hrithik Sharma 85, Biprodeep 37; Rex Singh 3-37) by 15 runs.

Vikash Cricket Ground, Bhubaneshwar, October 22: Nagaland 236/7 in 50 overs (Vipul Kapoor 87, Hem 56; Thanzuala 3-35) beat **Mizoram** 74 in 28 overs (Daniel 6-15, Chiranjivi 2-16, Yash Tandon 2-16) by 162 runs.

Railway Stadium, Bhubaneshwar, October 22: Sikkim 59 in 22 overs (Jagmohan Nagarkoti 6-20, Harman 4-26) lost to **Uttarakhand** 65/1 in 5.5 overs (Avneesh Sudha 42*) by nine wickets.

Vikash Cricket Ground, Bhubaneshwar, October 24: Mizoram 53 in 28.5 overs (Paramjeet Singh 4-16, Shivam Kumar 3-5) lost to **Bihar** 55 for no loss in 7 overs (Piyush Singh 32*) by 10 wickets.

Railway Stadium, Bhubaneshwar, October 24: Puducherry 185 in 49.4 overs (Nipun Gaikwad 112, Prashant 3-27, Abhishek 2-27) lost to **Meghalaya** 186/7 in 48.5 overs (Raghav Kapur 73, Anish Charak 29; Arbaaz Uddin 4-28) by three wickets.

KIIT Cricket Stadium, Bhubaneshwar, October 24: Uttarakhand 360/7 in 50 overs (Avneesh Sudha 95, Samarth 79*; Govind Mittal 2-67, Likha Tayo 2-80) beat **Arunachal Pradesh** 199 in 47.4 overs (Vishek Kumar 57, Abhi Singh 40; Sumit 3-30, Harman 3-63) by 161 runs.

Points table

Teams	M	W	L	D	T	N/R	Pts	NRR
Bihar	8	6	0	0	0	2	28	3.271
Nagaland	8	6	1	0	0	1	26	1.614
Uttarakhand	8	5	1	0	0	2	24	2.927
Manipur	8	5	2	0	0	1	22	1.563
Meghalaya	8	3	3	0	0	2	16	0.502
Arunachal Pradesh	8	3	4	0	0	1	14	-1.217
Mizoram	8	1	6	0	0	1	6	-2.731
Puducherry	8	1	6	0	0	1	6	-0.642
Sikkim	8	0	7	0	0	1	2	-3.867

Bihar qualified for the quarter-final

Quarter-finals

Vidarbha Cricket Association Stadium, Jamtha, Nagpur, October 29: Rajasthan 257 in 50 overs (SA Ahuja 77, HK Joshi 57; Sameer Choudhary 3-43, Mohit Jangra 3-46) beat **Uttar Pradesh** 197 in 48.1 overs (Aryan Sharma 44, Kritagya Singh 36; RM Bishnoi 5-30, RA Choudhary 3-38) by 60 runs.

VCA Stadium, Civil Lines, Nagpur, October 29: Andhra 263/7 in 50 overs (Yara Sandeep 71, Subramanyam 68; Shivam Kumar 2-43, Randhir Dubey 2-49) beat **Bihar** 248/8 in 50 overs (Akash Raj 60, Harsh Raj 47) by 15 runs.

Vidarbha Cricket Association Stadium, Jamtha, Nagpur, October 30: Madhya Pradesh 283/8 in 50 overs (Irfan Ali 78, Rahul Chandrol 60; Harsh Dubey 3-51, Rohit Dattatraya 2-65) lost to **Vidarbha** 284/2 in 45.5 overs (Mandar Mahale 108, Nayan Chavan 104*) by eight wickets.

VCA Stadium, Civil Lines, Nagpur, October 30: Delhi 169 in 43.5 overs (Vaibhav Kandpal 53, Priyansh Arya 35; Kishan Kumar 6-39, Yazh Arun 2-32) lost to **Tamil Nadu** 170/4 in 33.3 overs (Abhishek Selvakumar 61*, Sonu Yadav 50; Hrithik Shokeen 2-37) by six wickets.

Semi-finals

VCA Stadium, Civil Lines, Nagpur, November 1: Andhra 201/8 in 50 overs (Harsha Vardhan 56, Nithish Reddy 43; Mandar Mahale 4-25, Rohit Dattatraya 2-53) lost to **Vidarbha** 202/8 in 48.3 overs (A Mokhade 70, Sanket Khedkar 35; Satvik 2-33, Durgakumar 2-59) by two wickets.

Vidarbha Cricket Association Stadium, Jamtha, Nagpur, November 2: Rajasthan 148 in 39.2 overs (DR Gajraj 27; Yazh Arun 3-21, Kishan Kumar 3-30) lost to **Tamil Nadu** 150/8 in 38.1 overs (Abhishek Selvakumar 48; AM Singh 5-35, MJ Suthar 2-37) by two wickets.

Final: Vidarbha beat Tamil Nadu by 83 runs

VCA Stadium, Civil Lines, Nagpur, November 4: Vidarbha 297/6 in 50 overs (YV Rathod 104, A Mokhade 101; Trilok Nag 4-48) beat **Tamil Nadu** 214 in 45 overs (Praveen Kumar 48, Sonu Yadav 33; Rohit Dattatraya 5-37, Harsh Dubey 2-42) by 83 runs.

Winners: Vidarbha

Uttar Pradesh took a first-innings lead to dethrone Vidarbha in the Under-19 Cooch
Behar Trophy tournament. — *UPCA*

Under-19 Cooch Behar Trophy

Bountiful season for Rathod

For the second season in a row, Yash Rathod put up a stellar performance, scoring 1089 runs in 19 innings at an average of 57.38. His four hundreds and five half-centuries steered defending champions Vidarbha into the final, but this time, they lost to Uttar Pradesh on first-innings lead.

In the final, Aryan Juyal (94) and Priyam Garg (78) helped UP to 283 despite Nachiket Bhute, the tall bespectacled pacer, picking up five wickets. In response, Nayam Chavan and Rathod too scored half-centuries for Vidarbha but Purnank Tyagi's 7 for 65 meant they could manage only 251. Sameer Choudhary's 119 in UP's second innings ensured the game ended in a draw.

Last season, Rathod was the leading run-scorer of the tournament with 945 runs. This time, apart from him, Vathsal Govind (1235, average 123.50) of Kerala and Sanyam Arora (1080, average 108.00) of Uttarakhand also breached the 1000-run landmark. The two, however, faced relatively weaker opponents in Elite Group C and Plate Group respectively.

Arora's 347 against Pondicherry was the highest individual score of the tournament, while his team-mate Avneesh Sudha (339 v Bihar) and Govind (302 not out v Odisha) were the other triple-centurions. Arora was later banned by the BCCI for two years after being found guilty in a case of age-fudging.

Five bowlers — A Anand (of Bihar, 62 wickets), Manishi (Jharkhand, 57),

Rex Singh (Manipur, 56), Bhute (55) and Sumit Juyal (Uttarakhand, 53) — claimed 50 or more wickets. Rex's tally also included a perfect ten: 10 for 11 against Arunachal Pradesh.

In the **2017-18** season, where Rathod could manage just eight in the lone innings against Madhya Pradesh in the final, Vidarbha's captain Atharwa Taide plundered 320. This after Madhya Pradesh were all out for 289. Though Vidarbha ran out of time when Madhya Pradesh were 176 for 7 in their second innings, they lifted the trophy thanks to their massive 614.

Both Taide and Rathod travelled to Sri Lanka with the Under-19 team. While Taide scored two centuries in as many youth Tests, Rathod made a half-century in the 50-over game.

Ayush Jamwal, Himachal Pradesh's off-spinner, picked up four ten-wicket hauls in six matches, and also scored a handy 378 runs at 47.25.

	Most runs	**Most wickets**
2017-18	Yash Rathod (Vidarbha) (945 runs, 9 matches)	Ayush Jamwal (HP) (50 wickets, 6 matches)
2018-19	Vathsal Govind (Kerala) (1235 runs, 8 matches)	A Anand (Bihar) (62 wickets, 8 matches)

2018-19

Elite Group A

Vidarbha Cricket Association Stadium, Jamtha, Nagpur, November 19-22: Tamil Nadu 229 in 93 overs (Mokit Hariharan 57, Vignesh Iyer 46; Bhute 4-54, Tekan 2-26) and 176 in 66.4 overs (Sonu Yadav 40, Kishan Kumar 26*; Harsh Dubey 4-64, Rohit Dattatraya 3-51) drew with **Vidarbha** 526/8 dec. in 159.3 overs (Yash Kadam 141, YV Rathod 114; S Bhargav 3-102, Rahul D 2-82) by an innings and 121 runs.

Green Park Stadium, Kanpur, November 19-22: Chhattisgarh 149 in 65.3 overs (RV Sharma 39, AZ Samad 28; Kartik Tyagi 4-52, Purnank 3-39) and 208 in 76.1 overs (Ayush Pandey 62, Satya Sharma 43; K Tyagi 5-95, Sameer Choudhary 4-20) lost to **Uttar Pradesh** 510 in 141.5 overs (Dhruv Jurel 152, S Choudhary 99; Shashwat Mishra 5-136, Parivesh Dhar 3-88) by an innings and 153 runs.

MCA Cricket Stadium, Gahunje, Pune, November 19-22: Himachal Pradesh 354 in 99.3 overs (Vaibhav Sharma 181, Kushal Pal 55; RS Hangargekar 6-100, LG Sonawane) and 331/7 in 96 overs (SA Saran 145*, Deepinder Rana 70; RS Hangargekar 3-75) drew with **Maharashtra** 468 in 146.3 overs (SS Nawale 145, SA Veer 89; Himanshu Beck 5-99, Shivam Sharma 2-122). **Maharashtra** took first-innings lead.

Feroz Shah Kotla Stadium, New Delhi, November 19-22: Mumbai 453 in 136.1 overs (Divyaansh 211, Pragnesh Kanpillewar 56; Ayush Badoni 3-53, Hrithik Shokeen 3-131) and 155 in 72.1 overs (P Kanpillewar 26; H Shokeen 5-38, A Badoni 2-28) drew with **Delhi** 396 in 130.4 overs (Priyansh Arya 152, Gagan Vats 100; Arjun Tendulkar 5-98, Atharva Ankolekar 4-93) and 64/3 in 7.3 overs (A Badoni 40; Atharva Poojari 2-23). **Mumbai** took first-innings lead.

VCA Stadium, Civil Lines, Nagpur, November 26-29: Delhi 327 in 101 overs (Ayush Badoni 106, Anmol Sharma 49; Bhute 3-44, Tekan 3-59) and 301/4 dec. in 79 overs (Gagan Vats 92, Vaibhav Kandpal 61*, Anmol 61*; Harsh Dubey 2-72) beat **Vidarbha** 283 in 85.1 overs (YV Rathod 168, A Mokhade 30; Hrithik Shokeen 7-77, Anirudh Chowdhary 2-62) and 209 in

48.3 overs (Sandesh D 54, Bhute 30; Prince Choudhary 4-103, H Shokeen 3-66) by 236 runs.

NPR College Ground, Dindigul, November 26-29: Tamil Nadu 489 in 119.5 overs (Pradosh Paul 191, Praveen Kumar 84; Parikshit Kashyap 3-103, Himanshu Beck 3-126) drew with **Himachal Pradesh** 200 in 95.5 overs (Vaibhav Sharma 97, Kushal Pal 34; Sonu Yadav 3-41, S Bhargav 2-45) and 302/6 in 93.4 overs (SA Saran 102*, Deepinder Rana 60; S Bhargav 3-70). **Tamil Nadu** took first-innings lead.

MCA Cricket Stadium, Gahunje, Pune, November 26-29: Chhattisgarh 243 in 84 overs (Ayush Pandey 79, AG Rao 46; RS Hangargekar 5-67) and 325 in 106 overs (Kivnoor Singh 122, Satya Sharma 86; RS Hangargekar 3-61, SA Veer 3-88) lost to **Maharashtra** 314/9 dec. in 96 overs (PH Shah 92, SS Nawale 55; RT Taank 4-98, Kivnoor 2-4) and 258/3 in 50.1 overs (Om Bhosale 104*, AK Kale 68; Parivesh Dhar 2-58) by seven wickets.

Sachin Tendulkar Gymkhana, Kandivali, Mumbai, November 26-29: Baroda 139 in 41.5 overs (Ashutosh Das 34*, Shivang Sane 30; Atharva Poojari 4-38, Arjun Tendulkar 3-42) and 352 in 105 overs (Sumedh Marathe 89, VS Patil 85; Praful Devkate 5-88, A Poojari 3-67) lost to **Mumbai** 321 in 118.2 overs (Gautam Waghela 67, Vaibhav Kalamkar 59; Nisarg Patel 4-107, A Das 3-49) and 172/1 in 36.1 overs (Pragnesh Kanpillewar 112*, G Waghela 26*) by nine wickets.

Shaheed Veer Narayan Singh International Stadium, Raipur, December 3-6: Tamil Nadu 257 in 63.2 overs (Pradosh Paul 51, Mokit Hariharan 40; RT Taank 3-63, Anurag Yadav 2-41) and 135 in 46 overs (Nidhish Rajagopal 31, Sonu Yadav 30; Shashwat Mishra 4-43, RT Taank 3-38) lost to **Chhattisgarh** 177 in 50.1 overs (AG Rao 63, Satya Sharma 60; S Bhargav 3-37, Mohit Panghal 3-49) and 216/4 in 61.3 overs (AG Rao 126*, Ayush Pandey 59*; Yazh Arun 2-63) by six wickets.

Sharad Pawar Cricket Academy BKC, Mumbai, December 3-6: Uttar Pradesh 409 in 106.2 overs (Dhruv Jurel 147, Ansh Yadav 81; Atharva Ankolekar 4-95, Atharva Poojari 2-63) drew with **Mumbai** 155 in 61.5 overs (Divyaansh 93; Purnank Tyagi 3-31, Akshay Sain 3-39) and 450/8 in 172 overs (Manal Kawle 125*, Divyaansh 102; Mohit Jangra 3-63, Kartik Tyagi 3-82). **Uttar Pradesh** took first-innings lead.

Reliance cricket ground, Nagothane, December 3-6: Delhi 311 in 95.3 overs (Ayush Badoni 68, Gulzar Sandhu 66; RS Hangargekar 3-92, RA Daud 3-46) and 469/7 in 104.4 overs (Vaibhav Kandpal 215, Anmol Sharma 104*; RS Hangargekar 4-96, RA Daud 2-72) drew with **Maharashtra** 583/9 dec. in 137.5 overs (Om Bhosale 190, SS Nawale 116; Prince Choudhary 5-126, Anmol 2-31). **Maharashtra** took first-innings lead.

Alembic 2 Cricket Ground, Vadodara, December 3-6: Vidarbha 398 in 103.4 overs (Mandar Mahale 93, A Mokhade 65; Archan Kothari 4-85, Nisarg Patel 4-106) and 249/5 dec. in 55 overs (Harsh Dubey 103*, Yash Kadam 52*; A Kothari 3-62, N Patel 2-101) beat **Baroda** 198 in 59.5 overs (KT Marathe 48, Shashwat Rawat 39; Bhute 4-72, Rohit Dattatraya 3-32) and 174 in 59.2 overs (Shivang Sane 53*, VS Patil 27; Bhute 5-46, R Dattatraya 3-44) by 275 runs.

VCA Stadium, Civil Lines, Nagpur, December 10-13: Vidarbha 419 in 132 overs (Yash Kadam 131*, Harsh Dubey 88; Atharva Poojari 5-101, Uzair Khan 3-77) and 148/5 in 48 overs (Mandar Mahale 45, Nayan Chavan 36; Praful Devkate 3-63) drew with **Mumbai** 278 in 97.2 overs (Divyaansh 82, Pragnesh Kanpillewar 51; Tekan 6-66, Bhute 2-44). **Vidarbha** took first-innings lead.

ICL Sankar Nagar Ground, Tirunelveli, December 10-13: Tamil Nadu 132 in 48.3 overs (Nidhish Rajagopal 26; TS Jain 5-27, SA Veer 5-50) and 173 in 44.2 overs (N Rajagopal 84; TS Jain 4-50, SA Veer 3-63) lost to **Maharashtra** 148 in 48 overs (TS Jain 47*, SS Nawale 39; Pradosh Paul 6-52, S Bhargav 2-42) and 158/4 in 39.4 overs (SA Veer 66*; Kishan Kumar 2-46) by six wickets.

PCPA Stadium, Santokhgarh, December 10-13: Himachal Pradesh 184 in 65.1 overs (SA Saran 69; Parivesh Dhar 4-57, RT Taank 3-30) and 193/9 in 118 overs (Siddhant Dogra 70, Kushal Pal 47; Shashwat Mishra 5-46, RT Taank 2-58) drew with **Chhattisgarh** 308 in 83.4 overs (Kivnoor Singh 161, P Dhar 71; Parikshit Kashyap 4-51, Prashant Bakshi 2-51). **Chhat-**

tisgarh took first-innings lead.

Alembic 2 Cricket Ground, Vadodara, December 10-12: Uttar Pradesh 417 in 107 overs (Purnank Tyagi 73, Sameer Rizvi 68; Nisarg Patel 4-95, Archan Kothari 3-87) beat **Baroda** 132 in 50.4 overs (Kartik Tyagi 4-33, Mohit Jangra 2-28) and 122 in 58.3 overs (Shashwat Rawat 50; K Tyagi 4-35, Shivam Sharma 3-23) by an innings and 163 runs.

BSP Cricket Stadium, Bhilai, December 24-27: Mumbai 399 in 144.3 overs (Pragnesh Kanpillewar 130, Divyaansh 83; Vijay Yadav 3-32, Parivesh Dhar 2-62) and 182/4 in 27.4 overs (Yashasvi Jaiswal 100*, Varun Lavande 30; RT Taank) beat **Chhattisgarh** 224 in 73.2 overs (AG Rao 94, Ayush Pandey 37; Varun Jaijode 6-62, V Lavande 2-18) and 356 in 102.3 overs (A Pandey 79, RT Taank 44; Uzair Khan 3-71, Atharva Poojari 2-30) by six wickets.

Bhamashah Park Ground, Meerut, December 24-27: Uttar Pradesh 250 in 82.4 overs (Shivam Sharma 80, Purnank Tyagi 43; S Bhargav 3-41, Sonu Yadav 2-32) and 304/5 dec. in 68 overs (Ankur Malik 60*, Sameer Choudhary 56*; Yazh Arun 3-84) beat **Tamil Nadu** 99 in 44.2 overs (Tushar Raheja 29; Shivam 3-15, Kartik Tyagi 3-24, P Tyagi 3-31) and 119 in 44.5 overs (T Raheja 36, S Yadav 32*; P Tyagi 5-24, K Tyagi 2-38) by 336 runs.

PCPA Stadium, Santokhgarh, December 24-27: Vidarbha 606 (YV Rathod 257, Nayan Chavan 120; Shourya Garg 5-160, Rishi Mahajan 2-96) beat **Himachal Pradesh** 257 in 106 overs (SA Saran 79, Aryavrat Sharma 50; Rohit Dattatraya 6-64) and 238 in 88.4 overs (S Garg 96*, Aryavrat 79; Tekan 3-43, Harsh Dubey 3-45) by an innings and 111 runs.

St Stephens Ground, New Delhi, December 24-27: Baroda 170 in 58.2 overs (Ansh Patel 35*, VS Patil 28, Swapnil Ugle 28; Hrithik Shokeen 5-49, Saurav Dagar 3-31) and 259 in 88.4 overs (VS Patil 92, Shashwat Rawat 57; Prince Choudhary 5-51, S Dagar 2-44) lost to **Delhi** 355 in 90 overs (Vaibhav Kandpal 158, Mayank Bansal 72; Nisarg Patel 4-112, Archan Kothari 3-71) and 75 for no loss (S Dagar 43*, Gagan Vats 31*) by 10 wickets.

VCA Stadium, Civil Lines, Nagpur, December 31-January 3: Vidarbha 348 in 80.5 overs (Harsh Dubey 100, Nayan Chavan 84; Anurag Yadav 3-46, Binny Samuel 3-67, Shashwat Mishra 3-93) and 295/5 dec. in 82.1 overs (Yash Kadam 100*, N Chavan 90; S Mishra 3-82) beat **Chhattisgarh** 136 in 37.3 overs (Ayush Pandey 37, AG Rao 36; Bhute 5-32, Rohit Dattatraya 3-26) and 164 in 50.3 overs (S Mishra 35; R Dattatraya 4-57, Y Kadam 3-42) by 343 runs.

Sharad Pawar Cricket Academy BKC, Mumbai, December 31-January 3: Mumbai 407 in 118.5 overs (Vaibhav Kalamkar 110, Atharva Ankolekar 73; RV Chougule 3-81, RS Hangargekar 3-88) and 212/5 in 63 overs (Varun Lavande 124*; RV Chougule 4-66) drew with **Maharashtra** 586 in 153.2 overs (SS Nawale 154, PH Shah 103; Uzair Khan 4-98, A Ankolekar 2-141). **Maharashtra** took first-innings lead.

Jamia Milia Islamia, New Delhi, December 31-January 3: Uttar Pradesh 635/6 dec. in 180.1 overs (Sameer Rizvi 212, Anchit Yadav 134, Dhruv Jurel 100*; Hrithik Shokeen 2-101) beat **Delhi** 182 in 62.5 overs (Mayank Bansal 36, Dhruv 31; Shivam Sharma 4-25, Mohit Jangra 4-65) and 241 in 84.5 overs (Vaibhav Kandpal 85, Anmol Sharma 56; Vikas Singh 2-37, Shivam 2-48) by an innings and 212 runs.

Reliance Cricket Stadium, Vadodara, December 31-January 3: Himachal Pradesh 157 in 60.3 overs (Prashant Bakshi 53, Parikshit Kashyap 33*; Sachin Jha 5-25, Archan Kothari 3-51) and 319 in 124.1 overs (Kushal Pal 153, Deepinder Rana 58; S Jha 3-80, A Kothari 2-35) beat **Baroda** 142 in 45.1 overs (Shashwat Rawat 60; P Bakshi 8-66, P Kashyap 2-55) and 298 in 90.3 overs (Riyazhusen Diwan 78, Shivang Sane 54; Shivam Sharma 5-86, P Bakshi 4-54) by 36 runs.

Choudhary Charan Singh Sports Stadium, Muzaffarnagar, January 7-10: Vidarbha 177 in 48.5 overs (A Mokhade 43, Sanket Khedkar 38; Mohit Jangra 6-40, Kunal Yadav 3-42) and 220 in 66.5 overs (Mandar Mahale 61, A Mokhade 52; M Jangra 3-42, Purnank Tyagi 3-55) lost to **Uttar Pradesh** 246 in 85 overs (Ansh Yadav 72, Sameer Choudhary 46; Harsh Dubey 6-89, Tekan 2-59) and 155/2 in 52.2 overs (Aryan Sharma 78*, Dhruv Jurel 39*) by eight wickets.

Sachin Tendulkar Gymkhana, Kandivali, Mumbai, January 7-10: Mumbai 512/9 dec.

in 131 overs (Suved Parkar 136, Varun Lavande 104; Nidhish Rajagopal 4-96, Yazh Arun 3-130) drew with **Tamil Nadu** 308 in 90.3 overs (N Rajagopal 141, Tushar Raheja 33; Atharva Ankolekar 3-60, Arjun Tendulkar 3-73) and 411/7 in 118 overs (Mokit Hariharan 136, N Rajagopal 108; Praful Devkate 4-120). **Mumbai** took first-innings lead.

PCPA Stadium, Santokhgarh, January 7-10: Delhi 323 in 85.5 overs (Mayank Bansal 150, Priyansh Arya 88; Prashant Bakshi 4-54, Parikshit Kashyap 4-77) and 348/7 dec. in 114 overs (Saurav Dagar 87, Priyansh Arya 82; P Bakshi 3-77, Shivam Sharma 3-77) drew with **Himachal Pradesh** 462 in 136.4 overs (Kushal Pal 189, SA Saran 77; Dhruv Das 3-62, Mayank Rawat 2-68). **Himachal Pradesh** took first-innings lead.

Reliance Cricket Stadium, Vadodara, January 7-10: Maharashtra 241 in 49.5 overs (HA Kate 98*, SS Nawale 77; Archan Kothari 5-80, Ashutosh Das 2-55) and 466/3 dec. in 74 overs (PH Shah 200*, SA Veer 115*) beat **Baroda** 297 in 94 overs (P Patidar 58, VS Patil 55; PH Shah 3-45, RS Hangargekar 3-72, RV Chougule 3-80) and 291 in 100.3 overs (P Patidar 59, A Kothari 39*; SA Veer 2-32, HA Kate 2-33, LG Sonawane 2-33) by 119 runs.

TNCA Academy, Theni, January 14-17: Baroda 279 in 99 overs (P Patidar 83, Shivang Sane 48; Sonu Yadav 5-80, Trilok Nag 3-45) and 384/4 in 133 overs (Atharv Karulkar 169*, Shashwat Rawat 88) drew with **Tamil Nadu** 422 in 110 overs (Arjun Murthy 111*, S Yadav 80; P Patidar 4-101, Pahal Agarwal 2-67). **Tamil Nadu** took first-innings lead.

MCA Cricket Stadium, Gahunje, Pune, January 14-17: Maharashtra 253 in 76.3 overs (Om Bhosale 97, SA Veer 46; Sameer Choudhary 4-25) and 165 in 53.2 overs (SS Nawale 37, AK Kale 36; Shivam Sharma 6-41, Mohit Jangra 2-60) lost to **Uttar Pradesh** 374 in 133.5 overs (Ansh Yadav 132, Aniket Seth 82; RS Hangaregekar 4-115, RA Daud 3-84) and 49/1 in 7.2 overs (Dhruv Jurel 25*) by nine wickets.

PCPA Stadium, Santokhgarh, January 14-17: Mumbai 374 in 100.4 overs (Pragnesh Kanpillewar 147, Varun Lavande 104; Parikshit Kashyap 7-97, Harsh Jamwal 2-59) and 266 in 60.4 overs (P Kanpillewar 106, V Lavande 39; Shourya Garg 4-90, Shivam Sharma 3-58) beat **Himachal Pradesh** 245 in 69.3 overs (S Garg 84, SA Saran 37; Atharva Ankolekar 5-46, Arjun Tendulkar 3-45) and 233 in 86.4 overs (Vaibhav Sharma 100, S Garg 34; Praful Devkate 5-69, A Tendulkar 3-33) by 162 runs.

Feroz Shah Kotla Stadium, New Delhi, January 14-17: Chhattisgarh 174 in 66 overs (Satya Sharma 66; Ayush Badoni 3-19, Prince Choudhary 2-13) and 163 in 53 overs (Ayush Pandey 66, RV Sharma 30; A Badoni 4-11, Deepanshu Yadav 2-30) lost to **Delhi** 381 in 87 overs (Vaibhav Kandpal 111, Anuj Rawat 99; Shashwat Mishra 5-104, Anurag Yadav 2-54) by an innings and 44 runs.

Victoria Park Stadium, Meerut, January 21-24: Himachal Pradesh 138 in 73.1 overs (Shourya Garg 25; Vikas Singh 4-42, Shivam Sharma 3-22) drew with **Uttar Pradesh** 207/5 in 69 overs (Ansh Yadav 51*, Dhruv Jurel 45; Shivam 2-74). **Uttar Pradesh** took first-innings lead.

TNCA Academy, Theni, January 21-24: Tamil Nadu 274 in 99.3 overs (Pradosh Paul 101, Nidhish Rajagopal 43; Anirudh Choudhary 5-67) and 534 in 117.1 overs (P Paul 148, Vimal Khumar 90; Ayush Badoni 3-77, Prince Chaudhary 3-127) drew with **Delhi** 409 in 117.4 overs (Priyansh Arya 175, Vaibhav Kandpal 124; Trilok Nag 3-77, Yazh Arun 3-117). **Delhi** took first-innings lead.

Reliance cricket ground, Nagothane, January 21-23: Maharashtra 110 in 29.2 overs (HA Kate 38, SS Nawale 28; Bhute 6-27, Tekan 3-65) and 272 in 93.2 overs (TS Jain 59, SA Veer 57; Bhute 6-89, Tekan 3-74) beat **Vidarbha** 218 in 75.5 overs (Bhute 41*, Tekan 39; HA Kate 3-28, PH Shah 2-33) and 138 in 48.5 overs (Mandar Mahale 58; PH Shah 5-26, RV Chougule 4-44) by 26 runs.

SGSA Cricket Ground, Vadodara, January 21-23: Chhattisgarh 369 in 86.1 overs (Ayush Pandey 129, Kivnoor Singh 89; Nisarg Patel 5-92, Pahal Agarwal 4-65) and 233/9 dec. in 59.4 overs (AG Rao 80, A Pandey 55; Archan Kothari 6-66, N Patel 3-93) beat **Baroda** 113 in 37.3 overs (Shashwat Rawat 28; Shashwat Mishra 3-17, Binny Samuel 3-28, Parivesh Dhar 3-30) and 176 in 50 overs (S Rawat 86, L Mor 34; S Mishra 4-63, P Dhar 3-35) by 313 runs.

Elite Group B

Keenan Stadium, Jamshedpur, November 19-22: Jharkhand 131 in 58.4 overs (Ayush 34; Shubhang Hegde 5-36, Vidyadhar Patil 3-26) and 106 in 38 overs (Shresth Sagar 29; S Hegde 4-26, Rohit SSG 3-15) lost to **Karnataka** 474 in 117.3 overs (Aneesh KV 171, Luvnith Sisodia 88; Manishi 5-130, Pankaj Yadav 3-74) by an innings and 237 runs.

Dhruv Pandove Stadium, Patiala, November 19-22: Punjab 332 in 88.4 overs (Prabhsimran Singh 95; Jaish Jain 64; Suraj Suryal 5-89, Akash 3-97) and 246/6 dec. in 66 overs (Nehal Wadhera 77; Prabhsimran 58; P Hitanshu 3-30, SM Prajapati 2-31) drew with **Gujarat** 272 in 139.4 overs (Sunpreet Bagga 147*, LM Kocher 62; Sumit Sharma 4-33, Deepin Chitkara 3-48) and 162/6 in 70 overs (Priyesh 55, Smit Patel 25*; Harit Sachar 4-22, Deepanshu Chadha 2-47). **Punjab** took first-innings lead.

Teri Cricket Ground, Teri, November 19-21: Haryana 111 in 38.1 overs (Sagar Dahiya 31; RM Bishnoi 4-20, AM Singh 3-32) and 329 in 117.5 overs (S Dahiya 141, DA Thakral 80; HD Sharma 3-50, RM Bishnoi 3-77) lost to **Rajasthan** 312 in 114.5 overs (DR Gajraj 189, RA Chaudhary 45; Yashraj Bathara 3-69, Neeraj Rathee 3-91) and 129/3 in 35.2 overs (HK Joshi 77*; AS Sandhu 3-36) by seven wickets.

Bengal Cricket Academy Ground, Kalyani, November 19-22: Hyderabad 263 in 112 overs (Nitish Reddy 69, Divesh 54; Prabhat Maurya 4-71, Arka Sarkar 3-67) and 170 in 89.3 overs (N Reddy 48, Varun 39; Karan Lal 5-27, P Maurya 3-55) drew with **Bengal** 263 in 94.3 overs (Shakir Gandhi 50, Abhijeet Bhagat 47; Ajay Goud 7-73, CTL Rakshan 2-81) and 144/8 in 57 overs (Ankit Shukla 37; Hitesh Yadav 4-38, A Goud 3-37). Tied on first innings.

JSCA International Stadium Complex, Ranchi, November 26-29: Madhya Pradesh 230 in 89.1 overs (Mohammad Baggad 50, Suraj Vashisht 37; Manishi 7-70, Yuvraj Kumar 3-43) and 216 in 89.2 overs (S Vashisht 101*; Manishi 6-51, Sushant Mishra 3-52) beat **Jharkhand** 85 in 36.5 overs (Y Kumar 38; Omkar Singh 6-10, Ishan Afridi 4-25) and 219 in 89.1 overs (Ayush 44, Sahil Raj 42; Adheer Singh 5-50, I Afridi 3-39) by 142 runs.

KL Saini Stadium, Jaipur, November 26-29: Hyderabad 274 in 110.3 overs (Tilak Varma 147, Varun 37; RM Bishnoi 3-58, AM Singh 3-59, RA Choudhary 3-59) and 316 in 109.4 overs (T Varma 103, Sagar Chaurasia 51; MJ Suthar 3-75, RA Choudhary 2-31) drew with **Rajasthan** 333 in 119 overs (KG Baniwal 80, DR Gajraj 62; Rathan Teja 5-98, Ajay Goud 2-44) and 15/2 in 6.5 overs. **Rajasthan** took first-innings lead.

IS Bindra Cricket Stadium, PCA, Mohali, November 26-29: Bengal 254 in 113.2 overs (Aishik 72, Sourav Paul 41; Sumit Sharma 3-54, Amit Shukla 3-55) and 375/9 in 98 overs (Diganta Neogi 172, Karan Lal 52; A Shukla 5-119, Pukhraj Mann 3-14) drew with **Punjab** 422/8 dec. in 125 overs (Salil Arora 98, Arjun Azad 80; K Lal 4-93). **Punjab** took first-innings lead.

Lalbhai Contractor Stadium, Surat, November 26-29: Gujarat 212 in 94.3 overs (LM Kocher 52, Sunpreet Bagga 47; Neeraj Rathee 5-52, Anshul Kamboj 2-43) and 135 in 74 overs (Umang 42, Smit Patel 40; A Kamboj 6-36, Yashjeet Balhara 2-17) beat **Haryana** 189 in 77.2 overs (DA Thakral 72, Aman Sahrawat 31; SM Prajapati 4-56) and 58 in 22.1 overs (P Hitanshu 8-17) by 100 runs.

MPCA Cricket Ground, Sagar, December 3-6: Madhya Pradesh 453 in 142.3 overs (Rishabh Chouhan 109, Dev Barnale 90; Yuvraj Choudhary 4-89, Sumit Sharma 3-92) drew with **Punjab** 291 in 98.5 overs (Pukhraj Mann 76, Y Choudhary 68*; Adheer Singh 3-62, Ishan Afridi 2-42) and 319/8 in 98 overs (Salil Arora 104*, Anshul Chaudhary 69; Prankesh Rai 5-72, Adheer 2-98). **Madhya Pradesh** took first-innings lead.

KSCA Stadium, Hubli, December 3-6: Rajasthan 438 in 165.4 overs (HK Joshi 126, DR Gajraj 103; Shubhang Hegde 6-69, Venkatesh M 2-97) drew with **Karnataka** 212 in 74.5 overs (Smaran R 95; RA Choudhary 3-37, MJ Suthar 3-40) and 261/5 in 103 overs (Smaran R 131*, Kruthik Krishna 63*; AM Singh 3-38). **Rajasthan** took first-innings lead.

Teri Cricket Ground, Teri, December 3-6: Bengal 395 in 115.1 overs (Ankit Shukla 129, Aishik 105; Anshul Kamboj 5-100, Neeraj Rathee 4-91) and 231/5 in 70.1 overs (Abhijeet Bhagat 101*, Karan Lal 78; N Rathee 4-74) drew with **Haryana** 434 in 154.3 overs (A Kamboj

Domestic review

Sameer Rizvi struck a double-century for UP against Delhi. — UPCA

98, AS Sandhu 74; Prabhat Maurya 3-97, Iman Dutta 2-51). **Haryana** took first-innings lead.

Lalbhai Contractor Stadium, Surat, December 3-6: Gujarat 203 in 73 overs (Umang 43, Jaymeet Patel 41*; Sushant Mishra 5-61, Manishi 3-52) and 203 in 74.5 overs (Suraj Suryal 86, J Patel 35; Yuvraj Kumar 4-40, Manishi 4-59) beat **Jharkhand** 120 in 55 overs (Ayush 29, Y Kumar 26; Dhruvang Patel 4-25, J Patel 3-12) and 199 in 52.3 overs (Shresth Sagar 108, Marwah 29, Ayush 29; P Hitanshu 6-67) by 87 runs.

Bengal Cricket Academy Ground, Kalyani, December 10-13: Rajasthan 216 in 72.4 overs (KG Baniwal 35, SN Kulsreshtha 33; Prabhat Maurya 4-56, Kunal Kumar 2-55) and 57 in 42.3 overs (K Kumar 4-20, Karan Lal 2-6) beat **Bengal** 224 in 61.4 overs (Diganta Neogi 51, K Lal 34; AM Singh 5-68, AM Mathur 3-78) and 50/1 in 12 overs by nine wickets.

Gandhi Ground, Amritsar, December 10-13: Punjab 318 in 103.2 overs (Nehal Wadhera 125, Yuvraj Choudhary 69; Neeraj Rathee 4-74, Naman Bansal 3-57, Bhuwan Rohilla 3-83) drew with **Haryana** 148 in 65.4 overs (Sachin Choudhary 36, Sagar Dahiya 29; Amit Shukla 4-33, Deepin Chitkara 3-38) and 170/9 in 79 overs (Treyaksh Bali 53*, Yuvraj Singh 51; A Shukla 3-27, D Chitkara 2-27). **Punjab** took first-innings lead.

MPCA Cricket Ground, Sagar, December 10-13: Gujarat 78 in 53.2 overs (Ishan Afridi 4-16, Rishabh Chouhan 2-1) and 331 in 88.5 overs (Priyesh 156, Umang 27; Prankesh Rai 5-85, Mohammad Baggad 2-53) lost to **Madhya Pradesh** 348 in 116.5 overs (Rahul Chandrol 159, Dev Barnale 60; Dhruvang Patel 5-89, SM Prajapati 3-99) and 64/2 in 15.5 overs (D Barnale 43*) by eight wickets.

NFC Ground, Hyderabad, December 10-13: Hyderabad 457 in 166.1 overs (Ajay Goud 96, Tilak Varma 88; Shaun Joseph 2-60, Rohit SSG 2-74) and 260/4 in 75 overs (T Varma 119, Varun 52; Shubhang Hegde 2-53) drew with **Karnataka** 313 in 98.5 overs (Aneesh KV 89, Lochan Gowda 0; A Goud 3-64, Rathan Teja 3-68). **Hyderabad** took first-innings lead.

KL Saini Stadium, Jaipur, December 24-27: Rajasthan 345 in 121.1 overs (DA Agarwal 116, HK Joshi 107; Akash 7/92) and 193/3 dec. in 59 overs (SA Ahuja 78*, SN Kulsreshtha 30; Suraj Suryal 2-66) beat **Gujarat** 219 in 86.5 overs (MR Vachheta 57, Sunpreet Bagga 56; RM Bishnoi 5-56, RA Choudhary 2-24) and 270 in 78.5 overs (Priyesh 113, Umang 59; AM Mathur 4-42, RM Bishnoi 3-45) by 49 runs.

Dhruv Pandove Stadium, Patiala, December 24-27: Jharkhand 329 in 96 overs (Sahil Raj 108, Shresth Sagar 65; Amit Shukla 6-104, Arjun Pappal 3-61) and 294 in 104.3 overs (S Raj 84, S Sagar 81; Sumit Sharma 3-67, A Pappal 3-67, A Shukla 3-71) beat **Punjab** 292 in 81.4 overs (Salil Arora 103, Sumit 100; Sushant Mishra 5-75, Yuvraj Kumar 4-84) and 196 in 50.3 overs (Nehal Wadhera 59, Arjun Azad 46, S Arora 46; Amit Kumar 4-4, S Mishra 2-41) by 135 runs.

SDNRW Ground, Mysore, December 24-27: Karnataka 299 in 142.2 overs (Smaran R 66, Rohan Nayakar 64; SK Ajharuddin 3-36, Karan Lal 3-88) and 189/5 dec. in 57 overs (Aneesh KV 81, Munim Mehdi 49; Karan Lal 2-75) drew with **Bengal** 159 in 60.5 overs (Ankit Shukla 48, Aishik 25; Paras Arya 4-46, Shubhang Hegde 4-60) and 281/6 in 95 overs (Sourav Paul

134*, Aishik 82*; S Hegde 4-54). **Karnataka** took first-innings lead.

Gymkhana Ground, Hyderabad, December 24-27: Hyderabad 333 in 127.4 overs (Tilak Varma 104, Santosh Goud 72; Omkar Singh 5-72, Rishabh Chouhan 3-40) and 197 in 84.2 overs (Alankrit 61, S Goud 54; Omkar 4-51, Prankesh Rai 3-33) drew with **Madhya Pradesh** 326 in 102 overs (Irfan Ali 125*, Rahul Chandrol 40; Hitesh Yadav 4-74, CTL Rakshan 3-75) and 68/2 in 8.5 overs (I Ali 35, Dev Barnale 26*; CTL Rakshan 2-30). **Hyderabad** took first-innings lead.

BSL Cricket Stadium., Bokaro, December 31-January 3: Bengal 314 in 101.4 overs (Kaushik Maity 145*, Shakir Gandhi 80; Yuvraj Kumar 6-58) and 275/9 dec. in 83 overs (Karan Lal 67, Sourav Paul 49; Manishi 4-94, Sushant Mishra 2-66) drew with **Jharkhand** 287 in 118.4 overs (Pankaj Kumar 123, Ankit 54; Prabhat Maurya 5-66, SK Ajharuddin 2-52) and 249/2 in 56 overs (P Kumar 120, Shresth Sagar 73*). **Bengal** took first-innings lead.

Emerald Heights International School Ground, Indore, December 31-January 3: Rajasthan 179 in 53.3 overs (SA Ahuja 56, HK Joshi 30; Shivam Dwivedi 5-43, Amarjeet Singh 3-60) and 397/8 dec. in 110 overs (Karan Lamba 118, SA Ahuja 112; Adheer Singh 4-72, Rishabh Chouhan 3-78) drew with **Madhya Pradesh** 238 in 94.4 overs (Dev Barnale 79, Vikrant Bhadoriya 79; RM Bishnoi 6-78, RA Choudhary 3-61) and 256/4 in 83 overs (D Barnale 87, Irfan Ali 79*). **Madhya Pradesh** took first-innings lead.

Rajiv Gandhi International Stadium, Hyderabad, December 31-January 3: Haryana 400 in 142.2 overs (Sagar Dahiya 173, Ayush Negi 56; Rathan Teja 4-99, Hitesh Yadav 4-111) beat **Hyderabad** 164 in 78.2 overs (H Yadav 46, Divesh 40; Anshul Kamboj 5-30, AS Sandhu 2-16) and 153 in 84.4 overs (Santosh Goud 55, M Pratyush 35; Bhuwan Rohilla 5-28, A Kamboj 2-30) by an innings and 83 runs.

Sardar Patel Stadium, Valsad, December 31-January 3: Gujarat 356 in 141.2 overs (LM Kocher 136, Vardhman Shah 70; Shubhang Hegde 3-76, Vidyadhar Patil 3-80) and 145/3 in 72 overs (V Shah 46*, Sunpreet Bagga 44*; Paras Arya 2-48) drew with **Karnataka** 326 in 131.1 overs (S Hegde 82, Rohan Nayakar 76; Rutvik Kumar 3-53, Akash 3-86). **Gujarat** took first-innings lead.

Bengal Cricket Academy Ground, Kalyani, January 7-10: Bengal 401 in 111.3 overs (Ankit Shukla 115, Sourav Paul 74; JK Bhatt 3-77, Akash 3-94, SM Prajapati 3-96) drew with **Gujarat** 185 in 110.5 overs (JK Bhatt 34, Vardhman Shah 31; Prabhat Maurya 4-63, Abhijeet Bhagat 2-11) and 244/7 in 117 overs (LM Kocher 61, Sunpreet Bagga 54; Arka Sarkar 2-32, Karan Lal 2-54). **Bengal** took first-innings lead.

BSL Cricket Stadium., Bokaro, January 7-10: Hyderabad 302 in 88.3 overs (Varun 154, M Pratyush 71; Amit Kumar 4-92, Manishi 4-110) and 270 in 108.4 overs (Varun 165*, Santosh Goud 35; Manishi 4-110, Sushant Mishra 2-16) drew with **Jharkhand** 371 in 127 overs (Pankaj Kumar 106, Satya Setu 99; Hitesh Yadav 7-109, Akhilesh Reddy 2-55) and 109/4 in 24 overs (P Kumar 49; A Reddy 3-33). **Jharkhand** took first-innings lead.

MPCA Cricket Ground, Sagar, January 7-10: Madhya Pradesh 431 in 115.1 overs (Vikrant Bhadoriya 137, Rahul Chandrol 116; Anshul Kamboj 4-78, Yashjeet Balhara 3-98) and 228 in 73.1 overs (R Chandrol 38, Suraj Vashisht 34, Prankesh Rai 34; Y Balhara 8-65) beat **Haryana** 369 in 77.2 overs (Treyaksh Bali 102, Sagar Dahiya 65; Adheer Singh 3-30, P Rai 3-70) and 171 in 37.5 overs (A Kamboj 46*, T Bali 34; P Rai 7-54) by 119 runs.

KSCA Navale Stadium, Shimoga, January 7-10: Punjab 81 in 32.5 overs (Venkatesh M 5-34, Munim Mehndi 2-8) and 235 in 68.3 overs (Sumit Sharma 73, Salil Arora 52; Santokh Singh 4-70, Venkatesh M 3-63) lost to **Karnataka** 516/9 dec. in 136.3 overs (Luvnith Sisodia 236, Rohan Nayakar 86; Ketan Mankotia 2-88, Yuvraj Choudhary 2-92) by an innings and 200 runs.

Balurghat Stadium, Balurghat, January 14-17: Madhya Pradesh 225 in 87.1 overs (Irfan Ali 110, Rishabh Chouhan 51; Prayas Ray Barman 4-58, Karan Lal 4-73) and 195 in 93.2 overs (Suraj Vashisht 85, R Chouhan 39; P Ray Barman 5-58, K Lal 2-72) lost to **Bengal** 148 in 52.4 overs (Sourav Paul 52, Prabhat Maurya 28*; Prankesh Rai 4-36, Ishan Afridi 2-19) and

276/6 in 85.4 overs (Ankit 111*, K Lal 49*; I Afridi 2-49, Adheer Singh 2-65) by four wickets.

KL Saini Stadium, Jaipur, January 14-17: Rajasthan 293 in 89 overs (Karan Lamba 80, DA Agarwal 51; Sahil Raj 4-72, Manishi 3-58) and 229 in 75.3 overs (SN Kulsreshtha 47, MJ Suthar 44; Nitya 6-78, Manishi 3-72) drew with **Jharkhand** 221 in 66.1 overs (Ayush 86, Ankit 62; RA Choudhary 3-26, AM Singh 2-24) and 285/7 in 124 overs (Ankit 106, Satya Setu 79*; MJ Suthar 2-41, AM Mathur 2-59). **Rajasthan** took first-innings lead.

Gymkhana Ground, Hyderabad, January 14-17: Hyderabad 210 in 81.3 overs (Santosh Goud 63, Ajay Goud 47; Sumit Sharma 4-26, Vashish Mehra 2-49, Amit Shukla 2-49) and 135 in 45 overs (Tilak Varma 69*; Sumit 6-39, Ketan Mankotia 3-34) lost to **Punjab** 411 in 103.5 overs (Prabhsimran Singh 102, Salil Arora 101; A Goud 4-63, Amith Singh 2-50) by an innings and 66 runs.

Chaudhry Bansi Lal Cricket Stadium, Lahli, January 14-17: Haryana 126 in 37.2 overs (SR Singroha 26; Venkatesh M 5-63, Vidyadhar Patil 3-27) and 115 in 45.1 overs (Sachin Choudhary 40; Venkatesh M 4-45, Shubhang Hegde 3-19) lost to **Karnataka** 137 in 32.5 overs (Devdutt Padikkal 82; Anshul Kamboj 5-67, Neeraj Rathee 4/35) and 108/5 in 27.4 overs (D Padikkal 74*; A Kamboj 2-31, N Rathee 2-49) by five wickets.

KL Saini Stadium, Jaipur, January 21-24: Rajasthan 291 in 92.4 overs (RA Choudhary 65, Karan Lamba 64; Sumit Sharma 5-89, Ketan Mankotia 2-44) and 60/4 in 14.2 overs (K Mankotia 2-30) beat **Punjab** 59 in 22.2 overs (Arjun Azad 27; AM Singh 5-22, RM Bishnoi 4-14) and 289 in 62.2 overs (A Azad 115, Prabhsimran Singh 44; RM Bishnoi 5-86, MJ Suthar 2-35) by six wickets.

KSCA Stadium, Belgaum, January 21-24: Madhya Pradesh 275 in 107 overs (Dev Barnale 105, Irfan Ali 62; Venkatesh M 3-50, Chinmay NA 2-23) and 344/4 dec. in 124.4 overs (Suraj Vashisht 125, D Barnale 83) drew with **Karnataka** 189 in 83.1 overs (Shubhang Hegde 39, Devdutt Padikkal 36; Ishan Afridi 5-43, Prankesh Rai 2-27) and 70/1 in 23 overs (Luvnith Sisodia 39*, Rohan Nayakar 30*). **Madhya Pradesh** took first-innings lead.

Chaudhry Bansi Lal Cricket Stadium, Lahli, January 21-23: Haryana 145 in 38.1 overs (Treyaksh Balti 27; Manishi 6-43, Amit Kumar 2-38) and 52 in 38.2 overs (Manishi 4-6, Yuvraj Kumar 3-24) lost to **Jharkhand** 106 in 32.2 overs (Ayush 32; Yashjeet Balhara 4-42, Neeraj Rathee 2-9) and 95/6 in 26.1 overs (Ayush 29*; Y Balhara 5-20) by four wickets.

Lalbhai Contractor Stadium, Surat, January 21-23: Gujarat 133 in 59.3 overs (Sunpreet Bagga 52, Akash 37; Kavin Gupta 5-23, Ajay Goud 3-23) and 161 in 59.2 overs (SM Prajapati 29*, S Bagga 27; Hitesh Yadav 7-47, Ashish Srivastav 2-22) lost to **Hyderabad** 165 in 52.1 overs (Tilak Varma 80, Sagar Chaurasia 40; Akash 5-67, Dhruvang Patel 3-46) and 133/5 in 35.4 overs (Varun 81*; MR Vachheta 3-17) by five wickets.

Elite Group A and B points table

Teams	M	W	L	D	T	N/R	Pts	Quotient
Uttar Pradesh	8	6	0	2	0	0	45	2.370
Maharashtra	8	4	1	3	0	0	33	1.205
Vidarbha	8	4	3	1	0	0	29	1.435
Madhya Pradesh	8	3	1	4	0	0	28	1.250
Rajasthan	8	3	1	4	0	0	28	1.101
Karnataka	8	3	0	5	0	0	27	1.178
Mumbai	8	3	0	5	0	0	27	1.079
Delhi	8	3	1	4	0	0	26	1.081
Bengal	8	2	0	6	0	0	22	1.085

Gujarat	8	2	3	3	0	0	17	0.842
Jharkhand	8	2	3	3	0	0	17	0.930
Punjab	8	1	3	4	0	0	17	0.990
Chhattisgarh	8	2	5	1	0	0	15	0.771
Hyderabad	8	1	2	5	0	0	15	0.887
Himachal Pradesh	8	1	2	5	0	0	13	0.729
Haryana	8	1	5	2	0	0	11	0.828
Tamil Nadu	8	0	4	4	0	0	8	0.709
Baroda	8	0	7	1	0	0	1	0.589

UP, Maharashtra, Vidarbha, MP, Rajasthan qualified for quarter-finals

Elite Group C

MBB Stadium, Agartala, November 19-21: Andhra 133 in 38.5 overs (Nithish Reddy 49, Vamsi Krishna 29; Saruk Hossain 8-45) and 317 in 86.4 overs (V Krishna 104, Dheeraj Kumar 90; Amit Ali 5-58, Ashish Yadav 3-82) beat **Tripura** 155 in 58.4 overs (Babul Dey 29, Sankar Paul 29; Vasu 3-12, Durgakumar 3-23) and 151 in 71.5 overs (Sridam Paul 67, Bikram Das 30; Durgakumar 4-43, Subramanyam 2-16) by 144 runs.

Bokakhat District Sports Association Ground, Bokakhat, November 19-21: Kerala 133 in 57 overs (Vathsal 50; Hira Chettry 6-39, Biki Singh 2-26) and 239 in 99.4 overs (Vathsal 78, Akshay Manohar 61; Amlanjyoti Das 4-70, H Chettry 2-43) beat **Assam** 96 in 46 overs (Kiran Sagar 6-26, A Manohar 3-36) and 127 in 40.2 overs (Akhil Kalita 49, H Chettry 27; Abhijith K 5-35, Nakson Rahul 2-8) by 149 runs.

Saurashtra Cricket Association Stadium, Rajkot, November 19-22: Jammu and Kashmir 327 in 111 overs (Vivrant Sharma 77, Abdul Samad 72; Yuvrajsinh Shinol 3-54, Rishi Patel 2-48) and 139 in 49.5 overs (A Samad 44, Qamran Iqbal 36; Rahul Vankani 3-24, Dev Dand 3-48) lost to **Saurashtra** 553 in 159.3 overs (Siddhant Rana 133, R Patel 117; Vivrant 4-56, Govind Sharma 3-135) by an innings and 87 runs.

Margao Cricket Club, Margao, November 19-22: Odisha 368 in 128.4 overs (Anil Parida 107, Raghunath Malla 73; SA Mishra 4-82, Shanu Vantamuri 2-60) and 2/0 in 0.2 overs beat **Goa** 104 in 51.1 overs (S Vantamuri 39, Rahul Mehta 30; Shankar Majhi 4-29, Biswajit Mallick 2-26) and 264 in 105 overs (Piyush Yadav 95, Mohit Redkar 47; NB Bhuyan 3-61, R Malla 2-13) by 10 wickets.

MBB Stadium, Agartala, November 26-29: Tripura 139 in 79.1 overs (Amit Ali 49, Babul Dey 29; Yuvrajsinh Shinol 5-20, Dev Dand 3-42) and 121 in 67.3 overs (Bikram Das 64; Y Shinol 6-30, D Dand 3-29) lost to **Saurashtra** 230 in 93.1 overs (Jay Gohil 56, Rishi Patel 40; A Ali 4-59, Saruk Hossain 3-36) and 33/1 in 5.5 overs by nine wickets.

Bokakhat District Sports Association Ground, Bokakhat, November 26-27: Assam 182 in 63.1 overs (Denish Das 118; Durgakumar 4-57, Vasu 3-36) and 57 in 27.5 overs (Yara Sandeep 6-6, Vasu 4-13) lost to **Andhra** 124 in 45.5 overs (Y Sandeep 42; Amlanjyoti 5-26, Biki Singh 3-37) and 119/6 in 38.1 overs (Nitish Reddy 46, Y Sandeep 31; B Singh 4-36, A Das 2-39) by four wickets.

Veer Surendra Sai Stadium, Sambalpur, November 26-29: Kerala 651/5 dec. in 159 overs (Vathsal 302*, Ashwin Anand 203; Biswajit Mallick 3-185, Shekhar Majhi 2-120) beat **Odisha** 330 in 125 overs (Ayush Naik 116, Raghunath Malla 39; Nakson Rahul 3-51, Kiran Sagar 3-71) and 183 in 76 overs (R Malla 47, Swastik Samal 46; K Sagar 5-71, Akshay Manohar 4-71) by an innings and 138 runs.

Govt Gandhi Memorial Science College ground, Jammu, November 26-28: Goa 182 in

65.3 overs (Udit Yadav 66*, Ruthvik Naik 48; Rasikh Salam 6-39, Javid Ahmad 2-39) and 93 in 45.1 overs (Shubham Gajinkar 27, Alam Khan 26; Vivrant Sharma 4-14, Govind Sharma 4-25) lost to **Jammu and Kashmir** 351 in 120.4 overs (Kanhaiya Wadhawan 117, Musaif Ajaz 100*; R Naik 6-65, Chauhan 2-38) by an innings and 76 runs.

Dr PVG Raju ACA Sports Complex, Vizianagaram, December 3-6: Odisha 124 in 61.2 overs (Manas Nayak 40, Ayush Naik 32; Santhosh Kumar 3-19, Nithish Reddy 3-24) and 320 in 135.1 overs (Anil Parida 140, Swastik Samal 50; S Kumar 5-74, A Pranaykumar 4-71) lost to **Andhra** 407 in 125.1 overs (Subramanyam 164, Yara Sandeep 148; Umesh Yadav 4-48, Shekhar Majhi 4-130) and 39/1 in 7.2 overs (Vamsi Krishna 28*) by nine wickets.

Railway Cricket Ground, Rajkot, December 3-6: Saurashtra 298 in 147.5 overs (HS Kotak 71, Rishi Patel 58; Amlanjyoti Das 3-54, Hira Chettry 3-58) and 100/8 in 58 overs (Jay Gohil 37, HS Kotak 28; H Chettry 5-42, Hrishikesh Borah 2-13) drew with **Assam** 235 in 136.3 overs (Denish Das 62, Aman Chettry 33; Rahul Vankani 5-85, Dev Dand 4-36). **Saurashtra** took first-innings lead.

SD College, Alappuzha, December 3-6: Kerala 356 in 126.2 overs (Vathsal 146, Akshay Manohar 64; SA Mishra 4-62, Ruthvik Naik 3-75) and 191/8 dec. in 54.2 overs (Vathsal 59, Nikhil T 45; R Naik 3-28, Shanu Vantamuri 3-49) beat **Goa** 253 in 111.4 overs (Rahul Mehta 60, Piyush Yadav 58; A Manohar 3-40, Muhammed Afriedh 2-28) and 135 in 54.4 overs (Alam Khan 47; A Manohar 3-10, Kiran Sagar 3-39) by 159 runs.

Country Cricket Stadium Gharota, Jammu, December 3-6: Jammu and Kashmir 232 in 66.4 overs (Musaif Ajaz 61, Jiyaad Magrey 51; Amit Ali 3-42, Parvez Sultan 2-4) and 328 in 89.3 overs (Kanhaiya Wadhwan 77, M Ajaz 56; A Ali 3-74, P Sultan 2-45) beat **Tripura** 148 in 58.2 overs (Riaz Uddain 45, Arup Datta 33; Javid Ahmad 5-23, Mujtaba Yousuf 4-42) and 165 in 61 overs (Babul Dey 28; Govind Sharma 5-47, J Ahmad 2-27) by 247 runs.

Barsapara Cricket Stadium, Guwahati, December 10-13: Jammu and Kashmir 196 in 56.2 overs (Vivrant Sharma 64, Qamran Iqbal 42; Hira Chettry 5-46, Sunil Lachit 2-41) and 171 in 67.2 overs (Q Iqbal 80, Abdul Samad 42; Amlanjyoti Das 6-42, Hrishikesh Borah 2-20) lost to **Assam** 255 in 75 overs (Sourav Saha 60, Shivam Mittal 40; Vivrant 3-22, Govind Sharma 3-62) and 114/5 in 24.3 overs (Aman Chettry 64*, Denish Das 25; Vivrant 2-24, Rasikh Salam 2-38) by five wickets.

Gandhi Stadium, Balangir, December 10-13: Tripura 65 in 27.4 overs (Shekhar Majhi 5-20, Umesh Yadav 3-26) and 132 in 54.3 overs (Babul Dey 34, Sridam Paul 27; Biswajit Mallick 5-14, Ankitkar Jaiswal 4-44) lost to **Odisha** 264 in 125.1 overs (Raghunath Malla 102, Binit Mohanty 53; Ashish Yadav 3-74, Parvez Sultan 2-18) by an innings and 67 runs.

SD College, Alappuzha, December 10-13: Saurashtra 286 in 147.5 overs (Jay Gohil 61, Karan Lagariya 57; Nirmal Jaimon 3-52, Ananthakrishnan J 2-7) and 130/4 in 60 overs (Rishi Patel 54*, K Lagariya 28; N Jaimon 2-34) drew with **Kerala** 450/9 dec. in 143 overs (). **Kerala** took first-innings lead.

Margao Cricket Club, Margao, December 10-12: Goa 227 in 109.5 overs (Alam Khan 96, Krishna Thakur 43; A Pranaykumar 5-41, Yara Sandeep 2-8) and 153 in 86.5 overs (Ruthvik Naik 50, Mohit Redkar 29; Durgakumar 2-21, Vasu 2-41) lost to **Andhra** 483 in 134.4 overs (Nithish Reddy 155, Y Sandeep 74; Shadab Khan 3-80, Rahul Mehta 2-39) by an innings and 103 runs.

Nurul Amin Stadium, Nagaon, December 24-26: Assam 149 in 49.5 overs (Shivam Mittal 42, Ruhinandan Pegu 27; Ruthvik Naik 6-56, Sachin Mishra 2-50) and 79 in 27.5 overs (Amlanjyoti Das 30; S Mishra 3-5, R Naik 3-32) beat **Goa** 129 in 45.5 overs (Alam Khan 34; A Das 5-42, Hrishikesh Borah 3-44) and 78 in 40.4 overs (Rahul Mehta 25; H Borah 5-25, A Das 4-33) by 21 runs.

Saurashtra Cricket Association Stadium, Rajkot, December 24-27: Saurashtra 505 in 166 overs (Siddhant Rana 231, P Rana 103*; Raghunath Malla 3-72, Binit Mohanty 2-51) drew with **Odisha** 244 in 116.3 overs (Swastik Samal 132, Kunal Mallick 38; Dev Dand 4-61, Rahul Vankani 2-68) and 156/2 in 66 overs (R Malla 85, B Mohanty 52*). **Saurashtra** took first-innings lead.

SD College, Alappuzha, December 24-27: Tripura 271 in 146 overs (Riaz Uddain 78*, Arup Datta 59; Nirmal Jaimon 4-55, Akshay Manohar 2-69) and 135/5 in 79 overs (Babul Dey 53) drew with **Kerala** 402/5 dec. in 139.5 overs (Varun Nayanar 159, Amal CA 77; Parvez Sultan 2-101). **Kerala** took first-innings lead.

Jammu, December 24-27: Andhra 335 in 93.5 overs (Mohammed Raza 112, Vamsi Krishna 64; Mujtaba Yousuf 3-47, Abdul Samad 3-69) and 129/5 in 37.3 overs (Yara Sandeep 39; Rasikh Salam 2-22) beat **Jammu and Kashmir** 157 in 34.4 overs (Musaif Ajaz 67*; A Pranaykumar 4-55, Durgakumar 3-33) and 304 in 80 overs (Kanhaiya Wadhawan 89, M Yousuf 58*; Vasu 4-60, Santhosh Kumar 2-50) by five wickets.

BOSE Ground, Cuttack, December 31-January 2: Odisha 127 in 56.3 overs (Anil Parida 50, Aditya Rout 34; Sunil Lachit 5-32, Akash Chetri 3-26) and 230 in 77.1 overs (Swastik Samal 121; S Lachit 4-66, A Chetri 2-38) beat **Assam** 240 in 78.2 overs (Nibir Deka 55, Denish Das 33, Shivam Mittal 33, Gunjanjyoti Deka 33; Binit Mohanty 4-52, Ankitkar Jaiswal 4-82) and 112 in 40.2 overs (D Das 25; B Mohanty 5-37, A Jaiswal 3-34) by five runs.

SD College, Alappuzha, December 31-January 2: Kerala 377 in 116.2 overs (Vathsal 94, Amal CA 76; Mujtaba Yousuf 3-54, Vivrant Sharma 3-81) beat **Jammu and Kashmir** 83 in 33.2 overs (Vivrant Sharma 26; Akshay Manohar 6-29, Nirmal Jaimon 2-32) and 234 in 59.2 overs (Jiyaad Magrey 59, Vivrant 50; Kiran Sagar 4-43, N Jaimon 2-43) by an innings and 60 runs.

Margao Cricket Club, Margao, December 31-January 2: Goa 80 in 34.5 overs (Saruk Hossain 6-29) and 119 in 67.5 overs (Digesh Raikar 34, Alam Khan 27; Amit Ali 5-54, Parvez Sultan 3-20) lost to **Tripura** 295 in 117.5 overs (Arup Datta 84, Bikram Das 60; Rahul Mehta 4-56, Sachin Mishra 2-36) by an innings and 96 runs.

CSR Sharma College Ground, Ongole, December 31-January 3: Andhra 293 in 114.1 overs, (Subramanyam 107, Yara Sandeep 53; Yuvrajsinh Shinol 5-68, Rahul Vankani 4-92) and 313/8 in 104 overs (Dheeraj Kumar 91, Y Sandeep 61; Dev Dand 6-79) drew with **Saurashtra** 283 in 121.1 overs (Bhagyarajsinh Chudasama 42, Jay Gohil 42; Vasu 4-76, Y Sandeep 3-9). **Andhra** took first-innings lead.

MBB Stadium, Agartala, January 21-24: Assam 136 in 53.3 overs (Vikram Rawat 33, Shivam Mittal 28; Amit Ali 4-31, Ashish Yadav 2-23) and 349 in 110.3 overs (S Mittal 80, Nasir Ullah 80; Saruk Hossain 3-67, A Ali 3-110) lost to **Tripura** 432 in 146.1 overs (Bikram Das 197, Riaz Uddain 66; Hrishikesh Borah 3-66, Gunjanjyoti Deka 2-52) and 55/1 in 19.2 overs (Babul Dey 37*) by nine wickets.

Country Cricket Stadium Gharota, Jammu, January 21-24: Jammu and Kashmir 289 in 66.2 overs (Jiyaad Magrey 79, Qamran Iqbal 75; Ankitkar Jaiswal 6-82, Binit Mohanty 2-64) drew with **Odisha** 18 for no loss in 16 overs.

Goa Cricket Association Academy, Porvorim, January 21-24: Saurashtra 517/9 dec. in 166.2 overs (Siddhant Rana 155, P Rana 99; Ruthvik Naik 3-133, Mohit Redkar 2-86) and 80/3 in 29 overs (Prasham Rajdev 30*, Jay Gohil 26*; M Redkar 2-29) drew with **Goa** 278 in 144.1 overs (Alam Khan 149, Digesh Raikar 36; Rahul Vankani 5-96, Dev Dand 4-72). **Saurashtra** took first-innings lead.

CSR Sharma college ground, Ongole, January 21-24: Kerala 339 in 99 overs (Vathsal 139, Varun Nayanar 74; Santhosh Kumar 4-89, A Pranaykumar 3-74) and 313 in 110.5 overs (Vathsal 116, Nikhil T 65; S Kumar 4-63, A Pranaykumar 3-47, Sai Karthik Rao 3-81) drew with **Andhra** 335 in 109.5 overs (Harsha Vardhan 75, Subramanyam 57; Nirmal Jaimon 3-51, Akshay Manohar 3-70) and 100/2 in 21 overs (H Vardhan 44, Vamsi Krishna 33). **Kerala** took first-innings lead.

Elite Group C points table

Teams	M	W	L	D	T	N/R	Pts	Quotient
Andhra	7	5	0	2	0	0	35	1.441
Kerala	7	4	0	3	0	0	35	1.778
Saurashtra	7	2	0	5	0	0	24	1.303
Odisha	7	3	2	2	0	0	22	0.879
Jammu and Kashmir	7	2	4	1	0	0	14	0.889
Tripura	7	2	4	1	0	0	14	0.788
Assam	7	2	4	1	0	0	13	0.876
Goa	7	0	6	1	0	0	1	0.505

Andhra and Kerala qualified for the quarter-finals

Plate group

Jalan Outdoor Stadium, Dibrugarh, November 19-20: Mizoram 53 in 25.4 overs (Aryan 5-12, Abhishek 3-24) and 55 in 28.1 overs (Aryan 6-18, Swastic 3-4) lost to **Meghalaya** 265 in 79.3 overs (Ankit Singh 88, Swastic 67; Dina 4-57, Thanzuala 2-38) by an innings and 157 runs.

Moin-ul-Haq stadium, Patna, November 19-21: Bihar 364 in 94.1 overs (Akash Raj 110, Piyush Singh 87; Govind Mittal 3-86, Tsering Thapkey 2-16) beat **Arunachal Pradesh** 195 in 65.1 overs (Shashank Verma 48, MD Bilal 26; Amod Yadav 6-55, Suraj Kashyap 2-35) and 148 in 61 overs (Vishek Kumar 55, Shivender Sharma 31; A Anand 3-88, S Kashyap 2-9) by an innings and 21 runs.

Highlanders Sports Academy, Kashipur, November 19-22: Manipur 177 in 53.1 overs (Shubham Chauhan 131; Jagmohan Nagarkoti 4-29, Anveesh Sudha 2-11) and 200 in 42.3 overs (S Chauhan 88, Hrithik Kanojia 37; J Nagarkoti 4-73, Aman Negi 2-16) lost to **Uttarakhand** 549/6 dec. in 119 overs (Tanush Gusain 172, Akhil Rawat 126; Rex Singh 3-73) by an innings and 172 runs.

Palmyra Cricket Ground, Puducherry, November 19-22: Puducherry 247/8 in 91 overs (Arbaaz Uddin 142*, Rishab Belavadi 26; Rohin Limboo 3-27, Arif Ansari 3-36) drew with **Sikkim**.

Nagaland Cricket Stadium, Sovima, November 26-28: Manipur 212 in 73.3 overs (Gajendra 88, Abhijeet 30; Chiranjivi 3-24, Yash Tandon 3-51) and 120 in 60 overs (Shubham Chauhan 45; Chiranjivi 6-37, Aditya 3-25) lost to **Nagaland** 344 in 108.4 overs (Vipul Kapoor 70, Upanshu Verma 60; Abhijeet 3-75, KL Meitei 2-17) by an innings and 12 runs.

Jalan Outdoor Stadium, Dibrugarh, November 26-27: Mizoram 88 in 37 overs (Atul Singh 25; Shashank Verma 4-25, Govind Mittal 3-13) and 85 in 39.2 overs (G Mittal 5-22, D Bagra 3-36) lost to **Arunachal Pradesh** 335/9 dec. in 94.1 overs (MD Bilal 103, Shivender Sharma 81; Naveen 2-38, Sahil 2-43) by an innings and 162 runs.

Highlanders Sports Academy, Kashipur, November 26-28: Uttarakhand 515 in 150.5 overs (Avneesh Sudha 339, Tanush Gusain 49; Amod Yadav 3-128, Randhir Dubey 2-55) beat **Bihar** 234 in 69.5 overs (Harsh Raj 65, Suraj Kashyap 64; S Juyal 4-65, A Sudha 2-12) and 91 in 38 overs (Prakash 37; Harman 4-22, Janmejay 2-11) by an innings and 190 runs.

ASA Stadium, Anantapur, November 26-29: Puducherry 188 in 83.4 overs (Nipun Gaikwad 45, S Sanjay 39; Abhishek 5-47, Bipin 2-33) and 150 in 98 overs (Arbaaz Uddin 49, Sugadev 37; Abhishek 4-48, Bipin 2-28) beat **Meghalaya** 325 in 145.1 overs (Raghav Kapur

115, Ankit Singh 69; A Uddin 5-109, KSS Varma 3-34) and 14/2 in 2.5 overs (Nithishkumar 2-2) by eight wickets.

DN Singha Stadium, Goalpara, December 3-4: Meghalaya 176 in 59.1 overs (Ankit Singh 69, Bibek 46; Govind Mittal 4-12, Shashank Verma 3-43) and 88 in 28.5 overs (Ankit 26; G Mittal 3-22, D Bagra 3-23) beat **Arunachal Pradesh** 54 in 31.4 overs (Abhishek 6-15, Sudhir Sahani 2-20) and 146 in 54.4 overs (G Mittal 46, Abhi Singh 36; S Sahani 4-24, Aryan 4-33) by 64 runs.

Highlanders Sports Academy, Kashipur, December 3-4: Mizoram 91 in 60.5 overs (Jagmohan Nagarkoti 4-29, S Juyal 2-9) and 20 in 8.1 overs (S Juyal 6-12, J Nagarkoti 3-8) lost to **Uttarakhand** 449 in 106.1 overs (Sanyam 141, Gaurav Joshi 108; Shubham Yadav 3-77, Debojyoti Chanda 2-2) by an innings and 338 runs.

CAP Siechem Ground, Puducherry, December 3-5: Nagaland 186 in 57.5 overs (Rishabh 52, Aditya 35; Arbaaz Uddin 7-59) and 315/9 dec. (Vipul Kapoor 78, Joshua 77; A Uddin 3-117, Nipun Gaikwad 2-52) beat **Puducherry** 124 in 67.5 overs (Logesh 32; Chiranjivi 5-19, Yash Tandon 2-30) and 99 in 37.5 overs (Logesh 35, A Uddin 31; Y Tandon 7-31) by 278 runs.

Rural Development Trust Stadium, Anantapur, December 3-6: Sikkim 138 in 99.2 overs (Saurav Prasad 31; Rex Singh 3-31, Abhijeet 2-10) and 174 in 82.4 overs (Anwesh 68, Om Saini 61; Rex 7-36, Abhijeet 3-35) lost to **Manipur** 311 in 102.1 overs (Abhijeet 110, Rex 61; O Saini 4-55, Bhim 2-13) and 2 for no loss in 0.3 overs by 10 wickets.

Mahabir Chilarai Stadium, Abhayapuri, December 10-11: Nagaland 302 in 53.3 overs (Rishabh 93, Chiranjivi 51; Deepak Mahato 6-91, Anwesh 2-96) beat **Sikkim** 148 in 60.5 overs (Anwesh 34, Saurav Prasad 25; Aditya 5-45, Chiranjivi 4-30) and 140 in 60.1 overs (Rahul 57; Yash Tandon 4-64, Aditya 3-22) by an innings and 14 runs.

Energy Stadium Rajbansi Nagar, Patna, December 10-11: Mizoram 82 in 54.4 overs (Shubham Yadav 25; A Anand 5-24, Shivam Kumar 3-35) and 68 in 31.3 overs (Lalhriatrenga 28; A Anand 5-16, S Kumar 4-14) lost to **Bihar** 245 in 76.4 overs (Piyush Singh 81, Akash Raj 51; Naveen 5-86, Tluanga 2-74) by an innings and 95 runs.

Tanush Academy Ground, Dehradun, December 10-11: Uttarakhand 537/6 dec. in 109.4 overs (Avneesh Sudha 221, Sanyam 176; Abhishek 3-163, Bipin 2-87) beat **Meghalaya** 133 in 41.5 overs (Raghav Kapur 50, Hrithik Sharma 31, Ankit Singh 31; Harman 5-21, A Sudha 2-16) and 52 in 18.5 overs (S Juyal 5-33, Harman 3-4) by an innings and 352 runs.

Rural Development Trust Stadium, Anantapur, December 10-13: Arunachal Pradesh 138 in 54.5 overs (Govind Mittal 32*, Avinash Yadav 31; Rex Singh 5-33, KL Meitei 2-16) and 36 in 18.5 overs (Rex 10-11) lost to Manipur 122 in 49.1 overs (Abhijeet 48; G Mittal 5-50, D Bagra 4-25) and 55 for no loss (Shubham Chauhan 32*) by 10 wickets.

DN Singha Stadium, Goalpara, December 24-25: Meghalaya 281 in 72.1 overs (Ankit Singh 128, Raghav Kapur 65; Rex Singh 5-115, Johnson 3-72) beat **Manipur** 33 in 22.5 overs (Abhishek 9-11) and 75 in 31.1 overs (Bidash 42; Aryan 4-22, Bipin 3-21) by an innings and 173 runs.

Energy Stadium Rajbansi Nagar, Patna, December 25-27: Bihar 219 in 63.1 overs (Akash Raj 78, Amod Yadav 75; Om Saini 4-63, Adars 2-20) beat **Sikkim** 69 in 34.5 overs (Saurav Prasad 25; A Anand 4-15, Shivam Kumar 3-13) and 84 in 42.1 overs (O Saini 36; A Anand 5-4) by an innings and 66 runs.

Tanush Academy Ground, Dehradun, December 24-26: Nagaland 251 in 68.3 overs (Rishabh 64, Joshua 60; Avneesh Sudha 3-51, S Juyal 3-59) and 173 in 45.4 overs (Aditya 80, Shamphri 25; A Sudha 3-24, Jagmohan Nagarkoti 3-48) lost to **Uttarakhand** 561/6 dec. in 147.1 overs (Sanyam 112, Manish 92; Aditya 3-156) by an innings and 137 runs.

Palmyra Cricket Ground, Puducherry, December 24-27: Puducherry 333 in 89 overs (Sugadev 107, Logesh 54; Dina 8-71) beat **Mizoram** 102 in 35.2 overs (Arbaaz Uddin 5-32, Aryan Bangar 2-19) and 87 in 31.2 overs (Lalhriatrenga 43; A Bangar 5-26, A Uddin 3-15) by an innings and 144 runs.

Golaghat DSA Ground, Golaghat, December 31-January 2: Mizoram 113 in 33.4 overs

(Atul Singh 68, Aditya 5-33, Chiranjivi 3-14) and 76 in 33.1 overs (Aditya 5-42, Chiranjivi 4-18) lost to **Nagaland** 211 in 45.4 overs (Rishabh 62, Tepuchiba 48; Dina 8-69) by an innings and 22 runs.

Energy Stadium, Rajbansi Nagar, Patna, December 31-January 2: Bihar 404 in 113.2 overs (Piyush Singh 175, Harsh Raj 74; Abhishek 5-89, Sudhir Sahani 4-117) beat **Meghalaya** 183 in 73 overs (Ankit Singh 98, Hrithik Sharma 25, Raghav Kapur 25; A Anand 6-51, Malay Raj 2-40) and 43 in 21.5 overs (Amod Yadav 6-18, A Anand 2-6) by an innings and 178 runs.

Tanush Academy Ground, Dehradun, December 31-January 2: Sikkim 167 in 70.2 overs (Anwesh 61, Saurav Prasad 36; S Juyal 5-30, Jagmohan Nagarkoti 5-30) and 93 in 43.3 overs (Om Saini 55; S Juyal 5-47, Irfan 3-7) lost to **Uttarakhand** 395/4 dec. in 84.4 overs (Manish 203, Sanyam 131; Adars 2-71) by an innings and 135 runs.

Palmyra Cricket Ground, Puducherry, December 31-January 2: Puducherry 500/9 dec. in 119.5 overs (Aryan Bangar 149, Arbaaz Uddin 119, Logesh 104*; Shashank Verma 5-168, Govind Mittal 2-99) beat **Arunachal Pradesh** 165 in 49.5 overs (MD Bilal 85, G Mittal 39; A Uddin 7-73, A Bangar 3-46) and 187 in 54.4 overs (Shivender Sharma 43, MD Bilal 40; A Uddin 4-31, A Bangar 3-30) by an innings and 148 runs.

Jorhat DSA Stadium, Jorhat, January 7-9: Nagaland 188 in 57.3 overs (Shamphri 63, Joshua 34; Aryan 3-53, Sudhir Sahani 2-23) and 363/8 dec. in 94 overs (Aditya 89, Rishabh 78, Joshua 78; Bipin 2-58, Abhishek 2-77, S Sahani 2-77) beat **Meghalaya** 100 in 44.4 overs (Raghav Kapur 44; Yash Tandon 3-17, Chiranjivi 3-32) and 99 by 352 runs.

Energy Stadium Rajbansi Nagar, Patna, January 7-10: Bihar 160 in 38.1 overs (A Anand 68, Amod Yadav 43; Rex Singh 6-68, Bidash 2-16) and 334 in 106.1 overs (Suraj Kashyap 78, Akash Raj 55; Rex 6-98, Abhijeet 3-103) beat **Manipur** 161 in 57.3 overs (Shubham Chauhan 70, Aditya Verma 43*; A Anand 7-75, S Kashyap 2-13) and 208 in 92.5 overs (S Chauhan 116, Abhijeet 34; A Anand 5-63, Malay Raj 4-28) by 125 runs.

Goalpara Salmara Ground, Goalpara, January 7-10: Arunachal Pradesh 168 in 53.1 overs (MD Bilal 68, Vishek Kumar 40; Deepak Mahato 5-60, Arif Ansari 4-51) and 170 in 43.3 overs (Govind Mittal 34*, Tsering Thapkey 32; D Mahato 3-48, Bhim 2-19) lost to **Sikkim** 144 in 41.2 overs (Anwesh 61, Saurav Prasad 29; Shashank Verma 7-44) and 195/7 in 69 overs (Rahul 96, Om Saini 40; S Verma 3-69, Neelam Joseph 2-22) by three wickets.

Highlanders Sports Academy, Kashipur, January 7-9: Uttarakhand 664/3 dec. in 135 overs (Sanyam 347, Avneesh Sudha 189, Gaurav Joshi 101*) beat **Puducherry** 112 in 40.1 overs (Logesh 40; Janmejay 4-28, S Juyal 3-17) and 159 in 54.1 overs (Arbaaz Uddin 36, Rishab Belavadi 33; S Juyal 5-37, Irfan 2-18) by an innings and 393 runs.

Nagaland Cricket Stadium, Sovima, January 14-16: Nagaland 190 in 59.5 overs (Aditya 73, Vipul Kapoor 57; Amod Yadav 7-34) and 189 in 57.1 overs (Rishabh 44, V Kapoor 35; A Anand 8-51) beat **Bihar** 89 in 45.5 overs (Harsh Raj 31, Rishav Rakesh 30; Mukul 5-12, Abhishek 2-16) and 121 in 75.2 overs (Piyush Singh 34; Aditya 6-54, Mukul 4-32) by 169 runs.

Jorhat DSA Stadium, Jorhat, January 14-16: Sikkim 221 in 70.2 overs (Om Saini 84, Arif Ansari 43; Dina 4-43, Sahil 3-31) and 245/8 dec. in 61 overs (Rahul 107, Deepak Mahato 31; Nunfela 4-67, Naveen 2-41) beat **Mizoram** 114 in 48 overs (Atul Singh 64; O Saini 4-37, D Mahato 2-9) and 67 in 44.1 overs (Anwesh 2-0, Bhim 2-3) by 285 runs.

Abhimanyu Cricket Academy, Dehradun, January 14-16: Arunachal Pradesh 130 in 43.5 overs (Govind Mittal 39, MD Bilal 38; Jagmohan Nagarkoti 5-34, Harman 4-37) and 125 in 44 overs (Shivender Sharma 42, G Mittal 40; Sumit 3-19, S Juyal 3-38, J Nagarkoti 3-42) lost to **Uttarakhand** 284 in 75.4 overs (Tanush Gusain 97, Sanyam 53; Shivender 5-61, Shashank Verma 3-107) by an innings and 29 runs.

Palmyra Cricket Ground, Puducherry, January 14-16: Puducherry 185 in 58.2 overs (Aryan Bangar 54, Nipun Gaikwad 33; Abhijeet 6-38, Vishal 3-50) and 202 in 54 overs (A Bangar 85, N Gaikwad 39; Rex Singh 4-78, Vishal 3-47) lost to **Manipur** 290 in 94.1 overs (Abhijeet 71, Rex 50; Arbaaz Uddin 5-121, A Bangar 3-98) and 99/4 in 20.4 overs (Abhijeet 58; A Bangar 2-51) by six wickets.

Nagaland Cricket Stadium, Sovima, January 21-23: Nagaland 479/9 dec. in 116.3 overs (Joshua 125, Rishabh 100; Shashank Verma 5-160, Shivender Sharma 3-86) beat **Arunachal Pradesh** 139 in 39 overs (Shubham Patel 62; Aditya 6-44, Chiranjivi 3-33) and 158 in 51.1 overs (Shivender 50; Yash Tandon 3-46, Abhishek 2-19) by an innings and 182 runs.

MCA Cricket Ground, Polo Ground, Shillong, January 21-22: Meghalaya 192 in 54.4 overs (Raghav Kapur 91*, Ankit Singh 35; Deepak Mahato 7-57) and 237 in 53.4 overs (R Kapur 86, Kush Agarwal 46; D Mahato 4-75, Adars 2-31) beat **Sikkim** 109 in 32.2 overs (Saurav Prasad 72; Bipin 6-32, Abhishek 3-14) and 126 in 37.4 overs (Om Saini 39; Aryan 5-35, Sudhir Sahani 3-25) by 194 runs.

Jorhat DSA Stadium, Jorhat, January 21-22: Manipur 386 in 82 overs (Johnson 176*, Nawaz 70; Dina 4-79, Nunfela 3-116) beat **Mizoram** 117 in 47.4 overs (Sahil 27; Shubham Chauhan 5-22) and 62 in 25.1 overs (Rex Singh 5-34, Vishal 3-10) by an innings and 207 runs.

Palmyra Cricket Ground, Puducherry, January 21-23: Bihar 465/9 dec. in 114.2 overs (Akash Raj 156, Rishav Rakesh 125; Arbaaz Uddin 4-125, Thamizh Azhagan 2-90) beat **Puducherry** 154 in 48 overs (Rishab Belavadi 46, Sugadev 25; Sabir Khan 5-31, A Anand 2-44) and 205 in 54.3 overs (Arbaaz Uddin 45, Aryan Bangar 42; A Anand 7-63, Shivam Kumar 3-115) by an innings and 106 runs.

Plate group points table

Teams	M	W	L	D	T	N/R	Pts	Quotient
Uttarakhand	8	8	0	0	0	0	56	5.209
Nagaland	8	7	1	0	0	0	46	1.746
Bihar	8	6	2	0	0	0	41	1.504
Meghalaya	8	5	3	0	0	0	32	0.895
Manipur	8	4	4	0	0	0	27	0.915
Puducherry	8	2	5	1	0	0	15	0.700
Sikkim	8	2	5	1	0	0	13	0.639
Arunachal Pradesh	8	1	7	0	0	0	7	0.626
Mizoram	8	0	8	0	0	0	0	0.258

Uttarakhand qualified for the quarter-finals

Quarter-finals

Bharat Ratna Shri Atal Bihari Vajpayee Ekana Cricket Stadium, Lucknow, January 28-29: Uttarakhand 101 in 44.5 overs (Devesh 31, Akhil Rawat 27; Shivam Sharma 3-20, Kartik Tyagi 3-21) and 86 in 31.1 overs (Shivam 4-10, Purnank Tyagi 3-16) lost to **Uttar Pradesh** 272 in 76.1 overs (Sameer Rizvi 88, Mohit Jangra 58*; S Juyal 5-88, Irfan 3-46) by an innings and 85 runs.

SD College, Alappuzha, January 28-February 1: Maharashtra 502 in 128.2 overs (Om Bhosale 174, PH Shah 96; Muhammed Afriedh 5-87, Akshay Manohar 2-98) and 318 in 82.2 overs (SA Veer 107, O Bhosale 60; A Manohar 5-111, M Afriedh 2-80) drew with **Kerala** 266 in 88.5 overs (Varun Nayanar 136, Ashwin Anand 46; PH Shah 6-48, RS Hangargekar 4-68) and 211/3 in 40 overs (Vathsal 105*, Ashwin Anand 53*). **Maharashtra** took first-innings lead.

CSR Sharma College Ground, Ongole, January 28-31: Andhra 138 in 43.1 overs (Subramanyam 33, Vamsi Krishna 30; Bhute 5-40, Harsh Dubey 2-1) and 181 in 60.2 overs (Subramanyam 36, V Krishna 33; Gulam Ali 4-45, Tekan 3-59, Bhute 3-61) lost to **Vidarbha** 173 in 54.1 overs (YV Rathod 72; Santhosh Kumar 4-51, A Pranaykumar 2-29) and 147/3 in 36.5 overs (Mandar Mahale 58, BK Naidu 33*; Nithish Reddy 2-8) by seven wickets.

KL Saini Stadium, Jaipur, January 28-February 1: Rajasthan 281 in 99.4 overs (SA Ahuja 83, SV Joshi 56; Prankesh Rai 4-69, Ishan Afridi 4-76) and 407 in 136.4 overs (SA Ahuja 115, SV Joshi 110; Rishabh Chouhan 3-77, I Afridi 2-63) drew with **Madhya Pradesh** 254 in 88.3 overs (Rahul Chandrol 113*, R Chouhan 35; RM Bishnoi 3-51, AM Singh 2-44) and 34/1 in 10 overs. **Rajasthan** took first-innings lead.

Semi-finals

KL Saini Stadium, Jaipur, February 4-6: Rajasthan 114 in 41.2 overs (SN Kulsreshtha 35, MJ Suthar 25; Shivam Sharma 3-13, Kartik Tyagi 3-38) and 102 in 34.2 overs (SA Ahuja 36; K Tyagi 5-24, Mohit Jangra 4-21) lost to **Uttar Pradesh** 273 in 105.1 overs (Sameer Rizvi 51, Dhruv Jurel 37; RM Bishnoi 5-71, MJ Suthar 3-49) by an innings and 57 runs.

VCA Stadium, Civil Lines, Nagpur, February 4-7: Vidarbha 653 in 192 overs (Nayan Chavan 145, Yash Kadam 110, YV Rathod 103; RV Chougule 3-114, RS Hangargekar 3-136) and 138/6 dec. in 45 overs (Sandesh D 38, A Mokhade 29; RV Chougule 3-17) in drew with **Maharashtra** 239 in 82.2 overs (SA Veer 81, PH Shah 48; Rohit Dattatraya 6-90, Harsh Dubey 3-45) and 43/3 in 20 overs (H Dubey 2-11). **Vidarbha** took first-innings lead.

Final

VCA Stadium, Civil Lines, Nagpur, February 11-14: Uttar Pradesh 283 in 101.2 overs (Aryan Juyal 94, Priyam Garg 78; Bhute 5-59, Harsh Dubey 3-81) and 305 in 124.2 overs (Sameer Choudhary 119, Aryan Sharma 52; H Dubey 4-97, Yash Kadam 2-14) drew with **Vidarbha** 251 in 95.2 overs (Nayan Chavan 75, YV Rathod 59; Purnank Tyagi 7-65) and 53/1 in 15 overs (A Mokhade 36*). **Uttar Pradesh** took first-innings lead.

Winners: Uttar Pradesh

2017-18

Group A

Bokaro Steel Limited Cricket Stadium, Bokaro, November 5-8: Delhi 383 in 121.5 overs (Mayank Rawat 157, Sanat Sangwan 73; Amar Chaudhary 5-97, Pankaj Yadav 2-111) and 95/2 in 39.5 overs (Ayush Badoni 56*, Sanat Sangwan 29*) lost to **Jharkhand** 73 in 40.3 overs (Bhanu Anand 20; Harsh Tyagi 7-7, M Rawat 2-27) and404 in 150.1 overs (f/o) (Shresht Sagar 146. Aditya Singh 106; H Tyagi 6-115) by eight wickets.

Ravenshaw College Ground, Cuttack, December 8-11: Saurashtra 473 in 146 overs (Sachin Mevada 88, Bhavin Engle 68; Krishna Palai 3-117, Umesh Yadav 2-78) drew with **Odisha** 220 in 89.5 overs (Raghunath Malla 68*, Kunal Mallick 58; Sachin Parmar 5-86, Bhavyesh Donga 2-16) and 241/5 in 106 overs (f/o) (R Malla 110*, Aakash Nayak 67; Diprajsinh 2-34). Saurashtra won on first-innings lead.

Dhruve Pandove Stadium, Patiala, November 5-8: Tamil Nadu155 in 65.4 overs (Aditya Barooah 60, Sundaraman Radhakrishnan 38; Rohit Kumar 3-39, Rahul Kashyap 3-57) and 232 in 92.2 overs (A Barooah 67, S Radhakrishnan 48; R Kashyap 6-92, Prerit Dutta 2-46) lost to **Punjab** 215 in 66.5 overs (Nehal Wadhera 50, Jaish Jain 40; Uthirakumar Mukilesh 3-39, Ajith Ram 3-46) and 174/5 in 43.5 overs (Deepin Chitkara 65*, Prabsimran Singh 26; S Kishankumar 2-37) by five wickets.

BSP Cricket Stadium, Bhilai, November 12-15: Delhi 470/8 dec in 175 overs (Sanat Sang-

A prolific Yash Rathod led Vidarbha to the Cooch Behar Trophy, continuing the state's season of plenty. — *VCA*

wan 158, Harsh Tyagi 132*; Snehil Chadda 4-133, Naman Dhruw 3-87) and 86/1 in 21.5 overs (S Sangwan 35*, Samarth Seth 30*) drew with **Chhattisgarh** 415 in 146.5 overs (Harsh Sharma 100, Sanidhav Hurkat 75; H Tyagi 6-119, Lovnish Singh 3-89). Delhi took first-innings lead.

JSCA International Stadium Complex, Ranchi, November 12-15: Jharkhand 216 in 78.5 overs (Shresht Sagar 49, Yuvraj Kumar 32; Prerit Dutta 4-43, Rohit Kumar 3-45) and 100 in 58.1 overs (Sahil Raj 25; Rohit 5-36, Rahul Kashyap 4-30) lost to **Punjab** 281 in 108.3 overs (Arjun Verma 84, Jaish Jain 71*; Amar Chaudhary 6-56, Chandan 3-60) and 36/0 in 10.5 overs by ten wickets.

NPR College Ground, Dindigul, November 12-15: Saurashtra 253 in 111 overs (Siddhant Rana 80,Sachin Mevada 39; Ajith Ram S 3-63, E Yazh Arunmozhi 3-66) and 148 in 85 overs (S Mevada 58, Diprajsinh 36*; A Ram 6-38, Sundaraman Radhakrishnan 2-13) lost to **Tamil Nadu**348 in 104.4 overs (Aditya Barooah 95, R Sonu Yadav 93; Parnav Karia 3-89, Sachin Parmar 2-26) and55/2 in 21.1 overs (A Barooah 25*; P Karia 2-18) by eight wickets.

BSL Cricket Stadium., Bokaro, November 19-22: Jharkhand 195 in 69.3 overs (Aditya Singh 71, Aryaman Sen 30; Ajith Ram S 6-43) and 295 in 96.5 overs (Bhanu Anand 68, Shresht Sagar 45; E yazh Arunmozhi 4-105, S Krishnakumar 3-34) lost to **Tamil Nadu** 302 in 106 overs (Pradosh Paul 195, A Ram 27; Aditya 3-59, Amar Chaudhary 2-57) and 189/6 in 54.1 overs (Pradosh Paul 61, Tushar Raheja 36; A Chaudhary 2-19, Pankaj Yadav 2-64) by four wickets.

BSP Cricket Stadium, Bhilai, November 19-22: Odisha 65 in 22.5 overs (Rajesh Mohanty 24, Kshyamasagar Bal 21; Rohan Taank 6-27, Naman Dhruw 3-26) and 221 in 107.1 overs (Aakash Nayak 88, Raghunath Malla 46; Parvesh Dhar 3-53, R Taank 2-29) lost to **Chhattisgarh** 239 in 79.5 overs (Naved Ali 71, Sanidhav Hurkat 36; Krishna Palai 3-57, R Malla 2-28) and48/0 in 7.4 overs (Prateek Yadav 41*) by ten wickets.

New Delhi, November 19-22: Delhi 520 in 135.3 overs (Majot Kalra 173, Priyansh Arya 93; Rahul Kashyap 3-108, Rohit Kumar 2-87) and 25/2 in 4.2 beat **Punjab** 204 in 79.4 overs (Nehal Wadhera 61, Arjun Verma 33; Harsh Tyagi 5-49, Hrithik Shokeen 3-53) and 338 in 134.4 overs (f/o) (Prabhsimran Singh 111, Jagmeet Singh 65; H Tyagi 5-104, Mayank Rawat 2-52) by eight wickets.

Gandhi Ground, Amritsar, December 8-11: Odisha 155 in 65.4 overs (Jyoti Behera 34*, Swastik Samal 29; Rahul Kashyap 3-19, Rohit Kumar 3-41) and 172 in 68.5 overs (Manas Nayak 41, Raghunath Malla 34; Prerit Dutta 4-30, Rohit 3-37) lost to **Punjab** 452/9 dec in 100 overs (Jagmeet Singh 98, Arjun Verma 87; Krishna Palai 5-124, Biswajit Mallick 2-88) by an innings and 125 runs

St Stephen's Ground, New Delhi, December 8-11: Delhi 417 in 139.2 overs (Sanat Sangwan 119, Gulzar Sandhu 86; Uthirakumar Mukilesh 3-52, R Sonu Yadav 3-77, RS Jaganathsinivas 3-110) and 243/6 in 61 overs (Mayank Rawat 85, Harsh Tyagi 51; Sonu 2-41, Jaganathsinivas 2-43) drew with **Tamil Nadu** 338 in 103.2 overs (Pradosh Paul 74, Jaganathsinivas 46; Lovnish Singh 5-113, H Tyagi 3-90). Delhi took first-innings lead.

Railway Cricket Ground, Rajkot, December 8-11: Saurashtra 267 in 99.3 overs (Tarang Gohel 73, Pranav Karia 71; Rohan Taank 4-75, Sourabh Solanki 3-53) and 184 in 77 overs (Pratik Mandalia 66, Siddhant Rana 43; Harsh Sharma 4-44, S Solanki 2-31) lost to **Chhattisgarh** 262 in 105.5 overs (Sanidhav Hurkat 107, Harsh 31; Sachin Parmar 4-54, Pranav Savjani 2-53) and 192/1 in 41.3 overs (Prateek Yadav 99*, S Hurkat 85*) by nine wickets

Vikash ground, Bargarh, December 17-20: Jharkhand 276 in 102 overs (Sushant Mishra 61*, Amar Chaudhary 48; Rajesh Mohanty 5-73, Binit Mohanty 2-23) and 218/9 dec in 68.2 overs (Aditya Singh 82, Atul Surwar 65; R Mohanty 3-32, Jyoti Behera 2-17) beat **Odisha** 96 in 35.2 overs (S Mishra 4-24, Junaid Ashraf 3-36) and 204 in 61.3 overs (J Behera 61, Kunal Mallick 57; S Mishra 5-39, Vivek Tiwari 4-109) by 194 runs

Shaheed Veer Narayan Singh International Stadium, Raipur, December 17-20: Tamil Nadu 375 in 129.5 overs (Pradosh Paul 189, RS Jaganathsinivas 62; Naman Dhruw 4-97, Rohan Taank 2-52) drew with **Chhattisgarh** 201 in 85.1 overs (Naved Ali 47,Anand Rao 31; Ajith Ram S 4-38, Lokesh Raj 3-39, R Sonu Yadav 3-67) and 428/4 in 130 overs (f/o) (Sanidhav Hurkat 196, Harsh Sharma 106*; Jaganathsinivas 2-54). Tamil Nadu took first-innings lead.

St Stephen's Ground, New Delhi, December 17-20: Delhi 511 in 136.5 overs (Priyansh Arya 271, Ayush Badoni 73; Pranav Karia 4-161, Dev Dand 3-93) beat **Saurashtra** 181 in 59.4 overs (Bhavin Engle 43, Tarang Gohel 39; Harsh Tyagi 6-47, Mayank Rawat 2-18) and 257 in 70.5 overs (f/o) (T Gohel 46, Pranav Savjani 36; M Rawat 3-57, Lovnish Singh 2-26) by an innings and 73 runs.

Shaheed Veer Narayan Singh International Stadium, Raipur, December 25-29: Punjab 106 in 37 overs (Gaurav Choudhary 21*; Naman Dhruw 5-28, Snehil Chadda 2-26) and 357 in 92.4 overs (Prabhisimran Singh 158, Rahul Kashyap 59; Anand Rao 3-101, S Chadda 2-44) lost to **Chhattisgarh** 213 in 78.1 overs (Harsh Sharma 55, Gunjan Singh 49; Mandeep Singh 4-83, R Kashyap 3-51) and 251/2 in 71.4 overs (Sanidhav Hurkat 137*, Prateek Yadav 47) by eight wickets

TNCA Academy, Theni, December 25-29: Tamil Nadu 600/4 dec in 136 overs (Pradosh Paul 229*, Aditya Barooah 176) drew with **Odisha** 411 in 179 overs (Raghunath Malla 154, Jyoti Behera 118; E Yazh Arunmozhi 5-113, S Kishankumar 3-86) and 74/3 in 28 overs (f/o) (Swastik Samal 41). Tamil Nadu took first-innings lead.

Railway Cricket Ground, Rajkot, December 25-29: Jharkhand 602/5 dec in 169.5 overs (Adtiya Singh 215, V Vishal 168; Sachin Parmar 2-77) beat **Saurashtra** 252 in 83.2 overs (Tarang Gohel 93, Sachin Mevada 41; Sushant Mishra 4-36, Junaid Ashraf 2-35) and 146 in 87.4 overs (f/o) (Pratik Mandalia 60; S Mishra 3-25, Vivek Tiwari 3-37) by an innings and 204 runs.

Barabati Stadium, Cuttack, January 2-5: Delhi 244 in 70.4 overs (Sanat Sangwan 121, Vaibhav Kandpal 50; Krishna Palai 5-33, Ayaskant Sahu 4-64) and 364 in 106.5 overs (S Sangwan 73, Anuj Rawat 69; Shibasish Sahoo 3-71, K Palai 3-90) beat **Odisha** 225 in 96.4 overs (Jyoti Behera 41, Shekhar Majhi 41; Harsh Tyagi 5-56, Lovnish Singh 4-85) and 130 in 45.1 overs (J Behera 30, S Sahoo 30*; Nikhil Kumar 4-38, Lovnish 3-52) by 253 runs.

Railway Stadium, Dhanbad, Raipur, January 2-5: Chhattisgarh 521 in 146.3 overs (Anand Rao 123, Prateek Yadav 121; Amar Choudhary 5-147) and 113/9 dec in 20.3 overs (Prateek 50,

Naved Ali 32; Junaid Ashraf 3-45, Aditya Singh 2-18) lost to **Jharkhand** 373 in 147.1 overs (Atul Surwar 139, Bhanu Anand 104; Shaashwat Mishra 5-86, Rohan Taank 4-117) and 264/3 in 44.4 overs (Shresht Sagar 110, Aryaman Sen 103) by seven wickets

Dhruv Pandove Stadium, Patiala, January 2-5: Saurashtra 48 in 32.5 overs (Prerit Dutta 4-10, Rahul Kashyap 4-12) and 87 in 47.1 overs (Siddhant Rana 33; Rohit Kumar 5-25, P Dutta 2-20) lost to **Punjab** 327 in 71.4 overs (Prabhsimran Singh 103, Gaurav Choudhary 71; Kushal Shah 4-24, Parshwarajsinh Rana 2-75) by an innings and 192 runs.

Group A points table

Teams	M	W	L	D	T	N/R	Pts.	NRR
Delhi	6	4	0	2	0	0	31	+0.549
Punjab	6	4	2	0	0	0	27	+0.619
Chhattisgarh	6	3	1	2	0	0	21	+0.256
Jharkhand	6	3	3	0	0	0	19	-0.049
Tamil Nadu	6	2	1	3	0	0	19	+0.402
Saurashtra	6	0	5	1	0	0	3	-0.704
Odisha	6	0	4	2	0	0	2	-1.122

Delhi and Punjab qualified for the knock-outs

Group B

DSA Ground, Mangoldoi, November 5-6: Madhya Pradesh 269 in 85 overs (Ankush Singh 110, Yash Dubey 74; Mukhtar Hussain 4-70, Abir Chakraborty 2-13) beat **Assam** 68 in 44.5 overs (Aman Chhetry 43; Shivam Dwivedi 5-25, Rajarshi Srivastava 2-6) and 101 in 41.4 overs (f/o) (Jitumoni Kalita 27, Abdul Kuraishi 20; R Srivastava 6-49, Ritesh Shakya 4-28) by an innings and 100 runs

KSCA Ground No 3, Alur, November 5-8: Andhra 246 in 114.2 overs (P Girinath Reddy 117, S Ashish 33*; Shubhang Hegde 4-68, BM Shreyas 3-80) and 111 in 48 overs (Vinay 50, Ashish 29; S Hegde 5-33, Vidwath Kaverappa 2-11) lost to **Karnataka** 339 in 120 overs (Devdutt Padikkal 114, Luvnith Sisodia 83, Shaikh Mohd Rafi 4-58, Girinath Reddy 2-37) and 22/0 in 3.5 overs by ten wickets.

Sachin Tendulkar Gymkhana Ground, Mumbai, November 5-6: Gujarat 322 in 164.2 overs (Vardhman Shah 119, Sunpreet Bagga 101; Saksham 3-49, Atharva Ankolekar 2-43) and 193/4 dec in 69 overs (Abhishek Desai 53, Laxya Kocher 50*; Vignesh Solanki 2-45) beat **Mumbai** 148 in 57 overs (Suved Parkar 58, Divyansh Saxena 42; Kush Patel 5-58, Suraj Suryal 4-31) and 165 in 70.5 overs (Saksham 61, D Saxena 30; Priyajeet Jadeja 4-30, S Suryal 4-41) by 202 runs

Jalan Nagar Stadium, Dibrugarh, November 12-15: Railways 212 in 73.1 overs (Om Jadhav 92, Vikas Choudhary 43; Abir Chakraborty 4-36, Hrishikesh Borah 3-47, Mukhtar Hussain 3-52) and 202 in 75.2 overs (Nikhil Singh 43, Prakash Shroti 40; Jitumoni Kalita 3-48, M Hussian 2-32) lost to **Assam** 294 in 89.3 overs (Ishan Ahmed 128, H Borah 48; Sanket Yashwante 6-113, Madan Kumar 3-64) and 122/7 in 52.2 overs (M Hussain 32, Danish Ahmed 27; Madan 2-26, Vikas Singh 2-30) by three wickets.

Shambhubhai V Patel Stadium, Nadiad, November 12-15: Gujarat 247 in 137.3 overs (Vardhman Shah 63, Het Patel 39; Rajarshi Srivastava 5-72, Harshvardhan Singh 2-42) and 174 in 113.3 overs (Suraj Suryal 44, Laxya Kocher 38; Ritesh Shakya 4-47, R Srivastava 4-67) lost to **Madhya Pradesh** 348 in 106.1 overs (Irfan Ali 145, R Srivastava 49; Kush Patel

6-105, Akash Pandey 2-46) and77/0 in 4.1 overs (Rishabh Chouhan 36*, Ankush Singh 35*) by ten wickets.

Dr PVG Raju Andhra Cricket Association Sports Complex Ground, Vizianagram, November 12-15: Mumbai 326 in 129.2 overs (Suved Parkar 152, Nakul 32; S Ashish 3-63, Shaik Basha 2-23) and 22/0 in 3.2 overs drew with **Andhra** 371 in 130 overs (Vamsi Krishna 124, Mohammed Raza 77; Atharva Ankolekar 4-68, Saksham 3-112). Andhra took first-innings lead.

Jalan Outdoor Stadium, Dibrugarh, November 19-22: Assam 149 in 66.1 overs (Niraj Yadav 41, Hrishikesh Borah 34; Suraj Suryal 5-51, Kush Patel 4-34) and 107 in 55.2 overs (Gunjandeka 49; S Suryal 5-32, Hitanshu Pandya2-4) lost to **Gujarat** 174 in 79.1 overs (Smit Patel 55, Laxya Kocher 25; Mukhtar Hussain 6-56, Ridip Mohan 2-51) and 83/2 in 25.1 overs (Abhishek Desai 37*, Het Patel 20) by eight wickets.

KSCA Navale Stadium, Shimoga, November 19-22: Railways 163 in 60.5 overs (Om Jadhav 55*, Vaibhav Lande 46; Shubhang Hegde 3-33, Adtiya Goyal 3-37) and 331 in 92.4 overs (Nikhil Singh 114, Prakash Shroti 69; S Hegde 4-72, Manoj Bhandage 3-32) lost to **Karnataka** 618/4 dec in 132 overs (Abhiram 158, Devdutt Padikkal 148, S Nikin Jose 138, Luvnith Sisodia 107; Madan Kumar 2-74) by an innings and 124 runs

Sharad Pawar Cricket Academy BKC, Mumbai, November 19-22: Madhya Pradesh 361 in 92.5 overs (Yash Dubey 103, Rishabh Chouhan 92; Anjdeep Lad 7-118, Saksham 2-47) and 411/8 dec in 105 overs (R Chouhan 124, Rahul Chandrol 63; Arjun Tendulkar 5-95) drew with-**Mumbai**506 in 135.5 overs (Yashasvi Jaiswal 155, Suved Parkar 83; Amarnath Yadav 3-107, Ritesh Shakya 2-101) and 47/1 in 15 overs (S Parkar 26*). Mumbai took first-innings lead.

SDNRW Ground, Mysore, December 8-11: Gujarat 217 in 95.2 overs (Vardhman Shah 61, Smit Patel 43; Vidwath Kaverappa 4-40, Shubhang Hegde 4-44) and 265 in 114 overs (Laxya Kocher 88*, Suraj Suryal 39; S Hegde 6-53, Aditya Goyal 2-15) drew with **Karnataka** 163 in 76.4 overs (S Hegde 61*, BM Shreyas 23; Kush Patel 4-49, Hitanshu Pandya 3-40) and 106/7 in 69 overs (S Suryal 3-28, H Pandya 3-32). Gujarat took first-innings lead.

Sharad Pawar Cricket Academy BKC, Mumbai, December 8-11: Assam 94 in 46 overs (Sourav Saha 52*; Sidak Singh 5-33, Sylvester Dsouza 3-11) and 109 in 38.4 overs (Aman Chhetry 25, Mukhtar Hussain 20; Arjun Tendulkar 4-44, Tanush Kotian 3-0) lost to **Mumbai** 357 in 73.3 overs (Varun Lavande 118, Karan Shah 76; Mukhtar Hussin 6-126, Abir Chakraborty 2-51) by an innings and 154 runs

Karnail Singh Stadium, New Delhi, December 8-11: Andhra 337 in 96.5 overs (Vamsi Krishna 106, Girinath Reddy 89; Rizwan Ali Khan 5-82, Nikhil Singh 2-71) beat **Railways** 140 in 46.4 overs (Om Jadhav 54, Nikhil 43; S Ashish 5-19, Shaikh Mohd Rafi 3-20) and 99 in 41.1 overs (f/o) (Prakash Shroti 28; Ashish 4-22, Girish Reddy 3-25) by an innings and 98 runs

Emerald Heights International School Ground, Indore, December 17-20: Madhya Pradesh 394 in 151.2 overs (Yash Dubey 144, Dev Barnale 68; Shubhang Hegde 3-91, Vidwath Kaverappa 2-72) drew with **Karnataka** 420/7 in 195 overs (Manoj Bhandage 100*, S Hegde 100*; Adarsh Singh 4-100). Karnataka took first-innings lead.

Sachin Tendulkar Gymkhana, Kandivili, Mumbai, December 17-20: Mumbai 389 in 93 overs (Yashasvi Jaiswal 218, Sidak Singh 63; Rizwan Ali Khan 4-71, Sanket Yashwante 3-66) beat **Railways**150 in 42.3overs (Vaibhav Lande 44, Vikas Choudhary 43; A Vashishtha 8-30, Tanush Kotian 2-33) and 136 in 41.2 overs (f/o) (S Yashwante 38, V Lande 34; Arjun Tendulkar 5-44, Sidak Singh 3-17) by an innings and 103 runs.

CSR Sharma college ground, Ongole, December 17-20: Andhra 253 in 62.4 overs (KN Prudhvi Raj 64, CH Jogesh 48; Mukhtar Hussain 4-90, Bibhakar Nag 3-52) and 282/8 dec in 88.4 overs (K Mohan Kumar 52, Vinay 50*; Hrishikesh Borah 3-72, B Nag 2-41) beat **Assam** 106 in 46 overs (Jitumoni Kalita 50*, B Nag 21; Girinath Reddy 4-33, S Ashish 2-9) and 172 in 74.2 overs (J Kalita 35, H Borah 32; G Reddy 4-44, Varshith Reddy 3-43) by 257 runs.

Sardar Patel Stadium, Valsad, December 25-29: Railways 135 in 50.3 overs (Prakash Shroti 32, Sanket Yashwante 28; Siddharth Desai 4-36, Hitanshu Pandya 3-21) and 222 in 86.2 overs

(P Shroti 69, Vaibhav Lande 45; S Desai 4-78, H Pandya 3-31) lost to **Gujarat** 220 in 97.2 overs (Smit Patel 60, S Desai 44; V Lande 2-17, Chinmay Thada 2-37) and 141/3 in 47.3 overs (Het Patel 49, Vimal Solanki 34; Pritish Yadav 3-47) by seven wickets

Sharad Pawar Cricket Academy BKC, Mumbai, December 25-29: Mumbai 336 in 100 overs (Suved Parkar 119, Divyansh Saxena 69; Vidwath Kaverappa 3-62, Shubhang Hegde 3-87) and 299 in 53.4 overs (Yashasvi Jaiswal 72, S Parkar 63; S Hegde 3-110, Manoj Bhandage 2-45) lost to **Karnataka** 456 in 119.4 overs (Devdutt Padikkal 181, Sujay Sateri 120; A Vashishtha 4-89, Saksham 2-74) and 180/2 in 31.5 overs (D Padikkal 75, Goutham Sagar 70*) by eight wickets

CSR Sharma college ground, Ongole, December 25-29: Andhra 196 in 54 overs (Girinath Reddy 52, KN Prudhvi Raj 33; Shivam Dwivedi 6-80, Rajarshi Srivastava 2-22) and 219 in 80.1 overs (Vinay 54, CH Jogesh 43; Adarsh Singh 4-63, S Dwivedi 4-67) lost to **Madhya Pradesh** 458 in 155.4 overs (Yash Dubey 137, Irfan Ali 100; Varshith Reddy 3-73, G Reddy 2-89) by an innings and 43 runs.

KSCA Navale Stadium, Shimoga, January 2-5: Karnataka 406 in 98.4 overs (Devdutt Padikkal 208, Shubhang Hegde 66; Mukhtar Hussain 7-72) beat **Assam** 99 in 63 overs (M Hussain 39, Jitumoni Kalita 29; S Hegde 5-16, Vidwath Kaverappa 2-17) and 120 in 61.5 overs (f/o) (Niraj Yadav 27, Sourav Saha 20; BM Shreyas 4-45, S Hegde 2-25) by an innings and 187 runs.

MPCA Cricket Ground, Sagar, January 2-5: Madhya Pradesh 541/8 dec in 124 overs (Rishabh Chouhan 212*, Yash Dubey 86; Rizwan Ali Khan 2-84, Pritish Yadav 2-127) beat **Railways** 155 in 47 overs (Anand 44, Vaibhav Lande 34; Mohammed Baggad 6-40, Rajarshi Srivastava 2-65) and 120 in 36.2 overs (f/o) (V Lande 41, Om Jadhav 34; M Baggad 3-16, Irfan Ali 2-6) by an innings and 266 runs.

Dr P.V.G. Raju ACA Sports Complex, Vizianagaram, January 2-5: Andhra201 in 55.3 overs (Vamsi Krishna 95, B Munish Varma 27; Kush Patel 3-34, Akash Pandey 3-69) and 179 in 65.5 overs (V Krishna 67, Harsha Vardhan 28; Suraj Suryal 3-26, Siddharth Desai 3-33, A Pandey 3-68) lost to **Gujarat** 318 in 143.3 overs (Vardhman Shah 68, MA Umrigar 49; S Ashish 6-73, BM Varma 2-44) and 66/2 in 24.1 overs (Het Patel 39*) by eight wickets

Group B points table

Teams	M	W	L	D	T	N/R	Pts.	NRR
Karnataka	6	4	0	2	0	0	31	+0.498
Madhya Pradesh	6	4	0	2	0	0	30	+0.969
Gujarat	6	4	1	1	0	0	27	-0.440
Mumbai	6	2	2	2	0	0	18	+0.389
Andhra	6	2	3	1	0	0	16	+0.384
Assam	6	1	5	0	0	0	6	-1.117
Railways	6	0	6	0	0	0	0	-0.659

Karnataka and Madhya Pradesh qualified for the knock-outs

Group C

Jadavpur University Second Campus Ground, Kolkata, November 5-8: Baroda 181 in 73.3 overs (Harsh Ghalimatte 41, Smith Thakar 41; Suraj Jaiswal 3-24, Akash Pandey 3-75) and 247 in 85.5 overs (Shivalik Sharma 80, Urvil Patel 51; A Pandey 5-86, S Jaiswal 3-55) lost to **Bengal** 238 in 93.4 overs (Sudip Gharami 65, Sayan Biswas 60; Safvan Patel 4-33, Mistry

Milan 2-31) and192/3 in 76.3 overs (Sourav Paul 92, Dibya 62) by seven wickets.

Goa, November 5-8: Rajasthan 240 in 81.2 overs (Suraj Ahuja 59, Kapil Beniwal 55; Ruthvik Naik 5-37, Balpreet Singh 2-60) and 178 in 65 overs (S Ahuja 69, Dhruv Dixit 27; Balpreet 5-60, Rahul Mehta 3-35) beat **Goa** 252 in 83.1 overs (Alam Khan 74, Manthan Khutkar 47; Manav Suthar 5-82, Sanjay Kumar 2-42) and 123 in 44.4 overs (Shanu Vantamuri 30, M Khutkar 26; M Suthar 5-50, Sanjay 3-20) by 43 runs

Virender Sehwag Cricket Academy Ground, Jhajjar, November 5-8: Haryana 221 in 87.4overs (Gaurav Gaur 64, Sahil Hooda 39; Ajith Jacob 4-66, TS Vinil 3-25) and 288/7 dec in 82.5 overs (Prashant Vashist 95, Akhil 67; A Jacob 2-47, Aravind Rajesh 2-68) beat **Kerala** 94 in 43.4 overs (Akhil Scaria 30; Yashjeet Balhara 4-35, S Hooda 3-14) and246 in 97.2 overs (Akshay Manohar 67, J Ananthakrishnan 51; Kamal Yadav 3-36, Y Balhara 3-57) by 169 runs

Deccan Gymkhana Cricket Ground, Pune, November 12-15: Bengal 344 in 116 overs (Abhijeet Bhagat 81, Sudip Gharami 55; Siddhesh Warghante 3-107, Paras Gawali 3-31) and 306/8 in 103 overs (Karan Lal 100, Sayan Biswas 75; S Warghante 4-84, Alouk Jadhav 2-43) drew with **Maharashtra** 283 in 126.4 overs (Atharva Kale 77, Siddhesh Veer 60; Prayas Burman 4-91, K Lal 2-41). Bengal took first-innings lead.

Sanatana Dharma College Ground, Alappuzha, November 12-15: Kerala 370 in 15.5 overs (Ashwin Anand 126, Shiv Ganesh 100; Ninad Rathva 5-99, Mohit Mongia 2-40) and 182/6 in 72 overs (J Ananthakrishnan 69, Akshay Manohar 22; Dharmendra Dodia 4-74) drew with **Baroda** 470 in 97.5 overs (M Mongia 260, Shivalik Sharma 76; Ajith Jacob 4-124, Vatsal Govind 2-39). Baroda took first-innings lead.

Sehwag International School, Jhajjar, November 12-15: Haryana 556/4 dec in 111 overs (Prashant Vashist 227*, Yashu Sharma 206; Tunish Sawkar 2-69, Savio Kaalko 2-108) beat **Goa** 212 in 83 overs (Alam Khan 91, Mohit Redkar 28; Kamal Yadav 3-32, Sahil Hooda 2-24) and219 in 95.2 overs (f/o) (Manthan Khutkar 54, Rahul Mehta 31; Kamal 4-44, Yashjeet Balhara 2-29) by an innings and 125 runs.

MCA Cricket Stadium, Gahunje, Pune, November 19-22: Rajasthan 311 in 102.3 overs (Suraj Ahuja 87, Kapil Beniwal 62; Siddhesh Warghante 5-104, Atman Pore 3-25) and 243 in 103 overs (S Ahuja 110*, Sumit Raj 70; S Warghante 5-73, Akshay Kalokhe 3-84) drew with **Maharashtra** 359 in 106 overs (Om Bhosale 106, A Pore 77; Manav Suthar 6-108, Deepak Kadwasara 2-53) and 147/4 in 57 overs (Siddhesh Veer 53, Swapnil Fulpagar 40*; M Suthar 2-66) Maharashtra took first-innings lead.

SD College, Alappuzah, November 19-22: Bengal 360 in 125.3 overs (Dibya 110, Sourav Paul 81; TS Vinil 5-63, Aravind Rajesh 3-77) beat **Kerala** 94 in 73.4 overs (Akshay Manohar 20; Karan Lal 4-30, Akash Pandey 3-27) and 237 in 148 overs (f/o) (Vatsal Govind 62, Shiv Ganesh 40; K Lal 5-64, A Pandey 3-43) by an innings and 29 runs.

Sehwag International School , Jhajjar, November 19-22: Haryana 255 in 95.1 overs (Gaurav Gaur 82, Prashant Vashist 54; Saurin Thakar 5-48, Aditya Rangwani 3-53) and 327/8 dec in 110 overs (Sourabh Singroha 96, G Gaur 76; S Thakar 5-78) drew with **Baroda** 209 in 66.2 overs (Mohit Mongia 53, Urvil Patel 37; Yashjeet Balhara 7-31, Kamal Yadav 2-91) and 264/2 in 84 overs (Urvil 129*, Shivalik Sharma 78*; Y Balhara 2-76). Haryana took first-innings lead.

KL Saini Stadium, Jaipur, December 8-11: Rajasthan 412 in 103.4 overs (Salman Khan 185, Rahul Chahar 80; Vishnu Kumar 4-131, Afrad Reshab 3-61) beat **Kerala** 72 in 23 overs (Himanshu Sharma 5-16, R Chahar 4-19) and 292 in 90.4 overs (f/o) (Vatsal Govind 122, Nikhil T 89; Manav Suthar 3-43, R Chahar 3-119) by an innings and 48 runs

Chaudhry Bansi Lal Cricket Stadium, Lahli, December 8-11: Bengal 207 in 100.2 overs (Dibya 45, Sayan Biswas 39; Treyaksh Bali 3-30, Uday Kundu 3-42, Sahil Hooda 3-48) and 238 in 87.2 overs (Sudip Gharami 109, Akash Pandey 25*; Neeraj Rathee 4-42, Yashjeet Balhara 3-69) drew with **Haryana** 70 in 46 overs (Sourabh Singroha 24; Suraj Jaiswal 5-32, A Pandey 2-6) and 251/4 in 100 overs (Prashant Vashist 80*, Gaurav Gaur 62; A Pandey 2-49). Bengal took first-innings lead.

MCA Cricket Stadium, Gahunje, Pune, December 8-11: Goa 215 in 92.3 overs (Heramb Parab 61, Mohit Redkar 36; Alouk Jadhav 3-32, Yatin Mangwani 2-24) and 239 in 96.1 overs (Saiesh Kamat 46, H Parab 41; Y Mangwani 5-34, Atman Pore 2-55) lost to **Maharashtra** 322 in 88 overs (Hrishikesh Motkar 127, Swapnil Fulpagar 47; H Parab 3-75, Ruthvik Naik 2-47) and 133/0 in 25 overs (H Motkar 78*, Pavan Shah 54*) by ten wickets.

JU Second Campus, Salt Lake, Kolkata, December 17-20: Goa 146 in 64 overs (Heramb Parab 44, Ruthvik Naik 27; Akash Pandey 6-59, Souvik Paul 2-39) and 90 in 42.4 overs (Saiesh Kamat 22; Suraj Jaiswal 4-25, A Pandey 4-32) lost to **Bengal** 158 in 60.4 overs (Abhijeet Bhagat 44, Sourav Paul 29; Ruthvik Naik 7-43) and 80/2 in 21.3 overs (S Paul 39*; R Naik 2-26) by eight wickets.

Chaudhry Bansi Lal Cricket Stadium, Lahli, December 17-20: Haryana 139 in 66.1 overs (Prashant Vashist 63; Atman Pore 3-27, Siddhesh Warghante 3-54) and 147 in 70.5 overs (Sahil Hooda 28*, Ajay Guliya 25; Akshay Kalokhe 5-53, S Warghante 4-53) lost to **Maharashtra** 340 in 120.3 overs (Hrishikesh Motkar 72, Atharva Kale 71; Neeraj Rathee 3-52, Yashjeet Balhara 3-93) by an innings and 54 runs.

Reliance Cricket Stadium, Vadodara, December 17-20: Rajasthan 353 in 105.5 overs (Suraj Ahuja 91, Deepak Kadwasara 58; Ninad Rathva 6-95) and 226 in 64.5 overs (Rahul Chahar 64, D Kadwasara 36; N Rathva 4-43, Aditya Rangwani 2-46) lost to **Baroda** 177 in 52.2overs (Urvil Patel 36, Kinit Patel 35; Manav Suthar 7-47) and 475 in 120 overs (f/o) (N Rathva 143, Mohit Mongia 115, Kinit 106; R Chahar 4-178) by 73 runs.

MCA Cricket Stadium, Gahunje, Pune, December 25-29: Maharashtra 332 in 100.2 overs (Atharva Kale 104, Om Bhosale 81; Vishnu Kumar 5-103, TS Vinil 2-45) and 287/3 dec in 54.2 overs (A Kale 112*, O Bhosale 94) drew with **Kerala** 206 in 96.3 overs (Vatsal Govind 59, Arjun Aji 47; Yatin Mangwani 5-62, Atman Pore 2-34) and 168/5 in 101 overs (Vatsal 72, Akshay Manohar 36). Maharashtra took first-innings lead.

Sawai Mansingh Stadium, Jaipur, December 25-29: Rajasthan 111 in 53.2 overs (Rahul Chahar 31; Neeraj Rathee 6-41, Yashjeet Balhara 2-27) and 191 in 56.4 overs (Salman Khan 44, Kapil Beniwal 39; N Rathee 3-46, Y Balhara 3-68) lost to **Haryana** 459 in 129.5overs (Prashant Vashist 78, Sahil Hooda 63*; R Chahar 7-171, Dhruv Dixit 2-56) by an innings and 43 runs.

GCA Academy, Porvorim, December 25-29: Goa 158 in 64 overs (Manthan Khutkar 44, Aditya Suryawanshi 32; Saurin Thakar 3-24, Balpreet Singh 2-21) and 185.3 overs (Rahul Mehta 73, Vrusaj Talaulikar 49; Kinit Patel 4-50, N Rathva 4-71) lost to **Baroda**453 in 103.2 overs (Mohit Mongia 118, Urvil Patel 90; Balpreet Singh 3-119, Heramb Parab 2-63) by an innings and 74 runs.

SMS Stadium, Jaipur, January 2-5: Bengal 196 in 75.4 overs (Arif Ansari 52, Karan Lal 45; Manav Suthar 4-77, Himanshu Sharma 3-17) and 457/5 in 157 overs (Sourav Paul 238, Abhijeet Bhagat 93; Rahul Chahar 2-76) drew with **Rajasthan** 225 in 108.3 overs (Suhail Khan 86, Salman Khan 68; Suraj Jaiswal 4-38, Prayas Burman 2-38). Rajasthan took first-innings lead.

MCA Cricket Stadium, Gahunje, Pune, January 2-5: Baroda 317 in 85.3 overs (Ninad Rathva 101, Urvil Patel 70; Akshay Kalokhe 2-38,Yatin Mangwani 2-49) and 190 in 67.5 overs (Shivalik Sharma 86*, Mohit Mongia 31; Y Mangwani 4-52, Tanmay Shirode 3-22) lost to **Maharashtra**541/3 dec in 139overs (Hrishikesh Motkar 179, Siddesh Veer 158, Atharva kale 105*) by an innings and 34 runs.

Goa, January 2-5: Kerala 260 in 130.1 overs (Krishna Prasad 94, Vatsal Govind 47; Rahul Mehta 3-25, Balpreet Singh 2-62) and 302/5 in 91 overs (Arjun Aji 89, Akshay Manohar 66; Balpreet 2-100) drew with **Goa** 356 in 132.1 overs (Aditya Suryawanshi 180, Manthan Khutkar 81; A Manohar 4-57, Vishnu Kumar 3-92). Goa took first-innings lead.

Group C points table

Teams	M	W	L	D	T	N/R	Pts.	NRR
Maharashtra	6	3	0	3	0	0	28	+0.793
Bengal	6	3	0	3	0	0	26	+0.630
Haryana	6	3	1	2	0	0	24	+0.391
Baroda	6	2	2	2	0	0	17	+0.669
Rajasthan	6	2	2	2	0	0	17	-0.255
Goa	6	0	5	1	0	0	3	-0.926
Kerala	6	0	3	3	0	0	3	-1.219

Maharashtra and Bengal qualified for the knock-outs

Group D

Atal Bihari Vajpayee Stadium, Amtar, November 5-8: Uttar Pradesh 202 in 75.1 overs (Kritagya Singh 49, Aryan Juyal 30; Apoorav Walia 4-72, Ayush Jamwal 3-59) and 322 in 126.3 overs (Aryan Sharma 67, Kritagya 62; A Jamwal 5-122, A Walia 3-8) beat **Himachal Pradesh** 273 in 61.4 overs (Prashant Tomar 85, Karmanya Verma 62; Mohit Jangra 4-75, Kunal Yadav 3-56) and 225 in 71 overs (A Jamwal 60, Shaurya Saran 36; M Jangra 7-82) by 26 runs

Rajiv Gandhi International Stadium, Uppal, Hyderabad, November 5-8: Vidarbha 343 in 109 overs (Akash Kumar 115, Yash Rathod 110; G Anikethreddy 4-60, N Anirudh 3-41, Ajay Dev Goud 3-78) and 218/6 dec in 63.4 overs (Anirudha Choudhari 57, Akash 34; Anikethreddy 3-85, AD Goud 2-40) drew with**Hyderabad**210 in 105.3 overs (Anikethreddy 46, Sohail Shaikh 37; Parth Rekhade 6-77, Rohit Dattatraya 3-75) and 241/5 in 80 overs (Varun Goud 100*, Pragnay Reddy 79; P Rekhade 2-54). Vidarbha took first-innings lead.

Sovima Cricket Stadium, Dimapur, November 5-8: Jammu & Kashmir 145 in 62.5 overs (Sahil Lotra 37, Tahsin Dar 25; Rohit Singh 4-48, Chandan Ray 3-15) and 345 in 134.1 overs (Kanhaiya Wadhawan 117, Qamran Iqbal 116; C Ray 4-111, Sankar Paul 2-106) lost to **Tripura** 264 in 75.5 overs (Riaz Uddain 68, Arup Datta 52; Javid Ahmad 3-43, Umar Majeed 3-46) and 227/4 in 46.5 overs (A Datta 114*, S Paul 33) by six wickets.

Atal Bihari Vajpayee Cricket Stadium, Amtar, November 12-15: Himachal Pradesh 556/9 dec in 116 overs (Mohammed Arslan Khan 124, Shaurya Saran 121; Sabir Khan 3-89, Aryan 2-88) beat **Associates & Affiliate Combined XI** 66 in 25 overs (Tahmeed 22*; Ayush Jamwal 6-20, Apoorav Walia 2-23) and 103 in 35.3 overs (f/o) (Harshraj 33; A Jamwal 6-13, A Walia 2-16) by an innings and 387 runs

VCA Ground, Nagpur, November 12-15: Uttar Pradesh 286 in 89.5 overs (Aryan Juyal 114, Aryan Sharma 64; Rohit Dattatraya 5-114, Anirudha Choudhari 3-26) and 329/8 dec in 90.1 overs (A Juyal 154, Sameer Choudhary 82; R Dattatraya 3-100, Sushrut Bhaiswar 2-41) drew with **Vidarbha** 295 in 98.2 overs (Nayan Chavan 80*, Yash Rathod 78; Akshay Sain 7-102, Kritagya Singh 2-42) and 214/4 in 80 overs (A Choudhari 104*, Akash Kumar 35; Kritagya 2-62). Vidarbha took first-innings lead.

Gymkhana Ground, Hyderabad, November 12-15: Hyderabad 633/4 dec in 155 overs (Pragnay Reddy 212, Varun Goud 165, Thakur Tilak Varma 133; Rohit Singh 2-83) drew with **Tripura** 155 in 78 overs (Tanmoy Das 68, Dipayan Debbarma 22; Rathan Teja 4-22, Ajay Dev Goud 3-47) and 329/7 in 125 overs (f/o) (Sankar Paul 79, D Debbarma 63; AD Goud 3-78, G Anikethreddy 2-73). Hyderabad took first-innings lead.

MCA Cricket Ground, Polo Ground, Shillong, November 19-22: Jammu & Kashmir 338

in 119.3 overs (Sahil Lotra 105, Qamran Iqbal 85; Paramjeet Singh 6-94, Akash Kumar 2-50) beat **Associates & Affiliate Combined XI** 91 in 36.2 overs (Harshraj 24; Javid Ahmad 4-7, Aditya Chib 3-13) and 183 in 60.4 overs (f/o) (Tahmeed 45, Paramjeet 41; Umar Majeed 6-32, Mujtaba Yousuf 3-33) by an innings and 64 runs.

Nagpur, November 19-22: Vidarbha 454 in 142.5 overs (Yash Rathod 223, Akash Kumar 53; Prikshit Kashyap 5-92, Shourya Garg 4-54) drew with **Himachal Pradesh** 219 in 69.3 overs (Apoorav Walia 67, Karmanya Verma 56; Atharva Taide 4-30, Anirudha Choudhari 3-49) and 502/7 in 134.1 overs (f/o) (Mohammed Arslan Khan 172, Sidhant Purohit 151*; Aditya Thakare 4-62, Rohit Dattatraya 3-109). Vidarbha took first-innings lead.

Hyderabad, November 19-22: Hyderabad 225 in 82.4 overs (Varun Goud 103, Sohail Shaikh 27; Kunal Yadav 4-48, Shiva Singh 2-42) and 299 in 138.5 overs (V Goud 127, Pragnay Reddy 38; Shiva 4-109, Kunal 3-44) drew with **Uttar Pradesh** 307 in 113 overs (Shantanu 94, Sameer Choudhary 76: Ajay Dev Goud 6-71, C Rakshann Readdi 2-76) and 58/1 in 16 overs (Kritagya Singh 26*). Uttar Pradesh took first-innings lead.

VCA Ground, Nagpur, December 8-11: Jammu & Kashmir 257 in 90.5 overs (Tahsin Dar 56*, Sahil Lotra 52; Parth Rekhade 4-54, Darshan Nalkande 2-72) and 326 in 119.5 overs (Vivrant Sharma 158, S Lotra 66; Sushrut Bhaiswar 3-27, Rohit Dattatraya 3-80) lost to **Vidarbha** 574/7 dec in 125 overs (Akash Kumar 143, Yash Rathod 121*, Avesh Shaikh 120; S Lotra 3-65, Umar Majeeb 3-98) and 11/0 in 2 overs by ten wickets.

Atal Bihari Vajpayee Cricket Stadium, Amtar, December 8-11: Himachal Pradesh 241 in 67.1 overs (Sidhant Purohit 100*, Apoorav Walia 50; G Anikethreddy 5-59, Rathan Teja 4-61) and 200 in 68.1 overs (Prashant Tomar 46, S Purohit 45; R Teja 4-60, Anikethreddy 4-87) beat **Hyderabad** 135 in 55.2 overs (Varun Goud 34; Ayush Jamwal 6-63, A Walia 3-57) and 184 in 74.5 overs (Samhith Reddy 50, V Goud 48; A Walia 7-62, A Jamwal 2-75) by 122 runs.

Agartala, December 8-11: Associates & Affiliate Combined XI 67 in 29.2 overs (Harshraj 34; Saruk Hossain 4-22, Rohit Singh 2-14) drew with **Tripura** 128/2 in 44 overs (Babul Dey 44*, Dipayan Debbarma 36*). Tripura took first-innings lead.

Rajiv Gandhi International Stadium, Hyderabad, December 17-20: Hyderabad 527/7 dec in 129 overs (Varun Goud 238, T Santosh Goud 65*; Alfred Hmar 2-115) beat **Associates & Affiliate Combined XI** 130 in 33.3 overs (Abhishek Anand 54, Sonu Gupta 30; Ajay Dev Goud 5-26, E Sanketh 5-59) and 72 in 28.5 overs (f/o) (RK Rex 24; AD Goud 6-20, Alankrit 2-16) by an innings and 325 runs.

Atal Bihari Vajpayee Cricket Stadium, Amtar, December 17-20: Himachal Pradesh 208 in 67.5 overs (Apoorav Walia 84, Mohammed Arslan Khan 45; Sankar Paul 5-72, Amaresh Das 3-63) and 314/6 dec in 70.5 overs (Mohammed Arslan 101, Sidhant Purohit 55*; S Paul 3-107, A Das 2-93) beat **Tripura** 99 in 55.3 overs (Babul Dey 34, S Paul 25; Ayush Jamwal 5-31, A Walia 4-41) and 78 in 40.1 overs (Riaz Uddain 21; A Jamwal 7-31) by 345 runs.

Bhamashah Park Ground, Meerut, December 17-20: Jammu & Kashmir 281 in 99.4 overs (Jiyaad Magrey 102, Qamran Iqbal 43; Akshay Sain 4-47, Vikas Singh 2-48) and 116 in 40.2 overs (Umar Majeed 39, Vivrant Sharma 28; Kritagya Singh 4-33, A Sain 4-45) lost to **Uttar Pradesh** 454 in 131.2 overs (Sameer Choudhary 100, Mohit Jangra 81; Javid Ahmad 5-95, U Majeed 2-93) by an innings and 57 runs.

VCA Stadium, Nagpur, December 25-29: Vidarbha 393 in 100 overs (Darshan Nalkande 76, Anirudha Choudhari 76; Abhishek Anand 3-45, RK Rex 2-62) beat **Associates & Affiliate Combined XI** 69 in 39.2 overs (A Anand 20; Parth Rekhade 4-21, D Nalkande 3-6) and 116 in 27.3 overs (f/o) (A Anand 52; D Nalkande 5-39, A Choudhari 3-20) by an innings and 208 runs.

Gymkhana Ground, Hyderabad, December 25-29: Jammu & Kashmir 352 in 102.3 overs (Jiyaad Magrey 131, Tashin Dar 113; E Sanketh 5-74, G Anikethreddy 3-90) and 144 in 61.3 overs (Qamran Iqbal 30, J Magrey 25; Anikethreddy 6-50, Rathan Teja 3-28) lost to **Hyderabad** 619/7 dec in 144 overs (Samhith Reddy 210*, Ajay Dev Goud 108; Brijesh Sharma 3-135) by an innings and 123 runs.

Jawahar Lal Nehru Stadium, Ghaziabad, December 25-29: Tripura 153 in 65.5 overs (Dipayan Debbarma 66, Babul Dey 22; Kritagya Singh 4-72, Mohit Jangra 3-23) and 133 in 47.3 overs (Arup Datta 44, Chiranjib Debnath 26; Rajat Nirwal 4-23, Kritagya 2-35) lost to **Uttar Pradesh** 354 in 87.3overs (Ankur Malik 90, Priyam Garg 68; Chandan Ray 5-93, Sankar Paul 4-113) by an innings and 68 runs.

Maharaja Bir Bikram College Stadium, Agartala, January 2-5: Vidarbha 341 in 89 overs (Nayan Chavan 107, Anirudha Choudhari 61; Chiranjib Debnath 4-60, Pritam Debnath 2-40) beat**Tripura**127 in 53.4 overs (Tanmoy Das 27, Arup Datta 23; Darshan Nalkande 5-45, Parth Rekhade 3-32) and 213 in 91.2 overs (f/o) (A Datta 49, Babul Dey 31; D Nalkande 5-57, Sushrut Bhaiswar 2-27) by an innings and 1 run.

Atal Bihari Vajpayee Cricket Stadium, Amtar, January 2-5: Jammu & Kashmir 228 in 58.2 overs (Umar Majeed 76, Junaid Farooq 60; Ayush Jamwal 5-107, Apoorva Walia 3-76) and 152 in 51.5 overs (Sahil Lotra 26, Tahsin Dar 23; A Jamwal 5-63, A Walia 4-27) lost to **Himachal Pradesh** 613/8 dec in 129.2overs (A Jamwal 151*, Mohammed Arslan Khan 106; Brijesh Sharma 3-117, U Majeed 3-137) by an innings and 233 runs.

Choudhary Charan Singh Sports Stadium, Muzzafarnagar, January 2-5: Uttar Pradesh 414/7 dec in 81.3 overs (Priyam Garg 110, Ankur Malik 103; Chand Sharma 2-75) beat **Associates & Affiliate Combined XI** 84 in 26 overs (NG Johnson 33, Abhishek Anand 28; Kritagya Singh 3-12, Akshay Sain 2-12) and 64 in 20.2 overs (f/o) (Kritagya 5-10, Rajat Nirwal 3-17) by an innings and 266 runs.

Group D points table

Teams	M	W	L	D	T	N/R	Pts.	NRR
Uttar Pradesh	6	4	0	2	0	0	31	+0.523
Vidarbha	6	3	0	3	0	0	30	+0.591
Himachal Pradesh	6	4	1	1	0	0	27	+1.186
Hyderabad	6	2	1	3	0	0	19	+0.242
Tripura	6	1	3	2	0	0	10	-0.822
Jammu & Kashmir	6	1	5	0	0	0	7	-1.190
Associates & Affiliate Combined XI	6	0	5	1	0	0	1	-1.109

Uttar Pradesh and Vidarbha qualified for the knock-outs

Quarter-finals

Green Park Stadium, Kanpur, January 11-14: Delhi 293 in 100.4 overs (Ayush Badoni 96, Yash Madan 53; Zeeshan Ansari 4-86, Kartik Tyagi 2-27) and 194/4 35.2 overs (Priyansh Arya 91, A Badoni 84) drew with **Uttar Pradesh** 477 in 147.2 overs (Priyam Garg 206, Aryan Sharma 94; Harsh Tyagi 4-145, Hrithik Shokeen 3-109). Uttar Pradesh qualified for semi-final on first-innings lead.

Holkar Stadium, Indore, January 11-14: Madhya Pradesh 491 in 170 overs (Dev Barnale 209, Irfan Ali 54; Akash Pandey 4-144, Roshan Singh 3-76) drew with **Bengal** 209 in 73 overs (Arif Ansari 86, Sayan Biswas 56; Rishabh Chouhan 4-44, I Ali 2-2) and 360/6 in 100 overs (f/o) (S Biswas 151*, Sourav Paul 89). Madhya Pradesh qualified for semi-final on first-innings lead.

Dhruv Pandove Stadium, Patiala, January 11-14: Punjab 540 in 158.5 overs (Gourav Choudhary 184, Jagmeet Singh 85; Akshay Kalokhe 6-160, Tanmay Shirode 2-76) and 300/8 dec in 97.2 overs (Rahul Kashyap 73, Nehal Wadhera 69; T Shirode 3-55, Kalokhe 3-76) beat **Maharashtra** 163 in 62.3 overs (Siddhesh Veer 53, Swapnil Fulpagar 28; Rohit Kumar 4-52,

Mandeep Singh 2-22) and 185 in 59 overs (Siddhesh Warghante 101, S Veer 24; Deepin Chitkara 5-32, Rohit 4-65) by 492 runs.

VCA Ground, Nagpur, January 11-14: Karnataka 132 in 68.5 overs (Sujay Sateri 27*, Shubhang Hegde 25; Rohit Battatraya 3-16, Parth Rekhade 3-28, Darshan Nalkande 3-54) and 328 in 87.5 overs (S Nikin Jose 73, Devdutt Padikkal 72; P Rekhade 5-93, R Dattatraya 4-43) lost to **Vidarbha** 395 in 131.1 overs (Yash Rathod 101, P Rekhade 57; BM Shreyas 5-58, Vidwath Kaverappa 2-80) and 66/1 in 12.2 overs (Avesh Shaikh 26*, Akash Kumar 22) by nine wickets.

Semi-finals

Kanpur, January 19-22: Uttar Pradesh 395 in 127 overs (Shivam Bansal 151, Aryan Sharma 111; Mohammed Baggad 7-105, Rajarshi Srivastava 2-116) and 243/4 dec in 41 overs (Ankur Malik 85*, Sameer Choudhary 82*; Adarsh Singh 3-53) drew with**Madhya Pradesh** 460 in 146.5 overs (Rishabh Chouhan 141, Yash Dubey 136; Kritagya Singh 3-124, Zeeshan Ansari 3-160) and 129/3 in 42 overs (Suraj Vashisht 79*, Rahul Chandrol 25*). Madhya Pradesh took first-innings lead.

Nagpur, January 19-22: Vidrabha440 in 165.4 overs (Atharva Taide 124, Akash Kumar 92; Rohit Kumar 3-107, Deepin Chitkara 2-61) and 294/5 dec in 90 overs (Yash Rathod 124*, Akash 73; Rohit 2-63) drew with**Punjab**199 in 62.4 overs (Nehal Wadhera 63, Gourav Choudhary 45; Rohit Dattatraya 3-13, Yash Thakur 2-39) and 95/6 in 24 overs (N Wadhera 51*; Anirudha Choudhari 4-40). Vidarbha took first-innings lead.

Final

VCA Ground, Nagpur, January 28-31: Madhya Pradesh 289 in 94.3 overs (Suraj Vashisht 75, Yash Dubey 55; Darshan Nalkande 4-48, Parth Rekhade 3-77, Yash Thakur 3-77) and 176/7 in 63 overs (Sanket Shrivastava 71*, Y Dubey 67; P Rekhade 3-48) drew with **Vidarbha** 614 in 183.4 overs (Atharva Taide 320, Nayan Chavan 107; Rishabh Chouhan 4-119, Mohammed Baggad 3-139). Vidarbha took first-innings lead.

Winners: Vidarbha

Under-19 Challenger Trophy

Reddy keeps Green unbeaten

India Green, led by Nitish Kumar Reddy, capped their unbeaten run in the Under-19 Challenger Trophy 2018-19 by beating the defending champions India Blue by six wickets in the final. Just like the previous season, the tournament was again a four-team contest, with India Yellow replacing Sri Lanka Board President XI.

Batting first in the final, Qamran Iqbal and Swastik Samal gave Blue a 65-run opening stand. Reddy broke the partnership with Samal's wicket, and once Iqbal was dismissed for a run-a-ball 63, wickets fell at regular intervals. Reddy finished with figures of 3 for 25.

Chasing 206, Arya Sethi set the platform with 73. He and wicketkeeper-batsman Suraj Ahuja added 58 for the third wicket. Captain Pradosh Ranjan Paul, who made a useful half-century, had Ahuja caught and bowled for 26, and when Sethi fell as the fourth wicket, Green were still 55 away from victory. Nehal Wadhera's unbeaten 51, though, ensured Green reached the target without further hiccups.

Apart from his half-century in the final, Paul also scored 126 not out against India Red and 92 not out against Yellow and finished as the leading run-scorer.

The **previous season**, Sri Lanka Board President XI, the first overseas team to compete with the regulars, reached the final where they lost to Blue by 95 runs.

Put in by Ayan Siriwardena, Blue were bowled out for 244 despite captain Himanshu Rana's 90-ball 78 and Manoj Bhandage's counterattacking 50-ball 53. For the visitors, Siriwardena picked up 4 for 36, while Ravindu Sanjana chipped in with 3 for 42.

Sri Lanka's chase never took off, with Shivam Mavi sending the top three back in quick time and at 54 for 5, the result was a foregone conclusion.

Riyan Parag of Red, with a hundred and two fifties in four innings, was the leading run-getter of the tournament, while Prithvi Shaw and Shubman Gill could manage only 88 (in three innings) and 24 runs (in two innings) respectively.

	Most runs	Most wickets
2017-18	Riyan Parag (India Red) (207 runs, 4 matches)	Pankaj Yadav (India Green) (9 wickets, 3 matches)
2018-19	Pradosh Ranjan Paul (India Blue) (286 runs, 4 matches)	RA Choudhary (India Green), (8 wickets, 3 matches)

2018-19

Ekana International Cricket Stadium, Lucknow, November 10: India Blue 280/6 in 50 overs (Pradosh Paul 126*, Swastik Samal 80; Sushant Mishra 3-60, AM Singh 2-59) beat **India Red** 170 in 38 overs (Nayan Chavan 41, SV Joshi 34; Trilok Nag 3-30, Yazh Arun 3-43) by 110 runs.

Ekana International Cricket Stadium B, Lucknow, November 10: India Green 198 in 49.3 overs (Rishabh Chouhan 50, SA Ahuja 48; Jaymeet Patel 4-24, Prabhat Maurya 4-37) beat **India Yellow** 173 in 46.4 overs (Priyansh Arya 44, Tilak Varma 38; RA Choudhary 3-18, R Chouhan 2-17) by 25 runs.

Ekana International Cricket Stadium, Lucknow, November 12: India Red 226/8 in 50 overs (Yashasvi Jaiswal 66, Abhishek Selvakumar 59; Anirudh Chowdhary 2-27, Atharva Poojari 2-41) lost to **India Green** 227/6 in 47.4 overs (Arya Sethi 58, Nehal Wadhera 48; Sushant Mishra 2-42) by four wickets.

Ekana International Cricket Stadium B, Lucknow, November 12: India Yellow 179 in 43.3 overs (Rahul Chandrol 64, DR Gajraj 30; AS Sandhu 5-26, RS Hangargekar 2-32) lost to **India Blue** 183/3 in 44.5 overs (Pradosh Paul 92*, Qamran Iqbal 25) by seven wickets.

Ekana International Cricket Stadium, Lucknow, November 14: India Red 158 in 44.5 overs (Shashwat Rawat 102*; Shubhang Hegde 5-30, Jaymeet Patel 3-21) lost to **India Yellow** 162/3 in 32.4 overs (Priyansh Arya 51, DR Gajraj 41; Harsh Dubey 2-52) by seven wickets.

Ekana International Cricket Stadium B, Lucknow, November 14: India Green 293/5 in 50 overs (SA Ahuja 95, Nehal Wadhera 51; Prashant Bhati 2-47, Akash Raj 2-60) beat **India Blue** 140 in 37.2 overs (Swastik Samal 40, Qamran Iqbal 28; Rohit Dattatraya 5-31, RA Choudhary 3-25) by 153 runs.

Points table

Teams	M	W	L	D	T	N/R	Pts	NRR
India Green	3	3	0	0	0	0	12	+1.269
India Blue	3	2	1	0	0	0	8	-0.117
India Yellow	3	1	2	0	0	0	4	+0.153
India Red	3	0	3	0	0	0	0	-1.440

India Green and India Blue qualified for the final

Final

Ekana International Cricket Stadium, Lucknow, November 16: India Blue 206 in 47.3 overs (Qamran Iqbal 63, Pradosh Paul 63; Nithish Reddy 3-25, Atharva Ankolekar 2-32) lost to **India Green** 209/4 in 43.4 overs (Arya Sethi 73, Nehal Wadhera 51*; AS Sandhu 3-39) by six wickets.

Winners: India Green

2017-18

Cricket Club of India, Mumbai, November 26: India Blue 286/9 in 50 overs (Manjot Kalra 72, Ninad Rathva 50*; Rahul Chahar 4-64, Shiva Singh 3-38) beat **India Red** 247 in 47 overs (Atharva Taide 104, Ayush Badoni 54; Aditya Thakare 3-37, Shivam Mavi 3-42) by 39 runs.

BKC Ground, Mumbai, November 26: Sri Lanka Board President XI 220 in 48.4 overs (Ayan Siriwardena 59, Ravindu Sanjana 49; Darshan Nalkande 5-18, Ishan Porel 2-17) lost to **India Green** 222/3 in 32.1 overs (Priyam Garg 64, Abhishek Sharma 52*) by seven wickets.

BKC Ground, Mumbai, November 28: India Green 235 in 49.4 overs (Abhishek Sharma 89, Harkant Desai 40; Harsh Tyagi 3-45, Ninad Rathva 3-50) lost to **India Blue** 236/6 in 39.3 overs (Himanshu Rana 69, N Rathva 55*; Pankaj Yadav 3-39) by four wickets.

Cricket Club of India, Mumbai, November 28: India Red 226 in 46.3 overs (Prithvi Shaw 63, Kamlesh Nagarkoti 51; Hareen Buddila 4-30, Ayan Siriwardena 4-34) lost to **Sri Lanka Board President XI** 231/6 in 48.4 overs (Santhush Gunatilleke 80, Nipun Dananjaya 43; K Nagarkoti 2-44) by four wickets.

BKC Ground, Mumbai, November 30: India Blue 203 in 46.3 overs (Om Bhosale 49, Shivam Mavi 44; Heshan Hettiarachchi 2-26, Hareen Buddila 2-43) lost to **Sri Lanka Board President XI** 204/4 in 44.2 overs (Nuwanidu Fernando 91, Nipun Dananjaya 65*; S Mavi 2-40) by six wickets.

Cricket Club of India, Mumbai, November 30: India Red 273/8 in 50 overs (Riyan Parag 100, Kamalesh Nagarkoti 35; Tanush Kotian 2-35, Ishan Porel 2-45) beat **India Green** 186 in 42.1 overs (Priyam Garg 50, Aryan Juyal 46; Arshdeep Singh 5-19) by 87 runs.

3rd place playoff: India Green won by 95 runs

Wankhede Stadium, Mumbai, December 2: India Green 285/6 in 50 overs (Aryan Juyal 73, Harkant Desai 66; Vivek Tiwari 2-42, Arshdeep Singh 2-61) beat **India Red** 264 in 48 overs (Anuj Rawat 97, Riyan Parag 50; Pankaj Yadav 5-57, Ishan Porel 3-62) by 21 runs.

Points table

Teams	M	W	L	D	T	N/R	Pts.	NRR
India Blue	3	2	1	0	0	0	9	+0.444
Sri Lanka Board President XI	3	2	1	0	0	0	8	-0.345
India Red	3	1	2	0	0	0	5	+0.245
India Green	3	1	2	0	0	0	5	-0.361

India Blue and Sri Lanka Board President XI qualified for the final

Final

Cricket Club of India, Mumbai, December 2: India Blue 244 in 50 overs (Himanshu Rana 78, Urvil Patel 57; Ayan Sisrwardena 4-36, Ravindu Sanjana 3-42) beat**Sri Lanka Board President XI**149 in 45.4 overs (Nishan Madushka 44, R Sanjana 28; Ninad Rathva 3-28, Shivam Mavi 3-15) by 95 runs.

Winners: India Blue

Under-16 Vijay Merchant Trophy

Reddy reaches 441

In Aryan Hooda and Abhishek, Jharkhand had the players who topped the batting and bowling charts respectively, but Haryana claimed the title on first-innings lead in the final. Abhishek's six-wicket haul kept Haryana to 247, but Haryana's new-ball pair of Vivek Kumar and Anuj Thakral took five wickets each to bowl Jharkhand out for 186. As Haryana piled on 507 runs in the second innings, Jharkhand's bowlers could do little to claw their way back.

Similarly, in **2017-18**, with 1237 runs in seven games at 176.71, Andhra's Nithish Kumar Reddy stole the limelight with two 300-plus scores — including a 366-ball 441 against Nagaland — but the trophy belonged to Punjab, who repeated their title run from 2015-16 season. They remained unbeaten and defeated Uttar Pradesh by six wickets in the final to lift the trophy.

Nithish Kumar Reddy's feats won him recognition at the BCCI awards.

Yuvraj Choudhary starred in the deciding match with a four-wicket haul and a crucial 50 not out. Only once did Punjab concede a first-innings lead; yet, they didn't have a single batsman in the top five.

	Most runs	Most wickets
2017-18	Nithish Reddy (Andhra) (1237 runs, 7 matches)	Reshu Raj (Baroda) (46 wickets, 6 matches)
2018-19	Aryan Hooda (Jharkhand) (903 runs, 9 matches)	Abhishek (Jharkhand) (46 wickets, 9 matches)

2018-19

North Zone

Sher-i-Kashmir Cricket Stadium, Srinagar, October 21-22: Haryana 462/3 dec. in 105.4 overs (Yuvraj Singh 218*, Ahaan Poddar 167) beat **Jammu and Kashmir** 161 in 73.2 overs (Mohammad Manzir 54, Aakash Bhat 33; Anuj Thakral 4-40, Mudit Pruthi 3-28) and 133 in 55.4 overs (A Thakral 5-42, M Pruthi 2-33) by an innings and 168 runs.
St Stephen's Ground, New Delhi, October 21-23: Delhi 544/3 dec. in 109 overs (Arpit Rana

247, Naman Tiwari 109, Yash Dhull 100*) beat **Himachal Pradesh** 240 in 74.4 overs (Amanpreet Singh 60, Ayush Dhiman 42; Masab Alam 3-31, Ruben Massey 3-49, Divij Mehra 3-75) and 140 in 45.4 overs (Deep Singh 26*; Aryan Tandon 4-34, M Alam 4-40) by an innings and 164 runs.

Luhnu Cricket Ground, Bilaspur, October 27-29: Himachal Pradesh 209 in 85.1 overs (Arnav Bhardwaj 59, Mridul Surroch 44; Anuj Thakral 3-61, Mudit Pruthi 2-18) and 163 in 68.1 overs (M Surroch 72; A Thakral 3-36, Vivek Kumar 2-21) lost to **Haryana** 421/9 dec. in 102.1 overs (Sarvesh Rohilla 89, Yuvraj Singh 77; Rhitwicq Sharma 2-54, Ritik Kumar 2-99) by an innings and 49 runs.

Gandhi Ground, Amritsar, October 27-29: Punjab 375 in 141.3 overs (Manroop Singh 90, Uday Sharan 84; Parth Bali 3-62, Yash Dhull 2-22) drew with **Delhi** 432/9 dec in 102.1 overs (Y Dhull 185, Shreeyans Mahey 38; Akshdeep Singh 3-106, Vanshish Verma 3-108). **Delhi** took first-innings lead.

St Stephen's Ground, New Delhi, November 2-4: Haryana 338 in 96.3 overs (Nishant Sindhu 106, Yuvraj Singh 90; Divij Mehra 4-65) and 152/4 dec. in 52.2 overs (Ahaan Poddar 65, Yuvraj 60*) drew with **Delhi** 146 in 51.4 overs (Parth Bali 34, Raghav 29*; N Sindhu 3-9, Anuj Thakral 3-40) and 173/5 in 62 overs (Arpit Rana 101*; Mudit Pruthi 2-25). **Haryana** took first-innings lead.

Gandhi Ground, Amritsar, November 2-4: Punjab 402/7 dec. in 113 overs (Uday Saharan 119*, Harnoor Pannu 88; Nityam Abrol 4-121, Ranjot Singh 2-91) drew with **Jammu and Kashmir** 207 in 106.3 overs (Aakash Bhat 66; Harjas Tandon 5-42, Emanjot Chahal 3-59) and 65/5 in 52 overs (E Chahal 2-12). **Punjab** took first-innings lead.

Teri Cricket Ground, Teri, November 12-14: Haryana 251 in 92.1 overs (Nishant Sindhu 84, Piyush Dahiya 36; Emanjot Chahal 3-41, Jaskirat Mehra 3-59) and 146/1 in 49 overs (Yuvraj Singh 102*, Mayank Shandilya 31) drew with **Punjab** 240 in 113.1 overs (Sanraj Rattanpal 75*, Dhruv Jindal 57; Anuj Thakral 5-63). **Haryana** took first-innings lead.

Sher-i-Kashmir Cricket Ground, Srinagar, November 12-14: Himachal Pradesh 306 in 84.1 overs (Mridul Surroch 146, Amanpreet Singh 68; Basit Bashir 5-56, Azhar Wani 2-57) drew with **Jammu and Kashmir** 10/2 in 5.2 overs (Hardik Sharma 2-4). No result.

Gandhi Ground, Amritsar, November 18-20: Punjab 234 in 90.3 overs (Shivein Rakheja 71, Sanraj Rattanpal 35; Ritik Kumar 4-77, Mridul Surroch 3-26) and 176/3 dec. in 60.4 overs (S Rakheja 68, Harnoor Pannu 47) drew with **Himachal Pradesh** 230 in 87.2 overs (Kabir Singh 77, Amanpreet Singh 52; Harjas Tandon 2-44, Emanjot Chahal 2-47) and 59/5 in 32 overs (Harshdeep Singh 3-14, E Chahal 2-16). **Punjab** took first-innings lead.

Gandhi Memorial Science College Ground, Jammu, November 18-19: Jammu and Kashmir 163 in 63.3 overs (Akshit Gandral 34, Udhay Pratap 26; Masab Alam 4-30, Yash Dhull 3-13) and 50 in 21.5 overs (Divij Mehra 6-34, M Alam 3-1) lost to **Delhi** 352 in 80.2 overs (Arpit Rana 191, Aryan Dalal 34; Basit Bashir 5-62, Nityam Abrol 3-90) by an innings and 139 runs.

North Zone points table

Teams	M	W	L	D	T	N/R	Pts	Quotient
Haryana	4	2	0	2	0	0	20	2.538
Delhi	4	2	0	2	0	0	18	1.520
Punjab	4	0	0	4	0	0	8	1.283
Himachal	4	0	2	2	0	0	2	0.403
Jammu and Kashmir	4	0	2	2	0	0	2	0.272

Haryana qualified for the quarter-final, Delhi for the pre-quarter-final

Central Zone

Sawai Mansingh Stadium, Jaipur, October 21-23: Rajasthan 380 in 137.2 overs (SB Jat 100, Karan Lamba 99; Deepak Yadav 2-31, Abhyuday Singh 2-57) and 11 for no loss in 6 overs drew with **Chhattisgarh** 300 in 112.2 overs (Gaurav Mishra 101, Sajal Chandrakar 33, D Yadav 33; DM Bhatia 4-88, K Lamba 2-25). **Rajasthan** took first-innings lead.

MPCA Cricket Ground, Sagar, October 21-23: Uttarakhand 270 in 103.4 overs (Anuj Giri 95, Shashwat Dangwal 44*; Aryan Pandey 3-49, Nihar Bhatt 2-30) and 219/9 in 101.5 overs (S Dangwal 82*, Yuvvraj 32; N Bhatt 2-23, Masoom Kaif 2-25) drew with **Madhya Pradesh** 384/6 dec. in 71 overs (Nishant Sachan 153, Shubham Kushwah 134; Kanhaiya Bhatt 3-79, Poorvansh Dhruv 2-42). **Madhya Pradesh** took first-innings lead.

Aligarh Muslim University Ground, Aligarh, October 21-23: Uttar Pradesh 199 in 78.1 overs (Satnam Singh 88, Aaqib Khan 34; Sahil Sheikh 4-39, Minar Sahare 2-37) and 141 in 67 overs (Aaradhya Yadav 58, Satnam 25, Shubhanker Shukla 25; S Sheikh 4-20, M Sahare 3-41) beat **Vidarbha** 143 in 64.2 overs (MD Faiz 33; Abhishek Tomar 6-65, Aaqib 2-24) and 99 in 66.1 overs (Avishkar Jadhao 38; Aaqib 4-31, Damandeep Singh 3-17) by 99 runs.

Madan Mohan Malviya Stadium, Allahabad, October 27-29: Madhya Pradesh 218 in 84.1 overs (Adarsh Dubey 52, Shubham Kushwah 50; Kunal Tyagi 5-53, Aaqib Khan 4-66) and 156/2 in 37 overs (A Dubey 57, S Kushwah 55*; K Tyagi 2-58) drew with **Uttar Pradesh** 406/6 dec. in 136 overs (Siddharth Yadav 238*, Shivam Kumar 68; Vineet Baghel 2-48, Aryan Pandey 2-80). **Uttar Pradesh** took first-innings lead.

Shaheed Veer Narayan Singh International Stadium, Raipur, October 27-29: Uttarakhand 94 in 42.1 overs (Sajal Chandrakar 3-5, Deepak Singh 3-14, Satyam Dubey 3-53) and 182 in 82.1 overs (Shashwat Dangwal 39*, Anuj Giri 31; S Chandrakar 4-27, Deepak 2-35) lost to **Chhattisgarh** 302/9 dec. in 102 overs (Pratham Thakur 76, Deepak 55*; Satyam Baaliyan 3-46, Arush 2-32) by an innings and 26 runs.

Vidarbha Cricket Association Ground, Kalamana, Nagpur, October 27-29: Rajasthan 328 in 91.3 overs (Karan Lamba 181, M Choudhary 45; Sahil Sheikh 6-97, Tejas Soni 2-52) and 172/5 in 60.3 overs (RP Garg 89, SS Mishra 37; Danish Malewar 3-31) drew with **Vidarbha** 252 in 105 overs (MD Faiz 44, Harshit Bawane 43; SR Kataria 4-52, A Khaliya 2-40). **Rajasthan** took first-innings lead.

Shaheed Veer Narayan Singh International Stadium, Raipur, November 2-3: Chhattisgarh 59 in 33.5 overs (Kunal Tyagi 5-22, Damandeep Singh 3-14) and 57 in 27.1 overs (Aaqib Khan 4-14, Abhishek Tomar 4-17) lost to **Uttar Pradesh** 372/5 dec. in 117 overs (Aaradhya Yadav 158, Sameer Rizvi 108; Vasudev Bareth 2-59) by an innings and 256 runs.

Jaipur, November 2-4: Uttarakhand 292 in 94.5 overs (Anuj Giri 84, Yuvvraj 59; A Khaliya 5-52, HV Meena 2-42) and 103/4 in 50 overs (Ishagra Jagoori 50*, Poorvansh Dhruv 36*; HV Meena 3-28) drew with **Rajasthan** 376/5 dec. in 117 overs (Karan Lamba 101, RP Garg 85). **Rajasthan** took first-innings lead.

Vidarbha Cricket Association Ground, Kalamana, Nagpur, November 2-4: Madhya Pradesh 230 in 80.2 overs (Akshat Raghuwanshi 110, Jatin Rajput 60; Minar Sahare 4-32, MS Thakur 2-29) and 201/9 dec. in 54.4 overs (Masoom Kaif 48, Adarsh Dubey 36; Harshit Bawane 5-54, M Sahare 2-71) drew with **Vidarbha** 154 in 56.1 overs (MD Faiz 79, Jagjot 28; Vineet Baghel 4-36; Aryan Pandey 2-11,) and 272/7 in 72 overs (MD Faiz 80, Abhishek Agarwal 62; V Baghel 4-74, A Pandey 2-44). **Madhya Pradesh** took first-innings lead.

Vidarbha Cricket Association Ground, Kalamana, Nagpur, November 12-14: Vidarbha 379 in 115 overs (Danish Malewar 250, Tejas Soni 30; Parikshit Garkoti 3-73, Satyam Baaliyan 2-63) beat **Uttarakhand** 150 in 50.3 overs (S Baaliyan 27, Yuvvraj 26; Minar Sahare 6-26, Manvir 2-13) and 112 in 46.5 overs (Divyam Rawat 51, Ishagra Jagoori 25; Sahil Sheikh 4-28, Manvir 3-21, M Sahare 3-39) by an innings and 117 runs.

KL Saini Stadium, Jaipur, November 12-14: Rajasthan 171 in 49.1 overs (SB Jat 78*, Karan Lamba 31; Aaqib Khan 6-71, Damandeep Singh 2-40) and 184 in 73.4 overs (SS Mishra 56, K Lamba 51; Aaqib 5-62, Abhishek Tomar 2-21) lost to **Uttar Pradesh** 381/8 dec. in

100 overs (Sameer Rizvi 150, Aaradhya Yadav 119; A Khaliya 3-82, PM Rathore 2-40) by an innings and 26 runs.

Gwalior, November 12-14: Chhattisgarh 173 in 76.5 overs (Sajal Chandrakar 50, Mayank Yadav 33; Masoom Kaif 3-22, Yuvraj Nema 3-34) and 215 in 76 overs (Deepak Yadav 58, M Yadav 57; Jatin Rajput 3-11, Sushant Nagar 3-58) lost to **Madhya Pradesh** 217/7 dec. in 71.5 overs (Parth Chaudhary 78, Akshat Raghuwanshi 63; Satyam Dubey 2-30, S Chandrakar 2-46) and 120/7 in 39.5 overs (Jatin Rajput 46*; Deepak Singh 3-36, Vasudev Bareth 3-36) by three wickets.

Bhamashah Park Ground, Meerut, November 18-20: Uttarakhand 227 in 86.5 overs (Ashar Khan 99, Shashwat Dangwal 44; Kunal Tyagi 6-60, Abhishek Tomar 2-40) and 120/5 in 43 overs (S Dangwal 51*; K Tyagi 4-50) drew with **Uttar Pradesh** 644/9 dec. in 142.2 overs (Sameer Rizvi 280, Satnam Singh 117; Ashar 4-138, Kanhaiya Bhatt 2-75). **Uttar Pradesh** took first-innings lead.

Gwalior, November 18-20: Rajasthan 371/9 dec. in 83.3 overs (Karan Lamba 211, SA Yadav 73; Yuvraj Nema 3-51, Rohit Singhal 2-51) and 111 for 6 dec. in (SA Yadav 30; Sushant Nagar 3-47, Aryan Pandey 2-52) lost to **Madhya Pradesh** 241 in 80.1 overs (Shubham Kushwah 86, Aryan Deshmukh 38; SB Jat 2-28, A Khaliya 2-51) and 242/3 in 59.2 overs (S Kushwah 84, Parth Chaudhary 75) by seven wickets.

Gwalior, November 18-20: Vidarbha 291 in 101.2 overs (Danish Malewar 117, Neel Athaley 49; Deepak Yadav 5-58, Vasudev Bareth 3-57) and 180/5 dec. in 34 overs (Abhishek Agarwal 48, D Malewar 45*; D Yadav 2-32) drew with **Chhattisgarh** 211 in 82.2 overs (Gaurav Mishra 79, V Bareth 44; Sahil Sheikh 5-45, Tejas Soni 4-57) and 137/8 in 50 overs (G Mishra 35; Minar Sahare 4-33, D Malewar 2-20). **Vidarbha** took first-innings lead.

Central Zone points table

Teams	M	W	L	D	T	N/R	Pts	Quotient
Uttar Pradesh	5	3	0	2	0	0	26	2.805
Madhya Pradesh	5	2	0	3	0	0	19	1.153
Vidarbha	5	1	1	3	0	0	12	1.202
Chhattisgarh	5	1	2	2	0	0	9	0.635
Rajasthan	5	0	2	3	0	0	9	0.983
Uttarakhand	5	0	2	3	0	0	3	0.376

Uttar Pradesh and Madhya Pradesh qualified for pre-quarter-final

West Zone

Deccan Gymkhana, Pune, October 21-23: Maharashtra 404/9 dec in 147 overs (Soham Shinde 121, KS Tambe 78; Krish Gupta 4-67, Ujjwal Bhagat 2-107) drew with **Gujarat** 306/5 in 122 overs (Krish Gupta 91, Aarya Desai 67*; RM Chaudhari 2-36, TJ Jadhav 2-53). No result.

Rajkot, October 21-23: Mumbai 380 in 139.3 overs (Himanshu 81*, Sai Chavan 71; Meet Chauhan 6-97, Kartik Gida 2-33) and 28 for no loss in 8 overs drew with **Saurashtra** 237 in 119.4 overs (Deep Baraiya 54, K Gida 42; Himanshu 5-73, Aayush Zimare 3-24). **Mumbai** took first-innings lead.

Rajkot, October 27-29: Saurashtra 371 in 145.4 overs (Bhagyarajsinh Chudasama 143, Raxit Mehta 87; Aarya Jadhav 4-61, NN Thakur 2-50) drew with **Maharashtra** 254 in 128 overs (TJ Jadhav 71, SS Dhas 54; Gajjar Sammar 4-68, Kalp Shah 3-26). **Saurashtra** took first-innings lead.

Valsad, October 27-29: Gujarat 193 in 75.5 overs (Karan Thakkar 52, Laay Bhaskar 38; AD Patel 4-34, Het Thakkar 2-43) and 212/3 in 67.4 overs (Ved Patel 98, Aarya Desai 52*; PN Prajapati 2-36) drew with **Baroda** 282 in 115.2 overs (Aditya Menon 131, Yash Patanwadia 42; Ujjwal Bhagat 4-52, UA Sharma 4-83). **Baroda** took first-innings lead.

Sharad Pawar Cricket Academy, BKC, Mumbai, November 2-4: Gujarat 273 in 124.1 overs (Karan Thakkar 86, SJ Patel 47; Himanshu 7-78) and 65/5 in 45 overs (SJ Patel 35*; Himanshu 3-17) drew with **Mumbai** 416/7 dec. in 100 overs (Suryansh Shedge 151, Jash Ganiga 131; Aarya Desai 2-47, Ujjwal Bhagat 2-76). **Mumbai** took first-innings lead.

Railway Ground, Vadodara, November 2-4: Baroda 130 in 43 overs (Tasmay Bedade 49*, Rachesh Thakur 32; NN Thakur 4-40, RM Chaudhari 2-12) and 134 in 49.5 overs lost to **Maharashtra** 172 in 71.4 overs (Soham Shinde 49, NN Thakur 29; Het Thakkar 4-29, PN Prajapati 4-46) and 95/2 in 30.5 overs (S Shinde 54*) by eight wickets.

Railway Ground, Vadodara, November 12-14: Saurashtra 402 in 118.1 overs (Gajjar Sammar 113, Bhagyarajsinh Chudasama 82; Het Thakkar 3-55, Harsh Desai 2-61) and 186/1 dec. in 34 overs (B Chudasama 101*, Kartik Gida 62) drew with **Baroda** 345 in 119.3 overs (Aditya Menon 93, PK Kapadia 75; Meet Chauhan 4-81, Manav Khunt 3-43). **Saurashtra** took first-innings lead.

Pune, November 12-14: Maharashtra 309 in 131.2 overs (SS Dhas 107, Praduemna Chavan 63; Divyanshu Singh 5-48, Aayush Zimare 2-57) drew with **Mumbai** 507/6 in 132 overs (Suryansh Shegde 194, Vedanta Ghadia 147; RM Chaudhari 2-52, OK Patkal 2-88). **Mumbai** took first-innings lead.

Sachin Tendulkar Gymkhana, Kandivali, Mumbai, November 16-18: Mumbai 501 in 111.4 overs (Musheer Khan 215, Aayush Zimare 81; AD Patel 2-101, Shailendra Yadav 2-99) beat **Baroda** 82 in 50.4 overs (Harsh Desai 39; A Zimare 5-20, Himanshu 5-22) and 220 in 73.5 overs (Yatharth Ghunchala 94, Aditya Menon 72; Divyanshu Singh 3-25, A Zimare 3-67) by an innings and 199 runs.

Shastri Maidan, Anand, November 16-18: Gujarat 345 in 149.2 overs (SJ Patel 102, UA Sharma 68; Raxit Mehta 3-54, Makwana Hiren 2-57) and 42 for no loss in 9 overs drew with **Saurashtra** 264 in 99 overs (Daksh Bhindi 72, Kartik Gida 58; UA Sharma 3-55, Yuvraj Singh 2-58). **Gujarat** took first-innings lead.

West Zone points table

Teams	M	W	L	D	T	N/R	Pts	Quotient
Mumbai	4	1	0	3	0	0	16	1.699
Maharashtra	4	1	0	3	0	0	9	1.576
Saurashtra	4	0	0	4	0	0	8	1.021
Gujarat	4	0	0	4	0	0	6	0.880
Baroda	4	0	2	2	0	0	4	0.519

Mumbai qualified for the quarter-final, Maharashtra qualified for the pre-quarter-final

East Zone

Mangaldai Sports Association Stadium, Mangaldai, October 21-23: Bihar 172 in 93.1 overs (Kanishk Kaustabh 82, Yashraj 37; Mayukh Hazarika 5-40, Pritish Raha Roy 2-31) and 125/8 in 60 overs (Sraman Nigrodh 40; Shivam Mittal 3-16, Jacky Ali 2-17) drew with **Assam** 197 in 102 overs (S Mittal 44, Dhruv Borah 26; Aarya Chaudhary 4-60, Reshu Raj 3-47). **Assam** took first-innings lead.

Jadavpur University Second Campus, Salt Lake, Kolkata, October 21-23: Odisha 165 in 67.5 overs (Jagyanjeet Sahu 25; Siddharth Singh 5-32, Jayesh 2-26) and 170 in 68.4 overs (Biswajit Patra 45, Sanket Behera 43; Rahul Chowdhary 3-11, Siddharth 3-45) lost to **Bengal** 224 in 74.4 overs (Abhishek Porel 102, Toufik Uddin 36; Ashutosh Chhuria 6-70, Sobhan Behera 2-31) and 112/1 in 25 overs (Toufik 80*) by nine wickets.

Birsa Munda Cricket Stadium, Chaibasa, October 21-23: Jharkhand 412/6 dec. in 120.2 overs (Himanshu 189, Aryan Hooda 182; Sahil Sultan 2-79, Parvez Sultan 2-92) beat **Tripura** 56 in 50.2 overs (Gaurav Mishra 3-13, A Hooda 2-6) and 137 in 60.5 overs (S Sultan 53*, Rahul Ghosh 48; Abhishek 4-26, A Hooda 3-13) by an innings and 219 runs.

Bengal Cricket Academy Stadium, Kalyani, October 27-29: Assam 134 in 50.5 overs (Reshabh Dipok 34, Mayukh Hazarika 30; Jayesh 4-43, Rahul Chowdhary 2-13) and 207 in 86.1 overs (Shivam Mittal 56, Nihar Narah 47; Siddharth Singh 5-40, Toufik Uddin 3-13) lost to **Bengal** 378/6 dec. in 85.4 overs (Abhishek Porel 133, Ayush Singh 111; M Hazarika 2-54) by an innings and 37 runs.

Energy Stadium, Rajbansi Nagar, Patna, October 27-29: Bihar 295 in 101.5 overs (Arnav Kishor 125, Raushan 56; Rahul Ghosh 4-45, Dipen Biswas 2-49) beat **Tripura** 73 in 40.4 overs (Anandh Bhowmik 32; Raushan 4-11, Aarya Chaudhary 2-7) and 102 in 62.1 overs (R Ghosh 35; A Chaudhary 4-27, Raushan 2-1) by an innings and 120 runs.

Cuttack, October 27-29: Jharkhand 315 in 95.4 overs (Sharandeep Singh 153, Sushant Verma 36; Ramesh Melaka 4-61, Ashutosh Chhuria 2-75) and 31 for no loss in 17 overs drew with **Odisha** 227 in 106.2 overs (Biswa Muduli 62, Dinesh Majhi 37; Abhishek 5-46, HD Gautam 3-47). **Jharkhand** took first-innings lead.

Police Training Academy Ground, Agartala, November 2-4: Bengal 91 in 36.5 overs (Soumyajyoti 26; Arkajit Das 4-5, Rahul Ghosh 3-31) and 266/3 dec. in 62 overs (Soumyajyoti 126*, Ayush Singh 55; Sahil Sultan 2-49) beat **Tripura** 105 in 52.1 overs (Akash Ahmed 29; Anish Pandey 4-15, Debopratim Halder 2-14) and 98 in 82 overs (Parvez Sultan 26; Siddharth Singh 6-24, Toufik Uddin 3-11) by 154 runs.

Bidanasi Ground, Cuttack, November 2-4: Assam 158 in 61.2 overs (Shivam Mittal 57, Saurav Dihingia 25; Sobhan Behera 3-35, Ashutosh Chhuria 3-40) and 261/5 dec. in 93.4 overs (S Mittal 69*, Nihar Narah 60; Ashutosh Samal 3-83) drew with **Odisha** 215 in 96 overs (Biswajit Patra 90, Surya Mohapatra 36, Reshabh Dipok 8-52) and 41 for no loss in 21 overs (Sanket Behera 27*). **Odisha** took first-innings lead.

Railway Stadium, Dhanbad, November 2-4: Jharkhand 420 in 104.3 overs (Rajan Deep 181, Aryan Hooda 130; Aarya Chaudhary 5-96, Reshu Raj 3-90) beat **Bihar** 86 in 44.2 overs (Abhishek 5-28, A Hooda 2-7) and 187 in 53 overs (Arnav Kishor 53, Rajesh 28; HD Gautam 3-54, Abhishek 2-19) by an innings and 147 runs.

Barsapara Cricket Stadium, Guwahati, November 12-14: Assam 116 in 55.3 overs (Nihar Narah 42, Shivam Mittal 34; Parvez Sultan 5-21, Pamir Debnath 3-28) and 100 in 51.2 overs (S Mittal 61; Arkajit Das 5-20, P Sultan 3-26) lost to **Tripura** 314 in 123.3 overs (Anandh Bhowmik 104, Sahil Sultan 64; Reshabh Dipok 3-71, S Mittal 2-6) by an innings and 98 runs.

Keenan Stadium, Jamshedpur, November 12-14: Bengal 536/9 dec. in 137.4 overs (Toufik Uddin 198, Ayush Singh 148; HD Gautam 4-132, Mohit Ray 3-116) and 6 for no loss in 3 overs drew with **Jharkhand** 300 in 118.3 overs (Aryan Hooda 174, Shikhar Mohan 35; Siddharth Singh 5-69, Toufik 2-43). **Bengal** took first-innings lead.

Cuttack, November 12-14: Bihar 165 in 67.1 overs (Kanishk Kaustabh 64, Aditya 28; Ashutosh Chhuria 3-35, Shresth Singh 2-31) and 231 in 76 overs (Arnav Kishor 59, Harshit 29; Shresth 6-76, Ashutosh Samal 2-38) drew with **Odisha** 250 in 109.3 overs (Ashutosh Sahoo 45, Ramesh Melaka 43; Raushan 3-49, Aditya 3-49) and 17 for no loss in 7 overs. **Odisha** took first-innings lead.

Mahabir Chilarai Stadium, Abhayapuri, November 18-20: Jharkhand 406/5 dec. in 101.2 overs (Aryan Hooda 182, Shikhar Mohan 118; Hemanta Taye 2-53) beat **Assam** 105 in 94.4 overs (Ankush Mazumder 37; Mohit Ray 4-34, HD Gautam 3-33) and 157 in 87.4 overs (Shi-

vam Mittal 45, Dhruv Borah 32; HD Gautam 6-31, Abhishek 2-5) by an innings and 144 runs.
Police Training Academy Ground, Agartala, November 18-20: Tripura 128 in 54.3 overs (Anandh Bhowmik 44, Nabarun Chakraborty 38; Shresth Singh 5-39, Surya Mohapatra 2-14) and 124 in 81.4 overs (Arkajit Das 33, N Chakraborty 26; R Melaka 3-24, Shresth 3-32) lost to **Odisha** 230 in 90.4 overs (Bibhansu Ray 111, Biswa Muduli 49; Rahul Ghosh 3-61, Diptanu Chakraborty 2-29) and 26 for no loss in 10.1 overs by ten wickets.
Jadavpur University Second Campus, Salt Lake, Kolkata, November 18-20: Bihar 153 in 69.5 overs (Sraman Nigrodh 54, Kanishk Kaustabh 29*; Debopratim Halder 4-20, Jayesh 3-27) and 121 in 47.3 overs (Raushan 30, K Kaustabh 26; D Halder 5-23, Anish Pandey 2-20) lost to **Bengal** 200 in 57.5 overs (Abhishek Porel 78, Soumyajyoti 28; Aditya 3-32, Reshu Raj 2-31) and 75/1 in 12.4 overs (Toufik Uddin 25) by nine wickets.

East Zone points table

Teams	M	W	L	D	T	N/R	Pts	Quotient
Bengal	5	4	0	1	0	0	28	2.338
Jharkhand	5	3	0	2	0	0	25	2.067
Odisha	5	1	1	3	0	0	14	0.971
Bihar	5	1	2	2	0	0	9	0.797
Tripura	5	1	4	0	0	0	7	0.485
Assam	5	0	3	2	0	0	4	0.501

Bengal qualified for quarter-final, Jharkhand qualified for pre-quarter-final

North-East Zone

Mahabir Chilarai Stadium, Abhayapuri, October 21-23: Nagaland 218 in 76 overs (Yugandhar 135; Bhatt 3-78, M Kumar 2-26) and 172/4 dec. in 38 overs (Yugandhar 62*, Yash 25; Bhatt 2-59) beat **Arunachal Pradesh** 104 in 66.4 overs (Bhatt 32, Dhruv 25; Ranjen 4-19, Arjun 3-18) and 99 in 55 overs (Bhatt 48; Arjun 5-25, Ranjen 3-30) by 187 runs.
Assam Valley School Ground, Tezpur, October 21-23: Meghalaya 228 in 88.1 overs (Prince Maurya 45, Bharali 34, Nirdesh Baisoya 34; Ruatfela 3-45, Sahil 3-49) beat **Mizoram** 52 in 34.2 overs (N Baisoya 4-9, Gavineal Marpna 4-11) and 34 in 18.5 overs (P Maurya 5-14, N Baisoya 4-5) by an innings and 142 runs.
Rural Development Trust Stadium, Anantapur, October 21-23: Manipur 119 in 57.2 overs (Pavan Yadav 43; Sunil Kumar 8-39) and 188 in 48.1 overs (Chauhan 87, Jotin Pheiroijam 52; Zakir 4-29) beat **Sikkim** 37 in 27.1 overs (P Yadav 4-4, J Pheiroijam 4-7) and 34 in 34.2 overs (J Pheiroijam 4-10, Chirag 2-2) by 236 runs.
Mahabir Chilarai Stadium, Abhayapuri, October 27-29: Arunachal Pradesh 192 in 71.3 overs (Bhatt 98, Dhruv 32; Priyansh 5-42, Sahil 3-56) and 151 in 61.1 overs (Kunal Rawat 50, Dhruv 37; Sahil 6-45, Priyansh 2-34) lost to **Mizoram** 209 in 89 overs (Jung 59, Sahil 28; Bhatt 5-49, M Kumar 2-13) and 135/5 in 48 overs (Sahil 51*, Jung 26; Bhatt 2-38, T Muri 2-44) by five wickets.
Vikash Cricket Ground, Bhubaneshwar, October 27-29: Nagaland 255 in 60.2 overs (Arjun 110, Yash 50; Zakir 6-54, Sunil Kumar 2-42) beat **Sikkim** 82 in 52.1 overs (Zakir 40; Odilemba 5-3, Ranjen 4-13) and 128 in 57.1 overs (Zakir 28; Yash 3-9, Ranjen 3-26) by an innings and 45 runs.
Rural Development Trust Stadium, Anantapur, October 27-29: Manipur 194 in 71.1 overs

(Chirag 47, Suresh Singh 44; Prince Maurya 4-27, Sudhir Sahani 2-41) and 130 in 64.3 overs (Ulenyai Khwairakpam 34, Champion 27; S Sahani 3-28, Nirdesh Baisoya 2-20) lost to **Meghalaya** 142 in 62.4 overs (Chauhan 6-38, Pavan Yadav 3-43) and 183/9 in 72.5 overs (N Baisoya 66*, S Sahani 31; P Yadav 3-37, Vivekananda 3-37) by one wicket.

Mangaldai Sports Association Stadium, Mangaldai, November 2-3: Arunachal Pradesh 81 in 49 overs (Bhatt 47; Jotin Pheiroijam 3-23, Joyraj 2-16) and 40 in 27.4 overs (Jotin Pheiroijam 3-7, Chauhan 3-17) lost to **Manipur** 124 in 52 overs (Biswajeet Debnath 4-38, K Roy 3-7) by an innings and 3 runs.

Assam Valley School Ground, Tezpur, November 2-4: Meghalaya 135 in 47.1 overs (Nirdesh Baisoya 42, Prince Maurya 33; Tarun Sharma 3-32, Karma Wangchuk 2-19) and 167/8 dec. in 47.2 overs (N Baisoya 50*, Josiah Momin 34; Zakir 3-36, Vivek KR 2-16) beat **Sikkim** 67 in 38 overs (Adiv 28; P Maurya 5-15, N Baisoya 3-26) and 51 in 21.3 overs (N Baisoya 4-24, Gavineal Marpna 2-3) by 184 runs.

Golaghat District Sports Association Ground, November 2-4: Mizoram 58 in 31.3 overs (Ranjen 5-7, Ezaz Ali 2-10) and 54 in 29.2 overs (Sanjeev 3-0, E Ali 3-20) lost to **Nagaland** 225/7 dec. in 58 overs (Yugandhar 66, Yash 57; Gilbert 2-18, Rinsanga 2-24) by an innings and 113 runs.

Golaghat District Sports Association Ground, November 12-13: Meghalaya 119 in 39.4 overs (Sudhir Sahani 27; Ranjen 4-27, Jatin Jatin 3-24) and 44 in 33.5 overs (Ranjen 7-12, J Jatin 3-19) beat **Nagaland** 69 in 16.2 overs (Aman Yadav 46; S Sahani 5-4, Prince Maurya 4-4) and 56 in 24.2 overs (Nirdesh Baisoya 8-23) by 38 runs.

Vikash Cricket Ground, Bhubaneshwar, November 12-14: Arunachal Pradesh 169 in 41.3 overs (Y Bhardwaj 64, Nikhil Singh 34; Tarun Sharma 3-25, Zakir 3-60) and 254/5 dec. in 62 overs (Dhruv 135*, Y Bhardwaj 31; Arun 2-16, Tarun 2-77) beat **Sikkim** 118 in 38.3 overs (Adiv 25; Y Bhardwaj 7-42, Bhatt 2-23) and 74 in 37.5 overs (Y Bhardwaj 4-23, Chiran 3-21) by 231 runs.

Suaka Cricket Ground, Sihhmui, Aizawl, November 12-13: Mizoram 87 in 41.1 overs (Priyansh 29; Chauhan 4-29, Jotin Pheiroijam 2-11) and 132 in 56.4 overs (Priyansh 42; Chauhan 6-37, J Pheiroijam 3-21) lost to **Manipur** 228 in 71.2 overs (Ulenyai Khwairakpam 57, Suresh Singh 35; Priyansh 6-56) by an innings and 9 runs.

Suaka Cricket Ground, Sihhmui, Aizawl, November 18-20: Sikkim 219 in 68.2 overs (Zakir 62, Tarun Sharma 44; Sahil 5-81, Malsawma 2-14) and 71 in 25.4 overs (Moses Gurung 26; Priyansh 4-25, Gilbert 2-9) lost to **Mizoram** 85 in 35 overs (Jung 33; Tarun 4-13, Sunil Kumar 3-1) and 206/8 in 55.4 overs (Priyansh 124*, Kumar 29; Prashant Rai 3-37, Tarun 2-41) by two wickets.

Mangaldai Sports Association Stadium, Mangaldai, November 18-20: Meghalaya 137 in 53.3 overs (Prince Maurya 50*, Sudhir Sahani 31; Y Bhardwaj 5-44, Chiran 2-21) and 173/9 dec. in 53.1 overs (Nirdesh Baisoya 100*; Y Bhardwaj 5-53, T Muri 2-50) beat **Arunachal Pradesh** 57 in 43.1 overs (N Baisoya 4-14, S Sahani 2-7) and 97 in 43 overs (S Sahani 7-30) by 156 runs.

DN Singha Stadium, Goalpara, November 18-20: Manipur 131 in 45.1 overs (Pavan Yadav 61, Dominic 28; Jatin Jatin 3-26, Arjun 3-33) and 73 in 43.5 overs (Ulenyai Khwairakpam 26, Chirag 25; J Jatin 5-11, Arjun 2-18) lost to **Nagaland** 178 in 66.5 overs (Yugandhar 45, J Jatin 30; Chauhan 8-70) and 29/1 in 4.5 overs by nine wickets.

North-East Zone points table

Teams	M	W	L	D	T	N/R	Pts	Quotient
Meghalaya	5	5	0	0	0	0	31	1.013
Nagaland	5	4	1	0	0	0	26	1.365
Manipur	5	3	2	0	0	0	20	1.416
Mizoram	5	2	3	0	0	0	12	0.576
Arunachal Pradesh	5	1	4	0	0	0	6	0.751
Sikkim	5	0	5	0	0	0	0	0.452

Meghalaya and Nagaland qualified for pre-quarter-final

South Zone

Goa Cricket Association Academy, Porvorim, October 21-23: Hyderabad 187 in 86 overs (P Shiva 79, Aditya Mangat 40; Sujay Naik 3-42, Suryesh Pagi 2-16) and 174/5 dec. in 61 overs (P Shiva 104*, A Mangat 27; Kushal Hattangadi 2-38, Manish Kakode 2-46) drew with **Goa** 153 in 89.5 overs (K Hattangadi 56, Lakhmesh Pawane 25; Nikhil S 6-55) and 48/2 in 24 overs. **Hyderabad** took first-innings lead.

NPR College Ground, Dindigul, October 21-23: Karnataka 112 in 67.5 overs (Siddharth Rao 54; B Aaditya 4-21, R Rajagiri 2-32) and 180/6 drew in 86 overs (Yashovardhan Parantap 45*, Aneeshwar Gautam 40*; R Rajagiri 3-44) with **Tamil Nadu** 222/8 dec. in 104 overs (Vimal Khumar 66, BV Kumar 46; Shashi Kumar 3-41, Ayush Barik 2-44). **Tamil Nadu** took first-innings lead.

Krishnagiri Stadium, Wayanad, October 21-23: Andhra 396 in 156 overs (SK Rasheed 156*, Revanth Reddy 57; Abi Biju 4-80, Sudhi Anil 4-82) and 4 for no loss in 5 overs drew with **Kerala** 249 in 101.3 overs (Niranjan Dev 77, Rohan Nair 59; Srikar 3-82, A Kiran 2-20). **Andhra** took first-innings lead.

Palmyra Cricket Ground, Puducherry, October 27-29: Hyderabad 197 in 85.4 overs (Sarthak Bhardwaj 45, Balaji Reddy 34; Yashwanth 5-73, Rohan S 2-45) and 190/2 dec. in 49 overs (P Shiva 100*, YS Varun 49*) drew with **Puducherry** 200 in 127.3 overs (Neyan Kangayan 51, Akash Pugazhanthi 51; P Shiva 3-32, Nikhil S 3-51) and 65/1 in 29 overs (N Kangayan 40*). **Puducherry** took first-innings lead.

ICL Shankar Nagar Cricket Ground, Tirunelveli, October 27-29: Kerala 75 in 47.4 overs (Shoun Roger 31; B Aaditya 6-21, Manav Parakh 2-12) and 169/4 in 112 overs (Krishna Narayan 78, Sharon SS 30; M Parakh 2-26) drew with **Tamil Nadu** 243 in 107.3 overs (Vimal Khumar 89, Amith Satvik 47; Sudhi Anil 4-53, Mohammed Zouhan 3-49, Abi Biju 3-76). **Tamil Nadu** took first-innings lead.

Alur Cricket Stadium II, Bengaluru, October 27-29: Andhra 362/7 dec. in 158 overs (SK Rasheed 125*, Revanth Reddy 57; Ayush Barik 2-65, Shashi Kumar 2-86) drew with **Karnataka** 290/8 in 124 overs (Smaran R 167*, Joy Borah 36, Yashovardhan Parantap 36; M Deepak 5-37). No result.

Gymkhana Ground, Hyderabad, November 2-4: Hyderabad 187 in 138.4 overs (Aditya Mangat 48, Balaji Reddy 35, P Shiva 35; Priyal Singh 3-20, Shashi Kumar K 3-36) and 99/4 in 49 overs (Venkat Karthik 33; Priyal 2-25) drew with **Karnataka** 270/6 dec. in 92 overs (Jay Borah 106*, Anirudh Srinivas 71; Nikhil S 3-87). **Karnataka** took first-innings lead.

YS Raja Reddy ACA Cricket Stadium, Kadapa, November 2-4: Andhra 416/5 dec. in 105 overs (P Roshanpavankumar 123*, Hemanth Reddy 95) and 66 for no loss dec. in 10 overs (KS Raju 33*) drew with **Goa** 280 in 129.5 overs (Kaushal Hattangadi 108, Lakhmesh Pawane 47; Srikar 4-91, M Deepak 4-102) and 74/2 in 38 overs (Chittem Devankumar 30*). **Andhra** took first-innings lead.

Palmyra Cricket Ground, Puducherry, November 3-4: Puducherry 189 in 118.3 overs (Neyan Kangayan 90; R Rajagiri 5-78) drew with **Tamil Nadu** 198/3 in 48 overs (Vimal Khumar 83, Saffin C 55). **Tamil Nadu** took first-innings lead.

Krishnagiri Stadium, Wayanad, November 12-14: Puducherry 250 in 92.1 overs (Neyan Kangayan 122, David Nishanth 53; Abi Biju 4-34, Mohit Shibu 3-89) and 71 in 35.5 overs (A Biju 3-9, Sudhi Anil 3-28) lost to **Kerala** 446/6 dec. in 104 overs (Varun Nayanar 104*, Shoun Roger 78; D Nishanth 3-153) by an innings and 125 runs.

Margao Cricket Club, Margao, November 12-13: Karnataka 371/5 dec. in 78 overs (Smaran R 203*, Chaitanya 74; Sujay Naik 3-54, Pradnyesh Gaonkar 2-75) beat **Goa** 164 in 64.4 overs (Deep Kasvankar 70*, Kaushal Hattangadi 44; Shashi Kumar 5-46, Sanjay Krishnamurthi 3-9) and 97 in 53 overs (P Gaonkar 33; S Kumar 5-18, Priyal Singh 2-22) by an innings and 110 runs.

Mulapadu, November 12-14: Hyderabad 165 in 67.1 overs (Rishith Reddy 41, Shashank Lokesh 35; N Madhav 5-27) and 197 in 97.4 overs (P Shiva 49, Kamal Sawariya 28; G Chanti 2-30, Srikar 2-34) lost to **Andhra** 305 in 86.4 overs (KS Raju 84, SK Rasheed 44; K Sawariya 5-77, Sarthak Bhardwaj 2-45) and 58 for no loss in 11.5 overs (Revanth Reddy 29*, KS Raju 26*) by 10 wickets.

Krishnagiri Stadium, Wayanad, November 18-19: Kerala 241 in 86.2 overs (Varun Nayanar 58, Shoun Roger 30, Mohit Shibu 30; Pradnyesh Gaonkar 3-37, Kaushal Hattangadi 2-44) and 172/5 dec. in 28.3 overs (V Nayanar 64, S Roger 50; Manish Kakode 3-42) beat **Goa** 185 in 67 overs (M Kakode 49, Lakhmesh Pawane 33; M Shibu 5-61, Abi Biju 3-47) and 114 in 48 overs (A Biju 5-34, Rahaan Raheem 3-14) by 114 runs.

Mysuru, November 18-19: Puducherry 84 in 45.4 overs (Aneeshwar Gautam 5-18, Shashi Kumar 2-33) and 91 in 23 overs (Priyal Singh 5-28, Yashovardhan Parantap 2-17) lost to **Karnataka** 380/4 dec. in 77.4 overs (Smaran R 150*, Jay Borah 76; Yashwanth 2-139). by an innings and 205 runs.

Wyre Sports Park, Tiruppur, November 18-20: Andhra 139 in 57.2 overs (SK Rasheed 33; VP Diran 5-47, B Aaditya 3-33) and 167 in 80.2 overs (KS Raju 35, S Akhil 31; VP Diran 4-30, B Aaditya 4-64) lost to **Tamil Nadu** 342/5 dec. in 84 overs (Vimal Khumar 148, Manav Parakh 94; N Madhav 2-94, Srikar 2-101) by an innings and 36 runs.

Palmyra Cricket Ground, Puducherry, November 24-26: Goa 274 in 111.4 overs (Kaushal Hattangadi 114, Deep Kasvankar 61; Rohan S 3-44, David Nishanth 2-75) drew with **Puducherry** 479/6 dec. in 164.2 overs (Neyan Kangayan 302*, Shashank 50; D Kasvankar 2-76). **Puducherry** took first-innings lead.

Gymkhana Ground, Hyderabad, November 24-26: Tamil Nadu 269 in 102.4 overs (Manav Parakh 80, Sri Abisek 66; Kamal Sawariya 5-56, Rishith Reddy 3-42) and 110/9 in 55 overs (BV Kumar 57; Pranav Varma 3-37, Aryan Cariappa 2-16) drew with **Hyderabad** 215 in 114.2 overs (Aryan Krishna 44, Aman Rao 42; B Aaditya 6-59, VP Diran 2-48). **Tamil Nadu** took first-innings lead.

Alur Cricket Stadium, Bengaluru, November 24-26: Kerala 167 in 102 overs (Varun Nayanar 89*; Aneeshwar Gautam 3-38, Shashi Kumar 3-47) and 153/4 in 61 overs (Riya Basheer 43, Shoun Roger 36; S Kumar 2-36) drew with **Karnataka** 235 in 125.3 overs (Jay Borah 117, Sanjay Krishnamurthi 30; Sudhi Anil 3-49, Mohit Shibu 3-62). **Karnataka** took first-innings lead.

NFC Ground, Hyderabad, November 30-December 1: Hyderabad 466/5 dec. in 150 overs (Aman Rao 238*, P Shiva 114; Abi Biju 3-109) drew with **Kerala** 458/9 in 144 overs (Varun Nayanar 173, Shoun Roger 127; Kamal Sawariya 5-109).

Margao Cricket Club, Margao, November 30-December 1: Tamil Nadu 362/7 dec. in 73 overs (Manav Parikh 155, BV Kumar 101; Manish Kakode 3-86, Kaushal Hattangadi 2-37) and 8 for no loss in 0.2 overs beat **Goa** 157 in 69.2 overs (Veer Yadav 44, K Hattangadi 32*; B Aaditya 4-35, Mohana Kumar 2-17) and 209 in 108.2 overs (Lakhmesh Pawane 35, Akash M 30; VP Diran 5-46, B Aaditya 3-69) by ten wickets.

YS Raja Reddy ACA Cricket Stadium, Kadapa, November 30-December 1: Puducherry 89 in 40.3 overs (David Nishanth 27; Srikar 6-38, SK Rasheed 2-20) and 95 in 56.1 overs (Neyan Kangayan 47; Srikar 5-45, Hemanth Reddy 3-9) lost to **Andhra** 429/8 dec. in 120.5 overs (SK Rasheed 200*, P Roshanpavankumar 95; Yashwanth 3-81, D Nishanth 2-118) by an innings and 245 runs.

South Zone points table

Teams	M	W	L	D	T	N/R	Pts	Quotient
Tamil Nadu	6	2	0	4	0	0	26	1.571
Karnataka	6	2	0	4	0	0	22	1.449
Andhra	6	2	1	3	0	0	21	1.643
Kerala	6	2	0	4	0	0	17	1.196
Hyderabad	6	0	1	5	0	0	7	0.945
Puducherry	6	0	3	3	0	0	7	0.377
Goa	6	0	3	3	0	0	3	0.399

Tamil Nadu qualified for the quarter-finals, Karnataka qualified for the pre-quarter-finals

Pre-quarter-finals

Railway Stadium, Dhanbad, December 8-9: Nagaland 157 in 38.3 overs (Yugandhar 53, Sujal Prasad 38; Anant Bhatnagar 3-15, Kunal Tyagi 2-27) and 134 in 33.1 overs (Yash 33; Damandeep Singh 3-15, A Bhatnagar 3-25, Aaqib Khan 3-56) lost to **Uttar Pradesh** 561/9 dec. in 98.5 overs (Deepanshu Chaudhary 191, Satnam Singh 173; Khrievitso 5-68) by an innings and 270 runs.
Krishnagiri Stadium, Wayanad, December 8-11: Karnataka 174 in 71.2 overs (Aneeshwar Gautam 71, Abhay Rangan 26; Abhishek 4-54, HD Gautam 2-30) and 318 in 117 overs (Yashovardhan Parantap 86, Priyal Singh 47; HD Gautam 4-75, Abhishek 4-96) lost to **Jharkhand** 518/9 dec. in 118 overs (Rajan Deep 209, Sharandeep Singh 121; Shashi Kumar 4-129, Priyal 3-112) by an innings and 26 runs.
Krishnagiri Stadium, Wayanad, December 15-18: Madhya Pradesh 316 in 82.3 overs (Aryan Deshmukh 79, Shubham Kushwah 56; Divij Mehra 5-64, Parth Bali 2-46) and 262 in 76.3 overs (Akshat Raghuwanshi 75, Adarsh Dubey 34; P Bali 3-41, Masab Alam 3-44) beat **Delhi** 285 in 81.3 overs (P Bali 68, Naman Tiwari 48; Sushant Nagar 3-50, Aryan Pandey 3-61) and 168 in 60 overs (P Bali 42, Yash Dhull 37; Yuvraj Nema 6-25, S Nagar 3-41) by 125 runs.
YS Raja Reddy ACA Cricket Stadium, December 15-17: Maharashtra 623/4 dec. in 163 overs (KS Tambe 300*, SS Dhas 155, Varad Kulkarni 101*) beat **Meghalaya** 65 in 52 overs (Vicky Ostwal 8-12) and 84 in 31.1 overs (NN Thakur 2-11, V Ostwal 2-18) by an innings and 474 runs.

Uttar Pradesh, Maharashtra, Jharkhand and Madhya Pradesh qualified for the quarter-finals

Quarter-finals

YS Raja Reddy ACA Cricket Stadium, December 22-24: Mumbai 113 in 51 overs (Damandeep Singh 5-21, Kunal Tyagi 2-29) and 265 in 106.5 overs (Sai Chavan 126, Himanshu 65; K Tyagi 5-72, Abhishek Tomar 2-32) lost to **Uttar Pradesh** 409 in 110.4 overs (Shivam Kumar 115, Siddharth Yadav 96; Musheer Khan 5-92, Aayush Zimare 3-57) by an innings and 31 runs.

Gokulbhai Somabhai Patel Stadium, Nadiad, December 22-25: Jharkhand 226 in 84.3 overs (Kumar Kushagra 71, Sharandeep Singh 35; B Aaditya 5-65, Manav Parakh 3-67) and 176 in 63.2 overs (Rajan Deep 50, Aryan Hooda 37; M Parakh 6-57, B Aaditya 2-63) beat **Tamil Nadu** 88 in 37 overs (Abhishek 5-35, Mohit Ray 3-0) and 229 in 113.1 overs (Vimal Khumar 107, Saffin C 43; M Ray 4-75, HD Gautam 2-38) by 85 runs.

Jadavpur University Campus, Kolkata, December 29-January 1: Madhya Pradesh 422 in 142 overs (Jatin Rajput 127, Aryan Deshmukh 58; Toufik Uddin 3-51, Deopratim Halder 3-92, Siddharth Singh 3-101) and 337 in 81.2 overs (Parth Chaudhary 96, Abhishek Mavi 52; D Halder 5-37, Toufik 2-78) beat **Bengal** 127 in 30.5 overs (Toufik 35, Soumyajyoti 30; Yuvraj Nema 3-1, Masoom Kaif 3-21, Sushant Nagar 3-53) and 228 in 81.2 overs (Toufik 122, Soumyajyoti 26; Y Nema 4-28, J Rajput 3-24) by 404 runs.

YS Raja Reddy ACA Cricket Stadium, December 29-31: Haryana 198 in 71.5 overs (Piyush Dahiya 64*, Anuj Thakral 43; RM Chaudhari 5-40, Vicky Ostwal 3-42) and 359 in 130.3 overs (A Thakral 71, Mudit Pruthi 57*; RM Chaudhari 3-87, OK Patkal 3-80) beat **Maharashtra** 96 in 50.5 overs (A Thakral 6-43, Vivek Kumar 2-15) and 140 in 55.3 overs (SS Dhas 51, TJ Jadhav 37; Nishant Sindhu 4-2, P Dahiya 2-26) by 321 runs.

Uttar Pradesh, Jharkhand, Madhya Pradesh and Haryana qualified for the semi-finals

Semi-finals

Gokulbhai Somabhai Patel Stadium, Nadiad, January 5-8: Haryana 480 in 159.4 overs (Yuvraj Singh 134, Parth Vats 125; Aaqib Khan 4-127, Damandeep Singh 3-125) and 255/4 in 76 overs (Nishant Sindhu 108*, Sarvesh Rohilla 55*; Anant Bhatnagar 2-38) drew with **Uttar Pradesh** 353 in 123.4 overs (Satnam Singh 78, Siddharth Yadav 72; N Sindhu 6-73, Piyush Dahiya 2-51). **Haryana** took first-innings lead.

Shastri Medan, Anand, January 5-8: Madhya Pradesh 236 in 73 overs (Akshat Raghuwanshi 70, Aryan Deshmukh 70; Mohit Ray 3-58, HD Gautam 3-82) and 363 in 75.1 overs (A Raghuwanshi 138, A Deshmukh 82; HD Gautam 4-116) drew with **Jharkhand** 383 in 142.4 overs (Himanshu 148, Kumar Kushagra 103; Yuvraj Nema 4-132, Masoom Kaif 3-74) and 196/3 in 79 overs (Rajan Deep 113*, Aryan Hooda 29). **Jharkhand** took first-innings lead.

Haryana and Jharkhand qualified for final

Final

Devineni Venkata Ramana Praneetha Ground, Mulapadu, January 12-15: Haryana 247 in 101.2 overs (Ahaan Poddar 57, Sarvesh Rohilla 40; Abhishek 6-48, Rajan Deep 2-27) and 502/9 dec. in 163.1 overs (Yuvraj Singh 93, Parth Vats 70; Shikhar Mohan 2-10, R Deep 2-76) drew with **Jharkhand** 186 in 66.1 overs (Aryan Hooda 83, Rishu 43*; Anuj Thakral 5-53, Vivek Kumar 5-59) and 93/3 in 20 overs (R Deep 44, Kumar Kushagra 26*; A Thakral 2-33). **Haryana** took first-innings lead.

Winners: Haryana

2017-18

North Zone

PCPA Stadium, Santoshgarh, December 1-3: Delhi 503/5 dec in 135.2 overs (Sumit Chhikara 261, Mayank Gusain 168; Rahul Kumar 3-111) drew with **Himachal Pradesh** 262 in 100.5 overs (Amanpreet Singh 109, Vaibhav Kalta 91; Shaurya Malik 4-37, Kamal Bairwa 4-93) and 63/1 in 19 overs (f/o) (Atul Jaswal 24*, Amanpreet 22*). Delhi took first-innings lead.

Gandhi Ground, Amritsar, December 1-3: Punjab 546/4 dec in 113 overs (Aditya Singh 237, Ridham Satyawan 148) beat **Jammu & Kashmir** 39 in 23 overs (Karanpreet Singh 6-15, Anurag Watts 2-1) and 92 in 35.3 overs (f/o) (Musaif Ajaz 42; A Watts 7-32, Anshul Negi 2-7) by an innings and 415 runs.

Patchy Greens, Teri, December 6-8: Himachal Pradesh 208 in 101.4 overs (Vaibhav Kalta 82, Atul Jaswal 72; Nishant Sindhu 5-52, Rudraksh Kaushik 2-28) and 199/4 in 69 overs (Amanpreet Singh 100*, V Kalta 60; Farid Khan 2-43, Harshvardhan Singh 2-44) drew with **Haryana** 356/9 dec in 107 overs (Sagar Dahiya 177, Harshit Tushir 54; Himanshu Beck 3-86, Rohan Kumar 3-101). Haryana took first-innings lead.

Airforce Complex Ground, Palam, New Delhi, December 6-8: Jammu & Kashmir 160 in 72.2 overs (Yuvraj Saini 40, Dhruv Gupta 34; Raghuv Nagpal 4-43, Kamal Bairwa 3-31) and 125 in 44.5 overs (Mohammad Manzir 55, Vinayak Gupta 31*; K Bairwa 4-9, R Nagpal 3-85) lost to **Delhi** 468/4 dec in 81 overs (Mayank Gusain 144*, Sumit Chhikara 113; Mohammad Yawar 2-60) by an innings and 183 runs.

Teri, December 11-13: Jammu & Kashmir 72 in 47.2 overs (Mohammad Manzir 24; Rudraksh Kaushik 2-2, Harshvardhan Singh 2-12) and 55 in 29.2 overs (Musaif Ajaz 34; Bhuwan Rohilla 4-15, Harshvardhan 3-18) lost to **Haryana** 403/1 dec in 78 overs (Sagar Dahiya 218*, Annam Rao 111*) by an innings and 276 runs.

Feroz Shah Kotla Stadium, New Delhi, December 11-13: Punjab 499/8 dec in 150 overs (Jaskaranvir Paul 175, Gagan Verma 152*; Shaurya Malik 3-106, Gourav Rana 2-44) drew with **Delhi** 315/8 in 120 overs (Yash Dhull 183*, Mayank Gusain 36; Karanpreet Singh 6-126). No result.

IS Bindra Cricket Stadium, PCA, Mohali, December 16-18: Punjab 320 in 131.4 overs (Yuvraj Choudhary 122, Harnoor Pannu 76; Akashdeep Bhakar 3-53, Farid Khan 3-65) drew with **Haryana** 348/8 in 140 overs (Sagar Dahiya 106, Harshvardhan Singh 70*; Anurag Watts 4-128, Karanpreet Singh 2-65) Haryana took first-innings lead.

HPCA Stadium, Dharamsala, December 16-18: Hiimachal Pradesh 330 in 97.4 overs (Abhishek Thakur 76*, Arshad Dhiman 58; Dhruv Gupta 3-50, Nityam Abrol 2-46) beat **Jammu & Kashmir** 109 in 55.3 overs (Suhaib Majeeb 31*, Musaif Ajaz 24; Himanshu Beck 3-21, Rishi Mahajan 2-8) and 208 in 103.5 overs (f/o) (M Ajaz 79, Mohammad Manzir 40; Sahil Kumar 4-59, Rahul Kumar 2-31) by an innings and 13 runs.

HPCA Stadium, Dharamsala, December 21-23: Punjab 407/8 dec in 111.5 overs (Jaskaranvir Singh 130, Yuvraj Choudhary 63; Himanshu Beck 5-115, Rishi Mahajan 2-73) beat **Himachal Pradesh** 140 in 56.1overs (R Mahajan 60; Karanpreet Singh 4-59, Anurag Watts 3-35, Ayush Goyal 3-38) and 121 in 44 overs (f/o) (Rahul Kumar 41, Arshad Dhiman 30; A Watts 4-25, Karanpreet 3-45) by an innings and 146 runs.

Chaudhry Bansi Lal Cricket Stadium, Lahli, December 21-23: Haryana 333 in 133.2 overs (Nishant Sindhu 122, Harshvardhan Singh 43; Shaurya Malik 3-70, Aayush Singh 2-52) drew with **Delhi** 162 in 95.3 overs (Sumit Chhikara 68, Gourav Rana 38; Bhuwan Rohilla 3-38, Akashdeep Bhakar 2-26) and 133/5 in 41 overs (f/o) (Mayank Gusain 51*, S Chhikara 44; N Sindhu 2-16, A Bhakar 2-21). Haryana took first-innings lead.

North Zone points table

Teams	M	W	L	D	T	N/R	Pts.	NRR
Punjab	4	2	0	2	0	0	16	+0.979
Haryana	4	1	0	3	0	0	16	+0.913
Delhi	4	1	0	3	0	0	12	+0.572
Himachal Pradesh	4	1	1	2	0	0	9	-0.374
Jammu & Kashmir	4	0	4	0	0	0	0	-2.637

Punjab and Haryana qualified for the knock-outs

Central Zone

Sector 10 Ground, Bhilai, December 1-3: Chhattisgarh 340 in 113.2 overs (Mayank Yadav 112, Kivnoor Singh 75*; Minar Sahare 3-76, Rahul Dongarwar 2-71) drew with **Vidarbha** 186 in 88.4 overs (Shivam Deshmukh 70, Harsh Dubey 41*; Sajal Chandrakar 5-31, Gurpreet Bagga 3-41) and 105/3 in 61 overs (f/o) (Satyam Bhoyar 30*, SR 23; Shubham Shukla 2-29). Chhattisgarh took first-innings lead.

MPCA Cricket Ground, Sagar, December 1-3: Uttar Pradesh 377 in 89.4 overs (Ansh Yadav 157, Ashish Chaudhary 73; Priyanshu Shukla 3-28, Akash Panika 3-68, Tripuresh Singh 3-73) and 216/4 in 50 oves (Sameer Rizvi 112*, Abhishek Kaushal 32) drew with **Madhya Pradesh** 317 in 117.2 overs (Sumit Kushwah 71, Vaidansh Vysa 69; Suryakant 6-83). Uttar Pradesh took first-innings lead.

Kamla Club Ground, Kanpur, December 7-9: Uttar Pradesh 401 in 97.3 overs (Sameer Rizvi 108, Aanjaneya Suryavanshi 67; Hemant Joshi 3-92, Chakravati Charan 2-57) and 55/0 in 11 oves (A Suryavanshi 26*, Abhishek Kaushal 25*) drew with **Rajasthan** 393 in 147.4 overs (Sachin Kakodia 154, Dharamveer Saini 72; Suryakant 6-126, Abhishek Tomar 2-78). Uttar Pradesh took first-innings lead.

MPCA Cricket Ground, Sagar, December 7-9: Vidarbha 127 in 63.4 overs (Yasharth Singh 38, Shivam Deshmukh 27; Tripuresh Singh 6-30) and 161 in 60.2 overs (Kenny Batra 36, Harsh Dubey 33; Tripuresh 4-38, Akash Panika 3-41) lost to **Madhya Pradesh** 269 in 75.1 overs (Akshat Raghuwanshi 73, Nihar Bhatt 55; Parth Doshi 3-32, H Dubey 3-70) and 20/0 in 4.4 overs by ten wickets.

Madan Mohan Malviya Stadium, Allahabad, December 13-15: Uttar Pradesh 417/8 dec in 124.3 overs (Aanjaneya Suryavanshi 117, Sameer Rizvi 80; Deepak Yadav 2-49, Gurpreet Bagga 2-79) drew with **Chhattisgarh** 230 in 115.3 overs (Ayush Pandey 86, Deepak 64; Suryakant 6-89, Abhishek Tomar 2-60) and 73/0 in 19 overs (f/o) (A Pandey 53*). Uttar Pradesh took first-innings lead.

SMS Stadium, Jaipur, December 13-15: Rajasthan 422/9 dec in 155.4 overs (Sachin Kakodia 126, Hemant Joshi 124; Shivang Kumar 3-58, Jatin Rajput 2-58) drew with **Madhya Pradesh** 284/9 in 118 overs (Vaidnash Vysa 92*, Shivang 47; Akash Singh 4-96, Chakravati Charan 3-65) No result.

Sector 10 Ground, Bhilai, December 19-21: Chhattigarh 101 in 32.3 overs (Akash Panika 3-19, Priyanshu Shukla 3-24, Tripuresh Singh 3-42) and 160 in 55 overs (Gurpreet Bagga 50, Anurag Mishra 31; Shivang Kumar 3-13, A Panika 2-21) drew with **Madhya Pradesh** 428/6 dec in 117overs (Shivang 174, Vaidansh Vysa 101*; Gaurav Chaturvedi 2-104, Sajal Chandrakar 2-115). Madhya Pradesh took first-innings lead.

VCA Ground, Nagpur, December 19-21: Vidarbha 215 in 77.1 overs (Harsh Dubey 59, Saurav Harmikar 42; Preetam Sheoran 3-24, AA Ahuja 3-70) and 183 in 69 overs (H Dubey 45, Satyam Bhoyar 35; Sheoran 5-64, Akash Singh 2-24) beat**Rajasthan**172 in 60.3overs

(Devprakash Firoda 39, Akash 35*; Ganesh Bhosle 4-49, H Dubey 4-60) and 136 in 58.1 overs (Karan Lamba 36, Rahul Garg 32; H Dubey 6-54, Minar Sahare 2-11) by 90 runs.

KL Saini Stadium, Jaipur, December 25-27: Rajasthan 352 in 136.5 overs (Hemant Joshi 100, Dharamveer Saini 98; Shubham Shukla 4-86, Devraj Sahu 3-51) drew with **Chhattisgarh** 279 in 121 overs (Vijay Yadav 85*, Kivnoor Singh 50; Akash Singh 4-52, Chakravati Charan 3-44, Preetam Sheoran 3-58). Rajasthan took first-innings lead.

VCA Ground, Nagpur, December 25-27: Vidarbha 122 in 55.3 overs (Harsh Dubey 84; Suryakant 5-28, Divyansh Joshi 3-3) and 116 in 50.5 overs (Ashutosh Ikhe 56, Saurav Harmikar 23; Abhishek Tomar 5-20, Damandeep Singh 3-27) lost to**Uttar Pradesh** 297 in 105.2 overs (Sameer Rizvi 99, Aanjaneya Suryavanshi 60; Ganesh Bhosle 6-95, H Dubey 4-103) by an innings and 59 runs.

Central Zone points table

Teams	M	W	L	D	T	N/R	Pts.	NRR
Madhya Pradesh	4	2	0	2	0	0	16	-0.036
Uttar Pradesh	4	1	0	3	0	0	16	+1.215
Vidarbha	4	1	2	1	0	0	7	-0.649
Chhattisgarh	4	0	1	3	0	0	5	-0.226
Rajasthan	4	0	1	3	0	0	5	-0.231

Madhya Pradesh and Uttar Pradesh qualified for the knock-outs

West Zone

GSFC Cricket ground, Baroda, December 1-3: Mumbai 515/2 dec in 120.3 overs (Pragnesh Kanpillewar 214*, Yashasvi Jaiswal 125*) drew with **Baroda** 437/8 in 149 overs (Ansh Patel 171, Lakshyajeetsinh Padhiar 100; Y Jaiswal 3-122, Musheer Khan 2-103). No result.

SCA Stadium, Rajkot, December 1-3: Saurashtra 198 in 128.4 overs (Prasham Rajdev 92, Aryan Malik 39; Kushan Patel 5-29, Shervil Rathod 2-29) and 116/4 in 52.2 overs (Harshvardhan Rana 46, Pruthvi Chauhan 40; S Rathod 2-28) drew with **Gujarat** 276/4 dec in 96 overs (Purav Patel 162*, Aryadevsinh Vaghela 27). Gujarat took first-innings lead.

SCA Stadium Khanderi -B Ground, Rajkot, December 7-9: Saurashtra 223 in 91.4 overs (Hetvik Kotak 47, Prasham Rajdev 43; Archan Kothari 5-50, Abhay Kurmi 2-18) and 165 in 71.3 overs (Pruthvi Chauhan 70, Adityasinh Jadeja 22*; Harsh Prajapati 4-38, Ansh Patel 3-29, A Kothari 3-51) lost to **Baroda** 325 in 80.3 overs (Lakshyajeetsinh Padhiar 93, Harsh Desai 91; Smit Desai 5-81, Aryan Malik 2-54) and 67/1 in 7.2 overs (L Padhiar 32, Parikshit Patidar 29*) by nine wickets.

Sachin Tendulkar Gymkhana, Kandivili, Mumbai, December 7-9: Maharashtra 255 in 100 overs (Shreyas Walekar 73, Prathamesh Bajari 71; Suryansh Shedge 5-43, Aman Manihar 2-59) drew with **Mumbai** 218/7 in 77 overs (Musheer Khan 54, S Shedge 43; Ismail Tambe 2-35). No result.

Sardar Patel Stadium, Valsad, December 13-15: Mumbai 352 in 105.1 overs (Sheesh Shetty 85, Musheer Khan 55; Chinmay Patel 4-84, Chandram Patel 2-46) and 33/0 in 8 overs (Pragnesh Kanipillewar 20*) drew with **Gujarat** 287 in 139 overs (Smit Patel 75, Aryadevsinh Vaghela 65; Yashasvi Jaiswal 4-91, Khan 2-44). Mumbai took first-innings lead.

Deccan Gymkhana Cricket Ground, Pune, December 13-15: Maharashtra 478 in 136 overs (Aniket Nalavade 128, Shreyas Walekar 88; Harsh Prajapati 5-87, Abhay Kurmi 2-83) drew with **Baroda** 355 in 121.4overs (Parikshit Patidar 99, Harsh Desai 80; Rajvardhan Hangargekar 5-62, Vicky Ostwal 4-66). Maharashtra took first-innings lead.

Deccan Gymkhana Cricket Ground, Pune, December 19-21: Maharashtra 467/5 dec. in 111.3 overs (Harshal Kate 205*, Atharva Dharmadhikari 94; Pruthvi Chauhan 4-71) drew with **Saurashtra** 213 in 66.5 overs (P Chauhan 101, Neel Pandya 22; Vicky Ostwal 4-70, Rajvardhan Hangargekar 3-20) and 305/9 in 89 overs (f/o) (Bhagyarajsinh Chudasama 73, D Adarsh 68; V Ostwal 3-74, Aviraj Gawade 3-80). Maharashtra took first-innings lead.

GSFC Cricket ground, Vadodara, December 19-21: Baroda 189 in 84.5 overs (Ansh Patel 64, Archan Kothari 48; Jaimeet Patel 5-41, Chinmay Patel 3-50) and 202 in 93.3 overs (Ansh 66, Lakshyajeetsinh Padhiar 40; Kushan Patel 4-54, Jaimeet 2-20) drew with **Gujarat** 223 in 82.2 overs (Purav Patel 105, Jeet Upadhyay 29; Ansh 4-50, Parikshit Patidar 3-28) and 29/0 in 4 overs (Purav 28*). Gujarat took first-innings lead.

Lalbhai Contractor Stadium, Surat, December 25-27: Gujarat 276 in 135.2 overs (Jaimeet Patel 63, Purav Patel 45; Vicky Ostwal 3-51, Aviraj Gawade 3-56) drew with **Maharashtra** 330/4 in 124 overs (Harshal Kate 162, Atharva Dharmadhikari 132; Saral Prajapati 3-127). Maharashtra took first-innings lead.

Sachin Tendulkar Gymkhana, Kandivili, Mumbai, December 25-27: Saurashtra 340 in 126.4 overs (Bhagyarajsinh Chudasama 179, Prasham Rajdev 44; Musheer Khan 5-79, Ajit Yadav 3-46) and 125/8 dec in 52.4 overs (B Chudasama 51, Hetvik Kotak 26; Khan 5-55, Ajit 3-15) drew with **Mumbai** 238 in 81.4 overs (Pragnesh Kanpillewar 44, Akshat Jain 40; Aditya Rathore 4-61, Smit Desai 3-58) and 30/4 in 9 overs (P Kanpillewar 23; Harshvardhan Rana 2-6). Saurashtra took first-innings lead.

West Zone points table

Teams	M	W	L	D	T	N/R	Pts.	NRR
Maharashtra	4	0	0	4	0	0	10	+0.454
Baroda	4	1	0	3	0	0	9	-0.293
Gujarat	4	0	0	4	0	0	8	+0.008
Mumbai	4	0	0	4	0	0	6	+0.908
Saurashtra	4	0	1	3	0	0	5	-1.154

Maharashtra and Baroda qualified for the knock-outs

South Zone

Gymkhana Ground, Hyderabad, December 1-3: Hyderabad 266 in 87.5 overs (Ilyaan Sathani 56, T Rohan 51; Abi Biju 3-54, M Kiran Sagar 3-54) and 160/3 dec in 56 oves (YS Varun 64, P Shiva 54*; A Biju 2-45) drew with **Kerala** 151 in 58.3 overs (Albin Binu 46, Omar Aboobacker 40; Rohan 5-39, Trishank Gupta 2-31) and 190/6 in 72 overs (A Binu 62, Rohan Nair 52*; D Sai Sragvi 2-25, Sai Purnanda Rao 2-41). Hyderabad took first-innings lead.

NFC Ground, Hyderabad, December 1-3: Andhra 509/4 dec in 127 overs (Nithish Reddy 301*, Dharani Kumar 101*) drew with **Tamil Nadu** 388/9 in 153 overs (Lakshay Jain 97, Manav Parakh 55; Y Vasu 3-109). No result.

ECIL Ground, Hyderabad, December 1-3: Goa 217 in 124 overs (Om Madgaonkar 38, Ayush Verlekar 38; Kushal Gowda 3-66, Paras Arya 2-14) and 131/3 in 68 oves (A Verlekar 35*, Kaushal Hattangadi 34) drew with **Karnataka** 348/3 dec in 80.5 overs (BN Yashwant 175, Amod Kaluve 128; Shadab Khan 2-77). Karnataka took first-innings lead.

NFC Ground, Hyderabad, December 5-7: Tamil Nadu 409 in 131.2 overs (Mohana Kumar 113, Lakshay Jain 110; Nirmal Jaimon 2-65) drew with **Kerala** 254 in 91.3 overs (Omar Aboobacker 77, TK Akshay 59; Nirmal Kumar 4-52, Adithya Geethan 3-43) and 109/3 in 36 overs (f/o) (Albin Binu 56*, Akshay 26). Tamil Nadu took first-innings lead.

Gymkhana Ground, Hyderabad, December 5-7: Goa 242 in 103.1 overs (Kaushal Hattangadi 89, Shubham Gajinkar 43; Sai Purnanand Rao 2-36, Ilyaan Sathani 2-45) and 120 in 55.4 overs (Sagar Vantamuri 26, Om Madgaonkar 20; T Rohan 5-22, Trishank Gupta 5-33)lost to **Hyderabad** 419/9 dec in 95.3 overs (YS Varun 157, P Shiva 133; Rohan Bogati 2-66, Shadab Khan 2-109) by an innings and 57 runs.

ECIL Ground, Hyderabad, December 5-7: Andhra 444 in 131.1 overs (Nithish Reddy 190, P Subramanyam 87; Paras Arya 5-78, NA Chinmay 4-94) drew with **Karnataka** 139 in 65.1 overs (Amod Kaluve 48, Y Vasu 5-33, Akshay Papasani 2-18) and 165/8 in 74.5 overs (f/o) (Chinmay 33, Akshan Rao 32; N Reddy 2-24, A Papasani 2-36). Andhra took first-innings lead.

NFC Ground, Hyderabad, December 10-12: Kerala138 in 67.5 overs (PS Rehan Sai 30, Omar Aboobacker 29; Y Vasu 5-59, Asif Hussain 3-11) and 135 in 51.4 overs (TK Akshay 55, VS Sreenath 22; Vasu 7-71)lost to **Andhra** 353/9 dec in 85 overs (Nithish Reddy 69, Dharani Kumar 66; Rehan Sai 3-50, Sreenath 3-95, M Kiran Sagar 3-108) by an innings and 57 runs.

ECIL Ground, Hyderabad, December 10-12: Hyderabad 257 in 101.3 overs (Ilyaan Sathani 103, Anirudh Raj 26; Kushal Gowda 4-74, Shashi Kumar 2-33) and 180/5 in 67 overs (YS Varun 57, Sai Purnanand Rao 30; Shashi 2-36) drew with **Karnataka** 357 in 90.2 overs (Akshan Rao 103, R Smaran 76; D Sai Sragvi 3-83, T Rohan 2-48). Karnataka took first-innings lead.

Gymkhana Ground, Hyderabad, December 10-12: Goa 266 in 113.3 overs (Shubham Gajinkar 93, Udit Yadav 35; Prashid Akash 3-44, Adhithya Muralidharan 2-51) and 117/4 in 22 overs (Anand Tendulkar 73*, Udit 29*; A Ranjan 3-61) drew with **Tamil Nadu** 353/7 dec in 122overs (Sai Sudharsan 102, Mohana Kumar 100*; Udit 2-92). Tamil Nadu took first-innings lead.

ECIL Ground, Hyderabad, December 14-16: Andhra 460 in 154.1 overs (P Subramanyam 124, Nithish Reddy 94; Sai Puranand Rao 4-87) drew with **Hyderabad** 304/5 in 118overs (Thakur Tilak Verma 166*, Sai Rao 52; Y Vasu 2-103). No result.

NFC Ground, Hyderabad, December 14-16: Karnataka 304 in 92.5 overs (Akshan Rao 114, NA Chinmay 78*; Manav Parakh 2-27, S Aditya Geethan 2-49) and 79/3 in 45 overs (Amod Kaluve 32) drew with **Tamil Nadu** 256 in 114.4 overs (M Parakh 66, Adhithya Muralidharan 51; Chinmay 4-49, Paras Arya 4-67). Karnataka took first-innings lead.

Gymkhana Ground, Hyderabad, December 14-16: Kerala 446/8 dec in 119 overs (Albin Binu 122, Varun Nayanar 88; Shadab Khan 3-158) beat **Goa** 130 in 51.4 overs (Shubham Gajinkar 55, Sanket Palkar 20; CN Jaseer 5-45, Srivardhan Murali 2-16) and 178 in 88.2 overs (f/o) (Kaushal Hattangadi 69, S Palkar 63; Jaseer 4-44, TK Akshay 3-15, Akhin 3-39) by an innings and 139 runs.

NFC Ground, Hyderabad, December 19-21: Andhra 340 in 96.1 overs (Nithish Reddy 134, Asif Hussain 38; Udit Yadav 4-40, Manish Kakode 4-109) beat **Goa** 110 in 48.2 overs (Anand Tendulkar 32; N Reddy 7-40, Asif 2-7) and 135 in 62.3 overs (f/o) (A Tendulkar 63, Kaushal Hattangadi 26; Y Vasu 5-40, N Reddy 2-13) by an innings and 95 runs.

ECIL Ground, Hyderabad, December 19-21: Kerala 146 in 60.2 overs (TK Akshay 56, Omar Abubacker 23; NA Chinmay 3-18, Kushal Gowda 2-34) and 198 in 59.5 overs (Aryan Kathuria 74, Rohan Nair 58; Paras Arya 5-64, Chinmay 2-44) lost to **Karnataka** 350 in 98.2overs (R Smaran 100, Chinmay 77; Srivardhan Murali 3-61, Abi Biju 2-90) by an innings and six runs.

Gymkhana Ground, Hyderabad, December 19-21: Hyderabad 161 in 68.2 overs (Thakur Tilak Verma 47, YS Varun 25; Manav Parakh 4-31, Adhithya Muralidharan 3-22) and 171 in 52 overs (Varun 62, P Shiva 55; M Parakh 5-47, A Muralidharan 2-52) lost to **Tamil Nadu** 186 in 79 overs (B Sai Sudharsan 75*, M Parakh 33; T Rohan 3-50, Anirudh Raj 2-27) and 147/4 in 50.3 overs (B Sudharsan 68*, M Parakh 25) by six wickets.

South Zone points table

Teams	M	W	L	D	T	N/R	Pts.	NRR
Andhra	5	2	0	3	0	0	19	+1.188
Karnataka	5	1	0	4	0	0	17	+0.665
Tamil Nadu	5	1	0	4	0	0	14	-0.366
Hyderabad	5	1	1	3	0	0	12	+0.175
Kerala	5	1	2	2	0	0	9	-0.217
Goa	5	0	3	2	0	0	2	-1.481

Andhra and Karnataka qualified for the knock-outs

East Zone

Maharaja Bir Bikram College Stadium, Agartala, December 1-3: Jharkhand 98 in 60.3 overs (Aryan Hooda 38, Kumar Kushagra 27; Amit Ali 6-26, Parvez Sultan 3-16) and 296/3 dec in 82 overs (Ankit 108*, A Hooda 95) beat **Tripura** 141 in 57 overs (Sridam Paul 33, Hrituraj Roy 22; Sahil Raj 4-22, Manishi 3-26) and 54 in 28.3 overs (Manishi 5-6, Amit Kumar 5-23) by 199 runs.

Satindra Mohan Dev Stadium, Silchar, December 1-3: Bengal 293 in 113.3 overs (Anuj Singh 64, Sahitya Hazra 64; Denish Das 3-55, Dasarath Kumar 3-66) beat **Assam** 87 in 50.3 overs (Nibir Deka 26; Diganta Das 4-14, S Hazra 3-18) and 183 in 80 overs (f/o) (N Deka 90, Nihar Narah 25; Toufik Uddin 5-47, Amanjyot 2-31) by an innings and 23 runs.

Keenan Stadium, Jamshedpur, December 7-9: Jharkhand 177 in 74.3 overs (Sahil Raj 53, Parmit Singh 39; Bikash Naik 5-35, Sushil Barik 2-39) and 162/4 dec in 41 overs (Kumar Kushagra 71*, Aryan Hooda 69; Subham Shree 2-39) beat **Odisha** 101 in 45.5 overs (S Barik 30, Anwesh Tripathy 21; Manishi 6-15, Mohit Ray 2-33) and 126 in 59 overs (S Barik 44, Biswajit Patra 31; Manishi 6-22) by 112 runs

Shahid Kajal Smriti Cricket Ground , Melaghar, December 7-9: Assam 198 in 94.2 overs (Denish Das 42, Nihar Narah 36; Rajib Hossain 3-18, Amit Ali 3-58) and 40/1 in 15 overs (N Narah 25) drew with **Tripura** 56 in 35.4 overs (Kokil Gogoi 3-18, Dasarath Kumar 3-27). Assam took first-innings lead.

Birsa Munda Cricket Stadium, Chaibasa, December 13-15: Jharkhand 269 in 87.4 overs (Ankit 161, Sahil Raj 51; Kokil Gogoi 5-49, Dasarath Kumar 3-55) beat **Assam** 106 in 48.4 overs (Rohan Hazarika 34, Nibir Deka 21; Manishi 5-24, Amit Kumar 2-13) and 63 in 27.3 overs (f/o) (Rituraj Biswas 20; Amit 4-28, A Lala 3-15) by an innings and 100 runs

B.O.S.E. GROUND, Cuttack, December 13-15: Bengal 263 in 94.5 overs (Toufik Uddin 95, Trishul 34*; Sushil Barik 3-59, Suraj Behera 2-55) and 153/6 in 61 overs (Sahitya Hazra 58, T Uddin 30; S Barik 3-21) drew with **Odisha** 264 in 97.3 overs (Binayak Mohanty 94, Sambit Baral 42; Diganta Das 4-50, S Hazra 3-43). Odisha took first-innings lead.

Bengal Cricket Academy Ground, Kalyani, December 19-21: Bengal 143 in 79 overs (Abishek Porel 28, Iman Chaudhuri 28; Sahil Raj 5-62, A Lala 3-36) drew with **Jharkhand** 205 in 87.3 overs (Ram Sharan 44, Satya Setu 40; Trishul 3-45, Amanjyot 2-22). Jharkhand took first-innings lead.

Nimpur Ground, Cuttack, December 19-21: Tripura 347 in 105.1 overs (Sridam Paul 172, Tanmoy Das 68; Sushil Barik 4-82, Bikash Naik 2-69) and 110/2 in 40 overs (Hrituraj Roy 38, Parvez Sultan 26; Sambit Baral 2-31) drew with **Odisha** 277 in 105.4 overs (S Barik 49, Binayak Mohanty 49; Parvez Sultan 5-75, Amit Ali 4-78). Tripura took first-innings lead.

Nurul Amin Stadium, Nagaon, December 25-27: Assam 74 in 38 overs (Shivam Mittal 21; Bikash Naik 4-12, Suraj Behera 3-19) and 252 in 98 overs (Denish Das 50, S Mittal 42; B Naik 5-88, Sushil Barik 4-64) beat **Odisha** 119 in 50.4 overs (Binayak Mohanty 34, Surya Mohapatra 26; Reshabh Dipok 4-44, Rituraj Biswas 3-16) and 193 in 75.4 overs (S Mohapatra 104, Sidhartha Nayak 30; D Das 6-38) by 14 runs.

Bengal Cricket Academy Ground, Kalyani, December 25-27: Tripura 299 in 100.1 overs (Rajib Hossain 71, Amit Ali 55; Trishul 6-73, Toufik Uddin 2-40) beat **Bengal** 91 in 46.4 overs (Iman Chaudhuri 30, T Uddin 25; Parvez Sultan 5-24, Rahul Murasing 3-30) and 207 in 92.2 overs (f/o) (T Uddin 72, Anuj Singh 41; Rahul Ghosh 3-31, Sahil Sultan 3-42, P Sultan 3-44) by an innings and one run.

East Zone points table

Teams	M	W	L	D	T	N/R	Pts.	NRR
Jharkhand	4	3	0	1	0	0	22	+0.662
Tripura	4	1	1	2	0	0	11	+0.317
Bengal	4	1	1	2	0	0	9	-0.137
Assam	4	1	2	1	0	0	9	-0.342
Odisha	4	0	2	2	0	0	4	-0.297

Jharkhand and Tripura qualified for the knock-outs

Associated Zone

MCA Cricket Ground, Polo Ground, Shillong, December 1-3: Sikkim 114 in 50 overs (Adarsh Kumar 23; Gavineal Marpna 4-26, Waldo 3-12) and 141 in 64.5 overs (Dhiraj Mahato 30; G Marpna 4-32, Kirtirajsinh Raulji 3-13) lost to **Meghalaya** 263 in 85.5 overs (Kush Agarwal 79, K Raulji 63*; Ingsho Limboo 4-55, Zakir 2-31) by an innings and eight runs.

Nagaland Cricket Stadium, Sovima, December 1-3: Nagaland 130 in 60.2 overs (Yugandhar 35, Sunjib 22; John Hmar 4-24, Jotin Pheiroijam 3-20) and 210 in 74 overs (Yugandhar 88, Tohuka 43; Ansh 4-36, Lishan 2-13) beat **Manipur** 126 in 59.4 overs (Ansh 41, Ulenyai Khwairakpam 32; Tohuka 5-27, Ranjen 5-40) and 119 in 53.3 overs (Ansh 53*, Daniel 4-29, Tohuka 3-27) by 95 runs.

Energy Stadium Rajbansinagar, Patna, December 1-3: Arunachal Pradesh 83 in 31 overs (Latyir Damin 34; Reshu Raj 7-14) and 54 in 33.5 overs (L Damin 31; R Raj 6-23, Suraj 3-11) lost to **Bihar** 1007/7 dec in 159.1 overs (Binny 358, Prakash 220, Arnav Kishor 161; A Sharma 4-276, Vijay 2-93) by an innings and 870 runs.

MCA Cricket Ground, Polo Ground, Shillong, December 7-9: Meghalaya 504/8 dec in 116 overs (Rushikesh Jadhav 107, Diskshit Parmar 106; Milon Dey 6-173) beat **Arunachal Pradesh** 116 in 69.3 overs (Sushovan Mazumder 36, Manoj Singh 23; R Jadhav 5-43, Gavineal Marpa 2-32) and 132 in 56.2 overs (f/o) (A Sharma 79*; Sudhir Sahani 3-8, R Jadhav 3-40) by an innings and 256 runs.

Nagaland Cricket Stadium, Sovima, December 7-9: Sikkim 170 in 60.5 overs (Robin Limboo 41*, Karan Gupta 38; Tohuka 5-50, Daniel 2-16) and 88 in 29.4 overs (Zakir 31; Tohuka 6-40, Ranjen 3-33) lost to **Nagaland** 440 in 103.3 overs (Tohuka 151, Arjun 106; Tarun Sharma 5-126, Adarsh Kumar 2-29) by an innings and 182 runs.

Energy Stadium Rajbansinagar, Patna, December 7-9: Bihar 473/8 dec in 123 overs (Adarsh 137*, Arnav Kishor 109; Jotin Pheiroijam 4-92, Utkarsh 3-147) beat **Manipur** 105 in 57.5 overs (Bablu 35, Ulenyai Khwairakpam 22; Aditya 5-15, Reshu Raj 3-55) and 98 in 34 overs (f/o) (Utkarsh 25, Ansh 22; A Kishor 4-17, Saurabh 3-32) by an innings and 270 runs.

MCA Cricket Ground, Polo Ground, Shillong, December 12-14: Manipur 119 in 72.4 overs (Ansh 20; Gavineal Marpna 4-14, Swastic 3-20) and 149 in 48.1 overs (Bablu 50, Raghav 23; Rushikesh Jadhav 4-32, Sudhir Sahani 4-41) beat **Meghalaya** 167 in 88 overs (Kush Agarwal 41, Mrinal Das 35; Jotin Pheiroijam 4-34, Utkarsh 3-35) and 74 in 50.5 overs (Dikshit Parmar 27, R Jadhav 27; Utkarsh 5-25, J Pheiroijam 3-18) by 27 runs.

Luwangpokpa Cricket Stadium, Imphal, December 13-15: Arunachal Pradesh v Sikkim. Match abandoned.

Nagaland Cricket Stadium, Sovima, December 13-15: Bihar 469/8 dec in 118 overs (Arnav Kishor 181, Binny 150; Odilemba 4-89, Ranjen 2-90) beat **Nagaland** 113 in 41 overs (Yugandhar 57, Cheide 20; Suraj 3-16, Aditya 3-19) and 80 in 36 overs (f/o) (Arjun 24; Reshu Raj 5-20, Aditya 4-37) by an innings and 276 runs.

MCA Cricket Ground, Polo Ground, Shillong, December 19-21: Bihar 299/9 dec in 90.5 overs (Arnav Kishor 62, Rajesh 49; Swastic 5-62, Sunvish Charak 2-48) and 199/4 dec in 50 overs (A Kishor 100*, Prakash 42; Rushikesh Jadhav 2-52) beat **Meghalaya** 75 in 38.4 overs (R Jadhav 29; Raushan 5-6, Reshu Raj 4-23) and 122 in 52.5 overs (R Jadhav 31, Mrinal Das 20; R Raj 7-24) by 301 runs.

Luwangpokpa Cricket Stadium, Imphal, December 19-21: Manipur 118 in 50.4 overs (Raghav 32, Utkarsh 24; Aman Sharma 3-12, Ingsho Limboo 2-15) and 227/7 dec in 59 overs (Bablu 86, Ulenyai Khwairakpam 49; Robin Limboo 3-24, Tarun Sharma 2-91) beat **Sikkim** 29 in 23.1 overs (Donadoni Tongbram 5-6, Dominic 2-5) and 34 in 31.5 overs (Jotin Pheiroijam 4-8, D Tongbram 3-14) by 282 runs.

Nagaland Cricket Stadium, Sovima, December 19-21: Arunachal Pradesh 119 in 53 overs (Rohan 44, Sushovn Mazumder 23; Tohuka5-49, Daniel 4-13) and 110 in 47.2 overs (Latyir Damin 30, Milon Dey 29; Ranjen 7-33) lost to **Nagaland** 197 in 51.4 overs (Tohuka 83, Yugandhar 25; Vijay 4-72, A Sharma 3-41) and 33/0 in 8.3 overs (Yugandhar 20*) by ten wickets.

Luwangpokpa Cricket Stadium, Imphal, December 25-27: Arunachal Pradesh 69 in 35.2 overs (Sushovan Mazumder 34; Utkarsh 8-14) and 73 in 45.3 overs (Milon Dey 20; Utkarsh 6-23, Ansh 2-6) lost to **Manipur** 215 in 74.2 overs (Utkarsh 81, Raghav 49; Vijay 3-29, A Sharma 3-79) by an innings and 73 runs.

Energy Stadium Rajbansinagar, Patna, December 25-27: Sikkim 44 in 24.3 overs (Reshu Raj 6-11, Arnav Kishor 2-18) and 55 in 23.2 overs (Karan Gupta 28; Saurabh 5-18, R Raj 4-19) lost to **Bihar** 510/7 dec in 122.4 overs (Binny 206, Adarsh 133, Prakash 103; Robin Limboo 3-117, Adarsh Kumar 2-74) by an innings and 411 runs.

MCA Cricket Ground, Polo Ground, Shillong, December 26-28: Meghalaya 250 in 87.1 overs (Diskshit Parmar 100, Mrinal Das 56; Daniel 2-27, Prasant 2-35) and 162/7 dec in 60 overs (D Parmar 48, Abhishek Gupta 36*; Prasant 3-45, Arjun 2-44) beat **Nagaland** 178 in 54 overs (Sunjib 46*, Prasant 46; Swastic 5-38, Sudhir Sahani 2-22) and 144 in 58.4 overs (Prasant 45, Yugandhar 27; Swastic 4-53, Kirtirajsinh Raulji 2-4) by 90 runs.

Associated Zone points table

Teams	M	W	L	D	T	N/R	Pts.	NRR
Bihar	5	5	0	0	0	0	34	+2.233
Nagaland	5	3	2	0	0	0	20	+0.293
Meghalaya	5	3	2	0	0	0	20	+0.204
Manipur	5	3	2	0	0	0	19	+0.136
Sikkim	5	0	4	0	0	1	1	-1.504
Arunachal Pradesh	5	0	4	0	0	1	1	-2.741

Bihar and Nagaland qualified for the knock-outs

Pre-quarter finals

Rajkot, January 3-5: Nagaland 56 in 23.3 overs (Arjun 29; Y Vasu 4-15, Nithish Reddy 3-24) and 67 in 35.2 overs (Tohuka 35, Arjun 20; Vasu 6-28, N Reddy 3-13) lost to **Andhra** 801/2 dec in 127 overs (N Reddy 441, B Yogananda 217, P Subramanyam 106*) by an innings and 678 runs.

Rajkot, January 3-5: Baroda 362 in 133.5 overs (Roshan 129, Archan Kothari 50; Kritik Gosain 4-113, Karanpreet Singh 3-48) and 150/7 in 59 overs (Ansh Patel 55*, VB Patel 32; Anurag Watts 2-27) drew with **Punjab** 423 in 156.1 overs (Harnoor Pannu 121, Ridham Satyawan 74; A Kothari 3-76, Harsh Prajapati 3-83, Ansh 3-129). Punjab took first-innings lead.

Railway Cricket Ground, Rajkot, January 9-11: Bihar 76 in 40 overs (Rajesh 20; Manishi 5-32, Amit Kumar 2-22) and 316 in 85.5 overs (Arnav Kishor 134, Ankush Raj 52; Manishi 8-70) lost to **Jharkhand** 609/9 dec in 168 overs (Ram Sharan 128, Ankit 126; Aditya 3-110, Suraj 3-122) by an innings and 217 runs.

GSFC Cricket ground, Vadodara, January 9-11: Maharashtra 426 in 153.1 overs (Atharva Dharmadhikari 178, Vicky Ostwal 94; NA Chinmay 6-103, Paras Arya 2-92) and 85/0 in 16 overs (Harshal Kate 68*) drew with **Karnataka** 362 in 160.1 overs (Akshan Rao 111, Chinmay 68; V Ostwal 5-63, Aviraj Gawade 2-68). Maharashtra took first-innings lead.

Andhra, Madhya Pradesh, Tripura, Punjab, Haryana, Jharkhand, Uttar Pradesh and Maharashtra qualified for the quarter-finals

Quarter-finals

Reliance Cricket Stadium, Vadodara, January 14-16: Andhra 45 in 23 overs (Tripuresh Singh 4-22, Nihar Bhatt 2-5) and 103 in 51 overs (Mahendra Reddy 23; Tripuresh 6-29, Akash Panika 4-21) lost to **Madhya Pradesh** 229 in 74.1 overs (Shivang Kumar 108, Tripuresh 88; Nithish Reddy 5-56, Akshay Papasani 2-42) by an innings and 81 runs.

GSFC Cricket ground, Vadodara, January 14-16: Tripura 197 in 70.2 overs (Sridam Paul 76, Swarab Sahani 23; Anurag Watts 4-73, Ayush Goyal 3-34) and 196 in 76.3 overs (Hrituraj Roy 53, Amit Ali 45; A Watts 6-73, Anshul Negi 2-39) lost to **Punjab** 385 in 174 overs (A Negi 87*, Aditya Singh 86; A Ali 4-107, S Sahani 2-49) and 10/0 in 0.5 overs by ten wickets

Pune, January 20-22: Haryana 120 in 59.1 overs (Piyush Dahiya 44, Naman Singh 21; Ankit Abhishek 3-25, Sahil Raj 3-50) and 338 in 104.5 overs (P Dahiya 99, Sagar Dahiya 82; Satya Setu 4-28, S Raj 3-64) beat **Jharkhand** 145 in 65.5 overs (Ankit 44, Ram Sharan 42; Bhuwan Rohilla 4-32, Nishant Sindhu 3-38) and 201 in 103.2 overs (Kumar Kushagra 43, S Setu 42; B Rohilla 5-60, Akashdeep Bhakar 3-24) by 112 runs.

Pune, January 20-22: Uttar Pradesh 585 in 163.4 overs (Ansh Yadav 269*, Pratham Mishra 114; Rajvardhan Hangargekar 5-118, Vicky Ostwal 3-99) and 353/7 dec in 76 overs (Divyansh Joshi 82, P Mishra 63*; Prathamesh Bajari 2-64, Aviraj Gawade 2-78) drew with **Maharashtra** 335 in 101 overs (Atharva Dharmadhikari 93, UZ Khan 57; Suryakant 5-116, Damandeep Singh 4-85). Uttar Pradesh took first-innings lead.

Punjab, MP, UP, Haryana qualified for the semi-finals

Semi-finals

Wankhede Stadium, Mumbai, January 26-28: Punjab 370 in 151.2 overs (Aditya Singh 62, Harnoor Pannu 56; Tripuresh Singh 3-92, Abhishek Mavi 2-32) and 67/1 in 24 overs (Aditya 34*) drew with **Madhya Pradesh** 325 in 169.4 overs (Nihar Bhatt 67, Shubham Kushwah 55; Anurag Watts 5-99, Kritik Gosain 2-48). Punjab took first-innings lead.

Sharad Pawar Cricket Academy BKC, Mumbai, January 26-28: Uttar Pradesh 170 in 60 overs (Divyansh Joshi 54, Aanjaneya Suryavanshi 51; Harshvardhan Singh 3-14, Akashdeep Bhakar 3-53, Bhuwan Rohilla 3-54) and 269 in 74.3 overs (D Joshi 94, Sumit Rathore 36; B Rohilla 4-98, A Bhakar 3-69) beat **Haryana** 163 in 58.1 overs (Piyush Dahiya 59, Ajay Nandal 37; Aaqib Khan 7-25, Suryakant Chauhan 3-57) and 145 in 56 overs (Naman Singh 51, Nishant Sindhu 25*; S Chauhan 5-46, Damandeep Singh 4-51) by 131 runs.

Punjab and Uttar Pradesh qualified for the final

Final

Wankhede Stadium, Mumbai, February 1-3: Uttar Pradesh 160 in 77.5 overs (Ansh Yadav 65, Suryakant Chauhan 30; Yuvraj Choudhary 4-40, Ayush Goyal 2-32) and 140 in 74.3 overs (Sameer Rizvi 80, Ansh 45; Anurag Watts 4-25, Jashan Pannu 3-22) lost to **Punjab** 189 in 80.3 overs (Jaskaranvir Paul 84, A Watts 30; Aaqib Khan 6-86, Divyansh Joshi 2-23) and 112/4 in 48.4overs (Yuvraj Choudhary 50*; S Chauhan 2-25) by six wickets.

Winners: Punjab

Vizzy Trophy (Inter-zonal University)

South end North's run

South Zone were unbeaten through the tournament, capping things off with an all-round show against North Zone, the defending champions, in the final. Abhirath Reddy, who led the batting charts, struck a half-century, as did K Shashank, the leading wicket-taker, who provided an early breakthrough before wrapping up the North Zone innings.

East Zone had a dismal campaign, losing all their three matches, while West Zone had just one win from three games.

North had dominated the tournament for three years until then. In **2017-18**, Shubham Dahiya's 112 had taken them to 273 in the final against West, before their bowlers hunted in a pack to bundle out the opposition for 204. Dahiya Dahiya also chipped in with the ball to be the competition's second-highest wicket-taker.

	Most runs	Most wickets
2017-18	Shubham Dahiya (North Zone) (183 runs, 2 matches)	Pranjul Puri (West Zone) (6 wickets, 2 matches)
2018-19	Abhirath Reddy (South Zone) (202 runs, 4 matches)	K Shashank (South Zone) (13 wickets, 4 matches)

2018-19

ITM University, Gwalior, March 17: North Zone 232 in 47.4 overs (YR Sharma 50, SP Kumar 29, Prerit Dutta 29; Abinash Kumar 3-31, Kartik Biswal 2-26) beat **East Zone** 187 in 46.4 overs (K Biswal 53*, Vipin Chandra 50; Shubham Dahiya 3-20, SP Kumar 3-41) by 45 runs.
Scindia School Cricket Ground, Gwalior, March 17: South Zone 266/9 in 50 overs (Abhirath Reddy 85, Venkatesh M 44; AJ Tandel 4-49, Rushikesh Jadhav 2-62) beat **West Zone** 200 in 43.4 overs (MI Sayyed 66, R Jadhav 38; K Shashank 4-24, Uav Varma 3-49) by 66 runs.
ITM University, Gwalior, March 19: West Zone 146 in 41.5 overs (Abhishek Bhandari 63, Ravi Sikarwar 24; SP Kumar 3-15, Akash Tomar 3-22) lost to **North Zone** 148/2 in 31 overs (SG Rohilla 68*, YR Sharma 37) by eight wickets.
Scindia School Cricket Ground, Gwalior, March 19: East Zone 191 in 45.1 overs (Rajesh Dhuper 90, Kartik Biswal 46; K Shashank 3-16, Uav Varma 3-34) lost to **South Zone** 192/7 in 43.5 overs (SM Rajkumar 60, Abhirath Reddy 51; Divyaprakash Singh 2-29, Vipin Chandra 2-45) by three wickets.
Scindia School Cricket Ground, Gwalior, March 21: South Zone 247 in 49.5 overs (S Aditya 8, Kishore Kamath 53; SP Kumar 3-48, Vikas Yadav 2-33) beat **North Zone** 242 in 48.4 overs (Shubham Dahiya 56, Marshal Bhagat 50; K Shashank 3-50) by five runs.
ITM University, Gwalior, March 21: West Zone 279 in 50 overs (Rudra Dhanday 98, MI Sayyed 87; Ashutosh Das 3-48, Arun Kumar Yadav 2-28) beat **East Zone** 95 in 25.4 overs (Vipin Chandra 29, Divyaprakash Singh 20; Rushikesh Jadhav 4-27, Umang Patel 3-14, Rajendra Pandey 3-49) by 184 runs.

Points table

Teams	M	W	L	T	N/R	Pts	NRR
South Zone	3	3	0	0	0	12	+0.682
North Zone	3	2	1	0	0	8	+0.881
West Zone	3	1	2	0	0	6	+0.281
East Zone	3	0	3	0	0	0	-1.734

South Zone and North Zone qualified for the final

Final

ITM University, Gwalior, March 23: South Zone 274/8 in 50 overs (Abhirath Reddy 65, Uav Varma 51; Shubham Dahiya 3-48, Vikas Yadav 2-43) beat **North Zone** 214 in 45.2 overs (YR Sharma 47, S Dahiya 45; K Shashank 3-25, Pranav Bhatia 3-32) by 64 runs.

Winners: South Zone Universities

2017-18

Semi-finals

KIIT Cricket Stadium, Bhubaneshwar, March 20: North Zone Universities 281/8 in 50 overs (Rohan Marwaha 105, Shubham Dahiya 68; Ankit 3-51, Kumar Rahul 2-42) beat **East Zone Universities** 168 in 35.2 overs (HN Singh 50, Rahul 27; S Dahiya 4-37, Faizan Alam 2-32) by 113 runs.

KIIT Cricket Stadium, Bhubaneshwar, March 21: West Zone Universities 242/9 in 50 overs (Manan Mehta 83, Pranjul Puri 66; Akhil Anil 4-53, Sijomon Joseph 2-36) beat **South Zone Universities** 196 in 44.1 overs (Sumant Jain 74, S Joseph 30; Sumit Patel 4-32, P Puri 2-30) by 46 runs.

North Zone Universities, West Zone Universities qualified for the final

Final

KIIT Cricket Stadium, Bhubaneshwar, March 23: North Zone Universities 273 in 49.4 overs (Shubham Dahiya 115, Abhishek Sangwan 45; Pranjul Puri 4-37, Manan Mehta 3-21) beat **West Zone Universities** 204 in 48 overs (M Mehta 48, Yash Chavan 42; Vijayant Yadav 3-36, Faizan Alam 2-26) by 69 runs.

Winners: North Zone Universities

U19 Vinoo Mankad Trophy 2017-18
League and Inter-zone

Roy, Taide shine

The tournament would get a revamp the following season, but for now, Jharkhand, Vidarbha and Delhi dominated East, Central and North Zones respectively by remaining unbeaten throughout the tournament. Central then went on to win the inter-zonal tournament.

Anukul Roy, who was the joint-highest wicket-taker at the Under-19 World Cup in New Zealand, was the star of Jharkhand's campaign. The left-arm spinner grabbed a wicket for every four runs conceded and ten balls bowled, and finished as the leading wicket-taker here as well, taking one five-wicket and three four-wicket hauls from four games.

Atharwa Taide's equally astonishing numbers with the bat were responsible for Vidarbha's success. The opener hit two centuries, two half-centuries, and an unbeaten 27 in five innings to end with an average of 195.50. His tally of 391 runs was bettered by only Aryan Juyal of Uttar Pradesh, who hit two hundred and three fifties in five matches. Uttar Pradesh won four out of their five matches, with their only defeat coming against Vidarbha.

The competition was stiffer in the other two zones. There was a three-way tie between Karnataka, Andhra and Hyderabad in South with Karnataka pipping the other two on net run-rate. Similarly, in West Zone, four teams were tied with two wins each but Baroda's net run-rate was far superior to others.

In the zonal tournament, Central Zone were clinical, winning all their games. Juyal continued his good form from the zonal league. The wooden spoon went to South Zone, whose batting let them down as they managed 200 only once and lost all their games.

Most runs (league): Aryan Juyal (Uttar Pradesh) (401 runs, 5 matches)
Most wickets (league): Anukul Roy (Jharkhand) (17 wickets, 4 matches)
Most runs (zone): Ayush Badoni (North Zone) (245 runs, 4 matches)
Most wickets (zone): Siddarth Desai (West Zone) (11 wickets, 4 matches)

North Zone
Patchy Greens, Teri, October 7: Haryana 139 in 42.1 overs (Prashant Vashist 38, Konark Dalal 31; Prashant Bakshi 3-20, Ayush Jamwal 2-15) lost to **Himachal Pradesh** 143/4 in 37.4 overs (Karmanya Verma 38, Sidhant Purohit 32; Ashok Sandhu 2-14) by six wickets.
Sehwag International School, Jhajjar, October 7: Delhi 280/8 in 50 overs (Manjot Kalra 71, Mayank Rawat 56; Sahil Lotra 3-33, Umar Majeed 2-59) beat **Jammu & Kashmir** 117 in 27.1 overs (Abdul Samad 26, S Lotra 22; Harsh Tyagi 7-33) by 163 runs.
Sehwag International School, Jhajjar, October 9: Jammu & Kashmir 240 in 50 overs (Jiyaad Magrey 72, Qamran Iqbal 43; Ayush Jamwal 3-44, Harsh Jamwal 2-8) beat **Himachal Pradesh** 189 in 44.3 overs (Karmanya Verma 53, Sidhant Purohit 41; Ankush Gill 4-40, Taizeem Tak 3-34) by 51 runs.

Teri Cricket Ground, Teri, October 9: Punjab 186 in 48.5 overs (Jagmeet Singh 41, Rahul Kashyap 26; Anshul Kamboj 5-42) lost to **Haryana** 190/7 in 47.2 overs (Prashant Vashist 83*, Ashok Sandhu 27; Mandeep Singh 3-18, Prerit Dutta 2-29) by three wickets.

Patchy Greens, Teri, October 11: Delhi 217 in 48.5 overs (Ayush Badoni 64, Anmol Sharma45; Sahil Hooda 3-37, Prashant Vashist 3-46) beat **Haryana** 191 in 48.1 overs (P Vashist 42, Yashu Sharma 33; Mayank Rawat 4-18, Lovnish Singh 2-36) by 26 runs.

Sehwag International School , Jhajjar, October 11: Himachal Pradesh 85 in 25.3 overs (Mohammed Arslan Khan 27; Arshdeep Singh 6-26, Deepin Chitkara 2-8) lost to **Punjab** 90/3 in 18.2 overs (Prabhsimran Singh 50, Jagmeet Singh 24*; Ayush Jamwal 2-18) by seven wickets.

Teri Cricket Ground, Teri, October 13: Jammu & Kashmir 165 in 42.5 overs (Vivrant Sharma 55, Kanhaiya Wadhawan 42; Prashant Vashist 4-38, Ashok Sandhu 3-27) lost to **Haryana** 168/4 in 36.2 overs (Yashu Sharma 69*, Mayank Dahiya 32*; Umar Majeed 2-42) by six wickets.

Sehwag International School , Jhajjar, October 13: Punjab 189/9 in 50 overs (Prerit Dutta 63, Deepin Chitkara 58; Lovnish Singh 3-35, Harsh Tyagi 2-28) lost to **Delhi** 191/7 in 43.1 overs (Mayank Rawat 90*, Anmol Sharma 37; Arshdeep Singh 2-36, Rahul Kashyap 2-38) by three wickets.

Sehwag International School, Jhajjar, October 15: Himachal Pradesh 147 in 42 overs (Mohammed Arslan Khan 66, Apoorav Walia 43; Nikhil Kumar 3-19, Lovnish Singh 3-31) lost to **Delhi** 148/4 in 35.2 overs (Manjot Kalra 53, Rishab Drall 35; Ayush Jamwal 2-42) by six wickets.

Teri Cricket Ground, Teri, October 15: Punjab 235 in 47.5 overs (Deepin Chitkara 62, Prabhsimran Singh 52; Umar Majeed 4-45, Aayush Singh 2-21) beat **Jammu &Kashmir**118 in 38.2 overs (Kanhaiya Wadhawan 39, Sahil Lotra 37; Arshdeep Singh 4-14, Sumit Sharma 2-14) by 117 runs.

North Zone points table

Teams	M	W	L	T	A/NR	Pts.	NRR
Delhi	4	4	0	0	0	16	+1.463
Punjab	4	2	2	0	0	8	+1.093
Haryana	4	2	2	0	0	8	-0.043
Himachal Pradesh	4	1	3	0	0	4	-1.010
Jammu & Kashmir	4	1	3	0	0	4	-1.480

Zone winners: Delhi

Central Zone

Scindia School Cricket Ground, Gwalior, October 7: Madhya Pradesh 219/9 in 50 overs (Pranjal Dixit 70, Rishabh Chouhan 62; Parivesh Dhar 3-44) beat **Chhattisgarh** 212/7 in 50 overs (Prateek Yadav 103, Sanidhay Hurkat 35; R Chouhan 3-38) by 7 runs.

Captain Roop Singh Stadium, Gwalior, October 7: Uttar Pradesh 269 in 49.3 overs (Kritagya Singh 61, Aryan Juyal 61; Madan Kumar 3-54, Vikas Singh 2-42) beat **Railways** 111 in 31.3 overs (Rizwan Ali Khan 32, Ravindra Chouhan 28; Mohit Jangra 5-28, Subhashish Biswas 3-13) by 158 runs.

Scindia School Cricket Ground, Gwalior, October 8: Rajasthan 148 in 43.3 overs (Divya Gajraj 53, Raju Joshi 33; Aditya Thakare 5-23, Atharva Taide 2-24) lost to **Vidarbha** 153/1 in

25.4 overs (A Taide 79*, Akash Kumar 55) by nine wickets.

Captain Roop Singh Stadium, Gwalior, October 8: Madhya Pradesh 313/7 in 50 overs (Ankush Singh 87, Sanket Shrivastava 72; Vikas Singh 3-49, Madan Kumar 3-61) beat **Railways** 209/8 in 50 overs (Nikhil Singh 78, Vaibhav Saini 36; Adarsh Singh 3-23, Ankush 3-50) by 104 runs.

Captain Roop Singh Stadium, Gwalior, October 9: Chhattisgarh 130 in 35 overs (Naved Ali 33, Anand Rao 30; Dhruv Dixit 3-17, Manav Suthar 3-33) beat **Rajasthan** 121 in 48.1 overs (Raju Joshi 30, Deepak Kadwasara 24; Rohan Taank 3-14, Harsh Sharma 2-16) by 9 runs.

Scindia School Cricket Ground, Gwalior, October 9: Uttar Pradesh 233/9 in 50 overs (Aryan Juyal 56, Shiva Singh 46*; Parth Rekhade 3-33, KP Datey 2-19) lost to **Vidarbha** 237/5 in 48.5 overs (Atharva Taide 130, Yash Rathod 28) by five wickets.

Captain Roop Singh Stadium, Gwalior, October 10: Chhattisgarh 318/6 in 50 overs (Satya Sharma 105, Sanidhay Hurkat 70*; Vikas Singh 3-67) beat **Railways** 139 in 48.4 overs (Ravindra Chouhan 38*, Vaibhav Saini 26; Parvesh Dhar 3-29, Harsh Sharma 3-32) by 179 runs.

Scindia School Cricket Ground, October 12: Railways 61 in 27.5 overs (Manav Suthar 5-24) lost to **Rajasthan** 62/1 in 12 overs (Suhail Khan 24*, Divya Gajraj 20) by nine wickets.

Captain Roop Singh Stadium, Gwalior, October 12: Madhya Pradesh 190/9 in 50 overs (Lokesh Rathore 39, Rahul Chandrol 28; Mohit Jangra 3-35, Shiva Singh 2-30) lost to **Uttar Pradesh** 191/4 in 39.2 overs (Amaan Razi 61, Aryan Juyal 57) by six wickets.

Captain Roop Singh Stadium, Gwalior, October 13: Chhattisgarh 186 in 45.5 overs (Shubham Maurya 52, Naved Ali 51; Darshan Nalkande 3-31, Atharva Taide 2-20) lost to **Vidarbha** 190/1 in 42.3 overs (A Taide 105*, Yash Rathod 60*) by nine wickets.

Scindia School Cricket Ground, Gwalior, October 13: Uttar Pradesh 279/6 in 50 overs (Aryan Juyal 112*, Priyam Garg 86; Dhruv Dixit 3-45) beat **Rajasthan** 190 in 42.2 overs (Suraj Ahuja 55, Divya Gajraj 51; Shivam Dixit 4-27, Shiva Singh 2-27) by 89 runs.

Captain Roop Singh Stadium, Gwalior, October 14: Rajasthan 200 in 47.4 overs (Rammohan Chauhan 61, Divya Gajraj 59; Adarsh Singh 3-23, Harshvardhan Singh 2-30) lost to **Madhya Pradesh** 201/3 in 40.4 overs (Ankush Singh 83, Rahul Chandrol 61*; Manav Suthar 2-56) by seven wickets.

Scindia School Cricket Ground, Gwalior, October 14: Railways 105 in 25 overs (Ravindra Chouhan 26, Basit 20; Darshan Nalkande 4-51, Parth Rekhade 3-7) lost to **Vidarbha** 106/0 in 14.4 overs (Akash Kumar 70*, Atharva Taide 27*) by ten wickets.

Captain Roop Singh Stadium, Gwalior, October 15: Vidarbha 252/7 in 50 overs (Nayan Chavan 70*, Atharva Taide 50; Rajashi Srivastava 3-36, Rishabh Chouhan 2-38) beat **Madhya Pradesh** 183 in 40 overs (Rahul Chandrol 71, Ankush Singh 35; Rohit Dattatraya 6-26, Parth Rekhade 2-29) by 69 runs.

Scindia School Cricket Ground, Gwalior, October 15: Uttar Pradesh 292/5 in 50 overs (Aryan Juyal 115*, Sameer Choudhary 52; Naman Dhruw 2-45) beat **Chhattisgarh** 247 in 45.3 overs (Sanidhay Hurkat 62, Prateek Yadav 57; Sameer Choudhary 3-41, Shivam Dixit 3-37) by 45 runs.

Central Zone points table

Teams	M	W	L	T	A/NR	Pts.	NRR
Vidarbha	5	5	0	0	0	20	+1.743
Uttar Pradesh	5	4	1	0	0	16	+1.363
Madhya Pradesh	5	3	2	0	0	12	+0.150
Chhattisgarh	5	2	3	0	0	8	+0.409
Rajasthan	5	1	4	0	0	4	-0.408
Railways	5	0	5	0	0	0	-3.545

Zone winners: Vidarbha

West Zone

BKC Ground, Mumbai, October 9: Mumbai 143 in 35.4 overs (Divyaansh Saxena 77, Tanush Kotian 20; Mistry Milan 3-21, Mohit Mongia 2-26) lost to **Baroda** 145/3 in 21.4 overs (M Mongia 55*, Urvil Patel 43) by seven wickets.

BKC Ground, Mumbai, October 10: Saurashtra 208/8 in 43 overs (Tarang Gohel 100, Harvik Desai 49; A Vashishtha 3-46, Tanush Kotian 2-23) lost to **Mumbai** 211/2 in 32.4 overs (Divyaansh Saxena 69*, Karan Shah 68) by eight wickets.

Sachin Tendulkar Gymkhana, Kandivili, Mumbai, October 12: Maharashtra 154 in 43.2 overs (Hrishikesh Motkar 27, Swapnil Fulpagar 27; Ninad Rathva 4-21, Safvan Patel 2-14) lost to **Baroda** 159/4 in 41 overs (Urvil Patel 54, Shivalik Sharma 46*; Akshay Kalokhe 2-22, Siddhesh Warghante 2-38) by six wickets.

Sharad Pawar Cricket Academy, BKC, Mumbai, October 12: Gujarat 184/9 in 50 overs (Hemang Patel 65*, Sunpreet Bagga 31; Tanush Kotian 6-31, Saksham 2-33) lost to **Mumbai** 184/4 in 34.2 overs (Divyaansh Saxena 69, Atharva Ankolekar 30*; Akash Pandey 2-19, Siddarth Desai 2-35) by six wickets.

Mumbai, October 13: Saurashtra 143 in 42.3 overs (Bhavin Engle 41, Siddhant Rana 22; Akash Pandey 4-27, Umang Kumar 3-8) lost to **Gujarat** 87/4 in 17.4 overs (Het Patel 38*) by six wickets (VJD method).

MIG Cricket Club, Mumbai, October 13: Maharashtra 211/8 in 50 overs (Om Bhosale 83, Paras Gawali 37; Sylvester Dsouza 4-56, Saksham 2-51) beat **Mumbai** 206 in 48 overs (Sagar Chhabria 85, Atharva Ankolekar 56; Atman Pore 3-42, Akshay Kalokhe 3-35) by 5 runs.

Sachin Tendulkar Gymkhana, Kandivili, Mumbai, October 14: Maharashtra 261/6 in 50 overs (Pavan Shah 114 rtd hrt, Om Bhosale 40) beat **Saurashtra** 173/5 in 38 overs (Devrajsinh 49*, Tarang Gohel 40; Alouk Jadhav 3-35) by 10 runs (VJD method).

MIG Cricket Club, Mumbai, October 14: Gujarat 222/8 in 50 overs (Laxya Kocher 84, Het Patel 47; Safvan Patel 3-43, Mohit Mongia 2-49) beat **Baroda** 116/4 in 32 overs (Vasudev Patil 67*, Shivalik Sharma 29) by ten runs (VJD method).

MIG Cricket Club, Mumbai, October 15: Baroda v **Saurashtra**. Match abandoned.

Sachin Tendulkar Gymkhana, Kandivili, Mumbai, October 15: Maharashtra v Gujarat. Match abandoned.

West Zone points table

Teams	M	W	L	T	A/NR	Pts.	NRR
Baroda	4	2	1	0	1	10	+1.025
Maharashtra	4	2	1	0	1	10	-0.200
Gujarat	4	2	1	0	1	10	-0.499
Mumbai	4	2	2	0	0	8	+0.143
Saurashtra	4	0	3	0	1	2	-0.822

Zone winners: Baroda

South Zone

Alur Cricket Stadium-II, Alur, October 7: Kerala 188/9 in 50 overs (Akhil Scaria 61*, Shiv Ganesh 39; Ajay Dev Goud 3-40, G Anikethreddy 2-23) lost to **Hyderabad** 192/3 in 44 overs (Thakur Tilak Varma 79*, A Varun Goud 72*; TS Vinil 2-29) by seven wickets.

Alur Cricket Stadium-III, Alur, October 7: Andhra 124 in 26 overs (Shaik Rafi 29, KN Prudhvi Raj 20; K Deeban Lingesh 3-26, Uthirakumar Mukilesh 3-28) beat **Tamil Nadu**115/7 in 26 overs (Praveen Kumar 38, Aditya Barooah 25) by nine runs.

Alur Cricket Stadium, Alur, October 7: Goa 185 in 38 overs (Rahul Mehta 77, Manthan Khutkar 40; Ruchir Joshi 3-39, Manoj Bhandage 2-41) lost to **Karnataka** 191/3 in 31.4 overs (Devdutt Padikkal 106*, B A Mohith 35) by seven wickets.

Alur Cricket Stadium-III, Alur, October 8: Tamil Nadu 130 in 34.4 overs (Uthirakumar Mukilesh 35, Pradosh Paul 27; TS Vinil 3-14, Aravind Rajesh 3-32, Vishnu Kumar 3-32) lost to **Kerala** 134/2 in 33.4 overs (Shiv Ganesh 51, J Ananthakrishnan 32) by eight wickets.

Alur Cricket Stadium-II, Alur, October 8: Goa 220/6 in 50 overs (Aditya Suryawanshi 75*, Heramb Parab 38*; G Anikethreddy 2-35, C Rakshann Readdi 2-36) lost to**Hyderabad**224/6 in 48 overs (Sohail Shaikh 76*, Mohammed Junaid 36; Balpreet Singh 2-46) by four wickets.

Alur Cricket Stadium, Alur, October 8: Andhra 183 in 48.4 overs (KN Prudhvi Raj 55, Yara Sandeep 29; Manoj Bhandage 3-32, Ruchir Joshi 2-40) lost to **Karnataka** 185/3 in 39.5 overs (Luvnith Sisodia 80, S Nikin Jose 59*) by seven wickets.

Alur Cricket Stadium-III, Alur, October 10: Andhra164/7 in 31 overs (K Maheep Kumar 53, Vamsi Krishna 32; Ajith Jacob 3-23, Aravind Rajesh 2-42) beat **Kerala** 109/7 in 31 overs (Akhil Scaria 51*; Shaik Rafi 2-12, Girinath Reddy 2-17) by 55 runs.

Alur Cricket Stadium, Alur, October 10: Karnataka 149/7 in 33 overs (Devdutt Padikkal 37, Manoj Bhandage 28; Hitesh Yadav 4-27) lost to **Hyderabad** 150/4 in 31.4 overs (Pragnay Reddy 79*; BM Shreyas 2-31) by six wickets.

Alur Cricket Stadium-II, Alur, October 10: Goa 87 in 36 overs (S Ram Ajith 3-8, S Krishankumar 3-9) lost to **Tamil Nadu** 88/4 in 26 overs (S Nidhish Rajagopal 23; Balpreet Singh 2-25, Shanu Vantamuri 2-35) by six wickets.

Alur Cricket Stadium, Alur, October 12: Andhra151 in 31 overs (Vamsi Krishna 37, Vinay 30; Ajay Dev Goud 4-30. G Anikethreddy 4-33) beat **Hyderabad** 99 in 26 overs (Thakur Tilak Varma 30,Sagar Chaurasia 22; Vinay 5-13, K Girish Reddy 2-21) by 52 runs.

Alur Cricket Stadium-II, Alur, October 12: Tamil Nadu 80 in 20.3 overs (BM Shreyas 4-17, Aman Khan 2-21) lost to **Karnataka** 81/2 in 18.3 overs (Dev Padikkal 43, S Nikin Jose 21*) by eight wickets.

Alur Cricket Stadium-III, Alur, October 12: Goa v Kerala. Match abandoned

Alur Cricket Stadium-III, Alur, October 14: Goa v Andhra. Match abandoned

Alur Cricket Stadium-II, Alur, October 14: Kerala 27/2 in 10.1 overs drew with **Karnataka.** No result.

Alur Cricket Stadium, Alur, October 14: Hyderabad 24/1 in 4.2 overs drew with **Tamil Nadu.** No result.

South Zone points table

Teams	M	W	L	T	A/NR	Pts.	NRR
Karnataka	5	3	1	0	1	14	+0.764
Andhra	5	3	1	0	1	14	+0.533
Hyderabad	5	3	1	0	1	14	-0.018
Kerala	5	1	2	0	2	8	-0.161
Tamil Nadu	5	1	3	0	1	6	-0.212
Goa	5	0	3	0	2	4	-1.005

Zone winners: Karnataka

East Zone

Railway Stadium, Dhanbad, October 14: Assam 86/8 in 20 overs (Suraj Jaiswal 2-8, Akash Pandey 2-17) lost to **Bengal** 87/1 in 15.2 overs (Sudip Gharami 48*, Soumyabrata Nath 26) by nine wickets.

TATA Digwadih Stadium, Dhanbad, October 14: Jharkand versus **Odisha.** Match awarded to Jharkhand.

Jawaharlal Nehru Stadium, Jealgora, Dhanbad, October 14: Tripura 159/7 in 21 overs (Bikramkumar Das 56, Sankar Paul 34; Abhishek Anand 3-25) beat **Associates & Affiliate Combined XI** 91 in 20.5 overs (Sonu Gupta 20; Amaresh Das 2-16, S Paul 24) by 68 runs.

Jawaharlal Nehru Stadium, Jealgora, Dhanbad, October 15: Jharkhand 142/5 in 24 overs (Bhanu Anand 34*, V Vishal 32; Sudip Gharami 2-27) beat **Bengal** 138/8 in 24 overs (S Gharami 33, Karan Lal 29; Anukul Roy 4-22, Pankaj Yadav 2-22) by 4 runs.

Railway Stadium, Dhanbad, October 15: Odisha 167/8 in 50 overs (Somen Chand 38*, Swastik Samal 38; Amaresh Das 3-28, Sujit Deb 2-25) lost to **Tripura** 171/7 in 45.1 overs (Dipayan Debbarma 73*, Sankar Paul 36; Krishna Palai 3-28, Shibasish Sahoo 2-35) by three wickets.

TATA Digwadih Stadium, Dhanbad, October 15: Associates & Affiliate Combined XI 175 in 48.5 overs (Paramjeet Singh 69, Sonu Gupta 45; Hirakjyoti Das 3-26, Hrishikesh Borah 2-34) beat **Assam** 135 in 44.3 overs (Danish Ahmed 54; Akash Kumar 3-27, Abhishek Anand 3-31) by 40 runs.

TATA Digwadih Stadium, Dhanbad, October 16: Assam 200 in 50 overs (Danish Ahmed 44, Abdul Kuraishi 29; Sankar Paul 3-41, Amaresh Das 3-33) beat **Tripura** 121 in 39.5 overs (Rohit Singh 51*, S Paul 23; Jitumoni Kalita 4-18, Mukhtar Hussain 3-23) by 79 runs.

Jawaharlal Nehru Stadium, Jealgora, Dhanbad, October 16: Odisha 75 in 39.3 overs (Kshyamasagar Bal 24; Abhijeet Bhagat 5-4) lost to **Bengal** 81/0 in 14.4 overs (Sourav Paul 56*) by ten wickets.

Railway Stadium, Dhanbad, October 16: Associates & Affiliate Combined XI 103 in 39.2 overs (NG Johnson 52; Anukul Roy 5-17, Aditya Singh 2-20) lost to **Jharkhand** 106/1 in 25.3 overs (V Vishal 40*, Shresht Sagar 37*) by nine wickets.

TATA Digwadih Stadium, Dhanbad, October 17: Assam 167 in 47.4 overs (Abdul Kuraishi 33, Ayush Agarwal 28; Anukul Roy 4-20, Sushant Mishra 3-42) lost to **Jharkhand** 173/2 in 34.2 overs (Atul Surwar 60*, V Vishal 52) by eight wickets.

Railway Stadium, Dhanbad, October 17: Tripura 188 in 49 overs (Bikramkumar Das 45, Dipayan Debbarma 44; Souvik Paul 2-25, Akash Pandey 2-27) beat **Bengal** 155/8 in 46 overs (Kaushik Maity 36, S Paul 30*; Saruk Hossain 4-24, Rohit Singh 2-29) by 20 runs (VJD method).

Jawaharlal Nehru Stadium, Jealgora, Dhanbad, October 17: Associates & Affiliate Combined XI 180 in 49.4 overs (RK Rex 60*, Akash Kumar 37; Satyam Bharadwaj 3-20, Krishna Palai 3-46) lost to **Odisha** 181/4 in 45.5 overs (Swastik Samal 63, Kunal Mallick 50; Abhishek Anand 2-35) by six wickets.

Railway Stadium, Dhanbad, October 18: Assam 196 in 43.2 overs (Riyan Parag 94, Jitumoni Kalita 22; Krishna Palai 3-29, Umesh Yadav 2-21) beat **Odisha** 125 in 38.3 overs (Nitish Samantaray 37, Kunal Mallick 23; Mukhtar Hussain 3-18, J Kalita 2-17) by 71 runs.

TATA Digwadih Stadium, Dhanbad, October 18: Tripura 121 in 36 overs (Bikramkumar Das 34, Souvik Paul 23; Anukul Roy 4-9, Vivek Tiwari 2-23) lost to **Jharkhand** 122/0 in 25.2 overs (Aryaman Sen 62*, V Vishal 51*) by ten wickets.

Jawaharlal Nehru Stadium, Jealgora, Dhanbad, October 18: Associates & Affiliate Combined XI 106 in 44.4 overs (BB Dasgupta 20; Kaushik Maity 4-24, Abhijeet Bhagat 2-8) lost to **Bengal** 109/2 in 18.3 overs (Sudip Gharami 43*, Pradunya Sarkar 34) by eight wickets.

East Zone points table

Teams	M	W	L	T	A/NR	Pts.	NRR
Jharkhand	5	5	0	0	0	20	+1.934
Bengal	5	3	2	0	0	12	+1.736
Tripura	5	3	2	0	0	12	-0.301
Assam	5	2	3	0	0	8	+0.153
Odisha	5	1	4	0	0	4	-1.131
Associates &Affiliate Combined XI	5	1	4	0	0	4	-1.326

Zone winners: Jharkhand

Inter-zone Tournament

Alur Cricket Stadium-III, Alur, October 24: Central Zone 245/6 in 50 overs (Aryan Juyal 82, Salman Khan 42; Safvan Patel 3-37, Siddarth Desai 2-41) beat **West Zone** 240/9 in 50 overs (Harsh Desai 68, Tanush Kotian 45; Mohit Jangra 2-45, Shiva Singh 2-47) by 5 runs.

Alur Cricket Stadium, Alur, October 24: North Zone 219/9 in 50 overs (Ayush Badoni 72, Abhishek Sharma 38; Vinay 2-25, Manoj Bhandage 2-41) beat **South Zone**191 in 46.1 overs (M Bhandage 46, Vinay 29; Arshdeep Singh 5-41, Harsh Tyagi 4-28) by 28 runs.

Alur Cricket Stadium-III, Alur, October 25: North Zone 291/9 in 50 overs (Majot Kalra 81, Abhishek Sharma 71; Ninad Rathva 2-44, Siddarth Desai 2-47) beat **West Zone** 278/9 in 50 overs (Om Bhosale 112, Desai 34*; Anshul Kamboj 2-33, Arshdeeop Singh 2-43) by 13 runs.

Alur Cricket Stadium, Alur, October 25: East Zone135 in 38.3 overs (Mukhtar Hussain 35, Sudip Gharami 30; Darshan Nalkande 3-20, Mohit Jangra 3-49) lost to **Central Zone** 139/3 in 36 overs (Atharva Taide 52*, Ankush Singh 46; Pankaj Yadav 3-43) by seven wickets.

Alur Cricket Stadium, Alur, October 27: East Zone 211 in 49.2 overs (Anukul Roy 60, V Vishal 43; Akhil Scaria 3-24, Manoj Bhandage 3-37) beat **South Zone** 162 in 48.3 overs (Uthirakumar Mukilesh 28, Pragnay Reddy 25; Ishan Porel 3-13, Riyan Parag 2-23) by 49 runs.

Alur Cricket Stadium-III, Alur, October 27: North Zone 249/7 in 50 overs (Ayush Badoni 88, Deepin Chitkara 68; Mohit Jangra 2-55) lost to **Central Zone** 253/3 in 46.5 overs (Ankush Singh 79, Priyam Garg 65*) by seven wickets.

Alur Cricket Stadium-III, Alur, October 28: South Zone 232/9 in 50 overs (A Varun Goud 46, Manoj Bhandage 35*; Siddarth Desai 3-34, Ninad Rathva 3-48) lost to **West Zone** 233/6 in 47.4 overs (Urvil Patel 88, Pavan Shah 54; M Bhandage 3-34, Bhanu Shreyas 2-42) by four wickets.

Alur Cricket Stadium, Alur, October 28: East Zone 215 in 49.5 overs (Riyan Parag 84, Anukul Roy 61; Harsh Tyagi 3-40, Arshdeep Singh 2-26) lost to **North Zone** 220/7 in 46.4 overs (Ayush Badoni 72, Anuj Rawat 70; Ishan Porel 4-37, A Roy 2-40) by three wickets.

Alur Cricket Stadium-III, Alur, October 30: East Zone 137 in 37.3 overs (Shresht Sagar 39, Arif Ansari 25; Siddarth Desai 4-37, Tanush Kotian 2-23) beat **West Zone** 107 in 31.2 overs (Ninad Rathva 27; Ishan Porel 3-28) by 30 runs.

Alur Cricket Stadium, Alur, October 30: South Zone 189 in 47.5 overs (A Varun Goud 84, Devdutt Padikkal 21; Shiva Singh 3-29, Darshan Nalkande 2-30) lost to **Central Zone** 191/8

Domestic review

in 45.4 overs (D Nalkande 39*, Aryan Juyal 37; Uthirakumar Mukilesh 3-45, R S Jaganathsinivas 2-26) by two wickets.

Points table

Teams	M	W	L	D	T	N/R	Pts.	NRR
Central Zone	4	4	0	0	0	0	16	+0.574
North Zone	4	3	1	0	0	0	12	+0.218
East Zone	4	2	2	0	0	0	8	+0.052
West Zone	4	1	3	0	0	0	4	-0.184
South Zone	4	0	4	0	0	0	0	-0.547

Winners: Central Zone

WOMEN'S CRICKET

ANANYA UPENDRAN

The Mithali Raj-led India Blue lifted the trophy with a narrow win in the final.

Senior Women's T20 Challenger Trophy

Lukewarm audition for T20 World Cup

The Senior T20 Challenger Trophy was an audition for aspirants ahead of the ICC Women's World T20 later in the year. However, no new player seized the stage, and veteran Jhulan Goswami saw enough to decide to bow out of the format in India colours.

India Blue, led by Mithali Raj, defeated Deepti Sharma's India Red by four runs in a thrilling final. Chasing 132, India Red slipped from 86 for no loss to 127 for 7 after Deepti (45) and Punam Raut (52) laid a solid foundation — the spin duo of Poonam Yadav (3 for 25) and Radha Yadav (2 for 20) triggering the collapse.

Shikha Pandey, who finished the tournament with seven wickets for India Red, bowled with great rhythm and control, unveiling a newly developed out-swinger. Her wicket tally was bettered by Anuja Patil, India Blue's off-spinner, who picked up eight wickets at an average of 8, including a best of 3 for 4 against India Green.

In a tournament where team totals were low and run rates slow, VR Vanitha (128 runs), India Blue's opener, and Deepti's (124 runs) intent with the bat stood out. Vanitha smashed six sixes, while Deepti, whose runs came at a strike rate of 107.82, showed a more aggressive version of herself, even playing the shot of the tournament: a slog sweep for six over deep backward square leg against Mansi Joshi.

India Green managed only one win in four matches, their results a reflection of the form of Jemimah Rodrigues, their batting centrepiece, who scored a total of 11 runs.

Most runs: Punam Raut (India Red) (135 runs in 5 matches)
Most wickets: Anuja Patil (India Blue) (8 wickets in 5 matches)

Alur Cricket Stadium III, August 14: India Blue 100/8 in 20 overs (Mithali Raj 51; Deepti Sharma 2-15, Tanuja Kanwer 2-16) lost to **India Red** 79/3 in 16.3 overs (D Sharma 45*) by seven runs (VJD method).
Alur Cricket Stadium III, August 15: India Blue 82/5 in 17 overs (VR Vanitha 35; Arundhati Reddy 2-13) lost to **India Green** 84/3 in 15.5 overs (Priya Punia 46*) by seven wickets.
Alur Cricket Stadium II, August 16: India Red 114/8 in 20 overs (Mona Meshram 33, Punam Raut 25; Sushree Dibyadarshini 4-19, Rajeshwari 2-16) beat **India Green** 106 in 19.4 overs (Veda Krishnamurthy 27, Arundhati Reddy 20; Shikha Pandey 2-11) by eight runs.
Alur Cricket Stadium, August 17: India Red 84/7 in 20 overs (Punam Raut 28; Dayalan Hemalatha 2-11, Anuja Patil 2-15) lost to **India Blue** 86/2 in 17.4 overs (VR Vanitha 51, Mithali Raj 23*) by eight wickets.
Alur Cricket Stadium III, August 18: India Green 46 in 19.4 overs (Preeti Bose 3-1, Anuja Patil 3-4) lost to **India Blue** 47/2 in 9.5 overs (Taniya Bhatia 29*; Rajeshwari Gayakwad 2-15) by eight wickets.
Alur Cricket Stadium II, August 19: India Green 51 in 18.4 overs (Reemalaxmi Ekka 3-6, Shikha Pandey 2-4) lost to **India Red** 52/1 in 9.2 overs (Punam Raut 26*. Harleen Deol 24*) by nine wickets.

Points table

Team	M	W	L	T	N/R	Pts	NRR
India Red	4	3	1	0	0	12	+0.750
India Blue	4	2	2	0	0	8	+0.654
India Green	4	1	3	0	0	4	-1.468

India Red and India Blue qualified for the final

Final
Alur Cricket Stadium II, August 21: India Blue 131/7 in 20 overs (Dayalan Hemalatha 48, Taniya Bhatia 28; Shikha Pandey 2-16) beat **India Red** 127/7 in 20 overs (Punam Raut 52, Deepti Sharma 45; Poonam Yadav 3-25, Radha Yadav 2-20) by four runs.

Winners: India Blue

Inter-State One-day Competition

Bengal dethrone Railways

Bengal clinched their maiden title with a thrilling ten-run win over Andhra in the final of the Senior Women's One-Day Championship. Having been sent in to bat, even contributions from the top order saw Bengal post 198 for 7, before Deepti Sharma (3-33) and Shubhlakshmi Sharma (2-29), aided by some spectacular fielding, combined to snatch what, at one stage, looked like an unlikely victory.

Deepti, who had joined Bengal the previous season, was their most consistent performer through the tournament, racking up 487 runs and picking up 22 wickets with her wily off-spin. Her run-tally included two centuries and two half-centuries — none more important than a 132-ball 85 that, along

India internationals Jhulan Goswami and Deepti Sharma helped Bengal end Railways' hold on the trophy. — *CAB*

with Shubhlakshmi's five-wicket haul, helped Bengal oust Railways in the semi-final and end their six-year hold on the trophy.

In what was a relatively high scoring season, there were as many as 23 centuries, and five batters crossed the 400-run mark. Batting-friendly conditions across the board meant chasing became the norm: 2018-19 saw 45% of the matches won by teams batting second. Unsurprisingly, eight of the top ten wicket-takers were spinners: Tarannum Pathan, the off-spinner from Baroda, sat pretty at the top of the charts with 24 wickets at an average of 9.70.

Of the nine new teams in the Plate Group, Uttarakhand and Pondicherry were the most impressive. Saee Purandhare of Meghalaya finished second on the batting charts with 462 runs at an incredible average of 154, while her teammate, Vandana Mahajan picked up 22 wickets in seven matches with her inswingers, including astounding figures of 8 for 4 against Mizoram.

Other notable performances included Shafali Verma's tally of 239 runs for Haryana that came at a strike rate of 152.22, including 11 sixes, Sandhya Kumari's 159 and 5 for 1 for Mizoram against Arunachal Pradesh, and Meghalaya's tie against Sikkim.

In the 2017-18 season, consistent performances from Sarika Koli, MD Thirushkamini and Mithali Raj, all of whom crossed the 220-run mark, had meant Railways went unchallenged to secure their 11th title.

In a season where the young brigade began to put their hands up, Delhi, with their core group of senior players, finished second. Rumeli Dhar, the 34-year-old allrounder, led their charge scoring 226 runs and taking nine wickets. She bowled intelligently with the new ball, picking up crucial top-order wickets. Andhra, playing in the Elite Division for the first time, put in some inspiring performances to qualify for the Super League.

Riding on a high from the World Cup, Shikha Pandey led Goa to the Plate Division championship, where they defeated Bengal by 37 runs in the final; the captain contributed a crucial half-century. Deepti amassed 312 runs at an average of 102, including five half-centuries to guide Bengal to the Elite Division, setting them on the path to history the following year.

Other notable performances included Komal Zanzad's incredible nine-wicket haul for Vidarbha in a knock-out match against Haryana; Monikha Das's knock of 151 for Assam and Punam Raut's blistering 36-ball 61 against Andhra.

	Most runs	**Most wickets**
2017-18	Deepti Sharma (Bengal) (312 runs in 6 matches)	Shikha Pandey (Goa) (18 wickets in 7 matches)
2017-18	Deepti Sharma (Bengal) (487 runs in 11 matches)	Tarannum Pathan (Baroda) (24 wickets in 9 matches)

2018-19

Elite Group A

Devineni Venkata Ramana Praneetha Ground, Mulapadu, December 1: Chhattisgarh 184/8 in 50 overs (Shivi Pandey 75, Mantravadi Shalini 30; Anuja Patil 4-24) lost to **Maharashtra** 187/5 in 40.3 overs (Devika Vaidya 85*, Shivali Shinde 71; Adila Khanam 3-53, Urmila Harina 2-28) by five wickets.

Andhra Cricket Association Women's Cricket Academy Ground, Guntur, December 1: Punjab 174/8 in 50 overs (Taniya Bhatia 66, Parveen Khan 43; CH Jhansi Lakshmi 3-31, V

Pushpa Latha 2-20) lost to **Andhra** 175/4 in 46.5 overs (CH Jhansi Lakshmi 100, N Anusha 22) by six wickets.

Chukkapalli Pitchaiah Cricket Ground, Mulapadu, December 1: **Railways** 244/4 in 50 overs (Punam Raut 104, Mithali Raj 62; Sanjula Naik 2-60) beat **Goa** 72 in 44.1 overs (Poonam Yadav 6-8) by 172 runs.

Chukkapalli Pitchaiah Cricket Ground, Mulapadu, December 2: **Maharashtra** 311/ 2 in 50 overs (Tejal Hasabnis 148, Mukta Magre 70) beat **Haryana** 128 in 33.5 overs (Shafali Verma 42, Bhawna Ohlan 29; Maya Sonawane 6-23) by 183 runs.

Andhra Cricket Association Women's Cricket Academy Ground, Guntur, December 2: **Andhra** 152 in 45.3 overs (N Anusha 45, E Padmaja 39; Komal Zanzad 4-25, Nupur Kohale 4-28) beat **Vidarbha** 135 in 43 overs (Bharati Fulmali 77, Latika Inamdar 23; G Chandra Lekha 3-15, CH Jhansi Lakshmi 2-43) by 17 runs.

Devineni Venkata Ramana Praneetha Ground, Mulapadu, December 2: **Saurashtra** 91 in 43.3 overs (Neha Chvada 20; Sonali Gaunder 2-5, Sanjula Naik 2-19) lost to **Goa** 92/2 in 32.5 overs (S Naik 34*, Sunanda Yetrekar 32*) by eight wickets.

Devineni Venkata Ramana Praneetha Ground, Mulapadu, December 3: **Haryana** 140 in 44.3 overs (Bhawna Ohlan 68; Mehak Kesar 3-18, Sunita Rani 2-26) lost to **Punjab** 141/5 in 41.2 overs (Taniya Bhatia 56*, Parveen Khan 32; Sheetal Rana 2-16, Suman Gulia 2-18) by five wickets.

Andhra Cricket Association Women's Cricket Academy Ground, Guntur, December 3: **Railways** 220/6 in 50 overs (Mona Meshram 92, Punam Raut 39; Disha Kasat 2-35, Kanchan Nagwani 2-37) beat **Vidarbha** 83 in 38.1 overs (Bharati Fulmali 35*, Harsha Bokade 25; Sneh Rana 4-17, Rajeshwari Gayakwad 2-8) by 137 runs.

Chukkapalli Pitchaiah Cricket Ground, Mulapadu, December 3: **Chhattisgarh** 170/6 in 50 overs (Mantravadi Shalini 59, Manpreet Kaur 40; Neha Chavda 3-26) beat **Saurashtra** 120/9 in 50 overs (Pooja Nimavat 21*; M Shalini 3-22, Shraddha Vaishnava 2-22) by 50 runs.

Andhra Cricket Association Women's Cricket Academy Ground, Guntur, December 5: **Railways** 231/6 in 50 overs (Veda Krishnamurthy 80, Arundhati Reddy 48*; Tejal Hasabnis 3-52, Priyanka Garkhede 2-26) beat **Maharashtra** 179/7 in 50 overs (Shweta Mane 55, Shivali Shinde 46; Poonam Yadav 3-46, Ekta Bisht 2-28) by 52 runs.

Devineni Venkata Ramana Praneetha Ground, Mulapadu, December 5: **Chhattisgarh** 174/5 in 50 overs (Shivi Pandey 60, Manpreet Kaur 49; Sanjula Naik 2-44) beat **Goa** 148/8 in 50 overs (Sunanda Yetrekar 40, Tejashwini Duragad 28; Urmila Harina 3-23, Shyla Alam 3-26) by 26 runs.

Chukkapalli Pitchaiah Cricket Ground, Mulapadu, December 5: **Punjab** 199/8 in 50 overs (Jasia Akhter 76, Taniya Bhatia 30; Reena Dabhi 3-18, Reena M 3-37) beat **Saurashtra** 108 in 42.3 overs (Riddhi Ruparel 27, Jayu Jadeja 22; Sunita Rani 2-5, Babita Meena 2-34) by 91 runs.

Andhra Cricket Association Women's Cricket Academy Ground, Guntur, December 6: **Andhra** 123/9 in 50 overs (E Padmaja 33, N Anusha 21; Sneh Rana 2-11, Ekta Bisht 2-23) lost to **Railways** 126/2 in 25.1 overs (Mithali Raj 63*, S Rana 25; CH Jhansi Lakshmi 2-43) by eight wickets.

Chukkapalli Pitchaiah Cricket Ground, Mulapadu, December 6: **Haryana** 186/9 in 50 overs (Sonia Khatri 52, Sheetal Rana 50*) lost to **Chhattisgarh** 187/0 in 46 overs (Shivi Pandey 104*, Mantravadi Shalini 71*) by 10 wickets.

Devineni Venkata Ramana Praneetha Ground, Mulapadu, December 6: **Punjab** 206/9 in 50 overs (Jasia Akter 62, Taniya Bhatia 33; Komal Zanzad 4-33, Nupur Kohale 3-39) beat **Vidarbha** 165 in 45.3 overs (Bharati Fulmali 55, Latika Inamdar 27; Komalpreet Kour 3-27, Neelam Bisht 2-13) by 41 runs.

Chukkapalli Pitchaiah Cricket Ground, Mulapadu, December 8: **Vidarbha** 135 in 47 overs (Kanchan Nagwani 46, Disha Kasat 23; Vanita Bhandari 3-24, Sonali Gaunder 2-37) beat **Goa** 58 in 35.2 overs (Komal Zanzad 2-5, K Nagwani 2-6) by 77 runs.

Devineni Venkata Ramana Praneetha Ground, Mulapadu, December 8: Saurashtra 88 in 35.2 overs (Priyanka Garkhede 3-10, Maya Sonawane 2-4) lost to **Maharashtra** 89/3 in 23.2 overs (Tejal Hasabnis 24, Mukta Magre 20) by seven wickets.

Andhra Cricket Association Women's Cricket Academy Ground, Guntur, December 8: Andhra 219/4 in 50 overs (N Anusha 72, G Sneha 45) beat **Haryana** 213/5 in 50 overs (Sheetal Rana 59, Bhawna Ohlan 41; K Jyothi 2-23, Saranya Gadwal 2-56) by six runs.

Andhra Cricket Association Women's Cricket Academy Ground, Guntur, December 10: Chhattisgarh 93 in 44.2 overs (Manpreet Kaur 39; V Pushpa Latha 3-18, K Jyothi 3-25) lost to **Andhra** 94/8 in 36.4 overs (K Anjali Sarvani 22; Adila Khanam 2-14, Pransu Priya 2-21) by two wickets.

Devineni Venkata Ramana Praneetha Ground, Mulapadu, December 10: Goa 173/9 in 50 overs (Sanjula Naik 45, Nikita Malik 43; Anuja Patil 5-25) beat **Maharashtra** 161 in 47.1 overs (Tejal Hasabnis 45, Poonam Khemnar 35; Rupali Chavan 3-30, Tejashwini Duragad 2-25) by 12 runs.

Chukkapalli Pitchaiah Cricket Ground, Mulapadu, December 10: Punjab 109/9 in 50 overs (Taniya Bhatia 33, Neelam Bisht 31; Ekta Bisht 4-24, Kavita Patil 2-20) lost to **Railways** 110/1 in 28.2 overs (Shweta Jadhav 44*, Sneh Rana 41*) by nine wickets.

Chukkapalli Pitchaiah Cricket Ground, Mulapadu, December 12: Punjab 187 in 49.1 overs (Taniya Bhatia 60, Babita Meena 31; Rupali Chavan 4-28, Sunanda Yetrekar 3-31) lost to **Goa** 190/2 in 42.4 overs (Vinavi Gurav 73*, Shikha Pandey 71*) by eight wickets.

Andhra Cricket Association Women's Cricket Academy Ground, Guntur, December 12: Andhra 203/8 in 50 overs (G Chandra Lekha 71, S Hima Bindu 41; Reena Dabhi 3-27, Neha Chavda 2-38) beat **Saurashtra** 141/9 in 50 overs (Mridula Jadeja 32, Pooja Nimavat 30; K Anjali Sarvani 3-30, E Padmaja 2-17) by 62 runs.

Devineni Venkata Ramana Praneetha Ground, Mulapadu, December 12: Vidarbha 142/9 in 50 overs (Bharati Fulmali 76*; Priya Khatkar 3-13, Mansi Joshi 3-18) lost to **Haryana** 145/5 in 33.4 overs (Shafali Verma 53, Sheetal Rana 34; Disha Kasat 2-26) by five wickets.

Chukkapalli Pitchaiah Cricket Ground, Mulapadu, December 14: Railways 251/5 in 50 overs (Punam Raut 136*, Shweta Jadhav 45; Reena Dabhi 2-42, Reena M 2-50) beat **Saurashtra** 88 in 39.1 overs (Pooja Nimavat 26; Sneh Rana 5-10, Rajeshwari Gayakwad 3-12) by 163 runs.

Andhra Cricket Association Women's Cricket Academy Ground, Guntur, December 14: Punjab 206/6 in 50 overs (Parveen Khan 71*, Ridhima Aggarwal 30; Shraddha Vaishnava 2-32, Adila Khanam 2-34) beat **Chhattisgarh** 160 in 49 overs (Deepika Tiwari 59, Shivi Pandey 36; Neelam Bisht 3-21, Babita Meena 2-20) by 46 runs.

Devineni Venkata Ramana Praneetha Ground, Mulapadu, December 14: Maharashtra 154 in 48.2 overs (Anuja Patil 28, Shivali Shinde 26; Komal Zanzad 2-13, Kanchan Nagwani 2-14) lost to **Vidarbha** 155/7 in 49.5 overs (Disha Kasat 38, Bharati Fulmali 34; A Patil 4-25) by three wickets.

Andhra Cricket Association Women's Cricket Academy Ground, Guntur, December 16: Goa 76 in 29.5 overs (Sunanda Yetrekar 24*; K Jyothi 3-25, K Anjali Sarvani 2-16) lost to **Andhra** 70/3 in 13.4 overs (CH Jhansi Lakshmi 36; Shikha Pandey 2-29) by seven wickets. (VJD method).

Devineni Venkata Ramana Praneetha Ground, Mulapadu, December 16: Saurashtra 77 in 49.3 overs (Mridula Jadeja 42; Shiva Prajapati 3-9, Priya Khatkar 3-10) v **Haryana**. No result.

Chukkapalli Pitchaiah Cricket Ground, Mulapadu, December 16: Chhattisgarh 93/9 in 50 overs (Mantravadi Shalini 48; Ekta Bisht 3-5, Rajeshwari Gayakwad 3-8) v **Railways**. No result.

Devineni Venkata Ramana Praneetha Ground, Mulapadu, December 18: Saurashtra 105/8 in 30 overs (Mridula Jadeja 22, Riddhi Ruparel 21; Reena Paul 4-24, Disha Kasat 2-9) lost to **Vidarbha** 110/2 in 26.2 overs (Latika Inamdar 50, D Kasat 30) by eight wickets.

Chukkapalli Pitchaiah Cricket Ground, Mulapadu, December 18: Marashtra 129/7 in 24 overs (Tejal Hasabnis 50, Devika Vaidya 29; Rajni Devi 3-16, Mehak Kesar 2-34) lost to **Punjab** 130/7 in 23.5 overs (Ridhima Aggarwal 29, Neelam Bisht 25) by three wickets.

Andhra Cricket Association Women's Cricket Academy Ground, Guntur, December 18: Haryana 147/4 in 30 overs (Sheetal Rana 51*, Shafali Verma 40; Nikita Malik 2-17) beat **Goa** 96 in 23.4 overs (Sanjula Naik 30, Shikha Pandey 20; Priya Khatkar 4-19) by 51 runs.

Devineni Venkata Ramana Praneetha Ground, Mulapadu, December 20: Chhattisgarh 128/9 in 50 overs (Mantravadi Shalini 56, Shivi Pandey 36; Disha Kasat 3-17, Reena Paul 3-27) lost to **Vidarbha** 129/6 in 38.4 overs (D Kasat 54; Adila Khanam 2-27) by four wickets.

Chukkapalli Pitchaiah Cricket Ground, Mulapadu, December 20: Haryana 157/8 in 50 overs (Shafali Verma 49, Bhawna Ohlan 29; Ekta Bisht 2-18, Poonam Yadav 2-25) lost to **Railways** 158/4 in 42.5 overs (Mithali Raj 42, Veda Krishnamurthy 40; Suman Gulia 2-27) by six wickets.

Andhra Cricket Association Women's Cricket Academy Ground, Guntur, December 20: Maharashtra 187/9 in 50 overs (Shweta Mane 56*, Tejal Hasabnis 42; K Anjali Sarvani 2-27) beat **Andhra** 188/2 in 48.1 overs (V Pushpa Latha 82*, CH Jhansi Lakshmi 48) by eight wickets.

Elite Group A points table

Team	M	W	L	T	N/R	Pts	NRR
Railways	8	7	0	0	1	30	+2.205
Andhra	8	7	1	0	0	28	+0.453
Punjab	8	5	3	0	0	20	+0.259
Vidarbha	8	4	4	0	0	16	-0.320
Chhattisgarh	8	3	4	0	1	14	-0.220
Goa	8	3	5	0	0	12	-0.941
Maharashtra	8	3	5	0	0	12	+0.701
Haryana	8	2	5	0	1	10	-0.485
Saurashtra	8	0	7	0	1	2	-1.703

Railways and Andhra qualified for the knock-outs

Elite Group B

Alur Cricket Stadium III, Bangalore, December 1: Karnataka 117/9 in 50 overs (Monica Patel 24*, Rakshitha Krishnappa 24; Shrayosi Aich 4-28, Nisha Maji 3-25) lost to **Bengal** 118/2 in 35.4 overs (Deepti Sharma 62*, Paramita Roy 26*) by eight wickets.

Alur Cricket Stadium, Bangalore, December 1: Kerala 105 in 44.5 overs (Sajeevan Sajana 31, Jincy George 21; Radha Yadav 3-20, Tarannum Pathan 2-16) lost to **Baroda** 106/3 in 39 overs (Palak Patel 42, Binaisha Surti 41; S Asha Joy 2-22) by seven wickets.

Alur Cricket Stadium II, Bangalore, December 1: Mumbai 197/8 in 50 overs (Vrushali Bhagat 76, Manali Dakshini 33*; Soni Yadav 2-41, Lalita Sharma 2-44) lost to **Delhi** 198/5 in 49 overs (Ayushi Soni 83, Mandeep Kaur 37; Prakashika Naik 2-38, Saima Thakor 2-40) by five wickets.

Alur Cricket Stadium II, Bangalore, December 2: Gujarat 168/8 in 50 overs (Renuka Chaudhari 38, Simran 34; Chandu V 3-24, C Pratyusha 2-42) lost to **Karnataka** 169/6 in 47.5 overs (Rakshitha Krishnappa 74*, VR Vanitha 31; Sarvi 3-19) by four wickets.

Alur Cricket Stadium III, Bangalore, December 2: Baroda 190 in 50 overs (Hrutu Patel 33,

Tarannum Pathan 33; Sweety Sinha 3-31, Priyanka Acharjee 2-27) beat **Tripura** 133/9 in 50 overs (Rizu Saha 52; Gayatri Naik 3-19, Pragya Rawat 2-11) by 57 runs.

Alur Cricket Stadium, Bangalore, December 2: Delhi 261/6 in 50 overs (Priya Punia 143, Reema Malhotra 51*; SB Keerthana 3-31) beat **Tamil Nadu** 143/8 in 50 overs (Dayalan Hemalatha 30, MD Thirushkamini 30; Babita Negi 3-22, Lalita Sharma 2-20) by 118 runs.

Alur Cricket Stadium II, Bangalore, December 3: Gujarat 98 in 47.3 overs (S Asha Joy 3-12, Mrudhula VS 3-28) lost to **Kerala** 103/4 in 32 overs (JS Deepthi 24, S Asha Joy 23*; Krutika Chaudhari 2-20, Retal Patel 2-22) by six wickets.

Alur Cricket Stadium III, Bangalore, December 3: Tripura 129 in 48.1 overs (Mouchaity Debnath 58, Rizu Saha 37; Humaira Kazi 2-11, Saima Thakor 2-14) lost to **Mumbai** 133/6 in 43.5 overs (Jemimah Rodrigues 32, Hemali Borwankar 32; Annapurna Das 3-26, Priyanka Acharjee 2-18) by four runs.

Alur Cricket Stadium, Bangalore, December 3: Tamil Nadu 195/8 in 50 overs (Niranjana Nagarajan 100, MD Thirushkamini 25; Shrayosi Aich 2-27, Nisha Maji 2-39) beat **Bengal** 159 in 42.4 overs (Mandira Mahapatra 37, Neha Maji 25; SB Keerthana 3-41, KN Ramyashri 2-17) by 36 runs.

Alur Cricket Stadium, Bangalore, December 5: Karnataka 125 in 43.4 overs (Rakshitha Krishnappa 32, G Divya 32; Saima Thakor 4-28, Jemimah Rodrigues 2-15) lost to **Mumbai** 126/3 in 31.5 overs (J Rodrigues 78*, Hemali Borwankar 27; Sahana Pawar 2-13) by seven wickets.

Alur Cricket Stadium III, Bangalore, December 5: Bengal 178 in 49.4 overs (Mandira Mahapatra 57*, Tanusree Sarkar 35; Mandeep Kaur 4-29, Lalita Sharma 3-36) beat **Delhi** 154 in 48 overs (Priya Punia 47, M Kaur 43; Shubhlakshmi Sharma 4-33, Jhulan Goswami 3-17) by 24 runs.

Alur Cricket Stadium II, Bangalore, December 5: Tamil Nadu 186/7 in 50 overs (Dayalan Hemalatha 67, Niranjana Nagarajan 40; Minnu Mani 2-46) beat **Kerala** 166 in 49.2 overs (S Asha Joy 36, Sajeevan Sajana 25; KV Ramyashri 4-37, SB Keerthana 3-32) by 20 runs.

Alur Cricket Stadium II, Bangalore, December 6: Mumbai 217 in 49.4 overs (Jemimah Rodrigues 104, Humaira Kazi 24; Radha Yadav 4-38, Tarannum Pathan 2-34) beat **Baroda** 176/9 in 49 overs (T Pathan 53, R Yadav 31; H Kazi 4-22, J Rodrigues 3-37) by 36 runs. (VJD method).

Alur Cricket Stadium, Bangalore, December 6: Gujarat 54 in 40.3 overs (Deepti Sharma 4-12, Shrayosi Aich 4-14) lost to **Bengal** 56/1 in 15.1 overs (D Sharam 34*, Dipali Shaw 20) by nine wickets.

Alur Cricket Stadium III, Bangalore, December 6: Tripura 131/7 in 50 overs (Mouchaity Debnath 54, Rizu Saha 25; S Asha Joy 3-21) beat **Kerala** 122 in 42.5 overs (Sajeevan Sajana 30, Deepthi JS 26; Suravi Roy 4-21, Priyanka Acharjee 3-27) by nine runs.

Alur Cricket Stadium, Bangalore, December 8: Tripura 92 in 47 overs (Sulakshana Roy 22, Mouchaity Debnath 21; Babita Negi 4-21, Lalita Sharma 2-10) lost to **Delhi** 93/6 in 30 overs (Arushi Goel 27, Laxmi Yadav 26; Priyanka Acharjee 2-18, Annapurna Das 2-21) by four wickets.

Alur Cricket Stadium III, Bangalore, December 8: Karnataka 202/5 in 50 overs (Shubha Sateesh 72, VR Vanitha 47; Niranjana Nagarajan 2-28, KN Ramyashri 2-41) beat **Tamil Nadu** 153 in 46.2 overs (Dayalan Hemalatha 49, N Nagarajan 27; C Pratyusha 3-35, Chandu V 2-36) by 49 runs.

Alur Cricket Stadium II, Bangalore, December 8: Gujarat 78 in 37 overs (Renuka Chaudhari 25, Pragna Chaudhari 21; Tarannum Pathan 5-26, Nancy Patel 3-6) lost to **Baroda** 79/0 in 14.2 overs (Yastika Bhatia 45*, Palak Patel 30*) by 10 wickets.

Alur Cricket Stadium III, Bangalore, December 10: Bengal 221/2 in 50 overs (Deepti Sharma 106*, Tanusree Sarkar 81*) beat **Baroda** 91 in 37.3 overs (Tarannum Pathan 23; Priya Pandey 3-12, T Sarkar 2-16) by 130 runs.

Alur Cricket Stadium II, Bangalore, December 10: Delhi 157/9 in 50 overs (Reema Malhotra 42, Mandeep Kaur 26; Sahana Pawar 4-30, Monica Patel 2-42) beat **Karnataka** 129/9 in 50 overs (Chandu V 22*, Akanksha Kohli 22; Simran Bahadur 4-14, M Kaur 2-27) by 28 runs.

Alur Cricket Stadium, Bangalore, December 10: Mumbai 180/8 in 50 overs (Shweta Haranhalli 58, Vrushali Bhagat 27; T Shani 3-25, S Asha Joy 2-22) lost to **Kerala** 184/9 in 49.4 overs (Akshaya A 55*, Jincy George 30; Jemimah Rodrigues 3-29) by one wicket.

Alur Cricket Stadium III, Bangalore, December 12: Delhi 143 in 45.2 overs (Priya Punia 46, Ayushi Soni 27; Minnu Mani 4-32, Mrudhula VS 3-34) lost to **Kerala** 144/7 in 49 overs (Jincy George 46, T Shani 40; Lalita Sharma 3-23) by three wickets.

Alur Cricket Stadium, Bangalore, December 12: Tamil Nadu 120 in 46.5 overs (MD Thirushkamini 63; Radha Yadav 3-20, Nancy Patel 2-17) lost to **Baroda** 121/4 in 36 overs (Yastika Bhatia 55, R Yadav 35*; KN Ramyashri 2-19) by six wickets.

Alur Cricket Stadium II, Bangalore, December 12: Tripura 118 in 48.3 overs (Mouchaity Debnath 33; Toral Patel 3-22, Renuka Chaudhari 2-25) beat **Gujarat** 58 in 43.1 overs (Sweety Sinha 2-9, Priyanka Acharjee 2-9) by 60 runs.

Alur Cricket Stadium II, Bangalore, December 14: Tamil Nadu 151 in 49.1 overs (L Nethra Iyer 44, SB Keerthana 34; Humaira Kazi 3-12, Prakashika Naik 3-20) lost to **Mumbai** 152/5 in 42.2 overs (Vrushali Bhagat 41*, Mugdha Joshi 31; S Anusha 3-20) by five wickets.

Alur Cricket Stadium, Bangalore, December 14: Bengal 224/4 in 50 overs (Deepti Sharma 102*, Dipali Shaw 36; Sajeevan Sajana 2-35) beat **Kerala** 150/9 in 50 overs (S Asha Joy 88, Jipsa Joseph 20*; D Sharma 4-12, Shubhlakshmi Sharma 3-23) by 74 runs.

M. Chinnaswamy Stadium, Bangalore December 14: Karnataka 219/7 in 50 overs (Shubha Sateesh 60, VR Vanitha 35; Priyanka Acharjee 3-36) beat **Tripura** 162/5 in 50 overs (Rizu Saha 51*, Indra Rani Jamatia 32) by 57 runs.

Alur Cricket Stadium II, Bangalore, December 16: Baroda 188/8 in 50 overs (Palak Patel 80, Yastika Bhatia 37; Mandeep Kaur 3-28) beat **Delhi** 166 in 48 overs (Neha Tanwar 40, Arushi Goel 29; Tarannum Pathan 4-29, Radha Yadav 3-45) by 22 runs.

Alur Cricket Stadium III, Bangalore, December 16: Tamil Nadu 137/8 in 50 overs (L Nethra Iyer 34, MD Thirushkamini 25; Renuka Chaudhari 2-23, Retal Patel 2-30) beat **Gujarat** 114/8 in 50 overs (Simran 51, IM Patel 27; KN Ramyashri 2-21) by 23 runs.

M. Chinnaswamy Stadium, Bangalore December 16: Bengal 193 in 49.5 overs (Prativa 80, Jhulan Goswami 43; Jemimah Rodrigues 3-23, Sheryl Rozario 3-31) lost to **Mumbai** 194/2 in 38.5 overs (J Rodrigues 133*, Mugdha Joshi 32*) by eight wickets.

Alur Cricket Stadium II, Bangalore, December 18: Tripura 172/9 in 50 overs (Mouchaity Debnath 88, Rizu Saha 25; KN Ramyashri 3-23, SB Keerthana 3-36) lost to **Tamil Nadu** 174/4 in 46.1 overs (MD Thirushkamini 72, Dayalan Hemalatha 53; Sweety Sinha 2-21) by six wickets.

M. Chinnaswamy Stadium, Bangalore December 18: Kerala 117 in 49.3 overs (Minnu Mani 44*, C Pratyusha 2-17, Sahana Pawar 2-24) lost to **Karnataka** 118/7 in 34.4 overs (VR Vanitha 27, C Pratyusha 25*; S Asha Joy 5-27) by three wickets.

Alur Cricket Stadium III, Bangalore, December 18: Delhi 207/6 in 50 overs (Priya Punia 125, Neha Tanwar 33; Renuka Chaudhari 3-28, Krutika Chaudhari 2-30) beat **Gujarat** 110/9 in 50 overs (R Chaudhari 24, Sarvi 23; Lalita Sharma 3-34, Babita Negi 2-23) by 97 runs.

Alur Cricket Stadium III, Bangalore, December 20: Mumbai 199/6 in 50 overs (Shweta Haranhalli 56, Vrushali Bhagat 45; Pragna Chaudhari 3-34) beat **Gujarat** 74 in 31 overs (Renuka CHaudhari 22; Sayali Satghare 3-25, Prakashika Naik 2-10) by 125 runs.

M. Chinnaswamy Stadium, Bangalore December 20: Baroda 136 in 49.1 overs (Radha Yadav 43, Tarannum Pathan 29; Sahana Pawar 3-19, Akanksha Kohli 2-19) beat **Karnataka** 129 in 44.4 overs (VR Vanitha 36, Monica Patel 21; R Yadav 4-20, T Pathan 3-29) by seven runs.

Alur Cricket Stadium II, Bangalore, December 20: Tripura 63 in 37 overs (Deepti Sharma 3-4, Jhulan Goswami 2-10) lost to **Bengal** 64/2 in 16.1 overs (Tanusree Sarkar 31*) by eight wickets.

Elite Group B points table

Team	M	W	L	T	N/R	Pts	NRR
Mumbai	8	6	2	0	0	24	+0.822
Bengal	8	6	2	0	0	24	+1.208
Baroda	8	6	2	0	0	24	+0.296
Delhi	8	5	3	0	0	20	+0.679
Karnataka	8	4	4	0	0	16	+0.064
Tamil Nadu	8	4	4	0	0	16	-0.382
Kerala	8	3	5	0	0	12	-0.308
Tripura	8	2	6	0	0	8	-0.632
Gujarat	8	0	8	0	0	0	-1.568

Mumbai, Bengal and Baroda qualified for the knock-outs

Elite Group C

Sunshine Ground, Cuttack, December 1: Jharkhand 104 in 48.2 overs (Rashmi 39; Harleen Deol 4-23, Tanuja Kanwer 2-11) lost to **Himachal Pradesh** 107/1 in 21.5 overs (Nikita Chauhan 56, H Deol 36*) by nine wickets.

Bhubananda Orissa School of Engineering Ground, Cuttack, December 1: Assam 76 in 32.2 overs (Anita Lodhi 37; Poonam Soni 3-16, Nidhi Buley 2-3) lost to **Madhya Pradesh** 77/5 in 30.3 overs by five wickets.

Nimpur Ground, Cuttack, December 1: Hyderabad 183/7 in 50 overs (SK Sravanthi Naidu 49*, G Trisha 47; Madhusmita Behera 2-25, Sushree Dibyadarshini 2-35) beat **Odisha** 155/8 in 50 overs (S Dibyadarshini 50*, Pragyan Mohanty 43; G Trisha 2-23, Himani Yadav 2-27) by 28 runs.

Sunshine Ground, Cuttack, December 2: Jharkhand 253/4 in 50 overs (Durga Kumari Murmu 80, Kavita Roy 61*; Bismah Hassan 2-41) beat **Jammu & Kashmir** 121/8 in 50 overs (Meenu Salathia 36; Arti 3-30) by 132 runs.

Bhubananda Orissa School of Engineering Ground, Cuttack, December 2: Uttar Pradesh 227/4 in 50 overs (Muskan Malik 98, Aditi Sharma 67*; Shanti Rai 2-43) beat **Assam** 125 in 42.3 overs (Anita Lodhi 42, Rajni Lodhi 30; Tanu Kala 4-20, Rashi Kanojiya 3-18) by 102 runs.

Nimpur Ground, Cuttack, December 2: Hyderabad 207/5 in 50 overs (Mamtha Kanojia 88, G Trisha 52; Ayushi Garg 2-25) beat **Rajasthan** 129 in 49.1 overs (A Garg 61, Suman Meena 32; G Trisha 5-17, Bhogi Shravani 2-13) by 78 runs.

Sunshine Ground, Cuttack, December 3: Madhya Pradesh 155/8 in 50 overs (Babita Mandlik 44, Pallavi Bharadwaj 21; Nadia Chowdhary 3-28, Sandhya Balkar 3-37) beat **Jammu & Kashmir** 70 in 41.3 overs (Meenu Salathia 24; Aparna Shrivastava 5-8, Varsha Choudhary 2-23) by 85 runs.

Bhubananda Orissa School of Engineering Ground, Cuttack, December 3: Uttar Pradesh 141/8 in 50 overs (Aditi Sharma 44*, Muskan Malik 32; Madhusmita Behera 4-13, Priyanka Priyadarshini 2-20) lost to **Odisha** 142/4 in 44.1 overs (M Behara 50, Sarita Meher 34; Rashi Kanojiya 3-21) by six wickets.

Nimpur Ground, Cuttack, December 3: Rajasthan 121 in 49.1 overs (Tanuja Vaishnav 29, JD Choudhary 20; Tanuja Kanwer 2-12, Anisha Ansari 2-21) lost to **Himachal Pradesh** 124/6 in 45.2 overs (SM Singh 33*, Nikita Chauhan 32; SS Kalal 3-23) by four wickets.

Sunshine Ground, Cuttack, December 5: Odisha 68 in 36.4 overs (Kavita Roy 3-0, Arti

2-12) lost to **Jharkhand** 72/3 in 24.3 overs (Priyanka Sawaiyan 29) by seven wickets.

Bhubananda Orissa School of Engineering Ground, Cuttack, December 5: Hyderabad 148 in 49.5 overs (Vanka Pooja 34, Mamtha Kanojia 30; Renuka Singh 2-20, Harleen Deol 2-33) lost to **Himachal Pradesh** 152/6 in 37.5 overs (Neena Chaudhary 49*, Nikita Chauhan 25; Himani Yadav 3-27) by four wickets.

Nimpur Ground, Cuttack, December 5: Madhya Pradesh 202/3 in 50 overs (Babita Mandlik 81, Varsha Choudhary 37; Shweta Bishnoi 2-38) beat **Rajasthan** 64 in 40.2 overs (Priyanka Sharma 29*; Varsha Choudhary 2-6, Pallavi Bharadwaj 2-10) by 138 runs.

Sunshine Ground, Cuttack, December 6: Odisha 182/5 in 50 overs (Madhuri Meheta 93, Sarita Meher 37) beat **Assam** 116 in 38.4 overs (Anita Lodhi 32; Sushree Dibyadarshini 3-7, Reemalaxmi Ekka 3-22) by 66 runs.

Bhubananda Orissa School of Engineering Ground, Cuttack, December 6: Jammu & Kashmir 79 in 37.4 overs (Rubia Syed 29, Jaspreet Kour 20; Sushmita Kumari 3-15, Tanuja Kanwer 3-23) lost to **Himachal Pradesh** 80/1 in 16.2 overs (Nikita Chauhan 35*, Neena Chaudhary 30*) by nine wickets.

Nimpur Ground, Cuttack, December 6: Uttar Pradesh 133/8 in 50 overs (Kshama 35*, Sweta Verma 30; Pallavi Bharadwaj 2-29) beat **Madhya Pradesh** 126 in 49.4 overs (Tamanna Nigam 58, Ruchita Buley 31; Anjali Singh 3-4, Aditi Sharma 2-30) by seven runs.

Sunshine Ground, Cuttack, December 8: Hyderabad 211/3 in 50 overs (Mamtha Kanojia 69*, G Trisha 69; Tanu Kala 2-38) beat **Rajasthan** 158 in 44.4 overs (Kshama 28, Neetu Gaur 26; Himani Yadav 4-25, G Trisha 3-11) by 53 runs.

Bhubananda Orissa School of Engineering Ground, Cuttack, December 8: Jharkhand 173/8 in 50 overs (Priyanka Sawaiyan 34, Rashmi 30; Shweta Bishnoi 2-20, SS Kalal 2-24) beat **Rajasthan** 92 in 38.2 overs (Ayushi Garg 36; Devyani Prasad 3-19, Niharika Prasad 2-12) by 81 runs.

Nimpur Ground, Cuttack, December 8: Assam 160/9 in 50 overs (Anita Lodhi 68, Rashmi Dey 28*; Bismah Hassan 3-30) beat **Jammu & Kashmir** 105 in 41.5 overs (Rubia Syed 54*; A Lodhi 2-14, R Dey 2-15) by 55 runs.

Sunshine Ground, Cuttack, December 10: Assam 105 in 49.1 overs (Renuka Singh 4-33, Suhsmita Kumari 2-20) lost to **Himachal Pradesh** 109/1 in 26.2 overs (Harleen Deol 62*, Neena Chaudhary 32*) by nine wickets.

Bhubananda Orissa School of Engineering Ground, Cuttack, December 10: Hyderabad 155/8 in 50 overs (Mamtha Kanojia 72*, Rachna Kumar 31; Mamta Paswan 3-45, Kavita Roy 2-13) beat **Jharkhand** 131 in 47.5 overs (Niharika Prasad 38; Yashasri 2-7, R Kumar 2-13) by 24 runs.

Nimpur Ground, Cuttack, December 10: Odisha 164/6 in 50 overs (Madhuri Meheta 47, Sarita Meher 46; Nidhi Buley 2-31) beat **Madhya Pradesh** 156 in 49.5 overs (Babita Mandlik 44, Ruchita Buley 33; Madhusmita Behera 4-29, Sushree Dibyadarshini 3-31) by eight runs.

Sunshine Ground, Cuttack, December 12: Hyderabad 148/8 in 50 overs (Himani Yadav 40, Doli Ramya 28; Varsha Choudhary 3-22, Salonee Dangore 2-49) lost to **Madhya Pradesh** 149/6 in 48.3 overs (Tamanna Nigam 54, V Choudhary 40; H Yadav 3-33) by four wickets.

Bhubananda Orissa School of Engineering Ground, Cuttack, December 12: Rajasthan 110/8 in 50 overs (Ayushi Garg 30, Jwala Bijarnya 22; Rekharani Bora 2-16) lost to **Assam** 113/8 in 37.2 overs (Rajni Lodhi 25, Monikha Das 23; SS Kalal 3-24, Poonam Yadav 2-12) by two wickets.

Nimpur Ground, Cuttack, December 12: Jammu & Kashmir 98/7 in 50 overs (Meenu Salathia 42, Rashi Kanojiya 2-14, Tanu Kala 2-20) lost to **Uttar Pradesh** 99/2 in 29 overs (Aditi Sharma 51*, T Kala 28*; Sarla Devi 2-24) by eight wickets.

Sunshine Ground, Cuttack, December 14: Rajasthan 107 in 47.2 overs (Suman Meena 51*, Priyanka Sharma 24; Priyanka Priyadarshini 4-24, Sushree Dibyadarshini 2-27) lost to **Odisha** 108/7 in 46.2 overs (Sarita Meher 46*; S Meena 4-21, KP Dangi 2-16) by three wickets.

Bhubananda Orissa School of Engineering Ground, Cuttack, December 14: Himachal

Pradesh 129 in 48.5 overs (SM Singh 25, Chitra Singh Jamwal 21; Nidhi Buley 3-25, Varsha Choudhary 2-21) beat **Madhya Pradesh** 89 in 44.1 overs (Tamanna Nigam 22; Nikita Chauhan 2-5) by 40 runs.

Nimpur Ground, Cuttack, December 14: Uttar Pradesh 169 in 47.5 overs (Ekta Singh 84, Neetu Gaur 29; Kavita Roy 3-29, Ashwani Kumari 2-20) beat **Jharkhand** 155 in 49.1 overs (Rashmi 50, Indrani Roy 41; Aditi Sharma 2-35) by 14 runs.

Bhubananda Orissa School of Engineering Ground, Cuttack, December 16: Rajasthan 130 in 39.2 overs (Priyanka Sharma 24, Ayushi Garg 21; Rubia Syed 3-22, Sarla Devi 3-30) beat **Jammu & Kashmir** 103 in 48.4 overs (Jaspreet Kour 25; Shweta Bishnoi 3-12, SS Kalal 2-18) by 27 runs.

Nimpur Ground, Cuttack, December 16: Odisha 72 in 36.3 overs (Madhuri Meheta 32; Renuka Singh 5-17, Anisha Ansari 2-8) lost to **Himachal Pradesh** 76/2 in 18.1 overs (Harleen Deol 38*; Priyanka Priyadarshini 2-23) by eight wickets.

Sunshine Ground, Cuttack, December 16: Assam 205 in 49.2 overs (Rajni Lodhi 61, Monikha Das 38; Bhogi Shravani 3-44, Himani Yadav 2-38) beat **Hyderabad** 190/8 in 50 overs (Vanka Pooja 42, Sunitha Anand 41; Anita Lodhi 2-17) by 15 runs.

Sunshine Ground, Cuttack, December 18: Uttar Pradesh 107/4 in 20 overs (Muskan Malik 59*, Shashi Mathur 29) beat **Rajasthan** 69/7 in 20 overs (Kshama 4-7) by 38 runs.

Bhubananda Orissa School of Engineering Ground, Cuttack, December 18: Jharkhand v **Madhya Pradesh**. Match abandoned without a ball being bowled.

Nimpur Ground, Cuttack, December 18: Hyderabad v **Jammu & Kashmir**. Match abandoned without a ball being bowled.

Sunshine Ground, Cuttack, December 20: Himachal Pradesh 140 in 47.1 overs (Sushma Verma 38, Tanuja Kanwer 32; Tanu Kala 2-17, Aditi Sharma 2-22) beat **Uttar Pradesh** 133 in 49.2 overs (Kshama 36; T Kanwer 3-14, Sushmita Kumari 2-42) by seven runs.

Bhubananda Orissa School of Engineering Ground, Cuttack, December 20: Jammu & **Kashmir** 45 in 19.1 overs (Sujata Mallik 4-14, Priyanka Priyadarshini 3-0) lost to **Odisha** 46/5 in 7.4 overs (Bismah Hassan 3-18, Sarla Devi 2-24) by five wickets.

Nimpur Ground, Cuttack, December 20: Jharkhand 159/9 in 50 overs (Sonia 26, Ashwani 21; Rashmi Dey 2-13, Kakoli Saikia 2-43) beat **Assam** 101 in 37.3 overs (Anita Lodhi 26; Santi Kumari 3-21, Niharika Prasad 2-29) by 58 runs.

Elite Group C points table

Team	M	W	L	T	N/R	Pts	NRR
Himachal Pradesh	8	8	0	0	0	32	+1.322
Odisha	8	5	3	0	0	20	+0.076
Uttar Pradesh	8	5	3	0	0	20	+0.417
Madhya Pradesh	8	4	3	0	1	18	+0.660
Hyderabad	8	4	3	0	1	18	+0.340
Jharkhand	8	4	3	0	1	18	+0.700
Assam	8	3	5	0	0	12	-0.664
Rajasthan	8	1	7	0	0	4	-1.036
Jammu & Kashmir	8	0	7	0	1	2	-1.874

Himachal Pradesh and Odisha qualified for the knock-outs

Plate Group

Ravenshaw University Ground 1, Cuttack, December 1: Mizoram 287/4 in 50 overs (Sandhya Kumari 159, MP Singson 44; Kipa Mero 2-49) beat **Arunachal Pradesh** 91 in 26.5 overs (S Kumari 5-1, Rosie Hmar 2-26) by 196 runs.

Ravenshaw University Ground 2, December 1: Nagaland 203/5 in 50 overs (V Karuna Jain 85, Zehen 24; Rachana Kumari 3-33) beat **Bihar** 79 in 26.2 overs (Elina 3-16, Ayantika 2-18) by 124 runs.

KIIT Cricket Stadium, Bhubaneshwar, December 1: Manipur 190/8 in 50 overs (Monica 35*, Chingkhei M 28; Ashtalakshmi A 2-40) lost to **Pondicherry** 191/3 in 42.3 overs (Anagha Deshpande 64*, Gouher Sultana 36*) by seven wickets.

Ravenshaw University Ground 1, Cuttack, December 2: Mizoram 11 in 13 overs (Vandana Mahajan 8-4, Trisha Bera 2-5) lost to **Meghalaya** 14/0 in 3 overs by 10 wickets.

Ravenshaw University Ground 2, Cuttack, December 2: Bihar 75 in 34.4 overs (Syed Nishat Fatma 37; Madhwal 3-15, R Rai 2-31) lost to **Uttarakhand** 77/2 in 23.4 overs (Madhwal 25; Shraddha 2-22) by eight wickets.

KIIT Cricket Stadium, Bhubaneshwar, December 2: Manipur 233/5 in 50 overs (Ganga Waikom 113*, Ranita 37; Priyanka Acharya 3-30) beat **Sikkim** 180/7 in 50 overs (Archana Das 87*, Ananya Upendran 27; Milan Y 4-33) by 53 runs.

Ravenshaw University Ground 1, Cuttack, December 3: Meghalaya 152 in 48.1 overs (Saee Purandare 84, Trisha Bera 33; V Karuna Jain 2-10, J Rameshwari 2-22) beat **Nagaland** 129 in 45.5 overs (Munia 38, M Soujanya Nath 23; Vandana Mahajan 4-23, Pinky Chanda 3-32) by 23 runs.

Ravenshaw University Ground 2, Cuttack, December 3: Uttarakhand 138 in 46.2 overs (Mamta Kothiyal 36, Madhwal 22; Gouher 4-13) beat **Pondicherry** 122 in 45.1 overs (Anagha Deshpande 29, Gouher Sultana 29; Manisha Pradhan 4-24, R Rai 2-31) by 16 runs.

KIIT Cricket Stadium, Bhubaneshwar, December 3: Arunachal Pradesh 243/4 in 50 overs (Suvalaxmi Rout 100, Neelam Rajput 78; Ananya Upendran 2-37) beat **Sikkim** 209 in 42 overs (Tshering Ongmu Lepcha 60, Tabita Subba 34*; Nabam Yapu 2-28, Varsha Patel 2-35) by 34 runs.

Ravenshaw University Ground 1, Cuttack, December 5: Pondicherry 319/4 in 50 overs (Latika Kumari 122, Ramya Maharajan 102; Iram Khan 2-53) beat **Mizoram** 87 in 41.2 overs (I Khan 33*; Gouher Sultana 4-19, Divya Shanmugam 2-11) by 232 runs.

Ravenshaw University Ground 2, Cuttack, December 5: Manipur 198/9 in 50 overs (Ganga Waikom 42, Ranita 25; Neelam Rajput 3-27, T Doimari 2-40) beat **Arunachal Pradesh** 44 in 31.4 overs (Saba Siddiqui 4-6, Monica 2-16) by 154 runs.

KIIT Cricket Stadium, Bhubaneshwar, December 5: Nagaland 214/7 in 50 overs (V Karuna Jain 98, Kashish 26; Priyanka Acharya 2-34) beat **Sikkim** 160 in 47.5 overs (Archana Das 34, Ananya Upendran 23; Ayantika 4-28) by 54 runs.

Ravenshaw University Ground 1, Cuttack, December 6: Bihar 68 in 27 overs (Ashtalakshmi 4-8, Gouher Sultana 3-3) lost to **Pondicherry** 69/1 in 22.5 overs (Latika Kumari 41*) by nine wickets.

Ravenshaw University Ground 2, Cuttack, December 6: Meghalaya 291/3 in 50 overs (Saee Purandhare 153*, Trisha Bera 66) beat **Arunachal Pradesh** 82 in 41.2 overs (Neelam Rajput 34; T Bera 3-11, Debasmita Dutta 2-19) by 209 runs.

KIIT Cricket Stadium, Bhubaneshwar, December 6: Uttarakhand 213/6 in 50 overs (Megha Saini 72, Kanchan Parihar 40; Rupsena 2-46) beat **Nagaland** 165/9 in 50 overs (Zehen 58*, V Karuna Jain 29; Rekha 3-28, Madhwal 2-19) by 48 runs.

Ravenshaw University Ground 1, Cuttack, December 8: Manipur 118 in 49.3 overs (Chingkhei M 20; Nisha Mishra 4-21, R Rai 4-26) lost to **Uttarakhand** 119/7 in 36 overs (Mamta Kothiyal 31, Radha Chand 29*) by three wickets.

Ravenshaw University Ground 2, Cuttack, December 8: Sikkim 260/7 in 50 overs (Priyanka Acharya 82*, Tshering Ongmu Lepcha 48; Iram Khan 3-40) beat **Mizoram** 44 in 19 overs

(Dichen Ongmu Lepcha 5-14, Priyanka Acharya 2-5) by 216 runs.

KIIT Cricket Stadium, Bhubaneshwar, December 8: Bihar 104 in 43.4 overs (Syed Nishat Fatma 39; Trisha Bera 4-16, Debasmita Dutta 3-16) lost to **Meghalaya** 107/0 in 23 overs (Saee Purandhare 59*, D Dutta 39*) by 10 wickets.

Ravenshaw University Ground 1, Cuttack, December 10: Bihar 225/6 in 50 overs (Beauty Kumari 77*, Syed Nishat Fatma 24; Mari Ado 3-24) beat **Arunachal Pradesh** 53 in 31.4 overs (Pooja Kumari 3-18, Rachana Kumari 2-6) by 172 runs.

Ravenshaw University Ground 2, Cuttack, December 10: Manipur 245/6 in 50 overs (Chingkhei M 48, Ganga Waikom 46; Sandhya Kumari 2-27) beat **Mizoram** 27 in 21.3 overs (Monica 5-4, G Waikom 2-2) by 218 runs.

KIIT Cricket Stadium, Bhubaneshwar, December 10: Nagaland 194/6 in 50 overs (M Soujanya Nath 44*, Kashish 35; Ashtalakshmi A 2-29, Rebecca 2-30) lost to **Pondicherry** 195/2 in 36.4 overs (Latika Kumari 90*, Anagha Deshpande 84*; Merensola 2-30) by eight wickets.

Ravenshaw University Ground 1, Cuttack, December 12: Nagaland 172/9 in 50 overs (J Rameshwari 96; Roshni 3-15, Chingkhei M 3-27) beat **Manipur** 139 in 42.4 overs (Ganga Waikom 60, Milan Y 31; J Rameshwari 3-25, Merensola 2-22) by 33 runs.

Ravenshaw University Ground 2, Cuttack, December 12: Sikkim 176 in 49.1 overs (Archana Das 82, Ananya Upendran 26; Anamika 3-17, Beauty Kumari 2-28) beat **Bihar** 98 in 35.5 overs (Rachana Kumari 29, Syed Nishat Fatma 26; Priyanka Acharya 5-12, A Das 2-14) by 78 runs.

KIIT Cricket Stadium, Bhubaneshwar, December 12: Uttarakhand 101 in 40.4 overs (Manisha Pradhan 31, Rekha 25*; Vandana Mahajan 4-13, Trisha Bera 2-10) lost to **Meghalaya** 103/0 in 30 overs (Saee Purandhare 62*, Debasmita Dutta 34*) by 10 wickets.

Ravenshaw University Ground 1, Cuttack, December 14: Sikkim 198/6 in 50 overs (Ananya Upendran 92, Sunita Rai 37) lost to **Pondicherry** 199/4 in 39.1 overs (Anagha Deshpande 114*, Gouher Sultana 37*; Priyanka Acharya 2-15) by six wickets.

Ravenshaw University Ground 2, Cuttack, December 14: Arunachal Pradesh 110/8 in 50 overs (Neelam Rajput 29, Varsha Patel 24; Kashish 3-22, Merensola 2-14) lost to **Nagaland** 111/2 in 18.5 overs (V Karuna Jain 39*, Kashish 32*) by eight wickets.

KIIT Cricket Stadium, Bhubaneshwar, December 14: Uttarakhand 355/8 in 50 overs (Mamta Kothiyal 112, Kanchan Parihar 103; Iram Khan 3-54) beat **Mizoram** 114 in 46 overs (Sandhya Kumari 79*; Jyoti Giri 4-11, Nisha Mishra 2-15) by 241 runs.

Ravenshaw University Ground 1, Cuttack, December 16: Bihar 119 in 36.1 overs (Amisha Kumari Anshu 39, Anamika 31; Roshni 3-25, Ganga Waikom 2-15) lost to **Manipur** 120/6 in 44.1 overs (G Waikom 48, Ranita 33*; Shraddha 3-21, Anamika 2-25) by four wickets.

Ravenshaw University Ground 2, Cuttack, December 16: Sikkim 203 in 50 overs (Ananya Upendran 157*; Vandana Mahajan 4-42, Debasmita Dutta 2-26) tied with **Meghalaya** 203/6 in 50 overs (Saee Purandhare 68; D Dutta 43; Pranita Chhetri 2-25, A Upendran 2-35).

KIIT Cricket Stadium, Bhubaneshwar, December 16: Arunachal Pradesh 131/7 in 50 overs (Neelam Rajput 61, B Ritu 26; Gouher Sultana 4-15, Divya Shanmugam 2-27) lost to **Pondicherry** 132/2 in 25.2 overs (Latika Kumari 60, Ashtalakshmi A 38*) by eight wickets.

Ravenshaw University Ground 2, Cuttack, December 18: Uttarakhand 137/3 in 22 overs (Kanchan Parihar 57*, Megha Saini 55; Priyanka Acharya 2-27) beat **Sikkim** 85/8 in 20 overs (Archana Das 26, Ananya Upendran 22; Nisha Mishra 5-13, R Rai 2-16) by 42 runs. (VJD method).

Ravenshaw University Ground 2, Cuttack, December 18: Mizoram 32/8 in 22 overs (J Rameshwari 3-1) lost to **Nagaland** 36/3 in 15.1 overs (Sandhya Kumari 2-12) by seven wickets.

KIIT Cricket Stadium, Bhubaneshwar, December 18: Manipur v **Meghalaya**. Match abandoned without a ball being bowled.

Ravenshaw University Ground 1, Cuttack, December 20: Uttarakhand 300/7 in 50 overs (Radha Chand 104*, Jyoti Giri 45; Neelam Rajput 2-40) beat **Arunachal Pradesh** 75 in 35.2 overs (N Rajput 27; J Giri 4-2, R Chand 2-5) by 225 runs.

Ravenshaw University Ground 2, Cuttack, December 20: Meghalaya 167/7 in 50 overs (Debasmita Dutta 51, Vandana Mahajan 40; Radhi 3-31, Rebecca 2-37) lost to **Pondicherry** 168/5 in 44.5 overs (Gouher Sultana 69, Anagha Deshpande 38; Trisha Bera 2-22) by five wickets.

KIIT Cricket Stadium, Bhubaneshwar, December 20: Mizoram 78 in 38.3 overs (Beauty Kumari 3-13, Pooja Kumari 2-17) lost to **Bihar** 80/2 in 18.1 overs (B Kumari 34*, Amisha Kumari Anshu 24) by eight wickets.

Plate Group points table

Team	M	W	L	T	N/R	Pts	NRR
Uttarakhand	8	7	1	0	0	28	+1.889
Pondicherry	8	7	1	0	0	28	+1.548
Meghalaya	8	5	1	1	1	24	+1.737
Nagaland	8	5	3	0	0	20	+0.654
Manipur	8	4	3	0	1	18	+1.018
Sikkim	8	2	5	1	0	10	+0.186
Bihar	8	2	6	0	0	8	-0.512
Mizoram	8	1	7	0	0	4	-3.061
Arunachal Pradesh	8	1	7	0	0	4	-3.021

Uttarakhand qualified for the knock-outs

Quarter-finals

Just Cricket, Bangalore, December 26: Uttarakhand 62 in 37.5 overs (Poonam Yadav 5-8, Ekta Bisht 2-4) lost to **Railways** 64/0 in 8.2 overs (Mona Meshram 37*, Sneh Rana 20*) by 10 wickets.

M. Chinnaswamy Stadium, Bangalore, December 26: Odisha 160 in 50 overs (Sushree Dibyadarshini 46, Madhuri Meheta 42; G Chandra Lekha 2-16, E Padmaja 2-25) lost to **Andhra** 161/7 in 46.5 overs (CH Jhansi Lakshmi 75, E Padmaja 21; Priyanka Priyadarshini 2-17, S Dibyadarshini 2-28) by three wickets.

Alur Cricket Stadium II, Bangalore, December 27: Mumbai 138 in 36.4 overs (Mugdha Joshi 42, Humaira Kazi 30; Tanuja Kanwer 2-17, Anisha Ansari 2-24) lost to **Himachal Pradesh** 140/4 in 42.4 overs (Harleen Deol 74*, Nikita Chauhan 40) by six wickets.

Alur Cricket Stadium III, Bangalore, December 27: Bengal 174 in 48.2 overs (Prativa 37, Deepti Sharam 33; Tarannum Pathan 3-25, Nancy Patel 3-34) beat **Baroda** 97/9 in 50 overs (Tanusree Sarkar 3-19, Nisha Maji 2-13) by 77 runs.

Railways, Andhra, Himachal Pradesh, Bengal qualified for semi-finals

Semi-finals

M Chinnaswamy Stadium, Bangalore, December 29: Bengal 211/7 in 50 overs (Deepti Sharma 85, Jhulan Goswami 50*; Ekta Bisht 2-34) beat **Railways** 190 in 49 overs (Nuzhat Parween 74, Mithali Raj 37; Shubhlakshmi Sharma 5-48, J Goswami 3-9) by 21 runs.

Just Cricket, Bangalore, December 29: Himachal Pradesh 194/3 in 50 overs (Neena

Chaudhary 79, Sushma Verma 59) lost to **Andhra** 195/6 in 48.3 overs (G Chandra Lekha 49, S Hima Bindu 45; Renuka Singh 2-29) by four wickets.

Bengal and Andhra qualified for the final

Final: Bengal beat Andhra by 10 runs

Just Cricket, Bangalore, December 31: Bengal 198/7 in 50 overs (Mandira Mahapatra 39*, Deepti Sharma 34; CH Jhansi Lakshmi 3-40) beat **Andhra** 188 in 49.1 overs (N Anusha 60, E Padmaja 40; D Sharma 3-33, Shubhlakshmi Sharma 2-29) by 10 runs.

Winners: Bengal

2017-18

Elite Group A

Railways Recreation Club Ground, Secunderabad, December 6: Madhya Pradesh 150/9 in 50 overs (Nidhi Buley 33, Mamta Sharma 26; Swagatika Rath 3-25) lost to **Railways** 151/4 in 45.4 overs (Sarika Koli 41, Mithali Raj 38*; N Buley 2-21) by six wickets.

Army Ordinance Centre Cricket Ground, Secunderabad, December 6: Andhra 176/9 in 50 overs (N Anusha 41, E Padmaja 29*; Vellore Mahesh Kavya 4-32, Himani Yadav 2-21) beat **Hyderabad** 125 in 38.2 overs (Mamtha Kanojia 34, Pranathi Reddy 21; E Padmaja 4-25, Mallika Thalluri 2-19) by 51 runs.

Rajiv Gandhi International Stadium, Hyderabad, December 8: Madhya Pradesh 116 in 44.2 overs (Tamanna Nigam 28, Mamta Sharma 22; Nikita Chauhan 4-19, Tanuja Kanwer 3-7) beat **Himachal Pradesh** 113 in 49.5 overs (Vandna Rana 25, N Chauhan 23; Nidhi Buley 2-12, Pooja Vastrakar 2-21) by three runs.

Army Ordinance Centre Cricket Ground, Secunderabad, December 8: Railways 226/3 in 50 overs (Sarika Koli 71, Mithali Raj 55 retd hurt) beat **Hyderabad** 220/8 in 50 overs (Himani Yadav 54, Sravanthi Naidu 39; Rajeshwari Gayakwad 4-52, Ekta Bisht 2-37) by six runs.

Railways Recreation Club Ground, Secunderabad, December 10: Himachal Pradesh 144 in 48.2 overs (Nikita Chauhan 46, Chitra Singh Jamwal 26; V Pushpa Latha 4-20, CH Jhansi Lakshmi 2-26) lost to **Andhra** 145/5 in 47 overs (N Anusha 52, M Durga 23) by five wickets.

Army Ordinance Centre Cricket Ground, Secunderabad, December 10: Hyderabad 191/8 in 50 overs (Sravanthi Naidu 39, Sneha More 38; Aparna Shrivastava 3-29, Nikita Singh 2-29) beat **Madhya Pradesh** 166 in 49.1 overs (Priti Yadav 46; Vellore Mahesh Kavya 3-35, Gouher Sultana 2-27) by 25 runs.

Railways Recreation Club Ground, Secunderabad, December 12: Andhra 156/8 in 50 overs (S Hima Bindu 53, PV Sudharani 28; Sukanya Parida 2-19, Poonam Yadav 2-30) lost to **Railways** 157/4 in 42 overs (MD Thirushkamini 39, Punam Raut 34; Mallika Thalluri 2-44) by six wickets.

Army Ordinance Centre Cricket Ground, Secunderabad, December 12: Hyderabad 202 in 48.3 overs (Sneha More 35, Vellore Mahesh Kavya 33; Nikita Chauhan 2-22, Harleen Deol 2-31) lost to **Himachal Pradesh** 203/4 in 49.3 overs (H Deol 79, Neena Chaudhary 43; Gouher Sultana 3-34) by six wickets.

Army Ordinance Centre Cricket Ground, Secunderabad, December 14: Andhra 224/9 in 50 overs (CH Jhansi Lakshmi 65, V Pushpa Latha 56: Nidhi Buley 3-38, Priti Yadav 2-31) beat **Madhya Pradesh** 170 in 39.5 overs (Ruchita Buley 58, Deepika Shakya 33; Mallika Thalluri 3-35, E Padmaja 2-26) by 54 runs.

Railways Recreation Club Ground, Secunderabad, December 14: Himachal Pradesh 109 in 47.2 overs 109 (Harleen Deol 27, Kashish Verma 26; Ekta Bisht 5-18) lost to **Railways** 112/5 in 31.2 overs (Nuzhat Parween 34, MD Thiruskhamini 26; Susmita Kumari 3-28) by five wickets.

Elite Group A points table

Team	M	W	L	T	N/R	Pts	NRR
Railways	4	4	0	0	0	16	+0.647
Andhra	4	3	1	0	0	12	+0.454
Hyderabad	4	1	3	0	0	4	-0.175
Himachal Pradesh	4	1	3	0	0	4	-0.372
Madhya Pradesh	4	1	3	0	0	4	-0.460

Railways and Andhra qualified for the Super League

Elite Group B

Gujarat State Fertilizer Corporation Ground, Vadodara, December 6: Maharashtra 224/5 in 50 overs (Smriti Mandhana 98, Shivali Shinde 36*; Rumeli Dhar 2-24) beat **Delhi** 188/7 in 50 overs (Latika Kumari 76, Reema Malhotra 39*; Nikita Bhor 2-32, Mukta Magre 2-37) by 36 runs.

Reliance Cricket Stadium, Vadodara, December 6: Baroda 125 in 47.3 overs (Pragya Rawat 35; Fatima Jaffer 4-16, Shweta Haranhalli 2-25) lost to **Mumbai** 126/1 in 36.1 overs (Hemali Borwankar 52*, Sheral Rozario 35*) by nine wickets.

Reliance Cricket Stadium, Vadodara, December 8: Uttar Pradesh 199/8 in 50 overs (Shashi Mathur 69, Nishu Choudhary 45*; Maya Sonawane 3-34) beat **Maharashtra** 127/9 in 50 overs (Shweta Jadhav 63*; Aditi Sharma 2-22, Apurwa Bharadwaj 2-23) by 72 runs.

Gujarat State Fertilizer Corporation Ground, Vadodara, December 8: Delhi 232/7 in 50 overs (Rumeli Dhar 91, Latika Kumari 64; Radha Yadav 4-61) beat **Baroda** 231/9 in 50 overs (Binaisha Surti 52, Heena Patel 40*; Babita Negi 5-45, Mandeep Kaur 2-48) by one run.

Gujarat State Fertilizer Corporation Ground, Vadodara, December 10: Uttar Pradesh 126/9 in 50 overs (Nishu Choudhary 32*, Neetu Singh 20; Fatima Jaffer 5-19, Sheral Rozario 2-28) lost to **Mumbai** 127/1 in 26 overs (Hemali Borwankar 61*, S Rozario 57*) by nine wickets.

Reliance Cricket Stadium, Vadodara, December 10: Maharashtra 200/7 in 50 overs (Smriti Mandhana 69, Shweta Mane 42*; Jaya Mohite 2-54) lost to **Baroda** 202/6 in 48.2 overs (Yastika Bhatia 49, Palak Patel 34; Tejal Hasabnis 2-27) by four wickets.

Reliance Cricket Stadium, Vadodara, December 12: Mumbai 190/9 in 50 overs (Humaira Kazi 46, Mugdha Joshi 45; Arti Dhama 3-38, Rumeli Dhar 2-34) lost to **Delhi** 191/4 in 48.4 overs (Neha Tanwar 61, Priya Punia 51; Sheral Rozario 2-45) by six wickets.

Gujarat State Fertilizer Corporation Ground, Vadodara, December 12: Uttar Pradesh 89 in 30.4 overs (Nishu Choudhary 37*, Muskan Malik 20; Pragya Rawat 3-17, Jaya Mohite 2-17) lost to **Baroda** 92/3 in 31.4 overs (Palak Patel 31, Heena Patel 23*; Shefali Sahu 2-12) by seven wickets.

Gujarat State Fertilizer Corporation Ground, Vadodara, December 14: Maharashtra 219 in 49.5 overs (Shweta Jadhav 101, Priyanka Garkhede 37; Vrushali Bhagat 3-28, Fatima Jaffer 3-32) beat **Mumbai** 198 in 48.5 overs (Shweta Haranhalli 55, Humaira Kazi 30; Utkarsha Pawar 3-32, Maya Sonawane 2-32) by 21 runs.

Reliance Cricket Stadium, Vadodara, December 14: Uttar Pradesh 190/7 in 50 overs

(Muskan Malik 81, Vishwamohini Mishra 36; Mandeep Kaur 3-36) lost to **Delhi** 193/4 in 46.3 overs (Priya Punia 79*, Latika Kumari 59; Anshu Tiwari 2-29) by six wickets.

Elite Group B points table

Team	M	W	L	T	N/R	Pts	NRR
Delhi	4	3	1	0	0	12	-0.055
Mumbai	4	2	2	0	0	8	+0.626
Baroda	4	2	2	0	0	8	+0.136
Maharashtra	4	2	2	0	0	8	-0.118
Uttar Pradesh	4	1	3	0	0	4	-0.476

Delhi and Mumbai qualified for the Super League

Plate Group A

Dhaneshwar Rath Institute of Engineering and Management Sciences, Cuttack, December 6: Suarashtra 144/7 in 50 overs (Reena Dabhi 34*, Mridula Jadeja 33; Shiva Prajapati 3-18) lost to **Haryana** 145/0 in 34 overs (Sheetal Rana 76*, Bhawna Ohlan 65*) by 10 wickets.
Nimpur Sports and Cricket Club Ground, Cuttack, December 6: Tamil Nadu 144 in 45.2 overs (Niranjana Nagarajan 54, SB Keerthana 24; C Pratyusha 4-23, Sahana Pawar 3-24) lost to **Karnataka** 145/4 in 46.1 overs (Karuna Jain 61, Shubha Sateesh 36) by six wickets
Ravenshaw College Ground, Cuttack, December 6: Odisha 169/6 in 50 overs (Madhusmita Behara 41, Sushree Dibyadarshini 31*; Sneh Rana 2-46) beat **Punjab** 126 in 42.2 overs (Taniya Bhatia 70; Reemalaxmi Ekka 2-17, S Dibyadarshini 2-23) by 43 runs.
Nimpur Sports and Cricket Club Ground, Cuttack, December 8: Saurashtra 109 in 45.2 overs (Neha Chavda 31*, Bhakti Shastri 29; Madhusmita Behara 3-20, Sushree Dibyadarshini 2-19) v **Odisha**. No result.
Ravenshaw College Ground, Cuttack, December 8: Karnataka v **Haryana**. Match abandoned without a ball being bowled.
Dhaneshwar Rath Institute of Engineering and Management Sciences, Cuttack, December 8: Punjab v **Tamil Nadu**. Match abandoned without a ball being bowled.
Ravenshaw College Ground, Cuttack, December 10: Karnataka 140 in 48.4 overs (Rakshitha Krishnappa 36, C Pratyusha 21; Rasanara Parwin 4-28, Sushree Dibyadarshini 3-22) beat **Odisha** 65 in 31 overs (Madhuri Meheta 32; C Pratyusha 3-4, Rameshwari Gayakwad 2-10) by 75 runs.
Dhaneshwar Rath Institute of Engineering and Management Sciences, Cuttack, December 10: Tamil Nadu 151/7 in 50 overs (Niranjana Nagarajan 37, Vilasini V 26; Savita Malik 5-26) lost to **Haryana** 152/3 in 43.2 overs (Sonia Khatri 51*, Sheetal Rana 35) by seven wickets.
Nimpur Sports and Cricket Club Ground, Cuttack, December 10: Punjab 108 in 44.3 overs (Sneh Rana 32, Harpreet Dhillon 25; Neha Chavda 5-18, Reena Dabhi 4-9) lost to **Saurashtra** 111/7 in 43.5 overs (Jayu Jadeja 25; Mehak Kesar 2-13, S Rana 2-28) by three wickets.
Dhaneshwar Rath Institute of Engineering and Management Sciences, Cuttack, December 12: Karnataka 155/3 in 50 overs (Karuna Jain 55, G Divya 28; Nirali Oza 2-25) lost to **Suarashtra** 156/8 in 49.3 overs (Bhakti Shastri 50, Krishna Anovadia 28; C Pratyusha 3-45) by two wickets.
Nimpur Sports and Cricket Club Ground, Cuttack, December 12: Odisha 124 in 41.5

overs (Madhusmita Behara 33, Pragyan Mohanty 28; Nida Rehman 3-12, V Vilasini 2-17) lost to **Tamil Nadu** 125/8 in 41.5 overs (Niranjana Nagarajan 32, V Vilasini 21; Sujata Mallik 3-25, Sushree Dibyadarshini 2-21) by two wickets.

Ravenshaw College Ground, Cuttack, December 12: Punjab 103 in 46.2 overs (Sneh Rana 25, Jasia Akhter 23; Sheetal Rana 2-11, Priyanka Sharma 2-19) beat **Haryana** 84 in 39.4 overs (Bhawna Ohlan 38; Sneh Rana 5-15, Neelam Bisht 2-5) by 19 runs.

Nimpur Sports and Cricket Club Ground, Cuttack, December 14: Tamil Nadu 160/6 in 50 overs (Niranjana Nagarajan 76, L Nethra Iyer 35; Reena Dabhi 2-28, Neha Chavda 2-29) lost to **Suarashtra** 161/7 in 49.4 overs (Jayu Jadeja 66, R Dabhi 26; Vilasini V 2-46) by three wickets.

Ravenshaw College Ground, Cuttack, December 14: Odisha 152/9 in 50 overs (Kadambini Mohakhud 48, Priyanka Priyadarshini 22; Suman Gulia 3-34, Priyanka Sharma 2-32) lost to **Haryana** 153/8 in 49.2 overs (Sonia Khatri 50, Lasika Jangra 24; Rasanara Parwin 3-22, Sujata Mallik 2-28) by two wickets.

Dhaneshwar Rath Institute of Engineering and Management Sciences, Cuttack, December 14: Punjab 181 in 49.4 overs (Ridhima Aggarwal 66, Amarpal Kaur 42; Sahana Pawar 2-16, Monica Patel 2-24) lost to **Karnataka** 182/6 in 48.5 overs (G Divya 67*, Sanjana Batni 35; Sunita Rani 2-21) by four wickets.

Plate Group A points table

Team	M	W	L	T	N/R	Pts	NRR
Karnataka	5	3	1	0	1	14	+0.453
Haryana	5	3	1	0	1	14	+0.273
Saurashtra	5	3	1	0	1	14	-0.209
Punjab	5	1	3	0	1	6	-0.177
Tamil Nadu	5	1	3	0	1	6	-0.189
Odisha	5	1	3	0	1	6	-0.189

Karnataka and Haryana qualified for the Plate Knock-out

Plate Group B

Jharkhand State Cricket Association Oval Ground, Ranchi, December 6: Kerala 176/6 in 50 overs (S Asha 51*, Farha Sherin 45) beat **Assam** 88 in 32.2 overs (Rekharani Bora 22; Sajeevan Sajana 2-12, T Shani 2-14) by 88 runs.

Jharkhand State Cricket Association International Stadium, Ranchi, December 6: Vidarbha 96 in 44 overs (Kalyani Chawarkar 20; Devyani Prasad 3-18, Shannti Kumari 2-11) beat **Jharkhand** 85 in 39.4 overs (Priyanka Sawaiyan 26; Kanchan Nagwani 4-4, Priyanka Acharya 2-14) by 11 runs.

Jharkhand State Cricket Association International Stadium, Ranchi, December 8: Gujarat 146 in 48.2 overs (Poonam Khemnar 26, SA Shah 23; Sajeevan Sajana 3-31, Minnu Mani 2-11) lost to **Kerala** 147/6 in 43.4 overs (A Akshaya 59*, S Asha 31; Krutika Chaudhari 3-22) by four wickets.

Jharkhand State Cricket Association Oval Ground, Ranchi, December 8: Vidarbha 194/7 in 50 overs (Bharti Fulmali 59, Disha Kasat 48; Monikha Das 3-26, Suporna Sinha 2-27) beat **Assam** 158 in 46 overs (M Das 74, Sapna Choudhary 20; Kalyani Chawarkar 5-30, Nupur Kohale 3-36) by 36 runs.

Jharkhand State Cricket Association International Stadium, Ranchi, December 10: Gujarat 163/8 in 50 overs (Darshan Rajput 73, SS Patel 45; Mamta Paswan 3-24, Durga Kumari

Murmu 3-26) beat **Jharkhand** 88 in 42.1 overs (DK Murmu 37*; TD Patel 2-10, SA Shah 2-17) by 75 runs.

Jharkhand State Cricket Association Oval Ground, Ranchi, December 10: Kerala 113 in 45 overs (Sajeevan Sajana 45; Kalyani Chawarkar 3-17, Priyanka Acharya 2-8) lost to **Vidarbha** 117/3 in 26 overs (Disha Kasat 47*, K Chawarkar 22*; Minnu Mani 2-17) by seven wickets.

Jharkhand State Cricket Association International Stadium, Ranchi, December 12: **Jharkhand** 155/8 in 50 overs (Durga Kumari Murmu 58, Priyanka Hawaiian 27; Genevie Pando 2-16, Shanti Rai 2-40) lost to **Assam** 119 in 45.4 overs (Sapna Choudhary 39, Monikha Das 27; Shannti Kumari 4-21, Kavita Roy 2-14) by 36 runs.

Jharkhand State Cricket Association Oval Ground, Ranchi, December 12: Vidarbha 173/9 in 50 overs (Kanchan Nagwani 48, Harsha Bokde 31; TD Patel 3-25) lost to **Gujarat** 176/4 in 47.1 overs (Renuka Chaudhari 62*, SA Shah 37) by six wickets.

Jharkhand State Cricket Association International Stadium, Ranchi, December 14: **Jharkhand** 131 in 43.3 overs (Priyanka Hawaiian 35, Sonia 27; S Asha 4-29, Keerthy James 3-25) lost to **Kerala** 137/5 in 46.5 overs (S Asha 43*, Minnu Mani 21*) by five wickets.

Jharkhand State Cricket Association Oval Ground, Ranchi, December 14: Assam 257/8 in 50 overs (Monikha Das 151, Sapna Choudhary 61; Krutika Chaudhari 2-39, Renuka Chaudhari 2-39) beat **Gujarat** 209 in 44.2 overs (Anagha Deshpande 91, R Chaudhari 70; M Das 3-17, Genevie Pando 3-33) by 48 runs.

Plate Group B points table

Team	M	W	L	T	N/R	Pts	NRR
Vidarbha	4	3	1	0	0	12	+0.597
Kerala	4	3	1	0	0	12	+0.269
Gujarat	4	2	2	0	0	8	+0.086
Jharkhand	4	1	3	0	0	4	-0.321
Assam	4	1	3	0	0	4	-0.560

Vidarbha and Kerala qualified for the Plate Knock-out.

Plate Group C

Bengal Cricket Academy Ground, Kalyani, December 6: Jammu & Kashmir 96 in 48.4 overs (Neeru Manhas 36, Sarla Devi 20; Nisha Maji 5-19) lost to **Bengal** 98/0 in 19.3 overs (Deepti Sharma 55*, Aparna Mondal 35*) by 10 wickets.

Jadavpur University Second Campus Ground, Kolkata, December 6: Tripura 185/6 in 50 overs (Mouchaity Debnath 75, Moutushi Day 46*) beat **Rajasthan** 143 in 40.5 overs (Sofi Siddhu 24, PY Yadav 22; Suravi Roy 4-34, M Day 2-12) by 42 runs.

Eden Gardens, Kolkata, December 6: Chhattisgarh 104/9 in 50 overs (Yashi Pandey 36; Rupali Chavan 4-8, Shikha Pandey 4-26) lost to **Goa** 105/8 in 42.2 overs (Bharati Gaonkar 22; Adila Khanam 4-13) by two wickets.

Jadavpur University Second Campus Ground, Kolkata, December 8: Chhattisgarh 218/4 in 50 overs (Yashi Pandey 82*, Priya Verma 36*) beat **Jammu & Kashmir** 56 in 29.2 overs (Rubia Syed 32; Adila Khanam 3-5, Pransu Priya 2-7) by 162 runs.

Bengal Cricket Academy Ground, Kalyani, December 8: Tripura 185/8 in 50 overs (Mouchaity Debnath 56, Indra Rani Jamatia 33; Nisha Maji 3-32) beat **Bengal** 176 in 49.1 overs (Deepti Sharma 77, Mandira Mahapatra 33; Annapurna Das 3-32, Moutushi Day 3-36) by nine runs.

Eden Gardens, Kolkata, December 8: Rajasthan 139 in 49.3 overs (Priyanka Sharma 27, Sangeeta Kumawat 21; Sunanda Yetrekar 3-33) lost to **Goa** 140/2 in 37.5 overs (S Yetrekar 58*, Vinavi Gurav 42) by eight wickets.

Jadavpur University Second Campus Ground, Kolkata, December 10: Chhattisgarh v Tripura. Match abandoned without a ball being bowled.

Bengal Cricket Academy Ground, Kalyani, December 10: Bengal v Rajasthan. Match abandoned without a ball being bowled.

Eden Gardens, Kolkata, December 10: Goa v Jammu & Kashmir. Match abandoned without a ball being bowled.

Eden Gardens, Kolkata, December 12: Jammu & Kashmir 72 in 35.5 overs (Sapna Jamwal 20; Moutushi Dey 4-13, Sweety Sinha 3-12) lost to **Tripura** 76/0 in 12.2 overs (Indra Rani Jamatia 33*, Mouchaity Debnath 31*) by 10 wickets.

Jadavpur University Second Campus Ground, Kolkata, December 12: Rajasthan 113 in 43.4 overs (Shweta Bishnoi 27, Priyanka Sharma 25; Adila Khanam 5-29) lost to **Chhattisgarh** 114/2 in 41.2 overs (Shivi Pandey 48, Shalini Mantravadi 42) by eight wickets.

Bengal Cricket Academy Ground, Kalyani, December 12: Goa 137/9 in 50 overs (Shikha Pandey 43, Sugandha Ghadi 24*; Saika Ishaque 4-27, Deepti Sharma 3-29) lost to **Bengal** 138/3 in 37.2 overs (D Sharma 60*, Tanusree Sarkar 39; S Pandey 2-24) by seven wickets.

Jadavpur University Second Campus Ground, Kolkata, December 14: Rajasthan 169 in 49.5 overs (Babita Meena 58, Priyanka Sharma 39; Neeru Manhas 3-17, Asra Shafi 2-20) beat **Jammu & Kashmir** 120 in 41.4 overs (Rubia Syed 52; B Meena 2-21, Sofi Siddhu 2-26) by 49 runs.

Bengal Cricket Academy Ground, Kalyani, December 14: Chhattisgarh 119 in 48 overs (Yashi Pandey 50; Saika Ishaque 3-20, Tanusree Sarkar 2-20) lost to **Bengal** 120/2 in 32.2 overs (T Sarkar 54*, Deepti Sharma 51*) by eight wickets.

Eden Gardens, Kolkata, December 14: Tripura 63 in 28.5 overs (Shiuli Chakraborty 21; Shikha Pandey 6-10) lost to **Goa** 64/9 in 21.3 overs (Moutushi Dey 5-13) by one wicket.

Plate Group C points table

Team	M	W	L	T	N/R	Pts	NRR
Bengal	5	3	1	0	1	14	+1.138
Goa	5	3	1	0	1	14	+0.571
Tripura	5	3	1	0	1	14	+0.482
Chhattisgarh	5	2	2	0	1	10	+0.645
Rajasthan	5	1	3	0	1	6	-0.300
Jammu & Kashmir	5	0	4	0	1	2	-2.535

Bengal and Goa qualified for the Plate Knock-out

Plate knock-out

1st quarter-final: Jadavpur University Second Campus Ground, Kolkata, December 21: Haryana 31 in 18.4 overs (Komal Zanzad 9-8) lost to **Vidarbha** 33/0 in 4.4 overs (LM Inamdar 30*) by 10 wickets.

2nd quarter-final: Jadavpur University Second Campus Ground, Kolkata, December 22: Goa 122 in 43.2 overs (Sanjula Naik 43*, Shikha Pandey 29; Sajeevan Sajana 3-33, Keerthy James 2-16) beat **Kerala** 51 in 31 overs (Sunanda Yetrekar 4-12, S Pandey 4-17) by 71 runs.

1st semi-final: Eden Gardens, Kolkata, December 24: Bengal 210/6 in 50 overs (Paramita Roy 57, Deepti Sharma 53; Nupur Kohale 3-37, Kalyani Chawarkar 2-35) beat **Vidarbha**

173 in 49.5 overs (Bharti Fulmali 59, Harsha Bokde 23; D Sharma 3-26, Nisha Maji 3-29) by 37 runs.

2nd semi-final: Jadavpur University Second Campus Ground, Kolkata, December 24: Karnataka 102 in 36.4 overs (Sanjana Batni 24; Santoshi Rane 4-16, Rupali Chavan 4-17) lost to **Goa** 103/7 in 35 overs (Sunanda Yetrekar 47*; Monica Patel 2-27) by three wickets.

Final: Goa beat Bengal by 37 runs

Eden Gardens, Kolkata, December 26: Goa 147/9 in 50 overs (Shikha Pandey 66, Bharati Gaonkar 32*; Nisha Maji 3-31, Gayatri Mal 2-20) beat **Bengal** 110 in 43.5 overs (Paramita Roy 42, G Mal 20; Sunanda Yetrekar 3-13, Santoshi Rane 3-24) by 37 runs.

Winners: Goa
Elite Group Super League

Moti Bagh Stadium, Vadodara, December 21: Railways 229/6 in 50 overs (Meghana Sabbineni 67, Mithali Raj 51; Jemimah Rodrigues 3-52, Prakashika Naik 2-41) beat **Mumbai** 133 in 44.3 overs (Sheral Rozario 49, Hemali Borwankar 24; Ekta Bisht 3-17, Poonam Yadav 3-25) by 96 runs.

Railway Ground, Vadodara, December 21: Delhi 124/9 in 50 overs (Reema Malhotra 42*, Neha Tanwar 28; K Anjali Sarvani 2-16, CH Jhansi Lakshmi 2-16) lost to **Andhra** 126/2 in 30.1 overs (V Pushpa Latha 40*, S Hima Bindu 32*) by eight wickets.

Railway Ground, Vadodara, December 23: Railways 303/6 in 50 overs (MD Thirushkamini 139, Punam Raut 61*; Mallika Thalluri 2-40, G Sindhuja 2-64) beat **Andhra** 116/9 in 50 overs (S Hima Bindu 29; Poonam Yadav 4-22, Sukanya Parida 2-28) by 187 runs.

Moti Bagh Stadium, Vadodara, December 23: Mumbai 192/8 in 50 overs (Sheral Rozario 38, Vrushali Bhagat 34; Rumeli Dhar 3-43, Neelam Yadav 2-28) lost to **Delhi** 193/6 in 48.2 overs (Rumeli Dhar 79, Neha Tanwar 53*; Manji 2-36) by four wickets.

Moti Bagh Stadium, Vadodara, December 25: Delhi 166/5 in 50 overs (Priya Punia 64, Reema Malhotra 30*; Mona Meshram 2-37, Rajeshwari Gayakwad 2-38) lost to **Railways** 170/5 in 46.2 overs (Mithali Raj 49*, MD Thirushkamini 35; Sonia Lohiya 3-37) by five wickets.

Railway Ground, Vadodara, December 25: Andhra 165/8 in 50 overs (K Anjali Sarvani 25*, CH Jhansi Lakshmi 25; Fatima Jaffer 2-19) lost to **Mumbai** 166/6 in 47 overs (Shweta Haranhalli 50*, Sheral Rozario 30; M Bhavana 2-16, G Sindhuja 2-28) by four wickets.

Elite Group Super League points table

Team	M	W	L	T	N/R	Pts	NRR
Railways	3	3	0	0	0	12	+2.031
Delhi	3	1	2	0	0	4	-0.602
Mumbai	3	1	2	0	0	4	-0.610
Andhra	3	1	2	0	0	4	-0.915

Winners: Railways

Senior Women's One-day Challenger Trophy

Pandey takes five, youngsters impress

Shikha Pandey's five-wicket haul inspired India Red to a 15-run win against India Blue in the final of the Senior Women's One-Day Challenger Trophy. Having suffered a shocking one-wicket loss at the hands of the same opposition in the league phase, India Red's bowlers showed great character under pressure to thwart Blue's title hopes.

In the absence of many of India's more established players, youngsters were given an opportunity to showcase their skills. Of the lot, Harleen Deol, the right-hand batter (118 runs); Manali Dakshini, the medium-pacer (80 runs and four wickets); Komal Zanzad, the left-arm seamer (six wickets); and Bharati Fulmali, the right-hand batter (114 runs) were the most impressive. Manali's unbeaten knock of 49 from No.8 guided Blue to an unlikely victory against Red in the first match. This after Zanzad's opening burst, in which she took three wickets in her first over, had left them tottering at 24 for 8. Harleen showed great temperament, playing some ferocious cut shots and elegant cover drives, as she consistently anchored the team's innings.

Shikha Pandey took five wickets in the final.

The **previous season**, Jemimah Rodrigues, the 17-year-old 'wunderkid' had lit up the tournament with 174 runs in three outings, including a sparkling 84 in India Green's opening match against India Red. Her textbook technique, coupled with the ability to score at a brisk pace, captured the imagination of a country that has slowly begun to warm up to the women's game.

Punam Raut, her India Green opening partner, made one of only two centuries in the tournament. The pair were prolific, stitching together three century partnerships. Their heroics, however, were not enough, as India Green stumbled to a 33-run loss in the final against India Blue.

	Most runs	Most wickets
2017-18	Punam Raut (India Green) (273 runs in 3 matches)	Anuja Patil (India Green) (7 wickets in 3 matches)
2018-19	Harleen Deol (India Red) (118 runs in 3 matches)	Shikha Pandey (India Red) (8 wickets in 3 matches)

Deviñeni Venkata Ramana Praneetha Ground, Mulapadu, January 3: **India Red** 129 in 45 overs (Veda Krishnamurthy 27, Radha Yadav 21; Tanuja Kanwer 2-20, Reemalaxmi Ekka 2-26) lost to **India Blue** 130/9 in 45.5 overs (Manali Dakshini 49*, R Ekka 29*; Komal Zanzad 3-12, R Yadav 3-26) by one wicket.

Deviñeni Venkata Ramana Praneetha Ground, Mulapadu, January 4: **India Green** 149 in 44.4 overs (Dayalan Hemalatha 35, Arundhati Reddy 28; Manali Dakshini 3-34, Tanuja Kanwer 2-22) lost to **India Blue** 150/4 in 39.1 overs (Bharati Fulmali 45*, Priya Punia 41) by six wickets.

Deviñeni Venkata Ramana Praneetha Ground, Mulapadu, January 5: **India Red** 199/9 in 50 overs (Harleen Deol 57, N Anusha 48; SB Keerthana 3-33, Dayalan Hemalatha 2-28) beat **India Green** 189 in 49.3 overs (Tejal Hasabnis 65, D Hemalatha 50; Shikha Pandey 2-32, Komal Zanzad 2-36) by 10 runs.

points table

Team	M	W	L	T	N/R	Pts	NRR
India Blue	2	2	0	0	0	8	+0.514
India Red	2	1	1	0	0	4	-0.049
India Green	2	0	2	0	0	0	-0.534

India Blue and India Red qualified for the final

Final

Deviñeni Venkata Ramana Praneetha Ground, Mulapadu, January 6: **India Red** 183 in 49.2 overs (Veda Krishnamurthy 46, Harleen Deol 42; Tanusree Sarkar 3-22, Reemalaxmi Ekka 2-21) beat **India Blue** 168 in 47.2 overs (Bharati Fulmali 69, Manali Dakshini 31; Shikha Pandey 5-33, Tarannum Pathan 3-22) by 15 runs.

Winners: India Red

2017-18

Holkar Stadium, Indore, January 4: **India Red** 199 in 49.5 overs (Mithali Raj 72, Sushma Verma 30; Rajeshwari Gayakwad 2-23, Radha Yadav 2-38) lost to **India Blue** 200/2 in 46.1 overs (Smriti Mandhana 100*, Mona Meshram 44*) by eight wickets.

Holkar Stadium, Indore, January 7: **India Red** 217/6 in 50 overs (Deepti Dharma 76, Priya Punia 51; Anuja Patil 2-42) lost to **India Green** 219/2 in 42.4 overs (Punam Raut 84*, Jemimah Rodrigues 84; D Sharma 2-47) by eight wickets.

Holkar Stadium, Indore, January 6: **India Green** 232/8 in 50 overs (Punam Raut 101, Jemimah Rodrigues 52; Radha Yadav 3-39) beat **India Blue** 196/7 in 50 overs (Mona Meshram 56, Tanusree Sarkar 43; Anuja Patil 2-37) by 36 runs.

Points table

Team	P	W	L	Pts	NRR
India Green	2	2	0	8	+0.737
India Blue	2	1	1	4	-0.192
India Red	2	0	2	0	-0.557

India Green and India Blue qualified for the final

Final

Holkar Stadium, Indore, January 8: India Blue 207/9 in 50 overs (Mona Meshram 63, Smriti Mandhana 58; S Asha 3-29, Anuja Patil 3-42) beat **India Green** 174 in 45.2 overs (Punam Raut 88, Jemimah Rodrigues 43; C Pratyusha 4-23) by 33 runs.

Winners: India Blue

Punjab remained unbeaten in the tournament. — *BCCI*

Senior Women's Inter-state T20 Competition

Punjab hold nerve in thriller

Neelam Bisht scripted Punjab's thrilling four-run win over Karnataka in the final of the Senior Inter-State T20 tournament. The all-rounder first scored a crucial 14-ball 27 after Jasia Akhter (56) made Karnataka pay for some sloppy fielding to lift the score to 131, and then held her nerve to defend six runs in the last over, picking up two wickets and conceding only one run.

Punjab rode on the performances of Akhter (355 runs), Amarpal Kaur (205 runs), Sunita Rani and Bisht (both 14 wickets) to remain unbeaten through the tournament.

Dropped from the Indian T20I team, Delhi's Priya Punia topped the batting charts. She was closely followed by Sushma Verma (372 runs), the Himachal Pradesh captain, who was dismissed only once in nine innings. Four centuries were scored this edition — the most in any season — and while all of them came against this year's new entrants from the north-east, it was Shefali Verma's hundred that stood out. The 14-year-old Haryana opener blasted a 56-ball 128 against Nagaland — the highest T20 score by an Indian woman. The knock included 20 fours and six sixes. Her tournament strike-rate of

187.87 was evidence of that ferocious striking power.

As is the case every year, it was pace off the ball that did the trick; Assam skipper Monikha Das was the only pacer to feature among the top ten wicket-takers.

Other notable performances include Nancy Patel's spell of 5 for 7 against Bihar, V R Vanitha's tally of 15 sixes, Punjab's win over Tripura in a Super Over and Saee Purandhare's unbeaten 64 in Meghalaya's team total of 78 against Mumbai.

Punjab's win meant it was the second year running that the tournament had a winner other than Railways. In **2017-18**, back-to-back defeats in the group stage to Delhi and Maharashtra meant that for the first time since the tournament's inception, Railways failed to get their hands on the trophy. Delhi's senior duo of Neha Tanwar and Rumeli Dhar secured their team's tournament triumph.

Carrying her good form through the season, Shikha Pandey almost single-handedly led Goa into the Super Leagues. The skipper smashed 163 runs in only three innings, including a belligerent, unbeaten 92 against Bengal.

Odisha went undefeated through their campaign in the Plate Group.

	Most runs	Most wickets
2017-18	Neha Tanwar (Delhi) (189 runs in 7 matches)	Keerthy James (Kerala) (17 wickets in 7 matches)
2018-19	Priya Punia (Delhi) (382 runs in 10 matches)	Priyanka Priyadarshini (Odisha) (17 wickets in 11 matches)

2018-19

Group A

Sharad Pawar Cricket Academy (SPCA), BKC, Mumbai, February 20: Delhi 104/6 in 20 overs (Priya Punia 65; G Chandra Lekha 2-19, CH Jhansi Lakshmi 2-20) beat **Andhra** 79 in 20 overs (S Hima Bindu 49*; Mandeep Kaur 3-19) by 25 runs.

Sachin Tendulkar Gymkhana, Kandivili, Mumbai, February 20: Manipur 45/9 in 20 overs (Roshni 25*; Manali Dakshini 2-1, Pashte Monika 2-3) lost to **Mumbai** 46/2 in 5.4 overs (Vrushali Bhagat 31*; Monica 2-20) by eight wickets.

SPCA, BKC, Mumbai, February 20: Meghalaya 78/5 in 20 overs (Saee Purandhare 64*; Prachi Chauhan 2-9) lost to **Himachal Pradesh** 82/3 in 12.3 overs (Sushma Verma 29*) by seven wickets.

Sachin Tendulkar Gymkhana, Kandivili, Mumbai, February 21: Delhi 146/3 in 20 overs (Priya Punia 77*, Neha Tanwar 22) beat **Manipur** 16/9 in 20 overs (Soni Yadav 3-2) by 130 runs.

SPCA, BKC, Mumbai, February 21: Tamil Nadu 111/5 in 20 overs (L Nethra Iyer 39, Niranjana Nagarajan 27; Humaira Kazi 2-25) lost to **Mumbai** 113/1 in 16 overs (Vrushali BHagat 48*, Mugdha Joshi 33*) by nine wickets.

Sachin Tendulkar Gymkhana, Kandivili, Mumbai, February 21: Andhra 125/3 in 20 overs (N Anusha 56*, CH Jhansi Lakshmi 28) beat **Meghalaya** 24 in 16.3 overs (CH Jhansi Lakshmi 2-5) K Anjali Sarvani 2-10) by 101 runs.

SPCA, BKC, Mumbai, February 23: Manipur 49/7 in 20 overs (K Jyothi 2-3) lost to

Andhra 50/2 in 7 overs by eight wickets.

Sachin Tendulkar Gymkhana, Kandivili, Mumbai, February 23: Tamil Nadu 92/7 in 20 overs (Vilasini Nair 28*, Niranjana Nagarajan 26; Tanuja Kanwer 3-16) lost to **Himachal Pradesh** 94/1 in 17 overs (Sushma Verma 35*, Kashish Verma 32*) by nine wickets.

SPCA, BKC, Mumbai, February 23: Delhi 154/2 in 20 overs (Neha Tanwar 74, Priya Punia 70*) beat **Meghalaya** 53 in 19 overs (Lalita Sharma 3-8, Babita Negi 2-6) by 101 runs.

Sachin Tendulkar Gymkhana, Kandivili, Mumbai, February 24: Andhra 135/6 in 20 overs (CH Jhansi Lakshmi 78*, G Sneha 22; Renuka Singh 2-20, Anisha Ansari 2-31) lost to **Himachal Pradesh** 139/3 in 17.3 overs (Sushma Verma 56*, Nikitha Chauhan 51) by seven wickets.

SPCA, BKC, Mumbai, February 24: Manipur 93/8 in 20 overs (Monica 24, Chingkhei M 23; Niranjana Nagarajan 2-4) lost to **Tamil Nadu** 94/1 in 11 overs (MD Thirushkamini 69*) by nine wickets.

Sachin Tendulkar Gymkhana, Kandivili, Mumbai, February 24: Mumbai 137/5 in 20 overs (Humaira Kazi 55, Mugdha Joshi 41) beat **Meghalaya** 58/6 in 20 overs (Sejal Raut 3-1) by 79 runs.

SPCA, BKC, Mumbai, February 26: Delhi 97/4 in 20 overs (Neha Tanwar 34*, Arushi Goel 26*; Pashte Monika 2-16) lost to **Mumbai** 99/4 in 19.2 overs (Vrushali Bhagat 35*, Shweta Haranhalli 23; Babita Negi 2-20) by six wickets.

Sachin Tendulkar Gymkhana, Kandivili, Mumbai, February 26: Manipur 75/7 in 20 overs (Chingkhei M 25; Prachi Chauhan 2-8, Tanuja Kanwer 2-17) lost to **Himachal Pradesh** 76/0 in 6.5 overs (Nikita Chauhan 63*) by 10 wickets.

SPCA, BKC, Mumbai, February 26: Andhra 115/7 in 20 overs (N Anusha 26, K Anjali Sarvani 25; SB Keerthana 2-20, L Nethra Iyer 2-26) beat **Tamil Nadu** 100/9 in 20 overs (MD Thirushkamini 43; K Anjali Sarvani 214, CH Jhansi Lakshmi 2-19) by 15 runs.

Sachin Tendulkar Gymkhana, Kandivili, Mumbai, February 27: Himachal Pradesh 140/2 in 20 overs (Neena Chaudharu 63*, Sushma Verma 56*) beat **Mumbai** 99/7 in 20 overs (Saniya Raut 35*, Manali Dakshini 24; Anisha Ansari 4-10) by 41 runs.

SPCA, BKC, Mumbai, February 27: Meghalaya 109/6 in 20 overs (Debasmita Dutta 59; Monica 2-13) beat **Manipur** 64 in 18.4 overs (Pinky Chanda 3-17, Vandana Mahajan 2-8) by 45 runs.

Sachin Tendulkar Gymkhana, Kandivili, Mumbai, February 27: Tamil Nadu 74/6 in 20 overs (L Nethra Iyer 25; Lalita Sharma 2-11) lost to **Delhi** 75/4 in 16.4 overs (Priya Punia 30; Niranjana Nagarajan 2-15) by six wickets.

SPCA, BKC, Mumbai, March 1: Mumbai 140/6 in 20 overs (Shweta Haranhalli 48, Humaira Kazi 37; K Anjali Sarvani 2-20) beat **Andhra** 127/8 in 20 overs (N Anusha 48; H Kazi 2-15, Saniya Raut 2-24) by 13 runs.

Sachin Tendulkar Gymkhana, Kandivili, Mumbai, March 1: Tamil Nadu 172/2 in 20 overs (Niranjana Nagarajan 67*, MD Thirushkamini 66) beat **Meghalaya** 45 in 20 overs (SB Keerthana 3-3, MD Thirushkamini 2-1) by 127 runs.

SPCA, BKC, Mumbai, March 1: Delhi 118/7 in 20 overs (Arti Dhama 59, Neha Tanwar 38; Anisha Ansari 2-13) beat **Himachal Pradesh** 116/8 in 20 overs (Tanuja Kanwer 54*; Sonia Lohiya 3-13, Soni Yadav 2-13) by two runs.

Group A points table

Team	M	W	L	T	N/R	Pts	NRR
Delhi	6	5	1	0	0	20	+2.287
Himachal Pradesh	6	5	1	0	0	20	+1.920
Mumbai	6	5	1	0	0	20	+1.461
Andhra	6	3	3	0	0	12	+1.165

Tamil Nadu	6	2	4	0	0	8	+0.914
Meghalaya	6	1	5	0	0	4	-3.466
Manipur	6	0	6	0	0	0	-4.540

Delhi and Himachal Pradesh qualified for the Super League

Group B

Shaheed Veer Narayan Singh International Stadium, Raipur, February 20: Assam 72 in 20 overs (Adila Khanam 3-13) lost to **Chhattisgarh** 73/1 in 16.2 overs (Mantravadi Shalini 35*, Shivi Pandey 20) by nine wickets.

Raipur District Cricket Association Ground, Raipur, February 20: Haryana 221/2 in 20 overs (Shafali Verma 128, Sonia Khatri 53*) beat **Nagaland** 58/9 in 20 overs (Preeti Bose 3-8, Shiva Prajapati 2-12) by 163 runs.

Shaheed Veer Narayan Singh International Stadium, Raipur, February 20: Gujarat 66/9 in 20 overs (Mukta Magre 3-26, SB Pokharkar 2-7) lost to **Maharashtra** 67/5 in 18.3 overs (Toral Patel 2-10) by five wickets.

Raipur District Cricket Association Ground, Raipur, February 21: Assam 83/8 in 20 overs (Anita Lodhi 21; Anuja Patil 2-11) beat **Maharashtra** 82/9 in 20 overs (Anuja Patil 31*, SA Lonkar 30; Monikha Das 2-13) by one run.

Shaheed Veer Narayan Singh International Stadium, Raipur, February 21: Haryana 120/5 in 20 overs (Shivangi Chauhan 34*, Sonia Khatri 30; Adila Khanam 3-25) lost to **Chhattisgarh** 121/6 in 19.5 overs (Shivi Pandey 47, Mantravadi Shalini 31; Shiva Prajapati 3-39) by four wickets.

Shaheed Veer Narayan Singh International Stadium, Raipur, February 21: Nagaland 117/7 in 20 overs (V Karuna Jain 34, Rupsena 27; Priyanka Acharya 3-25) lost to **Sikkim** 118/3 in 19.2 overs (Ananya Upendran 63, Archana Das 40; Sheetal 2-23) by seven wickets.

Raipur District Cricket Association Ground, Raipur, February 23: Haryana 79 in 20 overs (Sonia Khatri 21; Monikha Das 4-6, Urmila Chatterjee 2-22) lost to **Assam** 81/5 in 15.5 overs (M Das 28, Anita Lodhi 23; Suman Gulia 2-7) by five wickets.

Shaheed Veer Narayan Singh International Stadium, Raipur, February 23: Maharashtra 127/6 in 20 overs (Shweta Mane 42*, Anuja Patil 35; Adila Khanam 2-22, Shyla Alam 2-34) beat **Chhattisgarh** 99 in 18.5 overs (Shilpa Sahu 30, Shivani Krishna 30; A Patil 3-20, Devika Vaidya 2-16) by 28 runs.

Shaheed Veer Narayan Singh International Stadium, Raipur, February 23: Gujarat 133/5 in 20 overs (Krutika Chaudhari 57*, Renuka Chaudhari 35; Priyanka Acharya 2-19) beat **Sikkim** 91/6 in 20 overs (Ananya Upendran 41, Archana Das 23; Toral Patel 3-17, Pragna Chaudhari 2-12) by 42 runs.

Shaheed Veer Narayan Singh International Stadium, Raipur, February 24: Assam 103/6 in 20 overs (Shanti Rai 22*, Rekharani Bora 22; Renuka Chaudhari 2-17, Toral Patel 2-19) beat **Guajarat** 101/7 in 20 overs (Hani Patel 24; Monikha Das 2-19, R Bora 2-22) by two runs.

Raipur District Cricket Association Ground, Raipur, February 24: Haryana 140/3 in 20 overs (Sheetal Rana 77, Preeti Bhatiwal 34; Priyanka Acharya 2-14) beat **Sikkim** 92/8 in 20 overs (Ananya Upendran 33, Archana Das 21; Divya 2-3, Priya Khatkar 2-11) by 48 runs.

Shaheed Veer Narayan Singh International Stadium, Raipur, February 24: Maharashtra 178/3 in 20 overs (Shweta Mane 51*, Tejal Hasabnis 39; J Rameshwari 2-29) beat **Nagaland** 38 in 13.5 overs (Devika Vaidya 3-2, SB Porkhankar 3-6) by 140 runs.

Shaheed Veer Narayan Singh International Stadium, Raipur, February 26: Assam 130/6 in 20 overs (Rekharani Bora 29, Rajni Lodhi 24; Diki Lepcha 2-27) beat **Sikkim** 55/6 in 20 overs (Monikha Das 3-12, Urmila Chatterjee 2-7) by 75 runs.

Raipur District Cricket Association Ground, Raipur, February 26: Nagaland 45/7 in 20 overs (Pransu Priya 3-8) lost to **Chhattisgarh** 46/1 in 5.1 overs by nine wickets.

Shaheed Veer Narayan Singh International Stadium, Raipur, February 26: Gujarat 83 in 19 overs (Krutika Chaudhari 20; Priya Khatkar 4-11, Divya 2-4) lost to **Haryana** 84/4 in 18.1 overs (Sonia Khatri 36, Bhawna Ohlan 25*; Sarvi 2-18) by six wickets.

Shaheed Veer Narayan Singh International Stadium, Raipur, February 27: Sikkim 34/9 in 20 overs lost to **Chhattisgarh** 35/1 in 5.3 overs by nine wickets.

Raipur District Cricket Association Ground, Raipur, February 27: Haryana 99/5 in 20 overs (Sheetal Rana 22, Shafali Verma 21; Anuja Patil 3-12, SB Porkhankar 2-16) lost to **Maharashtra** 100/1 in 13.2 overs (Devika Vaidya 46*, Tejal Hasabnis 26) by nine wickets.

Shaheed Veer Narayan Singh International Stadium, Raipur, February 27: Gujarat 121/5 in 20 overs (Simran 53, Hani Patel 52*) beat **Nagaland** 80/4 in 20 overs (V Karuna Jain 44; Retal Patel 2-22) by 41 runs.

Shaheed Veer Narayan Singh International Stadium, Raipur, March 1: Assam 154/7 in 20 overs (Anita Lodhi 50, Monikha Das 26; Sheetal 3-30) beat **Nagaland** 85/3 in 20 overs (V Karuna Jain 55*) by seven wickets.

Raipur District Cricket Association Ground, Raipur, March 1: Gujarat 119/4 in 20 overs (Bhavana Goplani 45*, Simran 44; Adila Khanam 2-21) beat **Chhattisgarh** 74/7 in 20 overs (Retal Patel 2-11, Pragna Chaudhari 2-13) by 45 runs.

Shaheed Veer Narayan Singh International Stadium, Raipur, March 1: Maharashtra 189/2 in 20 overs (Tejal Hasabnis 58, Mukta Magre 55*) beat **Sikkim** 108/5 in 20 overs (Ananya Upendran 51*) by 81 runs.

Group B Points Table

Team	M	W	L	T	N/R	Pts	NRR
Assam	6	5	1	0	0	20	+1.295
Maharashtra	6	5	1	0	0	20	+2.535
Chhattisgarh	6	4	2	0	0	16	+0.851
Haryana	6	3	3	0	0	12	+1.379
Gujarat	6	3	3	0	0	12	+0.915
Sikkim	6	1	5	0	0	4	-2.879
Nagaland	6	0	6	0	0	0	-4.494

Assam and Maharashtra qualified for the Super League

Group C

Vidarbha Cricket Association (VCA) Stadium, Civil Lines, Nagpur, February 20: Arunachal Pradesh 39/8 in 20 overs (Gayatri Naik 2-2, Kesha 2-6) lost to **Baroda** 40 /1 in 3.2 overs by nine wickets.

VCA Kalamna, Nagpur, February 20: Uttar Pradesh 90 in 18.2 overs (Shashi Mathur 38; Kavita Roy 3-23) lost to **Jharkhand** 91/8 in 19.3 overs (K Roy 21; Shefali Sahu 2-13) by two wickets.

VCA Stadium, Civil Lines, Nagpur, February 20: Bihar 44/8 in 20 overs (Kavita Patil 3-12, Arundhati Reddy 2-7) lost to **Railways** 45/0 in 3 overs (Sabbineni Meghana 30*) by 10 wickets.

VCA Kalamna, Nagpur, February 21: Arunachal Pradesh 37 in 13.11 overs (Sneh Rana 4-6, Meghna Singh 3-7) lost to **Railways** 38/1 in 3.3 overs by nine wickets.

VCA Stadium, Civil Lines, Nagpur, February 21: Uttar Pradesh 89/8 in 20 overs (Arti Singh 26, Kshama 21) lost to **Vidarbha** 90/5 in 16.3 overs (Bharati Fulmali 41, Disha Kasat 31; Kshama 2-5) by five wickets.

VCA Kalamna, Nagpur, February 21: Jharkhand 101/6 in 20 overs (Reena Singh 45; Tarannum Pathan 3-11) beat **Baroda** 70 in 18.4 overs (Karishma Tank 20; Ritu Kumari 4-5, Durga Kumari Murmu 2-7) by 31 runs.

VCA Stadium, Civil Lines, Nagpur, February 23: Jharkhand 165/3 in 20 overs (Rashmi 53, Ruma Mahato 41) beat **Arunachal Pradesh** 34 in 19.3 overs (Ritu Kumari 4-9, Kavita Roy 2-3) by 131 runs.

VCA Kalamna, Nagpur, February 23: Bihar 38 in 14.5 overs (Vaishnavi 4-6, Disha Kasat 2-2) lost to **Vidarbha** 40/3 in 8.5 overs by seven wickets.

VCA Stadium, Civil Lines, Nagpur, February 23: Baroda 72/8 in 20 overs (Radha Yadav 27; Sneh Rana 5-13) lost to **Railways** 73/2 in 12.5 overs (Shweta Jadhav 42*) by eight wickets.

VCA Kalamna, Nagpur, February 24: Bihar 124/3 in 20 overs (Syed Nishat Fatma 26, Beauty Kumari 23; Neelam Rajput 2-19) beat **Arunachal Pradesh** 64/8 in 20 overs (Kumari 2-7) by 60 runs.

VCA Stadium, Civil Lines, Nagpur, February 24: Railways 125/5 in 20 overs (Veda Krishnamurthy 55, Shweta Jadhav 24; Tanu Kala 2-15) beat **Uttar Pradesh** 79/7 in 20 overs (Ekta Singh 25; Swagatika Rath 4-16) by 46 runs.

VCA Kalamna, Nagpur, February 24: Jharkhand 78/8 in 20 overs (Kavita Roy 30; Komal Zanzad 2-11) lost to **Vidarbha** 79/3 in 12.1 overs (Disha Kasat 22) by seven wickets.

VCA Stadium, Civil Lines, Nagpur, February 26: Vidarbha 201/4 in 20 overs (Disha Kasat 113*, Knachan Nagwani 50; Neelam Rajput 2-58) beat **Arunachal Pradesh** 62/6 in 20 overs (Suvalaxmi Rout 25; Reena Paul 3-4) by 139 runs.

VCA Kalamna, Nagpur, February 26: Bihar 15 in 14 overs (Niharika Prasad 4-5) lost to **Jharkhand** 18/1 in 1.5 overs by nine wickets.

VCA Stadium, Civil Lines, Nagpur, February 26: Baroda 99/9 in 20 overs (Radha Yadav 40; Shefali Sahu 2-13, Tanu Kala 2-23) beat **Uttar Pradesh** 98/8 in 20 overs (Aditi Sharma 30; Tarannum Pathan 3-12) by one run.

VCA Stadium, Civil Lines, Nagpur, February 27: Baroda 110/5 in 20 overs (Radha Yadav 43, Yastika Bhatia 31; Nupur Kohale 2-26) beat **Vidarbha** 95 in 18.4 overs (Bharati Fulmali 28; Kesha 3-6, Tanvir Shaikh 3-12) by 15 runs.

VCA Kalamna, Nagpur, February 27: Jharkhand 131/8 in 20 overs (Indrani Roy 39, Rashmi 26; Arundhati Reddy 3-33, Sneh Rana 2-23) lost to **Railways** 132/6 in 19.1 overs (A Reddy 54*, Shweta Jadhav 40; Ashwani Kumari 3-14, Ritu Kumari 2-34) by four wickets.

VCA Kalamna, Nagpur, February 27: Uttar Pradesh 141/5 in 20 overs (Tanu Kala 33*, Shashi Mathur 30; Apurva 2-15) beat **Bihar** 29 in 18.2 overs (Rashi Kanojiya 3-3, Kashama 3-8) by 112 runs.

VCA Kalamna, Nagpur, March 1: Uttar Pradesh 186/0 in 20 overs (Shashi Mathur 103*, Ekta Singh 61*) beat **Arunachal Pradesh** 71 in 20 overs (Varsha Patel 25, Suvalaxmi Rout 21; Kshama 3-11, Tanu Kala 3-16) by 115 runs.

VCA Stadium, Civil Lines, Nagpur, March 1: Vidarbha 50/9 in 20 overs (Meghna Singh 2-3) lost to **Railways** 51/2 in 8.3 overs (Nishu Choudhary 23; Sayali Kamone 2-5) by eight wickets.

VCA Stadium, Civil Lines, Nagpur, March 1: Baroda 180/9 in 20 overs (Palak Patel 38, Karishma Tank 37; Apurva 3-34, Shraddha 3-36) beat **Bihar** 47 in 17.5 overs (Nancy Patel 5-7, Kesha 2-9) by 133 runs.

Group C points table

Team	M	W	L	T	N/R	Pts	NRR
Railways	6	6	0	0	0	24	+3.484
Jharkhand	6	4	2	0	0	16	+1.991
Vidarbha	6	4	2	0	0	16	+1.748
Baroda	6	4	2	0	0	16	+1.511
Uttar Pradesh	6	2	4	0	0	8	+1.338
Bihar	6	1	5	0	0	4	-4.149
Arunachal Pradesh	6	0	6	0	0	0	-6.125

Railways and Jharkhand qualified for the Super League

Group D

MBB Stadium, Agartala, February 20: Hyderabad 107/8 in 20 overs (Anitha Kotha 37, Mamtha Kanojia 27; Sunanda Yetrekar 3-32, Rupali Chavan 2-22) beat **Goa** 97/9 in 20 overs (Nikita Malik 22, Shreya Parab 21; SK Sravanthi Naidu 2-31) by 10 runs.

Police Training Academy Ground, Agartala, February 20: Tripura 41 in 15.3 overs (Akanksha Kohli 3-13, Sahan Pawar 2-7) lost to **Karnataka** 43/3 in 7.5 overs by seven wickets.

MBB Stadium, Agartala, February 20: Jammu & Kashmir 61/7 in 20 overs (Neelam Bisht 2-9) lost to **Punjab** 62/1 in 9 overs (Jasia Akhter 32*, Amarpal Kaur 28*) by nine wickets.

Police Training Academy Ground, Agartala, February 21: Hyderabad 115/7 in 20 overs (Mamtha Kanojia 40, SK Sravanthi Naidu 27; G Divya 2-14, Chandu V 2-26) lost to **Karnataka** 116/5 in 17.4 overs (C Pratyusha 35, K Pratyoosha 32*; Himani Yadav 2-41) by five wickets.

MBB Stadium, Agartala, February 21: Punjab 101/7 in 20 overs (Babita Meena 43*; Rupali Chavan 2-10) beat **Goa** 74 in 18.5 overs (Sunita Rani 4-4, Neelam Bisht 3-17) by 27 runs.

Police Training Academy Ground, Agartala, February 21: Uttarakhand 75 in 20 overs (Madhwal 20; Suravi Roy 2-12, Sweety Sinha 2-15) lost to **Tripura** 76/4 in 15.5 overs (Mouchaity Debnath 28, Rizu Saha 21*; Madhwal 2-13) by six wickets.

MBB Stadium, Agartala, February 23: Karnataka 74 in 18.5 overs (Akanksha Kohli 25, M Sowmya 24; Sonali Gaunder 3-12, Nikita Malik 2-10) beat **Goa** 73 in 19.5 overs (Sahana Pawar 2-6, Chandu V 2-8) by one run.

Police Training Academy Ground, Agartala, February 23: Jammu & Kashmir 100/5 in 20 overs (Rubia Syed 27*) lost to **Uttarakhand** 101/7 in 18.3 overs (AN Tomar 35, Tara 20*; Sandhya 5-15) by three wickets.

MBB Stadium, Agartala, February 23: Punjab 124/6 in 20 overs (Jasia Akhter 60, Neelam Bisht 20; Anitha Kotha 2-13, Himani Yadav 2-22) beat **Hyderabad** 101/7 in 20 overs (SK Sravanthi Naidu 29; N Bisht 2-18, Mehak Kesar 2-22) by 23 runs.

Police Training Academy Ground, Agartala, February 24: Goa 137/5 in 20 overs (Nikita Malik 44, Sunanda Yetrekar 39; Sandhya 2-9) beat **Jammu & Kashmir** 59/8 in 20 overs (Rupali Chavan 2-4, S Yetrekar 2-9) by 78 runs.

MBB Stadium, February 24: Uttarakhand 57 in 19.3 overs (Sahana Pawar 2-7, Akanksha Kohli 2-18) lost to **Karnataka** 61/2 in 12.1 overs (Shubha Sateesh 36*) by eight wickets.

Police Training Academy Ground, Agartala, February 24: Tripura 101/3 in 20 overs (Jhumki Debnath 41*, Rizu Saha 33; Komalpreet Kour 2-11) tied with **Punjab** 101/9 in 20 overs (Jasia Akhter 55, Amarpal Kaur 25; MK Rabidas 3-19, Suravi Roy 2-13). Super Over: Punjab 13/1 in 1 over beat Tripura 10/0 in 1 over.

MBB Stadium, Agartala, February 26: Karnataka 70/4 in 7 overs (VR Vanitha 44) beat **Jammu & Kashmir** 22/6 in 7 overs (C Pratyusha 2-3) by 48 runs.

Police Training Academy Ground, Agartala, February 26: Tripura 56/8 in 8 overs (Varsha Rajak 3-4, Bhogi Shravani 2-12) lost to **Hyderabad** 58/4 in 7.2 overs by six wickets.

MBB Stadium, Agartala, February 26: Goa 85/8 in 20 overs (Bharati Gaonkar 36; Manisha Pradhan 3-9, Madhwal 2-19) beat **Uttarakhand** 42 in 15.2 overs (Nikita Malik 3-7, Rupali Chavan 3-13) by 43 runs.

Police Training Academy Ground, Agartala, February 27: Jammu & Kashmir v **Tripura**. Match abandoned without a ball being bowled.

MBB Stadium, Agartala, February 27: Karnataka v **Punjab**. Match abandoned without a ball being bowled.

Police Training Academy Ground, Agartala, February 27: Hyderabad v **Uttarakhand**. Match abandoned without a ball being bowled.

MBB Stadium, Agartala, March 1: Jammu & Kashmir 95/4 in 20 overs (Sarla Devi 53*; Bhogi Shravani 2-10) beat **Hyderabad** 96/3 in 14 overs (Himani Yadav 44*, Ramya 24; Bismah Hassan 2-25) by seven wickets.

Police Training Academy Ground, Agartala, March 1: Goa 103/8 in 20 overs (Shreya Parab 33, Sweety Sinha 2-20) lost to **Tripura** 104/3 in 18 overs (Jhumki Debnath 32*, Mouchaity Debnath 29; Vanita Bhandari 2-20) by seven wickets.

MBB Stadium, March 1: Punjab 123/4 in 20 overs (Amarpal Kaur 56*, Priyanka Malik 30) beat **Uttarakhand** 71/6 in 20 overs (Mehak Kesar 3-8, Komalpreet Kour 2-20) by 52 runs.

Group D points table

Team	M	W	L	T	N/R	Pts	NRR
Karnataka	6	5	0	0	1	22	+2.089
Punjab	6	5	0	0	1	22	+1.662
Hyderabad	6	3	2	0	1	14	+0.168
Tripura	6	2	3	0	1	10	-0.436
Goa	6	2	4	0	0	8	+0.615
Uttarakhand	6	1	4	0	1	6	-1.544
Jammu & Kashmir	6	0	5	0	1	2	-2.929

Karnataka and Punjab qualified for the Super League

Group E

Palmyra Cricket Ground, Puducherry, February 20: Pondicherry 106/8 in 20 overs (Latika Kumari 42, Gouher Sultana 24; Shrayosi Aich 3-16) lost to **Bengal** 107/3 in 17.4 overs (Prativa 55*, Paramita Roy 25) by seven wickets.

Cricket Association of Pondicherry (CAP) Siechem Ground, Puducherry, February 20: Mizoram 24 in 16.2 overs (S Asha Joy 2-1, Keerthy James 2-1) lost to **Kerala** 27/0 in 2.3 overs by 10 wickets.

Palmyra Cricket Ground, Puducherry, February 20: Rajasthan 108/5 in 20 overs (SR Jat 42, Priyanka Sharma 24; Salonee Dangore 2-19, Nidhi Buley 2-26) lost to **Madhya Pradesh** 109/3 in 18.3 overs (Neha Badwaik 35*, Babita Mandlik 28) by seven wickets.

CAP Siechem Ground, Puducherry, February 20: Odisha 104/4 in 20 overs (Madhuri Meheta 51*; Reena M 2-16) lost to **Saurashtra** 73/9 in 20 overs (Neha Chavda 23; Sushree Dibyadarshini 4-20) by 31 runs.

Palmyra Cricket Ground, Puducherry, February 21: Saurashtra 105/6 in 20 overs (Mridula Jadeja 38) lost to **Bengal** 106/2 in 15.2 overs (Paramita Roy 61*, Tanusree Sarkar 27*; Baldha 2-23) by eight wickets.

CAP Siechem Ground, Puducherry, February 21: Kerala 90/6 in 20 overs (Jincy George 26; Rinku Tank 3-28) lost to **Rajasthan** 91/6 in 19.5 overs (AK Saini 21*, Shweta Bishnoi 21) by four wickets.

Palmyra Cricket Ground, Puducherry, February 21: Mizoram 9 in 13.5 overs (Tarang Jha 4-2, Salonee Dangore 2-0) lost to **Madhya Pradesh** 10/0 in 1 over by ten wickets.

CAP Siechem Ground, Puducherry, February 21: Odisha 131/5 in 20 overs (Madhusmita Behera 38, Madhuri Meheta 28; Ashtalakshmi A 5-27) beat **Pondicherry** 67 in 19.4 overs (Reemalaxmi Ekka 3-7, Sushree Dibyadarshini 2-4) by 64 runs.

Palmyra Cricket Ground, Puducherry, February 23: Kerala 109/6 in 20 overs (Jincy George 41, S Asha Joy 21; Shubhlakshmi Sharma 2-10) beat **Bengal** 102/8 in 20 overs (Paramita Roy 24, Aneena Mathews 2-18, S Asha Joy 2-23) by seven overs.

CAP Siechem Ground, Puducherry, February 23: Odisha 95/7 in 20 overs (Madhuri Meheta 23; Salonee Dangore 2-17, Nidhi Buley 2-18) lost to **Madhya Pradesh** 96/2 in 17.2 overs (Babita Mandlik 64*, Varsha Choudhary 23*) by eight wickets.

Palmyra Cricket Ground, Puducherry, February 23: Saurashtra 192/1 in 20 overs (Jayu Jadeja 104*, Pooja Nimavat 42) beat **Mizoram** 37/8 in 20 overs (Apurwa Bharadwaj 27; Neha Chavda 3-2, P Modhwadia 2-3) by 155 runs.

CAP Siechem Ground, Puducherry, February 23: Pondicherry 98/5 in 20 overs (Anagha Deshpande 42, Gouher Sultana 21; SS Kalal 2-13) lost to **Rajasthan** 99/5 in 18.5 overs (Shweta Bishnoi 23; Ashtalakshmi A 2-22) by five wickets.

Palmyra Cricket Ground, Puducherry, February 24: Odisha 117/4 in 20 overs (Madhuri Meheta 51*, Sushree Dibyadarshini 43*) beat **Bengal** 97 in 19.1 overs (Tanusree Sarkar 39, Paramita Roy 24; Priyanka Priyadarshini 3-20, Reemalaxmi Ekka 2-19) by 20 runs.

CAP Siechem Ground, February 24: Kerala 54 in 19.1 overs (Varsha Choudhary 3-16, Tarang Jha 2-9) lost to **Madhya Pradesh** 55/3 in 16.1 overs (T Jha 29) by seven wickets.

Palmyra Cricket Ground, February 24: Rajasthan 166/1 in 20 overs (SR Jat 65*, Priyanka Sharma 57*) beat **Mizoram** 28 in 19.4 overs (KP Dangi 3-5, Sofi Siddhu 2-1) by 138 runs.

CAP Siechem Ground, Puducherry, February 24: Pondicherry 76/9 in 20 overs (Gouher Sultana 23*; Reena Dabhi 2-8, Neha Chavda 2-10) lost to **Saurashtra** 79/4 in 18.4 overs (Riddhi Ruparel 30, Bhakti Shastri 22; Kani 2-6) by six wickets.

Palmyra Cricket Ground, Puducherry, February 26: Mizoram 29/9 in 20 overs (Shrayosi Aich 4-14) lost to **Bengal** 32/0 in 4.2 overs by 10 wickets.

CAP Siechem Ground, Puducherry, February 26: Kerala 118/4 in 20 overs (Jincy George 49, T Shani 30; Ashtalakshmi 2-27) beat **Pondicherry** 69 in 18.2 overs (Anagha Deshpande 31*; Sajeevan Sajana 2-6, Keerthy James 2-22) by 49 runs.

Palmyra Cricket Ground, Puducherry, February 26: Saurashtra 91/7 in 20 overs (Jayu Jadeja 27, Bhakti Shastri 25*; Nidhi Buley 3-18) lost to **Madhya Pradesh** 92/3 in 17.4 overs (Tarang Jha 32, Pooja Choudhary 24; Neha Chavda 2-18) by seven wickets.

CAP Siechem Ground, Puducherry, February 26: Odisha 123/3 in 20 overs (Madhuri Meheta 69*, Sarita Meher 22) beat **Rajasthan** 95/7 in 20 overs (Priyanka Sharma 24; Madhusmita Behera 3-21, Rasanara Parwin 2-18) by 28 runs.

Palmyra Cricket Ground, Puducherry, February 27: Bengal 91/9 in 20 overs (Tanusree Sarkar 20; Babita Mandlik 2-5, Nidhi Buley 2-14) lost to **Madhya Pradesh** 92/4 in 19.1 overs (Neha Badwaik 37*, Pooja Choudhary 35; Nisha Maji 2-18, T Sarkar 2-26) by six wickets.

CAP Siechem Ground, Puducherry, February 27: Kerala 109/8 in 20 overs (Jincy George 40; Rasanara Prwin 3-21) beat **Odisha** 61/6 in 20 overs (Madhusmita Behera 23; Minnu Mani 2-11, S Asha Joy 2-16) by 48 runs.

Palmyra Cricket Ground, Puducherry, February 27: Pondicherry 164/8 in 20 overs (Latika Kumari 63, Gouher Sultana 30; Sandhya Kumari 3-24) beat **Mizoram** 81/8 in 20 overs (Apurwa Bharadwaj 45; Ashtalakshmi A 4-9) by 83 runs.

CAP Siechem Ground, Puducherry, February 27: Rajasthan 91/6 in 20 overs (SR Jat 29) lost to **Saurashtra** 92/6 in 18.5 overs (Mridula Jadeja 27, Bhakti Shastri 30; SS Kalal 2-14) by four wickets.

Palmyra Cricket Ground, Puducherry, March 1: Bengal 107/9 in 20 overs (Antara Jana 39, Tanusree Sarkar 21; VD Singh 2-6, SS Kala 2-18) beat **Rajasthan** 81/8 in 20 overs (Paramita Roy 3-18, T Sarkar 2-14) by 26 runs.

CAP Siechem Ground, Puducherry, March 1: Kerala 68/9 in 20 overs (P Modhiwadia 2-9, Neha Chvada 2-13) lost to **Saurashtra** 72/5 in 18.4 overs (Jayu Jadeja 32; Sajeevan Sajana 2-15) by five wickets.

CAP Siechem Ground, Puducherry, March 1: Pondicherry 56/7 in 20 overs (Tarang Jha 2-9) lost to **Madhya Pradesh** 59/1 in 10.1 overs (Tamanna Nigam 27*) by nine wickets.

Palmyra Cricket Ground, Puducherry, March 1: Mizoram 11 in 9.5 overs (Priyanka Priyadarshini 3-2, Sujata Mallik 3-8) lost to **Odisha** 12/0 in 1.2 overs by 10 wickets.

Group E points table

Team	M	W	L	T	N/R	Pts	NRR
Madhya Pradesh	7	7	0	0	0	28	+1.530
Odisha	7	5	2	0	0	20	+1.309
Kerala	7	4	3	0	0	16	+1.174
Bengal	7	4	3	0	0	16	+0.880
Saurashtra	7	4	3	0	0	16	+0.854
Rajasthan	7	3	4	0	0	12	+0.560
Pondicherry	7	1	6	0	0	4	-0.835
Mizoram	7	0	7	0	0	0	-7.154

Madhya Pradesh and Odisha qualified for the Super League

Super League Group A

SPCA, BKC, Mumbai, March 5: Delhi 88/5 in 20 overs (Priya Punia 41, Lalita Sharma 21*; Devika Vaidya 3-18) lost to **Maharashtra** 90/3 in 15.1 overs (Shivali Shinde 37, D Vaidya 27; Neha Chhillar 2-16) by seven wickets.

SPCA, BKC, Mumbai, March 5: Railways 146/4 in 20 overs (Sabbineni Meghana 52, Punam Raut 49) lost to **Punjab** 147/6 in 19.4 overs (Riddhima Aggarwal 50, Jasia Akhter 37; Rajeshwari Gayakwad 2-18, Swagatika Rath 2-26) by four wickets.

SPCA, BKC, Mumbai, March 6: Delhi 91/5 in 20 overs (Mandeep Kaur 20) lost to **Railways** 92/4 in 12.5 overs (Nuzhat Parween 38*, Punam Raut 25; Lalita Sharma 2-23) by six wickets.

SPCA, BKC, Mumbai, March 6: Punjab 103/8 in 20 overs (Parveen Khan 43; Varsha Choudhary 3-14, Salonee Dangore 2-22) beat **Madhya Pradesh** 95 in 19.1 overs (Nishi Buley 34, V Choudhary 22; Sunita Rai 2-14, Komalpreet Kour 2-26) by eight runs.

SPCA, BKC, Mumbai, March 8: Madhya Pradesh 108/5 in 20 overs (Varsha Choudhary 47) lost to **Maharashtra** 109/4 in 14.3 overs (Tejal Hasabnis 38, Shivali Shinde 28) by six wickets.

SPCA, BKC, Mumbai, March 8: Delhi 125/3 in 20 overs (Priya Punia 61, Neha Tanwar 38; Sunita Rani 2-24) lost to **Punjab** 126/8 in 19.2 overs (Jasia Akhter 39, Parveen Khan 27; N Tanwar 2-19, Soni Yadav 2-27) by two wickets.

SPCA, BKC, Mumbai, March 9: Maharashtra 157/4 in 20 overs (Devika Vaidya 51, Shivali Shinde 47; Sneh Rana 2-13, Rajeshari Gayakwad 2-41) lost to **Railways** 158/7 in 19 overs (Sabbineni Meghana 39, Punam Raut 32; D Vaidya 2-39) by three wickets.

SPCA, BKC, Mumbai, March 9: Delhi 107/6 in 20 overs (Priya Punia 21, Deeksha Singh 20; Charu Joshi 2-13) beat **Madhya Pradesh** 103/8 in 20 overs (Neha Badwaik 33, Nidhi Buley 31; Lalita Sharma 3-15, Soni Yadav 2-18) by four runs.

Wankhede Stadium, Mumbai, March 11: Maharashtra 120 in 19.3 overs (Shivali Shinde 48, Tejal Hasabnis 34; Mehak Kesar 3-13, Neelam Bisht 3-17) lost to **Punjab** 121/3 in 19 overs (Jasia Akhter 38, Amarpal Kaur 27*; Devika Vaidya 3-19) by seven wickets.

Wankhede Stadium, Mumbai, March 11: Madhya Pradesh 56/8 in 20 overs (Pooja Choudhary 23; Arundhati Reddy 2-7, Poonam Yadav 2-12) lost to **Railways** 60/0 in 7.4 overs (Sabbineni Meghana 40*) by 10 wickets.

Group A Super League points table

Team	M	W	L	T	N/R	Pts	NRR
Punjab	4	4	0	0	0	16	+0.297
Railways	4	3	1	0	0	12	+2.003
Maharashtra	4	2	2	0	0	8	+0.743
Delhi	4	1	3	0	0	4	-0.966
Madhya Pradesh	4	0	4	0	0	0	-1.572

Punjab qualified for the final

Super League Group B

Sachin Tendulkar Gymkhana, Kandivili, Mumbai, March 5: Assam 99/6 in 20 overs (Anita Lodhi 43; Tanuja Kanwer 3-16) lost to **Himachal Pradesh** 102/1 in 18.3 overs (SM Singh 35*, Sushma Verma 33*) by nine wickets.

Sachin Tendulkar Gymkhana, Kandivili, Mumbai, March 5: Jharkhand 114/9 in 20 overs (Rashmi 36, Reena Singh 30; Chandu V 4-18, Akanksha Kohli 2-25) lost to **Karnataka** 115/1 in 18.1 overs (VR Vanitha 76*, Rakshitha Krishnappa 31*) by nine wickets.

Sachin Tendulkar Gymkhana, March 6: Jharkhand 154/3 in 20 overs (Reena Singh 49, Kavita Roy 40*; Prachi Chauhan 2-11) lost to **Himachal Pradesh** 158/6 in 19.2 overs (Sushma Verma 84*, Vandna Rana 27; Ashwani Kumari 2-32, K Roy 2-24) by four wickets.

Sachin Tendulkar Gymkhana, Mumbai, March 6: Odisha 106/4 in 20 overs (Madhusmita Behera 38, Sarita Meher 25*; Akanksha Kohli 2-27) lost to **Karnataka** 107/7 in 19.3 overs (Rakshitha Krishnappa 34*, G Divya 32; Priyanka Priyadarshini 2-26) by three wickets.

Sachin Tendulkar Gymkhana, Kandivili, Mumbai, March 8: Assam 103/9 in 20 overs (Anita Lodhi 31; Priyanka Priyadarshini 2-9, Sushree Dibyadarshini 2-22) lost to **Odisha** 104/5 in 19 overs (Pragyan Mohanty 45, Sarita Meher 30*) by five wickets.

Sachin Tendulkar Gymkhana, Kandivili, Mumbai, March 8: Himachal Pradesh 133/3 in 20 overs (Nikita Chauhan 66, SM Singh 32) lost to **Karnataka** 134/4 in 18.2 overs (VR Vanitha 84, Rakshitha Krishnappa 23*; Tanuja Kanwer 2-15) by six wickets.

Sachin Tendulkar Gymkhana, Kandivili, Mumbai, March 9: Jharkhand 112/9 in 20 overs (Indrani Roy 48, Priyanka Sawaiyan 22; Anita Lodhi 2-9, Genevie Pando 2-19) lost to **Assam** 113/7 in 19.2 overs (Monikha Das 49, Ruhina Pegu 21; Durga Kumari Murmu 3-25, Kavita Roy 2-14) by three wickets.

Sachin Tendulkar Gymkhana, Kandivili, Mumbai, March 9: Odisha 93 in 19.3 overs (Sarita Meher 32, Madhusmita Behera 24; Sushmita Kumari 4-9) lost to **Himachal Pradesh** 96/7 in 18.3 overs (Sushma Verma 43*, Nikita Chauhan 34, Priyanka Priyadarshini 3-13, Rasanara Parwin 2-21) by three wickets.

Sachin Tendulkar Gymkhana, Kandivili, Mumbai, March 11: Karnataka 115/6 in 20 overs (Rakshitha Krishnappa 29, Shubha Sateesh 27; Shanti Rai 2-17, Ruhina Pegu 2-21) lost to **Assam** 116/3 in 19.1 overs (Anita Lodhi 64*, Suporna Sinha 24) by seven wickets.

Sachin Tendulkar Gymkhana, Kandivili, Mumbai, March 11: Odisha 119/6 in 20 overs (Madhusmita Behera 55, Madhuri Meheta 30; Devyani Prasad 2-25) lost to **Jharkhand** 122/2 in 16.4 overs (Rashmi 61*, Reena Singh 35; M Behera 2-9) by eight wickets.

Group B Super League points table

Team	M	W	L	T	N/R	Pts	NRR
Karnataka	4	3	1	0	0	12	+0.273
Himachal Pradesh	4	3	1	0	0	12	+0.278
Assam	4	2	2	0	0	8	-0.097
Jharkhand	4	1	3	0	0	4	-0.025
Odisha	4	1	3	0	0	4	-0.390

Karnataka qualified for the final

Final

Wankhede Stadium, Mumbai, March 13: Punjab 131/7 in 20 overs (Jasia Akhter 56, Neelam Bisht 27; G Divya 2-24, Simren Henry 2-26) beat **Karnataka** 127/7 in 20 overs (G Divya 41, C Pratyusha 35; Sunita Rani 2-19, Komalpreet Kour 2-22) by four runs.

Winners: Punjab

2017-18

Elite Group A

Goa Cricket Association (GCA) Academy Ground, Porvorim, January 13: Madhya Pradesh 86 in 19.4 overs (Priti Yadav 25; Jhulan Goswami 2-8, Paramita Roy 2-11) lost to **Bengal** 87/0 in 16.2 overs (Deepti Sharma 40*, P Roy 39*) by ten wickets.

GCA Academy Ground, Porvorim, January 13: Uttar Pradesh 42 in 14.3 overs (Sunanda Yetrekar 3-8, Nikita Malik 2-6) lost to **Goa** 45/1 in 9.3 overs (S Yetrekar 22*, Sanjula Naik 20*) by nine wickets.

GCA Academy Ground, Porvorim, January 14: Madhya Pradesh 97/8 in 20 overs (Charu Joshi 29, Pooja Vastrakar 23; Tarannum Pathan 2-9, Tanvir Shaikh 2-14) lost to **Baroda** 98/7 in 19.2 overs (T Pathan 61*; C Joshi 3-9) by three wickets.

GCA Academy Ground, Porvorim, January 14: Uttar Pradesh 94/7 in 20 overs (Muskan Malik 38, Shashi Mathur 23; Priya Pandey 2-10, Nisha Maji 2-27) lost to **Bengal** 95/1 in 19 overs (Deepti Sharma 46, Paramita Roy 37*) by nine wickets.

GCA Academy Ground, Porvorim, January 15: Baroda 126/5 in 20 overs (Binaisha Surti 31, Yastika Bhatia 23) beat **Goa** 102/9 in 20 overs (Bharati Gaonkar 24; Shalini Sharma 3-14, Nancy Patel 2-12) by 24 runs.

GCA Academy Ground, Porvorim, January 15: Uttar Pradesh 105/5 in 20 overs (Shobha Devi 60; Aparna Shrivastava 3-15) beat **Madhya Pradesh** 104/4 in 20 overs (Pooja Vastrakar 47, Pallavi Bharadwaj 22) by one run.

GCA Academy Ground, Porvorim, January 16: Bengal 123/4 in 20 overs (Deepti Sharma 42, Mandira Mahapatra 28*; Rupali Chavan 2-23) lost to **Goa** 124/2 in 19.4 overs (Shikha Pandey 92*) by eight wickets.

GCA Academy Ground, Porvorim, January 16: Uttar Pradesh 70/9 in 20 overs (Shobha Devi 31; Shalini Sharma 3-10, Radha Yadav 2-5) lost to **Baroda** 75/2 in 15 overs (Binaisha Surti 28, Yastika Bhatia 27*) by eight wickets.

GCA Academy Ground, Porvorim, January 17: Madhya Pradesh 75/5 in 20 overs (Nidhi Buley 27*, Pallavi Bharadwaj 25; Santoshi Rane 2-7) lost to **Goa** 77/4 in 15.5 overs (Shikha Pandey 55*; Tamanna Nigam 2-6) by six wickets.

GCA Academy Ground, Porvorim, January 17: Bengal 103/6 in 20 overs (Deepti Sharma 42, Tanusree Sarkar 29; Radha Yadav 3-21) lost to **Baroda** 104/4 in 19.3 overs (Palak Patel 36, Yastika Bhatia 31; Nisha Maji 2-13) by six wickets.

Elite Group A points table

Team	M	W	L	T	N/R	Pts	NRR
Baroda	4	4	0	0	0	16	+0.808
Goa	4	3	1	0	0	12	+0.793
Bengal	4	2	2	0	0	8	+0.251
Uttar Pradesh	4	1	3	0	0	4	-1.136
Madhya Pradesh	4	0	4	0	0	0	-0.608

Baroda and Goa qualified for the Elite Super Leagues

Elite Group B

SPCA Ground, Mumbai, January 13: Hyderabad 107/9 in 20 overs (Doli Ramya 57, Himani Yadav 23; Mona Meshram 3-28) lost to **Railways** 109/2 in 17.4 overs (Mithali Raj 55*; M Meshram 24*) by eight wickets.

SPCA Ground, Mumbai, January 13: Maharashtra 173/4 in 20 overs (Devika Vaidya 54, Tejal Hasabnis 43; Saima Thakor 2-17) beat **Mumbai** 155/8 in 20 overs (Jemimah Rodrigues 53, Mugdha Joshi 37; Utkarsha Pawar 2-16, D Vaidya 2-19) by 18 runs.

Sachin Tendulkar Gymkhana Ground, Mumbai, January 14: Railways 130/8 in 20 overs (Sarika Koli 41; Mandeep Kaur 2-20, Neha Tanwar 2-20) lost to **Delhi** 135/7 in 20 overs (Rumeli Dhar 38, Priya Punia 35; Poonam Yadav 2-18, Rajeshwari Gayakwad 2-23) by three wickets.

Sachin Tendulkar Gymkhana Ground, Mumbai, January 14: Maharashtra 97 in 19.1 overs (Devika Vaidya 27; G Trisha 3-10, Gouher Sultana 2-13) beat **Hyderabad** 85 in 20 overs (Ananya Upendran 35; D Vaidya 3-14, Kavita Patil 2-5) by 12 runs.

SPCA Ground, Mumbai, January 15: Delhi 91 in 19.5 overs (Arushi Goel 32, Latika Kumari 21; Prakashika Naik 3-14, Sheral Rozario 2-12) beat **Mumbai** 85 in 19.1 overs (Mugdha Joshi 24; Neha Tanwar 3-14, Babita Negi 2-15) by six runs.

SPCA Ground, Mumbai, January 15: Railways 131/7 in 20 overs (Punam Raut 52, Sarika Koli 38; Mukta Magre 2-16) lost to **Maharashtra** 134/3 in 19.1 overs (Smriti Mandhana 67, Anuja Patil 41*) by seven wickets.

Sachin Tendulkar Gymkhana Ground, Mumbai, January 16: Hyderabad 67 in 2 overs (Sheral Rozario 4-10, Prakashika Naik 3-10) lost to **Mumbai** 69/2 in 15.5 overs (Mugdha Joshi 26*) by eight wickets.

Sachin Tendulkar Gymkhana Ground, Mumbai, January 16: Maharashtra 154/5 in 20 overs (Tejal Hasabnis 71, Shweta Jadhav 46; Rumeli Dhar 2-18) beat **Delhi** 112/6 in 20 overs (Neha Tanwar 26, Ayushi Soni 25*; Devika Vaidya 2-16) by 42 runs.

SPCA Ground, Mumbai, January 17: Hyderabad 98/6 in 20 overs (Himani Yadav 33, Doli Ramya 26; Ayushi Soni 4-15) lost to **Delhi** 99/4 in 17.5 overs (Neha Tanwar 51*, Rumeli Dhar 34) by six wickets.

SPCA Ground, Mumbai, January 17: Mumbai 45 in 17.5 overs (Rajeshwari Gayakwad 5-11, Ekta Bisht 3-8) lost to **Railways** 49/0 in 9.4 overs (Mithali Raj 30*) by 10 wickets.

Elite Group B points table

Team	M	W	L	T	N/R	Pts	NRR
Maharashtra	4	4	0	0	0	16	+1.011
Delhi	4	3	1	0	0	12	-0.223
Railways	4	2	2	0	0	8	+0.905
Mumbai	4	1	3	0	0	4	-0.786
Hyderabad	4	0	4	0	0	0	-0.780

Maharashtra and Delhi qualified for the Elite Super Leagues

Plate Group A

Karnataka State Cricket Association (KSCA) Ground, Alur, January 13: Vidarbha 111/7 in 20 overs (Disha Kasat 58*; C Pratyusha 2-10, Monica Patel 2-12) tied with **Karnataka** 111/9 in 20 overs (Rakshitha Krishnappa 32; Nupur Kohale 2-15, Ankita Guha 2-19). Super Over: Karnataka 10/0 in 1 over beat Vidarbha 7/1.

KSCA Ground, Alur, January 13: Assam 91 in 19.3 overs (Monikha Das 24, Sapna Choudhury 20; TD Patel 2-14, Poonam Khemnar 2-15) beat **Gujarat** 90 in 19.1 overs (SA Shah 33, Renuka Chaudhari 20; M Das 3-17, Rekharani Bora 2-13) by one run.

KSCA Ground, Alur, January 13: Andhra 81/9 in 20 overs (S Hima Bindu 37; Keerthy James 4-9, Aneena Mathews 2-23) lost to **Kerala** 82/4 in 16 overs (A Akshaya 23*; K Anjali Sarvani 2-8) by six wickets.

KSCA Ground, Alur, January 14: Assam 132/7 in 20 overs (Monikha Das 41; V Chandu 2-25) lost to **Karnataka** 136/3 in 19.2 overs (VR Vanitha 59*, Rakshitha Krishnappa 39) by seven wickets.

KSCA Ground, Alur, January 14: Andhra 72/7 in 20 overs (G Sneha 26; SA Shah 3-18, Krutika Chaudhari 2-10) lost to **Gujarat** 73/5 in 18 overs (Poonam Khemnar 23) by five wickets.

KSCA Ground, Alur, January 14: Vidarbha 72 in 19.5 overs (Disha Kasat 24; Keerthy James 3-19, Minnu Mani 2-12) lost to **Kerala** 76/6 in 19 overs (Nupur Kohale 3-16) by four wickets.

KSCA Ground, Alur, January 15: Karnataka 77/8 in 20 overs (Akanksha Kohli 22*; Krutika Chaudhari 207, Renuka Chaudhari 2-9) beat **Gujarat** 58 in 18.3 overs (G Divya 2-9, C Pratyusha 2-9) by 19 runs.

KSCA Ground, Alur, January 15: Vidarbha 87/9 in 20 overs (Shivani Dharne 25; K Anjali Sarvani 2-16, M Bhavana 2-21) lost to **Andhra** 88/3 in 17.2 overs (S Hima Bindu 39*, C Jhansi Lakshmi 32*) by seven wickets.

KSCA Ground, Alur, January 15: Assam 88/9 in 20 overs (Papori Gogoi 32*; Keerthy

James 3-14, Minnu Mani 2-9) lost to **Kerala** 89/7 in 19.3 overs (M Mani 23*; Shanti Rai 3-12) by three wickets.

KSCA Ground, Alur, January 16: Gujarat 77/9 in 20 overs (Poonam Khemnar 25, Darshana Rajput 24; Ankita Guha 2-9, Nupur Kohale 2-14) lost to **Vidarbha** 79/3 in 18.3 overs (Disha Kasat 38*) by seven wickets.

KSCA Ground, Alur, January 16: Assam 98/8 in 20 overs (Monikha Das 64; M Bhavana 3-12) beat **Andhra** 79/6 in 20 overs (S Hima Bindu 20; M Das 2-16) by 19 runs.

KSCA Ground, Alur, January 16: Karnataka 110/5 in 20 overs (Shubha Sateesh 41, Rakshitha Krishnappa 33; Minnu Mani 2-24) lost to **Kerala** 111/3 in 19.4 overs (K Jincy George 55, IV Drishya 21) by seven wickets.

KSCA Ground, Alur, January 17: Assam 102/9 in 20 overs (Uma Chetry 20, Ruhina Pegu 20; Ankita Guha 2-15, Harsha Bokade 2-17) beat **Vidarbha** 97/5 in 20 overs (Disha Kasat 43; Rashmi Dey 2-12) by five runs.

KSCA Ground, Alur, January 17: Andhra 48 in 16.3 overs (Sahana Pawar 3-7, C Pratyusha 3-7) lost to **Karnataka** 52/5 in 14.1 overs (C Jhansi Lakshmi 2-11) by five wickets.

KSCA Ground, Alur, January 17: Gujarat 57 in 18.3 overs (Minnu Mani 3-11, T Shani 2-5) lost to **Kerala** 58/4 in 15 overs (Sajeevan Sajana 34*; Renuka Chaudhari 2-12) by six wickets.

Plate Group A points table

Team	M	W	L	T	N/R	Pts	NRR
Kerala	5	5	0	0	0	20	+0.585
Karnataka	5	4	1	0	0	16	+0.582
Assam	5	3	2	0	0	12	+0.142
Vidarbha	5	1	4	0	0	4	-0.185
Gujarat	5	1	4	0	0	4	-0.410
Andhra	5	1	4	0	0	4	-0.665

Kerala and Karnataka qualified for the Plate knock-out

Plate Group B

Saurashtra Cricket Association (SCA) Stadium B, Rajkot, January 12: Haryana 117/2 in 20 overs (Bhawna Ohlan 52*, Sonia Khatri 48) tied with **Saurashtra** 117/6 in 20 overs (Mridula Jadeja 33, Jayu Jadeja 26). Super Over: Saurashtra 3/2 in 0.4 overs lost to Haryana 4/0 in 1 over.

SCA Stadium B, Rajkot, January 12: Rajasthan 115/5 in 20 overs (Shweta Bishnoi 33, Priyanka Sharma 32) lost to **Himachal Pradesh** 117/2 in 17.1 overs (Neena Choudhary 46*, Nikita Chauhan 40) by eight wickets.

SCA Stadium B, Rajkot, January 13: Himachal Pradesh 141/4 in 20 overs (Nikita Chauhan 60, Harleen Deol 55*; Sheetal Rana 2-27) beat **Haryana** 94/9 in 20 overs (S Rana 38, Sonia Khatri 21; H Deol 4-18, Tanuja Kanwer 2-9) by 47 runs.

SCA Stadium B, Rajkot, January 13: Saurashtra 131/6 in 20 overs (Bhakti Shastri 33, Mridula Jadeja 28; Kavita Roy 2-21) lost to **Jharkhand** 132/2 in 19 overs (Reena Singh 61*, K Roy 39*) by eight wickets.

SCA Stadium B, Rajkot, January 15: Rajasthan 79/8 in 20 overs (Shweta Bishnoi 32, SR Jat 21; Mamta Paswan 4-9, Niharika Prasad 2-8) lost to **Jharkhand** 80/5 in 17.4 overs (Ritu Kumari 22*, Priyanka Sawaiyan 22; Babita Meena 2-16) by five wickets.

SCA Stadium B, Rajkot, January 15: Himachal Pradesh 129/5 in 20 overs (Tanuja Kanwer

29, Sushma Verma 24) beat **Saurashtra** 89/9 in 20 overs (Mridula Jadeja 34; T Kanwer 4-12) by 40 runs.

SCA Stadium B, Rajkot, January 16: HP 117/6 in 20 overs (Sushma Verma 41, Nikita Chauhan 24; Mamta Paswan 2-19, Kavita Roy 2-23) lost to **Jharkhand** 118/5 in 20 overs (Priyanka Sawaiyan 50, Durga Kumari Murmu 35; Susmita Kumari 2-25) by five wickets.

SCA Stadium B, Rajkot, January 16: Rajasthan 116/3 in 20 overs (SR Jat 38, Priyanka Sharma 37) beat **Haryana** 92/5 in 20 overs (Sonia Khatri 31, Sheetal Rana 27; Shweta Bishnoi 2-19, MS Gurjar 2-22) by 24 runs.

SCA Stadium B, Rajkot, January 17: Rajasthan 105/9 in 20 overs (Priyanka Sharma 33, Babita Meena 21*) beat **Saurashtra** 104/8 in 20 overs (Mridula Jadeja 43, Bhakti Shastri 36; Suman Meena 4-23, B Meena 2-14) by one run.

SCA Stadium B, Rajkot, January 17: Haryana 87/5 in 20 overs (Suman Gulia 39, Sonia Khatri 38*) lost to **Jharkhand** 88/5 in 17.4 overs (Niharika Prasad 26*, Reena Singh 25; Urvashi Saini 2-9, Preeti Bose 2-10) by five wickets.

Plate Group B points table

Team	M	W	L	T	N/R	Pts	NRR
Jharkhand	4	4	0	0	0	16	+0.448
Himachal Pradesh	4	3	1	0	0	12	+1.331
Rajasthan	4	2	2	0	0	8	-0.064
Haryana	4	1	3	0	0	4	-1.073
Saurashtra	4	0	4	0	0	0	-0.601

Jharkhand and Himachal Pradesh qualified for the Plate Knock-out

Plate Group C

TI Cycles Ground, Murugappa, Chennai, January 13: Chhattisgarh 107/7 in 20 overs (Mantravadi Shalini 32, Manpreet Kaur 24*; Bushra Ashraf 3-9, Nadia Chouwdhary 2-17) beat **Jammu & Kashmir** 79/8 in 20 overs (Meenu Salathia 35; Anupriya Mandal 2-19) by 28 runs.

MA Chidambaram Stadium, Chepauk, Chennai, January 13: Tamil Nadu 120/7 in 20 overs (L Nethra Iyer 40, Niranjana Nagarajan 35; Suravi Roy 2-28) beat **Tripura** 89/8 in 20 overs (Mouchaity Debnath 20; N Iyer 4-22) by five wickets.

TI Cycles Ground, Murugappa, Chennai, January 13: Punjab 122/3 in 20 overs (Taniya Bhatia 85*) lost to **Odisha** 126/3 in 17.3 overs (Pragyan Mohanty 50*, Sarita Meher 21) by seven wickets.

TI Cycles Ground, Murugappa, Chennai, January 14: Tripura 131/7 in 20 overs (Indra Rani Jamatia 52, Rizu Saha 26) beat **Chhattisgarh** 99/9 in 20 overs (Pransu Priya 25*; Moutushi Dey 3-15) by 32 runs.

MA Chidambaram Stadium, Chepauk, Chennai, January 14: Odisha 130/8 in 20 overs (Madhuri Meheta 40, Sarita Meher 30; Bismah Hassan 5-19) beat **Jammu & Kashmir** 72/6 in 20 overs (Rubia Syed 33; Madhusmita Behara 2-10) by 58 runs.

MA Chidambaram Stadium, Chepauk, Chennai, January 14: Tamil Nadu 68 in 20 overs (Deksha Dogra 2-4, Sneh Rana 2-10) beat **Punjab** 65/9 in 20 overs (S Rana 25; Hemalatha Dayalan 2-6, K Ramyashri 2-7) by three runs.

MA Chidambaram Stadium, Chepauk, Chennai, January 15: Chhattisgarh 100/6 in 20 overs (Priya Verma 35*, Mantravadi Shalini 25; K Ramyashri 2-8) beat **Tamil Nadu** 97/7 in 20 overs (Hemalatha Dayalan 46) by three runs.

TI Cycles Ground, Murugappa, Chennai, January 15: Tripura 110/6 in 20 overs (Mouchaity Debnath 42, Indra Rani Jamatia 37; Rasanara Parwin 2-21) lost to **Odisha** 112/2 in 18.2 overs (Madhusmita Behara 45, Madhuri Meheta 32) by eight wickets.

MA Chidambaram Stadium, Chepauk, Chennai, January 15: Jammu & Kashmir 100/5 in 20 overs (Rubia Syed 50*; Mehek Kesar 2-24) beat **Punjab** 94 in 19.3 overs (Kanika Ahuja 21; Sandhya Balkar 4-9) by six runs.

TI Cycles Ground, Murugappa, Chennai, January 16: Tamil Nadu 152/3 in 20 overs (Hemalatha Dayalan 90*, Niranjana Nagarajan 32) beat **Jammu & Kashmir** 49 in 19.3 overs (L Nethra Iyer 3-12, Nida Rehman 2-1) by 103 runs.

TI Cycles Ground, Murugappa, Chennai, January 16: Punjab 116 in 20 overs (Ridhima Aggarwal 32, Sneh Rana 26; Sweety Sinha 2-14, Annapurna Das 2-31) beat **Tripura** 66 in 19.1 overs (S Rana 3-19, Komalpreet Kour 2-6) by 50 runs.

MA Chidambaram Stadium, Chepauk, Chennai, January 16: Chhattisgarh 104/4 in 20 overs (Manpreet Kaur 28*, Shivi Pandey 24; Rasanara Parwin 2-18) beat **Odisha** 103/8 in 20 overs (Sarita Meher 42*) by one run.

TI Cycles Ground, Murugappa, Chennai, January 17: Tripura 159/3 in 20 overs (Mouchaity Debnath 47, Indra Rani Jamatia 37; Sarla Devi 2-26) beat **Jammu & Kashmir** 64/7 in 20 overs (Neeru Manhas 29; Sweety Sinha 2-4) by 95 runs.

MA Chidambaram Stadium, Chepauk, Chennai, January 17: Punjab 55 in 16.4 overs (Harina 2-6, Vaishnava 2-8) lost to **Chhattisgarh** 56/1 in 14.5 overs (Mantravadi Shalini 37*) by nine wickets.

MA Chidambaram Stadium, Chepauk, Chennai, January 17: Tamil Nadu 108/8 in 20 overs (Hemalatha Dayalan 28; Sushree Dibyadarshini 2-16) tied with **Odisha** 108/8 in 20 overs (Madhuri Meheta 37, Sarita Meher 23). Super Over: Odisha 5/2 in 0.5 overs beat Tamil Nadu 4/2 in 1 over.

Plate Group C points table

Team	M	W	L	T	N/R	Pts	NRR
Odisha	5	4	1	0	0	16	+0.882
Chhattisgarh	5	4	1	0	0	16	+0.264
Tamil Nadu	5	3	2	0	0	12	+1.340
Tripura	5	2	3	0	0	8	+0.353
Punjab	5	1	4	0	0	4	+0.015
Jammu & Kashmir	5	1	4	0	0	4	-2.780

Odisha and Chhattisgarh qualified for the Plate Knock-out

Plate knock-out

1st quarter-final: KSCA Ground No.2, Alur, January 23: Chhattisgarh 71 in 19.2 overs (Shivi Pandey 27; Niharika Prasad 3-4, Devyani Prasad 2-14) lost to **Jharkhand** 75/3 in 14.5 overs (Kavita Roy 38*, Priyanka Sawaiyan 23) by seven wickets.

2nd quarter-final: KSCA Ground No.2, Alur, January 23: Karnataka 127/3 in 20 overs (Shubha Sateesh 61, Rakshitha Krishnappa 30) beat **Himachal Pradesh** 87 in 19 overs (Nikita Chauhan 30; V Chandu 4-18, Sahana Pawar 2-12) by 40 runs.

Semi-finals

1st semi-final: KSCA Ground No.2, Alur, January 25: Kerala 132/6 in 20 overs (Sajeevan Sajana 46, T Shani 32; Niharika Prasad 3-30) beat **Jharkhand** 90 in 18.3 overs (Kavita Roy

32; T Shani 3-12, Keerthy James 3-15) by 42 runs.

2nd semi-final: KSCA Ground No.2, Alur, January 25: Karnataka 85 in 18.1 overs (G Divya 32; Priyanka Priyadarshini 5-12) lost to **Odisha** 89/2 in 19 overs (Pragyan Mohanty 31*, Sarita Meher 23*) by eight wickets.

Finals

KSCA Ground No.2, Alur, January 27: Odisha 108/5 in 20 overs (Madhuri Meheta 28, Madhusmita Behara 26; Keerthy James 2-21) beat **Kerala** 100 in 19.2 overs (T Shani 48, Minnu Mani 20; Sushree Dibyadarshini 2-15, Sujatha Mallik 2-21) by eight runs.

Winners: Odisha

Elite Group Super League

Sachin Tendulkar Gymkhana Ground, Mumbai, January 23: Delhi 109/7 in 20 overs (Priya Punia 20, Latika Kumari 20; Shalini Sharma 3-27) lost to **Baroda** 110/2 in 19.1 overs (Palak Patel 47*, Binaisha Surti 44) by eight wickets.

Sachin Tendulkar Gymkhana Ground, Mumbai, January 23: Maharashtra 107/7 in 20 overs (Shweta Jadhav 40, Anuja Patil 23; Sanjula Naik 2-12) beat **Goa** 56/9 in 20 overs (Devika Vaidya 3-8, Utkarsha Pawar 2-2) by 51 runs.

Sachin Tendulkar Gymkhana Ground, Mumbai, January 25: Goa 104/8 in 20 overs (Sugandha Ghadi 31, Sanjula Naik 24; Jaya Mohite 2-6, Tarannum Pathan 2-16) lost to **Baroda** 105/9 in 19.3 overs (Binaisha Surti 32; Sunanda Yetrekar 2-8, S Naik 2-14) by one wicket.

Sachin Tendulkar Gymkhana Ground, Mumbai, January 25: Maharashtra 58/9 in 20 overs (Shweta Mane 22*; Rumeli Dhar 4-14, Ankita Sinha 2-12) lost to **Delhi** 61/3 in 14.4 overs (Neha Tanwar 22; Mukta Magre 2-9) by seven wickets.

Sachin Tendulkar Gymkhana Ground, Mumbai, January 27: Maharashtra 109/5 in 20 overs (Shweta Jadhav 34, Shweta Mane 26*; Radha Yadav 2-22, Tarannum Pathan 2-23) beat **Baroda** 95/9 in 20 overs (Yastika Bhatia 24; Devika Vaidya 4-11, Anuja Patil 3-18) by 14 runs.

Sachin Tendulkar Gymkhana Ground, Mumbai, January 27: Goa 96/5 in 20 overs (Sanjula Naik 34*, Tejaswini Duragad 24, Ankita Sinha 2-11) lost to **Delhi** 100/1 in 13.5 overs (Neha Tanwar 63*) by nine wickets.

Elite Super League points table

Team	M	W	L	T	N/R	Pts	NRR
Delhi	3	2	1	0	0	8	+1.105
Maharashtra	3	2	1	0	0	8	+0.689
Baroda	3	2	1	0	0	8	-0.083
Goa	3	0	3	0	0	0	-1.583

Winners: Delhi

Women's T20 Challenge

Harmanpreet fires up final

There was still no full-fledged women's IPL, but the one-off exhibition game held in 2018 was expanded to a three-team affair, with a round-robin group stage and a final, and all games having official T20 status. The BCCI had learnt from the criticisms of the previous year, when the match was held on a weekday afternoon in Mumbai, ahead of the IPL play-offs. They moved it to Jaipur and played it under lights. The crowds turned up, and the action and the reception was a reminder of the possibilities of this tournament.

The IPL has been a platform for showcasing local talent, and so it was again. Shafali Verma, all of 14, had been lighting up the domestic circuit with her hard hitting — now she was on TV and making sure people knew what she could do. Radha Yadav, another teenager, got a taste of playing under pressure. Having lost Harmanpreet Kaur, whose 37-ball 51 had taken them close, in the final over, she held her nerve to strike the last ball for four and seal the win. New Zealand's Lea Tahuhu was so excited, she hurt her shoulder while celebrating.

Sawai Mansingh Stadium, Jaipur, May 6: Trailblazers 140/5 in 20 overs (Smriti Mandhana 90, Harleen Deol 36; Radha Yadav 2-28) beat **Supernovas** 138/6 in 20 overs (Harmanpreet Kaur 46*, Sophie Devine 32; Sophie Ecclestone 2-11, Rajeshwari Gayakwad 2-17) by two runs. *PoM:* Smriti Mandhana.
Sawai Mansingh Stadium, Jaipur, May 8: Trailblazers 112/6 in 20 overs (Harleen Deol 43, Suzie Bates 26; Amelia Kerr 2-21, Koman Zanzad 2-23) lost to **Velocity** 113/7 in 18 overs (Danni Wyatt 46, Shafali Verma 34; Deepti Sharma 4-14) by three wickets. *PoM:* Danni Wyatt.
Sawai Mansingh Stadium, Jaipur, May 9: Supernovas 142/3 in 20 overs (Jemimah Rodrigues 77, Chamari Athapathu 31; Amelia Kerr 2-21) beat **Velocity** 130/3 in 20 overs (Danni Wyatt 43, Mithali Raj 40*) by 12 runs. *PoM:* Jemimah Rodrigues.

Final: Supernovas beat Velocity by four wickets
Sawai Mansingh Stadium, Jaipur, May 11: Velocity 121/6 in 20 overs (Sushma Verma 40*, Amelia Kerr 36) lost to **Supernovas** 125/6 in 20 overs (Harmanpreet Kaur 51, Priya Punia 29; Jahanara Alam 2-21, Amelia Kerr 2-29) by four wickets runs. *PoM:* Harmanpreet Kaur. *PoS:* Jemimah Rodrigues.

Winners: Supernovas

Under-23 T20 Challenger Trophy

Runs hard to come by

India Green cantered to a comfortable eight-wicket over India Blue in the final of the inaugural Under-23 T20 Challenger Trophy in Mysore. Having lost their league encounter against the same opposition, Disha Kasat's unbeaten 43 helped India Green, led by Sabbineni Meghana, overhaul India Blue's total of 70 with 7.1 overs to spare. Kasat was the leading run-scorer in the series with 89 runs, closely followed by Priya Punia of India Blue with 83 runs— her tally including a total of three sixes. Constant rain, heavy outfields and slow pitches meant the batters struggled in difficult conditions. Runs were hard to come by, and only once in eight innings did a team cross the 100-run mark— India Blue scoring 114 in their opening encounter against India Red. Sushree Dibyadarshini, the off-spinner from India Green, led the bowling charts with 6 wickets, while Renuka Chaudhari, their left-arm spinner, registered the best figures of the tournament— 4 for 18 against India Blue in the final.

Best batter: Disha Kasat (India Green) (89 runs in 3 matches)
Best bowler: Sushree Dibyadarshini (6 wickets in 3 matches)

Srikantadatta Narasimha Raja Wadeyar Ground, Mysore, October 4: India Blue 114/5 in 20 overs (Devika Vaidya 43, Priya Punia 30) beat **India Red** 95/6 in 20 overs (Harleen Deol 23, Nuzhat Parween 21; Nisha Maji 2-11, Tanuja Kanwer 2-18) by 19 runs.
Srikantadatta Narasimha Raja Wadeyar Ground, Mysore, October 5: India Green 89/6 in 20 overs (Disha Kasat 29; Reemalaxmi Ekka 2-12) lost to **India Blue** 64/0 in 10 overs (Priya Punia 31*, Devika Vaidya 28*) by 10 wickets. (VJD method).
Srikantadatta Narasimha Raja Wadeyar Ground, Mysore, October 6: India Red 75 in 17.4 overs (Minnu Mani 25; Shannti Kumari 3-10, Sushree Dibyadarshini 3-14) lost to **India Green** 79/1 in 16.3 overs (Sabbineni Meghana 34*, Nikita Chauhan 22) by nine wickets.

Points table

Team	M	W	L	T	N/R	Pts	NRR
India Blue	2	2	0	0	0	8	+1.667
India Green	2	1	1	0	0	4	-0.407
India Red	2	0	2	0	0	0	-1.038

India Blue and India Green qualified for the final

Final

Srikantadatta Narasimha Raja Wadeyar Ground, Mysore, October 8: India Blue 70 in 17.4 overs (Priya Punia 22; Renuka Chaudhari 4-18, Sushree Dibyadarshini 3-10) lost to **India Green** 72/2 in 12.5 overs (Disha Kasat 43*) by eight wickets.

Winners: India Green

Women's Under-23 Inter-state T20 Competition

Railways take honours, Devika shines

Railways maintained their unbeaten run in the tournament fending off challenges from Gujarat, Jharkhand and Mumbai in the Super League, to ultimately beat Maharashtra by three wickets in a close final. R Kalpana's 19-ball 25 and her 44-run sixth-wicket partnership with Dipa Das (22) in Railways' pursuit of 117 were enough to trump the efforts of Devika Vaidya (50*) and Tejal Hasabnis (52*) for Maharashtra.

Vaidya led her team's charge to the final, topping the batting charts with 395 runs, including four half-centuries, and also chipping in with 13 crucial wickets. She was ably assisted by Maya Sonawane, the leg-spinner, who finished as the highest wicket-taker with 22 scalps, including an incredible spell of 5 for 0 against Sikkim.

With relatively low scoring games and many close finishes, bowlers showed great character. The spinners in the top five wicket-takers' list conceded less than 4.2 runs an over. As many as eight five-wicket hauls were taken, with G Chandra Lekha, the off-spinner from Andhra, registering best figures of 6 for 7 against Gujarat. Shafali Verma, the opening batter from Haryana, continued her blazing form smashing 215 runs at a strike-rate of 169.29, including a best of 132 off 63 balls against Bihar — one of only five

Shafali Verma of Haryana had a best of 132 off just 63 balls, against Bihar. — *BCCI*

centuries scored in the tournament.

Other impressive performances include Tripura's incredible victory over Himachal Pradesh in a count back of the Super Over, Kajal Jena's tally of 311 runs at an average of 104 for Odisha and Arundhati Reddy's unbeaten 36-ball 79 against Saurashtra that included six sixes.

The **previous year**, in the tournament's inaugural edition, Kerala calmly chased down 115 against Maharashtra in the final. In a relatively low-scoring tournament with only 15 scores over 130 in 81 matches, Kerala out-bowled and out-fielded all their opponents. As a team, they effected 25 run-outs in nine matches, and three of their bowlers, Aneena Mathews, the leg-spinner, Sajeevan Sajana, the off-spinner (both 12 wickets), and Minnu Mani, the off-spinner (11 wickets) were in the top ten wickets-takers.

CH Jhansi Lakshmi, the left-hand opening batter from Andhra, showcased her full array of strokes as she racked up 244 runs at an average of 40.67. Nikita Singh, the Madhya Pradesh captain, was hot on her heels, collecting 235 runs, including two impressive half-centuries. Although her team failed to win a single match, Rubia Syed, Jammu and Kashmir captain, showed her ability to clear the field, with a total of eight sixes in only four matches — the highest by any single player.

	Most runs	**Most wickets**
2017-18	CH Jhansi Lakshmi (Andhra) (244 runs in 9 matches)	Charu Joshi (Madhya Pradesh) (17 wickets 9 matches)
2018-19	Devika Vaidya (Maharashtra) (395 runs in 10 matches)	Maya Sonawane (Maharashtra) (22 wickets in 10 matches)

2018-19

Group A

St Paul's College Ground Kalamassery, Kochi, January 14: Baroda 134/4 in 20 overs (Yastika Bhatia 89*, Karishma Tank 30) beat **Goa** 72 in 19.4 overs (Sanjula Naik 29; Radha Yadav 5-11) by 62 runs.

Rajagiri College of Engineering and Technology Ground, Kochi, January 14: Manipur 41 in 17.3 overs (Sunita Rani 3-0, Komalpreet Kour 3-8) lost to **Punjab** 42/0 in 5 overs by 10 wickets.

St Paul's College Ground Kalamassery, Kochi, January 14: Kerala 158/3 in 20 overs (Jilu George 56, Deepthi JS 45; Deiphi 2-42) beat **Meghalaya** 22 in 16.1 overs (Annena Mathews 2-2, Mrudhula VS 2-5) by 136 runs.

RCET Ground, Kochi, January 15: Uttar Pradesh 99/8 in 20 overs (Aditi Sharma 32*; Kanika Ahuja 2-12, Amanjot Kaur 2-24) lost to **Punjab** 101/8 in 19.4 overs (Neelam Bisht 40*, Riddhima Agarwal 21; Rashi Kanojiya 3-19) by two wickets.

St Paul's College Ground Kalamassery, Kochi, January 15: Meghalaya 38/8 in 20 overs lost to **Baroda** 39/2 in 6.1 overs by eight wickets.

St Paul's College Ground Kalamassery, Kochi, January 15: Manipur 44/9 in 20 overs (Kabia Badoni 21; Tejashwini Duragad 3-2, Vanita Bhandari 2-3) lost to **Goa** 45/0 in 4.2 overs (T Duragad 25*) by 10 wickets.

Rajagiri College of Engineering and Technology Ground, Kochi, January 17: Uttar Pradesh 112/4 in 20 overs (Aditi Sharma 41, Shobha Devi 35*) lost to **Kerala** 113/4 in 19.2 overs (Deepthi JS 45, Minnu Mani 43*) by six wickets.

St Paul's College Ground Kalamassery, Kochi, January 17: Manipur 15 in 17.1 overs (Gayatri Naik 3-0, Jaya Mohite 3-3) lost to **Baroda** 16/0 in 1.3 overs by 10 wickets.

St Paul's College Ground Kalamassery, Kochi, January 17: Goa 120/4 in 20 overs (Vinavi Gurav 46*, Shindiya Naik 36; Deiphi 2-21) beat **Meghalaya** 35/9 in 20 overs (Gawde Diksha 2-3) by 85 runs.

St Paul's College Ground Kalamassery, Kochi, January 18: Kerala 58 in 19.2 overs (Radha Yadav 2-8, Charmi 2-18) lost to **Baroda** 61/2 in 13.1 overs (R Yadav 22*) by eight wickets.

Rajagiri College of Engineering and Technology Ground, Kochi, January 18: Meghalaya 27/8 in 20 overs (Sunita Rani 2-1, Neelam Bisht 2-7) lost to **Punjab** 28/0 in 7 overs by 10 wickets.

St Paul's College Ground Kalamassery, Kochi, January 18: Manipur 21 in 12.5 overs (Bhawana Rathaur 4-5, Kshama 2-12) lost to **Uttar Pradesh** 22/0 in 2.2 overs by 10 wickets.

Rajagiri College of Engineering and Technology Ground, Kochi, January 20: Kerala 192/5 in 20 overs (IV Drishya 115, Sayoojya Salilan 27; VR Dharani 2-24, Linthoingambi Rajkumari 2-32) beat **Manipur** 45/7 in 20 overs (Kabia Badoni 21*; Keerthy James 3-9) by 147 runs.

St Paul's College Ground Kalamassery, Kochi, January 20: Baroda 112/6 in 20 overs (Radha Yadav 39, Yastika Bhatia 27; Rashi Kanojiya 2-20) beat **Uttar Pradesh** 89/7 in 20 overs (Shivpriya Pandey 40; R Yadav 2-11) by 23 runs.

St Paul's College Ground Kalamassery, Kochi, January 20: Punjab 94/7 in 20 overs (Srishti Rajput 31, Ridhima Aggarwal 27; Vanita Bhandari 3-12, Tejashwini Duragad 2-19) beat **Goa** 66 in 16.1 overs (Neelam Bisht 3-11, Rajni Devi 3-15) by 28 runs.

RCET Ground, Kochi, January 21: Manipur 103/6 in 20 overs (Linthoingambi Rajkumari 21; Debasmita Dutta 2-2) lost to **Meghalaya** 105/6 in 19.4 overs (D Dutta 39*; VR Dharani 2-14) by four wickets.

St Paul's College Ground Kalamassery, Kochi, January 21: Goa 71/9 in 20 overs (Sanjula Naik 25; Rashi Kanojiya 4-13, Kshama 2-4) lost to **Uttar Pradesh** 72/3 in 16.3 overs (Shivpriya Pandey 34, Muskan Malik 31*) by seven wickets.

St Paul's College Ground Kalamassery, Kochi, January 21: Punjab 76/8 in 20 overs (Amarpal Kaur 25; Mrudhula VS 3-16, Jipsa Joseph 2-10) beat **Kerala** 57 in 16.2 overs (Jisna Joseph 31*; Komalpreet Kour 4-14, Rajni Devi 3-6) by 19 runs.

Rajagiri College of Engineering and Technology Ground, Kochi, January 23: Meghalaya 59/9 in 20 overs (Aditi Sharma 2-10) lost to **Uttar Pradesh** 60/1 in 5 overs (Shivpriya Pandey 48*) by nine wickets.

St Paul's College Ground Kalamassery, Kochi, January 23: Baroda 98/7 in 20 overs (Yastika Bhatia 23; Sunita Rani 2-14, Rajni Devi 2-25) beat **Punjab** 62/9 in 20 overs (Kanika Ahuja 21; Pragya Rawat 2-6) by 36 runs.

St Paul's College Ground Kalamassery, Kochi, January 23: Kerala 75 in 19.4 overs (Diksha Gawde 4-5, Sanjula Naik 2-13) beat **Goa** 58 in 18.3 overs (Tejashwini Duragad 20; Aneena Mathews 4-3, Keerthy James 2-10) by 17 runs.

Group A Points Table

Team	M	W	L	T	N/R	Pts	NRR
Baroda	6	6	0	0	0	24	+2.907
Punjab	6	5	1	0	0	20	+1.163
Kerala	6	4	2	0	0	16	+2.167
Uttar Pradesh	6	3	3	0	0	12	+1.407

Goa	6	2	4	0	0	8	+0.244
Meghalaya	6	1	5	0	0	4	-4.109
Manipur	6	0	6	0	0	0	-5.746

Baroda and Punjab qualified for the Super Leagues

Group B

Rajasthan Cricket Association Academy Ground, Jaipur, January 15: Maharashtra 174/0 in 20 overs (Devika Vaidya 90*, Shivali Shinde 70*) beat **Sikkim** 20 in 15.1 overs (Maya Sonawane 5-0, Devika Vaidya 2-1) by 154 runs.

Jaipuria Vidhyalaya Ground, Jaipur, January 15: Assam 69 in 19.2 overs (Rashmi Dey 23) lost to **Hyderabad** 70/1 in 16.1 overs (Sneha More 31*) by nine wickets.

Jaipuria Vidhyalaya Ground, Jaipur, January 15: Jharkhand 153/6 in 20 overs (Indrani Roy 44, Rashmi 24; Ayantika 2-20) beat **Nagaland** 54/8 in 20 overs (Vaincy Chaudhary 34; Devyani Prasad 4-6, Shanti Kumari 2-1) by 99 runs.

Jaipuria Vidhyalaya Ground, Jaipur, January 16: Maharashtra 138/3 in 20 overs (Shivali Shinde 52, Tejal Hasabnis 47; G Trisha 2-14) beat **Hyderabad** 93/9 in 20 overs (G Trisha 23; Maya Sonawane 4-20, Devika Vaidya 2-22) by 45 runs.

Jaipuria Vidhyalaya Ground, Jaipur, January 16: Rajasthan 133/1 in 20 overs (SR Jat 64*, Ayushi Garg 33*) beat **Sikkim** 32/8 in 20 overs (SS Kalal 3-2, Suman Meena 3-5) by 101 runs.

Rajasthan Cricket Association Academy Ground, Jaipur, January 16: Assam 105/7 in 20 overs (Rashmi Dey 35; Ayantika 2-18, Rinki Biswas 2-27) beat **Nagaland** 75/5 in 20 overs (Nazma Khan 36; Bedashree Borpatragohain 3-19) by 30 runs.

Jaipuria Vidhyalaya Ground, Jaipur, January 18: Rajasthan 91/5 in 20 overs (Suman Meena 38; Devyani Prasad 3-16) lost to **Jharkhand** 94/2 in 18.5 overs (Rashmi 55*) by eight wickets.

Rajasthan Cricket Association Academy Ground, Jaipur, January 18: Maharashtra 141/6 in 20 overs (Devika Vaidya 74, Shivali Shinde 36; Rashmi Dey 2-15) beat **Assam** 78/7 in 20 overs (Ruhina Pegu 21) by 63 runs.

Jaipuria Vidhyalaya Ground, Jaipur, January 18: Nagaland 73/5 in 20 overs (Nazma Khan 23; Anitha Kotha 2-13) lost to **Hyderabad** 75/1 in 11.3 overs (Sneha More 34*, Doli Ramya 23*) by nine wickets.

Jaipuria Vidhyalaya Ground, Jaipur, January 19: Maharashtra 107/6 in 20 overs (Devika Vaidya 32, CD Charmy 28; Suman Meena 3-16) lost to **Rajasthan** 110/7 in 20 overs (SR Jat 31; Utkarsha Pawar 2-18) by three wickets.

Rajasthan Cricket Association Academy Ground, Jaipur, January 19: Assam 119/7 in 20 overs (Ruhina Pegu 40) beat **Jharkhand** 115/6 in 20 overs (Sonia 44, Priyanka Sawaiyan 49) by four wickets.

Jaipuria Vidhyalaya Ground, Jaipur, January 19: Nagaland 153/1 in 20 overs (Vaincy Chaudhary 58, Tulika 42*) beat **Sikkim** 44 in 16 overs (Rinki Biswas 3-7) by 109 runs.

Jaipuria Vidhyalaya Ground, Jaipur, January 21: Hyderabad 176/1 in 20 overs (Sneha More 88*, Vanka Pooja 49) beat **Sikkim** 45/9 in 20 overs (Anitha Kotha 3-6) by 131 runs.

Rajasthan Cricket Association Academy Ground, Jaipur, January 21: Assam 82/8 in 20 overs (Priyanka Boruah 29; Rinku Tank 2-19) lost to **Rajasthan** 86/6 in 19 overs (Ayushi Garg 36, Jyoti Choudhary 24; Rashmi Dey 2-19) by four wickets.

Jaipuria Vidhyalaya Ground, Jaipur, January 21: Maharashtra 76 in 20 overs (SA Lonkar 20; Mamta Paswan 3-16, Shanti Kumari 2-9) beat **Jharkhand** 75/8 in 20 overs (Aditi Gaikwad 2-14, SB Porkharkar 2-14) by one run.

Rajasthan Cricket Association Academy Ground, Jaipur, January 22: Maharashtra 115/4 in 20 overs (Tejal Hasabnis 51, SA Lonkar 27; Sariba 2-20, Rinki Biswas 2-22) beat **Nagaland** 43 in 13 overs (Maya Sonawane 4-4) by 72 runs.

Jaipuria Vidhyalaya Ground, Jaipur, January 22: Hyderabad 120/4 in 20 overs (G Trisha 42, Sneha More 32) beat **Rajasthan** 101 in 19.3 overs (Suman Meena 20; Bhogi Shravani 4-16) by 19 runs.

Jaipuria Vidhyalaya Ground, Jaipur, January 22: Sikkim 10 in 14.3 overs (Shanti Kumari 3-0, Mamta Paswan 3-0) lost to **Jharkhand** 11/1 in 1.2 overs by nine wickets.

Rajasthan Cricket Association Academy Ground, Jaipur, January 23: Assam 154/3 in 20 overs (Rashmi Dey 70*, Priyanka Boruah 60; Tabita Subba 2-28) beat **Sikkim** 37/8 in 20 overs (Kakoli Saikia 3-9, R Dey 2-13) by 117 runs.

Jaipuria Vidhyalaya Ground, Jaipur, January 23: Nagaland 48/9 in 20 overs (Tulika 23; Rinku Tank 2-6, Suman Meena 2-11) lost to **Rajasthan** 51/2 in 7.1 overs (Jyoti Choudhary 24*; Sheetal 2-20) by eight wickets.

Jaipuria Vidhyalaya Ground, Jaipur, January 24: Jharkhand 128/5 in 20 overs (Rashmi 42, Indrani Roy 38) beat **Hyderabad** 94/8 in 20 overs (Doli Ramya 21; Durga Kumari Murmu 3-13, Shanti Kumari 2-15) by 34 runs.

Group B Points Table

Team	M	W	L	T	N/R	Pts	NRR
Maharashtra	6	5	1	0	0	20	+2.938
Jharkhand	6	4	2	0	0	16	+2.050
Hyderabad	6	4	2	0	0	16	+1.216
Rajasthan	6	4	2	0	0	16	+1.323
Assam	6	3	3	0	0	12	+0.508
Nagaland	6	1	5	0	0	4	-1.977
Sikkim	6	0	6	0	0	0	-6.338

Maharashtra and Jharkhand qualified for the Super Leagues

Group C

Airforce Complex Ground, Palam II, New Delhi Services, January 14: Mumbai 104/6 in 20 overs (Sejal Raut 37, Vrushali Bhagat 22; Suman Hingra 5-13) beat **Haryana** 94/6 in 20 overs (Shivangi Chauhan 31; Manali Dakshini 2-12, Fatima Jaffer 2-15) by 10 runs.

Airforce Complex Ground, Palam, New Delhi Services, January 14: Arunachal Pradesh 22 in 12.5 overs (Apurva 5-9) lost to **Bihar** 23/0 in 4.5 overs by 10 wickets.

Airforce Complex Ground, Palam, New Delhi Services, January 14: Delhi 87/9 in 20 overs (Simran Dil Bahadur 22; Tanuja Kanwer 4-10) lost to **Himachal Pradesh** 91/2 in 18.5 overs (Harleen Deol 42*, Vandna Rana 23*; Ayushi Soni 2-14) by eight wickets.

Airforce Complex Ground, Palam II, New Delhi Services, January 15: Tripura 83/9 in 20 overs (Ambika Debnath 22; Samruddhi Rawool 3-1, Fatima Jaffer 2-12) lost to **Mumbai** 85/2 in 17.3 overs (Aachal Valanju 43*, Vrushali Bhagat 25*) by eight wickets.

Airforce Complex Ground, Palam, New Delhi Services, January 15: Arunachal Pradesh 14 in 11 overs (Prachi Chauhan 4-1, Renuka Singh 2-4) lost to **Himachal Pradesh** 17/0 in 1.2 overs by 10 wickets.

Airforce Complex Ground, Palam, New Delhi Services, January 15: Haryana 203/3 in 20 overs (Shafali Verma 132, Bhawna Ohlan 43) beat **Bihar** 43 in 16 overs (Apurva Kumari 22; Priya Khatkar 2-1, Diksha Sharma 2-5) by 160 runs.

Airforce Complex Ground, Palam II, New Delhi Services, January 17: Tripura 77/6 in 20 overs (Ambika Debnath 27; Ria Sharma 3-11) lost to **Delhi** 79/1 in 17.3 overs (Priya Punia 45*) by nine wickets.

Airforce Complex Ground, Palam, New Delhi Services, January 17: Arunachal Pradesh 15 in 16.4 overs (Priya Khatkar 4-6, Sheetal Rana 2-0) lost to **Haryana** 19/0 in 1 over by 10 wickets.

Airforce Complex Ground, Palam, New Delhi Services, January 17: Himachal Pradesh 137/4 in 20 overs (SM Singh 65*, Vandna Rana 21) beat **Bihar** 26 in 19.3 overs (Sushmita Kumari 3-3) by 111 runs.

Airforce Complex Ground, Palam II, New Delhi Services, January 18: Mumbai 101/4 in 17 overs (Sayali Satghare 22*) beat **Himachal Pradesh** 87/9 in 17 overs (Tanuja Kanwer 25*, Kashish Verma 23; Jagravi Pawar 2-16) by 14 runs.

Airforce Complex Ground, Palam, New Delhi Services, January 18: Arunachal Pradesh 26/9 in 17 overs (Simral Dil Bahadur 5-6, Ria Sharma 2-0) lost to **Delhi** 28/0 in 4.1 overs by 10 wickets.

Airforce Complex Ground, Palam, New Delhi Services, January 18: Tripura 84/9 in 20 overs (Nikita 27; Sheetal Rana 3-17, Priya Khatkar 2-5) lost to **Haryana** 85/2 in 13.2 overs (Shafali Verma 48; Antara Das 2-9) by eight wickets.

Airforce Complex Ground, Palam II, New Delhi Services, January 20: Delhi 136/1 in 20 overs (Priya Punia 55*, Laxmi Yadav 52) beat **Haryana** 92/8 in 20 overs (Bhawna Ohlan 31; Ayushi Soni 2-12, Ria Sharma 2-21) by 44 runs.

Airforce Complex Ground, Palam, New Delhi Services, January 20: Arunachal Pradesh 39/5 in 20 overs lost to **Tripura** 40/0 in 6 overs (Nikitha Debnath 20*) by 10 wickets.

Airforce Complex Ground, Palam, New Delhi Services, January 20: Mumbai 140/4 in 20 overs (Aachal Valanju 55, Vrushali Bhagat 29; Kumari 2-26) beat **Bihar** 39 in 19.5 overs (Sana Ali 20; Sayali Satghare 3-3, Fatima Jaffer 2-4) by 101 runs.

Airforce Complex Ground, Palam II, New Delhi Services, January 21: Haryana 117/4 in 20 overs (Shetal Rana 33*, Shafali Verma 28) lost to **Himachal Pradesh** 119/9 in 20 overs (Harleen Deol 57, SM Singh 29; Suman Hingra 4-19, S Rana 2-27) by one wicket.

Airforce Complex Ground, Palam, New Delhi Services, January 21: Bihar 50/9 in 20 overs (MK Rabidas 4-0) lost to **Tripura** 52/3 in 10.5 overs by seven wickets.

Airforce Complex Ground, Palam, New Delhi Services, January 21: Delhi 18/0 in 1.5 overs v **Mumbai**. No result.

Airforce Complex Ground, Palam II, New Delhi Services, January 23: Himachal Pradesh 81/3 in 14 overs (SM Singh 27, Kashish Verma 26) tied with **Tripura** 81/5 in 14 overs (Rizu Saha 35*, Jhumki Debnath 27). Super Over: Tripura 6/1 in 1 over tied with Himachal Pradesh 6/2 in 1 over. Tripura won by count back of Super Over.

Airforce Complex Ground, Palam, New Delhi Services, January 23: Arunachal Pradesh 40/9 in 12 overs (Saniya Raut 4-6, Fatima Jaffer 3-9) lost to **Mumbai** 41/0 in 4.2 overs (Sejal Raut 25*) by 10 wickets.

Airforce Complex Ground, Palam, New Delhi Services, January 23: Bihar 66/4 in 20 overs (Sana Ali 36*) lost to **Delhi** 67/1 in 11 overs (Priya Punia 34*) by nine wickets.

Group C points table

Team	M	W	L	T	N/R	Pts	NRR
Mumbai	6	5	0	0	1	22	+2.121
Delhi	6	4	1	0	1	18	+1.790
Himachal Pradesh	6	4	2	0	0	16	+1.998
Haryana	6	3	3	0	0	12	+2.291
Tripura	6	3	3	0	0	12	+0.496
Bihar	6	1	5	0	0	4	-3.742
Arunachal Pradesh	6	0	6	0	0	0	-6.323

Mumbai and Delhi qualified for the Super Leagues

Group D

Gokulbhai Somabhai Patel Stadium, Nandiad, January 15: Tamil Nadu 91/7 in 20 overs (SB Keerthana 32, S Anusha 28; Krutika Chaudhari 2-11) lost to **Gujarat** 92/8 in 19.4 overs (K Chaudhari 35*; Meenakshi 2-11, KN Ramyashri 2-12) by two wickets.

Shastri Medan, Anand, January 15: Bengal 102/7 in 20 overs (Tanusree Sarkar 34, Pravita 25; K Anjali Sarvani 3-17, G Chandra Lekha 2-15) beat **Andhra** 95 in 19.5 overs (V Pushpa Latha 28, K Anjali Sarvani 21; Nisha Maji 3-12, Saika Ishaque 2-16) by seven runs.

Shastri Medan, Anand, January 15: Chhattisgarh 79/7 in 20 overs (Shivi Pandey 21; SR Patil 2-15) lost to **Karnataka** 83/0 in 14.3 overs (G Divya 49*, Shubha Sateesh 33*) by 10 wickets.

Shastri Medan, Anand, January 16: Uttarakhand 102/3 in 20 overs (Ankita Dhami 38, Megha Saini 33) beat **Tamil Nadu** 96/9 in 20 overs (C Shushanthika 48; Rekha 2-16) by six runs.

Gokulbhai Somabhai Patel Stadium, Nandiad, January 16: Karnataka 85 in 18.3 overs (Shubha Sateesh 24; Saranya Gadwal 2-7, M Bhavana 2-8) lost to **Andhra** 86/7 in 17.5 overs (K Anjali Sarvani 36*; Sahana Pawar 4-4) by three wickets

Gokulbhai Somabhai Patel Stadium, Nandiad, January 16: Gujarat 92/5 in 20 overs (Simran 28, Krutika 20*; Saika Ishaque 2-16) lost to **Bengal** 93/3 in 18.3 overs (Pama Paul 39*, Tanusree Sarkar 23*) by seven wickets.

Gokulbhai Somabhai Patel Stadium, Nandiad, January 18: Chhattisgarh 107 in 19.5 overs (Shivi Pandey 40, Deepika Tiwari 20; Riya Rawat 3-11, Dimpal Kandari 2-17) beat **Uttarakhand** 106 in 19.5 overs (Shraddha Vaishnava 3-11, Ritu Meshram 3-23) by one run.

Shastri Medan, Anand, January 18: Gujarat 71 in 18.4 overs (Simran 27, IM Patel 20; G Chandra Lekha 6-7) beat **Andhra** 63 in 19 overs (V Pushpa Latha 21; Muskan Vasava 2-10, Hiral Solanki 2-11) by seven runs.

Shastri Medan, Anand, January 18: Karnataka 69 in 18.4 overs (D Vrinda 25*; Saika Ishaque 2-12, Nisha Maji 2-12) lost to **Bengal** 73/9 in 17.4 overs (Sahana Pawar 3-11, SR Patil 2-17) by one wicket.

Shastri Medan, Anand, January 19: Tamil Nadu 85/5 in 20 overs (S Anusha 42, SB Keerthana 30; Monica Patel 2-9, C Pratyusha 2-17) lost to **Karnataka** 86/4 in 14.5 overs (Shubha Sateesh 36, D Vrinda 27; SB Keerthana 2-18) by six wickets.

Gokulbhai Somabhai Patel Stadium, Nandiad, January 19: Andhra 108/7 in 20 overs (N Anusha 53, K Anjali Sarvani 27; Mamta Bhagat 2-19) beat **Chhattisgarh** 105/7 in 20 overs (Shivi Pandey 44, Deepika Tiwari 21; Saranya Gadwal 2-20, G Chandra Lekha 2-22) by three runs.

Gokulbhai Somabhai Patel Stadium, Nandiad, January 19: Uttarakhand 48 in 16.3 overs (Muskan Vasava 3-17, Hiral Solanki 2-2) lost to **Gujarat** 50/0 in 8.1 overs (Simran 37*) by 10 wickets.

Gokulbhai Somabhai Patel Stadium, Nandiad, January 21: Gujarat 100 in 19.5 overs (Renuka Chaudhari 46; Ritu Mehsram 2-13, Dipti Dhimar 2-19) beat **Chattisgarh** 78/9 in 20 overs (Manpreet Kaur 28; Hani Patel 2-4, Hiral Solanki 2-17) by 22 runs.

Shastri Medan, Anand, January 21: Andhra 145/4 in 20 overs (N Anusha 77, V Pushpa Latha 41; Pooja Raj 3-24) beat **Uttarakhand** 37/9 in 20 overs (G Chandra Lekha 4-7, K Anjali Sarvani 2-8) by 108 runs.

Shastri Medan, Anand, January 21: Bengal 125/3 in 20 overs (Pravita 38, Sushmita Ganguly 28*) beat **Tamil Nadu** 106/6 in 20 overs (Meenakshi 32*, C Shushanthika 23; Tanusree Sarkar 3-27, Saika Ishaque 2-16) by 19 runs.

Shastri Medan, Anand, January 22: Gujarat 135/ 1 in 20 overs (Simran 78, Hani Patel 51*) beat **Karnataka** 75 in 20 overs (PA Talpada 3-6, Krutika Chaudhari 2-9) by 60 runs.

Gokulbhai Somabhai Patel Stadium, Nandiad, January 22: Uttarakhand 66/5 in 20 overs (Ankita Dhami 26; Shreya Karar 2-9) lost to **Bengal** 69/1 in 13.5 overs (Pama Paul 39*) by nine wickets.

Gokulbhai Somabhai Patel Stadium, Nandiad, January 22: Chattisgarh 62 in 16.4 overs (Manpreet Kaur 28; MS Aishwarya 3-5, S Anusha 3-16) lost to **Tamil Nadu** 63/7 in 18.3 overs (M Kaur 2-10) by three wickets.

Gokulbhai Somabhai Patel Stadium, Nandiad, January 24: Uttarakhand 33 in 17.3 overs (SR Patil 4-10, Sahana Pawar 2-6) lost to **Karnataka** 34/3 in 7.5 overs (Rekha 2-11) by seven wickets.

Shastri Medan, Anand, January 22: Tamil Nadu 107/4 in 20 overs (S Anusha 41*, Meenakshi 25*; E Padmaja 2-17) lost to **Andhra** 108/4 in 18.4 overs (N Anusha 56*) by six wickets.

Shastri Medan, Anand, January 24: Chhattisgarh 75/9 in 20 overs (Shivi Pandey 22; Mouli Mondal 3-10, Shreya Karar 2-13) lost to **Bengal** 76/6 in 18.4 overs by four wickets.

Group D points table

Team	M	W	L	T	N/R	Pts	NRR
Bengal	6	6	0	0	0	24	+0.759
Gujarat	6	5	1	0	0	20	+1.227
Andhra	6	4	2	0	0	16	+0.968
Karnataka	6	3	3	0	0	12	+0.195
Tamil Nadu	6	1	5	0	0	4	-0.457
Chhattisgarh	6	1	5	0	0	4	-0.583
Uttarakhand	6	1	5	0	0	4	-2.310

Bengal and Gujarat qualified for the Super League

Group E

Saurashtra Cricket Association Stadium Khanderi B Ground, Rajkot, January 15: Saurashtra 99/7 in 20 overs (Tanya Rao 31; Payal Balmik 2-11, Khushboo Verma 2-14) beat **Pondicherry** 51/8 in 20 overs (Reena M 3-8) by 48 runs.

Saurashtra Cricket Association Stadium, Rajkot, January 15: Railways 187/5 in 20 overs (Sabbineni Meghana 55, Nuzhat Parween 37; Sadiya Wani 2-22, Heena Kouser 2-48) beat

Jammu & Kashmir 60/9 in 20 overs (Sonika 20*; Bharti Bawa 5-7, S Meghana 2-14) by 127 runs.

Saurashtra Cricket Association Stadium Khanderi B Ground, Rajkot, January 15: Mizoram 27 in 16.2 overs (Vaishnavi Khandkar 4-1, MS Bodkhe 2-6) lost to **Vidarbha** 30/0 in 2.2 overs by 10 wickets.

Saurashtra Cricket Association Stadium, Rajkot, January 15: Madhya Pradesh 89/6 in 20 overs (Anshula Rao 25*; Louisa Dash 2-14) lost to **Odisha** 90/2 in 18.2 overs (Kajal Jena 42*, Sushree Dibyadarshini 32*) by eight wickets.

Saurashtra Cricket Association Stadium Khanderi B Ground, Rajkot, January 16: Odisha 221/2 in 20 overs (Kajal Jena 112*, Rani Tudu 30) beat **Mizoram** 17 in 12.3 overs (Louisa Dash 3-0, Indrani Chhatria 2-4) by 204 runs.

Saurashtra Cricket Association Stadium, Rajkot, January 16: Saurashtra 111/7 in 20 overs (Riddhi Ruparel 65; Nadia Chowdhary 2-13) beat **Jammu & Kashmir** 91/4 in 20 overs (Sonika 39*, N Chowdhary 21; T Dharani 3-22) by 20 runs.

Saurashtra Cricket Association Stadium Khanderi B Ground, Rajkot, January 16: Pondicherry 44 in 19.3 overs (Bharti Bawa 2-6, Archana Dutta 2-11) lost to **Railways** 48/0 in 4.1 overs (Sabbineni Meghana 39*) by 10 wickets.

Saurashtra Cricket Association Stadium, Rajkot, January 16: Madhya Pradesh 85/8 in 20 overs (Soniya Sharma 31; Nupur Kohale 2-16, Vaishnavi Khandkar 2-17) lost to **Vidarbha** 89/1 in 12.3 overs (Latika Inamdar 39, Rohini More 27*) by nine wickets.

Saurashtra Cricket Association Stadium Khanderi B Ground, Rajkot, January 18: Vidarbha 117/6 in 20 overs (Disha Kasat 45, Rohini More 28; Arundhati Reddy 2-16) lost to **Railways** 120/2 in 18.1 overs (Sabbineni Meghana 61*, A Reddy 33*) by eight wickets.

Saurashtra Cricket Association Stadium, Rajkot, January 18: Jammu & Kashmir 53 in 15.1 overs (Soumya Tiwari 3-9) lost to **Madhya Pradesh** 55/3 in 10.4 overs by seven wickets.

Saurashtra Cricket Association Stadium Khanderi B Ground, Rajkot, January 18: Odisha 123/2 in 20 overs (Sushree Dibyadarshini 42*, Anjali Singh 39; T Dharani 2-16) beat **Saurashtra** 74/8 in 20 overs (Drashti Somaiya 20; Indrani Chhatria 3-7, S Dibyadarshini 2-17) by 49 runs.

Saurashtra Cricket Association Stadium, Rajkot, January 18: Pondicherry 181/2 in 20 overs (R Sandhya Mounika 107*, Payal Balmik 42*) beat **Mizoram** 31/9 in 20 overs (Khushboo Verma 3-5, P Balmik 2-1) by 150 runs.

Saurashtra Cricket Association Stadium Khanderi B Ground, Rajkot, January 19: Odisha 71 in 20 overs (MS Bodkhe 3-13, Vaishnavi Khandkar 2-11) lost to **Vidarbha** 76/4 in 15.1 overs (Disha Kasat 50*) by six wickets.

Saurashtra Cricket Association Stadium, Rajkot, January 19: Madhya Pradesh 212/0 in 20 overs (Soniya Sharma 105*, Kalpana Yadav 89*) beat **Mizoram** 19 in 12.5 overs (Srashti 5-2, Charu Joshi 2-1) by 193 runs.

Saurashtra Cricket Association Stadium Khanderi B Ground, Rajkot, January 19: Railways 159/3 in 20 overs (Arundhati Reddy 79*, Sabbineni Meghana 30) beat **Saurashtra** 67/3 in 20 overs (Pallavi Hudda 20*) by 92 runs.

Saurashtra Cricket Association Stadium, Rajkot, January 19: Pondicherry 113/4 in 20 overs (R Sandhya Mounika 55) beat **Jammu & Kashmir** 103 in 19.4 overs (Iqra Rasool 28, Sonika 21; Moumee Sasmal 2-17, Khushboo Verma 2-22) by 10 runs.

Saurashtra Cricket Association Stadium Khanderi B Ground, Rajkot, January 21: Saurashtra 174/2 in 20 overs (Riddhi Ruparel 79*, Reena Savasadiya 62) beat **Mizoram** 31/8 in 20 overs (S Yadav 23; M Tanna 3-4, Reena M 2-5) by 143 runs.

Saurashtra Cricket Association Stadium, Rajkot, January 21: Madhya Pradesh 80/7 in 20 overs (Kalpana Yadav 23; Pushpa Kiresur 2-13) lost to **Railways** 81/5 in 18.4 overs (R Kalpana 35*, Arundhati Reddy 25; Poonam Soni 2-12, Anshula Rao 2-14) by five wickets.

Saurashtra Cricket Association Stadium Khanderi B Ground, Rajkot, January 21:

Pondicherry 33 in 18.5 overs (Gargi Wankar 3-5, Vaishnavi Khandkar 2-8) lost to **Vidarbha** 34/0 in 7.3 overs (Latika Inamdar 26*) by 10 wickets.

Saurashtra Cricket Association Stadium, Rajkot, January 21: Odisha 160/0 in 20 overs (Anjali Singh 97*, Kajal Jena 56*) beat **Jammu & Kashmir** 74/9 in 19.1 overs (Humaira Farooq 41; Barsarani Singh 3-10, Rajashree Swain 2-2) by 86 runs.

Saurashtra Cricket Association Stadium Khanderi B Ground, Rajkot, January 22: Odisha 102/4 in 20 overs (Kajal Jena 66; Bharti Bawa 2-14, Archana Dutta 2-20) lost to **Railways** 106/1 in 18 overs (V Sneha Deepthi 59*, Nuzhat Parveen 38*) by nine wickets.

Saurashtra Cricket Association Stadium, Rajkot, January 22: Madhya Pradesh 141/6 in 20 overs (Charu Joshi 43, Nikita Singh 34; Khushboo Verma 3-21) beat **Pondicherry** 60/5 in 20 overs (Ramya Maharajan 33*; N Singh 2-2) by 81 runs.

Saurashtra Cricket Association Stadium Khanderi B Ground, Rajkot, January 22: Saurashtra 66/6 in 20 overs (Riddhi Ruparel 30*; Disha Kasat 2-14) lost to **Vidarbha** 67/2 in 8.2 overs (D Kasat 32*) by eight wickets.

Saurashtra Cricket Association Stadium, Rajkot, January 22: Jammu & Kashmir 191/4 in 20 overs (Nadia Chowdhary 87, Bismah Hassan 34*) beat **Mizoram** 68/6 in 20 overs (S Yadav 23, Sandhya Kumari 22; Heena Kouser 4-9) by 123 runs.

Saurashtra Cricket Association Stadium Khanderi B Ground, Rajkot, January 24: Odisha 130/2 in 20 overs (Anjali Singh 76, Sumitra Sahoo 39*) beat **Pondicherry** 78/6 in 20 overs (Payal Balmik 33*; Rajashree Swain 3-10, Indrani Chhatria 2-16) by 52 runs.

Saurashtra Cricket Association Stadium, Rajkot, January 24: Saurashtra 89/5 in 20 overs (Riddhi Ruparel 25*; Charu Joshi 2-14, Poonam Soni 2-17) lost to **Madhya Pradesh** 91/4 in 17.5 overs (Nikita Singh 38; T Dharani 2-19) by six wickets.

Saurashtra Cricket Association Stadium Khanderi B Ground, Rajkot, January 24: Mizoram 17 in 16.5 overs (V Sneha Deepthi 2-1) lost to **Railways** 18/0 in 1.2 overs by 10 wickets.

Saurashtra Cricket Association Stadium, Rajkot, January 24: Vidarbha 163/8 in 20 overs (Latika Inamdar 77, Rohini More 24; Heena Kouser 3-36, Sadiya Wani 2-30) beat **Jammu & Kashmir** 60/9 in 20 overs (Gargi Wankar 4-8, Vaibhavi Sonwane 2-16) by 103 runs.

Group E points table

Team	M	W	L	T	N/R	Pts	NRR
Railways	7	7	0	0	0	28	+3.698
Vidarbha	7	6	1	0	0	24	+3.367
Odisha	7	5	2	0	0	20	+2.600
Madhya Pradesh	7	4	3	0	0	16	+2.146
Saurashtra	7	3	4	0	0	12	-0.002
Pondicherry	7	2	5	0	0	8	-1.248
Jammu & Kashmir	7	1	6	0	0	4	-2.026
Mizoram	7	0	7	0	0	0	-8.415

Railways and Vidarbha qualified for the Super Leagues

Group A Super League

Sawai Mansingh Stadium, Jaipur, January 28: Jharkhand 123/5 in 20 overs (Sonia 48, Indrani Roy 25) beat **Baroda** 100/9 in 20 overs (Hrutu Patel 33; Durga Kumari Murmu 3-19, Ashwani 2-15) by 23 runs.

Sawai Mansingh Stadium, Jaipur, January 28: Mumbai 94/5 in 20 overs (Aachal Valanju 36, Vrushali Bhagat 23; Renuka Chaudhari 2-21) lost to **Gujarat** 95/6 in 19.4 overs (Simran 25; Samruddhi Rawool 3-14) by four wickets.

Sawai Mansingh Stadium, Jaipur, January 29: Baroda 94/9 in 20 overs (Yastika Bhatia 42, Hrutu Patel 21) lost to **Mumbai** 95/4 in 16.3 overs (Sejal Raut 39, Vrushali Bhagat 27*; Kesha 2-21) by six wickets.

Sawai Mansingh Stadium, Jaipur, January 29: Gujarat 99/6 in 20 overs (Hani Patel 39*, Renuka Chaudhari 26; Bharti Bawa 3-18) lost to **Railways** 100/6 in 18 overs (Sabbineni Meghana 31, Nuzhat Parween 25; Krutika Chaudhari 2-17, R Chaudhari 2-26) by four wickets.

Sawai Mansingh Stadium, Jaipur, January 31: Jharkhand 104/6 in 20 overs (Indrani Roy 33, Rashmi 27; Bharti Bawa 2-19) lost to **Railways** 105/4 in 19.1 overs (Nuzhat Parween 39*, V Sneha Deepthi 28) by six wickets.

Sawai Mansingh Stadium, Jaipur, January 31: Baroda 62 in 19.5 overs (PA Talpada 3-9, Hiral Solanki 2-14) lost to **Gujarat** 65/5 in 18 overs (Hani Patel 36*; Jaya Mohite 2-14) by five wickets.

Sawai Mansingh Stadium, Jaipur, February 1: Jharkhand 93/9 in 20 overs (Indrani Roy 40; Samruddhi Rawool 3-21, Manali Dakshini 2-12) lost to **Mumbai** 94/4 in 19.2 overs (Sejal Raut 32, Manjiri Gawade 23) by six wickets.

Sawai Mansingh Stadium, Jaipur, February 1: Baroda 106/6 in 20 overs (Hrutu Patel 31, J Fernandes 29; Archana Dutta 2-14) lost to **Railways** 107/2 in 10 overs (V Sneha Deepthi 56, Nuzhat Parween 27*) by eight wickets.

Sawai Mansingh Stadium, Jaipur, February 3: Gujarat 46/9 in 20 overs (Devyani Prasad 3-8, Mamta Paswan 2-8) lost to **Jharkhand** 47/4 in 12.4 overs (Priyanka Sawaiyan 22) by six wickets.

Sawai Mansingh Stadium, Jaipur, February 3: Mumbai 88/9 in 20 overs (Vrushali Bhagat 26; Sabbineni Meghana 2-16, Nirupama Baro 2-19) lost to **Railways** 89/6 in 19.4 overs (Priyanka Bala 28; Saima Thakor 4-12) by four wickets.

Super League Group A points table

Team	M	W	L	T	N/R	Pts	NRR
Railways	4	4	0	0	0	16	+0.308
Jharkhand	4	2	2	0	0	8	+0.656
Mumbai	4	2	2	0	0	8	+0.342
Gujarat	4	2	2	0	0	8	-0.361
Baroda	4	0	4	0	0	0	-0.710

Railways qualified for the final

Group B Super League

Jaipuria Vidhyalaya Ground, Jaipur, January 28: Maharashtra 134/3 in 20 overs (Tejal Hasabnis 43*, Shivali Shinde 39) beat **Punjab** 84/8 in 20 overs (Ridhima Aggarwal 20; Devika Vaidya 3-8) by 50 runs.

Jaipuria Vidhyalaya Ground, Jaipur, January 28: Delhi 96/3 in 20 overs (Laxmi Yadav 60, Ayushi Soni 20) lost to **Bengal** 97/2 in 18.3 overs (Kashish Agarwal 47, Prativa 39*) by eight wickets.

Jaipuria Vidhyalaya Ground, Jaipur, January 29: Delhi 86/7 in 20 overs (Arti Dhama 22, Simran Dil Bahadur 22; Rajni Devi 2-12, Sunita Rani 2-21) beat **Punjab** 83/8 in 20 overs (Ridhima Aggarwal 51*; Ayushi Soni 2-10, SD Bahadur 2-12) by three runs.

Jaipuria Vidhyalaya Ground, Jaipur, January 29: Bengal 109/5 in 20 overs (Prativa 56, Aparna Mondal 26*; Vaishnavi Khandkar 2-15) beat **Vidarbha** 99/9 in 20 overs (Shivani Dharne 38, V Khandkar 20; Nisha Maji 2-11, Shrayosi Aich 2-21) by 10 runs.

Jaipuria Vidhyalaya Ground, Jaipur, January 31: Maharashtra 127/4 in 20 overs (Devika Vaidya 51, Tejal Hasabnis 42; Vaibhavi Sonwane 2-18) beat **Vidarbha** 80 in 18.5 overs (Maya Sonawane 4-15, D Vaidya 2-18) by 47 runs.

Jaipuria Vidhyalaya Ground, Jaipur, January 31: Bengal 103/7 in 20 overs (Tanusree Sarkar 37*; Sunita Rani 4-15) beat **Punjab** 75/9 in 20 overs (Shrey Karar 4-15) by 28 runs.

Jaipuria Vidhyalaya Ground, Jaipur, February 1: Delhi 102/3 in 20 overs (Laxmi Yadav 63*) lost to **Maharashtra** 103/4 in 18.1 overs (Devika Vaidya 62*, Priyanka Ghodke 20; Ria Sharma 2-18) by six wickets.

Jaipuria Vidhyalaya Ground, Jaipur, February 1: Punjab 94/6 in 20 overs (Ridhima Aggarwal 30, Priyanka Malik 21*; MS Bodkhe 2-12) tied with **Vidarbha** 94/5 in 20 overs (Disha Kasat 37, Shivani Dharne 25; Sunita Rani 2-14). Super Over: Vidarbha 14/0 in 1 over beat Punjab 3/0 in 1 over.

Jaipuria Vidhyalaya Ground, Jaipur, February 3: Maharashtra 91/8 in 20 overs (Tanusree 2-10, Shreya 2-22) beat **Bengal** 60 in 16.3 overs (Saika Ishaque 23; Devika Vaidya 2-12, SB Porkharkar 2-12) by 31 runs.

Jaipuria Vidhyalaya Ground, Jaipur, February 3: Delhi 84/3 in 20 overs (Ayushi Soni 26*, Rupali Sati 26) beat **Vidarbha** 83/8 in 20 overs (Disha Kasat 46; Ria Sharma 2-15) by one run.

Super League Group B points table

Team	M	W	L	T	N/R	Pts	NRR
Maharashtra	4	4	0	0	0	16	+1.746
Bengal	4	3	1	0	0	12	+0.188
Delhi	4	2	2	0	0	8	-0.261
Vidarbha	4	1	3	0	0	4	-0.950
Punjab	4	0	4	0	0	0	-1.013

Maharashtra qualified for the final

Final

Sawai Mansingh Stadium, Jaipur, February 5: Maharashtra 116/2 in 20 overs (Tejal Hasabnis 52*, Devika Vaidya 50*) lost to **Railways** 117/7 in 18.3 overs (R Kalpana 25, Sabbineni Meghana 23; Aditi Gaikwad 2-19) by three wickets.

Winners: Railways

2017-18

North Zone

Himachal Pradesh Cricket Association Stadium, Dharamsala, March 17: Delhi 138/4 in 20 overs (Ayushi Soni 51*, Arushi Goel 30; Asra Shafi 2-12) beat **Jammu & Kashmir** 90/7 in 20 overs (Bismah Hassan 35; Vaishali Mathur 2-12) by 48 runs.

Himachal Pradesh Cricket Association Stadium, Dharamsala, March 17: Punjab 148/5 in 20 overs (Ridhima Aggarwal 64, Neelam Bisht 28*) beat **Haryana** 104/7 in 20 overs (Shivangi

37*, Shafali Verma 22; Sunita Rani 3-13, Bharti Bawa 2-18) by 44 runs.

Himachal Pradesh Cricket Association Stadium, Dharamsala, March 18: Jammu & Kashmir 87/8 in 20 overs (Rubia Syed 44, Bismah Hassan 21; Susmita Kumari 3-14) lost to **Himachal Pradesh** 88/2 in 15 overs (Kashish Verma 32*, Monika Devi 29) by eight wickets.

Himachal Pradesh Cricket Association Stadium, Dharamsala, March 18: Delhi 90/9 in 20 overs (Vaishali Mathur 25; Diksha Sharma 4-16, Urvashi Saini 2-12) lost to **Haryana** 94/6 in 20 overs (Susmita Kumari 25, Lasika Jangra 22) by four wickets.

Himachal Pradesh Cricket Association Stadium, Dharamsala, March 20: Himachal Pradesh 114/7 in 20 overs (Monika Devi 42*, Nikita Chauhan 42; Bharti Bawa 2-23) lost to **Punjab** 115/6 in 17.4 overs (Neelam Bisht 54, Amanjot Kaur 22*; Susmita Kumari 2-19, VS Fishta 2-26) by four wickets.

Himachal Pradesh Cricket Association Stadium, Dharamsala, March 20: Haryana 143/3 in 20 overs (Bhawna Ohlan 59*, Shafali Verma 49; Sapna Jamwal 2-23) beat **Jammu & Kashmir** 109/6 in 20 overs (Rubia Syed 59*; Shweta Sharma 2-21) by 34 runs.

Himachal Pradesh Cricket Association Stadium, Dharamsala, March 21: Punjab v **Delhi**. Match abandoned without a ball being bowled.

Himachal Pradesh Cricket Association Stadium, Dharamsala, March 21: Himachal Pradesh 65/6 in 11 overs (Kashish Verma 23; Priyanka Sharma 3-13) lost to **Haryana** 71/3 in 11 overs (Shafali Verma 29*, Bhawna Ohlan 21) by seven wickets.

Himachal Pradesh Cricket Association Stadium, Dharamsala, March 22: Jammu & Kashmir 73 in 19 overs (Rubia Syed 21, Nadia Chowdhary 21; Neelam Bisht 5-3, Sunita Rani 3-13) lost to **Punjab** 77/6 in 16.4 overs (N Bisht 24, Akanksha 2-10) by four wickets.

Himachal Pradesh Cricket Association Stadium, Dharamsala, March 22: Himachal Pradesh 99/8 in 20 overs (Nikita Chauhan 30; Ayushi Soni 3-15, Vandana Chaturvedi 2-13) lost to **Delhi** 100/9 in 20 overs (V Chaturvedi 30*, Laxmi Yadav 22; VS Fishta 2-15, Susmita Kumari 2-20) by one wicket.

North Zone points table

Team	M	W	L	T	N/R	Pts	NRR
Punjab	4	3	0	0	1	14	+1.325
Haryana	4	3	1	0	0	12	+0.000
Delhi	4	2	1	0	1	10	+0.750
Himachal Pradesh	4	1	3	0	0	4	+0.113
Jammu & Kashmir	4	0	4	0	0	0	-1.679

Punjab and Haryana qualified for the Super League

Central Zone

Neemkheda Stadium 2, Jabalpur, March 17: Railways 138/3 in 20 overs (V Sneha Deepthi 53, Rajni Lodhi 41) beat **Vidarbha** 134/5 in 20 overs (Bharti Fulmali 70, Disha Kasat 40; R Lodhi 2-6) by four runs.

Neemkheda Stadium, Jabalpur, March 17: Uttar Pradesh 112/7 in 20 overs (Shashi Mathur 38, Kshama 25; Dipti Dhimar 2-19) beat **Chhattisgarh** 84/6 in 20 overs (Yashi Pandey 36*) by 28 runs.

Neemkheda Stadium 2, Jabalpur, March 17: Rajasthan 110/9 in 20 overs (Aditi Garg 31, SR Jat 23; Charu Joshi 3-30) lost to **Madhya Pradesh** 113/1 in 16.5 overs (Tarang Jha 49*, Tamanna Nigam 43*) by nine wickets.

Neemkheda Stadium 2, Jabalpur, March 18: Chhattisgarh 76/5 in 20 overs (Yashi Pandey

39*; Pushpa Kiresur 2-5) lost to **Railways** 77/0 in 7.5 overs (V Sneha Deepthi 53*, Anita Lodhi 20*) by 10 wickets.

Neemkheda Stadium, Jabalpur, March 18: Rajasthan 92 in 18.4 overs (Sangeeta Kumawat 32; Kshama 2-17, Arju 2-23) lost to **Uttar Pradesh** 93/3 in 17.3 overs (Aditi Sharma 35*, Shivpriya Pandey 24) by seven wickets.

Neemkheda Stadium, Jabalpur, March 18: Madhya Pradesh 93 in 19.5 overs (Gargi Wankar 3-24, Nupur Kohale 2-11) lost to **Vidarbha** 92/7 in 20 overs (AS Bhongade 23; Priti Yadav 3-11) by three wickets.

Neemkheda Stadium, Jabalpur, March 19: Railways 121/4 in 20 overs (Nuzhat Parween 45*, Priyanka Bala 27; Kshama 2-15) beat **Uttar Pradesh** 91/8 in 20 overs (Shobha Devi 25; Suchi Kaushik 3-21, Sarika Koli 2-16) by 30 runs.

Neemkheda Stadium 2, Jabalpur, March 19: Vidarbha 130/5 in 20 overs (Disha Kasat 62*, Shivani Dharne 22; SS Kalal 2-24) beat **Rajasthan** 67/5 in 20 overs (Vaishnavi Khandkar 2-8) by 63 runs.

Neemkheda Stadium 2, Jabalpur, March 19: Chhattisgarh 86/6 in 20 overs (Kajal Meshram 28; Anshula Rao 2-12, Priyanka Koushal 2-22) lost to **Madhya Pradesh** 88/3 in 18.4 overs (Tamanna Nigam 40, Tarang Jha 23) by seven wickets.

Neemkheda Stadium 2, Jabalpur, March 21: Chhattisgarh 114/5 in 20 overs (Shilpa Sahu 39, Shivi Pandey 29) lost to **Vidarbha** 115/3 in 17.1 overs (Shivani Dharne 45*, Disha Kasat 25) by seven wickets.

Neemkheda Stadium 2, Jabalpur, March 21: Railways 126/7 in 20 overs (Nuzhat Parween 21; Suman Meena 2-21, Ruby Choudary 2-26) beat **Rajasthan** 91/7 in 20 overs (SR Jat 30, JU Bijarnya 25; Anita Lodhi 3-20, Sarika Koli 2-14) by 35 runs.

Neemkheda Stadium, Jabalpur, March 21: Uttar Pradesh 116/6 in 20 overs (Shashi Mathur 55, Aditi Sharma 25; Priyanka Koushal 2-23) lost to **Madhya Pradesh** 117/2 in 19.3 overs (Nikita Singh 56*, Tarang Jha 24; Anjali Singh 2-14) by eight wickets.

Neemkheda Stadium 2, Jabalpur, March 22: Uttar Pradesh 119/5 in 20 overs (Aditi Sharma 59*; MS Bodkhe 2-12) beat **Vidarbha** 91 in 18.3 overs (Shivani Dharne 48; Rashi Kanojiya 4-17, Tanu Kala 3-17) by 28 runs.

Neemkheda Stadium 2, Jabalpur, March 22: Chhattisgarh 106/5 in 20 overs (Yashi Pandey 39, Shivi Pandey 29; Sofi Sidhu 2-32) tied with **Rajasthan** 106/9 in 20 overs (SR Jat 39; Dipti Dhimar 2-18). Super Over: Rajasthan 10/1 in 1 over beat Chhattisgarh 2/2 in 0.2 overs.

Neemkheda Stadium, Jabalpur, March 22: Railways 142/7 in 20 overs (Meghana Sabbineni 50, Anita Lodhi 45; Charu Joshi 4-29) beat **Madhya Pradesh** 133/2 in 20 overs (Tarang Jha 58*, Tamanna Nigam 37) by nine runs.

Central Zone points table

Team	M	W	L	T	N/R	Pts	NRR
Railways	5	5	0	0	0	20	+1.627
Madhya Pradesh	5	4	1	0	0	16	+0.266
Uttar Pradesh	5	3	2	0	0	12	+0.371
Vidarbha	5	2	3	0	0	8	+0.474
Rajasthan	5	1	4	0	0	4	-1.361
Chhattisgarh	5	0	5	0	0	0	-1.292

Railways and Madhya Pradesh qualified for the Super League
West Zone

Gujarat College Ground, Ahmedabad, March 17: Mumbai 115/8 in 20 overs (Hemali Borwankar 46; Shalini Sharma 2-19, Kesha Patel 2-21) beat **Baroda** 82 in 19.4 overs (Saima Thakor 3-16, Janhvi Kate 2-12) by 33 runs.

Gujarat College Ground, Ahmedabad, March 17: Gujarat 105/7 in 20 overs (SS Patel 28, Retal Patel 23; Dharani 3-19) beat **Saurashtra** 69/9 in 20 overs (Hira Modhwadia 20) by 36 runs.

Gujarat College Ground, Ahmedabad, March 18: Baroda 124/7 in 20 overs (Tanvir Shaikh 53, J Fernandes 29; Pooja Nimavat 2-24) beat **Saurashtra** 61/6 in 20 overs (Riddhi Ruparel 28; Shalini Sharma 3-9) by 63 runs.

Gujarat College Ground, Ahmedabad, March 18: Maharashtra 98/7 in 20 overs (Tejal Hasabnis 44, Mukta Magre 20; Janhvi Kate 3-19) lost to **Mumbai** 99/7 in 19.5 overs (Fatima Jaffer 30; T Hasabnis 2-19) by three wickets.

Gujarat College Ground, Ahmedabad, March 20: Mumbai 105/8 in 20 overs (Sejal Raut 25, Manali Dakshini 20*; HR Solanki 3-22, Hani Patel 2-17) beat **Gujarat** 80/7 in 20 overs (SS Patel 27; Fatima Jaffer 2-21) by 25 runs.

Gujarat College Ground, Ahmedabad, March 20: Maharashtra 113/7 in 20 overs (Mukta Magre 57, Nikita Bhor 44; Charmi 2-10, Shalini Sharma 2-26) beat **Baroda** 54 in 15.2 overs (Maya Sonawane 4-14, Aditi Gaikwad 2-6) by 59 runs.

Gujarat College Ground, Ahmedabad, March 21: Saurashtra 55 in 19.5 overs (Nikita Bhor 2-15) lost to **Maharashtra** 57/3 in 13.1 overs (Tejal Hasabnis 30*) by seven wickets.

Gujarat College Ground, Ahmedabad, March 21: Baroda 78/9 in 20 overs (HR Solanki 3-13, Reeta Patel 2-8) lost to **Gujarat** 82/4 in 16.4 overs (SS Patel 45*) by six wickets.

Gujarat College Ground, Ahmedabad, March 22: Maharashtra 125/2 in 20 overs (Devika Vaidya 40*, Mukta Magre 35) beat **Gujarat** 94/7 in 20 overs (SS Patel 36; Tejal Hasabnis 2-15, Maya Sonawane 2-16) by 31 runs.

Gujarat College Ground, Ahmedabad, March 22: Mumbai 112/5 in 20 overs (Sayali Satghare 29*, Hemali Borwankar 24; T Dharani 3-15) beat **Saurashtra** 43/8 in 20 overs (JR Pawar 2-5) by 69 runs.

West Zone points table

Team	M	W	L	T	N/R	Pts	NRR
Mumbai	4	4	0	0	0	16	+1.611
Maharashtra	4	3	1	0	0	12	+1.588
Guajarat	4	2	2	0	0	8	-0.004
Baroda	4	1	3	0	0	4	-0.614
Saurashtra	4	0	4	0	0	0	-2.590

Mumbai and Maharashtra qualified for the Super League

South Zone

Chukkapalli Pitchaiah Cricket Ground, Mulapadu, March 17: Kerala 130/4 in 20 overs (Aarthy Jayapal 64*, Aswathy Babu 22) beat **Hyderabad** 46 in 17.2 overs (Minnu Mani 2-4, Aneena Mathews 2-16) by 84 runs.

Devineni Venkata Ramana Praneetha Ground, Mulapadu, March 17: Tamil Nadu 32 in 18 overs (K Anjali Sarvani 3-7, K Dhatri 3-10) lost to **Andhra** 33/0 in 6.4 overs (CH Jhansi Lakshmi 20*) by 10 wickets.

Devineni Venkata Ramana Praneetha Ground, Mulapadu, March 17: Karnataka 88 in 17.5 overs (K Pratyoosha 22; Vanita Bhandari 2-13, Diksha Gawde 2-15) beat **Goa** 59 in 17.3

Minnu Mani was one of the big performers for Kerala on their way to the title.

overs (G Divya 2-12, C Pratyusha 2-15) by 29 runs.

Chukkapalli Pitchaiah Cricket Ground, Mulapadu, March 18: Kerala 160/3 in 20 overs (Minnu Mani 58*, Sajeevan Sajana 35*; PB Swetha 2-38) beat **Tamil Nadu** 41 in 19.5 overs (Jipsa Joseph 2-4, Keerthy James 2-12) by 119 runs.

Chukkapalli Pitchaiah Cricket Ground, Mulapadu, March 18: Andhra 90/5 in 20 overs (V Pushpa Latha 44*; G Divya 2-19) beat **Karnataka** 89 in 19.5 overs (K Pratyoosha 29; G Chandralekha 3-17) by one run.

Devineni Venkata Ramana Praneetha Ground, Mulapadu, March 18: Goa 74 in 19.1 overs (G Trisha 3-9, Rachna Kumar 2-12) lost to **Hyderabad** 75/2 in 15.5 overs (G Trisha 36*, Doli Ramya 33) by eight wickets.

Chukkapalli Pitchaiah Cricket Ground, Mulapadu, March 20: Kerala 49 in 16.1 overs (Aarthy Jayapal 26*; K Anjali Sarvani 5-8) lost to **Andhra** 50/1 in 11.1 overs (N Anusha 23*) by nine wickets.

Devineni Venkata Ramana Praneetha Ground, Mulapadu, March 20: Karnataka 63 in 19 overs (C Prtyusha 21; Rachna Kumar 2-7, G Trisha 2-11) lost to **Hyderabad** 64/2 in 14.5 overs (Pranathi Reddy 24*) by eight wickets.

Devineni Venkata Ramana Praneetha Ground, Mulapadu, March 20: Tamil Nadu 78/7 in 20 overs (S Anusha 32*; Sanjula Naik 2-7) lost to **Goa** 80/6 in 17.4 overs (S Naik 27; Thenmozhi M 3-16, Nida Rehman 2-8) by four wickets.

Chukkapalli Pitchaiah Cricket Ground, Mulapadu, March 21: Kerala 81/9 in 20 overs (Minnu Mani 23; Sanjula Naik 4-14, Diksha Gawde 2-11) beat **Goa** 63 in 19.4 overs (Aneena Mathews 3-13, Sajeevan Sajana 2-7) by 18 runs.

Devineni Venkata Ramana Praneetha Ground, Mulapadu, March 21: Hyderabad 57 in 18.4 overs (E Padmaja 3-4, K Dhatri 2-16) lost **Andhra** 60/1 in 16.3 overs (CH Jhansi Lakshmi 31*, N Anusha 23) by nine wickets.

Devineni Venkata Ramana Praneetha Ground, Mulapadu, March 21: Tamil Nadu 53 in 18.5 overs (S Anusha 24; G Divya 4-5, Monica Patel 2-10) lost to **Karnataka** 55/0 in 7.2 overs (G Divya 42*) by 10 wickets.

Chukkapalli Pitchaiah Cricket Ground, Mulapadu, March 23: Tamil Nadu 57 in 19.5 overs (S Anusha 30; Rachna Kumar 3-6, Bhogi Shravani 3-9) lost to **Hyderabad** 58/4 in 10 overs (G Trisha 22; Nida Rehman 2-12) by six wickets.

Devineni Venkata Ramana Praneetha Ground, Mulapadu, March 23: Karnataka 82/7 in 20 overs (G Divya 35, D Vrinda 25; Aneena Mathews 3-14) lost to **Kerala** 83/5 in 16 overs (A Akshaya 44; G Divya 2-17, Rameshwari Gayakwad 2-24) by five wickets.

Devineni Venkata Ramana Praneetha Ground, Mulapadu, March 23: Andhra 110/7 in 20 overs (CH Jhansi Lakshmi 43, E Padmaja 20; Vanita Bhandari 2-18, Tejaswini Duragad 2-26) beat **Goa** 77 in 17.5 overs (Sanjula Naik 30; E Padmaja 3-14) by 33 runs.

South Zone points table

Team	M	W	L	T	N/R	Pts	NRR
Andhra	5	5	0	0	0	20	+1.574
Kerala	5	4	1	0	0	16	+2.146
Hyderabad	5	3	2	0	0	12	-0.260
Karnataka	5	2	3	0	0	8	+0.475
Goa	5	1	4	0	0	4	-0.893
Tamil Nadu	5	0	5	0	0	0	-3.649

Andhra and Kerala qualified for the Super League

East Zone

Barsapara Cricket Stadium, Guwahati, March 17: Tripura 50 in 18.1 overs (Suravi Roy 25; Urmila Chatterjee 3-9, Nibedita Baruah 2-7) lost to **Assam** 51/4 in 15 overs by six wickets.

Barsapara Cricket Stadium, Guwahati, March 17: Odisha 92/9 in 20 overs (Silpa Swain 46; Shrayosi Aich 4-20, Nisha Maji 3-7) lost to **Bengal** 95/2 in 17.1 overs (Ambika Guha 27, Parna Paul 21*; Louisa Dash 2-14) by eight wickets.

Barsapara Cricket Stadium, Guwahati, March 18: Odisha 56 in 18.5 overs (Rashmi Dey 2-6, Shanti Rai 2-14) lost to **Assam** 58/6 in 17.3 overs (D Janaki Reddy 2-8, Reemalaxmi Ekka 2-10) by four wickets.

Barsapara Cricket Stadium, March 18: Tripura 62 in 17 overs (Mamta Paswan 3-4, Anjali 3-19) lost to **Jharkhand** 63/3 in 14.5 overs (Durga Kumari Murmu 34*) by seven wickets.

Barsapara Cricket Stadium, Guwahati, March 20: Jharkhand 91/7 in 20 overs (Ruma Kumari Mahato 35; Shrayosi Aich 2-15, Nisha Maji 2-24) lost to **Bengal** 92/6 in 18.5 overs (Richa 34, Prativa 30*; Mamta Paswan 3-14) by four wickets.

Barsapara Cricket Stadium, Guwahati, March 20: Tripura 90/9 in 20 overs (Jhumki Debnath 23, Nikita Debnath 23; Sangeeta Khadia 4-7) lost to **Odisha** 91/5 in 18.5 overs (Sasmita Mahalik 34, Reemalaxmi Ekka 25*) by five wickets.

Barsapara Cricket Stadium, Guwahati, March 21: Jharkhand 56 in 16.5 overs (Rashmi Dey 3-3, Shanti Rai 2-6) lost to **Assam** 57/3 in 15.3 overs by seven wickets.

Barsapara Cricket Stadium, Guwahati, March 21: Tripura 54/9 in 20 overs (Shrayosi Aich 2-10, Nisha Maji 2-11) lost to **Bengal** 56/5 in 13.2 overs (Parna Paul 20) by five wickets.

Barsapara Cricket Stadium, Guwahati, March 23: Bengal 91/7 in 20 overs (Ambika Guha 29; Rekharani Bora 2-18, Rashmi Dey 2-21) beat **Assam** 74/8 in 20 overs (R Bora 24; Richa 2-9, Priya Pandey 2-13) by 17 runs.

Barsapara Cricket Stadium, March 23: Jharkhand 49 in 18.4 overs (Reemalaxmi Ekka 3-7, Louisa Dash 2-9) lost to **Odisha** 50/2 in 14.1 overs (Sasmita Mahalik 30) by eight wickets.

East Zone points table

Team	M	W	L	T	N/R	Pts	NRR
Bengal	4	4	0	0	0	16	+0.930
Assam	4	3	1	0	0	12	+0.367
Odisha	4	2	2	0	0	8	+0.048
Jharkhand	4	1	3	0	0	4	-0.349
Tripura	4	0	4	0	0	0	-1.010

Bengal and Assam qualified for the Super League

Group A Super League

Sachin Tendulkar Gymkhana Ground, Mumbai, March 28: Haryana 75 in 19.5 overs (Susmita Kumari 29; K Anjali Sarvani 2-12) lost to **Andhra** 76/1 in 12.2 overs (V Pushpa Latha 34*, N Anusha 24*) by nine wickets.

Sachin Tendulkar Gymkhana Ground, Mumbai, March 28: Maharashtra 151/2 in 20 overs (Mukta Magre 54, Devika Vaidya 52*) beat **Assam** 86/9 in 20 overs (Rekharani Bora 20; Aditi Gaikwad 3-15, D Vaidya 3-16) by 65 runs.

Sachin Tendulkar Gymkhana Ground, Mumbai, March 29: Assam 115/4 in 20 overs (Sapna Choudhary 46, Rekharani Bora 39) lost to **Railways** 119/4 in 19 overs (Meghana Sabbineni 34, Sarika Koli 28*; Shanti Rai 2-25) by six wickets.

Sachin Tendulkar Gymkhana Ground, Mumbai, March 29: Haryana 86/9 in 20 overs (Shafali Verma 22, Bhawna Ohlan 20; Aditi Gaikwad 3-11) lost to **Maharashtra** 87/4 in 18.4 overs (Devika Vaidya 25*, Mukta Magre 24; Priyanka Sharma 2-10) by six wickets.

Sachin Tendulkar Gymkhana Ground, Mumbai, March 31: Railways 139/6 in 20 overs (Meghana Sabbineni 53, Sarika Koli 53; K Dhatri 2-24) lost to **Andhra** 140/6 in 19.3 overs (CH Jhansi Lakshmi 53, V Pushpa Latha 25; Anita Lodhi 2-13, M Sabbineni 2-28) by four wickets.

Sachin Tendulkar Gymkhana Ground, Mumbai, March 31: Haryana 93 in 19.5 overs (Shafali Verma 61; Hemalata Payeng 2-10, Anamika Bori 2-15) lost to **Assam** 95/3 in 16.3 overs (Ume Chetry 36, Sapna Choudhary 33) by seven wickets.

Sachin Tendulkar Gymkhana Ground, Mumbai, April 1: Maharashtra 88/8 in 20 overs (SA Lonkar 35; Nirupama Baro 3-11, Pushpa Kiresur 3-17) lost to **Railways** 89/3 in 13.5 overs (Anita Lodhi 43, Meghana Sabbineni 20) by seven wickets.

Sachin Tendulkar Gymkhana Ground, Mumbai, April 1: Assam 108/9 in 20 overs (Sapna Choudhary 31, Urmila Chatterjee; E Padmaja 3-15, G Chandralekha 2-20) lost to **Andhra** 109/1 in 16.4 overs (CH Jhansi Lakshmi 58*, V Pushpa Latha 24*) by nine wickets.

Sachin Tendulkar Gymkhana Ground, Mumbai, April 2: Railways 126/5 in 20 overs (Meghana Sabbineni 41, Anita Lodhi 24; Urvashi Saini 2-29) lost to **Haryana** 128/2 in 19.4 overs (Susmita Kumari 47*, Bhawna Ohlan 41*; Sarika Koli 2-23) by eight wickets.

Sachin Tendulkar Gymkhana Ground, Mumbai, April 2: Maharashtra 115/8 in 20 overs (Priyanka Ghodke 49, Tejal Hasabnis 35; G Chandralekha 2-10, K Dhatri 2-19) beat **Andhra** 74 in 19.1 overs (Utkarsha Pawar 3-21, Maya Sonawane 2-10) by 41 runs.

Super League Group A points table

Team	M	W	L	T	N/R	Pts	NRR
Maharashtra	4	3	1	0	0	12	+1.069
Andhra	4	3	1	0	0	12	+0.362
Railways	4	2	2	0	0	8	+0.545
Haryana	4	1	3	0	0	4	-0.894
Assam	4	1	3	0	0	4	-0.957

Maharashtra qualified for the final

Group B Super League

Bandra Kurla Complex (BKC), Mumbai, March 28: Punjab 87 in 19.5 overs (Bharti Bawa 21; Sourabhya P 2-12, Sajeevan Sajana 2-19) lost to **Kerala** 90/3 in 15.3 overs (Jilu George 41*; Komalpreet Kour 2-12) by seven wickets.

BKC, Mumbai, March 28: Bengal 90/6 in 20 overs (Shrayosi Aich 32*, Richa 22) lost to **Mumbai** 91/7 in 19.4 overs (Sayali Satghare 38*) by three wickets.

BKC, Mumbai, March 29: Bengal 66 in 17.5 overs (Charu Joshi 3-6) lost to **Madhya Pradesh** 67/6 in 15.1 overs (Nikita Singh 37; Ahireeta 2-6, Priya Pandey 2-17) by four wickets.

BKC, Mumbai, March 29: Mumbai 132/2 in 20 overs (Hemali Borwankar 48, Sejal Raut 36) beat **Punjab** 88/6 in 20 overs (Manisha Badhan 29, Renu 23; Manali Dakshini 2-20, Prakashika Naik 2-20) by 44 runs.

BKC, Mumbai, March 31: Madhya Pradesh 76/6 in 20 overs (Soniya Sharma 24; Sajeevan Sajana 3-12) lost to **Kerala** 77/9 in 18.4 overs (Minnu Mani 38, A Akshaya 21; Charu Joshi 3-19) by one wicket.

BKC, Mumbai, March 31: Punjab 116 in 19.4 overs (Taniya Bhatia 65; Nisha Maji 3-15, Priya Pandey 2-17) lost to **Bengal** 118/5 in 19.2 overs (Prativa 40*, Mita Paul 31; Manisha Badhan 2-17) by five wickets.

BKC, Mumbai, April 1: Madhya Pradesh 95/7 in 20 overs (Nikita Singh 44; Saima Thakor 2-8) lost to **Mumbai** 96/4 in 18.4 overs (Sejal Raut 33, Fatima Jaffer 30; Poonam Soni 2-13) by six wickets.

BKC, Mumbai, April 1: Kerala 136/2 in 20 overs (Minnu Mani 46*, A kshaya 30; Nisha Maji 3-18) beat **Bengal** 108/8 in 20 overs (Parna Paul 26, Richa 23; Sajeevan Sajana 3-19, M Mani 2-18) by 28 runs.

BKC, Mumbai, April 2: Punjab 113/5 in 20 overs (Taniya Bhatia 42*; Charu Joshi 2-26) lost to **Madhya Pradesh** 116/1 in 19.3 overs (Nikita Singh 59, Tamanna Nigam 55*) by nine wickets.

BKC, Mumbai, April 2: Kerala 89/9 in 20 overs (IV Drishya 25*, Jilu George 23; Vrushali Bhagat 3-16, Janhvi Kate 2-13) beat **Mumbai** 85 in 19.5 overs (Keerthy James 3-11, Minnu Mani 2-16) by four runs.

Super League Group B points table

Team	M	W	L	T	N/R	Pts	NRR
Kerala	4	4	0	0	0	16	+0.835
Mumbai	4	3	1	0	0	12	+0.632
Madhya Pradesh	4	2	2	0	0	8	+0.189
Bengal	4	1	3	0	0	4	-0.664
Punjab	4	0	4	0	0	0	-1.085

Kerala qualified for the final

Final

Bandra Kurla Complex, Mumbai, April 4: **Maharashtra** 114/4 in 20 overs (Mukta Magre 33, Priyanka Ghodke 24) lost to **Kerala** 115/5 in 19.5 overs (A Akshaya 37, Sajeevan Sajana 24*) by five wickets.

Winners: Kerala

Under-23 Inter-State One-Day Competition

Deepti inspires Bengal to title

Deepti Sharma's three-wicket haul and her unbeaten 105 in pursuit of Mumbai's 179 allowed Bengal to seal a two wicket win in the final of the Under-23 Inter-State One-Day championship. The victory meant Bengal swept the one-day tournaments across age-groups, having secured the senior and Under-19 championships earlier. Deepti's third century of the tournament took her tally to 701 runs in 11 matches at an average of 71.89 to go along with the 23 wickets she picked up with her off-spin. Her efforts with the bat, however, were overshadowed by Jemimah Rodrigues's scintillating run for Mumbai.

Deepti Sharma's move to Bengal has been a fruitful one.

The right-hander smashed 960 runs at a Bradman-esque average of 137.14, including four centuries. Rodrigues had saved her best for last with scores of 140 not out, 185 not out and 55 in the knock-outs.

Saniya Raut, Mumbai's left-arm spinner, was outstanding in the knock-out stage, picking up consecutive five-wicket hauls in the semi-finals and finals.

Shafali Verma, Haryana's 14-year-old opening batter, finished the season with a bang: her 543 runs, including three hundreds, came at a strike-rate of 198.17. No other batter who scored more than 150 runs had a strike-rate over 100.

Other notable performances included Debasmita Dutta's haul of 9 for 3 against Mizoram, Nisha Mishra's four five-wicket hauls, Tanusree Sarkar's unbeaten 129 that led Bengal to victory against Railways, and Punjab's tie with Odisha.

The **2017-18** edition saw relatively low scores, but the gap between the less fancied teams and the traditional power houses was closing swiftly. Haryana beat Delhi, Vidarbha pipped Madhya Pradesh, Gujarat trounced Baroda and Goa snuck passed Karnataka in nail-biting contests. Seven centuries were scored across the tournament, with Priya Punia's unbeaten 124 against Jammu Kashmir the highest of the lot.

N Anusha, Andhra's opening batter, continued her good run through the season, collecting the bulk of her runs with crisp drives through the off side. While Sonia Lohiya of Delhi and Keerthy James of Kerala finished top of the bowling lists with 12 wickets apiece, Sunita Rani's figures really stood out. The left-arm spinner from Punjab picked up ten wickets in four matches at an incredible average of 2.30 and scarcely believable economy rate of 0.87; her tally including a scintillating spell of 8-8-0-4 against Haryana.

	Most runs	**Most wickets**
2017-18	N Anusha (Andhra) (279 runs in 5 matches)	Sonia Lohiya (Delhi) (12 wickets in 4 matches)
2018-19	Jemimah Rodrigues (Mumbai) (960 runs in 11 matches)	Nisha Mishra (Uttarakhand) (31 wickets in 8 matches)

Elite Group A

Lalbhai Contractor Stadium, Surat, March 17: Odisha 181/9 in 50 overs (Kajal Jena 51, Poonam Nayak 46; Hiral Solanki 3-36, Krutika Chaudhari 2-25) beat **Gujarat** 144 in 47.3 overs (Renuka Chaudhari 66, Hani Patel 27; Sushree Dibyadarshini 3-17, Barsarani Sigh 3-24) by 37 runs.

CB Patel Ground, Surat, March 17: Punjab 114 in 44.4 overs (Taniya Bhatia 47; Shrayosi Aich 3-18, Nisha Maji 2-20) lost to **Bengal** 115/3 in 35.2 overs (Tanusree Sarkar 59*, Richa 31; Sunita Rani 2-23) by seven wickets.

CK Pithawala Ground, Surat, March 17: Railways 139 in 50 overs (Nuzhat Parween 73; Sahana Pawar 4-16, C Pratyusha 2-26) lost to **Karnataka** 142/2 in 34.2 overs (G Divya 53, Shubha Sateesh 51*) by eight wickets.

Lalbhai Contractor Stadium, Surat, March 18: Kerala 185/6 in 50 overs (IV Drishya 54*, Akshaya A 37) beat **Odisha** 124/8 in 50 overs (Sushree Dibyadarshini 42, Sunita Murmu 20; Jipsa 3-10, Minnu Mani 2-21) by 61 runs.

CK Pithawala Ground, Surat, March 18: Uttar Pradesh 191/5 in 50 overs (Muskan Malik 73, Ekta Singh 71; Sushmita Ganguly 2-30) lost to **Bengal** 195/3 in 35.1 overs (Deepti Sharma 95, Richa 59; Aditi Sharma 2-38) by seven wickets.

CB Patel Ground, Surat, March 18: Tamil Nadu 91 in 42.5 overs (Meenakshi 22, C Sushanthika 20; G Divya 2-15, Monica Patel 2-15) lost to **Karnataka** 92/4 in 19.2 overs (C Pratyusha 33; KN Ramyashri 2-31) by six wickets.

CK Pithawala Ground, Surat, March 19: Punjab 193/5 in 50 overs (Amarpal Kaur 69, Amanjot Kaur 53*; Jipsa Joseph 3-32) lost to **Kerala** 196/6 in 48.2 overs (Akshaya A 81, IV Drishya 50*; Komalpreet Kour 2-12, Neelam Bisht 2-33) by four wickets.

Lalbhai Contractor Stadium, Surat, March 19: Uttar Pradesh 130/9 in 50 overs (Sabbineni Meghana 2-16, Papori Gogoi 2-30) lost to **Railways** 132/2 in 30.5 overs (V Sneha Deepthi 53, S Meghana 44) by eight wickets.

CB Patel Ground, Surat, March 19: Tamil Nadu 92 in 45.1 overs (Yogya Kosuri 35*; Renuka Chaudhari 3-12, Hiral Solanki 2-20) lost to **Gujarat** 95/3 in 23.5 overs (Itisha Patel 21*) by seven wickets.

CB Patel Ground, Surat, March 21: Odisha 123 in 48.4 overs (Rani Tudu 28; Sabbineni Meghana 3-14, Arundhati Reddy 3-21) lost to **Railways** 127/2 in 32 overs (S Meghana 41, A Reddy 39*) by eight wickets.

Lalbhai Contractor Stadium, Surat, March 21: Gujarat 63 in 28.5 overs (Sahana Pawar 4-20, C Pratyusha 2-9) lost to **Karnataka** 64/2 in 16.5 overs (Shubha Sateesh 28*, C Pratyusha 24*; Krutika Chaudhari 2-26) by eight wickets.

CK Pithawala Ground, Surat, March 21: Tamil Nadu 158/9 in 50 overs (S Anusha 67, SB

530 Domestic review

Keerthana 26; Rajni Devi 2-45) lost to **Punjab** 161/5 in 39.5 overs (Amanjot Kaur 51*, Taniya Bhatia 23; S Anusha 2-30) by five wickets.

CK Pithawala Ground, Surat, March 22: Bengal 223/6 in 50 overs (Tanusree Sarkar 129*, Prativa Rana 32; Sabbineni Meghana 5-39) beat **Railways** 123 in 37.1 overs (Arundhati Reddy 32, Nuzhat Parween 26; Sushmita Ganguly 3-15, T Sarkar 2-15) by 100 runs.

CB Patel Ground, Surat, March 22: Kerala 154/9 in 50 overs (IV Drishya 67*, Ansu Sunil 26; Renuka Chaudhari 2-20, Hiral Solanki 2-27) beat **Gujarat** 146/8 in 50 overs (R Chaudhari 31, Bhavana Goplani 30; Mrudhula VS 4-30) by eight runs.

Lalbhai Contractor Stadium, Surat, March 22: Punjab 188/8 in 50 overs (Priyanka Malik 50, Amarpal Kaur 48; Kajal 2-28, Shilpi Yadav 2-29) lost to **Uttar Pradesh** 193/5 in 38.4 overs (Ekta Singh 93, Kshama 50; A Kaur 3-43) by five wickets.

Lalbhai Contractor Stadium, Surat, March 24: Karnataka 79 in 33.4 overs (C Pratyusha 23; Rashi Kanojiya 3-17, Anjali Singh 2-13) lost to **Uttar Pradesh** 80/6 in 34.3 overs (Ekta Singh 22, Shivpriya Pandey 21; G Divya 3-15) by four wickets.

CK Pithawala Ground, Surat, March 24: Odisha 200/4 in 50 overs (Poonam Nayak 58*, Sushree Dibyadarshini 48; Yogya Kosuri 2-32) beat **Tamil Nadu** 126 in 44.1 overs (S Anusha 71; Louisa Dash 4-28, Indrani Chhatria 3-19) by 74 runs.

CB Patel Ground, Surat, March 24: Kerala 128 in 45.3 overs (Akshaya A 42, Minnu Mani 29; Deepti Sharma 3-22, Shreya Karar 3-29) lost to **Bengal** 132/7 in 43.2 overs (D Sharma 46, Aparna Mondal 22*; Darsana Mohanan 3-28, Jipsa Joseph 2-28) by three wickets.

CK Pithawala Ground, Surat, March 26: Gujarat 119 in 44.1 overs (Simran 45; Shrayosi Aich 4-17, Tanusree Sarkar 2-21) lost to **Bengal** 120/1 in 29.2 overs (Deepti Sharma 54*, T Sarkar 41*) by nine wickets.

CB Patel Ground, Surat, March 26: Karnataka 114 in 40.3 overs (Shubha Sateesh 51; Sushree Dibyadarshini 4-19, Barsarani Singh 3-26) beat **Odisha** 81 in 34.5 overs (C Pratyusha 3-14, Shreyanka Patil 3-16) by 33 runs.

Lalbhai Contractor Stadium, Surat, March 26: Punjab 152 in 44.3 overs (Taniya Bhatia 54*, Neelam Bisht 46; Arundhati Reddy 4-44, Papori Gogoi 2-14) lost to **Railways** 153/4 in 44.2 overs (A Reddy 54*, Nuzhat Parween 30) by six wickets.

CB Patel Ground, Surat, March 28: Karnataka 168 in 50 overs (G Divya 69, Simren Henry 25; Amanjot Kaur 3-27, Neelam Bisht 3-27) beat **Punjab** 129 in 38.3 overs (Ridhima Aggarwal 46*, Taniya Bhatia 23; C Pratyusha 4-29, Sahana Pawar 2-19) by 39 runs.

Lalbhai Contractor Stadium, Surat, March 28: Bengal 303/7 in 50 overs (Prativa Rana 89, Tanusree Sarkar 88; KN Ramyashri 3-52) beat **Tamil Nadu** 88 in 41.4 overs (A Eloksi 27; Deepti Sharma 4-9, Shreya Karar 3-25) by 215 runs.

CK Pithawala Ground, Surat, March 28: Kerala 170/8 in 50 overs (Akshaya A 70, IV Drishya 33*; Anjali Singh 3-36, Shilpi Yadav 2-27) beat **Uttar Pradesh** 145 in 46.3 overs (Ekta Singh 50, Muskan Malik 25;Sourabhya 2-22, Minnu Mani 2-28) by 25 runs.

Lalbhai Contractor Stadium, Surat, March 30: Railways 248/5 in 50 overs (Sabbineni Meghana 59, Nuzhat Parween 54; Thenmozhi M 2-27) beat **Tamil Nadu** 133/7 in 50 overs (SB Keerthana 40, Meenakshi 37*; Bharti Bawa 3-12) by 115 runs.

CK Pithawala Ground, Surat, March 30: Gujarat 103 in 35 overs (Simran 40, Renuka Chaudhari 30; Sunita Rani 3-16, Manpreet Kaur 2-18) lost to **Punjab** 104/3 in 40.3 overs (Taniya Bhatia 53*, Amanjot Kaur 30*) by seven wickets.

CB Patel Ground, Surat, March 30: Odisha 76 in 48.4 overs (Kshama 4-24, Shilpi Yadav 2-10) lost to **Uttar Pradesh** 79/1 in 16.3 overs (Kshama 32*, Ekta Singh 28) by nine wickets.

CB Patel Ground, Surat, April 1: Bengal 240/7 in 50 overs (Deepti Sharma 123, Prativa Rana 32; Simren Henry 3-28, Sahana Pawar 2-40) beat **Karnataka** 42 in 31.1 overs (Shrayosi Aich 2-0, D Sharma 2-4) by 198 runs.

Lalbhai Contractor Stadium, Surat, April 1: Kerala 149 in 49.1 overs (Minnu Mani 69; SB Keerthana 4-23, KN Ramyashri 2-17) beat **Tamil Nadu** 103 in 39 overs (A Eloksi 42, S Anusha 31; Darasana Mohanan 4-3, M Mani 2-11) by 46 runs.

CK Pithawala Ground, Surat, April 1: Railways 253/7 in 50 overs (Priyanka Bala 105, Sabbineni Meghana 75; Krutika Chaudhari 2-34, Renuka Chaudhari 2-41) beat **Gujarat** 175/9 in 50 overs (Simran 72, K Chaudhari 26; Arundhati Reddy 2-22, Bhrati Bawa 2-29) by 78 runs.

CB Patel Ground, Surat, April 3: Tamil Nadu 152 in 46.4 overs (S Anusha 82, A Eloksi 26; Rashi Kanojiya 2-10, Shilpi Yadav 2-25) beat **Uttar Pradesh** 144 in 41.2 overs (Ekta Singh 32, Shobha Devi 27; KN Ramyashri 3-34, MS Aishwarya 2-16) by eight wickets.

Lalbhai Contractor Stadium, Surat, April 3: Odisha 115 in 46.3 overs (Anjali Singh 29, Sushree Dibyadarshini 27; Rajni Devi 3-24, Amanjot Kaur 2-13) tied with **Punjab** 115 in 35.5 overs (Priyanka Malik 34, Amarpal Kaur 32; S Dibyadarshini 4-25, Barsarani Singh 2-25).

CK Pithawala Ground, Surat, April 3: Karnataka 178 in 49.3 overs (G Divya 71, C Pratyusha 24; Keerthy James 3-30, Darasana Mohanan 2-23) beat **Kerala** 133 in 49.3 overs (Jipsa Joseph 34, IV Drishya 25; Shubha Sateesh 2-14, Sahana Pawar 2-19) by 45 runs.

CB Patel Ground, Surat, April 5: Uttar Pradesh 160/8 in 50 overs (Sweta 52*, Shobha Devi 36; PA Talpada 2-32, Renuka Chaudhari 2-41) beat **Gujarat** 122 in 45.5 overs (Bhavana Goplani 43, Hani Patel 27; Shilpi Yadav 3-18, Aditi 2-20) by 38 runs.

CK Pithawala Ground, Surat, April 5: Kerala 142/8 in 50 overs (Minnu Mani 31, Ansu Sunil 27; Nirupama Baro 2-24, Archana Dutta 2-25) beat **Railways** 131 in 43.3 overs (Nuzhat Parween 64, V Sneha Deepthi 21; Mrudhula 3-21, Jipsa Joseph 3-32) by 11 runs.

Lalbhai Contractor Stadium, Surat, April 5: Bengal 234/7 in 50 overs (Deepti Sharma 104, Prativa Rana 43; Louisa Dash 3-36, Sushree Dibyadarshini 2-43) beat **Odisha** 154/9 in 50 overs (Anjali Singh 37, S Dibyadarshini 21; Tanusree Sarkar 2-18, D Sharma 2-19) by 80 runs.

Elite Group A points table

Team	M	W	L	T	N/R	Pts	NRR
Bengal	8	8	0	0	0	32	+2.154
Karnataka	8	6	2	0	0	24	+0.256
Kerala	8	6	2	0	0	24	+0.227
Railways	8	5	3	0	0	20	+0.482
Uttar Pradesh	8	4	4	0	0	16	+0.248
Punjab	8	2	5	1	0	10	-0.225
Odisha	8	2	5	1	0	10	-0.590
Gujarat	8	1	7	0	0	4	-0.764
Tamil Nadu	8	1	7	0	0	4	-1.823

Bengal and Karnataka qualified for the knock-outs

Elite Group B

Vidarbha Cricket Association Stadium, Jamtha, Nagpur, March 17: Madhya Pradesh 152 in 50 overs (Soniya Sharma 63, Bharti Choudhary 23; Priya Mishra 2-20, Ria Sharma 2-31) lost to **Delhi** 156/8 in 49 overs (Simran Dil Bahadur 48, Ayushi Soni 37*; Nikita Singh 3-23) by two wickets.

Vidarbha Cricket Association Stadium, Civil Lines, Nagpur, March 17: Andhra 105 in 42.2 overs (K Anjali Sarvani 39; Tejal Hasabnis 3-22, Devika Vaidya 2-13) lost to **Maharashtra** 106/7 in 32.2 overs (T Hasabnis 41*) by three wickets.

Vidarbha Cricket Association Kalamna, Nagpur, March 17: Mumbai 224/8 in 50 overs (Jemimag Rodrigues 93, Vrushali Bhagat 42; Renuka Singh 2-57) lost to **Himachal Pradesh**

225/5 in 49.3 overs (Harleen Deol 88, Kashish Verma 55; J Rodrigues 2-36) by five wickets.

Vidarbha Cricket Association Stadium, Jamtha, Nagpur, March 18: Hyderabad 132/8 in 50 overs (Rachna Kumar 39*, G Trisha 23; Poonam Soni 3-11) lost to **Madhya Pradesh** 135/8 in 45.2 overs (Soumya Tiwari 36*, Salonee Dangore 33; Lakshmi Prasanna 2-21, Bhogi Shravani 2-22) by two wickets.

Vidarbha Cricket Association Stadium, Civil Lines, Nagpur, March 18: Vidarbha 133 in 50 overs (Disha Kasat 40, Vaidhnavi Khandkar 22; Saranya Gadwal 3-31, CH Jhansi Lakshmi 2-17) lost to **Andhra** 137/1 in 32.4 overs (N Anusha 55*, CH Jhansi Lakshmi 42) by nine wickets.

Vidarbha Cricket Association Kalamna, Nagpur, March 18: Tripura 108 in 45.5 overs (Rizu Saha 50; Tanuja Kanwer 5-11) lost to **Himachal Pradesh** 109/7 in 38.2 overs (Chitra Singh Jamwal 25; Suravi Roy 2-29) by three wickets.

Vidarbha Cricket Association Stadium, Jamtha, Nagpur, March 19: Maharashtra 219/7 in 50 overs (Shivali Shinde 59, Tejal Hasabnis 47*; Keerthi Reddy 4-38) beat **Hyderabad** 158 in 49 overs (G Trisha 47, Lakshmi Prasanna 32*; Devika Vaidya 4-17, T Hasbanis 3-34) by 61 runs.

Vidarbha Cricket Association Stadium, Civil Lines, Nagpur, March 19: Mumbai 175 in 49.2 overs (Jemimah Rodrigues 106; MS Bodkhe 4-24) beat **Vidarbha** 132 in 44.5 overs (Latika Inamdar 31, Nupur Kohale 28; J Rodrigues 3-27, Manali Dakshini 2-31) by 43 runs.

Vidarbha Cricket Association Kalamna, Nagpur, March 19: Tripura 147/7 in 50 overs (Rizu Saha 38, Jhumki Debnath 33; Ayushi Soni 2-15, Madhu 2-31) lost to **Delhi** 150/2 in 32 overs (Priya Punia 86*, Simran Dil Bahadaur 37*; Puja Das 2-28) by eight wickets.

Vidarbha Cricket Association Stadium, Jamtha, Nagpur, March 22: Andhra 196/7 in 50 overs (N Anusha 73, CH Jhansi Lakshmi 52; Manali Dakshini 2-40) beat **Mumbai** 175 in 49.3 overs (Jemimah Rodrigues 34, M Dakshini 33; K Anjali Sarvani 3-28, E Padmaja 2-45) by 21 runs.

Vidarbha Cricket Association Kalamna, Nagpur, March 22: Hyderabad 87 in 37.3 overs (Trisha Poojitha 20; Priya Mishra 2-10) lost to **Delhi** 88/4 in 25.3 overs (Priya Punia 23; G Trisha 2-16) by six wickets.

Vidarbha Cricket Association Stadium, Civil Lines, Nagpur, March 22: Vidarbha 148/9 in 50 overs (Nupur Kohale 39*, Saloni Allot 24; Maya Sonawane 2-19, Devika Vaidya 2-31) lost to **Maharashtra** 149/7 in 47.4 overs (Tejal Hasabnis 50*, D Vaidya 23) by three wickets.

Vidarbha Cricket Association Stadium, Civil Lines, Nagpur, March 24: Vidarbha 51 in 30.3 overs (Sushmita Kumari 4-5, VS Fishta 2-18) lost to **Himachal Pradesh** 52/1 in 17.1 overs (SM Singh 37*) by nine wickets.

Vidarbha Cricket Association Stadium, Jamtha, Nagpur, March 24: Tripura 111 in 48.4 overs (Rizu Saha 69; Salonee Dangore 4-19) lost to **Madhya Pradesh** 112/1 in 36.3 overs (Soniya Sharma 56*, Soumya Tiwari 22*) by nine wickets.

Vidarbha Cricket Association Kalamna, Nagpur, March 24: Andhra 247/3 in 50 overs (CH Jhansi Lakshmi 126, V Pushpa Latha 69*) beat **Hyderabad** 171 in 41.4 overs (Anuradha Nayak 38, Himani Yadav 31; K Anjali Sarvani 3-35, E Padmaja 2-37) by 76 runs.

Vidarbha Cricket Association Stadium, Jamtha, Nagpur, March 25: Madhya Pradesh 149 in 47.5 overs (Soumya Tiwari 43, Charu Joshi 28; Saniya Raut 3-30, Manali Dakshini 2-17) lost to **Mumbai** 150/3 in 34.3 overs (Jemimah Rodrigues 100*, Vrushali Bhagat 33) by seven wickets.

Vidarbha Cricket Association Stadium, Civil Lines, Nagpur, March 25: Delhi 142 in 49.5 overs (Priya Punia 48, Laxmi Yadav 26*; VS Fishta 3-21, Tanuja Kanwer 3-30) lost to **Himachal Pradesh** 144/3 in 35.1 overs (SM Singh 76*, T Kanwer 40*) by seven wickets.

Vidarbha Cricket Association Kalamna, Nagpur, March 25: Maharashtra 279/5 in 50 overs (Tejal Hasabnis 75*, Devika Vaidya 64) beat **Tripura** 121 in 41.1 overs (Rizu Saha 57; Maya Sonawane 4-30, T Hasabnis 2-18) by 158 runs.

Vidarbha Cricket Association Stadium, Jamtha, Nagpur, March 26: Delhi 139/9 in 50 overs (Ayushi Soni 32, Priya Punia 24; CH Jhansi Lakshmi 3-26) beat **Andhra** 100 in 45 overs (G Sneha 25, K Anjali Sarvani 23; A Soni 3-13, Simran Dil Bahadur 3-17) by 39 runs.

Vidarbha Cricket Association Stadium, Civil Lines, Nagpur, March 26: Himachal Pradesh 103 in 46 overs (Kashish Verma 37; Soumya Tiwari 4-2, Charu Joshi 4-20) lost to **Himachal** 92 in 46.4 overs (Nikita Singh 30*; Tanuja Kanwer 3-13, PG Kahlon 2-7) by 11 runs.

Vidarbha Cricket Association Kalamna, Nagpur, March 26: Mumbai 220 in 49.4 overs (Jemimah Rodrigues 69, Manali Dakshini 49; Tejal Hasbnis 4-47, Aditi Gaikwad 2-19) beat **Maharashtra** 142 in 42.1 overs (Devika Vaidya 34, SA Lonkar 24; Saniya Raut 4-24, M Dakshini 2-21) by 79 runs.

Vidarbha Cricket Association Kalamna, Nagpur, March 28: Maharashtra 71 in 31.5 overs (Renuka Singh 5-12, Sushmita Kumari 3-11) lost to **Himachal Pradesh** 73/2 in 20.3 overs (SM Singh 26, Harleen Deol 25*) by eight wickets.

Vidarbha Cricket Association Stadium, Jamtha, Nagpur, March 28: Tripura 62 in 34.4 overs (K Dhatri 4-20, E Padmaja 3-2) lost to **Andhra** 63/5 in 13.1 overs (V Pushpa Latha 28; Puja Das 2-10, Suravi Roy 2-32) by five wickets.

Vidarbha Cricket Association Stadium, Civil Lines, Nagpur, March 28: Hyderabad 79 in 39 overs (Trisha Poojitha 20; Vaishnavi Khandkar 5-18, Disha Kasat 2-10) lost to **Vidarbha** 80/1 in 19.3 overs (D Kasat 37*, Latika Inamdar 31*) by nine wickets.

Vidarbha Cricket Association Stadium, Jamtha, Nagpur, March 30: Tripura 85 in 49.4 overs (Saniya Raut 5-18, Jagravi Pawar 2-9) lost to **Mumbai** 89/1 in 14.2 overs (Jemimah Rodrigues 51*, Riya Chaudhari 31*) by nine wickets.

Vidarbha Cricket Association Kalamna, Nagpur, March 30: Delhi 155 in 49.1 overs (Priya Punia 41; Devika Vaidya 2-15) beat **Maharashtra** 142 in 44 overs (D Vaidya 45, SA Lonkar 30; Madhu 3-15, Ayushi Soni 2-22) by 13 runs.

Vidarbha Cricket Association Stadium, Civil Lines, Nagpur, March 30: Vidarbha 107 in 47.5 overs (Nupur Kohale 29; Bharti Choudhary 3-23, Salonee Dangore 2-12) beat **Madhya Pradesh** 108/9 in 49.3 overs (Nikita Singh 46; Vaishnavi Khandkar 4-16, Disha Kasat 2-12) by one wicket.

Vidarbha Cricket Association Stadium, Jamtha, Nagpur, April 1: Andhra 138 in 46 overs (V Pushpa Latha 50*, G Sneha 21; Sushmita Kumari 3-23, Tanuja Kanwer 3-29) lost to **Himachal Pradesh** 139/6 in 46.3 overs (Harleen Deol 55, Kashish Verma 35) by four wickets.

Vidarbha Cricket Association Stadium, Civil Lines, Nagpur, April 1: Tripura 101 in 43.4 overs (Rizu Saha 40; Rachna Kumar 4-19, G Trisha 3-6) lost to **Hyderabad** 104/3 in 30.2 overs (Himani Yadav 41, Anuradha Nayak 24*) by seven wickets.

Vidarbha Cricket Association Kalamna, Nagpur, April 1: Mumbai 229 in 50 overs (Jemimah Rodrigues 74, Vrushali Bhagat 64; Ria Sharma 2-35, Simran Dil Bahadur 2-57) beat **Delhi** 202/9 in 50 overs (SD Bahadur 69, Neha Chhillar 35*; Saniya Raut 3-34, Manjiri Gawade 2-22) by 27 runs.

Vidarbha Cricket Association Stadium, Civil Lines, Nagpur, April 3: Tripura 113/9 in 50 overs (Shiuli Chakraborty 34*, MK Rabidas 33; Vaishnavi Khandkar 2-32) lost to **Vidarbha** 114/4 in 33.4 overs (Disha Kasat 55*; MK Rabidas 2-24, Puja Das 2-47) by six wickets.

Vidarbha Cricket Association Stadium, Jamtha, Nagpur, April 3: Maharashtra 191/6 in 50 overs (Devika Vaidya 57*, Shivali Shinde 54; Salonee Dangore 5-30) beat **Madhya Pradesh** 82 in 25.3 overs (Maya Sonawane 3-9) by 109 runs.

Vidarbha Cricket Association Kalamna, Nagpur, April 3: Hyderabad 156/9 in 50 overs (Anuradha Nayak 73*, Trisha Poojiha 32; Renuka Singh 3-19, Tanuja Kanwer 3-29) lost to **Himachal Pradesh** 157/4 in 47.4 overs (Kashish Verma 64*, Harleen Deol 53; Rachna Kumar 3-31) by six wickets.

Vidarbha Cricket Association Stadium, Civil Lines, Nagpur, April 5: Vidarbha 150/8 in 50 overs (Disha Kasat 87; Ria Sharma 2-36, Simran Dil Bahadur 2-49) lost to **Delhi** 152/5 in 48.3 overs (SD Bahadur 50, Priya Punia 41; Viashnavi Khandkar 2-32) by five wickets.

Vidarbha Cricket Association Stadium, Jamtha, Nagpur, April 5: Mumbai 158/9 in 50

overs (Jemimah Rodrigues 53, Vrushali Bhagat 22; Rachna Kumar 3-18, Bhogi Shravani 2-31) beat **Hyderabad** 146 in 49.2 overs (Lakshmi Prasanna 65*; Jagravi Pawar 3-14) by 12 runs.
Vidarbha Cricket Association Kalamna, Nagpur, April 5: Andhra 140 in 45.4 overs (K Hepsiba 27, N Anusha 21; Salonee Dangore 3-23, Charu Joshi 3-33) beat **Madhya Pradesh** 134 in 47.1 overs (Soniya SHarma 47, Nikita Singh 41; D Pravallika 2-17, CH Jhansi Lakshmi 2-19) by six runs.

Elite Group B points table

Team	M	W	L	T	N/R	Pts	NRR
Himachal Pradesh	8	8	0	0	0	32	+0.834
Mumbai	8	6	2	0	0	24	+0.873
Delhi	8	6	2	0	0	24	+0.347
Maharashtra	8	5	3	0	0	20	+0.552
Andhra	8	5	3	0	0	20	+0.460
Madhya Pradesh	8	3	5	0	0	12	-0.314
Vidarbha	8	2	6	0	0	8	-0.202
Hyderabad	8	1	7	0	0	4	-0.790
Tripura	8	0	8	0	0	0	-1.987

Himachal Pradesh, Mumbai and Delhi qualified for the knock-outs

Elite Group C

Saurashtra Cricket Association Stadium Khanderi B Ground, Rajkot, March 17: Baroda 305/7 in 50 overs (Yastika Bhatia 145, Radha Yadav 68; Diksha Sharma 2-54, Suman Hingra 2-57) beat **Haryana** (Shafali Verma 110, Divya 20; R Yadav 2-24, Jaya Mohite 2-56) by 83 runs.
Saurashtra Cricket Association Stadium, Rajkot, March 17: Jammu & Kashmir 139 in 46.4 overs (Nadia Chowdhary 28, Farkhanda Aziz Khan 25; Kakoli Saikia 3-26, Gayatri Gurung 2-26) lost to **Assam** 141/9 in 43.1 overs (Priyanka Boruah 29, Uma Chetry 24; Bismah Hassan 4-29, N Chowdhary 3-13) by one wicket.
Railway Cricket Ground, Rajkot, March 17: Chhattisgarh 183/5 in 50 overs (Deepika Tiwari 63, Shivani Krishna 44; Shanti Kumari 3-44) lost to **Jharkhand** 186/4 in 41.2 overs (Indrani Roy 64, Sonia 58) by six wickets.
Saurashtra Cricket Association Stadium Khanderi B Ground, Rajkot, March 18: Goa 243/5 in 50 overs (Purvaja Verlekar 71, Vinavi Gurav 64; Versha Bhatiwal 2-4) beat **Haryana** 76 in 25.5 overs (Shivangi Chauhan 26; Sanjula Naik 2-2, Diksha Gawde 2-16) by 167 runs.
Saurashtra Cricket Association Stadium, Rajkot, March 18: Assam 126 in 44.1 overs (Rashmi Dey 32; Suman Meena 3-23, SR Choudhary 2-15) beat **Rajasthan** 100 in 44.2 overs (Kakoli Saikia 4-8, Ruhina Pegu 2-17) by 26 runs.
Railway Cricket Ground, Rajkot, March 18: Chhattisgarh 208/6 in 50 overs (Manpreet Kaur 58, Vidya Verma 58; P Modhwadia 2-34) beat **Saurashtra** 97 in 44.4 overs (Garima Janghel 4-17) by 111 runs.
Saurashtra Cricket Association Stadium Khanderi B Ground, Rajkot, March 19: Jammu & Kashmir 86 in 34 overs (Bismah Hassan 47*; Diksha Gawde 3-17, Rakshanda Pilankar 2-9) beat **Goa** 58 in 25.2 overs (Nadia Chowdhary 6-8, Bismah Hassan 3-24) by 28 runs.
Saurashtra Cricket Association Stadium, Rajkot, March 19: Rajasthan 217/4 in 50 overs (Jyoti Choudhary 83*, SR Jat 52; Mamta Paswan 3-34) lost to **Jharkhand** 218/4 in 47.5 overs

(Priyanka Sawaiyan 60*, Ruma 47*) by six wickets.

Railway Cricket Ground, Rajkot, March 19: Saurashtra 95 in 45.1 overs (Pragya Rawat 4-29, Gayatri Naik 2-11) lost to **Baroda** 96/1 in 15.1 overs (Yastika Bhatia 44*, Amrita Joseph 35*) by nine wickets.

Saurashtra Cricket Association Stadium Khanderi B Ground, Rajkot, March 21: Haryana 177 in 50 overs (Shafali Verma 98; Devyani Prasad 4-29, Ritu Kumari 2-26) lost to **Jharkhand** 178/5 in 46.4 overs (Priyanka Sawaiyan 71*, Durga Kumari Murmu 55*; Suman Gulia 2-42) by five wickets.

Saurashtra Cricket Association Stadium, Rajkot, March 21: Chhattisgarh 127/7 in 50 overs (Deepika Tiwari 39, Sanjana Pardi 22; Kesha 2-13, Pragya Rawat 2-34) lost to **Baroda** 128/1 in 28.3 overs (Amrita Jospeh 57*, Karishma Tank 48*) by nine wickets.

Railway Cricket Ground, Rajkot, March 21: Saurashtra 177/8 in 50 overs (Riddhi Ruparel 67, Drashti Somaiya 22; Nadia Chowdhary 2-16, Sadiya Wani 2-23) beat **Jammu & Kashmir** 112 in 40.2 overs (N Chowdhary 21; P Modhwadia 4-8) by 65 runs.

Saurashtra Cricket Association Stadium Khanderi B Ground, Rajkot, March 22: Assam 129 in 43.3 overs (Ruhina Pegu 50; Ashwani 3-18, Ritu Kumari 2-17) lost to **Jharkhand** 130/2 in 34.5 overs (Indrani Roy 60, Rashmi 33) by eight wickets.

Saurashtra Cricket Association Stadium, Rajkot, March 22: Baroda 95 in 34 overs (Karishma Tank 20; Tejashwini Duragad 2-15, Kalangutker Avisha Gurudas 2-27) lost to **Goa** 97/3 in 30.1 overs (Shindiya Naik 41*, Shreya Parab 38) by seven wickets.

Railway Cricket Ground, Rajkot, March 22: Jammu & Kashmir 59 in 29.1 overs (Sweety Siddhu 3-14, SR Choudhary 2-5) lost to **Rajasthan** 60/0 in 15.5 overs (SR Jat 32*, TB Vaishnav 22*) by 10 wickets.

Saurashtra Cricket Association Stadium Khanderi B Ground, Rajkot, March 24: Rajasthan 222/6 in 50 overs (Suman Meena 80, Ayushi Garg 61) beat **Chhattisgarh** 98/9 in 50 overs (ASP Maheshwari 2-8, SP Sharma 2-14) by 124 runs.

Saurashtra Cricket Association Stadium, Rajkot, March 24: Haryana 272/8 in 50 overs (Shafali Verma 80, Parmila Kumari 52; T Dharani 4-22) beat **Saurashtra** 128/8 in 50 overs (Sarasvati 46, P Modhwadia 20; Sheetal Rana 3-30, Priya Khatkar 2-19) by 144 runs.

Railway Cricket Ground, Rajkot, March 24: Goa 139/9 in 50 overs (Shindiya Naik 39, Vinavi Gurav 20; Rashmi Dey 2-11, Ruhina Pegu 2-17) lost to **Assam** 142/8 in 43.3 overs (R Dey 46*; Tejashwini Duragad 2-30) by two wickets.

Saurashtra Cricket Association Stadium Khanderi B Ground, Rajkot, March 26: Baroda 216/7 in 50 overs (Amrita Joseph 87, Hrutu Patel 38; Bedashree Bopatragohain 2-21, Ruhina Pegu 2-34) lost to **Assam** 217/3 in 46.2 overs (R Pegu 63*, Gayatri Gurung 58; Charmi 2-38) by seven wickets.

Saurashtra Cricket Association Stadium, Rajkot, March 26: Haryana 205 in 48.1 overs (Sheetal Rana 54, Shafali Verma 42; Shraddha Vaishnava 2-15, Dipti Dhimar 2-46) beat **Chhattisgarh** 143/8 in 50 overs (Manpreet Kaur 40, Sanjana Pardi 26; Suman Gulia 3-24, Parmila Kumari 2-20) by 62 runs.

Railway Cricket Ground, Rajkot, March 26: Jammu & Kashmir 93 in 33.3 overs (Nadia Chowdhary 33, Rudrakshi Chib 24; Devyani Prasad 5-38, Ashwani Kumari 2-17) lost to **Jharkhand** 94/3 in 18 overs (Ritu Kumari 32*, Sonia 31) by seven wickets.

Railway Cricket Ground, Rajkot, March 28: Rajasthan 256/5 in 50 overs (Ayushi Garg 127, SR Jat 78; Diksha Gawde 2-52) beat **Goa** 152 in 42.5 overs (Sugandha Ghadi 35, Vinavi Gurav 32; Suman Meena 5-32) by 104 runs.

Saurashtra Cricket Association Stadium Khanderi B Ground, Rajkot, March 28: Jammu & Kashmir 123 in 48.4 overs (Nadia Chowdhary 34*; Shraddha Vaishnava 3-14, Manpreet Kaur 3-18) lost to **Chhattisgarh** 127/6 in 38.1 overs (M Kaur 50; Bismah Hassan 3-49, Sadiya Wani 2-21) by four wickets.

Saurashtra Cricket Association Stadium, Rajkot, March 28: Saurashtra 134/7 in 50 overs (Riddhi Ruparel 30, Reena Savasadiya 29; Bedashree Borpatragohain 3-22, Ruhina Pegu 3-28) beat **Assam** 114 in 43.4 overs (Rashmi Dey 23, Priyanka Boruah 23; Hira Modhwadia 3-17, T Dharani 3-28) by 20 runs.

Saurashtra Cricket Association Stadium Khanderi B Ground, Rajkot, March 30: Jharkhand 236/5 in 50 overs (Sonia 87, Ruma 48; M Tanna 2-21) beat **Saurashtra** 124/8 in 50 overs (Tanya Rao 58, Sujan Sama 20; Shanti Kumari 3-13, Mamta Paswan 2-17) by 112 runs.

Saurashtra Cricket Association Stadium, Rajkot, March 30: Jammu & Kashmir 66 in 32.2 overs (Bansi 5-9, Radha Yadav 2-17) lost to **Baroda** 70/1 in 12.2 overs (Yastika Bhatia 37*) by nine wickets.

Railway Cricket Ground, Rajkot, March 30: Haryana 238/8 in 50 overs (Suman Gulia 72*, Sheetal Rana 38; SP Sharma 2-28, SS Kalal 2-42) beat **Rajasthan** 207 in 43.3 overs (Ayushi Garg 75, Sangeeta Kumawat 51; Bhawna Ohlan 3-34, Priya Khatkar 2-44) by 31 runs.

Saurashtra Cricket Association Stadium Khanderi B Ground, Rajkot, April 1: Chhattisgarh 124/9 in 50 overs (Manpreet Kaur 54, Sanjana Pardi 24; Hemalata Payeng 4-19) beat **Assam** 85 in 41.2 overs (Bedashree Borpatragohain 34; Ritu Meshram 4-11, Mamta Bhagat 3-17) by 39 runs.

Saurashtra Cricket Association Stadium, Rajkot, April 1: Goa 234/6 in 50 overs (Purvaja Verlekar 57, Shindiya Naik 46; Sujan Sama 2-31, P Modhwadia 2-39) beat **Saurashtra** 121/9 in 50 overs (Tejashwini Duragad 3-20, Snehal Shet 2-22) by 113 runs.

Railway Cricket Ground, Rajkot, April 1: Baroda 190/9 in 50 overs (Amrita Joseph 31, Radha Yadav 30; Devyani Prasad 3-31, Ritu Kumari 2-30) beat **Jharkhand** 108 in 36 overs (R Kumari 32, D Prasad 20; R Yadav 3-23, Gayatri Naik 3-37) by 82 runs.

Saurashtra Cricket Association Stadium Khanderi B Ground, Rajkot, April 3: Rajasthan 235/5 in 50 overs (Ayushi Garg 82, Suman Meena 71*) beat **Saurashtra** 111 in 45.1 overs (Riddhi Ruparel 41; SR Choudhary 3-25, SP Sharma 2-18) by 124 runs.

Saurashtra Cricket Association Stadium, Rajkot, April 3: Haryana 341/7 in 50 overs (Shafali Verma 100, Shivangi Chauhan 96; Nadia Chowdhary 3-65) beat **Jammu & Kashmir** 102 in 39.5 overs (N Chowdhary 27; Bhawna Ohlan 2-8, Sheetal Rana 2-8) by 239 runs.

Railway Cricket Ground, Rajkot, April 3: Goa 174/9 in 50 overs (Vinavi Gurav 38, Tejashwini N Duragad 37; Durgesh Nandani Sahu 3-44, Dipti Dhimar 2-44) beat **Chhattisgarh** 65 in 35.1 overs (Manpreet Kaur 22; Sanjula Naik 3-10, Diksha Gawde 2-16) by 109 runs.

Saurashtra Cricket Association Stadium Khanderi B Ground, Rajkot, April 5: Rajasthan 156 in 49.2 overs (Suman Meena 50, Sangeeta Kumawat 44; Jaya Mohite 5-25) lost to **Baroda** 160/4 in 34.1 overs (Hrutu Patel 84*, Radha Yadav 27*) by six wickets.

Saurashtra Cricket Association Stadium, Rajkot, April 5: Jharkhand 240/9 in 50 overs (Rashmi 126, Indrani Roy 51; Snehal Shet 4-41, Tejashwini Duragad 3-32) beat **Goa** 145 in 41.3 overs (Vinavi Gurav 54, T Duragad 20; Devyani Prasad 4-30, Mamta Paswan 2-36) by 95 runs.

Railway Cricket Ground, Rajkot, April 5: Haryana 317/8 in 50 overs (Shafali Verma 102, Suman Gulia 71; Anamika Bori 5-51, Ruhina Pegu 2-36) beat **Assam** 221 in 44.3 overs (Gayatri Gurung 75, Jyoti Devi 33; Priya Khatkar 2-29, Sheetal Rana 2-31) by 96 runs.

Elite Group C point table

Team	M	W	L	T	N/R	Pts	NRR
Jharkhand	8	7	1	0	0	28	+0.959
Baroda	8	6	2	0	0	24	+1.453
Haryana	8	5	3	0	0	20	+0.770
Assam	8	4	4	0	0	16	-0.308

Team	M	W	L	T	N/R	Pts	NRR
Rajasthan	8	4	4	0	0	16	+0.930
Goa	8	4	4	0	0	16	+0.520
Chhattisgarh	8	3	5	0	0	12	-0.529
Saurashtra	8	2	6	0	0	8	-1.659
Jammu & Kashmir	8	1	7	0	0	4	-1.899

Jharkhand and Baroda qualified for the knock-outs

Plate Group

Ravenshaw University Ground 1, Cuttack, March 17: Mizoram 86 in 40.2 overs (Sandhya Kumari 23; M Kalra 4-9, K Kaithl 3-12) lost to **Arunachal Pradesh** 87/6 in 29.4 overs (S Kumari 3-16) by four wickets.

KIIT Cricket Stadium, Bhubaneswar, March 17: Bihar 121 in 47.2 overs (Sikha Singh 45, Harshita 20; Sariba 4-35, Priyanka Karmakar 2-15) beat **Nagaland** 98 in 45.2 overs (Elina 24; Apurva Kumari 2-14, Nivedita 2-15) by 23 runs.

Vikash Cricket Ground, Bhubaneswar, March 17: Manipur 138/8 in 50 overs (Kabia Badoni 32*; Janaki 2-24) beat **Pondicherry** 122 in 43.2 overs (Soundharya 21*, Nandhini C 21; VR Dharani 3-10, Linthoingambi Rajkumari 3-11) by 16 runs.

Ravenshaw University Ground 1, Cuttack, March 18: Mizoram 43 in 21 overs (Sandhya Kumari 26; Debasmita Dutta 9-3) lost to **Meghalaya** 44/2 in 14.3 overs (D Dutta 21*) by eight wickets.

KIIT Cricket Stadium, Bhubaneswar, March 18: Uttarakhand 217/9 in 50 overs (Radha Chand 66, Megha Saini 32; Kumari 4-29, Apurva Kumari 2-29) beat **Bihar** 102 in 39.1 overs (Sana Ali 54; Dimpal Kandari 2-18, Rekha 2-29) by 115 runs.

Vikash Cricket Ground, Bhubaneswar, March18: Sikkim 143/6 in 50 overs (Pretika Chhetri 42, Nandita 33; Ronibala Thokchom 3-36, Linthoingambi Rajkumari 2-11) beat **Manipur** 76 in 31 overs (Seterny 23; Neema Yanki Lepcha 5-27) by 67 runs.

Ravenshaw University Ground 1, Cuttack, March 19: Nagaland 128 in 42.2 overs (Vaincy Chaudhary 58; Debasmita Dutta 5-20, Deiphi 3-21) beat **Meghalaya** 65 in 30.5 overs (D Dutta 30; Sariba 4-18, Sheetal 2-9) by 63 runs.

KIIT Cricket Stadium, Bhubaneswar, March 19: Uttarakhand 246/8 in 50 overs (Megha Saini 56, Ankita Dhami 48; Payal Balmik 3-35, Nandhini C 2-42) beat **Pondicherry** 84 in 38.5 overs (R Sandhya Mounika 39; Nisha Mishra 4-14, Rekha 4-20) by 162 runs.

Vikash Cricket Ground, Bhubaneswar, March 19: Sikkim 111/8 in 50 overs (K Kaithl 3-16, M Kalra 2-13) lost to **Arunachal Pradesh** 114/4 in 34.4 overs (Itee Yadav 37, Megha Sharma 35*) by six wickets.

Ravenshaw University Ground 1, Cuttack, March 21: Pondicherry 255/5 in 50 overs (R Sandhya Mounika 111*, Moumee Sasmal 36) beat **Mizoram** 46 in 31 overs (M Sasmal 4-7, Rebecca 4-12) by 209 runs.

KIIT Cricket Stadium, Bhubaneswar, March 21: Arunachal Pradesh 157 in 48.5 overs (Rishika Kumari 39, K Kaithl 28; VR Dharani 5-30) beat **Manipur** 86 in 34.1 overs (VR Dharani 23; Itee Yadav 2-10, Rishika Kumari 2-11) by 71 runs.

Vikash Cricket Ground, Bhubaneswar, March 21: Sikkim 59 in 35.5 overs (Sariba 5-11, Trishna Nair 2-15) lost to **Nagaland** 60/1 in 13.5 overs (Nazma Khan 40*) by nine wickets.

Ravenshaw University Ground 1, Cuttack, March 23: Pondicherry 111 in 44.4 overs (Ramya Maharajan 32; Apurva 4-31, Nivedita 3-23) lost to **Bihar** 112/6 in 42.1 overs (Aradhya Raj 21, Sana Ali 20) by four wickets.

KIIT Cricket Stadium, Bhubaneswar, March 23: Meghalaya 110/9 in 50 overs (Razia

Ahmed 24, Banri Wahlang 20*; Megha Sharma 3-28, RIshika Kumari 2-12) lost to **Arunachal Pradesh** 111/5 in 45.2 overs (M Kalra 21*; Deiphi 2-20) by five wickets.

Vikash Cricket Ground, Bhubaneswar, March 23: Uttarakhand 284/5 in 50 overs (Kanchan Parihar 107*, Radha Chand 74; Priyanka Karmakar 2-17) beat **Nagaland** 56 in 31 overs (Pooja Raj 5-16, Rekha 2-18) by 228 runs.

Ravenshaw University Ground 1, Cuttack, March 24: Manipur 43 in 27 overs (Nisha Mishra 6-8, Pooja Raj 2-8) lost to **Uttarakhand** 44/2 in 7.2 overs (Kanchan Parihar 22*; VR Dharani 2-6) by eight wickets.

KIIT Cricket Stadium, Bhubaneswar, March 24: Sikkim 209/3 in 50 overs (Nandita 65, Samayita 64*) beat **Mizoram** 88 in 34 overs (Neema Yanki Lepcha 3-22, Tabita Subba 2-13) by 121 runs.

Vikash Cricket Ground, Bhubaneswar, March 24: Bihar 174/9 in 50 overs (Sana Ali 55, Apurva Kumari 27; Debasmita Dutta 2-25) beat **Meghalaya** 39 in 28.5 overs (Apurva 3-7, Kumari 3-17) by 135 runs.

Ravenshaw University Ground 1, Cuttack, March 26: Arunachal Pradesh 52 in 36.1 overs (Apurva 7-23) lost to **Bihar** 53/1 in 22.2 overs (Apurva Kumari 23*) by nine wickets.

KIIT Cricket Stadium, Bhubaneswar, March 26: Manipur 136/9 in 50 overs (Linthoingambi Rajkumari 47, VR Dharani 31; Sawmi 3-55, S Yadav 2-12) beat **Mizoram** 94 in 38 overs (Sandhya Kumari 39; Priyangka 4-15, L Rajkumari 4-20) by 42 runs.

Vikash Cricket Ground, Bhubaneswar, March 26: Nagaland 216/1 in 50 overs (Nazma Khan 121*, Tulika 49) beat **Pondicherry** 179 in 49.5 overs (Moumee Sasmal 63, R Sandhya Mounika 40; Sariba 2-29, Trishna Nair 2-31) by 37 runs.

Ravenshaw University Ground 1, Cuttack, March 28: Manipur 44 in 32.4 overs (Sheetal 3-18, Priyanka Karmakar 2-4) lost to **Nagaland** 45/0 in 12 overs by 10 wickets.

KIIT Cricket Stadium, Bhubaneswar, March 28: Sikkim 77 in 39.1 overs (Pretika Chettri 20; Apurva 3-28, Apurva Kumari 2-8) lost to **Bihar** 81/1 in 29.1 overs (Sana Ali 47*) by nine wickets.

Vikash Cricket Ground, Bhubaneswar, March 28: Uttarakhand 275/5 in 50 overs (Raghvi 127*, Jyoti Giri 48; Debasmita Dutta 3-26) beat **Meghalaya** 38 in 23 overs (Pooja Raj 5-10, Nisha Mishra 3-6) by 237 runs.

Ravenshaw University Ground 1, Cuttack, March 30: Sikkim 95/9 in 50 overs (Nandita 38; Payal Balmik 2-10, Rebecca 2-13) lost to **Pondicherry** 96/4 in 28.4 overs (Ramya Maharajan 33, Moumee Sasmal 22; Pranita Chettri 2-28) by six wickets.

KIIT Cricket Stadium, Bhubaneswar, March 30: Arunachal Pradesh 112/9 in 50 overs (Megha Sharma 35, K Kaithl 25; Tulika 2-20) lost to **Nagaland** 115/1 in 21.1 overs (Nazma Khan 55*, Vaincy Chaudhary 42*) by nine wickets.

Vikash Cricket Ground, Bhubaneswar, March 30: Mizoram 53 in 18.3 overs (Nisha Mishra 5-7, Pooja Raj 3-12) lost to **Uttarakhand** 57/1 in 6.5 overs (Neelam 43*) by nine wickets.

Ravenshaw University Ground 1, Cuttack, April 1: Manipur 42 in 41 overs (Nivedita 3-3, Tejashwi 3-17) lost to **Bihar** 43/2 in 15.2 overs (Linthoingambi Rajkumari 2-13) by seven wickets.

KIIT Cricket Stadium, Bhubaneswar, April 1: Sikkim 65 in 34.1 overs (Tabita Subba 29; Debasmita Dutta 5-23) lost to **Meghalaya** 66/4 in 23.1 overs (D Dutta 48*; Neema Yanki Lepcha 2-18) by six wickets.

Vikash Cricket Ground, Bhubaneswar, April 1: Arunachal Pradesh 56 in 29 overs (Payal Balmik 3-8, Nandhini C 2-19) lost to **Pondicherry** 57/4 in 30 overs (M Kalra 2-10, K Kaithl 2-15) by six wickets.

Ravenshaw University Ground 1, Cuttack, April 3: Sikkim 42 in 29.1 overs (Nisha Mishra 7-7, Rekha 2-19) lost to **Uttarakhand** 43/0 in 8.1 overs (Megha Saini 20*) by 10 wickets.

KIIT Cricket Stadium, Bhubaneswar, April 3: Mizoram 80 in 47.4 overs (Sariba 4-25, Sheetal 3-5) lost to **Nagaland** 82/1 in 18.2 overs (Tulika 32*) by nine wickets.

Vikash Cricket Ground, Bhubaneswar, April 3: Manipur 141/7 in 50 overs (Kabia Badoni

54, Linthoingambi Rajkumari 20*; Debasmita Dutta 3-14, Daikia 2-34) lost to **Meghalaya** 144/4 in 46.1 overs (D Dutta 69*; VR Dharani 2-19) by six wickets.

Ravenshaw University Ground 1, Cuttack, April 5: Arunachal Pradesh 42 in 19.2 overs (Nisha Mishra 6-2, Rekha 2-12) lost to **Uttarakhand** 43/1 in 10.3 overs by nine wickets.

KIIT Cricket Stadium, Bhubaneswar, April 5: Pondicherry 105 in 45.5 overs (Payal Balmik 38, Reena T 26; Debasmita Dutta 4-17, Deiphi 2-13) lost to **Meghalaya** 106/1 in 39.4 overs (L Tamang 37, D Dutta 27*) by nine wickets.

Vikash Cricket Ground, Bhubaneswar, April 5: Bihar 222/1 in 50 overs (Sana Ali 118, Aradhya 75*) beat **Mizoram** 70 in 42.4 overs (S Yadav 29*; Nivedita 5-9, Tejaswi 3-19) by 152 runs.

Plate Group points table

Team	M	W	L	T	N/R	Pts	NRR
Uttarakhand	8	8	0	0	0	32	+4.303
Bihar	8	7	1	0	0	28	+1.174
Nagaland	8	6	2	0	0	24	+0.655
Arunachal Pradesh	8	4	4	0	0	16	-0.300
Meghalaya	8	4	4	0	0	16	-0.744
Pondicherry	8	3	5	0	0	12	+0.155
Sikkim	8	2	6	0	0	8	-0.614
Manipur	8	2	6	0	0	8	-1.055
Mizoram	8	0	8	0	0	0	-2.654

Uttarakhand qualified for the knock-outs

Quarter-finals

VCA, Civil Lines, Nagpur, April 9: Uttarakhand 102 in 48.5 overs (Deepti Sharma 4-17, Shreya Karar 3-19) lost to **Bengal** 103/3 in 22.5 overs (D Sharma 46, Tanusree Sarkar 40*; Jyoti Giri 2-17) by seven wickets.

VCA Kalamna, Nagpur, April 9: Baroda 222/8 in 50 overs (Yastika Bhatia 82, Hrutu Patel 69; Renuka Singh 3-32, Sushmita Kumari 2-39) lost to **Himachal Pradesh** 223/6 in 48.1 overs (Tanuja Kanwer 64, Chitra Singh Jamwal 44; Radha Yadav 3-49, Gayatri Naik 2-23) by four wickets.

VCA, Civil Lines, Nagpur, April 10: Mumbai 273/6 in 50 overs (Jemimah Rodrigues 140*, Manjiri Gawade 39; Devyani Prasad 2-46) beat **Jharkhand** 200 in 46 overs (Indrani Roy 91, Ritu 30; Manali Dakshini 2-19, Saniya Raut 2-38) by 73 runs.

VCA Kalamna, Nagpur, April 10: Delhi 187/9 in 50 overs (Arushi Goel 45, Simran Dil Bahadur 30; Sahana Pawar 3-18, Monica Patel 2-41) beat **Karnataka** 145 in 49.1 overs (Simren Henry 46, D Vrinda 34; SD Bahadur 5-24, Ria Sharma 3-25) by 42 runs.

Bengal, Himachal Pradesh, Mumbai, Delhi qualified for the semi-finals

Semi-finals

VCA, Civil Lines, Nagpur, April 12: Bengal 203/9 in 50 overs (Deepti Sharma 57, Richa 44; Sonia Lohiya 4-41, Madhu 2-37) beat **Delhi** 146/9 in 50 overs (Neha Chhillar 41, Ayushi Soni 38; Sushmita Ganguly 3-16, Nisha Maji 2-24) by 57 runs.

VCA Kalamna, Nagpur, April 12: Mumbai 263/4 in 50 overs (Jemimah Rodrigues 185*, Vrushali Nhagat 40) beat **Himachal Pradesh** 125 in 36.2 overs (Harleen Deol 21; Saniya Raut 5-19, Jagravi Pawar 2-26) by 138 runs.

Bengal and Mumbai qualified for the final

Final

VCA, Civil Lines, Nagpur, April 14: Mumbai 179 in 49.1 overs (Jemimah Rodrigues 55, Vrushali Bhagat 40; Deepti Sharma 3-35, Tanusree Sarkar 2-26) lost to **Bengal** 181/8 in 44 overs (D Sharma 105*, T Sarkar 33; Saniya Raut 5-34) by two wickets.

Winners: Bengal

2017-18

North Zone

Chaudhary Bansi Lal Cricket Stadium, Lahli, February 23: Himachal Pradesh 180 in 49.4 overs (Kashish Verma 42, Tanuja Kanwer 40; PD Sharma 3-28, Sheetal Rana 3-34) beat **Haryana** 113 in 43.5 overs (Shivangi 27, Shafali Verma 25; Nikita Chauhan 5-16, Susmita Kumari 2-14) by 67 runs.

Virender Sehwag Cricket Academy Ground, Jhajjar, February 23: Delhi 246/7 in 50 overs (Priya Punia 124*, Arushi Goel 31; Bushra Ashraf 3-31, Aditi Aryan 2-21) beat **Jammu & Kashmir** 117 in 38.1 overs (Rubia Syed 42; Kirti Arya 4-25, Ayushi Soni 2-10) by 129 runs.

Chaudhary Bansi Lal Cricket Stadium, Lahli, February 25: Delhi 102 in 48.5 overs (Tanuja Kanwer 3-11, Renuka Singh 2-28) lost to **Himachal Pradesh** 105/6 in 25.5 overs (Nikita Chauhan 53, Harleen Deol 22; Sonia Lohiya 2-14, Ayushi Soni 2-20) by four wickets.

Virender Sehwag Cricket Academy Ground, Jhajjar, February 25: Jammu & Kashmir 80 in 41.4 overs (Neelam Bisht 4-21, Sunita Rani 3-10) lost to **Punjab** 81/1 in 24.3 overs (Manisha Badha 28*, Priya Kumari 27*) by nine wickets.

Chaudhary Bansi Lal Cricket Stadium, Lahli, February 27: Haryana 120 in 45.1 overs (Sheetal Rana 46, PD Sharma 20; Rubia Syed 3-17, Sapna Jamwal 3-17) beat **Jammu & Kashmir** 50 in 24.5 overs (Suman Gulia 3-17, Urvashi Saini 2-12) by 70 runs.

Virender Sehwag Cricket Academy Ground, Jhajjar, February 27: Punjab 76 in 26.4 overs (Sonia Lohiya 5-14, Kirti Arya 2-5) lost to **Delhi** 78/4 in 37.2 overs (Ayushi Soni 22*; Amanjot Kaur 2-20) by six wickets.

Chaudhary Bansi Lal Cricket Stadium, Lahli, March 1: Haryana 59 in 35.3 overs (Sunita Rani 4-0, Amanjot Kaur 2-14) lost to **Punjab** 60/2 in 18.1 overs (Taniya Bhatia 26*) by eight wickets.

Virender Sehwag Cricket Academy Ground, Jhajjar, March 1: Himachal Pradesh 295/4 in 50 overs (Harleen Deol 119, Tanuja Kanwer 55*; Bismah Hassan 2-35) beat **Jammu & Kashmir** 74 in 41.2 overs (Sapna Jamwal 20; T Kanwer 5-4, Susmita Kumari 2-13) by 221 runs.

Virender Sehwag Cricket Academy Ground, Jhajjar, March 3: Himachal Pradesh 100 in 36.1 overs (Tanuja Kanwer 31, Harleen Deol 23; Bharti Bawa 4-12, Sunita Rani 2-7) lost to **Punjab** 101/7 in 48 overs (Susmita Kumari 3-25, H Deol 2-15) by three wickets.

Chaudhary Bansi Lal Cricket Stadium, Lahli, March 3: Haryana 132/8 in 50 overs (Suman Gulia 49*; Sonia Lohiya 4-20) beat **Delhi** 121 in 48.4 overs (Laxmi Yadav 43*, Pratika Rawal 22; Priya Khatkar 5-25, PD Sharma 2-15) by 11 runs.

North Zone points table

Team	M	W	L	T	N/R	Pts	NRR
Himachal Pradesh	4	3	1	0	0	12	+1.898
Punjab	4	3	1	0	0	12	+0.568
Delhi	4	2	2	0	0	8	+0.474
Haryana	4	2	2	0	0	8	-0.324
Jammu & Kashmir	4	0	4	0	0	0	-2.647

Zone winners: Himachal Pradesh

Central Zone

Shaheed Veer Narayan Singh International Cricket Stadium (SVNS stadium), Naya Raipur, February 23: Vidarbha 177 in 48.1 overs (LM Inamdar 32, Krutika Pophali 26; Garima Janghel 4-25, Shivi Pandey 2-30) lost to **Chhattisgarh** 180/2 in 45.2 overs (S Pandey 101*, Shilpa Sahu 31) by eight wickets.

Bhilai Steel Plant Cricket Club Ground, Bhilai, February 23: Uttar Pradesh 137 in 46 overs (Sweta Verma 26, Shashi Mathur 23; Priti Yadav 3-22, Priyanka Koushal 2-18) lost to **Madhya Pradesh** 138/4 in 42.5 overs (Nikita Singh 57, Soniya Sharma 22) by six wickets.

Shaheed Veer Narayan Singh International Cricket Stadium, Naya Raipur, February 24: Chhattisgarh 83 in 43 overs (Shivi Pandey 33, Deepika Tiwari 21; SS Kalal 3-17, Rinku Tank 2-26) lost to **Rajasthan** 85/2 in 32.2 overs (SR Jat 34*, Sangeeta Kumawat 24*) by eight wickets.

Bhilai Steel Plant Cricket Club Ground, Bhilai, February 24: Railways 250/9 in 50 overs (Sarika Koli 63, Neha Badwaik 42; Krutika Pophali 2-44) beat **Vidarbha** 106 in 32.3 overs (LM Inamdar 35; S Koli 3-8, Suchi Kaushik 3-31) by 144 runs.

SVNS stadium, Naya Raipur, February 25: Railways 228/6 in 50 overs (Neha Badwaik 48, V Sneha Deepthi 42; Charu Joshi 3-49, Priti Yadav 2-39) beat **Madhya Pradesh** 75 in 31.4 overs (Soniya Sharma 31; Suchi Kaushik 3-18, Sarika Koli 2-6) by 153 runs.

Bhilai Steel Plant Cricket Club Ground, Bhilai, February 25: Uttar Pradesh 208/7 in 50 overs (Anjali Singh 53, Shobha Devi 48; Suman Meena 2-34) beat **Rajasthan** 160 in 50 overs (Tanuja Vaishnav 43*, JU Bijarnya 25; Arju 2-24, Kshama 2-38) by 48 runs.

SVNS stadium, Naya Raipur, February 26: Railways 257/7 in 50 overs (Arundhati Reddy 57*, V Sneha Deepthi 50; Pratigya Singh 2-40) beat **Chhattisgarh** 124/7 in 50 overs (Shivi Pandey 58, P Singh 27*) by 133 runs.

Bhilai Steel Plant Cricket Club Ground, Bhilai, February 26: Madhya Pradesh 100 in 47.2 overs (Gargi Wankar 2-5, Vaishnavi Khandkar 2-14) lost to **Vidarbha** 101/5 in 37 overs (LM Inamdar 28, Bharati Fulmali 23; Charu Joshi 2-10) by five wickets.

SVNS stadium, Naya Raipur, February 28: Vidarbha 166/9 in 50 overs (Disha Kasat 43, Bharati Fulmali 31; Anjali Singh 2-12, Rashi Kanojiya 2-21) lost to **Uttar Pradesh** 167/8 in 48.4 overs (Aditi Sharma 85*; Krutika Pophali 2-29, Nupur Kohale 2-34) by two wickets.

SVNS stadium, Naya Raipur, March 1: Railways 226/9 in 50 overs (Neha Badwaik 77, Anita Lodhi 51; Sofi Sidhu 3-49) beat **Rajasthan** 49 in 30.5 overs (JU Bijarnya 20; Arundhati Reddy 5-10, Sarika Koli 3-6) by 177 runs.

Bhilai Steel Plant Cricket Club Ground, Bhilai, March 1: Chhattisgarh 142/3 in 50 overs (Kajal Meshram 49*, Manpreet Kaur 41*; Priti Yadav 2-16) lost to **Madhya Pradesh** 144/3 in 37.2 overs (Tamanna Nigam 57*, Tarang Jha 50; Mamta Bhagat 2-16) by seven wickets.

SVNS stadium, Naya Raipur, March 2: Uttar Pradesh 192/8 in 50 overs (Aditi Sharma

The gap between the traditionally strong teams and the rest of the field has been closing. — *UPCA*

90*, Ekta Singh 49; Meghana Sabbineni 3-33, Arundhati Reddy 2-33) lost to **Railways** 193/7 in 46.3 overs (M Sabbineni 69, V Sneha Deepthi 49; Anshu Tiwari 3-29, Anjali Singh 2-38) by seven wickets.

Bhilai Steel Plant Cricket Club Ground, Bhilai, March 2: Rajasthan 156 in 47.4 overs ((Aditi Garg 59, Suman Meena 51; Vaishanvi Khandkar 3-44, Gargi Wankar 2-27) lost to **Vidarbha** 157/1 in 35.4 overs (Disha Kasat 80*, V Khandkar 50*) by nine wickets.

SVNS stadium, Naya Raipur, March 3: Uttar Pradesh 165 in 48.3 overs (Aditi Sharma 35, Shobha Devi 33; Mamta Bhagat 2-28) beat **Chhattisgarh** 160/8 in 50 overs (Shivi Pandey 58, Deepika Tiwari 39; Rashi Kanojiya 2-24, Anshu Tiwari 2-26) by two wickets.

Bhilai Steel Plant Cricket Club Ground, Bhilai, March 3: Rajasthan 90 in 44 overs (Suman Meena 20; Priti Yadav 2-6, Saloni Dangore 2-6) lost to **Madhya Pradesh** 91/6 in 30.1 overs (Nikita Singh 33, Tamanna Nigam 26; MS Gurjar 3-13, Sofi Sidhu 2-33) by four wickets.

Central Zone points table

Team	M	W	L	T	N/R	Pts	NRR
Railways	5	5	0	0	0	20	+2.498
Uttar Pradesh	5	3	2	0	0	12	+0.081
Madhya Pradesh	5	3	2	0	0	12	-0.340
Vidarbha	5	2	3	0	0	8	-0.321
Chhattisgarh	5	1	4	0	0	4	-0.961
Rajasthan	5	1	4	0	0	4	-1.220

Zone winners: Railways

West Zone

Western Railway Ground, Rajkot, February 23: Gujarat 197/7 in 50 overs (Renuka Chaudhari 63, Hani Patel 32; Kesha Patel 3-26, Jaya Mohite 3-30) beat **Baroda** 62 in 24.1 overs (Hrutvisha Patel 33; Krutika Chaudhari 5-18) by 135 runs.

SCA Stadium, Rajkot, February 23: Saurashtra 111 in 45.2 overs (Pooja Nimavat 53; Saniya Raut 3-14, Manali Dakshini 3-35) lost to **Mumbai** 112/1 in 26.5 overs (Hemali Borwankar 57*, Sejal Raut 24) by nine wickets.

Western Railway Ground, Rajkot, February 24: Mumbai 245/7 in 50 overs (Sayali Satghare 78, Prakashika Naik 40; Tanvir Shaikh 2-36, Jaya Mohite 2-45) beat **Baroda** 132 in 43 overs (Hrutvisha Patel 43, J Mohite 22; Manali Dakshini 4-22, P Naik 3-30) by 113 runs.

SCA Stadium, Rajkot, February 24: Gujarat 154/4 in 50 overs (Hani Patel 62*, Krutika Chaudhari 47) lost to **Maharashtra** 155/5 in 37.5 overs (Devika Vaidya 67*, Priyanka Ghodke 35; TD Patel 2-37) by five wickets.

Western Railway Ground, February 26: Saurashtra 86/9 in 50 overs (Reta Patel 3-20, Renuka Chaudhari 2-9) lost to **Gujarat** 87/6 in 29 overs (P Modhwadia 2-17) by four wickets.

SCA Stadium, Rajkot, February 26: Maharashtra 233/7 in 50 overs (Devika Vaidya 69, Mukta Magre 57; Nancy Patel 3-41, Ridhi Maurya 2-44) beat **Baroda** 184/6 in 50 overs (Hrutvisha Patel 73, N Patel 27*) by 49 runs.

Western Railway Ground, Rajkot, February 27: Mumbai 231/4 in 50 overs (Jemimah Rodrigues 73, Fatima Jaffer 50*; Aditi Gaikwad 2-48) beat **Maharashtra** 160 in 42.2 overs (Tejal Hasabnis 38, Devika Vaidya 28; Saima Thakor 4-48, Manali Dakshini 2-21) by 71 runs.

SCA Stadium, Rajkot, February 27: Baroda 204/9 in 50 overs (Amrita Joseph 73, P Modhwadia 3-29, Pooja Nimavat 2-30) beat **Saurashtra** 119/5 in 50 overs (Riddhi Ruparel 26, Megha Chauhan 23; Ridhi Maurya 2-24) by 85 runs.

Western Railway Ground, Rajkot, March 1: Maharashtra 287/2 in 50 overs (Tejal Hasabnis 117*, Devika Vaidya 108; M Tanna 2-33) beat **Saurashtra** 116 in 41.3 overs (Riddhi Ruparel 25; Maya Sonawane 3-12, Mukta Magre 3-16) by 171 runs.

SCA Stadium, Rajkot, March 1: Mumbai 176 in 49.5 overs (Fatima Jaffer 50, Shaheen 37; Renuka Chaudhari 2-23, Krutika Chaudhari 2-34) beat **Gujarat** 105/9 in 50 overs (R Chaudhari 50; Saniya Raut 5-12) by 71 runs.

West Zone points table

Team	M	W	L	T	N/R	Pts	NRR
Mumbai	4	4	0	0	0	16	+1.780
Maharashtra	4	3	1	0	0	12	+1.020
Gujarat	4	2	2	0	0	8	+0.483
Baroda	4	1	3	0	0	4	-1.060
Saurashtra	4	0	4	0	0	0	-2.268

Zone winners: Mumbai

South Zone

Army Ordinance Centre Cricket Ground, Secunderabad, February 23: Hyderabad 137 in 48.1 overs (G Trisha 39, Doli Ramya 32; P Sourabhya 4-23, Keerthy James 3-22) lost to **Kerala** 139/7 in 48.1 overs (IV Drishya 76*; Bhogi Shravani 4-13, V Lakshmi Prasanna 3-23) by three wickets.

Nuclear Fuel Complex Cricket Ground, Hyderabad, February 23: Andhra 153/8 in 50 overs (N Anusha 30; L Nethra Iyer 3-31, KN Ramyashri 2-8) lost to **Tamil Nadu** 154/2 in 34.3 overs (Hemalatha Dayalan 88*, LN Iyer 39) by eight wickets.

Electronic Corporation of India Limited (ECIL) Ground, Hyderabad, February 23: Karnataka 100 in 37.2 overs (Rameshwari Gayakwad 33, G Divya 30; Diksha Gawde 3-15, Rakshanda Pilankar 2-5) lost to **Goa** 102/8 in 42.2 overs (Sanjula Naik 29, Purvaja 26; Sahana Pawar 4-29, G Divya 2-25) by two wickets.

ECIL Ground, Hyderabad, February 24: Tamil Nadu 204/4 in 50 overs (L Nethra Iyer 108*, Hemalatha Dayalan 58) lost to **Kerala** 205/9 in 48.5 overs (Sajeevan Sajana 72*, Jipsa Joseph 34; H Dayalan 3-38, KN Ramyashri 2-27) by one wicket.

Nuclear Fuel Complex Cricket Ground, Hyderabad, February 24: Hyderabad 220 in 48.3 overs (Rachna Kumar 65, Pranathi Reddy 45; Sanjula Naik 3-30, Diksha Gawde 2-43) beat **Goa** 96 in 25.4 overs (S Naik 54; R Kumar 3-5, V Lakshmi Prasanna 3-19) by 124 runs.

Army Ordinance Centre Cricket Ground, Secunderabad, February 24: Andhra 229/5 in 50 overs (K Anjali Sarvani 82*, N Anusha 62; C Pratyusha 2-25, G Divya 2-59) beat **Karnataka** 84 in 34.2 overs (K Dhatri 4-37, E Padmaja 2-6) by 145 runs.

ECIL Ground, Hyderabad, February 26: Andhra 114 in 49.1 overs (N Anusha 49; Keerthy James 4-30, P Sourabhya 3-15) beat **Kerala** 89 in 35.4 overs (Sajeevan Sajana 44, A Akshaya 22; CH Jhansi Lakshmi 4-20, G Chandralekha 2-10) by 25 runs.

Nuclear Fuel Complex Cricket Ground, Hyderabad, February 26: Karnataka 158 in 46.3 overs (G Divya 76; Bhogi Shravani 3-26, G Trisha 3-27) beat **Hyderabad** 97 in 40.2 overs (Sneha More 25; Sahana Pawar 3-20) by 61 runs.

Army Ordinance Centre Cricket Ground, Secunderabad, February 26: Goa 124 in 38.3 overs (Vinavi Gurav 40, Vanita Bhandari 23; Hemalatha Dayalan 3-11, S Anusha 2-15) lost to **Tamil Nadu** 125/4 in 38 overs (S Anusha 48*, L Nethra Iyer 27; Sanjula Naik 2-39) by six wickets.

Nuclear Fuel Complex Cricket Ground, Hyderabad, February 27: Hyderabad 163 in 45.2 overs (Doli Ramya 60, Rachna Kumar 35; G Chandralekha 5-34, K Dhatri 3-34) lost to **Andhra** 164/3 in 31.2 overs (CH Lhansi Lakshmi 65*, E Padmaja 31*) by seven wickets.

Gymkhana Ground, Hyderabad, February 27: Karnataka 152/9 in 50 overs (D Vrinda 50, Rameshwari Gayakwad 36; Manju Ganesan 2-16) beat **Tamil Nadu** 38 in 26.3 overs (R Gayakwad 4-1, C Pratyusha 2-19) by 114 runs.

Army Ordinance Centre Cricket Ground, Secunderabad, February 27: Goa 107 in 43.1 overs (Sugandha Ghadi 34; Sajeevan Sajana 4-39, Minnu Mani 3-26) lost to **Kerala** 108/5 in 33.5 overs (IV Drishya 32, Jipsa Hoseph 27*; Vanita Bhandari 3-10) by five wickets.

Nuclear Fuel Complex Cricket Ground, Hyderabad, March 1: Andhra 243/5 in 50 overs (N Anusha 108, E Padmaja 39; Pratiksha Gadekar 2-45) beat **Goa** 62 in 29 overs (K Jyoti 3-6, K Anjali Sarvani 3-28) by 181 runs.

Army Ordinance Centre Cricket Ground, Secunderabad, March 1: Kerala 157/9 in 50 overs (Sajeevan Sajana 46, A Akshaya 39; C Pratyusha 4-33) beat **Karnataka** 76 in 29.2 overs (C Pratyusha 20; Minnu Mani 5-12, Keerthy James 3-9) by 81 runs.

Gymkhana Ground, Hyderabad, March 1: Hyderabad 186/9 in 50 overs (Doli Ramya 80, Sneha More 52; Hemalatha Dayalan 3-39, S Anusha 2-22) beat **Tamil Nadu** 165/9 in 50 overs (H Dayalan 49, L Nethra Iyer 45; Rachna Kumar 3-28, Bhogi Shravani 2-26) by 21 runs.

South Zone points Table

Team	M	W	L	T	N/R	Pts	NRR
Andhra	5	4	1	0	0	16	+1.550
Kerala	5	4	1	0	0	16	+0.472
Hyderabad	5	2	3	0	0	8	+0.066
Tamil Nadu	5	2	3	0	0	8	-0.212
Karnataka	5	2	3	0	0	8	-0.291
Goa	5	1	4	0	0	4	-1.562

Zone winners: Andhra

East Zone

Jadavpur University Second Campus Ground, Kolkata, February 23: Assam 140 in 46.5 overs (Kalpana Shoutal 37, Gayatri Gurung 25; Devyani Prasad 2-14, Mamta Paswan 2-20) lost to **Jharkhand** 141/6 in 45.3 overs (Durga Kumari Murmu 45, Ruma Kumari Mahato 42; Kakoli Saikia 4-21) by four wickets.

Eden Gardens, Kolkata, February 23: Tripura 119/8 in 50 overs (Jhumki Debnath 48, Shiuli Chakraborty 22; Shrayosi Aich 4-19) lost to **Bengal** 120/4 in 33.3 overs (Prativa Rana 37, Tanusree Sarkar 31*; MK Rabidas 2-22) by six wickets.

Eden Gardens, Kolkata, February 25: Assam 118/9 in 50 overs (Sapna Choudhary 53; Saika Ishaque 3-27) lost to **Bengal** 121/2 in 30.1 overs (Tanusree Sarkar 55*, Richa 41*) by eight wickets.

Jadavpur University Second Campus Ground, Kolkata, February 25: Odisha 170/7 in 50 overs (Sumitra Sahoo 40*, Sasmita Mahalik 30; Devyani Prasad 2-23) beat **Jharkhand** 73 in 29 overs (Reemalaxmi Ekka 3-16, Louisa Dash 2-7) by 97 runs.

Jadavpur University Second Campus Ground, Kolkata, February 27: Tripura 175/5 in 50 overs (Rizu Saha 68*, Suravi Roy 22; Urmila Chatterjee 2-22) beat **Assam** 120 in 43.3 overs (Papori Gogoi 37, Kalpana Shoutal 21; Sweety Sinha 3-22, MK Rabidas 2-18) by 55 runs.

Eden Gardens, Kolkata, February 27: Odisha 157 in 49.4 overs (Sushree Dibyadarshini 70, Sangeeta Khadia 50; Tanusree Sarkar 4-33, Nisha Maji 2-21) lost to **Bengal** 158/4 in 40 overs (T Sarkar 63*, Richa 34; S Dibyadarshini 3-42) by six wickets.

Jadavpur University Second Campus Ground, Kolkata, February 28: Odisha 121 in 44.5 overs (Sumitra Sahoo 29, Sasmita Mahalik 20; Shanti Rai 3-12, Urmila Chatterjee 2-23) beat **Assam** 67 in 23 overs (Sushree Dibyadarshini 5-32, D Janaki Reddy 2-4) by 54 runs.

Eden Gardens, Kolkata, February 28: Jharkhand 155/9 in 50 overs (Devyani Prasad 70*, Ruma Kumari Mahato 24; Suravi Roy 4-27, Sweety Sinha 2-20) lost to **Tripura** 158/8 in 49.4 overs (Rizu Saha 81*, Rita Debbarma 32; Shannti Kumari 3-16) by two wickets.

Eden Gardens, Kolkata, March 3: Bengal 174 in 49.4 overs (Deepti Sharma 40, Aparna Mondal 28; Apurva 4-35, Ritu Kumari 2-14) beat **Jharkhand** 96 in 47.3 overs (Priyanka Sawaiyan 27, Durga Kumari Murmu 22*; Saika Ishaque 2-3, Shrayosi Aich 2-10) by 78 runs.

Jadavpur University Second Campus Ground, Kolkata, March 3: Tripura 139 in 48.2 overs (Rizu Saha 60, Rita Debbarma 39; Rajashree Swain 4-21, Louisa Dash 3-31) beat **Odisha** 137/9 in 50 overs (Sushree Dibyadarshini 24, Silpa Swain 22*; Gangati Tripura 2-21, R Debbarma 2-26) by two runs.

East Zone points table

Team	M	W	L	T	N/R	Pts	NRR
Bengal	4	4	0	0	0	16	+1.263
Tripura	4	3	1	0	0	12	+0.061
Odisha	4	2	2	0	0	8	+0.633
Jharkhand	4	1	3	0	0	4	-0.837
Assam	4	0	4	0	0	0	-0.951

Zone winners: Bengal

Under-23 One-Day Challenger Trophy

Shafali, Arundhati impress

Priya Punia's consistency caught the eye of the national selectors.

Devika Vaidya's India Blue defeated India Green in the final by five wickets to maintain a clean slate in the inaugural Under-23 Challenger Trophy. Having won the toss, India Green elected to bat, but failed to find any momentum in their innings as India Blue's bowlers chipped away. Shafali Verma's 32-ball 40 on a deteriorating surface guided the chase of 118.

Verma's knock meant she finished at the top of the batting charts with 114 runs, beating out Priya Punia of India Green who scored 110 runs. Her tournament strike rate of 139.02 was head and shoulders above the rest.

In conditions where the batters struggled, only Nuzhat Parween and Punia managed half centuries. Arundhati Reddy, the fast bowler from India Red, attacked the stumps on the slow, low surfaces in Ranchi, forcing the batters to play at every delivery and using her out-swinger to good effect. Her figures of 4 for 25 against India Blue was the best in the tournament, but her efforts were not enough to give India Red a single win.

Most runs: Shafali Verma (India Blue) (114 runs in 3 matches)
Most wickets: Arundhati Reddy (India Red) (7 wickets in 2 matches)

Jharkhand State Cricket Association International Stadium Complex, Ranchi, April 20: **India Red** 149 in 49.5 overs (Harleen Deol 46, Rizu Saha 21; Simran Dil Bahadur 2-20, Tanuja Kanwer 2-23) lost to **India Blue** 152/7 in 45.2 overs (Nuzhat Parween 51, Shafali Verma 37; Arundhati Reddy 4-25) by three wickets.
Jharkhand State Cricket Association International Stadium Complex, Ranchi, April 21: **India Green** 185/6 in 50 overs (Priya Punia 48, S Anusha 41*; Tanusree Sarkar 2-29, Tanuja Kanwer 2-34) lost to **India Blue** 186/6 in 47.4 overs (Simran Dil Bahadur 42*, Vrushali Bhagat 40; Radha Yadav 3-38) by four wickets.
Jharkhand State Cricket Association International Stadium Complex, Ranchi, April 22: **India Green** 195/9 in 50 overs (Priya Punia 52, Shivali Shinde 39; Arundhati Reddy 3-21, CH Jhansi Lakshmi 2-43) beat **India Red** 100 in 31.4 overs (R Kalpana 25; Sushree Dibyadarshini 3-13, K Anjali Sarvani 2-17) by 95 runs.

Points table

Team	M	W	L	T	N/R	Pts	NRR
India Blue	2	2	0	0	0	8	+0.294
India Green	2	1	1	0	0	4	+0.872
India Red	2	0	2	0	0	0	-1.150

India Blue and India Green qualified for the final

Final

Jharkhand State Cricket Association International Stadium Complex, Ranchi, April 24: India Green 117 in 44 overs (Radha Yadav 23, Yastika Bhatia 20; Tanusree Sarakar 2-17, Devika Vaidya 2-17) lost to **India Blue** 120/5 in 28.4 overs (Shafali Verma 40, Nuzhat Parween 20; R Yadav 2-30) by five wickets.

Winners: India Blue

Under-19 Inter-State T20 Tournament

Shobha Devi, Anjali Singh power UP

Uttar Pradesh claimed the inaugural edition of the Under-19 Inter-State Twenty20 championship defeating Andhra by 18-runs in the final in Guntur. Shobha Devi, the opening batter, and Anjali Singh were Uttar Pradesh's best performers with bat and ball, topping the charts with 404 runs and 20 wickets, respectively. The pair were well complemented by Muskan Malik (378 runs), Rishika Yadav and Sonam Yadav (both 13 wickets). Sonam's tally included a crucial three-wicket haul in the final.

Bowlers kept a tight leash on proceedings through much of the tournament, with team scores generally hovering between the 80-90-run mark. The 200-run barrier was crossed five times. However, teams chasing generally struggled to get anything beyond 100 runs: 122 was the highest total batting second, while 113 for 3 from Bengal was the highest successful chase.

It was not all doom and gloom for the batters, however, with four centuries in the tournament. Amanjot Kaur, the right-hander from Punjab, reached a high of 121 not out.

Other notable performances included Sayali Satghare's 6 for 2 for Mumbai against Manipur, IV Drishya's 385 runs at an average of 96 for Kerala, Andhra's mauling of Sikkim by 199 runs, and Tejashwini Duragad's tally of 14 wickets in six matches for Goa.

Most runs: Shobha Devi (Uttar Pradesh) (404 runs in 11 matches)
Most wickets: Anjali Singh (Uttar Pradesh) (20 wickets in 11 matches)

Group A

ACA Women's Academy, Guntur, October 14: Punjab 95/8 in 20 overs (Kanika Ahuja 43, Raman Preet Kaur 22; Lakshmi Prasanna 2-14) beat **Hyderabad** 91/6 in 20 overs (Trisha Poojitha 22, G Trisha 21; Raman Preet Kaur 2-13, K Ahuja 2-14) by four runs.

J Narendranath ACA Cricket Ground, Perecherla, October 14: Meghalaya 91/4 in 20 overs (Hajong 28*) lost to **Sikkim** 80/5 in 18.3 overs (Pretika Chettri 21, Tshering Yangden Lepcha 20; Deiphi 2-11, Thymmei 2-15) by one run. (VJD method).

ACA Women's Academy, Guntur, October 14: Andhra v **Gujarat**. Match abandoned without a ball being bowled.

J Narendranath ACA Cricket Ground, Perecherla, October 15: Gujarat 138/2 in 20 overs (Anjali Patel 43, Aruja Wadhwa 40) beat **Meghalaya** 35/9 in 20 overs (Devanshi Prajapati 3-6, HR Solanki 2-4) by 103 runs.

ACA Women's Academy, Guntur, October 15: Tamil Nadu 192/3 in 20 overs (C Shushanthika 87, SB Keerthana 43) beat **Sikkim** 33 in 14.4 overs (A Eloksi 3-7) by 159 runs.

ACA Women's Academy, Guntur, October 15: Andhra v **Punjab**. Match abandoned without a ball being bowled.

J Narendranath ACA Cricket Ground, Perecherla, October 17: Gujarat 65/8 in 20 overs (Parul 3-12, Nandani Sharma 2-5) lost to **Punjab** 66/2 in 14.3 overs (Amanjot Kaur 36*,

Uttar Pradesh topped the individual charts for batting and bowling on their way to the Under-19 T20 title. — *UPCA*

Kanika Ahuja 24*) by eight wickets.

ACA Women's Academy, Guntur, October 17: Andhra 198/1 in 20 overs (V Pushpa Latha 84, E Padmaja 55*) beat **Meghalaya** 13/6 in 11 overs (G Sindhuja 3-0, k Dhatri 2-4) by 116 runs. (VJD method).

ACA Women's Academy, Guntur, October 17: Hyderabad 72/2 in 8 overs (G Trisha 40, Trisha Poojitha 27; SB Keerthana 2-16) beat **Tamil Nadu** 27/7 in 8 overs (G Trisha 2-6) by 45 runs.

ACA Women's Academy, Guntur, October 18: Andhra 112/4 in 17 overs (V Pushpa Latha 39, A Sireesha 24*) v **Hyderbad**. Match abandoned.

J Narendranath ACA Cricket Ground, Perecherla, October 18: Punjab v **Sikkim**. Match abandoned without a ball bowled.

ACA Women's Academy, Guntur, October 18: Meghalaya 25 in 11.5 overs (KN Ramyashri 3-3, Ramya Rajaram 2-4) lost to **Tamil Nadu** 26/1 in 5.3 overs by nine wickets.

J Narendranath ACA Cricket Ground, Perecherla, October 20: Tamil Nadu 74/9 in 20 overs (Saranya Gadwal 2-16) lost **Andhra** 76/1 in 11.3 overs (V Pushpa Latha 32*, E Padmaja 26*) by nine wickets.

ACA Women's Academy, Guntur, October 20: Gujarat 118/6 in 20 overs (PA Talpada 26*, Muskan Vasava 21; Nur Pandi Lepcha 2-16) beat **Sikkim** 29/7 in 20 overs (Ruhita Thaker 2-2) by 89 runs.

ACA Women's Academy, Guntur, October 20: Hyderabad 221/5 in 20 overs (G Trisha 49, Trisha Poojitha 48; Thymmei 2-38, Dasan 2-40) beat **Meghalaya** 23 in 15.3 overs (Yashasri 3-1, Vanka Pooja 2-5) by 198 runs.

J Narendranath ACA Cricket Ground, Perecherla, October 21: Sikkim 20 in 13.1 overs (Vanka Pooja 3-6, G Trisha 2-2) lost to **Hyderabad** 21/0 in 3.1 overs by 10 wickets.

ACA Women's Academy, Guntur, October 21: Punjab 203/4 in 20 overs (Amanjot Kaur 121*, Gazala Naj 39) beat **Meghalaya** 35/5 in 20 overs (Nandani Sharma 2-5) by 168 runs.

ACA Women's Academy, Guntur, October 21: Gujarat 86/7 in 20 overs (Itisha Patel 28) lost to **Tamil Nadu** 91/6 in 19.2 overs (SB Keerthana 25; Aruja Wadhwa 2-14) by four wickets.

J Narendranath ACA Cricket Ground, Perecherla, October 23: Gujarat 83/7 in 20 overs beat **Hyderabad** 72 in 18.2 overs (Keerthi Reddy 23; SD Jani 3-15) by 11 runs.

ACA Women's Academy, Guntur, October 23: Punjab 114/8 in 20 overs (Srishti Rajput 42, Amanjot Kaur 39; SB Keerthana 3-23, Meenakshi 2-21) beat **Tamil Nadu** 83 in 17.3 overs (Kanika Ahuja 3-12, Nandani Sharma 2-12) by 31 runs.

ACA Women's Academy, Guntur, October 23: Andhra 207/5 in 20 overs (Saranya Gadwal 72*, V Pushpa Latha 42) beat **Sikkim** 8 in 8.5 overs (S Sailakshmi 5-6, G Sindhuja 3-1) by 199 runs.

Group A points table

Team	M	W	L	T	N/R	Pts	NRR
Punjab	6	4	0	0	2	20	+2.991
Andhra	6	3	0	0	3	18	+7.831
Gujarat	6	3	2	0	1	14	+1.777
Hyderabad	6	3	2	0	1	14	+3.884
Tamil Nadu	6	3	3	0	0	12	+1.230
Sikkim	6	1	4	0	1	6	-5.829
Nagaland	6	0	6	0	0	0	-6.479

Punjab and Andhra qualified for the Super Leagues

Group B

Ravenshaw University Ground 1, Cuttack, October 14: Arunachal Pradesh 23 in 19.4 overs (Ayushi Soni 3-2, Mallika Khatri 2-5) lost to **Delhi** 24/1 in 3 overs by nine wickets.

Nimpur Ground, Cuttack, October 14: Maharashtra 71 in 19.1 overs (Sakshi Kanadi 23; Janhvi Kate 3-12, Sayali Satghare 2-6) lost to **Mumbai** 72/3 in 18.5 overs (Aachal Valanju 20*) by seven wickets.

Ravenshaw University Ground 1, Cuttack, October 14: Manipur 19 in 16.4 overs (Taranna Pradhan 3-4) lost to **Odisha** 23/0 in 4.2 overs by 10 wickets.

Ravenshaw University Ground 1, Cuttack, October 15: Arunachal Pradesh 18 in 13.3 overs (Tanvi Parab 2-0, Savesharvi Suhas 2-3) lost to **Mumbai** 19/1 in 2.5 overs by nine wickets.

Nimpur Ground, Cuttack, October 15: Delhi 184/1 in 20 overs (Ayushi Soni 79*, Trisha Chaudhary 50*) beat **Manipur** 42/4 in 20 overs by 142 runs.

Ravenshaw University Ground 1, Cuttack, October 15: Odisha 93/7 in 20 overs (Rasmita Chinhara 37) beat **Tripura** 27 in 15.4 overs (Taranna Pradhan 2-4) by 66 runs.

Ravenshaw University Ground 1, Cuttack, October 17: Arunachal Pradesh 66/5 in 20 overs (VR Dharani 3-2) lost to **Manipur** 67/2 in 13.2 overs (VR Dharani 27*) by eight wickets.

Nimpur Ground, Cuttack, October 17: Delhi 95/5 in 20 overs (Ayushi Soni 33, Simran Dil Bahadur 20; Janhvi Kate 2-10) beat **Mumbai** 60 in 19.1 overs (Aachal Valanju 21; Priya Mishra 3-11, Shweta Sehrawat 2-3) by 35 runs.

Ravenshaw University Ground 1, Cuttack, October 17: Tripura 58/6 in 20 overs (Aditi Gaikwad 2-9) lost to **Maharashtra** 61/5 in 16.2 overs (SS Kanadi 22; Puja Das 3-8) by five wickets.

Ravenshaw University Ground 1, Cuttack, October 18: Arunachal Pradesh 18 in 18 overs (Aditi Gaikwad 3-2, SB Waghmode 3-4) lost to **Maharashtra** 21/0 in 2 overs by 10 wickets.

Nimpur Ground, Cuttack, October 18: Tripura 114/3 in 20 overs (Ambika Debnath 34, Puja Das 22) beat **Manipur** 39/8 in 20 overs (Antara Das 3-7, Sebika Das 2-8) by 75 runs.

Ravenshaw University Ground 1, Cuttack, October 18: Odisha 92/3 in 20 overs (Poonam Nayak 41*, Subhra Nirjharini Swain 30) beat **Mumbai** 90/8 in 20 overs (Sejal Raut 37; Sonali Hembram 3-13, Kalpana Nayak 2-16) by two runs.

Nimpur Ground, Cuttack, October 20: **Tripura** 123/5 in 20 overs (Puja Das 30, Puja Paul 24) beat **Arunachal Pradesh** 44 in 19.2 overs (Gangati Tripura 4-9, Sebika Das 2-3) by 79 runs.

Ravenshaw University Ground 1, Cuttack, October 20: **Odisha** 92/8 in 20 overs (Kajal Jena 25; Ayushi Soni 2-13, Madhu 2-15) lost to **Delhi** 94/3 in 16.3 overs (A Soni 27*, Mallika Khatri 26) by seven wickets.

Nimpur Ground, Cuttack, October 20: **Maharashtra** 121/7 in 20 overs (Aditi Gaikwad 32, KN Mulla 29; Linthoingambi Rajkumari 4-19) beat **Manipur** 34 in 15.4 overs (Priyanka Ghodke 3-3, A Gaikwad 2-6) by 87 runs.

Nimpur Ground, Cuttack, October 21: **Tripura** 42 in 19.4 overs (Ayushi Soni 3-7, Simran Dil Bahadur 3-8) lost to **Delhi** 43/2 in 8.5 overs (A Soni 24*; Puja Das 2-14) by eight wickets.

Ravenshaw University Ground 1, Cuttack, October 21: **Maharashtra** 88/5 in 20 overs (Priyanka Ghodke 26*; Taranna Pradhan 3-12) lost to **Odisha** 89/3 in 16.3 overs (Subhra Nirjharini Swain 38*) by seven wickets.

Nimpur Ground, Cuttack, October 21: **Mumbai** 184/5 in 20 overs (Sejal Raut 92, Simran Shaikh 30*) beat **Manipur** 9 in 6.3 overs (Sayali Satghare 6-2, Tanvi Parab 2-2) by 175 runs.

Nimpur Ground, Cuttack, October 23: **Odisha** 176/0 in 20 overs (Kajal Jena 108*, Subhra Nirjharini Swain 60*) beat **Arunachal Pradesh** 22 in 19.1 overs (Sonali Hembram 4-2, Kalpana Nayak 2-4) by 154 runs.

Ravenshaw University Ground 1, Cuttack, October 23: **Maharashtra** 60/8 in 20 overs (Neha Bhargava 2-12) lost to **Delhi** 61/3 in 13.4 overs (Ayushi Soni 22*) by seven wickets.

Nimpur Ground, Cuttack, October 23: **Tripura** 71/4 in 20 overs (Ambika Debnath 29; Tanvi Parab 3-22) lost to **Mumbai** 72/2 in 12.4 overs (Sejal Raut 33*, Aachal Valanju 31) by eight wickets.

Group B points table

Team	M	W	L	T	N/R	Pts	NRR
Delhi	6	6	0	0	0	24	+3.451
Odisha	6	5	1	0	0	20	+2.685
Mumbai	6	4	2	0	0	16	+2.302
Maharashtra	6	3	3	0	0	12	+1.246
Tripura	6	2	4	0	0	8	+0.027
Manipur	6	1	5	0	0	4	-4.780
Arunachal Pradesh	6	0	6	0	0	0	-5.438

Delhi and Odisha qualified for the Super Leagues

Group C

HPCA Stadium, Dharamsala, October 14: **Goa** 97/7 in 20 overs (Purvaja Verlekar 36, Tejashwini Duragad 28) beat **Haryana** 95/8 in 20 overs (Shafali Verma 29, Pramila Kumari 23; Shindiya Naik 3-9) by two runs.

Atal Bihari Vajpayee Cricket Stadium, Amtar, October 14: **Kerala** 108/5 in 20 overs (IV Drishya 53*, Jisna Joseph 26; Nancy Sharma 2-26) lost to **Himachal Pradesh** 109/1 in 18.3 overs (SM Singh 46*, Chitra Singh Jamwal 45*) by nine wickets.

HPCA Stadium, Dharamsala, October 14: Nagaland 77/4 in 20 overs (Antima Teotia 32; P Priya 2-21) lost to **Jharkhand** 78/2 in 14.3 overs (Anamika Kumari 26, Jaya 21*) by eight wickets.

HPCA Stadium, Dharamsala, October 15: Jharkhand 91/8 in 20 overs (Anamika Kumari 50*, Sandhya Kumari 21) lost to **Haryana** 92/5 in 14.3 overs (Shafali Verma 68; Anjali Das 3-22) by five wickets.

Atal Bihari Vajpayee Cricket Stadium, Amtar, October 15: Kerala 100/5 in 20 overs (IV Drishya 33*, Sayoojya Salilan 25; Tejashwini Duragad 2-10) beat **Goa** 88/8 in 20 overs (Darasana Mohanan 3-9, Ajanya TP 2-9) by 12 runs.

HPCA Stadium, Dharamsala, October 15: Uttarakhand 141/6 in 20 overs (Ruchi Chauhan 22*; Sapna 2-16) beat **Nagaland** 90/5 in 20 overs (Antima Teotia 23, Reety Biswas 21; Radha Chand 3-11) by 51 runs.

HPCA Stadium, Dharamsala, October 17: Uttarakhand 56/9 in 20 overs (Nancy Sharma 3-20) lost to **Himachal Pradesh** 57/1 in 11.5 overs (SM Singh 32*, Chitra Singh Jamwal 24*) by nine wickets.

Atal Bihari Vajpayee Cricket Stadium, Amtar, October 17: Goa 91/9 in 20 overs (Anjali Das 2-6, Khushbu Kumari 2-11) beat **Jharkhand** 80 in 19 overs (Pratiksha Gautam 21; Tejashwini Duragad 3-17, Poorva Bhaidkar 2-17) by 11 runs.

HPCA Stadium, Dharamsala, October 17: Haryana 98 in 19.2 overs (Tannu Joshi 32, Parmila Kumari 20; Darasana P 2-13, Darasana Mohanan 2-26) lost to **Kerala** 99/3 in 17.2 overs (IV Drishya 27*, Sayoojya Salilan 24) by seven wickets.

HPCA Stadium, Dharamsala, October 18: Goa 80/8 in 20 overs (Purvaja Verlekar 26, Shindiya Naik 20) lost to **Himachal Pradesh** 81/6 in 19.2 overs (Tejashwini Duragad 2-10, Diksha Gawde 2-17) by four wickets.

Atal Bihari Vajpayee Cricket Stadium, Amtar, October 18: Uttarakhand 87/8 in 20 overs (Kanchan Parihar 24; Anjali Das 3-14) tied with **Jharkhand** 87 in 19.5 overs (Anamika Kumari 42; Anjali Goswami 3-14, Nisha Mishra 2-17). Super Over: Jharkhand 1/2 in 0.3 overs lost to Uttarakhand 2/0 in 0.4 overs.

HPCA Stadium, Dharamsala, October 18: Kerala 204/3 in 20 overs (IV Drishya 63, Sayoojya Salilan 53*; Sapna 2-25) beat **Nagaland** 28 in 11 overs (Sandra Suren 5-4, Sourabhya P 2-5) by 176 runs.

HPCA Stadium, Dharamsala, October 20: Goa 123/2 in 20 overs (Tejashwini Duragad 81*) beat **Uttarakhand** 109/6 in 20 overs (Kanchan Parihar 46*, Radha Chand 24; T Duragad 3-28) by 14 runs.

Atal Bihari Vajpayee Cricket Stadium, Amtar, October 20: Nagaland 68 in 18.4 overs (Reety Biswas 31; Suman Hingra 2-5, NB Jangra 2-13) lost to **Haryana** 69/1 in 7.1 overs (Shafali Verma 42*) by nine wickets.

HPCA Stadium, Dharamsala, October 20: Jharkhand 60/9 in 20 overs (Sandhya Kumari 25; VS Fishta 3-7, Nancy Sharma 2-15) lost to **Himachal Pradesh** 63/3 in 14.4 overs (SM Singh 33*) by seven wickets.

HPCA Stadium, Dharamsala, October 21: Uttarakhand 63/6 in 20 overs lost to **Haryana** 64/1 in 8.1 overs (Shafali Verma 26) by nine wickets.

Atal Bihari Vajpayee Cricket Stadium, Amtar, October 21: Jharkhand 68/8 in 20 overs (Sourabhya P 2-9, Aleena Surendran 2-18) lost to **Kerala** 69/8 in 19 overs (Jisna Joseph 23; Manisha Tigga 2-7) by two wickets.

HPCA Stadium, Dharamsala, October 21: Nagaland 26 in 18.4 overs (PG Kahlon 3-6, VS Fishta 2-3) lost to **Himachal Pradesh** 30/0 in 3 overs by 10 wickets.

HPCA Stadium, Dharamsala, October 23: Nagaland 51/8 in 20 overs (Tejashwini Duragad 3-3, Purvaja 2-12) lost to **Goa** 53/1 in 7.1 overs (Purvaja Verlekar 30*) by nine wickets.

Atal Bihari Vajpayee Cricket Stadium, Amtar, October 23: Uttarakhand 98/7 in 20 overs (Raghvi 22, Kanchan Parihar 20) lost to **Kerala** 100/2 in 16.3 overs (IV Drishya 57*, Sayoojya Salilan 37*) by eight wickets.

HPCA Stadium, Dharamsala, October 23: Himachal Pradesh 70 in 18.3 overs (Pooja Negi 20, Sonal Thakur 20; Suman Hingra 3-11, DP Sharma 3-20) beat **Haryana** 67 in 19.5 overs (Natasha Negi 2-12, Nancy Sharma 2-19) by three runs.

Group C points table

Team	M	W	L	T	N/R	Pts	NRR
Himachal Pradesh	6	6	0	0	0	24	+1.386
Kerala	6	5	1	0	0	20	+1.900
Goa	6	4	2	0	0	16	+0.640
Haryana	6	3	3	0	0	12	+1.240
Uttarakhand	6	2	4	0	0	8	-0.782
Jharkhand	6	1	5	0	0	4	-0.376
Nagaland	6	0	6	0	0	0	-5.171

Himachal Pradesh and Kerala qualified for the Super Leagues

Group D

MPCA Cricket Ground 1, Nimkheda, Jabalpur, October 14: Assam 84/7 in 20 overs (Gayatri Gurung 32) lost to **Bengal** 85/4 in 18.2 overs (Ankita Chakraborty 47*; Rashmi Dey 2-16) by six wickets.

MPCA Cricket Ground 2, Nimkheda, Jabalpur, October 14: Bihar 140/6 in 20 overs (Harshita 44*, Sikha Singh 27; Ananya Halder 2-33) beat **Pondicherry** 53/4 in 20 overs (Sumi Dutta 21) by 87 runs.

MPCA Cricket Ground 1, Nimkheda, Jabalpur, October 14: Madhya Pradesh 71 in 19.5 overs (SR Choudhary 2-25) beat **Rajasthan** 46 in 15.2 overs (Anita Choudhary 21*; Sapna Jadhav 3-12, Srashti Nagpure 2-6) by 25 runs.

MPCA Cricket Ground 2, Jabalpur, October 15: Pondicherry 31/8 in 20 overs (Bedashree Borpatragohain 2-4, Gayatri Gurung 2-4) lost to **Assam** 35/1 in 6 overs by nine wickets.

MPCA Cricket Ground 2, Nimkheda, Jabalpur, October 15: Rajasthan 114/3 in 20 overs (Jyoti Choudhary 33*, RS Tinker 30) beat **Vidarbha** 80/8 in 20 overs (ASP Maheshwari 2-11, Suman Meena 2-25) by 34 runs.

MPCA Cricket Ground 1, Nimkheda, Jabalpur, October 15: Madhya Pradesh 81/8 in 20 overs (Shreya Karar 2-14) lost to **Bengal** 82/2 in 16.5 overs (Shara Gujjar 40*, Piyali Ghosh 23*) by eight wickets.

MPCA Cricket Ground 2, Nimkheda, Jabalpur, October 17: Vidarbha 97 in 19.3 overs (Latika Inamdar 36; Tejeshwi 3-13, Rohini Raj 2-15) beat **Bihar** 82/6 in 20 overs (Aachal Shahu 2-16) by 15 runs.

MPCA Cricket Ground 1, Nimkheda, Jabalpur, October 17: Bengal 179/4 in 20 overs (Ankita Chakraborty 68, Santhita Biswas 42; Ananya Halder 2-30, Suni Dutta 2-34) beat **Pondicherry** 34 in 13.2 overs (Piyali Ghosh 4-4) by 145 runs.

MPCA Cricket Ground 1, Nimkheda, Jabalpur, October 17: Madhya Pradesh 77/6 in 20 overs (Reena Yadav 20) lost to **Assam** 80/1 in 12 overs (Gayatri Gurung 42, Uma Chetry 29*) by nine wickets.

MPCA Cricket Ground 2, Nimkheda, Jabalpur, October 18: Pondicherry 47/4 in 20 overs (Ananya Halder 26) lost to **Rajasthan** 50/3 in 11.5 overs (Ayushi Garg 20*) by seven wickets.

MPCA Cricket Ground 2, Nimkheda, Jabalpur, October 18: Madhya Pradesh 115/9 in 20 overs (Sanjana Awase 41; Tanvi Pavitrkar 2-19, Aachal Shahu 2-21) beat **Vidarbha** 59 in 19.3

overs (Latika Inamdar 26; Srashti Nagpure 3-11, Poonam Soni 2-4) by 56 runs.

MPCA Cricket Ground 1, Nimkheda, Jabalpur, October 18: Bihar 82/6 in 20 overs (Shruti 30; Kakoli Saikia 4-10, Bedashree Borpatragohain 2-14) lost to **Assam** 83/9 in 19.4 overs (B Borpatragohain 21; Rohini Raj 3-15, Apurva 2-12) by one wicket.

MPCA Cricket Ground 2, Nimkheda, Jabalpur, October 20: Madhya Pradesh 113/4 in 20 overs (Nitya Tiwari 48*, Reena Yadav 38; Sikha Singh 2-24, Apurva 2-31) beat **Bihar** 74 in 16.3 overs (Harshita 25, Apurva 22; Srashti Nagpure 4-14) by 39 runs.

MPCA Cricket Ground 1, Nimkheda, Jabalpur, October 20: Vidarbha 58/6 in 20 overs lost to **Assam** 59/1 in 9.4 overs (Gayatri Gurung 41*) by nine wickets.

MPCA Cricket Ground 1, Nimkheda, Jabalpur, October 20: Rajasthan 75/5 in 20 overs (Jyoti Choudhary 27*, Ayushi Garg 21; Priyanka Sarkar 3-13) lost to **Bengal** 76/3 in 16.2 overs (Dhara Gujjar 33*, Mamata 21*) by seven wickets.

MPCA Cricket Ground 2, Nimkheda, Jabalpur, October 21: Pondicherry 36 in 19.4 overs (Nitya Tiwari 5-11, Srashti Nagpure 2-10) lost to **Madhya Pradesh** 39/4 in 7 overs (Divya Shanmugam 2-13) by six wickets.

MPCA Cricket Ground 2, Nimkheda, Jabalpur, October 21: Vidarbha 48 in 19.5 overs (Sushmita Ganguly 4-9, Piyali Ghosh 2-13) lost to **Bengal** 49/0 in 7.3 overs (Ankita Chakraborty 31*) by 10 wickets.

MPCA Cricket Ground 1, Nimkheda, Jabalpur, October 21: Rajasthan 91/5 in 20 overs (Jyoti Choudhary 28*, AR Choudhary 22; Dipa Kumari 2-16) beat **Bihar** 72/7 in 20 overs (Apurva 21*; AK Choudhary 2-12) by 19 runs.

MPCA Cricket Ground 1, Nimkheda, Jabalpur, October 23: Rajasthan 100/9 in 20 overs (AK Garg 42) beat **Assam** 93/8 in 20 overs (Bedashree Borpatragohain 33*, Rashmi Dey 27; Pooja Choudhary 2-12, Suman Meena 2-16) by seven runs.

MPCA Cricket Ground 2, Nimkheda, Jabalpur, October 23: Vidarbha 173/2 in 20 overs (Latika Inamdar 103*, MS Bodkhe 21) beat **Pondicherry** 55/9 in 20 overs (Janhvi Ranganathan 3-6, Monika Gohate 2-5) by 118 runs.

MPCA Cricket Ground 1, Nimkheda, Jabalpur, October 23: Bengal 156/4 in 20 overs (Ankita Chakraborty 51, Mamata 28*) beat **Bihar** 58 in 19.5 overs (Puja Rajak 3-21, Mouli Mondal 2-4) by 98 runs.

Group D points table

Team	M	W	L	T	N/R	Pts	NRR
Bengal	6	6	0	0	0	24	+3.167
Assam	6	4	2	0	0	16	+1.310
Madhya Pradesh	6	4	2	0	0	16	+1.172
Rajasthan	6	4	2	0	0	16	+0.483
Vidarbha	6	2	4	0	0	8	-0.587
Bihar	6	1	5	0	0	4	-0.722
Pondicherry	6	0	6	0	0	0	-5.128

Bengal and Assam qualified for the Super Leagues

Group E

SCA Stadium, Rajkot, October 14: Chhattisgarh 87/6 in 20 overs (Manpreet Kaur 34; Ridhi Maurya 2-9, Jaya Mohite 2-18) lost to **Baroda** 93/1 in 15.5 overs (Hrutvisha Patel 54*, Amrita Joseph 31*) by nine wickets.

SCA Stadium Khanderi B Ground, Rajkot, October 14: Karnataka 141/3 in 20 overs (Shishira Gowda 52, D Vrinda 46*) beat **Saurashtra** 65 in 18.5 overs (Tanya Rao 22; D Vrinda 2-15, Anagha M 2-16) by 76 runs.

SCA Stadium, Rajkot, October 14: Jammu & Kashmir 116/4 in 20 overs (Iqra Rasool 37; Srilekha Roy 2-10) beat **Mizoram** 52 in 16 overs (Sagarika Sengupta 28; Rehana Bano 3-7, I Rasool 2-7) by 64 runs.

SCA Stadium, Rajkot, October 15: Karnataka 94/5 in 20 overs (D Vrinda 34*, Niki Prasad 22; Manpreet Kaur 2-14) beat **Chhattisgarh** 56/9 in 20 overs (Anagha M 2-12, D Vrinda 2-16) by 38 runs.

SCA Stadium Khanderi B Ground, Rajkot, October 15: Uttar Pradesh 159/2 in 20 overs (Shobha Devi 78, Muskan Malik 65*) beat **Saurashtra** 65/5 in 20 overs (Tanya Rao 30*; Pratibha Bharti 2-7, Anjali Singh 2-13) by 94 runs.

SCA Stadium, Rajkot, October 15: Baroda 185/1 in 20 overs (Hrutvisha Patel 110*, Amrita Joseph 57*) beat **Mizoram** 33 in 19.4 overs (Jaya Mohite 4-7) by 152 runs.

SCA Stadium, Rajkot, October 17: Mizoram 53/7 in 20 overs (Sagarika Sengupta 21; Shivani Yadav 2-12, Gunnaj Qurishi 2-15) lost to **Chhattisgarh** 54/1 in 10.1 overs (Manpreet Kaur 26*) by nine wickets.

SCA Stadium Khanderi B Ground, Rajkot, October 17: Uttar Pradesh 180/3 in 20 overs (Neetu Gaur 73*, Shobha Devi 60) beat **Jammu & Kashmir** 59 in 17 overs (Anjali Singh 3-14) by 121 runs.

SCA Stadium, Rajkot, October 17: Karnataka 74/6 in 20 overs (Aditi Rajesh 36*; K Vasava 3-13, Ridhi Maurya 2-9) lost to **Baroda** 75/4 in 16.5 overs (Amrita Joseph 24; Anagha M 2-9) by six wickets.

SCA Stadium, Rajkot, October 18: Jammu & Kashmir 32 in 18.5 overs (Richa Ajay Patel 3-5, Ridhi Maurya 2-3) lost to **Baroda** 34/1 in 5.4 overs (Amrita Joseph 26*) by nine wickets.

SCA Stadium Khanderi B Ground, Rajkot, October 18: Mizoram 70/6 in 20 overs (Swati Shah 27; T Dharani 3-8, Sujan Sharma 2-18) lost to **Saurashtra** 71/1 in 12.1 overs (P Kanojiya 42*) by nine wickets.

SCA Stadium, Rajkot, October 18: Karnataka 62/9 in 20 overs (Niki Prasad 21; Rishika Yadav 3-8, Falak Naz 2-9) lost to **Uttar Pradesh** 65/1 in 15.2 overs (Shobha Devi 21*, Anjali Singh 20*) by nine wickets.

SCA Stadium, Rajkot, October 20: Uttar Pradesh 93/4 in 20 overs (Shobha Devi 49*, Neetu Gaur 22; Pragya Rawat 2-16) beat **Baroda** 69/8 in 20 overs (Rishika Yadav 3-13, Anjali Singh 2-24) by 24 runs.

SCA Stadium Khanderi B Ground, Rajkot, October 20: Jammu & Kashmir 75/9 in 20 overs (Nancy Gill 21; Sneha Jagadish 2-5, Aditi Rajesh 2-6) lost to **Karnataka** 78/3 in 13.2 overs (Shishira Gowda 27, D Vrinda 21*; Rudrakshi 2-21) by seven wickets.

SCA Stadium, Rajkot, October 20: Chhattisgarh 90/4 in 20 overs (Manpreet Kaur 30) beat **Saurashtra** 58/8 in 20 overs (Mamta Bhagat 3-11, M Kaur 2-10) by 32 runs.

SCA Stadium, Rajkot, October 21: Uttar Pradesh 121/5 in 20 overs (Muskan Malik 39, Shobha Devi 29; Anjali Thakur 2-23, Shivani Yadav 2-31) lost to **Chhattisgarh** 70/4 in 20 overs (Manpreet Kaur 28) by six wickets.

SCA Stadium Khanderi B Ground, Rajkot, October 21: Mizoram 50/7 in 20 overs (Swati Sah 23; Sneha Jagadish 3-7) lost to **Karnataka** 51/4 in 11.3 overs (Niki Prasad 23*) by six wickets.

SCA Stadium, Rajkot, October 21: Jammu & Kashmir 99/5 in 20 overs (Rudrakshi Chib 27, Iqra Rasool 26*) lost to **Saurashtra** 100/3 in 19.5 overs (Tanya Rao 42*, P Kanojiya 30) by seven wickets.

SCA Stadium, Rajkot, October 23: Saurashtra 57/6 in 20 overs (Tanya Rao 38*; Rathod Janki 2-6, Pragya Rawat 2-8) lost to **Baroda** 61/2 in 16.1 overs (Hrutvisha Patel 25*, Amrita Joseph 20) by eight wickets.

SCA Stadium Khanderi B Ground, Rajkot, October 23: Uttar Pradesh 201/2 in 20 overs (Shobha Devi 84*, Muskan Malik 74) beat **Mizoram** 56/3 in 20 overs (Swati Sah 23) by 145 runs.

SCA Stadium, Rajkot, October 23: Chhattisgarh 140/6 in 20 overs (Manpreet Kaur 68, Kriti Gupta 33; Sadiya Wani 2-20) beat **Jammu & Kashmir** 64/4 in 20 overs (Sonika 26*; Mamta Bhagat 2-10) by 76 runs.

Group E points table

Team	M	W	L	T	N/R	Pts	NRR
Uttar Pradesh	6	6	0	0	0	24	+3.926
Baroda	6	5	1	0	0	20	+2.338
Karnataka	6	4	2	0	0	16	+1.328
Chhattisgarh	6	3	3	0	0	12	+0.342
Saurashtra	6	2	4	0	0	8	-1.623
Jammu & Kashmir	6	1	5	0	0	4	-2.201
Mizoram	6	0	6	0	0	0	-4.609

Uttar Pradesh and Baroda qualified for the Super Leagues

Group A Super League

Chukkapalli Pitchaiah Cricket Ground, Mulapadu, October 26: Odisha 76/7 in 20 overs (Taranna Pradhan 22*, Kajal Jena 21; Parul 2-17) lost to **Punjab** 79/3 in 15.4 overs (Srishti Rajput 33*) by seven wickets.

Chukkapalli Pitchaiah Cricket Ground, Mulapadu, October 26: Assam 98/6 in 20 overs (Uma Chetry 37, Rashmi Dey 33) beat **Himachal** 96/5 in 20 overs (SM Singh 32; Hemalata Payeng 2-16) by two runs.

Chukkapalli Pitchaiah Cricket Ground, Mulapadu, October 27: Uttar Pradesh 125/3 in 20 overs (Muskan Malik 74, Neetu Gaur 27) beat **Assam** 77 in 20 overs (Rashmi Dey 22; Anjali Singh 4-14) by 48 runs.

Chukkapalli Pitchaiah Cricket Ground, Mulapadu, October 27: Punjab 131/5 in 20 overs (Amanjot Kaur 77*, Raman Preet Kaur 29; PG Kahlon 2-22) beat **Himachal Pradesh** 122/4 in 20 overs (Chitra Singh Jamwal 67, SM Singh 20; A Kaur 2-16) by nine runs.

Chukkapalli Pitchaiah Cricket Ground, Mulapadu, October 29: Assam 105/8 in 20 overs (Gayatri Gurung 42, Priyanka Boruah 26; Kanika Ahuja 3-8, Kashvee Gautam 2-16) beat **Punjab** 78/9 in 20 overs (Rashmi Dey 3-13) by 27 runs.

Chukkapalli Pitchaiah Cricket Ground, Mulapadu, October 29: Uttar Pradesh 116/6 in 20 overs (Anjali Singh 45, Shipra Giri 29; Sonali Hembram 2-24) beat **Odisha** 85/9 in 20 overs (Subhra Nirjharini Swain 42; A Singh 3-10) by 31 runs.

Chukkapalli Pitchaiah Cricket Ground, Mulapadu, October 30: Odisha 69/9 in 20 overs (PG Kahlon 2-7, NM Chauhan 2-16) lost to **Himachal Pradesh** 70/5 in 17.3 overs (Sonal Thakur 27, Chitra Singh Jamwal 23; Sonali Hembram 2-9) by five wickets.

Chukkapalli Pitchaiah Cricket Ground, Mulapadu, October 30: Punjab 104/8 in 20 overs (Amanjot Kaur 50, Anjali 22; Anjali Singh 3-11, Rishika Yadav 3-18) lost to **Uttar Pradesh** 105/3 in 20 overs (Shobha Devi 35, Neetu Gaur 31; Avreet 2-21) by seven wickets.

Chukkapalli Pitchaiah Cricket Ground, Mulapadu, November 1: Uttar Pradesh 115/3 in 20 overs (Muskan Malik 56, Neetu Gaur 36) beat **Himachal Pradesh** 79 in 20 overs (Sonam Yadav 2-11, Falak Naz 2-16) by 36 runs.

Chukkapalli Pitchaiah Cricket Ground, Mulapadu, November 1: Odisha 91/6 in 20 overs (Kajal Jena 30, Subhra Nirjharini Swain 20) lost to **Assam** 92/3 in 18 overs (Gayatri Gurung 31) by seven wickets.

Super League Group A points table

Team	M	W	L	T	N/R	Pts	NRR
Uttar Pradesh	4	4	0	0	0	16	+1.598
Assam	4	3	1	0	0	12	-0.106
Punjab	4	2	2	0	0	8	-0.050
Himachal Pradesh	4	1	3	0	0	4	-0.427
Odisha	4	0	4	0	0	0	-1.004

Uttar Pradesh qualified for the final

Group B Super League

ACA Women's Academy, Guntur, October 26: Delhi 89/8 in 20 overs (Simran Dil Bahadur 21; Ayushi Soni 20; V Pushpa Latha 2-9) beat **Andhra** 91/5 in 16.1 overs (E Padmaja 27, M Durga 20; Priya Mishra 2-16) by five wickets.

ACA Women's Academy, Guntur, October 26: Kerala 111/6 in 20 overs (IV Drishya 35, Jisna Joseph 35; Sushmita Ganguly 3-13) lost to **Bengal** 113/3 in 17.5 overs (Richa 43, Ankita Chakraborty 26) by seven wickets.

ACA Women's Academy, Guntur, October 27: Baroda 80 in 20 overs (Richa Patel 24, Hrutvisha Patel 21; Shreya Karar 3-14, Kashish Agarwal 2-10) lost to **Bengal** 81/7 in 19.1 overs (Mamata 35*; Jaya Mohite 2-15) by three wickets.

ACA Women's Academy, Guntur, October 27: Kerala 54 in 14.5 overs (IV Drishya 25; Saranya Gadwal 4-6, G Sindhuja 3-19) lost to **Andhra** 55/2 in 12.3 overs (E Padmaja 35*; Sandra Suren 2-17) by eight wickets.

ACA Women's Academy, Guntur, October 29: Andhra 110/6 in 20 overs (E Padmaja 36, G Sindhuja 23; Mouli Mondal 2-18) beat **Bengal** 100/7 in 20 overs (Richa 26, Ankita Chakraborty 22; Saranya Gadwal 2-6, S Sailakshmi 2-14) by 10 runs.

ACA Women's Academy, Guntur, October 29: Delhi 112/3 in 20 overs (Simran Dil Bahadur 56*, Riti Tomar 25*) beat **Baroda** 99/5 in 20 overs (Purab 42, Amrita Joseph 24; Ayushi Soni 3-20) by 13 runs.

ACA Women's Academy, Guntur, October 30: Delhi 105/8 in 20 overs (Simran Dil Bahadur 29, Ayushi Soni 22; Sourabhya P 2-26) lost to **Kerala** 109/3 in 19.1 overs (IV Drishya 54*, Jisna Joseph 37) by seven wickets.

ACA Women's Academy, Guntur, October 30: Andhra 124/5 in 20 overs (V Ramya Deepika 39, Saranya Gadwal 23*; Ridhi Maurya 2-22) beat **Baroda** 68 in 17.5 overs (Jaya Mohite 25, Camy Desai 21; K Dhatri 4-1, E Padmaja 3-14) by 56 runs.

ACA Women's Academy, Guntur, November 1: Baroda 100/8 in 20 overs (Hrutvisha Patel 29; Aleena Surendran 3-25) tied with **Kerala** 100/5 in 20 overs (IV Drishya 28*, Ansu Sunil 24). Super Over: Kerala 10/0 in 1 over lost to Baroda 11/1 in 1 over.

ACA Women's Academy, Guntur, November 1: Delhi 68 in 19.3 overs (Mouli Mondal 3-6, Anindita Nath 3-10) lost to **Bengal** 69/3 in 16.2 overs (Dhara Gujjar 27*, Mamata 23*; Priya Mishra 2-19) by seven wickets.

Super League Group B points table

Team	M	W	L	T	N/R	Pts	NRR
Andhra	4	4	0	0	0	16	+1.646
Bengal	4	3	1	0	0	12	+0.338
Delhi	4	1	3	0	0	4	-0.460
Kerala	4	1	3	0	0	4	-0.579
Baroda	4	1	3	0	0	4	-0.930

Andhra qualified for the final

Final

ACA Women's Academy, Guntur, November 3: Uttar Pradesh 103/9 in 20 overs (Humaira Rais 25, Muskan Malik 21; E Padmaja 3-14, B Anusha 3-27) beat **Andhra** 85 in 20 overs (E Padmaja 21; Sonam Yadav 3-8, Juhi Pandey 3-11) by 18 runs.

Winners: Uttar Pradesh

Under-19 T20 Challenger Trophy

All-rounder Shafali stars for India Red

The theory goes in the Senior Women's Challenger Trophy that the winner in the league stage is often the loser in the final. In keeping with that trend, India Red struggled to a three-wicket win over India Blue in the first Under-19 T20 Challenger Trophy, after having failed to defend 122 in their opening encounter against the same opposition.

A disciplined bowling effort in the final by Neetu Gaur's team meant India Blue were kept to a meagre 82 for 6, before Red recovered from a middle-order collapse to chase down the target with 14 balls to spare.

Chasing was the preferred tactic through the tournament — India Green were the only team that successfully defended a score when they held on for a four-run win over Blue. E Padmaja, captain of Blue, was the most impressive batter, collecting 89 runs at an average of 44.50. Simran Dil Bahadur, the top-order batter from Red, managed the only half-century of the tournament: her unbeaten 31-ball 52 was studded with four fours and four sixes.

E Padmaja topped the batting charts.

Simran's tournament strike rate of 131.91 was only bettered by Shafali Verma, the opener from Green, who scored at 154.28. While Shafali's big hitting was kept under control through the tournament, the right-hander — normally a wicket-keeper — showcased her skills with the ball, topping the charts with five wickets in two matches. Her figures of 3 for 21 against Blue came second to Sayali Satghare's 3 for 12 against Green, in a performance that pushed Red into the final.

Best batter: E Padmaja (India Blue) (89 runs in 3 matches)
Best bowler: Shafali Verma (India Green) (5 wickets in 2 matches)

Andhra Cricket Association Women's Academy, Guntur, November 12: India Red 122/4 in 20 overs (Simran Dil Bahadur 52*, Manpreet Kaur 21) lost to **India Blue** 123/4 in 19.5 overs (E Padmaja 32, Latika Inamdar 21) by six wickets.
Andhra Cricket Association Women's Academy, Guntur, November 13: India Green 120/4 in 20 overs (Amanjot Kaur 29, IV Drishya 28*; Suman Meena 2-27) beat **India Blue**

114/7 in 20 overs (E Padmaja 31, SB Keerthana 27; Shefali Verma 3-21) by six runs.
Andhra Cricket Association Women's Academy, Guntur, November 14: India Green 78 in 19.4 overs (Shafali Verma 33; Sayali Satghare 3-12, Tejashwini Duragad 2-15) lost to **India Red** 79/2 in 13.4 overs (SM Singh 45*) by eight wickets.

Points table

Team	M	W	L	T	N/R	Pts	NRR
India Red	2	1	1	0	0	4	+0.753
India Blue	2	1	1	0	0	4	-0.254
India Green	2	1	1	0	0	4	-0.783

India Red and India Blue qualified for the final

Final
Andhra Cricket Association Women's Academy, Guntur, November 16: India Blue 85/6 in 20 overs (E Padmaja 26; Manpreet Kaur 2-10) lost to **India Red** 83/7 in 17.4 overs (M Kaur 20*; SB Keerthana 3-22, Anjali Singh 2-19) by three wickets.

Winners: India Red

Under-19 Inter-state One-day Tournament

Bengal claim maiden title

Having defeated Mumbai in a close semi-final, Bengal overcame a resurgent Delhi by 26 runs in the rain-interrupted final of the Under-19 Inter-State One-Day tournament. Ankita Chakraborty (49), the Bengal captain, and Kashish Agarwal (40) made crucial contributions at the top of the order, before the bowlers, led by Sushmita Ganguly (2-20), combined to tie Delhi down.

Mamta (368 runs), Chakraborty (269 runs) and Agarwal (262 runs) were Bengal's most consistent batters, while Shreya Karar (17 wickets), Mouli Mondal (16) and Ganguly (14) led their charge with the ball. Karar's tally included a fine spell of 6 for 12 in the quarter-final against Uttarakhand, one of 21 five-wicket hauls taken in this edition.

Despite slightly tough batting conditions, as many as 14 centuries were scored this time around, beating the previous best tournament tally of eight. Sejal Raut, Mumbai's opener, scored two of those. Raut, a small-built right-

Bengal would go on to claim the one-day title across age groups. — *ACA*

hander, was the only batter to cross the 400-run mark. She drove with authority off the front foot and, most impressively, showed great intent between the wickets. In stark contrast to her approach — Raut's run tally included only 36 boundaries — was Shafali Verma, Haryana's 14-year-old opening batter, who clobbered 376 runs in only five matches, including two centuries and an unbeaten 98. Her runs came at an incredible strike-rate of 172.47 and included 64 fours and three sixes.

Formerly a team that struggled at age-group level, Goa sprung quite a surprise, dominating through the league stage to qualify for the knock-outs. Tejashwini Duragad, the captain, led from the front picking up 26 wickets with her leg-spin at an average of 4.30 and was well supported by Diksha Gawde, the off-spinner, who took 21 wickets. Other impressive performances included Niki Prasad's spell of 7 for 21 for Karnataka against Himachal Pradesh, Raghvi's unbeaten 168 for Uttarakhand against Pondicherry, and Himachal Pradesh's tie with Assam.

In **2017-18**, Jemimah Rodrigues, Mumbai's 17-year-old batting star, captured the imagination of the country to become India's first women's domestic superstar. The right-hander amassed 1013 runs in 11 matches at 112.56, including six centuries and one half-century. She became only the second woman, after Smriti Mandhana to score a double-century in an Under-19 tournament when she smashed an unbeaten 202 against Saurashtra. Rodrigues also showcased her ability with the ball, picking up 19 wickets with her off-spin. She even defended six runs in the final over in Mumbai's league match against arch-rivals, Maharashtra.

Fatima Jaffer complemented Rodrigues's efforts as she picked up 28 wickets through the tournament. A classical left-arm spinner who is quite slow through the air, Jaffer can extract turn from any surface. Despite the duo's efforts, though, Mumbai were beaten in the final by a resurgent Andhra, who won their second title in four years.

Six new teams — Arunachal Pradesh, Bihar, Manipur, Meghalaya, Nagaland and Sikkim — made their first appearance this season and competed admirably.

	Most runs	**Most wicket**
2017-18	Jemimah Rodrigues (Mumbai) (1017 runs in 11 matches)	Fatima Jaffer (Mumbai) (28 wickets in 10 matches)
2018-19	Sejal Raut (Mumbai) (440 runs in 10 matches)	Tejashwini Duragad (Goa) (26 wickets in 8 matches)

Elite Group A

Bokakhat District Sports Association (DSA) Ground, February 10: Himachal Pradesh 54 in 29.5 overs (Priya Mishra 3-11, Madhu 3-12) lost to **Delhi** 55/3 in 19.1 overs (Ayushi Soni 23*, Simran Dil Bahadur 21; VS Fishta 2-7) by seven wickets.

Golaghat DSA Ground, February 10: Karnataka 49 in 24 overs (Juhi Pandey 3-3, Archana Devi 2-17) lost to **Uttar Pradesh** 50/2 in 15.5 overs (Muskan Malik 26*) by eight wickets.

Jorhat DSA Stadium, February 10: Assam 52 in 17.5 overs (Priyanka Boruah 21; Saranya Gadwal 4-6, S Sailakshmi 2-7) lost to **Andhra** 53/5 in 19.4 overs (Anamika Bori 2-8, Rashmi Dey 2-12) by five wickets.

Golaghat DSA Ground, February 11: Uttar Pradesh 192/8 in 50 overs (Neetu Gaur 48, Anjali Singh 35; AK Choudhary 2-34, SR Choudhary 2-45) beat **Rajasthan** 103 in 42.4 overs (Suman Meena 28; A Singh 5-24, Archana Devi 2-15) by 89 runs.

Jorhat DSA Stadium, February 11: Andhra 184/8 in 50 overs (A Sireesha 47*, E Padmaja 36; Anju Rajan 2-32) beat **Kerala** 92 in 45.2 overs (Saranya Gadwal 3-18, M Bhavana 2-6) by 92 runs.

Bokakhat DSA Ground, February 11: Maharashtra 109 in 49.3 overs (KN Mulla 23; Madhu 5-19, Priya Mishra 2-24) lost to **Delhi** 110/5 in 43.5 overs (Simran Dil Bahadur 31; Aditi Gaikwad 2-22, Nikita Aage 2-22) by five wickets.

Golaghat DSA Ground, February 12: Rajasthan 57 in 28.2 overs (Ayushi Garg 25; Sneha Jagadish 3-11, Shreyanka Patil 2-4) lost to **Karnataka** 60/3 in 36.4 overs (K Shubhashree 20; AK Choudhary 2-9) by seven wickets.

Jorhat DSA Stadium, February 12: Kerala 39 in 31.3 overs (Kakoli Saikia 3-12, Bedashree Borpatragohain 3-12) lost to **Assam** 40/5 in 14 overs (Anju Rajan 3-18) by five wickets.

Bokakhat DSA Ground, February 12: Maharashtra 92/9 in 50 overs (SS Waghmode 31, Nikita Aage 20; VS Fishta 4-8, LS Dutta 2-17) lost to **Himachal Pradesh** 94/3 in 38.4 overs (SM Singh 49) by seven wickets.

Bokakhat DSA Ground, February 14: Rajasthan 130/8 in 50 overs (Suman Meena 44*; Sandra Suren 3-24) beat **Kerala** 101 in 47.1 overs (Ansu Sunil 61; ASP Maheshwari 4-13, S Meena 3-25) by 29 runs.

Jorhat DSA Stadium, February 14: Karnataka 39 in 34 overs (Rashmi Dey 2-7, Bedashree Borpatragohain 2-9) lost to **Assam** 40/5 in 11.1 overs (Shreyanka Patil 3-16, Aditi Rajesh 2-10) by five wickets.

Golaghat DSA Ground, February 14: Uttar Pradesh 132 in 40.2 overs (Ayushi Srivastava 58, Neetu Gaur 21; Saranya Gadwal 3-32, B Anusha 2-10) beat **Andhra** 69 in 40.5 overs (Sonam Yadav 4-15, Anjali Singh 2-12) by 63 runs.

Golaghat DSA Ground, February 15: Uttar Pradesh 81 in 35.4 overs (Shobha Devi 36; Madhu 5-16, Saumya 3-4) lost to **Delhi** 82/4 in 36.1 overs (Neha Bhargava 22; Sonam Yadav 2-15) by six wickets.

Jorhat DSA Stadium, February 15: Himachal Pradesh 126 in 46.3 overs (Chitra Singh Jamwal 45*, Sonal Thakur 22; Niki Prasad 7-12, Shreyanka Patil 2-16) beat **Karnataka** 92 in 44.3 overs (D Vrinda 24; LS Dutta 3-28) by 34 runs.

Bokakhat DSA Ground, February 15: Rajasthan 151/8 in 50 overs (Suman Meena 37*, Ayushi Garg 29; Priyanka Ghodke 2-27, Aarati Kedar 2-28) beat **Maharashtra** 85 in 36.1 overs (A Kedar 29*; SR Choudhary 4-7, S Meena 2-14) by 66 runs.

Golaghat DSA Ground, February 17: Delhi 146/9 in 50 over (Mallika Khatri 44, Ayushi Soni 21; G Sindhuja 2-13, Saranya Gadwal 2-21) beat **Andhra** 131 in 42.1 overs (E Padmaja 24, K Hamsa 21; Simran Dil Bahadur 3-11, Priya Mishra 2-25) by four runs. (VJD method).

Jorhat DSA Stadium, February 17: Himachal Pradesh 79 in 43 overs (Sonal Thakur 30*; Rashmi Dey 3-15, Kakoli Saikia 2-13) tied with **Assam** 79 in 42 overs (PG Kahlon 3-14, LS Dutta 3-25).

Bokakhat DSA Ground, February 17: Maharashtra 81 in 41.1 overs (Darsana Mohanan 3-22, Sandra Suren 3-26) lost to **Kerala** 82/9 in 29 overs (Sourabhya P 25*; Priyanka Ghodke 3-12, Aditi Gaikwad 3-19) by one wicket.

Golaghat DSA Ground, February 19: Assam v **Delhi**. Match abandoned.

Jorhat DSA Stadium, February 19: Karnataka 82/6 in 28 overs (D Vrinda 48*) lost to **Maharashtra** 83/2 in 23.4 overs (Nikita Aage 25*, Hrutuja Deshmukh 25*) by eight wickets.

Bokakhat DSA Ground, February 19: Uttar Pradesh 90/8 in 20 overs (Muskan Malik 30, Ayushi Srivastava 20; IV Drishya 2-8, Ajanya TP 2-11) beat **Kerala** 71/8 in 20 overs (IV Drishya 31; Archana Devi 3-8, Anjali Singh 3-23) by 19 runs.

Golaghat DSA Ground, February 21: Delhi 228/6 in 50 overs (Simran Dil Bahadur 88, Ayushi Soni 58; Shanu 2-29, DR Kanwar 2-36) beat **Rajasthan** 66/8 in 31 overs (Jyoti Choudhary 25; Neha Bhargava 3-5, Madhu 2-13) by 133 runs. (VJD method).

Jorhat DSA Stadium, February 21: Andhra 184/6 in 20 overs (E Padmaja 65*, M Durga 28; Aditi Rajesh 2-32) beat **Karnataka** 105 in 47.4 overs (A Rajesh 29, D Vrinda 23; Saranya Gadwal 3-11, E Padmaja 2-11) by 79 runs.

Bokakhat DSA, February 21: Kerala 88 in 46.5 overs (PG Kahlon 2-11, VS Fishta 2-12) lost to **Himachal Pradesh** 89/2 in 25.4 overs (SM Singh 64*) by eight wickets.

Golaghat DSA Ground, February 23: Rajasthan 83 in 42 overs (Jyoti Choudhary 29; Anamika Bori 4-16, Kakoli Saikia 2-9) lost to **Assam** 84/4 in 29.5 overs (Uma Chetry 22; AP Bharadwaj 2-15) by six wickets.

Jorhat DSA Stadium, February 23: Andhra 112/4 in 28 overs (E Padmaja 39, M Durga 25; Priyanka Ghodke 2-26) beat **Maharashtra** 64 in 21.4 overs (Nikita Aage 21; Saranya Gadwal 4-12, E Padmaja 3-12) by 48 runs.

Bokakhat DSA, February 23: Uttar Pradesh 81 in 43.3 overs (Anjali Singh 35; VS Fishta 4-7, LS Dutta 2-6) lost to **Himachal Pradesh** 82/8 in 36.1 overs (SM Singh 24; Archana Devi 2-14, Anjali Singh 2-15) by two wickets.

Golaghat DSA Ground, February 25: Andhra 162 in 47.3 overs (M Durga 34, K Hamsa 24; SP Sharma 3-28, ASP Maheshwari 2-31) beat **Rajasthan** 47 in 30 overs (Saranya Gadwal 3-8, A Sireesha 2-5) by 115 runs.

Jorhat DSA Stadium, February 25: Assam 137/9 in 50 overs (Sudha Shukla 5-22, Sonam Yadav 2-15) lost to **Uttar Pradesh** 138/4 in 37.2 overs (Shobha Devi 47, Muskan Malik 33*; Rashmi Dey 2-21) by six wickets.

Bokakhat DSA Ground, February 25: Kerala 77/9 in 24 overs (Anagha M 2-10, Aditi Rajesh 2-11) beat **Karnataka** 60/9 in 24 overs (Shreyanka Patil 20*; Darsana Mohanan 2-4, Ajanya TP 2-5) by 17 runs.

Golaghat DSA Ground, February 27: Andhra 189/8 in 50 overs (A Sireesha 53, E Padmaja 42; LS Dutta 4-49, PG Kahlon 2-30) beat **Himachal Pradesh** 69 in 35.5 overs (Chitra SIngh Jamwal 24; Saranya Gadwal 4-10, M Bhavana 2-11)by 120 runs.

Jorhat DSA Stadium, February 27: Maharashtra 73 in 22.3 overs (Aditi Gaikwad 31*; Falak Naz 5-22, Anjali Singh 2-7) lost to **Uttar Pradesh** 75/4 in 23.3 overs (Muskan Malik 22*; BM Mirajkar 2-20) by six wickets.

Bokakhat DSA, February 27: Delhi 138/9 in 50 overs (Nain 56, Ishika 40; D Vrinda 2-19, Shreyanka Paril 2-28) beat **Karnataka** 54 in 34 overs (Neha Bhargava 2-5, Saumya 2-9) by 84 runs.

Golaghat DSA Ground, March 1: HP 68/8 in 24 overs (SM Singh 32; SP Sharma 2-14) lost to **Rajasthan** 69/2 in 22.2 overs (RS Tinker 30*, Ayushi Garg 20) by eight wickets.

Jorhat DSA Stadium, March 1: Assam 95 in 36.4 overs (Gayatri Gurung 29, Bedashree Borpatragohain 21*; BM Mirajkar 5-15) beat **Maharashtra** 93/9 in 50 overs (Rashmi Dey 3-15, Anamika Bori 2-15) by two runs.

Bokakhat DSA Ground, March 1: Delhi 78 in 47.4 overs (Sourabhya P 4-14, Ajanya TP 2-7) lost to **Kerala** 79/8 in 30.3 overs (IV Drishya 32; Shweta Sehrawat 3-7, Priya Mishra 3-15) by two wickets.

Elite Group A points table

Team	M	W	L	T	N/R	Pts	NRR
Delhi	8	6	1	0	1	26	+1.005
Uttar Pradesh	8	6	2	0	0	24	+0.835
Andhra	8	6	2	0	0	24	+1.158
Assam	8	4	2	1	1	20	+0.555
Himachal Pradesh	8	4	3	1	0	18	-0.145
Rajastan	8	3	5	0	0	12	-0.920
Kerala	8	3	5	0	0	12	-0.646
Maharashtra	8	1	7	0	0	4	-0.780
Karnataka	8	1	7	0	0	4	-1.088

Delhi and Uttar Pradesh qualified for the knock-outs

Elite Group B

Reliance Cricket Stadium, Vadodara, February 10: Madhya Pradesh 165/8 in 50 overs (Soumya Tiwari 62, Reena Yadav 46) beat **Chhattisgarh** 47 in 39 overs (Srashti Nagpure 3-3, Poonam Soni 3-11) by 118 runs.

GSFC Cricket Ground, Vadodara, February 10: Baroda 190/9 in 50 overs (Hrutu Patel 71, Amrita Joseph 60; Sandhya Kumari 3-21) beat **Jharkhand** 86 in 35.4 overs (S Kumari 34; Bansi 2-8, Rathod Janki 2-12) by 104 runs.

Alembic 2 Cricket Ground, Vadodara, February 10: Hyderabad 160 in 49.2 overs (Trisha Poojitha 29, Lakshmi Prasanna 29; Sushmita Ganguly 2-17, Mouli Mondal 2-29) lost to **Bengal** 161/3 in 41.1 overs (Dhara Gujjar 66, Ankita Chakraborty 58*) by seven wickets.

Alembic 2 Cricket Ground, Vadodara, February 11: Mumbai 195/7 in 50 overs (Sejal Raut 70, Sayali Satghare 27; Duregesh Nandani Sahu 3-33, Jyoti Nat 2-28) beat **Chhattisgarh** 70 in 41.1 overs (Manpreet Kaur 23; S Satghare 2-3, Simran Shaikh 2-5) by 125 runs.

Reliance Cricket Stadium, Vadodara, February 11: Punjab 178 in 49.2 overs (Kanika Ahuja 64, Shabnam Thakur 23; Pragya Rawat 2-29) lost to **Baroda** 179/5 in 47.5 overs (Hrutu Patel 89*, Amrita Joseph 27; Parul 2-29) by five wickets.

GSFC Cricket Ground, Vadodara, February 11: Haryana 237/9 in 50 overs (Shafali Verma 125, Versha Bhatiwal 37; Keerthi Reddy 4-30, Merlyn 2-39) beat **Hyderabad** 200 in 29.4 overs (Lakshmi Prasanna 76, G Trisha 67; Pramila Kumari 3-29, Nisha Jangra 3-30) by 37 runs.

Reliance Cricket Stadium, Vadodara, February 12: Mumbai 179/6 in 50 overs (Sejal Raut 69, Aachal Valanju 63; Shreya Karar 2-33) lost to **Bengal** 183/8 in 48.1 overs (Mamata 77*, Richa 39; Jagravi Pawar 2-31) by two wickets.

GSFC Cricket Ground, Vadodara, February 12: Madhya Pradesh 130 in 46.1 overs (Sanjana Awase 27, Aashna Patidar 25; Shbnam Thakur 2-12, Parul 2-13) lost to **Punjab** 131/6 in 47.2 overs (Pragati Singh 29*, Kanika Ahuja 26; Soumya Tiwari 2-16, Shashi Kala Yadav 2-20) by four wickets.

Alembic 2 Cricket Ground, Vadodara, February 12: Jharkhand 123 in 48.5 overs (Khushbu Kumari 32, Laxmi Kumari Murmu 29; Parmila Kumari 3-25, Suman Hingra 2-13) lost to **Haryana** 124/3 in 19.2 overs (Shafali Verma 98*) by seven wickets.

GSFC Ground, Vadodara, February 14: Jharkhand 40 in 27.4 overs (Sayali Satghare 4-12, Vidhi Mathuria 3-0) lost to **Mumbai** 41/2 in 25.1 overs (Shaheen 24*) by eight wickets.

Alembic 2 Cricket Ground, Vadodara, February 14: Bengal 189 in 45.2 overs (Ankita Chakraborty 68, Mamata 30; Durgesh Nandani Sahu 4-26, Jyoti Nat 2-32) beat **Chhattisgarh** 68 in 31.3 overs (Aishwarya Singh 28; Mouli Mondal 2-0, Megha Ghosh 2-1) by 121 runs.

Reliance Cricket Stadium, Vadodara, February 14: Hyderabad 132 in 47.4 overs (G Trisha 44, Trisha Poojitha 31; Nitya Tiwari 5-24, Srashti Nagpure 2-30) lost to **Madhya Pradesh** 135/5 in 47.4 overs (Ananya Dubey 43*, Sanjana Awase 26) by five wickets.

GSFC Cricket Ground, Vadodara, February 15: Jharkhand 147 in 50 overs (Jaya 28, Payel Ghosh 25; Avreet 2-32) lost to **Punjab** 151/6 in 46.2 overs (Kanika Ahuja 45*, Gazala Naj 35*; Mamta Paswan 2-18) by four wickets.

Reliance Cricket Stadium, Vadodara, February 15: Haryana 216/9 in 50 overs (Shafali Verma 101, Parmila Kumari 37) beat **Bengal** 201/9 in 50 overs (Mamata 47, Kashish Agarwal 38; Sarita Bhumbak 3-37, Suman Hingra 2-36) by 15 runs.

Alembic 2 Cricket Ground, Vadodara, February 15: Madhya Pradesh 116 in 45.5 overs (Reena Yadav 27, Nitya Tiwari 23; Jaya Mohite 3-24, Pragya Rawat 2-20) beat **Baroda** 68 in 36 overs (P Rawat 31; Srashti Nagpure 6-15, N Tiwari 2-14) by 48 runs.

GSFC Cricket Ground, Vadodara, February 17: Haryana 189/8 in 50 overs (Versha Bhatiwal 67, Nitika 36; Bansi 3-25, Pragya Rawat 2-23) beat **Baroda** 141/9 in 50 overs (P Rawat 25, Hrutu Patel 24; Suman Hingra 4-17, Parmila Kumari 2-25) by 48 runs.

Reliance Cricket Stadium, Vadodara, February 17: Hyderabad 121/8 in 50 overs (Lakshmi Prasanna 36, GK Sravya 23; Sayali Satghare 2-10) lost to **Mumbai** 122/3 in 35.5 overs (Aachal Valanju 47*, Shaheen 35) by seven wickets.

Alembic 2 Cricket Ground, Vadodara, February 17: Chhattisgarh 96 in 41.1 overs (Sanjita Patel 33; Kanika Ahuja 2-9, Parul 2-16) lost to **Punjab** 98/6 in 34 overs (Gazala Naj 28*, Amanjot Kaur 21; Durgesh Nandani Sahu 3-32) by four wickets.

GSFC Cricket Ground, Vadodara, February 19: Madhya Pradesh 137 in 49.1 overs (Soumya Tiwari 46; Mamta Paswan 3-34, Anjali 2-17) beat **Jharkhand** 69 in 27.3 overs (Sandhya Kumari 28*; Nitya Tiwari 3-12, Poonam Soni 2-19) by 68 runs.

Alembic 2 Cricket Ground, Vadodara, February 19: Hyderabad 221 in 49.5 overs (Lakshmi Prasanna 66, Trisha Poojitha 65; Durgesh Nandani Sahu 2-30, Anjali Thakur 2-40) beat **Chhattisgarh** 65/9 in 50 overs (Suvartha 3-17, L Prasanna 2-6) by 156 runs.

Reliance Cricket Stadium, February 19: Baroda 128/9 in 50 overs (Jaya Mohite 35*, Hrutu Patel 23; Sushmita Ganguly 3-28, Piyali Ghosh 2-13) lost to **Bengal** 129/8 in 39 overs (Santhita Biswas 31, Kashish Agarwal 21; J Mohite 3-25, Pragya Rawat 2-29) by two wickets.

Reliance Cricket Stadium, Vadodara, February 21: Haryana 105 in 48.2 overs (Jigyasha Siwach 21*; Kanika Ahuja 5-18) lost to **Punjab** 108/4 in 38.4 overs (Anjali 31*; Parmila Kumari 2-22) by six wickets.

GSFC Cricket Ground, Vadodara, February 21: Mumbai 187/8 in 50 overs (Sejal Raut 102*, Shaheen 22; Bansi 3-41, Jaya Mohite 2-38) beat **Baroda** 101 in 41.1 overs (Pragya Rawat 29, Bansi 20; Sayali Satghare 4-28, Jagravi Pawar 3-15) by 86 runs.

Alembic 2 Cricket Ground, Vadodara, February 21: Jharkhand 180 in 50 overs (Sandhya Kumari 37, Jaya 32; Jyoti Nat 3-32) beat **Chhattisgarh** 75/8 in 50 overs (Anjali 2-9, P Priya 2-10) by 105 runs.

Reliance Cricket Stadium, February 23: Punjab 205/4 in 50 overs (Gazala Naj 57, Anjali 42*) beat **Hyderabad** 65 in 35.2 overs (Raman Preet Kaur 6-13, Parul 3-7) by 141 runs.

GSFC Cricket Ground, Vadodara, February 23: Bengal 212/9 in 50 overs (Kashish Agarwal 83, Mamata 55; Mamta Paswan 3-38, Priti Kumari 2-40) beat **Jharkhand** 89/8 in 50 overs (Sandhya Kumari 23; Mouli Mondal 3-11) by 123 runs.

Alembic 2 Cricket Ground, Vadodara, February 23: Madhya Pradesh 117/9 in 50 overs (Ananya Dubey 58*; Jagravi Pawar 2-11) lost to **Mumbai** 118/9 in 48.1 overs (Sejal Raut 22, Aachal Valanju 22; Nitya Tiwari 3-24) by one wicket.

Alembic 2 Cricket Ground, Vadodara, February 25: Bengal 106/8 in 50 overs (Tithi Das 44, Priyanka Sarkar 22*; Nitya Tiwari 4-13, Srashti Nagpure 3-13) beat **Madhya Pradesh** 79 in 46 overs (Aashna Patidar 32; Sushmita Ganguly 4-18, Shreya Karar 2-15) by 27 runs.

GSFC Cricket Ground, Vadodara, February 25: Mumbai 256/5 in 50 overs (Sejal Raut 112, Riya Chaudhari 91; Suman Hingra 2-30) beat **Haryana** 65 in 23.5 overs (Tanvi Parab 3-0, Savesharvi Suhas 3-20) by 191 runs.

Reliance Cricket Stadium, Vadodara, February 25: Baroda 230/2 in 50 overs (Hrutu Patel 125*, Jaya Mohite 44*) beat **Chhattisgarh** 96 in 44.4 overs (Sanjana Pardi 29; Diksha 5-18, Bansi 2-18) by 134 runs.

Reliance Cricket Stadium, Vadodara, February 27: Haryana 196/5 in 50 overs (Versha Bhatiwal 101*, Nisha Jangra 27) beat **Chhattisgarh** 144/8 in 50 overs (Yeesha Bharti Dewangan 23, Kriti Gupta 23) by 52 runs.

GSFC Cricket Ground, Vadodara, February 27: Hyderabad 142/8 in 50 overs (GK Sravya 44, G Trisha 21; Mamta Paswan 4-11) lost to **Jharkhand** 143/0 in 43.5 overs (Payel Ghosh 76*, Kumaari Sabita 52*) by 10 wickets.

Alembic 2 Cricket Ground, Vadodara, February 27: Mumbai 136 in 47 overs (Aachal Valanju 42; Pragati Singh 4-36, Parul 3-17) lost to **Punjab** 137/4 in 47.5 overs (Shabnam Thakur 40, Srishti Rajput 29; Jagravi Pawar 2-22) by six wickets.

Reliance Cricket Stadium, Vadodara, March 1: Baroda 152/6 in 50 overs (R Patel 37*, K Vasava 36*; Kranthi Reddy 3-22) lost to **Hyderabad** 153/3 in 47.2 overs (Trisha Poojitha 66, Keerthi Reddy 43*) by seven wickets.

Alembic 2, Vadodara, March 1: Madhya Pradesh 176/9 in 50 overs (Soumya Tiwari 83, Ananya Dubey 22; Sarka Bhumbak 3-27, Suman Hingra 2-31) beat **Haryana** 140 in 43.3 overs (Nitika 42, Pallavi 25; Shivani Santore 3-16, Srashti Nagpure 2-34) by 36 runs.

GSFC Cricket Ground, Vadodara, March 1: Bengal 208/8 in 50 overs (Santhita Biswas 51, Mamata 38*; Pragati Singh 3-34, Parul 2-39) beat **Punjab** 117 in 43.2 overs (Kanika Ahuja 61; Mouli Mondal 4-24) by 91 runs.

Elite Group B points table

Team	M	W	L	T	N/R	Pts	NRR
Bengal	8	7	1	0	0	28	+1.081
Punjab	8	6	2	0	0	24	+0.412
Mumbai	8	6	2	0	0	24	+1.428
Madhya Pradesh	8	5	3	0	0	20	+0.602
Haryana	8	5	3	0	0	20	-0.027
Baroda	8	3	5	0	0	12	+0.053
Jharkhand	8	2	6	0	0	8	-1.013
Hyderabad	8	2	6	0	0	8	-0.308
Chhattisgarh	8	0	8	0	0	0	-2.186

Bengal, Punjab and Mumbai qualified for the knock-out

Elite Group C

Goa Cricket Association Academy, Porvorim, February 10: Odisha 204/6 in 20 overs (Kajal Jena 74, Poonam Nayak 67; MS Bodkhe 2-24) beat **Vidarbha** 65 in 29.3 overs (Sonali Hembram 3-7, Indrani Chhatria 3-12) by 139 runs.

Sanguem Cricket Ground, February 10: J&K 27 in 22.4 overs (KN Ramyashri 4-6, SB Keerthana 2-1) lost to **Tamil Nadu** 28/0 in 3.5 overs (A Eloksi 21*) by 10 wickets.

GCA Academy, Porvorim, February 11: Goa 236/5 in 50 overs (Diksha Amonkar 71, Diksha Gawde 50*; Ambika Debnath 2-41) beat **Tripura** 105 in 50 overs (Antara Das 42; D Gawde 4-18, Tejashwini Duragad 2-22) by 131 runs.

Sanguem Cricket Ground, Sanguem, February 11: Vidarbha 132 in 42.2 overs (Latika Inamdar 33, SS Sadaf 28; M Modhvadiya 3-24, S Jethva 2-29) lost to **Saurashtra** 133/7 in 47 overs (Tanya Rao 42, Sujan Sama 23*; Aachal Shahu 4-35) by three wickets.

GCA Academy, Porvorim, February 12: Tamil Nadu 162 in 50 overs (SB Keerthana 76*; Subhra Nirjharini Swain 2-24) lost to **Odisha** 164/8 in 48.4 overs (Sweet Beura 44*, Poonam Nayak 33; KN Ramyashri 3-27) by two wickets.

Margao CC, February 12: Gujarat 146/7 in 50 overs (Itisha Patel 46, Tanya Patel 22*; Tumpa Das 2-16) beat **Tripura** 64 in 36.3 overs (Hiral Solanki 4-9, PA Talpada 2-11) by 82 runs.

Sanguem Cricket Ground, Sanguem, February 13: Tamil Nadu 276/6 in 50 overs (SB Keerthana 114, C Shushanthika 70; Sujan Sama 2-55, T Dharani 2-64) beat **Saurashtra** 105 in 42.3 overs (T Dharani 32; MS Aishwarya 2-15, A Eloksi 2-16) by 171 runs.

GCA Academy, Porvorim, February 13: Gujarat 101 in 31.3 overs (Itisha Patel 25; Ananaya Sharma 2-20, Absar Ul Huda 2-23) beat **Jammu & Kashmir** 21 in 10.3 overs (Tanya Patel 5-5, Muskan Vasava 3-10) by 80 runs.

Margao Cricket Club, Margao, February 13: Goa 137/9 in 50 overs (Diksha Gawde 42, Tanaya Nayak 26*; Aachal Shahu 3-26, MS Bodkhe 2-21) beat **Vidarbha** 67 in 28.5 overs (Latika Inamdar 30; D Gawde 4-7, Tejashwini Duragad 2-2) by 70 runs.

Sanguem Cricket Ground, Sanguem, February 14: Odisha 168/8 in 50 overs (Poonam Nayak 35, Indrani Chhatria 29*; T Dharani 2-36, M Modhvadiya 2-40) beat **Saurashtra** 57 in 29.4 overs (Sonali Hembram 2-6) by 111 runs.

Margao Cricket Club, February 14: Tripura 251/6 in 50 overs (Ambika Debnath 84, Puja Paul 44; Arti 2-27) beat **J&K** 61 in 30.3 overs (Hiramani 3-6, Puja Das 3-18) by 190 runs.

GCA Academy, Porvorim, February 15: Goa 207/7 in 50 overs (Purvaja Verlekar 61, Tanaya Naik 29; Stuti Jani 2-23) beat **Gujarat** 99 in 47.2 overs (Anjali Patel 31, S Jani 29; Tejashwini Duragad 4-13, Diksha Gawde 2-16) by 108 runs.

Sanguem Cricket Ground, Sanguem, February 16: Odisha 289/6 in 50 overs (Indrani Chhatria 51*, Poonam Nayak 45; Ronaq Jahan 2-58, Rudrakshi Chib 2-62) beat **Jammu & Kashmir** 91 in 32.3 overs (Rani Kumari Prasad 3-13) by 198 runs.

Margao Cricket Club, Margao, February 16: Tamil Nadu 99 in 45.5 overs (C Shushanthika 22, A Eloksi 21; Tejashwini Duragad 4-19, Diksha Gawde 2-6) lost to **Goa** 100/5 in 30.1 overs (T Duragad 45, Tanaya Naik 20) by five wickets.

GCA Academy, Porvorim, February 17: Tripura 166/6 in 50 overs (Ambika Debnath 120*; Monika Gohate 2-21, Aachal Shahu 2-38) lost to **Vidarbha** 168/3 in 41.4 overs (Latika Inamdar 86*, Sayali Rajendra Shinde 22*) by seven wickets.

Sanguem Cricket Ground, February 18: J&K 59 in 21 overs (Iqra Rasool 29; Diksha Gawde 5-18, Shindiya Naik 2-13) lost to **Goa** 60/0 in 9.3 overs (Purvaja Verlekar 30*, S Naik 23*) by ten wickets.

Goa Cricket Association Academy, Porvorim, February 18: Tamil Nadu 217/8 in 50 overs (C Shushanthika 75, R Abarna 28*; Sebika Das 3-63, Krittika Karmakar 2-47) beat **Tripura** 36 in 25.1 overs (KN Ramyashri 6-5, Priyanshi Pande 2-10) by 181 runs.

Margao Cricket Club, Margao, February 18: Gujarat 162/8 in 50 overs (Muskan Vasava 57*, Aruja Wadhwa 32; Tanaya Rao 4-17, M Modhvadiya 2-37) beat **Saurashtra** 62 in 36.5 overs (Hiral Solanki 3-10) by 100 runs.

Sanguem Cricket Ground, Sanguem, February 20: Vidarbha 80 in 41.5 overs (KN Ramyashri 5-11, MS Aishwarya 2-20) lost to **Tamil Nadu** 81/5 in 27.5 overs (S Swathi 27*; Aachal Shahu 2-28) by five wickets.

GCA Academy, Porvorim, February 20: Saurashtra 199/9 in 50 overs (Tanya Rao 105, T Dharani 24; Sonika 4-35, Sadiya Wani 2-34) beat **Jammu & Kashmir** 58 in 24.3 overs (Lalita 20; T Dharani 2-13, Hira V 2-10) by 141 runs.

Margao Cricket Club, Margao, February 20: Odisha 225/5 in 50 overs (Rasmita Chinhara 62, Swwet Beura 55; Tanya Patel 3-39) beat **Gujarat** 95 in 49.4 overs (Anjali Patel 31; Poonam Nayak 3-11) by 130 runs.

Sanguem Cricket Ground, February 22: Vidarbha 165/9 in 50 overs (Latika Inamdar 47, Sayali Rajendra Shinde 21*; Devanshi Prajapati 3-23, Tanya Patel 2-27) lost to **Gujarat** 166/6 in 48.5 overs (T Patel 62*, Hiral Solanki 26*; Monika Gohate 3-27) by four wickets.

GCA Academy, Porvorim, February 22: Tripura 150/9 in 50 overs (Ambika Debnath 71; Sonali Hembram 2-23, Rani Kumari Prasad 2-25) lost to **Odisha** 151/6 in 46.2 overs (Rasmita Chinhara 41, Sweet Beura 39*; Sebika Das 2-29) by four wickets.

Margao Cricket Club, February 22: Saurashtra 49 in 38.1 overs (Tejashwini Duragad 5-3) lost to **Goa** 50/2 in 14.2 overs (Purvaja Verlekar 22, Shindiya Naik 21*) by eight wickets.

Sanguem Cricket Ground, Sanguem, February 24: Vidarbha 236 in 50 overs (Aayushi Thakre 70, MS Bodkhe 57; Rudrakshi Chib 3-46, Ananaya Sharma 2-41) beat **Jammu & Kashmir** 62 in 30.3 overs (Jahnvi Ranganathan 3-3) by 174 runs.

Margao Cricket Club, Margao, February 24: Gujarat 208/4 in 50 overs (Anjali Patel 69, Muskan Vasava 50*) beat **Tamil Nadu** 167 in 41.3 overs (S Swathi 35, A Eloksi 30; Hiral Solanki 2-35, Tanya Patel 2-46) by 41 runs.

Sanguem Cricket Ground, Sanguem, February 26: Tripura 110 in 43.4 overs (Puja Paul 45; T Dharani 6-27) lost to **Saurashtra** 112/4 in 42.2 overs (P Kanojiya 34*; Gangati Tripura 2-23, Sebika Das 2-24) by six wickets.

Margao Cricket Club, Margao, February 26: Odisha 114 in 44.4 overs (Poonam Nayak 31, Sweet Beura 25; Tejashwini Duragad 4-20, Tanaya Naik 2-16) beat **Goa** 107 in 41.3 overs (T Duragad 32, Diksha Amonkar 26; P Nayak 3-20, Kalpana Nayak 2-11) by seven runs.

Elite Group C points table

Team	M	W	L	T	N/R	Pts	NRR
Odisha	7	7	0	0	0	28	+1.734
Goa	7	6	1	0	0	24	+1.840
Gujarat	7	5	2	0	0	20	+0.198
Tamil Nadu	7	4	3	0	0	16	+1.465
Saurashtra	7	3	4	0	0	12	-0.928
Vidarbha	7	2	5	0	0	8	-0.258
Tripura	7	1	6	0	0	4	-0.783
Jammu & Kashmir	7	0	7	0	0	0	-3.337

Odisha and Goa qualified for the knock-out

Plate Group

SelaQui International School, Dehradun, February 10: Pondicherry 131/7 in 50 overs (Ananya Halder 28, Yuvashri 21; Priti Tarkar 3-16) lost to **Manipur** 132/8 in 42.4 overs (VR Dharani 37; A Halder 2-18, Divya Shanmugam 2-28) by two wickets.

Tanush Academy Ground, Dehradun, February 10: Nagaland 145 in 48.2 overs (Sentilemla 24, Antima Teotia 23; Rishika Kumari 3-13, Shivangi Tyagi 3-39) beat **Arunachal Pradesh** 135 in 48.2 overs (S Tyagi 24; Gunjan 4-16, Sariba 2-25) by 10 runs.

Abhimanyu Cricket Academy, Dehradun, February 10: Mizoram 68 in 35.1 overs (Swati Sah 28; Aarya 4-4, Apurva Kumari 4-7) lost to **Bihar** 69/0 in 20.2 overs (A Kumari 41*, Shruti 21*) by ten wickets.

Abhimanyu Cricket Academy, Dehradun, February 11: Manipur 140 in 49.3 overs (Linthoingambi Rajkumari 25, VR Dharani 20; Neema Yanki Lepcha 3-29, Pranita Chettri 2-12) beat **Sikkim** 111/9 in 50 overs (Pretika Chettri 25, Nandita 21; Priyangka 3-18, Priti Tarkar 2-25) by 29 runs.

SelaQui International School, Dehradun, February 11: Arunachal Pradesh 80/9 in 50 overs (Shivangi Tyagi 29; Jyoti Giri 4-14, Nisha Mishra 2-8) lost to **Uttarakhand** 81/0 in 12.5 overs (Raghvi 45*, Kanchan Parihar 27*) by 10 wickets.

Tanush Academy Ground, Dehradun, February 11: Mizoram 95 in 33.2 overs (Swati Sah 36*; Deiphi 3-7, Wahlang 2-7) lost to **Meghalaya** 96/2 in 34.5 overs (Hajong 28, Rubi Chetri 22*) by eight wickets.

Tanush Academy Ground, Dehradun, February 12: Bihar 191 in 45.1 overs (Apurva Kumari 42, Dipa Kumari 40*; Nur Pandi Lepcha 5-49) beat **Sikkim** 39 in 24.4 overs (Aarya 3-14, Rohini Raj 2-5) by 152 runs.

Abhimanyu Cricket Academy, Dehradun, February 12: Uttarakhand 282/5 in 50 overs (Raghvi 168*, Jyoti Giri 44; Yuvashri 2-29, Sumi Dutta 2-51) beat **Pondicherry** 97 in 47 overs (Ananya Halder 23; Radha Chand 2-11, Pooja Raj 2-17) by 185 runs.

SelaQui International School, Dehradun, February 12: Nagaland 211/7 in 50 overs (Antima Teotia 100*, Sentilemla 37; Dasan 2-27, Deiphi 2-32) beat **Meghalaya** 71 in 38.4 overs (Sapna 4-17, Elina 2-8) by 140 runs.

SelaQui International School, Dehradun, February 14: Nagaland v **Sikkim**. Match abandoned without a ball being bowled.

Abhimanyu Cricket Academy, Dehradun, February 14: Bihar v **Manipur**. Match abandoned without a ball being bowled.

Tanush Academy Ground, Dehradun, February 14: Mizoram v **Pondicherry**. Match abandoned without a ball being bowled.

SelaQui International School, Dehradun, February 15: Nagaland v **Uttarakhand**. Match abandoned without a ball being bowled.

Abhimanyu Cricket Academy, Dehradun, February 15: Bihar v **Meghalaya**. Match abandoned without a ball being bowled.

Tanush Academy Ground, Dehradun, February 15: Arunachal Pradesh v **Pondicherry**. Match abandoned without a ball being bowled.

Tanush Academy Ground, Dehradun, February 17: Arunachal Pradesh 93 in 42.1 overs (Dasan 4-19, Deiphi 2-17) lost to **Meghalaya** 94/7 in 36.5 overs (Shivangi Tyagi 3-23, K Kaithl 2-14) by three wickets.

Abhimanyu Cricket Academy, Dehradun, February 17: Mizoram 125 in 37.2 overs (Omoni 29; Pramila 2-12) beat **Sikkim** 108 in 45.4 overs (Swati Sah 4-14) by 17 runs.

SelaQui International School, Dehradun, February 17: Uttarakhand 342/3 in 50 overs (Kanchan Parihar 131*, Radha Chand 112*; Priyangka 2-56) beat **Manipur** 78 in 39.5 overs (VR Dharani 39*; Dimpal Kandari 4-19, Ruhi Chauhan 2-6) by 264 runs.

SelaQui International School, Dehradun, February 19: Nagaland v **Pondicherry**. Match abandoned without a ball being bowled.

Abhimanyu Cricket Academy, Dehradun, February 19: Arunachal Pradesh v **Bihar**. Match abandoned without a ball being bowled.

Tanush Academy Ground, Dehradun, February 19: Manipur v **Mizoram**. Match abandoned without a ball being bowled.

SelaQui International School, Dehradun, February 21: Meghalaya 57 in 41.1 overs (Dimapl Kandari 4-14, Nisha Mishra 3-6) lost to **Uttarakhand** 58/1 in 12.5 overs (Kanchan Parihar 31*) by nine wickets.

Abhimanyu Cricket Academy, Dehradun, February 21: Arunachal Pradesh v **Sikkim**. Match abandoned without a ball being bowled.

Tanush Academy Ground, Dehradun, February 21: Manipur 143/6 in 39 overs (Seterny 22) beat **Nagaland** 124 in 37.4 overs (Nabila 25*; VR Dharani 2-23, Kiranbala Haorungbam 2-24) by 19 runs.

Abhimanyu Cricket Academy, Dehradun, February 23: Uttarakhand 296/8 in 50 overs (Raghvi 112, Kanchan Parihar 55; Swati Sah 3-49, Srilekha Roy 2-43) beat **Mizoram** 70 in 35.5 overs (S Sah 22; Nisha Mishra 4-11, Pooja Raj 3-15) by 226 runs.

SelaQui International School, Dehradun, February 23: Nagaland 82 in 35.4 overs (Reety Biswas 20; Rohini Raj 4-21, Aarya 2-15) lost to **Bihar** 85/2 in 16.5 overs (Apurva Kumari 38*) by eight wickets.

Tanush Academy Ground, Dehradun, February 23: Sikkim 96 in 45.1 overs (Pranita Chettri 29, Nandita 23; Sumi Dutta 3-16, Yuvashri 2-4) beat **Pondicherry** 89 in 40.1 overs (Ananya Halder 30; Simran Gurung 3-8, Samayita 2-36) by seven runs.

Tanush Academy Ground, Dehradun, February 25: Pondicherry 110/8 in 50 overs (Tanishka Sen 40*, Sumi Dutta 25; Apurva Kumari 3-10, Rohini Raj 2-29) lost to **Bihar** 111/1 in 22.2 overs (Shruti 45*, Aarya 39*) by nine wickets.

Abhimanyu Cricket Academy, Dehradun, February 25: Sikkim 124/8 in 50 overs (Samayita 50*; N Roy 2-14, Rubi Chetri 2-18) beat **Meghalaya** 100 in 44.1 overs (Pranita Chettri 3-9, Nur Pandi Lepcha 2-19) by 24 runs.

SelaQui International School, Dehradun, February 25: Manipur 144 in 43 overs (Seterny 37, Ronibala Thokchom 28; Shivangi Tyagi 4-36, A Priyedarshni 3-30) beat **Arunachal Pradesh** 115 in 42.4 overs (S Tyagi 45*, Meghna Sharma 22; VR Dharani 4-9, Priyangka 2-17) by 29 runs.

Abhimanyu Cricket Academy, Dehradun, February 27: Manipur v **Meghalaya**. Match abandoned without a ball being bowled.

Tanush Academy Ground, Dehradun, February 27: Mizoram 89 in 30.5 overs (Swati Sah 40; Ritu 5-10, Gunjan 2-12) lost to **Nagaland** 85/3 in 20.3 overs (Reety Biswas 29*; Zuali 3-21) by seven wickets. (VJD method).

SelaQui International School, February 27: Sikkim 54 in 39.4 overs (Dimpal Kandari 3-16, Pooja Raj 2-6) lost to **Uttarakhand** 55/2 in 5.4 overs (Raghvi 31) by eight wickets.

Tanush Academy Ground, Dehradun, March 1: Arunachal Pradesh 119/7 in 50 overs (Shivani Tyagi 44; Sagarika Sengupta 2-9, Swati Sah 2-14) lost to **Mizoram** 120/8 in 45.4 overs (S Sah 64*; K Kaithl 3-12, A Priyedarshni 3-30) by two wickets.

SelaQui International School, Dehradun, March 1: Pondicherry 101 in 38 overs (Sumi Dutta 49; Dasan 2-13, Rubi Chetri 2-21) lost to **Meghalaya** 102/9 in 47.3 overs (Sanchisa 22; Divya Shanmugam 3-9, Sumi Dutta 2-17) by one wicket.

Abhimanyu Cricket Academy, March 1: Bihar 53 in 25.1 overs (Nisha Mishra 3-13, Ritika 2-9) lost to **Uttarakhand** 54/2 in 16.3 overs (Kanchan Parihar 21*) by eight wickets.

Plate Group points table

Team	M	W	L	T	N/R	Pts	NRR
Uttarakhand	8	7	0	0	1	30	+4.491
Bihar	8	4	1	0	3	22	+1.561
Manipur	8	4	1	0	3	22	-0.912
Nagaland	8	3	2	0	3	18	+0.276
Meghalaya	8	3	3	0	2	16	-0.508
Mizoram	8	2	4	0	2	12	-1.046
Sikkim	8	2	4	0	2	12	-0.953
Arunachal Pradesh	8	0	5	0	3	6	-0.778
Pondicherry	8	0	5	0	3	6	-1.475

Uttarakhand qualified for the knock-out

Quarter-finals

Abhimanyu Cricket Academy, Dehradun, March 6: Bengal 224/7 in 50 overs (Richa 60, Ankita Chakraborty 36; Raghvi 2-19, Nisha Mishra 2-29) beat **Uttarakhand** 57 in 38.4 overs (Shreya Karar 6-12) by 167 runs.

Tanush Academy Ground, Dehradun, March 6: Odisha 140 in 47.3 overs (Kajal Jena 34, Poonam Nayak 31; Sudha Shukla 3-20, Falak Naz 2-14) lost to **Uttar Pradesh** 143/7 in 36.1 overs (Shipra Giri 44*, Muskan Malik 38; P Nayak 4-14, Kalpana Nayak 2-22) by three wickets.

Abhimanyu Cricket Academy, Dehradun, March 7: Goa 73 in 31.3 overs (Tejashwini Duragad 23; Simran Dil Bahadur 3-9, Ayushi Soni 2-2) lost to **Delhi** 74/6 in 25.3 overs (SD Bahadur 22; T Duragad 4-19) by four wickets.

Tanush Academy Ground, Dehradun, March 7: Punjab 164/9 in 50 overs (Amanjot Kaur 58, Kanika Ahuja 40; Sayali satghare 3-24, Jagravi Pawar 3-31) lost to **Mumbai** 165/5 in 49.1 overs (Shaheen 66*, Aachal Valanju 30; K Ahuja 3-27, A Kaur 2-33) by five wickets.

Bengal, Uttar Pradesh, Delhi and Mumbai qualified for the semi-finals

Semi-finals

Abhimanyu Cricket Academy, Dehradun, March 9: Bengal 150 in 49.2 overs (Mamata 42, Richa 32; Tanvi Parab 4-30, Jagravi Pawar 3-25) beat **Mumbai** 130 in 46.2 overs (Sayali Satghare 20; Priyanka Sarkar 3-11, Shreya Karar 2-20) by 20 runs.

Tanush Academy Ground, Dehradun, March 9: Delhi 172/9 in 50 overs (Shweta Sehrawat 46, Ayushi Soni 38; Sonam Yadav 3-21, Anjali Singh 3-33) beat **Uttar Pradesh** 81 in 32.4 overs (Priya Mishra 3-15, A Soni 2-7) by 91 runs.

Bengal and Delhi qualified for the final

Final

Abhimanyu Cricket Academy, Dehradun, March 11: Bengal 181 in 50 overs (Kashish Agarwal 49, Ankita Chakraborty 40; Madhu 3-33) beat **Delhi** 110/5 in 38 overs (Simran Dil Bahadur 47*; Sushmita Ganguly 2-20) by 26 runs. (VJD method).

Winners: Bengal

2017-18

North Zone

Paramount Cricket Promotion Association Ground (Paramount ground), Santokhgarh, November 1: Himachal Pradesh 115 in 42.1 overs (Chitra Singh Jamwal 48; Simran 3-7) lost to **Delhi** 116/4 in 41 overs (Pratika Rawal 30*, Neha Bhargava 27; Nikita Chauhan 2-24) by six wickets.

Jawaharlal Navoday Vidhyalay Stadium, Una, November 1: Jammu & Kashmir 53 in 41.5 overs (Parul 2-6, Rajni Devi 2-8) lost to **Punjab** 56/1 in 13.2 overs (Srishti Rajput 20*) by nine wickets.

Paramount ground, Santokhgarh, November 3: Haryana 169/8 in 50 overs (Suman Gulia 55*, Bhawna Ohlan 51; Prachi Chauhan 3-15, Sonal Thakur 2-22) lost to **Himachal Pradesh** 170/8 in 49.1 overs (Preeti Kahlon 39*, S Thakur 31) by two wickets.

Jawaharlal Navoday Vidhyalay Stadium, Una, November 3: Jammu & Kashmir 107 in 47 overs (Tanisha Sharma 33; Pratika Rawal 2-14, Ayushi Soni 2-20) lost to **Delhi** 108/0 in 26.1 overs (Jyoshi Nain 54*, Mansi Sharma 36*) by 10 wickets.

Paramount ground, Santokhgarh, November 5: Jammu & Kashmir 55 in 32.4 overs (Parmila Kumari 4-2, Priya Kumari 2-6) lost to **Haryana** 60/0 in 7.3 overs (Bhawna Ohlan 45*) by 10 wickets.

Jawaharlal Navoday Vidhyalay Stadium, Una, November 5: Delhi 126/9 in 50 overs (Ayushi Soni 51, Jyoshi Nain 33; Nandani Sharma 4-16, Rajni Devi 2-40) beat **Punjab** 109 in 46.3 overs (Kanika Ahuja 44; Simran 4-21, Neha Bhargava 3-16) by 17 runs.

Paramount ground, Santokhgarh, November 7: Himachal Pradesh 73 in 25.1 overs (Rajni Devi 4-9, Nandani Sharma 3-20) lost to **Punjab** 74/0 in 34.1 overs (Shabnam Thakur 35*, Amanjot Kaur 32*) by 10 wickets.

Jawaharlal Navoday Vidhyalay Stadium, Una, November 7: Delhi 172/5 in 50 overs (Ayushi Soni 59*, Mansi Sharma 33) beat **Haryana** 105 in 40 overs (Neha Bhargava 3-26, Shreeya 2-17) by 67 runs.

Jawaharlal Navoday Vidhyalay Stadium, Una, November 9: Punjab 159/6 in 50 overs (Kanika Ahuja 71*, Raman Preet Kaur 23; Anjali 2-14, Bhawna Ohlan 2-27) beat **Haryana** 144 in 46.5 overs (B Ohlan 43, Suman Gulia 24; Rajni Devi 5-18, K Ahuja 3-31) by 15 runs.

Paramount ground, Santokhgarh, November 9: Jammu & Kashmir 60 in 29.3 overs (Nikita Chauhan 3-14, Kahlon 3-18) lost to **Himachal Pradesh** 61/0 in 8.3 overs (SM Singh 37*) by 10 wickets.

North Zone points table

Team	M	W	L	T	N/R	Pts	NRR
Delhi	4	4	0	0	0	16	+0.943
Punjab	4	3	1	0	0	12	+0.718
Himachal Pradesh	4	2	2	0	0	8	+0.265
Haryana	4	1	3	0	0	4	+0.243
Jammu & Kashmir	4	0	4	0	0	0	-3.760

Delhi and Punjab qualified for the Super League

Central Zone

Kamla Club Sports Ground, Kanpur, November 4: Uttar Pradesh 223/6 in 50 overs (Ekta Singh 103*, Kshama Singh 37;) beat **Madhya Pradesh** 135/8 in 50 overs (Pooja Vastrakar 32, Bharti Choudhary 31; Anjali Singh 4-37, Tanu Kala 2-24) by 88 runs.

Green Park Stadium, Kanpur, November 4: Rajasthan 263/9 in 50 overs (Suman Meena 91, Ayushi Garg 62; Aayushi Thakre 2-34) beat **Vidarbha** 127/3 in 50 overs (LM Inamdar 66, SA Borekar 25) by 136 runs.

Kamla Club Sports Ground, Kanpur, November 5: Uttar Pradesh 346/3 in 50 overs (Shobha Devi 113*, Ekta Singh 69) beat **Vidarbha** 109/8 in 50 overs (LM INamdar 34; Rishika Yadav 2-10, Kshama 2-18) by 237 runs.

Modi Stadium, Kanpur, November 5: Chhattisgarh 120/6 in 50 overs (Yashi Pandey 58*, Deepika Tiwari 20; Srashti Nagpure 3-17, Rajak 2-16) beat **Madhya Pradesh** 79 in 38.1 overs (Nadani Sahu 4-27, Y Pandey 2-6) by 41 runs.

Green Park Stadium, Kanpur, November 6: Chhattisgarh 147/8 in 50 overs (Manpreet Kaur 75; PM Choudhary 3-17, Ruby Choudary 2-27) lost to **Rajasthan** 149/0 in 33.3 overs (Ayushi Garg 74, Jyoti Choudhary 48*) by 10 wickets.

Kamla Club Sports Ground, Kanpur, November 7: Vidarbha 90 in 45 overs (MS Bhodkhe 23; Bharti Choudhary 3-2, Ananya Dubey 3-18) lost to **Madhya Pradesh** 94/2 in 25.3 overs (Pooja Vasttrakar 58*, Soniya Sharma 26) by eight wickets.

Kamla Club Sports Ground, Kanpur, November 8: Madhya Pradesh 168/9 in 50 overs (Pooja Vastrakar 84, Soniya Sharma 29; MS Gurjar 2-26) beat **Rajasthan** 82 in 37.4 overs (Ayushi Garg 23; Bharti Choudhary 3-11, S Sharma 2-7) by 86 runs.

Green Park Stadium, Kanpur, November 8: Chhattisgarh 159/8 in 50 overs (Deepika Tiwari 54, Yashi Pandey 50; Tanu Kala 5-10) lost to **Uttar Pradesh** 160/0 in 38 overs (Muskan Malik 72*, Ekta Singh 66*) by 10 wickets.

Kamla Club Sports Ground, Kanpur, November 9: Chhattisgarh 244/7 in 50 overs (Yashi Pandey 75, Manpreet Kaur 69) beat **Vidarbha** 185 in 49.3 overs (LM Inamdar 74, MS Bhodkhe 40; Mamta Bhagat 3-25, Y Pandey 2-40) by 59 runs.

Green Park Stadium, Kanpur, November 9: Rajasthan 165/8 in 50 overs (Jyoti Choudhary 42, AR Choudhary 21; Tanu Kala 3-21) lost to **Uttar Pradesh** 171/7 in 45 overs (Ekta Singh 57, Shobha Devi 37; Ruby Choudary 3-26) by three wickets.

Central Zone points table

Team	M	W	L	T	N/R	Pts	NRR
Uttar Pradesh	4	4	0	0	0	16	+2.078
Rajasthan	4	2	2	0	0	8	+0.448
Madhya Pradesh	4	2	2	0	0	8	+0.137

Team	M	W	L	T	N/R	Pts	NRR
Chhattisgarh	4	2	2	0	0	8	+0.009
Vidarbha	4	0	4	0	0	0	-2.841

Uttar Pradesh and Rajasthan qualified for the Super League

West Zone

Marathwada Sanskrit Mandal Ground, Aurangabad, November 1: Baroda 219/7 in 50 overs (Jaya Mohite 52*, Radha Yadav 35; T Dharani 4-31, Tanya Rao 2-41) beat **Saurashtra** 48 in 28 overs (Meghna Jambucha 21; Charmi Shah 3-20, R Yadav 2-2) by 171 runs.

Aurangabad DCA Ground, November 1: Mumbai 323/3 in 50 overs (Jemimah Rodrigues 178, Pooja Yadav 87; Anjali Patel 2-51) beat **Gujarat** 61 in 36.2 overs (BS Goplani 20; Sayali Satghare 5-19, Janhvi Kate 3-3) by 262 runs.

Marathwada Sanskrit Mandal Ground, Aurangabad, November 2: Gujarat 111 in 43 overs (Itisha Patel 30; T Dharani 3-10, Jethva 3-27) beat **Saurashtra** 107 in 48.1 overs (Tanya Rao 28, JH Makwana 28; PA Talpada 4-8, Anjali Patel 3-28) by four runs.

Aurangabad DCA Ground, November 2: Baroda 264/2 in 50 overs (Yastika Bhatia 131, Radha Yadav 91*) beat **Maharashtra** 160 in 48.5 overs (Priyanka Ghodke 51, Aditi Gaikwad 26; Charmi Shah 4-32, Jaya Mohite 3-43) by 104 runs.

Marathwada Sanskrit Mandal Ground, November 4: Baroda 204/6 in 50 overs (Yastika Bhatia 60, Hrutvisha Patel 55; Fatima Jaffer 2-34) beat **Mumbai** 171/9 in 50 overs (Vrushali Bhagat 61, Riya Chaudhari 31; Radha Yadav 5-20, Pragya Rawat 2-35) by 33 runs.

Jemimah Rodrigues' double-century made her a star across the country.

Aurangabad DCA Ground, November 4: Saurashtra 50 in 31 overs (Maya Sonawane 4-2, Nikita Aage 2-6) lost to **Maharashtra** 52/0 in 8 overs (Priyanka Ghodke 30*, M Sonawane 22*) by ten wickets.

Marathwada Sanskrit Mandal Ground, Aurangabad, November 5: Gujarat 84 in 49.1 overs (Aruja Wadhwa 36; Maya Sonawane 4-18, Nikita Aage 2-8) lost to **Maharashtra** 86/2 in 26.3 overs (M Sonawane 34*, Hrutuja Deshmukh 23; HR Solanki 2-20) by eight wickets.

Aurangabad DCA Ground, November 5: Mumbai 347/2 in 50 overs (Jemimah Rodrigues 202*, Sejal Raut 98) beat **Saurashtra** 62 in 39.4 overs (Meghna Jambucha 25; Sayali Satghare 3-20, Fatima Jaffer 2-10) by 285 runs. **Marathwada Sanskrit Mandal Ground, Aurangabad, November 7: Mumbai** 112 in 38.1 overs (Jemimah Rodrigues 27; Priyanka Ghodke 3-18, Nikita Aage 2-10) beat **Maharashtra** 107 in 37 overs (Aditi Gaikwad 32; J Rodrigues 4-28, Janhvi Kate 3-23) by five runs.

Aurangabad DCA Ground, November 7: Gujarat 56 in 29.5 overs (Radha Yadav 3-4, Jaya Mohite 3-19) lost to **Baroda** 59/1 in 13.3 overs (Yastika Bhatia 27*, Amrita Joseph 24) by nine wickets.

West Zone points table

Team	M	W	L	T	N/R	Pts	NRR
Baroda	4	4	0	0	0	16	+2.388
Mumbai	4	3	1	0	0	12	+2.595
Maharashtra	4	2	2	0	0	8	+0.461
Gujarat	4	1	3	0	0	4	-2.547
Saurashtra	4	0	4	0	0	0	-3.279

Baroda and Mumbai qualified for the Super League

South Zone

J Narendranath ACA Ground, Perecherla, November 1: Kerala 151/8 in 50 overs (Malavika Sabu 26, Minnu Mani 24; G Trisha 3-9, Bhavya Mahati 2-27) beat **Hyderabad** 147/9 in 50 overs (Vanka Pooja 38*, G Trisha 29; M Mani 2-18, Biby Sebastin 2-30) by four runs.

RVRJCE Ground, Guntur, November 1: Andhra 209 in 49.4 overs (Miriyala Durga 80, V Pushpa Latha 42; Nida Rehman 4-30, KN Ramyashri 2-34) beat **Tamil Nadu** 51 in 27.2 overs (B Anusha 5-9) by 158 runs.

JKC College, Guntur, November 1: Goa 85 in 31 overs (Tejaswini Duragad 43; D Vrinda 2-14, S Chaitra 2-15) lost to **Karnataka** 86/1 in 14 overs (D Vrinda 51*, K Pratyoosha 21) by nine wickets.

RVRJCE Ground, Guntur, November 2: Tamil Nadu 81 in 32.2 overs (Aswathi Shankar 34; Minnu Mani 5-9, Biby Sebastin 2-16) lost to **Kerala** 82/4 in 29.5 overs (Malavika Sabu 27, Jisna Joseph 23; Nida Rehman 2-22) by six wickets.

J Narendranath ACA Ground, Perecherla, November 2: Hyderabad 272 in 49.4 overs (Trisha Poojitha 104, Kameswara Sravya 68; Tejashwini Duragad 3-62, Diksha Gawde 2-28) beat **Goa** 166 in 49.5 overs (Sugandha Ghadi 48, T Duragad 34; Lakshmi Prasanna 4-11, G Trisha 2-9) by 106 runs.

JKC College, Guntur, November 2: Andhra 234/7 in 50 overs (V Pushpa Latha 102, G Sindhuja 47*; M Anagha 3-49, Monica Patel 2-42) beat **Karnataka** 129 in 41.3 overs (K Pratyoosha 32, D Vrinda 25; K Dhatri 4-24, E Padmaja 3-16) by 105 runs.

JKC College, Guntur, November 4: Kerala 101/9 in 50 overs (Aleena Surendran 20, Jisna Joseph 20; M Bhavana 2-13, G Sindhuja 2-20) lost to **Andhra** 102/7 in 38.3 overs (Miriyala Durga 29; Anju Rajan 2-29) by three wickets.

RVRJCE Ground, Guntur, November 4: Karnataka 122 in 38.5 overs (Aditi Rajesh 55*; G Trisha 4-18, Vanka Pooja 2-32) lost to **Hyderabad** 123/3 in 26.4 overs (G Trisha 52, Trisha Poojitha 22; M Anagha 2-35) by seven wickets.

J Narendranath ACA Ground, Perecherla, November 4: Tamil Nadu 205/4 in 50 overs (S Pavithra Sridharan 75*, Aswathi Shankar 46; Diksha Gawde 2-34) beat **Goa** 91 in 36.2 overs (KN Ramyashri 4-34, Nida Rehman 2-16) by 114 runs.

JKC College, Guntur, November 5: Hyderabad 123/8 in 50 overs (Lakshmi Prasanna 30, Anitha Kotha 20; K Devika 3-26, V Pushpa Latha 2-14) lost to **Andhra** 124/2 in 30.4 overs (Miriyala Durga 64*, E Padmaja 29*) by eight wickets.

RVRJCE Ground, Guntur, November 5: Tamila Nadu 90 in 34.2 overs (SB Keerthana 40; Monica Patel 4-9, Sneha Jagadish 3-29) lost to **Karnataka** 91/4 in 28.4 overs (K Pratyoosha 42; KN Ramyashri 2-21) by six wickets.

J Narendranath ACA Ground, Perecherla, November 5: Goa 132 in 47.1 overs (Shindiya Naik 33, Purvaja 20; TP Sruthy 2-11, Sandra Suren 2-12) lost to **Kerala** 133/3 in 36.3 overs (Malavika Sabu 38, Minnu Mani 29*) by seven wickets.

J Narendranath ACA Ground, Perecherla, November 7: Andhra 274/3 in 50 overs (E Padmaja 93*, V Pushpa Latha 82*) beat **Goa** 147/2 in 50 overs (Purvaja 68*, Tejashwini Duragad 40*; G Sindhuja 2-37) by 127 runs.

JKC College, Guntur, November 7: Karnataka 150/9 in 50 overs (D Vrinda 38, Monica Patel 30*; Sandra Suren 4-19, Minnu Mani 3-30) lost to **Kerala** 151/4 in 44.4 overs (IV Drishya 67, M Mani 31) by six wickets.

RVRJCE Ground, Guntur, November 7: Hyderabad 231/6 in 50 overs (Lakshmi Prasanna 79, Vanka Pooja 57; A Eloksi 2-34) beat **Tamil Nadu** 129 in 46.1 overs (SB Keerthana 46; G Trisha 4-5, Merlyn John 3-20) by 102 runs.

South Zone points table

Team	M	W	L	T	N/R	Pts	NRR
Andhra	5	5	0	0	0	20	+2.099
Kerala	5	4	1	0	0	16	+0.363
Hyderabad	5	3	2	0	0	12	+0.953
Karnataka	5	2	3	0	0	8	-0.086
Tamil Nadu	5	1	4	0	0	4	-1.152
Goa	5	0	5	0	0	0	-2.354

Andhra and Kerala qualified for the Super League

East Zone

Jharkhand State Cricket Association (JSCA) International Stadium Complex, Ranchi, November 1: Tripura 87/6 in 50 overs (P Radha Jamatia 20; Anjali Das 2-12) lost to **Jharkhand** 88/2 in 21.3 overs (Payel Ghosh 32*) by eight wickets.

JSCA Oval Ground, Ranchi, November 1: Assam 109 in 49.1 overs (Ruhina Pegu 22; Tapati Paul 3-13, N Khatun 2-15) lost to **Bengal** 113/1 in 31.2 overs (Richa 53*, Ankita Chakraborty 32*) by nine wickets.

JSCA International Stadium Complex, Ranchi, November 3: Jharkhand 154 in 49.3 overs (Durga Kumari Murmu 42, Suvecha Mondal 21; Kakoli Saikia 4-21, Priyanka Baruah 3-20) beat **Assam** 92 in 41 overs (Rashmi Dey 20; Anjali Das 6-17, Mamta Paswan 2-12) by 62 runs.

JSCA Oval Ground, Ranchi, November 3: Odisha 218/3 in 50 overs (Kajal Jena 69, Rasmita Chinhara 47; Antara Das 2-31) beat **Tripura** 91 in 46 overs (P Radha Jamatia 27, Ambika Debnath 21; Kalpana Nayak 2-11, Nirjharini Swain 2-17) by 127 runs.

JSCA Oval Ground, Ranchi, November 5: Odisha 138/7 in 50 overs (Taranna Pradhan 41, Indrani Chhatria 25*; Mamta Paswan 3-25, P Priya 2-28) lost to **Jharkhand** 139/3 in 39.3 overs (Durga Kumari Murmu 51*, Sonia 35*; Kalpana Nayak 2-26) by seven wickets.

JSCA Complex, Ranchi, November 5: Tripura 136/9 in 50 overs (Shiuli Chakraborty 29, Ambika Debnath 26; Sushmita Ganguly 2-15, N Khatun 2-17) lost to **Bengal** 137/6 in 41.3 overs (Mamata 48*, Dhara Gujjar 21; Puja Das 2-28) by four wickets.

JSCA Complex, Ranchi, November 8: Bengal 95/9 in 50 overs (Mamata 27, Dhara Gujjar 22; Shannti Kumari 2-22, P Priya 2-29) lost to **Jharkhand** 96/2 in 29.2 overs (Payel Ghosh 46*, Sonia 29*; Salma Khatun 2-18) by eight wickets.

JSCA Oval Ground, Ranchi, November 8: Odisha 165/4 in 50 overs (Sangeeta Khadia 54*, Kajal Jena 50) lost to **Assam** 166/5 in 41.2 overs (Gayatri Gurung 39, Ruhina Pegu 38; GM Alakananda 3-41) by five wickets.

JSCA Oval Ground, Ranchi, November 10: Tripura 116 in 48.4 overs (SH Chakraborty 35; Kakoli Saikia 3-13) lost to **Assam** 117/1 in 33 overs (Gayatri Gurung 48*, Priyanka Boruah 33) by nine wickets.

JSCA International Stadium Complex, Ranchi, November 10: Odisha 77 in 49.1 overs (P Choudhary 2-10, Jhumpa Roy 2-15) lost to **Bengal** 79/1 in 22 overs (Richa 44*, Ankita Chakraborty 25*) by nine wickets.

East Zone points table

Team	M	W	L	T	N/R	Pts	NRR
Jharkhand	4	4	0	0	0	16	+1.339
Bengal	4	3	1	0	0	12	+0.597
Assam	4	2	2	0	0	8	-0.246
Odisha	4	1	3	0	0	4	-0.118
Tripura	4	0	4	0	0	0	-1.686

Jharkhand and Bengal qualified for the Super League

North East and Bihar

Tata Digwadi Stadium, November 1: Meghalaya 80 in 22.4 overs (Neema Yanki Lepcha 6-16, Archana Limbu 2-25) lost to **Sikkim** 81/5 in 24.5 overs (Monica 3-19) by five wickets.

Railway Stadium, Dhanbad, November 1: Arunachal Pradesh 124/9 in 50 overs (M Kalra 60; Sikha Singh 3-17, Tejeshwi 2-24) lost to **Bihar** 125/4 in 25 overs (Kumari 26, Apurva 25; Kalra 2-26) by five wickets.

Jawaharlal Nehru Stadium, Dhanbad, November 1: Nagaland 215 in 38 overs (Mushkan 54, Pori 24; Linthoingambi Rajkumari 4-34) beat **Manipur** 98 in 27.3 overs (Ronibala Thokchom 24; Pori 5-16, Arpana 3-16) by 117 runs.

Jawaharlal Nehru Stadium, Dhanbad, November 3: Meghalaya 37 in 12.2 overs (R Yadav 7-6) lost to **Arunachal Pradesh** 39/1 in 6.5 overs by nine wickets.

Railway Stadium, Dhanbad, November 3: Nagaland 167 in 48 overs (Priyanka Karmakar 24, Mushkan 24; Archana Limbu 4-28) beat **Sikkim** 47 in 32 overs (Arpana 7-3) by 120 runs.

Tata Digwadi Stadium, Jamadoba, November 3: Bihar 327/6 in 50 overs (Mansi Kashyap 96*, Soni 32; Linthoingambi Rajkumari 3-47) beat **Manipur** 53 in 19 overs (Sapna Kumari 4-16, Sikha Singh 3-14) by 274 runs.

Jawaharlal Nehru Stadium, Dhanbad, November 5: Manipur 99 in 23.4 overs (Daiaka 6-34, Smriti 2-11) lost to **Meghalaya** 103/4 in 13.5 overs (Smriti 38*; Palujam Kiranbala 4-22) by six wickets.

Railway Stadium, Dhanbad, November 5: Arunachal Pradesh 157 in 34.4 overs (M Kalra 38, K Kaithl 31; Tshering Chokey Lepcha 2-7, Neema Yanki Lepcha 2-17) beat **Sikkim** 77 in 33.3 overs (K Kaithl 4-5, R Yadav 4-19) by 80 runs.

Tata Digwadi Stadium, Jamadoba, November 5: Nagaland 133/9 in 50 overs (Elina 32, Kanika 20; Kumari 3-12, Apurva 3-22) lost to **Bihar** 134/7 in 37.4 overs (Tejashwi 25*, Kumari 20; Mushkan 5-21, Arpana 2-34) by three wickets.

Railway Stadium, Dhanbad, November 7: Bihar 384/5 in 50 overs (Apurva 108, Soni 51*; Lasiewspah 2-58) beat **Meghalaya** 18 in 11 overs (Kumari 5-8, Sikha Singh 3-9) by 366 runs.

Tata Digwadi Stadium, Jamadoba, November 7: Sikkim 121/4 in 50 overs (Pinky Keithellakpam 2-23) lost to **Manipur** 122/8 in 44.5 overs (Khumbongmayum Bidyarani 20; Simran Gurung 4-14) by two wickets.

Jawaharlal Nehru Stadium, Dhanbad, November 7: AP 48 in 27.4 overs (Arpana 5-7, Mushkan 3-19) lost to **Nagaland** 49/2 in 11.3 overs (Mushkan 2-9) by eight wickets.

Jawaharlal Nehru Stadium, Dhanbad, November 9: Bihar 265/6 in 50 overs (Apurva 99, Soni 42; Tshering Chokey Lepcha 2-45) beat **Sikkim** 18 in 24 overs (Sikha Singh 8-6, Apurva 2-0) by 247 runs.

Railway Stadium, Dhanbad, November 9: Nagaland 149 in 35.1 overs (Sariba 31; Daiaka 2-25, Shhilpa 2-30) beat **Meghalaya** 17 in 13 overs (Arpana 7-5, Pori 2-12) by 132 runs.
Tata Digwadi Stadium, Jamadoba, November 9: Arunachal Pradesh 161 in 44.1 overs (M Kalra 25; Linthoingambi Rajkumari 3-30, Palujam Kiranbala 3-38) beat **Manipur** 80 in 30.2 overs (Ronibala Thokchom 32; M Kalra 4-8, R Yadav 4-18) by 81 runs.

North East and Bihar points table

Team	M	W	L	T	N/R	Pts	NRR
Bihar	5	5	0	0	0	20	+4.423
Nagaland	5	4	1	0	0	16	+1.924
Arunachal Pradesh	5	3	2	0	0	12	+0.584
Sikkim	5	1	4	0	0	4	-1.701
Manipur	5	1	4	0	0	4	-2.489
Meghalaya	5	1	4	0	0	4	-2.947

Bihar and Nagaland qualified for the Super League

Group A Super League

Keenan Stadium, Jamshedpur, November 15: Punjab 70/5 in 36 overs (Kanika Ahuja 25*; K Dhatri 2-11, B Anusha 2-12) lost to **Andhra** 85/4 in 26.2 overs (Miriyala Durga 40*, N Anusha 26) by six wickets (VJD method).
Shaheed Nirmal Mahato Stadium, Jamshedpur, November 15: Baroda 143/9 in 45 overs (Yastika Bhatia 40, Amrita Joseph 23; Shreya Karar 3-25, Tapati Paul 3-26) beat **Bengal** 90 in 37.2 overs (Richa 51; Pragya Rawat 4-14, Kesha Patel 2-11) by 53 runs.
Keenan Stadium, Jamshedpur, November 16: Bihar 46 in 43 overs (MS Gurjar 3-7, Suman Meena 2-11) lost to **Rajasthan** 44/1 in 7.1 overs by nine wickets.
Shaheed Nirmal Mahato Stadium, November 17: Bengal 218/4 in 49 overs (Richa 94, Dhara Gujjar 52; Rajni Devi 2-59) lost to **Punjab** 118 in 45.2 overs (Kanika Ahuja 29, Amanjot Kaur 22; Jhumpa Roy 3-12, Tapati Paul 3-19) by 100 runs.
Keenan Stadium, Jamshedpur, November 17: Rajasthan 62 in 34.5 overs (AR Choudhary 30; G Sindhuja 4-20, E Padmaja 3-9) lost to **Andhra** 63/2 in 31.5 overs (N Anusha 25*, V Pushpa Latha 20) by eight wickets.
Keenan Stadium, Jamshedpur, November 18: Bihar 56 in 35.4 overs (Radha Yadav 5-15) lost to **Baroda** 57/2 in 12 overs (Yastika Bhatia 25*; Apurva 2-10) by eight wickets.
Shaheed Nirmal Mahato Stadium, November 19: Punjab 227/7 in 50 overs (Amanjot Kaur 102*, Kanika Ahuja 64; Sikha Singh 2-39) beat **Bihar** 108/7 in 50 overs (S Singh 40) by 119 runs.
Keenan Stadium, Jamshedpur, November 19: Bengal 124/6 in 50 overs (Dhara Gujjar 31; G Sindhuja 2-21) lost to **Andhra** 125/5 in 46.2 overs (Miriyala Durga 37, G Sindhuja 24; P Choudhary 2-20, Tapati Paul 2-27) by five wickets.
Keenan Stadium, Jamshedpur, November 20: Baroda 147/9 in 50 overs (Jaya Mohite 39, Yastika Bhatia 34; Ruby Choudhary 3-21, PM Choudhary 2-24) lost to **Rajasthan** 150/6 in 49.4 overs (RS Tinker 53, Ayushi Garg 45; J Mohite 2-37) by four wickets.
Keenan Stadium, Jamshedpur, November 21: Baroda 157 in 48.2 overs (Yastika Bhatia 55, Radha Yadav 50; Kanika Ahuja 3-27, Rajni Devi 3-29) beat **Punjab** 136/8 in 50 overs (K Ahuja 42, Amanjot Kaur 31; R Yadav 3-14, Ridhi Maurya 2-23) by 21 runs.
Shaheed Nirmal Mahato Stadium, November 21: Bihar 61/7 in 50 overs (V Pushpa Latha 2-3, A Sireesha 2-7) lost to **Andhra** 63/1 in 10.5 overs (N Anusha 31*) by nine wickets.
Shaheed Nirmal Mahato Stadium, Jamshedpur, November 22: Bengal 99 in 44.1 overs

(Dhara Gujjar 22; MS Gurjar 3-18) lost to **Rajasthan** 100/2 in 42 overs (Sangeeta Kumawat 46*, Jyoti Choudhary 38*) by eight wickets.

Keenan Stadium, Jamshedpur, November 22: Andhra 138/9 in 50 overs (G Sindhuja 63, A Sireesha 35; Pragya Rawat 3-12, Radha Yadav 3-16) beat **Baroda** 71 in 41 overs (Camy Desai 20; Divya 4-3, G Sindhuja 3-20) by 67 runs.

Keenan Stadium, Jamshedpur, November 23: Punjab 159/9 in 50 overs (Kanika Ahuja 73, Rajni Devi 32; Rinku Tank 4-43, Suman Meena 2-33) lost to **Rajasthan** 160/5 in 43.5 overs (Sangeeta Kumawat 52*, Aditi Garg 29; R Devi 3-44) by five wickets.

Keenan Stadium, Jamshedpur, November 24: Bihar 21 in 13.4 overs (N Khatun 3-9, Priyanka Sarkar 3-10) lost to **Bengal** 22/1 in 12.4 overs by nine wickets.

Super League Group A points table

Team	M	W	L	T	N/R	Pts	NRR
Andhra	5	5	0	0	0	20	+1.149
Rajasthan	5	4	1	0	0	16	+0.405
Baroda	5	3	2	0	0	12	+0.399
Bengal	5	2	3	0	0	8	+0.494
Punjab	5	1	4	0	0	4	-0.214
Bihar	5	0	5	0	0	0	-3.243

Andhra and Rajasthan qualified for the semi-finals

Group B Super League

Jagarlamudi Kuppuswamy Choudary (JKC) College, Guntur, November 16: Delhi 142 in 49.2 overs (Ayushi Soni 62, Simran 39; Sandra Suren 3-18) lost to **Kerala** 143/5 in 42.4 overs (Aleena Surendran 40*, Jisna Joseph 30) by five wickets.

Rayapati Venkata Rangarao and Jagarlamudi Chandramouli College of Engineering (RVRJCE) Ground, Guntur, November 16: Mumbai 230/5 in 50 overs (Jemimah Rodrigues 107, Vrushali Bhagat 57; Shannti Kumari 2-44) beat **Jharkhand** 134 in 40.2 overs (Sonia 45, Durga Kumari Murmu 30; J Rodrigues 3-26, Fatima Jaffer 3-27) by 96 runs.

J Narendranath ACA Cricket Ground, Perecherla, November 16: Nagaland 37 in 30.3 overs (Anjali Singh 4-2, Tanu Kala 3-1) lost to **Uttar Pradesh** 40/0 in 5.1 overs (Ekta Singh 22*) by 10 wickets.

JKC College, Guntur, November 18: Delhi 179/5 in 50 overs (Neha Bhargava 46*, Jyoshi Nain 43) lost to **Uttar Pradesh** 183/4 in 46.5 overs (Ekta Singh 55, Tanu Kala 35) by six wickets.

RVRJCE Ground, Guntur, November 18: Nagaland 22 in 18 overs (Fatima Jaffer 4-5, Sayali Satghare 4-11) lost to **Mumbai** 26/0 in 3.2 overs by 10 wickets.

J Narendranath Andhra Cricket Association Cricket Ground, Perecherla, November 18: Kerala 98/9 in 50 overs (Sandra Suren 24*, P Sourabhya 21; Durga Kumari Murmu 3-15, Mondal 2-30) lost to **Jharkhand** 99/9 in 50 overs (Sonia 23, P Priya 22; TP Sruthy 3-16, Minnu Mani 2-12) by one wicket.

JKC College, Guntur, November 20: Nagaland 40 in 27 overs (Ayushi Soni 5-11, Jasleen Khokhar 2-5) lost to **Delhi** 46/0 in 5.2 overs (A Soni 37*) by 10 wickets.

RVRJCE Ground, Guntur, November 20: Jharkhand 141/8 in 50 overs (Durga Kumari Murmu 25, Sonia 20; Tanu Kala 2-20) beat **Uttar Pradesh** 119 in 40.4 overs (Muskan Malik 31, Shobha Devi 22; Shannti Kumari 4-33, Mamta Paswan 2-15) by 22 runs.

J Narendranath ACA Cricket Ground, Perecherla, November 20: Mumbai 150 in 49.5 overs (Jemimah Rodrigues 75, Vrushali Bhagat 34; Sandra Suren 2-21, Biby Sebastin 2-36) beat **Kerala** 76 in 46.2 overs (Malavika Sabu 21; V Bhagat 2-6, Fatima Jaffer 2-10) by 74 runs.

RVRJCE Ground, Guntur, November 22: Jharkhand 316/7 in 50 overs (Sonia 128, Sunita Kumari Murmu 75; Joyshree 3-62, Priyanka Karmakar 2-30) beat **Nagaland** 48 in 36.6 overs (Anjali 2-6, Suvecha Mondal 2-9) by 268 runs.

J Narendranath ACA Cricket Ground, November 22: Mumbai 230/8 in 50 overs (Jemimah Rodrigues 100, Pooja Yadav 60; Rupali 3-49, Neha Bhargava 2-34) beat **Delhi** 144 in 43.3 overs (N Bhargava 27, Jyoshi Nain 25; Fatima Jaffer 4-26, Vrushali Bhagat 3-26) by 86 runs.

JKC College, Guntur, November 22: Kerala 87 in 41.3 overs (Minnu Mani 21, Jisna Joseph 21; Anjali Singh 3-17, Ekta Singh 3-21) lost to **Uttar Pradesh** 88/0 in 19 overs (Muskan Malik 43*, E Singh 42*) by 10 wickets.

RVRJCE Ground, Guntur, November 24: Jharkhand 141/6 in 41 overs (Sonia 66*, P Priya 21*; Simran 2-23) beat **Delhi** 131 in 40.5 overs (Ayushi Soni 82*, Simran 20; Mamta paswan 2-28) by 10 runs.

J Narendranath ACA Cricket Ground, Perecherla, November 24: Mumbai 198/8 in 50 overs (Jemimah Rodrigues 128, Vrushali Bhagat 31; Tanu Kala 3-41, Rishika Yadav 2-39) beat **Uttar Pradesh** 169 in 49.4 overs (Ekta Singh 58, Muskan Malik 46) by 29 runs.

JKC College, Guntur, November 24: Nagaland 2 in 17 overs (Minnu Mani 4-0, P Sourabhya 2-0) lost to **Kerala** 5/0 in 0.1 overs by 10 wickets.

Super League Group B points table

Team	M	W	L	T	N/R	Pts	NRR
Mumbai	5	5	0	0	0	20	+1.922
Jharkhand	5	4	1	0	0	16	+0.851
Uttar Pradesh	5	3	2	0	0	12	+0.935
Kerala	5	2	3	0	0	8	-0.075
Delhi	5	1	4	0	0	4	+0.073
Nagaland	5	0	5	0	0	0	-6.170

Mumbai and Jharkhand qualified for the semi-finals

Semi-finals

JKC College, Guntur, November 28: Andhra 191/4 in 50 overs (V Pushpa Latha 72, E Padmaja 63*; Durga Kumari Murmu 2-23) beat **Jharkhand** 176 in 47.4 overs (DK Murmu 64*, P Priya 28; G Sindhuja 2-27) by 15 runs.

J Narendranath ACA Cricket Ground, Perecherla, November 28: Mumbai 240/7 in 50 overs (Jemimah Rodrigues 153) beat **Rajasthan** 85 in 32.4 overs (Sangeeta Kumawat 21; Fatima Jaffer 4-15, J Rodrigues 2-8) by 155 runs.

Andhra and Mumbai qualified for the final

Final: Andhra beat Mumbai by 47 runs

JKC College, Guntur, November 30: Andhra 192 in 49.5 overs (E Padmaja 73, V Pushpa Latha 34; Jemimah Rodrigues 3-51, Vrushali Bhagat 2-22) beat **Mumbai** 145 in 43.4 overs (Sayali Satghare 42*, J Rodrigues 26; A Sireesha 2-11, M Bhavana 2-19) by 47 runs.

Senior Inter-zonal Three-day Tournament 2017-18

End of the road for tourney?

Having successfully led Delhi to second place in the one-day format, and as winners in the T20s, Reema Malhotra added another feather to her cap, leading North Zone to the Inter-Zonal Three-Day championship. Preeti Bose, their left-arm spinner, picked up 21 wickets in three matches.

Spinners dominated on the slow, low pitches in Trivandrum, with nine of the top ten wicket-takers being tweakers. There were six outright results — the most in any long-format women's tournament. While North Zone dominated the championship, South overcame a disappointing start to finish second. M D Thirushkamini of Central was the only batter to cross the 300-run mark.

The BCCI chose not to continue with the tournament from the following season. It meant that no nation's female players had a taste of days' cricket at the domestic level. With women's Tests practically non-existent but for the one-off Ashes every couple of years, this came as another blow to the women's red-ball ambitions.

Best Batter: MD Thirushkamini (Central Zone) (353 runs in 4 matches)
Best Bowler: Preeti Bose (North Zone) (21 wickets in 3 matches)

St Xavier's KCA Cricket Ground, Trivandrum, March 18-20: South Zone 203 in 99.4 overs (S Asha 63,T Shani 28; Renuka Chaudhari 4-17, Shweta Haranhalli 2-20) and 89 in 50.3 overs (Niranjana Nagarajan 26; R Chaudhari 3-8, Sania Raut 3-35) lost to **West Zone** 212 in 101 overs (Shweta Jadhav 81, Mugdha Joshi 73; Gouher Sultana 3-70, Ananya Upendran 2-5) and 82/0 in 13 overs (Palak Patel 46*, Binaisha Surti 29*) by 10 wickets.
Greenfield Stadium, Trivandrum, March 18-20: East Zone 54 in 36.1 overs (Mouchaity Debnath 22; Renuka Singh 6-23, Sneh Rana 2-4) and 305/7 in 131 overs (Madhusmita Behara 114*, Tanusree Sarkar 99; Tanuja Kanwer 3-60) drew with **North Zone** 194 in 93.5 overs (Priya Punia 73, Mandeep Kaur 30*; Devyani Prasad 3-43, Saika Ishaque 2-25). North Zone took first-innings lead.
St Xavier's KCA Cricket Ground, Trivandrum, March 22-24: South Zone 204 in 93.3 overs (S Asha 55, Niranjana Nagarajan 53; Tanuja Kanwer 3-52, Harleen Deol 2-24) and 96/4 in 63 overs (Hemalatha Dayalan 31, Ananya Upendran 28*; H Deol 3-22) drew with **North Zone** 218/9 decl. in 93.1 overs (Mandeep Kaur 65, H Deol 38; N Nagarajan 4-52, A Upendran 2-22). North Zone took first-innings lead.
Greenfield Stadium, Trivandrum, March 22-24: Central Zone 155 in 58.5 overs (Punam Raut 55, MD Thirushkamini 34; Devyani Prasad 4-27, Madhusmita Behara 2-25) and 151/5 in 60 overs (Shweta Bishnoi 48, MD Thirushkamini 40; Sushree Dibyadarshini 2-17) drew with **East Zone** 248 in 137 overs (Tanusree Sarkar 84, Priyanka Priyadarshini 34; Priti Yadav 3-42, Meghna Singh 2-44). East Zone took first-innings lead.
St Xavier's KCA Cricket Ground, Trivandrum, March 26-28: West Zone 131 in 63.4 overs (Palak Patel 32; Preeti Bose 3-31, Tanuja Kanwer 3-37) and 104 in 63.4 overs (Shweta

Jadhav 35; P Bose 5-26, T Kanwer 3-29) lost to **North Zone** 243 in 85.5 overs (Neha Tanwar 82, Reema Malhotra 72; Renuka Chaudhari 4-60, Krutika Chaudhari 3-39) by an innings and eight runs.

Greenfield Stadium, Trivandrum, March 26-28: South Zone 125 in 59.3 overs (Hemalatha Dayalan 32, S Hima Bindu 22; Meghna Singh 3-20, Shivangi Raj 3-28) and 154 in 86 overs (Niranjana Nagarajan 47, S Hima Bindu 33; Shivangi Raj 4-42, Sukanya Parida 3-19) beat **Central Zone** 100 in 59.3 overs (Shweta Bishnoi 29; SK Sravanthi Naidu 6-7) and 74 in 31.4 overs (N Nagarajan 3-12, H Dayalan 3-23) by 105 runs.

St Xavier's KCA Cricket Ground, Trivandrum, March 30- April 1: West Zone 190 in 94.5 overs (Prajakta Shirwadkar 45, Renuka Chaudhari 42; Monikha Das 7-23) and 140/8 decl. in 60 overs (Palak Patel 42, Shweta Haranhalli 26*; Devyani Prasad 4-47, Priyanka Priyadarshini 2-16) drew with **East Zone** 106 in 59.1 overs (Tanusree Sarkar 23, Priyanka Sawaiyan 23; R Chaudhari 7-40, Krutika Chaudhari 2-20) and 126/2 in 42.2 overs (T Sarkar 61*, Madhuri Meheta 46). West Zone took first-innings lead.

Greenfield Stadium, Trivandrum, March 30- April 1: Central Zone 140 in 46.3 overs (MD Thirushkamini 55, Meghna Singh 41; Tanuja Kanwer 5-36, Preeti Bose 4-43) and 92 in 46.1 overs (MD Thirushkamini 36, Sukanya Parida 20; P Bose 7-32, Sneh Rana 2-24) lost to **North Zone** 183 in 107.1 overs (Renuka Singh 44, Priya Punia 38; Shivangi Raj 4-52, Priti Yadav 2-38) and 50/1 in 13.4 overs (Priya Punia 28*) by nine wickets.

St Xavier's KCA Cricket Ground, Trivandrum, April 3-5: West Zone 137 in 80.4 overs (Binaisha Surti 42, Renuka Chaudhari 32; Shweta Bishnoi 4-31, Priti Yadav 3-21) and 188 in 87.1 overs (Humaira Kazi 81*, R Chaudhari 34; Shivangi Raj 5-46, Meghna Sigh 2-28) lost to **Central Zone** 183 in 65.2 overs (MD Thirushkamini 80, Nishu Choudhary 47; Krutika Chaudhari 5-61, H Kazi 2-15) and 143/2 in 26.5 overs (MD Thirushkamini 91*, Disha Kasat 27; K Chaudhari 2-40) by eight wickets.

Greenfield Stadium, Trivandrum, April 3-5: South Zone 216 in 111 overs (L Nethra Iyer 65, Niranjana Nagarajan 52*; Saika Ishaque 4-49, Madhusmita Behara 2-27) and 107/6 decl in 42.4 overs (LN Iyer 71*; Sushree Dibyadarshini 2-26, S Ishaque 2-29) beat **East Zone** 99 in 46.3 overs (Monikha Das 23, Madhuri Meheta 21; Gouher Sultana 7-36, SK Sravanthi Naidu 3-4) and 105 in 38 overs (M Meheta 50; Ananya Upendran 3-16, Nikita Malik 2-16) by 119 runs.

Points table

Team	M	W	L	D	T	A	Pts	Q
North Zone	4	2	0	2	0	0	19	+0.185
South Zone	4	2	1	1	0	0	13	-0.354
West Zone	4	1	2	1	0	0	10	-0.445
Central Zone	4	1	2	1	0	0	7	+0.729
East Zone	4	0	1	3	0	0	5	-0.084

Winners: North Zone

Inter-zonal U23 One-day Tournament 2017-18

East Zone take the honours

Having started their campaign with a thrilling one-wicket win over North Zone, East Zone carried the momentum to be crowned champions in the Inter-Zonal Under-23 One-Day competition. While their batting line-up shared equal responsibility through the team's unbeaten run, Anjali Singh was their standout with 145 runs in three innings at an average of 72.50.

Hemali Borwankar, West Zone's wicketkeeper, scored the only century of the tournament: her 110 headlined West Zone's nail-biting chase of 244 against Central Zone.

Seven of the ten matches were won by teams chasing, a result of the rather flat, unresponsive pitches in Vadodara. While the bowlers largely struggled, Radha Yadav, the left-arm spinner and West Zone's captain, topped the charts with ten wickets at an average of 12.30, and most impressively, an economy rate of 3.51.

Arundhati Reddy's credentials as a hard hitting all-rounder continued to rise, as the fast bowler from Central Zone picked up nine wickets and scored 83 runs at a strike-rate of 96.51 coming in down the order.

L Nethra Iyer, the right-hand batter, finished atop the batting charts, but her performances were not enough to win a single match for South Zone.

Most runs: L Nethra Iyer (South Zone) (167 runs in 4 matches)
Most wickets: Radha Yadav (West Zone) (10 wickets in 4 matches)

Alembic Cricket Ground, Vadodara, March 9: West Zone 194 in 50 overs (Hrutvisha Patel 53, Manali Dakshini 28; Minnu Mani 3-26, C Pratyusha 2-28) beat **South Zone** 180/7 in 50 overs (Sanjula Naik 71*, L Nethra Iyer 38; Jaya Mohite 2-18, Radha Yadav 2-36) by 14 runs.
Gujarat State Fertiliser Corporation Ground, Vadodara, March 9: North Zone 183/7 in 50 overs (Taniya Bhatia 50, Suman Gulia 30; Reemalaxmi Ekka 2-26, Durga Kumari Murmu 2-29) lost to **East Zone** 184/9 in 49.3 overs (Sushree Dibyadarshini 40*, DK Murmu 39; Renuka Singh 3-30, Ayushi Soni 2-16) by one wicket.
Alembic Cricket Ground, Vadodara, March 10: South Zone 221/8 in 50 overs (L Nethra Iyer 42, N Anusha 36; Nikita Chauhan 2-23, Tanuja Kanwer 2-25) lost to **North Zone** 224/5 in 46.4 overs (Taniya Bhatia 71*, Harleen Deol 64; Sajeevan Sajana 2-28) by five wickets.
Gujarat State Fertiliser Corporation Ground, Vadodara, March 10: Central Zone 213/6 in 50 overs (Sarika Koli 61, V Sneha Deepthi 46; Tanusree Sarkar 2-20) lost to **East Zone** 214/5 in 47.2 overs (Anjali Singh 80, Durga Kumari Murmu 44; S Koli 2-29, Aditi Sharma 2-38) by five wickets.
Gujarat State Fertiliser Corporation Ground, Vadodara, March 11: North Zone 193/8 in 50 overs (Ayushi Soni 59*, Harleen Deol 29; Saima Thakor 3-23, Radha Yadav 3-30) beat **West Zone** 112 in 38.1 overs (Fatima Jaffer 42, Mukta Magre 39; Sheetal Rana 4-21, H Deol 3-23) by 81 runs.

Alembic Cricket Ground, Vadodara, March 11: Central Zone 214/6 in 50 overs (Aditi Sharma 49*, Nuzhat Parween 31; Sajeevan Sajana 2-46) beat **South Zone** 133 in 38.3 overs (L Nethra Iyer 42, G Divya 35; A Sharma 3-5, Arundhati Reddy 3-18) by 81 runs.

Alembic Cricket Ground, Vadodara, March 12: West Zone 105 in 46.3 overs (Tanusree Sarkar 3-14, Sushree Dibyadarshini 3-23) lost to **East Zone** 106/1 in 28.4 overs (Anjali Singh 50*, T Sarkar 33*) by nine wickets.

Gujarat State Fertiliser Corporation Ground, Vadodara, March 12: North Zone 190/8 in 50 overs (Priya Punia 84, Taniya Bhatia 33; Anjali Singh 2-24, Sarika Koli 2-36) lost to **Central Zone** 194/8 in 49.4 overs (Nuzhat Parween 35, S Koli 30*) by two wickets.

Alembic Cricket Ground, Vadodara, March 13: Central Zone 243/8 in 50 overs (Nuzhat Parween 53, Meghana Sabbineni 50; Radha Yadav 4-34, Saima Thakor 3-65) lost to **West Zone** 244/7 in 49.4 overs (Hemali Borwankar 110, R Yadav 38; Arundhati Reddy 3-56, Aditi Sharma 2-49) by three wickets.

Gujarat State Fertiliser Corporation Ground, Vadodara, March 13: South Zone 167 in 43.5 overs (L Nethra Iyer 45, Sanjula Naik 27; Shantti Kumari 3-32, Mamta Paswan 2-32) lost to **East Zone** 171/0 in 38.2 overs (Richa 88*, Sapna Choudhary 71*) by 10 wickets.

Points table

Team	M	W	L	T	N/R	Pts	NRR
East Zone	4	4	0	0	0	16	+0.780
North Zone	4	2	2	0	0	8	+0.447
Central Zone	4	2	2	0	0	8	+0.363
West Zone	4	2	2	0	0	8	-0.761
South Zone	4	0	4	0	0	0	-0.836

Winners: East Zone

Inter-zonal U19 Two-day Competition 2017-18

Consecutive titles for West Zone

For the second consecutive year West Zone dominated the Inter-Zone Under-19 Two-Day Competition. Leading in the absence of Jemimah Rodrigues, Yastika Bhatia, the left-hand opening batter, stepped up, making 256 runs, including three half-centuries. She batted with authority, driving the pacers beautifully through cover and down the ground, and unveiling an array of sweep shots against the slower bowlers.

Chitra Singh Jamwal of North Zone (253 runs), who scored the only century of the tournament, and Ekta Singh of Central Zone (221 runs) were the only other batters to cross the 200-run mark.

Much like the previous years, it was the spinners who did the bulk of the work through the tournament, with only two of the top ten wickets-takers being medium-pacers. As many as eight five-wicket hauls were taken across the ten matches — six of those by tweakers. In the only outright result of the tournament Sayali Satghare (5 for 42), the medium pacer, and Maya Sonawane (6 for 29), the leg spinner, combined to lead West Zone's demolition of East Zone by an innings and 32 runs.

Most runs: Yastika Bhatia (West Zone) (256 runs in 4 matches)
Most wickets: Tanu Kala (Central Zone) (14 wickets in 4 matches)

MIG Cricket Club, Mumbai, February 5-6: South Zone 165 in 56.1 overs (N Anusha 48, G Trisha 33; Janhvi Kate 2-7, Utkarsha Pawar 2-23) and 28/1 in 13 overs drew with **West Zone** 224 in 94.4 overs (Fatima Jaffer 74, Yastika Bhatia 47; Minnu Mani 4-74, G Trisha 2-11). West Zone took first-innings lead.
Mumbai, February 5-6: East Zone 276/4 decl. in 81 overs (Durga Kumari Murmu 72*, Richa 61) drew with **North Zone** 251 in 95.5 overs (Suman Gulia 67, Chitra Singh Jamwal 58; Shannti Kumari 5-57, Mamta Paswan 4-40). East Zone took first-innings lead.
Mumbai, February 8-9: South Zone 171 in 71.3 overs (N Anusha 38, Tejashwini Duragad 36; Ayushi Soni 3-34) and 19/1 in 6 overs drew with **North Zone** 267 in 90 overs (Chitra Singh Jamwal 109, A Soni 52; Monica Patel 3-42, Nida Rehman 3-55). North Zone took first-innings lead.
Mumbai, February 8-9: Central Zone 171 in 71.2 overs (Ekta SIngh 42, Tanu Kala 33; Anjali 3-34, Mamta paswan 3-46) and 12/1 in 5 overs drew with **East Zone** 161 in 86.1 overs (Dhara Gujjar 41, Durga Kumari Murmu 33; Poonam Soni 5-54, T Kala 3-28). Central Zone took first-innings lead.
Mumbai, February 11-12: West Zone 214 in 98.4 overs (Yastika Bhatia 53, Vrushali Bhagat 51; Simran 5-32, Amanjot Kaur 2-17) drew with **North Zone** 204 in 72.5 overs (Chitra Singh Jamwal 70, Ayushi Soni 51; Jaya Mohite 2-30, Utkarsha Pawar 2-34). West Zone took first-innings lead.
MIG Cricket Club, Mumbai, February 11-12: Central Zone 217 in 88.2 overs (Ekta Singh 63, Shobha Devi 47; Nida Rehman 3-34, Minnu Mani 3-41) drew with **South Zone** 89 in 55.2

overs (N Anusha 34, K Sravya 23*; Anjali Singh 6-31, Poonam Soni 3-25) and 37/3 in 17 overs (Tanu Kala 2-9). Central Zone took first-innings lead.

Mumbai, February 14-15: East Zone 112 in 53.3 overs (Durga Kumari Murmu 41, Sangeeta Khadia 30; Sayali Satghare 5-42, Jaya Mohite 3-27) and 98 in 38.1 overs (DK Murmu 30, Richa 28; Maya Sonawane 6-29, Fatima Jaffer 2-6) lost to **West Zone** 242/5 decl. in 73 overs (Yastika Bhatia 98, J Mohite 56; Kakoli Saikia 2-60) by an innings and 32 runs.

MIG Cricket Club, Mumbai, February 14-15: North Zone 166 in 84.1 overs (Pratika Rawal 29, Simran 27; Tanu Kala 5-32, Poonam Soni 2-44) drew with **Central Zone** 201/8 in 79 overs (Ekta Singh 67, Anjali Singh 58, Diksha Sharma 3-28). Central Zone took first-innings lead.

Mumbai, February 17-18: Central Zone 141 in 52 overs (Ekta Singh 49, LM INamdar 28; Maya Sonawane 4-22, Sayali Satghare 3-32) drew with **West Zone** 194/8 in 118 overs (Yastika Bhatia 58, Priyanka Ghodke 37; Tanu Kala 3-31). West Zone took first-innings lead.

MIG Cricket Club, Mumbai, February 17-18: East Zone 120 in 88.1 overs (Richa 34, Kajal Jena 26; Nida Rehman 4-15, Monica Patel 2-11) and 31/2 in 22 overs drew with **South Zone** 73 in 53.2 overs (Kakoli Saikia 5-34, Mamta Paswan 2-19). East Zone took first-innings lead.

Points table

Team	M	W	L	D	T	A	Pts	Q
West Zone	4	1	0	3	0	0	16	-0.344
Central Zone	4	0	0	4	0	0	10	+0.716
East Zone	4	0	1	3	0	0	7	-0.347
North Zone	4	0	0	4	0	0	6	-0.031
South Zone	4	0	0	4	0	0	4	-0.105

Winners: West Zone

PART FOUR
International Series

INDIA INTERNATIONALS 2018-19

West Indies in India

Kohli's men extend home dominance

DEBASISH DUTTA

Five years earlier, West Indies made a hastily arranged visit to India for the sole purpose of providing two matches in which Sachin Tendulkar could reach 200 Tests and bow out in front of his adoring public. With Ganguly, Laxman and Dravid already retired, it marked the end of a dynasty. Fast-forward to this series, and India had moved decisively into the Virat Kohli era.

For West Indies, however, nothing much seemed to have changed. In 2013, they were twice thrashed by an innings in three days; this time they lost by an innings and ten wickets. Green shoots are occasionally visible in West Indian cricket, but tours such as this mean they are usually trampled underfoot. Nor was there any solace in the limited-overs matches. They won one 50-over international and tied another, but otherwise were left with individual scraps: Roston Chase hit a century in the Second Test, Shimron Hetmyer and Shai Hope made white-ball runs, and Jason Holder again showed maturity as a leader.

If nothing else, the series underlined India's dominance at home. They had now won ten home Test series off the reel (including two single-Test visits by Bangladesh and Afghanistan), equalling the world record set twice by Australia. And they had now won seven in a row, home and away, against West Indies, stretching back to 2002-03.

West Indies coach Stuart Law was suspended from the first two ODIs: he was given three demerit points and fined his match fee for making "inappropriate comments" about the third and fourth umpires after Kieran Powell had been given out to a low catch by Ajinkya Rahane during the Second Test in Hyderabad. Perhaps fired by indignation, the West Indian batsmen produced their best displays of the series.

For India, the victories served as a morale booster after their 4–1 Test defeat in England. Their batsmen were dominant: they lost just 19 wickets in the two Tests, and four players averaged over 90. It gave them a chance to hand a first cap to the 18-year-old opener Prithvi Shaw, who responded with a century on debut. Umesh Yadav was the most successful bowler with 11 wickets at 15, including a match-winning performance in the Second Test, when injury to his new-ball partner Shardul Thakur left him with extra responsibility.

In the 50-over series, Kohli reeled off three hundreds, while Rohit Sharma proved as insatiable as he had been in the Asia Cup. The Tests were again played in front of largely empty stands, which led to questions about the scheduling of the tour, but India had at least built their confidence before the trip to Australia.

	Tests	ODIs	T20Is
Most runs	Prithvi Shaw (India) (237 runs, 2 matches)	Virat Kohli (India) (453 runs, 5 matches)	Shikhar Dhawan (India) (138 runs, 3 matches)
Most wickets	Umesh Yadav (India) (11 wickets, 2 matches)	Kuldeep Yadav (India) (9 wickets, 5 matches)	Kuldeep Yadav (India) (5 wickets, 2 matches)

Tour match

Reliance Stadium, Vadodara, September 29-30: Indian Board President's XI 360/6 dec. in 90 overs (Ankit Bawne 116*, Mayank Agarwal 90; Devendra Bishoo 3-104, Shannon Gabriel 2-41) drew with **West Indians** 366/7 dec. in 89 overs (Sunil Ambris 114*, Shane Dowrich 65; Avesh Khan 4-60, Saurabh Kumar 2-126).

Test series (2): India 2 West Indies 0

1ˢᵗ Test: India won by an innings and 272 runs

As the records piled up, the extent of India's dominance and West Indies' humiliation became starker. India's biggest innings win, and West Indies' second-heaviest defeat, never remotely resembled a contest. Kohli did not need to pull off any tactical masterstrokes: he won the toss, made the largest contribution to a huge total, then let his bowlers loose. Fourteen West Indies wickets fell on the third day — most in attempting ill-judged attacking shots

Prithvi Shaw became the fourth-youngest to hit a Test century on debut, against the West Indies in Rajkot. — *Getty Images*

— and their two innings did not add up to 100 overs.

West Indies were without captain Holder, who had suffered an ankle injury at the pre-tour camp in Dubai, and Kemar Roach, who flew home after the death of his grandmother. It left their attack short of experience. Kraigg Brathwaite took over the captaincy, but the seam bowling was entrusted to Shannon Gabriel, Keemo Paul, in only his second Test, and debutant Sherman Lewis.

After opting not to blood him in England, India gave Shaw a first cap. He disappointed no one. After K L Rahul had been dismissed by Gabriel for a duck in the first over, Shaw eased towards his hundred as if it were preordained. Attacking mainly off the back foot, he reached 50 in 56 balls, and a century off 99. He became the fourth-youngest to hit a Test century on debut, and the third-fastest recorded by balls faced. Shaw received a congratulatory message from Sachin Tendulkar, still India's youngest centurion, while coach Ravi Shastri did not shy away from comparisons: he said there "was a bit of Viru [Sehwag] and the Master" in the innings.

Shaw and Cheteshwar Pujara added 206 for the second wicket to put India in control and, though Pujara fell 14 short of a century on his home ground, to no surprise, Kohli completed his 24th Test hundred. In England, India had been let down by their lower-middle order, but there were no such failings here against a wilting attack. Pant freewheeled to 92, at one point looking as if he might beat Kohli to three figures, and Jadeja added an entertaining first Test hundred, at which point Kohli declared at India's highest score against West Indies, beating 644 for 7 at Kanpur in 1978-79.

With temperatures soaring, it was soon clear the tourists had no stomach for a fight: five batsmen were gone before the total reached 50. With the deficit an eye-watering 468, the follow-on was a no-brainer. Powell survived a skittish start, but most of his team-mates appeared to think the white-ball matches had already started. Kohli gave an extended bowl to Kuldeep Yadav, who was rewarded with his first Test five-for, and became the seventh to take international five-wicket hauls in three formats.

India's biggest innings victories

Inns & 272 runs	**India (649-9 dec) v West Indies (181 & 196), Rajkot, 2018-19**
Inns & 262 runs	**India (474) v Afghanistan (109 & 103), Bangalore, 2018**
Inns & 239 runs	India (610-3 dec) v Bangladesh (118 & 253), Mirpur, 2007
Inns & 239 runs	**India (610-6 dec) v Sri Lanka (205 & 166), Nagpur, 2017-18**
Inns & 219 runs	India (633-5 dec) v Australia (233 & 181), Calcutta, 1997-98

Saurashtra Cricket Association Stadium, Rajkot, October 4-6: India 649/9 dec. in 149.5 overs (Virat Kohli 139, Prithvi Shaw 134, Ravindra Jadeja 100*; Devendra Bishoo 4-217, Shermon Lewis 2-93) beat **West Indies** 181 in 48 overs (Roston Chase 53, Keemo Paul 47; R Ashwin 4-37, Mohammed Shami 2-22) and 196 in 50.5 overs (Kieran Powell 83; Kuldeep Yadav 5-57, R Jadeja 3-35) by an innings and 272 runs. *PoM:* Prithvi Shaw.

2ⁿᵈ Test: India won by ten wickets

Umesh Yadav joined elite company in another crushing victory that wrapped up the series in six days. He became only the third Indian seamer to take ten wickets in a home Test, after Kapil Dev (twice) and Javagal Srinath.

Emerging from the wreckage of Rajkot, West Indies showed some overdue competitive spirit before collapsing in a heap. Only six teams have won by ten wickets after gaining a smaller first-innings lead than India's 56.

On a pitch expected to help the spinners later on, the returning Holder was happy to bat first. And when Thakur limped off with a groin injury ten balls into his debut, the cards seemed to be falling for West Indies. But their top order was again unable to find the right blend of attack and defence. They were saved from another lightweight total only by Chase and Holder, who put on 104 for the seventh wicket. Chase completed his fourth Test century next morning, but West Indies were in the field within 40 minutes of the start. Umesh finished with a Test-best 6 for 88.

Shaw picked up where he had left off in the First Test, with 70 off 53 balls, although the match then deviated from its expected course. When Holder removed Kohli for 45, India were 162 for 4 and by no means in command. Ajinkya Rahane, adapting his game to the pace of the pitch, and the more aggressive Pant put on 152 to steady the ship, with the help of some shoddy West Indies fielding: Pant was reprieved on 24. Holder became the first West Indies seamer to take a five-for in India since Kenny Benjamin at Mohali in 1994-95. Pant departed for 92 for the second successive innings, and India's lead was a slender 28 when the ninth wicket fell. Thakur hobbled out to join Ashwin, and helped double the advantage and deflate West Indian morale. Just how much was demonstrated when four wickets fell before the visitors had wiped off the arrears.

Umesh and Ashwin offered contrasting challenges. After two days in which 14 wickets fell, 16 crashed on a frantic third. "We didn't expect that in the morning," said Kohli. "A three-day finish was not part of the plan."

Rajiv Gandhi International Stadium, Uppal, Hyderabad, October 12-14: West Indies 311 in 101.4 overs (Roston Chase 106, Jason Holder 52; Umesh Yadav 6-88, Kuldeep Yadav 3-85) and 127 in 46.1 overs (Sunil Ambris 38, Shai Hope 28; U Yadav 4-45, Ravindra Jadeja 3-12) lost to **India** 367 in 106.4 overs (Rishabh Pant 92, Ajinkya Rahane 80; J Holder 5-56, Shannon Gabriel 3-107) and 75 for no loss in 16.1 overs (Prithvi Shaw 33*, KL Rahul 33*) by ten wickets. *PoM:* Umesh Yadav. *PoS:* Prithvi Shaw.

ODI series (5): India 3 West Indies 1

1ˢᵗ ODI: India won by eight wickets

A sell-out crowd for the Barsapara Stadium's first ODI were treated to a thrilling match-winning partnership of 246 between Rohit Sharma and Virat Kohli. At times the batsmen appeared to be competing more with each other than the West Indies bowlers. It was their fifth double-century stand, improving their own world record, and India's highest for any wicket batting second. Kohli's 36th ODI century — his 20th in a successful chase — needed only 88 balls. Sharma became the fourth-fastest player to 20 hundreds, and the first to reach 150 six times, eclipsing Tendulkar and David Warner.

Earlier, Hetmyer had taken advantage of the absence of Kuldeep, who had dismissed him three times in the Tests, to hit his third ODI century. But not even West Indies' highest score against India since January 2007 could prevent defeat.

Barsapara Cricket Stadium, Guwahati, October 21: West Indies 322/8 in 50 overs (Shimron Hetmyer 106, Kieran Powell 51; Yuzvendra Chahal 3-41, Ravindra Jadeja 2-66) lost to **India** 326/2 in 42.1 overs (Rohit Sharma 152*, Virat Kohli 140) by eight wickets. *PoM:* Virat Kohli.

2nd ODI: Match tied

When Umesh ran in to bowl the last ball of the match to Hope, West Indies needed five and appeared to have made a mess of the final stages of their chase. But Hope carved a full, wide delivery past point to secure the 37th ODI tie — India's second inside a month.

The headlines seemed set to be about Kohli reaching 10,000 ODI runs, knocking 54 innings off Tendulkar's record. His second successive century came after a stand of 139 with Ambati Rayudu, who looked as if he might provide a solution to India's problem No.4 spot. Kohli smashed 48 off his last 17 balls to complete what looked a formidable total. But with Hetmyer leading the charge, West Indies were not intimidated. The youngster followed up his hundred in Guwahati with a fearless 94 off 64 balls, including seven sixes, and put on 143 with Hope. Hope's century was his second in ODIs, but the first since his second appearance.

Dr YS Rajasekhara Reddy ACA-VDCA Cricket Stadium, Visakhapatnam, October 24: **India** 321/6 in 50 overs (Virat Kohli 157*, Ambati Rayudu 73; Ashley Nurse 2-46, Obed McCoy 2-71) tied with **West Indies** 321/7 in 50 overs (Shai Hope 123*, Shimron Hetmyer 94; Kuldeep Yadav 3-67). *PoM:* Virat Kohli.

3rd ODI: West Indies won by 43 runs

It was either tactical genius or outrageous good fortune, but Holder's introduction of the part-time off-spin of Marlon Samuels in the 42nd over turned the match in West Indies' favour and squared the series. With his third ball, Samuels bowled the well-set Kohli — who had become the tenth man to score three successive ODI centuries, but the first for India — and added two more cheap wickets to complete his best ODI figures. In all, the last seven wickets fell for 68.

West Indies were again indebted to the cool Hope, although they needed a late blast from Ashley Nurse — 40 off 22 balls — to set a challenging total. Jasprit Bumrah's four wickets included a beauty to remove Hope as he closed in on another hundred.

Maharashtra Cricket Association, Pune, October 27: West Indies 283/9 in 50 overs (Shai Hope 95, Ashley Nurse 40; Jasprit Bumrah 4-35, Kuldeep Yadav 2-52) beat **India** 240 in 47.4 overs (Virat Kohli 107, Shikhar Dhawan 35; Marlon Samuels 3-12, Obed McCoy 2-38) by 43 runs. *PoM:* Ashley Nurse.

4ᵗʰ ODI: India won by 224 runs

India ruthlessly reasserted themselves to take a 2–1 lead into the final match. It was their third-largest win by runs — the biggest against a Full Member — and West Indies' second-heaviest defeat. Hosting its first men's ODI for 12 years, the Brabourne Stadium was reduced to silence when Kohli fell well short of a fourth successive hundred, but Sharma — going past 150 for the seventh time — and Rayudu raised spirits during a third-wicket partnership of 211 in 27.1 overs. Rayudu's century was the first for India by a batsman outside the top three in 21 months. Kohli's hunch that bowling under lights would help his seamers proved correct. From 56 for 6, only Holder's unbeaten half-century prevented an even bigger humiliation.

Brabourne Stadium, Mumbai, October 29: India 377/5 in 50 overs (Rohit Sharma 162, Ambati Rayudu 100; Kemar Roach 2-74) beat **West Indies** 153 in 36.2 overs (Jason Holder 54*; Khaleel Ahmed 3-13, Kuldeep Yadav 3-42) by 224 runs. *PoM:* Rohit Sharma.

5ᵗʰ ODI: India won by nine wickets

The public at Greenfield Stadium's first ODI were entitled to feel cheated by a contest that lasted less than half its scheduled duration. With a chance to make it 2–2, West Indies folded limply after failing to come to terms with the slowness of the pitch. India won in less than 15 overs — an anti-climactic end to a series that had been boiling up nicely. India's seamers had West Indies in trouble from the start, but the main beneficiary of their befuddled approach was Jadeja, who took his second four-wicket haul since returning to the team at the Asia Cup. Oshane Thomas provided a crumb of comfort for West Indies: his pace was too hot for Shikhar Dhawan, and he also had Kohli dropped.

Greenfield International Stadium, Thiruvananthapuram, November 1: West Indies 104 in 31.5 overs (Jason Holder 25; Ravindra Jadeja 4-34, Jasprit Bumrah 2-11) lost to **India** 105/1 in 14.5 overs (Rohit Sharma 63*, Virat Kohli 33*) by nine wickets. *PoM:* Ravindra Jadeja. *PoS:* Virat Kohli.

T20I series (3): India 3 West Indies 0

1ˢᵗ T20I: India won by five wickets

• India's victory looks more comfortable than it was. • In their first home T20I without M S Dhoni, India can choose from two wicketkeepers: Dinesh Karthik takes the gloves, while Pant fields in the deep. • West Indies are unable to fathom the Indian spinners, especially the miserly Kuldeep. • Fabian Allen top-scores on debut from No.8. • Thomas, on debut, and captain Carlos

Brathwaite reduce them to 45 for 4, with Thomas making the top order jump around. • But West Indies have too few to defend, and Manish Pandey and Karthik calm any flutters.

Eden Gardens, Kolkata, November 4: West Indies 109/8 in 20 overs (Fabian Allen 27; Kuldeep Yadav 3-13) lost to **India** 110/5 in 17.5 overs (Dinesh Karthik 31*; Carlos Brathwaite 2-11, Oshane Thomas 2-21) by five wickets. *PoM:* Kuldeep Yadav.

2nd T20I: India won by 71 runs

• Sharma illuminates India's first visit to the Ekana Stadium by becoming the first batsman to make four T20I hundreds. • He bats through for 111 not out, hitting eight fours and seven sixes. • He puts on 123 for the first wicket with Dhawan, who cannot find his usual fluency. • West Indies' top order struggles again. • The menacing Khaleel removes Hope and Hetmyer. • The visitors can only scrap into three figures.

Bharat Ratna Shri Atal Bihari Vajpayee Ekana Cricket Stadium, Lucknow, November 6: India 195/2 in 20 overs (Rohit Sharma 111*, Shikhar Dhawan 43) beat **West Indies** 124/9 in 20 overs (Bhuvneshwar Kumar 2-12, Jasprit Bumrah 2-20) by 71 runs. *PoM:* Rohit Sharma.

3rd T20I: India won by six wickets

• A last-ball howler by Allen denies West Indies the chance of a consolation victory. • Bowling the final over, has brought his team back into it with a fourth-ball dot, followed by the wicket of Dhawan. • Needing one to win, Pandey hits the final delivery to Allen's right, but he fails to collect it cleanly, allowing Pandey and Karthik to scamper the winning single. • West Indies bat more sensibly than in previous matches. • In an unbroken stand of 87, Darren Bravo plays conventionally, while Nicholas Pooran improvises for his first international fifty. • The bedrock of India's response is a partnership of 130 for the third wicket between Dhawan and the innovative Pant.

MA Chidambaram Stadium, Chepauk, Chennai, November 11: West Indies 181/3 in 20 overs (Nicholas Pooran 53*, Darren Bravo 43*; Yuzvendra Chahal 2-28) lost to **India** 182/4 in 20 overs (Shikhar Dhawan 92, Rishabh Pant 58; Keemo Paul 2-32) by six wickets. *PoM:* Shikhar Dhawan. *PoS:* Kuldeep Yadav.

Series averages

India

Player	M	I	NO	Batting R	HS	Avge	100s/50s
P Shaw	2	3	1	237	134	118.50	1/1
R Jadeja	2	2	1	100	100*	100.00	1/0
V Kohli	2	2	0	184	139	92.00	1/0
R Pant	2	2	0	184	92	92.00	0/2

A Rahane	2	2	0	121	80	60.50	0/1
C Pujara	2	2	0	96	86	48.00	0/1
R Ashwin	2	2	0	42	35	21.00	0/0
KL Rahul	2	3	1	37	33*	18.50	0/0
U Yadav	2	2	0	24	22	12.00	0/0
K Yadav	2	2	0	18	12	9.00	0/0
S Thakur	1	1	1	4	4*	-	0/0
M Shami	1	1	1	2	2*	-	0/0

Bowling and fielding

Player	M	W	R	BBI	BBM	Avge	5wI/10wM	Ct/St
U Yadav	2	11	169	6-88	10-133	15.36	1/1	1/-
M Shami	1	2	33	2-22	2-33	16.50	0/0	0/-
R Jadeja	2	7	138	3-12	4-57	19.71	0/0	2/-
R Ashwin	2	9	181	4-37	6-108	20.11	0/0	1/-
K Yadav	2	10	249	5-57	6-119	24.90	1/0	1/-
S Thakur	1	0	9	-	-	-	0/0	0/-
V Kohli	2	-	-	-	-	-	-/-	0/-
R Pant	2	-	-	-	-	-	-/-	5/2
C Pujara	2	-	-	-	-	-	-/-	2/-
A Rahane	2	-	-	-	-	-	-/-	3/-
KL Rahul	2	-	-	-	-	-	-/-	1/-
P Shaw	2	-	-	-	-	-	-/-	2/-

West Indies

Batting

Player	M	I	NO	R	HS	Avge	100s/50s
R Chase	2	4	0	185	106	46.25	1/1
J Holder	1	2	0	71	52	35.50	0/1
K Paul	1	2	0	62	47	31.00	0/0
K Powell	2	4	0	106	83	26.50	0/1
S Hope	2	4	0	91	36	22.75	0/0
D Bishoo	2	4	2	38	17*	19.00	0/0
S Dowrich	2	4	1	56	30	18.66	0/0
S Ambris	2	4	0	68	38	17.00	0/0
J Warrican	1	2	1	15	8*	15.00	0/0
S Hetmyer	2	4	0	50	17	12.50	0/0
K Brathwaite	2	4	0	26	14	6.50	0/0
S Lewis	1	2	0	4	4	2.00	0/0
S Gabriel	2	4	0	6	4	1.50	0/0

Player	M	W	R	BBI	BBM	Avge	5wI/10wM	Ct/St
				Bowling and fielding				
J Holder	1	5	73	5-56	5-73	14.60	1/0	0/-
S Lewis	1	2	93	2-93	2-93	46.50	0/0	1/-
S Gabriel	2	4	191	3-107	3-107	47.75	0/0	0/-
J Warrican	1	2	101	2-84	2-101	50.50	0/0	0/-
K Brathwaite	2	1	53	1-47	1-47	53.00	0/0	0/-
D Bishoo	2	4	314	4-217	4-217	78.50	0/0	2/-
R Chase	2	1	173	1-137	1-137	173.00	0/0	0/-
K Paul	1	0	61	-	-	-	0/0	1/-
S Ambris	2	-	-	-	-	-	-/-	0/-
S Dowrich	2	-	-	-	-	-	-/-	3/0
S Hetmyer	2	-	-	-	-	-	-/-	2/-
S Hope	2	-	-	-	-	-	-/-	1/-
K Powell	2	-	-	-	-	-	-/-	0/-

Squads

India: Virat Kohli (capt), Ajinkya Rahane (vice-capt), Mayank Agarwal, R Ashwin, Ravindra Jadeja, Kuldeep Yadav, Mohammed Shami, Mohammed Siraj, Rishabh Pant (wk), Cheteshwar Pujara, KL Rahul, Prithvi Shaw, Shardul Thakur, Hanuma Vihari, Umesh Yadav.

West Indies: Jason Holder (capt), Sunil Ambris, Devendra Bishoo, Kraigg Brathwaite, Roston Chase, Shane Dowrich (wk), Shannon Gabriel, Jahmar Hamilton, Shimron Hetmyer, Shai Hope, Shermon Lewis, Keemo Paul, Kieran Powell, Kemar Roach, Jomel Warrican, Alzarri Josepsh (withdrawn).

Debasish Dutta is a cricket writer based in Kolkata.

End of a long wait: India's maiden Test series triumph Down Under had taken 12 attempts and 70 years. — *Getty Images*

India in Australia

Pujara, pacers end India's long wait

R KAUSHIK

Since the beginning of 2018, those invested in Indian cricket were excited. Three overseas Test tours were lined up: to South Africa at the start of the year, to England in the summer and to Australia at the very end. There was genuine belief that, finally, India could compete with these powerhouses in their own backyard on an equal footing. That belief stemmed from the quality and, more significantly, the depth of the Indian pace-bowling department. Historically driven by their spinners, India had started off with an obvious handicap in these alien territories because, despite the presence of gun batsmen, they didn't have a bunch of fast bowlers who could hustle the opposition collectively. By the time of the tour of South Africa, India had a plethora of highly skilled, and supremely fit, quicks — Ishant Sharma, Mohammed Shami, Bhuvneshwar Kumar, Umesh Yadav and Jasprit Bumrah, with Hardik Pandya as an adequate back-up — with which to hit back at their opponents.

However, let down by their experienced and widely-travelled batting group, India courted familiar failure in South Africa (1-2) and England (1-4), going shoulder-to-shoulder in both series until letting key moments slip.

Even so, for the first time in their history, India arrived in Australia as favourites to secure their maiden Test series triumph, not just because of the resources they possessed, but also because of the disarray the hosts found themselves in.

In the aftermath of the 'sandpaper' fiasco in Cape Town in March, Australia were without Steve Smith, David Warner and Cameron Bancroft. They had lost not just their captain, vice-captain, their coach and a host of administrative bigwigs, but also two of their next three Tests and looked ripe for the taking.

Still, India could not expect to merely turn up to get the job done. No Australian side rolls over and dies, and while Tim Paine didn't have the most experienced or accomplished batting line-up at his disposal, he still had a world-beating attack of Mitchell Starc, Josh Hazlewood, Pat Cummins and Nathan Lyon.

India needed someone to not merely score heavily, but also run this heavy-duty attack to the ground. They found their hero in Cheteshwar Pujara. Out of favour not so long ago owing to reasons best known to the team management, the Saurashtra batsman amassed 521 runs in four Tests. Equally crucially, he occupied the crease for more than 31 hours — that's more than the duration of an entire Test match — while negotiating 1258 deliveries, which is almost 210 overs, all on his own.

Until Mayank Agarwal made a roaring start to his Test career with successive half-centuries, India struggled with their openers. Virat Kohli wasn't quite the influential force he was expected to be, though his magnificent 123 in the Perth Stadium's inaugural Test was easily the knock of the series. Rishabh Pant did his burgeoning reputation no harm at all with 350 bruising runs. But it was Pujara who held India together, diligently and without fuss, setting the tone with a wonderful 123 under huge pressure on day one of the series in Adelaide, and backing it up with hundreds in Melbourne and Sydney.

Unsurprisingly, the pacers stepped up to the plate. Between them, Bumrah (21), Shami (16) and Ishant (11) accounted for 48 wickets, harrying Australia with pace, bounce, movement and intelligence. They were well backed up by Pant, who finished with 20 dismissals behind the stumps. The Perth defeat was an aberration, no matter how crushing it was. Indeed, had it not been for the weather that allowed just over 25 overs on the last two days in Sydney, India might have ended up with a 3-1 scoreline that would have been a more appropriate reflection of the difference in quality of cricket from the two sides.

Rain in the second game had almost certainly denied India the chance to clinch the preceding T20I, but there was no stopping Kohli's men in the subsequent ODI series as they rallied from 0–1 behind to complete a 2–1 triumph. For the first time ever, a team emerged from a tour of Australia unbeaten across formats. India's maiden Test series triumph Down Under had taken 12 attempts and 70 years, but the wait was well worth it.

Most Test wickets by a pace trio in a calendar year

Bowlers	Year	Wickets
Jasprit Bumrah, Ishant Sharma, Mohammed Shami	2018	130
Joel Garner, Michael Holding, Malcolm Marshall	1984	130
Morne Morkel, Makhaya Ntini, Dale Steyn	2008	123

	T20Is	Tests	ODIs
Most runs	Shikhar Dhawan (India) (117 runs, 3 matches)	Cheteshwar Pujara (India) (521 runs, 4 matches)	Shaun Marsh (Australia) (224 runs, 3 matches)
Most wickets	Krunal Pandya (India) (5 wickets, 3 matches)	Jasprit Bumrah (India) (21 wickets, 4 matches)	Bhuvneshwar Kumar (India) (8 wickets, 3 matches)

T20I series (3): Australia 1 India 1

1ˢᵗ T20I: Australia won by four runs (DLS)

• Australia make a conservative start on being put in, reaching 38 for the loss of D'Arcy Short at the end of the powerplay. • Chris Lynn gets the show going with four towering sixes in a 20-ball 37 to set the stage for a grandstand finish. • Glenn Maxwell, with four sixes, and Marcus Stoinis with a bruising 33 muscle the hosts to 158 for 4 in 17 overs after an hour-long break for rain. • Chasing a revised target of 174 from 17, India's chase is fuelled by opener Shikhar Dhawan's pyrotechnics. • However, with little of note from the middle order, the visitors find themselves in a hole until Dinesh Karthik cuts loose with 30 off 13. • With 13 needed off the final over, Stoinis nips out Karthik and Krunal Pandya as Australia sneak home.

Brisbane Cricket Ground, Woolloongabba, November 21: Australia 158/4 in 17 overs (Glenn Maxwell 46, Chris Lynn 37; Kuldeep Yadav 2-24) beat **India** 169/7 in 17 overs (Shikhar Dhawan 77, Dinesh Karthik 30; Adam Zampa 2-22, Marcus Stoinis 2-27) by four runs (DLS method). *PoM:* Adam Zampa.

2ⁿᵈ T20I: No result

• Melbourne is hit by heavy showers and strong winds, with more rain forecast. • Australia lose Aaron Finch in the first over to Bhuvneshwar Kumar. • India's bowlers are impeccable in their disciplines with Bhuvneshwar and Bumrah stymieing momentum. • Ben McDermott patiently holds the innings together when the skies open up to halt Australia's innings after 19 overs. • India's target is revised four times between spells of intermittent rainfall. • But with no time left for even the five overs needed to constitute a game, the match is abandoned.

Melbourne Cricket Ground, Melbourne, November 23: Australia 132/7 in 19 overs (Ben McDermott 32*; Bhuvneshwar Kumar 2-20, Khaleel Ahmed 2-39) v **India**. No result.

3rd T20I: India won by six wickets

• Batting first by choice for the first time in the series, Australia begin promisingly with Short and Finch adding 68 for the first wicket. • The introduction of spin hurts them, as Kuldeep Yadav stifles the flow of runs and Krunal picks up important wickets. • Kuldeep concedes just 19 in his four overs. • Dhawan makes the most of form and Rohit holds his own to put on 67 for the opening wicket in a mere 33 deliveries. • Kohli, the master of the chase, then assumes command. • The skipper and Karthik add 60 in quick time to reach their target with two deliveries to spare.

Sydney Cricket Ground, Sydney, November 25: Australia 164/6 in 20 overs (D'Arcy Short 33, Aaron Finch 28; Krunal Pandya 4-36) lost to **India** 168/4 in 19.4 overs (Virat Kohli 61*, Shikhar Dhawan 41) by six wickets. *PoM:* Krunal Pandya.

Tour match

Sydney Cricket Ground, Sydney, November 28-December 1: Indians 358 in 98 overs (Prithvi Shaw 66, Virat Kohli 64; Aaron Hardle 4-50) and 211/2 in 43.4 overs (M Vijay 129, KL Rahul 62) drew with **Cricket Australia XI** 544 in 151.1 overs (Harry Nielsen 100, A Hardle 86; Mohammed Shami 3-97, R Ashwin 2-122).

Test series (4): India 2 Australia 1

1st Test: India won by 31 runs

A familiar tale of unchecked Indian implosion on the opening day of an overseas Test series appeared to be unfolding until Pujara stepped up with a magnificent 16th century that drove Australia to their knees.

Batting with scant regard for context and the quality of the opposition bowling, India's top order embraced disaster at the Adelaide Oval with a series of poor strokes. If, from the low of 41 for 4 in the first session of the game, they managed to close out a 31-run win in the final session of the last day, it was largely on the back of their solid No.3. The drop-in pitch held few demons, though its slowness discouraged free stroke-making. Even as batsmen from both sides struggled to make the necessary adjustments, Pujara rode on customary patience and innate composure to tower above the rest.

Once he had allowed India to grab the upper hand, the bowlers stepped in to deliver the knockout blows. The pacers were always going to have a massive say, but India received an unexpected bonus from R Ashwin, whose off-spin yielded three first-innings wickets to go with as many in the second.

Even when India were bowled out for 250 off the first ball of the second morning, it was obvious that the total was worth more than its numerical value. If not for an old failing — the inability to winkle out the lower order rapidly — and the common-sense approach of Travis Head, India would have opened up a more substantial lead than 15 as the last four Australian

Solid defence: Cheteshwar Pujara occupied the crease for more than 31 hours through the series. — *Getty Images*

wickets realised 108. Pujara was again central to India's second-innings performance, putting on 87 for the fourth wicket with Ajinkya Rahane. A dramatic late collapse triggered by Lyon and Starc that saw the last five wickets go down for just 25 runs meant Australia's target was 323; still, no team had successfully chased down as many at the Adelaide Oval ever.

Shami did his reputation as a second-innings destroyer no harm at all and Bumrah continued to harry the Aussies, making sure that despite their bizarre decision to use Ashwin as a defensive option on a day-five track, India made deep inroads. Like in the first innings, the Australian lower order outdid the top, the last four wickets yielding 135 and the last pair putting on 32. But India were never seriously threatened and, when Ashwin dismissed last-man Josh Hazlewood, they went 1-0 up after the first Test of a series on Aussie soil for the first time.

Adelaide Oval, Adelaide, December 6-10: India 250 in 88 overs (Cheteshwar Pujara 123, Rohit Sharma 37; Josh Hazlewood 3-52, Pat Cummins 2-49) and 307 in 106.5 overs (C Pujara 71, Ajinkya Rahane 70; Nathan Lyon 6-122, Mitchell Starc 3-40) beat **Australia** 235 in 98.4 overs (Travis Head 72, Peter Handscomb 34; Jasprit Bumrah 3-47, R Ashwin 3-57) and 291 in 119.5 overs (Shaun Marsh 60, Tim Paine 41; Mohammed Shami 3-65, J Bumrah 3-68, R Ashwin 3-92) by 31 runs. *PoM:* Cheteshwar Pujara.

2nd Test: Australia won by 146 runs

For a large part of the early 2000s, India failed to build on gains overseas, losing a Test match immediately on the heels of a victory. It happened in Zimbabwe (2001), the West Indies (2002), Australia (2003), Pakistan (2004) and South Africa (2006).

History repeated itself in Australia in 2018 when, in the first Test match at Perth's swank new Optus Stadium — sadly, the authorities felt the iconic WACA ground had outlived its utility — the hosts roared back in pacer-friendly conditions to square the series.

The match was in the balance for three days after Kohli conjured one of his best hundreds, but Australia sped away on day four and needed a mere 45 minutes on the final morning to complete the formalities.

Kohli's ton was a fabulous compilation on a surface with searing pace, considerable lateral movement and, gradually, inconsistent bounce. It wasn't vintage Kohli in that he didn't dominate like he usually does. Instead, in deference to the conditions and Australia's fiery pace attack, the Indian captain opted to bat out of character, setting ego aside and grinding his way to a five-hour, 214-ball hundred.

With an abdominal strain keeping Ashwin out of the mix, India went with an all-pace attack, but with Umesh Yadav, the off-spinner's replacement, particularly profligate and the others not making the openers play as much as they should have, Aaron Finch and Marcus Harris put on 112 for the first wicket. India pulled up their socks thereafter with Ishant leading the way, and recovered from a poor start with three successive half-century partnerships in which Kohli was the constant. While Australia's fast bowlers threatened, it was offie Lyon who reaped the rewards, with his second successive five-wicket haul of the series.

Usman Khawaja, thriving in Ashwin's absence, drove Australia's lead beyond India's reach, though Shami kept India interested with another telling second-innings burst to ensure the target was under 300. In no time, India were reduced to 13 for 2 — including Pujara for four — and when Lyon forced Kohli to edge to slip, India's chase was stymied.

Starc, his struggles for rhythm notwithstanding, led the way, while Hazlewood and Cummins kept up the pressure and Lyon flourished at India's expense. That Lyon snared the match award in conditions more suited to his pace colleagues only gave fuel to questions about Kohli's team selection.

Perth Stadium, Perth, December 14-18: Australia 326 in 108.3 overs (Marcus Harris 70, Travis Head 58; Ishant Sharma 4-41, Jasprit Bumrah 2-53, Hanuma Vihari 2-53) and 243 in 93.2 overs (Usman Khawaja 72, Tim Paine 37; Mohammed Shami 6-56, J Bumrah 3-39) beat **India** 283 in 105.5 overs (Virat Kohli 123, Ajinkya Rahane 51; Nathan Lyon 5-67, Josh Hazlewood 2-66) and 140 in 56 overs (A Rahane 30, Rishabh Pant 30; N Lyon 3-39, Mitchell Starc 3-46) by 146 runs. *PoM:* Nathan Lyon.

3rd Test: India won by 137 runs

Utilising the week between the Second and Third Tests to good effect, India rang in tactical and personnel changes that, coupled with a sub-continent-type surface, Kohli's luck with the coin and stirring individual performances, helped them secure their first Boxing Day Test win at the MCG since 1980-81.

Agarwal showed there was more to him than sheer weight of runs in domestic and A cricket, Pujara again blunted Australia's increasingly dispirited attack and Bumrah reaffirmed his standing as among the premier new-ball bowlers in world cricket. While these were the principal performers, others made handy contributions, not least the skipper himself. Australia, by contrast, had little to fall back on beyond the heroics of Cummins, who brought up his best figures and highest score in Test cricket on the same day. Given this massive dichotomy, India's commanding win was no surprise.

When Agarwal and G Hanuma Vihari walked out in front of 73,516 fans on the first morning, it marked the first time in 82 years that both Indians were in their maiden stints as Test openers. Their stand was worth only 40, but spanned 18.5 overs; Vihari's 8 off 66 was a sig-

Spearhead: Bumrah bowled with fire, control and intent on a two-paced Melbourne surface. — *Getty Images*

nificant hand because it kept the home pace attack at bay, after which Pujara took over with another telling exhibition of determination, focus and hunger. With Agarwal, who systematically dismantled Lyon's threat, Pujara put on 83, then realised a spirit-shattering 170 alongside his captain. His eight-hour 106 was complemented by cameos from the middle order.

Bumrah, bowling with fire, control and intent on a two-paced surface of indifferent bounce, carved through Australia's hesitant batting, his working over of opener Harris as compelling as the slower delivery last ball before lunch on day three that accounted for a completely befuddled Shaun Marsh.

Cummins blasted out the Indian top order, but armed with a lead of 292, the visitors were in little danger of frittering away their advantage. The paceman, who had finished with 6 for 27 in India's second innings, then took it upon himself to keep Australia's fight going after they slumped to 215 for 8 in quest of 399. Showcasing skills that ought to have shamed the misfiring top order, he pushed the game to the final day in the company of an obdurate Lyon. The artificial excitement generated by rain, which pushed back the start of play on day five by two hours and 25 minutes, however, lasted just 22 minutes and 27 deliveries, Ishant formalising the lead-snatching win by having Lyon caught behind.

Melbourne Cricket Ground, December 26-30: India 443/7 dec. in 169.4 overs (Cheteshwar Pujara 106, Virat Kohli 82; Pat Cummins 3-72, Mitchell Starc 2-87) and 106/8 dec. in 37.3 overs (Mayank Agarwal 42, Rishabh Pant 33; P Cummins 6-27, Josh Hazlewood 2-22) beat **Australia** 151 in 66.5 overs (Jasprit Bumrah 6-33, Ravindra Jadeja 2-45) and 261 in 89.3 overs (P Cummins 63, Shaun Marsh 44; J Bumrah 3-53, R Jadeja 3-82) by 137 runs. *PoM:* Jasprit Bumrah.

> Rishabh Pant's 20 dismissals against Australia are the most by an Indian wicket-keeper in a series. Naren Tamhane (1954-55) and Syed Kirmani (1979-80) both had 19 in series against Pakistan.

4th Test: Match drawn

Not even the anti-climactic end, with rain consigning the final Test of the series to a watery grave, took the sheen off India's tryst with history. India settled for a 2–1 scoreline after just 25.2 overs of play was possible on the fourth day and none at all on the fifth. There were no glum faces, however: Kohli's men were delighted at being the first Indian team to secure a Test series triumph in Australia, Paine's beleaguered troops were relieved at having got out of jail.

Pujara again proffered a magnificent compilation, occupying the crease for a staggering nine hours and eight minutes and seeing off 373 deliveries in working his way to 193. It was the cornerstone around which India erected a monumental 622 for 7 declared, his single-mindedness paving the way for the ebullient Pant to pile the misery with a spectacular unbeaten 159, off just 189 deliveries. In easily the truest batting surface of the series, India scored at a rapid clip after Kohli's luck with the coin held. Agarwal reiterated his international credentials with another sparkling half-century during a stand of 116 with Pujara and Ravindra Jadeja provided the late flourish in Pant's company as 204 were realised for the seventh wicket.

India's spinners, led by the recalled Kuldeep, enjoyed much better returns than Lyon. Australia had worked their way to 128 for 1 on the back of two solid half-century alliances when Kuldeep and Jadeja got into the act. In his first bowl in a Test in Australia, the left-arm wrist-spinner finished with a five-wicket haul. Jadeja, the left-arm orthodox spinner, backed him up as the hosts were bowled out for 300, and that because the last four wickets put on 102. With the surface expected to assist spinners more and the threat of rain genuine, Kohli enforced the follow-on, the first time since January 1988 that Australia were facing such an ignominy on home patch. Had the weather not intervened, India would have fancied their chances.

Sydney Cricket Ground, Sydney, January 3-7: India 622/7 dec. in 167.2 overs (Cheteshwar Pujara 193, Rishabh Pant 159*; Nathan Lyon 4-178, Josh Hazlewood 2-105) drew with **Australia** 300 in 104.5 overs (Marcus Harris 79, Marnus Labuschagne 38; Kuldeep Yadav 5-99, Mohammed Shami 2-58) and 6/0 in 4 overs. *PoM:* Cheteshwar Pujara. *PoS:* Cheteshwar Pujara.

Historic: India were in with a good chance to make it 3-1 in Sydney before rain intervened to force a draw. — *Getty Images*

Most balls faced by a batsman in an away series of four matches or fewer

Batsman	Series	M/I	R	Avge	BF
Rahul Dravid	England, 2002	4/6	602	100.33	1336
Alastair Cook	India, 2012-13	4/8	562	80.28	1285
Cheteshwar Pujara	Australia, 2018-19	4/7	521	74.42	1258
Bert Sutcliffe	Australia, 1928-29	4/7	355	50.71	1237
Brian Lara	Sri Lanka, 2001-02	3/6	688	114.76	1226

ODI series (3): India 2 Australia 1

1st ODI: Australia won by 34 runs

Rohit uncorked a punishing 22nd ODI hundred, but Jhye Richardson carried the night. A competent rather than muscular display from the top order, which bore an uncanny resemblance to their Test line-up, had lifted Australia to a competitive total, with Khawaja, Shaun Marsh and Peter Handscomb making differently paced half-centuries, and Stoinis applying the finishing touches with a breezy knock.

India lost Dhawan in the first over to Jason Behrendorff, but it was Richardson who drove the dagger deep by dismissing Kohli and Ambati Rayudu in three deliveries in the fourth over of the chase. Rohit, typically punishing, batted with customary freedom despite the situation, while Mahendra Singh

Dhoni's painstaking 51 off 96 deliveries in a stabilising stand of 137 again whipped up frenzied debate.

Sydney Cricket Ground, Sydney, January 12: Australia 288/5 in 50 overs (Peter Handscomb 73, Usman Khawaja 59; Kuldeep Yadav 2-54, Bhuvneshwar Kumar 2-66) beat **India** 254/9 in 50 overs (Rohit Sharma 133, MS Dhoni 51; Jhye Richardson 4-26, Jason Behrendorff 2-39) by 34 runs. *PoM:* Jhye Richardson.

2nd ODI: India won by six wickets

Within three nights of his laborious half-century, Dhoni reiterated his value to the Indian side, steering the visitors to a series-levelling win. Marsh made his fourth hundred in eight innings, Kohli continued his mastery of the 50-over game with a fabulous 39th century and Bhuvneshwar rediscovered his white-ball mojo, but it was Dhoni who walked away with the accolades after a decisive unbeaten fifty and a match-sealing stand of 57 in just 34 deliveries with Karthik.

Australia seemed set to post a total in excess of 300 with a well-set Marsh and Maxwell in the middle, when Bhuvneshwar sent them both back in the 48th over and India fought back. They then began the chase brightly, before Kohli's brilliance got them close, and Dhoni and Karthik sealed the deal.

Adelaide Oval, Adelaide, January 15: Australia 298/9 in 50 overs (Shaun Marsh 131, Glenn Maxwell 48; Bhuvneshwar Kumar 4-45, Mohammed Shami 3-58) lost to **India** 299/4 in 49.2 overs (Virat Kohli 104, MS Dhoni 55*) by six wickets. *PoM:* Virat Kohli.

3rd ODI: India won by seven wickets

Playing his first match of the series, leggie Yuzvendra Chahal bamboozled Australia with a career-best 6 for 42, but India still had to work hard on a sluggish pitch to complete a historic come-from-behind 2-1 series triumph.

Chahal's dismissal of form batsman Marsh with his second ball meant from 100 for 2 after 23 overs, Australia were rolled over for 230 with eight deliveries left unutilised. A potentially straightforward chase was made trickier by the slowness of the pitch. Kohli laid the platform, leaving it to Dhoni, with his third fifty on the trot, and Kedar Jadhav, who like Chahal was in his first outing, to get the job done. As is his wont, Dhoni took it deep, though Jadhav made up with cheeky innovation. When victory arrived, the pair had put on 121.

Melbourne Cricket Ground, January 18: Australia 230 in 48.4 overs (Peter Handscomb 58, Shaun Marsh 39; Yuzvendra Chahal 6-42, Bhuvneshwar Kumar 2-28) lost to **India** 234/3 in 49.2 overs (MS Dhoni 87*, Kedar Jadhav 61*) by seven wickets. *PoM:* Yuzvendra Chahal. *PoS:* MS Dhoni.

Divisive style: Dhoni brought up three half-centuries, not everyone agreed with his methods. — *Getty Images*

Series averages

Australia

Batting

Player	M	I	NO	R	HS	Avge	100s/50s
M Labuschagne	1	1	0	38	38	38.00	0/0
M Harris	4	8	1	258	79	36.85	0/2
T Head	4	7	0	237	72	33.85	0/2
U Khawaja	4	8	1	198	72	28.28	0/1
S Marsh	4	7	0	183	60	26.14	0/1
T Paine	4	7	0	174	41	24.85	0/0
M Starc	4	7	2	117	29*	23.40	0/0
P Cummins	4	7	0	163	63	23.28	0/1
P Handscomb	3	5	0	105	37	21.00	0/0
N Lyon	4	7	3	83	38*	20.75	0/0
A Finch	3	6	0	97	50	16.16	0/1
J Hazlewood	4	7	2	51	21	10.20	0/0
M Marsh	1	2	0	19	10	9.50	0/0

Bowling and fielding

Player	M	W	R	BBI	BBM	Avge	5wI/10wM	Ct/St
P Cummins	4	14	389	6-27	9-99	27.78	1/0	1/-
N Lyon	4	21	639	6-122	8-106	30.42	2/0	2/-
J Hazlewood	4	13	398	3-52	4-90	30.61	0/0	0/-
M Starc	4	13	449	3-40	5-103	34.53	0/0	4/-
A Finch	3	0	8	-	-	-	0/0	7/-
T Head	4	0	35	-	-	-	0/0	1/-
U Khawaja	4	0	4	-	-	-	0/0	6/-
M Labuscha-gne	1	0	76	-	-	-	0/0	1/-
M Marsh	1	0	51	-	-	-	0/0	0/-
P Handscomb	3	-	-	-	-	-	-/-	6/-
M Harris	4	-	-	-	-	-	-/-	6/-
S Marsh	4	-	-	-	-	-	-/-	2/-
T Paine	4	-	-	-	-	-	-/-	16/0

India

Batting

Player	M	I	NO	R	HS	Avge	100s/50s
C Pujara	4	7	0	521	193	74.42	3/1
M Agarwal	2	3	0	195	77	65.00	0/2
R Pant	4	7	1	350	159*	58.33	1/0
V Kohli	4	7	0	282	123	40.28	1/1
R Sharma	2	4	1	106	63*	35.33	0/1
A Rahane	4	7	0	217	70	31.00	0/2
R Jadeja	2	3	0	90	81	30.00	0/1
H Vihari	3	5	0	111	42	22.20	0/0
R Ashwin	1	2	0	30	25	15.00	0/0
M Vijay	2	4	0	49	20	12.25	0/0
KL Rahul	3	5	0	57	44	11.40	0/0
U Yadav	1	2	1	6	4*	6.00	0/0
J Bumrah	4	4	2	4	4	2.00	0/0
M Shami	4	5	2	6	6	2.00	0/0
I Sharma	3	4	0	5	4	1.25	0/0
K Yadav	1	-	-	-	-	-	-/-

Bowling and fielding

Player	M	W	R	BBI	BBM	Avge	5wI/10wM	Ct/St
J Bumrah	4	21	357	6-33	9-86	17.00	1/0	0/-
K Yadav	1	5	99	5-99	5-99	19.80	1/0	1/-
I Sharma	3	11	262	4-41	5-86	23.81	0/0	2/-
R Ashwin	1	6	149	3-57	6-149	24.83	0/0	0/-
M Shami	4	16	419	6-56	6-136	26.18	1/0	1/-
R Jadeja	2	7	200	3-82	5-127	28.57	0/0	0/-
H Vihari	3	2	94	3-53	2-84	47.00	0/0	1/-
U Yadav	1	2	139	2-78	2-139	69.50	0/0	0/-
M Vijay	2	0	31	-	-	-	0/0	1/-
M Agarwal	2	-	-	-	-	-	-/-	3/-
V Kohli	4	-	-	-	-	-	-/-	5/-
R Pant	4	-	-	-	-	-	-/-	20/0
C Pujara	4	-	-	-	-	-	-/-	3/-
A Rahane	4	-	-	-	-	-	-/-	6/-
KL Rahul	3	-	-	-	-	-	-/-	1/-
R Sharma	2	-	-	-	-	-	-/-	1/-

Squads

Australia: Tim Paine (capt & wk), Pat Cummins, Aaron Finch, Peter Handscomb, Marcus Harris, Josh Hazlewood, Travis Head, Usman Khawaja, Marnus Labuschagne, Nathan Lyon, Mitchell Marsh, Shaun Marsh, Peter Siddle, Mitchell Starc, Chris Tremain.

India: Virat Kohli (capt), Ajinkya Rahane (vice-capt), Mayank Agarwal, R Ashwin, Jasprit Bumrah, Ravindra Jadeja, Kuldeep Yadav, Bhuvneshwar Kumar, Mohammad Shami, Hardik Pandya, Rishabh Pant (wk), Parthiv Patel (wk), Cheteshwar Pujara, KL Rahul, Ishant Sharma, Rohit Sharma, M Vijay, Umesh Yadav, Hanuma Vihari, Prithvi Shaw (withdrawn).

India in New Zealand

Candidates line up for World Cup spots

The limited-overs series in New Zealand was supposed to help India get a few answers ahead of the World Cup. While it did allow candidates on the fringe to make a case for themselves — Mohammed Shami stormed back into white-ball contention in the absence of the rested Jasprit Bumrah — it only served to confirm what India already knew: Their top order holds them up, their middle is soft; Hardik Pandya makes them a better team; Ambati Rayudu and Vijay Shankar are their best candidates for the troublesome No.4 spot.

New Zealand, the No.3 side with an eye-catching record at home, were expected to pose the sternest test yet for India. So, the mismatches early on came as a surprise. As did those occasions when things went horribly wrong for India — such as when they were bundled out for 92. The surprise was in how quickly things had turned, but perhaps not as much in the top order's troubles against the moving ball.

India began without Pandya, who had been suspended for his comments on a talk show that were deemed sexist and racist. When the all-rounder joined them midway, his suspension lifted pending investigation, he quickly showed his utility.

New Zealand had problems of their own over the off-field behaviour of their players. Scott Kuggeliejn was the subject of protest posters following his trial in a rape case; while he had admitted in court that the woman said 'no', he was found not guilty.

	ODIs	T20Is
Most runs	Ambati Rayudu (India) (190 runs, 5 matches)	Tim Seifert (New Zealand) (139 runs, 3 matches)
Most wickets	Trent Boult (New Zealand) (12 wickets, 5 matches)	Daryl Mitchell (New Zealand) (4 wickets, 3 matches)

ODI series (5): New Zealand 1 India 4

1st ODI: India won by eight wickets (DLS method)

The talk before the series was about how New Zealand's tendency to post tall totals will pose a challenge for India. The visitors needed 38 overs to pooh-pooh that idea. Shami broke open the door, and India's wrist-spinning duo feasted. The India seamer got the ball to move both ways in an excellent opening spell, and exposed the New Zealand openers' shortcomings in reducing them to 18 for 2. In his 56th ODI, he became the fastest Indian to 100 wickets. Yuzvendra Chahal and Kuldeep Yadav, reunited after a while, played on the middle order's impatience, before the left-armer ran through the tail. Even Williamson was drawn into an early shot trying to clear the field. Shikhar Dhawan found his rhythm to be joint fifth-fastest to 5000 ODI runs with Brian Lara, in 118 innings. The only delay for India was when the setting sun stopped play — the McLean Park pitch, uniquely, runs from east to west.

Seam-bowling excellence: Mohammed Shami got the ball to move both ways and was a constant threat.
— *Getty Images*

McLean Park, Napier, January 23: New Zealand 157 in 38 overs (Kane Williamson 64; Kuldeep Yadav 4-39, Mohammed Shami 3-19) lost to **India** 156/2 in 34.5 overs (Shikhar Dhawan 75*, Virat Kohli 45) by eight wickets (DLS method). *PoM:* Mohammed Shami.

2nd ODI: India won by 90 runs

India's middle order did little to change the school of thought that the team was unduly reliant on the top three. Rohit and Dhawan had blazed away to 154 at the halfway mark, but with ten overs to go, India were just 238/3. Ish Sodhi conceded only a single boundary in his ten-over spell. M S Dhoni and Kedar Jadhav made amends at the death, taking 14 off the penultimate over and 21 off the final to push the total past 320. Martin Guptill survived a run-out chance first ball, and was dropped; Williamson came out all guns blazing, smashing Shami for a sequence of six, six, four. However, the luck of both batsmen ran out quickly. With Shami and Bhuvneshwar a handful with the new ball, and the spinners cleaning up the rest, it was all over in the 41st. Doug Bracewell's 58-run stand for the ninth wicket with Lockie Ferguson was cosmetic.

Bay Oval, Mount Maunganui, January 26: India 324/4 in 50 overs (Rohit Sharma 87, Shikhar Dhawan 66; Trent Boult 2-66, Lockie Ferguson 2-81) beat **New Zealand** 234 in 40.2 overs (Doug Bracewell 57, Tom Latham 34; Kuldeep Yadav 4-45, Bhuvneshwar Kumar 2-42) by 90 runs. *PoM:* Rohit Sharma.

3rd ODI: India won by seven wickets

New Zealand finally showed intent in taking on the Indian spinners. But another batting collapse, this time losing their last seven for just 65, meant they could only post another middling total. And despite the slow nature of the surface, captain Kohli and his vice-captain Rohit had no real trouble in sealing the series for India. The second-wicket pair was cautious in adding 113, before Rayudu and Dinesh Karthik were brisk in wrapping up the chase.

India benefitted from the return of Pandya, who not only took an excellent catch to send back Williamson, but also chipped in with two lower-middle-order wickets. Taylor's 119-run stand with Tom Latham went in vain.

Bay Oval, Mount Maunganui, January 28: New Zealand 243 in 49 overs (Ross Taylor 93, Tom Latham 51; Mohammed Shami 3-41, Hardik Pandya 2-45) lost to **India** 245/3 in 43 overs (Rohit Sharma 62, Virat Kohli 60; Trent Boult 2/40) by seven wickets. *PoM:* Mohammed Shami.

4th ODI: New Zealand won by eight wickets

Captain in his 200th ODI, there was little for Rohit to celebrate. With Kohli rested and Dhoni injured, India fell apart against a searing test of swing bowling, failing to get into triple-figures and consigned to their biggest loss in terms of balls remaining. Trent Boult bowled unchanged for incredible figures of 10-4-21-5. It began in the fifth over, with Dhawan trapped lbw with an inswinger. Colin de Grandhomme too joined in the fun, picking up Rayudu and Karthik in his first, and India were 55 for 8 in 20. Taylor slammed three sixes to finish the game in a hurry.

Seddon Park, Hamilton, January 31: India 92 in 30.5 overs (Trent Boult 5/21, Colin de Grandhomme 3-26) lost to **New Zealand** 93/2 in 14.4 overs (Ross Taylor 37*, Henry Nicholls 30*; Bhuvneshwar Kumar 2-25) by eight wickets. *PoM:* Trent Boult.

5th ODI: India won by 35 runs

At 18 for 4, India seemed on course for another low total. Rayudu and Vijay, however, dug in, doing their case for selection for the World Cup no harm. On 7 off 36 balls before he hit his first four, Rayudu steadily upped his scoring, adding 98 with a calm Vijay and 74 with Kedar Jadhav. Pandya's burst at the death, including three sixes in the 47th off Todd Astle, made for a challenging total on a tricky surface. Williamson tried to replicate Rayudu's plan, but was out for 39 off 72 when he tried to get a move on. Jimmy Neesham got a reminder of why Dhoni's the best at what he does: in the middle of an lbw appeal he strayed out of his crease, not realising the ball had rolled to Dhoni, who, even as he appealed for the lbw, quickly completed the run-out.

Westpac Stadium, Wellington, February 3: India 252 in 49.5 overs (Ambati Rayudu 90, Vijay Shankar 45, Hardik Pandya 45; Matt Henry 4-35, Trent Boult 3-39) beat **New Zealand** 217 in 44.1 overs (Jimmy Neesham 44, Kane Williamson 39; Yuzvendra Chahal 3-41, Mohammed Shami 2-35) by 35 runs. *PoM:* Ambati Rayudu. *PoS:* Mohammed Shami.

T20 series (3): New Zealand 2 India 1

1st T20I: New Zealand won by 80 runs

• Tim Seifert quickly takes to his new spot as opener. • He and Colin Munro, who has found his touch after an indifferent ODI series, add 66 in the powerplay. • A combination of innovative shots and positive cricket brings up Seifert's fifty in 30 balls, and he tees off to reach 84 in 43, with six sixes. • Only West Indies (245 for 6) have made a higher total against India, and never before have three Indian bowlers gone for more than 45 each in a T20I. • India lose Rohit early, but the real damage happens when they go from 51 for 1 to 77 for 6. • It is India's worst defeat in terms of runs in a T20I.

Westpac Stadium, Wellington, February 3: New Zealand 219/6 in 20 overs (Tim Seifert 84, Colin Munro 34, Kane Williamson 34; Hardik Pandya 2-51) beat **India** 139 in 19.2 overs (MS Dhoni 39, Shikhar Dhawan 29; Tim Southee 3-17, Lockie Ferguson 2-22) by 80 runs. *PoM:* Tim Seifert.

2nd T20I: India won by seven wickets

• The visiting bowlers bounce back strongly to give India their first T20I win in New Zealand. • The hosts can't repeat their top-order heroics from the previous match as Krunal Pandya strikes twice in his first over. • There's controversy as Daryl Mitchell is given out lbw on DRS although HotSpot shows a clear mark. • De Grandhomme's 50 off 28 balls gives his colleagues something to bowl at. • A half-century off 28 balls takes Rohit to the top of the all-time T20I batting charts. • Pant is typically ebullient as India complete a clinical chase.

Eden Park, Auckland, February 8: New Zealand 158/8 in 20 overs (Colin de Grandhomme 50, Ross Taylor 42; Krunal Pandya 3-28, Khaleel Ahmed 2-27) lost to **India** 162/3 in 18.5 overs (Rohit Sharma 50, Rishabh Pant 40*) by seven wickets. *PoM:* Krunal Pandya.

3rd T20I: New Zealand won by four runs

• Tim Southee defends 15 in the last over to give New Zealand the series. • All of the hosts' top six contribute, with Williamson's 27 off 21 the only score made at a rate less than 170. • Munro is especially punishing, striking three sixes in his 72 off 40. • Rohit plays anchor while Shankar (43 off 28), Pant (28 off 12) and Hardik (21 off 11) hit out. • Karthik and Krunal need 68 off 28 when they combine. • Six sixes between them keeps the target in sight, but Karthik cannot do a repeat of the Nidahas final.

Seddon Park, Hamilton, February 10: New Zealand 212/4 in 20 overs (Colin Munro 72, Tim Seifert 43; Kuldeep Yadav 2-26) beat **India** 208/6 in 20 overs (Vijay Shankar 43, Rohit Sharma 38; Daryl Mitchell 2-27, Mitchell Santner 2-32) by four runs. *PoM:* Colin Munro. *PoS:* Tim Seifert.

Australia in India

Glenn Maxwell's authoritative hundred in the second T20I in Bengaluru included some fantastic sixes. — *Getty Images*

Spirited turnaround from Finch's men

T20I series (2): Australia 2 India 0

1ˢᵗ T20I: Australia won by three wickets

• Jasprit Bumrah concedes just two runs in the penultimate over, rounding off his spell with wickets off his last two balls. • All Umesh Yadav has to do is defend 14 off the last over with two new batsmen at the crease. • But Pat Cummins and Jhye Richardson throw their bats around to chase a target they ought to have cruised to in the first place. • At one stage, Australia need 38 in 40 balls with eight wickets in hand, but they nearly lose track once Glenn Maxwell holes out to long-off. • India have done the same earlier in the day: K L Rahul and Virat Kohli took them to 69 for 1 before Nathan Coulter-Nile scythed through a weak lower-middle order. • MS Dhoni had no option but to keep denying singles to ensure India bat the full quota of overs.

Dr YS Rajasekhara Reddy ACA-VDCA Cricket Stadium, Visakhapatnam, February 24: **India** 126/7 in 20 overs (KL Rahul 50, MS Dhoni 29*; Nathan Coulter-Nile 3-26) lost to **Australia** 127/7 in 20 overs (Glenn Maxwell 56, D'Arcy Short 37; Jasprit Bumrah 3-16) by three wickets. *PoM:* Nathan Coulter-Nile.

2nd T20I: Australia won by seven wickets

• An authoritative 55-ball unbeaten 113 from Maxwell helps Australia clinch their first bilateral T20I series against India. • Along with D'Arcy Short, he lifts Australia from 22 for 2. • The most spectacular of Maxwell's nine sixes, an incredible bottom-handed scoop of sorts of Siddarth Kaul, soars over the bowler's head. • Vijay Shankar, brought into the side to reduce the length of the ridiculously long tail, takes two of the three wickets. • Earlier, Kohli has dazzled during his 38-ball 72 not out, while Rahul and Dhoni hit out brutally for their forties. • Unfortunately, none of their team-mates score even 15 runs in the entire series.

M Chinnaswamy Stadium, Bengaluru, February 27: India 190/4 in 20 overs (Virat Kohli 72*, KL Rahul 47) lost to **Australia** 194/3 in 19.4 overs (Glenn Maxwell 113*, D'Arcy Short 40; Vijay Shankar 2-38) by seven wickets. *PoM:* Glenn Maxwell. *PoS:* Glenn Maxwell.

ODI series (5): Australia 3 India 2

1st ODI: India won by six wickets

An unbeaten fourth-wicket stand between Dhoni and Kedar Jadhav helped India go one-up after they were reduced to 99 for 4 by Coulter-Nile and Adam Zampa. The chase had a familiar look to it, with Dhoni dropping anchor at one end as Jadhav played his strokes as the target came down. This was Dhoni's fourth consecutive fifty against Australia; he was not dismissed in the last three. Earlier, seven Australians scored between 19 and 50, but that was not enough for them to go past 236 for 7. Mohammed Shami bowled an excellent first spell where he was unfortunate to not get a wicket, but he broke through twice — including a gem to bowl Maxwell through the gate — later in the innings.

Rajiv Gandhi International Stadium, Uppal, Hyderabad, March 2: Australia 236/7 in 50 overs (Usman Khawaja 50, Glenn Maxwell 40; Mohammed Shami 2-44, Kuldeep Yadav 2-46) lost to **India** 240/4 in 48.2 overs (Kedar Jadhav 81*, MS Dhoni 59*, Nathan Coulter-Nile 2-46, Adam Zampa 2-49) by six wickets. *PoM:* Kedar Jadhav.

2nd ODI: India won by eight runs

India were as good as out of the hunt after 45 overs into the chase despite Kuldeep Yadav's three wickets. Australia needed a mere 29 at that point. Then Kohli decided to bowl out Bumrah's last two overs. Bumrah's last spell — 2-0-2-2 — turned the match on its head. Having to defend 11 off the last over, Vijay settled things with two wickets in three balls.

Before that, Kohli had himself carved out a hard-earned 116. Boundaries were not easy to come by — he got only ten of them — but he ran hard enough to score at a strike-rate of 97. He lifted India from 75 for 3, then 171 for 6; and the innings folded for 250 seven balls after he was the eighth to be dismissed.

Vidarbha Cricket Association Stadium, Jamtha, Nagpur, March 5: India 250 in 48.2 overs (Virat Kohli 116, Vijay Shankar 46; Pat Cummins 4-29, Adam Zampa 2-62) beat **Australia** 242 in 49.3 overs (Marcus Stoinis 52, Peter Handscomb 48; Kuldeep Yadav 3-54, V Shankar 2-15) by eight runs. *PoM:* Virat Kohli.

3ʳᵈ ODI: Australia win by 32 runs

Usman Khawaja's maiden ODI hundred and Aaron Finch's return-to-form 93 helped Australia register their first win of the series. The pair added 193 for the opening stand, and cameos from Maxwell, Marcus Stoinis and Alex Carey took the total to 313 for 5 despite Kuldeep's triple blow. The Indians, who had taken the field in army caps in honour of the Pulwama attack victims, had a terrible day in the field.

Kohli duly got a hundred — a 95-ball 123 out of the 208 India scored during his stay — but there was little support at the other end. Richardson and Cummins provided the early blows, while Zampa bowled intelligently later in the innings. The trio shared three wickets apiece as India collapsed.

JSCA International Stadium Complex, Ranchi, March 8: Australia 313/5 in 50 overs (Usman Khawaja 104, Aaron Finch 93; Kuldeep Yadav 3-64) beat **India** 281 in 48.2 overs (Virat Kohli 123, Vijay Shankar 32; Jhye Richardson 3-37, Pat Cummins 3-37, Adam Zampa 3-70) by 32 runs. *PoM: Usman Khawaja.*

4ᵗʰ ODI: Australia won by four wickets

Shikhar Dhawan finally returned to form with a dazzling exhibition of strokes en route a 115-ball 143, pushing Rohit Sharma into the background in an opening stand of 193. The middle order exploded in a flurry of shots, and it was only Cummins's five-wicket haul that pegged them back — if the phrase is applicable here — to 358 for 9. Bumrah rounded things off with a six off the last ball to raise both his career average and strike-rate by 50%, bringing the entire dressing room to its feet.

Australia lost two quick wickets before Khawaja and Peter Handscomb (117 in 105, his maiden ODI hundred) added 192 to set the platform for the final fireworks. The Mohali dew prevented Kuldeep and Yuzvendra Chahal from being their best, but the target still mounted to 62 in six overs.

India were stunned by Ashton Turner, drafted in for the injured Stoinis. Australia got there with 13 balls to spare, Turner converting a 31-ball 43 into a 43-ball unbeaten 84.

Punjab Cricket Association IS Bindra Stadium, Mohali, Chandigarh, March 10: India 358/9 in 50 overs (Shikhar Dhawan 143, Rohit Sharma 95; Pat Cummins 5-70, Jhye Richardson 3-85) lost to **Australia** 359/6 in 47.5 overs (Peter Handscomb 117, Usman Khawaja 91; Jasprit Bumrah 3-63) by four wickets. *PoM:* Ashton Turner.

5ᵗʰ ODI: Australia won by 35 runs

Australia provided the fifth instance of a team coming back from 0-2 to clinch an ODI series, while also winning their first series after losing six in a row. With a round 100, Khawaja finished the series with 383 runs, while

Cummins' haul of 14 wickets became a new record by anyone in a bilateral series against India in India.

Thanks to Khawaja, Australia countered some incisive bowling from Bhuvneshwar Kumar and Bumrah to post 272 for 9. The Indians lost too many wickets too early in their innings, and at 132 for 6 there could have been only one winner. Jadhav and Bhuvneshwar fought hard, but their 91-run stand did little beyond reducing the margin.

Feroz Shah Kotla, Delhi, March 13: Australia 272/9 in 50 overs (Usman Khawaja 100, Peter Handscomb 52; Bhuvneshwar Kumar 3-48, Ravindra Jadeja 2-45) beat **India** 237 in 50 overs (Rohit Sharma 56, B Kumar 46; Adam Zampa 3-46, Marcus Stoinis 2-31) by 35 runs. *PoM: Usman Khawaja. PoS: Usman Khawaja.*

	T20Is	**ODIs**
Most runs	Glenn Maxwell (Australia) (169 runs, 2 matches)	Usman Khawaja (Australia) (383 runs, 5 matches)
Most wickets	Nathan Coulter-Nile (Australia) (4 wickets, 2 matches)	Pat Cummins (Australia) (14 wickets, 5 matches)

INDIA INTERNATIONALS 2017-18

New Zealand in India

Bumrah, Chahal enjoy home comforts

ROSHAN THYAGARAJAN

After the one-sided results against West Indies and Sri Lanka on their shores, and then a drama-filled series against the Australians at home, spectators in India were left craving good, clean competition. Kane Williamson and his men promised to deliver, with their brand of fearless batting, disciplined bowling and world-class fielding.

New Zealand set the ball rolling with a morale-boosting victory in Mumbai, even in the face of a fantastic century from Virat Kohli. The hosts bounced back to level scores, with bowlers hogging the limelight for a change. The trend continued in the series decider as Yuzvendra Chahal and Jasprit Bumrah turned into aggressive defenders of a 338-run citadel built on centuries from Rohit Sharma and Kohli. The six-run win meant New Zealand had to wait longer to achieve their maiden ODI series win in India.

The high-scoring final contest set up an exciting exchange in the three-match T20I series. When India came away with 53-run win to stud Ashish Nehra's farewell match, there wasn't much to suggest that the visitors would put up a fight. Colin Munro, however, brought the visitors within one win of their second T20I series victory in India with an explosive ton.

India gave Ashish Nehra a send-off with a 53-run win. — *BCCI/Sportzpics*

It all came down to the contest in Thiruvananthapuram, and much to the dismay of everyone involved, the rain held sway for a significant portion of the day. When the game did get under way, it was an eight-over shoot-out. Once again, India's bowling unit kept their composure in what turned out to be yet another series win in a fruitful season.

	ODIs	**T20Is**
Most runs	Virat Kohli	Colin Munro
	(263 runs, 3 matches)	(123 runs, 3 matches)
Most wickets	Jasprit Bumrah	Trent Boult
	(6 wickets, 3 matches)	(6 wickets, 3 matches)

Tour matches

Brabourne Stadium, Mumbai, October 17: Indian Board President's XI 295/9 in 50 overs (Karun Nair 78, KL Rahul 68; Trent Boult 5-38, Mitchell Santner 2-40) beat **New Zealand** 265 in 47.4 overs (Tom Latham 59, Kane Williamson 47; Shahbaz Nadeem 3-41, Jaydev Unadkat 3-62) by 30 runs.

Brabourne Stadium, Mumbai, October 19: New Zealand 343/9 in 50 overs (Tom Latham 108 retd.out, Ross Taylor 102 retd.out; Jaydev Unadkat 4-57, Karn Sharma 2-45) beat **Indian Board President's XI** 310 in 47.1 overs (Gurkeerat Singh Mann 65, Karun Nair 53; Mitchell Santner 3-44, Tim Southee 2-22) by 33 runs.

ODI series (3): India 2 New Zealand 1

1st ODI: New Zealand won by six wickets

The Wankhede stood in awe as Kohli came up with another gem, this time a mature 121 in his 200th ODI, against a raging Tim Southee and Trent Boult. Although the pacemen dictated the tempo, Kohli maintained a decent flow to carry the home side to a sub-par total after opting to bat first — a not-so-wise decision given the extra grass on the surface. Martin Guptill and Munro provided a solid base to build on, but losing Williamson early to Kuldeep Yadav spiced things up, or so it seemed for a short while. Ross Taylor and Tom Latham added 200 runs, with Latham coming up with a momentum-dictating unbeaten 103 from 102 balls. That fourth-wicket alliance ruined Kohli's visions of victory in a milestone ODI.

Wankhede Stadium, Mumbai, October 22: India 280/8 in 50 overs (Virat Kohli 121, Dinesh Karthik 37; Trent Boult 4-35, Tim Southee 3-73) lost to **New Zealand** 284/4 in 49 overs (Tom Latham 103*, Ross Taylor 95) by six wickets. *MoM:* Tom Latham.

2nd ODI: India won by six wickets

Controversy clouded the start of the second ODI in Pune as Pandurang Salgaoncar, the curator, was dismissed by the BCCI for "malpractice". In a sting operation carried out by a local television channel, Salgaoncar was heard claiming that the pitch was certain to yield 337 and that 337 was chaseable.

The pitch was anything but that easy. New Zealand, who countered India's spin ploy with ease in the opener, couldn't handle the hosts' pace-fuelled aggression. With Bhuvneshwar Kumar, Bumrah and even Hardik Pandya to some degree using the pacy wicket to their advantage, India restricted the visitors to 230 for 9.

Rohit was dismissed early but Shikhar Dhawan offered India an anchor. Kohli suffered a rare failure, dismissed for 29 by Colin de Grandhomme, but Dinesh Karthik's unbeaten half-century and an atypically cautious knock from Pandya saw India level the series.

MCA Stadium, Pune, October 25: New Zealand 230/9 in 50 overs (Henry Nicholls 42, Colin de Grandhomme 41; Bhuvneshwar Kumar 3-45, Yuzvendra Chahal 2-36) lost to **India** 232/4 in 46 overs (Shikhar Dhawan 68, Dinesh Karthik 64*) by six wickets. *MoM:* Bhuvneshwar Kumar.

3rd ODI: India won by six runs

Although Kohli was back to century-scoring ways, it was Rohit and Bumrah who decided another series victory at home. Asked to bat, Kohli and Rohit put up their fourth double-century alliance to take the total past 330. The pitch was a good one to bat on and New Zealand's batsmen exploited the conditions with three of their top five, including Williamson, making half-centuries. New Zealand were on course, but Latham, who was enjoying a purple patch, couldn't see his side through after being run out with 13 balls left in the innings. Bumrah's discipline at the death and Chahal's incisiveness restricted the visitors to give India their seventh consecutive bilateral series win.

Green Park, Kanpur, October 29: India 337/6 in 50 overs (Rohit Sharma 147, Virat Kohli 113; Mitchell Santner 2-58, Adam Milne 2-64) beat **New Zealand** 331/7 in 50 overs (Colin Munro 75, Tom Latham 65; Jasprit Bumrah 3-47, Yuzvendra Chahal 2-47) by six runs. *MoM:* Rohit Sharma. *MoS:* Virat Kohli.

T20I series (3): India 2 New Zealand 1

1st T20I: India won by 53 runs

• After an injury-plagued career that lasted 18 years, Nehra gets the rare privilege of a farewell game — it is his 164th international. • He bows out with figures of 4-0-29-0. • Shreyas Iyer is handed his T20I debut, but the young Mumbaikar doesn't get a chance to bat. • Dhawan and Rohit both come away with 80 runs; Dhawan's are off 52 balls as opposed to Rohit's 55. • New Zealand lose Guptill and Munro early, and though Williamson and Latham resuscitate the innings, they don't find support from the lower-middle order. • While Nehra is restrictive, Chahal and Axar Patel make the most of the cracks on the track.

Feroz Shah Kotla, Delhi, November 1: India 202/3 in 20 overs (Shikhar Dhawan 80, Rohit Sharma 80; Ish Sodhi 2-25) beat **New Zealand** 149/8 in 20 overs (Tom Latham 39, Kane Williamson 28; Axar Patel 2-20, Yuzvendra Chahal 2-26) by 53 runs. *MoM:* Shikhar Dhawan.

2ⁿᵈ T20I: New Zealand won by 40 runs

• On an absolute belter of a strip in Rajkot, Williamson doesn't hesitate to bat and it proves to be a good toss to win. • Munro smashes an unbeaten 109 runs from 58 balls with seven fours and as many sixes; his 105-run alliance with Guptill is the basis for the total. • Mohammad Siraj goes for 53 runs from his four overs on debut, but does account for Williamson. • Openers Rohit and Dhawan depart with only 11 runs on the board, Boult scalping them both. • Iyer and Kohli add 54 runs for the third wicket, but losing Iyer and Pandya in quick succession hampers their chase. • An aggressive Boult gets MS Dhoni just short of his fifty when he is threatening to build on his start and India are restricted.

SCA Stadium, Rajkot, November 4: New Zealand 196/2 in 20 overs (Colin Munro 109*, Martin Guptill 45) beat **India** 156/7 in 20 overs (Virat Kohli 65, MS Dhoni 49; Trent Boult 4-34) by 40 runs. *MoM:* Colin Munro.

3ʳᵈ T20I: India won by six runs

• Conditions in Thiruvananthapuram are less than ideal, and it rains on the afternoon of the match. • The game is reduced to eight overs a side and India are asked to bat. • New Zealand put on a fine show with the ball: Southee and Ish Sodhi take two wickets apiece, but the efforts of Mitchell Santner, who also has a phenomenal day as a fielder, and Boult can't be discounted. • Chahal and Bumrah give away just 17 runs in four combined overs. • Manish Pandey, who top-scored, inflicts a couple of run-outs. • Pandya, left with 19 to defend in the final over, is struck for a six, but India hold their nerve to claim the thriller and the series.

Greenfield International Stadium, Thiruvananthapuram, November 7: India 67/5 in 8 overs (Tim Southee 2-13, Ish Sodhi 2-23) beat **New Zealand** 61/6 in 8 overs (Jasprit Bumrah 2-9) by six runs. *MoM:* Jasprit Bumrah. *MoS:* Jasprit Bumrah.

Roshan Thyagarajan (@RdT1969) is a sports writer in Bengaluru.

Sri Lanka in India

Lakmal fights, but Rohit, spinners prevail

R KAUSHIK

India had completed an unprecedented 9-0 rout on their tour of Sri Lanka just two months previously, so the possibility of another whitewash across formats loomed large during the return leg comprising three Tests, and as many ODIs and T20Is.

Those fears were unfounded as the visitors gave a far better account of themselves, securing creditable draws in two Tests and stunning the hosts in the first ODI when Suranga Lakmal feasted on pace-friendly conditions in Dharamsala. It was only in the T20Is that India overran their opponents, on the back of muscular batting and the wrist-spinning duo of Yuzvendra Chahal and Kuldeep Yadav.

India prevailed in all three series: 1-0 in the first Test series between the sides on Indian soil since December 2009, 2-1 in the ODIs and 3-0 in the T20Is; but Sri Lanka were far from disgraced.

The red-ball contest was dominated by the scything willow of Virat Kohli, who became the first batsman to score six double-hundreds as captain. Kohli's campaign got off to a miserable start when he was dismissed without scoring on the opening day of the series, but he finished strongly with 104*, 213, 243 and 50, giving him a series aggregate of 610 runs.

While Kohli comfortably topped the batting charts, R Ashwin was the leading wicket-taker with 12 strikes. This despite sending down just eight wicketless overs in the First Test in Kolkata, where fast bowlers from both teams made capital of overcast conditions and a grassy surface. Ashwin reached 300 Test wickets faster than any bowler in Test history, getting there in his 54th Test, though not even his skills could conquer the dead surface in New Delhi where Sri Lanka's young batsmen fought through to earn an honourable draw.

Sri Lanka have struggled to compete consistently, especially overseas, since the retirements of batting behemoths Kumar Sangakkara and Mahela Jayawardene. The gumption and skill shown by Dhananjaya de Silva and Roshen Silva, in particular, are encouraging signs for a side that had come to depend heavily on Dinesh Chandimal, the captain, Angelo Mathews, his predecessor who has been battling multiple injuries, and Dimuth Karunaratne, the phlegmatic opener.

The worst of the national capital was in evidence during the Kotla Test, which came close on the heels of Diwali. The already high levels of pollution spiked in the aftermath of the festival of crackers. Many of Sri Lanka's fielders threw up on the field and almost everyone donned protective masks on the second afternoon to guard against the poor quality of air, exposing the lack of foresight on the part of the BCCI's Tour, Fixture and Programme Committee.

With the tour of South Africa not far away, the Indian selectors rested Kohli for the white-ball games in a bid to manage his workload. Lakmal marred Rohit Sharma's debut as ODI skipper by blowing the Indians away in Dharamsala. In the process, however, he stirred a sleeping giant. Rohit responded with a blazing unbeaten 208 in the next game in Mohali, an unparalleled third ODI double-century, which he backed up with a record-equalling 35-ball hundred in the second T20I in Indore.

	Tests	ODIs	T20Is
Most runs	Virat Kohli (610 runs, 3 matches)	Rohit Sharma (217 runs, 3 matches)	Rohit Sharma (162 runs, 3 matches)
Most wickets	R Ashwin (12 wickets, 3 matches)	Yuzvendra Chahal (6 wickets, 3 matches)	Yuzvendra Chahal (8 wickets, 2 matches)

Tour match

Jadavpur University Campus 2nd Ground, Kolkata, November 11-12: Sri Lankans 411/9 dec in 88 overs (Sadeera Samarawickrama 74, Niroshan Dickwella 73*; Sandeep Warrier 2-60, Akash Bhandari 2-111) drew with **Indian Board President's XI** 287/5 in 75 overs (Sanju Samson 128, Rohan Prem 39; Lahiru Gamage 2-41).

Test series (3): India 1 Sri Lanka 0

1st Test: Match drawn

Only 11.5 overs of play was possible on the first day at Eden Gardens, but in unusually pacer-friendly conditions in the sub-continent, that was time enough for Lakmal to make a dramatic impact. After Chandimal put the hosts in on a grass-laden track under overcast skies, Lakmal left India in tatters at 17 for 3, including the scalps of K L Rahul off the first ball of the series and Kohli for a rare duck.

If India scrambled to 172, it was on the back of a typically pugnacious half-century, compiled in three hours, by Cheteshwar Pujara, backed up by handy contributions from a lower order.

As the dampness dissipated, Sri Lanka moved into the ascendancy on the back of half-centuries by Lahiru Thirimanne and Mathews, who put on 99 for the third wicket. Rangana Herath, batting at No.9, top-scored with an entertaining 67 as the tourists stopped a little short of 300. Ashwin and Ravindra Jadeja together bowled just nine overs for the innings and ten for the match for returns of 0 for 21, the first time India's spinners failed to take a wicket in a home Test.

With less than a day and a half left and despite being 122 in arrears, India took on the game. Rahul and Shikhar Dhawan restored normal service with 166 for the first wicket, and Kohli blasted to an unbeaten 104 off just 119 deliveries with 12 fours and a six, his 50th international hundred lifting India

Suranga Lakmal had incredible figures of 6-6-0-3 at the end of the first day of the
First Test in Kolkata. — *BCCI/Sportzpics*

to a lead of 230 when the declaration came, 45 minutes before tea on the
final evening.

A regulation hour and a half looked the most likely possibility until Bhuvneshwar Kumar and Mohammed Shami removed the openers in the eight
overs before the interval. Hesitant and tentative, Sri Lanka played right into
India's hands, losing three further wickets in 27 deliveries after tea with the
light rapidly fading.

Niroshan Dickwella frustrated India with his batting and his successful
efforts at wasting time, and when the umpires deemed that the light had
dimmed enough to pose physical danger to batsmen, Sri Lanka finished on
75 for 7, hanging on by the most slender of threads to scramble to a nervous
draw.

Eden Gardens, Kolkata, November 16-20: India 172 in 59.3 overs (Cheteshwar Pujara 52,
Wriddhiman Saha 29; Suranga Lakmal 4-26, Dilruwan Perera 2-19) and 352/8 dec. in 88.4
overs (Virat Kohli 104*, Shikhar Dhawan 94; Dasun Shanaka 3-76, S Lakmal 3-93) drew with
Sri Lanka 294 in 83.4 overs (Rangana Herath 67, Angelo Mathews 52; Bhuvneshwar Kumar
4-88, Mohammed Shami 4-100) and 75/7 in 26.3 overs (Niroshan Dickwella 27; B Kumar 4-8,
M Shami 2-34). *PoM:* Bhuvneshwar Kumar.

2ⁿᵈ Test: India won by an innings and 239 runs

The seam and swing of Kolkata gave way to the more familiar slow and
dry at the VCA Stadium, facilitating India's joint-biggest victory in Test
cricket. The innings-and-239-run margin was also Sri Lanka's heaviest Test
drubbing.

Having played no more than a bit part in the First Test, Ashwin and Jadeja accounted for 13 wickets, including seven on a first-day surface. In his 54th game, Ashwin broke Dennis Lillee's mark of 56 to become the fastest to 300 Test wickets. He chopped Sri Lanka down for 205 in their first dig, during which Karunaratne, the opener, completed 1000 runs for the calendar year.

India responded with a powerhouse batting display studded by centuries galore and a string of massive partnerships. M Vijay and Pujara made up for Rahul's early dismissal with a second-wicket alliance of 209, and Pujara put on a further 183 for the third with Kohli. Rohit, playing his first Test for 13 months, became the fourth centurion of the innings while realising 173 for the fifth wicket with his skipper. Kohli's 213 was his fifth double-hundred as captain; it was also his 12th century while at the helm, a new Indian record.

When Kohli applied the declaration late on the third evening, India's lead was 405 and Sri Lanka had toiled without reward for more than 12 hours. The events that followed were both predictable and inevitable. Sadeera Samarawickrama's second-ball dismissal, offering no stroke to a delivery from Ishant Sharma that cut back in, summed up the visitors' state of mind, and India needed no second invitation.

Chandimal made a second attractive half-century of the game, but the skipper was waging a lone battle. Like he had in the first innings, Ashwin befuddled the Sri Lankans to pick up four wickets again on his way to match figures of 8 for 130. Sri Lanka, competitive for so long in the First Test in conditions somewhat alien to both teams, capitulated without a fight as their winless record on Indian patch continued.

Vidarbha Cricket Association Stadium, Jamtha, Nagpur, November 24-27: Sri Lanka 205 in 79.1 overs (Dinesh Chandimal 57, Dimuth Karunaratne 51; R Ashwin 4-67, Ishant Sharma 3-37, Ravindra Jadeja 3-56) and 166 in 49.3 overs (D Chandimal 61, Suranga Lakmal 31*; R Ashwin 4-63, R Jadeja 2-28) lost to **India** 610/6 dec. in 176.1 overs (Virat Kohli 213, Cheteshwar Pujara 143, M Vijay 128, Rohit Sharma 102*; Dilruwan Perera 3-202) by an innings and 239 runs. *PoM:* Virat Kohli.

Fewest Tests to 300 wickets

R Ashwin	54
Dennis Lillee	56
Muttiah Muralitharan	58
Richard Hadlee, Malcolm Marshall, Dale Steyn	61

3rd Test: Match drawn

Sri Lankan cricket received a shot in the arm as the young guns put their hand up to secure a creditable draw under immense pressure, baulking India's designs of a second successive victory with a battling batting display on the final day.

Chasing an improbable 410 to level the series, Sri Lanka looked headed for familiar embarrassment at 35 for 4, half an hour into day five, when Dhananjaya led a stirring fightback in the company of Roshen, the debutant, and Dickwella. Using the flat, slow deck at the Feroz Shah Kotla to their advantage, they held firm in the face of another searching examination from India's relentless spin duo of Ashwin and Jadeja.

Dhananjaya's 119, his third Test hundred, was more remarkable because he battled cramps towards the second half of his knock. Eventually, he was forced to retire hurt with more than two hours remaining, but Roshen, stodgily, and Dickwella, with typical enterprise, saw them through to safety at 299 for 5.

The alarming air quality in the Indian capital tested Sri Lanka's character as much as the opposition did. Lakmal and Lahiru Gamage, the fast bowlers, were the most affected, throwing up on the field on the second afternoon and breathing off oxygen tanks in the dressing-room as long hours of physical exertion courtesy another strong Indian batting performance began to catch up.

India's 536 for 7 — Kohli enforced the declaration in the middle of a protracted discussion between the umpires and the coaches over the suitability of the atmospheric conditions for play to continue — was built around a third-wicket association of 283 between Vijay and the skipper. Vijay's 155 was measured only in comparison with Kohli's blazing 243, off a mere 287 deliveries with 25 fours. The Indian captain became just the sixth batsman to make double-hundreds in successive games as he hurtled past 5000 Test runs.

Sri Lanka replied in kind through Chandimal and Mathews, who put on 181 for the fourth wicket and made feisty hundreds. The four-man Indian attack toiled away for 135.3 overs before securing a lead of 163, on which the batsmen built rapidly while scoring at 4.7 to the over in the second dig.

By stumps on day four, Sri Lanka had imploded to 31 for 3, but with the young turks embracing responsibility, only two further wickets fell on the final day as the Test meandered into a stalemate.

Feroz Shah Kotla, Delhi, December 2-6: India 539/7 dec. in 127.5 overs (Virat Kohli 243, M Vijay 155; Lakshan Sandakan 4-167, Lahiru Gamage 2-95) and 246/5 dec. in 52.2 overs (Shikhar Dhawan 67, Rohit Sharma 50*) drew with **Sri Lanka** 373 in 135.3 overs (Dinesh Chandimal 164, Angelo Mathews 111; R Ashwin 3-90, Ishant Sharma 3-98) and 299/5 in 103 overs (Dhananjaya de Silva 119rh, Roshen Silva 74; Ravindra Jadeja 3-81). *PoM:* Virat Kohli. *PoS:* Virat Kohli.

ODI series (3): India 2 Sri Lanka 1

1st ODI: Sri Lanka won by seven wickets

Lakmal gorged on the generous assistance from moisture in the air and grass on the track to destroy the Indian top order as Sri Lanka snapped a 12-match losing streak in ODI cricket. Bowling a fuller length and letting the conditions do the rest, Lakmal sent India tumbling to 29 for 7 on Rohit's debut as 50-over skipper, before the calm of Mahendra Singh Dhoni temporarily arrested the slide. Dhoni farmed the strike in making an intelligent 65, but Lakmal's unchanged burst of 10-4-13-4 had made sure that the most India could manage was 112.

Sri Lanka were themselves in a spot at 19 for 2, but Upul Tharanga wrested the initiative back with a counter-punching knock just short of a fifty. Mathews and Dickwella settled any nerves in the dressing-room by putting on 49, and Sri Lanka cruised home with a massive 176 deliveries to spare.

HPCA Stadium, Dharamsala, December 10: India 112 in 38.2 overs (MS Dhoni 65; Suranga Lakmal 4-13, Nuwan Pradeep 2-37) lost to Sri Lanka 114/3 in 20.4overs (Upul Tharanga 49, Niroshan Dickwella 26*) by seven wickets. *PoM:* Suranga Lakmal.

2nd ODI: India won by 141 runs

Rohit bounced back at the PCA Stadium on his way to becoming the first batsman to score three double-hundreds in ODI cricket. After a circumspect start that saw them score just 33 in the first ten overs, India went into overdrive. Dhawan and Shreyas Iyer made blazing half-centuries, but Rohit was the main act, raining fours and sixes while muscling to 208. His first hundred came off 115 deliveries, the second off a mere 36, studded by one four and six giant sixes.

Sri Lanka had little hope of scaling down 392 for 4. All that was left after the first half was to ascertain the margin of India's victory. Mathews conjured a stylish unbeaten century, but like everything else on the day, it was just a footnote to the Rohit masterclass.

PCA IS Bindra Stadium, Mohali, December 13: India 392/4 in 50 overs (Rohit Sharma 208*, Shreyas Iyer 88; Thisara Perera 3-80) beat **Sri Lanka** 251/8 in 50 overs (Angelo

Another double: Rohit Sharma's first hundred at Mohali came off 115 deliveries, the second off a mere 36. — *BCCI/Sportzpics*

Mathews 111*, Asela Gunaratne 34; Yuzvendra Chahal 3-60, Jasprit Bumrah 2-43) by 141 runs. *PoM:* Rohit Sharma.

3rd ODI: India won by eight wickets

Through Tharanga's extraordinary ball-striking, Sri Lanka appeared headed for a massive total in the decider when Kuldeep lured the left-handed opener forward and Dhoni completed a quicksilver stumping. That precipitated a stunning collapse, the visitors losing their last eight for a mere 55 runs.

Dhawan led India's assault on a modest target with his 12th ODI hundred, steering the team home with nearly 18 overs in the bag. The come-from-behind 2-1 victory was India's eighth successive series triumph, the second-longest winning streak in ODI history.

Tharanga had stormed to 95 off just 82 deliveries and, at 160 for 2 after 27, seemed to have given Sri Lanka the perfect platform from which to launch. Once Kuldeep outwitted him, the left-arm wrist-spinner linked up with Chahal, the leggie, for combined figures of 6 for 88 in 20 overs.

Dr Y S Rajasekhara Reddy ACA-VDCA Cricket Stadium, Visakhapatnam, December 17: Sri Lanka 215 in 44.5 overs (Upul Tharanga 95, Sadeera Samarawickrama 42; Kuldeep Yadav 3-42, Yuvendra Chahal 3-46) lost to **India** 219/2 in 32.1 overs (Shikhar Dhawan 100*, Shreyas Iyer 65) by eight wickets. *PoM:* Kuldeep Yadav. *PoS:* Shikhar Dhawan.

T20I series (3): India 3 Sri Lanka 0

1st T20I: India won by 93 runs

• Rahul leads India's charge on being put in, with a powerful 61 that includes seven fours and a six. • Sri Lanka's pace-heavy attack struggles to cope with the wet ball due to the early onset of dew, allowing India to build through the middle stages. • Dhoni and Manish Pandey provide a grandstand finish with 68 off just 33 deliveries. • Jaydev Unadkat packs off Dickwella in the second over. • Chahal and Kuldeep take over, together finishing with 6 for 41 in eight overs and ensuring that no one apart from Tharanga tops 20. • Pandya lops off the tail, and India's 93-run victory is their biggest in T20Is.

Barabati Stadium, Cuttack, December 20: India 180/3 in 20 overs (KL Rahul 61, MS Dhoni 39*) beat **Sri Lanka** 87 in 16 overs (Upul Tharanga 23; Yuzvendra Chahal 4-23, Hardik Pandya 3-29) by 93 runs. *PoM:* Yuzvendra Chahal.

2nd T20I: India won by 88 runs

• Old nemesis Rohit returns to haunt Sri Lanka, dominating a stand of 165 with Rahul; it is India's highest opening partnership in the format. • Rohit blazes to his century in 35 deliveries, the joint-fastest alongside David Miller in all T20Is. • Rahul extends his good form with a belligerent 85, and India's 260 for 5 is a true reflection of the Holkar Stadium surface and the small boundaries. • Tharanga keeps Sri Lanka in the hunt with a 29-ball 47, before

Kusal Perera briefly ignites visions of a dramatic finale. • Perera smashes four fours and seven sixes in racing to 77 off 37 when Kuldeep forces him to hole out to long-off. • Kuldeep and Chahal leak runs but also account for seven wickets.

Holkar Cricket Stadium, Indore, December 22: India 260/5 in 20 overs (Rohit Sharma 118, KL Rahul 89; Thisara Perera 2-49, Nuwan Pradeep 2-61) beat **Sri Lanka** 172 in 17.2 overs (Kusal Perera 77, Upul Tharanga 47; Yuzvendra Chahal 4-52, Kuldeep Yadav 3-52) by 88 runs. *PoM:* Rohit Sharma.

3rd T20I: India won by five wickets

• Unadkat makes the most of the unexpectedly grassy Wankhede strip to fire out openers Dickwella and Tharanga inside the first four overs. • Sri Lanka find no *PoM*entum through the middle even though Samarawickrama and Gunaratne briefly steady the ship with a stand of 38. • Dasun Shanaka's late flourish lifts them, but the total is well below par despite the seam-friendly conditions. • After losing Rahul and Rohit, India make no more than measured progress through Iyer and Pandey. • Pandey's dismissal at the start of the 17th over leaves the hosts needing 28 off 23, a tricky ask under the circumstances. • Dinesh Karthik and Dhoni adroitly steer the team home with four deliveries to spare, capping India's 16th successive home series win across formats.

Wankhede Stadium, Mumbai, December 24: Sri Lanka **135/7** in 20 overs (Asela Gunaratne 36, Dasun Shanaka 29*; Jaydev Unadkat 2-15, Hardik Pandya 2-25) lost to **India** 139/5 in 19.2 overs (Manish Pandey 32, Shreyas Iyer 30; Dushmantha Chameera 2-22, Dasun Shanaka 2-27) by five wickets. *PoM:* Jaydev Unadkat. *PoS:* Jaydev Unadkat.

Sri Lanka in India

India

Batting

Player	M	I	NO	R	HS	Avge	100s/50s
R Sharma	2	3	2	217	102*	217.00	1/2
V Kohli	3	5	1	610	243	152.50	3/1
M Vijay	2	3	0	292	155	97.33	2/0
C Pujara	3	5	0	289	143	57.80	1/1
S Dhawan	2	4	0	192	94	48.00	0/2
M Shami	2	2	1	36	24	36.00	0/0
KL Rahul	2	3	0	86	79	28.66	0/1
W Saha	3	4	2	44	29	22.00	0/0
R Jadeja	3	4	2	40	22	20.00	0/0
B Kumar	1	2	0	21	13	10.50	0/0

R Ashwin	3	4	0	20	7	5.00	0/0
A Rahane	3	5	0	17	10	3.40	0/0
U Yadav	2	1	1	6	6*	-	0/0
I Sharma	2	-	-	-	-	-	-/-

Bowling and fielding

Player	M	W	R	BBI	BBM	Avge	5wI/10wM	Ct/St
B Kumar	1	8	96	4-8	8-96	12.00	0/0	0/-
R Jadeja	3	10	259	3-56	5-84	25.90	0/0	1/-
I Sharma	2	8	210	3-37	5-80	26.25	0/0	1/-
M Shami	2	9	269	4-100	6-134	29.88	0/0	1/-
R Ashwin	3	12	359	4-63	8-130	29.91	0/0	1/-
U Yadav	2	5	177	2-30	3-104	35.40	0/0	0/-
M Vijay	2	0	3	-	-	-	0/0	1/-
V Kohli	3	0	6	-	-	-	0/0	3/-
S Dhawan	2	-	-	-	-	-	-/-	2/-
C Pujara	3	-	-	-	-	-	-/-	1/-
A Rahane	3	-	-	-	-	-	-/-	5/-
KL Rahul	2	-	-	-	-	-	-/-	2/-
W Saha	3	-	-	-	-	-	-/-	9/0
R Sharma	2	-	-	-	-	-	-/-	1/-

Sri Lanka

Batting

Player	M	I	NO	R	HS	Avge	100s/50s
D de Silva	1	2	1	120	119*	120.00	1/0
R Silva	1	2	1	74	74*	74.00	0/1
D Chandimal	3	6	0	366	164	61.00	1/2
A Mathews	3	6	0	196	111	32.66	1/1
N Dickwella	3	6	1	134	44*	26.80	0/0
R Herath	2	4	1	71	67	23.66	0/1
L Thirimanne	2	4	0	90	51	22.50	0/1
S Lakmal	3	5	1	69	31*	17.25	0/0
D Karunaratne	3	6	0	91	51	15.16	0/1
D Perera	3	5	0	62	42	12.40	0/0
S Samarawickrama	3	6	0	74	33	12.33	0/0
D Shanaka	2	4	1	25	17	8.33	0/0
L Gamage	3	4	2	1	1	0.50	0/0
L Sandakan	1	1	1	0	0*	-	0/0

Bowling and fielding

Player	M	W	R	BBI	BBM	Avge	5wI/10wM	Ct/St
D Shanaka	2	6	215	3-76	5-112	35.83	0/0	1/-
L Sandakan	1	5	217	4-167	5-217	43.40	0/0	1/-
S Lakmal	3	8	370	4-26	7-119	46.25	0/0	2/-
L Gamage	3	7	396	2-59	3-143	56.57	0/0	0/-
D Perera	3	8	469	3-202	3-68	58.62	0/0	4/-
D de Silva	1	1	79	1-31	1-79	79.00	0/0	0/-
R Herath	2	1	115	1-81	1-81	115.00	0/0	0/-
D Karunaratne	3	0	25	-	-	-	0/0	2/-
D Chandimal	3	-	-	-	-	-	-/-	0/-
N Dickwella	3	-	-	-	-	-	-/-	6/3
A Mathews	3	-	-	-	-	-	-/-	2/-
S Samarawickrama	3	-	-	-	-	-	-/-	2/-
R Silva	1	-	-	-	-	-	-/-	0/-
L Thirimanne	2	-	-	-	-	-	-/-	2/-

Squads

India: Virat Kohli (capt), Ajinkya Rahane (vice-capt), R Ashwin, Shikhar Dhawan, Ravindra Jadeja, Bhuvneshwar Kumar, Hardik Pandya (withdrawn), Cheteshwar Pujara, KL Rahul, Wriddhiman Saha (wk), Mohammed Shami, Ishant Sharma, Rohit Sharma, M Vijay, Kuldeep Yadav, Umesh Yadav, Vijay Shankar.

Sri Lanka: Dinesh Chandimal (capt), Dhananjaya de Silva, Niroshan Dickwella (wk), Vishwa Fernando, Lahiru Gamage, Rangana Herath, Dimuth Karunarathne, Suranga Lakmal, Angelo Mathews, Dilruwan Perera, Sadeera Samarawickrema, Lakshan Sandakan, Dasun Shanaka, Roshen Silva, Lahiru Thirimanne, Jeffrey Vandersay.

India in South Africa

Kohli, de Villiers sublime against pace

SAURABH SOMANI

This was among India's most successful tours of South Africa. A narrow 2-1 loss in the Tests, an obliterating 5-1 win in the ODIs and a tight 2-1 triumph in the T20Is. Whether it was the most successful ever, as coach Ravi Shastri claimed, is debatable. The 2010-11 tour, where the Test series was drawn 1-1 — the only time an Indian team has drawn a Test series in the country — and the tourists won the lone T20I while losing the ODI series 3-2, was arguably a greater success. Despite the limited-overs results in 2018, the tour will be measured by how the Test series went. And what will rankle India is that they could have well ended up winning all three formats.

Debate over decisions taken in the longest format will continue. There was an opportunity to send a bulk of the squad well in advance to prepare for the conditions, but Shastri startlingly claimed that logistics would have been an issue with half the team in South Africa and the other half still engaged in limited-overs contests against Sri Lanka. To suggest that the BCCI, the game's richest and most influential body, would have found it difficult to arrange proper practice matches and facilities for a chunk of its Test players stretches credibility. As it was, the entire team travelled together — the captain newly married, and his team-mates having attended his reception — but they had less than a week between landing in South Africa and playing the First Test. They opted for intensive practice sessions leading up to the Test, cancelling a scheduled two-day match.

In the Tests, particularly in Cape Town and Johannesburg, India faced some of the most seam-friendly conditions they have ever seen. In Cape Town, the bowlers were profligate in South Africa's first innings, which eventually decided the match. Tellingly, that waywardness wasn't seen the rest of the tour, which raised the question of how the attack would have done if they had the chance to train and play in South Africa for a bit longer. Or for that matter, if the batsmen could have adjusted better.

India also picked Shikhar Dhawan and Rohit Sharma on form shown at home against an insipid Sri Lankan attack, ahead of K L Rahul and Ajinkya Rahane. If Dhawan was fortunate to be picked, he was also unfortunate to be axed after just one Test. Rohit played two, before Rahane came back and made a vital contribution towards India winning the third. Quite apart from Rahane's batting, his catching would have been sorely missed, especially in the Second Test when India put down as many as seven chances.

The cricket itself was compelling. South Africa had a dream pace attack of Dale Steyn, Kagiso Rabada, Vernon Philander and Morne Morkel for the First Test. Steyn's ill-luck with injuries continued to haunt him, though: after

A B de Villiers's continuing comeback after a self-imposed break featured the sort of shot-making in hostile conditions that few others are capable of. — *Getty Images*

a year of rehab and waiting to come back, he limped off, heel caught in a foothole, and his Test summer reduced to less than one full match. Lungi Ngidi proved to be a potent replacement. A B de Villiers's continuing comeback to Tests after a self-imposed break went off rather better. He seized the moment at crucial points in the first two Tests, with the sort of shot-making in the face of hostile conditions that few others are capable of.

But the batting star of the tour was Kohli. The India captain settled the debate of what happens when an irresistible force meets an immovable object by becoming both, all through the Tests and the ODIs. Given the pitches and the bowling attack, Kohli's mastery settled the argument over who in world cricket was the best batsman across formats.

Kohli the captain was more up and down. And Kohli the antagonist was never far away. He had his tempestuous moments on the field — an argument with the umpires in the Second Test earned him a fine — and after play, when he responded with biting aggression to questions he didn't like, and even a siege-like dismissal of praise when India had won the ODI series.

The ODI triumph itself was notable for India's complete domination of the hosts. South Africa won a close Pink ODI, but in the others, they didn't even come close. The T20Is were more evenly fought, but the tourists proved to have just that much more at the crunch moments. Kohli merely kicked on a gear from his Test form, and the spin duo of Kuldeep Yadav and Yuzvendra Chahal, having already supplanted more senior spinners as the preferred duo for limited-overs cricket, cemented their places with this series. South Africa's batsmen were befuddled almost from start to finish.

There was no clear answer to India's middle-order problems, but with the World Cup 2019 looming, South Africa had far deeper issues. Without Faf du Plessis and de Villiers, the batting looked orphaned in ODIs. De Villiers's international retirement a few months after this match-up means South Africa's batting looks far from assured.

	Tests	**ODIs**	**T20Is**
Most runs	Virat Kohli (286 runs, 3 matches)	Virat Kohli (558 runs, 6 matches)	Shikhar Dhawan (143 runs, 3 matches)
Most wickets	Vernon Philander (15 wickets, 3 matches)	Kuldeep Yadav (17 wickets, 6 matches)	Bhuvneshwar Kumar (7 wickets, 3 matches)

Test series (3): South Africa 2 India 1

1st Test: South Africa won by 72 runs

Technically, this Test went four days, but that was only because the third was completely washed out. The relatively short period of play was compensated for by the action in it. The rained out day too, was a blessing in the larger scheme, with the city of Cape Town reeling under one of its most severe droughts. Water in every home was strictly rationed: two-minute showers and signs at the airport saying 'If it's brown, flush it down, if it's yellow, let it mellow' told a grim tale, if with ghoulish humour.

The Test itself had plenty of colour before it began. Steyn was match-fit after more than a year out of the game and just four shy of Shaun Pollock's South Africa record of 421 Test wickets. De Villiers had made a soft return to the longest format against Zimbabwe a week earlier, but this would be a much sterner examination. India had put together arguably the best fast-bowling unit they ever had. A scheduled two-day practice game was cancelled with the team opting to focus on intensive nets sessions. The upshot was optional practice on the eve of the Test, which every single Indian squad member opted not to attend.

On a spicy pitch, Bhuvneshwar Kumar reduced South Africa to 12 for 3 in the first half-hour. That was followed by something no bowling attack in the world could have planned for: a de Villiers counter-attack. Among all the players on the park, it was perhaps he alone who had the mix of audacity and outrageous skill to go after the bowlers with his side in such trouble. But after he became Jasprit Bumrah's maiden Test wicket, India's attack seemed to lose radar.

None of the batsmen who followed had the whirring shot-making skills of de Villiers, and the first-day pitch was at its most bowler friendly, but South Africa's last five wickets more than doubled the score.

They were still bowled out well inside the first day, which meant India had to bat for almost half a session at the end. The key was to survive. But M Vijay wafted at one he should have left alone, Dhawan was undone by a ball climbing on him, and most crucial of all, Kohli poked outside off early in his stay, all before stumps.

Those wickets on day one meant whatever advantage India had of batting on a strip that had eased out a mite on the second day was negated. There was no respite for the batsmen, until Hardik Pandya came in at No.7 and rode his luck. In Bhuvneshwar he found a solid ally.

At tea on the second day, perhaps the most cruel blow of the match landed: Steyn, who had added another wicket to move within two of Pollock, pulled up in his run-up and hobbled off the field. It was a freak injury, his left heel caught in one of the footholes while running in. Steyn had handled his bowling load comfortably, but heart-breakingly had to hobble off midway through a comeback he had waited more than a year to make.

A rained out third day meant India's bowlers got the best of bowling conditions on day four too, and this time, they found their zip to run through South Africa. The victory target of 208 seemed in reach, but Philander gave a masterclass in the art of bowling on a seaming pitch, keeling the Indians over for 135. His working over of Kohli was particularly impressive, dragging the bat away from body with a succession of away-going deliveries before jagging one back in to have him plumb. That wicket sealed the match for South Africa, with India left to ponder what might have been.

Newlands, Cape Town, January 5-8: South Africa 286 in 73.1 overs (AB de Villiers 65, Faf du Plessis 62; Bhuvneshwar Kumar 4-87, R Ashwin 2-21) and 130 in 41.2 overs (AB de Villiers 35, Aiden Markram 34; Mohammed Shami 3-28, Jasprit Bumrah 3-39) beat **India** 209 in 73.4 overs (Hardik Pandya 93, Cheteshwar Pujara 26; Vernon Philander 3-33, Kagiso Rabada 3-34) and 135 in 42.4 overs (R Ashwin 37, Virat Kohli 26; V Philander 6-42, Morne Morkel 2-39) by 72 runs. *PoM:* Vernon Philander.

2nd Test: South won by 135 runs

Kohli the batsman was sublime, Kohli the captain was tetchy. India let slip another potential win, surrendering the series to South Africa. The home side found a hero in Ngidi, who took six wickets on debut.

Kohli played an innings for the ages in the first essay, and the bowlers had moments of brilliance. But dropped catches and some amateurish run-outs meant South Africa escaped with their own errors. Du Plessis had won the toss and batted again. That R Ashwin bowled 31 of the 90 overs sent down on the first day at the Highveld spoke for how atypical a Centurion track this was.

India had gone into this Test without Bhuvneshwar, a controversial decision given he had taken the most wickets and made valuable lower-order runs in Cape Town. They also dropped Dhawan and brought in K L Rahul, while an injured Wriddhiman Saha made way for Parthiv Patel. This was thus the 34th straight Test since the start of Kohli's leadership that India changed a playing XI from one match to the next. When asked if that affected team stability, Kohli bristled with barely concealed anger.

India found some inspiration in the day's 81st over. Pandya showed his athleticism, running down the pitch after bowling to pick up the ball, turn and hit the stumps direct, catching Hashim Amla well short. One brought three, and a day that South Africa had dominated ended up even. But in what had become a recurring theme, India let the door slam shut. The next morning, South Africa added 66 runs — aided by a slew of dropped chance.

Cheteshwar Pujara was run out off his very first ball, going for a non-existent single to mid-on. But Kohli was batting with a mastery over the conditions and bowlers, and Vijay seemed to be finding his groove. Both were still together when the final session began, and looking comfortable — until South Africa prised out three quick wickets near stumps.

If India had hoped for a tail-end resistance like South Africa's, the third morning didn't start promisingly. Pandya was run-out in a shockingly careless manner, ambling back into his crease without looking at ball or fielder, and holding his bat in his hands. Ashwin gave Kohli the support he needed, before Kohli began farming the strike until he was last man out for a colossal — in skill as well as runs — 153. He had dragged India to within 28 runs of South Africa. They had visions of victory when Bumrah took two wickets inside six overs, but once again de Villiers stood in their way.

Alongside him was Dean Elgar, playing as often as missing. Du Plessis shepherded the tail again and South Africa set India a stiff target of 287.

That might have as well been 487, because before stumps on the fourth day, India had lost Kohli to Ngidi. The next day, Pujara was run out again and Pandya was caught behind attempting a ramp. Ngidi cleaned house, leading to long celebrations in the South African dressing room and a rendering of the team song mid-pitch when the crowds had cleared.

SuperSport Park, Centurion, January 13-17: **South Africa** 335 in 113.5 overs (Aiden Markram 94, Hashim Amla 82; R Ashwin 4-113, Ishant Sharma 3-46) and 258 in 91.3 overs (AB de Villiers 80, Dean Elgar 61; Mohammed Shami 4-49, Jasprit Bumrah 3-70) beat **India** 307 in 92.1 overs (Virat Kohli 153, M Vijay 46; Morne Morkel 4-60) and 151 in 50.2 overs (Rohit Sharma 47, M Shami 28; Lungi Ngidi 6-39, Kagiso Rabada 3-47) by 135 runs. *PoM: Lungi Ngidi.*

3rd Test: India won by 63 runs

Both teams went into the match with an all-seam attack. On the third evening, the umpires called off play 19 minutes before scheduled stumps, when a back-of-length delivery from Bumrah hit Elgar's grille. There was some debate on whether the Test would resume, to much outrage from India, who had batted twice on that pitch and weathered its blows to get into a winning position. Play did get under way on the fourth day, and India did go on to win. It didn't affect the series result, but 2–1 was a much fairer reflection than 2–0 or 3–0 would have been.

Pujara got together with Kohli to face extravagant seam movement. The combination of one man smarting from two run-outs and the other being the best batsman in the series on either side gave India an important partnership. While Pujara took a patience-defying 53 balls before he finally got off the mark, Kohli seemed to transcend the conditions and never let what the previous ball had done affect his sure-footed leaving or shot-making.

Bhuvneshwar Kumar pitched in with early wickets and lower-order runs, yet was controversially dropped for the Second Test. — *Getty Images*

There was some luck, too. South Africa didn't take a review when Pujara was rapped on the pads on nought, replays showing three reds on DRS. Kohli had a chance dropped at slip, which fractured de Villiers's finger in the bargain.

Once South Africa broke the stand, only Bhuvneshwar — back in the team again — offered any meaningful runs.

South Africa's first innings almost mirrored India's, with two good scores in the top four and one lower-order contribution. Hashim Amla's 61 was the fulcrum, but the other contribution came from Rabada, who was nightwatchman at No.3. Bumrah got his first five-wicket haul, his action and bowling uniquely suited to extracting all the pitch's variable bounce. Despite Mohammed Shami being completely off radar in his first spell, all South Africa had was a lead of seven runs.

With a one-innings shootout now, Vijay finally rediscovered the calm that had made him India's most valuable opener in tough conditions, leaving the ball with unerring judgement. Kohli was magnificent again and Rahane proved just why his omission in the first two Tests had caused an uproar.

On the fourth morning, the pitch behaved markedly better than it had previously. India, however, were patient, even as Elgar scrapped away and Amla got his second half-century of the match. However, once Ishant broke through, India quickly kept their unbeaten Wanderers record intact.

New Wanderers, Johannesburg, January 24-27: India 187 in 76.4 overs (Virat Kohli 54, Cheteshwar Pujara 50; Kagiso Rabada 3-39, Andile Phehlukwayo 2-25) and 247 in 80.1 overs (Ajinkya Rahane 48, V Kohli 41; Morne Morkel 3-47, Vernon Philander 3-61, K Rabada 3-69) beat **South Africa** 194 in 65.5 overs (Hashim Amla 61, V Philander 35; Jasprit Bumrah 5-54,

Bhuvneshwar Kumar 3-44) and 177 in 73.3 overs (Dean Elgar 86*, H Amla 52; Mohammed Shami 5-28, Ishant Sharma 2-31) by 63 runs. *PoM:* Bhuvneshwar Kumar. *PoS:* Vernon Philander.

ODI series (6): India 5 South Africa 1

1st ODI: India won by six wickets

India had decided to give Rahane a run at the problematic No.4 spot and he came good. But his effort was eclipsed by both captains: du Plessis almost single-handedly dragged South Africa to a respectable total. The spin duo of Kuldeep Yadav and Yuzvendra Chahal were notable in reining South Africa in, and against Kohli, the master of the chase who was in command from the moment he walked out, the total was never going to be enough. This set a recurring pattern for Kuldeep, Chahal and Kohli in the series. It was also India's first win at Kingsmead in eight matches, while South Africa lost at home in an ODI after nearly two years.

Kingsmead, Durban, February 1: South Africa 269/8 in 50 overs (Faf du Plessis 120, Chris Morris 37; Kuldeep Yadav 3-34, Yuzvendra Chahal 2-45) lost to **India** 270/4 in 45.3 overs (Virat Kohli 112, Ajinkya Rahane 79; Andile Phehlukwayo 2-42) by six wickets. *PoM:* Virat Kohli.

2nd ODI: India won by nine wickets

Chahal had his first five-wicket haul in ODIs, while Kuldeep took three as South Africa were bowled out for their lowest total at home. India waltzed

Virat Kohli's 558 runs in six matches against South Africa are the most by any batsman in a bilateral series. — *Getty Images*

home in 20.3 overs in a match that lasted barely more than a full ODI innings, at 52.5 overs. Two wrist-spinners starring in successive matches together is rare enough in the subcontinent; in South Africa it was remarkable. It was a harsh captaincy initiation for Aiden Markram, with du Plessis out of the series with a broken finger. To general bemusement, lunch was taken with India two runs from victory. Kohli and Dhawan walked off, then came back after lunch to quickly seal victory.

SuperSport Park, Centurion, February 4: South Africa 118 in 32.2 overs (JP Duminy 25, Khaya Zondo 25; Yuzvendra Chahal 5-22, Kuldeep Yadav 3-20) lost to **India** 119/1 in 20.3 overs (Shikhar Dhawan 51*, Virat Kohli 56*) by nine wickets. *PoM:* Yuzvendra Chahal.

3ʳᵈ ODI: India won by 124 runs

Kohli almost carried his bat while taking India to a 3-0 lead with South Africa outclassed. The home bowlers had no answer to the Indian captain, while the batsmen still couldn't figure out Kuldeep and Chahal, who took four wickets each this time. Kohli wasn't at his fluent best, but he was at his most determined. He pushed past the pain and exhaustion of his longest ODI innings while at the crease for 49 overs on a two-paced pitch in searing heat. It was his 12th hundred as captain, the most for India. Dhawan had made a smooth 76 at the top, but none of the other batsmen, from either side, could dominate. South Africa had started brightly, but once the spinners were introduced, the innings unravelled in familiar fashion. Ngidi's ODI debut was considerably more forgettable than his Test entry.

Newlands, Cape Town, February 7: India 303/6 in 50 overs (Virat Kohli 160*, Shikhar Dhawan 76; JP Duminy 2-60) beat **South Africa** 179 in 40 overs (Duminy 51, Aiden Markram 32; Kuldeep Yadav 4-23, Yuzvendra Chahal 4-46) by 124 runs. *PoM:* Virat Kohli.

4ᵗʰ ODI: South Africa won by five wickets (DLS method)

South Africa received a shot in the arm with de Villiers declared fit, but their unbeaten record in Pink ODIs was preserved thanks to Heinrich Klaasen and David Miller. Dhawan made the century he had been threatening to, and Kohli a half-century, but with both men out by the 36th over, the middle and lower order had its first real test — and stuttered.

India still seemed to have enough and rain made South Africa's target steeper, but Klaasen and Miller — who was dropped and bowled off a no-ball early on — combined for a game-changing 72 runs in 41 balls. Klaasen used the sweep to great effect, giving Kuldeep and Chahal their first poor outing. Andile Phehlukwayo hit three sixes and a four in five balls to hasten the end.

New Wanderers Stadium, Johannesburg, February 10: India 289/7 in 50 overs (Shikhar Dhawan 109, Virat Kohli 75; Lungi Ngidi 2-52, Kagiso Rabada 2-58) lost to **South Africa** 207/5 in 25.3 overs (Heinrich Klaasen 43*, David Miller 39; Kuldeep Yadav 2-51) by five wickets (DLS method). *PoM:* Heinrich Klaasen.

5ᵗʰ ODI: India won by 73 runs

Rohit shrugged off poor returns in the first four ODIs to hit a superbly paced century, giving India a first-ever bilateral ODI series win in South Africa. For the first time, neither of Dhawan or Kohli got a fifty, but Rohit ensured that didn't hurt India. This was despite another middle-order failure.

Kuldeep and Chahal had a bit of their mystique broken in the fourth ODI, but while South Africa played them with more confidence, they couldn't stop them taking wickets. The bowling hero was Pandya, who not only maintained an impeccable line and length, but also ran out Amla with a direct hit.

St George's Park, Port Elizabeth, February 13: India 274/7 in 50 overs (Rohit Sharma 115, Virat Kohli 36; Lungi Ngidi 4-51) beat **South Africa** 201 in 42.2 overs (Hashim Amla 71, Heinrich Klaasen 39; Kuldeep Yadav 4-57, Hardik Pandya 2-30) by 73 runs. *PoM:* Rohit Sharma.

6ᵗʰ ODI: India won by eight wickets

Kohli became the first man to aggregate more than 500 runs in a bilateral ODI series, completing his utter mastery of South Africa with a scintillating century. Both teams had made changes with the series already decided. Only Khaya Zondo crossed fifty and no batsman could dominate for any extended time. In contrast, Kohli scored at more than eight per over without looking in a hurry. The bowlers had kept South Africa to a below-par total again, but with the ball not coming on to the bat, South Africa might have expected to make India work for their victory. Kohli rendered that moot. He ended the series with 558 runs. It had been a captaincy baptism by fire for Markram, on the wrong end of a 5–1 scoreline.

SuperSport Park, Centurion, February 16: South Africa 204 in 46.5 overs (KhayaZondo 54, AndilePhehlukwayo 24; Shardul Thakur 4-52, JaspritBumrah 2-24) lost to **India** 206/2 in 32.1 overs (Virat Kohli 129*, AjinkyaRahane 34*; Lungi Ngidi 2-54) by eight wickets. *PoM:* Virat Kohli. *PoS:* Virat Kohli.

T20I series (3): India 2 South Africa 1

1ˢᵗ T20I: India won by 28 runs

• Rohit clatters 18 runs in the first over to set the tone. • Dhawan gets into the groove despite two early wickets as India make 78 in the powerplay. • India lose steam after Dhawan falls, but still end up with more than 200. • Bhuvneshwar strikes in the third over. • Regular wickets send the asking rate soaring. • Bhuvneshwar returns to spark a collapse and take five wickets, sealing a comfortable win.

New Wanderers Stadium, Johannesburg, February 18: India 203/5 in 20 overs (Shikhar Dhawan 72, Manish Pandey 29*; Junior Dala 2-47) beat **South Africa** 175/9 in 20 overs (Reeza Hendricks 70, Farhaan Behardien 39; Bhuvneshwar Kumar 5-24) by 28 runs. *PoM:* Bhuvneshwar Kumar.

2ⁿᵈ T20I: South Africa won by six wickets

• South Africa take out Rohit, Dhawan and Kohli inside the powerplay. • Manish Pandey and M S Dhoni come together when the run-rate is good but India are four down. • The pair lays into the bowling in an unbeaten 98-run stand. • South Africa lose their openers in five overs, even as a steady drizzle comes down. • Klaasen hits two sixes in his first over, powering ahead with JP Duminy. • Klaasen falls after a 93-run stand, but Duminy holds firm.

SuperSport Park, Centurion, February 21: India 188/4 in 20 overs (Manish Pandey 79*, MS Dhoni 52*; Junior Dala 2-28) lost to **South Africa** 189/4 in 18.4 overs (Heinrich Klaasen 69, JP Duminy 64*; Jaydev Unadkat 2-42) by six wickets. *PoM:* Heinrich Klaasen.

3ʳᵈ T20I: India won by seven runs

• Rohit leads with Kohli sitting out due to a stiff back. • South Africa's bowlers keep the top order from exploding. • India take 36 runs off the last three overs to end up with a competitive total. • India's pacers strangle the hosts, who reach only 52 for 2 in ten overs. • With 53 needed off 18 balls, debutant Christiaan Jonker smashes two sixes and three fours. • South Africa bring the equation to 12 needed off three balls, but fall short.

Newlands, Cape Town, February 24: India 172/7 in 20 overs (Shikhar Dhawan 47, Suresh Raina 43; Junior Dala 3-35, Chris Morris 2-43) beat **South Africa** 165/6 in 20 overs (JP Duminy 55, Christiaan Jonker 49; Bhuvneshwar Kumar 2-24) by seven runs. *PoM:* Suresh Raina. *MoS:* Bhuvneshwar Kumar.

India in South Africa

South Africa

Batting

Player	M	I	NO	R	HS	Avge	100s/50s
D Elgar	3	6	1	207	86*	41.40	0/2
AB de Villiers	3	6	0	211	80	35.16	0/2
H Amla	3	6	0	203	82	33.83	0/3
F du Plessis	3	6	0	183	63	30.50	0/2
A Markram	3	6	0	140	94	23.33	0/1
K Maharaj	2	4	0	74	35	18.50	0/0
V Philander	3	6	0	94	35	15.66	0/0
K Rabada	3	6	0	76	30	12.66	0/0
Q de Kock	3	6	0	71	43	11.83	0/0
M Morkel	3	6	2	29	10*	7.25	0/0
A Phehlukwayo	1	2	0	9	9	4.50	0/0
L Ngidi	2	4	1	6	4	2.00	0/0
D Steyn	1	2	2	16	16*	-	0/0

Bowling and fielding

Player	M	W	R	BBI	BBM	Avge	5wI/10wM	Ct/St
V Philander	3	15	238	6-42	9-75	15.86	1/0	1/-
L Ngidi	2	9	155	6-39	7-90	17.22	1/0	0/-
M Morkel	3	13	260	4-60	5-94	20.00	0/0	3/-
A Phehlukwayo	1	2	40	2-25	2-40	20.00	0/0	1/-
K Rabada	3	15	304	3-34	6-108	20.26	0/0	3/-
D Steyn	1	2	51	2-51	2-51	25.50	0/0	1/-
K Maharaj	2	1	125	1-67	1-93	125.00	0/0	1/-
H Amla	3	-	-	-	-	-	-/-	1/-
Q de Kock	3	-	-	-	-	-	-/-	17/0
AB de Villiers	3	-	-	-	-	-	-/-	6/-
F du Plessis	3	-	-	-	-	-	-/-	7/-
D Elgar	3	-	-	-	-	-	-/-	2/-
A Markram	3	-	-	-	-	-	-/-	2/-

India

Batting

Player	M	I	NO	R	HS	Avge	100s/50s
V Kohli	3	6	0	286	153	47.66	1/1
B Kumar	2	4	1	101	33	33.66	0/0
A Rahane	1	2	0	57	48	28.50	0/0
R Ashwin	2	4	0	90	38	22.50	0/0
H Pandya	3	6	0	119	93	19.83	0/1
R Sharma	2	4	0	78	47	19.50	0/0
M Vijay	3	6	0	102	46	17.00	0/0
C Pujara	3	6	0	100	50	16.66	0/1
S Dhawan	1	2	0	32	16	16.00	0/0
M Shami	3	6	1	72	28	14.40	0/0
P Patel	2	4	0	56	19	14.00	0/0
KL Rahul	2	4	0	30	16	7.50	0/0
I Sharma	2	4	2	14	7*	7.00	0/0
W Saha	1	2	0	8	8	4.00	0/0
J Bumrah	3	6	2	4	2	1.00	0/0

Bowling and fielding

Player	M	W	R	BBI	BBM	Avge	5wI/10wM	Ct/St
M Shami	3	15	256	5-28	6-74	17.06	1/0	0/-
I Sharma	2	8	150	3-46	5-86	18.75	0/0	0/-
B Kumar	2	10	203	4-87	6-120	20.30	0/0	2/-
J Bumrah	3	14	353	5-54	7-111	25.21	1/0	2/-
R Ashwin	2	7	215	4-113	5-191	30.71	0/0	0/-
H Pandya	3	3	162	2-27	3-80	54.00	0/0	3/-
S Dhawan	1	-	-	-	-	-	-/-	0/-
V Kohli	3	-	-	-	-	-	-/-	3/-
P Patel	2	-	-	-	-	-	-/-	10/0
C Pujara	3	-	-	-	-	-	-/-	1/-
A Rahane	1	-	-	-	-	-	-/-	2/-
KL Rahul	2	-	-	-	-	-	-/-	1/-
W Saha	1	-	-	-	-	-	-/-	10/0
R Sharma	2	-	-	-	-	-	-/-	1/-
M Vijay	3	-	-	-	-	-	-/-	4/-

Squads

South Africa: Faf du Plessis (capt), Hashim Amla, Temba Bavuma, Theunis de Bruyn, Quinton de Kock (wk), AB de Villiers, Dean Elgar, Keshav Maharaj, Aiden Markram, Morne Morkel, Chris Morris, Andile Phehlukwayo, Vernon Philander, Kagiso Rabada, Dale Steyn, Lungi Ngidi, Duanne Olivier.

India: Virat Kohli (capt), Ajinkya Rahane (vice-capt), R Ashwin, Jasprit Bumrah, Shikhar Dhawan, Ravindra Jadeja, Bhuvneshwar Kumar, Hardik Pandya, Parthiv Patel (wk), Cheteshwar Pujara, KL Rahul, Wriddhiman Saha (wk), Mohammed Shami, Ishant Sharma, Rohit Sharma, M Vijay, Umesh Yadav, Dinesh Karthik.

Afghanistan in India

Initiation by fire

KARUNYA KESHAV

Afghanistan, for all their inspired and impatient gallop up the ranks of cricket, weren't expected to win their first ever Test. No story could be that magical, could it? But they were expected to be more competitive than they proved, collapsing twice in one day in a Test that lasted a mere two days.

The welcome party at the start struck all the right dramatic notes and the sense of occasion lingered over the M Chinnaswamy stadium. The bright red caps were laid out in rows, waiting to be handed out along with framed commemorative ones. Salim Durani, the 83-year-old former India all-rounder, was invited to be a part of a day when he, finally, would no longer be the only Afghanistan-born Test cricketer. The presence of high-ranking government officials was a reminder and a reality check that perhaps the No.1 Test side weren't playing the newest kids on the block out of the goodness of their hearts.

India treated the opposition with respect, not getting drawn into a battle of words with Asghar Stanikzai (now Asghar Afghan), the captain, about who had the best spin attack. Virat Kohli, the regular captain, was not part of a historic contest: he had been set to miss this match while he played county cricket in England to prepare for the five-Test series there, but ended up missing it because of a back injury. But, overall, the Ajinkya Rahane-led side was a strong one and the Afghans were chastened.

Yamin Ahmadzai bowled Afghanistan's first ball in Test cricket — on his second attempt, having pulled out at the last minute the first time — and lanky Wafadar got good movement when not being inconsistent with his lengths. While M Vijay was streaky, Shikhar Dhawan was impudent against the debutants, becoming the first Indian and only the sixth batsman ever to make a century before lunch in the opening session of a Test, off just 87 balls. Virender Sehwag, who made 99 before lunch against the Windies in 2006, is the only other Indian batsman to have come close to the feat.

The much-heralded Afghan spin attack came into their own in the second half of the day. Rashid Khan, already feared in limited overs, had a rocky initiation to Tests. His first ten-over spell resulted in 75 runs, before the morning's nerves made way for a final spell that read 9-2-15-1 — although the number could well have been higher in the wickets column.

India's last four added 140 to the total, and chasing a strong 474, Afghanistan began as shakily with the bat as they had with the ball. Mohammad Shahzad's four through gully and backward point put their first runs on the board, but there was little to celebrate. The new-ball pair of Umesh Yadav and Ishant Sharma were disciplined, and R Ashwin won the battle of the

Bowled out twice in a day, Afghanistan got a reality check against a clinical Indian attack. — *BCCI/Sportzpics*

spinners. The debutants were bowled out inside a session, and then were bowled out again.

Asked to follow on, they came out more circumspect and lasted a little longer: 38.4 overs as compared to the 27.5 the first time, but couldn't make too much more and had little to offer against Ravindra Jadeja's leggies. A day that had begun with Eid-ul-Fitr festivities had a subdued finish.

The capitulation was fodder for those arguing that cricket at the highest levels — in Tests and World Cups — should be played only about the best and that two-day drubbings did the game a disservice. But to whom really was the disservice? The joy with which this Test was played is everything idealised about cricket. Afghanistan came into the match with no four-day practice; they didn't play another Test for a while afterwards. Should India (and other countries) do more — including them in the first-class system perhaps? This Test was, in so many ways, just the smallest of starts.

Chinnaswamy Stadium, Bengaluru, June 14-15: India 474 in 104.5 overs (Shikhar Dhawan 107, M Vijay 105; Yamin Ahmadzai 3-51, Wafadar Momand 2-100) beat **Afghanistan** 104 in 27.5 overs (R Ashwin 4-27, Ravindra Jadeja 2-18) and 103 in 38.4 overs (Hashmatullah Shahidi 36*, Asghar Afghan 25; R Jadeja 4-17, Umesh Yadav 3-26) by an innings and 262 runs. *PoM:* Shikhar Dhawan.

Alastair Cook signed off with 218 runs in the final Test at The Oval, becoming only the fifth player to score a century in both his first and last Tests. — *Getty Images*

India in England

Kohli's lost chance, Cook's farewell

LAWRENCE BOOTH

India arrived in England with high hopes of disproving old stereotypes about their phobia of the moving ball, and left nursing another Test series defeat away from home. If the 4-1 margin was cruel, including as it did a pair of narrow losses in Birmingham and Southampton, then it also reflected a fundamental truth: when the pressure was on, England responded with more vigour than India. Luck was against the tourists, for they lost all five tosses. But, too often, their resolve deserted them at the crucial moment.

For Virat Kohli in particular, the result was tough to take. His haul of 593 runs was 244 clear of the next best on either side, Jos Buttler. At both Edgbaston and Trent Bridge, he totalled precisely 200, and not until the finale at The Oval, where he made his first golden duck in Tests in four years, did England appear to break his spirit. Not once did he fall to Jimmy Anderson, his nemesis from 2014. And while he needed some good fortune along the way, how he ticked the final box on his CV was one of the stories of the summer.

So too were India's seamers. Ishant Sharma was rarely less than outstanding, especially from round the wicket to England's battery of left-handers. It was no coincidence that Alastair Cook's best day of the series — when he signed off from Test cricket with an emotional 147 at The Oval — came with Ishant off the field nursing an ankle injury. Mohammed Shami deserved much better than a series average of 38, beating the bat so regularly that he might have wondered which god he had had upset. Jasprit Bumrah was often outstanding; among seamers on both sides, only Anderson had a meaner economy-rate than Bumrah's 2.72. Hardik Pandya, meanwhile, picked up a cheap five-for in India's win at Trent Bridge, though didn't always provide the control offered by his three colleagues.

The quartet persuaded Ravi Shastri, the coach, bullish after victory in Nottingham, to label them the best group of fast bowlers in India's history. Had Bhuvneshwar Kumar been fit, they might have been even better.

But India had too many problems to mount a sustained challenge, even against an England side who were unusually vulnerable at home. Kohli's excellence masked deficiencies in others. Until K L Rahul and the precocious Rishabh Pant made hundreds on the last day of the series in a brave but futile chase of 464, the only Indian other than Kohli to reach three figures was Cheteshwar Pujara, in Southampton. Too often, the batting was blown away. M Vijay was ditched after a pair at Lord's, Shikhar Dhawan failed to reach 50, and Ajinkya Rahane averaged 25. Even with his last-gasp 149, Rahul averaged below 30.

England's lower-order firepower ultimately proved the difference. In Buttler and Sam Curran, the hosts had cricketers capable of turning a game in a session. The template was set at Edgbaston, where Curran's second-innings 63 rescued England from the depths of 87 for 7, leaving India with a chase that proved just beyond them. In the Fourth Test, he hit 78 after England had slipped to 86 for 6 on the first day. And at The Oval, Buttler — who had registered a maiden Test hundred in Nottingham — turned a scoreline of 181 for 7 into 332.

If only the Indian selectors had been more in tune with the needs of the side. In the First Test, they were a spinner short, well though R Ashwin bowled. In the second, under gloomy skies, they added Kuldeep Yadav to their XI; predictably, he barely bowled a ball. Then, after the fillip of victory at Trent Bridge, they selected an unfit Ashwin ahead of Ravindra Jadeja. Ashwin was comfortably outbowled on a turning track by Moeen Ali, and Jadeja enjoyed success with bat and ball in his only outing of the series at The Oval.

Shastri and Kohli seemed determined to stick to a narrative that wasn't entirely borne out by events: their team, they insisted, was the best Indian touring side there had been. This despite the fact that it was only 11 years since an Indian team had won in England. Yet, they couldn't take advantage of a shaky England — or at least a shaky England top order.

Keaton Jennings was awful throughout, but hung on to his place mainly because his opening partner, Cook, couldn't buy a run until The Oval, which became a prolonged farewell after he announced the Test would be his last. Typically, he signed off with 218 runs in the game, becoming only the fifth player to score a century in both his first and last Tests. Joe Root, meanwhile, lost out in comparison with Kohli, eventually moving down a spot to No.4, from where he did at least make a hundred in his final innings. Without the class of Buttler and the chutzpah of Curran, England would have regretted the uncertainty up the order.

Their bowling, though, was often irresistible. Anderson led the way, taking nine wickets in the thrashing at Lord's, and finishing things off at The Oval by overhauling Glenn McGrath's tally of 563 Test wickets, until then the most by a seamer. He managed 24 in the series at 18 apiece, and was not flattered by his figures. Everyone chipped in.

England were not always good, but they were usually good enough.

The blood-and-guts nature of the Test series meant the white-ball matches that preceded it almost disappeared from memory. India won the T20 series 2-1 amid a heat wave that seemed to bode well for their chances in the longer formats. And when Kuldeep continued his torment of English batsmen in the first ODI, India looked set to win that series too. But a pair of centuries from Root inspired the hosts, and deflated India at the just the wrong moment.

	Tests	ODIs	T20Is
Most runs	Virat Kohli	Joe Root	Rohit Sharma
	(593 runs, 5 matches)	(216 runs, 3 matches)	(137 runs, 3 matches)
Most wickets	James Anderson	Kuldeep Yadav	Hardik Pandya
	(24 wickets, 5 matches)	(9 wickets, 3 matches)	(6 wickets, 3 matches)

T20I series (3): England 1 India 2

1st T20I: India won by eight wickets

• Jason Roy and Buttler get England off to a flyer, putting on 50 in five overs before Umesh Yadav bowls Roy. • Kuldeep removes Alex Hales for a sluggish 18-ball 8 and dismantles England's middle order. • Both Root and Jonny Bairstow are stumped first ball, giving MS Dhoni a world-record 33 stumpings in T20Is, beating Pakistan's Umar Akmal. • Buttler is Kuldeep's final victim, for a ferocious 46-ball 69, but England's total looks below par. • David Willey bowls Dhawan with the fifth ball of India's chase, but Rohit Sharma and Rahul thrash 123 for the second wicket at quicker than ten an over. • Rahul finishes with an unbeaten 101 from 54 balls as India waltz home.

Old Trafford, Manchester, July 3: England 159/8 in 20 overs (Jos Buttler 69, Jason Roy 30; Kuldeep Yadav 5-24, Umesh Yadav 2-21) lost to **India** 163/2 in 18.2overs (KL Rahul 101*, Rohit Sharma 32) by eight wickets. *MoM:* Kuldeep Yadav.

2nd T20I: England won by five wickets

• India stumble early, losing three wickets in five overs, including Dhawan, run out after dropping his bat. • Kohli rebuilds the innings, assisted by Suresh

Raina and Dhoni, but progress is slow on a grabby surface. • Liam Plunkett finishes with 1 for 17, and Willey 1 for 18, the most-economical figures of his T20I career. • Kuldeep removes both openers, and when Yuzvendra Chahal's googly proves too good for Root, England are an unsteady 44 for 3 in the seventh over. • Hales atones for his Manchester nightmare, adding 48 with Eoin Morgan, then 34 with Bairstow, who slog-sweeps Kuldeep for two sixes in two balls. • Needing 12 off Bhuvneshwar's final over (his first three cost only seven), Hales launches the first ball for a straight six, and finishes with a series-levelling 58 not out from 41.

Sophia Gardens, Cardiff, July 6: India148/5 in 20 overs (Virat Kohli 47, MS Dhoni 32*) lost to **England** 149/5 in 19.4overs (Alex Hales 58*, Jonny Bairstow 28; Umesh Yadav 2-36) by five wickets. *MoM:* Alex Hales.

3rd T20I: India won by seven wickets

• Once again, Roy and Buttler go berserk, crashing 94 inside eight overs on the small Nevil Road Ground. • But both fall in quick succession — Roy for a 31-ball 67, including seven sixes, equalling the England record for a T20 innings. • Pandya's first over cost 22, but a career-best 4 for 38, including Ben Stokes, back after injury, derails England's innings. • Dhoni holds five catches as they finish at least 20 short of par. • Willey again disposes of Dhawan, but Rohit eases his way to an undefeated century from just 56 deliveries. • Kohli's knock and Pandya's late flourish — 33 not out from 14 — clinch the match, and the series, with eights balls in hand.

County Ground, Bristol, July 8: England 198/9 in 20 overs (Jason Roy 67, Jos Buttler 34; Hardik Pandya 4-38, Siddarth Kaul 2-35) lost to **India** 201/3 in 18.4overs (Rohit Sharma 100*, Virat Kohli 43) by seven wickets. *MoM:* Rohit Sharma. *MoS:* Rohit Sharma.

ODI series (3): England 2 India 1

1st ODI: India won by eight wickets

After wreaking havoc in the first T20I, Kuldeep repeated the trick, taking the best figures by a spinner in an ODI in England, to set up a straightforward chase for India's batsmen. From 71 for none after ten overs, his impact was immediate. Roy reverse-swept his second ball to cover, Root was pinned by his seventh and Bairstow lbw to his 11th, a googly. Only Buttler played with any certainty, before becoming Kuldeep's fourth victim, while Stokes ate up 103 balls over his 50 before becoming his fifth. On a ground where England had broken the world record twice in three summers, their total of 268 felt anti-climactic.

The chase was more of a stroll. Rohit finished with his second unbeaten hundred in five days, adding 167 for the second wicket with Kohli. It was the 39th win in Kohli's 50 games as captain.

Joe Root sealed the ODI series for England, brought up his England record 13th ODI hundred, and celebrated it all with an impulsive bat drop. — *Getty Images*

Trent Bridge, Nottingham, July 12: England 268 in 49.5 overs (Jos Buttler 53, Ben Stokes 50; Kuldeep Yadav 6-25, Umesh Yadav 2-70) lost to **India** 269/2 in 40.1overs (Rohit Sharma 137*, Virat Kohli 75) by eight wickets. *MoM:* Kuldeep Yadav.

2nd ODI: England won by 86 runs

England squared the series with a hundred from Root. Kuldeep managed three more wickets, but conceded 68 against batsmen determined not to let him dictate terms. From 239 for 6 in the 42nd over, England received a late injection from Root and Willey, who compiled his maiden international fifty, from just 30 balls.

India threw away a sound start to lose three wickets in 16 deliveries. The key, though, was when Moeen trapped Kohli short of his fifty and Raina, in his first ODI in almost three years, was bowled by Rashid. The asking-rate climbed, and Dhoni was powerless to intervene, eventually falling for 37 from 59 balls amid jeers from a disappointed crowd.

Lord's, London, July 14: England 322/7 in 50 overs (Joe Root 113*, Eoin Morgan 53; Kuldeep Yadav 3-68) beat **India** 236 in 50 overs (Suresh Raina 46, Virat Kohli 45; Liam Plunkett 4-46, Adil Rashid 2-38) by 86 runs. *MoM:* Joe Root.

3rd ODI: England won by eight wickets

This decider was memorable for two gestures. The first came when Rashid produced a snorter of a leg-break to bowl Kohli, leaving India's captain wide-eyed and open-mouthed at the impudence of it all. The second occurred once Root had sealed the series for England with the boundary that also took him to a national-record 13th ODI hundred, one clear of Marcus Trescothick. Mimicking the mic-drop gesture beloved of musicians and comedians, he dropped his bat. Watching on in the background, Kohli made a mental note. But he knew his side had been outplayed from start to finish.

Unable to make much headway against Willey and Rashid, who shared six wickets, India were then unable to separate Root and Morgan, whose third-wicket stand of 186 not out was an England record for any wicket against India. The result condemned Kohli to his first defeat as captain in eight bilateral one-day series.

Headingley, Leeds, July 17: India 256/8 in 50 overs (Virat Kohli 71, Shikhar Dhawan 44; David Willey 3-40, Adil Rashid 3-49) lost to **England** 260/2 in 44.3 overs (Joe Root 100*, Eoin Morgan 88*) by eight wickets. *MoM:* Adil Rashid. *MoS:* Joe Root.

1st Test: England beat India by 31 runs

The series began with a classic to mark England's 1000th men's Test, and it was thanks largely to two men. For India, Kohli was a colossus, single-handedly keeping them in the match with a superlative first-innings 149, then holding the key to their fourth-innings chase. For England, the star was Curran, who knocked over India's top order on the second day, then saved their bacon with the bat on the third.

When play resumed on the fourth, it was anyone's game. India needed 84 runs, England five wickets — but Kohli was still there on 43, apparently immovable. Anderson dispatched Dinesh Karthik with the sixth ball of the day, but Kohli and Pandya took India to within 53 of victory when Stokes entered the attack. His third ball was full and straight. For once, Kohli missed a work to leg and was plumb lbw. Shami followed three balls later, Ishant was trapped by Rashid's googly and Stokes wrapped up England's win when Pandya was caught behind. Spectators had barely caught their breath.

Kohli, who lacked support from his batsmen, hardly deserved to lose. Even without a bat in his hand, he hogged centre stage. On the first afternoon, with England cruising at 216 for 3, he produced a direct hit from midwicket to run out Root after Bairstow called him back for a second; the Indian captain was unable to resist mocking Root's mic-drop celebration in the ODI. The wicket triggered a collapse of 7 for 71, with Ashwin claiming four.

Dhawan and Vijay put on a fluent 50, before the first of Curran's interventions. Playing only his second Test, he found swing with his left-armers and picked up three wickets in eight balls.

India regrouped. Then, with the score on 100 came a series of mini-dramas. Rahane was caught in the slips off Stokes, who then bowled Karthik for a duck and won a leg-before shout against Pandya. India asked for a review — and the ball was missing leg stump. Malan at second slip then dropped Kohli, on 21, off Anderson. Next ball, unbelievably, Cook dropped Pandya at first slip off Stokes. The total was still 100, the tension unremitting.

India slipped to 182 for 8, only for Kohli to supervise a stunning fightback, helping add a further 92 while ticking off his first Test hundred in England, and reducing the deficit to 13. Shell shocked, England promptly lost Cook before stumps, bowled by a beauty from Ashwin for the second time in the game.

Wickets cascaded on the third, including three in an Ishant over interrupted by lunch. That left England seven down and only 100 ahead. India were nearly there. But Curran had other ideas, belting sixes off Ashwin and Ishant on his way to a 65-ball 63. Suddenly, India needed 194.

Broad removed both openers, Stokes took out Rahul, and it was 78 for 5 when Anderson bagged Ashwin. The fourth day was set up perfectly — and England squeezed home.

Edgbaston, Birmingham, August 1-4: England 287 in 89.4 overs (Joe Root 80, Jonny Bairstow 70; R Ashwin 4-62, Mohammed Shami 3-64) and 180 in 53 overs (Sam Curran 63, J Bairstow 28; Ishant Sharma 5-51, R Ashwin 3-59) beat **India** 274 in 76 overs (Virat Kohli 149, Shikhar Dhawan 26; S Curran 4-74, Adil Rashid 2-31) and 162 in 54.2 overs (V Kohli 51, Hardik Pandya 31; Ben Stokes 4-40, Stuart Broad 2-43) by 31 runs. *PoM:* Sam Curran.

2nd Test: England won by an innings and 159 runs

If Edgbaston provided a reminder of Kohli's importance to India, Lord's was the flipside. When he failed twice, the tourists had nowhere to go, and lost all 20 wickets in the equivalent of less than a day's play. It's true that the conditions played with uncanny precision into England's hands: stormy when they bowled, sunny when they batted. But India, the world's No.1 team, were supposed to cope with the discomfort. Instead, Kohli suffered his first innings defeat as captain.

After the first day was lost to rain, the second belonged to England's seamers. Root stuck India in under glowering skies and Anderson slipped an awayswinger on to Vijay's off stump with his fifth ball. Rahul followed, and when Pujara — back in place of Dhawan — was run out after a horrible mix-up with Kohli, India went into a long rain break at 15 for 3. The weather relented long enough for England to skittle them for 107 by stumps, Anderson collecting five in 13.2 overs of wonderful skill and craft. But it was Woakes — playing because Stokes was answering a charge of affray at Bristol Crown Court — who bagged the prize: Kohli caught at second slip by Buttler, the ball after Buttler had dropped him.

England began their reply on the third morning, but didn't have it all their own way. Shami won three leg-before appeals, including Root for a laborious 19, and Pandya got the debutant, Ollie Pope, for a promising 28. At 131 for 5, England were not yet in the clear. Bairstow and Woakes changed all that in a forthright partnership of 189, England's highest for the sixth wicket against India.

Woakes brought up a popular maiden Test hundred that evening, moments before Bairstow was caught behind for 93. By stumps, England led by 250,

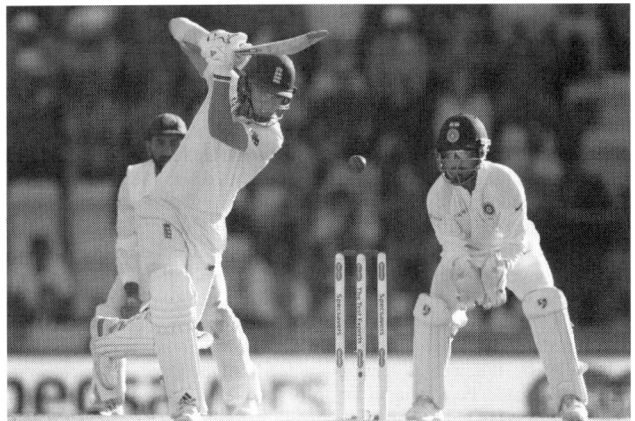

Sam Curran was a thorn in the side for the Indians both with his game-changing wickets and lower-order runs. — *Getty Images*

with power to add. Some critics grumbled that they already had enough, but there were two days to go, and Root had no intention of batting again. Curran reached a brisk 40 on the fourth morning, and India were left needing 289 to avoid an innings defeat.

Their task was immediately put into context. When Anderson inflicted a pair on Vijay, this time thanks to an inswinger that took the inside edge, it was his 550th Test wicket, of which precisely 100 had now come at Lord's. But the main damage was wrought by Broad, who produced a pre-tea spell of 7-4-7-4. Kohli, wincing through every shot and single after aggravating an old back complaint, was among his victims, caught at short leg as he gloved an unconvincing pull.

From 61 for 6, Pandya and Ashwin — who top-scored in both Indian innings — added 55, but the kill proved swift. Woakes and Anderson, who finished with enviable match figures of 9 for 43, claimed two apiece, and England were 2-0 up with three to play. Talk turned to 5-0, and only Kohli contested it with much conviction.

Lord's, London, August 9-12: India 107 in 35.2 overs (R Ashwin 29; James Anderson 5-20, Chris Woakes 2-19) and 130 in 47 overs (R Ashwin 33, Hardik Pandya 26; J Anderson 4-23, Stuart Broad 4-44) lost to **England** 396/7 dec. (C Woakes 137*, Jonny Bairstow 93; H Pandya 3-66, Mohammed Shami 3-96) by an innings and 159 runs. *PoM: Chris Woakes.*

3rd Test: India won by 203 runs

This time, unlike at Edgbaston, Kohli's match haul of 200 runs was not in vain. Root's decision to bowl seemed reasonable enough on a cloudy Midlands morning, but Anderson and Broad could not locate the fuller length that conditions demanded, and it was up to Woakes — with three pre-lunch wickets — to justify his captain's move. Then Kohli and Rahane took over.

While they added 159, batting looked as serene as at any time so far in the series, and Rahane could hardly believe his bad luck when Cook, part of England's fallible cordon, clung on to a one-handed screamer at first slip. Kohli followed soon after just short of a century, edging a Rashid leg-break to slip, and Anderson had 100 wickets against India when Pandya fell to the last ball of the day. But 307 for 6 was a decent retort to being asked to bat.

Broad and Anderson polished things off on the second morning, but England's promising opening stand of 54 proved entirely illusory. One by one, they found ways of getting out. In a collapse of ten for 107, Buttler top-scored for 39, and it was not lost on England fans that Curran, omitted here to accommodate Stokes after his not-guilty verdict, had just made 40 for Surrey.

India led by 168, with all tension drained from the game. But there were points to be made. Pujara dug in for his best score of a difficult summer with both Yorkshire and India, while Kohli made up for his first-innings near-miss with a ton — though he was dropped on 93 by Jennings off an inconsolable Anderson. India eventually called it a day on the third evening, setting England a notional 521.

At 62 for 4 next morning, a massacre beckoned, but Pant, keeping wicket in place of Karthik, dropped Buttler on one off Bumrah. It felt trivial at the time, but less so when, after tea, Buttler brought up his maiden Test hundred with a trio of leg-side fours in one over off Shami. The second new ball did the trick, though. Buttler padded up fatally to Bumrah to end a stand of 169 in 57 overs with Stokes, and Bairstow, demoted after fracturing his left middle finger while keeping wicket, was bowled first ball.

Bumrah quickly bounced out Woakes to pick up his fifth wicket, and a four-day defeat beckoned, but Rashid and Broad put on 50 for the ninth wicket, and the game dragged on to the fifth morning. With the 17th delivery of the last day, Ashwin removed Anderson, and India had their seventh Test win in England. More importantly, they were still in the series.

Trent Bridge, Nottingham, August 18-22: India 329 in 94.5 overs (Virat Kohli 97, Ajinkya Rahane 81; James Anderson 3-64, Stuart Broad 3-72, Chris Woakes 3-75) and 352/7 dec. in 110 overs (V Kohli 103, Cheteshwar Pujara 72; Adil Rashid 3-101, Ben Stokes 2-68) beat **England** 161 in 38.2 overs (Jos Buttler 39, Alastair Cook 29; Hardik Pandya 5-28, Ishant Sharma 2-32) and 317 in 104.5 overs (J Buttler 106, B Stokes 62; Jasprit Bumrah 5-85, Ishant 2-70) by 203 runs. *PoM:* Virat Kohli.

4th Test: England won by 60 runs

For the second time in the series, India emerged on the wrong end of a thriller. And, once more, the pivotal moment was the fourth-innings dismissal of Kohli. While he and Rahane were adding a restorative 101 for the fourth wicket in 42 careful overs, India's pursuit of 245 to take matters to a decider at The Oval looked plausible. But Moeen, back in England's Test side for the first time all summer, had Kohli caught at short leg after his fifty, and India folded in an ungainly heap, their last seven falling for 71. Another series in England had passed them by.

There had been another familiar plotline, too. At 86 for 6 on the first day, England looked to have thrown away the advantage of winning their fourth toss in a row. But, as at Edgbaston, Curran organised a recovery, adding 81 with Moeen, then 63 with Broad. When Ashwin bowled Curran for 78, England had 246. On a pitch already offering turn, they were in the game.

Broad removed both Indian openers, before Pujara, drawing confidence from his performance in Nottingham, and Kohli asserted their class. At 142 for 2, India held the aces, only for Curran to persuade Kohli into a loose drive outside off stump. As if to prefigure events later in the game, his departure triggered a collapse, as Moeen knocked over the lower-middle order, including Pant, for a torturous 29-ball duck.

But this series was nothing if not full of twists, and from 195 for 8, Pujara batted as Kohli had done in the first innings at Edgbaston, easing to his first Test century in England and squeezing 78 out of the last two wickets to earn India an unexpected lead of 27.

Which way would the pendulum swing now? At first, it kept swinging towards India. Shami trapped Jennings with the last ball before lunch on the third day, then bowled Bairstow with the first ball after it. When Root was run out by Shami's direct hit from mid-on, England were 122 for 5, only 95 ahead.

What followed felt — for India, at least — grimly inevitable, as Buttler made 69 and Curran 46. Ashwin bowled 37 overs for a single wicket — a poor return on a helpful surface on which Moeen, his supposed inferior, had already taken five. It looked as if he was struggling with a groin injury. The upshot was that Kohli's men needed more than they had ever made in the fourth innings to win a Test in England.

Anderson and Broad reduced them to 22 for 3, before Kohli and Rahane staunched the bleeding. But it was never easy, as Moeen unerringly located the rough outside the right-hander's off stump. Kohli was fortunate not to be given lbw on nine; when he finally went, gloving an off-break, the dam burst. Moeen finished with nine in the match, and England headed to The Oval relieved to have the series in the bag.

Rose Bowl, Southampton, August 30-September 2: England 246 in 76.4 overs (Sam Curran 78, Moeen Ali 40; Jasprit Bumrah 3-46, Ishant Sharma 2-26) and 271 in 96.1 overs (Jos Buttler 69, Joe Root 48; Mohammed Shami 4-57, Ishant 2-36) beat **India** 273 in 84.5 overs (Cheteshwar Pujara 132*, Virat Kohli 46; M Ali 5-63, Stuart Broad 3-63) and 184 in 69.4 overs (V Kohli 58, Ajinkya Rahane 51; M Ali 4-71, James Anderson 2-33) by 60 runs. *PoM:* Moeen Ali.

5th Test: England won by 118 runs

There were moments in this game when it was easy to forget that a Test match was taking place, and not a benefit game for Cook. On at least a dozen occasions, a packed ground rose to show their appreciation for England's all-time leading run-scorer following his announcement three days before the start that this Test would be his 161st and last. Cook rose to the occasion too, hitting 71 and 147. There was barely a dry eye in the house.

It was not the only cause for English celebration. With the last ball of the game, Anderson bowled Shami to collect his 564th Test wicket, one more than McGrath and thus the most by any fast bowler.

When Root won his fifth toss in a row, the stage was set for the first of Cook's standing ovations, accompanied by a guard of honour from the Indians, who were nothing but gentlemen throughout. He began by taking part in England's highest opening stand of the summer: 60, before Jennings tickled Jadeja to leg slip. Progress by Cook and Moeen was slow after lunch against some outstanding seam bowling, but at 133 for 1, the hard work seemed to have been done.

India's best fourth-innings partnerships			
Batsmen	**Wicket**	**Runs**	**Match details**
Chetan Chauhan, Sunil Gavaskar	1	213	v England, The Oval, 1979
KL Rahul, Rishabh Pant	6	204	v England, The Oval, 2018
Rahul Dravid, Sourav Ganguly	3	194	v New Zealand, Hamilton, 1999
Virat Kohli, M Vijay	3	185	v Australia, Adelaide, 2014
Deep Dasgupta, Rahul Dravid	2	171	v South Africa, Port Elizabeth, 2001

Then, to groans, Bumrah bowled Cook off an inside edge, setting off a collapse. Root and Bairstow both fell for ducks, and when the probing Ishant removed Curran for another, it was 181 for 7. But India's problem all series had been finishing their opponents off, and so it proved once more. Buttler led the revival this time: when he was last out for 89, England had more than 300.

India replied with 292, a disappointment from 101 for 2, but an improvement on 160 for 6. On day three, Jadeja came to the fore with a combative unbeaten 86, which reduced the deficit to 40. And when England lost Jennings and Moeen with 62 on the board, India were still in the hunt.

Then came the biggest partnership of the series, an untroubled 259 between Cook, determined to make up for his first-innings near miss, and Root, determined to make up for a mediocre summer. After overhauling Kumar Sangakkara's tally of 12,400 to become Test cricket's highest-scoring left-hander, Cook moved to his 33rd — and most emotional — hundred courtesy of four overthrows from Bumrah. Root soon ticked off No.14. Both eventually fell in successive balls to debutant Hanuma Vihari, and India were set 464 in 108 overs.

A thrashing looked inevitable when Anderson and Broad reduced them to 2 for 3 on the fourth evening, including Kohli for a golden duck. But Rahul found two willing partners. First he added 118 for the fourth wicket with Rahane, then a stirring 204 for the sixth with Pant, who became the first Indian wicketkeeper to score a Test hundred in England.

At 325 for 5, India began to entertain notions of the impossible. But Rashid, after a quiet series, bowled Rahul with a wicked leg-break, then had Pant caught at long-off. Armed with the second new ball, Curran picked up a couple, before Anderson's coup de grace knocked back Shami's middle stump — a stirring end to a superb series.

The Oval, London, September 7-11: England 332 in 122 overs (Jos Buttler 89, Alastair Cook 71; Ravindra Jadeja 4-79, Ishant Sharma 3-62, Jasprit Bumrah 3-83) and 423/8 dec. in 112.3 overs (A Cook 147, Joe Root 125; Hanuma Vihari 3-37, R Jadeja 3-179) beat **India** 292 in 95 overs (R Jadeja 86*, H Vihari 56; Moeen Ali 2-50, James Anderson 2-54) and 345 in 94.3 overs (KL Rahul 149, Rishabh Pant 114; J Anderson 3-45, Sam Curran 2-23) by 118 runs. *PoM:* Alastair Cook. *PoS:* Sam Curran (England), Virat Kohli (India).

Alistair Cook's records on his retirement

• Fifth-highest run-getter in Tests, first among left-handers with his 12,472 runs from 291 innings.

• One of only five batsmen to make centuries in both his first and last Tests.

• Only the second batsman after South Africa's Bruce Mitchell to make half-centuries in both innings of both his first and last Tests. He had made 60 and 104 not out on debut in 2006.

• His 15 centuries in his team's second innings are the most for any cricketer, one more than Kumar Sangakkara.

• 159 consecutive Test appearances, the most by any player

• 26,562 balls faced — since his debut, no other player has faced as many deliveries, with only Hashim Amla's 17,806 after him.

India in England

England

Batting

Player	M	I	NO	R	HS	Avge	100s/50s
C Woakes	2	3	1	149	137*	74.50	1/0
S Curran	4	7	0	272	78	38.85	0/2
J Buttler	5	9	0	349	106	38.77	1/2
A Cook	5	9	0	327	147	36.33	1/1

J Root	5	9	0	319	125	35.44	1/1
M Ali	2	4	0	119	50	29.75	0/1
J Bairstow	5	9	0	230	93	25.55	0/2
B Stokes	4	8	0	200	62	25.00	0/1
A Rashid	5	8	2	119	33*	19.83	0/0
K Jennings	5	9	0	163	42	18.11	0/0
O Pope	2	3	0	54	28	18.00	0/0
J Anderson	5	7	6	15	11	15.00	0/0
D Malan	1	2	0	28	20	14.00	0/0
S Broad	5	7	0	87	38	12.42	0/0

Bowling and fielding

Player	M	W	R	BBI	BBM	Avge	5wI/10wM	Ct/St
J Anderson	5	24	435	5-20	9-43	18.12	1/0	1/-
C Woakes	2	8	167	3-75	4-43	20.87	0/0	0/-
M Ali	2	12	252	5-63	9-134	21.00	1/0	1/-
S Curran	4	11	259	4-74	5-92	23.54	0/0	0/-
B Stokes	4	14	408	4-40	6-113	29.14	0/0	2/-
S Broad	5	16	475	4-44	5-81	29.68	0/0	3/-
A Rashid	5	10	309	3-101	4-147	30.90	0/0	1/-
K Jennings	5	0	4	-	-	-	0/0	3/-
J Root	5	0	26	-	-	-	0/0	3/-
J Bairstow	5	-	-	-	-	-	-/-	14/1
J Buttler	5	-	-	-	-	-	-/-	5/0
A Cook	5	-	-	-	-	-	-/-	13/-
D Malan	1	-	-	-	-	-	-/-	3/-
O Pope	2	-	-	-	-	-	-/-	2/-

India

Batting

Player	M	I	NO	R	HS	Avge	100s/50s
R Jadeja	1	2	1	99	86*	99.00	0/1
V Kohli	5	10	0	593	149	59.30	2/3
CA Pujara	4	8	1	278	132*	39.71	1/1
KL Rahul	5	10	0	299	149	29.90	1/0
H Vihari	1	2	0	56	56	28.00	0/1
R Pant	3	6	0	162	114	27.00	1/0
A Rahane	5	10	0	257	81	25.70	0/2

Player							
H Pandya	4	8	1	164	52*	23.42	0/1
R Ashwin	4	8	2	126	33*	21.00	0/0
S Dhawan	4	8	0	162	44	20.25	0/0
M Vijay	2	4	0	26	20	6.50	0/0
I Sharma	5	9	1	42	14	5.25	0/0
D Karthik	2	4	0	21	20	5.25	0/0
M Shami	5	10	1	27	10*	3.00	0/0
J Bumrah	3	5	2	6	6	2.00	0/0
K Yadav	1	2	0	0	0	0.00	0/0
U Yadav	1	2	2	1	1*	-	0/0

Bowling and fielding

Player	M	W	R	BBI	BBM	Avge	5wI/10wM	Ct/St
H Vihari	1	3	38	3-37	3-38	12.66	0/0	0/-
I Sharma	5	18	437	5-51	6-97	24.27	1/0	0/-
H Pandya	4	10	247	5-28	6-50	24.70	1/0	0/-
U Yadav	1	3	76	2-20	3-76	25.33	0/0	0/-
J Bumrah	3	14	363	5-85	7-122	25.92	1/0	1/-
R Ashwin	4	11	360	4-62	7-121	32.72	0/0	1/-
R Jadeja	1	7	258	4-79	7-258	36.85	0/0	0/-
M Shami	5	16	622	4-57	6-108	38.87	0/0	2/-
K Yadav	1	0	44	-	-	-	0/0	0/-
S Dhawan	4	-	-	-	-	-	-/-	2/-
D Karthik	2	-	-	-	-	-	-/-	5/0
V Kohli	5	-	-	-	-	-	-/-	4/-
R Pant	3	-	-	-	-	-	-/-	15/0
C Pujara	4	-	-	-	-	-	-/-	0/-
A Rahane	5	-	-	-	-	-	-/-	4/-
KL Rahul	5	-	-	-	-	-	-/-	14/-
M Vijay	2	-	-	-	-	-	-/-	0/-

Squads

England: Joe Root (capt), Moeen Ali, James Anderson, Jonny Bairstow (wk), Stuart Broad, Jos Buttler (wk), Alastair Cook, Sam Curran, Keaton Jennings, Dawid Malan, Jamie Porter, Adil Rashid, Ben Stokes, Ollie Pope, Chris Woakes, James Vince.

India: Virat Kohli (capt), Ajinkya Rahane (vice-capt), R Ashwin, Jasprit Bumrah, Shikhar Dhawan, Ravindra Jadeja, Dinesh Karthik (wk), Karun Nair, Hardik Pandya, Rishabh Pant (wk), Cheteshwar Pujara, KL Rahul, Mohammed Shami, Ishant Sharma, Shardul Thakur, M Vijay, Kuldeep Yadav, Umesh Yadav, Prithvi Shaw, Hanuma Vihari.

MULTI-NATION TOURNAMENTS

Nidahas Trophy 2018

Dinesh Karthik slammed 29 in eight balls, including a winning six off the last ball to claim the Nidahas Trophy. — *Getty Images/AFP*

Karthik steals last-ball win

SA'ADI THAWFEEQ

Sri Lanka were excluded from their own party when they failed to reach the final of a T20 tournament organised to celebrate 70 years of independence. India left five leading players at home, but underlined their bench strength by winning a pulsating final against Bangladesh. The hosts, in their first home assignment under new coach Chandika Hathurusingha, could only look on enviously.

Bangladesh battled hard, but made themselves deeply unpopular at the conclusion of their victory over Sri Lanka in the last game of the league stage. It was marred by ugly scenes, in part a result of bad feeling during the series in Bangladesh the previous month. The teams riled each other by trading versions of the '*nagin*' snake dance at the fall of wickets, and the rancour spilled over in the last over of what amounted to a semi-final. With Bangladesh needing 12 off four balls, Shakib Al Hasan — in charge for the first time in the tournament after injury — briefly tried to call his batsmen off in protest at the umpires' failure to award a no-ball on height. Bangladesh substitute Nurul Hasan exchanged angry words with Sri Lanka's stand-in captain Thisara Perera, before Mahmudullah channeled his fury, rounding off his 43 from 18 balls with a match-winning six off the penultimate delivery. It also emerged that a glass door in the Bangladesh dressing-room had been smashed after the match. Shakib and Nurul were fined and given demerit points, while the Bangladesh board issued a statement rebuking the players.

The kerfuffle meant India received enthusiastic support in the final. Rohit proved good at extracting the most from his players. Washington Sundar, an 18-year-old off-spinner with just two previous international appearances, was the Player of the Tournament, with eight wickets at 14.

1ˢᵗ match: Sri Lanka beat India by five wickets

• Sri Lanka launch their campaign with an assured victory, with Kusal Perera hogging the headlines for his 66 off 37 balls. • He slams 26 off the third over of the chase, from seamer Shardul Thakur. • Thisara calms nerves at the death with a well-judged unbeaten 22. • India slip to 9 for 2 after two overs, and a modest 40 after the powerplay. • But they reached a challenging total thanks to Shikhar Dhawan's 90 off 49 balls, his best T20I score.

R Premadasa Stadium, Colombo, March 6: India 174/5 in 20 overs (Shikhar Dhawan 90, Manish Pandey 37; Dushmantha Chameera 2-33) lost to **Sri Lanka** 175/5 in 18.3 overs (Kusal Perera 66, Thisara Perera 22*; Washington Sundar 2-28, Yuzvendra Chahal 2-37) by five wickets. *MoM:* Kusal Perera.

2ⁿᵈ match: India beat Bangladesh by six wickets

• Dhawan's second successive fifty guides India to a comfortable win in a lacklustre encounter. • Bangladesh's total would have been feebler but for some generous Indian fielding: three catches were dropped from medium-pacer Vijay Shankar, including one by the bowler himself. • He still wins the match award, after removing the dangerous duo of Mushfiqur Rahim and Mahmudullah. • Liton Das is put down twice on his way to a top score. • But, from 107 for 4 after 15 overs, Bangladesh never seem likely to go too hard.

R Premadasa Stadium, Colombo, March 8: Bangladesh 139/8 in 20 overs (Liton Das 34, Sabbir Rahman 30; Jaydev Unadkat 3-38, Vijay Shankar 2-32) lost to **India** 140/4 in 18.4 overs (Shikhar Dhawan 55, Suresh Raina 28; Rubel Hossain 2-24) by six wickets. *MoM:* Vijay Shankar.

3ʳᵈ match: Bangladesh beat Sri Lanka by five wickets

• The 215 they are set is 22 higher than Bangladesh have ever made in a T20 innings. • They are given a flying start by Tamim Iqbal and Liton, who is promoted to open. • Mushfiqur joins in with a dazzling 72 not out off 35 balls, equally severe on seam and spin. • He secures the fourth-highest successful chase in T20Is in the final over. • Sri Lanka's total, their fourth-highest, has leaned heavily on Kusal Mendis (57 off 30) and Kusal Perera (74 off 48).

R Premadasa Stadium, Colombo, March 10: Sri Lanka 214/6 in 20 overs (Kusal Perera 74, Kusal Mendis 57; Mustafizur Rahman 3-48, Mahmudullah 2-15) lost to **Bangladesh** 215/5 in 19.4overs (Mushfiqur Rahim 72*, Tamim Iqbal 47; Nuwan Pradeep 2-37) by five wickets. *MoM:* Mushfiqur Rahim.

4th match: India beat Sri Lanka by six wickets

• Thakur bounces back from his mauling in the opening match. • His four wickets put India within touching distance of the final. • He deploys his variations to good effect, while teenage off-spinner Washington claims two victims in inexpensive overs. • In a match reduced to 19 overs, Sri Lanka — without captain Dinesh Chandimal, who is suspended for two matches because of a slow over-rate — move brightly to 96 for 2 in the 11th over. • A partnership of 62 between Kusal Mendis and Upul Tharanga brings them there. • India stumble to 85 for 4, but Manish Pandey and Dinish Karthik guide them home.

R Premadasa Stadium, Colombo, March 12: Sri Lanka 152/9 in 19 overs (Kusal Mendis 55, Upul Tharanga 22; Shardul Thakur 4-27, Washington Sundar 2-21) lost to **India** 153/4 in 17.3 overs (Manish Pandey 42*, Dinesh Karthik 39*; Akila Dananjaya 2-19) by six wickets. *MoM:* Shardul Thakur.

5th match: India beat Bangladesh by 17 runs

• India continue their improvement since their opening defeat and book their place in the final. • On a slow pitch, they advance cautiously, before going at ten an over in the second half of their innings. • Rohit top-scores with 89 off 61 balls, including five sixes. • He gets good support from Dhawan and Suresh Raina. • Bangladesh's response is holed below the waterline by Sundar, who strikes three times in the powerplay. • Mushfiqur continues his rich vein of form with 72 not out off 55, but lacks assistance.

R Premadasa Stadium, Colombo, March 14: India 176/3 in 20 overs (Rohit Sharma 89, Suresh Raina 47; Rubek Hossain 2-27) beat **Bangladesh** 159/6 in 20 overs (Mushfiqur Rahim 72*, Tamim Iqbal 27; Washington Sundar 3-22) by 17 runs. *MoM:* Rohit Sharma.

6th match: Bangladesh beat Sri Lanka by two wickets

• In a feverish atmosphere, Mahmudullah remains the coolest man. • He steers Bangladesh into the final with a six off the penultimate ball. • Earlier in the over, captain Shakib has emerged from the dressing-room and tried to take his batsmen off in protest at the umpires' failure to call a no-ball on height. • Substitute Nurul Hasan trades verbals with Thisara, and there is pushing and shoving. • When things calm down, Mahmudullah hits Isuru Udana for four, two and six to round off a match-winning 43 not out off 18 balls. • Sri Lanka's total has owed much to the Pereras — Kusal and Thisara.

R Premadasa Stadium, Colombo, March 16: Sri Lanka 159/7 in 20 overs (Kusal Perera 61, Thisara Perera 58; Mustafizur Rahman 2-39) lost to **Bangladesh** 160/8 in 19.5 overs (Tamim Iqbal 50, Mahmudullah 43*; Akila Dananjaya 2-37) by two wickets. *MoM:* Mahmudullah.

Points table

Teams	M	W	L	T	N/R	Pts.	NRR
India	4	3	1	0	0	6	+0.377
Bangladesh	4	2	2	0	0	4	-0.293
Sri Lanka	4	1	3	0	0	2	-0.085

India and Bangladesh qualified for the final

Final: India beat Bangladesh by four wickets

• Karthik faces just eight balls, but makes the biggest impact. • With five needed off the final ball, he clears the rope over cover with the third of his sixes. • Soumya Sarkar, a part-timer asked to defend 11 in the last over, is inconsolable. • This after Bangladesh are in control after the 18th over, a wicket-maiden for Mustafizur. • Vijay Shankar's struggles in his debut tournament are forgotten. • Bangladesh's total is down to Sabbir Rahman's 50-ball 77 and Mehidy's lower-order blows.

R Premadasa Stadium, Colombo, March 18: Bangladesh 166/8 in 20 overs (Dabbir Rahman 77, Mahmudullah 21; YuzvendraChahal 3-18, JaydevUnadkat 2-33) lost to **India** 168/6 in 20 overs (Rohit Sharma 56, Dinesh Karthik 29*; Rubel Hossain 2-35) by four wickets. *MoM:* Dinesh Karthik. *MoS:* Washington Sundar.

Winners: India

Asia Cup 2018

Rohit's men prevail in last-ball thriller

K R NAYAR

Defending champions India arrived for the Asia Cup with doubts over their ability to retain the title. They had suffered a demoralising defeat in England, losing the Test series 4-1 just four days before the start of the event. They had also rested Virat Kohli. Pakistan, as Champions Trophy winners and most familiar with the conditions in UAE, were seen as favourites.

There was an uproar over the scheduling: India had to play back-to-back matches against Hong and Pakistan, while the others were upset that India were playing all their matches in Dubai, and did not have to travel to Abu Dhabi.

The focus was on the India-Pakistan matches. For 12 years the two teams hadn't played here, after all. However, it was a one-sided contest both times the teams met, with Pakistan crumbling under pressure. By the end of the tournament, the contrast between the teams was stark: while stand-in captain Rohit Sharma was praised for his calm decisions and inclination to back his players, Sarfaraz Ahmed was tetchy, coming in for flak from several quarters.

Other matches, though, provided the surprises and entertainment. The pitches allowed for a contest between bat and ball, and there were no totals above 300. India's first match against Hong Kong was expected to be one sided, and they rested some regular players. However, Hong Kong's opening partnership of 174 between Nizakat Khan and Anshuman Rath made them sweat. For a side that had heart-breakingly lost their ODI status a few months before, that they could still feature in tournaments like this meant a lot.

Bangladesh captured everyone's attention with a 137-run victory over five-time champions Sri Lanka, before Afghanistan, displaying their indomitable spirit, completed their first victory over Sri Lanka in ODI cricket. The islanders became the first team to crash out of the tournament and captain Angelo Mathews lost his job and, temporarily, a place in the side.

Afghanistan thrashed Bangladesh in the group stage, threatened to upset both Pakistan and Bangladesh in the Super Four stage, and held India to a tie. They could walk away from the tournament holding their heads high.

Memories of the Nidahas Trophy were still fresh when India and Bangladesh played out another last-ball thriller in the final. It was a repeat of that result, with the bigger neighbour holding on.

Most runs: Shikhar Dhawan (India) (342 runs, 5 matches)
Most wickets: Rashid Khan (Afghanistan) (10 wickets, 5 matches)

Afghanistan enjoyed an excellent outing at the Asia Cup, knocking out Sri Lanka and challenging Bangladesh, Pakistan and India. — *Getty Images/AFP*

Group A

Dubai International Cricket Stadium, September 16: Hong Kong 116 in 37.1 overs (Aizaz Khan 27, Kinchit Shah 26; Usman Shinwari 3-19, Hasan Ali 2-19) lost to **Pakistan** 120/2 in 23.4 overs (Imam-ul-Haq 50*, Babar Azam 33; Ehsan Khan 2-34) by eight wickets. *PoM:* Usman Shinwari.

Dubai International Cricket Stadium, September 18: India 285/7 in 50 overs (Shikhar Dhawan 127, Ambati Rayudu 60; Kinchit Shah 3-39, Ehsan Khan 2-65) lost to **Hong Kong** 259/8 in 50 overs (Nizakat Khan 92, Anshuman Rath 73; Yuzvendra Chahal 3-46, Khaleel Ahmed 3-48) by 26 runs. *PoM:* Shikhar Dhawan.

Dubai International Cricket Stadium, September 19: Pakistan 162 in 43.1 overs (Babar Azam 47, Shoaib Malik 43; Bhuvneshwar Kumar 3-15, Kedar Jadhav 3-23) lost to **India** 164/2 in 29 overs (Rohit Sharma 52, Shikhar Dhawan 46) by eight wickets. *PoM:* Bhuvneshwar Kumar.

Points table

Teams	M	W	L	D	T	N/R	Pts	NRR
India	2	2	0	0	0	0	4	+1.474
Pakistan	2	1	1	0	0	0	2	+0.284
Hong Kong	2	0	2	0	0	0	0	-1.748

India and Pakistan qualified for Super Four

Group B

Dubai International Cricket Stadium, September 15: Bangladesh 261 in 49.3 overs (Mushfiqur Rahim 144, Mohammad Mithun 63; Lasith Malinga 4-23, Dhananjaya de Silva 2-38) beat **Sri Lanka** 124 in 35.3 overs (Dilruwan Perera 29, Upul Tharanga 27; Mustafizur Rahman 2-20, Mehidy Hasan 2-21) by 137 runs. *PoM:* Mushfiqur Rahim.

Sheikh Zayed Stadium, Abu Dhabi, September 17: Afghanistan 249 in 50 overs (Rahmat Shah 72, Ihsanullah 45; Thisara Perera 5-55, Akila Dananjaya 2-39) beat **Sri Lanka** 158 in

41.2 overs (Upul Tharanga 36, T Perera 28; Rashid Khan 2-26, Gulbadin Naib 2-29) by 91 runs. *PoM:* Rahmat Shah.

Sheikh Zayed Stadium, Abu Dhabi, September 20: Afghanistan 255/7 in 50 overs (Hashmatullah Shahidi 58, Rashid Khan 57*; Shakib Al Hasan 4-42, Abu Hider 2-50) beat **Bangladesh** 119 in 42.1 overs (S Al Hasan 32, Mahmudullah 27; Rashid 2-13, Mujeeb Ur Rahman 2-22) by 136 runs. *PoM:* Rashid Khan.

Points table

Teams	M	W	L	D	T	N/R	Pts	NRR
Afghanistan	2	2	0	0	0	0	4	+2.270
Bangladesh	2	1	1	0	0	0	2	+0.010
Sri Lanka	2	0	2	0	0	0	0	-2.280

Afghanistan and Bangladesh qualified for Super Four

Super Four

Match 1: India beat Bangladesh by seven wickets

Ravindra Jadeja's four wickets checked Bangladesh's run flow and helped India open with a win. Having landed in the UAE only the day before as a replacement for the injured Axar Patel, Jadeja carried the confidence and form from The Oval Test in England, where he had made an unbeaten 86 and taken seven for the match. It was his first ODI in 15 months. Mehidy Hasan and skipper Mashrafe Mortaza added 66 for the eighth wicket, but India were never tested by the small total. Rohit remained unbeaten on his second successive half-century.

Dubai International Cricket Stadium, September 21: Bangladesh 173 in 49.1 overs (Mehidy Hasan 42, Mashrafe Mortaza 26; Ravindra Jadeja 4-29, Bhuvneshwar Kumar 3-32) lost to **India** 174/3 in 36.2 overs (Rohit Sharma 83*, Shikhar Dhawan 40) by seven wickets. *PoM:* Ravindra Jadeja.

Match 2: Pakistan beat Afghanistan by three wickets.

Pakistan downed Afghanistan in a thriller, riding on Shoaib Malik's experience. Hashmatullah Shahidi missed out on a century, but he and Asghar Afghan's elegant fifty rescued Afghanistan after they had lost the first three wickets for 94 at the half-way mark. Pakistan lost opener Fakhar Zaman in the first over, but Babar Azam and Imam-ul-Haq added 154 runs. Once Rashid Khan had Babar stumped, Pakistan lost wickets regularly. Pakistan needed 10 runs in the last over. Malik, hitting Aftab Alam for a six off the second ball and a boundary off the third, won the match for his side.

Sheikh Zayed Stadium, Abu Dhabi, September 21: Afghanistan 257/6 in 50 overs (Hashmatullah Shahidi 97*, Asghar Afghan 67; Mohammad Nawaz 3-57, Shaheen Afridi 2-38) lost to **Pakistan** 258/7 in 49.3 overs (Imam-ul-Haq 80, Babar Azam 66; Rashid Khan 3-46, Mujeeb Ur Rahman 2-33) by three wickets. *PoM:* Shoaib Malik.

Match 3: India beat Pakistan by nine wickets.

For the second time in the tournament, the India-Pakistan match was a damp squib. In a brilliant exhibition of death bowling, the Indian bowlers gave away just 26 in the last five overs. Malik's 78 and 107-run fourth-wicket partnership with Sarfaraz propped up the total, and there were starts for Asif Ali and Fakhar, too; but overall, Pakistan's batting was unimpressive. Rohit and Shikhar Dhawan, on the other hand, posted 210 in 33.3 overs, exposing chinks in Pakistan's bowling. Both openers brought up centuries, as India won with 63 balls to spare.

Dubai International Cricket Stadium, September 23: Pakistan 237/7 in 50 overs (Shoaib Malik 78, Fakhar Zaman 31; Jasprit Bumrah 2-29, Kuldeep Yadav 2-41) lost to **India** 238/1 in 39.3 overs (Shikhar Dhawan 114, Rohit Sharma 111*) by nine wickets. *PoM:* Shikhar Dhawan.

Match 4: Bangladesh beat Afghanistan by three runs

Where against Pakistan, Afghanistan had been unable to defend ten runs in the final over, here, they couldn't get the eight runs they needed. Left-arm pacer Mustafizur Rahman proved again to be one of the best finishers with the ball.

Afghanistan again had Shahidi to thank. They lost their first two wickets for 26, and Mohammad Shahzad found the going tough till Shahidi brought them back into the game. For Bangladesh, Imrul Kayes and Mahmudullah made half-centuries after they had slipped to 87 for 5.

Sheikh Zayed Stadium, Abu Dhabi, September 23: Bangladesh 249/7 in 50 overs (Mahmudullah 74, Imrul Kayes 72*; Aftab Alam 3-54) beat **Afghanistan** 246/7 in 50 overs (Hashmatullah Shahidi 71, Mohammad Shahzad 53; Mustafizur Rahman 2-44, Mashrafe Mortaza 2-62) by three runs. *PoM: Mahmudullah.*

Match 5: Tied

India rested five players, including captain Rohit and vice-captain Dhawan, with Mahendra Singh Dhoni taking charge. The Afghan openers thrashed the Indian attack to bring up 124 runs, before the experienced Mohammad Nabi pushed the total past 250. Yet, India were sailing with a century stand of their own, through K L Rahul and Ambati Rayudu. Rashid, Nabi and Javed Ahmadi then turned the match. Needing seven to win, last man Khaleel Ahmad equalled the score. Jadeja hit the fifth ball from Rashid in the air and was caught, resulting in the 36th tie in an ODI.

Dubai International Cricket Stadium, September 25: Afghanistan 252/8 in 50 overs (Mohammad Shahzad 124, Mohammad Nabi 64; Ravindra Jadeja 3-46, Kuldeep Yadav 2-38) tied with **India** 252 in 47.5 overs (KL Rahul 60, Ambati Rayudu 57; M Nabi 2-40, Rashid Khan 2-41). *PoM: Mohammad Shahzad.*

Match 6: Bangladesh beat Pakistan by 37 runs

In a virtual semi-final, Pakistan pacers Junaid Khan and Shaheen Afridi began promisingly, removing the first three batsmen for single-digit scores.

But the in-form Mushfiqur and Mohammad Mithun lifted their team out of trouble. Fakhar and Babar fell for a run each and the pressure was on Pakistan. After the skipper too fell cheaply, Malik and Imam-ul-Haq fought hard. Mahmudullah, though, had Imam stumped for 83 to shatter Pakistan's hopes of reaching the final. Mustafizur continued to impress, this time taking four wickets.

Sheikh Zayed Stadium, Abu Dhabi, September 26: Bangladesh 239 in 48.5 overs (Mushfiqur Rahim 99, Mohammad Mithun 60; Junaid Khan 4-19, Shaheen Afridi 2-47) beat **Pakistan** 202/9 in 50 overs (Imam-ul-Haq 83, Asif Ali 37; Mustafizur Rahman 4-43, Mehidy Hasan 2-28) by 37 runs. *PoM:* Mushfiqur Rahim.

Points table

Teams	M	W	L	D	T	N/R	Pts	NRR
India	3	2	0	0	1	0	5	+0.863
Bangladesh	3	2	1	0	0	0	4	-0.156
Pakistan	3	1	2	0	0	0	2	-0.599
Afghanistan	3	0	2	0	1	0	1	-0.044

India and Bangladesh qualified for the final

Final: India beat Bangladesh by three wickets

India were crowned Asia Cup champion for the seventh time, but only after a nail-biting last-ball finis. Put in, Bangladesh opener Liton Das, through his maiden century, and Mehidy, who was promoted to open, put on 120 runs. Then Kedar Jadhav, known for his ability to force settled batsmen to commit mistakes, got Mehidy to hit an easy delivery into the hands of Rayudu to break the partnership. That choked the run flow. India began their chase confidently, but Bangladesh prevented any partnerships from flourishing. They pushed India to a stage where six runs were needed off the last over. Jadhav, who had retired due to a hamstring injury, hobbled back to win the match off a leg-bye off the last ball.

Dubai International Cricket Stadium, September 28: Bangladesh 222 in 48.3 overs (Liton Das 121, Soumya Sarkar 33; Kuldeep Yadav 3-45, Kedar Jadhav 2-41) lost to **India** 223/7 in 50 overs (Rohit Sharma 48, Dinesh Karthik 37; Rubel Hossain 2-26, Mustafizur Rahman 2-38) by three wickets. *PoM:* Liton Das. *PoS:* Shikhar Dhawan.

INDIA'S OTHER INTERNATIONALS

India A in England

Chahar, Shaw get call-ups

Once a reject at his state trials for not being tall enough, Rajasthan fast bowler Deepak Chahar was one of the biggest beneficiaries of the tour. The 25-year old picked up 13 wickets in five matches on his first tour with India A, including a best of 5 for 27 against West Indies A, to earn his T20I cap against England.

Krunal Pandya too earned a maiden call-up as an injury replacement, but couldn't break into India's XI. Mayank Agarwal smashed three hundreds in five innings on his first England tour. That he was picked across formats was a validation of the belief that he had matured to become an all-formats player. Prithvi Shaw and Shubman Gill seamlessly made the step up from the Under-19 level.

Shaw's big-match temperament and free-flowing run-scoring even earned him a maiden Test call-up for the last two Tests in England, after the selectors ran out of patience with M Vijay. G Hanuma Vihari, the Andhra captain, with the highest first-class average among current cricketers during the time, also finished as the highest run-scorer in the 50-overs leg. A subsequent half-century in swinging conditions in the four-dayers earned him a controversial Test debut at The Oval, where he leapfrogged Karun Nair, the tour's reserve batsman, for a middle-order berth. *SK*

Most runs: Sam Hain (England Lions) (356 runs, 5 matches)
Most wickets: Liam Dawson (England Lions) (14 wickets, 5 matches)

England A-team tri-series
County Ground, Derby, June 22: India A 232 in 46.3 overs (Rishabh Pant 64, Shreyas Iyer 42; Liam Dawson 4-30, Tom Helm 3-33) lost to **England Lions** 236/3 in 41.5overs (Nick Gubbins 128*, Sam Hain 54; Shardul Thakur 2-30) by seven wickets.
County Ground, Derby, June 23: England Lions 318/5 in 50 overs (Sam Hain 145*, Tom Kohler-Cadmore 67) beat **West Indies A** 231 in 44.4 overs (Rovman Powell 55, Jason Mohammad 52; Liam Dawson 4-27, Chris Jordan 3-25, Reece Topley 3-54) by 87 runs.
Grace Road, Leicester, June 25: West Indies A 221 in 49.1 overs (Devon Thomas 64*, Chandrapaul Hemraj 45; Deepak Chahar 5-27) lost to **India A** 222/3 in 38.1overs (Mayank Agarwal 112, Shubman Gill 58*; Dominic Drakes 2-37) by seven wickets.
Grace Road, Leicester, June 26: India A 309/6 in 50 overs (Mayank Agarwal 112, Shubman Gill 72; Ed Barnard 2-51, Mathew Fisher 2-58) beat **England Lions** 207 in 41.3 overs (Liam Dawson 38, Ben Foakes 32; Shardul Thakur 3-53, Khaleel Ahmed 2-30) by 109 runs.
County Ground, Northampton, June 28: West Indies A 162 in 44.3 overs (Devon Thomas 45, Sunil Ambris 27; Reece Topley 4-16, Liam Dawson 4-21) lost to **England Lions** 163/1 in 25overs (Tom Kohler-Cadmore 80*, Sam Hain 48*) by nine wickets.

County Ground, Northampton, June 29: India A 354/6 in 50 overs (Hanuma Vihari 147, Prithvi Shaw 102; Chemar Holder 3-70) beat **West Indies A** 151 in 37.4 overs (Chandrapaul Hemraj 43, Sunil Ambris 32; Axar Patel 4-34, Deepak Chahar 2-21) by 203 runs.

Points table

Teams	M	W	L	T	N/R	Pts.	NRR
India A	4	3	1	0	0	6	+1.688
England Lions	4	3	1	0	0	6	+0.868
West Indies A	4	0	4	0	0	0	-2.653

India A and England Lions qualified for the final

Final: India A beat England Lions by five wickets

Kennington Oval, London, July 2: England Lions 264/9 in 50 overs (Sam Hain 108, Liam Livingstone 83; Khaleel Ahmed 3-48, Deepak Chahar 3-58) lost to **India A** 267/5 in 48.2 overs (Rishabh Pant 64*, Shreyas Iyer 44; Liam Dawson 2-37) by five wickets.

Winners: India A

South Africa A in India

Fruitful series for Agarwal

In terms of results, this was a disastrous tour for South Africa, looking for middle-order reinforcements in the wake of AB de Villiers' retirement. Over a month, they managed a solitary win across six matches.

Their loss in the first four-day fixture was the most heart-breaking, as they came within 1.1 overs of batting out a hard-fought draw on a wearing Chinnaswamy surface, only to be thwarted by Mohammad Siraj's maiden first-class ten-for.

Prithvi Shaw and Mayank Agarwal, who were successful in the away leg of this match-up, applied further pressure on the Indian national team's top order. Chief selector MSK Prasad was in attendance, watching the duo peel off effortless centuries in a double-century opening stand. Agarwal progressed to his second 200-plus score in less than a year: he had hit an unbeaten 304 against Maharashtra in the Ranji Trophy in 2017. *SK*

Most runs: Mayank Agarwal (248 runs, 2 matches)
Most wickets: Mohammad Siraj (14 wickets, 2 matches)

Tour match

M Chinnaswamy Stadium, Bengaluru, July 30 – August 1: South Africa A 473/4dec in 115.1 overs (Sarel Erwee 117 retd.hurt, Zubayr Hamza 104 retd.hurt; Jalaj Saxena 2-54) and 69/2 in 17.3 overs (Dwaine Pretorius 30*; Mihir Hirwani 2-35) drew with**Indian Board Presidents XI**397/6 dec in 108 overs (Dhruv Shorey 101, Ricky Bhui 91; Shaun von Berg 3-62).

Unofficial Test series (2): India A 1 South Africa A 0

M Chinnaswamy Stadium, Bengaluru, August 4-7: South Africa A 246 in 88.3 overs (Rudi Second 94, Sarel Erwee 47; Mohammad Siraj 5-56, Rajneesh Gurbani 2-47) and 308 in 128.5 overs (R Second 94. Zubayr Hamza 63; M Siraj 5-73, R Gurbani 2-45) lost to **India A** 584/8 dec in 129.4overs (Mayank Agarwal 220, Prithvi Shaw 136; Beuran Hendricks 3-98, Duanne Olivier 2-88) by an innings and 30 runs. *PoM:* Tom Latham.
KSCA Cricket Ground, Alur, August 10-13: India A 345 in 101 overs (Hanuma Vihari 148, Ankit Bawne 80; Duanne Olivier 6-63, Anrich Nortje 2-69) and 181/4 in 51 overs (Shrayas Iyer 65, A Bawne 64*; D Olivier 2-24, Senuran Muthusamy 2-45) drew with **South Africa A** 319 in 98.2 overs (Zubayr Hamza 93, Sarel Erwee 58; Mohammad Siraj 4-72, Ankit Rajpoot 3-52). *PoM:* Tom Latham.

'A' Team Quadrangular Series

Pandey leads from the front

India B, under Manish Pandey's captaincy, clinched the series. Pandey finished the tournament with unbeaten scores of 95, 21, 117 and 73. In all, his 306 runs came at a strike-rate of 99.15. The series also marked Ambati Rayudu's return to competitive cricket after he was withdrawn from the tour of England for failing the yo-yo test. Bhuvneshwar Kumar, who missed the entire Test series in England because of a lower-back injury, returned to action after a month-long rehabilitation programme at the National Cricket Academy.

Australia will remember the series for Jack Wildermuth's Miandad moment, when he hit a six off the final ball to win a thriller.   *SK*

Most runs: Manish Pandey (India B) (306 runs, 4 matches)
Most wickets: Shreyas Gopal (India B) (9 wickets, 4 matches)

Devineni Venkata Ramana Praneetha Ground, Mulapadu, Krishna, Andhra Pradesh, August 17: India A v **Australia A.** Match abandoned.
Dr Gokaraju Liala Gangaraju ACA Cricket Ground, Vijayawada, August 17: India B v **South Africa A.** Match abandoned.
Devineni Venkata Ramana Praneetha Ground, Mulapadu, Krishna, Andhra Pradesh, August 19: India A v **India B.** Match abandoned.
Dr Gokaraju Liala Gangaraju ACA Cricket Ground, Vijayawada, August 19: Australia A v **South Africa A.** Match abandoned.
M Chinnaswamy Stadium, Bengaluru, August 23: Australia A 151 in 31.4 overs (Ashton Agar 34, Travis Head 28; Mohammad Siraj 4-68, K Gowtham 3-31) lost to **India A** 152/5 in

Manish Pandey (left) led India B to the quadrangular series title. — *BCCI*

38.3 overs (Ambati Rayudu 62*, Krunal Pandya 49; Jhye Richardson 3-27) by five wickets. *PoM:* Ambati Rayudu.

KSCA Cricket Ground, Alur, August 23: South Africa A 231 in 47.3 overs (Senuran Muthusamy 55, Farhaan Behardien 43; Prasidh Krishna 4-49, Shreyas Gopal 3-42) lost to **India B** 214/5 in 40.3 overs (Manish Pandey 95*, Shubman Gill 42; Dane Paterson 2-33) by 30 runs (D/L method).

KSCA Cricket Ground, Alur, August 25: India A 217 in 49 overs (Ambati Rayudu 48, K Gowtham 35; Prasidh Krishna 4-50, Shreyas Gopal 2-38) lost to **India B** 218/3 in 41.1 overs (Mayank Agarwal 124, Shubman Gill 42; Khaleel Ahmed 2-33) by seven wickets. *PoM:* Mayank Agarwal.

M Chinnaswamy Stadium, Bengaluru, August 25: Australia A 322/5 in 50 overs (Travis Head 110, Marnus Labuschagne 65; Sisanda Magala 2-59) beat **South Africa A** 290 in 48.4 overs (Khaya Zondo 117, Gihahn Cloete 50; Mitchell Swepson 3-40, T Head 2-25) by 32 runs. *PoM:* Travis Head.

M Chinnaswamy Stadium, Bengaluru, August 27: India A 157 in 37.3 overs (Deepak Chahar 38, Sanju Samson 36; Dane Paterson 5-19, Robert Frylinck 2-36) lost to **South Africa A** 159/6 in 37.4 overs (Pieter Malan 47, Gihahn Cloete 24; Khaleel Ahmed 3-45, Krunal Pandya 2-37) by four wickets. *PoM:* Dane Paterson.

KSCA Cricket Ground, Alur, August 27: India B 276/6 in 50 overs (Manish Pandey 117*, Mayank Agarwal 36; Michael Neser 3-47) lost to **Australia A** 248/5 in 40 overs (Usman Khawaja 101*, Jack Wildermuth 62*; Jalaj Saxena 2-48) by five wickets (D/L method). *PoM:* Usman Khawaja.

KSCA Cricket Ground, Alur, August 29: India A 275/7 in 50 overs (Shreyas Iyer 67, Ambati Rayudu 66; Beuran Hendricks 3-39, Robert Frylinck 2-35) beat **South Africa A** 151 in 37.1 overs (Senuran Muthusamy 40, Farhaan Behardien 38*; Bhuvneshwar Kumar 3-33, Mayank Markande 2-30) by 124 runs.

Points table

Teams	M	W	L	T	N/R	Pts.	NRR
India B	5	2	1	0	2	12	+0.599
Australia A	5	2	1	0	2	12	-0.204
South Africa A	5	1	2	0	2	9	+0.006
India A	5	1	2	0	2	9	-0.3

India B and Australia A qualified for the final

Final: India B beat Australia A by nine wickets

M Chinnaswamy Stadium, Bengaluru, August 29: Australia A 225 in 47.5 overs (D'Arcy Short 72, Alex Carey 53; Shreyas Gopal 3-50, Siddarth Kaul 2-24) lost to **India B** 230/1 in 36.3 overs (Manish Pandey 73*, Mayank Agarwal 69) by nine wickets. *PoM:* Manish Pandey

Winners: India B

Australia A in India

Labuschagne, Khawaja conquer spin

This was a tour to test the readiness of Australia's next-gen in Steven Smith and David Warner's absence, ahead of the series against Pakistan in UAE. By the end of it, Travis Head, a South Australian, and Marnus Labuschagne, a South African-born Queenslander, took strides towards the baggy green. Head, captain on tour, manoeuvred spin expertly in the middle overs to finish as the second-highest run-getter in the quadrangular one-day series and the highest for Australia A in the two four-day fixtures. Labuschagne, meanwhile, exhibited the kind of poise rarely seen from Australia batsmen in the subcontinent recently. Usman Khawaja too banished his old demons against spin and displayed the kind of fleet-footedness he would use to his benefit during a monumental match-saving effort on the final day of a Dubai turner against Pakistan.

For India, the biggest gainer was Mohammad Siraj, whose polished red-ball efforts earned him a maiden Test call-up when West Indies toured India for two Tests in October. Siraj picked up 11 wickets in the only game he played, including an eight-for during which his ability to wildly reverse the old ball — a prospect that could make him lethal on dead tracks at home — surfaced.   *SK*

Most runs: Travis Head (206 runs, 2 matches)
Most wickets: Kuldeep Yadav (12 wickets, 2 matches)

Unofficial Test series (2): India A 1 Australia A 1

M Chinnaswamy Stadium, Bengaluru, September 2-5: Australia A 243 in 75.3 overs (Usman Khawaja 127, Marnus Labuschagne 60; Mohammed Siraj 8-59, Kuldeep Yadav 2-63) and 292 in 83.5 overs (Travis Head 87, U Khawaja 40; M Siraj 3-77, Kuldeep 2-51) beat **India A** 274 in 83.1overs (Ankit Bawne 91*, Mayank Agarwal 47; Michael Neser 4-61, Jon Holland 3-89) and 163 in 59.3 overs (M Agarwal 80, Shreyas Iyer 28; J Holland 6-81, Brendon Doggett 2-26) by 98 runs.

KSCA Cricket Ground, Alur, September 8-11: Australia A 346 in 109 overs (Mitchell Marsh 113*, Travis Head 68; Kuldeep Yadav 5-91, Shahbaz Nadeem 3-90) and 213 in 102.5 overs (Peter Handscomb 56, T Head 47; K Gowtham 3-39, Kuldeep 3-46) lost to **India A** 505 in 144overs (Srikar Bharat 106, Abhimanyu Easwaran 86; Chris Tremain 3-41, Ashton Agar 3-87) and 55/4 in 6.2 overs (Ankit Bawne 28*; C Tremain 2-26, Michael Nesar 2-28) by six wickets.

ACC Emerging Teams Cup

Sri Lanka snap India's winning streak

In a tournament marred by scheduling problems and issues with the playing conditions, co-hosts Sri Lanka walked away with the honours after a nervy three-run win over India in the final. Pakistan was to host the entire tournament, but after India refused to play in the country citing security concerns, six group stage matches were awarded to Colombo.

India advanced to the semi-final having won all their group stage matches, aided as much by centuries from Deepak Hooda, Himmat Singh as by Mayank Markande's four-wicket burst. Sri Lanka was the other team that qualified from Group A, while Pakistan and Bangladesh made the cut from Group B.

In the first semi-final, India rode on Markande's four-wicket haul and half-centuries from Himmat and Nitish Rana to trump Pakistan by seven wickets. Sri Lanka scaled Bangladesh's 238-run target in the second semi-final thanks to Kamindu Mendis's measured 91. Sri Lanka snapped India's winning streak by triggering a top-order wobble in pursuit of 271. A rearguard half-century from Jayant Yadav, the captain, wasn't enough and Sri Lanka pulled off a narrow win.

Mayank Markande topped the wickets charts. — *ACC*

DS

Most runs: Kamindu Mendis (Sri Lanka Emerging Team) (310 runs, 5 matches)
Most wickets: Mayank Markande (India Emerging Team) (12 wickets, 5 matches)

Group A

Colombo Cricket Club Ground, Colombo, December 7: India Emerging Team 281/8 in 50 overs (Deepak Hooda 105, Ankush Bains 34; Fazal Haque 3-54, Karim Janat 2-49) beat **Afghanistan Emerging Team** 207 in 44.4 overs (K Janat 58, Shahidullah Kamal 47; Jayant Yadav 3-37, Mayank Markande 3-41) by 74 runs.

R Premadasa Stadium, Khettarama, Colombo, December 7: Sri Lanka Emerging Team 324/5 in 50 overs (Hasitha Boyagoda 80, Kamindu Mendis 75; Jay Odedra 3-47, Bilal Khan 2-61) beat **Oman Emerging Team** 215/8 in 50 overs (Jatinder Singh 36, Ajay Lalcheta 34; Shammu Ashan 2-34, Shehan Madushanka 2-45) by 109 runs.

Colombo Cricket Club Ground, Colombo, December 7: Afghanistan Emerging Team 210 in 47.5 overs (Karim Janat 68, Shahidullah Kamal 38; Lasith Embuldeniya 3-35, Kamindu Mendis 3-46) lost to **Sri Lanka Emerging Team** 211/9 in 49.2 overs (K Mendis 71, Avishka Fernando 34, Shammu Ashan 34; Zia-ur-Rehman 3-33, K Janat 2-30) by one wicket.

R Premadasa Stadium, Khettarama, Colombo, December 7: Oman 203 in 44.2 overs (Aqib Ilyas 117, Ajay Lalcheta 25; Mayank Markande 4-41, Jayant Yadav 3-33) lost to **India Emerging Team Emerging Team** 206/4 in 41.1 overs (Ankush Bains 83, Himmat Singh 63; Jay Odedra 3-38) by six wickets.

R Premadasa Stadium, Khettarama, Colombo, December 7: Sri Lanka Emerging Team 260/7 in 50 overs (Avishka Fernando 80, Asela Gunaratne 67*; Shivam Mavi 3-62, Prasidh Krishna 2-47) lost to **India Emerging Team** 261/6 in 47.3 overs (Himmat Singh 126*, Ruturaj Gaikwad 67; Kamindu Mendis 3-51, Asitha Fernando 2-20) by four wickets.

Colombo Cricket Club Ground, Colombo, December 7: Afghanistan Emerging Team 252 in 49.1 overs (Najibullah Zadran 83, Qais Ahmed 66; Kaleemullah 3-39, Bilal Khan 2-31) beat **Oman Emerging Team** 140 in 39.5 overs (Moonamchery Michal 54, Jatinder Singh 30; Karim Janat 2-9, N Zadran 2-16) by 112 runs.

Points table

Teams	M	W	L	D	T	N/R	Pts	NRR
India Emerging Team	3	3	0	0	0	0	6	+0.928
Sri Lanka Emerging Team	3	2	1	0	0	0	4	+0.673
Afghanistan Emerging Team	3	1	2	0	0	0	2	+0.228
Oman Emerging Team	3	0	3	0	0	0	0	-1.820

India Emerging, Sri Lanka Emerging qualified for the semi-final

Group B

Southend Club Cricket Stadium, Karachi, December 6: UAE Emerging Team 267 in 49.4 overs (Ashfaq Ahmed 98, Ghulam Shabber 52; Shoriful Islam 4-55, Khaled Ahmed 3-65) beat **Bangladesh Emerging Team** 170 in 36.5 overs (Mizanur Rahman 43, Shafiul Islam 32; Imran Haider 4-35, Ahmed Raza 4-50) by 97 runs. *PoM: Ashfaq Ahmed.*

National Stadium, Karachi, December 6: Pakistan Emerging Team 366/3 in 50 overs (Sahibzada Farhan 130, Ali Imran 107; Aizaz Khan 2-92) beat **Hong Kong Emerging Team** 141 in 34 overs (Shahid Wasif 59, Nizakat Khan 25; Mohammad Ilyas 5-35, Khushdil Shah 2-5) by 225 runs. *PoM: Mohammad Ilyas.*

Southend Club Cricket Stadium, Karachi, December 7: Bangladesh Emerging Team

286/8 in 50 overs (Mosaddek Hossain 100, Zakir Hasan 49; Aizaz Khan 3-62, Ehsan Nawaz 2-48) beat **Hong Kong Emerging Team** 258/7 in 50 overs (Nizakat Khan 92, Babar Hayat 91; M Hossain 2-23, Khaled Ahmed 2-69) by 28 runs.

National Stadium, Karachi, December 7: UAE Emerging Team 233/9 in 50 overs (Ashfaq Ahmed 69, Muhammad Usman 51*; Ashiq Ali 3-34, Khushdil Shah 2-29) lost to **Pakistan Emerging Team** 235/1 in 39 overs (Hussain Talat 116*, Sahibzada Farhan 104*) by nine wickets.

National Stadium, Karachi, December 10: Bangladesh Emerging Team 309/5 in 50 overs (Mosaddek Hossain 85*, Zakir Hasan 69; Khushdil Shah 3-48, Muhammad Musa 2-55) beat **Pakistan** 225 in 46.5 overs (K Shah 61, Zeeshan Malik 47; Nayeem Hasan 3-36, M Hossain 2-32) by 84 runs. *PoM: Mosaddek Hossain.*

Southend Club Cricket Stadium, Karachi, December 10: Hong Kong Emerging Team 87/4 in 31 overs (Babar Hayat 45*) v **UAE Emerging Team**. No result.

Points table

Teams	M	W	L	D	T	N/R	Pts	NRR
Pakistan Emerging Team	3	2	1	0	0	0	4	+1.389
Bangladesh Emerging Team	3	2	1	0	0	0	4	+0.100
UAE Emerging Team	3	1	1	0	0	1	3	+0.449
Hong Kong Emerging Team	3	0	2	0	0	1	1	-2.530

Pakistan Emerging, Bangladesh Emerging qualified for the semi-final

Semi-finals

Colombo Cricket Club Ground, Colombo, December 13: Pakistan Emerging Team 172 in 44.4 overs (Mohammad Rizwan 67, Saud Shakeel 62; Mayank Markande 4-38, Ankit Rajpoot 2-19) lost to **India Emerging Team** 178/3 in 27.3 overs (Nitish Rana 60*, Himmat Singh 59*) by seven wickets.

R Premadasa Stadium, Khettarama, Colombo, December 13: Bangladesh Emerging Team 237 in 49.1 overs (Mizanur Rahman 72, Yasir Ali 66; Chamika Karunaratne 4-31, Asitha Fernando 2-50) lost to **Sri Lanka Emerging Team** 241/6 in 48.2 overs (Kamindu Mendis 91*, Sandun Weerakkody 47; Shoriful Islam 2-50) by six wickets.

Final

R Premadasa Stadium, Khettarama, Colombo, December 13: Sri Lanka Emerging Team 270/7 in 50 overs (Kamindu Mendis 61, Hasitha Boyagoda 54; Ankit Rajpoot 2-61) beat **India Emerging Team** 267/9 in 50 overs (Jayant Yadav 71, Shams Mulani 46; Asela Gunaratne 3-38, Lasith Embuldeniya 2-37) by three runs. *PoM: Kamindu Mendis. PoS: Kamindu Mendis.*

India A in New Zealand

Nair, Pandey make merry

The first four-day game was supposed to provide valuable match practice for the Australia-bound trio of Ajinkya Rahane, Rohit Sharma and M Vijay. Rohit, initially named captain for the Mount Maunganui fixture, was eventually rested due to workload concerns. Rahane, who led the side instead, and Vijay struggled even as the rest of the side put up a dominant show in the first innings. The duo, however, was among the runs in the second hit as India A drew the game.

Karun Nair took over the reins for the next two four-dayers that met a similar fate. Will Young's century headlined the severely rain-affect second match in Hamilton. Rain affected the third drawn game too, where Cam Fletcher's century and K Gowtham's six-wicket haul were the highlights.

Led by Manish Pandey, India A swept the one-day leg 3–0. In a high scoring match at Mount Maunganui, Vijay Shankar's unbeaten 87 and his 116-run fifth-wicket stand with Ishan Kishan steered India A to victory with an over to spare. The next game, Pandey's unbeaten 111 pipped Will Young's 102 as India A chased the 300-run target with ease. In the third one-dayer, Siddharth Kaul's 4 for 37 triggered a middle-order collapse and sealed the sweep.

DS

	First-class	List A
Most runs	Will Young (New Zealand A) (189 runs, 3 matches)	Vijay Shankar (India A) (188 runs, 3 matches)
Most wickets	K Gowtham (India A) (9 wickets, 2 matches)	Siddharth Kaul (India A) (7 wickets, 3 matches)

Unofficial Tests (3): New Zealand A 0 India A 0

Bay Oval, Mount Maunganui, November 16-19: India A 467/8 dec. in 122.1 overs (Parthiv Patel 94, Hanuma Vihari 86; Blair Tickner 4-80) and 247/3 in 65 overs (M Vijay 60, H Vihari 51*) drew with **New Zealand A** 458/9 dec. in 134 overs (Hamish Rutherford 114, Seth Rance 69*; K Gowtham 3-107, Deepak Chahar 2-51).

Seddon Park, Hamilton, November 23-26: New Zealand A 303/7 dec. in 106 overs (Will Young 123, Theo van Woerkom 54; Mohammed Siraj 4-59, Rajneesh Gurbani 2-60) drew with **India A** 159/2 in 46 overs (Ravikumar Samarth 50*, Abhimanyu Easwaran 47).

Cobham Oval, Whangarei, November 30-December 3: India A 323 in 89 overs (Vijay Shankar 71, Shubman Gill 62; Doug Bracewell 5-78, Lockie Ferguson 4-88) and 38/1 in 14 overs (Ravikumar Samarth 27*) drew with **New Zealand A** 398 in 131.4 overs (Cam Fletcher 103, Tim Seifert 86; K Gowtham 6-139, Mohammed Siraj 2-82).

One-dayers (3): India A 3 New Zealand A 0

Bay Oval, Mount Maunganui, December 7: New Zealand A 308/6 in 50 overs (Jimmy Neesham 79*, Hamish Rutherford 70; Siddharth Kaul 2-74) lost to **India A** 311/6 in 49 overs

(Vijay Shankar 87*, Shreyas Iyer 54; Hamish Bennett 2-65, Lockie Ferguson 2-75) by four wickets.

Bay Oval, Mount Maunganui, December 9: New Zealand A 299/9 in 50 overs (Will Young 102, George Worker 99; Khaleel Ahmed 2-65, Navdeep Saini 2-68) lost to **India** 300/5 in 49 overs (Manish Pandey 111*, Shreyas Iyer 59, Vijay Shankar 59; Cole McConchie 2-39, Hamish Bennett 2-45) by five wickets.

Bay Oval, Mount Maunganui, December 11: India A 275/8 in 50 overs (Anmolpreet Singh 75, Ankit Bawne 48; Seth Rance 3-49, Lockie Ferguson 2-20) beat **New Zealand A** 200 in 44.2 overs (Tim Seifert 55, Daryl Mitchell 30; Siddharth Kaul 4-37, K Gowtham 2-40) by 75 runs.

England Lions in India

Hosts' depth on display

KL Rahul, struggling for form and the subject of much public criticism for his comments with Hardik Pandya on a talk show, was handed a chance to find a path to redemption in Thiruvananthapuram under the steady gaze of Rahul Dravid. He overcame a patchy start to contribute to India's series wins with three fifties across formats.

Ben Duckett, on a redemption journey of his own, and Sam Billings fought for England, but India's batting was too strong. Ajinkya Rahane in the one-dayers, and double-centurion Priyank Panchal in the first-class game dominated, while bowlers Navdeep Saini and Mayank Markande put them to the sword.

For England, there was a sour note before the tour began: Joe Clarke and Tom Kohler-Cadmore were dropped from the squad, following revelations about their role in a 'game' about their sexual escapades, details of which emerged during the rape trial of their former Worcestershire team-mate, Alex Hepburn.

	List A	**First-class**
Most runs	Sam Billings (England Lions) (156 runs, 5 matches)	Priyank Panchal (India A) (256 runs, 2 matches)
Most wickets	Axar Patel (India A) (8 wickets, 4 matches)	Navdeep Saini (India A) (9 wickets, 2 matches)

Tour matches

St Xavier's College Ground, Thumba, Thiruvananthapuram, January 18: England Lions 255/6 in 50 overs (Alex Davies 100, Sam Hain 31, Sam Billings 31; Mayank Markande 3-41) lost to **India A** 256/6 in 49.2 overs (Ruturaj Gaikwad 110, Ricky Bhui 93*; Zak Chappell 3-53) by four wickets.

St Xavier's College Ground, Thumba, Thiruvananthapuram, January 20: England Lions 104 in 22.3 overs (Sam Billings 52; Pankaj Jaiswal 4-16, Navdeep Saini 4-32) lost to **India A** 105/5 in 21.2 overs (Deepak Hooda 36*, Ishan Kishan 34; Jamie Porter 5-36) by five wickets.

One-day series (5): India A 4 England Lions 1

Greenfield International Stadium, Thiruvananthapuram, January 23: England Lions 285/7 in 50 overs (Sam Billings 108*, Alex Davies 54; Mayank Markande 2-45, Axar Patel 2-52) lost to **India A** 288/7 in 49.1 overs (Ajinkya Rahane 59, Ishan Kishan 57*; Zak Chappell 3-84, Danny Briggs 2-31) by three wickets. *PoM:* Ishan Kishan.

Greenfield stadium, Thiruvananthapuram, January 25: India A 303/6 in 50 overs (Hanuma Vihari 92, Ajinkya Rahane 91; Zak Chappell 2-47, Lewis Gregory 2-61) beat **England Lions** 165 in 37.4 overs (Alex Davies 48, L Gregory 39*; Mayank Markande 3-32, Axar Patel 2-13) by 138 runs. *PoM:* Hanuma Vihari.

Greenfield International Stadium, Thiruvananthapuram, January 27: India A 172 in 47.1 overs (Deepak Chahar 39, Ishan Kishan 30; Jamie Overton 3-34, Matthew Carter 2-23) beat **England Lions** 112 in 30.5 overs (Ben Duckett 39, Ollie Pope 27; Krunal Pandya 4-21, Navdeep Saini 2-21) by 60 runs. *PoM:* Krunal Pandya.

Ishan Kishan was a regular of the A tours. — *KCA*

Greenfield International Stadium, Thiruvananthapuram, January 29: England Lions 221/8 in 50 overs (Ollie Pope 65, Steven Mullaney 58*; Shardul Thakur 4-49, Rahul Chahar 2-38) lost to **India A** 222/4 in 46.3 overs (Rishabh Pant 73*, Deepak Hooda 47*; Will Jacks 2-35) by six wickets. *PoM:* Rishabh Pant.

Greenfield International Stadium, Thiruvananthapuram, January 31: India A 121 in 35 overs (Siddhesh Lad 36; Jamie Overton 3-24, Tom Bailey 2-23) lost to **England Lions** 125/9 in 30.3 overs (Ben Duckett 70*; Deepak Chahar 3-25, Rahul Chahar 3-43) by one wicket. *PoM:* Ben Duckett.

Tour match

St Xavier's College Ground, Thumba, Thiruvananthapuram, February 3-4: **England Lions** 145/6 in 60 overs (Sam Hain 40*, Max Holden 38; Ankit Rajpoot 4-20) and 83/2 in 30 overs (Sam Billings 36*) lost to **Indian Board President's XI** 134/5 in 30 overs (Ishan Kishan 40*, Siddhesh Lad 27; Jamie Porter 2-22, Zak Chappell 2-23) and 246/6 in 60 overs (I Kishan 55*, Ricky Bhui 51rh; Danny Briggs 2-40, Dom Bess 2-51) by 152 runs.

Unofficial Tests (2): India A 1 England Lions 0

Krishnagiri Stadium, Wayanad, February 7-10: **England Lions** 340 in 104.3 overs (Ben Duckett 80, Will Jacks 63; Navdeep Saini 5-79, Shardul Thakur 2-77) and 214/5 in 83 overs (Ollie Pope 63, Sam Hain 57; Jalaj Saxena 2-41, Shahbaz Nadeem 2-56) drew with **India A** 540/6 dec. in 134.5 overs (Priyank Panchal 206, Srikar Bharat 142; Zak Chappell 3-105, Danny Briggs 2-144).

Krishnagiri Stadium, Wayanad, February 13-15: **India A** 392 in 114.4 overs (Abhimanyu Easwaran 117, KL Rahul 81; Zak Chappell 4-60, Danny Briggs 3-71) beat **England Lions** 144 in 48.4 overs (Ollie Pope 25; Navdeep Saini 3-30, Shahbaz Nadeem 3-32) and 180 in 53.3 overs (Ben Duckett 50, Lewis Gregory 44; Mayank Markande 5-31, Jalaj Saxena 2-40) by an innings and 68 runs.

Sri Lanka A in India

Visitors come back from behind

After being brushed aside by India A in the unofficial 'Tests', Sri Lanka A came back from 0-2 to level the one-day series. India A set the tone of the first-class game on the first day, with Abhimanyu Easwaran posting a colossal 352-run stand with captain Priyank Panchal. Anmolpreet Singh also joined in the fun, following which the tourists sank under the sheer volume of runs. The seamers provided early breakthroughs, and Rahul Chahar's leg-breaks did the rest.

Sri Lanka A did better in the second match. Lahiru Kumara dismissed both Indian openers for ducks, but Chahar followed his 84 with five fourth-innings wickets.

Till a point it seemed that the one-day games would follow the same track. In the first match, Ruturaj Gaikwad's incredible 136-ball unbeaten 187 took India A to 317 for 4 — that too in a match reduced to 42 overs a side. Sri Lanka A were never in the hunt, despite Shehan Jayasuriya's 108.

An inspired new-ball spell by Ishan Porel and Tushar Deshpande left Sri Lanka A reeling at 16 for 3 in the next match. Jayasuriya scored another hundred in the rescue, but then, so did Gaikwad, in response. The hero of the chase, however, was Shubman Gill, who had to retire with cramps with 109.

The turnaround began in the third match, where India A took field without both Gaikwad and Gill. This time Prashant Chopra got the hundred, but Chamika Karunaratne took five wickets and fifties from Niroshan Dickwella, Sangeeth Cooray, and Jayasuriya saw them through.

A sixth match was added after rain prevented the next two matches from producing results. Akila Dananjaya and Lakshan Sandakan, left out of Sri Lanka's World Cup squad, prevented the Indian middle order from putting up big partnerships. Dickwella and Cooray put on 165 for the first wicket, and Sri Lanka A won with 14 balls to spare.

	First-class	List A
Most runs	Anmolpreet Singh (India A) (241 runs, 2 matches)	Ruturaj Gaikwad (India A) (470 runs, 5 matches)
Most wickets	Rahul Chahar (India A) (14 wickets, 2 matches)	Chamika Karunaratne (Sri Lanka A) (7 wickets, 4 matches)

First-class matches (2): India A 2 Sri Lanka A 0

Union Gymkhana Ground, Belgaum, May 25-27: India A 622/5 dec. in 142 overs (Abhimanyu Easwaran 233, Priyank Panchal 160, Anmolpreet Singh 116*; Vishwa Fernando 2-83) beat **Sri Lanka A** 232 in 63.4 overs (Niroshan Dickwella 103, Ashan Priyanjan 49; Rahul

Chahar 4-78, Shivam Dube 2-19) and 185 in 52.3 overs (Sadeera Samarawickrama 48, A Priyanjan 39; R Chahar 4-45, Ankit Rajpoot 2-11) by an innings and 205 runs. *PoM:* Abhimanyu Easwaran.

Nehru Stadium, Hubli, May 31-June 3: India A 269 in 69.1 overs (Srikar Bharat 117, Anmolpreet Singh 65; Lahiru Kumara 4-53, Lakshan Sandakan 4-64) and 372 in 82.2 overs (Rahul Chahar 84, Anmolpreet 60, S Bharat 60; Vishwa Fernando 3-68, L Sandakan 3-87) beat **Sri Lanka A** 212 in 60 overs (Kamindu Mendis 68, Niroshan Dickwella 39; Jayant Yadav 3-24, Sandeep Warrier 2-32) and 277 in 66.4 overs (Bhanuka Rajapaksa 110, K Mendis 46; R Chahar 5-112, Shivam Dube 2-26) by 152 runs. *PoM:* Srikar Bharat.

List A matches (6): India A 2 Sri Lanka A 2

Union Gymkhana Ground, Belgaum, June 6: India A 317/4 in 42 overs (Ruturaj Gaikwad 187*, Anmolpreet Singh 65; Lahiru Kumara 3-65) beat **Sri Lanka A** 269/6 in 42 overs (Shehan Jayasuriya 108*, Dasun Shanaka 44; Mayank Markande 2-66) by 48 runs. *PoM:* Ruturaj Gaikwad.

Union Gymkhana Ground, Belgaum, June 8: Sri Lanka A 242/7 in 50 overs (Shehan Jayasuriya 101, Ishan Jayaratne 79*; Shivam Dube 2-47, Tushar Deshpande 2-51) lost to **India A** 243 for no loss in 33.3 overs (Ruturaj Gaikwad 125*, Shubman Gill 109) by ten wickets. *PoM:* Shubman Gill.

Union Gymkhana Ground, Belgaum, June 10: India A 291/8 in 50 overs (Prashant Chopra 129, Deepak Hooda 53; Chamika Karunaratne 5-36) lost to **Sri Lanka A** 266/4 in 43.5 overs (Sangeeth Cooray 88, Shehan Jayasuriya 66*; Shivam Dube 2-27) by six wickets (DLS Method). *PoM:* Chamika Karunaratne.

Nehru Stadium, Hubli, June 13: India A 208/4 in 22 overs (Anmolpreet Singh 85*, Ruturaj Gaikwad 84; Lahiru Kumara 2-34) v **Sri Lanka** 10/1 in 1.5 overs. No result.

Nehru Stadium, Hubli, June 14: Sri Lanka A 22/1 in 3.3 overs v **India A**. No result.

Nehru Stadium, Hubli, June 13: India A 259 in 50 overs (Ruturaj Gaikwad 74, Ricky Bhui 38; Akila Dananjaya 3-51, Ashan Priyanjan 2-23) lost to **Sri Lanka** 260/3 in 47.4 overs (Niroshan Dickwella 111, Sangeeth Cooray 61; Shreyas Gopal 3-49) by seven wickets. *PoM:* Niroshan Dickwella.

India Under-19s remained unbeaten through the touranament. — *ACC*

ACC Under-19 Asia Cup 2018

Jaiswal carries India U19 to title

Close on the heels of India's Under-19 World Cup triumph came another piece of silverware: the Asia Cup claimed by overwhelming Sri Lanka. Harsh Tyagi's six-wicket haul confirmed a one-sided contest, after Yashasvi Jaiswal's measured 113-ball 85 at the top of the order and half-centuries from Anuj Rawat, Prab Simran Singh and Ayush Badoni set the tone for their sixth Asia Cup title. Jaiswal was prolific throughout, registering scores of 104, 92 and 37 prior to the final. His form coincided with India's unbeaten run through the round-robin stage before advancing to the final with a two-run win over Bangladesh.

Afghanistan, the defending champions, won two of their three group stage matches, but a batting collapse in the semi-final against Sri Lanka brought an early end to their campaign. Sri Lanka, who were unbeaten until the final, had no answer against a spirited Indian side. Bangladesh couldn't make the most of home advantage in the play-off. *DS*

Most runs: Yashasvi Jaiswal (India U19) (214 runs, 3 matches)
Most wickets: Harsh Tyagi (India U19) (11 wickets, 3 matches)

Group A

Bangladesh Krira Shikkha Protisthan No. 4 Ground, Savar, September 29: UAE Under-19s 140 in 43.5 overs (Brandon Adam 25; Qais Ahmed 4-40) lost to **Afghanistan Under-19s** 144/5 in 27 overs (Azmatullah Omarzai 50; KR Meiyappan 2-39) by five wickets. *PoM:* Azmatullah Omarzai.

Bangladesh Krira Shikkha Protisthan No. 3 Ground, Savar, September 29: India Under-19s 304/9 in 50 overs (Yashasvi Jaiswal 104, Simran Singh 82; Bhim Sharki 4-42, Rashid Khan 2-45) beat **Nepal Under-19s** 133 in 36.5 overs (Aasif Sheikh 25; Siddharth Desai 3-19, Harsh Tyagi 3-21) by 171 runs. *PoM:* Yashasvi Jaiswal.

Bangladesh Krira Shikkha Protisthan No. 3 Ground, Savar, September 30: India Under-19s 354/6 in 50 overs (Devdutt Padikkal 121, Anuj Rawat 102; Alishan Sharafu 2-46, Aaron Benjamin 2-88) beat **UAE Under-19s** 127 in 33.5 overs (Ali Mirza 41; Siddharth Desai 6-25) by 227 runs. *PoM:* Devdutt Padikkal.

Bangladesh Krira Shikkha Protisthan No. 4 Ground, Savar, October 1: Nepal Under-19s 131 in 38.3 overs (Rohit Paudel 46, Rashid Khan 30; Azmatullah Omarzai 4-14, Abdul Rahman 2-21) lost to **Afghanistan Under-19s** 136/7 in 37.3 overs (Rahmanullah Gurbaz 26; Surya Tamang 4-36) by three wickets. *PoM:* Azmatullah Omarzai.

Bangladesh Krira Shikkha Protisthan No. 3 Ground, Savar, October 1: India Under-19s 221 in 45.3 overs (Yashasvi Jaiswal 92, Ayush Badoni 65; Qais Ahmed 3-46, Abid Mohammadi 2-28) beat **Afghanistan Under-19s** 170 in 45.4 overs (Riaz Hussain 47, Rahmanullah Gurbaz 37; Siddharth Desai 4-37, Harsh Tyagi 3-40) by 41 runs. *PoM:* Yashasvi Jaiswal.

Bangladesh Krira Shikkha Protisthan No. 4 Ground, Savar, October 2: UAE Under-19s 268/8 in 50 overs (Fahad Nawaz 83, Ansh Tandon 68; Pawan Sarraf 2-43, Nandan Yadav 2-51, Rashid Khan 2-51) lost to **Nepal Under-19s** 274/7 in 49.1 overs (Rohit Paudel 91, Sundeep Jora 67; Aaron Benjamin 2-23, Aryan Lakra 2-37) by three wickets. *PoM:* Rohit Paudel.

Points table

Teams	M	W	L	D	T	N/R	Pts	NRR
India Under-19s	3	3	0	0	0	0	6	+2.993
Afghanistan Under-19s	3	2	1	0	0	0	4	+0.650
Nepal Under-19s	3	1	2	0	0	0	2	-1.544
UAE Under-19s	3	0	3	0	0	0	0	-2.544

India Under-19s and Afghanistan Under-19s qualified for the semi-final

Group B

Zohur Ahmed Chowdhury Stadium, Chittagong, September 29: Bangladesh Under-19s 141 in 46.4 overs (Towhid Hridoy 35; Shashika Dulshan 2-11, Dulith Wellalage 2-21) lost to **Sri Lanka Under-19s** 144/4 in 37.5 overs (Nuwanidu Fernando 64*, Pasindu Sooriyabandara 36; Shoriful Islam 2-29) by six wickets. *PoM:* Nuwanidu Fernando.

MA Aziz Stadium, Chittagong, September 29: Hong Kong Under-19s 77 in 33 overs (Haroon Arshed 36; Naseem Shah 5-13, Junaid Khan 3-23) lost to **Pakistan Under-19s** 78/1 in 14.4 overs (Mohsin Khan 32*) by nine wickets. *PoM:* Naseem Shah.

Zohur Ahmed Chowdhury Stadium, Chittagong, September 30: Hong Kong Under-19s 56 in 33.1 overs (Shashika Dulshan 5-19, Dulith Wellalage 2-5) **lost to Sri Lanka Under-19s**

57 for no loss in 9.2 overs (Nipun Dananjaya 35*) by ten wickets. *PoM:* Shashika Dulshan.

MA Aziz Stadium, Chittagong, October 1: Pakistan Under-19s 187 in 45.2 overs (Waqar Ahmed 67, Saim Ayub 49; Rishad Hossain 3-53, Shoriful Islam 2-20) lost to **Bangladesh Under-19s** 191/7 in 47.2 overs (Shamim Hossain 65rh, Prantik Nawroz 58; Muhammad Musa 3-24) by three wickets. *PoM:* Shamim Hossain.

Zohur Ahmed Chowdhury Stadium, Chittagong, October 2: Hong Kong Under-19s 91 in 46.5 overs (Rishad Hossain 3-11, Mrittunjoy Chowdhury 2-16) lost to **Bangladesh Under-19s** 92/5 in 11.2 overs (Mahmudul Hasan 32*, Akbar Ali 25; Narsulla Rana 4-39) by five wickets. *PoM:* Rishad Hossain.

MA Aziz Stadium, Chittagong, October 2: Sri Lanka Under-19s 200 in 49.4 overs (Kalana Perera 51, Nipun Dananjaya 33; Arshad Iqbal 6-34, Bilal Javed 2-25) beat **Pakistan Under-19s** 177/8 in 50 overs (Awaiz Zafar 43, A Iqbal 26*; Navod Paranavithana 2-27, Dulith Wellalage 2-28) by 23 runs. *PoM:* Arshad Iqbal.

Points table

Teams	M	W	L	D	T	N/R	Pts	NRR
Sri Lanka Under-19s	3	3	0	0	0	0	6	+1.644
Bangladesh Under-19s	3	2	1	0	0	0	4	+0.840
Pakistan Under-19s	3	1	2	0	0	0	2	+0.678
Hong Kong Under-19s	3	0	3	0	0	0	0	-4.959

India Under-19s and Afghanistan Under-19s qualified for the semi-final

Semi-finals

Sher-e-Bangla National Stadium, Mirpur, October 4: India Under-19s 172 in 49.3 overs (Yashasvi Jaiswal 37, Anuj Rawat 35; Shoriful Islam 3-16, Towhid Hridoy 2-4) beat **Bangladesh Under-19s** 170 in 46.2 overs (Shamim Hossain 59, Akbar Ali 45; Mohit Jangra 3-25, Siddharth Desai 3-35) by two runs. *PoM:* Mohit Jangra.

Sher-e-Bangla National Stadium, Mirpur, October 5: Sri Lanka Under-19s 209/7 in 50 overs (Nuwanidu Fernando 111, Nipun Dananjaya 27; Abdul Rahman 3-42) beat **Afghanistan Under-19s** 178 in 48.3 overs (Rahmanullah Gurbaz 46, Ijaz Ahmad 37; Shashika Dulshan 4-24, Navod Paranavithana 2-17) by 31 runs. *PoM:* Nuwanidu Fernando.

Final

Sher-e-Bangla National Stadium, Mirpur, October 7: India Under-19s 304/3 in 50 overs (Yashasvi Jaiswal 85, Simran Singh 65*) beat **Sri Lanka Under-19s** 160 in 38.4 overs (Navod Paranavithana 48, Pasindu Sooriyabandara 31; Harsh Tyagi 6-38, Siddharth Desai 2-37) by 144 runs. *PoM:* Harsh Tyagi. *PoS:* Yashasvi Jaiswal.

Winners: India Under-19s

South Africa Under-19s in India

Visitors crumble against spin

The off-spin of Hrithik Shokeen proved too much for the South African batsmen, who couldn't cross 200 in any of their innings. India had to bat just thrice, one of those to chase 37. The left-arm spin of Manishi and medium-pace of Anshul Kamboj offered Shokeen good support. Yashasvi Jaiswal's high score of 173 in the second match was one of three centuries for India, Divyaansh Saxena and Vaibhav Kandpal accounting for the others. Bryce Parsons, with two half-centuries, offered some resistance for South Africa.

Most runs: Yashasvi Jaiswal (India Under-19s) (197 runs, 2 matches)
Most wickets: Hrithik Shokeen (India Under-19s) (10 wickets, 2 matches)

Youth Test series (2): India U19 2 South Africa U19 0
Greenfield International Stadium, Thiruvananthapuram, February 20-22: South Africa Under-19s 197 in 67.5 overs (Bryce Parsons 58, Matthew Montgomery 57; Hrithik Shokeen 4-50, Anshul Kamboj 2-28) and 167 in 66 overs (Bonga Makhakha 74, Andile Mokgakane 30; Manav Suthar 3-44, H Shokeen 3-52) lost to **India Under-19s** 330 in 92.3 overs (Divyaansh Saxena 122, Suraj Ahuja 57; B Parsons 6-77, Lifa Ntanzi 2-56) and 37/1 in 7.5 overs by nine wickets. *PoM:* Divyaansh Saxena.
Greenfield International Stadium, Thiruvananthapuram, February 20-22: South Africa Under-19s 152 in 54.4 overs (Bryce Parsons 64, Ruan Terblanche 51; Manishi 5-58, Hrithik Shokeen 2-44) and 85 in 45.4 overs (Matthew Montgomery 36; Rex Singh 4-18, Anshul Kamboj 3-20) lost to **India Under-19s** 395 in 101.2 overs (Yashasvi Jaiswal 173, Vaibhav Kandpal 120; Lifa Ntanzi 4-90, M Montgomery 3-49) by an innings and 158 runs. *PoM:* Yashasvi Jaiswal.

Quadrangular Under-19 series in India

Chandrol takes India B to honours

It was an all-India final. India B' captain Rahul Chandrol's second half-century of the tournament came at the opportune time. With Sameer Rizvi supporting him in a 99-run fourth-wicket stand, the duo overcame a wobbly start before Sushant Mishra's double-strike in the fourth over to send back the India A openers struck a blow that the opposition could not recover from.

South Africa could take comfort in individual honours, while Harsh Dubey's 3 for 7 in the first match was another highlight for India A.

Most runs: Andile Mokgakane (South Africa Under-19s) (140 runs, 4 matches)
Most wickets: Marco Jansen (South Africa Under-19s) (8 wickets, 4 matches)

League

Greenfield International Stadium, Thiruvananthapuram, March 5: India A Under-19s 251 in 50 overs (Shashwat Rawat 64, Qamran Iqbal 60; Marco Jansen 4-30, Nonelela Yikha 2-37) beat **South Africa Under-19s** 94 in 35.4 overs (M Jansen 33; Harsh Dubey 3-7, Ravi Bishnoi 3-27-) by 157 runs. *PoM:* Qamran Iqbal.

St Xavier's College Ground, Thumba, March 5: Afghanistan Under-19s 106 in 47.3 overs (Jamshid Khan 28; Purnank Tyagi 4-36, Prayas Ray Barman 3-10) lost to **India B Under-19s** 107/3 in 22.5 overs (Rahul Chandrol 56*, Tilak Varma 44*; Abdul Rahman 2-28) by seven wickets. *PoM:* Purnank Tyagi.

Greenfield International Stadium, Thiruvananthapuram, March 7: India A Under-19s 252 in 47.4 overs (Siddhesh Veer 81, Shashwat Rawat 45; Shafiqullah Ghafari 4-35, Arif Khan 2-4) beat **Afghanistan Under-19s** 160 in 48.4 overs (Arif 33, Farhan Zakhil 28, S Ghafari 28; Yuvraj Chaudhary 3-24, S Veer 2-11) by 91 runs. *PoM:* Siddhesh Veer.

St Xavier's College Ground, Thumba, March 7: India B Under-19s 198 in 49.1 overs (Pragnesh Kanpillewar 42, Sameer Rizvi 40; Siya Plaatjie 3-40, Bryce Parsons 2-41) beat **South Africa Under-19s** 197/9 in 50 overs (Ruan Terblanche 73, Andile Mokgakane 64; Sumit Juyal 2-18, Karan Lal 2-29) by one run. *PoM:* Andile Mokgakane.

St Xavier's College Ground, Thumba, March 9: India A Under-19s 129 in 40.3 overs (Dhruv Jurel 40, Yashasvi Jaiswal 30; Shivam Sharma 3-15, Karan Lal 2-18) lost to **India B Under-19s** 130/7 in 41.4 overs (Arya Sethi 51, Atharva Ankolekar 29*; Yuvraj Chaudhary 2-18, Shubhang Hegde 2-20) by one wicket. *PoM:* Shivam Sharma.

Greenfield International Stadium, Thiruvananthapuram, March 9: South Africa Under-19s 200 in 49.5 overs (Luke Beaufort 40, Bryce Parsons 40; Riaz Hussan 3-26, Shafiqullah Ghafari 2-24) beat **Afghanistan** 191 in 48.3 overs (Farhan Zakhil 63, R Hussan 35; Marco Jansen 4-23, B Parsons 2-32) by nine runs. *PoM:* Bryce Parsons.

Points table

Teams	M	W	L	D	T	N/R	Pts	NRR
India B Under-19s	3	3	0	0	0	0	13	+0.919
India A Under-19s	3	2	1	0	0	0	10	+1.503
South Africa Under-19s	3	1	2	0	0	0	4	-0.993
Afghanistan Under-19s	3	0	3	0	0	0	0	-1.504

India A Under-19s and India B Under-19s qualified for the final

3rd place play-off

St Xavier's College Ground, Thumba, March 11: South Africa Under-19s 231/8 in 50 overs (Matthew Montgomery 73, Bryce Parsons 44; Abdullah Tarakhail 3-25, Fazal Haque 2-45) beat **Afghanistan Under-19s** 176 in 45 overs (Ijaz Ahmad 70*; Kgaudisa Molefe 4-31, Andile Mokgakane 3-24) by 55 runs. *PoM:* Matthew Montgomery.

Final: India B U19 beat India A U19 by 72 runs

Greenfield International Stadium, Thiruvananthapuram, March 11: India B Under-19s 232/9 in 50 overs (Rahul Chandrol 70, Sameer Rizvi 67; Kartik Tyagi 3-33, Shubhang Hegde 2-35) beat **India A Under-19s** 160 in 38.3 overs (S Hegde 42, Yashasvi Jaiswal 27, Shashwat Rawat 27; Sushant Mishra 4-41, Kunal Lal 3-25) by 72 runs. *PoM:* Rahul Chandrol.

Afghanistan's win in the Under-19 Asia Cup 2017 was emphatic. — *ACC*

2017-18

Under-19 Asia Cup 2017

Mujeeb headlines Afghanistan's rise

The tournament stood out for one big reason: the rise of Afghanistan. The ICC's newest Full Member has been making waves at senior level for the best part of a decade, but the U19 Asia Cup in Malaysia was the first instance in which the trickle-down effect on their junior side was evident. The way Afghanistan secured their maiden Asia Cup title stood out. Apart from a loss to Sri Lanka, they dominated ever match they played, including the final in which they beat Pakistan handsomely by 185 runs.

Observers got the first whiff of some of Afghanistan's future stalwarts, including Mujeeb Ur Rahman, who went on to make his international debut within a year of the tournament. Mujeeb's 5 for 13 helped Afghanistan bundle out Pakistan for 63 in just 22.1 overs in the final, after Ikram Ali Khil's 107 not out helped them set a 249-run target.

Bangladesh, unbeaten till then, may well have displaced Pakistan in the final had they won a thrilling semi-final: Pakistan claimed it by two runs on DLS. Nepal showed promise, finishing above third-placed India — even accounting for the fact that the sub-continent giants played a second-string side. *MN*

Most runs: Mohammad Taha (Pakistan Under-19) (250 runs, 5 matches)
Most wickets: Mujeeb Ur Rahman (Afghanistan Under-19) (20 wickets, 5 matches)

Group A

Team	M	W	L	Pts	NRR
Bangladesh U19	3	3	0	6	2.377
Nepal U19	3	2	1	4	0.889
India U19	3	1	2	2	1.257
Malaysia U19	3	0	3	0	-4.757

Group B

Team	M	W	L	Pts	NRR
Afghanistan U19	3	2	1	4	2.853
Pakistan U19	3	2	1	4	1.24
Sri Lanka U19	3	2	1	4	-0.988
UAE U19	3	0	3	0	-4.964

Bangladesh U19, Nepal U19, Afghanistan U19, Pakistan U19 qualified for the semi-final; Afghanistan U19 and Pakistan U19

Final: Afghanistan U19 beat Pakistan U19 by 185 runs

Kinrara Academy Oval, Kuala Lumpur, November 19: Afghanistan U19 248/7 in 50 overs (Ikram Ali Khil 107*, Rahmanullah Gurbaz 40; Muhammad Musa 3-46, Shaheen Shah Afridi 2-42) beat **Pakistan U19** 63 in 22.1 overs (Mujeeb Ur Rahman 5-13, Qais Ahmad 3-18) by 185 runs. *PoM:* Ikram Ali Khil.

Winners: Afghanistan Under-19

Shubman Gill's century in the semi-final against Pakistan was a sign of his maturity.
— *ICC*

Under-19 World Cup 2018

Gill, Shaw hold mirror to the future

MANOJ NARAYAN

It was only when the dust settled after India's triumph and Prithvi Shaw posed at the beach, with the gorgeous Mount Maunganui in the backdrop, that it began to sink in: India's fourth junior World Cup triumph was no ordinary feat. They beat Australia in the final by eight wickets, their worst winning margin in the whole tournament. Every other win was by ten wickets or at least 100 runs.

Every side had talented boys, but India's professionalism set them apart. This was a well-oiled, well-drilled machine. Their lifting of the trophy was the culmination of an 18-month effort, and quite simply, they were groomed to win this tournament. None of the other 15 teams even came close in terms of preparation.

None of which is to say this was cold-blooded unit. No, there was plenty of emotion in the side. A few hours after the final was won and the Bay Oval was nearly deserted, the whole Indian team, backroom staff and all, led by coach Rahul Dravid, walked out to the middle. There they formed a huddle for a deeply private moment. When they disengaged, there was pandemonium. They were teenagers again, after a tournament as pretend-men, and the spirit in the side that powered their tittle charge was evident.

The experience gained from this tournament was immense. Take Afghanistan. They finished ninth in the 2016 edition. This time, they reached the semi-finals. It's not necessarily because they had a better pool of players, but because the management learned their lessons, and made it a point to make their systems more professional. The day isn't far an Afghanistan wins one of these tournaments.

Kohli always speaks of how modern youngsters are already well-rounded players in their teens, more than what his generation was at the same stage. That was evident in the way Prithvi Shaw and Shubman Gill showed different facets of their batting, the way Lloyd Pope demolished England to raise hopes for leg-spin, and how some of these youngsters handled the media.

Most runs: Alick Athanaze (West Indies Under-19) (418 runs, 6 matches)
Most wickets: Anukul Roy (India Under-19) (14 wickets, 6 matches)

Final: India U19 beat Australia U19 by eight wickets
Bay Oval, Mount Maunganui, February 3: Australia U19 216 in 47.2 overs (Jonathan Merlo 76, Param Uppal 34; Ishan Porel 2-30, Anukul Roy 3-32) lost to **India U19** 220/2 in 38.5 overs (Manjot Kalra 101*, Harvik Desai 47*) by eight wickets. *PoM:* Manjot Kalra. *PoS:* Shubman Gill.

India Under-19 in Sri Lanka 2018

Shah double-ton leads Indian charge

A 'Tendulkar' was again a part of an India squad. Sachin's son, Arjun, was named for the four-dayers in Sri Lanka, but there was more to the series than him, of course. It was India's first outing since their triumph at the ICC Under-19 World Cup in New Zealand, and Rahul Dravid's policy of shifting players on after a World Cup meant this was a fresh squad.

Expectations were high after that World Cup win, and India more than matched them: they dominated the two four-day matches, winning both by an innings, but had a tougher time in the five one-day matches, although they came through the series with a 3–2 victory.

Pawan Shah was a stand-out in the four-dayers; he scored a 332-ball 282 in the first innings of the second match, while Atharwa Taide, the opener, impressed as well with centuries in each match. Mohit Jangra, the left-arm pacer, took 5 for 72 in the first match.

The Indian squad came back from behind to take the one-dayers, with Shah again the top scorer. *MN*

	Youth Tests	**Youth ODIs**
Most runs	Pawan Shah (India) (320 runs, 2 matches)	Pawan Shah (India) (210 runs, 5 matches)
Most wickets	Mohit Jangra (India) (11 wickets, 2 matches)	Ajay Dev Goud (India) (8 wickets, 4 matches)

INTERNATIONAL CRICKET

Pakistan v Australia in UAE

Usman Khawaja played the reverse sweep freely and nailed it almost every time.
— *Getty Images*

Khawaja defiant for new Australia

GEOFF LEMON

Australia's Test side took the field for the first time since the ball-tampering tour of South Africa six months earlier. Steve Smith and David Warner were suspended, and it was less a case of the new team containing a few holes, than of a series of holes being stitched together by a few new players. Tim Paine, Smith's replacement as captain, had promised a reformation of on-field behaviour. The times, they had a-changed, but no one knew what shape the new era would assume.

By rights, the 2018-19 visiting team should have been smashed hard. It was an inexperienced team, with three of the top six making their debuts, two of the three first-choice pace bowlers injured, and a new coach, Justin Langer, in his first major engagement. All the distractions and ferment of the previous six months made it hard to focus on the cricket. This was an Australian team as green and unsteady as a newly hatched mantis; add in the punishing climate, and there should have been no chance to stand firm at all.

So, to fight out a heroic draw from a hopeless position in Dubai was a superb performance, of the type even the great Australian teams of recent years had never produced in Asia. It was built around Usman Khawaja's epic century, but plenty of others contributed. In the end, though, the blame belonged to Australia's double batting failure in the Second Test, which allowed Pakistan to complete their biggest win by runs.

For the hosts, the series — which marked the Wisden website's first foray into audio broadcasting, after securing commentary rights to the Tests and covering them live from the grounds — was no less important. Sarfaraz Ahmed was still finding his way as Test captain, and recovering from a dire Asia Cup. But after letting a win slip in Dubai, he rallied his team in Abu Dhabi with a fearless counter-attack. That gave Pakistan the momentum going into the T20 series.

	Tests	**T20Is**
Most runs	Usman Khawaja (Australia) (229 runs, 2 matches)	Babar Azam (Pakistan) (163 runs, 3 matches)
Most wickets	Mohammad Abbas (Pakistan) (17 wickets, 2 matches)	Shadab Khan (Pakistan) (6 wickets, 3 matches)

Tour match

ICC Academy, Dubai, September 29-October 2: Pakistan A 278 in 99.1 overs (Abid Ali 85, Sami Aslam 51; Nathan Lyon 8-103) and 261/7 in 85 overs (Asad Shafiq 69, A Ali 52; Jon Holland 5-79) drew with **Australians** 494/4 dec. in 170 overs (Mitchell Marsh 162, Shaun Marsh 94; Waqas Maqsood 2-66, Iftikhar Ahmed 2-149).

Test series (2): Pakistan 1 Australia 0

1st Test: Match drawn

This match will be remembered for the heroic resistance of Khawaja. His second innings ended at 141, but that does not convey the full scope of the 302 balls he faced, nor the nearly nine hours he spent at the crease in conditions so enervating he thought he had heatstroke on the final day, before carrying on for another session and a half.

Such an innings had not seemed possible in a match Pakistan should have won inside four days. On each of those days, they dominated two sessions before Australia found a way to pull things back. The first day belonged to Mohammad Hafeez, recalled to the Test team, at the age of 37, for the first time in two years after some blazing domestic form. His century, a mixture of doggedness and sporadic aggression, helped build an intimidating first-wicket partnership of 205 with Imam-ul-Haq. On the second day, it was Haris Sohail's turn for a century, his first in Tests.

Australia's openers reached stumps, then lunch next day, while adding a patient 142. Aaron Finch, making his Test debut after 135 white-ball internationals (and 13 centuries), scored 62. But after he and Khawaja were parted, a shocking collapse saw all ten wickets cascade for 60. Mohammad Abbas's 80mph deliveries landed with suffocating accuracy and a touch of movement from a perfectly presented seam, while the 33-year-old Bilal Asif, Pakistan's own debutant, found huge bounce from an action that produced over-spin; he picked off the left-handers with turn. He finished with 6 for 36, the best figures by a debutant against Australia.

The eventual closure came after lunch, with the lead restricted to 461. That still left Australia the best part of five sessions to survive — a big ask. The first-wicket pair again started brightly and another slide was averted by Travis Head, Australia's third debutant, but Khawaja was in the throes of a left-hander's masterclass. He started reverse-sweeping Yasir Shah's leg-breaks out of the rough from round the wicket. He played the stroke more than 20 times, and nailed almost every one.

When Paine arrived with nearly four hours left, the draw was still unlikely. But he absorbed plenty of the strike, helping his exhausted partner push into the final hour. Khawaja was finally trapped by Yasir after 522 minutes, equalling the second-longest vigil in the fourth innings of a Test, behind only Michael Atherton's 643 in Johannesburg in 1995-96. Hearts were in mouths through a tense final hour: But Paine saw out 220 minutes and 194 deliveries, while Nathan Lyon survived for 50 and 34. This was no ordinary draw.

Dubai International Cricket Stadium, Dubai, October 7-11: Pakistan 482 in 164.2 overs (Mohammad Hafeez 126, Haris Sohail 110; Peter Siddle 3-58, Nathan Lyon 2-114) and 181/6 dec. in 57.5 overs (Imam-ul-Haq 48, Asad Shafiq 41; Jon Holland 3-83, N Lyon 2-58) drew with **Australia** 202 in 83.3 overs (Usman Khawaja 85, Aaron Finch 62; Bilal Asif 6-36, Mohammad Abbas 4-29) and 362/8 in 139.5 overs (U Khawaja 141, Tim Paine 61*; Yasir Shah 4-114, M Abbas 3-56). *PoM: Usman Khawaja.*

2nd Test: Pakistan won by 373 runs

If Dubai was Australia's get-out-of-jail card, Abu Dhabi was the equivalent for Pakistan. They looked doomed here following a spectacular collapse, but Sarafraz hit back, and Australia's batting misfired again.

Lyon produced a stunning pre-lunch spell of four wickets without conceding a run: in the space of six balls, he caught and bowled Azhar Ali, had Haris Sohail held at silly point and Asad Shafiq at short leg after a review, then bowled Babar Azam on the charge. Pakistan had spiralled from 57 for 1 to 57 for 5. But Sarfraz countered without recklessness in a sparkling display. Rather than slamming boundaries, he kept the score ticking over by manipulating the field, backing away to cut off the stumps, or moving across to work to leg. His first 58 came at a run a ball, and relieved the pressure on Fakhar Zaman, who was making his debut after Imam broke a finger fielding in Dubai. As the runs flowed in the middle session, Australia lost the plot. If conditions had helped Lyon, they were a gift to Abbas. The extra grass here made him almost unstoppable: he moved the ball away, swung it, reversed it, and produced a succession of edges and lbws.

Fakhar and Sarfaraz each made another half-century. Babar had his own moment of drama. A star in limited-overs matches, he had never scored a

The conditions in Abu Dhabi were a gift to Mohammad Abbas, who took ten wickets in the match. — *Getty Images*

Test hundred. That remained the case when he was out for 99, trapped by Mitchell Marsh after becoming becalmed by a strangling field. Still, Babar had helped Pakistan towards a lead of 537 by the time Sarfaraz declared late on the third day.

Australia had other problems: Khawaja, the saviour in Dubai, had injured his knee during the morning warm-up, and would not bat. Abbas feasted again, taking five more wickets to make it ten in the match. His ten-Test career had yielded 59 wickets at 15. For Pakistan, it was their biggest win by runs in Tests, eclipsing the thrashing by 356 of the Australians on the same ground four years previously.

Sheikh Zayed Stadium, Abu Dhabi, October 16-19: Pakistan 282 in 81 overs (Fakhar Zaman 94, Sarfaraz Ahmed 94; Nathan Lyon 4-78, Marnus Labuschagne 3-45) and 400/9 dec. in 120 overs (Babar Azam 99, S Ahmed 81; N Lyon 4-135, M Labuschagne 2-74) beat **Australia** 145 in 50.4 overs (Aaron Finch 39, Mitchell Starc 34; Mohammad Abbas 5-33, Bilal Asif 3-23) and 164 in 49.4 overs (M Labuschagne 43, Travis Head 36; M Abbas 5-62, Yasir Shah 3-45) by 373 runs. *PoM:* Mohammad Abbas. *PoS:* Mohammad Abbas.

One-off T20I v UAE: Australia won by seven wickets
Sheikh Zayed Stadium Nursery 1, Abu Dhabi, October 22: UAE 117/6 in 20 overs (Shaiman Anwar 41, Mohammad Naveed 27*; Nathan Coulter-Nile 2-20, Billy Stanlake 2-20) lost to **Australia** 119/3 in 16.1 overs (D'Arcy Short 68*; Amir Hayat 2-26) by seven wickets. *PoM:* D'Arcy Short.

T20I series (3): Pakistan 3 Australia 0

1st T20I: Pakistan won by 66 runs
• Some say T20 matches are meaningless, others argue they are cricket's future; having a trophy shaped like a biscuit rather favours the first. • The first

match is not exactly a cracker. • Azam and Hafeez are criticised for a 73-run partnership that uses up nearly ten overs, and is followed by a collapse of 7 for 28. • Australia have chosen to chase, but Imad Wasim bowls both openers in the first over. • The rest can't work out their timing, several dismissed trying to force the pace on a relatively slow surface. • Australia are soon 22 for 6, and limp to 89, which equals their third-lowest in T20 internationals.

Sheikh Zayed Stadium, Abu Dhabi, October 24: Pakistan 155/8 in 20 overs (Babar Azam 68*, Mohammad Hafeez 39; Billy Stanlake 3-21, Andrew Tye 3-24) beat **Australia** 89 in 16.5 overs (Nathan Coulter-Nile 34; Imad Wasim 3-20, Faheem Ashraf 2-10) by 66 runs. *PoM:* Imad Wasim.

2nd T20I: Pakistan won by 11 runs

• Azam and Hafeez put on 70 in ten overs, then a few wickets and some late hitting. • Australia are set back by three tight overs at the start. • There is a moment of magic when Zaman collects the ball in his left hand at mid-off, and throws back-handed while swan-diving in mid-air, without looking at the stumps, to run out Craig McDermott. • At the other end is Glenn Maxwell, improvising his way to 52 from 37 balls, dragging Australia back in the game. • They need 23 from Shaheen Shah Afridi's final over, but Maxwell falls to a mis-hit, and Pakistan take their tenth consecutive T20 series win.

Dubai International Cricket Stadium, Dubai, October 26: Pakistan 174/6 in 20 overs (Babar Azam 45, Mohammad Hafeez 40; Nathan Coulter-Nile 3-18, Billy Stanlake 2-36) beat **Australia** 136/8 in 20 overs (Glenn Maxwell 52, N Coulter-Nile 27; Shadab Khan 2-30, Shaheen Afridi 2-35) by 38 runs. *PoM:* Imad Wasim.

3rd T20I: Pakistan won by 33 runs

• Another day, another mid-range total defended with ease. • This time Azam's accomplice is the 22-year-old Sahibzada Farhan, the support act in an opening partnership of 93, which takes nearly 13 overs. • Lyon and Nathan Coulter-Nile suffer particular punishment, but once Adam Zampa and D'Arcy Short slow things up with their varying wrist-spin, the wickets begin to drop. • Australia have been unable to score off Wasim in the first two games, but now the promoted Alex Carey savages his first over for two sixes and two fours. • But just as the tourists' fortunes seem to have changed, Finch and Carey give soft catches in the circle, while McDermott is run out for the third time out of three. • Pakistan take ten wickets for the 27th time in T20Is — way ahead of the next best, Australia's 19.

Dubai International Cricket Stadium, Dubai, October 28: Pakistan 150/5 in 20 overs (Babar Azam 50, Sahibzada Farhan 29; Mitchell Marsh 2-6) beat **Australia** 117 in 19.1 overs (Shadab Khan 3-19, Hasan Ali 2-14) by 33 runs. *PoM:* Shadab Khan. *PoS:* Babar Azam.

Geoff Lemon (@GeoffLemonSport) is a cricket writer and commentator. His book Steve Smith's Men *was released in 2018.*

Zimbabwe in South Africa

Steyn's triumphant comeback

LUNGANI ZAMA

As thoughts turned towards the World Cup in England in 2019, South Africa took the chance to test their one-day bench strength during this low-key series against their neighbours. Zimbabwe competed bravely at times, but were predictably outclassed, and saved from a 6–0 whitewash only by the rain that ruined the final match.

It meant a white-ball recall for Test opener Dean Elgar, a rare chance for reserve wicketkeeper Heinrich Klaasen, and another for the 32-year-old Christiaan Jonker. South Africa also welcomed back Dale Steyn, injury-free after a spell with Hampshire. Steyn entered the series with a point to prove to those who had written off his international prospects, and did well with the ball. He also turned one game with the bat.

The matches were spread around South Africa's lesser international venues, but the early-season pitches could have been better: the highest total in the 50-over series was a modest 231. The track at Kimberley, especially, was capricious: low and slow one minute, wicked bounce the next. South Africa's top order struggled and without Steyn's surprise batting intervention, Zimbabwe might well have won the second ODI. In his first ODI in two years, Steyn clobbered a maiden fifty, in his 117th match. He put on 75 with Andile Phehlukwayo to give himself something to bowl at — then ripped out two quick wickets. Zimbabwe made it to 43 for 2, only to lose 8 for 35, six to Tahir, whose haul included South Africa's fourth ODI hat-trick.

There was a dream start for Rassie van der Dussen, who smacked 56 from 44 balls in the first T20I, while the home seamers throttled the opposition in the second match.

For the visitors, Kyle Jarvis was a threat, while his new-ball partner Tendai Chatara took six wickets in the one-day series. Tahir, though, matched that in one game, finishing with 15 at 7.60 in all and won both series awards.

	ODIs	T20Is
Most runs	Heinrich Klaasen (South Africa) (104 runs, 3 matches)	Rassie van der Dussen (South Africa) (69 runs, 2 matches)
Most wickets	Imran Tahir (South Africa) (10 wickets, 3 matches)	Imran Tahir (South Africa) (5 wickets, 2 matches)

ODI series (3): South Africa 3 Zimbabwe 0

Diamond Oval, Kimberley, September 30: Zimbabwe 117 in 34.1 overs (Elton Chigumbura 27, Hamilton Masakadza 25; Lungi Ngidi 3-19, Andile Phehlukwayo 2-22) lost to **South Africa** 119/5 in 26.1 overs (Heinrich Klaasen 44, Aiden Markram 27; Tendai Chatara 2-22,

Wellington Masakadza 2-26) by five wickets. *PoM:* Lungi Ngidi.

Mangaung Oval, Bloemfontein, October 3: South Africa 198 in 47.3 overs (Dale Steyn 60, Aiden Markram 35; Tendai Chatara 3-42, Kyle Jarvis 2-26) beat **Zimbabwe** 78 in 24 overs (Hamilton Masakadza 27; Imran Tahir 6-24, D Steyn 2-19) by 120 runs. *PoM:* Dale Steyn.

Boland Park, Paarl, October 6: Zimbabwe 228 in 49.3 overs (Sean Williams 69, Brendan Taylor 40; Dale Steyn 3-29, Kagiso Rabada 3-32) lost to **South Africa** 231/6 in 45.5 overs (Reeza Hendricks 66, Heinrich Klaasen 59; Donald Tiripano 2-35) by four wickets. *PoM:* Heinrich Klaasen. *PoS:* Imran Tahir.

T20I series (2): South Africa 2 Zimbabwe 0

Buffalo Park, East London, October 9: South Africa 160/6 in 20 overs (Rassie van der Dussen 56, David Miller 39; Kyle Jarvis 3-37, Christopher Mpofu 2-24) beat **Zimbabwe** 126 in 17.2 overs (Peter Moor 44, Brandon Mavuta 28; Imran Tahir 5-23, Junior Dala 2-25, Andile Phehlukwayo 2-25) by 34 runs. *PoM:* Imran Tahir.

Senwes Park, Potchefstroom, October 12: Zimbabwe 132/7 in 20 overs (Sean Williams 41, Brendon Taylor 29; Robbie Frylinck 2-20, Dane Paterson 2-22) lost to **South Africa** 135/4 in 15.4 overs (JP Duminy 33*, Quinton de Kock 26; S Williams 2-25) by six wickets. *PoM:* Dane Paterson.

Willowmoore Park, Benoni, October 14: South Africa vs **Zimbabwe** abandoned without a ball bowled. No toss. *PoS:* Imran Tahir.

Lungani Zama (@whamzam17) is a sports and travel writer.

Zimbabwe in Bangladesh

Visiting spinners spring surprise

MOHAMMAD ISAM

Tour match
Bangladesh Krira Shikkha Protisthan No. 4 Ground, Savar, October 19: Zimbabweans
178 in 45.2 overs (Hamilton Masakadza 102, Elton Chigumbura 47; Ebadat Hossain 5-19,
Mohammad Saifuddin 3-32) lost to **Bangladesh Cricket Board XI** 181/2 in 39 overs (Soumya
Sarkar 102*, Mosaddek Hossain 33rh) by eight wickets.

ODI series (3): Bangladesh 3 Zimbabwe 0

1st ODI: Bangladesh won by 28 runs

Bangladesh, without the injured Tamim Iqbal and Shakib, were in trouble at 139 for 6 in the 30th over before Kayes, who clobbered six sixes in
his highest score, put on a national-record 127 for the seventh wicket with
Mohammad Saifuddin, who hit a maiden half-century. Brendan Taylor took
five catches behind the stumps. Zimbabwe found it hard to push the scoring
along, and when Raza fell, it was 88 for 4 after 21 overs. Kyle Jarvis hit 37 at
No.10, his highest score in ODIs, to follow his best bowling figures.

Sher-e-Bangla National Stadium, Mirpur, Dhaka, October 21: Bangladesh 271/8 in 50
overs (Imrul Kayes 144, Mohammad Saifuddin 50; Kyle Jarvis 4-37, Tendai Chatara 3-55)
beat **Zimbabwe** 243/9 in 50 overs (Sean Williams 50*, K Jarvis 37; Mehidy Hasan 3-46,
Nazmul Islam 2-38) by 28 runs. *PoM:* Imrul Kayes.

Highest ODI scores for Bangladesh		
Score	**Player**	**Match**
154	Tamim Iqbal	v Zimbabwe, Bulawayo, 2009
144	Mushfiqur Rahim	v Sri Lanka, Dubai, 2018-19
144	Imrul Kayes	v Zimbabwe, Mirpur, 2018-19
134*	Shakib Al Hasan	v Canada, Antigua, 2006-07
132	Tamim Iqbal	v Pakistan, Mirpur, 2014-15

2nd ODI: Bangladesh won by seven wickets

Bangladesh's victory never looked in doubt once Kayes and Liton Das
raced out of the blocks with 148 in 24 overs. Kayes fell within sight of another century. Earlier, a bright innings from Taylor had given Zimbabwe
some impetus, but only 58 came from the last 12 overs. Saifuddin followed
a half-century in the first match with three wickets for his medium-pacers.

Zahur Ahmed Chowdhury Stadium, Chattogram, October 24: Zimbabwe 246/7 in 50 overs (Brendan Taylor 75, Sikandar Raza 49; Mohammad Saifuddin 3-45) lost to **Bangladesh** 250/3 in 44.1 overs (Imrul Kayes 90, Liton Das 83; S Raza 3-43) by seven wickets. *PoM:* Mohammad Saifuddin.

3rd ODI: Bangladesh won by seven wickets

Liton fell to the first ball of the chase, but then Kayes and Soumya Sarkar sprinted away. After the ten-over powerplay, Bangladesh had 80 for 1 — Zimbabwe were 35 for 2 — and they eventually put on 220, a national second-wicket record, beating 207 by Iqbal and Shakib against West Indies in Providence three months earlier. Kayes took his aggregate to 349 runs, the second-highest for any three-match ODI series, after Babar Azam's 360 for Pakistan v West Indies in the UAE in 2016-17. Sarkar's century was his second in ODIs, following only 47 runs in six innings. Bangladesh completed a 3–0 clean sweep with 47 balls to spare, even though Zimbabwe set a stiff target, thanks mainly to a third-wicket stand of 132 between Taylor and Williams, who also hit his second ODI hundred.

Zahur Ahmed Chowdhury Stadium, Chattogram, October 26: Zimbabwe 286/5 in 50 overs (Sean Williams 129*, Brendan Taylor 75; Nazmul Islam 2-58) lost to **Bangladesh** 288/3 in 42.1 overs (Soumya Sarkar 117, Imrul Kayes 115) by seven wickets. *PoM:* Soumya Sarkar. *PoS:* Imrul Kayes.

Tour match
Zahur Ahmed Chowdhury Stadium, Chattogram, October 29-31: Zimbabweans 145/5 dec. in 48 overs (Hamilton Masakadza 39rh, Sikandar Raza 32*; Ebadat Hossain 2-13) drew with **Bangladesh Cricket Board XI** 56/2 in 18 overs.

Test matches (2): Bangladesh 1 Zimbabwe 1

1st Test: Zimbabwe won by 151 runs

Zimbabwe will long remember the inaugural Test at the pretty Sylhet Stadium in the north-east of Bangladesh. The 116th ground to stage a Test boasts a ceremonial tea garden, and there was even a Lord's-style bell to start proceedings with a flourish. Zimbabwe enjoyed the trappings, easing to their first victory in an overseas Test for 17 years, and only their 12th anywhere in 107 attempts. And they did it with spin, their inexperienced trio faring better than Bangladesh's much-hyped battalion.

The hosts were handicapped by the absence of their leading wicket-taker Shakib, but had still been expected to rule the roost. Instead it was the skiddy off-breaks of Raza, supported by the debutants Mavuta and Wellington, which proved more incisive.

In their first Test of the year, Zimbabwe's batsmen also worked hard. Hamilton and Williams made half-centuries. But when Chakabva fell — one of six victims for the hard-working slow left-armer Taijul Islam — the last five wickets added only 21. That looked plenty, though, when Bangladesh dipped to 19 for 4, the lively new-ball pair of Jarvis and Chatara doing the damage. Mushfiqur and Ariful Haque — chosen for his debut a month after making 231 in a domestic game — papered over the cracks, but three wickets for Raza left Bangladesh staring at a deficit of 139.

Zimbabwe craved a big score to put themselves out of reach, but instead lost regular wickets to the spinners. Bangladesh's eventual target was 321: tough on a pitch taking turn, but not impossible. Everything in the tea garden looked rosy as openers Liton and Kayes put on 56, but Raza pinned Liton, and Zimbabwe started to tighten the screw. Mominul Haque's indifferent run continued when he was castled by Jarvis, then Raza removed Kayes and Mahmudullah,

Mushfiqur Rahim: 219 not out in Mirpur.
— *Getty Images/AFP*

and Mavuta extracted four wickets with his leg-breaks. Finally, Wellington persuaded Ariful to sky a catch, which 'keeper Regis Chakabva clasped to spark Zimbabwean celebrations.

Sylhet International Cricket Stadium, Sylhet, November 3-6: Zimbabwe 282 in 117.3 overs (Sean Williams 88, Peter Moor 63*; Taijul Islam 6-108, Nazmul Islam 2-49) and 181 in 65.4 overs (Hamilton Masakadza 48, Sikandar Raza 25; T Islam 5-62, Mehidy Hasan 3-48) beat **Bangladesh** 143 in 51 overs (Ariful Haque 41*, Mushfiqur Rahim 31; Tendai Chatara 3-19, S Raza 3-35) and 169 in 63.1 overs (Imrul Kayes 43, A Haque 38; Brandon Mavuta 4-21, S Raza 3-41) by 151 runs. *PoM:* Sean Williams.

2nd Test: Bangladesh won by 218 runs

Bangladesh levelled the series with an emphatic victory at the Sher-e-Bangla Stadium, which was fast becoming their stronghold. It was set up by big innings from Mominul and Mushfiqur, and rammed home by the spinners, who shared 16 wickets to thwart a pair of hundreds from Taylor.

The Bangladeshis had not passed 200 in their previous eight Test innings and looked on course for another disappointment when they lurched to 26 for 3 in the first hour. But that was the end of the good news for Zimbabwe. The spinners, so potent in Sylhet, were neutralised by a slower pitch. Mominul, who had scored only 69 runs in eight Test innings since his twin hundreds against Sri Lanka at Chittagong in January, was quickly into his stride, showing improved footwork. He purred to his eighth Test century, and it was a surprise when he fell to the new ball shortly before stumps for a superb 161. His stand with Mushfiqur was eventually worth 266, a record for Bangladesh's fourth wicket in Tests, beating 180 by Mominul and Liton against Sri Lanka in that match at Chittagong.

Next day, Mushfiqur carried on serenely towards his second Test double-century. Not content with the fourth-wicket record, he broke the eighth-wicket record too, putting on 144 with Mehidy Hasan. Mahmudullah eventually called a halt after Mushfiqur reclaimed the record for Bangladesh's highest Test score, passing Shakib's 217 in Wellington in 2016-17.

Zimbabwe were up against it, but Taylor kept their heads above water with a defiant century, his fifth in Tests but first away from home. Reining in his attacking instincts, he put on 139 for the sixth wicket with Peter Moor.

But the spinners worked their way through, Taijul finishing with a third successive five-for as the innings ended just before stumps on the third day. Zimbabwe had kept Bangladesh in the field for more than 105 overs, so Mahmudullah waived what would have been his side's first follow-on, despite a lead of 218. Embarrassment loomed at 25 for 4, but Mohammad Mithun and Mahmudullah stopped the rot with a stand of 118. The captain declared shortly after reaching his second Test century, nearly nine years after the first.

Zimbabwe were left with a mountain to climb: 443 to win or, more realistically, 120 overs to draw. Taylor at least reached the foothills, and was undefeated with 106 — it was the second time he had scored two hundreds in a Test. But he was alone: after the openers put on 68, no one else managed more than 13 as off-spinner Mehidy winkled out the tail.

Shere Bangla National Stadium, Mirpur, Dhaka, November 11-15: Bangladesh 522/7 dec. (Mushfiqur Rahim 219*, Mominul Haque 161; Kyle Jarvis 5-71) and 224/6 dec. in 54 overs (Mahmudullah 101*, Mohammad Mithun 67; K Jarvis 2-27, Donald Tiripano 2-31) beat **Zimbabwe** 304 in 105.3 overs (Brendon Taylor 110, Peter Moor 83; Taijul Islam 5-107, Mehidy Hasan 3-61) and 224 in 83.1 overs (B Taylor 106*, Brian Chari 43; M Hasan 5-38, T Islam 2-93) by 218 runs. *PoM:* Mushfiqur Rahim. *PoS:* Taijul Islam.

	ODIs	**T20Is**
Most runs	Imrul Kayes (Bangladesh) (349 runs, 3 matches)	Mushfiqur Rahim (Bangladesh) (270 runs, 2 matches)
Most wickets	Kyle Jarvis (Zimbabwe) (5 wickets, 3 matches)	Taijul Islam (Bangladesh) (18 wickets, 2 matc0hes)

Mohammad Isam (@isam84) is Bangladesh correspondent for ESPNcricinfo.

England, as if swinging machetes at the undergrowth, swept, reverse-swept, then swept again to a series win. — *Getty Images*

England in Sri Lanka

Root's new approach scripts sweep

NEIL MANTHORP

Eyebrows were raised by England's pre-tour talk of a "brave and bold" approach to the Test series. But as a delighted Joe Root said afterwards: "We walked the talk, and it paid off with a victory we can all be very proud of for the rest of our careers."

There was almost constant collateral damage whenever they batted, but the loss of wickets was a price worth paying: their overall run-rate of 3.66 was their second-highest in a series on the subcontinent. Root, inspired by the positivity of ODI captain Eoin Morgan, didn't simply challenge England's past approach: he challenged the traditional approach to Test cricket. In all three matches, England won the toss, batted, and reached three figures by lunch, improving as they went on: 113 for 5 in Galle, 120 for 4 in Pallekele, 102 for two in Colombo. Even when they were five down in the First Test, it was obvious they had rattled Sri Lanka, who retreated into caution and defence, and allowed England, thanks to a superb debut century from Ben Foakes, to recover.

England did not maintain the tempo for the Second Test: they upped it. A plan to upset Sri Lanka's spinners produced over 200 sweeps, almost as many reverse as conventional. It was more than had been played in an entire series — by anyone, anywhere — since shot selection was first accurately recorded in 2006. Jos Buttler led the way, but nearly everyone followed. It became impossible for Sri Lanka to set a field, since bowling one side of the wicket was insufficient.

Sri Lanka were sloppy, most damningly when spinner Lakshan Sandakan was twice denied the wicket of Ben Stokes in Colombo because of overstepping. More than that, England beat the hosts at their own game: not only did they match Sri Lanka's spinners, but they outperformed them. Slow bowlers on both sides claimed 100 of the 116 wickets to fall. The probing Dilruwan Perera topped the list with 22, but next for Sri Lanka came fellow off-spinner Akila Dananjaya, with ten. (Dananjaya's action was reported after Galle, and he missed Colombo to have it tested at Brisbane's National Cricket Centre, where it was deemed illegal.) By contrast, England's trio — left-armer Jack Leach, off-spinner Moeen Ali and leg-spinner Adil Rashid — prided themselves on working as a team, celebrating others' wickets as much as their own. Between them, they collected 48 wickets.

If Sri Lanka were often a shambles on the field, they were even worse off it. Their best cricketer, Angelo Mathews, had been omitted from the one-day squad (which he had captained until September) to work on his fitness, according to coach Chandika Hathurusinghe, who also muttered bleakly about his running between the wickets. Veteran spinner Rangana Herath announced that the First Test, his 93rd, would be his last, and signed off by dismissing Root twice. Mathews, recalled for the Tests, contributed to the leadership vacuum by cutting a lone figure in the field, and signalled his dissatisfaction with his treatment by the selectors by pointing to his bat and making a chatting gesture after reaching both his half-centuries in Galle; unfortunately, Sri Lanka needed his bat to do more talking than 52 and 53. When injury ruled Dinesh Chandimal out after Galle, the captaincy passed to fast bowler Suranga Lakmal, whose aptitude for it was matched by his peripheral role with the ball.

	ODIs	**T20I**	**Tests**
Most runs	Eoin Morgan (England) (195 runs, 4 matches)	Jason Roy (England) (69 runs, 1 match)	Ben Foakes (England) (277 runs, 3 matches)
Most wickets	Akila Dananjaya (Sri Lanka) (9 wickets, 5 matches)	Joe Denly (England) (4 wickets, 1 match)	Dilruwan Perera (Sri Lanka) (22 wickets, 3 matches)

Tour matches

P Sara Oval, Colombo, October 5: Sri Lanka Board XI 287/9 in 50 overs (Dinesh Chandimal 77, Kamindu Mendis 61; Moeen Ali 3-42, Ben Stokes 2-33) lost to **England** 215/2 in 35.3 overs (Eoin Morgan 91*, Joe Root 90*) by 43 runs (DLS method).

P Sara Oval, Colombo, October 6: Sri Lanka Board XI vs England. No result.

ODI series (5): England 3 Sri Lanka 1

NICK HOULT

1st ODI: No result

Only 15 overs were possible before the monsoon arrived, with England — already short of match practice because of the weather — 92 for two. During a 49-run opening stand, Jason Roy and Bairstow became the first England partnership to reach 1,000 runs in a calendar year. Earlier, Warwickshire seamer Olly Stone had been presented with his first one-day cap by Darren Gough, as England looked to add raw pace to their World Cup options.

Rangiri Dambulla International Stadium, Dambulla, October 10: England 92/2 in 15 overs (Joe Root 25*, Jonny Bairstow 25) vs **Sri Lanka**. No result.

2nd ODI: England won by 31 runs (DLS)

Lasith Malinga delivered a classic spell of death bowling, but it was not enough to affect the result of a rain-shortened match. He took 5 for 44, his best one-day international haul since August 2011, to prevent a late charge from England after they had been put in. Ali, bowled first ball with a dipping yorker, was his 500th international wicket. But Morgan's well-crafted 92 from 91 balls had given his team a platform. Niroshan Dickwella ramped Chris Woakes for four in a first over which also brought the wicket of Upul Tharanga, but was then bounced out by the lively Stone, who touched 90mph. Woakes claimed three in a probing burst, before England's spinners whizzed through their overs to ensure the 20 needed to enact DLS.

Rangiri Dambulla International Stadium, Dambulla, October 13: England 278/9 in 50 overs (Eoin Morgan 92, Joe Root 71; Lasith Malinga 5-44) beat **Sri Lanka** 140/5 in 29 overs (Thisara Perera 44*, Dhananjaya de Silva 36*; Chris Woakes 3-26) by 41 runs (DLS method). *PoM:* Eoin Morgan.

3rd ODI: England won by seven wickets

Tom Curran's slower balls and Rashid's wrist-spin helped England to a 2–0 lead in a game shortened by rain to 21 overs. After a bright start, Sri Lanka failed to adapt to the conditions, holding back the dangerous hitters Thisara and Dasun Shanaka. Rashid combined accuracy with penetration to claim four wickets. Chandimal's lack of urgency — he made 34 off 42 balls — put pressure on the others. Bairstow and Root fell early to slow left-armer Amila Aponso as England set about chasing 151, but Roy looked more comfortable against spin than in previous innings, and Morgan stroked the ball around. The best shots, however, came from Stokes, who had spent 45 minutes on the eve of the game working on his ramp. The preparation paid off when he scooped Nuwan Pradeep for six, and England cruised home with 15 balls to spare.

Pallekele International Cricket Stadium, Pallekele, Kandy, October 17: Sri Lanka 150/9 in 21 overs (Niroshan Dickwella 36, Sadeera Samarawickrama 35; Adil Rashid 4-36, Tom Curran 3-17) lost to **England** 153/3 in 18.3 overs (Eoin Morgan 58*, Jason Roy 41; Amila Aponso 2-27) by seven wickets. *PoM:* Adil Rashid.

4th ODI: England won by 18 runs (DLS)

The target of 274 was always going to be subject to DLS recalculations and England stayed in control under the clouds to seal their ninth bilateral series in a row. Malinga's first over included two sets of four byes and cost 12 in all. And, thanks to Roy's hitting and Morgan's ability to find the gaps off the spinners, they stayed comfortably ahead. Sri Lanka thought they had dismissed the patient Root on 22, when he was caught on the sweep at short fine top-edging a full toss. But square-leg umpire Lyndon Hannibal had spotted there were too few fielders inside the ring, and called no-ball as the stroke was played. It was a lack of awareness that summed up Sri Lanka's series. Sri Lanka had at least batted with some consistency. Shanaka clouted five sixes in a run-a-ball 66 and the fifth, sixth and seventh wickets all added at least 50. It represented progress, but it was not enough.

Pallekele International Cricket Stadium, Pallekele, Kandy, October 20: Sri Lanka 273/7 in 50 overs (Dasun Shanaka 66, Niroshan Dickwella 52; Moeen Ali 2-55) lost to **England** 132/2 in 27 overs (Jason Roy 45, Joe Root 32*; Akila Dananjaya 2-27) by 18 runs (DLS method). *PoM:* Eoin Morgan.

5th ODI: Sri Lanka won by 219 runs (DLS)

England slumped to their heaviest one-day defeat by runs, having made three changes to their series-winning side. Liam Plunkett returned after cutting short his honeymoon, while Mark Wood came in for Stone and Morgan rested himself to make room for Sam Curran. Sam and Tom became the first brothers to play for England together since another Surrey duo, Adam and Ben Hollioake, in February 1999. But England, led by Buttler, were sloppy in the field, and their seamers poor; worse, on a humid night in Colombo, they at times lost their cool with each other.

After putting on 137 in 19 overs for the first wicket with Samarawick-rama, Dickwella was set for Sri Lanka's first one-day hundred of the year, but exhaustion set in and he holed out for 95. Chandimal, put down by Tom off Moeen on six, recovered to make his first fifty of the series, while Kusal Mendis made his first ODI half-century in 24 innings. Sri Lanka's 366 for 6 was their highest against England. Within ten balls of the reply, England were reeling at 4 for 3.

R Premadasa Stadium, Khettarama, Colombo, October 23: Sri Lanka 366/6 in 50 overs (Niroshan Dickwella 95, Dinesh Chandimal 80; Moeen Ali 2-57, Tom Curran 2-71) beat **England** 132/9 in 26.1 overs (Ben Stokes 67, M Ali 37; Akila Dananjaya 4-19, Dushmantha Chameera 3-20) by 219 runs (DLS method). *PoM:* Niroshan Dickwella. *PoS:* Eoin Morgan.

One-off T20I: England won by 30 runs

• More than eight years after his previous international, Joe Denly takes four wickets with his reinvigorated leg-spin — and, after England ease to victory, the match award. • Having hit 20 off 17 balls in an imposing total of 187 for 8, Denly opens the bowling, removes Mendis with his sixth ball and Dickwella with his 11th, and returns at the end to grab two more. • With the superb Rashid taking a career-best 3 for 11, the tourists' leg-spinners bag seven. • England's innings centres on Roy's mercurial 69. • Roy is badly dropped in the deep three times, on 34, 41 and 53, and ought to have persuaded Hales to review his lbw verdict; he also plays a part in the run-out of Morgan. • England are comfortable against the 20-year-old debutant Kamindu Mendis, who bowls slow left-arm to the right-handed Roy, and off-breaks to the left-handed Stokes.

R Premadasa Stadium, Khettarama, Colombo, October 27: England 187/8 in 20 overs (Jason Roy 69, Moeen Ali 27; Amila Aponso 2-29, Lasith Malinga 2-30) beat **Sri Lanka** 157 in 20 overs (Thisara Perera 57, Dinesh Chandimal 26; Joe Denly 4-19, Adil Rashid 3-11) by 30 runs. *PoM:* Joe Denly.

Tour matches

Nondescripts Cricket Club Ground, Colombo, October 30-31: Sri Lanka Board XI 392/9 dec. in 89.5 overs (Kaushal Silva 62rh, Manoj Sarathchandra 59*; Moeen Ali 2-64) drew with **England** 365/7 in 90 overs (Joe Root 100rh, M Ali 60; Nishan Peiris 3-108).
Colombo Cricket Club Ground, Colombo, November 1-2: England 210/6 dec. in 50 overs (Ben Stokes 53rh, Sam Curran 48*; Lahiru Kumara 3-19) drew with **Sri Lanka Board XI** 200/7 in 50 overs (Charith Asalanka 68rh, Avishka Fernando 47).

Test matches (3): England 3 Sri Lanka 0

1st Test: England won by 211 runs

Herath has never looked like much of an athlete, yet he turned himself into one of Sri Lanka's greatest cricketers. This was his last Test, and it was practically a testimonial.

It was also a party Ben Foakes never thought he'd be invited to. Foakes was making his debut in Herath's backyard — and England were in trouble. But the wicketkeeper batsman had spent time in Sri Lanka, with England Under-19s and the Lions, and a couple of matches for Colombo's Colts CC. He had visited the place so many times he probably had a flat there. And that is how he played, as if these were his home conditions. While his teammates attacked recklessly after Root had won the toss, Foakes batted like the only adult in the room. After 43, he had only nine. Then he started driving the spinners through cover. But mostly he waited for poor deliveries, which came often, and clinically put them away. By the end of the first day, he had turned 103 for 5 into 321 for 8. The only time his century looked anything but assured was when he had 95, and Leach was ninth out, a fifth wicket for Perera. But Anderson survived the rest of the over, before Foakes hit two boundaries in three balls from Lakmal to pick up only the second hundred on debut by an England wicketkeeper.

In reply, Sri Lanka collapsed to 40 for four before lunch. For a while, Mathers and Chandimal played as sensibly as Foakes. But once Mathews fell to Moeen first ball after tea, the tail offered little. Sri Lanka trailed by 139.

Jennings had looked the most composed top-order player in the first innings, and now cashed in. He is a peculiar batsman: he seems to have too many limbs, and plays fast bowling like it is booby-trapped, but he's superb against spin, even if his reverse sweep resembles a praying mantis going through puberty. And he manipulated an already chaotic Sri Lankan field: Chandimal was off injured, leaving the ineffectual Lakmal in charge; Herath occasionally weighed in, and Mathews moped.

England were able to set Sri Lanka 462 in two days plus seven overs. They couldn't have chased it in two lifetimes.

As for Herath, he reached 100 wickets at the ground when he dismissed Root in the first innings, and passed Richard Hadlee's Test tally of 431 when he added him in the second. His final wicket, Buttler, moved him to joint-eighth on the all-time list with Broad, who had been left out here, and one behind Kapil Dev. Mathews had made headlines for being dropped. Sanath Jayasuriya was in hot water for not handing his mobile phone over to the ICC's anti-corruption unit. And the minister for petroleum, Arjuna Rana-tunga, had been briefly arrested on charges relating to murder. Three of Sri Lanka's greatest cricketers were in the news, the country was in a constitutional crisis, and yet for a week the nation stopped to pay tribute to the wizard of Galle. When Herath had come on to bowl on the first day, there were fireworks over the Galle Fort. It was touching, yet ridiculous: fireworks in the daytime can hardly be seen. When they finished, Herath bowled. Just as he let the ball go, and Jennings leaned forward, there was one last, huge firework. His career might have come late, but it came with a bang. After England had won, he quietly collected his trophies and headed back to the bank.   *Jarrod Kimber*

Galle International Stadium, Galle, November 6-9: England 342 in 97 overs (Ben Foakes 107, Sam Curran 48; Dilruwan Perera 5-75, Suranga Lakmal 3-73) and 222/6 dec. in 93 overs (Keaton Jennings 146*, Ben Stokes 62; Rangana Herath 2-59, D Perera 2-94) beat **Sri Lanka** 203 in 68 overs (Angelo Mathews 52, Dinesh Chandimal 33; Moeen Ali 4-66, Adil Rashid 2-30) and 250 in 85.1 overs (A Mathews 53, Kusal Mendis 45; M Ali 4-71, Jack Leach 3-60) by 211 runs. *PoM:* Ben Foakes.

2nd Test: England won by 57 runs

England's approach was simple, but brutal: as if swinging machetes at the undergrowth, they swept, reverse-swept, then swept again — all the way to their first series win in Sri Lanka since Nasser Hussain's team 17 years earlier. England's tactics peaked during a sparkling 124 from 146 balls by Root, batting as inventively as any of his compatriots can ever have done in Asia.

The First Test was Rangana Herath's last, and his final wicket moved him to joint-eighth on the all-time charts. — *Getty Images/AFP*

Others needed little encouragement to follow their leader. In all, England's second innings produced 84 sweeps of various genres, for a return of 122 runs, of which Root contributed 47; only Curran, out first ball, and Rashid didn't play the shot. And while those 84 also included the first seven wickets, the rewards were clear. If the pragmatism was unsparing, the flair was outrageous. This was one of their most watchable wins in years.

Their spinners, too, rose to the occasion. For the first time since Jim Laker's Test at Old Trafford in 1956, England won without a wicket from a seamer.

Root won another toss and, again, England almost squandered the advantage. Jennings nibbled tamely at Lakmal — the only wicket in the Test for a seamer — and Stokes was unconvincing in his new position of No.3. From 225 for 9, Curran, who had 16 from 65 deliveries, took off. From his next 38 deliveries, he plundered six sixes, moving to fifty with the fifth. That made him the first player to reach his first three Test half-centuries with a six. England had added 60 for the last wicket in 11 overs, and Anderson had faced just 12 balls.

Roshen Silva, playing instead of Chandimal, took on the England spinners and gave Sri Lanka a lead of 46. But England returned to score briskly. Root moved to his 15th Test hundred, just his fourth overseas. Foakes and Anderson extended their last-wicket stand to 41 on the fourth morning, setting Sri Lanka 301 to square the series. And when, in a trice, Leach reduced them to 26 for 3, it looked as if there wouldn't be a fifth day. The first show of resistance came from Dimuth Karunaratne and Mathews, who put on 77, before Silva added 73 with Mathews. At 219 for 5, both sides fancied their chances. Instead, Moeen immediately trapped Mathews for 88 and the rain dragged the game into a final day, with Sri Lanka seven down and 75 adrift. Root later said he had managed only three hours' sleep, though he needn't have fretted. Moeen and Leach required barely half an hour to wrap things up, completing a Sri Lankan collapse of 5 for 22, and leaving Leach with a maiden Test five-for.   *Lawrence Booth*

Pallekele International Cricket Stadium, Pallekele, Kandy, November 14-18: England 290 in 75.4 overs (Sam Curran 64, Jos Buttler 63; Dilruwan Perera 4-61, Malinda Pushpakumara 3-89) and 346 in 80.4 overs (Joe Root 124, Ben Foakes 65*; Akila Dananjaya 6-115, D Perera 3-96) beat **Sri Lanka** 336 in 103 overs (Roshen Silva 85, Dimuth Karunaratne 63; Jack Leach 3-70, Adil Rashid 3-75) and 243 in 74 overs (Angelo Mathews 88, D Karunaratne 57; J Leach 5-83, Moeen Ali 4-72) by 57 runs. *PoM:* Joe Root.

3rd Test: England won by 42 runs

England claimed their first whitewash in Asia in a series of three Tests or more, and only their third away from home. With Anderson rested, and Curran missing because of a side injury, they had the luxury of bringing in replacements with 182 Tests between them. Both Broad and Bairstow had a point to prove. In Bairstow's case, it was done emphatically, with his sixth Test hundred — and probably his most challenging.

Coming in at No.3, a drive for four through extra cover from his first ball spoke of a purpose Bairstow carried through to lunch. His 42 from 58 deliveries included a slog-swept six off Pushpakumara. A paddle to fine leg from his 165th delivery took him to three figures, followed by a celebration aimed, it seemed, at everyone and no one.

England's last seven fell for 101; Sandakan finished with a Test best 5 for 95. England's collapse looked particularly damaging while Karunaratne and de Silva took Sri Lanka to 173 for 1. Stokes persisted with some testing short-pitched bowling, hitting Karunaratne in the ribs and Mendis on the right hand, before Rashid ended a second-wicket stand of 142 shortly before tea as de Silva tickled him to Jennings at short leg. Karunaratne followed in the first over after the break and, as England grew in confidence, Sri Lanka lost their heads. In all, nine wickets tumbled for 67 in 18 overs, Rashid collecting his best Test figures of 5 for 49, and Jennings holding on to four close catches. From nowhere, England led by 96.

Early on the third, England found themselves 39 for 4. It would have been worse for England had Sandakan not overstepped twice: once when Stokes slapped him to cover on 29, then when he edged to slip on 32. Those were two of 13 uncalled no-balls *Sky Sports* picked up during Sandakan's spell. Stokes was eventually dismissed for 42, but by then he and Buttler had added 89, quelling Sri Lanka's enthusiasm and tipping the game back England's way. The lead was 326 when Perera wrapped up the innings, claiming his eighth five-wicket haul.

Sri Lanka's chase was hampered by a woeful start late on the third day. A probing spell from Moeen accounted for both left-handed openers and they closed on 53 for 4. Mendis and the classy Silva diligently added 102. It needed a rocket of a throw from deep square leg by Leach to end their alliance. It took the puff out of the hosts: soon it was 226 for 9, and victory beckoned with more than four sessions to spare. Instead, Pushpakumara threatened to knock England off kilter, thrashing 42 from 40 balls and leading Sri Lanka to tea with 43 needed. But the break allowed the tourists to take stock. Four balls after the restart, Leach trapped Lakmal, and the review proved in vain. The finale was a fitting microcosm of the series: England's spinners outbowled Sri Lanka's, while Sri Lanka's batsmen outcollapsed England's.

Vithushan Ehantharajah

Sinhalese Sports Club Ground, Colombo, November 23-26: England 336 in 92.5 overs (Jonny Bairstow 110, Ben Stokes 57; Lakshan Sandakan 5-95, Dilruwan Perera 3-113) and 230 in 69.5 overs (Jos Buttler 64, B Stokes 42; D Perera 5-88, Malinda Pushpakumara 3-28) beat **Sri Lanka** 240 in 65.5 overs (Dimuth Karunaratne 83, Dhananjaya de Silva 73; Adil Rashid 5-49, B Stokes 3-30) and 284 in 86.4 overs (Kusal Mendis 86, Roshen Silva 65; Jack Leach 4-72, Moeen Ali 4-92) by 42 runs. *PoM:* Jonny Bairstow. *PoS:* Ben Foakes.

Neil Manthorp (@NeilManthorp) is a sports writer based in Cape Town.

Pakistan v New Zealand in UAE

Williamson outsmarts Sarfaraz

MAZHER ARSHAD

New Zealand had not played for seven months before this tour. They showed some rust in the white-ball games, but atoned in the Tests, where they came from behind twice for stirring victories — the first by just four runs — to clinch their first away win over Pakistan for nearly half a century (Graham Dowling's side had triumphed 1–0 in 1969-70).

Kane Williamson, New Zealand's captain, had a memorable time in the Tests. In three matches on sluggish pitches, he amassed 386 runs at 77, including 89 and 139 in the Third Test, before a familiar last-day collapse by Pakistan. It moved Williamson up to second in the ICC rankings, not far behind Virat Kohli. "Beating Pakistan in their backyard is very tough," he said. "This will be one the guys remember for a long time."

Williamson's captaincy outshone Sarfaraz Ahmed's: the New Zealander bravely threw uncapped spinners Ajaz Patel and Will Somerville into the mix, and they responded with crucial performances in the two Test victories on their debuts. There were also important runs from left-hander Henry Nicholls, who made his first overseas century in the Third Test.

Sarfaraz blamed the defeat on a lack of input from the tail. In the two defeats, both in Abu Dhabi, Pakistan lost 6 for 53, 7 for 41, then 7 for 62 and all ten for 137 on the final day of the series.

New Zealand's two victories sandwiched a huge Pakistan win in the Second Test, in Dubai, where leg-spinner Yasir Shah was unstoppable. Disconcerting the batsmen with bounce and extravagant turn, he claimed 14 wickets, and went on to zip past 200 in the final Test, his 33rd — it made him the fastest to the landmark.

Pakistan also unleashed an exciting prospect in Shaheen Shah Afridi, a slippery left-arm seamer. Only 18, he was fast-tracked into the Test squad after doing well in the limited-overs games. Mohammad Hafeez, 20 years Afridi's senior, announced his retirement from Test cricket before the decider, to concentrate on white-ball formats.

In the T20Is, Pakistan continued their terrific run of form. It was their 11th successive T20 series win since Sarfaraz took over the captaincy in 2016. New Zealand hit back in the first ODI — their 12th successive win over Pakistan in the format — but Fakhar Zaman ensured that run soon ended.

Tour match
Sheikh Zayed Stadium, Abu Dhabi, October 28: New Zealand 161/4 in 20 overs (Glenn Phillips 48, Mark Chapman 36) beat **UAE** 124/8 in 20 overs (Ish Sodhi 2-11, Tim Southee 2-24) by 37 runs.

	T20Is	**ODIs**	**Tests**
Most runs	Mohammad Hafeez (Pakistan) (132 runs, 3 matches)	Ross Taylor (New Zealand) (166 runs, 3 matches)	Kane Williamson (New Zealand) (386 runs, 3 matches)
Most wickets	Adam Milne (New Zealand) (4 wickets, 2 matches)	Lockie Ferguson (New Zealand) (11 wickets, 3 matches)	Yasir Shah (Pakistan) (29 wickets, 2 matches)

T20I series (3): Pakistan 3 New Zealand 0

1st T20I: Pakistan won by two runs

• The match can go to a super over if Ross Taylor hits Afridi's last ball for six — but he can only despatch a full toss to long-off for four. • From 10 for 2 in the fourth, Asif Ali and Mohammad Hafeez add 67 for Pakistan. • Later, from a dicey 123 for 6, the team conjure 25 from the last two overs, with Imad Wasim carting Tim Southee for four and six to end the innings. • Colin Munro ignites the chase with 58 from 42 balls before falling to leg-spinner Shadab Khan. • After a miserly spell from Hafeez (3–10–13–0), the odds are stacked against New Zealand, which means 17 are needed off the last. • Taylor, whose 26-ball 42* contains only three boundaries, muscles them close.

Sheikh Zayed Stadium, Abu Dhabi, October 31: Pakistan 148/6 in 20 overs (Mohammad Hafeez 45, Sarfaraz Ahmed 34; Adam Milne 2-28) beat **New Zealand** 146/6 in 20 overs (Colin Munro 58, Ross Taylor 42*; Hasan Ali 3-35) by two runs. *PoM:* Mohammad Hafeez.

2nd T20I: Pakistan won by six wickets

• The result is in the balance when Pakistan need 40 from four overs, but Hafeez takes 17 off the 17th, from Ish Sodhi. • He finishes with 34* from 21 balls, as Pakistan clinch their 11th successful chase in a row. • Earlier, Munro gives New Zealand another turbocharged start. • Glenn Phillips makes only five of the opening stand of 50. • But, with Afridi bowling tightly (4–12–20–3), the runs dry up. • It is 83 for 4 in the 13th over, before Corey Anderson clouts 44* from 25 to set up a more challenging target.

Dubai International Cricket Stadium, Dubai, November 2: New Zealand 153/7 in 20 overs (Corey Anderson 44*, Colin Munro 44; Shaheen Afridi 3-20) lost to **Pakistan** 154/4 in 19.4 overs (Babar Azam 40, Asif Ali 38; Adam Milne 2-25) by six wickets. *PoM:* Shaheen Afridi.

3rd T20I: Pakistan won by 47 runs

• Pakistan complete a 3–0 sweep thanks to Babar Azam. • He consolidates his place on top of the T20 batting rankings with 79 from 58 balls during a second-wicket stand of 94 with Hafeez. • Azam's 48th run is his 1,000th in T20Is in his 26th innings, beating Kohli's record by one. • New Zealand are always up against it once big hitters Munro and Colin de Grandhomme fall in single figures. • Williamson crashes 60 from 38 balls, but he is the first of eight wickets to tumble for 23. • Waqas Maqsood, a 31-year-old left-arm seamer, is the first man to make his T20I debut on his birthday; he ends with two wickets in his second over.

Dubai International Cricket Stadium, Dubai, November 4: Pakistan 166/3 in 20 overs (Babar Azam 79, Mohammad Hafeez 53*; Colin de Grandhomme 2-41) beat **New Zealand** 119 in 16.5 overs (Kane Williamson 60, Glenn Phillips 26; Shadab Khan 3-30, Waqas Maqsood 2-21) by 47 runs. *PoM:* Babar Azam. *PoS:* Mohammad Hafeez.

ODI series (3): Pakistan 1 New Zealand 1

1st ODI: New Zealand won by 47 runs

A change of format worked wonders for New Zealand, who breezed to their 12th successive ODI victory over Pakistan. Their hero was Trent Boult, who set back the chase with a high-class hat-trick — Zaman, Azam and Hafeez — to reduce Pakistan to 8 for 3. A workmanlike innings from Sarfraz Ahmed and Imad patched things up, but there was too much to do. A fourth-wicket partnership of 130 between Taylor and Tom Latham had been the bedrock of New Zealand's competitive total. Shadab just missed a hat-trick of his own, taking three wickets in four balls as New Zealand lurched from 208 for 3 to 210 for 7.

Sheikh Zayed Stadium, Abu Dhabi, November 7: New Zealand 266/9 in 50 overs (Ross Taylor 80, Tom Latham 68; Shadab Khan 4-38, Shaheen Afridi 4-46) beat **Pakistan** 219 in 47.2 overs (Sarfaraz Ahmed 64, Imad Wasim 50; Lockie Ferguson 3-36, Trent Boult 3-54) by 47 runs. *PoM:* Trent Boult.

2nd ODI: Pakistan won by six wickets

Zaman's return to form, after a lacklustre Asia Cup, helped Pakistan end their losing run. He made an even 88 and put on 101 with Azam after Imam-ul-Haq retired hurt on being clonked on the helmet by Callum Ferguson, who also took three wickets. But New Zealand's under-par total, in which the only substantial partnership was 75 between Taylor (who hit just three fours and a six from 120 balls) and Nicholls, never looked enough. They were not helped when Williamson was run out for one by a fingertip deflection by Afridi, after a George Worker straight-drive.

Sheikh Zayed Stadium, Abu Dhabi, November 9: New Zealand 209/9 in 50 overs (Ross Taylor 86*, Henry Nicholls 33; Shaheen Afridi 4-38, Hasan Ali 2-59) lost to **Pakistan** 212/4 in 40.3 overs (Fakhar Zaman 88, Babar Azam 46; Lockie Ferguson 3-60) by six wickets. *PoM:* Shaheen Afridi.

3rd ODI: No result.

Pakistan gave themselves a chance of a series win after Azam thumped 92 and put on 108 for the third wicket with Haris Sohail. The hostile Ferguson completed his maiden international five-for, but Boult finished with chastening figures of 1-80. New Zealand's quest for 280 started badly, when Munro was bowled by Afridi for a duck, but the rain came before enough overs had been bowled to constitute a match. This was the 332nd official ODI in the UAE, but only the second to end without a result.

Dubai International Cricket Stadium, November 11: Pakistan 279/8 in 50 overs (Babar Azam 92, Fakhar Zaman 65; Lockie Ferguson 5-45) vs **New Zealand** 35/1 in 6.5 overs. No result. *PoM:* Lockie Ferguson. *PoS:* Shaheen Afridi.

Test matches (3): New Zealand 2 Pakistan 1

1st Test: New Zealand won by four runs

Pakistan seemed to be heading for a routine win as they chased just 176. But a collapse, in which the last seven wickets crashed for 41, allowed New Zealand to pull off an improbable victory. It was only their fourth win away from home against Pakistan, who stumbled to their second defeat in 12 Tests at the Sheikh Zayed Stadium (another would soon follow). The win was sealed by Ajaz Patel, an Indian-born slow left-armer making his debut. Ajaz claimed 5 for 59 in the second innings, the last four for seven in 41 balls.

Pakistan had gone to lunch on the fourth day at 130 for 4. Asad Shafiq had just departed, but they needed only 46 more. Instead, Azam was run out from short fine leg after a mix-up with Azhar Ali, then Sarfaraz was given out on review, with New Zealand certain he had tickled Ajaz to BJ Watling while trying to sweep. Panic set in, and the next three all failed to score. Azhar had tried to farm the strike during the later stages of his fighting 65, but finally pushed forward to Ajaz and was struck on the pad.

The scoring rate hovered around two and a half an over throughout, as New Zealand struggled to 153, the lowest opening innings in a Test in Abu Dhabi. Mohammad Abbas conceded only 13 runs in 12 overs. Not long after lunch on the second day, Pakistan looked in total charge, already in front with only four wickets down, but once Shafiq departed — one of four victims for Boult — the innings faded. The last six wickets fell for 53. Yet, a lead of 74 looked decisive on a difficult surface.

Jeet Raval and Williamson dug deep, before Nicholls and Watling shared the only century partnership of the match. Three quick strikes from Ajaz and leg-spinner Sodhi on the fourth morning gave New Zealand hope, but Azhar and Shafiq seemed to snuff that out in a stand of 82. And then came the sensational session.

Sheikh Zayed Stadium, Abu Dhabi, November 16-19: New Zealand 153 in 66.3 overs (Kane Williamson 63, Henry Nicholls 28; Yasir Shah 3-54, Haris Sohail 2-11) and 249 in 100.4 overs (BJ Watling 59, H Nicholls 55; Hasan Ali 5-45, Y Shah 5-110) beat **Pakistan** 227 in 83.2 overs (Babar Azam 62, Asad Shafiq 43; Trent Boult 4-54, Colin de Grandhomme 2-30) and 171 in 58.4 overs by (Azhar Ali 65, A Shafiq 45; Ajaz Patel 5-59, Neil Wagner 2-27) four runs. *PoM:* Ajaz Patel.

2ⁿᵈ Test: Pakistan won by an innings and 16 runs

After Pakistan's batsmen had made a hash of things in Abu Dhabi, Yasir made sure they would not have the chance to do so in Dubai, taking 14 wickets in an innings victory. It was a superb performance, which answered critics who had wondered whether his powers were on the wane after a troublesome hip injury. Only Imran Khan, with 14 for 116 against Sri Lanka in Lahore in 1981-82, had returned better match figures for Pakistan.

Before Yasir got going, though, Pakistan's batsmen had given him a sizeable total to bowl at. Azhar unrolled another patient innings; he and Haris Sohail ground out 126 in more than 61 overs. Then, Sohail, dropped by Watling off Sodhi when 37, and Azam batted into the final session of the second day, adding 186 for the fifth wicket. Sohail reached his second Test century, and Babar his first. Wagner kept things tight, but he and Boult proved toothless on the sluggish surface, and the spinners found little assistance.

New Zealand reached 50 the next day, before Yasir uncorked the genie. Williamson became a spectator, finishing with 28 not out from No.3. There were a record equalling six ducks as the last eight in the order managed just five runs between them. Yasir, often spinning the ball the width of the stumps or more, had a spell of 8 for 17 in 42 balls, including a triple-wicket maiden. And he was not done. Pakistan enforced the follow-on (for the first time in seven UAE Tests in which they had the option), and he claimed two more wickets before the close, including Williamson, done in by one that spat sideways and kissed the outside edge. That gave him ten on the third day alone.

New Zealand batted much better second time around, but it was only a matter of time. Pakistan squared the series late on the fourth day.

Dubai International Cricket Stadium, Dubai, November 24-27: Pakistan 418/5 dec. in 167 overs (Haris Sohail 147, Babar Azam 127*; Colin de Grandhomme 2-44) beat **New Zealand** 90 in 35.3 overs (Jeet Raval 31, Kane Williamson 28*; Yasir Shah 8-41) and 312 in 112.5 overs (Ross Taylor 82, Henry Nicholls 77; Y Shah 6-143, Hasan Ali 3-46) by an innings and 16 runs. *PoM:* Yasir Shah.

3ʳᵈ Test: New Zealand won by 123 runs

In the First Test, New Zealand had overturned a first-innings deficit of 74 to win in Abu Dhabi. Now they did it again, to complete their first series victory over Pakistan away from home since 1969-70, and only the second by a visiting team, after Sri Lanka two years earlier, since Pakistan made the UAE their home in 2010.

Like the first match, this one owed much to a debutant spinner: 34-year-old Will Somerville, who earlier in the year had been representing New South Wales. After returning to play for Auckland in his native New Zealand, he was called up as a replacement for this tour — and took seven wickets, including three important strikes as Pakistan's chase foundered.

Amid the Kiwi celebrations there was another landmark for Yasir, whose fifth wicket in the match (Somerville in the second innings) was his 200th in

On sluggish pitches, Kane Williamson played gritty knocks, including for a centuriy in the Third Test. — *Getty Images*

Tests, in only his 33rd match. He was easily the fastest to the mark.

As was the case for most of the series, runs were hard to come by. Williamson was determined, Watling gritty. In Pakistan's reply, Hafeez, who had announced his Test retirement before the match, fell for a duck to Boult. Azhar and Shafiq dropped anchor, putting on 201 in 76 overs, by which time Pakistan were in the lead. But another tepid lower-order display kept the advantage within bounds.

New Zealand lost early wickets, but the fifth-wicket pair booked in for the rest of the fourth day. Williamson took the eye, cover-driving off front foot and back during an excellent century, his 19th in Tests and one of the most valuable. Nicholls marched on to his own hundred, his first away from home, before a declaration left Pakistan a tantalising 280 in 79 overs. They never threatened.

From 55 for 5, Azam and Sarfaraz resisted for an hour, but ultimately, for the sixth time since August 2016 Pakistan surrendered all ten wickets on the final day to lose a Test.

Sheikh Zayed Stadium, Abu Dhabi, December 3-7: New Zealand 274 in 116.1 overs (Kane Williamson 89, BJ Watling 77*; Bilal Asif 5-65, Yasir Shah 3-75) and 353/7 dec. in 113 overs (K Williamson 139, Henry Nicholls 126*; Y Shah 4-129, Shaheen Afridi 2-85) beat **Pakistan** 348 in 135 overs (Azhar Ali 134, Asad Shafiq 104; William Somerville 4-75, Trent Boult 2-66) and 156 in 56.1 overs (Babar Azam 51, Sarfaraz Ahmed 28; Tim Southee 3-42, Ajaz Patel 3-42, W Somerville 3-52) by 123 runs. *PoM:* Kane Williamson. *PoS:* Yasir Shah.

Mazher Arshad (@MazherArshad) is a cricket statistician and writer.

South Africa in Australia

Du Plessis piles on Aussie woes

BEN HORNE

Faf du Plessis must wonder how many times he can stand at the other end while Australian cricket self-destructs. On South Africa's previous visit, in late 2016, Australia's national selector Rod Marsh and half a dozen players were axed after the Test side were steamrollered in Hobart. That defeat, and the ensuing panic, led to the relaunch of their attack-dog approach. The chickens had come home to roost in March 2018, when David Warner, Steve Smith and Cameron Bancroft conspired to use sandpaper to alter the condition of the ball in the Third Test at Cape Town. With Australia already flat out on the canvas, it was going to be difficult for du Plessis to inflict another knockout when he arrived for four limited overs matches in November. But what he did prove by winning the 50-over games 2–1, as well as the lone T20 match — reduced to ten overs by rain — was just how long the Australians' road to redemption might be.

There were other humiliations en route. Photos appeared on social media revealing the catch phrases plastered on the dressing-room wall. One of them, "elite honesty", created an internet storm and became yet another way to parody an organisation that, in the wake of their crushing independent cultural review, had done a pretty good job of it themselves.

Once the cricket started, things didn't get much better. Batting first in Perth under a new one-day captain in Aaron Finch — Tim Paine had been jettisoned after the whitewash in England, along with his deputy, Mitchell Marsh — Australia didn't last 40 overs. In the second match, in Adelaide, they recovered some respect after their bowlers defended a mediocre total to end a seven-match losing streak. Ultimately South Africa were too good, but Australia were far from disgraced in the decider in Hobart, clinched by du Plessis's spectacular hundred.

For South Africa, Dale Steyn made a triumphant return, but they looked fragile, and were too reliant for runs on du Plessis and David Miller.

	ODIs	T20I
Most runs	David Miller (South Africa) (192 runs, 3 matches)	Glenn Maxwell (Australia) (69 runs, 2 match)
Most wickets	Marcus Stoinis (Australia) (8 wickets, 3 matches)	Chris Morris (South Africa) (2 wickets, 1 match)

Tour match

Manuka Oval, Canberra, October 31: South Africans 173 in 42 overs (Aiden Markram 47, David Miller 45; Usman Qadir 3-28, Jason Behrendorff 3-35) lost to **Prime Minister's XI** 174/6 in 36.3 overs (Josh Phillippe 57, George Bailey 51; Lungi Ngidi 2-16, Kagiso Rabada 2-41) by four wickets.

ODI series (3): South Africa 2 Australia 1

Perth Stadium, Perth, November 4: Australia 152 in 38.1 overs (Nathan Coulter-Nile 34, Alex Carey 33; Andile Phehlukwayo 3-33, Dale Steyn 2-18) lost to **South Africa** 153/4 in 29.2 overs (Quinton de Kock 47, Reeza Hendricks 44; Marcus Stoinis 3-16) by six wickets. *PoM:* Dale Steyn.

Adelaide Oval, Adelaide, November 9: Australia 231 in 48.3 overs (Alex Carey 47, Chris Lynn 44; Kagiso Rabada 4-54, Dwaine Pretorius 3-32) beat **South Africa** 224/9 in 50 overs (David Miller 51, Faf du Plessis 47; Marcus Stoinis 3-35, Josh Hazlewood 2-42) by seven runs. *PoM:* Aaron Finch.

Bellerive Oval, Hobart, November 11: South Africa 320/5 in 50 overs (David Miller 139, Faf du Plessis 125; Mitchell Starc 2-57, Marcus Stoinis 2-70) beat **Australia** 280/9 in 50 overs (Shaun Marsh 106, M Stoinis 63; Kagiso Rabada 3-40, Dale Steyn 3-45) by 40 runs. *PoM:* David Miller. *PoS:* David Miller.

Tour match

Allan Border Field, Brisbane, November 14: South Africans 201/5 in 20 overs (Aiden Markram 45, Heinrich Klaasen 41) beat **Cricket Australia XI** 160/7 in 20 overs (Alex Ross 40, Max Bryant 36; Chris Morris 2-35) by 41 runs.

Only T20I: South Africa won by 21 runs

Carrara Oval, Carrara, November 17: South Africa 108/6 in 10 overs (Faf du Plessis 27; Andrew Tye 2-18, Nathan Coulter-Nile 2-19) beat **Australia** 87/7 in 10 overs (Glenn Maxwell 38; Chris Morris 2-12, Lungi Ngidi 2-16) by 21 runs. *PoM:* Tabraiz Shamsi.

Ben Horne (@BenHorne8) is a sports journalist with the Daily Telegraph.

West Indies in Bangladesh

Home spinners take all 40 wickets

MOHAMMAD ISAM

West Indies had won both Tests easily when Bangladesh toured the Caribbean earlier in 2018, taking their overall record against them to ten victories out of 14. But the boot was firmly on the other foot when the teams reconvened on spin-friendly subcontinental surfaces. The West Indians had expected a trial by turn, but the scale of it probably surprised them. Uniquely, the Bangladesh spinners took all 40 wickets in the two Tests, with the only pace bowling coming from Mustafizur Rahman, who sent down just four overs at Chittagong.

Mehidy Hasan took a national record 12-117 in the Second Test. — *Getty Images*

The visiting batsmen kept trying to play the spinners off the back foot, with little success: on average, they lost a wicket every 29 deliveries. Only Shane Dowrich played an innings that lasted more than 100. Off-spinner Mehedi Hasan led the way with 15 wickets, including 12 in the Second Test in Mirpur, where he broke his own national record for Bangladesh's best match figures. In Chittagong, 17-year-old off-spinner Nayeem Hasan had taken 5 for 61 in the first innings, watched by his parents and childhood coach.

Bangladesh won the one-day series as well, but West Indies fought back to take a T20 series marred by umpiring errors.

There was much interest in Bangladesh in the position of Mashrafe bin Mortaza, the long-serving one-day captain, who had announced his intention to run for parliament as part of the ruling Awami League just before the series; shortly after it, he was elected in his native Narail with 96% of the vote.

	Tests	**ODIs**	**T20Is**
Most runs	Shimron Hetmyer (222 runs, 2 matches)	Shai Hope (297 runs, 3 matches)	Shai Hope (114 runs, 3 matches)
Most wickets	Mehidy Hasan (15 wickets, 2 matches)	Mehidy Hasan (6 wickets, 3 matches)	Shakib Al Hasan (8 wickets, 3 matches)

Tour match

MA Aziz Stadium, Chattogram, November 18-19: West Indians 303/7 dec. in 86.3 overs (Shai Hope 88rh, Kieran Powell 72; Nayeem Hasan 2-104) drew with **Bangladesh Cricket Board XI** 232/5 in 75 overs (Soumya Sarkar 78, Shadman Islam 73; Shannon Gabriel 2-24).

Test series (2): Bangladesh 2 West Indies 0

1st Test: Bangladesh won by 64 runs

Bangladesh needed only three days to complete their first victory at home against West Indies. The spinners did all the damage, and also combined to score some important first-innings runs, when a collapse would have undone much of Mominul Haque's good work in making 120.

Mominul's century was his eighth in Tests, six of them on this ground, where he now averaged 83. He played conservatively, cashing in only when the bowlers pitched short or wide. Just before he was out, Bangladesh were riding high at 222 for 3 after winning the toss, but four wickets in 15 balls from the fiery Shannon Gabriel reduced them to 235 for 7. Nayeem, a local teenager making his debut, hung around for more than two hours, sharing a ninth-wicket stand of 65 with Taijul Islam, who went on to his highest Test score as Bangladesh batted into the second day.

Then began West Indies' trial by spin: Taijul started the slide, and before long it was 88 for 5. Shimron Hetmyer counter-attacked spectacularly, adding 92 in 14 overs with Dowrich; they hit seven sixes in all. But it couldn't last: Hetmyer tickled Mehedi to the keeper, and although Dowrich inched the total to 246, a deficit of 78 was daunting on a turning pitch. Off-spinner Nayeem became the third-youngest to take a five-for in a Test.

West Indies turned to their own spinners after a solitary over from Kemar Roach, which cost 11. The hosts struggled against Roston Chase and Devendra Bishoo, who claimed seven for 44 between them. In all, 17 wickets tumbled on the second day.

A target of 204 looked attainable for West Indies — but not for long. They were soon in disarray at 11 for 4. First to go was Kieran Powell, who missed a slog and was stumped first ball for a duck. That was a unique dismissal for an opener in Tests, and a landmark victim for Shakib in his 54th match: the first Bangladeshi to 200 Test wickets, and the fastest of any nationality to combine that with 3,000 runs, beating Ian Botham, who needed 55. Taijul's figures of 6 for 33 are the best for Bangladesh in the fourth innings.

Zahur Ahmed Chowdhury Stadium, Chattogram, November 22-24: Bangladesh 324 in 92.4 overs (Mominul Haque 120, Imrul Kayes 44; Jomel Warrican 4-62, Shannon Gabriel 4-70) and 125 in 35.5 overs (Mahmudullah 31; Devendra Bishoo 4-26, Roston Chase 3-18) beat **West Indies** 246 in 64 overs (Shimron Hetmyer 63, Shane Dowrich 63; Nayeem Hasan 5-61, Shakib Al Hasan 3-43) and 139 in 35.2 overs (Sunil Ambris 43, J Warrican 41; Taijul Islam 6-33, Mehidy Hasan 2-27) by 64 runs. *PoM:* Mominul Haque.

2ⁿᵈ Test: Bangladesh won by an innings and 184 runs

Bangladesh wrapped up the series with their first innings win. This one, while pressed home by the spinners, was set up by a huge total in which West Indies' own spinners failed to make much impression.

First to lay down a marker was Shadman Islam, a solid 23-year-old opener, who became Bangladesh's eighth new cap in their eight Tests in 2018, after replacing the injured Imrul Kayes. He bedded down for most of the first two sessions, hitting just six fours from 199 balls in a patient display. It looked as if his good work might be in vain when Mushfiqur Rahim, just after completing 4,000 Test runs, fell to Shermon Lewis. But skipper Shakib put on 111 with Mahmudullah, who batted for more than six hours before being last out with his third Test century. With everyone reaching double figures, Bangladesh made 508.

West Indies started their innings after tea on the second day, and by the close were in trouble at 75 for 5. The top five were all bowled — the first such instance in a Test since 1890. The procession continued next morning, when Mehedi shot them out for their lowest total against this opposition. A massive 397 runs ahead, Shakib enforced the follow-on, the first time Bangladesh had done so.

Total embarrassment for West Indies was averted by an astonishing innings from Hetmyer, who blasted nine sixes and a solitary four. Few would have begrudged him a maiden century, but he holed out at long-on for 93, from 92 balls. He was one of 12 wickets in the match for Mehedi, who improved his own national record for the best match figures (previously 12 for 157, against England in 2016-17).

Sher-e-Bangla National Stadium, Mirpur, Dhaka, November 30-December 2: Bangladesh 508 in 154 overs (Mahmudullah 136, Shakib Al Hasan 80; Kraigg Brathwaite 2-57, Kemar Roach 2-61) beat **West Indies** 111 in 36.4 overs (Shimron Hetmyer 39, Shane Dowrich 37; Mehidy Hasan 7-58, S Al Hasan 3-27) and 213 in 59.2 overs (S Hetmyer 93, K Roach 37*; M Hasan 5-59, Taijul Islam 3-40) by an innings and 184 runs. *PoM:* Mehidy Hasan. *PoS:* Shakib Al Hasan.

Tour match

Khan Saheb Osman Ali Stadium, Fatullah, December 6: West Indians 331/8 in 50 overs (Shai Hope 81, Roston Chase 65*; Rubel Hossain 2-55, Nazmul Islam 2-61) lost to **Bangladesh Cricket Board XI** 314/6 in 41 overs (Tamim Iqbal 107, Soumya Sarkar 103*; R Chase 2-57, Devendra Bishoo 2-81) by 51 runs (DLS method).

ODI series (3): Bangladesh 2 West Indies 1

1ˢᵗ ODI: Bangladesh won by five wickets

West Indies' batting problems continued, against a combination of spin and the wily seam of Mortaza. They struggled to 127 for 6 in the 40th over, before Chase and Keemo Paul put on 51. But Mustafizur, one of the best death bowlers around, took three wickets in nine balls to keep the total under 200. Liton Das gave the chase a quick start, then Mushfiqur eased Bangladesh home.

Sher-e-Bangla National Stadium, Mirpur, Dhaka, December 9: West Indies 195/9 in 50 overs (Shai Hope 43, Keemo Paul 36; Mashrafe Mortaza 3-30, Mustafizur Rahman 3-35) lost to **Bangladesh** 196/5 in 35.1 overs (Mushfiqur Rahim 55*, Liton Das 41; Roston Chase 2-47) by five wickets. *PoM:* Mashrafe Mortaza.

2ⁿᵈ ODI: West Indies won by four wickets

Bangladesh seemed to have the series in the bag when West Indies slipped to 185 for 6 after 39 overs, chasing 256. But Shai Hope was still there, approaching a third ODI century, and he dominated an unbroken seventh-wicket stand of 71 with Paul, whose contribution was 18, to pull off a sensational last-over victory. Hope's career-best 146 not out came from 144 balls.

Bangladesh's total included half-centuries from their three senior batsmen, but only 64 came from the last ten overs.

Shere Bangla National Stadium, Mirpur, Dhaka, December 11: Bangladesh 255/7 in 50 overs (Shakib Al Hasan 65, Mushfiqur Rahim 62; Oshane Thomas 3-54) lost to **West Indies** 256/6 in 49.4 overs (Shai Hope 146*, Darren Bravo 27; Rubel Hossain 2-57, Mustafizur Rahman 2-63) by four wickets. *PoM:* Shai Hope.

3ʳᵈ ODI: Bangladesh won by eight wickets

Bangladesh made sure of the ODI series with disciplined bowling, again restricting West Indies to under 200. That included another century from Hope, who batted through the 50 overs, but received little support: the next-highest score was 19, by Marlon Samuels. Mehedi took the first two wickets and finished with four, although the West Indians were annoyed about his dismissal of their captain, Rovman Powell, as they claimed there were too many fielders (six) on the leg side; the third umpire reviewed footage, but was unable to find a clear shot of the whole ground.

Tamim Iqbal and Soumya Sarkar (who launched five sixes) made light of the chase with a second-wicket stand of 131 in 25 overs.

Sylhet International Cricket Stadium, Sylhet, December 14: West Indies 198/9 in 50 overs (Shai Hope 108*; Mehidy Hasan 4-29, Mashrafe Mortaza 2-34) lost to **Bangladesh** 202/2 in 38.3 overs (Tamim Iqbal 81*, Soumya Sarkar 80; Keemo Paul 2-38) by eight wickets. *PoM:* Mehidy Hasan. *PoS:* Shai Hope.

T20I (3): West Indies 2 Bangladesh 1

1ˢᵗ T20I: West Indies won by eight wickets

• Bangladesh misfire against the pacy left-armer Sheldon Cottrell. • He performs his signature salute celebration (he was formerly in the Jamaican army) four times on a bouncy track. • Despite Shakib's half-century, it is a middling score. • Hope then smashes six sixes from 23 balls as West Indies saunter home. • The start time was brought forward twice: first from 5pm to 2pm to avoid early evening dew, then to 12.30 after a floodlight failed.

Sylhet International Cricket Stadium, Sylhet, December 17: Bangladesh 129 in 19 overs (Shakib Al Hasan 61; Sheldon Cottrell 4-28, Keemo Paul 2-23) lost to **West Indies** 130/2 in 10.5 overs (Shai Hope 55*, K Paul 28*) by eight wickets. *PoM:* Sheldon Cottrell.

2ⁿᵈ T20I: Bangladesh won by 36 runs

• Bangladesh square the series largely thanks to their captain Shakib. • The skipper follows a brisk 42 not out with 5 for 20. • Those are his country's second-best T20 figures, behind Elias Sunny's 5 for 13 against Ireland in Belfast in 2012. • With Liton blazing 60 from 34, Bangladesh's total proves more than enough. • Even a dew-laden ball can't hamper their bowlers. • The West Indies can't last their quota of overs.

Shere Bangla National Stadium, Mirpur, Dhaka, December 20: Bangladesh 211/4 in 20 overs (Liton Das 60, Mahmudullah 43*; Sheldon Cottrell 2-38) beat **West Indies** 175 in 19.2 overs (Rovman Powell 50, Shai Hope 36; Shakib Al Hasan 5-20, Mustafizur Rahman 2-50) by 36 runs. *PoM:* Shakib Al Hasan.

3ʳᵈ T20I: West Indies won by 50 runs

• West Indies take the series, after a match marred by umpiring errors. • In the fourth over of the chase, Tanvir calls Thomas twice for overstepping, only for replays to show both are legal deliveries: Liton Das is caught at mid-off from the second, and both calls result in free hits that go for six. • The game is held up for ten minutes while West Indies' captain Carlos Brathwaite discusses it with the umpires and match referee Jeff Crowe, but to no avail. • West Indies regroup well, sending Bangladesh plummeting from 65 for 1 to 96 for 8. • Paul polishes off the innings with his side's best T20 figures, and only their second five-for, after Darren Sammy's 5 for 26 against Zimbabwe at Port-of-Spain in 2009-10. • Earlier, Evin Lewis has clattered 89 from 36 balls, with eight sixes.

Shere Bangla National Stadium, Mirpur, Dhaka, December 22: West Indies 190 in 19.2 overs (Evin Lewis 89, Nicholas Pooran 29; Mahmudullah 3-18, Mustafizur Rahman 3-33, Shakib Al Hasan 3-37) beat **Bangladesh** 140 in 17 overs (Liton Das 43; Keemo Paul 5-15, Fabian Allen 2-19) by 50 runs. *PoM:* Evin Lewis. *PoS:* Shakib Al Hasan.

Sri Lanka in New Zealand

Sparks can't ignite win for visitors

MARK GEENTY

Some belligerent and occasionally brutal Sri Lankan batting meant this tour didn't quite provide the mismatch expected. Even so, New Zealand assumed a familiarly dominant position at home in front of sun-drenched, holidaying crowds, leaving the tourists winless throughout their five-week visit.

It would be a stretch to say Sri Lanka's hopes were high, after a 3–0 home defeat by England. Then, early in the tour, news broke that batting coach Thilan Samaraweera was being shown the door after the Tests, to be replaced by the former Durham coach Jon Lewis. Kusal Mendis pointedly paid a glowing tribute to Samaraweera after he helped save the Wellington Test with an unbeaten 141, in concert with 120 not out from Angelo Mathews — the high point of Sri Lanka's trip.

New Zealand had returned less than a week before the First Test following a memorable 2–1 win over Pakistan in the UAE. Having scrapped hard on turning pitches, the batsmen relished home climes and true bounce — notably opener Tom Latham. He carried his bat for 264 on a friendly Wellington surface, and amassed 450 runs in the two games, nearly half Sri Lanka's entire tally of 909.

A fresher pitch at Christchurch showed up the visitors' technique against swing and bounce. New Zealand's new-ball duo, Trent Boult and Tim Southee, took 14 wickets, with Boult picking up six for four in 15 balls to destroy Sri Lanka's first innings. Latham and Henry Nicholls batted them out of the game, before New Zealand completed a fourth successive series win for the first time.

The one-day internationals reflected the rankings — New Zealand third, Sri Lanka eighth — despite some whirlwind hitting from Niroshan Dickwella, Kusal Perera and Thisara Perera, whose breath-taking 57-ball hundred got Sri Lanka within 22 runs in the second match. But the bowling, led by the veteran Lasith Malinga, was toothless on dream batting surfaces, and Ross Taylor led the run-feast as New Zealand averaged 351 across the three games. After himself averaging 91 in ODIs in 2018, Taylor began World Cup year with scores of 54, 90 and 137.

The return of all-rounder Jimmy Neesham, 18 months after his last international, and his six-hitting duel with Thisara was the abiding memory of the ODIs. Neesham crashed Thisara's medium-pace over the rope five times in one over at Bay Oval, before Perera managed four off an over from Southee two days later. But Neesham's bowling was more effective, and helped New Zealand close out victories.

	Tests	ODIs	T20I
Most runs	Tom Latham (450 runs, 2 matches)	Ross Taylor (281 runs, 3 matches)	Doug Bracewell (44 runs, 1 match)
Most wickets	Tim Southee (13 wickets, 2 matches)	Ish Sodhi (8 wickets, 3 matches)	Lockie Ferguson (3 wickets, 1 match)

Tour match

McLean Park, Napier, December 8-10: Sri Lankans 210/9 dec. in 59 overs (Angelo Mathews 128*, Dinesh Chandimal 26; Blake Coburn 3-44, Peter Younghusband 2-25) and 321/5 dec. in 80 overs (Danushka Gunathilaka 83, Kusal Mendis 72; P Younghusband 2-48, B Coburn 2-77) drew with **New Zealand XI** 270/8 dec. in 82 overs (Sandeep Patel 69, Katene Clarke 46; Dilruwan Perera 2-30, Lakshan Sandakan 2-67) and 139/2 in 28.3 overs (William O'Donnell 52*, Dale Phillips 39*).

Test series (2): New Zealand 1 Sri Lanka 0

1st Test: Match drawn

By the close on the third evening, it was one-way traffic, a finish apparently imminent as Sri Lanka's top order crumbled again. Teetering at 20 for 3, they were still 276 behind. Latham's epic unbeaten 264 in 11 hours 34 minutes — the sixth-highest and third-longest by a New Zealander — looked certain to lead them to a tenth successive victory in an early-season (November or December) home Test.

Angelo Mathews, who had a point to prove, marked his century with a flurry of press-ups and a glare to the dressing-room. — *Getty Images*

Not so fast, said two Sri Lankans with a point to prove. Still just 23, Mendis had endured a lean trot against South Africa and England, his breakthrough 176 against Australia in 2016 a distant memory. Mathews, meanwhile, was still pained by his axing from the one-day captaincy amid questions over his fitness. His batting had a steely, defiant edge, and he had already top-scored in the first innings, when the pitch was at its trickiest. What followed was the first wicketless full day of Test cricket since South African openers

Graeme Smith and Neil McKenzie batted through the first in Chittagong in February 2008. In almost 89 years of Tests in New Zealand, it had never happened before.

The batsmen reined in their instincts and when the weather had the final say, 274 runs and nearly seven and a half hours after the pair united, they had secured a draw. It was Sri Lanka's highest second-innings stand, beating an unbroken 240 between Asanka Gurusinha and Arjuna Ranatunga against Pakistan at Colombo's P Sara Oval in March 1986. Mendis had his sixth Test century, and Mathews his ninth, which he celebrated with a flurry of press-ups and a glare to the dressing-room.

New Zealand felt they hadn't bowled badly, but were frustrated by the pitch. Southee had been outstanding early on, generating swing on a calm first day to snare six, even as Dimuth Karunaratne and Mathews added 133 from the depths of 9 for 3. Then it was the Latham show. Only one other New Zealander, Glenn Turner (twice), had carried his bat through a Test innings. Latham's was a classic opener's knock, leaving well, avoiding risk, and text-book cover-driving. Williamson unfurled another gem, an effortless 91 off 93 balls and, after he surprised everyone on a sun-drenched Sunday afternoon by getting out, Latham took over. He passed Alastair Cook's 244 in Melbourne in 2017-18 as the highest Test innings by an opener carrying his bat.

Basin Reserve, Wellington, December 15-19: Sri Lanka 282 in 90 overs (Angelo Mathews 83, Niroshan Dickwella 80*; Tim Southee 6-68, Neil Wagner 2-75) and 287/3 in 115 overs (Kusal Mendis 141*, A Mathews 120*; T Southee 2-52) drew with **New Zealand** 578 in 157.3 overs (Tom Latham 264*, Kane Williamson 91; Lahiru Kumara 4-127, Dhananjaya de Silva 2-54). *PoM:* Tom Latham.

2nd Test: New Zealand won by 423 runs

If the pitch at the Basin Reserve was not to New Zealand's liking, the one at Hagley Oval was the perfect Christmas present. Another Latham marathon — a mere nine and a half hours this time — was backed up by another busy century from Nicholls, then by a swing clinic from Boult and an award-winning performance from Southee.

The result looked comprehensive, but it had taken a while for New Zealand to assert themselves. Suranga Lakmal put in a superb display of swing bowling: around the wicket, and hooping it in to the left-handers, he swept through the top order to have them 36 for 4. When Taylor was run out at the non-striker's end, 150 looked a lofty goal. But Southee's gung-ho approach of 68 off 65 balls was a telling contribution. Then, by stumps, he quickly removed Sri Lanka's top three. Although 14 wickets had tumbled, the tourists still looked likely to overhaul New Zealand's 178.

That all changed next morning in 15 balls from Boult. After ten wicketless overs on day one, he scythed through Sri Lanka with a stunning spell. The last four fell lbw for ducks as Boult's inswing looked almost unplayable, and he walked off with Test-best figures of 6 for 30. From there, Sri Lanka were never in it.

Latham's eighth Test century was a formality. Nicholls joined in the fun with his former schoolboy rival, notching his third century of a year in which he averaged 73. He and Latham, who were sharing a car to the ground each morning, added 214, before Colin de Grandhomme, with an undefeated 71 off 45 balls, joined him for 124 in less than 15 overs. Sri Lanka lasted 106 overs, but couldn't replicate their Wellington heroics.

It was easily New Zealand's biggest Test victory by runs.

Hagley Oval, Christchurch, December 26-30: New Zealand 178 in 50 overs (Tim Southee 68, BJ Watling 46; Suranga Lakmal 5-54, Lahiru Kumara 3-49) and 585/4 dec. in 153 overs (Tom Latham 176, Henry Nicholls 162*; L Kumara 2-134) beat **Sri Lanka** 104 in 41 overs (Angelo Mathews 33*; Trent Boult 6-30, T Southee 3-35) and 236 in 106.2 overs (Kusal Mendis 68, Dinesh Chandimal 56; Neil Wagner 4-48, T Boult 3-77) by 423 runs. *PoM:* Tim Southee.

ODI series (3): New Zealand 3 Sri Lanka 0

1st ODI: New Zealand won by 45 runs

Two returnees did most of the damage after New Zealand ran up 371, their fourth-highest ODI total at home. Martin Guptill, missing through injury for ten months, hit a run-a-ball 138, which set the stage for a brutal late onslaught from Neesham, out of form and favour since the 2017 Champions Trophy. He smashed the first five deliveries of a Thisara over for six; with the over including a no-ball, it cost 34 in all. His 47 not out needed only 13 deliveries.

Sri Lanka replied boldly, with Dickwella reverse-lapping the faster bowlers during a perky opening stand of 119 with Danushka Gunathilaka. But Neesham removed both in the space of four balls and, although Kusal Perera made his fourth one-day hundred, the mountain was too high to climb.

Bay Oval, Mount Maunganui, January 3: New Zealand 371/7 in 50 overs (Martin Guptill 138, Kane Williamson 76; Nuwan Pradeep 2-72, Lasith Malinga 2-78) beat **Sri Lanka** 326 in 49 overs (Kusal Perera 102, Niroshan Dickwella 76; Jimmy Neesham 3-38, Trent Boult 2-65, Lockie Ferguson 2-65) by 45 runs. *PoM:* Martin Guptill.

2nd ODI: New Zealand won by 21 runs

It's rare to score 140 from 74 balls and lose, but it happened to Thisara. He arrived at 121 for 5, which soon became 128 for 7, but stunned spectators — and the New Zealand bowlers — by clouting 13 sixes and eight fours. The fielding disintegrated, with six chances going down; there were four sixes in the 46th over, bowled by Southee. Thisara put on 75 with Malinga (17), 51 with Lakshan Sandakan (6) and 44 with last man Nuwan Pradeep (3*), before Boult finally clung on to a catch.

New Zealand were grateful they had again comfortably exceeded 300, mainly thanks to a third-wicket stand of 112 between Colin Munro and Taylor, and another late blitz from Neesham — 64 off 37 this time.

Bay Oval, Mount Maunganui, January 5: New Zealand 319/7 in 50 overs (Ross Taylor 90, Colin Munro 87; Lasith Malinga 2-45) beat **Sri Lanka** 298 in 46.2 overs (Thisara Perera 140, Danushka Gunathilaka 71; Ish Sodhi 3-55, Jimmy Neesham 2-48) by 21 runs. *PoM:* Thisara Perera.

3rd ODI: New Zealand won by 115 runs

New Zealand completed a clean sweep after a three-match run-fest. Taylor followed innings of 54 and 90 with a superb 137, his 20th one-day century, putting on 116 for the third wicket with Williamson, and 154 for the fourth in 20 overs with Nicholls, who reached his maiden ODI hundred from 71 balls. Malinga started with two early wickets, but lost the plot at the end, his first spell of 5–1–21–2 morphing into 10–1–93–3. Sri Lanka began well once more, and New Zealand were looking anxious when Thisara got going again, on his way to 80 from 63 balls. But he fell to Lockie Ferguson, who unleashed a heady combination of raw pace, precision yorkers and slower bouncers to take four wickets.

Saxton Oval, Nelson, January 8: New Zealand 364/4 in 50 overs (Ross Taylor 137, Henry Nicholls 124*; Lasith Malinga 3-93) beat **Sri Lanka** 249 in 41.4 overs (Thisara Perera 80, Niroshan Dickwella 46; Lockie Ferguson 4-40, Ish Sodhi 3-40) by 115 runs. *PoM:* Ross Taylor.

One-off T20I: New Zealand won by 35 runs

• When New Zealand slip to 55 for 5 after ten overs, bothered by the bounce at Eden Park, it seems Sri Lanka might finally register a win. • But Doug Bracewell, playing only because Neesham has tweaked a hamstring, crashes five sixes from 26 balls. • Then the debutant Scott Kuggeleijn adds 35 from 15, with three sixes. • It is still gettable on a small ground. • But Bracewell removes the dangerous Dickwella, and catches Kusal and Thisara. • The last six wickets tumble for 26.

Eden Park, Auckland, January 11: New Zealand 179/7 in 20 overs (Doug Bracewell 44, Scott Kuggeleijn 35*; Kasun Rajitha 3-44, Lasith Malinga 2-24) beat **Sri Lanka** 144 in 16.5 overs (Thisara Perera 43; Lockie Ferguson 3-21, Ish Sodhi 3-30) by 35 runs. *PoS:* Doug Bracewell.

Pakistan in South Africa

The fleeting star of Olivier

LUNGANI ZAMA

Pakistan arrived with serious skill, the chutzpah of youth and a coach, Mickey Arthur, who knew local conditions better than most. But there was a caveat: they would have to score enough runs for their bowlers to work with — and South Africa has become the most unforgiving country in the world for batsmen. That view was only strengthened by what happened here. Hard though they fought, Pakistan couldn't overcome a barrage of nasty quick bowling.

Dale Steyn had begun the series with a bit of history, overhauling Shaun Pollock's national-record 421 Test wickets on the first morning at Centurion. But the real damage was done by Duanne Olivier, whose previous five Tests had been spread across two years. He made himself undroppable, and finished with 24 wickets at 14. Rapid, mean and partial to the bouncer, Olivier was central to South Africa's 3–0 win.

It was their seventh Test series victory in a row at home, equalling the national record, set between March 1998 and November 2001. However, two Tests later, he'd abandon his international career to go Kolpak.

Duanne Olivier: Rapid, mean and partial to the bouncer. — *Getty Images*

Babar Azam had a good tour and Shan Masood was belligerent. Imam-ul-Haq occasionally sparkled — mainly in the one-dayers — but South Africa always won the big moments. The result was tough on Pakistan, but they bowled better than they batted, with left-arm quicks Mohammad Amir and newcomer Shaheen Shah Afridi especially impressive.

The find of the ODIs for South Africa was Rassie van der Dussen, who struck three half-centuries to complicate selection for the World Cup.

For a while, the cricket took a

back seat, as the authorities considered how to deal with comments made during the second game by Pakistan captain Sarfraz Ahmed. With Andile Phehlukwayo leading South Africa's chase, Sarfraz was caught on the stump mike referring to him, in Urdu, as "black guy". He later apologised, both to Phehlukwayo and to "the people of South Africa", prompting Faf du Plessis to say: "We forgive him because he said sorry." But the ICC punished Sarfraz anyway, banning him for four white-ball matches.

Pakistan ended a tough but entertaining visit by winning the last of the three T20I games, but not before they had suffered their first series defeat in the format since visiting New Zealand early in 2016.

	Tests	ODIs	T20Is
Most runs	Quinton de Kock (251 runs, 3 matches)	Imam-ul-Haq (271 runs, 5 matches)	Babar Azam (151 runs, 3 matches)
Most wickets	Duanne Olivier (24 wickets, 3 matches)	Andile Phehlukwayo (8 wickets, 5 matches)	Beuran Hendricks (8 wickets, 3 matches)

Tour match

Willowmoore Park, Benoni, December 19-21: Cricket South Africa Invitation XI 318/7 dec. in 84.3 overs (Marques Ackerman 103*, Joshua Richards 98; Azhar Ali 2-19, Faheem Ashraf 2-45) and 182/7 dec. in 50.3 overs (Neil Brand 71, Onke Nyaku 37; Mohammad Amir 3-35) lost to **Pakistanis** 306/7 dec. in 78.2 overs (Babar Azam 104*, A Ali 100; Thandolwethu Mnyaka 3-45) and 195/4 in 40.2 overs (Haris Sohail 73*, Imam-ul-Haq 66; Kyle Simmonds 2-79) by six wickets.

Test series (3): South Africa 3 Pakistan 0

1ˢᵗ Test: South Africa won by six wickets

Steyn broke Pollock's national record of 421 Test wickets on the ground where his career first took flight. After Pakistan elected to bat, Kagiso Rabada trapped Imam in the second over, before Steyn had Fakhar Zaman taken at third slip, to spark celebrations from the players and an appreciative audience.

But the remaining headlines belonged to another South African fast bowler. Olivier. Bowling fast and short, he helped himself to his first Test haul of more than three and confirmed the rise of the Bloemfontein Bone Collector, a nickname bestowed by his team-mate, Dean Elgar.

Pakistan only made 181 thanks to a ninth-wicket stand of 67 in less than ten overs between Babar and Hasan Ali. In response, South Africa faced a skilful Pakistani attack. Locating good lengths and meticulous lines, left-armers Amir and Afridi, in only his second Test, struck regularly. The hosts required resolute knocks from Temba Bavuma and Quinton de Kock to gain a first-innings lead of 42.

Pakistan moved 59 in front with nine wickets in hand. But Olivier rushed through the defences of Imam, before bouncing out Azhar Ali in his next over, a taste of what awaited him in the rest of the series. He had prised open the middle order, and the rest of his gang poured through. From 101 for 1, Pakistan had limped to 190.

South Africa were unlikely to be pushed by a target of 149, but there were a few hairy moments. Aiden Markram fell for a duck, before the out-of-form Hashim Amla was dropped at third slip on eight by Fakhar. In the next over, Pakistan were fuming when third umpire Joel Wilson ruled Azhar had failed to get his fingers under the ball at first slip after Elgar edged Afridi. Coach Arthur stormed into Wilson's room to remonstrate, earning a demerit point for his troubles. But slowly, the batsmen asserted themselves.

SuperSport Park, Centurion, December 26-28: Pakistan 181 in 47 overs (Babar Azam 71, Azhar Ali 36; Duanne Olivier 6-37, Kagiso Rabada 3-59) and 190 in 56 overs (Shan Masood 65, Imam-ul-Haq 57; D Olivier 5-59, K Rabada 3-47) lost to **South Africa** 223 in 60 overs (Temba Bavuma 53, Quinton de Kock 45; Mohammad Amir 4-62, Shaheen Afridi 4-64) and 151/4 in 50.4 overs (Hashim Amla 63*, Dean Elgar 50) by six wickets. *PoM:* Duanne Olivier.

2nd Test: South Africa won by nine wickets

Newlands traditionally brings spinners into the game, but that didn't stop South Africa from sacrificing slow left-armer Keshav Maharaj for the fit-again Vernon Philander. And while the pacer managed only two wickets, a four-pronged attack proved too strong for Pakistan.

Pakistan were 54 for 5 inside 20 overs, before Sarfraz showed what was possible during a roguish half-century that took them to 177.

Unpredictable bounce would become a theme of the match, and from 149 for 4, the innings was rebuilt by du Plessis and Bavuma. It wasn't always pretty, as balls spat from a length, but their alliance of 156 in 53 overs sealed the series. De Kock added gloss with 59, and although Amir and Afridi both claimed first-innings four-fors for the second match running, South Africa led by 254. Having been given a breather of 124 overs, their fast bowlers charged in once more. Steyn and Rabada made early breaches, before Masood and Asad Shafiq added a spirited 132. But Steyn induced an edge from Masood and the Pakistan crumble was on. Despite a brilliant innings from Babar, whose 72 included 15 fours, their last seven fell for 100.

A tetchy Sarfraz was left to bemoan the difference in pace between the teams, suggesting the hosts' attack was "fitter than us".

Newlands, Cape Town, January 3-6: Pakistan 177 in 51.1 overs (Sarfaraz Ahmed 56, Shan Masood 44; Duanne Olivier 4-48, Dale Steyn 3-48) and 294 in 70.4 overs (Asad Shafiq 88, Babar Azam 72; Kagiso Rabada 4-61, D Steyn 4-85) lost to **South Africa** 431 in 124.1 overs (Faf du Plessis 103, Aiden Markram 78; Mohammad Amir 4-88, Shaheen Afridi 4-123) and 43/1 in 9.5 overs by nine wickets. *PoM:* Faf du Plessis.

3rd Test: South Africa won by 107 runs

South Africa made it seven home Test wins in a row against Pakistan, and 11 out of 12, as their fast bowlers again outgunned the tourists' batsmen.

With du Plessis suspended, the captaincy passed to Elgar for the second time. And while Elgar, after winning the toss under sunny skies, was caught behind off Abbas in the second over, Markram cover-drove imperiously during a second-wicket stand of 126 with Amla. At 229 for 3, South Africa had a chance to bat Pakistan out of the game, but the last seven fell for 33 in 15 overs — including Zubayr Hamza, their 100th Test cricketer since readmission.

Thanks to Philander and his trademark relentlessness, however, Pakistan's top order were in the mire before the first-day close. Sarfraz got his one-day practice in early, spanking eight fours in a 40-ball 50, but the last five crashed for 16, leaving Olivier with another five-for.

Walking out to bat at 93 for 5, only 170 in front, de Kock fought fire with fire. Amla stood vigil, methodically grinding down the bowlers' resolve, but de Kock dazzled, striding to his first Test century in two years. By the time he fell for a startling 129 off 138 balls, the game was beyond Pakistan's reach.

New Wanderers, Johannesburg, January 11-14: South Africa 262 in 77.4 overs (Aiden Markram 90, Theunis de Bruyn 49; Faheem Ashraf 3-57, Mohammad Amir 2-36) and 303 in 80.3 overs (Quinton de Kock 129, Hashim Amla 71; Shadab Khan 3-41, F Ashraf 3-42) beat **Pakistan** 185 in 49.4 overs (Sarfaraz Ahmed 50, Babar Azam 49; Duanne Olivier 5-51, Vernon Philander 3-43) and 273 in 65.4 overs (Asad Shafiq 65, Shadab 47*; D Olivier 3-74, Kagiso Rabada 3-75) by 107 runs. *PoM:* Quinton de Kock. *PoS:* Duanne Olivier.

ODI series (5): South Africa 3 Pakistan 2

1st ODI: Pakistan won by five wickets

Rassie van der Dussen, a stalwart of domestic cricket, wasted little time getting comfortable: he made an even-paced 93 before falling to a full toss, and put on 155 for the second wicket with Amla, who reached his 27th ODI century. But, on a slow surface, neither could quite hit the accelerator. With powerhouses like David Miller lying in wait, South Africa's 266 for 2 felt like a missed opportunity. Their total was soon exposed as pedestrian. The arrival of Mohammad Hafeez and Shoaib Malik had galvanised Pakistan and, after Imam hit a half-century, Hafeez struck a pugnacious unbeaten 71 from 63 balls to lead his side home with five balls to spare. This was Pakistan's highest successful chase away to South Africa.

St George's Park, Port Elizabeth, January 19: South Africa 266/2 in 50 overs (Hashim Amla 108*, Rassie van der Dussen 93) lost to **Pakistan** 267/5 in 49.1 overs (Imam-ul-Haq 86, Mohammad Hafeez 71*; Duanne Olivier 2-73) by five wickets. *PoM:* Mohammad Hafeez.

2nd ODI: South Africa won by five wickets

South Africa's series-squaring win was overshadowed by comments made in the field by Sarfraz to Phehlukwayo, who was riding his luck as he took his side to victory with a maiden ODI fifty. On his home ground, Phehlukwayo had helped rescue South Africa from 80 for 5 in pursuit of 204, putting on an

Andile Phehlukwayo followed up a career-best 4 for 22 with his maiden ODI fifty in the second ODI. — *Getty Images*

unbroken 124 with van der Dussen after three early wickets for Afridi and two in two balls for Shadab. Earlier, Phehlukwayo had made good use of the slower ball on a clammy Kingsmead surface to help reduce Pakistan to 112 for 8. Their eventual 203 owed much to a cheeky 59 from 45 balls by No.10 Hasan, who became Phehlukwayo's fourth victim — also an ODI best.

Kingsmead, Durban, January 22: Pakistan 203 in 45.5 overs (Hasan Ali 59, Sarfaraz Ahmed 41; Andile Phehlukwayo 4-22, Tabraiz Shamsi 3-56) lost to **South Africa** 207/5 in 42 overs (Rassie van der Dussen 80*, A Phehlukwayo 69*; Shaheen Afridi 3-44, Shadab Khan 2-46) by five wickets. *PoM:* Andile Phehlukwayo.

3rd ODI: South Africa won by 13 runs (DLS)

A savage Gauteng storm interrupted an engaging match, with South Africa ahead on DLS. The day had begun with a tweet from Sarfraz, this time a photo of him shaking hands with, and apologising to, Phehlukwayo for his comments during the second ODI. Two days later, Sarfraz was found guilty by the ICC of breaching their anti-racism code, and banned for four matches. Before all that, Imam celebrated a brilliant century by making a chatting gesture with his hands, then putting a finger to his lips. It was aimed, he said, at those who believed he owed his place in the side to his uncle, Pakistan's chief selector Inzamam-ul-Haq, a suggestion that had "really pissed me off". Babar made a sweet half-century, as did Hafeez, before Imad Wasim clubbed 43 from 23 balls at the death. South Africa initially needed 318 on a good track, before rain interrupted the innings at 88 for 2 in the 17th. Hendricks decided it would be best to stay ahead on DLS, in case bad weather returned. When it did, after 33, he had added 58 from 57 balls, and 108 for the third wicket with du Plessis.

SuperSport Park, Centurion, January 25: **Pakistan** 317/6 in 50 overs (Imam-ul-Haq 101, Babar Azam 69; Dale Steyn 2-43, Kagiso Rabada 2-57) lost to **South Africa** 187/2 in 33 overs (Reeza Hendricks 83*, Faf du Plessis 40*) by 13 wickets (DLS method). *PoM:* Reeza Hendricks.

4ᵗʰ ODI: Pakistan won by eight wickets

This was the first Pink Day fixture lost by the hosts. Left-arm seamer Usman Shinwari took four wickets, including three in four balls, as South Africa failed to build on half-centuries from Amla and du Plessis, who added 101 for the third wicket. The last eight went down for 45. Imam put on 70 for the first wicket with Fakhar, and 94 for the second with Babar. Shoaib Malik had walked out for the toss, leading his country in an ODI for the first time for ten years.

New Wanderers, Johannesburg, January 27: **South Africa** 164 in 41 overs (Hashim Amla 59, Faf du Plessis 57; Usman Shinwari 4-35, Shaheen Afridi 2-24) lost to **Pakistan** 168/2 in 31.3 overs (Imam-ul-Haq 71, Fakhar Zaman 44) by eight wickets. *PoM:* Usman Shinwari.

5ᵗʰ ODI: South Africa won by seven wickets

At the end of a fluctuating series, South Africa prevailed after a disciplined performance from their bowlers was followed by a reminder of the talents of de Kock. The only real threat came from Fakhar, who made a run-a-ball 70. Imad gave them a late boost with 47 not out off 31, but middle-order sluggishness — their No. 4-7 managed only 77 off 144 balls between them — cost them. De Kock was caught at cover off Shinwari on 12, only for replays to reveal a no-ball. He went on to a fearless 83 from 58, before du Plessis and van der Dussen each hit 50 not out as South Africa cantered to victory.

Newlands, Cape Town, January 30: **Pakistan** 240/8 in 50 overs (Fakhar Zaman 70, Imad Wasim 47*; Andile Phehlukwayo 2-42, Dwaine Pretorius 2-46) lost to **South Africa** 241/3 in 40 overs (Quinton de Kock 83, Faf du Plessis 50*, Rassie van der Dussen 50*) by seven wickets. *PoM:* Quinton de Kock. *PoS:* Imam-ul-Haq.

T20I series (2): South Africa 2 Pakistan 1

1ˢᵗ T20I: South Africa won by six runs

• After his grafting century in the Test here, du Plessis pummels 78 from 45 balls. • Adding a festive 131 in 12 overs with the in-form Hendricks (74 from 41), he paves the way for a record T20I score at Newlands. • This despite South Africa losing five from the last 29 balls for 35 runs, three to Shinwari. • Set more than 9.5 an over, Babar (38 from 27) and Hussain Talat (40 from 32) get the ball rolling, before Shoaib takes the chase deep. • But with 14 needed off three balls, he swings wildly to provide a fourth catch for Miller, who also ran out Babar and Mohammad Rizwan, and wins the match award for his fielding. • South Africa are grateful for the nerve of Phehlukwayo, whose slower balls keep Pakistan guessing.

Newlands, Cape Town, February 1: South Africa 192/6 in 20 overs (Faf du Plessis 78, Reeza Hendricks 74; Usman Shinwari 3-31) beat **Pakistan** 186/9 in 20 overs (Shoaib Malik 49, Hussain Talat 40; Tabraiz Shamsi 2-33, Chris Morris 2-39) by six runs. *PoM:* David Miller.

2nd T20I: South Africa win by seven runs

• South Africa begin by clattering 188 for 3, the acceleration coming first from van der Dussen (45 from 27 balls, with four sixes), then from Miller, who is captaining for the first time. • Miller blasts 65 not out from 29, with five sixes, three in a traumatic 20th over from Shinwari, which costs 29. • His four overs leak 63, in contrast to the left-arm spin of Imad, who has gone for just nine. • Chasing a big total, Pakistan need instant aggression and Babar supplies it, with a blistering 90 from 58 balls. • Talat (55 from 41) helps add 102 for the second wicket. • But the middle order has no answer to Phehluk-wayo's relish for the death overs and the knuckle ball. • He takes three as Pakistan lose six for 33.

New Wanderers, Johannesburg, February 3: South Africa 188/3 in 20 overs (David Miller 65*, Rassie van der Dussen 45) beat **Pakistan** 181/7 in 20 overs (Babar Azam 90, Hussain Talat 55; Andile Phehlukwayo 3-36, Beuran Hendricks 2-30) by seven runs. *PoM:* David Miller.

3rd T20I: Pakistan won by 27 runs

• Babar drills five fours in an 11-ball 23. • Beuran Hendricks returns career-best figures of 4 for 14, and Chris Morris chipps in with two. • The others come in for stick, though, as Pakistan take advantage of an inexperienced attack. • Imad is tidy again, going for 19 from four overs. • And, with a rash of established stars rested, only van der Dussen stands firm in the top order. • That left too much to do at the back end, though Morris blazes a maiden T20I half-century, from 29 balls.

SuperSport Park, Centurion, February 6: Pakistan 168/9 in 20 overs (Mohammad Rizwan 26, Asif Ali 25; Beuran Hendricks 4-14, Chris Morris 2-27) beat **South Africa** 141/9 in 20 overs (C Morris 55*, Rassie van der Dussen 41; Mohammad Amir 3-27, Shadab Khan 2-34) by 27 runs. *PoM:* Shadab Khan. *PoS:* David Miller.

Kemar Roach scythed through the England line-up in the First Test to bundle them out for 77. — *CWI*

England in West Indies

Visiting batsmen chastened

England conceded the Test series to West Indies before they could find their groove. They had only three innings in excess of forty in the first two Tests as Kemar Roach, Shannon Gabriel, Jason Holder, and Alzarri Joseph kept peppering them with bouncers on lively pitches, while Roston Chase had a spell of 8 for 60. England managed 77, 246, 187 and 132 in the in first four innings of the series.

Kraigg Brathwaite and debutant John Campbell converted their first four opening stands into fifties, while Holder slammed an unbeaten 202 to add an unbroken 395 for the seventh wicket in the First Test. If any indication was needed that England's low scores were down to the batsmen, not the pitch, this was it.

Mark Wood's late inclusion, combined with Holder's one-Test suspension for slow over-rate, helped the visitors pull off a consolation win. Brathwaite led in the absence of Holder, and England's long wait for a Test series win in the West Indies — they have only one there since 1968 — continued.

The first three ODIs were marked by some serious hitting, followed by one where England were bowled out for 113 and West Indies won before lunch to level the series.

Chris Gayle set a new series record by smashing 39 sixes, bettering his own record of 26, set in the 2015 World Cup, by some distance. Gayle's 162 from 97 in Grenada was the perfect response to Jos Buttler's incredible

150 from 77 balls, which included the Englishman going from 50 to 150 in a mere 31 deliveries. The Jamaican claimed he would retire after the World Cup, but that knock seemed to have him pondering "un-retirement". Having become only the second West Indian batsman after Brian Lara to reach 10,000 ODI runs, he was keen to add more to the tally.

The hosts had the World Cup on their mind when they chose their T20 squad. But the tour ended anticlimactically, with West Indies getting bowled out for 45 and 71 in the last T20Is to lose the series 0–3.

	Tests	ODIs	T20Is
Most runs	Jason Holder (229 runs, 2 matches)	Chris Gayle (424 runs, 5 matches)	Jonny Bairstow (117 runs, 3 matches)
Most wickets	Kemar Roach (18 wickets, 3 matches)	Adil Rashid (9 wickets, 5 matches)	Chris Jordan (6 wickets, 3 matches)

Tour matches

Three Ws Oval, Cave Hill, Barbados, January 15-16: England 317/10 dec. in 87 overs (Joe Root 87, Ben Stokes 56; Bryan Charles 5-100, Chemar Holder 3-67) drew with **West Indies President's XI** 203 in 79.5 overs (Vishaul Singh 35+ and 25+, Jahmar Hamilton 25; James Anderson 4-12, Stuart Broad 4-19).

Three Ws Oval, Cave Hill, Barbados, January 17-18: England 379 in 86.4 overs (Jonny Bairstow 98, Rory Burns 68; Raymon Reifer 3-39, John Campbell 3-58) drew with **West Indies President's XI** 233/11 in 73 overs (Sunil Ambris 94; Chris Woakes 3-31, Stuart Broad 2-33).

+ *In both matches, batsmen of both sides were allowed to bat again till the day's play got over.*

Test series (3): West Indies 2 England 1

1st Test: West Indies won by 381 runs

Kensington Oval, Bridgetown, Barbados, January 23-26: West Indies 289 in 101.3 overs (Shimron Hetmyer 81, Shai Hope 57; James Anderson 5-46, Ben Stokes 4-59) and 415/6 dec. in 103.1 overs (Jason Holder 202*, Shane Dowrich 116*; Moeen Ali 3-78, B Stokes 2-81) beat **England** 77 in 30.2 overs (Kemar Roach 5-17, J Holder 2-15) and 246 in 80.4 overs (Rory Burns 84, B Stokes 34; Roston Chase 8-60) by 381 runs. *PoM:* Jason Holder.

2nd Test: West Indies won by ten wickets

Sir Vivian Richards Stadium, North Sound, Antigua, January 31-February 2: England 187 in 61 overs (Moeen Ali 60, Jonny Bairstow 52; Kemar Roach 4-30, Shannon Gabriel 3-45) and 132 in 42.1 overs (Jason Holder 4-43, K Roach 4-52) lost to **West Indies** 306 in 131 overs (Darren Bravo 50, Kraigg Brathwaite 49; Stuart Broad 3-53, M Ali 3-62) and 17 for no loss in 2.1 overs by ten wickets. *PoM:* Kemar Roach.

3rd Test: England won by 232 runs

Darren Sammy National Cricket Stadium, Gros Islet, St Lucia, February 9-12: England 277 in 101.5 overs (Ben Stokes 79, Jos Buttler 67; Kemar Roach 4-48, Shannon Gabriel 2-49) and 361/5 dec. in 105.2 overs (Joe Root 122, Joe Denly 69; S Gabriel 2-95) beat **West Indies** 154 in 47.2 overs (John Campbell 41, Shane Dowrich 38; Mark Wood 5-41, Moeen Ali 4-36) and 252 in 69.5 overs (Roston Chase 102*, Alzarri Joseph 34; James Anderson 3-27, M Ali 3-99) by 232 runs. *PoM:* Mark Wood. *PoS:* Kemar Roach.

Tour match

Three Ws Oval, Cave Hill, Barbados, February 17: England 371/7 in 50 overs (Joe Root 114, Jason Roy 110; Yannick Ottley 2-64) beat **UW Vice Chancellor's XI** 200 in 43.5 overs (Nicholas Kirton 37, Kyle Corbin 35, Amir Jangoo 35; Adil Rashid 2-21, Chris Woakes 2-28) by 171 runs.

ODI series (5): West Indies 2 England 2

Kensington Oval, Bridgetown, Barbados, February 20: West Indies 360/8 in 50 overs (Chris Gayle 135, Shai Hope 64; Ben Stokes 3-37, Adil Rashid 3-74) lost to **England** 364/4 in 48.4 overs (Jason Roy 123, Joe Root 102; Jason Holder 2-63) by six wickets. *PoM:* Jason Roy.

Kensington Oval, Bridgetown, Barbados, February 22: West Indies 289/6 in 50 overs (Shimron Hetmyer 104*, Chris Gayle 50) beat **England** 263 in 47.4 overs (Ben Stokes 79, Eoin Morgan 70; Sheldon Cottrell 5-46, Jason Holder 3-53) by 26 runs. *PoM:* Shimron Hetmyer.

National Stadium, St George's, Granada, February 25: West Indies v **England**. No play after England won toss.

National Stadium, St George's, Granada, February 27: England 418/6 in 50 overs (Jos Buttler 150, Eoin Morgan 103; Carlos Brathwaite 2-69, Oshane Thomas 2-84) beat **West Indies** 389 in 48 overs (Chris Gayle 162, Darren Bravo 61; Adil Rashid 5-85, Mark Wood 4-60) by 29 runs. *PoM:* Jos Buttler.

Darren Sammy National Cricket Stadium, Gros Islet, St Lucia, March 2: England 113 in 28.1 overs (Oshane Thomas 5-21, Carlos Brathwaite 2-17) lost to **West Indies** 115/3 in 12.1 overs (Chris Gayle 77; Mark Wood 2-55) by seven wickets. *PoM:* Oshane Thomas. *PoS:* Chris Gayle.

T20I series (3): England 3 West Indies 0

Darren Sammy National Cricket Stadium, Gros Islet, St Lucia, March 2: West Indies 160/8 in 20 overs (Nicholas Pooran 58, Darren Bravo 28; Tom Curran 4-36, Chris Jordan 2-16) lost to **England** 161/6 in 18.5 overs (Jonny Bairstow 68, Joe Denly 30; Sheldon Cottrell 3-29) by four wickets. *PoM:* Jonny Bairstow.

Warner Park, Basseterre, March 8: England 182/6 in 20 overs (Sam Billings 87, Joe Root 55; Fabian Allen 2-29) beat **West Indies** 45 in 11.5 overs (Chris Jordan 4-6, Liam Plunkett 2-8) by 137 runs. *PoM:* Sam Billings.

Warner Park, Basseterre, March 10: West Indies 71 in 13 overs (David Willey 4-7, Mark Wood 3-9) lost to **England** 72/2 in 10.3 overs (Jonny Bairstow 37*) by eight wickets. *PoM:* David Willey. *PoS:* Chris Jordan.

Sri Lanka in Australia

Cummins, Starc rip through Sri Lanka

The Australians shrugged off their defeat at home against India with comfortable innings wins against Sri Lanka to regain the Warne-Muralitharan Trophy.

Pat Cummins tore through Sri Lanka in Brisbane for match figures of 10 for 62, while debutant Jhye Richardson had 5 for 45. Bowled out for 144, Sri Lanka, spearheaded by Suranga Lakmal, who picked up five wickets, reduced Australia to 82 for 4 before Travis Head and Marnus Labuschagne took the match away from them.

Pat Cummins continued his excellent form from the India series, setting the tone with a ten-wicket haul in the First Test in Brisbane. — *Getty Images*

Joe Burns, Head, Kurtis Patterson and Usman Khawaja all got hundreds in the Second Test, the first ever at Manuka Oval, Canberra. This time, Mitchell Starc, who had reached the 200-wicket mark in Test cricket in Brisbane, took 10 for 100.

Angelo Mathews missed out on the tour because of a hamstring injury. Sri Lanka were also without Nuwan Pradeep due to a hamstring injury. Then Lahiru Kumara pulled his hamstring as well, Dushmantha Chameera fractured his ankle, while Lakmal's back pain did not heal. They were forced to field a second-string attack in Canberra, where Kusal Perera was forced to retire in the first innings after being hit on the helmet by Richardson, though he batted in the second. It only added to the woes of a team already seeing too much off-field drama: the coach was removed as selector-on-tour, and Thisara Perera got into a social media tiff with Lasith Malinga's wife.

Throughout the series, their batsmen failed to demonstrate the doggedness that had helped them save the Wellington Test a month previously. They crossed 150 only once in four attempts, and their batsmen managed only two half-centuries between them, neither of which was over 65.

Most runs: Travis Head (Australia) (304 runs, 2 matches)
Most wickets: Pat Cummins (Australia) (14 wickets, 2 matches)

Tour match
Bellerive Oval, Hobart, January 17-19: Cricket Australia XI 316/5 dec. in 75 overs (Kurtis Patterson 157*, Jake Doran 102*; Dushmantha Chameera 3-57, Kasun Rajitha 2-71) and 224/3 dec. in 59 overs (K Patterson 102*, Marnus Labuschagne 50) drew with **Sri Lankans** 176/5 dec. in 75 overs (Dimuth Karunaratne 44, Roshen Silva 36*; M Labuschagne 2-27, Scott Boland 2-37) and 131/6 in 51 overs (Lahiru Thirimanne 46; Jon Holland 4-28, Michael Neser 2-8).

Test series (2): Australia 2 Sri Lanka 0
Brisbane Cricket Ground, Woolloongabba, Brisbane, January 24-26: Sri Lanka 144 in 56.4 overs (Niroshan Dickwella 64; Pat Cummins 4-39, Jhye Richardson 3-26) and 139 in 50.5 overs (Lahiru Thirimanne 32; P Cummins 6-23, J Richardson 2-19) lost to **Australia** 323 in 106.2 overs (Travis Head 84, Marnus Labuschagne 81; Suranga Lakmal 5-75, Dilruwan Perera 2-84) by an innings and 40 runs.
Manuka Oval, Canberra, February 1-4: Australia 534/5 dec. in 132 overs (Joe Burns 180, Travis Head 161, Kurtis Patterson 114*; Vishwa Fernando 3-126) and 196/3 dec. in 47 overs (Usman Khawaja 101*, T Head 59*; Kasun Rajitha 2-64) beat **Sri Lanka** 215 in 68.3 overs (Dimuth Karunaratne 59, Lahiru Thirimanne 41; Mitchell Starc 5-54, Nathan Lyon 2-70) and 149 in 51 overs (Kusal Mendis 42, L Thirimanne 30; M Starc 5-46, Pat Cummins 3-15) by 366 runs. *PoM:* Mitchell Starc. *PoS:* Pat Cummins.

Kusal Perera's remarkable 153 not out to pull off a one-wicket win will go down in history as one of the all-time great innings. — *Getty Images*

Sri Lanka in South Africa

Kusal Perera writes a classic

South Africa did a clean sweep of the limited-overs leg of the tour, winning all five ODIs and all three T20Is. However, whether these wins were enough to erase the scar of the 0–2 whitewash in the Tests is debatable. This was also their first series loss at home after winning seven on the trot.

Kusal Perera was Sri Lanka's star in Durban for his 51 and 153 not out, the second innings enough to find a place in the pantheon of the all-time great Test innings. At Port Elizabeth, the visitors put up a more clinical performance, turning a first-innings deficit into a comfortable eight-wicket win. Their young brigade of Vishwa Fernando, Oshada Fernando and Lasith Embuldeniya were impressive enough throughout the Test series for Sri Lanka to count on a bright future in the long format under Dimuth Karunaratne, their newly appointed captain.

Unfortunately, they were hardly the same side in the shorter formats. They failed to contain Quinton de Kock and Faf du Plessis — or, in the T20Is, Reeza Hendricks; neither could they stand up against Kagiso Rabada, Lungi Ngidi, Anrich Nortje and Imran Tahir, all of whom took at least eight wickets at under 19 while conceding below five an over.

The surprise package was Isuru Udana (242 runs at 80.67, strike-rate 141, 19 fours, 15 sixes in ODIs and T20Is). He even won the match award in the fourth ODI despite South Africa's convincing win.

	Tests	**ODIs**	**T20Is**
Most runs	Kusal Perera (224 runs, 2 matches)	Quinton de Kock (353 runs, 5 matches)	Reeza Hendricks (139 runs, 3 matches)
Most wickets	Vishwa Fernando (12 wickets, 2 matches)	Imran Tahir (9 wickets, 5 matches)	Andile Phehlukwayo (7 wickets, 3 matches)

Test series (2): Sri Lanka 2 South Africa 0

1st Test: Sri Lanka won by one wicket

Over years, analysts and historians will determine whether Kusal Perera's unbeaten 153 during Sri Lanka's chase was the greatest in history. As for fans, they have watched the highlights enough to narrate to their grandchildren tales of his two sixes over square leg off Dale Steyn, the one over fine leg off Rabada, the fact that he added 78 for the last wicket to seal a Test against a quality attack at their den … Perera's unbroken stand with Vishwa Fernando is the highest ever in a successful chase. Vishwa's own contribution was all of six, four of those runs coming in overthrows. Perera's knock is also the highest by a Sri Lankan in a successful chase.

There were also the bowlers: left-arm seamer Vishwa, in his fourth Test, took four wickets in each innings; debutant Embuldeniya followed a gritty cameo with a five-wicket haul; Kasun Rajitha was sharp and incisive; and Suranga Lakmal was backbreakingly persistent. But in the end, the Test will be remembered as Perera's.

Kingsmead, Durban, February 13-16: South Africa 235 in 59.4 overs (Quinton de Kock 80, Temba Bavuma 47; Vishwa Fernando 4-62, Kasun Rajitha 3-68) and 259 in 79.1 overs (Faf du Plessis 90, Q de Kock 55; Lasith Embuldeniya 5-66, V Fernando 4-71) lost to **Sri Lanka** 191 in 59.2 overs (Kusal Perera 51, Dimuth Karunaratne 30; Dale Steyn 4-48, Vernon Philander 2-32) and 304/9 in 85.3 overs (K Perera 153*, Dhananjaya de Silva 48; Keshav Maharaj 3-71, Duanne Olivier 2-35) by one wicket. *PoM:* Kusal Perera.

2nd Test: Sri Lanka won by eight wickets

Sri Lanka beat South Africa by eight wickets despite conceding a 68-run lead and getting reduced to ten men.

De Kock counterattacked against Vishwa and Rajitha to lift South Africa from 15 for 3 to 222 on a grassy pitch. Embuldeniya was ruled out of the rest of the Test with a dislocated finger, but Dhananjaya de Silva stepped in with match figures of 5 for 51.

Sri Lanka were rescued by Niroshan Dickwella after Rabada and Duanne Olivier had reduced them to 97 for 6. Then Lakmal finally did justice by converting his probing bowling into a game-changing spell of 4 for 15, even as Faf du Plessis stood tall with an unbeaten fifty. Sri Lanka slipped to 34 for 2 in pursuit of 197, but Kusal Mendis and young Oshada made sure there were no further hiccups.

St George's Park, Port Elizabeth, February 21-23: South Africa 222 in 61.2 overs (Quinton de Kock 86, Aiden Markram 60; Vishwa Fernando 3-62, Kasun Rajitha 3-67) and 128 in 44.3 overs (Faf du Plessis 50*, Hashim Amla 32; Suranga Lakmal 4-39, Dhananjaya de Silva 3-36) lost to **Sri Lanka** 154 in 37.4 overs (Niroshan Dickwella 42, Lahiru Thirimanne 29; Kagiso Rabada 4-38, Duanne Olivier 3-61) and 197/2 in 45.4 overs (Kusal Mendis 84*, Oshada Fernando 75*) by eight wickets. *PoM:* Kusal Mendis. *PoS:* Kusal Perera.

Tour match

St George's Park, Port Elizabeth, January 19: Cricket South Africa Invitation XI 304 in 48 overs (Raynard van Tonder 164, Marques Ackerman 42; Lasith Malinga 5-35, Kasun Rajitha 2-36) lost to **Sri Lankans** 307/4 in 41 overs (Avishka Fernando 82, Oshada Fernando 63; Okuhle Cele 2-37) by six wickets.

ODI series (5): South Africa 5 Sri Lanka 0

New Wanderers, Johannesburg, January 27: Sri Lanka 231 in 47 overs (Kusal Mendis 60, Oshada Fernando 49; Imran Tahir 3-26, Lungi Ngidi 3-60) lost to **South Africa** 232/2 in 38.5 overs (Faf du Plessis 112*, Quinton de Kock 81) by eight wickets. *PoM:* Faf du Plessis.

SuperSport Park, Centurion, January 25: South Africa 251 in 46.1 overs (Quinton de Kock 94, Faf du Plessis 57; Thisara Perera 3-26, Lasith Malinga 2-39) beat **Sri Lanka** 138 in 32.2 overs (Oshada Fernando 31; Kagiso Rabada 3-43, Lungi Ngidi 2-14) by 113 runs. *PoM:* Quinton de Kock.

Kingsmead, Durban, January 22: South Africa 331/5 in 50 overs (Quinton de Kock 121, Rassie van der Dussen 50; Isuru Udana 2-50) beat **Sri Lanka** 121/5 in 24 overs (Kusal Mendis 41, Oshada Fernando 25; Imran Tahir 2-19) by 71 runs (DLS method). *PoM:* Quinton de Kock.

St George's Park, Port Elizabeth, January 19: Sri Lanka 189 in 39.2 overs (Isuru Udana 78, Avishka Fernando 29; Anrich Nortje 3-57, Andile Phehlukwayo 2-21) lost to **South Africa** 190/4 in 32.5 overs (Quinton de Kock 51, Faf du Plessis 43; Dhananjaya de Silva 3-41) by six wickets. *PoM:* Isuru Udana.

Newlands, Cape Town, January 30: Sri Lanka 225 in 49.3 overs (Kusal Mendis 56, Priyamal Perera 33; Kagiso Rabada 3-50, Imran Tahir 2-33) lost to **South Africa** 135/2 in 28 overs (Aiden Markram 67*, Rassie van der Dussen 28*) by 41 runs (DLS method). *PoM:* Aiden Markram. *PoS:* Quinton de Kock.

T20I series (3): South Africa 3 Sri Lanka 0

Newlands, Cape Town, February 1: Sri Lanka 134/7 in 20 overs (Kamindu Mendis 41; Andile Phehlukwayo 3-25) lost to **South Africa** 134/8 in 20 overs (David Miller 41, Rassie van der Dussen 34; Lasith Malinga 2-11) by two wickets. *PoM:* David Miller.

SuperSport Park, Centurion, February 6: South Africa 180/3 in 20 overs (Reeza Hendricks 65, Rassie van der Dussen 64) beat **Sri Lanka** 164/9 in 20 overs (Isuru Udana 84*; Chris Morris 3-32, Tabraiz Shamsi 2016) by 16 runs. *PoM:* Rassie van der Dussen.

New Wanderers, Johannesburg, February 3: South Africa 198/2 in 20 overs (Dwaine Pretorius 77*, Reeza Hendricks 66) beat **Sri Lanka** 137 in 15.4 overs (Niroshan Dickwella 38, Isuru Udana 36; Andile Phehlukwayo 4-24, Lutho Simpala 2-22) by 45 runs (DLS method). *PoM:* Dwaine Pretorius. *PoS:* Reeza Hendricks.

Bangladesh in New Zealand

Terror cuts short tour

Terror struck Christchurch and the Bangladesh team found themselves traumatically close to it. Ahead of the final Test, a group of players and support staff were going to a mosque close to the Hagley Oval for Friday afternoon prayers when their bus was flagged down by a good Samaritan yards away from the mosque where a shooting was unfolding. Witness to the carnage, the contingent took refuge in the bus for a while, before making a dash for safety to the ground and their hotel, where the horror of what they'd just been through and the reality of their own fortunate escape sunk in. Expectedly, the tour was called off as the players made their way home.

The incident slightly consigned to the background the on-field action till then, where Bangladesh were still denied in their quest for a win in any format in New Zealand. Martin Guptill's back-to-back centuries gave the hosts an unassailable lead in the ODIs, before Tim Southee's six wickets meant Sabbir Rahman's maiden hundred came in a losing cause.

Tamim Iqbal found his touch in the Tests after disappointing outings with the white ball, and Bangladesh adapted to the short-ball barrage that greeted them. Yet, they found no joy as they were batted out of the game. The hosts had to bat just twice in the two completed Tests. Kane Williamson and Ross Taylor made a double-hundred each in successive matches, while Jeet Raval and Tom Latham added 254 for the first wicket in the First Test in Hamilton.

It was New Zealand's record fifth consecutive series win.

	ODIs	Tests
Most runs	Martin Guptill (New Zealand) (264 runs, 3 matches)	Tamim Iqbal (Bangladesh) (278 runs, 2 matches)
Most wickets	Tim Southee (New Zealand) (6 wickets, 3 matches)	Neil Wagner (New Zealand) (16 wickets, 2 matches)

Tour match

Bert Sutcliffe Oval, Lincoln, February 10: Bangladeshis 247 in 46.1 overs (Mahmudullah 72, Mushfiqur Rahim 62; Ian McPeake 4-38, Rachin Ravindra 2-34) lost to **New Zealand XI** 251/8 in 48.1 overs (Andrew Fletcher 92, Jeet Raval 52; Mustafizur Rahman 2-33, Mahmudullah 2-37) by two wickets.

ODI series (3): New Zealand 3 Bangladesh 0

McLean Park, Napier, February 13: Bangladesh 232 in 48.5 overs (Mohammad Mithun 62, Mohammad Saifuddin 41; Trent Boult 3-40, Mitchell Santner 3-45) lost to **New Zealand** 233/2 in 44.3 overs (Martin Guptill 117*, Henry Nicholls 53) by eight wickets. *PoM:* Martin Guptill.

Hagley Oval, Christchurch, February 15: Bangladesh 226 in 49.4 overs (Mohammad Mithun 57, Sabbir Rahman 43; Lockie Ferguson 3-43, Jimmy Neesham 2-21) lost to **New Zealand** 229.2 in 36.1 overs (Martin Guptill 118, Kane Williamson 65*; Mustafizur Rahman 2-42) by eight wickets. *PoM:* Martin Guptill.

University Oval, Dunedin, February 20: New Zealand 330/6 in 50 overs (Ross Taylor 69, Tom Latham 59; Mustafizur Rahman 2-93) beat **Bangladesh** 242 in 47.2 overs (Sabbir Rahman 102, Mohammad Saifuddin 44; Tim Southee 6-65, Trent Boult 2-37) by 88 runs. *PoM:* Tim Southee. *PoS:* Martin Guptill.

Tour match

Bert Sutcliffe Oval, Lincoln, February 23-24: Bangladeshis 411 in 96.1 overs (Shadman Islam 67, Liton Das 62rh; Blake Coburn 2-92) drew with **New Zealand XI** 57/2 in 12 overs (Andrew Fletcher 43*).

Test series (2): New Zealand 2 Bangladesh 0

Seddon Park, Hamilton, February 28-March 3: Bangladesh 234 in 59.2 overs (Tamim Iqbal 126, Liton Das 29; Neil Wagner 5-47, Tim Southee 3-76) and 429 in 103 overs (Soumya Sarkar 149, Mahmudullah 146; Trent Boult 5-123, T Southee 3-98) lost to **New Zealand** 715/6 dec. in 163 overs (Kane Williamson 200*, Tom Latham 161, Jeet Raval 132; S Sarkar 2-68, Mehidy Hasan 2-246) by an innings and 52 runs. *PoM:* Kane Williamson.

Basin Reserve, Wellington, March 8-12: Bangladesh 211 in 61 overs (Tamim Iqbal 74, Liton Das 33; Neil Wagner 4-28, Trent Boult 3-38) and 209 in 56 overs (Mahmudullah 67, Mohammad Mithun 47; N Wagner 5-45, T Boult 4-52) lost to **New Zealand** 432/6 dec. in 84.5 overs (Ross Taylor 200, Henry Nicholls 107; Abu Jayed 3-94, Taijul Islam 2-99) by an innings and 12 runs. *PoM:* Ross Taylor.

Hagley Oval, Christchurch, March 16-20: New Zealand v **Bangladesh** called off. No toss.

Afghanistan v Ireland in India

Zazai, Rahmat raise the bar

The fortunes of cricket's two newest Full Members seem to have taken divergent paths in recent times, and the trend continued in Dehradun. Afghanistan extended their dominance over Ireland in the T20Is, before going on to claim their first Test win, in just their second Test.

Both teams had spent time in the months leading up to the multi-format fixtures getting used to the conditions in India. Ireland, having focused on playing spin, began well, reducing the opposition to 50 for 5 in defending 132 and had a strong appeal for lbw against Mohammad Nabi. But that was when their luck turned: Nabi went on to put in an all-round show and Ireland found little respite the rest of the series.

Hazratullah Zazai — him of the six sixes in an over and joint-fastest T20 fifty — clattered a record 16 hits over the fence, including four off Kevin O'Brien's 17th. His 162 off 62 balls is the second-highest T20I score, behind Aaron Finch's 172 against Zimbabwe in 2018. Usman Ghani's impressive 73 off 48 was consigned to a footnote in the opening stand of 236 — the highest for any wicket in T20s, beating the 229 between Virat Kohli and AB de Villiers in IPL 2016.

Records broken in the 2nd T20I

- 278 — Highest total in T20s
- 162* — Second-highest individual score in T20Is
- 16 — Most sixes in a T20I innings
- 236 — First-wicket stand between Zazai and Ghani, the most for any wicket in T20s.
- 91 — Paul Stirling's score, the highest individual score for Ireland

---

It only got more impressive: Nabi slammed 81 off 36 in the final match and Rashid Khan — fresh off the Big Bash League, where he had performed through the pain of losing his father — took a remarkable four in four.

Andy Balbirnie figured out a way to negate the spin threat, following up his century with a fifty to level the ODIs, but a batting collapse proved costly in the Tests. Tim Murtagh scored a half-century from No.11, leading a recovery from 69 for 8 to 172, adding 87 for the last wicket with George Dockrell. But with Afghanistan adopting a cautious approach — even the cavalier Mohammad Shahzad learning from his adventurism of their maiden Test — their bowlers couldn't make inroads.

Rahmat Shah fell two agonizing runs short of becoming his country's first centurion, chopping on off Murtagh. But he had set the platform before a

Hazratullah Zazai was explosive at the top for Afghanistan. — *ACB*

collapse of 226 for 3 to 280 for 8 was blunted by an aggressive fifty from captain Asghar Afghan — you couldn't tell that he was battling a painful shoulder.

Rashid, the No.1 in T20Is, showed his red-ball chops in ignoring a finger niggle to pick up five wickets. Another half-century stand for the last wicket gave Ireland hope, but Rahmat's second fifty of the game saw the modest target of 147 overhauled.

There was exuberance, but there was also a new maturity and a seriousness. Afghanistan turned out for the presentation in dapper jackets, sending out a message. Said Afghan: "It is a historic day for Afghanistan, for Afghanistan people, for our team, for our cricket board."

	T20Is	ODIs	Test
Most runs	Hazratullah Zazai (204 runs, 3 matches)	Asghar Afghan (226 runs, 5 matches)	Rahmat Shah (174 runs, 1 match)
Most wickets	Rashid Khan (11 wickets, 3 matches)	George Dockrell (8 wickets, 5 matches)	Rashid Khan (7 wickets, 1 match)

T20I series (3): Afghanistan 3 Ireland 0

Rajiv Gandhi International Cricket Stadium, Dehradun, February 21: Ireland 132/6 in 20 overs (George Dockrell 34*, Stuart Poynter 31*; Mohammad Nabi 2-16, Rashid 2-21) lost to **Afghanistan** 136/5 in 19.2 overs (M Nabi 49*, Najibullah Zadran 40*; Boyd Rankin 2-39) by five wickets. *PoM:* Mohammad Nabi.

Rajiv Gandhi International Cricket Stadium, Dehradun, February 23: Afghanistan 278/3 in 20 overs (Hazratullah Zazai 162*, Usman Ghani 73) beat Ireland 194/6 in 20 overs (Paul Stirling 91, Kevin O'Brien 37; Rashid Khan 4-25) by 84 runs. *PoM:* Hazratullah Zazai.

Rajiv Gandhi International Cricket Stadium, Dehradun, February 24: Afghanistan 210/7 in 20 overs (Mohammad Nabi 81, Hazratullah Zazai 31; Boyd Rankin 3-53) beat Ireland 178/8 in 20 overs (Kevin O'Brien 74, Andy Balbirnie 47; Rashid Khan 5-27, Ziaur Rahman 2-42) by 32 runs. *PoM:* Mohammad Nabi. *PoS:* Mohammad Nabi.

ODI series (5): Afghanistan 2 Ireland 2

Rajiv Gandhi International Cricket Stadium, Dehradun, February 28: Ireland 161 in 49.2 overs (Paul Stirling 89, George Dockrell 37; Mujeeb Ur Rahman 3-14, Dawlat Zadran

3-35) lost to **Afghanistan** 165/5 in 41.5 overs (Gulbadin Naib 46, Mohammad Shahzad 43; Boyd Rankin 2-48) by five wickets. *PoM:* Gulbadin Naib.

Rajiv Gandhi International Cricket Stadium, Dehradun, March 2: Afghanistan 250/7 in 48.3 overs (Hazratullah Zazai 67, Rahmat Shah 54; George Dockrell 3-51, Andy McBrine 2-43) vs **Ireland**. No result.

Rajiv Gandhi International Cricket Stadium, Dehradun, March 5: Afghanistan 256/8 in 50 overs (Najibullah Zadran 104*, Asghar Afghan 75; Boyd Rankin 2-56, Tim Murtagh 2-60) lost to **Ireland** 260/6 in 49 overs (Andy Balbirnie 145*, George Dockrell 54; Dawlat Zadran 2-52) by four wickets. *PoM:* Andy Balbirnie.

Rajiv Gandhi International Cricket Stadium, Dehradun, March 8: Afghanistan 223 in 49.1 overs (Mohammad Nabi 64, Asghar Afghan 54; James Cameron-Dow 3-32, Andy McBrine 2-37) beat **Ireland** 114 in 35.3 overs (Kevin O'Brien 26; Aftab Alam 4-25, Rashid Khan 2-22) by 109 runs. *PoM:* Rashid Khan.

Rajiv Gandhi International Cricket Stadium, Dehradun, March 10: Afghanistan 216/6 in 50 overs (Asghar Afghan 82rh, Mohammad Nabi 40; George Dockrell 2-46) lost to **Ireland** 219/5 in 47.2 overs (Paul Stirling 70, Andy Balbirnie 68; Zahir Khan 2-55) by five wickets. *PoM:* Asghar Afghan. *PoS:* Andy Balbirnie.

Only Test: Afghanistan won by seven wickets

Rajiv Gandhi International Cricket Stadium, Dehradun, March 15-18: Ireland 172 in 60 overs (Tim Murtagh 54*, George Dockrell 39; Mohammad Nabi 3-36, Yamin Ahmadzai 3-41) and 288 in 93 overs (Andy Balbirnie 82, Kevin O'Brien 56; Rashid Khan 5-82, Y Ahmadzai 3-52) lost to **Afghanistan** 314 in 106.3 overs (Rahmat Shah 98, Asghar Afghan 67; Stuart Thompson 3-28, G Dockrell 2-63) and 149/3 in 47.5 overs (R Shah 76, Ihsanullah 65*) by seven wickets. *PoM:* Rahmat Shah.

Pakistan v Australia in UAE

Finch finds form to settle sweep

For a while, even before the Newlands scandal that saw David Warner and Steve Smith banned, there were concerns about Australia's limited-overs form. Few would have considered the reigning champions among the favourites for the World Cup, but a dominant series sweep of Pakistan — their first 5-0 scoreline since 2008 — was a warning to the other teams that Australians simply know how to raise their game when the World Cup draws near.

Aaron Finch shook off a horror run of form during which he hadn't got into triple digits in 30 innings across formats to lead the resurgence. He fell ten runs short of an Australian record third ton in a row. Usman Khawaja and Glenn Maxwell both fell just short of centuries too; Maxwell sealed the sweep with a blazing 70 off 33 balls in his 100th ODI.

Jhye Richardson's injury in the second match, which would rule him out of the World Cup, was a black spot on an otherwise stellar tour.

Pakistan used the occasion to test their bench. Haris Sohail and Mohammad Rizwan both had two hundreds against their name — the first two of their ODI careers — while Abid Ali claimed one more on debut, but they all went in losing causes. Shoaib Malik stood in for the rested Sarfaraz Khan as captain, but after he too suffered a bruised rib, Imad Wasim found himself deputising.

Most runs: Aaron Finch (Australia) (451 runs, 5 matches)
Most wickets: Nathan Coulter-Nile (Australia) (7 wickets, 3 matches)

ODI series (5): Australia 5 Pakistan 0

Sharjah Cricket Stadium, Sharjah, March 22: Pakistan 280/5 in 50 overs (Haris Sohail 101*, Umar Akmal 48; Nathan Coulter-Nile 2-61) lost to **Australia** 281/1 in 49 overs (Aaron Finch 116, Shaun Marsh 91*) by nine wickets. *PoM:* Aaron Finch.

Sharjah Cricket Stadium, Sharjah, March 24: Pakistan 284/7 in 50 overs (Mohammad Rizwan 115, Shoaib Malik 60; Jhye Richardson 2-16, Nathan Coulter-Nile 2-52) lost to **Australia** 285/2 in 47.5 overs (Aaron Finch 153*, Usman Khawaja 88) by eight wickets. *PoM:* Aaron Finch.

Sheikh Zayed Stadium, Abu Dhabi, March 27: Australia 266/6 in 50 overs (Aaron Finch 90, Glenn Maxwell 71) beat **Pakistan** 186 in 44.4 overs (Imam-ul-Haq 46, Imad Wasim 43; Adam Zampa 4-43, Pat Cummins 3-23) by 80 runs. *PoM:* Pat Cummins.

Dubai International Cricket Stadium, Dubai, March 29: Australia 277/7 in 50 overs (Glenn Maxwell 98, Usman Khawaja 62; Mohammad Hasnain 2-52, Imad Wasim 2-56) beat **Pakistan** 271/8 in 50 overs (Abid Ali 112, Mohammad Rizwan 104; Nathan Coulter-Nile 3-53, Marcus Stoinis 2-20) by six runs. *PoM:* Glenn Maxwell.

Dubai International Cricket Stadium, Dubai, March 31: Australia 327/7 in 50 overs (Usman Khawaja 98, Glenn Maxwell 70; Usman Shinwari 4-49, Junaid Khan 3-73) beat **Pakistan** 307/7 in 50 overs (Haris Sohail 130, Imad Wasim 50*; Jason Behrendorff 3-63) by 20 runs. *PoM:* Glenn Maxwell. *PoS:* Aaron Finch.

Three matches of scorching pace and canny variations were enough for England selectors to decide on Jofra Archer's worth. — *Getty Images*

Pakistan in England

Archer auditions amid run-fest

Pakistan arrived in England before others to get accustomed to the conditions before the World Cup. They did an excellent job in the tour matches before losing to England in all four completed ODIs as well as the only T20I.

The ODIs followed a similar pattern. Pakistan reached 340 thrice in four attempts and were bowled out for 297 in the other, but England's heavy artillery turned out to be too much for their bowlers. Nothing exemplified this more than the third match, where England chased down a target of 359 inside 45 overs.

Pakistan's top three — Imam-ul-Haq, Fakhar Zaman and Babar Azam — all did well, as did Sarfraz Ahmed and the belligerent Asif Ali, but their bowlers had no answer to the English onslaught, match after match. Shadab Khan's absence owing to illness did not help their cause.

The run-fest fluctuated between mind-boggling and crudeness. The four completed matches witnessed 240 fours and 74 sixes being hit. Every batsman with two or more outings for England in the series had a strike rate of 98 or more. Jos Buttler struck at 158, while Jonny Bairstow and Eoin Morgan both topped the 130-mark.

Fast-tracked into the international side, Jofra Archer was closely monitored by the team management. Three matches of scorching pace and canny variations were enough for them to decide his worth. He found a place in the World Cup squad.

	T20I	**ODIs**
Most runs	Babar Azam (Pakistan) (65 runs, 1 match)	Jason Roy (England) (277 runs, 3 matches)
Most wickets	Jofra Archer (England) (2 wickets, 1 match)	Chris Woakes (England) (10 wickets, 4 matches)

Tour matches

The Kent County Cricket Ground, Beckenham, April 27: Pakistanis 358/7 in 50 overs (Imad Wasim 117*, Fakhar Zaman 76; Imran Qayyum 4-45) beat **Kent** 258 in 44.1 overs (Alex Blake 89, Ollie Robinson 49; Yasir Shah 3-90, Faheem Ashraf 2-16) by 100 runs.

County Ground, Northampton, April 29: Northamptonshire 273/6 in 50 overs (Josh Cobb 146*, Brett Hutton 27*) lost to **Pakistanis** 275/2 in 41 overs (Fakhar Zaman 101, Imam-ul-Haq 71) by eight wickets.

Grace Road, Leicester, May 1: Pakistanis 200/6 in 20 overs (Babar Azam 101, Fakhar Zaman 52; Ben Mike 3-38, Dieter Klein 2-31) beat **Leicestershire** 142 in 19.2 overs (B Mike 37, Callum Parkinson 27; Shaheen Shah Afridi 2-12, Imad Wasim 2-19) by 58 runs.

Only T20I: England won by seven wickets

Sophia Gardens, Cardiff, May 5: Pakistan 173/6 in 20 overs (Babar Azam 65, Haris Sohail 50; Jofra Archer 2-29) lost to **England** 175/3 in 19.2 overs (Eoin Morgan 57*, Joe Root 47) by seven wickets. *PoM:* Eoin Morgan.

ODI series (5): England 4 Pakistan 0

The Oval, London, May 8: Pakistan 80/2 in 19 overs (Imam-ul-Haq 42*) vs **England**. No result.

The Rose Bowl, Southampton, May 11: England 373/3 in 50 overs (Jos Buttler 110*, Jason Roy 87) beat **Pakistan** 361/7 in 50 overs (Fakhar Zaman 138, Babar Azam 51, Asif Ali 51; David Willey 2-57, Liam Plunkett 2-64) by 12 runs. *PoM:* Jos Buttler.

County Ground, Bristol, May 14: Pakistan 358/9 in 50 overs (Imam-ul-Haq 151, Asif Ali 52; Chris Woakes 4-67, Tom Curran 2-74) beat **England** 359/4 in 44.5 overs (Jonny Bairstow 128, Jason Roy 76) by six wickets. *PoM:* Jonny Bairstow.

Trent Bridge, Nottingham, May 17: Pakistan 340/7 in 50 overs (Babar Azam 115, Mohammad Hafeez 59; Tom Curran 4-59, Mark Wood 2-71) lost to **England** 341/7 in 49.3 overs (Jason Roy 114, Ben Stokes 71*; Imad Wasim 2-62, Mohammad Hasnain 2-80) by three wickets. *PoM:* Jason Roy.

Headingley, Leeds, May 19: England 351/9 in 50 overs (Joe Root 84, Eoin Morgan 76; Shaheen Shah Afridi 4-82, Imad Wasim 2-53) beat **Pakistan** 297 in 46.5 overs (Sarfaraz Ahmed 97, Babar Azam 80; Chris Woakes 5-54, Adil Rashid 2-54) by 54 runs. *PoM:* Chris Woakes. *PoS:* Jason Roy.

England in Ireland

Only ODI: England won by four wickets

The Village, Malahide, Dublin, May 3: Ireland 198 in 43.1 overs (Paul Stirling 33, Mark Adair 32; Liam Plunkett 4-35, Tom Curran 3-35) lost to **England** 199/6 in 42 overs (Ben Foakes 61*, T Curran 47*; Josh Little 4-45) by four wickets. *PoM:* Ben Foakes.

Bangladesh and West Indies in Ireland

Historic win for Bangladesh

Bangladesh won a historic first ODI series final after going through the tri-series unbeaten. Set 210 to chase in 24 overs in the rain-hit final, they did so with seven balls to spare. Soumya Sarkar slammed three sixes and nine fours in his 66 off 56 balls at the top of the order before Mossadek Hossain raced to his fifty off just 23 balls to seal the chase. West Indies accounted for four of the six centuries made in the tournament, including two for Shai Hope and a 148 for Sunil Ambris, which helped them to their highest successful chase, hunting down Ireland's 327/5 with plenty to spare.

Most runs: Shai Hope (West Indies) (470 runs, 5 matches)
Most wickets: Shannon Gabriel (West Indies) (8 wickets, 4 matches)

Castle Avenue, Dublin, May 5: West Indies 381/3 in 50 overs (John Campbell 179, Shai Hope 170; Barry McCarthy 2-76) beat **Ireland** 185 in 34.4 overs (Kevin O'Brien 68, Gary Wilson 30; Ashley Nurse 4-51, Shannon Gabriel 3-44) by 196 runs. *PoM:* John Campbell.
Castle Avenue, Dublin, May 7: West Indies 261/9 in 50 overs (Shai Hope 109, Roston Chase 51; Mashrafe Mortaza 3-49, Mohammad Saifuddin 2-47) lost to **Bangladesh** 264/2 in 45 overs (Tamim Iqbal 80, Soumya Sarkar 73) by eight wickets. *PoM:* Shai Hope.
The Village, Malahide, Dublin, May 9: Ireland vs **Bangladesh**. No toss.
The Village, Malahide, Dublin, May 11: Ireland 327/5 in 50 overs (Andy Balbirnie 135, Paul Stirling 77; Shannon Gabriel 2-47) lost to **West Indies** 331/5 in 47.5 overs (Sunil Ambris 148, Roston Chase 46; Boyd Rankin 3-65) by five wickets. *PoM:* Sunil Ambris.
The Village, Malahide, Dublin, May 13: West Indies 247/9 in 50 overs (Shai Hope 87, Jason Holder 62; Mustafizur Rahman 4-43, Mashrafe Mortaza 3-60) lost to **Bangladesh** 248/5 in 47.2 overs (Mushfiqur Rahim 63, Soumya Sarkar 54; Ashley Nurse 3-53) by five wickets. *PoM:* Mustafizur Rahman.
Castle Avenue, Dublin, May 15: Ireland 292/8 in 50 overs (Paul Stirling 130, William Porterfield 94; Abu Jayed 5-58, Mohammad Saifuddin 2-43) lost to **Bangladesh** 294/4 in 43 overs (Liton Das 76, Tamim Iqbal 57; Boyd Rankin 2-48) by six wickets. *PoM:* Abu Jayed.

Teams	M	W	L	T	N/R	Pts	NRR
Bangladesh	4	3	0	0	1	14	+0.622
West Indies	4	2	0	0	0	9	+0.843
Ireland	4	0	3	0	1	2	-1.743

Bangladesh and West Indies qualify for the final

Final: Bangladesh won by five wickets

Castle Avenue, Dublin, May 17: West Indies 152/1 in 24 overs (Shai Hope 74, Sunil Ambris 69*) lost to **Bangladesh** 213/5 in 22.5 overs (Soumya Sarkar 66, Mosaddek Hossain 52*; Raymon Reifer 2-23, Shannon Gabriel 2-30) by five wickets (DLS method). *PoM:* Mosaddek Hossain. *PoM:* Shai Hope.

Afghanistan in Scotland

ODI series (2): Afghanistan 1 Scotland 0

Grange Cricket Club, Raeburn Place, Edinburgh, May 8: Scotland v **Afghanistan.** No toss.
Grange Cricket Club, Raeburn Place, Edinburgh, May 10: Scotland 325/7 in 50 overs
(Calum MacLeod 100, Kyle Coetzer 79; Gulbadin Naib 3-72, Hamid Hassan 2-55) lost to
Afghanistan 269/3 in 44.5 overs (Rahmat Shah 113, Hashmatullah Shahidi 59*) by seven
wickets (DLS method). *PoM:* Rahmat Shah.

Sri Lanka in Scotland

ODI series (2): Sri Lanka 1 Scotland 0

Grange Cricket Club, Edinburgh, May 18: Sri Lanka vs **Afghanistan.** No toss.
Grange Cricket Club, Raeburn Place, Edinburgh, May 21: Sri Lanka 322/8 in 50 overs
(Dimuth Karunaratne 77, Avishka Fernando 74; Brad Wheal 3-49, Safyaan Sharif 2-76) beat
Scotland 199 in 33.2 overs (George Munsey 61, Matthew Cross 55; Nuwan Pradeep 4-34,
Suranga Lakmal 2-55) by 35 runs (DLS method). *PoM:* Nuwan Pradeep.

Afghanistan in Ireland

ODI series (2): Ireland 1 Afghanistan 1

Civil Service Cricket Club, Stormont, Belfast, May 19: Ireland 210 in 48.5 overs (Paul
Stirling 71, William Porterfield 53; Aftab Alam 3-28, Dawlat Zadran 3-35) beat **Afghanistan**
138 in 35.4 overs (Asghar Afghan 29; Mark Adair 4-19, Boyd Rankin 3-40) by 72 runs.
Civil Service Cricket Club, Stormont, Belfast, May 21: Afghanistan 305/7 in 50 overs
(Mohammad Shahzad 101, Rahmat Shah 62; Mark Adair 3-71, Andy McBrine 2-43) beat **Ireland** 179 in 41.2 (Paul Stirling 50, Gary Wilson 34; Gulbadin Naib 6-43) by 126 runs.

Zimbabwe in the Netherlands

ODI series (2): Netherlands 2 Zimbabwe 1

Sportpark Het Schootsveld, Deventer, June 19: Zimbabwe 205/8 in 47 overs (Brendan
Taylor 71, Kyle Jarvis 32*; Fred Klaassen 2-29, Paul van Meekeren 2-30) lost to **Netherlands**
208/3 in 42.4 overs (Max O'Dowd 86*, Wesley Barresi 39*; Sean Williams 2-38) by seven
wickets.
Sportpark Het Schootsveld, Deventer, June 21: Zimbabwe 290/6 in 50 overs (Sikandar
Raza 85*, Craig Ervine 84; Fred Klaassen 2-53) lost to **Netherlands** 291/7 in 49.2 overs
(Max O'Dowd 59, Roelof van der Merwe 57; Sean Williams 4-43, Donald Tiripano 2-62) by
three wickets.

Most runs: Max O'Dowd (Netherlands) (145 runs, 2 matches)
Most wickets: Sean Williams (Zimbabwe) (6 wickets, 2 matches)

T20I series (2): Netherlands 1 Zimbabwe 1

Hazelaarweg, Rotterdam, June 23: Netherlands 199/7 in 20 overs (Roelof van der Merwe 75*, Ben Cooper 54; Christopher Mpofu 2-38) beat **Zimbabwe** 150 in 19.5 overs (Craig Ervine 59; Brandon Glover 3-20, Pieter Seelaar 3-28, Fred Klaassen 3-36) by 49 runs.

Hazelaarweg, Rotterdam, June 25: Netherlands 152/8 in 20 overs (Max O'Dowd 56, Pieter Seelaar 29; Sean Williams 2-28, Christopher Mpofu 2-39) tied with **Zimbabwe** 152 in 20 overs (Brendan Taylor 40, Craig Ervine 29, Elton Chigumbura 29; Roelof van der Merwe 4-35, Paul van Meekeren 3-25). **Super Over: Zimbabwe** 18 for no loss in 1 over beat **Netherlands** 9/1 in 1 over by nine runs.

Most runs: Craig Ervine (Zimbabwe) (88 runs, 2 matches)
Most wickets: Roelof van der Merwe (Netherlands) (5 wickets, 2 matches)

Zimbabwe in Ireland

Tour match

Woodvale Road, Eglinton, June 29: Ireland A 283/9 in 50 overs (Simi Singh 90, Harry Tector 36; Kyle Jarvis 2-41, Sean Williams 2-54, Ryan Burl 2-54) beat **Zimbabwe** 256 in 47.2 overs (S Williams 104, Solomon Mire 35; Peter Chase 3-44, Barry McCarthy 2-46) by 27 runs.

ODI series (3): Ireland 3 Zimbabwe 0

Bready Cricket Club, Magheramason, Bready, July 1: Zimbabwe 254/9 in 50 overs (Craig Ervine 105, Ryan Burl 49*; Mark Adair 4-73, Shane Getkate 2-33) lost to **Ireland** 258/6 in 48.3 overs (Andy Balbirnie 101, Paul Stirling 57; Tendai Chatara 3-36, Kyle Jarvis 2-43) by four wickets.

Civil Service Cricket Club, Stormont, Belfast, July 4: Ireland 242/9 in 50 overs (James McCollum 73, Lorcan Tucker 52; Sikandar Raza 2-28, Sean Williams 2-43) beat **Zimbabwe** 237/9 in 50 overs (S Williams 58, Ryan Burl 53; Tim Murtagh 5-21, Shane Getkate 2-57) by five runs.

Civil Service Cricket Club, Stormont, Belfast, July 7: Zimbabwe 190 in 46.5 overs (Sean Williams 67, Richmond Mutumbami 28, Kyle Jarvis 28; Tim Murtagh 3-39, Shane Getkate 2-30) lost to **Ireland** 191/4 in 41.2 overs (James McCollum 54, William Porterfield 49) by six wickets. *PoS: Tim Murtagh.*

T20I series (3): Ireland 1 Zimbabwe 1

Civil Service Cricket Club, Stormont, Belfast, July 10: Ireland v **Zimbabwe**. No toss.

Bready Cricket Club, Magheramason, Bready, July 12: Zimbabwe 132/8 in 13 overs (Craig Ervine 55, Sean Williams 34; Mark Adair 4-40, Craig Young 2-20) lost to **Ireland** 134/1 in 10.5 overs (Paul Stirling 83*, Andy Balbirnie 28*) by nine wickets.

Bready Cricket Club, Magheramason, Bready, July 14: Ireland 171/9 in 20 overs (Gary Wilson 47, Mark Adair 38; Kyle Jarvis 3-38, Tendai Chatara 2-35) lost to **Zimbabwe** 172/2 in 16.4 overs (Craig Ervine 68*, Sean Williams 58*) by eight wickets.

	ODIs	T20Is
Most runs	Craig Ervine (Zimbabwe) (156 runs, 3 matches)	Craig Ervine (Zimbabwe) (123 runs, 2 matches)
Most wickets	Tim Murtagh (Ireland) (9 wickets, 3 matches)	Mark Adair (Ireland) (4 wickets, 2 matches)

INTERNATIONAL CRICKET 2017-18

Bangladesh in South Africa

Visitors steamrolled

NEIL MANTHORP

When Bangladesh first toured South Africa in 2002-03, they were given manufactured assurances of respect, but were twice thrashed by an innings. This time, the respect was genuine. In the preceding 12 months, Bangladesh had won Tests against England, Sri Lanka and Australia, and in 2015 had clinched the most recent ODI series between these teams. But the result was the same: a South African clean sweep across the formats.

While the home side were flourishing in a honeymoon period under new coach Ottis Gibson, the tourists were a rabble. It emerged that their own coach, Chandika Hathurusinghe, the most successful in their history, had handed in his resignation halfway through the trip. Captain Mushfiqur Rahim threw a strop in the Second Test, fielding in the deep for a session. He was upset by low wages, players not pulling their weight, and the criticism levelled at him for twice bowling first on flat pitches. Nazmul Hassan, the Bangladesh Cricket Board president, patronisingly described him as "an emotional personality". Also harming morale was Shakib Al Hasan's request to miss the Tests. Many interpreted his wish to spend time with his family as a distaste for Test cricket. In all, the tourists were steamrolled.

In the First Test, they lost their last seven wickets in an hour to be dismissed for 90. Mushfiqur's decision to bowl baffled everybody. Frost had covered the outfield just two days before the start, and the pitch was lifeless after a bitter winter. Aiden Markram, making his debut six days before his 23rd birthday, lived up to his reputation as an uncomplicated, technically correct player, armed with a pleasing on-drive. Markram was 97 when opening partner Dean Elgar, on 99, made a false start for a single and the youngster was run out. Elgar was eventually dismissed for 199, prompting observations about cricket's version of natural justice.

Mominul Haque made a combative 77 before Faf du Plessis left his bowlers four and a half sessions to win the game, and Bangladesh a notional 424 runs — Mehedi had bowled 67-5-247-0, the third-most expensive none-for in history. Kagiso Rabada bullied away the middle order, and Keshav Maharaj cleaned up the tail.

As if to prove his idiotic decision to bowl first at Potchefstroom was not a one-off, Mushfiqur did it again. It was only the second time South Africa had four centuries in the same innings, after Antigua in 2004-05. Elgar and Markram — who did now manage a maiden hundred — put on 243 while

Bangladesh were steamrolled, and had few answers to the South African pacers.
— *Getty Images*

Hashim Amla and du Plessis's fourth-wicket partnership reached 247. It set up South Africa's biggest Test victory.

Across three innings, the hosts had scored 1316 runs for the loss of 13 wickets. Rabada was younger than most of the Bangladesh side, but still appeared a man against boys: he was too quick, too smart and too determined.

In the ODIs, Mushfiqur's meticulous century underpinned a respectable total in the first game, only for Quinton de Kock and Amla to cruise to the third-highest opening partnership in ODIs, and the highest successful chase without losing a wicket. AB de Villiers joined the party, reaching 100 in 68 balls in the next match.

David Miller was on 57 with 12 balls remaining in the second T20I; he went on to finish with 101 not out. He hit the first five deliveries of the penultimate over, bowled by Saifuddin, for six. The hundred came in 35 balls, comfortably the fastest in T20Is, beating 45 by compatriot Richard Levi against New Zealand in Hamilton in 2011-12. Bangladesh had let it happen: Mushfiqur had dropped him on nought.

Tour match

Willowmoore Park, Benoni, September 21-23: Bangladesh 306/7 dec in 74.1 overs (Mominul Haque 68, Mushfiqur Rahim 63; Michael Cohen 4-23) and 235/9 dec in 63 overs (Sabbir Rahman 67, Imrul Kayes 51; Shaun von Berg 4-77, Leus du Plooy 2-51) drew with **Cricket South Africa Invitation XI** 313/8 dec in 91 overs (S Berg 62*, Zubayr Hamza 60; Shafiul Islam 2-61).

Test series (2): South Africa 2 Bangladesh 0

Senwes Park, Potchefstroom, September 28 - October 2: South Africa 496/3 dec in 146 overs (Dean Elgar 199, Hashim Amla 137) and 247/6 dec in 56 overs (Faf du Plessis 81, Temba Bavuma 71; Mominul Haque 3-27, Mustafizur Rahman 2-30) beat **Bangladesh** 320 in 89.1 overs (M Haque 77, Mahmudullah 66; Keshav Maharaj 3-92, Morne Morkel 2-51) and 90 in 32.4 overs (Imrul Kayes 32; K Maharaj 4-25, Kagiso Rabada 3-33) by 333 runs. *MoM:* Dean Elgar.

Mangaung Oval, Bloemfontein, October 6-8: South Africa 573/4 dec in 120 overs (Aiden Markram 143, Faf du Plessis 135*, Hashim Amla 132, Dean Elgar 113; Subashis Roy 3-118) beat **Bangladesh** 147 in 42.5 overs (Liton Das 70, Imrul Kayes 26; Kagiso Rabada 5-33, Duanne Olivier 3-40) and 172 in 42.4 overs (f/o) (Mahmudullah 43, I Kayes 32; K Rabada 5-30, Andile Phehlukwayo 3-36) by an innings and 254 runs. *MoM:* Kagiso Rabada. *MoS:* Dean Elgar.

Tour match

Mangaung Oval, Bloemfontein, October 12: Bangladesh 255 in 48.1 overs (Shakib Al Hasan 68, Sabbir Rahman 52; Robbie Frylinck 2-25, Mbulelo Budaza 2-41) lost to **Cricket South Africa Invitation XI** 257/4 in 46.3 overs (Aiden Markram 82, Matthew Breetzke 71; Mahmudullah 2-13) by six wickets.

ODI series (3): South Africa 3 Bangladesh 0

Diamond Oval, Kimberley, October 15: Bangladesh 278/7 in 50 overs (Mushfiqur Rahim 110*, Imrul Kayes 31; Kagiso Rabada 4-43, Dwaine Pretorius 2-48) lost to **South Africa** 282/0 in 42.5 overs (Quinton de Kock 168*, Hashim Amla 110*) by ten wickets. *MoM:* Quinton de Kock.

Boland Park, Paarl, October 18: South Africa 353/6 in 50 overs (AB de Villiers 176, Hashim Amla 85; Rubel Hossain 4-62, Shakib Al Hasan 2-60) beat **Bangladesh** 249 in 47.5 overs (Imrul Kayes 68, Mushfiqur Rahim 60; Andile Phehlukwayo 4-40, Imran Tahir 3-50) by 104 runs. *MoM:* AB de Villiers.

Buffalo Park, East London, October 22: South Africa 369/6 in 50 overs (Faf du Plessis 91 retd. hurt, Quinton de Kock 73; Mehidy Hasan Miraz 2-59, Taskin Ahmed 2-66) beat **Bangladesh** 169 in 40.4 overs (Shakib Al Hasan 63, Sabbir Rahman 39; Dane Paterson 3-44, Aiden Markram 2-18) by 200 runs. *MoM:* Faf du Plessis. *MoS:* Quinton de Kock.

T20I series (2): South Africa 2 Bangladesh 0

Mangaung Oval, Bloemfontein, October 26: South Africa 195/4 in 20 overs (Quinton de Kock 59, AB de Villiers 49; Mehidy Hasan Miraz 2-31) beat **Bangladesh** 175/9 in 20overs (Soumya Sarkar 47, Mohammad Saifuddin 39*; Dane Paterson 2-29, Andile Phehlukwayo 2-25) by 20 runs. *MoM:* AB de Villiers

Senwes Park, Potchefstroom, October 26: South Africa 224/4 in 20 overs (David Miller 101*, Hashim Amla 85; Shakib Al Hasan 2-22, Mohammad Saifuddin 2-53) beat **Bangladesh** 141 in 18.3 overs (Soumya Sarkar 44, Mahmudullah 24; JP Duminy 2-23, Aaron Phangiso 2-31) by 83 runs. *MoM:* David Miller. *MoS:* David Miller.

	Tests	ODIs	T20Is
Best batsman	Dean Elgar (330 runs, 2 matches)	Quinton de Kock (287 runs, 3 matches)	David Miller (126 runs, 2 matches)
Best bowler	Kagiso Rabada (15 wickets, 2 matches)	Imran Tahir (6 wickets, 3 matches)	Robbie Frylinck (3 wickets, 2 matches)

Sri Lanka in UAE and Pakistan

Misbah, Younis missed

OSMAN SAMIUDDIN

This was Sri Lanka's third tour of the UAE since 2011 — the most by any opponent. Pakistan have also toured Sri Lanka three times since then, so there was a distinct feeling that had this series not happened, no one would have minded.

This was the first time a Test had begun in the UAE in September, when daytime temperatures can top 40°C. The second match was day/night, despite there being no real justification: crowds don't turn up for Test cricket here, regardless of the time of day. It was appropriate that, during the tour, the ICC finalised plans for a new Test championship, to give more meaning to contests such as this. Still, in their own Emirati way, where matters tend to drift aimlessly, then hurtle towards a taut conclusion, the Tests were compelling.

This was Pakistan's first Test foray after the Misbah-ul-Haq/Younis Khan era, and it was frightening, with batting failures commonplace. Losing a first Test series in the UAE since 2002-03, to beleaguered opponents, drove home the impact of their exits. For Sri Lanka, it was brief respite from a turbulent year in which they had burned through captain after captain and lurched from one embarrassing defeat to the next. But a wipeout in the limited-overs leg only restored the doom and gloom.

There were mitigating circumstances, though, for the T20 defeats. As Sri Lanka Cricket had agreed to play the last match in Lahore — where their team had been attacked by terrorists in March 2009 — only those willing to travel to Pakistan were picked for the overall squad. A demoralised side already missing the injured Angelo Mathews were thus deprived of Dinesh Chandimal, Akila Dananjaya, Niroshan Dickwella and Upul Tharanga; Tissara Perera, who had been part of the World XI side in September, now took over as captain. The huge security operation was comparable to a state visit. But none of that mattered to a packed Gaddafi Stadium crowd.

Test series (2): Sri Lanka 2 Pakistan 0

1st Test: Sri Lanka won by 21 runs

Somehow, after four meandering days, the match arrived at a dead-eyed shootout: Rangana Herath versus Pakistan. The last time they had met in Tests, in 2015, Pakistan devised a strategy. They had used their feet and they swept, restricting Herath to two wickets across two matches. They figured it would work again. After all, Herath was older, and had endured a poor series against India. But he had a plan of his own: He did for them when they used

Rangana Herath consigned Pakistan to their first series loss in UAE since 2003-04.
— *Getty Images*

their feet, he did for them when they swept. He did for them every which way, in fact, and led Sri Lanka's defence of 136, the lowest target they had protected in Tests.

The result was unexpected: Pakistan had never tasted Test defeat in Abu Dhabi, while Sri Lanka had lost nine out of nine in all formats at home to India, and had been without an away Test victory against top-eight opposition since beating England in Leeds in 2014.

Herath's second-innings six-for, to go with five in the first, included his 100th against Pakistan, making him their biggest destroyer (Kapil Dev had 99). Humble to his very last molecule, he said he had got there simply because he had played them 20 times. He also became, at 39, the first left-arm spinner to reach 400 Test scalps, with half coming after turning 35.

Earlier, Chandimal, a captain setting the tone for the series, hit a nine-hour 155 not out. But Pakistan grabbed a three-run lead, with Azhar Ali passing 5000 Test runs, and Haris Sohail making an attractive 76 on debut. When yet another Yasir Shah five-for scuttled Sri Lanka on the fifth morning, the stage was set for a Pakistan victory. Apparently.

Sheikh Zayed Stadium, Abu Dhabi, September 28 - October 2: Sri Lanka 419 in 154.5 overs (Dinesh Chandimal 155*, Dimuth Karunaratne 93; Mohammad Abbas 3-75, Yasir Shah 3-120) and 138 in 66.5 overs (Niroshan Dickwella 40*, Kaushal Silva 25; Y Shah 5-51, M Abbas 2-22) beat **Pakistan** 422 in 162.3 overs (Azhar Ali 85, Haris Sohail 76; Rangana Herath 5-93, Suranga Lakmal 2-42) and 114 in 47.4 overs (H Sohail 34, Asad Shafiq 20; R Herath 6-43, Dilruwan Perera 3-46) by 21 runs. *MoM:* Rangana Herath.

2nd Test: Sri Lanka won by 68 runs

Since moving their base to the UAE in 2010, Pakistan had not lost a Test series here. But the fortress now fell. On the final afternoon of Dubai's second day/night Test, but Sri Lanka's first, Pakistan could still have saved their proud record. Asad Shafiq and Sarfraz Ahmed were at the crease, and a target of 317 was less than a hundred away. But after another collapse, Sarfraz was left to acknowledge that Test captaincy was tough.

Dimuth Karunaratne's career-best 196 in nine and a quarter hours was the kind of knock he had played often in 2017: barely noticeable, never vulnerable. The middle order gave strong support, while Yasir picked up another six, to become the first spinner to collect a five-for or better in five successive Tests (and the fourth in all, after Charlie Turner, SF Barnes and Alec Bedser).

Pakistan's response was inadequate and Sri Lanka's bowlers did enough to secure a 220-run lead. That should have been that. But they were unused to winning positions, and by stumps were 34 for 5. Wahab Riaz hurtled in and discomfited Sri Lanka with pace and hostility, claiming three wickets that evening, and another next day, when Sohail picked up three in an over to wrap things up at 96. The 386-run gap between their two innings was a Sri Lankan record.

Pakistan then went nowhere for 33 overs, scoring just 52 for the loss of five wickets. Shafiq, who crafted a majestic hundred, and Sarfraz injected life into the innings. But once Dilruwan Perera had induced a sweep from Sarfraz to deep square leg, ending a 173-run stand, Pakistan imploded from 225 for 5 to 248.

Dubai International Cricket Stadium, October 6-10: Sri Lanka 482 in 159.2 overs (Dimuth Karunaratne 196, Dinesh Chandimal 62; Yasir Shah 6-184, Mohammad Abbas 2-100) and 96 in 26 overs (Kusal Mendis 29, Niroshan Dickwella 21; Wahab Riaz 4-41, Haris Sohail 3-1) beat **Pakistan** 262 in 90.3overs (Azhar Ali 59, H Sohail 56; Dilruwan Perera 3-72, Rangana Herath 3-84) and 248 in 90.2 overs (Asad Shafiq 112, Sarfraz Ahmed 68; D Perera 5-98, R Herath 2-57) by 68 runs. MoM: Dimuth Karunaratne. MoS: Dimuth Karunaratne

ODI series (5): Pakistan 5 Sri Lanka 0

1st ODI: Pakistan won by 83 runs

Babar Azam's sixth ODI hundred, from just 32 innings, provided the platform for a comfortable victory. Upul Tharanga had surprisingly chosen to bowl, and Babar initially looked out of sorts, carrying over his red-ball hesitancy. But as the surface settled, so did he. He took his time, building his innings on elegant strokeplay and good running. Shoaib Malik brought the ammunition in a 61-ball 81 that drove Pakistan close to 300. And after Dickwella and Chandimal fell in successive Rumman Raees overs, Hasan Ali grabbed two wickets in the 16th over, leaving Sri Lanka 67 for 5. Akila Dananjaya hit a maiden one-day half-century, but it was academic.

Dubai International Cricket Stadium, October 13: Pakistan 292/6 in 50 overs (Babar

Azam 103, Shoaib Malik 81; Suranga Lakmal 2-47) beat **Sri Lanka** 209/8 in 50 overs (Lahiru Thirimanne 53, Akila Dananjaya 50*; Hasan Ali 3-36, Rumman Raees 3-49) by 83 runs. *MoM:* Shoaib Malik.

2nd ODI: Pakistan won by 32 runs

Another Babar hundred — his fifth in a row in the UAE — set up another home victory. But his was not the critical performance. That came from Shadab Khan. After an early collapse, Shadab put on 109 with Babar for the seventh wicket and kept him company from the 28th over until the last. There was no flashiness, just a steady supply of ones and twos. Then, after Junaid Khan and Hasan struck top-order blows, he took three wickets in three overs to send Sri Lanka into a tailspin. The first two were treats, Chandimal and Milinda Siriwardene undone by googlies. At 93 for 7, complacency crept in, and Tharanga and Jeffrey Vandersay bedded down for a stand of 76. Pakistan missed chances from Tharanga, who eventually reached a classy hundred but, just as they started to panic, Raees dismissed Vandersay for 22, and the game was up.

Sheikh Zayed Stadium, Abu Dhabi, October 16: Pakistan 219/9 in 50 overs (Babar Azam 101, Shadab Khan 52*; Lahiru Gamage 4-57, Thisara Perera 2-34) beat **Sri Lanka** 187 in 48 overs (Upul Tharanga 112*, Jeffrey Vandersay 22; Shadab 3-47) by 32 runs. *MoM:* Shadab Khan.

3rd ODI: Pakistan won by seven wickets

There were charges of nepotism when bespectacled opener Imam-ul-Haq was picked — uncle Inzamam was the chief selector — but his performance silenced them. He became only the second Pakistani to hit a century on ODI debut, after Salim Elahi against Sri Lanka at Gujranwala in 1995-96. Imam's style bore no similarity to Inzamam's: left-handed and unafraid to go aerial, even on the off side. When he fell a ball after reaching three figures, Pakistan were only six runs away from securing the series. Sri Lanka had been tied down by the spinners and taken apart by Hasan. Aiming at the stumps with the pace — and changes in it — that has marked him out as Pakistan's star limited-overs bowler, he became the ninth to pick up three five-fors in a year.

Sheikh Zayed Stadium, Abu Dhabi, October 18: Sri Lanka 208 in 48.2 overs (Upul Tharanga 61, Thisara Perera 38; Hasan Ali 5-34, Shadab Khan 2-37) lost to **Pakistan** 209/3 in 42.3 overs (Imam-ul-Haq 100, Mohammad Hafeez 34*) by seven wickets. *MoM:* Imam-ul-Haq.

4th ODI: Pakistan won by seven wickets

After the latest crushing victory, Sarfraz said Pakistan had the best attack in the world. Here they showed their depth, drafting in Usman Shinwari — yet another left-arm seamer — and Imad Wasim, in place of Raees and Fahim Ashraf, with no discernible dip in performance. Shinwari took a wicket with his second ball in ODIs, a ripper that skidded through Tharanga's gate, while Imad took 2 for 13 off seven. Lahiru Thirimanne apart, Sri Lanka were

Hasan Ali was an important reason why Pakistan captain Sarfaraz Ahmed claimed they had the best attack in the world. — *Getty Images*

hapless. Pakistan's task was simple and, after they slipped to 58 for 3, Babar saw them home.

Sharjah Cricket Stadium, October 20: Sri Lanka 173 in 43.4 overs (Lahiru Thirimanne 62, Suranga Lakmal 23*; Hasan Ali 3-37, Imad Wasim 2-13) lost to **Pakistan** 177/3 in 39 overs (Shoaib Malik 69*, Babar Azam 69*) by seven wickets. *MoM:* Babar Azam.

5th ODI: Pakistan won by nine wickets

Shinwari secured five wickets in his first 21 balls, the third-quickest after Sri Lanka's Chaminda Vaas (16) against Bangladesh in the 2003 World Cup and the Netherlands' Timm van der Gugten (20) against Canada in 2013. It was a very Pakistani spectacle: extravagant early swing, energetic pace and smashed stumps. Sri Lanka were blown out of the game, even if 103 all out represented a recovery from 20 for 5. This was their 12th ODI defeat in a row, and third 5–0 whitewash in 2017, after losing to South Africa and India.

Sharjah Cricket Stadium, October 23: Sri Lanka 103 in 26.2 overs (Thisara Perera 25; Usman Khan 5-34, Hasan Ali 2-19) lost to **Pakistan** 105/1 in 202 overs (Fakhar Zaman 48, Imam-ul-Haq 45*) by nine wickets. *MoM:* Usman Khan. *MoS:* Hasan Ali.

T20I series (3): Pakistan 3 Sri Lanka 0

1st T20I: Pakistan won by seven wickets

• Sri Lanka are a different side from the ODIs, but the result is the same. • Only two batsmen cross 20. • Pakistan's attack, with every angle and genre covered, is once again too much. • Shinwari receives the match award for his two wickets, but it could easily have been Hasan. • Pakistan stutter in reply, falling to 18 for 2. • But once Mohammad Hafeez and Shoaib settle, it is over quickly.

Sheikh Zayed Stadium, Abu Dhabi, October 26: Sri Lanka 102 in 18.3 overs (Seekkuge Prasanna 23*, Sadeera Samarawickrama 23; Hasan Ali 3-23, Mohammad Hafeez 2-10) lost to **Pakistan** 103/3 in 17.2 overs (Shoaib Malik 42*, M Hafeez 25*; Vikum Sanjaya 2-20) by seven wickets. *MoM:* Usman Khan.

2nd T20I: Pakistan won by two wickets

• Finally, a contest: Sri Lanka slug it out to the end, but it is settled in Pakistan's favour by the nerveless boy wonder Shadab. • Off the fourth ball of the final over, he punches a six down the ground, then pushes two more in the same direction to clinch the series. • Earlier, Sri Lanka are well placed at 106 for 1, with four overs left and two batsmen set. • Then lose eight for 18, including a hat-trick for Fahim Ashraf, the first for Pakistan in the format. • Sri Lanka defend through Tissara Perera and might have won had Dhanushka Gunathilleke held on to a difficult chance from Hasan in the last over. • But his drop allows three runs and, crucially, Shadab to regain the strike.

Sheikh Zayed Stadium, Abu Dhabi, October 27: Sri Lanka 124/9 in 20 overs (Danushka Gunathilaka 51, Sadeera Samarawickrama 32; Faheem Ashraf 3-16, Hasan Ali 2-31) lost to **Pakistan** 125/8 in 19.5 overs (Sarfraz Ahmed 28, Ahmed Shehzad 27; Thisara Perera 3-24) by two wickets. *MoM:* Shadab Khan.

3rd T20I: Pakistan won by 36 runs

• Those at Gaddafi Stadium have memories of a grand occasion to take back with them, if not a competitive one. • The packed crowd welcomes back the team who in 2009 were attacked barely a kilometre from the ground. • Shoaib's 24-ball 51 gives a strong Pakistan batting performance a final flourish. • A familiar collapse shatters any hopes of a Sri Lankan consolation. • Mohammad Amir does most damage, with a T20-best in his first international game on home turf after 97 elsewhere.

Gaddafi Stadium, Lahore, October 29: Pakistan 180/3 in 20 overs (Shoaib Malik 51, Umar Amin 45) beat **Sri Lanka** 144/9 in 20 overs (Dasun Shanaka 54, Chaturanga de Silva 21; Mohammad Amir 4-13, Faheem Ashraf 2-19) by 36 runs. *MoM:* Shoaib Malik. *MoS:* Shoaib Malik.

	Tests	**ODIs**	**T20Is**
Best batsman	Dimuth Karunaratne (306 runs, 2 matches)	Babar Azam (303 runs, 5 matches)	Shoaib Malik (102 runs, 3 match)
Best bowler	Rangana Herath (16 wickets, 2 matches)	Hasan Ali (14 wickets, 5 matches)	Faheem Ashraf (6 wickets, 3 match)

West Indies in Zimbabwe

Bishoo bests placid pitch

West Indies bested Zimbabwe in a short series in Bulawayo, where lifeless pitches meant hard graft for bowlers and batsmen alike. Yet there were bright moments in both matches, and the teams looked evenly matched.

Zimbabwe had the leading run-scorers in Hamilton Masakadza and Sikandar Raza. For West Indies, Devendra Bishoo shone after a nondescript tour of England. Not far behind his 13 wickets was Zimbabwe's captain Graeme Cremer. In conditions heavily weighted towards the slow men, the two leggies took 22 of the 64 wickets to fall to bowlers, while spin accounted for 43 overall. The series marked the return of Kyle Jarvis, back after a four-year Kolpak stint with Lancashire, as well as Brendan Taylor, the former Zimbabwe captain, who cut short his stay with Nottinghamshire for family reasons.

For West Indies, consistency in both performance and selection was their watchword for the tour. A settled group performed well, and they registered their first series win under Jason Holder. Importantly, they also gained experience in conditions some of them would encounter again at the World Cup qualifying tournament in March 2018.

These were West Indies' first Tests in Zimbabwe since 2003-04, when Brian Lara's 191 in Bulawayo set up another overall win. It is unclear when, if ever, they will be back for more: Soon after, the impecunious Zimbabwean board announced they would scale back on home Tests.

Best batsman: Hamilton Masakadza (251 runs, 2 matches)
Best bowler: Devendra Bishoo (13 wickets, 2 matches)

Tour match
Bulawayo Athletic Club, October 15-17: West Indies 336/7 dec in 97.1 overs (Shai Hope 85 retd.out, Roston Chase 79 retd.out; Michael Chinouya 2-55, William Mashinge 2-71) and 263/5 dec in 68 overs (Kieran Powell 77 retd.out, Kyle Hope 61 retd.out) drew with **Zimbabwe A** 143 in 44.1 overs (Peter Moor 32, Chamu Chibhabha 27; Devendra Bishoo 3-28, Shannon Gabriel 2-5) and 70/4 in 27 overs (C Chibhabha 24).

Test series (2): West Indies 1 Zimbabwe 0
Queens Sports Club, Bulawayo, October 21-24: West Indies 219 in 82.5 overs (Shai Hope 90*, Kieran Powell 56; Graeme Cremer 4-64, Sean Williams 3-20) and 373 in 126 overs (Roston Chase 95, Kraigg Brathwaite 86; G Cremer 4-114, S Williams 3-91) beat **Zimbabwe** 159 in 61.3 overs (Hamilton Masakadza 42, Craig Ervine 39; Devendra Bishoo 5-79, Kemar Roach 2-23) and 316 in 90.4 overs (Brendan Taylor 73, H Masakadza 57; D Bishoo 4-105, R Chase 2-61) by 117 runs. *MoM:* Devendra Bishoo.
Queens Sports Club, Bulawayo, October 29 – November 2: Zimbabwe 326 in 109.1 overs (Hamilton Masakadza 147, Sikandar Raza 80; Kemar Roach 3-44, Shannon Gabriel 2-64) and 301/7 in 144 overs (S Raza 89, Regis Chakabva 71*; S Gabriel 2-34, K Roach 2-37) drew with **West Indies** 448 in 178.2overs (Jason Holder 110, Shane Dowrich 103; S Raza 5-99, Tendai Chisoro 3-113). *MoM:* Sikandar Raza. *MoS:* Devendra Bishoo.

England in Australia

Smith supreme, drama dreary

TIM WIGMORE

In 1993, the Australian prime minister Paul Keating was asked by the leader of the opposition why he had not called an early election. "Because I want to do you slowly," Keating responded.

It could have been an epitaph for Australia's triumph in the 2017-18 Ashes, as the broadcaster Ed Smith observed. For all the predictions of Australia's pace trio wreaking havoc on rapid pitches in front of braying crowds — egged on by Cricket Australia, which marketed the duels as the series of #BeatEngland, the slogan ubiquitous at grounds during the games — all five Tests went to the fifth day. Australia chiselled and clinically dissected England en route to their 4-0 triumph; the series run-rate was only 2.95, the slowest since the 1990s. They did England slowly.

No one did it better than Steve Smith. By the end of the series, Smith had made 22 hundreds in his last 83 Test innings, entering such rarefied territory that, according to the ICC's historical player rankings, he became the second best batsman of all time, behind only Donald Bradman. The similarities in how the two play — the Australian spirit of self-reliance and autodidactic method, with a bottom-handed backlift that lifts the bat unusually towards gully while waiting for each ball — became increasingly notable. And, more than anything, so did the sheer volume of their runs, and the adaptability with which they made them. Smith followed up the slowest century of his Test career — a 261-ball hundred in Brisbane, channelling the spirit of Keating — with the quickest, a 138-ball dash in the WACA's final Test, which was a mere staging post to his 239 there. Another century followed in Melbourne, and when he was done, Smith had amassed 687 runs at 137.40, every run pushing England a little closer to despair.

While England had only slingshots in their armoury — though James Anderson again showed himself the craftiest slinger and swinger around — Australia had bazookas. Three of them: Pat Cummins, Mitchell Starc and Josh Hazlewood, who were persistent menaces and each regularly topped 145kmph, while the six fast bowlers England used seldom crept over 135kmph.

Unlike in the 2013-14 whitewash, England were seldom blown away. Instead, they were slowly worn down. Batsmen consistently got in, and there were few trademark collapses, but the sheer mental and physical exertion of withstanding Australia's battery proved too much; often it was Nathan Lyon, who took 21 wickets to Moeen Ali's five, who benefited.

Joe Root made five half-centuries, yet never made it past 83, his score on the opening day in Sydney when he flicked Mitchell Starc to square leg in the

The #BeatEngland slogan was ubiquitous at grounds and Cricket Australia's marketing department did their bit to rub in the final scoreline. – *Getty Images*

dying embers of the day. As he lay slouched on the floor for several seconds, disbelieving of his shot, it felt like a metaphor for England's tour. While Root got in a lot without making a decisive score, Alastair Cook failed a lot and only made one major score: the 244 at Melbourne which inoculated England against a whitewash. At least Dawid Malan, who made a fine century at Perth, had a breakthrough tour.

All the while Ben Stokes, who was absent after a late-night altercation in Bristol, which was being investigated by the police, loomed as the ghost at the feast. His teammates would have been entitled to feel let down, even if the gap between the sides felt much larger than the Stokes-shaped chasm. Indeed, Australia's much-derided Marsh brothers scored more centuries between them than all England's players managed together.

The focus on Stokes was emblematic of a series in which off-field shenanigans often seemed to leave the cricket itself peripheral. This reached a nadir during the soporific MCG Test, when Cricket Australia's own media arm helped circulate bogus stories about ball-tampering, and Stuart Broad's admission that he had bowled poorly at Perth was misrepresented to attack him for not trying enough.

The wider worry was that the Ashes — and, by extension, Test cricket — was becoming far too predictable. This was the eighth Ashes out of nine to be won by a home team.

Over the last 25 years, the erosion of perceived home-team umpiring advantage — due to the introduction of neutral umpires, and then the Decision Review System — has helped away teams. But, the recalibration of touring schedules has done even more to help home teams. England's preparations here consisted of a match against a Western Australian XI, and then two thoroughly unsatisfactory games against a Cricket Australia XI — essentially, a coalition of the unwanted, cobbled together from Sheffield Shield discards. And they only played a solitary tour game — a futile two-day game against, yep, another Cricket Australia XI — once the Tests had begun, rendering it almost impossible to get back into form or for players outside the first choice XI to play any meaningful cricket. The upshot was that once Australia had converted three tight days in the opening Test in Brisbane into a resounding ten-wicket win, England only fleetingly hinted at being able to win Tests thereafter.

   Did this lack of competitiveness and excitement matter? On one level the answer was a resounding no. While Australian tickets and TV audiences against, say, Pakistan or Sri Lanka tend to be higher if the series are competitive, Aussies love little more than bashing the Poms. This was the second best attended Ashes series in history. Those who came got to see Australia #BeatEngland, all right. But too few saw Test cricket at anything like its best.

Tour matches

W.A.C.A. Ground, Perth, November 4-5: England 349/6 dec in 91 overs (Mark Stoneman 85, James Vince 82; Aaron Hardie 2-46) drew with **Western Australia XI** 342 in 86 overs (Josh Philippe 88, Clint Hinchliffe 75; James Anderson 4-27, Craig Overton 2-70).

Adelaide Oval, November 8-11: England 293 in 95 overs (Dawid Malan 63, Mark Stoneman 61; Daniel Fallins 5-73, Jackson Coleman 3-72) and 207 in 67.4 overs (Jonny Bairstow 61*, M Stoneman 51; Simon Milenko 5-34, Gurinder Sandhu 2-47) beat **Cricket Australia XI** 233/9 dec in 76 overs (Tim Paine 52, S Milenko 50; Mason Crane 3-78, James Anderson 2-30) and 75 in 40.1 overs (Matthew Short 28; Chris Woakes 4-17, James Anderson 3-12, Craig Overton 3-15) by 192 runs.

Tony Ireland Stadium, Townsville, November 15-18: Cricket Australia XI 250 in 91.3 overs (Matthew Short 51, Jake Carder 39; Chris Woakes 6-57, Stuart Broad 2-29) and 364/4 in 110 overs (M Short 134*, Jason Sangha 133; Moeen Ali 2-88, Mason Crane 2-97) drew with **England** 515 in 142.5 overs (Mark Stoneman 111, Dawid Malan 109; M Short 4-103, Daniel Fallins 3-127).

Test series (5): Australia 4 England 0

1st Test: Australia won by ten wickets

Finally, the copious hype gave way to the actual cricket. And it was of a sort that was out of kilter with all expectations of a fast pitch and frenetic pace. Instead, the Gabba was host to a throwback to Test cricket at a more genteel pace.

   Few had anticipated England reaching 127 for 1 after 54 overs; fewer still that James Vince, a controversial selection, would make their top score. His dismissal, run-out for 83 by Lyon's direct hit, was later identified by Smith as the turning point in the series. Still, at 246 for 4, with Malan and Moeen having withstood the second new ball, England had designs on the sort of score that would have ensured they did not lose at Australia's fortress. Instead, their last six wickets succumbed for 56.

   Before the series, Broad had declared that England intended to bore Aus-

Steve Smith was magnificent in leading Australia to victory in the Ashes. – *Getty Images*

tralia out. At 76 for 4, they were doing just that, aided by the enterprising decision to allow Moeen to bowl at Usman Khawaja, often vulnerable against off-spin, early on. Though Shaun Marsh made an austere half-century, Smith was in danger of receiving inadequate support as Australia slipped to 209 for 7 in the second over against the second new ball. Yet Cummins, extraordinarily accomplished for a No.9 batsman, added 69 with Smith at barely two an over. Not only did England fail to get Smith out, but, as they bowled wide outside off stump, they gave the impression of having stopped trying.

A lead of 26 was useful, but far from decisive. Australia had a golden final hour on the third day to bowl at England. They took two wickets, including Cook to an aberrant hook shot, and scented more. Those came on the fourth day, as no England batsman could top Root's 51 — though Moeen was unlucky to be stumped to a borderline call. A target of 170 did not appear taxing, but few expected Australia to waltz to victory, as three tense days gave way to a ten-wicket romp.

Brisbane Cricket Ground, Woolloongabba, Brisbane, November 23-27: England 302 in 116.4 overs (James Vince 83, Dawid Malan 56; Mitchell Starc 3-77, Pat Cummins 3-85) and 195 in 71.4 overs (Joe Root 51, Jonny Bairstow 42; Josh Hazlewood 3-46, M Starc 3-51, Nathan Lyon 3-67) lost to **Australia** 328 in 130.3overs (Steven Smith 141*, Shaun Marsh 51; Stuart Broad 3-49, James Anderson 2-50) and 173/0 in 50 overs (David Warner 87*, Cameron Bancroft 82*) by ten wickets. *MoM:* Steven Smith.

2nd Test: Australia won by 120 runs

At times, the first Ashes day-night Test appeared to be simmering towards being a classic. Yet, the desperation for an epic Ashes Test perhaps concealed that England's task — to score 354 to win in their second innings — was always fanciful. At 169 for 3 on the fourth evening, the travelling Barmy

Army were daring to dream, delighting in Smith having used up both of Australia's reviews.

Alas, they were not necessary: Cummins curved a ball in to uproot Malan's off stump, and Hazlewood's venomous spell the following morning accounted for Chris Woakes and Root within his opening two overs.

In hindsight, the tale of the Test had been written long before — though less by Root's decision to bowl first, which was not without rationale, than by England's tame bowling on the first day, in conditions that were well-suited to English seam and swing. Two Australian returnees — Shaun Marsh, with a wonderful maiden Ashes hundred, and Tim Paine, with an elegant counter-punching half-century on the second morning — and Cummins hauled Australia up to 442 when Smith declared to allow his bowlers to enjoy the new ball under lights. The evening rain limited Australia to one wicket then, but England seemed overwhelmed by Australia's relentlessness as Craig Overton top scored on debut.

An engrossing passage, with England hooping the pink ball around under lights, followed. But the excellence of Anderson, who took his maiden five-wicket haul in Australia, and Woakes was a couple of days too late.

Adelaide Oval, December 2-6: Australia 442/8 dec in 149 overs (Shaun Marsh 126*, Tim Paine 57; Craig Overton 3-105, Stuart Broad 2-72) and 138 in 58 overs (Usman Khawaja 20, Mitchell Starc 20; James Anderson 5-43, Chris Woakes 4-36) beat **England** 227 in 76.1 overs (C Overton 41*, Alastair Cook 37; Nathan Lyon 4-60, M Starc 3-49) and 233 in 84.2 overs (Joe Root 67, Jonny Bairstow 36; M Starc 5-88, N Lyon 2-45) by 120 runs. *MoM*: Shaun Marsh.

Tour match 4

Richardson Park, Perth, December 9-10: England XI 314/9 dec in 69.2 overs (Keaton Jennings 80, Tom Curran 77*; Macalister Wright 2-19, Nick Buchanan 2-79) and 130/3 dec in 20 overs (Moeen Ali 47, Gary Balance 45*; Gabe Bell 2-29) drew with **Cricket Australia XI** 151/4 dec in 50 overs (M Wright 36*, Clint Hinchliffe 35*; Mark Wood 2-25, T Curran 2-28) and 269/8 in 36.5 overs (Travis Dean 100, William Bosisto 50; Jack Leach 4-104, T Curran 3-28).

3rd Test: Australia won by an innings and 41 runs

At 3.46pm local time, an edge from Woakes sparked delirium: after 863 days without it, Australia had regained the Ashes urn. If the scene was not the packed out WACA Australia might have envisaged — because of a combination of the match taking place on the fifth day, on a Monday, and unseasonal rain that delayed the start by three hours — Australia were in no mood to complain.

In a deeper sense, the ending was fitting. The last Ashes Test at the WACA was on a surface with some extra pace and bounce — as well as a crack that accounted for Vince in the second innings — and Australia's pace trio evoked some of the scenes here in the 1970s and 1980s. If Hazlewood, with eight wickets in the match, was the main beneficiary, emphatically this was a triumph of the collective.

For England, it should not have been this way. Malan and Jonny Bairstow withstood a pace barrage to score centuries in the first innings, lifting England to 368 for 4, a position from which it required all of England's ingenuity to lose. Manage it they did.

First, their last six second-innings wickets fell for just 35, their tail seeming hapless against Australia's remorseless pace once more. Then, England were again clueless against Smith; this time, they didn't even have the solace of making him score slowly, as he flew to his quickest Test century. That became a gargantuan 239, while Mitchell Marsh converted a maiden Test century into 181, as Australia extended their lead to 259.

Vince and Malan were both gutsy and resourceful in the second innings. But they lacked support from the senior players and only the rain threatened to delay Smith's recapture of the urn. An hour after it was all confirmed, as if to mock England, Perth experienced a bout of unseasonal torrential rain.

W.A.C.A. Ground, Perth, December 14-18: England 403 in 115.1 overs (Dawid Malan 140, Jonny Bairstow 119; Mitchell Starc 4-91, Josh Hazlewood 3-92) and 218 in 72.5 overs (James Vince 55, D Malan 54; J Hazlewood 5-48, Nathan Lyon 2-42) lost to **Australia** 662/9 dec in 179.3 overs (Steven Smith 239, Mitchell Marsh 181; James Anderson 4-116, Craig Overton 2-110) by an innings and 41 runs. *MoM:* Steven Smith.

4th Test: Match drawn

For Cook, who had failed to reach even 40 while the series was still live, the Boxing Day Test brought redemption and personal glory: a chanceless 244 not out, which was the highest score by a visiting batsman at the MCG, and meant that Cook replaced Viv Richards on the honours board in the members' bar.

For the ground itself, the Boxing Day Test brought ignominy. The soporific pitch sucked all life out of the game, rendering the members' bar far more entertaining than the cricket itself. The ICC later rated the pitch 'poor', which was a generous way to describe an anaemic surface in which only 24 wickets fell over the five days. Still, that amounted to better news for England than Australia: at least they could avoid a third Ashes whitewash in four tours.

Broad located greater zip than in the first three Tests, and with Root and him scoring fifties in support of Cook's marathon, England built to a position from which they appeared to be mounting a victory push.

Such analysis, though, was reckoning without the pitch. Smith calmly amassed a match-saving hundred and Warner was only denied one by an impetuous shot on 86. But it drained the spirit not just from England, but from the 14,000 at the ground on the final day. For one of world cricket's great grounds, this was a nadir and humiliation.

Melbourne Cricket Ground, December 26-30: Australia 327 in 119 overs (David Warner 103, Steven Smith 76; Stuart Broad 4-51, James Anderson 3-61) and 263/4 dec in 124.2 overs (S Smith 102*, D Warner 86) drew with **England** 491 in 144.1 overs (Alastair Cook 244*, Joe Root 61; Pat Cummins 4-117, Josh Hazlewood 3-95, Nathan Lyon 3-109). *MoM:* Alastair Cook.

Joe Root's reaction summed up the series for England. — *Getty Images*

5th Test: Australia won by an innings and 123 runs

In 2014, England arrived in Sydney demoralised. In their panic and desperation, they selected three debutants — two of whom never played again — and suffered ignominious defeat. This time was both different, in that England's spirit remained far more redoubtable, and depressingly familiar: England still lost by an innings and 123 runs.

There had been little hint of the evisceration to come when England, blooding Mason Crane for the injured Woakes, but leaving their team otherwise unchanged, reached 228 for 3 on the first evening. Root and Malan, their two most consistent batsmen all tour, had added 133 and seemed largely unperturbed. Then, with the third delivery of the second new ball, Root flicked Starc to square leg; the picture of him slouched on his knees in anguish provided one of the images of the tour. In the next over, the day's very last, Bairstow nicked Hazlewood behind, and a day's admirable grind had been squandered in five minutes.

England's tail slashed and dashed their way up to 346 and, when Broad bowled Bancroft in the second over, England could be excused for dreams of a cathartic SCG victory. Instead, they endured three days being roasted in heat, culminating in forlornly waiting for Australia to declare on the fourth day, the hottest day of Test cricket ever recorded here. They eventually did so on 649 for 7, after the lack of variety and potency in England's attack had again been hopelessly exposed. The Marsh brothers, who began the series mocked, ended it by celebrating their centuries in the middle together — the second of the series for both — after Khawaja compiled a delicious hundred.

Thereafter, the only question was how long England would survive. Despite Root's guts — he returned to the field after suffering food poisoning, which may have been exacerbated by the heat, before going off again — they managed just under 90 overs before Anderson, again enduring a barrage of short bowling after the result had long since been inevitable, was dismissed. It was the fourth time that England had won the toss, batted first and lost by an innings in their last seven away Tests.

Sydney Cricket Ground, January 4-8: England 346 in 112.3 overs (Joe Root 83, Dawid Malan 62; Pat Cummins 4-80, Josh Hazlewood 2-65) and 180 in 88.1 overs (J Root 58 retd.ill, Jonny Bairstow 38; P Cummins 4-39, Nathan Lyon 3-54) lost to **Australia** 649/7 dec in 193 overs (Usman Khawaja 171, Shaun Marsh 156, Mitchell Marsh 101; Moeen Ali 2-170) by an innings and 123 runs. *MoM:* Pat Cummins. *MoS:* Steven Smith.

Tour match
Drummoyne Oval, Sydney, January 11: Cricket Australia XI 258/9 in 50 overs (Travis Dean 62, Mackenzie Harvey 59; Adil Rashid 3-45, Moeen Ali 2-28) lost to **England** 259/5 in 40.5 overs (Eoin Morgan 81*, Alex Hales 52; Gabe Bell 2-35, Daniel Fallins 2-56) by five wickets.

ODI series (5): England 4 Australia 1
MCG, January 14: Australia 304/8 in 50 overs (Aaron Finch 107, Marcus Stoinis 60; Liam Plunkett 3-71, Adil Rashid 2-73) lost to **England** 308/5 in 48.5 overs (Jason Roy 180, Joe Root 91*; Pat Cummins 2-63, Mitchell Starc 2-71) by five wickets. *MoM:* Jason Roy.
Brisbane Cricket Ground, January 19: Australia 270/9 in 50 overs (Aaron Finch 106, Mitchell Marsh 36; Joe Root 2-31, Adil Rashid 2-71) lost to **England** 274/6 in 44.2overs (Jonny Bairstow 60, Alex Hales 57; Mitchell Starc 4-59, Jhye Richardson 2-57) by four wickets. *MoM:* Joe Root.
Sydney Cricket Ground, January 21: England 302/6 in 50 overs (Jos Buttler 100*, Chris Woakes 53; Josh Hazlewood 2-58) beat **Australia** 286/6 in 50 overs (Aaron Finch 62, Marcus Stoinis 56; Mark Wood 2-46, Adil Rashid 2-51) by 16 runs. *MoM:* Jos Buttler.
Adelaide Oval, January 26: England 196 in 44.5 overs (Chris Woakes 78, Tom Curran 35; Pat Cummins 4-24, Andrew Tye 3-33, Josh Hazlewood 3-39) lost to **Australia** 197/7 in 37 overs (Travis Head 96, Mitchell Marsh 32; Adil Rashid 3-49) by three wickets. *MoM:* Pat Cummins.
Perth Stadium, January 28: England 259 in 47.4 overs (Joe Root 62, Jason Roy 49; Andrew Tye 5-46, Mitchell Marsh 2-24) beat **Australia** 247 in 48.2overs (Marcus Stoinis 87, Glenn Maxwell 34; Tom Curran 5-35, Moeen Ali 3-55) by 12 runs. *MoM:* Tom Curran. *MoS:* Joe Root.

	Tests	ODIs
Best batsman	Steven Smith (687 runs, 5 matches)	Aaron Finch (275 runs, 3 matches)
Best bowler	Pat Cummins (23 wickets, 5 matches)	Adil Rashid (10 wickets, 5 matches)

Tim Wigmore (@timwig) is a freelance cricket writer and author of Second XI: Cricket In Its Outposts.

Trans-Tasman T20 Tri-series

Warner leads T20 turnaround

Australia began the series ranked No.7. They finished it unbeaten and a fraction below Pakistan at No.1. While that may suggest an anomaly in the rankings system, it should take nothing away from the exciting cricket played by what can only be called a specialist T20 team.

The World T20 is the one trophy missing from Australia's cabinet, and their plan to get better in the format had included bringing in Ricky Ponting as batting coach and Mark Waugh as T20 selector, and stacking their squad with BBL-proven firepower. Besides, with several Test and one-day regulars rested after an exhausting Ashes, it allowed a bright, new-look side to express themselves.

David Warner, the one all-format shoo-in, displayed astute captaincy — given he'd already won the IPL, his credentials weren't really in doubt. Billy Stanlake, Kane Richardson and Andrew Tye offered a variety of bowling options ranging from pace and canny variations. D'Arcy Short fired at the top, while Glenn Maxwell, overlooked for the ODIs, was in fine form. In the first match against England, Maxwell dominated the chase with his second T20I century, a 58-ball effort, striking the winning runs and reaching his hundred with a six. This after taking 3 for 10 in two overs.

It all came together at Eden Park, when they completed the highest ever T20 chase of a target of 244 in just 18.5 overs against New Zealand.

England, perhaps drained out after a long tour, struggled, as did New Zealand, who made it to the final on net run-rate. Martin Guptill brought up a ton at Eden Park against Australia, also becoming the top T20I run-scorer ahead of Brendon McCullum's 2140, in his 73rd match.

		Highest successful T20 chases	
Target	**Match**	**Venue**	**Balls left**
244	Australia v New Zealand	Auckland, Feb 2018	7
232	West Indies v South Africa	Johannesburg, Jan 2015	4
230	England v South Africa	Mumbai (Wankhede), Mar 2016	2
226	Sussex v Essex	Chelmsford, Jul 2014	9
225	Nottinghamshire v Yorkshire	Nottingham, July 2017	5

Best batsman: Martin Guptill (New Zealand) (258 runs, 5 matches)
Best bowler: Andrew Tye (Australia) (10 wickets, 5 matches)

Tour match

Manuka Oval, Canberra, February 2: Prime Minister's XI 136/8 in 20 overs (Peter Handscomb 43, Seb Gotch 22; Liam Dawson 3-16, David Willey 3-32) lost to **England XI** 139/2 in 12.4 overs (D Willey 79, James Vince 26; Mitchell Swepson 2-33) by eight wickets

Group stage

Sydney Cricket Ground, February 3: New Zealand 117/9 in 20 overs (Colin de Grandhomme 38*, Ross Taylor 24; Andrew Tye 4-23, Billy Stanlake 3-15) lost to **Australia** 96/3 in 11.3 overs (Chris Lynn 44, Glenn Maxwell 40*; Trent Boult 2-14) by seven wickets (DLS method). *MoM:* Billy Stanlake.

Bellerive Oval, Hobart, February 7: England 155/9 in 20 overs (Dawid Malan 50, Eoin Morgan 22; Glenn Maxwell 3-10, Ashton Agar 2-15) lost to **Australia** 161/5 in 18.3 overs (G Maxwell 103*, D'Árcy Short 30; David Willey 3-28) by five wickets. *MoM:* Glenn Maxwell.

Melbourne Cricket Ground, February 10: England 137/7 in 20 overs (Jos Buttler 46, Sam Billings 29; Kane Richardson 3-33, Billy Stanlake 2-28) lost to **Australia** 138/3 in 14.3 overs (Glenn Maxwell 39, D'Arcy Short 36*; Chris Jordan 2-26) by seven wickets. *MoM:* Kane Richardson.

Westpac Stadium, Wellington, February 13: New Zealand 196/5 in 20 overs (Kane Williamson 72, Martin Guptill 65; Adil Rashid 2-36, Mark Wood 2-51) beat **England** 184/9 in 20 overs (Dawid Malan 59, Alex Hales 47; Mitchell Santner 2-29, Trent Boult 2-46) by 12 runs. *MoM:* Kane Williamson.

Eden Park, Auckland, February 16: New Zealand 243/6 in 20 overs (Martin Guptill 105, Colin Munro 76; Kane Richardson 2-40, Andrew Tye 2-64) lost to **Australia** 245/5 in 18.5 overs (D'Arcy Short 76, David Warner 59) by five wickets. *MoM:* D'Arcy Short.

Seddon Park, Hamilton, February 18: England 194/7 in 20 overs (Eoin Morgan 80*, Dawid Malan 53; Trent Boult 3-50, Tim Southee 2-22) beat **New Zealand** 192/4 in 20 overs (Martin Guptill 62, Colin Munro 57) by 2 runs. *MoM:* Eoin Morgan.

Points table

Teams	M	W	L	T	N/R	Pts.	NRR
Australia	4	4	0	0	0	8	+1.719
New Zealand	4	1	3	0	0	2	-0.556
England	4	1	3	0	0	2	-1.036

Australia and New Zealand qualified for the final

Final: Australia beat New Zealand by 19 runs (DLS method)

Eden Park, Auckland, February 21: New Zealand 150/9 in 20 overs (Ross Taylor 43*, Colin Munro 29; Ashton Agar 3-27, Andrew Tye 2-30, Kane Richardson 2-30) lost to **Australia** 121/3 in 14.4 overs (D'Arcy Short 50, David Warner 25) by 19 runs (DLS method). *MoM:* Ashton Agar. *MoS:* Glenn Maxwell.

Winners: Australia

England in New Zealand

New low of 58 all out

Smarting from their 0-4 drubbing in the Ashes just across the Tasman Sea, England arrived in New Zealand looking to rediscover confidence. Instead, they were decimated in the opening Test, a day-night game in Auckland, by the wonderful left-arm swing of Trent Boult. Boult's remarkable 6 for 32 in 10.4 unchanged overs sent England tumbling to 58 all out in a mere 20.4 overs, the visitors managing to avoid their worst Test total by a mere 13 runs.

It was a long road back from that ignominy, and even though England pushed the game to the final session, it was primarily because only 26 overs of play was possible on days two and three combined.

Centuries by the admirable Kane Williamson and Henry Nicholls powered the hosts to a 369-run lead, the declaration coming midway through the fourth evening. England batted with far greater composure the second time around, but the determination and short-ball proclivity of Neil Wagner saw the hosts through to an innings-and-49-run victory.

Wagner was to play another significant hand late in the Second Test in

Trent Boult's remarkable 6 for 32 in 10.4 unchanged overs sent England tumbling to 58 all out in Auckland. — *Getty Images*

Christchurch a week later, associating himself in a terrific rearguard stand with Ish Sodhi, which frustrated England's designs of a series-levelling victory. After four absorbing days, the visitors were on course when New Zealand, chasing 382 for victory, subsided to 219 for 7 with more than 30 overs remaining. The feisty Wagner dug in alongside the equally dour Sodhi in an eighth-wicket stand that was worth only 37, but ate up 189 deliveries. Wagner was eventually dismissed for a 103-ball seven, by which time the light had faded enough for the umpires to pull out the stumps.

The results underlined the gulf between England's white and red-ball teams. Although the Black Caps were more competitive than the Australians overall, with Ross Taylor and Williamson adding to a long list of reasons to look at them as New Zealand legends, Eoin Morgan's men eased to their sixth ODI series win on the trot.

ODI series (5): England 3 New Zealand 2

Seddon Park, Hamilton, February 25: England 284/8 in 50 overs (Jos Buttler 79, Joe Root 71; Mitchell Santner 2-54, Ish Sodhi 2-63) lost to **New Zealand** 287/7 in 49.2 overs (Ross Taylor 113, Tom Latham 79; Ben Stokes 2-43, Chris Woakes 2-47) by three wickets. *MoM:* Ross Taylor.

Bay Oval, Mount Maunganui, February 28: New Zealand 223 in 49.4 overs (Mitchell Santner 63*, Martin Guptill 50; Moeen Ali 2-33, Ben Stokes 2-42) lost to **England** 225/4 in 37.5 overs (B Stokes 63*, Eoin Morgan 62; Trent Boult 2-46) by six wickets. *MoM:* Ben Stokes.

Westpac Stadium, Wellington, March 3: England 234 (Eoin Morgan 48, Ben Stokes 39; Ish Sodhi 3-53, Trent Boult 2-47) beat **New Zealand** 230/8 in 50 overs (Kane Williamson 112*, Colin Munro 49; Moeen Ali 3-36, Adil Rashid 2-34) by 4 runs. *MoM:* Moeen Ali.

University Oval, Dunedin, March 7: England 335/9 in 50 overs (Jonny Bairstow 138, Joe Root 102; Ish Sodhi 4-58, Colin Munro 2-53) lost to **New Zealand** 339/5 in 49.3 overs (Ross Taylor 181*, Tom Latham 71; Tom Curran 2-57) by five wickets. *MoM:* Ross Taylor.

Hagley Oval, Christchurch, March 10: New Zealand 223 in 49.5 overs (Mitchell Santner 67, Henry Nicholls 55; Chris Woakes 3-32, Adil Rashid 3-42) lost to **England** 229/3 in 32.4 overs (Jonny Bairstow 104, Alex Hales 61) by seven wickets. *MoM:* Jonny Bairstow. *MoS:* Chris Woakes.

Tour matches

Seddon Park, Hamilton, March 14-15: New Zealand XI 376 in 90 overs (Tom Blundell 131*, Kyle Jamieson 101 retd.out; James Anderson 4-56, Mark Wood 2-80) drew with **England** 319/9 in 90 overs (Liam Livingstone 88, Joe Root 51*).

Seddon Park, Hamilton, March 16-17: New Zealand XI 287/13 in 90 overs (Martin Guptill 73, Kyle Jamieson 38; Joe Root 3-23, Moeen Ali 3-67) drew with **England** 353/9 in 90 overs (J Root 115, Mark Stoneman 48; Scott Kuggeleijn 3-67, Logan van Beek 2-30).

Test series (2): New Zealand 1 England 0

Eden Park, Auckland, March 22-26: England 58 in 20.4 overs (Craig Overton 33*; Trent Boult 6-32, Tim Southee 4-25) and 320 in 126.1 overs (Ben Stokes 66, Mark Stoneman 55; Todd Astle 3-39, T Boult 3-67, Neil Wagner 3-77) lost to **New Zealand** 427/8 dec in 141overs (Henry Nicholls 145*, Kane Williamson 102; Stuart Broad 3-78, James Anderson 3-87) by an innings and 49 runs. *MoM:* Trent Boult.

Hagley Oval, Christchurch, March 30 – April 3: England 307 in 96.5 overs (Jonny Bairstow 101, Mark Wood 52; Tim Southee 6-62, Trent Boult 4-87) and 352/9 dec in 106.4 overs (James Vince 76, Mark Stoneman 60; Colin de Grandhomme 4-94, Neil Wagner 2-51) drew with **New Zealand** 278 in 93.3overs (BJ Watling 85, de Grandhomme 72; Stuart Broad 6-54, James Anderson 4-76) and 256/8 in 124.4 overs (Tom Latham 83, Ish Sodhi 56*; M Wood 2-45, Jack Leach 2-61). *MoM:* Tim Southee. *MoS:* Trent Boult.

	Tests	**ODIs**
Best batsman	Jonny Bairstow (163 runs, 2 matches)	Ross Taylor (304 runs, 3 matches)
Best bowler	Trent Boult (15 wickets, 2 matches)	Chris Woakes (10 wickets, 5 matches)

West Indies in New Zealand

Wagner, Boult make short work of visitors

MARK GEENTY

West Indies arrived without a Test win in New Zealand for nearly 23 years, but with reason for optimism. A stable line-up under coach Stuart Law and captain Jason Holder had won a match in England, then, less surprisingly, a series in Zimbabwe, and looked battle-hardened; New Zealand hadn't played a Test in eight months. But the tourists' confidence evaporated during a first day collapse in Wellington. Five weeks later, they were on the plane home after defeats in every completed game of the tour.

With the exception of opener Kraigg Brathwaite, the ill discipline of West Indies' batting was alarming. They could not handle the steep New Zealand bounce, nor the skill and variety of the home pace attack. Neil Wagner's prolonged short-pitched assaults, and Trent Boult's swing and speed, over-whelmed batsmen itching for the million-dollar shot.

Meanwhile, the hitting power of the Colins — de Grandhomme in the Tests, Munro elsewhere — was too much for any West Indian to match, or

Despite not having played a Test in eight months, New Zealand were clinical in brushing aside West Indies. — *Getty Images*

quell. Ross Taylor was another New Zealand batsman in superb touch.

After an innings defeat in the First Test, Holder was banned in Hamilton for a slow over-rate. Brathwaite took the reins, but couldn't inspire others to follow his lead: the 444 balls he faced across the series was more than double any of his teammates.

Sunil Ambris made one of the more unfortunate starts to a Test career: In Wellington, facing his first ball in Test cricket, he trod on his stumps. Then, after his first scoring shot in the second innings was a top-edged six, he was again dismissed hit wicket at Hamilton. His tour was ended abruptly by a Wagner bouncer, which broke his left forearm.

Chris Gayle's arrival for the white-ball matches was cause for renewed hope, particularly after two whirlwind centuries in the Bangladesh Premier League. But he was anonymous. Fielding a full-strength side remained a challenge for West Indies. The all-rounder Dwayne Bravo was at Australia's Big Bash League, and said he was unlikely to play international cricket again. Sunil Narine and Kieron Pollard withdrew late, while Evin Lewis missed the T20Is, all for personal reasons.

Tour match

Bert Sutcliffe Oval, Lincoln, November 25-27: West Indians 451/9 dec in 90 overs (Sunil Ambris 153, Shai Hope 110; Lockie Ferguson 5-67, Logan van Beek 2-60) and 186 in 53 overs (Kraigg Brathwaite 88 retd.out, Shane Dowrich 47; Hamish Bennett 3-50, James Neesham 2-16) drew with **New Zealand A** 237 in 61.4 overs (Todd Astle 68, Tom Bruce 46; Roston Chase 2-7, Raymon Reifer 2-27) and 72/0 in 29 overs (Jeet Raval 32*, Tom Latham 28*).

Test series (2): New Zealand 2 West Indies 0

Basin Reserve, Wellington, December 1-4: West Indies 134 in 45.4 overs (Kieran Powell 42, Kraigg Brathwaite 24; Neil Wagner 7-39, Trent Boult 2-36) and 319 in 106 overs (K Brathwaite 91, Shimron Hetmyer 66; Matt Henry 3-57, Colin de Grandhomme 2-40) lost to **New Zealand** 520/9 dec in 148.4 overs (Tom Blundell 107*, de Grandhomme 105; Kemar Roach 3-85, Miguel Cummins 2-92) by an innings and 67 runs. *MoM:* Neil Wagner.

Seddon Park, Hamilton, December 9-12: New Zealand 373 in 102.2 overs (Jeet Raval 84, Colin de Grandhomme 58; Shannon Gabriel 4-119, Kemar Roach 3-58) and 291/8 dec in 77.4 overs (Ross Taylor 107*, Kane Williamson 54; Miguel Cummins 3-69, Roston Chase 2-51) beat **West Indies** 221 in 66.5 overs (Kraigg Brathwaite 66, Shane Dowrich 35; Trent Boult 4-73, Tim Southee 2-34) and 203 in 63.5 overs (R Chase 64, K Roach 32; Neil Wagner 3-42, Mitchell Santner 2-13) by 240 runs. *MoM:* Ross Taylor.

Tour match

Cobham Oval (New), Whangarei, December 16: West Indians 288 in 48.4 overs (Kyle Hope 94 retd.out, Shai Hope 69; Aniket Parikh 4-47) lost to **New Zealand XI** 289/4 in 48.3 overs (Jeet Raval 169, Bharat Popli 62) by six wickets.

ODI series (3): New Zealand 3 West Indies 0

Cobham Oval (New), Whangarei, December 20: West Indies 248/9 in 50 overs (Evin Lewis 76, Rovman Powell 59; Doug Bracewell 4-55, Todd Astle 3-33) lost to **New Zealand** 249/5 in 46overs (George Worker 57, Ross Taylor 49*; Jason Holder 2-52, Ashley Nurse 2-55) by five wickets. *MoM:* Doug Bracewell.

Hagley Oval, Christchurch, December 23: New Zealand 325/6 in 50 overs (Henry Nicholls 83*, George Worker 58; Sheldon Cottrell 3-62, Jason Holder 2-52) beat **West Indies** 121 in 28 overs (Ashley Nurse 27, Shai Hope 23; Trent Boult 7-34, Lockie Ferguson 3-17) by 204 runs. *MoM:* Trent Boult.

Hagley Oval, Christchurch, December 26: New Zealand 131/4 in 23 overs (Ross Taylor 47*, Tom Latham 37; Sheldon Cottrell 2-19) beat **West Indies** 99/9 in 23 overs (Jason Holder 34, Nikita Miller 20*; Mitchell Santner 3-15, Trent Boult 3-18) by 66 runs (DLS method). *MoM:* Ross Taylor. *MoS:* Trent Boult.

T20I series (3): New Zealand 2 West Indies 0

Saxton Oval, Nelson, December 29: New Zealand 187/7 in 20 overs (Glenn Phillips 56, Colin Munro 53; Carlos Brathwaite 2-38, Jerome Taylor 2-41) beat **West Indies** 140 in 19 overs (Andre Fletcher 27, C Brathwaite 21; Seth Rance 3-30, Tim Southee 3-36) by five wickets. *MoM:* Glenn Phillips.

Bay Oval, Mount Maunganui, January 1: New Zealand 102/4 in 9 overs (Colin Munro 66) v **West Indies.** No result.

Bay Oval, Mount Maunganui, January 3: New Zealand 243/5 in 20 overs (Colin Munro 104, Martin Guptill 63; Carlos Barthwaite 2-50) beat **West Indies** 124 in 16.3 overs (Andre Fletcher 46; Tim Southee 3-21, Ish Sodhi 2-25) by five wickets. *MoM:* Colin Munro. *MoS:* Colin Munro.

	Tests	ODIs	T20Is
Best batsman	Ross Taylor	Ross Taylor	Colin Munro
	(216 runs, 2 matches)	(153 runs, 3 matches)	(223 runs, 3 match)
Best bowler	Neil Wagner	Trent Boult	Tim Southee
	(14 wickets, 2 matches)	(10 wickets, 3 matches)	(6 wickets, 3 matches)

Mark Geenty (@mark_geenty) is cricket writer for Stuff.

Afghanistan v Ireland in UAE

Stirling fashions comeback

IAN CALLENDER

In the squabble over who was the pre-eminent Associate Member, Afghanistan had won across all three formats at Greater Noida earlier in the year. In UAE, Ireland snapped back. Rashid Khan, the leg-spinner, proved dangerous throughout, but they were caught on the hop by another teenager, Mujeeb Ur Rahman, a genre-busting slow bowler who became the first male international born in this century. He took four wickets in his first seven overs in ODIs, as Ireland were dismissed for their fifth-lowest total in the format.

But Ireland developed plans, inspired by opener Paul Stirling, easily the best batsman on either side. He started the comeback with 82, putting on 115 for the first wicket with William Porterfield, before Barry McCarthy killed off any Afghanistan hope with three wickets in eight balls for his maiden ODI five-for. Stirling then lit up the decider with a brilliant century. The bowlers had set it up, dismantling Afghanistan for 177. Then, Andy Balbirnie and Gary Wilson stuck around with Stirling as he went from 81 to 101 in four balls off Shapoor Zadran. It was his tenth century for Ireland, two and a half years after his ninth.

ODI series (3): Ireland 2 Afghanistan 1

Sharjah Cricket Association Stadium, Sharjah, December 5: Afghanistan 238/9 in 50 overs (Rahmat Shah 50, Nasir Ahmadzai 53; Tim Murtagh 3-28, Boyd Rankin 4-44) beat **Ireland** 100 in 31.4 overs (Mujeeb Zadran 4-24, Rashid Khan 3-28) by 138 runs. *MoM:* Mujeeb Zadran

Sharjah Cricket Association Stadium, Sharjah, December 7: Ireland 271/9 in 50 overs (Paul Stirling 82, George Dockrell 62*) beat **Afghanistan** 220 in 45.2 overs (Barry McCarthy 5-46). *MoM:* Barry McCarthy.

Sharjah Cricket Association Stadium, Sharjah, December 10: Afghanistan 177 in 48.2 overs (George Dockrell 4-28, Barry McCarthy 3-32) lost to **Ireland** 180/5 in 38 overs (Paul Stirling 101). *MoM:* Paul Stirling. *MoS:* P Stirling.

Ian Callender (@Ian_Callender) is a cricket writer based in Northern Ireland.

Zimbabwe in South Africa

Mismatch under lights

TELFORD VICE

Africa's first day-night Test was also the first anywhere since February 1973 to be scheduled for four days. The venue for this experiment — which had the blessing of the ICC — was Port Elizabeth, where, in March 1889, Aubrey Smith's England had played the first Test in South Africa. Like that one, this sped to a conclusion inside two days.

The notion of lopping a day off Test matches is worthy of consideration. Play them from Thursday to Sunday — and, most importantly, play more of them. But against Zimbabwe, who hardly play under lights at all, much less

with a pink ball? Against an attack bristling with some of the best fast bowlers around? Even in ordinary circumstances, this would have been a mismatch. In this pink-ball game, the chasm between the teams widened to tragicomic proportions.

Thirteen wickets fell on the first day (nine in the third session), and 16 on the second. Zimbabwe were put out of their misery for 68, asked to follow on, and bundled out again inside three hours. Such was the abruptness of the second day that the floodlights, upgraded at a cost of £1.6m, were not needed. The match lasted a total of 907 deliveries — the third-shortest Test since the Second World War.

Even in broad daylight, the ball moved appreciably off the seam. But it did not

Morne Morkel picked up his first five-for in 36 Tests, against Zimbabwe at Paarl. — *Getty Images* move enough to prevent Aiden Markram from showing off his rare talent for his second century, in his third Test. AB de Villiers, playing his first Test since January 2016, after choosing to sit out 17, was temporary captain because a virus had hindered Faf du Plessis's recovery from back and shoulder injuries. Few teams would have found an answer to Markram's unimpeachable orthodoxy and de Villiers's profane innovation, and the Zimbabweans didn't come close.

It might have been a short game, but it was an eventful one for de Villiers: he also had to keep wicket, after Quinton de Kock strained a hamstring while batting, and held on to eight catches. Morne Morkel's picked up his first five-for in 36 Tests, but the main destroyer in the second innings was slow left-armer Keshav Maharaj.

For all the cynicism sparked by these not-quite-two days of not-quite-day-night Test cricket, no one could say they hadn't seen 907 eventful balls. Progress, they call it.

Tour match

Boland Park, Paarl, December 20-22: Zimbabwe 196 in 71.5 overs (Hamilton Masakadza 79, Ryan Burl 26; Lizaad Williams 3-12, Michael Cohen 3-21, Shaun von Berg 3-64) and 243 in 74.3 overs (Chamu Chibhabha 55, Ryan Burl 51; L Williams 4-47, von Berg 3-57) lost to **Cricket South Africa Invitation XI** 287 in 78 overs (Temba Bavuma 70, Dayyaan Galiem 57; Graeme Cremer 4-67, Chris Mpofu 2-30) and 154/5 in 38.2 overs (Ricardo Vasconcelos 57*, Isaac Dikgale 26; G Cremer 4-44) by five wickets.

Test series (1): South Africa 1 Zimbabwe 0

1st Test: South Africa won by an innings and 120 runs

St George's Park, Port Elizabeth, December 26-27: South Africa 309/9 dec in 78.3 overs (Aiden Markram 125, AB de Villiers 53; Kyle Jarvis 3-57, Chris Mpofu 3-58) beat **Zimbabwe** 68 in 30.1 overs (K Jarvis 23; Morne Morkel 5-21, Kagiso Rabada 2-12) and 121 in 42.3 overs (f/o) (Craig Ervine 23; Keshav Maharaj 5-59, Andile Phephlukwayo 3-13) by an innings and 120 runs. *MoM:* Aiden Markram.

Best batsman: Aiden Markram (125 runs, 1 match)
Best bowler: Andile Phehlukwayo (5 wickets, 1 match)

Telford Vice (@TelfordVice) is a sports writer from South Africa.

Pakistan in New Zealand

T20I antidote to tourists' ODI woes

Pakistan finished the tour as the No.1 ranked T20I side, and the reiteration that in the young blood of batsmen Fakhar Zaman and Babar Azam, and bowlers Hasan Ali and Shadab Khan they had a group of match-winners who could deliver under pressure. That was some consolation for being imperiously swept aside in the ODIs.

New Zealand's power proved too much for Pakistan in the 50-over game. Centuries by Kane Williamson and Martin Guptill, who was returning from injury, bookended the series, with Colin de Grandhomme's blazing 74 not out off 40 balls lighting up the chase in the fourth game.

Throughout, the visitors' batting faltered. Only Zaman reached 150 runs — yet it was less than half of what Martin Guptill finished with. The 74 all out in 27.2 overs was the lowest total by a team visiting New Zealand. But that was only the worst in a worrying sequence that read 54 for 5, 39 for 3, 32 for 8, 11 for 2, and 57 for 5 at the starts of the five matches.

Coach Mickey Arthur blamed T20 leagues and poor fitness for their reverse. "I saw that players returned in a far worse state physically and technically when they were away from us for five weeks," he told *ESPNcricinfo*. "Of course, I want our players to make extra money, so I will be reasonable with our management plan. But some players came back far worse from T20 competitions in all departments."

Tour match

Saxton Oval, Nelson, January 3: Pakistan 341/9 in 50 overs (Fakhar Zaman 106 retd.out, Azhar Ali 104 retd.out; Aniket Parikh 3-74, Mark Craig 2-51) beat **New Zealand XI** 221 in 47.1 overs (Michael Davidson 54, Matt McEwan 28; Shadab Khan 4-52, Faheem Ashraf 2-21) by 120 runs.

ODI series (5): New Zealand 5 Pakistan 0

Basin Reserve, Wellington, January 6: New Zealand 315/7 in 50 overs (Kane Williamson 115, Colin Munro 58; Hasan Ali 3-61) beat **Pakistan** 166/6 in 30.1overs (Fakhar Zaman 82*, Shadab Khan 28; Tim Southee 3-22, Trent Boult 2-35) by 61 runs (DLS method). *MoM:* Kane Williamson.

Saxton Oval, Nelson, January 9: Pakistan 246/9 in 50 overs (Mohammad Hafeez 60, Shadab Khan 52; Lockie Ferguson 3-39, Todd Astle 2-50) lost to **New Zealand** 151/2 in 23.5 overs (Martin Guptill 86*, Ross Taylor 45*) by eight wickets (DLS method). *MoM:* Martin Guptill.

University Oval, Dunedin, January 13: New Zealand 257 in 50 overs (Kane Williamson 73, Ross Taylor 52; Rumman Raees 3-51, Hasan Ali 3-59) beat **Pakistan** 74 in 27.2 overs (Trent Boult 5-17, Colin Munro 2-10) by 183 runs. *MoM:* Trent Boult.

Seddon Park, Hamilton, January 16: Pakistan 262/8 in 50 overs (Mohammad Hafeez 81, Fakhar Zaman 54; Tim Southee 3-44, Kane Williamson 2-32) lost to **New Zealand** 263/5 in

Pakistan won the T20I series and rose to No.1 in the world. — *Getty Images*

45.5 overs (Colin de Grandhomme 74*, Colin Munro 56; Shadab Khan 3-42) by five wickets. *MoM:* Colin de Grandhomme.

Basin Reserve, Wellington, January 19: New Zealand 271/7 in 50 overs (Martin Guptill 100, Ross Taylor 59; Rumman Raees 3-67, Faheem Ashraf 2-49) beat **Pakistan** 256 in 49 overs (Haris Sohail 63, Shadab Khan 54; Matt Henry 4-53, Mitchell Santner 3-40) by 15 runs. *MoM:* Martin Guptill. *MoS:* Martin Guptill.

T20I series (3): Pakistan 2 New Zealand 1

Westpac Stadium, Wellington, January 22: Pakistan 105 in 19.4 overs (Babar Azam 41, Hasan Ali 23; Tim Southee 3-13, Seth Rance 3-26) lost to **New Zealand** 106/3 in 15.5 overs (Colin Munro 49*, Tom Bruce 26; Rumman Raees 2-24) by seven wickets. *MoM:* Colin Munro.

Eden Park, Auckland, January 25: Pakistan 201/4 in 20 overs (Fakhar Zaman 50, Babar Azam 50*; Ben Wheeler 2-36) beat **New Zealand** 153 in 18.3 overs (Mitchell Santner 37, B Wheeler 30; Faheem Ashraf 3-22, Mohammad Amir 2-28) by 48 runs. *MoM:* Fakhar Zaman.

Bay Oval, Mount Maunganui, January 28: Pakistan 181/6 in 20 overs (Fakhar Zaman 46, Sarfraz Ahmed 29; Mitchell Santner 2-24, Ish Sodhi 2-47) beat **New Zealand** 163/6 in 20 overs (Martin Guptill 59, Ross Taylor 25; Shadab Khan 2-19) by 18 runs. *MoM:* Shadab Khan. *MoS:* Mohammad Amir

	ODIs	T20Is
Best batsman	Martin Guptill (310 runs, 5 matches)	Babar Azam (109 runs, 3 matches)
Best bowler	Trent Boult (9 wickets, 4 matches)	Shadab Khan (5 wickets, 3 matches)

Bangladesh Tri-nation Series 2018

Sri Lanka come from behind to win

The chinks in the Sri Lankan armour — the unsettled batting foremost among them — were exposed early as they failed to chase Zimbabwe's 290 and were bundled out for 157 by Bangladesh in their first two games. However, they came back strongly to win the title round.

Much of the hard work was done by Thisara Perera, the all-rounder. He gave the innings vital boosts when the rest of the batting looked shaky, did more than his share with the ball and was lively on the field. By the latter half of the tournament, the bowling was coming together nicely. The second time they met Bangladesh — days after being taken for 320 — Suranga Lakmal reduced them for 16 for 3, before Perera, Dushmantha Chameera and Lakshan Sandakan routed the hosts for 82. Frontline spinner Akila Dananjaya didn't bowl at all in the game that lasted all of 35.5 overs.

In the final against the same side, Shehan Madushanka took a hat-trick on debut, putting the finishing touches on work begun by Chameera and Dananjaya.

Having Chandika Hathurusingha as coach — he had been with the Bangladesh side just three months before — undoubtedly helped Sri Lanka, but they can take claim for the attitude with which they pulled off the turnaround.

Meanwhile, Bangladesh, ruing their luckless run in big matches, had the added concern of an injury to Shakib Al Hasan. The problematic finger would come to haunt them for months following the series.

Best batsman: Tamim Iqbal (Bangladesh) (252 runs, 5 matches)
Best bowler: Thisara Perera (Sri Lanka) (11 wickets, 5 matches)

1st match: Bangladesh beat Zimbabwe by eight wickets
Sher-e-Bangla National Stadium, Mirpur, Dhaka, January 15: Zimbabwe 170 in 49 overs (Sikandar Raza 52, Peter Moor 33; Shakib Al Hasan 3-43, Rubel Hossain 2-24) lost to **Bangladesh** 171/2 in 28.3 overs (Tamim Iqbal 84*, Shakib 37; S Raza 2-53) by eight wickets. *MoM:* Shakib Al Hasan.

2nd match: Zimbabwe beat Sri Lanka by 12 runs
Sher-e-Bangla National Stadium, Mirpur, Dhaka, January 17: Zimbabwe 290/6 in 50 overs (Sikandar Raza 81*, Hamilton Masakadza 73; Asela Gunaratne 3-37, Thisara Perera 2-43) beat **Sri Lanka** 278 in 48.1 overs (Kusal Perera 80, T Perera 64; Tendai Chatara 4-33, Kyle Jarvis 2-56) by 12 runs. *MoM:* Sikandar Raza.

3rd match: Bangladesh beat Sri Lanka by 163 runs
Sher-e-Bangla National Stadium, Mirpur, Dhaka, January 19: Bangladesh 320/7 in 50 overs (Tamim Iqbal 84, Shakib Al Hasan 67; Thisara Perera 3-60, Nuwan Pradeep 2-66) beat

Sri Lanka 157 in 32.2overs (T Perera 29, Dinesh Chandimal 28; Shakib 3-47, Rubel Hossain 2-20) by 163 runs. *MoM:* Shakib Al Hasan.

4ᵗʰ match: Sri Lanka beat Zimbabwe by five wickets

Sher-e-Bangla National Stadium, Mirpur, Dhaka, January 21: Zimbabwe 198 in 44 overs (Brendan Taylor 58, Graeme Cremer 34; Thisara Perera 4-33, Nuwan Pradeep 3-28) lost to **Sri Lanka** 202/5 in 44.5 overs (Kusal Perera 49, T Perera 39*; Blessing Muzarabani 3-52) by five wickets. *MoM:* Thisara Perera.

5ᵗʰ match: Bangladesh beat Zimbabwe by 91 runs

Sher-e-Bangla National Stadium, Mirpur, Dhaka, January 23: Bangladesh 216/9 in 50 overs (Tamim Iqbal 76, Shakib Al Hasan 51; Graeme Cremer 4-32, Kyle Jarvis 3-42) beat **Zimbabwe** 125 in 36.3 overs (Sikandar Raza 39, G Cremer 23; Shakib 3-34, Mustafizur Rahman 2-16) by 91 runs. *MoM:* Tamim Iqbal.

6ᵗʰ match: Sri Lanka beat Bangladesh by ten wickets

Sher-e-Bangla National Stadium, Mirpur, Dhaka, January 25: Bangladesh 82 in 24 overs (Mushfiqur Rahim 26; Suranga Lakmal 3-21, Dushmantha Chameera 2-6) lost to **Sri Lanka** 83/0 in 11.5 overs (Upul Tharanga 39*, Danushka Gunathilaka 35*) by ten wickets. *MoM:* Suranga Lakmal.

Points table

Teams	M	W	L	T	N/R	Pts.	NRR
Bangladesh	4	3	1	0	0	15	+1.114
Sri Lanka	4	2	2	0	0	9	+0.146
Zimbabwe	4	1	3	0	0	4	-1.087

Bangladesh and Sri Lanka qualified for the final

Final: Sri Lanka beat Bangladesh by 79 runs

Shere Bangla National Stadium, Mirpur, Dhaka, January 27: Sri Lanka 221 in 50 overs (Upul Tharanga 56, Dinesh Chandimal 45; Rubel Hossain 4-46, Mustafizur Rahman 2-29) beat **Bangladesh** 142 in 41.1 overs (Mahmudullah 76, Mushfiqur Rahim 22; Shehan Madushanka 3-26, Dushmantha Chameera 2-17) by 79 runs. *MoM:* Upul Tharanga. *MoS:* Thisara Perera.

Winners: Sri Lanka

Sri Lanka in Bangladesh

Hathurusingha era begins well

MOHAMMAD ISAM

Sri Lanka had a successful tour, winning all three trophies in Bangladesh. After their excellent bounce-back in the tri-nation ODI series in Dhaka, they won the Test and T20I series with some ease. It was the best start new coach Chandika Hathurusingha could have hoped for, having spent the previous four years in the same role in Bangladesh.

The hosts were without Shakib Al Hasan after the tri-nation final, where he suffered a finger injury. The selectors called upon six specialist spinners in the 16-man squad for the First Test in Chittagong. But the curator delivered a pitch where batsmen, from both sides, put together the highest run aggregates in the last three years.

Mominul Haque made 176 and 105 to become the first Bangladeshi batsman to score hundreds in each innings of a Test match. Kusal Mendis, Dhananjaya de Silva and Roshen Silva were not going to be left behind, batting long and scoring big as Sri Lanka took a 200-run lead. Mominul held them back on the final day, adding 180 for the fourth wicket with Liton Das. The 1533 runs scored in Chittagong was the highest aggregate in a Test match in three years.

Mominul Haque became the first Bangladeshi batsman to score hundreds in each innings of a Test. — *Getty Images*

But the batting festivities were over in the Dhaka Test, where the teams lasted just two and a half days. Bangladesh were woeful against Sri Lanka's spin trio of Rangana Herath, Dilruwan Perera and Akila Dananjaya, who finished with 8 for 44 on debut. Herath went past Wasim Akram's 414 wickets to become the highest Test wicket-taker among left-arm bowlers.

The T20I series was also the visitors' domain as they first chased down a stiff 193 quite comfortably, before posting a 200-plus total in the second game in Sylhet, which Bangladesh couldn't get near. It was a disappointing home season, and one that had started so brightly in January.

Test series (2): Sri Lanka 1 Bangladesh 0

Zahur Ahmed Chowdhury Stadium, Chittagong, January 31 – February 4: Bangladesh 513 in 129.5 overs (Mominul Haque 176, Mushfiqur Rahim 92; Suranga Lakmal 3-68, Rangana Herath 3-150) and 307/5 dec in 100 overs (M Haque 105, Liton Das 94, R Herath 2-80) drew with **Sri Lanka** 713/9 dec in 199.3 overs (Kusal Mendis 196, Dhananjaya de Silva 173, Roshen Silva 109; Taijul Islam 4-219, Mehidy Hasan Miraz 3-174). *MoM:* Mominul Haque.

Sher-e-Bangla National Stadium, Mirpur, Dhaka, February 8-10: Sri Lanka 222 in 65.3 overs (Kusal Mendis 68, Roshen Silva 56; Abdus Razzak 4-63, Taijul Islam 4-83) and 226 in 73.5 overs (R Silva 70*, Dimuth Karunaratne 32; T Islam 4-76, Mustafizur Rahman 3-49) beat **Bangladesh** 110 in 45.4 overs (Mehidy Hasan Miraz 38*, Liton Das 25; Akila Dananjaya 3-20, Suranga Lakmal 3-25) and 123 in 29.3 overs (Mominul Haque 33, Mushfiqur Rahim 25; A Dananjaya 5-24, Rangana Herath 4-49) by 215 runs. *MoM:* Roshen Silva. *MoS:* Roshen Silva.

T20I series (2): Sri Lanka 2 Bangladesh 0

Sher-e-Bangla National Stadium, Mirpur, Dhaka, February 15: Bangladesh 193/5 in 20 overs (Mushfiqur Rahim 66*, Soumya Sarkar 51; Jeevan Mendis 2-21) lost to **Sri Lanka** 194/4 in 16.4overs (Kusal Mendis 53, Dasun Shanaka 42*; Nazmul Islam 2-25) by six wickets. *MoM:* Kusal Mendis.

Sylhet International Cricket Stadium, February 18: Sri Lanka 210/4 in 20 overs (Kusal Mendis 70, Danushka Gunathilaka 42) beat **Bangladesh** 135 in 18.4 overs (Mahmudullah 41, Tamim Iqbal 29; D Gunathilaka 2-3, Shehan Madushanka 2-23) by 75 runs. *MoM:* Kusal Mendis. *MoS:* Kusal Mendis.

	Tests	T20Is
Best batsman	Mominul Haque (314 runs, 2 matches)	Kusal Mendis (123 runs, 2 matches)
Best bowler	Taijul Islam (12 wickets, 2 matches)	Danushka Gunathilaka (3 wickets, 2 matches)

Afghanistan v Zimbabwe in UAE

Rashid, Mujeeb rule Sharjah

First they combined to take seven wickets in the T20Is. Then they together had 28 from five ODIs. Afghanistan's spin sensations Rashid Khan and Mujeeb Ur Rahman rattled Zimbabwe as the Asian side won six of the seven games across formats.

Throw in Mohammad Nabi's all-round efforts and Afghanistan's classic template for victory appears; but, in fact, there was more to their game. Rahmat Shah showed the batting could keep up with the world-class bowlers with a hundred that set up their second-highest ODI total of 333/5 — only behind their 338 made against Ireland in Greater Noida the previous year — and another fifty later on.

They could, of course, have used more consistency. On the one occasion that the spinners couldn't check the scoring, Zimbabwe too reached the exact same 333/5, through Brendan Taylor's ton. In reply, Dawlat Zadran made 47 not out from No.10, yet Afghanistan crumbled to their second-biggest defeat.

T20I series (2): Afghanistan 2 Zimbabwe 0

1st T20I: Afghanistan won by five wickets

Sharjah Cricket Stadium, February 5: Zimbabwe 120/9 in 20 overs (Solomon Mire 34, Malcolm Waller 27*; Rashid Khan 3-19, Sharafuddin Ashraf 2-31) lost to **Afghanistan** 121/5 in 14.4 overs (Mohammad Nabi 40*, Mohammad Shahzad 20; Blessing Muzarabani 2-36) by five wickets. *MoM:* Mohammad Nabi.

2nd T20I: Afghanistan won by 17 runs

Sharjah Cricket Stadium, February 6: Afghanistan 158/9 in 20 overs (Mohammad Nabi 45, Karim Sadiq 28; Tendai Chatara 3-20, Graeme Cremer 2-20) beat **Zimbabwe** 141/5 in 20 overs (Sikandar Raza 40, Ryan Burl 30; Mujeeb Ur Rahman 2-21, Rashid Khan 2-23) by 17 runs. *MoM:* Mohammad Nabi.

ODI series (5): Afghanistan 4 Zimbabwe 1

1st ODI: Afghanistan won by 154 runs

Sharjah Cricket Stadium, February 9: Afghanistan 333/5 in 20 overs (Rahmat Shah 114, Najibullah Zadran 81*; Graeme Cremer 3-47) beat **Zimbabwe** 179 in 34.4 overs (Solomon Mire 34, Craig Ervine 33; Rashid Khan 4-26, Mujeeb Ur Rahman 2-41) by 154 runs. *MoM:* Rahmat Shah.

2nd ODI: Zimbabwe won by 154 runs

Sharjah Cricket Stadium, February 11: Zimbabwe 333/5 in 20 overs (Brendan Taylor 125, Sikandar Raza 92; Rashid Khan 2-36) beat **Afghanistan** 179 in 30.1 overs (Dawlat Zadran

47*, Rahmat Shah 43; Graeme Cremer 4-41, Tendai Chatara 3-24) by 154 runs. *MoM:* Brendan Taylor.

3rd ODI: Afghanistan won by six wickets

Sharjah Cricket Stadium, February 13: Zimbabwe 154 in 34.3 overs (Craig Ervine 39, Sikandar Raza 38; Rashid Khan 5-24, Mujeeb Ur Rahman 3-45) lost to **Afghanistan** 158/4 in 27.3 overs (Rahmat Shah 56, Nasir Jamal 51; Tendai Chatara 2-18) by six wickets. *MoM:* Rashid Khan.

4th ODI: Afghanistan won by ten wickets

Sharjah Cricket Stadium, February 16: Zimbabwe 134 in 38 overs (Craig Ervine 54*, Brendon Taylor 30; Mujeeb Ur Rahman 5-50, Mohammad Nabi 2-18) lost to **Afghanistan** 135/0 in 21.1 overs (Mohammad Shahzad 75*, Ihsanullah 51*) by ten wickets. *MoM:* Mujeeb Ur Rahman.

5th ODI: Afghanistan won by 146 runs

Sharjah Cricket Stadium, February 19: Afghanistan 241/9 in 50 overs (Javed Ahmadi 76, Rahmat Shah 59; Sikandar Raza 2-41, Tendai Chatara 2-42) beat **Zimbabwe** 95 in 32.1 overs (Craig Ervine 34, Brendon Taylor 27; Rashid Khan 3-13, Sharafuddin Ashraf 2-15) by 146 runs. *MoM:* Sharafuddin Ashraf. *MoS:* Rashid Khan.

	ODIs	T20Is
Best batsman	Rahmat Shah (272 runs, 5 matches)	Mohammad Nabi (85 runs, 2 matches)
Best bowler	Rashid Khan (16 wickets, 5 matches)	Rashid Khan (5 wickets, 2 matches)

De Villiers provided the star turn bat in what would prove to be his final series for the Proteas. — *Getty Images*

Australia in South Africa

Sandpaper rubs sheen off de Villiers finale

GEOFF LEMON

Let's be blunt. Australia's tour of South Africa will forever be remembered for one scandal that began on the field, crossed the boundary and raced around the globe. When the touring team was caught on camera during the Third Test in Cape Town grinding sandpaper on the match ball to produce reverse swing, the reaction had a ferocity and intensity that no other ball-tampering case has come close to producing. Perhaps only match-fixing revelations have provoked a response more severe. An investigation from Cricket Australia concluded that vice-captain David Warner had concocted the plan, his young opening partner Cameron Bancroft had carried it out, and captain Steve Smith was cognisant of their intentions. All three received lengthy bans from international and domestic cricket.

That the series is most associated with Australia's cheating is a shame for their opponents, who not only beat Australia in South Africa for the first time since readmission to international cricket in the 1990s, but who did so with one of the great Test performances. After a thumping loss in the opening match, South Africa swept back to win the next three in a row, something only done before by the great 1950 West Indies team that toured England with the storied talents of Weekes, Worrell, Walcott, Ramadhin and Valentine.

The talents of AB de Villiers are no less storied, while those of Kagiso Rabada will be the same should the rest of his career follow its vaulting early trajectory. De Villiers provided the star turn with the bat in what would prove to be his final series for the Proteas, while Rabada matched him with the ball. But the result took a varied effort across a changing XI: stifling the current best Test batsman in the world after Smith's devastating Ashes in which he had made centuries at will; resisting three of the most rapid and dangerous fast bowlers in the world operating in concert; and neutralising a spinner who during the course of the series took his 300th Test wicket and moved to sixth on his country's all-time list.

After the cheating was exposed, a distracted Australian team was no longer able to compete. But the match and series had already all but slipped away, with an exhausted touring side wilting in hostile environs. A heated dressing-room argument between Warner and South African wicketkeeper Quinton de Kock had been leaked to the media via CCTV footage during the First Test, after which portions of the local crowd subjected the partners and children of Australian players to relentless abuse. This ill-will and aggression all fed the poisonous atmosphere in which the decision to cheat was taken.

There was little sympathy for Australian players when the truth was revealed. Longstanding resentment of the aggression of Australian teams over at least 20 years, coming from opposition countries and from Australians alike, was coupled with a resentment of sanctimony from those same teams who had lectured others about the spirit of cricket.

At the time of writing, six months on, there are plenty of unanswered questions about how things reached this point, where responsibility lies, and what must change. The governing body seems keen to avoid ask-

Cameron Bancroft was caught on camera covering up evidence that cheating happening. — *Getty Images*

ing or answering these questions, while the suspended players will resume their careers with no incentive to say any more about it. The claim that Cape Town was the first time any Australian player had tampered with the ball is especially dubious, with plenty of evidence suggesting otherwise.

The age-old Australian claim of playing "hard but fair" is now mothballed; anyone uttering it could have others justifiably laugh in their face. Things fade in their intensity, and after some years this saga will become another story from cricket's past rather than an indictment on its present. But for at least a couple of decades, anyone debating the ethics or spirit of an Australian team will only have to mention sandpaper to have a conquering rebuttal. Remarkable that a mere few strokes with fine-grit abrasive can leave such a deep and lasting impression.

Tour match

Willowmoore Park, Benoni, February 22-24: South Africa A220 in 58.5 overs (Theunis de Bruyn 46, Zubayr Hamza 44; Pat Cummins 4-32, Josh Hazlewood 3-40) and 248 in 72.5 overs (Shaun von Berg 52, Pieter Malan 34; Mitchell Starc 4-46, Steven Smith 2-22) lost to **Australia**329 in 90.4 overs (P Cummins 59*, Cameron Bancroft 45; Beuran Hendricks 5-83, Duanne Olivier 2-37) and 140/5 in 29.3 overs (Shaun Marsh 39*, S Smith 25; D Olivier 4-74) by five wickets.

Test series (4): South Africa 3 Australia 1

1st Test: Australia won by 118 runs

Seven visits to South Africa since readmission had brought Australia five series wins and two draws. The First Test of 2018 suggested that success would continue.

Australia batted through an attritional opening day on an abrasive surface. Wickets were a matter of discipline. Key batsmen Warner and Smith made 51 and 56, but South Africa were able to cut them off before too much damage was done. At 225 for 5 at stumps, the game was anyone's. But Mitchell Marsh settled in the next day to play his most important Test innings, building partnerships with the lower order. Pat Cummins blocked 11 overs of the new ball, Mitchell Starc thrashed 35 runs off 25 balls before lunch, then an energised Marsh whacked 36 from 26 balls afterwards, having only made 28 in the previous session. He was second-last out, trying to drag Philander over mid-on for a century, but his efforts saw Australia register an imposing 351.

South Africa's reply fell apart. De Villiers's unbeaten half-century was full of sparkling strokes, but wickets crashed around him. Nathan Lyon did the early damage with his off-breaks and a new ball, taking Dean Elgar and Hashim Amla within an over to go past Craig McDermott's mark of 291 wickets for Australia. Then Starc produced a spell of wicked destructiveness after tea.

Five wickets in 34 balls, costing 15 runs. He used savage reverse swing away from the edge to nick off three right-handers, then inswing to bowl two lefties. Questions would later be asked about how that reverse swing was obtained, though South Africa had got the ball to swerve equally early when they had bowled.

Australia's lead of 189 extended to 416 on day three as Bancroft showed composure with a half-century. The game should have been over on day four when South Africa lost four wickets quickly, including de Villiers for a diamond duck. But a brilliant counterpunching century from the young Aiden Markram brought the home team belief and joy, with Theunis de Bruyn and de Kock working in a rare display of cooperation alongside. With 134 to get and five wickets in hand, a miracle was possible. But the late-day dismissal of the weary Markram, on a ground that had only once seen a fourth-innings century, ended the spree.

The last-wicket pair survived a stint of spin in the darkness, but were wrapped up early on day five. Before they were out, so was the video footage of Warner's verbal brawl with de Kock, and a bad-tempered series was locked in.

Kingsmead, Durban, March 1-5: Australia 351 in 110.4 overs (Mitchell Marsh 96, Steven Smith 56; Keshav Maharaj 5-123, Vernon Philander 3-59) and 227 in 74.4 overs (Cameron Bancroft 53, S Smith 38; K Maharaj 4-102, Morne Morkel 3-47) beat **South Africa** 162 in 51.4 overs (AB de Villiers 71*, Aiden Markram 32; Mitchell Starc 5-34, Nathan Lyon 3-50) and 298 in 92.4 overs (A Markram 143, Quinton de Kock 83; M Starc 4-75, Josh Hazlewood 3-61) by 118 runs. *MoM:* Mitchell Starc.

2nd **Test: South Africa won by six wickets**

Taking heart from the fightback late in the Durban Test, it was in the second match that de Villiers and Rabada swung the series for South Africa. The batsman made what may well have been the best century of his career, while the bowler took 11 wickets with an aggressive display of pace, swing and reverse swing, while at times unable to contain his rage at his opponents.

Warner threatened to antagonise the home crowd with a century, but the new inclusion Lungi Ngidi bowled him after lunch on the first day with a peach of a ball that clipped the bails after cutting the batsman in half. Morne Morkel had announced that he would retire after the series, but it didn't save him from being dropped for Ngidi after a poor outing at Durban.

Rabada roared through the gap made by Ngidi with five wickets, and bumped shoulders with Smith after dismissing him. He would be suspended for two Tests by the referee after the match, then have that ban overturned on appeal.

On the second day, with the ball reversing constantly, Elgar and Amla battled through 46.2 overs for 88 runs. They didn't damage the scoreboard, but they put miles into the bowlers.

That set the stage for de Villiers at his most audacious. As wickets began to fall after tea, he took control, playing shots of outrageous control and inventiveness against the hooping ball. Five of his teammates were out for a combined 19 runs, even as he wiped off the deficit by stumps. He continued on his merry way in the morning with the tail, raising his 22nd Test century. His mark of six against Australia was the most by any South African. By the time he ran out of partners, having pasted the ball stylishly to all corners, the lead was 136.

Khawaja battled hard for an Australian lead, but was out to Rabada in the dying minutes of the third day, while Mitchell Marsh had also fought but was gone early the next morning. Again, the bowler's sharp movement and accuracy was irresistible. Rabada cleaned up once more, including drawing another disciplinary charge for shouting at Warner after dismissing him, and South Africa cantered home against a small target. The series had been flipped on its head in the most impressive fashion.

St George's Park, Port Elizabeth, March 9-12: Australia 243 in 71.3 overs (David Warner 63, Cameron Bancroft 38; Kagiso Rabada 5-96, Lungi Ngidi 3-51) and 239 in 79 overs (Usman Khawaja 75, Mitchell Marsh 45; K Rabada 6-54, L Ngidi 2-24) lost to **South Africa** 382 in 118.4 overs (AB de Villiers 126*, Dean Elgar 57; Pat Cummins 3-79, M Marsh 2-26) and 102/4 in 22.5 overs (de Villiers 28, Hashim Amla 27; Nathan Lyon 2-44) by six wickets. *MoM:* Kagiso Rabada.

3rd Test: South Africa won by 322 runs

By the post-lunch session of the third day, when television cameras spotted Bancroft using a yellow object on the ball, the match was already slipping from Australia's grasp. Bancroft shoved the object down his trousers when the first batch of incriminating footage was shown on the ground's big screen, but of course the same cameras also captured his attempt to hide the evidence. The umpires didn't find it at the time, but the jig was well and truly up.

Elgar had gone from a thorn in the Australian side to a dagger in the ribs in the first innings, carrying his bat for the third time in Test cricket to match the record held only by the great Barbadian opener Cuthbert Gordon Greenidge. Without him South Africa wouldn't have made half of their score of 311, with de Villiers's 64 the only other contribution of note.

With the frustration at letting that opportunity slip, the siege mentality of constant abuse and conflict, and the infuriation that Rabada's suspension had been overturned between matches, Australia's mental demons were finding voice. Warner set out to destroy Rabada, slamming 30 from 13 balls before the bowler inevitably destroyed his stumps. Smith looked his worst at the crease for years, fencing at a wide trash delivery from the recalled Morkel to nick for 5. Only Bancroft's unexpected maturity took Australia within reach of parity.

The deficit was back out to 121 with only one wicket down when the cameraman sprung their trap and caught Bancroft. From that point, concentration wandered. De Villiers made another fifty by stumps, after which Smith and Bancroft gave a press conference which was supposedly a confession,

In a subdued press conference, Cameron Bancroft and Steve Smith confessed to tampering the ball, left out key parts of the story. — *Getty Images*

although they were lying about key parts of the tampering story to make it seem less grave, including attempting to conceal Warner's involvement.

By the next morning, Smith and Warner had stood down as captain and vice-captain, with wicketkeeper Tim Paine asked to lead the side.

South Africa's lower order frolicked against a broken team, who then had to bat after lunch chasing 430. Bancroft, at the centre of the storm, held things together for a partnership of 57, but after a frazzled Warner ran him out, all ten wickets fell for 50 runs. This quickly and easily, Australia's tour had fallen apart.

Newlands, Cape Town, March 22-25: South Africa 311 in 97.5 overs (Dean Elgar 141*, AB De Villiers 64; Pat Cummins 4-78, Nathan Lyon 2-43) and 373 in 112.2 overs (Aiden Markram 84, Quinton de Kock 65; P Cummins 3-67, Josh Hazlewood 3-69, N Lyon 3-102) beat **Australia** 255 in 69.5 overs (Cameron Bancroft 77, N Lyon 47; Morne Morkel 4-87, Kagiso Rabada 4-91) and 107 in 39.4 overs (David Warner 32, C Bancroft 26; M Morkel 5-23, Keshav Maharaj 2-32) by 322 runs. *MoM:* Morne Morkel.

4th Test: South Africa won by 492 runs

The final Test at the Wanderers was a curious exercise. Smith, Warner and Bancroft had been sent home. Paine was officially captain, having six months previously been nowhere near the side. Matt Renshaw and Joe Burns were flown over from Australia, having just opened the batting in the Sheffield Shield final for Queensland. Starc had a shin injury, so Chadd Sayers made his long-awaited debut. But after a frenzied week of global condemnation, it was strange to be playing cricket at all.

Australia's coach Darren Lehmann announced it would be his last Test in charge. At 2-1, his team had a nominal chance to square the series. But they were no chance really.

Cummins toiled impressively, as he had done in Cape Town, and took five wickets across 29 long overs. But Markram added 152 to an already impressive series. Temba Bavuma was stranded just short of a century, while de Villiers made his fifth score above fifty in six attempts.

Sayers bowled well to de Villiers with swing and control, eventually taking an inside edge for his debut wicket. But the feelgood stories for the tourists ended there. They were six down by stumps; Cummins and Paine mustered some resistance on the third morning, but that just meant South Africa didn't enforce the follow-on. The Australians would live to regret that.

An initial deficit of 267 swelled to 612 by the fourth afternoon, thanks to Elgar's tortuous 81. Paine kept wicket with a broken thumb, refusing to leave the field while his team was suffering. Faf du Plessis hadn't passed 20 in the series but smashed a belligerent century despite Cummins smashing his finger. Australia lost three wickets by stumps, then Philander routed them on the final morning with a spell of 6 for 3.

Paine had led with class, asking that the teams shake hands, apologising for what had happened and saying publicly that an ugly behavioural culture had sprung up from players who weren't willing to listen to supporters who wanted better. Unlike the spiteful 2014 tour, the teams gathered for a drink in good spirits after play.

The South Africans understood the scale of their achievement, even if most eyes were on the other team. "I've played a lot of cricket against Australia and I've never been in the position where I can look up at the scoreboard and see a lead of 600," said du Plessis. "To win by 490 runs against any Australian team is an unbelievable performance, and I'm really proud of that."

The Wanderers Stadium, Johannesburg, March 30 – April 3: South Africa 488 in 136.5 overs (Aiden Markram 152, Temba Bavuma 95*; Pat Cummins 5-83, Nathan Lyon 3-182) and 344/6 dec in 105 overs (Faf du Plessis 120, Dean Elgar 81; P Cummins 4-58, N Lyon 2-116) beat **Australia** 221 in 70 overs (Tim Paine 62, Usman Khawaja 53; Vernon Philander 3-30, Kagiso Rabada 3-53, Keshav Maharaj 3-92) and 119 in 46.4 overs (Joe Burns 42, Peter Handscomb 24; V Philander 6-21, Morne Morkel 2-28) by 492 runs. *MoM:* Vernon Philander. *MoS:* Kagiso Rabada.

Best batsman: Aiden Markram (480 runs, 4 matches)
Best bowler: Kagiso Rabada (23 wickets, 4 matches)

West Indies in Pakistan

Azam swats away raw tourists

The No.1 T20I side, against the defending World T20 champions — Karachi's first taste of international cricket in nine years was quite the match-up. But, only on paper.

Despite the occasional tours and the stars who braved security fears to play the PSL, players were still wary to tour Pakistan, and it was an inexperienced 13-member West Indies squad led by Jason Mohammed and including four uncapped players that made the visit. The rawness told right from the start: 24 hours after they landed, when chasing Pakistan's then joint-highest T20I total of 203, the visitors crumbled to their lowest of 60, with Veerasammy Permaul injured and not batting. The next game, the hosts went one better, getting to a new record total of 205/3. Babar Azam took only eight runs off the last five balls he faced, to finish three short of a hundred. His 97 not out came off 58 balls and included 13 fours and a six.

Denesh Ramdin's unbeaten 42 off 18 balls propped up the West Indies' best batting performance of the tour, but it wasn't enough against a marauding Azam and Fakhar Zaman. As if the wins both on and off the field weren't enough cause for celebration for Pakistan, they also uncovered in debutant Hussain Talat a handy option in the top order.

> Six of Pakistan's top ten T20I totals have come since September 2017, including three of the top five.

T20I series (3): Pakistan 3 West Indies 0

ational Stadium, Karachi, April 1: Pakistan 203/5 in 20 overs (Hussain Talat 41, Fakhar Zaman 39) beat **West Indies** 60 in 13.4 overs (Mohammad Amir 2-3, Shoaib Malik 2-13) by 143 runs. *MoM:* Hussain Talat.

National Stadium, Karachi, April 2: Pakistan 205/3 in 20 overs (Babar Azam 97*, Hussain Talat 63) beat **West Indies** 123 in 19.2 overs (Chadwick Walton 40, Denesh Ramdin 21; Mohammad Amir 3-22, H Talat 2-12) by 82 runs. *MoM:* Babar Azam.

National Stadium, Karachi, April 3: West Indies 153/6 in 20 overs (Andre Fletcher 52, Denesh Ramdin 42*; Shadab Khan 2-27) lost to **Pakistan** 154/2 in 16.5 overs (Babar Azam 51, Fakhar Zaman 40) by eight wickets. *MoM:* Fakhar Zaman. *MoS:* Babar Azam.

Best batsman: Babar Azam (165 runs, 3 matches)
Best bowler: Mohammad Amir (5 wickets, 2 matches)

Pakistan in Ireland, England and Scotland

O'Brien, Buttler test impressive tourists

STEPHEN BRENKLEY

By the standards set on many of Pakistan's previous excursions to England, this was almost humdrum. There was no rancour, dispute or altercation. All that could be managed by way of controversy was some of the tourists being advised to remove their smart watches during the Test at Lord's. It was a delight to concentrate fully on the cricket and that was rarely less than captivating. Pakistan's raw squad played with verve and intelligence. In late spring conditions that were hardly natural to them, the manner of their play, not least their seam bowling, was often as smart as those discarded watches.

Before their arrival in England, the team had an historic assignment in Dublin, where they eventually overcame Ireland in an enthralling inaugural Test. Kevin O'Brien's defiant second-innings hundred for Ireland, which not only extended the match but also almost tipped the balance, was the stuff of sporting dreams. Although Pakistan's victory was, ultimately, comfortable, it was enough of a contest to justify Ireland's elevation to the group of Test-playing nations.

The match was also perfect preparation for the short series against England. Inexperienced as much of Pakistan's team were, they went to Lord's for the opening Test as a well-honed unit compared to their opponents. England were simply swept away, the home side as incompetent as the tourists were proficient. It was Pakistan's fifth Test victory at Lord's, their second in successive tours, and only Australia have a better record there.

Questions were already being asked about the composition and leadership of England's side following their heavy defeat in the Ashes. Another defeat in the Second Test at Headingley might have had far-reaching consequences.

As it was, fortunes were reversed. England, somewhat bizarrely, seemed to have learned from the opposition how English pitches in May should be approached and, without ever suggesting that world Test domination beckoned, they produced an efficient and well balanced display.

That it was a bowlers' series was enshrined in the batting figures. Jos Buttler's bravura innings of 80 not out at Headingley justified his recall to the England Test side. It was the highest individual innings in the series; there had not been a lower top score in a series in England since WG Grace's 75 not out against Australia at Lord's in 1890.

Fittingly, the bowling honours were divided. Pakistan coped better, much better, at Lord's, but England's vast experience shone through at Headingley. There was plenty to hearten Pakistan. Still becoming accustomed to life without the talismanic Misbah-ul-Haq, a record of two won, one lost was perfectly respectable.

In Mohammad Abbas, Pakistan unearthed a beguiling seam bowler who took 19 wickets in the three Tests, bowling below 130kph. He came made to measure for the time of year, seaming the ball here, cutting it there, and there can be no higher praise than to report that he lost nothing by comparison with England's master craftsman Jimmy Anderson. He may have to deduce what to do when batsmen decide to stand out of their crease to him, as Buttler did tellingly at Headingley, but Abbas and Mohammad Amir were a potent combination.

The captain, Sarfraz Ahmed, had a disturbingly quiet series with the bat, but was a deceptively spring-heeled wicketkeeping presence and his perky captaincy seemed to complement the engaging Mickey Arthur, who has never shed the capacity to wear his coach's heart on his sleeve.

Tour matches

St Lawrence Ground, Canterbury, April 28 – May 1: Pakistan 168 in 55.2 overs (Imam-ul-Haq 61, Hasan Ali 24; Will Gidman 547, Harry Podmore 2-35)drew with**Kent** 209/4 in 64 overs (Hoe Denly 113*, Sean Dickson 74; Shadab Khan 2-88).

County Ground, Northampton, May 4-7: Northamptonshire 259 in 73.4 overs (Adam Rossington 90, Rob Newton 35; Shadab Khan 6-77, Rahat Ali 2-25) and 301 in 95.5 overs (R Newton 118,Josh Cobb 52; Mohammad Abbas 4-62, Shadab 4-80) lost to **Pakistan** 428 in 116.3 overs (Asad Shafiq 186*, Haris Sohail 79; Steven Crook 4-89, Rob Keogh 4-111) and 134/1 in 27 overs (Imam-ul-Haq 59*, Haris 55*) by nine wickets.

Test series (1): Pakistan 1 Ireland 0

1st Test: Pakistan won by five wickets

Even 20 years before, the idea that Ireland would play in a Test match was so much stuff and nonsense. Now, it seemed that they were eating at the high table by perfect right. The justification was jubilantly present in a wonderfully dogged century from O'Brien, which began as a kind of defiant but futile resistance, but nearly tilted the match. Pakistan won it, but they knew they had been in a proper contest. At 14 for 3 in the second innings, still needing 146, the wires and social media were humming.

Ireland's elevation to Test status might have been all but forced on the ICC, but it was also a reward for the diligence and passion of a cricketing organisation that had begun from a low base and defied the indifference of most of the population to the sport of cricket. There has been a steady stream of skilful cricketers in the past decade or so, though it was a necessary quirk of selection that of the 2911 players to have appeared in Tests at the time, Ireland fielded the 19th, 55th and 61st oldest in Ed Joyce, Tim Murtagh and Niall O'Brien.

After the cruel disappointment of a first-day washout, there was a certain poetic justice that the first Test wicket for Ireland should be taken by Boyd Rankin. He had first played Test cricket for England, fearing that he would

Kevin O'Brien's century, which began as a kind of defiant but futile resistance, nearly tilted Ireland's maiden Test. — *Getty Images*

never have the chance to represent the country of his birth and upbringing. He became the 15th player to represent two countries and the sixth to have taken a wicket for both. To Peter Siddle, Rankin's sole victim in his only match for England, could now be added Azhar Ali.

Ireland, though, could not quite capitalise on that encouraging start and Pakistan had enough batsman who were prepared to remain patient against some characteristically insistent bowling from Rankin and Tim Murtagh.

When the debutants batted, it was as if they were not ready for this moment after all. Abbas was momentarily irrepressible: four wickets went down for seven. There was a show of spirit from Kevin, but it was insufficient to save the follow-on.

Ireland then demonstrated they had the mettle for this. Kevin, once scorer of a legendary World Cup hundred against England, was all jutting jaw and impassable bat. His 118 from 354 balls gave Ireland a lead. When Murtagh and Rankin set to work again, anything seemed possible, but Imam-ul-Haq and Babar Azam retained their composure.

The Village, Malahide, Dublin, May 11-15: Pakistan 310/9 dec in 96 overs (Faheem Ashraf 83, Asad Shafiq 62; Tim Murtagh 4-45, Stuart Thompson 3-62) and 160/5 in 45 overs (Imam-ul-Haq 74*, Babar Azam 59; T Murtagh 2-55) beat **Ireland** 130 in 47.2 overs (Kevin O'Brien 40, Gary Wilson 33*; Mohammad Abbas 4-44, Shadab Khan 3-31) and 339 in 129.3 overs (f/o) (K O'Brien 118, S Thompson 53; M Abbas 5-66, Mohammed Amir 3-63) by five wickets. *MoM:* Kevin O'Brien.

Best batsman: Kevin O'Brien (158 runs, 1 match)
Best bowler: Mohammad Abbas (9 wickets, 1 match)

Tour match
Grace Road, Leicester, May 19-20: Pakistan 321/9 dec in 89.5 overs (Azhar Ali 73, Fakhar Zaman 71; Aadil Ali 2-28, Ateeq Javid 2-42)drew with**Leicestershire** 226/6 in 75 overs (A Javid 54 retd.out, A Ali 41; Shadab Khan 2-32).

Test series (2): Pakistan 1 England 1

1ˢᵗ Test: Pakistan won by nine wickets

England were as abject as Pakistan were remorseless. The tourists had a plan and they never wavered from it. Their bowlers understood what it meant to bowl a full length, allowing the ball to do its work in helpful circumstances and ensuring that batsmen ignoring the requirements of Test cricket were never comfortable. By contrast, Pakistan's own batsmen were dutifully cautious by and large, playing for each other, while England's bowlers seemed to suppose they were operating on a different surface.

Pakistan's seam quartet was quite something and the slope at Lord's, which can be the undoing of those who know it not, was the making of them. Abbas — compelling at times, using the crease and with an endlessly flexible wrist — and Hasan Ali were to the fore, and no one allowed a hapless England to settle for long. An exception was Alastair Cook, his footwork determinedly fluent.

Four Pakistan batsman made fifties and three more passed 20. England pitched it too short and the lead looked to be quite enough.

Again Pakistan's bowling was persistent; again Abbas was compelling, this time with Amir as his thrilling chief cohort. Abbas finished with eight wickets, four in each innings and thus not enough, sadly, to have his name engraved on the Lord's dressing room honours board where this performance deserved to be enshrined.

There was a little more to cheer for England. Joe Root fetchingly fashioned his 17th fifty as England captain, but for the 15th time failed to convert.

At 110 for 6, an innings defeat loomed, but the recalled Buttler and the 19-year-old off-spinning debutant Dom Bess manufactured a partnership that demonstrated what was possible. On the third night, with the seventh-wicket stand unbroken on 125, all sorts of possibilities were being pondered. But only one run was added the next morning before Buttler fell, the last four wickets went for six runs in all and Pakistan deservedly won at a canter.

Lord's, London, May 24-27: England 184 in 58.2 overs (Alastair Cook 70, Ben Stokes 38; Mohammad Abbas 4-23, Hasan Ali 4-51) and 242 in 82.1 overs (Joe Root 68, Jos Buttler 67; Mohammad Amir 4-36, M Abbas 4-41) lost to **Pakistan** 363 in 114.3 overs (Babar Azam 68 retd.out, Asad Shafiq 59; B Stokes 3-73, James Anderson 3-82) and 66/1 in 12.4 overs (Haris Sohail 39*) by nine wickets. *MoM:* Mohammad Abbas.

2ⁿᵈ Test: England won by an innings and 55 runs

There had been exhibited an array of raised eyebrows when England's new chairman of selectors, Ed Smith, decided to recall Buttler to the Test team based in part on a spectacular run in the IPL. They were firmly lowered after the Second Test.

A wicketkeeper who was not keeping and instead batting as a specialist No.7 was verging on the wastefully extravagant. But Buttler had provided evidence of what Smith was getting at with a measured half-century in the

Mohammad Abbas was persistent and compelling, finishing with eight wickets for the match at Lord's. — *Getty Images*

Lord's match; now, he ratcheted it up a gear or two. His sterling 80 not out was the centrepiece of a vastly improved exhibition from England.

Pakistan were a trifle unfortunate that barely sooner had they chosen to bat than clouds appeared. This suited perfectly a four-man seam attack of which 19-year-old Sam Curran was the surprise newest member after Ben Stokes withdrew with a pulled hamstring. Stuart Broad was first up, with Anderson and Chris Woakes on hand to assist. The great majority of the wickets were taken by full deliveries. The bowlers had taken note.

With the ball still doing plenty, England had to rediscover a purpose and patience that had hitherto been absent for long periods. This they did to an extent: the first nine passed 17 or more, doubtless being helped by the fact that for once the first wicket, featuring the recalled Keaton Jennings, put on 53.

Briefly, it seemed as if this collective effort might not be enough. But Buttler, after surviving a chance to midwicket on 12, accelerated hungrily towards the end. Nobody does it better.

The lead was almost 200 and Pakistan batted as though they knew the game was up. All England's bowlers had wickets and there were three for Bess. If he was one of the most unlikely Test participants for many a year, he featured with bat, ball and in the field where he took a spectacular one-handed catch.

There was never a smidgen of doubt that England would win for the first time in eight Tests. By tea on the third day, the series was level.

Headingley, Leeds, June 1-3: Pakistan 174 in 48.4 overs (Shadab Khan 56, Haris Sohail 28;

Stuart Broad 3-38, James Anderson 3-43, Chris Woakes 3-55) and 134 in 46 overs (Imam-ul-Haq 34, Usman Salahuddin 33; S Broad 3-28, Dominic Bess 3-33) lost to **England** 363 in 106.2 overs (Jos Buttler 80*, D Bess 49; Faheem Ashraf 3-60, Mohammad Amir 2-72) by an innings and 55 runs. *MoM:* Jos Buttler. *MoS:* Mohammad Abbas.

Best batsman: Jos Buttler (161 runs, 2 matches)
Best bowler: Mohammad Abbas (10 wickets, 2 matches)

T20I series (2): Pakistan 2 Scotland 0

1st T20I: Pakistan won by 48 runs

• Having pulled off the giant-killers act against England, the No.1 ODI side, Scotland dream of upsetting the No.1 T20I side soon after. • Alasdair Evans is tight with the new ball, but Ahmed don't flag under pressure. • He anchors the innings with 89 not out off 49 balls, with Shoaib Malik adding 53 off 27 in a fourth-wicket partnership of 96. • The 204 for 4 is their second-highest T20I total. • Scotland's openers race along at over 10 an over in the first five. • But once Ali gets the breakthrough and Shadab turns the screws, the acceleration becomes a splutter.

Grange Cricket Club, Raeburn Place, Edinburgh, June 12: Pakistan 204/4 in 20 overs (Sarfraz Ahmed 89*, Shoaib Malik 53; Alasdair Evans 3-23) beat **Scotland** 156/6 in 20 overs (Michael Leask 38*, Kyle Coetzer 31; Shadab Khan 2-25, Hasan Ali 2-33) by 48 runs. *MoM:* Sarfraz Ahmed.

2nd T20I: Pakistan won by 84 runs

• Malik misses out on his second straight fifty, but his explosive last two overs change the rhythm of the game. • His five sixes in an unbeaten 22-ball 49 ruin the figures of bowlers who'd otherwise been disciplined. • Leask, the best of the home bowlers, puts Malik down in the penultimate over. • He makes them regret it, adding 14 in the final over, but even without that, it isn't close. • Usman Khan's opening spell makes sure of that. • A spate of run-outs highlights the difference between the sides.

Grange Cricket Club, Raeburn Place, Edinburgh, June 13: Pakistan 166/6 in 20 overs (Shoaib Malik 49*, Fakhar Zaman 33; Michael Leask 3-31, Chris Sole 2-38) beat **Scotland** 82 in 14.4 overs (Calum MacLeaod 25, Richie Berrington 20; Faheem Ashraf 3-5, Usman Khan 2-4) by 84 runs. *MoM:* Usman Khan.

Best batsman: Sarfraz Ahmed (103 runs, 2 matches)
Best bowler: Faheem Ashraf (3 wickets, 2 matches)

Stephen Brenkley (@stephenbrenkley) is cricket correspondent for
The Independent.

Sri Lanka in the West Indies

Chandimal penalty blot on keen contest

In many ways, this series between two competitive teams in the bottom half of the ICC rankings was a wonderful advertisement for Test cricket. Doughty and occasionally free-flowing batting was complemented by excellent fast bowling by both sides on helpful surfaces and snappy close-in catching. If there was one blot, it was the suspension of the visiting captain for the last Test in Bridgetown, the first day-night match in the Caribbean, for tampering with the ball.

Dinesh Chandimal was hauled up by the match officials just a couple of days after making a feisty unbeaten century in Sri Lanka's first innings in a game the visitors could not afford to lose. Outclassed in the First Test by 226 runs, Sri Lanka owed it to their skipper as they made a fist in St Lucia, only for Chandimal to fall foul of the authorities when he tried to artificially alter the condition of the ball. His protestations of innocence were shown up by damning evidence and he was banned for the final Test — subsequently, he received a six-match suspension for bringing the game into disrepute — but that somehow seemed to galvanise his side as a splendid rearguard batting display allowed them to escape with a hard-earned draw.

West Indies were by far the most consistent side, but they paid the penalty for one poor batting stint when they were blasted out for 93 in the second innings in the last Test at the Kensington Oval. With the conditions clearly loaded in favour of the faster bowlers, the hosts had a potentially decisive advantage of 50 in the first innings and looked on course for their first home series win in four years. But acting captain Suranga Lakmal, the increasingly impressive Lahiru Kumara and Kasun Rajitha joined forces to send them crashing to 93 all out, setting Sri Lanka 144 for a series-levelling win.

Jason Holder, the Windies skipper in the middle of a purple patch with the ball, threatened to derail a modest chase with 5 for 41, but the injured Kusal Perera and Dilruwan Perera saw a nervy chase to its logical conclusion by putting on 63 for the unfinished seventh wicket.

West Indies were clearly the superior side in the first game in Port of Spain, riding on a century from Shane Dowrich, the wicketkeeper-batsman, and the depth in their batting to recover from 147 for 5 to 414 for 8 declared. Sri Lanka were blown away by the quicks and found themselves chasing 453 for victory after another competent Windies batting display. Kusal Mendis, opening the batting, made a sparkling 102 but no one else touched 35 as Devendra Bishoo's leg-spin and Roston Chase's off-spin sent them tumbling from 175 for 3 to 226 all out.

West Indies were more consistent that Sri Lanka, but paid for one poor batting stint.
— *Getty Images*

Tour match

Brian Lara Stadium, Tarouba, Trinidad, May 30-June 1: Sri Lankan 428 in 119.4 overs (Dinesh Chandimal 108, Niroshan Dickwella 74; Jomel Warrican 4-81, Rahkeem Cornwall 3-124) and 135/0 in 33 overs (Kusal Mendis 60*, Kusal Perera 50 retd.hurt) drew with **West Indies President's XI** 272 in 77 overs (John Campbell 62, Kieran Powell 60; Akila Dananjaya 3-46, Lahiru Kumara 3-47, Dilruwan Perera 3-50).

Test series (3): West Indies 1 Sri Lanka 1

Queen's Park Oval, Port of Spain, Trinidad, June 14-18: West Indies 414/8 dec 154 overs (Shane Dowrich 125*, Shai Hope 44; Lahiru Kumara 4-95, Suranga Lakmal 2-55) and 223/7 dec in 72 overs (Kieran Powell 88, Jason Holder 39; L Kumara 3-40, Rangana Herath 2-52) beat **Sri Lanka** 185 in 55.4overs (Dinesh Chandimal 44, Niroshan Dickwella 31; Miguel Cummins 3-39, Kemar Roach 2-34) and 226 in 83.2 overs (Kusal Mendis 102, Angelo Mathews 31; Roston Chase 4-15, Devendra Bishoo 3-48) by 226 runs. *MoM:* Shane Dowrich.

Daren Sammy National Cricket Stadium, Gros Islet, St Lucia, June 6-10: Sri Lanka 253 in 79 overs (Dinesh Chandimal 119*, Kusal Mendis 45; Shannon Gabriel5-59, Kemar Roach 4-49) and 342 in 91.4 overs (K Mendis 87, Niroshan Dickwella 62; S Gabriel 8-62, K Roach 2-78) drew with **West Indies** 300 in 100.3 overs (Devon Smith 61, Shane Dowrich 55; Lahiru Kumara 4-86, Kasun Rajitha 3-49) and 147/5 in 60.3 overs (Kraigg Brathwaite 59*, Shai Hope 39; K Rajitha 2-23, Suranga Lakmal 2-48). *MoM:* Shannon Gabriel.

Kensington Oval, Bridgetown, Barbados, June 23-27: West Indies 204 in 69.3 overs (Jason Holder 74, Shane Dowrich 71; Lahiru Kumara 4-58, Kasun Rajitha 3-68) and 93 in 31.2 overs (Kemar Roach 23; K Rajitha 3-20, Suranga Lakmal 3-25) lost to **Sri Lanka** 154 in 59 overs (Niroshan Dickwella 42, Danushka Gunathilaka 29; J Holder 4-19, Shannon Gabriel 3-52) and 144/6 in 40.2 overs (Kusal Perera 28*, Kusal Mendis 25; J Holder 5-41) by four wickets. *MoM:* Jason Holder. *MoS:* Shane Dowrich.

Best batsman: Shane Dowrich (288 runs, 3 matches)
Best bowler: Shannon Gabriel (20 wickets, 3 matches)

ICC World XI v West Indies in England

Stars come out for hurricane relief

Hurricanes Irma and Maria had eight months previously wreaked havoc over several islands of the Caribbean. This match aimed to raise funds to repair and renovate cricket stadia in Anguilla, Antigua, Dominica, British Virgin Islands and St Martin.

The composition of the World XI remained in flux right till the end. Finally, it was Tamim Iqbal (Bangladesh), Luke Ronchi, Mitchell McClenaghan (New Zealand), Sam Billings, Tymal Mills (England), Dinesh Karthik (India), Shoaib Malik, Shahid Afridi (Pakistan), Thisara Perera (Sri Lanka), Rashid Khan (Afghanistan) and Sandeep Lamichhane who walked out as the XI. Nasser Hussain's presence as an on-field 'roving reporter' — an experiment by the broadcasters Sky, who were providing the feed for free — kindled suspicion that maybe this wasn't a serious game. Afridi's involvement for his 99th T20I almost confirmed it; he took his 98th wicket and benefitted from tweaked rules to have a runner while batting.

But the match indeed had official status, which meant it marked Andre Russell's return to international cricket after a year's suspension, and allowed Evin Lewis to add a half-century to his tally.

Only T20I: West Indies won by 72 runs
Lord's, London, May 31: West Indies 199/4 in 20 overs (Evin Lewis 58, Denesh Ramdin 44*; Rashid Khan 2-48) beat **ICC World XI** 127 in 16.4 overs (Thisara Perera 61; Kesrick Williams 3-42, Samuel Badree 2-4) by 45 runs. *MoM:* Evin Lewis.

Hurricanes Irma and Maria had eight months previously wreaked havoc over several islands of the Caribbean, including at stadiums. — *CWI*

Afghanistan v Bangladesh in India

Rashid unstoppable

Rashid Khan had played the World Cup qualifiers in Zimbabwe, the IPL across India, the Hurricane Relief Challenge at Lord's and was back in India, for Afghanistan's 'home' series against Bangladesh. Like most of his team-mates, he too was fasting. Yet, he showed no fatigue nor signs of too much cricket as he was the main magician in a marauding spin trio.

In the final game, he got just one wicket, but defended eight in the final over to seal the sweep.

Bangladesh had claimed they were the underdogs of the contest, and they were indeed brushed aside. They had few answers to spin, and where Afghanistan enjoyed timely power-hitting from their batsmen to complement the work of the bowlers, Bangladesh were left floundering for the same batting touches.

It was a great result for the winners, but the question remained: Why was a team playing their debut Test right after preparing for it with T20Is?

T20I series (3): Afghanistan 3 Bangladesh 0

Rajiv Gandhi International Cricket Stadium, Dehradun, June 3: Afghanistan 167/8 in 20 overs (Mohammad Shahzad 40, Samiullah Shenwari 36; Mahmudullah 2-1, Abul Hasan 2-40) beat **Bangladesh** 122 in 19 overs (Liton Das 30, Mahmudullah 29; Rashid Khan 3-13, Shapoor Zadran 3-40) by 45 runs. *MoM:* Rashid Khan.
Rajiv Gandhi International Cricket Stadium, Dehradun, June 5: Bangladesh 134/8 in 20 overs (Tamim Iqbal 43, Mushfiqur Rahim 22; Rashid Khan 4-12, Mohammad Nabi 2-19) lost to **Afghanistan** 135/4 in 18.5overs (Samiullah Shenwari 49, Mohammad Nabi 31*; Mosaddek Hossain 2-21) by six wickets. *MoM:* Rashid Khan.
Rajiv Gandhi International Cricket Stadium, Dehradun, June 7: Afghanistan 145/6 in 20 overs (Samiullah Shenwari 33*, Asghar Afghan 27; Nazmul Islam 2-18, Abu Jayed 2-27) beat **Bangladesh** 144/6 in 20 overs (Mushfiqur Rahim 46, Mahmudullah 45) by 1 run. *MoM:* Mushfiqur Rahim. *MoS:* Rashid Khan.

Best batsman: Samiullah Shenwari (118 runs, 3 matches)
Best bowler: Rashid Khan (8 wickets, 3 matches)

Australia in England

Paine's new era scarred by 481

Alex Hales did his bit in lifting England to a record 481 for 6. — *Getty Images*

England slammed 481 for 6 in the third ODI against Australia. It was, of course, the highest total in men's ODIs, ahead of the 444 the same team made against Pakistan at the same Trent Bridge ground. Jonny Bairstow and Alex Hales made hundreds, finishing with strike rates of over 150; it was Bairstow's fourth in six innings. Eoin Morgan made a 21-ball half-century, the fastest for England and becoming their highest run-getter in the format. A remarkable 21 sixes were struck.

And you didn't even need these kinds of numbers to recognise the gulf between these two limited-overs sides — it was remorselessly rubbed in in all five ODIs and one T20I.

In Australia's first assignment since the sandpaper scandal, with the Justin Langer-Tim Paine coach-captain combination in charge, a depleted side slipped to No.7 on the rankings and were reminded how far they were from being able to defend their world title the following year. Even when Aaron Finch and Shaun Marsh made hundreds, England chased down their 310 with a little over five overs remaining. When they reduced the hosts to 114 for 8 while defending 205, Jos Buttler pulled off one of the greatest escapes, adding 81 for the ninth wicket with Adil Rashid and completing his century in sealing a thrilling 5-0 sweep.

Tour matches

County Ground, Hove, June 7: Australia 277/9 in 50 overs (Marcus Stoinis 110, Aaron Finch 78; Jofra Archer 3-62, Danny Briggs 2-42) beat **Sussex** 220 in 42.3 overs (Philip Salt 62, Laurie Evans 57; Ashton Agar 3-64) by 57 runs.

Lord's, London, June 9: Australia 283/6 in 50 overs (Travis Head 106, Aaron Finch 54; Tom Barber 3-62) beat **Middlesex** 182 in 41 overs (Max Holden 71, Hilton Cartwright 31; Kane Richardson 3-31, Michael Neser 2-33) by 101 runs.

ODI series (5): England 5 Australia 0

Kennington Oval, London, June 13: Australia 214 in 47 overs (Glenn Maxwell 62, Ashton Agar 40; Liam Plunkett 3-42, Moeen Ali 3-43) lost to **England** 218/7 in 44overs (Eoin Morgan 69, Joe Root 50; Andrew Tye 2-42, Michael Neser 2-46) by three wickets. *MoM:* Moeen Ali.
Sophia Gardens, Cardiff, June 16: England 342/8 in 50 overs (Jason Roy 120, Jos Buttler 91*; Kane Richardson 2-56, Jhye Richardson 2-64) beat **Australia** 304 in 47.1overs (Shaun Marsh 131, Ashton Agar 46; Liam Plunkett 4-53, Adil Rashid 3-70) by 38 runs. *MoM:* Jason Roy.
Trent Bridge, Nottingham, June 19: England 481/6 in 50 overs (Alex Hales 147, Jonny Bairstow 139; Jhye Richardson 3-92) beat **Australia** 239 in 37 overs (Travis Head 51, Marcus Stoinis 44; Adil Rashid 4-47, Moeen Ali 3-28) by 242 runs. *MoM:* Alex Hales.
Riverside Ground, Chester-le-Street, June 21: Australia 310/8 in 50 overs (Shaun Marsh 101, Aaron Finch 100; David Willey 4-43, Mark Wood 2-49) lost to **England** 314/4 in 44.4 overs (Jason Roy 101, Jonny Bairstow 79; Ashton Agar 2-48) by six wickets. *MoM:* Jason Roy.
Old Trafford, Manchester, June 24: Australia 205 in 34.4 overs (Travis Head 56, D'Arcy Short 47*; Moeen Ali 4-46, Sam Curran 2-44) lost to **England** 208/9 in 48.3 overs (Jos Buttler 110*, Alex Hales 20; Billy Stanlake 3-35, Kane Richardson 3-51) by one wicket. *MoM:* Jos Buttler. *MoS:* Jos Buttler.

T20I series (1): England 1 Australia 0

Edgbaston, Birmingham, June 27: England 221/5 in 20 overs (Jos Buttler 61, Alex Hales 49; Mitchell Swepson 2-37) beat **Australia** 193 in 19.4 overs (Aaron Finch 84, Ashton Agar 29; Adil Rashid 3-27, Chris Jordan 3-42) by 28 runs. *MoM:* Adil Rashid.

	ODIs	T20Is
Best batsman	Jason Roy (304 runs, 5 matches)	Aaron Finch (84 runs, 1 match)
Best bowler	Moeen Ali (12 wickets, 5 matches)	Adil Rashid (3 wickets, 1 match)

Scotland's spirited performance helped them upset the No.1-ranked ODI side in the world. — *Getty Images*

England in Scotland

Associates shock No.1 side

Scotland had shown in the World Cup qualifiers just how entertaining an ODI side they could be. With that spirited performance, they didn't deserve to miss out on a World Cup spot, and by beating England, who were No.1 in ICC's ODI rankings, they highlighted just what the World Cup in England in 2019 would miss.

Calum MacLeod, who now has four of the top five individual scores for Scotland, got his second big one of the year: his 140 not out came off 94 balls, featuring 16 fours and three sixes. With Matthew Cross (48 off 39), Kyle Coetzer (58 off 49) and George Munsey (55 off 51) also showing the same fearless approach, the hosts posted their highest ODI total, way beyond their previous best of 341 against Canada in 2014. In fact, the 371 was the best by any Associate in ODIs.

England, to be fair, got close, riding on Jonny Bairstow's third consecutive century in the format — off 54 balls. But it was one of the greatest days for Scottish cricket, and for the Associates.

Only T20I: Scotland won by six runs

Grange Cricket Club, Edinburgh, June 10: Scotland 371/5 in 50 overs (Calum MacLeod 140*, Kyle Coetzer 58; Adil Rashid 2-72, Liam Plunkett 2-85) beat **England** 365 in 48.5 overs (Jonny Bairstow 105, Alex Hales 52; Mark Watt 3-55, Alasdair Evans 2-50) by six runs. *MoM:* Calum MacLeod.

Bangladesh in the West Indies and USA

Pacers provoke visitors' capitulation

For four years since their 2-0 conquest of Bangladesh in 2014, West Indies had endured an agonising wait for a home Test series win. Jason Holder's men finally got the monkey off the back by crushing the same opposition by an identical scoreline, winning both Tests inside three days in comprehensive fashion.

The skipper himself was in the forefront with 11 wickets in the Second Test in Kingston as the fast bowlers accounted for 38 of the 40 Bangladesh wickets to fall through the series. Despite Shakib Al Hasan's 6 for 33 in the second innings, which sent the hosts plummeting to 129 all out, West Indies packed far too many guns as they emerged victors by 166 runs following a second century in as many games by Kraigg Brathwaite, the opener.

Bangladesh had been humiliated in the First Test at North Sound by an innings and 219 runs, their capitulation triggered by a first-session meltdown when they were knocked over for 43, their lowest Test total. They lasted just 59 overs in two innings combined, the fewest a side had faced in 66 years while being bowled out twice in a Test. While Kemar Roach was in the middle of it all with 5 for 8 from five overs in the first essay, Shannon Gabriel ran riot in the second, finishing with 5 for 77.

The visitors redeemed themselves in the white-ball formats by winning both the 50-over and 20-over series 2-1. Tamim Iqbal was the hero in the ODIs with two centuries and a fifty, while Mashrafe Mortaza, the captain, joined the team late but produced a telling burst of 4 for 37 in the first game to ensure that, for a change, the Bangladeshi fast bowlers too made a significant contribution to overseas victories.

Tour match
Stanford Cricket Ground, Coolidge, Antigua, June 28-29: Bangladesh 403 in 84.2 overs (Tamim Iqbal 125 retd.out, Mahmudullah 102 redt.out; Alzarri Joseph 4-53) drew with **West Indies Cricket Board President XI** 310/8 in 85 overs (Shimron Hetmyer 123, Shamarh Brooks 72; Abu Jayed 2-39, Shafiul Islam 2-48).

Test series (2): West Indies 2 Bangladesh 0
Sir Vivian Richards Stadium, North Sound, Antigua, July 4-8: Bangladesh 43 in 18.4 overs (Liton Das 25; Kemar Roach 5-8, Miguel Cummins 3-11) and 144 in 40.2 overs (Nurul Hasan 64; Shannon Gabriel 5-77, Jason Holder 3-30) lost to **West Indies** 406 in 137.3 overs (Kraigg Brathwaite 121, Shai Hope 67; Abu Jayed 3-84, Mehidy Hasan 3-101) by an innings and 219 runs. *MoM:* Kemar Roach.
Sabina Park, Kingston, Jamaica, Julu12-16: West Indies 354 in 112 overs (Kraigg Brathwaite 110, Shimron Hetmyer 86; Mehidy Hasan Miraz 5-93, Abu Jayed 3-38) and 129 in 45 overs (Roston Chase 32; Shakib Al Hasan 6-33, Mehidy Hasan 2-45) beat **Bangladesh** 149 in 46.1overs (Tamim Iqbal 47, Shakib 32; Jason Holder 5-44, Shannon Gabriel 2-19) and 168

in 42 overs (Shakib 54, Liton Das 33; J Holder 6-59, R Chase 2-20) by 166 runs. *MoM:* Jason Holder. *MoS:* Jason Holder.

Tour match

Sabina Park, Kingston, Jamaica, July 19: UWI Vice Chancellors XI 227/9 in 50 overs (Yannick Ottley 58, Kavem Hodge 44; Mosaddek Hossain 4-14, Rubel Hossain 3-40) lost to **Bangladesh** 230/6 in 43.3 overs (Mushfiqur Rahim 75*, Liton Das 70; Rovman Powell 2-32) by four wickets.

ODI series (3): Bangladesh 2 West Indies 1

Providence Stadium, Guyana, July 22: Bangladesh 279/4 in 50 overs (Tamim Iqbal 130*, Shakib Al Hasan 97; Devendra Bishoo 2-52) beat **West Indies** 231/9 in 50overs (Shimron Hetmyer 52, Chris Gayle 40; Mashrafe Mortaza 4-37, Mustafizur Rahman 2-35) by 48 runs. *MoM:* Tamim Iqbal.

Providence Stadium, Guyana, July 25: West Indies 271 in 49.3 overs (Shimron Hetmyer 125, Rovman Powell 44; Rubel Hossain 3-61, Mustafizur Rahman 2-44) beat **Bangladesh** 268/6 in 50 overs (Mushfiqur Rahim 68, Shakib Al Hasan 56) by three runs. *MoM:* Shimron Hetmyer.

Warner Park, Basseterre, St Kitts, July 28: Bangladesh 301/6 in 50 overs (Tamim Iqbal 103, Mahmudullah 67*; Ashley Nurse 2-53, Jason Holder 2-55) beat **West Indies** 283/6 in 50 overs (Rovman Powell 74*, Chris Gayle 73; Mashrafe Mortaza 2-63) by 18 runs. *MoM:* Tamim Iqbal. *MoS:* Tamim Iqbal.

T20I series (3): Bangladesh 2 West Indies 1

Warner Park, Basseterre, St Kitts, July 31: Bangladesh 143/9 in 20 overs (Mahmudullah 35, Liton Das 24; Kesrick Williams 4-28, Ashley Nurse 2-6) lost to **West Indies** 93/3 in 9.1 overs (Andre Russell 35*, Marlon Samuels 26; Mustafizur Rahman 2-18) by seven wickets (D/L method). *MoM:* Andre Russell.

Central Broward Regional Park Stadium Turf Ground, Lauderhill, Florida, August 4: Bangladesh 171/5 in 20 overs (Tamim Iqbal 74, Shakib Al Hasan 60; Ashley Nurse 2-25, Keemo Paul 2-39) beat **West Indies** 159/9 in 20overs (Rovman Powell 43, Andre Fletcher 43; Nazmul Islam 3-28, Mustafizur Rahman 3-50) by 12 runs. *MoM:* Tamim Iqbal.

Central Broward Regional Park Stadium Turf Ground, Lauderhill, Florida, August 5: Bangladesh 184/5 in 20 overs (Liton Das 61, Mahmudullah 32*; Keemo Paul 2-26, Carlos Brathwaite 2-32) beat **West Indies** 135/7 in 17.1 overs (Andre Russell 47, Rovman Powell 23; Mustafizur Rahman 3-31) by 19 runs (DLS method). *MoM:* Liton Das. *MoS:* Shakib Al Hasan.

	Tests	ODIs	T20Is
Best batsman	Kraigg Barthwaite (239 runs, 2 matches)	Tamim Iqbal (287 runs, 3 matches)	Shakib Al Hasan (103 runs, 3 matches)
Best bowler	Jason Holder (16 wickets, 2 matches)	Mashrafe Mortaza (7 wickets, 3 matches)	Mustafizur Rahman (8 wickets, 3 matches)

Zimbabwe Tri-nation Series 2018

Finch dazzles, Fakhar stands firm

Aaron Finch's 172 was the highest individual score in T20Is, breaking a record held by … Aaron Finch. It came against Zimbabwe in a stand of 223 in 19.2 overs with D'Arcy Short — another T20I record, and short of Virat Kohli and AB de Villiers' 229 in all T20s. Incredibly, he made 75 per cent of the team's 229 for 2.

That, along with Billy Stanlake's spell of 4-0-8-4, and seeing Short and Glenn Maxwell among the runs gave Australia the confidence boost they so desperately needed after the debacle in England. But they couldn't dislodge Pakistan from the top spot. Undeterred by the cold, Fakhar Zaman went from

Aaron Finch's 172 is the highest individual score in T20Is. — *Getty Images*

strength to strength. He saved the best for the last, his 91 off 46 balls guiding his side's highest successful chase in the format.

As for hosts Zimbabwe, Solomon Mire's 94 off 63 balls was a national record, but it wasn't enough. With their campaign over before the other teams', they got a few extra days to watch the football World Cup that the rest of the world was following.

Highest T20I scores			
Batsman	**Runs**	**For v against**	**Details**
Aaron Finch	172	Australia v Zimbabwe	Harare, Jul 2018
Aaron Finch	156	Australia v England	Southampton, Aug 2013
Glenn Maxwell	145*	Australia v Sri Lanka	Pallekele, Sept 2016
Evin Lewis	125*	West Indies v India	Kingston, July 2017
Shane Watson	124*	Australia v India	Sydney, Jan 2016

1st match: Pakistan beat Zimbabwe by 74 runs

Harare Sports Club, Harare, July 1: Pakistan 182/4 in 20 overs (Fakhar Zaman 61, Asif Ali 41*; Tendai Chisoro 2-28) beat **Zimbabwe** 108 in 17.5 overs (Tarisai Musakanda 43, Solomon Mire 27; Mohammad Hafeez 2-3, Usman Khan 2-11) by 74 runs. *MoM:* Asif Ali.

2nd match: Australia beat Pakistan by nine wickets

Harare Sports Club, Harare, July 2: Pakistan 116 in 19.5 overs (Shadab Khan 29, Asif Ali 22; Billy Stanlake 4-8, Andrew Tye 3-38) lost to **Australia** 117/1 in 105 overs (Aaron Finch 68*, Travis Head 20*) by nine wickets. *MoM:* Billy Stanlake.

3rd match: Australia beat Zimbabwe by 100 runs

Harare Sports Club, Harare, July 3: Australia 229/2 in 20 overs (Aaron Finch 172, D'Arcy Short 46; Blessing Muzarabani 2-38) beat **Zimbabwe** 129/9 in 20 overs (Solomon Mire 28; Andrew Tye 3-12, Ashton Agar 2-16) by 100 runs. *MoM:* Aaron Finch.

4th match: Pakistan beat Zimbabwe by seven wickets

Harare Sports Club, Harare, July 4: Zimbabwe 162/4 in 20 overs (Solomon Mire 94, Tarisai Musakanda 33) lost to **Pakistan** 163/3 in 19.1overs (Fakhar Zaman 47, Hussain Talat 44) by seven wickets. *MoM:* Solomon Mire.

5th match: Pakistan beat Australia by 45 runs

Harare Sports Club, Harare, July 5: Pakistan 194/7 in 20 overs (Fakhar Zaman 73, Asif Ali 37*; Andrew Tye 3-35, Jhye Richardson 2-43) beat **Australia** 149/7 in 20overs (Alex Carey 37*, D'Arcy Short 28; Shaheen Afridi 3-37) by 45 runs. *MoM:* Fakhar Zaman.

6th match: Australia beat Zimbabwe by five wickets

Harare Sports Club, Harare, July 6: Zimbabwe 151/9 in 20 overs (Solomon Mire 63, Peter Moor 30; Andrew Tye 3-28, Billy Stanlake 2-21) lost to **Australia** 154/5 in 19.5overs (Glenn Maxwell 56, Travis Head 48; Blessing Muzarabani 3-21) by five wickets. *MoM:* Andrew Tye.

Points table

Teams	M	W	L	T	N/R	Pts.	NRR
Australia	4	3	1	0	0	12	+1.809
Pakistan	4	3	1	0	0	12	-0.707
Zimbabwe	4	0	4	0	0	0	-2.340

Australia and Pakistan qualified for the final

Final: Pakistan beat Australia six wickets

Harare Sports Club, Harare, July 8: Australia 183/8 in 20 overs (D'Arcy Short 76, Aaron Finch 47; Mohammad Amir 3-33, Shadab Khan 2-38) lost to **Pakistan** 187/4 in 19.2overs (Fakhar Zaman91, Shoaib Malik 43*; Glenn Maxwell 2-35) by six wickets. *MoM:* Fakhar Zaman. *MoS:* Fakhar Zaman.

Best batsman: Aaron Finch (Australia) (306 runs, 5 matches)
Best bowler: Andrew Tye (Australia) (12 wickets, 5 matches)

Pakistan in Zimbabwe

Fakhar reaps records out of mismatch

Brendan Taylor, Sikandar Raza and Graeme Cremer were among the big names missing from the Zimbabwe squad, their dispute with the board over contracts continuing. Hamilton Masakadza led a depleted side — and with records there for the taking, Pakistan feasted.

Fakhar Zaman's 210 in the fourth ODI was the pick of the lot, with Pakistan getting their first double-centurion. He finished the series with 515 runs, the most runs in a bilateral five-match ODI series and only after Virat Kohli's 558 runs from six matches against South Africa earlier in the year. It took him to 1000 career runs in a record 18 innings in the format — three fewer than anyone else.

Standing steadfastly by him was his fellow opener, Imam-ul-Haq. Their 304 in the fourth game was another one for the books, ahead of the 286 added by Sanath Jayasuriya and Upul Tharanga for Sri Lanka against England in 2006.

The bespectacled youngster, only nine ODIs old, took his tally of hundreds to four, while Babar Azam too came to the party in the final match. Faheem Ashraf, the pacer, was consistently probing, and the visitors' victory margins were embarrassingly comprehensive. It barely came as a surprise that they checked off another milestone for their highest ODI total of 399.

Most runs in a bilateral ODI series				
Player	R	Inns	Ave	Details
Virat Kohli	558	6	186.0	India in South Africa, 2017-18
Fakhar Zaman	515	5	257.5	Pakistan in Zimbabwe, 2018
Rohit Sharma	491	6	122.75	Australia in India, 2013-14
George Bailey	478	6	95.6	Australia in India. 2013-14
Hamilton Masakadza	467	5	116.75	Kenya in Zimbabwe, 2009-10

ODI series (5): Pakistan 5 Zimbabwe 0

Queens Sports Club, Bulawayo, July 13: **Pakistan** 308/7 in 50 overs (Imam-ul-Haq 128, Fakhar Zaman 60; Tendai Chatara 2-49, Donald Tiripano 2-66) beat **Zimbabwe** 107 in 35 overs (Ryan Murray 32*, Tarisai Musakanda 21; Shadab Khan 4-32, Faheem Ashraf 2-14) by 201 runs. *MoM:* Imam-ul-Haq.

Queens Sports Club, Bulawayo, July 16: Zimbabwe 194 in 49.2 overs (Hamilton Masakadza 59, Peter Moor 50; Usman Khan 4-36, Hasan Ali 3-32) lost to **Pakistan** 195/1 in 36 overs

Fakhar Zaman's 515 runs are the most in a bilateral five-match ODI series. — ZC

(Fakhar Zaman 117*, Imam-ul-Haq 44) by nine wickets. *MoM:* Fakhar Zaman.
Queens Sports Club, Bulawayo, July 18: Zimbabwe 67 in 25.1 overs (Faheem Ashraf 5-22, Junaid Khan 2-7) lost to **Pakistan** 69/1 in 9.5 overs (Fakhar Zaman 43*) by nine wickets. *MoM:* Faheem Ashraf.
Queens Sports Club, Bulawayo, July 20: Pakistan 399/1 in 50 overs (Fakhar Zaman 210*, Imam-ul-Haq 113) beat **Zimbabwe** 155 in 42.4 overs (Donald Tiripano 44, Elton Chigumbura 37; Shadab Khan 4-28, Faheem Ashraf 2-16) by 244 runs. *MoM:* Fakhar Zaman.
Queens Sports Club, Bulawayo, July 22: Pakistan 364/4 in 50 overs (Imam-ul-Haq 110, Babar Azam 106*) beat **Zimbabwe** 233/4 in 50 overs (Ryan Murray 47, Peter Moor 44*; Mohammad Nawaz 2-47, Hasan Ali 2-55) by 131 runs. *MoM:* Babar Azam. *MoS:* Fakhar Zaman.

Best batsman: Fakhar Zaman (515 runs, 5 matches)
Best bowler: Faheem Ashraf (9 wickets, 4 matches)

South Africa in Sri Lanka

Karunaratne soars in spin test

Until the end of the first decade of the new millennium, South Africa carried the not unfounded tag of being the best travellers to the Asian subcontinent. That reputation has taken a serious beating in the last few years, but even so, their 2-0 annihilation in Sri Lanka, masterminded by the spin trio of Rangana Herath, Dilruwan Perera and Akila Dananjaya, was surprising for the ease with which it unfolded.

In a series dominated entirely by the ball – the 300-run mark was breached just once in eight completed innings – Dimuth Karunaratne was the standout batsman with scores of 158 not out, 60, 53 and 85. With skipper Dinesh Chandimal serving out a six-match suspension, the experienced opener embraced responsibility, and his remarkable consistency against a strong South African attack, which welcomed back Dale Steyn, set the base from which the spinners could weave tantalising, wicked webs.

Keshav Maharaj battled on manfully for the South Africans, the left-arm spinner picking up an extraordinary 9 for 129 in the first innings of the Second Test. However, the pace attack was blunted by the slow, low, dry surfaces and the adhesiveness of the left-handed Karunaratne who, in the First Test in Galle, became only the fourth Sri Lankan to carry his bat.

Battered into submission in the three-Test series when they travelled to South Africa in late 2016, Sri Lanka turned the tables against batsmen clueless when confronted by the turning ball. Dilruwan feasted on their vulnerability against off-spin as he finished with 16 wickets, the canny Herath picked up 12 and Dananjaya, with his baffling mix of off-spin, leg-spin and the googly, grabbed seven wickets in his only appearance.

South Africa topped 150 only in their final innings, their misery highlighted by team totals of 126, 73 (their lowest score since readmission) and 124. Unsure of their defensive techniques, they tried to hit their way out of trouble, with predictably disastrous consequences against well-equipped bowlers made more dangerous by generous assistance from the surfaces.

The one-dayers that followed were a complete contrast. Kagiso Rabada, Lungi Ngidi and Andile Phehlukwayo ensured the Sri Lankans didn't reprise their batting competence of the Test matches, after left-arm wrist-spinner Tabraiz Shamsi set the ball rolling with 4 for 33 in the first game in Dambulla. Batting first or second, South Africa always were a few steps ahead of the opposition, most batsmen relishing a return to less arduous challenges.

Reeza Hendricks celebrated his belated ODI debut, at 29, in the third game with a spectacular 88-ball century, while old heads Hashim Amla, skipper

South Africa were clueless when confronted by the turning ball and Sri Lanka
completed two big Test match wins. — *Getty Images/AFP*

Faf du Plessis, JP Duminy and Quinton de Kock held their own with significant contributions in largely regulation run-chases.

It wasn't until South Africa had taken a commanding 4-0 lead in the five-
match showdown that Sri Lanka finally turned up. With only pride at stake,
skipper Angelo Mathews' unbeaten 97 finally gave their bowlers something
to play with. South Africa's chase of 300 came unstuck against Dananjaya,
whose mesmeric 6 for 29 reopened festering wounds from the drubbing in
the Tests.

In the one-off T20I too they crumbled against a trial by spin. Dhananjaya
de Silva, Akila Dananjaya and Lakshan Sandakan returned 7 for 56 in 12
overs, sending South Africa plummeting to 98 all out.

Tour match
P Sara Oval, Colombo, July 7-8: Sri Lanka Board President's XI 287 in 78.2 overs (An-
gelo Mathews 92, Kaushal Silva 76; Tabraiz Shamsi 5-45, Shaun von Berg 2-82) drew with
South Africa 338 in 73.5 overs (Faf du Plessis 79, Hashim Amla 78; Wanidu Hasaranga 3-79,
Dhananjaya de Silva 2-9).

Test series (2): Sri Lanka 2 South Africa 0
Galle International Stadium, Galle, July 12-16: Sri Lanka 287 in 78.4 overs (Dimuth
Karunaratne 158*, Danushka Gunathilaka 26; Kagiso Rabada 4-50, Tabraiz Shamsi 3-91) and
190 in 57.4 overs (D Karunaratne 60, Angelo Mathews 35; Keshav Maharaj 4-58, K Rabada
3-44) beat **South Africa** 126 in 54.3 overs (Faf du Plessis 49; Dilruwan Perera 4-46, Suranga
Lakmal 3-21) and 73 in 28.5 overs (Vernon Philander 22*; D Perera 6-32, Rangana Herath
3-38) by 278 runs. *MoM:* Dimuth Karunaratne.
Sinhalese Sports Club, Colombo, July 20-24: Sri Lanka 338 in 104.1 overs (Dhananjaya
de Silva 60, Danushka Gunathilaka 57; Keshav Maharaj 9-129) and 275/5 dec in 81 overs

(Dimuth Karunaratne 85, Angelo Mathews 71; K Maharaj 3-154) beat **South Africa** 124 in 34.5 overs (Faf du Plessis 48, Quinton de Kock 32; Akila Dananjaya 5-52, Dilruwan Perera 4-40) and 290 in 86.5 overs (Theunis de Bruyn 101, Temba Bavuma 63; Rangana Herath 6-98, A Dananjaya 2-67) by 199 runs. *MoM:* Dimuth Karunaratne. *MoS:* Dimuth Karunaratne.

Tour match

P Sara Oval, Colombo, July 26: South Africa 293 in 49.4 overs (Faf du Plessis 71, Reeza Hendricks 59; Prabath Jayasuriya 2-46, Nishan Peiris 2-47) beat **Sri Lanka Board President's XI** 230 in 44.1 overs (Isuru Udana 53, Dimuth Karunaratne 50; Williem Mulder 3-12, Tabraiz Shamsi 3-41) by 63 runs.

ODI series (5): South Africa 3 Sri Lanka 2

Rangiri Dambulla International Stadium, Dambulla, July 29: Sri Lanka 193 in 34.3 overs (Kusal Perera 81, Thisara Perera 49; Tabraiz Shamsi 4-33, Kagiso Rabada 4-41) lost to **South Africa** 196/5 in 31 overs (JP Duminy 53*, Faf du Plessis 47; Akila Dananjaya 3-50) by five wickets. *MoM:* Tabraiz Shamsi.

Rangiri Dambulla International Stadium, Dambulla, August 1: Sri Lanka 244/8 in 50 overs (Angelo Mathews 79*, Niroshan Dickwella 69; Andile Phehlukwayo 3-45, Lungo Ngidi 3-50) lost to **South Africa** 246/6 in 42.5 overs (Quinton de Kock 87, Faf du Plessis 49; Akila Dananjaya 3-60) by four wickets. *MoM:* Quinton de Kock.

Pallekele International Cricket Stadium, Pallekele, August 5: South Africa 363/7 in 50 overs (Reeza Hendricks 102, JP Duminy 92; Thisara Perera 4-75, Lahiru Kumara 2-67) beat **Sri Lanka** 285 in 45.2 overs (Dhananjaya de Silva 84, Akila Dananjaya 37; Lungi Ngidi 4-57, Andile Phehlukwayo 3-74) by 78 runs. *MoM:* Reeza Hendricks.

Pallekele International Cricket Stadium, Pallekele, August 8: Sri Lanka 306/7 in 39 overs (Dasun Shanaka 65, Kusal Perera 51; JP Duminy 2-35, Lungi Ngidi 2-65) beat **South Africa** 187/9 in 21overs (Hashim Amla 40, Duminy 38; Suranga Lakmal 3-46, Thisara Perera 2-32) by 3 runs (DLS method). *MoM:* Dasun Shanaka.

R Premadasa Stadium, Colombo, August 12: Sri Lanka 299/8 in 50 overs (Angelo Mathews 97*, Niroshan Dickwella 43; Willem Mulder 2-59, Andile Phehlukwayo 2-60) beat **South Africa** 121 in 24.4overs (Quinton de Kock 54, Aiden Markram 20; Akila Dananjaya 6-29, Lahiru Kumara 2-34) by 178 runs. *MoM:* Akila Dananjaya. *MoS:* JP Duminy.

R Premadasa Stadium, Colombo, August 14: South Africa 98 in 16.4 overs (Quinton de Kock 20; Lakshan Sandakan 3-19, Akila Dananjaya 2-15) lost to **Sri Lanka** 99/7 in 16 overs (Dinesh Chandimal 36*, Dhananjaya de Silva 31; Junior Dala 2-22, Kagiso Rabada 2-24) by three wickets. *MoM:* Dhananjaya de Silva.

	Tests	ODIs	T20Is
Best batsman	Dimuth Karunaratne (356 runs, 2 matches)	Angelo Mathews (235 runs, 5 matches)	Dinesh Chandimal (36 runs, 1 match)
Best bowler	Dilruwan Perera (16 wickets, 2 matches)	Akila Dananjaya (14 wickets, 5 matches)	Lakshan Sandakan (3 wickets, 1 match)

Afghanistan in Ireland

Zazai's bat backs spin trio

Another round in the all-two frequent match-ups between the two youngest Full Members, but this time the matches served a larger purpose for Afghanistan. Travelling to Ireland in summer, they got a taste of the conditions they could expect in England in the World Cup the following year.

Rashid Khan combined with Mohammad Nabi (six wickets) and Mujeeb Ur Rahman (two) to take 14 wickets in the 50-over games, while leading the way with seven of the 14 the trio took in the T20Is.

Perhaps most encouragingly for Afghanistan, their batsmen showed promise. In Hazratullah Zazai, the left-hand opening batsman, they found a fearless striker of the ball. Returning to the squad after his debut game in 2016, he struck 74 off 33 and 82 off 54 in the two 20-over games that saw play.

Their 100th ODI — Nabi had featured in every one of them — was the only match all tour that they lost. For Ireland, bundled out for 124 in the last match, it was a reminder of how far behind their limited-overs game had slipped.

T20I series (3): Afghanistan 2 Ireland 0

Bready Cricket Club, Northern Ireland, August 20: Afghanistan 160/7 in 18 overs (Hazratullah Zazai 74, Asghar Afghan 31; Joshua Little 2-20, Tyrone Kane 2-50) beat **Ireland** 144/9 in 18 overs (Gary Wilson 34, Paul Stirling 27; Rashid Khan 3-35, Mujeeb Ur Rahman 2-14) by 16 runs.

Bready, Northern Ireland, August 22: Afghanistan 160/8 in 20 overs (Hazratullah Zazai 82, Asghar Afghan 37; Peter Chase 3-35, Boyd Rankin 2-14) beat **Ireland** 79 in 15 overs (William Porterfield 33, Gary Wilson 22; Rashid Khan 4-17, Mujeeb Ur Rahman 3-17) by 81 runs.

Bready, Northern Ireland, August 24: Afghanistan v **Ireland. Match abandoned.**

ODI series (3): Afghanistan 2 Ireland 1

Civil Service Cricket Club, Belfast, August 27: Afghanistan 227/9 in 50 overs (Gulbadin Naib 64, Hashmatullah Shahidi 54; Tim Murtagh 4-31, Boyd Rankin 2-44) beat **Ireland** 198 in 48.3 overs (Andrew Balbirnie 55, Gary Wilson 38; Aftab Alam 2-34, Rashid Khan 2-41) by 29 runs.

CSCC, Belfast, August 29: Afghanistan 182/9 in 50 overs (Najibullah Nabi 42, Asghar Afghan 39; Tim Murtagh 4-30) lost to **Ireland** 183/7 in 43.5 overs (Andrew Balbirnie 60, Paul Stirling 39; Rashid Khan 3-37, Mohammad Nabi 2-38) by three wickets.

CSCC, Belfast, August 31: Ireland 124 in 36.1 overs (Gary Wilson 23; Rashid Khan 3-18, Aftab Alam 2-22) lost to **Afghanistan** 127/2 in 23.5 overs (Ihsanullah Janat 57*, Hashmatullah Shahidi 34*) by eight wickets. *MoS*: Rashid Khan

	ODIs	T20Is
Best Batsman	Andrew Balbirnie (132 runs, 3 matches)	Hazratullah Zazai (156 runs, 2 matches)
Best Bowler	Tim Murtagh (9 wickets, 3 matches)	Rashid Khan (7 wickets, 2 matches)

WOMEN'S CRICKET

India's new generation of batting stars, led by Jemimah Rodrigues, promise an exciting brand of cricket. — *BCCI*

India internationals

A new grammar

KARUNYA KESHAV

The last two seasons in women's cricket have been unlike any other. It was as if with the sold-out 2017 World Cup final, a switch was flipped.

In the first 13 years of women's T20Is, there were three centuries. But since that big Lord's final, that number has shot up to 11 among the top ten nations. Run-rates have risen from 5.84 an over before the World Cup, to 6.9 for the top six teams.

Three of the top four ODI totals came in 2018 — all, incidentally, for New Zealand. This included the record high of 491 for 4, led by 17-year-old Amelia Kerr's 232 not out off 145 balls displacing Belinda Clark's 229 not out in 1997.

The first ten months of the year had seven of the top eight T20I totals of all time — and three of the top four chases, with the other coming the previous November. India, for instance, made 198 for 4 in Mumbai in the tri-series, only to have England overhaul it with eight balls to spare. Less than a week later at the same ground, Australia posted only the second ever 200-plus total. New Zealand's record 216 for 1 against South Africa lasted only a few hours, before England smashed the same hapless Proteas for 250 for 3.

One reason for this drastic batting boost is the change in rules. New playing conditions stipulated two new balls in ODIs and four fielders outside the circle in limited overs. But as vital was the change in mindset: increasing professionalism and the knowledge that the world was now, finally, watching has pushed for new skills.

Initially, with the 2018 World T20 on the horizon, India always looked a step behind in the power game. A poor tri-series against England and Australia, and losses to Bangladesh — twice — for their first defeats in the Asia Cup did little to assuage these concerns. The domestic T20 Challenger Trophy, which was to serve as an audition for spots in the World T20, had only three batters make half-centuries; the highest individual score was 52 and the scoring was often glacial. 'Intent', that metric without a number, which is so integral to the 20-over game, seemed replaced by apprehension.

But then at the ICC Women's World T20, Harmanpreet Kaur set the tournament alight with her century in the opening game, becoming the first Indian to get to the three-figure mark. A young Indian team punched above their weight to reach the semi-final and exceed expectations.

Thankfully for India, Harmanpreet is not alone. Standing as an example for the others was also Mandhana. Putting her duck in the World Cup final behind her, she introspected and dug deep to find a new gear to her batting and enjoy her game. She became only the second woman after Mithali to make a T20 hundred, lighting up the Women's Cricket Super League in England, including with the joint record for the fastest fifty, off 18 balls. Since the World Cup, Mandhana has two ODI centuries and ten fifties from 18 matches.

As heartening was the prodigious Jemimah Rodrigues. Rewarded with a national call-up for a spectacular domestic season, the teenager was all maturity and verve. Like Mandhana had done a few years before, Rodrigues too came with the reputation of having struck a one-day double-century on the domestic circuit. But unlike Mandhana, she had the full glare of the nation's media on her; even ahead of her debut, her first press conference was packed, as she sat alone and poised under the spotlight.

In this fast-changing game, Jhulan Goswami saw she had no place. The veteran pacer bowed out of the shortest format, telling *ESPNcricinfo* with some candour, "Watching England and Australia and my own team-mates play in [the tri-series in Mumbai], I couldn't help but realise how fast the game has become. On my own part, though, I was evidently slow." It meant that soon Poonam Yadav, the leg-spinner, overtook her 56 wickets to be India's highest wicket-taker in the format.

The change in generation in women's cricket is evident. India's World T20 implosion was accompanied by a very public spat featuring Harmanpreet and coach Ramesh Powar on one side, and the experienced Mithali Raj on the other. Mithali had a strong average, but not an especially 'modern' strike-rate, and her style was seen as the antithesis of the new "freedom" with which India were playing. She didn't find a place in the World T20 semi-final that India lost. In the hands of a BCCI at war within itself, the women's stalwarts were pawns as mails exchanged were leaked and an ugly power game was played out. Powar, who came into the role after the players complained about Tushar Arothe (who in turn had been brought in when the players asked for a change from Purnima Rau), couldn't last long.

The Women's T20 Challenge on the sidelines of the IPL is a step towards a full-fledged women's IPL. — *BCCI/Sportzpics*

In this atmosphere, only results can bring the team back on track. India's batting was horribly exposed by England and New Zealand in the T20Is, making the case for a women's IPL more pressing. An exhibition T20 in 2018 was expanded to a three-team event in 2019 with considerable success. But there is still no full-fledged competition — something Australia's Ellyse Perry referred to as the "missing piece of the puzzle" of women's cricket.

On the domestic circuit, the hegemony of Railways was challenged. With opportunities opening up and their short-term financial future mostly secured, Harmanpreet and Sushma Verma quit Railways and returned to their state squads, while Deepti Sharma moved from Uttar Pradesh to became a professional for Bengal and guided them to the senior title in her second year there. Delhi showed they can be a T20 force, and for the first time in a while, it wasn't a Railways sweep. The number of tournaments were increased, but the absence of a multi-day competition was another sign of the receding importance of red-ball cricket in the women's game.

India in New Zealand

Mandhana sublime in historic win

Smriti Mandhana smashed 196 runs as India completed their first ever bilateral series win in New Zealand. WV Raman's tenure as coach got off to a positive start, and given the mud-slinging that led to his appointment, the women's team were finally in the news for the right reasons.

Mandhana, the 2018 Rachael Heyhoe-Flint medallist, began with her fourth ODI century, and a record 190-run opening partnership with Jemimah Rodrigues. She followed it up with an unbeaten 90, and a 151-run third-wicket association with Mithali Raj in the second. The left-hander cut, pulled and lofted with ferocious power, punishing New Zealand's bowlers whenever they erred even slightly. She thrived under the added responsibility of being the team's batting centrepiece, inspiring those around her to lift their game.

Although Mandhana stole the spotlight, it was India's bowlers who set up the victories: the spin trioka of Poonam Yadav, Deepti Sharma and Ekta Bisht picked up 14 wickets at an average of 7.36 between them.

Having swung the momentum in their favour in the final ODI, Amy Satterthwaite's team swept the three-match T20I series, thanks mostly to India's middle-order mess. Mandhana continued her sublime form, scoring 180 runs, including India's fastest T20I half-century, off 24 balls, in the first match, and her highest T20I score of 86 in the third. She was ably supported by Rodrigues, who collected 132 runs from three innings, but the rest of the line-up failed to make an impact.

Suzie Bates and Sophie Devine, the 'Smash Sisters', lived up to their reputation, making sure the Indian bowlers were unable to settle. Devine clobbered 153 runs at a strike-rate of 131.89, and also picked up four crucial wickets, proving to be the major difference between the two sides.   *AU*

Tour match
Nelson Park, Napier, January 18: India 217/9 in 50 overs (Mona Meshram 78*, Dayalan Hemalatha 36; Jess Watkin 4-34, Rosemary Mair 3-28) beat **Central Districts** 79 in 31.4 overs (Poonam Yadav 4-6, Mansi Joshi 2-8) by 138 runs.

ODI series (3): India 2 New Zealand 1

1st ODI: India win by nine wickets
McLean Park, Napier, January 24: New Zealand 192 in 48.4 overs (Suzie Bates 36, Amy Satterthwaite 31; Ekta Bisht 3-32, Poonam Yadav 3-42) lost to **India** 193/1 in 33 overs (Smriti Mandhana 105, Jemimah Rodrigues 81*) by nine wickets. *PoM*: Smriti Mandhana.

Smriti Mandhana thrived under the added responsibility of being the team's batting centrepiece, leading India to their first bilateral win in New Zealand. — *Getty Images*

2nd ODI: India win by eight wickets
Bay Oval, Mount Maunganui, January 29: New Zealand 161 in 44.2 overs (Amy Satterthwaite 71, Leigh Kasperek 21; Jhulan Goswami 3-23, Ekta Bisht 2-14) lost to **India** 166/2 in 35.2 overs (Smriti Mandhana 90*, Mithali Raj 63*) by eight wickets. *PoM:* Smriti Mandhana.

3rd ODI: New Zealand win by eight wickets
Seddon Park, Hamilton, February 1: India 149 in 44 overs (Deepti Sharma 52, Harmanpreet Kaur 24; Anna Peterson 4-28, Lea Tahuhu 3-26) lost to **New Zealand** 153/2 in 29.2 overs (Amy Satterthwaite 66*, Suzie Bates 57) by eight wickets. *PoM:* Anna Peterson. *PoS:* Smriti Mandhana.

T20I series (3): India 0 New Zealand 3

1st T20I: New Zealand win by 23 runs
Westpac Stadium, Wellington, February 6: New Zealand 159/6 in 20 overs (Sophie Devine 62, Amy Satterthwaite 33) beat **India** 136 in 19.1 overs (Smriti Mandhana 58, Jemimah Rodrigues 39, Lea Tahuhu 3-20, Leigh Kasperek 2-25) by 23 runs. *PoM:* Lea Tahuhu.

2nd T20I: New Zealand win by four wickets
Eden Park, Hamilton, February 8: India 135/6 in 20 overs (Jemimah Rodrigues 72, Smriti Mandhana 36; Rosemary Mair 2-17) lost to **New Zealand** 136/6 in 20 overs (Suzie Bates 62, Amy Satterthwaite 23; Arundhati Reddy 2-22, Radha Yadav 2-23) by four wickets. *PoM:* Suzie Bates.

3rd T20I: New Zealand win by two runs
Seddon Park, Hamilton, February 10: New Zealand 161/7 in 20 overs (Sophie Devine 72, Amy Satterthwaite 31; Deepti Sharma 2-28) beat **India** 159/4 in 20 overs (Smriti Mandhana 86, Mithali Raj 24*; S Devine 2-21) by two runs. *PoM:* Sophie Devine. *PoS:* Suzie Bates.

England in India

Hosts claim ODIs, but T20I woes continue

India carried their impressive ODI form from New Zealand, defeating England in a tightly contested three-match ODI series at home, 2-1. The victory saw them rise to second on the ICC Women's Championship table.

Contrary to expectation, and the traditional subcontinent conditions on offer, the fast-bowling pair of Jhulan Goswami and Shikha Pandey did the bulk of the damage.

Pandey bowled with a newfound confidence: her big, hooping inswingers pinging the batters on the pads and consistently challenging the stumps. Her wickets came at an impressive average of 9.12 and an economy rate of 2.60, and also included a career-best haul of 4 for 18 in the second ODI, a spell that ripped through England's batting line-up and helped India seal the series with a game to spare.

Despite the success of Smriti Mandhana, who topped the batting charts with 153 runs, the rest of the Indian batters struggled through the series. In the absence of Harmanpreet Kaur (ankle injury) the middle order was found wanting; none more so than in the final ODI, where Katherine Brunt's five-wicket haul meant India lost 6 for 21 in the middle overs — a collapse that saw England complete a nervy two-wicket win on the back of Danielle Wyatt's maiden ODI half-century.

With Harmanpreet ruled out, Mandhana got her first taste of captaincy in the T20I series, and it was baptism by fire as England bulldozed India 3-0. Tammy Beaumont and Wyatt headlined England victories in the first two matches with measured half-centuries, while Kate Cross made a memorable return to T20Is after an absence of four years with a match award in the final game. With India needing only three runs in the final over with six wickets in hand, the medium-pacer took two wickets and conceded only one run, all with Mithali Raj stranded at the other end, allowing England to pull off an unlikely victory.   *AU*

Tour match
Wankhede Stadium, Mumbai, February 18: Indian Board President's XI 154 in 49 overs (Minnu Mani 28, Bharati Fulmali 23; Anya Shrubsole 4-30, Georgia Elwiss 2-20) lost to **England** 157/8 in 37.3 overs (Heather Knight 64*, Lauren Winfield 23*; Komal Zanzad 3-14, Reemalaxmi Ekka 2-24) by two wickets.

ODI series (3): England 1 India 2

1st ODI: India win by 66 runs
Wankhede Stadium, Mumbai, February 22: India 202 in 49.1 overs (Jemimah Rodrigues 48, Mithali Raj 44; Sophie Ecclestone 2-27, Natalie Sciver 2-29) beat **England** 136 in 41

overs (N Sciver 44, Heather Knight 39; Ekta Bisht 4-25, Shikha Pandey 2-21) by 66 runs. *PoM:* Ekta Bisht.

2nd ODI: India win by seven wickets

Wankhede Stadium, Mumbai, February 25: England 161 in 43.3 overs (Natalie Sciver 85, Lauren Winfield 28; Shikha Pandey, Jhulan Goswami 4-30) lost to **India** 162/3 in 41.1 overs (Smriti Mandhana 63, Mithali Raj 47*; Anya Shrubsole 2-23) by seven wickets. *PoM:* Jhulan Goswami.

3rd ODI: England win by two wickets

Wankhede Stadium, Mumbai, February 28: India 205/8 in 50 overs (Smriti Mandhana 66, Punam Raut 56; Katherine Brunt 5-28) lost to **England** 208/8 in 48.5 overs (Danielle Wyatt 56, Heather Knight 47; Jhulan Goswami 3-41, Shikha Pandey 2-34) by two wickets. *PoM:* Katherine Brunt. *PoS:* Smriti Mandhana.

T20I series (3): England 3 India 0

1st T20I: England win by 41 runs

Barsapara Cricket Stadium, Guwahati, March 4: England 160/4 in 20 overs (Tammy Beaumont 62, Heather Knight 40; Radha Yadav 2-33) beat **India** 119/6 in 20 overs (Shikha Pandey 23*, Deepti Sharma 22*; Katherine Brunt 2-21, Linsey Smith 2-22) by 41 runs. *PoM:* Tammy Beaumont.

2nd T20I: England win by five wickets

Barsapara Cricket Stadium, Guwahati, March 7: India 111/8 in 20 overs (Mithali Raj 20; Katherine Brunt 3-17, Linsey Smith 2-11) lost to **England** 114/5 in 19.1 overs (Danielle Wyatt 64*, Lauren Winfield 29; Ekta Bisht 2-23) by five wickets. *PoM:* Danielle Wyatt.

3rd T20I: England win by one run

Barsapara Cricket Stadium, Guwahati, March 9: England 119/6 in 20 overs (Tammy Beaumont 29, Amy Jones 26; Anuja Patil 2-13, Harleen Deol 2-13) beat **India** 118/6 in 20 overs (Smriti Mandhana 58, Mithali Raj 30*; Kate Cross 2-18). *PoM:* Kate Cross. *PoS:* Danielle Wyatt.

	ODIs	T20Is
Best batter	Smriti Mandhana (153 runs, 3 matches)	Danielle Wyatt (123 runs, 3 matches)
Best bowler	Shikha Pandey (8 wickets, 3 matches)	Katherine Brunt (5 wickets, 2 matches)

2017-18

India in South Africa

Batters step up in double triumph

Playing their first series since the 2017 World Cup, India overcame an inconsistent South Africa to claim four important points in the ICC Women's Championship and seal the ODI series 2-1. Smriti Mandhana, India's left-hand opener, shook off any World Cup blues to headline the team's ODI campaign, smashing 219 runs, including a swashbuckling 135 in the second ODI — her highest ODI score. In conditions where only one other batter (Veda Krishnamurthy) managed to cross the 100-run mark, Mandhana cut, pulled and lofted with abandon.

Jhulan Goswami, the veteran pacer, checked off another milestone in her long career when she dismissed Laura Wolvaardt in the second game to become the first woman to take 200 ODI wickets.

Having sealed the series in the first two matches, India were chasing history in the third ODI — their maiden series whitewash in South Africa in the format — but a lower-order collapse and Mignon du Preez's unbeaten 90 meant the hosts were able to come away with pride and two points.

India completed an away series double, as they took the five-match T20I series 3-1. They unveiled a quartet of debutants: Jemimah Rodrigues, Pooja

Mithali Raj was in fine form against South Africa, bringing up three half-centuries at an average of 96. — *CSA*

Vastrakar, Radha Yadav and Taniya Bhatia. Rodrigues took to international cricket like fish to water, scoring a rapid 37 in her first outing, before ending the series with a 34-ball 44. Raj's credentials as a T20I opener continued to rise, as she amassed 192 runs at an astounding average of 96 with three half-centuries. Her unbeaten half-centuries in the first two matches guided India to comfortable victories, before Shabnim Ismail's fiery spell of 5 for 30 in the third allowed the hosts to claw their way back.

With the series on the line in the fifth T20I, Raj and Rodrigues combined to lift India to 166 for 4. Then, the pace duo of Shikha Pandey and Rumeli Dhar — Player of the Match in India's very first T20I back in 2006, this was her first series in seven years — picked up three wickets each.   *AU*

ODI series (3): India 2 South Africa 1

Diamond Oval, Kimberley, February 5: India 213/7 in 50 overs (Smriti Mandhana 84, Mithali Raj 45; Marizanne Kapp 2-26, Ayabonga Khaka 2-47) beat **South Africa** 125 in 43.2 overs (Dane van Niekerk 41, M Kapp 23; Jhulan Goswami 4-24, Shikha Pandey 3-23) by 88 runs. *PoM:* Smriti Mandhana.

Diamond Oval, Kimberley, February 7: India 302/3 in 50 overs (Smriti Mandhana 135, Harmanpreet Kaur 55*) beat **South Africa** 124 in 30.5 overs (Lizelle Lee 73; Poonam Yadav 4-24, Rajeshwari Gayakwad 2-14) by 178 runs. *PoM:* Smriti Mandhana.

Senwes Park, Potchefstroom, February 10: India 240 in 50 overs (Deepti Sharma 79, Veda Krishnamurthy 56; Shabnim Ismail 4-30, Chloe Tryon 2-48) lost to **South Africa** 241/3 in 49.2 overs (Mignon du Preez 90*, Laura Wolvaardt 59) by seven wickets. *PoM:* Mignon du Preez. *PoS:* Smriti Mandhana.

T20I series (5): India 3 South Africa 1

Senwes Park, Potchefstroom, February 13: South Africa 164/4 in 20 overs (Dane van Niekerk 38, Chloe Tryon 32*; Anuja Patil 2-23) lost to **India** 168/3 in 18.5 overs (Mithali Raj 54*, Veda Krishnamurthy 37*) by seven wickets. *PoM:* Mithali Raj.

Buffalo Park, East London, February 16: South Africa 142/7 in 20 overs (Sune Luus 33, Nadine de Klerk 26; Poonam Yadav 2-18, Anuja Patil 2-37) lost to **India** 144/1 in 19.1 overs (Mithali Raj 76*, Smriti Mandhana 57) by nine wickets.

The Wanderers Stadium, Johannesburg, February 18: India 133 in 17.5 overs (Harmanpreet Kaur 48, Smriti Mandhana 37; Shabnim Ismail 5- 30, Masabata Klaas 2-20) lost to **South Africa** 134/5 in 19 overs (Sune Luus 41, Chloe Tryon 34; Pooja Vastrakar 2-21) by five wickets. *PoM:* Shabnim Ismail.

SuperSport Park, Centurion, February 21: South Africa 130/3 in 15.3 overs (Lizelle Lee 58*, Dane van Niekerk 55, Deepti Sharma 2-33) v **India**. No result.

Newlands, Cape Town, February 21: India 166/4 in 20 overs (Mithali Raj 62, Jemimah Rodrigues 44) beat **South Africa** 112 in 18 overs (Marizanne Kapp 27, Chloe Tryon 25; Shikha Pandey 3-16, Rumeli Dhar 3-26) by 54 runs. *PoM:* Mithali Raj. *PoS:* Mithali Raj.

	ODIs	T20Is
Best batter	Smriti Mandhana	Mithali Raj
	(219 runs in 3 matches)	(192 runs in 5 matches)
Best bowler	Poonam Yadav	Shabnim Ismail
	(7 wickets in 3 matches)	(6 wickets in 5 matches)

Nicole Bolton began with a hundred in a series where the Australians underlined their dominance. — *BCCI/Sportzpics*

Australia in India

Bolton hands out payback

SNEHAL PRADHAN

Leading up to the first meeting between India and Australia since *that* 2017 World Cup semi-final, there was some talk of payback. In that game, India had ousted the defending champions thanks to the brilliance of Harmanpreet Kaur. Now, in India's own backyard and over more matches, Australia showed they were the better team, effecting a 3-0 whitewash in Vadodara.

Jhulan Goswami missed the series because of a heel injury, and Mithali Raj missed the first game due to a fever, marking only the second occasion in 14 years that India had played without both veterans. Against an Australian side with a score to settle, Harmanpreet received her first ODI loss as captain.

Nicole Bolton started the series with an even 100, unbeaten, to see Australia home in a chase of 201. Mithali's return in the next two games did little to halt the Australian run-machine, oiled by the new batting-friendly ICC playing conditions. Three half centuries, including 84 from Bolton, saw them to 287 and a 60-run win in the second ODI.

In the last game, the visitors racked up 332, courtesy Alyssa Healy's maiden century. It wasn't just Australia's highest score in almost 20 years: it was a statement.

Smriti Mandhana provided the only real resistance from India, accumulating 131 runs in the three games, mending her poor home record. The emergence of Pooja Vastrakar's all-round talent and the precocity of Jemimah Rodrigues notwithstanding, it was a bruising for the hosts. The fact that the Australian spinners took 18 wickets while India's took only six was the hardest pill to swallow.

The flat pitches at the IPCL stadium provided plenty of runs, but most came from foreign bats. Undeterred, an estimated 20,000 people attended the three games, including a full house for the third, on a Sunday. It was an exhibition of how well-marketed women's matches in Tier II cities can be a commercial success.

Best batter: Nicole Bolton (Australia) (195 runs in 3 matches)
Best bowler: Jess Jonassen (Australia) (8 wickets 3 matches)

Warm-up matches

Bandra Kurla Complex Ground, Mumbai, March 6: Australia 413/8 in 50 overs (Beth Mooney 115, Ashleigh Gardner 90; Sarika Koli 3-67, Kavita Patil 2-58) beat **India A** 92 in 29.5 overs (Megan Schutt 3-24, Amanda Jade Wellington 2-11) by 321 runs.

Bandra Kurla Complex Ground, Mumbai, March 8: India A 170 in 46.2 overs (Anuja Patil 49, D Hemalatha 37; Amanda Jade Wellington 3-30, Ashleigh Gardener 2-32) lost to **Australia** 171/3 in 26 overs (Meg Lanning 63, Ellyse Perry 38) by seven wickets.

ODI series (3): Australia 3 India 0

Reliance Stadium, Vadodara, March 12: India 200 in 50 overs (Pooja Vastrakar 51, Sushma Verma 41; Jess Jonassen 4-30, Amanda Jade Wellington 3-29) lost to **Australia** 202/2 in 32.1 overs (Nicole Bolton 100*, Alyssa Healy 38) by eight wickets. *PoM:* Nicole Bolton.

Reliance Stadium, Vadodara, March 15: Australia 287/9 in 50 overs (Nicole Bolton 84, Ellyse Perry 70*; Shikha Pandey 3-61, Poonam Yadav 2-52) beat **India** 227 in 49.2 overs (Smriti Mandhana 67, Pooja Vastrakar 30; Jess Jonassen 3-51, Amanda Jade Wellington 2-20) by 60 runs. *PoM:* Nicole Bolton.

Reliance Stadium, Vadodara, March 18: Australia 332/7 in 50 overs (Alyssa Healy 133, Rachel Haynes 43; Harmanpreet Kaur 2-51) beat **India** 235 in 44.4 overs (Smriti Mandhana 52, Jemimah Rodrigues 42; Ashleigh Gardner 3-40, Ellyse Perry 2-40) by 97 runs. *PoM:* Alyssa Healy.

Tri-nation T20I tournament

Schutt, Lanning set the bar

KARUNYA KESHAV

The two 2017 World Cup finalists, and the three-time World T20 winners. The tri-series in Mumbai with Australia, England and India promised the highest quality of cricket. And it did not disappoint.

It also was an opportunity for teams to see where they stood ahead of the World T20 later in the year. And it did: Australia seemed to have cracked a changing T20 game, England were fearless and intimidating with the bat on their day, and India had a way to go before they could match them.

For instance, in the hosts' second match, Smriti Mandhana continued her rich form smashing 76 off 40 balls. She and Mithali Raj added 129 for the opening wicket off just 12.5 overs, and India's 198 for 4 was their highest T20I total and the second-highest overall. But that record lasted only for a little more than an hour. Danni Wyatt made a mockery of scoreboard pressure with her second T20I century in six months; her 124 off 64 balls included five hits over the ropes. It seemed almost routine when England eased past the line with seven wickets and eight balls to spare.

While Mandhana continued to impress, young Jemimah Rodrigues earned praise from Meg Lanning. Veteran Jhulan Goswami returned from injury

Australia seemed to have cracked a changing T20 game to emerge winners in a high-scoring tri-series in Mumbai. — *BCCI*

to strike for three wickets in her first game back, but Harmanpreet Kaur, who herself had a frustrating series, made her displeasure at selection calls known, declaring, "We need fit players in the team … who can run all across the ground."

Meg Lanning came back hungrier than ever after her shoulder surgery, her sublime 88 not out off 45 balls in the final orchestrating the team's total of 209 for 4, the new world record. In conditions that offered bowlers little, Megan Schutt was clever with her variations and disciplined in her plans. She took a hat-trick against India and was ranked the No.1 bowler after the series.

Unfortunately, there were but a couple of hundred spectators enjoying the treat from the stands. Matches at 10am on weekdays and scarce promotional efforts meant the records were set in a mostly empty stadium.

Best batter: Danielle Wyatt (England) (213 runs in 5 matches)
Best bowler: Megan Schutt (Australia) (9 wickets in 5 matches)

Tour matches

Cricket Club of India, Mumbai, March 19: England 176/4 in 20 overs (Tammy Beaumont 57*, Heather Knight 52; Radha Yadav 2-37) beat **India A** 131 in 20 overs (Hemalatha Dayalan 41, VR Vanitha 23; Natasha Farrant 2-21, Anya Shrubsole 2-23) by 45 runs.
Cricket Club of India, Mumbai, March 20: India A 85/9 in 20 overs (VR Vanitha 40; Katie George 4-6, Danielle Wyatt 2-7) lost to **England** 210/4 in 20 overs (Natalie Sciver 54, D Wyatt 46; Shannti Kumari 2-34) by nine wickets. (England reached their target in 8.3 overs)

Tri-series

Group stage

Brabourne Stadium, Mumbai, March 22: India 152/5 in 20 overs (Smriti Mandhana 67, Anuja Patil 35; Ashleigh Gardner 2-22, Ellyse Perry 2-31) lost to **Australia** 156/4 in 18.1 overs (Beth Mooney 45, Elyse Villani 39; Jhulan Goswami 3-30) by six wickets. *PoM:* Ashleigh Gardner.

Brabourne Stadium, Mumbai, March 23: Australia 149/8 in 20 overs (Rachel Haynes 65, Alyssa Healy 31; Jenny Gunn 3-26, Natalie Sciver 2-29) lost to **England** 150/2 in 17 overs (Natalie Sciver 68*, Tammy Beaumont 58*) by eight wickets. *PoM:* Natalie Sciver.

Brabourne Stadium, Mumbai, March 25: India 198/4 in 20 overs (Smriti Mandhana 76, Mithali Raj 53; Natasha Farrant 2-32) lost to **England** 199/3 in 18.4 overs (Danielle Wyatt 124, Tammy Beaumont 35; Deepti Sharma 2-36) by seven wickets. *PoM:* Danielle Wyatt.

Brabourne Stadium, Mumbai, March 26: Australia 186/5 in 20 overs (Beth Mooney 71, Elyse Villani 61; Pooja Vastrakar 2-28) beat **India** 150/5 in 20 overs (Jemimah Rodrigues 50, Anuja Patil 38*; Megan Schutt 3-31) by 36 runs. *PoM:* Megan Schutt.

Brabourne Stadium, Mumbai, March 28: England 96 in 17.4 overs (Alice Davidson-Richards 24; Delissa Kimmince 3-20, Megan Schutt 2-13) lost to **Australia** 97/2 in 11.3 overs

Smriti Mandhana guided India to the second-highest women's T20I total, but the record only lasted a few hours as England's Danni Wyatt chased it down. — *BCCI*

Brabourne Stadium, Mumbai, March 29: England 107 in 18.5 overs (Danielle Wyatt 31; Anuja Patil 3-21, Radha Yadav 2-16) lost to **India** 108/2 in 15.4 overs (Smriti Mandhana 62*, Harmanpreet Kaur 20*; Daniella Hazell 2-17) by eight wickets. *PoM:* Anuja Patil.

Points table

Team	M	W	L	T	N/R	Pts	NRR
Australia	4	3	1	0	0	6	+1.323
England	4	2	2	0	0	4	-0.923
India	4	1	3	0	0	2	-0.399

Australia and England qualified for the final

Australia beat England by 57 runs

Brabourne Stadium, Mumbai, March 31: Australia 209/4 in 20 overs (Meg Lanning 88*, Elyse Villani 51; Jenny Gunn 2-38) beat **England** 152/9 in 20 overs (Natalie Sciver 50, Danielle Wyatt 34; Megan Schutt 3-14, Ashleigh Gardner 2-20) by 57 runs. *PoM:* Meg Lanning. *PoS:* Megan Schutt.

Winners: Australia

England in India

Mandhana, bowlers scrap to the finish

India somewhat put to bed the ghosts of the 2017 World Cup loss to England by holding their nerve in the next ODI meeting between the teams. They chased down a modest target of 208, with the last-wicket pair of Ekta Bisht and Poonam Yadav adding an thrilling 18 runs to pull off a scrappy win with five balls to spare. The duo had earlier combined to precipitate an England collapse from 71 for no loss to 102 for 5, before finishing with seven wickets between them.

On a tricky surface, Smriti Mandhana curbed her natural instincts to make a mature 86 off 109 balls (even though it did include four sixes). It left India comfortable needing 37 off 72 balls. But the middle order ate up too many dot balls, having no answer to Sophie Ecclestone, the young left-arm spinner.

Ecclestone followed up her four-wicket haul in the first game with a career-best 4 for 14 in the second to bundle India out for 113.

Another youngster, Amy Jones, the wicketkeeper-opener, held fort in the third ODI, even as the Indian spinners scythed through the English line-up. India, though, prevailed. Mithali Raj, who'd by then earned a reputation as Danielle Hazell's bunny, held off her nemesis to combine with Deepti Sharma to bring up her 56th ODI half-century — an all-time record — during a match-winning 103-run stand for the third wicket.

Best batter: Smriti Mandhana (India) (181 runs in 3 matches)
Best bowler: Sophie Ecclestone (England) (8 wickets in 3 matches)

Warm-up

Vidarbha Cricket Association Stadium, Nagpur, April 3: India A 211/4 in 50 overs (Devika Vaidya 104, Mona Meshram 31*; Sophie Ecclestone 2-24) lost to **England** 252 in 49.2 overs (Tammy Beaumont 52, Danielle Wyatt 43; Anuja Patil 3-33, Tanusree Sarkar 2-16) by 4 wickets. England chased down the target of 212/6 in 41 overs but batted the entire 50 overs.

ODI series (3): India 2 England 1

Vidarbha Cricket Association Stadium, Nagpur, April 6: England 207 in 49.3 overs (Fran Wilson 45, Tammy Beaumont 37; Poonam Yadav 4-30, Ekta Bisht 3-49) lost to **India** 208/9 in 49.1 overs (Smriti Mandhana 86, Deepti Sharma 24; Sophie Ecclestone 4-37, Georgia Elwiss 2-14) by one wicket. *PoM:* Smriti Mandhana.
Vidarbha Cricket Association Stadium, Nagpur, April 9: India 113 in 37.2 overs (Smriti Mandhana 42, Deepti Sharma 26*; Sophie Ecclestone 4-14, Danielle Hazell 4-32) lost to **England** 117/2 in 29 overs (Danielle Wyatt 47, Tammy Beaumont 39*; Ekta Bisht 2-44) by eight wickets. *PoM:* Sophie Ecclestone.
Vidarbha Cricket Association Stadium, Nagpur, April 12: England 201/9 in 50 overs (Amy Jones 94, Heather Knight 36; Rajeshwari Gayakwad 2-32, Deepti Sharma 2-35) lost to **India** 202/2 in 45.2 overs (Mithali Raj 74*, D Sharma 54*; Anya Shrubsole 2-37) by eight wickets. *PoM:* Deepti Sharma. *PoS:* Smriti Mandhana.

India in Sri Lanka

Next generation shows chutzpah

India held their nerve against an inconsistent Sri Lanka to claim four important ICC Championship points and take the ODI series 2-1. Playing their first series under Ramesh Powar, who replaced Tushar Arothe as head coach, India showed signs of a more attacking approach as the tour progressed.

Mansi Joshi made a successful return to international cricket after a knee injury had kept her out for 14 months. The fast bowler picked up seven wickets in three ODIs, including a career-best haul of 3 for 16 in the first match.

After a nine-wicket demolition, Sri Lanka came back strongly in the second ODI, almost chasing down a target of 220. Taniya Bhatia, India's wicketkeeper-batter, cut and swept her way to a maiden ODI fifty in her first innings. D Hemalatha, another debutant, also caught the eye with her fluent strokeplay.

Having conceded the series in the first two games, Sri Lanka hit back hard in the third to clinch a thrilling three-wicket win. Chamari Athapaththu's power-packed innings of 115 guided Sri Lanka to their highest successful ODI run-chase: 257 for 7. Her fine effort trumped Mithali Raj's unbeaten knock of 125.

Jemimah Rodrigues stole the show in the T20Is against Sri Lanka, her runs coming at a strike-rate of 155.28. — *SLC*

Through the course of the ODI series, Jhulan Goswami became the first woman to take 300 international wickets when she dismissed Nipuni Hansika with a brutal bouncer in the first ODI; Raj surpassed Charlotte Edwards (116) to become the most capped women's ODI captain that same game, and then notched up her 73rd victory as skipper to become the second-most successful women's ODI captain, behind Belinda Clark (83).

The T20I series was more one-sided, with India demolishing the hosts 4-0. After a promising start to the series, where Sri Lanka went down by only 13 runs, India dominated proceedings.

Teenage sensation Jemimah Rodrigues stole the show, leading India's charge with 191 runs at a strike-rate of 155.28. Her tally included two half-centuries and a blistering 15-ball 36 — a knock in which she carted Nilakshi de Silva for three consecutive sixes.

Athapaththu (107) and Shashikala Siriwardene (101) were the only other batters to cross the 100-run mark. Poonam Yadav continued to spin her web around Sri Lanka, picking up eight wickets through the series, thereby overtaking Goswami to become India's highest wicket-taker in T20Is.

ODI series (3): India 2 Sri Lanka 1

Galle International Stadium, September 11: Sri Lanka 98 in 35.1 overs (Chamari Athapaththu 33, Sripali Weerakkody 26; Mansi Joshi 3-16, Jhulan Goswami 2-13) lost to **India** 100/1 in 19.5 overs (Smriti Mandhana 76*, Punam Raut 24) by nine wickets.
Galle International Stadium, September 13: India 219 in 50 overs (Taniya Bhatia 68, Mithali Raj 52; Chamari Athapaththu 3-42, Sripali Weerakkody 2-36) beat **Sri Lanka** 212 in 48.1 overs (C Athapaththu 57, Shashikala Siriwardene 49; Rajeshwari Gayakwad 2-37, Mansi Joshi 2-49) by seven runs.
FTZ Sports Complex (BOI), Katunayake, September 16: India 253/5 in 50 overs (Mithali Raj 125, Smriti Mandhana 51) lost to **Sri Lanka** 257/7 in 49.5 overs (Chamari Athapaththu 115, Hasini Perera 45; Jhulan Goswami 2-39, Mansi Joshi 2-43) by three wickets. *PoS:* Chamari Athapaththu.

T20I series (5): India 4 Sri Lanka 0

FTZ Sports Complex (BOI), Katunayake, September 19: India 168/8 in 20 overs (Taniya Bhatia 46, Jemimah Rodrigues 36; Udeshika Prabodhani 2-18, Chamari Athapaththu 2-23) beat **Sri Lanka** 155 in 19.3 overs (Eshani Kaushalya 45, Yasoda Mendia 32; Poonam Yadav 4-26, Radha Yadav 2-15) by 13 runs.
Colts Cricket Club Ground, Colombo, September 21: Sri Lanka 49/3 in 7.5 overs (Chamari Athapaththu 21) v **India.** No result.
Colombo Cricket Club Ground, September 22: Sri Lanka 131/8 in 20 overs (Shashikala Siriwardene 35, Nilakshi de Silva 31; Harmanpreet Kaur 2-3, Arundhati Reddy 2-19) lost to **India** 132/5 in 18.2 overs (Jemimah Rodrigues 57, Harmanpreet Kaur 24; Chamari Athapaththu 2-29) by five wickets.
Colombo Cricket Club Ground, September 24: Sri Lanka 134/5 in 17 overs (Shashikala Siriwardene 40, Chamari Athapaththu 31; Anuja Patil 3-36) lost to **India** 137/3 in 15.4 overs (A Patil 54*, Jemimah Rodrigues 52*; Oshadi Ranasinghe 3-33) by seven wickets.
FTZ Sports Complex (BOI), Katunayake, September 25: India 156 in 18.3 overs (Har-

Smriti Mandhana's incredible run of form continued with another pair of fifties in the ODIs. — *SLC*

manpreet Kaur 63, Jemimah Rodrigues 46; Shashikala Siriwardene 3-19, Inoshi Priyadarshini 3-24) beat **Sri Lanka** 105 in 17.4 overs (Anushka Sanjeewani 29, S Siriwardene 22; Poonam Yadav 3-18, Radha Yadav 2-14) by 51 runs. *PoS:* Jemimah Rodrigues.

	ODIs	**T20Is**
Best batter	Chamari Athapaththu (205 runs, 3 matches)	Jemimah Rodrigues (191 runs, 5 matches)
Best bowler	Mansi Joshi (7 wickets, 3 matches)	Poonam Yadav (8 wickets, 5 matches)

MULTI-NATION TOURNAMENTS

ICC Women's World T20 2018

Healy lifts Australia to fourth title

KARUNYA KESHAV

The aura of Australian indomitability on a world stage had been broken in the previous two tournaments: a West Indian heist had denied them the T20 prize in 2016 and Harmanpreet Kaur had sent them packing from the 50-over World Cup in 2017. Coming to the Caribbean, Australia were ranked No.1, but were acutely aware that they were in possession of no trophy. That knowledge made them hungry, but it also unlocked in the players freedom, humility and a determination to enjoy every outing. India had shown in the group stages that Meg Lanning's side could be defeated, and the nerves showed in the final through uncharacteristic fielding fumbles. But ultimately, the depth in their squad and the cool heads from their next generation of players sealed an emotional victory.

Alyssa Healy was the face of their campaign. The colourful wicketkeeper-opening bat was in the form of her life, getting the team off to blazing starts all year. She picked up four match awards, including for a 21-ball fifty against Ireland. Australia were glad when she recovered from a concussion scare in the India game in time for the semi-final.

As the first standalone women's World T20, the pressure was on the ICC, the organisers and the players to deliver — and but for some nervous moments owing to the weather as well as obligations to play multiple matches a day on a single pitch, they did. On the opening day triple-header, Harmanpreet, leading an inexperienced India in the opener against New Zealand, smashed the first T20I century by an Indian before Deandra Dottin fed off the energy of the home crowd to take five wickets for five runs.

The hosts' fitness and fielding stood out, but they slipped in the semis against England, who came in loaded with spinners for the slow and low surfaces. India, undefeated in their group, found their campaign imploding in the semis under lights even as Mithali Raj was controversially left on the bench and divisions came out in the open. Pakistan ticked the boxes for several national records. South Africa, prone to collapses, took a step backwards, while Bangladesh too didn't do justice to potential. Ireland, in tears after their loss to Pakistan, stood as a reminder of the gulf between the top teams — whose players are on contracts — and the rest. "It's so incredibly frustrating," said Laura Delany, their captain, choking up. "Because if we were professional, I wonder what the score would've been."

Group A

Providence Stadium, Guyana, November 9: West Indies 106/8 in 20 overs (Kycia Knight 32, Stafanie Taylor 29; Jahanara Alam 3-23, Rumana Ahmed 2-16) beat **Bangladesh** 46 in 14.4 overs (Deandra Dottin 5-5, Shakera Selman 2-12) by 60 runs. *PoM:* Deandra Dottin.

Darren Sammy National Cricket Stadium, Gros Islet, St Lucia, November 10: England v **Sri Lanka.** Match abandoned without a ball being bowled.

Darren Sammy stadium, St Lucia, November 12: Bangladesh 76/9 in 20 overs (Ayasha Rahman 39; Kirstie Gordon 3-16) lost to **England** 64/3 in 9.3 overs (Amy Jones 28*, Natalie Sciver 23; Salma Khatun 2-17) by seven wickets (D/L method). *PoM:* Kirstie Gordon.

Darren Sammy stadium, St Lucia, November 12: Sri Lanka 99/8 in 20 overs (Shashikala Siriwardene 21, Dilani Manodara 20*; Shabnim Ismail 3-10) lost to **South Africa** 102/3 in 18.3 overs (Marizanne Kapp 38, Dane van Niekerk 33*) by seven wickets. *PoM:* Shabnim Ismail.

Darren Sammy stadium, St Lucia, November 14: Sri Lanka 97/7 in 20 overs (Shashikala Siriwardene 31; Jahanara Alam 3-21) beat **Bangladesh** 72 in 20 overs (Nigar Sultana 20; Chamari Athapaththu 3-17, Udeshika Prabodhani 2-6) by 25 runs. *PoM:* Shashikala Siriwardene.

Darren Sammy stadium, St Lucia, November 14: West Indies 107/7 in 20 overs (Kycia Knight 32, Natasha McLean 28; Shabnim Ismail 3-12, Dane van Niekerk 2-8) beat **South Africa** 76 in 18.4 overs (Marizanne Kapp 26, Lizelle Lee 24; Stafanie Taylor 4-12) by 31 runs. *PoM:* Stafanie Taylor.

Darren Sammy stadium, St Lucia, November 16: South Africa 85 in 19.3 overs (Chloe Tryon 27; Natalie Sciver 3-4, Anya Shrubsole 3-11) lost to **England** 87/3 in 14.1 overs (Danielle Wyatt 27, Tammy Beaumont 24; Dane van Niekerk 2-13) by seven wickets. *PoM:* Natalie Sciver.

Darren Sammy stadium, St Lucia, November 16: West Indies 187/5 in 20 overs (Hayley Matthews 62, Deandra Dottin 49) beat **Sri Lanka** 104 in 17.4 overs (Chamari Athapaththu 44; H Matthews 3-16) by 83 runs. *PoM:* Hayley Matthews.

Darren Sammy stadium, St Lucia, November 18: England 115/8 in 20 overs (Sophia Dunkley 35, Anya Shrubsole 29; Shakera Selman 2-15, Deandra Dottin 2-21) lost to **West Indies** 117/6 in 19.3 overs (D Dottin 46, Shemaine Campbelle 45; A Shrubsole 3-10) by four wickets. *PoM:* Deandra Dottin.

Darren Sammy stadium, St Lucia, November 18: South Africa 109/9 in 20 overs (Marizanne Kapp 25, Lizelle Lee 21; Salma Khatun 3-20, Khadija Tul Kubra 2-18) beat **Bangladesh** 79/5 in 20 overs (Rumana Ahmed 34*) by 30 runs. *PoM:* Marizanne Kapp.

Group A points table

Team	M	W	L	T	N/R	Pts	NRR
West Indies	4	4	0	0	0	8	+2.241
England	4	2	1	0	1	5	+1.317
South Africa	4	2	2	0	0	4	-0.277
Sri Lanka	4	1	2	0	1	3	-1.171
Bangladesh	4	0	4	0	0	0	-1.989

West Indies and England qualified for the semi-final

Group B

Providence Stadium, Guyana, November 9: India 194/5 in 20 overs (Harmanpreet Kaur 103, Jemimah Rodrigues 59; Lea Tahuhu 2-18) beat **New Zealand** 160/9 in 20 overs (Suzie Bates 67, Katey Martin 39; Dayalan Hemalatha 3-26, Poonam Yadav 3-33) by 34 runs. *PoM:* Harmanpreet Kaur.

Alyssa Healy (top) gave Australia explosive starts on which they could build; Harmanpreet Kaur became the first Indian woman to strike a T20I century. *– ICC*

Providence Stadium, Guyana, November 9: Australia 165/5 in 20 overs (Alyssa Healy 48, Beth Mooney 48; Aliya Riaz 2-25, Nashra Sandhu 2-43) beat **Pakistan** 113/8 in 20 overs (Bismah Maroof 26, Umaima Sohail 20; Megan Schutt 2-13, Georgia Wareham 2-18) by 52 runs. *PoM:* Alyssa Healy.

Providence Stadium, Guyana, November 11: Pakistan 133/7 in 20 overs (Bismah Maroof 53, Nida Dar 52; Poonam Yadav 2-22, Dayalan Hemalatha 2-34) lost to **India** 137/3 in 19 overs (Mithali Raj 56, Smriti Mandhana 26) by seven wickets. *PoM:* Mithali Raj.

Providence Stadium, Guyana, November 11: Ireland 93/6 in 20 overs (Kim Garth 24; El-lyse Perry 2-12) lost to **Australia** 94/1 in 9.1 overs (Alyssa Healy 56*) by nine wickets. *PoM:* Alyssa Healy.

Providence Stadium, Guyana, November 13: Pakistan 139/6 in 20 overs (Javeria Khan 74*, Ayesha Zafar 21; Lucy O'Reilly 3-19) beat **Ireland** 101/9 in 20 overs (Isobel Joyce 30, Claire Shillington 27; Nashra Sandhu 2-8, Aliya Riaz 2-16) by 38 runs. *PoM:* Javeria Khan.

Providence Stadium, Guyana, November 13: Australia 153/7 in 20 overs (Alyssa Healy 53, Rachel Haynes 29*; Leigh Kasperek 3-25, Sophie Devine 2-37) beat **New Zealand** 120 in 17.3 overs (Suzie Bates 48, Katey Martin 24; Megan Schutt 3-12, Sophie Molineux 2-20) by 33 runs. *PoM:* Alyssa Healy.

Providence Stadium, Guyana, November 15: India 145/6 in 20 overs (Mithali Raj 51, Smriti Mandhana 33; Kim Garth 2-22) beat **Ireland** 93/8 in 20 overs (Isobel Joyce 33, Claire Shillington 23; Radha Yadav 3-25, Deepti Sharma 2-15) by 52 runs. *PoM:* Mithali Raj.

Providence Stadium, Guyana, November 15: New Zealand 144/6 in 20 overs (Suzie Bates 35, Sophie Devine 32; Aliya Riaz 2-29, Sana Mir 2-35) beat **Pakistan** 90 in 18 overs (Javeria Khan 36; Jess Watkin 3-9, Amelia Kerr 3-21) by 54 runs. *PoM:* Jess Watkin.

Providence Stadium, Guyana, November 17: India 167/8 in 20 overs (Smriti Mandhana 83, Harmanpreet Kaur 43; Ellyse Perry 3-16, Ashleigh Gardner 2-25) beat **Australia** 119 in 19.4 overs (E Perry 39*, A Gardner 20; Anuja Patil 3-15, Radha Yadav 2-13) by 48 runs. *PoM:* Smriti Mandhana.

Providence Stadium, Guyana, November 17: Ireland 79/9 in 20 overs (Gaby Lewis 39; Leigh Kasperek 3-19, Lea Tahuhu 2-17) lost to **New Zealand** 81/2 in 7.3 overs (Sophie Devine 51) by eight wickets. *PoM:* Sophie Devine.

Group B points table

Team	M	W	L	T	N/R	Pts	NRR
India	4	4	0	0	0	8	+1.827
Australia	4	3	1	0	0	6	+1.515
New Zealand	4	2	2	0	0	4	+1.031
Pakistan	4	1	3	0	0	2	-0.987
Ireland	4	0	4	0	0	0	-3.525

India and Australia qualified for the semi-final

Knock-out

1st semi-final: Sir Vivian Richards Stadium, North Sound, Antigua, November 22: Australia 142/5 in 20 overs (Alyssa Healy 46, Meg Lanning 31) beat **West Indies** 71 in 17.3 overs (Ellyse Perry 2-2, Ashleigh Gardner 2-15) by 71 runs. *PoM:* Alyssa Healy.

2nd semi-final: Sir Vivian Richards Stadium, North Sound, Antigua, November 22: India 112 in 19.3 overs (Smriti Mandhana 34, Jemimah Rodrigues 26; Heather Knight 3-9, Kirstie Gordon 2-20) lost to **England** 116/2 in 17.1 overs (Amy Jones 53*, Natalie Sciver 52*) by eight wickets. *PoM:* Amy Jones.

Australia and England qualified for the final

Final: Australia beat England by eight wickets

Sir Vivian Richards Stadium, North Sound, Antigua, November 24: England 105 in 19.4 overs (Danielle Wyatt 43, Heather Knight 25; Ashleigh Gardner 3-22, Georgia Wareham 2-11) lost to **Australia** 106/2 in 15.1 overs (A Gardner 33*, Meg Lanning 28*) by eight wickets. *PoM:* Ashleigh Gardner. *PoT:* Alyssa Healy.

Asia Cup 2018

Bangladesh knock India off their perch

For the first time since the tournament's inception, India lost their hold on the Asia Cup trophy. The defending champions were beaten not once, but twice through their campaign, losing to Bangladesh on both occasions.

It didn't go unnoticed that the winning coach, assistant coach and physio were all from India: Anju Jain, the former wicketkeeper, Deivika Palshikaar, who also played for India, and Anuja Dalvi.

In the league phase, it was Fargana Hoque (52*) and Rumana Ahmed (42*) who helped their team chase down a target of 142 with seven wickets to spare, handing India their first ever loss in the tournament.

Despite the stumble, Harmanpreet Kaur's team were the favourites going into the final, while Bangladesh were expected to crumble under the pressure. Instead, Rumana's team rose to the occasion, first restricting the hosts to a meagre total of 112 for 9, before holding their nerve in an exhilarating chase to knock off nine runs from the final over. India's defensive mindset did not help their cause, often digging themselves into a hole against the spinners, and then getting out while trying to force the pace.

Harmanpreet (215 runs) was the only batter to cross the 200-run mark, with Mithali Raj (147 runs) the next best. For Bangladesh, the opening pair of Shamima Sultana (130) and Ayasha Rahman (101) did the bulk of the scoring, while Rumana (ten wickets), the leg-spinner, was their best bowler.

Bangladesh's win was not the only upset of the tournament: Thailand managed to beat Sri Lanka in another last-ball thriller. All the 'less fancied' teams showed vast improvement, indicating that the gap between the top eight and the Associate nations is closing. Sri Lanka, who were without Chamari Athapaththu, struggled through the tournament and Pakistan's inconsistency meant they fell short of another final.

Notable performances included Mithali's unbeaten 97 against Malaysia, Nida Dar's 5 for 21 against Sri Lanka and Wongpaka Liengprasert 5 for 12 in Thailand's win over Sri Lanka. *AU*

Best batter: Harmanpreet Kaur (India) (215 runs in 6 matches)
Best bowler: Nida Dar (Pakistan) (11 wickets in 5 matches)

Kinrara Academy Oval, Kuala Lumpur, June 3: India 169/3 in 20 overs (Mithali Raj 97*, Harmanpreet Kaur 32) beat **Malaysia** 27 in 13.4 overs (Pooja Vastrakar 3-6, Poonam Yadav 2-0) by 142 runs. *PoM:* Mithali Raj.
Royal Selangor Club, Kuala Lumpur, June 3: Bangladesh 63 in 19.3 overs (Sugandika Kumari 3-17, Udeshika Prabodhani 2-6) lost to **Sri Lanka** 64/4 in 14.3 overs (Nipuni Hansika

Bangladesh beat India not once but twice in the Asia Cup, holding their nerve in a thrilling final. — *ACC*

23, Yasoda Mendis 20; Khadija Tul Kubra 3-13) by six wickets. *PoM:* Sugandika Kumari.

Kinrara Academy Oval, Kuala Lumpur, June 3: Thailand 67/8 in 20 overs (Sana Mir 2-7) lost to **Pakistan** 70/2 in 13.1 overs (Nahida Khan 38*) by eight wickets. *PoM:* Nahida Khan.

Kinrara Academy Oval, Kuala Lumpur, June 4: Pakistan 95/5 in 20 overs (Sana Mir 21*; Nahida Akter 2-23) lost to **Bangladesh** 96/3 in 17.5 overs (Nigar Sultana 31*, Shamima Sultana 31) by seven wickets. *PoM:* Fahima Khatun.

Royal Selangor Club, Kuala Lumpur, June 4: India 132/4 in 20 overs (Mona Meshram 32, Smriti Mandhana 29; Wongpaka Liengprasert 2-16) beat **Thailand** 66/8 in 20 overs (Nattaya Boochatham 21; Harmanpreet Kaur 3-11, Deepti Sharma 2-16) by 66 runs. *PoM:* Harmanpreet Kaur.

Royal Selangor Club, Kuala Lumpur, June 4: Sri Lanka 136/3 in 20 overs (Yasoda Mendis 36, Hasini Perera 32) beat **Malaysia** 46/7 in 20 overs (Nilakshi de Silva 3-13, Shashikala Siriwardene 2-12) by 90 runs. *PoM:* Nilakshi de Silva.

Kinrara Academy Oval, Kuala Lumpur, June 6: Pakistan 136/4 in 20 overs (Bismah Maroof 60*, Nahida Khan 38; Sugandika Kumari 2-18) beat **Sri Lanka** 113/9 in 20 overs (Yasoda Mendis 25, Nipuni Hansika 24; Nida Dar 5-21) by 23 runs. *PoM:* Nida Dar.

Royal Selangor Club, Kuala Lumpur, June 6: Malaysia 36/8 in 20 overs (Wongpaka Liengprasert 2-10) lost to **Thailand** 37/1 in 9 overs (Naruemol Chaiwai 20*) by nine wickets. *PoM:* Wongpaka Liengprasert.

Kinrara Academy Oval, Kuala Lumpur, June 6: India 141/7 in 20 overs (Harmanpreet Kaur 42, Deepti Sharma 32; Rumana Ahmed 3-21) lost to **Bangladesh** 142/3 in 19.4 overs (Fargana Hoque 52*, Rumana Ahmed 42*) by seven wickets. *PoM:* Rumana Ahmed.

Kinrara Academy Oval, Kuala Lumpur, June 7: Thailand 60/8 in 20 overs (Salma Khatun 2-6, Nahida Akter 2-10) lost to **Bangladesh** 62/1 in 11.1 overs (Ayasha Rahman 25*, Nigar Sultana 25*) by nine wickets. *PoM:* Salma Khatun.

Royal Selangor Club, Kuala Lumpur, June 7: Pakistan 177/5 in 20 overs (Bismah Maroof

62, Nida Dar 42) beat **Malaysia** 30 in 18.4 overs (N Dar 4-5) by 147 runs. *PoM:* Nida Dar.
Royal Selangor Club, Kuala Lumpur, June 7: Sri Lanka 107/7 in 20 overs (Hasini Perera 46*, Yasoda Mendis 27; Ekta Bisht 2-20) lost to **India** 110/3 in 18.5 overs (Veda Krishnamurthy 29*, Harmanpreet Kaur 24) by seven wickets. *PoM:* Anuja Patil.
Kinrara Academy Oval, Kuala Lumpur, June 9: Pakistan 72/7 in 20 overs (Sana Mir 20*; Ekta Bisht 3-14) lost to **India** 75/3 in 16.1 overs (Smriti Mandhana 38, Harmanpreet Kaur 34*; Anam Amin 2-10) by seven wickets. *PoM:* Ekta Bisht.
Royal Selangor Club, Kuala Lumpur, June 9: Sri Lanka 104 in 20 overs (Anushka Sanjeewani 32, Yasoda Mendis 22; Wongpaka Liengprasert 5-12, Sornnarin Tippoch 2-19) lost to **Thailand** 105/6 in 20 overs (Naruemoi Chaiwai 43; Nilakshi de Silva 2-17) by four wickets. *PoM:* Wongpaka Liengprasert.
Royal Selangor Club, Kuala Lumpur, June 9: Bangladesh 130/4 in 20 overs (Shamima Sultana 43, Ayasha Rahman 31; Winifired Duraisingam 2-19) beat **Malaysia** 60/9 in 20 overs (Rumana Ahmed 3-8) by 70 runs. *PoM:* Shamima Sultana.

Points table

Teams	M	W	L	T	N/R	Pts	NRR
India	5	4	1	0	0	8	+2.446
Bangladesh	5	4	1	0	0	8	+1.116
Pakistan	5	3	2	0	0	6	+1.850
Sri Lanka	5	2	3	0	0	4	+0.891
Thailand	5	2	3	0	0	4	-1.026
Malaysia	5	0	5	0	0	0	-5.302

India and Bangladesh qualified for the final

Kinrara Academy Oval, Kuala Lumpur, June 10: India 112/9 in 20 overs (Harmanpreet Kaur 56; Rumana Ahmed 2-22, Khadija Tul Kubra 2-23) lost to **Bangladesh** 113/7 in 20 overs (Nigar Sultana 27, R Ahmed 23; Poonam Yadav 4-9, H Kaur 2-19) by three wickets. *PoM:* Rumana Ahmed. *PoS:* Harmanpreet Kaur.

Winners: Bangladesh

INDIA'S OTHER INTERNATIONALS

Australia A in India

Mithali cracks second T20 century

Punam Raut's India A team failed to put up much of a fight through the three-match one-day series against Australia A, with the visitors claiming an easy 3-0 victory.

Tahlia McGrath and Heather Graham were two of their best batters, scoring 167 and 116 runs respectively. McGrath's tally included two half-centuries and came at an impressive average of 55.66. For the hosts, Raut and Mona Meshram managed 162 and 144 runs respectively, but despite their contributions, India A managed to cross the 200-run mark only once. In batting-friendly conditions, Molly Strano was the most successful bowler, with the off-spinner picking up six wickets at an average of 11.50 and an economy rate of 3.13.

While the one-day matches worked as game-time for India hopefuls, the T20 series served as preparation for the World T20 in the Caribbean. 'A' only in name, the full-strength Indian squad dominated the series. Mithali Raj became the only Indian batter to score two T20 centuries when she struck an unbeaten 61-ball 105 in the second match. India's spin trio of Anuja Patil (6) Deepti Sharma and Poonam Yadav (5 each) kept the Australia A batters honest, their combined economy rate of 7.11 testament to that.   *AU*

One-day series (3): Australia A 3 India A 0

Bandra Kurla Complex, Mumbai, October 15: Australia A 271/8 in 50 overs (Tahlia McGrath 58, Heather Graham 48; Preeti Bose 3-42, Reemalaxmi Ekka 2-42) beat **India A** 180 in 46.2 overs (Preeti Bose 62*, Shikha Pandey 42; Molly Strano 3-23, Maitlan Brown 2-16) by 91 runs.

BKC, Mumbai, October 17: India A 197/7 in 50 overs (Punam Raut 64, Mona Meshram 59; Molly Strano 3-23, Tahlia McGrath 2-32) lost to **Australia A** 200/6 in 40.3 overs (Heather Graham 68*, T McGrath 47; Shikha Pandey 3-38, Rajeshwari Gayakwad 2-35) by four wickets.

BKC, Mumbai, October 19: India A 254/8 in 50 overs (Punam Raut 98, Mona Meshram 57; Amanda Wellington 3-59, Piepa Cleary 2-44) lost to **Australia A** 257/5 in 44.3 overs (Georgia Redmayne 98, Josephine Dooley 67; Tanusree Sarkar 2-30) by five wickets.

T20 series (3): Australia A 0 India A 3

BKC, Mumbai, October 22: Australia A 160/6 in 20 overs (Heather Graham 43, Naomi Stalenberg 39; Anuja Patil 2-22, Deepti Sharma 2-30) lost to **India A** 163/6 in 19 overs (Smriti Mandhana 72, Harmanpreet Kaur 45; Lauren Cheatle 2-18, Amanda Wellington 2-34) by four wickets.

BKC, Mumbai, October 24: India A 184/5 in 20 overs (Mithali Raj 105*, Harmanpreet Kaur 57*; Tahlia McGrath 2-36) beat **Australia A** 156/9 in 20 overs (T McGrath 47, Heather Graham 24; Poonam Yadav 2-29, Anuja Patil 2-31) by 28 runs.

BKC, Mumbai, October 26: India A 154/8 in 20 overs (Harmanpreet Kaur 41, Jemimah Rodrigues 38; Maitlan Brown 2-21, Molly Strano 2-25) beat **Australia A** 117 in 19.2 overs (Naomi Stalenberg 26, Heather Graham 20; Poonam Yadav 3-23, Pooja Vastrakar 2-21) by 37 runs.

	One-day	T20
Best batter	Tahlia McGrath (167 runs, 3 matches)	Harmanpreet Kaur (143 runs, 3 matches)
Best bowler	Molly Strano (6 wickets, 3 matches)	Anuja Patil (6 wickets, 3 matches)

Bangladesh A in India 2017-18

Anuja marshals young troops

In the introspection following the narrow 2017 World Cup loss in England arose the not particularly new idea that India need to strengthen their bench. The dust was shaken off the A set-up after a few years limited-overs series were organised against a competitive Bangladesh side with almost all their first-choice players.

Under the experienced leadership of Anuja Patil, youngsters such as Jemimah Rodrigues, Radha Yadav, Taniya Bhatia and Pooja Vastrakar showed more of that talent that would see them establish themselves in the senior team.

A nearly full-strength Bangladesh A would have been disappointed that they had to wait till the final match to get a win. Rumana Ahmed, though, was a constant threat with both bat and ball. After the series, she and fellow spinner Khadija Tul Kubra were to link up with Women's Big Bash League teams for a two-week rookie programme.   *KK*

Warm-up

Alur Cricket Stadium II, Alur, November 26: Karnataka 111 in 42.4 overs (Rakshitha Krishnappa 27; Jahanara Alam 2-17, Rumana Ahmed 2-20) lost to **Bangladesh A** 112/8 in 40.3 overs (Nigar Sultana Joty 23*, Lata Mondal 22; R Krishnappa 3-15, Rameshwari Gayakwad 2-23) by two wickets.

Alur Cricket Stadium II, Alur, November 28: Bangladesh A 166/7 in 50 overs (Fargana Hoque 51, Shamima Sultana 40*, Sahana Pawar 3-28, Rakshitha Krishnappa 2-35) beat **Karnataka** 137 in 45 overs (V Karuna Jain 87*, G Divya 29; Rumana Ahmed 4-22, Shaila Sharmin 2-13) by 29 runs.

India revived their 'A' team programme to boost their bench strength.

One-day series (3): India A 3 Bangladesh A 0

KSCA Stadium, Hubli, December 2: India A 215/9 in 50 overs (VR Vanitha 76, Anuja Patil 33; Nahida Akter 3-35, Shaila Sharmin 2-28) beat **Bangladesh A** 183/6 in 50 overs (Lata Mondal 45, Rumana Ahmed 39*; Devika Vaidya 2-35) by 32 runs.

KSCA Stadium, Hubli, December 5: Bangladesh A 195/7 in 50 overs (Lata Mondal 71, Rumana Ahmed 65) lost to **India A** 196/5 in 48.1 overs (Neena Chaudhary 56, Neha Tanwar 44) by five wickets.

KSCA Stadium, Hubli, December 7: Bangladesh A 116 in 42 overs (Rumana Ahmed 42, Murshida Khan 21; Anuja Patil 2-11, Preeti Bose 2-16) lost to **India A** 118/1 in 32.3 overs (Jemimah Rodrigues 56*, Devika Vaidya 30*) by nine wickets.

T20 series: India A 2 Bangladesh A 1

KSCA Stadium, Belgaum, December 12: Bangladesh A 57 in 17 overs (Rumana Ahmed 24; Radha Yadav 2-4, Anuja Patil 2-9) lost to **India A** 60/2 in 10.4 overs (S Meghana 30*) by eight wickets.

KSCA Stadium, Belgaum, December 14: India A 152/5 in 20 overs (Jemimah Rodrigues 63, Taniya Bhatia 35; Jahanara Alam 2-31) beat **Bangladesh A** 112/8 in 20 overs (Fargana Hoque 34, Murshida Khatun 31; Anuja Patil 2-19) by 40 runs.

KSCA Stadium, Belgaum, December 16: Bangladesh A 112/7 in 20 overs (Rumana Ahmed 46, Salma Khatun 21; Anuja Patil 2-17, Tanuja Kanwer 2-20) beat **India A** 73/8 in 20 overs (Nahida Akter 2-14) by 39 runs.

	ODIs	T20s
Best batter	Rumana Ahmed (146 runs, 3 matches)	Rumana Ahmed (79 runs, 3 matches)
Best bowler	Anuja Patil (4 wickets, 3 matches)	Anuja Patil (6 wickets, 3 matches)

OTHER INTERNATIONALS 2018-19

Pakistan in Bangladesh

Reality check for Bangladesh

Following the highs of the Asia Cup and the ICC World T20 Qualifier, Bangladesh crashed to a 3-0 T20I series defeat against Pakistan at home. It wasn't the defeat itself that would have hurt, but the manner in which their batters continually failed to come up with any substantial scores.

They began on a terrible note, faltering in pursuit of 88 to be dismissed for 30, their lowest ever T20I total. Anam Amin, Pakistan's left-arm spinner, finished with incredible figures of 3-3-0-3. After that, they stuttered to scores of 81 for 8 and 77.

While Javeria Khan — leading Pakistan while Bismah Maroof underwent surgery — topped the batting charts with 92 runs, it was Pakistan's spinners who set up the series win. Amin, Nida Dar (both five wickets) and Nashra Sandhu (four) finished with a combined series analysis of 26.5-4-84-14.

The hosts salvaged some pride in the one-off ODI, courtesy a six-wicket haul from Khadija Tul Kubra. The off-spinner's figures of 6 for 20 were the best by a Bangladesh bowler in ODIs. The victory was Bangladesh's eighth overall, third against Pakistan, and first since February 2017.

	ODI	**T20Is**
Best batter	Fargana Hoque (48 runs, 1 match)	Javeria Khan (92 runs, 3 matches)
Best bowler	Khadija Tul Kubra (6 wickets, 1 match)	Anam Amin (5 wickets, 3 matches)

T20I series (4): Bangladesh 0 Pakistan 3

Sheikh Kamal International Cricket Stadium, Cox's Bazar, October 2: Bangladesh v Pakistan. Match abandoned without a ball being bowled.
Sheikh Kamal International Cricket Stadium, Cox's Bazar, October 3: Pakistan 88/5 in 14 overs (Javeria Khan 25; Nahida Akter 2-19) beat **Bangladesh** 30 in 12.5 overs (Anam Amin 3-0, Nida Dar 2-4) by 58 runs. *PoM*: Anam Amin.
Sheikh Kamal International Cricket Stadium, Cox's Bazar, October 5: Bangladesh 81/8 in 20 overs (Nashra Sandhu 2-16, Nida Dar 2-16) lost to **Pakistan** 85/3 in 18.1 overs (Nahida Khan 33, Javeria Khan 31*) by seven wickets. *PoM*: Nahida Khan.
Sheikh Kamal International Cricket Stadium, Cox's Bazar, October 7: Bangladesh 77 in 20 overs (Rumana Ahmed 24; Natalia Pervaiz 3-20, Sana Mir 2-10) lost to **Pakistan** 78/3 in 14.5 overs (Javeria Khan 36*) by seven wickets. *PoM*: Natalia Pervaiz.

Only ODI: Bangladesh win by six wickets

Sheikh Kamal International Cricket Stadium, Cox's Bazar, October 8: Pakistan 94 in 34.5 overs (Javeria Khan 29; Khadija Tul Kubra 6-20, Rumana Ahmed 2-15) lost to **Bangla-**

desh 95/4 in 29 overs (Fargana Hoque 48, R Ahmed 34; Sana Mir 2-20) by six wickets. *PoM:* Khadija Tul Kubra.

Pakistan v Australia in Malaysia

Australian juggernaut gathers steam

Sophie Molinuex's career-best 4 for 14 sealed a series win for Australia. — *PCB*

Australia handed out a 3-0 thrashing in both the ODIs and T20Is in Malaysia. Meg Lanning's 12th ODI century sealed the series with a 150-run win in the second match. She shared a 181-run partnership with Rachael Haynes before Sophie Molineux and Ashleigh Gardner ripped through the Pakistan batting line-up. Molineux, filling in for Jess Jonassen, who was recovering from knee surgery, registered career-best figures of 4 for 14, after Nahida Khan, Pakistan's opener, scored a solid 66 — Pakistan's highest individual score against Australia.

In the final ODI, Alyssa Healy missed out on a century, but Gardner blasted her maiden fifty to lift Australia to a mammoth total of 324. Gardner plundered 90 runs from the last ten overs alongside Molineux and Nicola Carey. Her 37-ball 62 was studded with six fours and three sixes.

In reply, Pakistan managed their highest ODI score against Australia: 235 for 7. Sana Mir, who became the No.1 ranked ODI bowler, fittingly finished at the top of the bowling charts.

A change in format brought no change in fortune for Pakistan, as Healy and Gardner continued to assert their dominance at the top of the order and the bowlers kept it tight. Healy smashed 132 runs, including two half-centuries, at a strike-rate of 155.29, while Gardner collected her maiden T20I half-century in the first match — another blistering knock of 63 in 37 balls.

Umaima Sohail (72 runs) made a promising debut for the hosts, even scoring a highest of 43 in the second match.

ODI series (3): Australia 3 Pakistan 0

Kinrara Academy Oval, Kuala Lumpur, October 18: Pakistan 95 in 37.2 overs (Javeria Khan 21, Sana Mir 21; Megan Schutt 3-17, Nicola Carey 3-19) lost to **Australia** 95/5 in 22.2 overs (Alyssa Healy 26, Rachael Haynes 24; Sana Mir 3-26) by five wickets. (DLS method). *PoM:* Megan Schutt.

Kinrara Academy Oval, Kuala Lumpur, October 20: Australia 273/7 in 50 overs (Meg Lanning 124, Rachael Haynes 79; Nashra Sandhu 3-54, Diana Baig 2-40) beat **Pakistan** 123 in 40.1 overs (Nahida Khan 66; Sophie Molineux 4-14, Ashleigh Gardner 2-4) by 150 runs. *PoM:* Meg Lanning.

Kinrara Academy Oval, Kuala Lumpur, October 22: Australia 324/7 in 50 overs (Alyssa Healy 97, Ashleigh Gardner 62*; Sana Mir 3-53, Anam Amin 2-63) beat **Pakistan** 235/7 in 50 overs (Aliya Riaz 51, Sidra Ameen 41; A Gardner 3-44) by 89 runs. *PoM:* Ashleigh Gardner. PoS: Meg Lanning & Sana Mir.

T20I series (3): Australia 3 Pakistan 0

Kinrara Academy Oval, Kuala Lumpur, October 25: Australia 195/3 in 20 overs (Ashleigh Gardner 63*, Alyssa Healy 59) beat **Pakistan** 131/7 in 20 overs (Nahida Khan 43, Umaima Sohail 25; Sophie Molineux 4-16) by 64 runs. *PoM:* Sophie Molinex.

Kinrara Academy Oval, Kuala Lumpur, October 27: Pakistan 101 in 19.5 overs (Umaima Sohail 43, Javeria Khan 23; Georgia Wareham 3-12, Sophie Molineux 3-14) lost to **Australia** 104/4 in 17 overs (Beth Mooney 29, Elyse Villani 24*) by six wickets. *PoM:* Georgia Wareham.

Kinrara Academy Oval, Kuala Lumpur, October 29: Pakistan 97/8 in 20 overs (Bismah Maroof 34; Megan Schutt 2-15) lost to **Australia** 98/1 in 10.2 overs (Alyssa Healy 67*, Beth Mooney 21) by nine wickets. *PoM:* Alyssa Healy. *PoS:* Alyssa Healy & Umaima Sohail.

	ODIs	T20Is
Best batter	Meg Lanning (142 runs, 3 matches)	Alyssa Healy (132 runs, 3 matches)
Best bowler	Sana Mir (7 wickets, 3 matches)	Sophie Molineux (7 wickets, 3 matches)

Pakistan v West Indies in Pakistan & UAE

History, twice made

Ten months after the West Indies men's team travelled to Pakistan, the women's team followed suit for a three-match T20I series in Karachi. Deandra Dottin was at her belligerent best, pummelling 158 runs in three matches at a strike-rate of 139.82, as the visitors clinched the series 2-1. Dottin began with an unbeaten 90 in the opening encounter — her 109-run partnership with Chedean Nation headlining a comfortable win. In the following match, the Pakistan bowlers showed great discipline to force a tie, before 'Hurricane' Dottin struck again. She carted Sana Mir for 18 runs in the Super Over,

Pakistan were delighted to seal their first ODI series win against West Indies. — *PCB*

and then watched as Shakera Selman cleaned up Pakistan in three balls.

The final match was Mir's 100th T20I appearance for Pakistan, and her team marked the occasion with an exciting 12-run victory.

Buoyed by their success in the final T20I, Pakistan entered the three-match ODI series in Dubai with confidence. Although West Indies were strengthened by the return of their captain, Stafanie Taylor, who skipped the T20I series due to security concerns, Bismah Maroof's team refused the back down. They came back from a crushing 146-run loss in the first ODI to claim their first ODI series win against West Indies. This was thanks largely to excellent performances from Sidra Ameen (148 runs), Nida Dar (110 runs) and Diana Baig (seven wickets). Ameen scored back-to-back half-centuries — the first, a career-best 96. The series win helped push Pakistan past West Indies to fourth place on the ICC Women's Championship table, with 12 points.

T20I series (3): Pakistan 1 West Indies 2

Southend Club Cricket Stadium, Karachi, January 31: West Indies 160/2 in 20 overs (Deandra Dottin 90*, Chedean Nation 50*) beat **Pakistan** 89 in 18 overs (Bismah Maroof 38; Shamilia Connell 3-29, Shakera Selman 2-8). *PoM:* Deandra Dottin.
Southend Club Cricket Stadium, Karachi, February 1: Pakistan 132/4 in 20 overs (Bismah Maroof 31, Javeria Khan 26; Deandra Dottin 2-26) tied with **West Indies** 132/6 in 20 overs (Shemaine Campbell 41, Kycia Knight 32; Anam Amin 2-24). Super Over: West Indies 18/0 in 1 over beat Pakistan 1/2 in 0.3 overs. *PoM:* Shemaine Campbell.
Southend Club Cricket Stadium, Karachi, February 3: Pakistan 150/6 in 20 overs (Nida Dar 53, Umaima Sohail 28; Karishma Ramharack 2-20) beat **West Indies** 138/8 in 20 overs (Deandra Dottin 46, Natasha McLean 26; Anam Amin 3-34, Sana Mir 2-21) by 12 runs. *PoM:* Nida Dar. *PoS:* Deandra Dottin.

ODI series (3): Pakistan 2 West Indies 1

ICC Academy, Dubai, February 7: West Indies 216/5 in 50 overs (Deandra Dottin 96, Stafanie Taylor 58; Kainat Imtiaz 3-49) beat **West Indies** 70 in 29.5 overs (Nahida Khan 23, Javeria Khan 21; D Dottin 3-14, Afy Fletcher 3-17) by 146 runs. *PoM:* Deandra Dottin.

ICC Academy, Dubai, February 9: Pakistan 240 in 49.4 overs (Sidra Ameen 96, Nida Dar 81; Shakera Selman 2-33, Deandra Dottin 2-55) beat **West Indies** 206 in 49.4 overs (Natasha McLean 82, Stafanie Taylor 48; Diana Baig 4-34, Sana Mir 3-21) by 34 runs. *PoM:* Sidra Ameen.

ICC Academy, Dubai, February 11: Pakistan 159 in 47.3 overs (Stafanie Taylor 52, Deandra Dottin 28; Nashra Sandhu 3-21, Diana Baig 3-42) lost to **West Indies** 163/6 in 47.2 overs (Sidra Ameen 52, Nida Dar 26; S Taylor 2-17, Shakera Selman 2-24) by four wickets. *PoM:* Sidra Ameen. *PoS:* Sidra Ameen, Stafanie Taylor.

	ODIs	**T20Is**
Best batter	Stafanie Taylor (158 runs, 3 matches)	Deandra Dottin (158 runs, 3 matches)
Best bowler	Diana Baig (7 wickets, 3 matches)	Anam Amin (5 wickets, 3 matches)

Sri Lanka in South Africa

Luus regains touch

Keen to put their poor show in the 2018 World T20 behind them, South Africa crushed Sri Lanka 3-0 in the three-match T20I series at home. They made significant changes to their squad: Lizelle Lee (failed to meet fitness standards) and Laura Wolvaardt (poor form) were dropped, Chloe Tryon was missing due to injury and Nadine de Klerk earned a recall after impressive domestic performances. All with an aim to play more "aggressive and attacking" cricket.

They made that intent clear in the very first game when, having restricted Sri Lanka to 90 for 8, Dane van Niekerk blasted an unbeaten 55-ball 71. The South African captain finished as the highest run-getter in the series with 142 runs at a strike-rate of 137.86.

Sune Luus, not originally part of the squad, but roped in as a replacement for Tryon, made an emphatic return, picking up her second T20I five-for, in the second match. Her se-

Dane van Niekerk notched up her maiden ODI century, in the first ODI against Sri Lanka. — *CSA*

ries tally of six wickets came at an incredible average of 6.16 and economy rate of 4.82 — bettered only by Marizanne Kapp's economy rate of 3.80.

The hosts carried that aggressive style into the ODIs as well, completing another comfortable 3-0 sweep. Van Niekerk notched up her maiden ODI century in the first match, sharing a 117-run partnership with Andrie Steyn. She became only the fourth woman (after Lisa Sthalekar, Stafanie Taylor and Ellyse Perry) to complete the double of 2000 runs and 100 wickets in ODIs.

Kapp's unbeaten 69 off 34 deliveries, coupled with half-centuries from Wolvaardt and Lara Goodall, trumped Chamari Athapaththu's belligerent 74-ball 94 in the second ODI, before Luus — standing in as skipper for an injured van Niekerk (stress fracture) — and Mignon du Preez combined to complete a clean sweep in the final match. Du Preez became the first South African woman to score 3000 ODI runs.

T20I series (3): South Africa 3 Sri Lanka 0

Newlands, Cape Town, February 1: Sri Lanka 90/8 in 20 overs (Hasini Perera 27, Imalka Mendis 25*; Dane van Niekerk 3-12, Masabata Klaas 2-22) lost to **South Africa** 94/3 in 14.2 overs (D van Niekerk 71*) by seven wickets. *PoM:* Dane van Niekerk.

New Wanderers Stadium, Johannesburg, February 3: Sri Lanka 105 in 19.4 overs (Shashikala Siriwardene 38, Chamari Athapaththu 20; Sune Luus 5-14, Marizanne Kapp 3-17) lost to **South Africa** 107/8 in 19.5 overs (Dane van Niekerk 33; S Siriwardene 2-12, Inoka Ranaweera 2-15) by two wickets. *PoM:* Sune Luus.

SuperSport Park, Centurion, February 6: South Africa 163/5 in 20 overs (Dane van Niekerk 38, Tazmin Brits 36) beat **Sri Lanka** 124/8 in 20 overs (Chamari Athapaththu 43, Shashikala Siriwardene 29; Nadine de Klerk 3-27, Shabnim Ismail 2-11) by 39 runs. *PoM:* Sune Luus. *PoS:* Dane van Niekerk.

Tour matches

North-West University No.1 Ground, Potchefstroom, February 8: South Africa 197/9 in 50 overs (Mignon du Preez 78, Andrie Steyn 24; Hanno Swanepoel 3-14, Dylan Niemack 3-27) lost to **North West Under-17s** 221 in 44.3 overs (Caleb Seleka 57, Tebogo Mathe 55; Tumi Sekhukhune 3-67) by two wickets.

North-West University No.1 Ground, Potchefstroom, February 9: Sri Lanka 255/8 in 50 overs (Prasadani Weerakkody 64, Harshitha Madavi 59; E Olivier 2-56) beat **North West** 93 in 28.3 overs (Sinalo Jafta 20; Inoka Ranaweera 4-38, Nilakshi de Silva 2-4) by 162 runs.

ODI series (3): South Africa 3 Sri Lanka 0

Senwes Park, Potchefstroom, February 11: South Africa 225/7 in 48 overs (Dane van Niekerk 102, Andrie Steyn 75; Oshadi Ranasinghe 3-40, Udeshika Prabodhani 2-39) beat **Sri Lanka** 218/9 in 48 overs (Shashikala Siriwardene 49, Prasadani Weerakkody 47; Masabata Klaas 3-46, D van Niekerk 2-26) by seven runs. *PoM:* Dane van Niekerk.

Senwes Park, Potchefstroom, February 14: South Africa 268/7 in 50 overs (Marizanne Kapp 69*, Laura Wolvaardt 64; Kavisha Dilhari 2-34) lost to **Sri Lanka** 231 in 46.2 overs (Chamari Athapaththu 94, Anushka Sanjeewani 46; M Kapp 2-41, Tumi Sekhukhune 2-55) by 30 runs. (DLS method). *PoM:* Marizanne Kapp.

Senwes Park, Potchefstroom, February 17: Sri Lanka 139 in 44.2 overs (Anushka Sanjeewani 28, Harshitha Madavi 22; Sune Luus 4-30, Nadine de Klerk 2-30) lost to **South Africa** 141/4 in 38.2 overs (Mignon du Preez 61*, Lara Goodall 25; Inoka Ranaweera 3-23) by six wickets. *PoM:* Mignon du Preez. *PoS:* Andrie Steyn.

	ODIs	**T20Is**
Best batter	Andrie Steyn (115 runs, 3 matches)	Dane van Niekerk (142 runs, 3 matches)
Best bowler	Sune Luus (5 wickets, 2 matches)	Sune Luus (6 wickets, 2 matches)

New Zealand in Australia

Jonassen returns to dominate Rose Bowl

Determined to end their season on a high, Australia swept past New Zealand to extend their 20-year domination in the Rose Bowl trophy.

Jess Jonassen, the left-arm spinner who had spent much of the season recovering from a knee injury, and then warming the bench, made a roaring return to the XI in the absence of Sophie Molineux (shoulder injury). In the first ODI, the 26-year-old contributed a useful 32-ball 36 to push Australia's score past the 240-run mark, before she ripped through New Zealand's lower-middle order to hand the hosts a thrilling win. She followed that up with a career-best 5 for 27 in the second match — a spell that followed Ellyse Perry's long-awaited maiden ODI century. Jonassen's series haul of nine wickets came at an average of 12.22 and a strike rate of 18.6. She was well backed up by Georgia Wareham, Megan Schutt, Perry and Ashleigh Gardner who took 14 wickets between them. Wareham, the leg-spinner, was particularly impressive with her ability to extract turn on rather unhelpful surfaces.

For the visitors, Amy Satterthwaite and Sophie Devine held New Zealand's batting together, but failed to find much support. Australia on the other hand, managed to share the load: Perry, whose 167 runs came at an average of 167, Rachael Haynes, who revelled in her role as opener collecting 129 runs, Alyssa Healy (96 runs) and Beth Mooney, who averaged 45 in the middle order, all made crucial contributions.

Most runs: Amy Satterthwaite (New Zealand) (178 runs in 3 matches)
Most wickets: Jess Jonassen (Australia) (9 wickets in 3 matches)

ODI series (3): Australia 3 New Zealand 0

WACA Ground, Perth, February 22: Australia 241 in 49.4 overs (Rachael Haynes 67, Jess Jonassen 36; Sophie Devine 3-32, Hayley Jensen 2-34) beat **New Zealand** 236/9 in 50 overs (Amy Satterthwaite 92, Katie Perkins 48; J Jonassen 4-43, Ellyse Perry 2-39) by five runs. *PoM:* Jess Jonassen.

Karen Rolton Oval, Adelaide, February 24: Australia 247/7 in 50 overs (Ellyse Perry 107*, Alyssa Healy 46; Amelia Kerr 3-30, Anna Peterson 2-47) beat **New Zealand** 152 in 38 overs (Sophie Devine 47, Amy Satterthwaite 37; Jess Jonassen 5-27, Megan Schutt 2-33) by 95 runs. *PoM:* Ellyse Perry.

Tour match: Drummoyne Oval, Sydney, February 28: New Zealand 323/7 in 50 overs (Lauren Down 107, Katey Martin 76; Heather Graham 2-48) beat **Australia Governor-General's XI** 157 in 38.2 overs (Anabel Sutherland 32, Erin Burns 28; Anna Peterson 3-28, Amelia Kerr 2-23) by 166 runs.

Junction Oval, Melbourne, March 3: New Zealand 231/8 in 50 overs (Sophie Devine 58, Amy Satterthwaite 49; Ashleigh Gardner 3-49, Georgia Wareham 2-36) lost to **Australia** 233/3 in 47.5 overs (Ellyse Perry 54*, Meg Lanning 48; Leigh Kasperek 2-54) by seven wickets. *PoM:* Ashleigh Gardner. *PoS:* Jess Jonassen.

England in Sri Lanka

Jones makes it ten in a row

Amy Jones smashed three fifties in a row. — *SLC*

Amy Jones smashed three consecutive fifties as England completed a comfortable 3-0 series win over Sri Lanka in the three-match ODI series, thereby rising to second place in the ICC Women's Championship table. Jones took her chance at the top of the order accumulating 209 runs at a strike-rate of 124.40. She was well supported by Tammy Beaumont, her opening partner, who finished with 141 runs.

Sri Lanka were never in the hunt at any point, the England bowlers keeping them on a tight leash throughout. Anya Shrubsole, Alex Hartley and Kate Cross picked up 15 wickets between them.

The T20I series was equally one-sided as England completed ten consecutive victories across formats. Shrubsole surpassed Danielle Hazell (85) to become England's highest wicket-taker in T20Is, while Beaumont became the fifth England batter to score 1000 runs in T20Is — both players ticking off their respective milestones in the first match. Having secured the series with a commanding win in the second game, England proceeded to smash 204 for 2 in the final T20I — their highest ever total in T20Is in Sri Lanka — to finish the series on a high.

Tour match
P Sara Oval, Colombo, March 13: England 319/7 in 50 overs (Lauren Winfield 80, Heather

Knight 67; Madhushika Meththananda 2-58) beat **Sri Lanka Emerging Team** 166 in 40 overs (Harshitha Madavi 59, Hansima Karunaratne 28; H Knight 4-13, Laura Marsh 2-34) by 153 runs.

ODI series (3): England 3 Sri Lanka 0

Mahinda Rajapaksa International Stadium, Hambantota, March 16: England 331/7 in 50 overs (Natalie Sciver 93, Amy Jones 79; Oshadi Ranasinghe 2-71) beat **Sri Lanka** 159/8 in 40 overs (O Ranasinghe 51*, Nilakshi de Silva 45; Katherine Brunt 3-24, Kate Cross 2-33) by 154 runs. (DLS method).

Mahinda Rajapaksa International Stadium, Hambantota, March 18: Sri Lanka 187/9 in 50 overs (Harshitha Madavi 42, Hansima Karunaratne 28; Alex Hartley 3-36, Anya Shrubsole 2-21) lost to **England** 188/4 in 33.3 overs (Amy Jones 54, Lauren Winfield 44; Inoshi Priyadarshini 3-45) by six wickets.

FTZ Sports Complex, Katunayake, March 21: Sri Lanka 174 in 50 overs (Harshitha Madavi 42, Oshadi Ranasinghe 29; Kate Cross 2-25, Anya Shrubsole 2-30) lost to **England** 177/2 in 26.1 overs (Amy Jones 76, Tammy Beaumont 63; Shashikala Siriwardene 2-56) by eight wickets.

T20I series (3): England 3 Sri Lanka 0

Colts Cricket Club Ground, Colombo, March 24: Sri Lanka 94 in 19 overs (Oshadi Ranasinghe 20; Linsey Smith 3-18, Anya Shrubsole 2-20) lost to **England** 95/2 in 14.2 overs (Tammy Beaumont 50) by eight wickets.

Colts Cricket Club Ground, Colombo, March 26: Sri Lanka 108/6 in 20 overs (Chamari Athapaththu 24; Katherine Brunt 2-31) lost to **England** 109/2 in 13.5 overs (Danielle Wyatt 37, Amy Jones 36; Shashikala Siriwardene 2-26) by eight wickets.

P Sara Oval, Colombo, March 28: England 204/2 in 20 overs (Amy Jones 57, Danielle Wyatt 51; Oshadi Ranasinghe 2-28) beat **Sri Lanka** 108/6 in 20 overs (Hansima Karunaratne 44*; Kate Cross 2-20) by 96 runs.

	ODIs	T20Is
Best batter	Amy Jones (209 runs, 3 matches)	Amy Jones (111 runs, 3 matches)
Best bowler	Anya Shrubsole (5 wickets, 3 matches)	Linsey Smith (4 wickets, 3 matches)

Pakistan in South Africa

Lee, Dar star in see-saw contests

There was little to tell between the teams. After the ODI series was drawn 1-1, South Africa came from 0-1, then 1-2, to clinch the T20I series 3-2 — though it must be mentioned here that they missed the services of Dane van Niekerk, their regular captain and probably their most important cricketer, for the series.

Sana Mir got the tour off to a spectacular start. Her 4 for 11 helped Pakistan skittle the hosts for 63 in the first ODI, their second-lowest score. South Africa pulled one back in the second match and put up 265 for 6 in the third. Javeria Khan and Aliya Riaz led the Pakistan chase. They needed 11 off the last four balls with their last wicket standing, but Nashra Sandhu's six off Masabata Klaas in the penultimate ball ensured a tie.

All five T20Is were won by sides batting second, the targets varying between 120 and 173. Lizelle Lee made a strong return after complaints about her fitness. She was Player of the Match in all three games South Africa won, making three half-centuries in a row. Nida Dar's all-round performance (192 runs, strike-rate 152, five wickets) helped her clinch the series award.

Tour matches

North-West University No. 1 Ground, Potchefstroom, May 1: Pakistan Women 232/8 in 50 overs (Aliya Riaz 50, Bismah Maroof 39; Rameem Shamim 2-34, Hanno Swanepoel 2-37) beat **North West Under-17s** 96 in 27.3 overs (Waldo Kemp 25; Nashra Sandhu 3-7, Nida Dar 2-7) by 136 runs.

North-West University No. 1 Ground, Potchefstroom, May 3: North West Under-17s 191 in 38.2 overs (Mohamed Sidat 81, C Bester 34; Sana Fatima 4-60, Sana Mir 2-21) lost to **Pakistan Women** 192/4 in 34.2 overs (Umaima Sohail 53*, Kainat Imtiaz 39*; Tebogo Mathe 2/42) by six wickets.

ODI series (3): South Africa 1 Pakistan 1

Senwes Park, Potchefstroom, May 6: South Africa 63 in 22.5 overs (Sana Mir 4-11, Nashra Sandhu 2-8) lost to **Pakistan** 66/2 in 14.4 overs (Javeria Khan 34*) by eight wickets. *PoM:* Sana Mir.

Senwes Park, Potchefstroom, May 9: Pakistan 147 in 42 overs (Nahida Khan 37, Bismah Maroof 32; Masabata Klaas 3-27, Tumi Sekhukhune 2-24) lost to **South Africa** 148/2 in 36.4 overs (Laura Wolvaardt 74*, Lizelle Lee 40) by eight wickets. *PoM:* Masabata Klaas.

Willowmoore Park, Benoni, May 12: South Africa Women 265/6 in 50 overs (Sune Luus 80, Lizelle Lee 57; Aliya Riaz 2-49) tied with **Pakistan Women** 265/9 in 50 overs (Javeria Khan 74; A Riaz 71; Masabata Klaas 3-55, Marizanne Kapp 2-57). *PoM:* Aliya Riaz.

T20I series (5): South Africa 3 Pakistan 2

LD de Villiers Park, Pretoria, May 15: South Africa 119/7 in 20 overs (Chloe Tryon 43; Sana Mir 3-14, Nida Dar 2-30) lost to **Pakistan** 120/3 in 18 overs (Bismah Maroof 53*, N Dar 53) by eight wickets. *PoM:* Nida Dar.

City Oval, Pietermaritzburg, May 18: Pakistan 128/5 in 20 overs (Bismah Maroof 63*; Sune Luus 2-29) lost to **South Africa** 129/2 in 19.5 overs (Marizanne Kapp 56*, Lizelle Lee 56) by eight wickets. *PoM:* Lizelle Lee.

City Oval, Pietermaritzburg, May 19: South Africa 138/3 in 20 overs (Tazmin Brits 70*, Nadine de Klerk 36) lost to **Pakistan** 139/6 in 19.4 overs (Iram Javed 55, Nida Dar 32; Moseline Daniels 3-13, Shabnim Ismail 2-12) by four wickets. *PoM:* Iram Javed.

Willowmoore Park, Benoni, May 12: Pakistan 172/5 in 20 overs (Nida Dar 75, Bismah Maroof 37; Shabnim Ismail 2-22) lost to **South Africa** 174/6 in 19.1 overs (Lizelle Lee 60; Fatima Sana 3-27) by four wickets. *PoM:* Lizelle Lee.

Willowmoore Park, Benoni, May 12: Pakistan 125/5 in 20 overs (Nida Dar 28, Aliya Riaz 26) lost to **South Africa** 127/1 in 15.1 overs (Lizelle Lee 75*, Nadine de Klerk 37*) by nine wickets. *PoM:* Lizelle Lee. *PoS:* Nida Dar.

	ODIs	**T20Is**
Most runs	Laura Wolvaardt (South Africa) (134 runs, 3 matches)	Lizelle Lee (South Africa) (193 runs, 5 matches)
Most wickets	Masabata Klaas (South Africa) (6 wickets, 3 matches)	Shabnim Ismail (South Africa) (5 wickets, 3 matches)

West Indies in Ireland

T20I series (3): West Indies 3 Ireland 0

YMCA Cricket Club, Dublin, May 26: West Indies 139/4 in 20 overs (Stafanie Taylor 75) beat **Ireland Women** 75 in 18.4 overs (Kim Garth 46; Afy Fletcher 4-14, Chinelle Henry 2-15) by 64 runs.
Sydney Parade, Dublin, May 28: West Indies 157/6 in 20 overs (Stacy-Ann King 34, Hayley Matthews 33; Kim Garth 3-22) beat **Ireland** 112/6 in 20 overs (K Garth 51*; Mary Waldron 25; S-A King 2-15, Afy Fletcher 2-20) by 45 runs.
Sydney Parade, Dublin, May 29: West Indies 188/1 in 20 overs (Hayley Matthews 107*, Chedean Nation 63*) beat **Ireland** 116/3 in 20 overs (Mary Waldron 55*, Kim Garth 45; Stafanie Taylor 2-19) by 72 runs. *PoS:* Hayley Matthews.

Most runs: Hayley Matthews (West Indies) (143 runs, 3 matches)
Most wickets: Afy Fletcher (West Indies) (6 wickets, 3 matches)

West Indies in England

Jones, bowlers sweep Caribbean visitors

Fresh from their whitewash of Ireland, West Indies were in for a rude shock in England. They lost all three ODIs and the only T20I where play was possible. What made it worse was the margins of defeat: 208 runs, 121 runs, 135 runs and 42 runs.

England put up 318 for 9 in the first ODI, the highest total against West Indies by any side. The visitors' bowling was wayward, and taking full advantage, Amy Jones and Heather Knight raced to respective nineties. The West Indian middle order then crumbled against the slow bowlers.

Rain hit the next two ODIs. Anya Shrubsole threw her bat around for a 16-ball unbeaten 32 before removing both openers to seal the series, while Jones played her second big innings in the third match.

Even in their preferred 20-over format, the West Indies' fielding was below par, and Danni Wyatt, dropped by Chinelle Henry, made a delightful 81. They reached 96 for 3 in the 13th over in pursuit of 181, but their chase was derailed by a Katherine Brunt double-strike.

ODI series (3): England 3 West Indies 0

Grace Road, Leicester, June 6: England 318/9 in 50 overs (Heather Knight 94, Amy Jones 91; Hayley Matthews 4-57, Afy Fletcher 2-59) beat **West Indies** 110 in 36 overs (Chedean Nation 42*; Sophie Ecclestone 3-30, Laura Marsh 3-30) by 208 runs. *PoM:* Amy Jones.

New Road, Worcester, June 9: England 233/7 in 50 overs (Tammy Beaumont 61, Nat Sciver 35; Afy Fletcher 3-48) beat **West Indies** 87/6 in 28 overs (Shemaine Campbelle 29*; Kate Cross 2-4, Anya Shrubsole 2-12) by 121 runs (DLS method). *PoM:* Anya Shrubsole.

County Ground, Chelmsford, June 13: England 258/4 in 50 overs (Amy Jones 80, Sarah Taylor 70; Hayley Matthews 2-52) beat **West Indies** 131 in 37.4 overs (Kycia Knight 38, Stacy-Ann King 26; Kate Cross 2-16, Sophie Ecclestone 2-27) by 135 runs (DLS method). *PoM:* Amy Jones.

T20I series (3): England 1 West Indies 0

County Ground, Northampton, June 18: England v **West Indies**. No toss.

County Ground, Northampton, June 21: England 180/6 in 20 overs (Danni Wyatt 81, Amy Jones 37) beat **West Indies** 138/9 in 20 overs (Stacy-Ann King 43, Chedean Nation 32; Linsey Smith 2-22, Katherine Brunt 2-22) by 42 runs. *PoM:* Danni Wyatt.

County Ground, Derby, June 25: England v **West Indies**. No toss.

	ODIs	T20Is
Most runs	Amy Jones (England) (189 runs, 3 matches)	Danni Wyatt (England) (89 runs, 1 match)
Most wickets	Matthews (West Indies) (7 wickets, 3 matches)	Katherine Brunt (England) (2 wickets, 1 match)

OTHER INTERNATIONALS 2017-18

Deandra Dottin became the first woman to score two T20I centuries when she smashed 112 off 67 balls in the final T20I against Sri Lanka. — *CWI*

Sri Lanka in West Indies

Dottin makes history in whitewash

West Indies kicked off their ICC Women's Championship campaign in style, blanking Sri Lanka 3-0 in the ODI series before completing a double whitewash with 3-0 in the T20Is.

Stafanie Taylor led the way with a fabulous all-round performance in the ODIs, scoring 117 runs and taking eight wickets. Her off-spin took centre stage in the very first ODI, when she picked up three wickets to help dismiss the visitors for 136. Sri Lanka were unable to tackle West Indies' spin quartet of Afy Fletcher, Hayley Matthews, Anisa Mohammed and Taylor, who accounted for 21 out of 30 wickets in the ODIs, and 15 out of 22 wickets in the T20Is.

The T20I series proved as difficult for Sri Lanka, as they were unable to challenge West Indies' powerful batting line-up. Chasing 141 in the first match, they limped to 69 for 7 in reply. Although their graph seemed to show a slight upward turn in the second game, with the score at 84 for 3 in pursuit of 155, Fletcher, the leg-spinner, dismantled the middle order, picking up five wickets to trigger a collapse and seal the series for the hosts.

In the final match, Deandra Dottin became the first woman to score two T20I centuries when she smashed 112. Her 67-ball innings included nine fours and five towering sixes, and helped West Indies amass a total of 159 for 6.

Although Sri Lanka never came close to chasing down the target, they did put up their most impressive performance with the bat; Rebeca Vandort and Shashikala Siriwardene had identical scores of 50. There was not much else for the tourists to cheer about through the tour. Vandort (128 runs), the wicket-keeper batter, and Inoka Ranaweera (nine wickets), the left-arm spinner, were their best performers.

ODI series (3): Sri Lanka 0 West Indies 3

Brian Lara Stadium, Tarouba, Trinidad, October 11: Sri Lanka 136 in 49.4 overs (Yasoda Mendis 34, Dilani Manodara 28*; Hayley Matthews 3-18, Stafanie Taylor 3-24) lost to **West Indies** 138/4 in 39 overs (Merissa Aguilleira 32*, Chedean Nation 24; Inoka Ranaweera 2-27) by six wickets. *PoM:* Hayley Matthews.

Brian Lara Stadium, Tarouba, Trinidad, October 13: Sri Lanka 162 in 46.3 overs (Yasoda Mendis 34, Chamari Athapaththu 31; Afy Fletcher 3-24, Anisa Mohammed 2-16) lost to **West Indies** 163/3 in 39.4 overs (Stafanie Taylor 60*, Deandra Dottin 37*) by seven wickets. *PoM:* Stafanie Taylor.

Brian Lara Stadium, Tarouba, Trinidad, October 15: West Indies 182/8 in 45 overs (Stafanie Taylor 55, Hayley Matthews 41; Shashikala Siriwardene 3-26, Inoka Ranaweera 2-24) beat **Sri Lanka** 142 in 40.4 overs (Dilani Manodara 42, Rebeca Vandort 34; S Taylor 3-29, Shakera Selman 3-30) by 40 runs. *PoM:* Stafanie Taylor.

T20I series (3): Sri Lanka 0 West Indies 3

Stanford Cricket Ground, Coolidge, Antigua, October 19: West Indies 140/4 in 20 overs (Hayley Matthews 37, Stafanie Taylor 31; Inoka Ranaweera 2-35) beat **Sri Lanka** 69/7 in 20 overs (Shakera Selman 2-6, Anisa Mohammed 2-14) by 71 runs.

Stanford Cricket Ground, Coolidge, Antigua, October 21: West Indies 154/6 in 20 overs (Stafanie Taylor 49, Deandra Dottin 27; Inoka Ranaweera 2-47) beat **Sri Lanka** 107 in 19.4 overs (Chamari Athapaththu 30, Yasoda Mendis 22; Afy Fletcher 5-12, Hayley Matthews 2-25) by 47 runs. *PoM:* Afy Fletcher.

Stanford Cricket Ground, Coolidge, Antigua, October 22: West Indies 159/6 in 20 overs (Deandra Dottin 112, Hayley Matthews 34; Ama Kanchana 2-24) lost to **Sri Lanka** 128/5 in 20 overs (Rebeca Vandort 50, Shashikala Siriwardene 50; Hayley Matthews 4-18) by 31 runs. *PoM:* Deandra Dottin. *PoS:* Deandra Dottin.

	ODIs	T20Is
Best batter	Stafanie Taylor (117 runs, 3 matches)	DeandraDottin (154 runs, 3 matches)
Best bowler	Stafanie Taylor (8 wickets, 3 matches)	Hayley Matthews (7 wickets, 3 matches)

England in Australia

Perry, Schutt sparkle as Australia retain urn

Eager to shake off a disappointing World Cup campaign where they had lost to India in the semi-finals, Australia came hard at England in the multi-format Women's Ashes series at home. Despite conceding the T20I series and both teams finishing with eight points each, the hosts, as defending champions, maintained their hold on the wooden ball.

Without the services of their skipper Meg Lanning, who missed out on six months of cricket after having a shoulder surgery, Australia were led astutely by Rachael Haynes. Haynes — a bit of a left-field choice as skipper — quickly dispelled any doubts of her ability with the bat, smashing a belligerent half-century in the second ODI to give Australia an early lead in the series. Megan Schutt, who picked up 18 wickets, the most in the series, bowled intelligently and got the ball to swing at will. Her big, hooping in-swingers had the England top order tied in knots, and their inability to break free meant Australia were often not chasing very many.

The day-night Test match at North Sydney Oval proved to be Ellyse Perry's moment to shine. After several failed attempts through her career, the prolific all-rounder finally converted a fifty to a century, notching up her maiden international hundred. It went on to be a mammoth unbeaten 213, the highest Test score by an Australian woman and the third-highest Test score overall. Perry managed 351 runs through the series, and was closely followed by Heather Knight, who was often England's saviour with the bat, with 335 runs.

With the Ashes still wide open heading into the T20I leg, it was Beth Mooney's turn to step up for the hosts. Having lost her place in the ODI XI with Alyssa Healy being promoted to open the batting, the left-hander, determined to prove a point, smashed an unbeaten 86 in the first T20I to help Australia retain the Ashes. She backed up her half-century with another stunning knock of 117 in the final match of the series, but her efforts were trumped by a spectacular 56-ball 100 from Danielle Wyatt, which helped England chase down 179.

England showed flashes of brilliance through the series, but an inconsistent top order and no real support for Katherine Brunt with the ball meant they struggled to put consistent pressure on the Australians.

ODI series (3): Australia 2 England 1

Allan Border Field, Brisbane, October 22: England 228/9 in 50 overs (Lauren Winfield 48, Natalie Sciver 36; Ashleigh Gardner 3-47, Megan Schutt 2-44) lost to **Australia** 231/8 in 49.1 overs (Alex Blackwell 67*, Elyse Villani 38; Alex Hartley 2-40, Katherine Brunt 2-47) by two wickets. *PoM:* Alex Blackwell.
International Sports Stadium, Coffs Harbour, October 26: Australia 296/6 in 50 overs (Rachel Haynes 89*, Ellyse Perry 67; Jenny Gunn 4-55) beat **England** 209 in 42.2 overs

After 181 international appearances and an ODI average above 50, Ellyse Perry got her long-awaited maiden hundred, in the Ashes Test. She went on to make it a double. — *Getty Images*

(Katherine Brunt 52, Fran Wilson 37; Megan Schutt 4-26, Kristen Beams 2-38) by 75 runs. *PoM:* Rachel Haynes.

International Sports Stadium, Coffs Harbour, October 29: England 284/8 in 50 overs (Heather Knight 88*, Tammy Beaumont 74; Megan Schutt 4-44, Ellyse Perry 2-51) beat **Australia** 257/9 in 48 overs (Alyssa Healy 71, Nicole Bolton 62; Alex Hartley 3-45, Natalie Sciver 2-24) by 20 runs (DLS method). *PoM:* Heather Knight.

Tour matches

Manuka Oval, Canberra, November 3-5: Australia 272/8 in 78.1 overs (Beth Mooney 118, Ellyse Perry 58; Haley Jensen 5-26) and 287/9 decl in 94 overs (Elyse Villani 70, Alex Blackwell 45; Tahlia McGrath 3-8, Erin Osborne 2-33) drew with **Australian Capital Territory** 290/7 in 81 overs (Angela Reakes 103*, Marizanne Kapp 61; E Perry 2-45) and 68/3 in 41 overs (H Jensen 24*, E Osborne 23; Megan Schutt 2-9).

Blacktown International Sportspark, Sydney, November 3-5: England 231 in 71 overs (Lauren Winfield 82, Tammy Beaumont 28; Lauren Smith 3-18, Sophie Molineux 3-27) and 305/7 decl in 96 overs (Sarah Taylor 85*, Fran Wilson 35; Piepa Cleary 2-36) drew with **Cricket Australia XI** 271 in 93 overs (Naomi Stalenberg 114, Georgia Redmayne 36; Katherine Brunt 4-37, Kate Cross 2-36) and 182/7 in 40 overs (Nicola Carey 52, Heather Graham 40; Heather Knight 3-12, Laura Marsh 2-44).

Test match: Draw

North Sydney Oval, Sydney, November 9-12: England 280 in 116 overs (Tammy Beaumont 70, Heather Knight 62; Ellyse Perry 3-59, Tahlia McGrath 2-45) and 206/2 in 105 overs (H Knight 79*, Georgia Elwiss 41*) drew with **Australia** 448/9 decl in 166 overs (E Perry 213*, T McGrath 47; Sophie Ecclestone 3-107, Laura Marsh 3-109). *PoM:* Ellyse Perry.

Tour match

Drummoyne Oval, Sydney, November 15: England 146/5 in 20 overs (Sarah Taylor 93*; Erin Fazackerley 2-13) beat **Australia Governor-General's XI** 56 in 15.5 overs (Naomi Stalenberg 20; Jenny Gunn 2-4, Natalie Sciver 2-9) by 90 runs. *PoM:* Sarah Taylor.

T20I series (3): Australia 1 England 2

North Sydney Oval, Sydney, November 17: England 132/9 in 20 overs (Danielle Wyatt 50, Natalie Sciver 26; Megan Schutt 4-22, Ellyse Perry 2-26) lost to **Australia** 134/4 in 15.5 overs (Beth Mooney 86*) by six wickets. *PoM:* Beth Mooney.

Manuka Oval, Canberra, November 19: England 152/6 in 20 overs (Natalie Sciver 40, Katherine Brunt 32*; Megan Schutt 2-16) beat **Australia** 112 in 18 overs (Alyssa Healy 24; Jenny Gunn 4-13, K Brunt 2-10) by 40 runs. *PoM:* Katherine Brunt.

Manuka Oval, Canberra, November 21: Australia 178/2 in 20 overs (Beth Mooney 117*, Ellyse Perry 22*) lost to **England** 181/6 in 19 overs (Danielle Wyatt 100, Heather Knight 51; Jess Jonassen 2-25, Delissa Kimmince 2-30) by four wickets. *PoM:* Danielle Wyatt. *PoS:* Heather Knight.

	ODIs	Test	T20Is
Best batter	Alyssa Healy (145 runs, 3 matches)	Ellyse Perry (213 runs, 1 match)	Beth Mooney (220 runs, 3 matches)
Best bowler	Megan Schutt (10 wickets, 3 matches)	Tahlia McGrath (3 wickets, 1 match)	Megan Schutt (6 wickets, 3 matches)

New Zealand v Pakistan in UAE

Hosts make history, White Ferns win series

New Zealand registered a double series victory over Pakistan in the United Arab Emirates, winning a hard-fought ODI series 2-1, and sealing a comfortable 4-0 victory in the T20I series.

Pakistan pushed the visitors to the brink in the ODIs, putting up spirited performances across the three matches. They fell agonisingly short in the first ODI, suffering a dramatic collapse triggered by New Zealand's spin duo of Amelia Kerr (2 for 36) and Leigh Kasperek (2 for 35) to lose 5 for 15 at the back end of the innings, to lose by only eight runs.

Having conceded the series with a poor showing in the second match, the hosts bounced back strongly in the final ODI to register a historic five-wicket win — their first ODI victory against New Zealand in 13 attempts. Sana Mir, the wily off-spinner, was the architect of that victory, with her spell of 4 for 25 dismantling the top order.

For New Zealand, Sophie Devine, who was promoted to open the batting in the absence of Rachel Priest, grabbed her opportunity, smashing 167 runs, including her second ODI century: a 119-ball 103 in the first ODI.

The T20I series was more one-sided. New Zealand's powerful top order bludgeoned Pakistan into submission. Devine continued her good run at the top of the order, amassing 158 runs at a strike-rate of 162.88. She was well supported by Suzie Bates, the New Zealand skipper, who collected 123 runs, including an important half-century in a low-scoring third T20I. Hannah Rowe, the tall fast bowler, who mainly warmed the bench through the ODI series, took her opportunities in the T20Is, taking six wickets at an average of 6.66.

Pakistan's batters struggled to make much of an impression. Nahida Khan (89 runs) was the only one whose runs came at a strike-rate of over 100.

ODI series (3): Pakistan 1 New Zealand 2

Sharjah Cricket Association Stadium, October 31: New Zealand 240/9 in 50 overs (Sophie Devine 103, Suzie Bates 36; Sana Mir 3-33, Javeria Khan 2-36) beat **Pakistan** 232 in 48.3 overs (J Khan 55, Nahida Khan 51; Holly Huddleston 2-32, Leigh Kasperek 2-35) by eight runs. *PoM:* Sophie Devine.

Sharjah Cricket Association Stadium, November 2: Pakistan 147 in 49.1 overs (Nahida Kahn 39, Bismah Maroof 36; Amelia Kerr 3-35, Hannah Rowe 2-17) lost to **New Zealand** 148/3 in 24 overs (Sophie Devine 62, Suzie Bates 33; Javeria Khan 2-6) by seven wickets. *PoM:* Sophie Devine.

Sharjah Cricket Association Stadium, November 5: New Zealand 155 in 43.4 overs (Samantha Curtis 50, Maddy Green 26; Sana Mir 4-25, Sadia Yousuf 2-23) lost to **Pakistan** 156/5 in 48.5 overs (Bismah Maroof 36*, Sidra Ameen 32; Anna Peterson 2-25) by five wickets. *PoM:* Sana Mir.

T20I series (4): Pakistan 0 New Zealand 4

Sharjah Cricket Association Stadium, November 8: New Zealand 147/8 in 20 overs (Katey Martin 46, Sophie Devine 41; Sadia Yousuf 3-30) beat **Pakistan** 132/7 in 20 overs (Nahida Khan 34, Javeria Khan 27; Thamsyn Newton 2-22) by 15 runs. *PoM:* Katey Martin.

Sharjah Cricket Association Stadium, November 9: New Zealand 150/8 in 20 overs (Sophie Devine 70, Suzie Bates 52; Javeria Khan 2-23, Sadia Yousuf 2-37) beat **Pakistan** 111/7 in 20 overs (Aliya Riaz 23, Nahida Khan 22; Amy Satterthwaite 2-18) by 39 runs. *PoM:* Sophie Devine.

Sharjah Cricket Association Stadium, November 12: New Zealand 126/4 in 20 overs (Suzie Bates 65*, Katey Martin 25; Natalia Pervaiz 2-12) beat **Pakistan** 84 in 19 overs (Nahida Khan 23; Hanna Rowe 3-18, Amelia Kerr 2-8) by 42 runs. *PoM:* Suzie Bates.

Sharjah Cricket Association Stadium, November 14: Pakistan 89/8 in 20 overs (Javeria Khan 36; Hannah Rowe 3-22, Holly Huddleston 2-16) lost to **New Zealand** 93/3 in 11 overs (Sophie Devine 41, Amy Satterthwaite 35; Aiman Anwar 2-19) by seven wickets. *PoM:* Sophie Devine. *PoS:* Sophie Devine.

	ODIs	T20Is
Best batter	Sophie Devine (167 runs, 3 matches)	Sophie Devine (158 runs, 4 matches)
Best bowler	Sana Mir (7 wickets, 3 matches)	Hannah Rowe (6 wickets, 2 matches

West Indies in New Zealand

Devine, Kasperek blank tourists

New Zealand whitewashed an inconsistent West Indies in a three match ODI series, before completing the double series victory with a 4-0 win in the T20I series. The visitors started their tour on a spirited note, going down by just one run in pursuit of New Zealand's 278 in the first ODI. Sophie Devine scored her third ODI century, and second at the top of the order, to lead her team's charge before Leigh Kasperek, the off-spinner, defended ten runs in the final over to deny West Indies victory.

That was as close as West Indies would get to a win on tour, as New Zealand overpowered them in the next two matches. Suzie Bates smashed an 86-ball 101 in the second match and followed it up with 89 in the final ODI, taking her three-match tally to 234, marginally behind Devine's 261 runs.

Stafanie Taylor, the West Indies skipper, was the only opposition batter to show any fight, scoring 202 runs at an average of 67.33 including two half-centuries. New Zealand's 3-0 victory meant they climbed to the top of the Championship table with ten points in six matches.

Kasperek, who picked up seven wickets through the ODIs, continued her good run with the ball in the T20I series. The off-spinner spun a web around the visitors; her slow, well-flighted deliveries brought her ten wickets at an average of 9.8.

The T20I series also gave Katey Martin, the wicket-keeper, an opportunity to consolidate her position in the middle order. The right hander swept, cut and slogged her way to 180 runs at a strike-rate of 141.73, her belligerence only bettered by Devine whose 89 runs came at 171.15.

While New Zealand had the upper hand for a major part of the series, West Indies came close to victory in the third T20I, only to fall short by a single run, once again. This time, with five runs required off the final over, Anna Peterson, the off-spinner, picked up two wickets and inflicted a run out to maintain the home team's clean sheet and make sure West Indies left without having won a single international game on tour.

Tour match

Bert Sutcliffe Oval, Lincoln, March 1: Canterbury 216/5 in 50 overs (Evelyn Jones 98, Kate Broadmore 84; Afy Fletcher 3-44) lost to **West Indies** 220/3 in 34 overs (Kycia Knight 70*, Hayley Matthews 61; Gabby Sullivan 2-26) by seven wickets.

ODI series (3): New Zealand 3 West Indies 0

Bert Sutcliffe Oval, Lincoln, March 4: New Zealand 278/9 in 50 overs (Sophie Devine 108, Suzie Bates 44; Stafanie Taylor 3-54, Afy Fletcher 3-55) beat **West Indies** 277/9 in 50 overs (S Taylor 90, Kyshona Knight 44*; Holly Huddleston 2-40, Amelia Kerr 2-49) by 1 run. *PoM:* Sophie Devine.

Bert Sutcliffe Oval, Lincoln, March 8: West Indies 194 in 48.1 overs (Stafanie Taylor 86, Chedean Nation 35; Leigh Kasperek 4-44, Lea Tahuhu 3-42) lost to **New Zealand** 195/2 in 30.4 overs (Suzie Bates 101*, Sophie Devine 80; Afy Fletcher 2-47) by eight wickets. *PoM:* Suzie Bates.

Hagley Oval, Christchurch, March 11: New Zealand 310/5 in 50 overs (Suzie Bates 89, Sophie Devine 73*; Deandra Dottin 2-58) beat **West Indies** 105 in 34.5 overs (Stafanie Taylor 26, S Devine 3-24, Holly Huddleston 2-19) by 205 runs. *PoM:* Sophie Devine.

T20I series (5): New Zealand 4 West Indies 0

Bay Oval, Mount Maunganui, March 14: New Zealand 167/6 in 20 overs (Katey Martin 54, Suzie Bates 49; Deandra Dottin 2-23) beat **West Indies** 159/6 in 20 overs (Hayley Matthews 53, Stafanie Taylor 51*; Leigh Kasperek 3-35, Sophie Devine 2-27) by 8 runs. *PoM:* Katey Martin.

Bay Oval, Mount Maunganui, March 16: New Zealand 185/3 in 20 overs (Amy Satterthwaite 71*, Katey Martin 65) beat **West Indies** 79/8 in 20 overs (Kyshona Knight 20; Sophie Devine 3-12, Leigh Kasperek 2-13) by 106 runs. *PoM:* Amy Satterthwaite.

Pukekura Park, New Plymouth, March 20: New Zealand 134/7 in 20 overs (Suzie Bates 52*, Sophie Devine 41; Hayley Matthews 3-24, Deandra Dottin 2-23) beat **West Indies** 133/7 in 20 overs (Merissa Aguilleira 38*, Kycia Knight 26; Leigh Kasperek 3-31, Anna Peterson 2-25) by 1 run. *PoM:* Hayley Matthews.

Pukekura Park, New Plymouth, March 22: New Zealand v **West Indies.** Match abandoned without a ball being bowled.

Seddon Park, Hamilton, March 25: West Indies 139/5 in 20 overs (Stafanie Taylor 42, Hayley Matthews 40; Leigh Kasperek 2-19, Lea Tahuhu 2-27) lost to **New Zealand** 143/3 in 16.2 overs (Katey Martin 54*, Amy Satterthwaite 43*; Shamilia Connell 3-35) by seven wickets. *PoM:* Katey Martin.

	ODIs	**T20Is**
Best batter	Sophie Devine (261 runs, 3 matches)	Katey Martin (180 runs, 4 matches)
Best bowler	Leigh Kasperek (7 wickets, 3 matches)	Leigh Kasperek (10 wickets, 4 matches)

Pakistan in Sri Lanka

Pakistan register historic series wins

Bismah Maroof led Pakistan to their first ODI series win since October 2015. Pakistan's batting dominated the series, with the visitors consistently posting scores above 200. Javeria Khan's unbeaten 113 in the first ODI — her second ODI century — and Maroof's 89 in the second match propelled Pakistan to identical scores of 250 for 6, before a collective effort from the top order took them to 215 for 9 in the final ODI.

Sri Lanka failed to match the visitors' might with the bat; Chamari Athapaththu was their top run-getter with 70 runs in the series. Pakistan's spinners kept a tight leash on their scoring rates, with the home side labouring through the series at a little over three runs per over; the spinners also took 24 of the 30 Sri Lankan wickets to fall.

The three-match T20I series was a slightly better contest, but once the visitors took home the trophy. The 2-1 result marked their first T20I series win in three years. Once again Javeria showed her class, blasting a 36-ball 52 — Pakistan's fastest T20I half-century — in the team's nail-biting one-wicket win

Javeria Khan followed her second ODI century with Pakistan's fastest T20I century.
— *SLC*

in the first match. Shashikala Siriwardene led Sri Lanka's fightback with an incredible spell of 4 for 9, but with the series on the line, Sri Lanka's frailties with the bat were exposed once again.

ODI series (3): Pakistan 3 Sri Lanka 0

Ranagiri Dambulla International Stadium, March 20: Pakistan 250/6 in 50 overs (Javeria Khan 113*, Nida Dar 34; Shashikala Siriwardene 2-40, Chamari Athapaththu 2-48) beat **Sri Lanka** 181 in 45.2 overs (C Athapaththu 46, S Siriwardene 44; Bismah Maroof 3-17, Sana Mir 2-29) by 69 runs. *PoM:* Javeria Khan.

Ranagiri Dambulla International Stadium, March 22: Pakistan 250/6 in 50 overs (Bismah Maroof 89, Nida Dar 38; Sripali Weerakkody 2-46) beat **Sri Lanka** 156 in 37 overs (S Weerakkody 29*, Chamari Athapaththu 24; Sana Mir 4-32, N Dar 2-27) by 94 runs. *PoM:* Bismah Maroof.

Ranagiri Dambulla International Stadium, March 24: Pakistan 215/9 in 50 overs (Nahida Khan 46, Javeria Khan 30; Ama Kanchana 2-35, Shashikala Siriwardene 2-40) beat **Sri Lanka** 107 in 41.3 overs (Nipuni Hansika 35; Sana Mir 4-27, Nashra Sandhu 3-18) by 108 runs. *PoM:* Sana Mir.

T20I series (3): Pakistan 2 Sri Lanka 1

Sinhalese Sports Club, Colombo, March 28: Sri Lanka 129/6 in 20 overs (Anushka Sanjeewani 61, Nilaksi de Silva 35*; Diana Baig 2-18, Sana Mir 2-25) lost to **Pakistan** 133/9 in 19.5 overs (Javeria Khan 52, Bismah Maroof 42; Sugandika Kumari 3-23) by one wicket. *PoM:* Javeria Khan.

Nondescripts Cricket Club Ground, Colombo, March 30: Pakistan 72 in 18.4 overs (Bismah Maroof 20; Shashikala Siriwardene 4-9, Sugandika Kumari 2-15) lost to **Sri Lanka** 73/3 in 14.2 overs (Anushka Sanjeewani 20) by seven wickets. *PoM:* Shashikala Siriwardene.

Sinhalese Sports Club, Colombo, March 31: Pakistan 113/6 in 20 overs (Javeria Khan 38, Sidra Ameen 23; Sugandika Kumari 2-20, Oshadi Ranasinghe 2-23) beat **Sri Lanka** 75/8 in 20 overs (Imalka Mendis 25*; Bismah Maroof 2-14) by 38 runs. *PoM:* Javeria Khan.

	ODIs	**T20Is**
Best batter	Javeria Khan (159 runs, 3 matches)	Anushka Sanjeewani (95 runs, 3 matches)
Best bowler	Sana Mir (10 wickets, 3 matches)	Sugandika Kumari (7 wickets, 3 matches)

Bangladesh in South Africa

Pacers, Lee make it easy for hosts

South Africa's pace trio of Ayabonga Khaka (seven wickets), Marizanne Kapp and Shabnim Ismail (both five wickets), consistently ripped through Bangladesh's batting line-up to hand their team an easy 5-0 ODI series win at home. The hosts were rarely pushed through the series, as Bangladesh's batters regularly collapsed in a heap, often labouring through their innings at less than three runs an over. Lizelle Lee clobbered 244 runs at an average of 61.00, including two half-centuries. She became only the third South African woman to score 2000 ODI runs during her knock of 70 in the fourth match. Laura Wolvaardt and Chloe Tryon were the only other batters to cross the 100-run mark, with the latter's tally coming at a strike-rate of 141.05.

Bangladesh put up improved performances through the T20Is, with the shortness of the format giving them a chance to match up to their opponents, but still conceded the series 3-0. They ran them close in the first match, falling short by 17 runs. Shamima Sultana, in scoring their maiden T20I fifty, guided the team to their highest T20I score of 137 for 5 in the second match.

ODI series (5): Bangladesh 0 South Africa 5

Senwes Park, Potchefstroom, May 4: South Africa 270/9 in 50 overs (Chloe Tryon 65, Lizelle Lee 54; Nahida Akter 2-22, Fahima Khatun 2-53) beat **Bangladesh** 164 in 49.3 overs (Fargana Hoque 69*, Sanjida Islam 35; Dane van Niekerk 3-23, C Tryon 2-14) by 106 runs. *PoM:* Chloe Tryon.

Senwes Park, Potchefstroom, May 6: Bangladesh 89 in 39.5 overs (Panna Ghosh 20*; Aya-bonga Khaka 3-13, Raisibe Ntozakhe 3-16) lost to **South Africa** 90/1 in 17.1 overs (Laura Wolvaardt 37*, Lizelle Lee 32) by nine wickets. *PoM:* Ayabonga Khaka.

Diamond Oval, Kimberley, May 9: Bangladesh 71 in 36.5 overs (Nigar Sultana 33*; Aya-bonga Khaka 3-16, Marizanne Kapp 2-14) lost to **South Africa** 72/1 in 14.2 overs (Lizelle Lee 44*) by nine wickets. *PoM:* Lizelle Lee.

Diamond Oval, Kimberley, May 11: South Africa 230/7 in 50 overs (Lizelle Lee 70, Chloe Tryon 60; Nahida Akter 2-36, Jahanara Alam 2-54) beat **Bangladesh** 76 in 33.2 overs (Fargana Hoque 22; Shabnim Ismail 2-8, Raisibe Ntozakhe 2-10) by 154 runs. *PoM:* Chloe Tryon.

Mangaung Oval, Bloemfontein, May 14: Bangladesh 166/9 in 50 overs (Rumana Ahmed 74, Shamima Sultana 53; Shabnim Ismail 3-17, Marizanne Kapp 2-21) lost to **South Africa** 169/4 in 35 overs (Laura Wolvaardt 70*, Lizelle Lee 44; Khadija Tul Kubra 3-37) by six wick-ets. *PoM:* Laura Wolvaardt. *PoS:* Lizelle Lee.

T20I series (3): Bangladesh 0 South Africa 3

Diamond Oval, Kimberley, May 17: South Africa 127/6 in 20 overs (Lizelle Lee 46, Laura Wolvaardt 30; Khadija Tul Kubra 3-23, Rumana Ahmed 2-19) beat **Bangladesh** 110/5 in 20 overs (R Ahmed 36, Fargana Hoque 35; Shabnim Ismail 3-19) by 17 runs.

Mangaung Oval, Bloemfontein, May 19: South Africa 169/4 in 20 overs (Sune Luus 71, Dane van Niekerk 66; Nahida Akter 2-32, Panna Ghosh 2-32) beat **Bangladesh** 137/5 in 20 overs (Shamima Sultana 50, Fargana Hoque 37; Shabnim Ismail 2-29) by 32 runs. *PoM:* Dane van Niekerk.

Mangaung Oval, Bloemfontein, May 20: South Africa 64/4 in 9 overs (Tazmin Brits 29; Salma Khatun 2-18) beat **Bangladesh** 41/6 in 9 overs (Ayabonga Khaka 3-10, Marizanne Kapp 2-8) by 23 runs. *PoM:* Ayabonga Khaka. *PoS:* Shabnim Ismail.

	ODIs	T20Is
Best batter	Lizelle Lee (244 runs, 5 matches)	SuneLuus (104 runs, 3 matches)
Best bowler	RaisibeNtozakhe (8 wickets, 5 matches)	Shabnim Ismail (5 wickets, 3 matches)

New Zealand in Ireland

Kerr double-ton and five-for

Suzie Bates's New Zealand smashed the record books during their mauling of Ireland in a three-match ODI series ahead of their tour of England. The home team, who were without the services of some of their key players, including Kim Garth and Ciara Metcalfe, struggled to contain New Zealand's powerful batting line-up.

The visitors began the tour with a resounding ten-wicket win in the one-off T20I, where they chased down 136 in 11 overs. Jess Watkin, the debutant, quite easily overshadowed Bates through the partnership.

Through the ODI series, New Zealand notched up totals of 491 for 4 — the highest in men's and women's ODIs — 418 and 440 for 3, to become the first team to manage three consecutive score of 400-plus. Amelia Kerr, the 17-year-old all-rounder was the standout for the visitors, smashing 342 runs and taking eight wickets with her leg-spin. She clobbered an unbeaten 232 in the final game, the highest score in women's ODIs, beating Belinda Clark's 21-year-old record when she pummelled Amy Kenealy for six off the final ball of the innings. Kerr shared a 295-run stand with Leigh Kasperek — the highest partnership for the second wicket in ODIs — on her way to becoming the youngest ever double-centurion. She sealed her team's 305-run win with a fantastic spell of 5 for 17 to cap off a wonderful day.

Records broken in Kerr's unbeaten knock of 232

• Kerr's 232 not out is the highest individual score in women's ODIs, overtaking Belinda Clark's unbeaten 229 for Australia against Denmark in Mumbai, 1997.

• She became the youngest double-centurion across formats in international cricket at 17 years and 243 days. The record was previously held by Javed Miandad of Pakistan, who scored a double-century at 19 years and 140 days.

• Her innings consisted of 31 fours, the highest in women's cricket.

• Her 295-run partnership was the highest partnership for New Zealand for any wicket, and also the highest second-wicket partnership in women's ODIs.

Ireland's frailties with the ball were exposed through the series with as many as five New Zealanders scoring centuries. Bates, who scored a rapid 151 in the first ODI, passed Debbie Hockley's tally of 4064 to become New Zealand's highest run-scorer in the format. The skipper's efforts headlined the team's 346-run demolition of the hosts — the fourth biggest win in ODIs. In the second game, the White Ferns hit 50 fours in their total of 418 — only the third instance this has happened.

Suzie Bates became the highest run-scorer for New Zealand in ODIs during her 151 in the first match against Ireland. — *Cricket Ireland*

Only T20I: New Zealand won by ten wickets

YMCA Cricket Club, Dublin, June 6: Ireland 136/8 in 20 overs (Gaby Lewis 61, Cecilia Joyce 30; Leigh Kasperek 3-25, Lea Tahuhu 2-22) lost to **New Zealand** 142/0 in 11 overs (Jess Watkin 77*, Suzie Bates 63*) by ten wickets.

ODI series (3): Ireland 0 New Zealand 3

YMCA Cricket Club, Dublin, June 8: New Zealand 491/4 in 20 overs (Suzie Bates 151, Maddy Green 122; Cara Murray 2-119) beat **Ireland** 144 in 35.3 overs (Laura Delany 37, Jennifer Gray 35; Leigh Kasperek 4-17, Hannah Rowe 2-23) by 347 runs.

The Hills Cricket Club Ground, Dublin, June 10: New Zealand 418 in 49.5 overs (Sophie Devine 108, Maddy Green 50; Laura Maritz 4-58, Cara Murray 2-96) beat **Ireland** 112 in 35.3 overs (Laura Delany 33, Cecelia Joyce 26; Anna Peterson 2-12, Holly Huddleston 2-13) by 306 runs.

Castle Avenue, Dublin, June 13: New Zealand 440/3 in 50 overs (Amelia Kerr 232*, Leigh Kasperek 113) beat **Ireland** 135 in 44 overs (Una Raymond-Hoey 42, Shauna Kavanagh 29; A Kerr 5-17, Hannah Rowe 2-24) by 305 runs. *PoS:* Amelia Kerr.

	ODIs	**T20I**
Best batter	Amelia Kerr (342 runs, 3 matches)	Jess Watkin (77 runs, 1 match)
Best bowler	Amelia Kerr (8 wickets, 3 matches)	Leigh Kasperek (3 wickets, 1 match)

South Africa in England

Beaumont masterclass scripts fightback

Back-to-back hundreds from Tammy Beaumont ensured England maintained their clean sheet against South Africa to record a 2-1, come-from-behind ODI series win at home.

The visitors, who were keen to exact revenge for their heart-breaking semi-final loss in the previous year's World Cup, cantered to a convincing seven-wicket win in the first ODI on the back of Lizelle Lee's belligerent 92. England, however, fought their way back into the series through Beaumont, who continued her run fest at home, scoring 212 runs at an average of 70.67. The opener slapped South Africa's fiery attack into submission, first in the company of Sarah Taylor in the second ODI, and then alongside Heather Knight in a lop-sided final encounter.

England thus recorded their ninth consecutive series win against South Africa since the rivalry began in 1997.

Lee, who was South Africa's best batter by a distance, was hot on the heels of Beaumont, collecting 211 runs, including a 107-ball 117 in the second ODI. Her century gave South Africa hope in their chase of a massive 332, but it wasn't enough to get them over the line.

Their inconsistency with the ball was also a major let down. Having started the series brilliantly, restricting the hosts to 189 for 9, Dane van Niekerk's attack was unable to hit its stride in the next two games. Although Ayabonga Khaka was their highest wicket-taker with seven scalps, she went at 6.10 runs an over through the series, as compared to Sophie Ecclestone (four wickets at 3.73 rpo), Katherine Brunt (six wickets at 3.90 rpo) and Anya Shrubsole (four wickets at 4.14 rpo).

Best batter: Tammy Beaumont (England) (212 runs in 3 matches)
Best bowler: Ayabonga Khaka (South Africa) (7 wickets in 3 matches)

ODI series (3): England 2 South Africa 1

New Road, Worcester, June 9: England 189/9 in 50 overs (Katherine Brunt 72*; Shabnim Ismail 3-25, Ayabonga Khaka 3-42) lost to **South Africa** 193/3 in 45.3 overs (Lizelle Lee 92*, Dane van Niekerk 58; Anya Shrubsole 2-36) by seven wickets.

County Ground, Hove, June 12: England 331/6 in 50 overs (Sarah Taylor 118, Tammy Beaumont 101; Marizanne Kapp 2-48, Ayabonga Khaka 2-72) beat **South Africa** 262/9 in 50 overs (Lizelle Lee 117, Chloe Tryon 44; Sophie Ecclestone 3-54, Katherine Brunt 2-34) by 69 runs. *PoM:* Sarah Taylor.

St. Lawrence Ground, Canterbury, June 15: South Africa 228 in 49.5 overs (Dane van Niekerk 95, Laura Wolvaardt 64; Katherine Brunt 3-52, Laura Marsh 2-43) lost to **England** 232/3 in 44 overs (Tammy Beaumont 105, Heather Knight 80*; Ayabonga Khaka 2-63) by seven wickets. *PoM:* Tammy Beaumont.

Tammy Beaumont scored a 47-ball century against South Africa, powering England to 250 for 3, the highest total in T20Is. — *Getty Images*

England Tri-Nation T20 Series

Beaumont, Ecclestone shine as records fall

England overpowered New Zealand by seven wickets in the final of the tri-nation tournament that also involved South Africa. Tammy Beaumont and Sophie Ecclestone put in special performances, allowing the hosts to dominate the competition and gain momentum ahead of the World T20 in November.

Beaumont scored a 47-ball century on the first day of the tournament against South Africa, her 116 powering England to a mammoth 250 for 3 — the highest total in T20Is. That beating came on the back of another record-breaking innings earlier in the day: New Zealand had amassed 216 for 1 against South Africa, thanks to an unbeaten 124 from Suzie Bates and her 182-run opening partnership with Sophie Devine, also a world record.

South Africa managed to register a win after the pummelling they received in the first round of matches, but that was all they could manage. Lizelle Lee and Chloe Tryon, their most attacking batters, were inconsistent, Dane van Niekerk (180 runs) received no real support from the rest of the line-up, and Shabnim Ismail's injury worries meant they lacked any firepower with the ball.

On flat pitches that offered no assistance to the bowlers, Ecclestone showed the importance of varying pace and attacking the stumps. The left-arm spinner picked up ten wickets at an average of 13.40. She was well-assisted by the experienced pace duo of Anya Shrubsole and Katherine Brunt (both six wickets), who did well to keep the opposition batters in check, going at 5.42 and 6.36 runs per over respectively.

Amelia Kerr, New Zealand's 17-year-old leg-spinner also showed glimpses of brilliance. Her googlies to dismiss Sarah Taylor twice in two innings, including the final, were the standout.

Through the course of the tournament, Bates became the highest run-scorer in women's T20Is, surpassing Charlotte Edwards's tally of 2605, and also became only the second woman to play 100 internationals in the format.

Best batter: Tammy Beaumont (England) (256 runs in 5 matches)
Best bowler: Sophie Ecclestone (England) (10 wickets in 5 matches)

The Cooper Associates County Ground, Taunton, June 20: New Zealand 216/1 in 20 overs (Suzie Bates 124*, Sophie Devine 73) beat **South Africa** 150/6 in 20 overs (Dane van Niekerk 58, Mignon du Preez 36; Hayley Jensen 3-28) by 66 runs. *PoM:* Suzie Bates.
The Cooper Associates County Ground, Taunton, June 20: England 250/3 in 20 overs (Tammy Beaumont 116, Danielle Wyatt 56; Stacy Lackay 2-59) beat **South Africa** 129/6 in 20 overs (Dane van Niekerk 72, Mignon du Preez 25; Katherine Brunt 2-18, Danielle Hazell 2-35) by 121 runs. *PoM:* Tammy Beaumont.
The Cooper Associates County Ground, Taunton, June 23: England 160/5 in 20 overs (Tammy Beaumont 71, Heather Knight 35*; Shabnim Ismail 2-27, Zintle Mali 2-39) lost to **South Africa** 166/4 in 19.3 overs (Lizelle Lee 68, SuneLuus 63*; Anya Shrubsole 2-24, Sophie Ecclestone 2-35) by six wickets. *PoM:* SuneLuus.
The Cooper Associates County Ground, Taunton, June 23: England 172/8 in 20 overs (Natalie Sciver 59, Tammy Beaumont 22; Leigh Kasperek 3-35, Sophie Devine 2-42) beat **New Zealand** 118 in 18.3 overs (Maddy Green 23, Suzie Bates 23; Sophie Ecclestone 4-18, Heather Knight 2-17) by 54 runs. *PoM:* Sophie Ecclestone.
County Ground, Bristol, June 28: South Africa 148/6 in 20 overs (Chloe Tryon 35, Lizelle Lee 25; Hayley Jensen 2-24, Amelia Kerr 2-28) lost to **New Zealand** 151/2 in 15.2 overs (Sophie Devine 68*, Suzie Bates 62) by eight wickets. *PoM:* Sophie Devine.
County Ground, Bristol, June 28: New Zealand 129 in 18.1 overs (Sophie Devine 52, Amy Satterthwaite 37; Anya Shrubsole 3-16, Danielle Hazell 2-21) lost to **England** 130/3 in 15.5 overs (Sarah Taylor 51, Natalie Sciver 39*; Jess Watkin 2-27) by seven wickets. *PoM:* Anya Shrubsole.

Points table

Team	M	W	L	T	N/R	Pts	NRR
England	4	3	1	0	0	6	+2.571
New Zealand	4	2	2	0	0	4	+0.238
South Africa	4	1	3	0	0	2	-2.855

England and New Zealand qualified for the Final

Final: England beat New Zealand by seven wickets
County Ground, Chelmsford, July 1: New Zealand 137/9 in 20 overs (Sophie Devine 31, Suzie Bates 31; Danielle Hazell 2-20, Katherine Brunt 2-26) lost to **England** 141/3 in 17.1 overs (Danielle Wyatt 50, Tammy Beaumont 35; Amelia Kerr 2-22) by seven wickets. *PoM:* Katherine Brunt. *PoS:* Sophie Ecclestone.

Winners: England

Bangladesh in Ireland

Alam, Hoque make the difference

Ahead of the World T20 qualifiers in the Netherlands, Bangladesh stopped over in Ireland for a three-match T20I series. The visitors continued their incredible run in the shortest format, overcoming the hosts 2-1.

The first match was a thrilling encounter that Bangladesh won largely due to the efforts of Jahanara Alam and Fahima Khatun. Alam, the right-arm seamer, started the tour with an incisive spell of 5 for 28 to help restrict Ireland to 134 for 8, before Khatun struck an unbeaten 18-ball 26, including 11 runs off the final over, to take her side home.

Bangladesh, fast becoming masters of the chase, romped to another four-wicket win in the second T20I thanks to a steady half-century from Shamima Sultana.

Having conceded the series, the hosts bounced back in the final match to grab a consolation win despite Bangladesh's record-breaking efforts: they posted their highest team score, 151 for 4, and Fargana Hoque's 66 not out was their highest individual score. Despite the mountain in front of her, Gaby Lewis, the 17-year-old, led Ireland's charge, scoring her second T20I half-century in the company of Laura Delany (46) as the hosts snuck home off the final ball.

Best batter: Fargana Hoque (Bangladesh (115 runs in 3 matches)
Best bowler: Jahanara Alam (Bangladesh) (7 wickets in 3 matches)

T20I series (3): Bangladesh 2 Ireland 1
YMCA Cricket Club, Dublin, June 28: Ireland 134/8 in 20 overs (Isobel Joyce 41, Gaby Lewis 28; Jahanara Alam 5-28) lost to **Bangladesh** 135/6 in 20 overs (Nigar Sultana 46, Fahima Khatun 26*; Eimear Richardson 2-20, G Lewis 2-20) by four wickets.
The Village, Dublin, June 29: Ireland 124/8 in 20 overs (Cecilia Joyce 60, Laura Delany 20; Jahanara Alam 2-15, Nahida Akter 2-18) lost to **Bangladesh** 125/6 in 19.1 overs (Shamima Sultana 51, Fargana Hoque 36; L Delany 2-21, Ciara Metcalfe 2-26) by four wickets.
Pembroke Cricket Club, Dublin, July 1: Bangladesh 151/4 in 20 overs (Fargana Hoque 66*, Shamima Sultana 30) lost to **Ireland** 152/4 in 20 overs (Gaby Lewis 50, Laura Delany 46) by six wickets. *PoS:* Jahanara Alam

New Zealand in England

Knight's ladies cap off strong summer

England ended their home summer with a comfortable 2-1 ODI series win over a tired New Zealand. The visitors, who were coming to the end of a long tour of Ireland and England were plagued by batting collapses through the three-match series. Aside from Sophie Devine (162 runs), who was the highest run-getter in the series, none of the New Zealand batters scored more than 65 runs across three matches.

England kept a clean slate, collecting their third trophy of the home season. Tammy Beaumont (160 runs) continued her impressive run, forming a solid partnership with Amy Jones (161 runs) at the top. The pair combined for two century partnerships. In the absence of Anya Shrubsole, Katie George, the left-arm seamer, made her debut, bowling a lethal spell of 3 for 36 in the second ODI to trigger New Zealand's collapse. England's spin duo of Sophie Ecclestone and Laura Marsh picked up 11 wickets between them, keeping the visitors' batting line-up on a tight leash.

Having dominated the first two matches, Heather Knight's team stuttered in the final game of the series when Leigh Kasperek's five wickets and Devine's century combined to deliver New Zealand a consolation win.

Meanwhile, Katherine Brunt surpassed Jenny Gunn (135 wickets), to become England's highest wicket-taker when she dismissed Amy Satterthwaite in the final match.

Best batter: Sophie Devine (New Zealand) (164 runs in 3 matches)
Best bowler: Leigh Kasperek (New Zealand) (8 wickets in 3 matches)

ODI series (3): England 2 New Zealand 1

Headingley, Leeds, July 7: England 290/5 in 50 overs (Heather Knight 63, Amy Jones 63; Amelia Kerr 2-36, Lea Tahuhu 2-57) beat **New Zealand** 148 in 35.3 overs (Sophie Devine 33, Suzie Bates 28; Natalie Sciver 3-18, Laura Marsh 3-24) by 142 runs. *PoM:* Natalie Sciver.

County Ground, Derby, July 10: England 241 in 48 overs (Tammy Beaumont 67, Natalie Sciver 54; Sophie Devine 2-26, Jess Watkin 2-30) beat **New Zealand** 118 in 38 overs (Suzie Bates 24, Maddy Green 20; Sophie Ecclestone 3-14, Katie George 3-36) by 123 runs. *PoM:* Tammy Beaumont.

Grace Road, Leicester, July 13: England 219 in 47.4 overs (Amy Jones 78, Tammy Beaumont 53; Leigh Kasperek 5-39, Hayley Jensen 2-26) lost to **New Zealand** 224/6 in 44.4 overs (Sophie Devine 117*, Amy Satterthwaite 25; Sophie Ecclestone 2-39, Katherine Brunt 2-40) by four wickets. *PoM:* Sophie Devine.

Women's World T20 2018 Qualifier

Bangladesh, Ireland head to Caribbean

Hot on the heels of their Asia Cup success, Bangladesh defeated Ireland by 25 runs in the final to lift the ICC Women's World T20 Qualifier in the Netherlands. Panna Ghosh, the tall fast bowler, starred in the final, picking up five wickets for 16 runs.

After they were asked to bat first, Ayasha Rahman's steely 46 shepherded Bangladesh to 122 for 9, despite Lucy O'Reilly's career-best haul of 4 for 28. In reply, Ireland stumbled at the start, being reduced to 27 for 3 within the power play. Gaby Lewis attempted to get her team back on track, but Ghosh, Rumana Ahmed and Nahida Akter combined to wipe out Ireland's challenge.

By making it to the final, Ireland joined Bangladesh as the last two teams to qualify for the World T20 in the West Indies in November.

Unlike the previous edition of the tournament, where the top teams went unchallenged, this time, the likes of Papua New Guinea, Uganda, United Arab Emirates and even Thailand punched above their weight pulling off the odd upset. UAE played out a thrilling six-wicket win against the Netherlands in their opening match, before being defeated by PNG later in the tournament. PNG were the biggest surprise, reaching the semi-finals after defeating both UAE and the Netherlands. The hosts were unable to register a single win despite Sterre Kalis, their opening batter, having a superb tournament. She racked up 231 runs and was the only batter to cross the 200-run mark, at an average of 57.75, including two half-centuries.

Other notable performances included Fahima Khatun's hat-trick for Bangladesh against UAE, Uganda's defeat of Thailand and Kalis's unbeaten 68-ball 88 against UAE.

Best batter: Sterre Kalis (Netherlands) (231 runs in 5 matches)
Best bowler: Lucy O'Reilly (Ireland) (11 wickets in 4 matches)

The Netherlands' Sterre Kalis built on her reputation as a bit hitter. — *ICC*

Gaby Lewis, at just 17, stood tall to lead Ireland's charge. — *Cricket Ireland*

Group A

Sportpark Maarschalkerweerd, Utrecht, July 7: Netherlands 137/3 in 20 overs (Sterre Kalis 88*, Denise Hannema 23; Heena Hotchandani 2-18) lost to **United Arab Emirates** 138/4 in 19.4 overs (Nisha Ali 69, Chaya Mughal 36; Caroline de Fouw 3-31) by six wickets. *PoM:* Nisha Ali

VRA Cricket Ground, Amstelveen, July 7: Papua New Guinea 84/6 in 20 overs (Veru Frank 27, Tanya Ruma 23*; Panna Ghosh 2-15) lost to **Bangladesh** 86/2 in 14.5 overs (Shamima Sultana 35) by eight wickets. *PoM:* Shamima Sultana

Sportpark Maarschalkerweerd, Utrecht, July 8: Netherlands 42 in 18 overs (Rumana Ahmed 3-2, Fahima Khatun 3-3) lost to **Bangladesh** 44/3 in 7.5 overs (Cher van Slobbe 2-4) by seven wickets. *PoM:* Fahima Khatun

VRA Cricket Ground, Amstelveen, July 8: United Arab Emirates 83 in 20 overs (Subha Srinivasan 22; Sibona Jimmy 2-11) lost to **Papua New Guinea** 84/8 in 19.5 overs (S Srinivasan 3-13) by two wickets. *PoM:* Brenda Tau

Sportpark Maarschalkerweerd, Utrecht, July 10: United Arab Emirates 39 in 16.2 overs (Fahima Khatun 4-8, Nahida Akter 2-2) lost to **Bangladesh** 40/2 in 6.5 overs (Nigar Sultana 21*) by eight wickets. *PoM:* Fahima Khatun

VRA Cricket Ground, Amstelveen, July 10: Papua New Guinea 129/5 in 20 overs (Kopi John 40, Brenda Tau 34) beat **Netherlands** 85 in 16.4 overs (Denise Hannema 35; Mairi Tom 4-24, RavinaOa 2-11) by 44 runs. *PoM:* Mairi Tom

Group A points table

Teams	M	W	L	T	N/R	Pts	NRR
Bangladesh	3	3	0	0	0	6	+3.013
Papua New Guinea	3	2	1	0	0	4	+0.332
United Arab Emirates	3	1	2	0	0	2	-1.235
Netherlands	3	0	3	0	0	0	-2.147

Bangladesh and PNG qualified for the semi-finals
Group B

Sportpark Maarschalkerweerd, Utrecht, July 7: Thailand 92/7 in 20 overs (Nattaya Boochatham 41; Lucy O'Reilly 3-23, Isobel Joyce 2-12) lost to **Ireland** 93/3 in 16.2 overs (Clare Shillington 38; Sornnarin Tippoch 3-12) by seven wickets. *PoM:* Clare Shillington

VRA Cricket Ground, Amstelveen, July 7: Uganda 43 in 15.3 overs (Rachel Scholes 3-3, Abtaha Maqsood 3-8) lost to **Scotland** 47/1 in 6.5 overs (Sarah Bryce 36*) by nine wickets. *PoM:* Rachel Scholes

Sportpark Maarschalkerweerd, Utrecht, July 8: Thailand 67/9 in 20 overs (Nannapat Koncharoenkai 22; Immaculate Nakisuuyi 2-8, Getrude Candiru 2-11) lost to **Uganda** 68/6 in 18.1 overs (I Nakisuuyi 21; Suleeporn Laomi 3-17, Chanida Sutthiruang 2-11) by four wickets. *PoM:* Immaculate Nakisuuyi

VRA Cricket Ground, Amstelveen, July 8: Scotland 98/2 in 20 overs (Sarah Bryce 49*) lost to **Ireland** 99/1 in 15.4 overs (Clare Shillington 47, Cecilia Joyce 35*) by nine wickets. *PoM:* Clare Shillington

Sportpark Maarschalkerweerd, Utrecht, July 10: Scotland 97/7 in 20 overs (Kathryn Bryce 39*, Becky Glen 28; Nattaya Boochatham 3-16 beat **Thailand** 70 in 17.2 overs (Nannapat Koncharoenkai 22; Rachel Scholes 4-10, Katie McGill 2-4) by 27 runs. *PoM:* Kathryn Bryce

VRA Cricket Ground, Amstelveen, July 10: Uganda 78/8 in 20 overs (Ciara Metcalfe 3-8, Eimear Richardson 2-19) lost to **Ireland** 79/2 in 12.1 overs (Clare Shillington 27) by eight wickets. *PoM:* Ciara Metcalfe

Group B points table

Teams	M	W	L	T	N/R	Pts	NRR
Ireland	3	3	0	0	0	6	+1.669
Scotland	3	2	1	0	0	4	+1.359
Uganda	3	1	2	0	0	2	-1.699
Thailand	3	0	3	0	0	0	-0.917

Ireland and Scotland qualified for the Semi-Finals

1st playoff semi-final: Sportpark Maarschalkerweerd, Utrecht, July 12: Netherlands 118/3 in 20 overs (Heather Siegers 46, Sterre Kalis 43) lost to **Uganda** 119/4 in 18.3 overs (Getrude Candiru 43*, Immaculate Nakisuuyi 27) by six wickets. *PoM:* Getrude Candiru
2nd playoff semi-final: Sportpark Maarschalkerweerd, Utrecht, July 12: United Arab Emirates 50 in 18.1 overs (Chanida Sutthiruang 2-7, Suleeporn Laomi 2-10) lost to **Thailand**

51/3 in 15.3 overs (Subha Srinivasan 2-15) by seven wickets. *PoM:* Chanida Sutthiruang
1st semi-final: VRA Cricket Ground, Amstelveen, July 12: Ireland 113/6 in 20 overs (Gaby
Lewis 36, Laura Delany 21*; Vicky Araa 2-23) beat **Papua New Guinea** 86 in 19.2 overs
(Brenda Tau 22; Lucy O'Reilly 3-13, Laura Delany 2-15) by 27 runs. *PoM:* Lucy O'Reilly
2nd semi-final: VRA Cricket Ground, Amstelveen, July 12: Bangladesh 125/6 in 20 overs
(Nigar Sultana 31*, Shamima Sultana 22; Priyanaz Chatterji 2-17) beat **Scotland** 76/7 in 20
overs (Sarah Bryce 31, Kathryn Bryce 21; Rumana Ahmed 2-10, Nahida Akter 2-16) by 49
runs. *PoM:* Rumana Ahmed

Ireland and Bangladesh qualified for the final

7th place playoff: VRA Cricket Ground, Amstelveen, July 14:Netherlands 146/3 in 20
overs (Sterre Kalis 79, Denise Hannema 30) tied with **United Arab Emirates** 146/9 in 20
overs (Nisha Ali 37, Chaya Mughal 32; Lisa Klokgieters 3-43, Hether Siegers 2-25). United
Arab Emirates won the one-over eliminator. *PoM:* Sterre Kalis.
5th place playoff: VRA Cricket Ground, Amstelveen, July 14: Thailand 113/7 in 20 overs
(Nattakan Chantam 44, Nattaya Boochatham 38) beat **Uganda** 79/8 in 20 overs (Stephani
Nampiina 29*; Chanida Sutthiruang 2-7) by 34 runs. *PoM:* Nattaya Boochatham.
3rd place playoff: Sportpark Maarschalkerweerd, Utrecht, July 14: Papua New Guinea
101/6 in 20 overs (Veru Frank 28*, Sibona Jimmy 25; Hannah Rainey 2-22) lost to **Scotland**
102/0 in 17 overs (Kathryn Bryce 51*, Sarah Bryce 41*) by ten wickets, *PoM:* Kathryn Bryce.

Final: Sportpark Maarschalkerweerd, Utrecht, July 14: Bangladesh 122/9 in 20 overs
(Ayasha Rahman 46; Lucy O'Reilly 4-28, Ciara Metcalfe 2-24) beat **Ireland** 97 in 18.4 overs
(Gaby Lewis 26, Eimear Richardson 23; Panna Ghosh 5-16, Rumana Ahmed 2-14) by 25 runs.
PoM: Panna Ghosh.

Winners: Bangladesh

PART FIVE

Reviews & Records

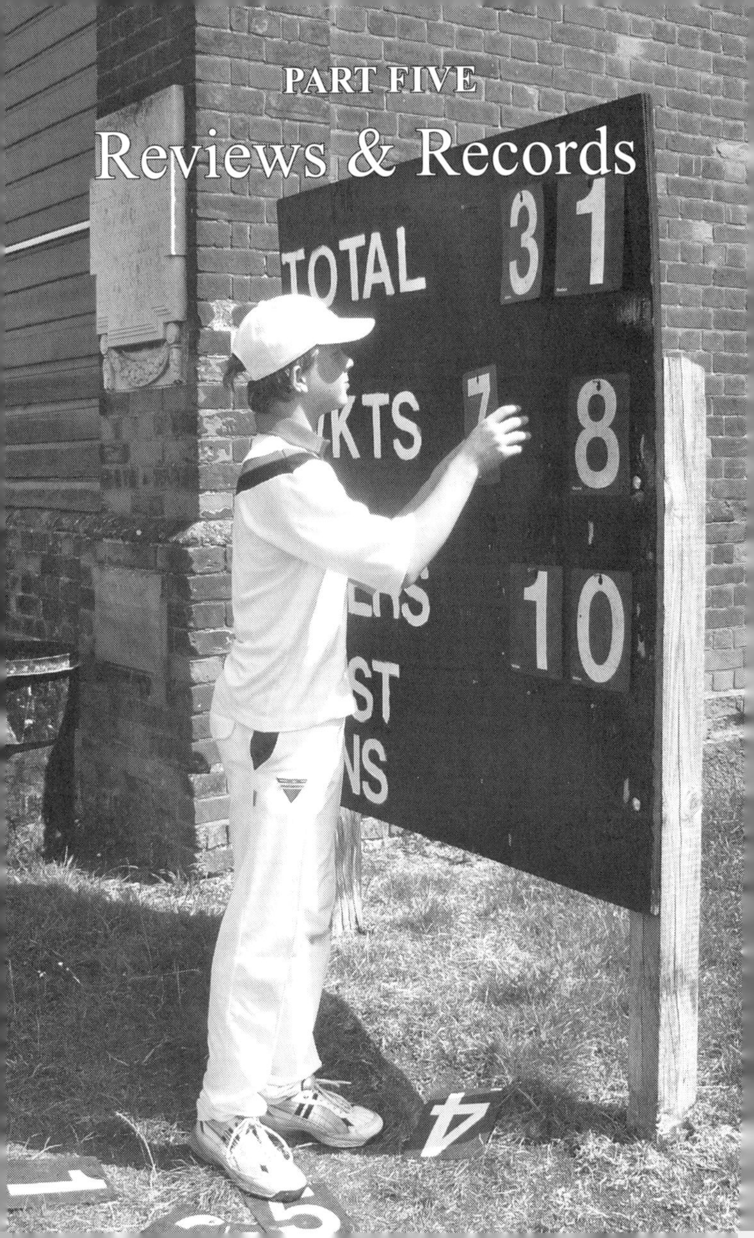

CRICKET BOOKS

ZENODOTUS

In the season of ghosted autobiographies by former Indian cricketers, Sanjay Manjrekar's **Imperfect** stood out. It wins over the reader early with a startling confession: "I played cricket not because I deeply loved the game … [but because] I wanted to be famous."

It is not the thought that is unique, but its admission. The tone is set: this is a book of searing honesty. The relationship with his father, the former Indian batsman Vijay Manjrekar, is troubled but crucial. There is suffering and embarrassment, but no complaint. Above all, there is gratitude and acceptance — not qualities one always finds in a cricketing memoir.

What went wrong with Manjrekar? At the dawn of the 1990s, his centuries in the West Indies and Pakistan, then teams with great fast bowlers, marked him out as a leader of India's batting for a generation. Yet it began to unravel steadily. Manjrekar blames himself. Perhaps he wasn't focused enough. Perhaps he was more concerned about how he looked than with scoring runs. Perhaps he didn't keep himself fit enough. Perhaps he relied on momentum rather than taking fresh guard, as it were. Perhaps he didn't seize his chances in the period before Rahul Dravid, Sourav Ganguly and V V S Laxman combined with Sachin Tendulkar to lock up the middle order. Manjrekar was finished at 33, after 37 Tests.

V V S Laxman's **281 and Beyond** is, like his batting, pleasing. Written engagingly by R Kaushik, a veteran of over 100 Tests as a journalist, it whispers rather than screams; but a clearer picture of a player tougher than his public image does emerge.

In the Tendulkar era, when India probably had the best batting line-up in the world, it was left to Laxman to play the defining innings. His epic 281 in Kolkata against Australia inaugurated the golden age of Indian cricket, and has been voted often as the finest by an Indian. People who had never met the man spoke of his gentleness, their opinion based on nothing more than his cover drive or the ability to play the leg glance. Laxman had substance to go with the style. He gives the reader a front row seat on a tour of his life and game. The most interesting, and touching portions reveal his vulnerabilities and self-doubt, his brushes with frustration and uncertainty.

It was never easy to be Sourav Ganguly, and reading his **A Century is not Enough: My Roller Coaster Ride to Success** you can discern why. The title is a wry reference to what more it takes to succeed.

When he started out, Ganguly was seen as a "quota" selection from the East. When he was made captain, it was seen as endorsement of the theory that captains usually came from the most powerful zone in the country, in this case thanks to Jagmohan Dalmiya. When he made everything look simple, he was accused of being too casual; when he dug in and defended, he was denying his natural game. Ganguly fought through all this, emerging as one of India's most elegant batsmen, and its toughest captain, with a shrewd understanding of where to look for talent and how to nurture it. His captaincy, he says in this memoir (rather intriguingly marketed as a "manual for living"), was based on "proper identification of talent, and then ensuring the young finds played fearless cricket".

As players emerged from the cricketing outposts of Ranchi, Jalandhar, Najafgarh, Kochi, Shrirampur, he built a team, injecting it with his own brand of self-belief. If Tiger Pataudi led the original self-respect movement in Indian cricket, Ganguly led the second. "While attempting to win, if I lost," he says, "I didn't mind. [I] absolutely detested draws."

Of the players of India's golden age, Ganguly was the most fascinating, and had to fight the hardest to make his name. But in the end, he changed the face of Indian cricket. The full details of that transformation are not in this book (written with veteran cricket writer Gautam Bhattacharya), but what is there is interesting enough.

Autobiography is seldom as interesting as biography, and the reason is simple. Life stories told from the inside do not join the dots to reveal character as definitively as those told by someone with the benefit of distance in time and space. The element of self-justification that tends to creep into autobiographies often ruins them, even if the ghost, as in the case of Shane Warne's **No Spin** is as fine a journalist as Mark Nicholas.

This is not a book of introspection; it is unlikely that Shane Warne understood himself better at the end of it. We certainly do not.

He tells us, sometimes in disjointed fashion, about his growing up years, his love affairs, his sexual escapades, his list of the best players and so on — standard issue autobiography, you might say.

When Warne turns his attention to leg-spin bowling, however, he is brilliant — in the book as in his career. It may not all have been his fault, but Warne was at the centre of some of the main issues of modern sport: match-fixing (he was reported for sharing information — however innocently — with a bookie in Sri Lanka), drugs (he was banned for a year after — innocently — taking a masking agent to reduce weight), sex (he was photographed in a threesome in England).

There are interesting vignettes about the IPL here: Shane Watson weeping in a corner of the dressing room after a Rajathan Royals defeat, or Lalit Modi meeting Warne in a "room as large as The Oval" while getting his feet massaged by "two people, one on each foot".

Harmanpreet Kaur's 171 in the World Cup against Australia has already assumed legendary, even mythical proportions. She had, according to **The Fire Burns Blue** (by Karunya Keshav and Sidhanta Patnaik), walked out to bat "with a serious expression, a clear mind, an aching shoulder and a borrowed bat". The marvellous economy, the telling detail and the research implied in that short sentence make for a wonderful introduction to the book. The qualities are sustained through this, the first history of women's cricket in India.

Awareness of context gives the book the feel of a Renaissance painting — where the background and foreground are both in focus; there is both depth and detail here.

It means when the large issues are discussed, they gain significance in the story of the individual, while an individual's story illustrates a bigger point. *The Fire Burns Blue* is the story of the players great and small and the gradual emergence of a sport from the sexist cartoons ("All they want during the drinks break is the make-up kit") to the back pages to the front pages and live television and the highest sign of acceptance today: social media trolling.

The stories of struggle — "Thoughts of suicide crossed my mind", confesses one player — and the sacrifices of the pioneers make the turnaround that much more rewarding and heart-warming.

It is a far cry today from when the women travelled in unreserved train compartments, learnt how to pull the chain without getting caught (to help those who rushed in late where the train stopped for a very short while) and time their run to the food carts on the platforms so they didn't have to get a team-mate to pull the chain. There was little administrative interest, hardly any money, few matches, fewer international engagements, but as one official said, "The girls just wanted to play." Still the fire burned.

The Fire Burns Blue is a book of unexpected gifts. Virginia Woolf puts in an appearance, as does Emily Dickinson. Women's issues seldom spoken about are discussed intelligently: menstruation, pregnancy, sexual harassment, sexual preferences. There is a plea for a progressive pregnancy policy. Post-career counseling is crucial too, as another former captain Pramila Bhatt says.

In 1911, the first 'All-India' team toured England for a series of matches, 14 of them first class. It was led by a 19-year-old prince, and comprised six Parsis, five Hindus, three Muslims and two Dalits. At least two earlier attempts had failed because the communal balance was deemed unsatisfactory. **Cricket Country: The Untold History of the First All India Team** by Prashant Kidambi superbly describes and analyses the tour and the politics that led up to it. The nation on the cricket field, Kidambi clarifies, was originally constituted by, and not against, the forces of empire.

Kidambi has deliberately used the title of a book written during the world war. Edmund Blunden's *Cricket Country* is both a lament on the passing of an age and a celebration of the timelessness of the game. While Blunden's book is about Englishness, Kidambi's is a tribute to the game's Indianness. "By a curious historical twist," he says, "a sport that defined the identity of the former colonisers is now the ruling passion of the country that they conquered." If Blunden was saying that cricket was authentic only when it was English, Kidambi is saying, clearing his throat gently, that the 'country' in the title is actually India.

Kidambi's research is deep and extensive. He clears misconceptions that have attached themselves to that 1911 team. It was not "organised and financed" by the skipper, Maharajah of Patiala Bhupinder Singh, a most colourful character who fathered 88 children (according to one estimate). The Parsi star Keki Mistry should have led, but Mistry worked for Bhupinder and would not have been granted permission to tour. Hence the ploy of getting a

19-year-old to lead so his employee could make the trip. Bhupinder "played in a manner that befitted his regal status: short, sharp bursts of flamboyant batting before boredom set in and induced a fatal error". A brilliant description of the cricket the princes played as well as the lifestyles they led.

All-India won two of 14 first-class matches and lost 10. Apart from psychological and geographical reasons, there were two sound cricketing ones too, Kidambi tells us. The weapons bowlers had developed recently, the outswinger and the googly, were a mystery to Indian batsmen.

Watching India playing in England with the crowd support suggesting they might be playing at home, it is useful to remember how it all began. *Cricket Country* tells that riveting story with passion and authority, which is why it is my **Wisden India Book of the Year**.

Alexander Pope, the 17th century English poet, has written about the tedium of the twice-told tale. Mihir Bose's second book on the history of Indian cricket, **The Nine Waves: The Extraordinary Story of Indian Cricket** is a journalist's rather than a historian's take on the eight decades from C K Nayudu to Virat Kohli. It has allowed him a greater latitude in dealing with the rumours and innuendos that have accompanied the game — and recording these without the pressure of having to ensure historical accuracy.

Did Tiger Pataudi's mother really write to Prime Minister Nehru asking that her son ought to be made captain ahead of Chandu Borde because he "belonged to a minority community"? Did Vijay Merchant really call the Kathiawar captain and ask him to concede the match, thus denying the Maharashtra batsman B B Nimbalkar, then batting on 443, a chance to overtake Don Bradman's world record of 452? Bose tells us these stories in a spirt of take-it-or-leave-it. To authenticate is the reader's responsibility.

The lite version of Bose's earlier tome is chattier, gossipy, anecdotal and joins the dots in a slightly different way, although the narrative is chronological and repeats some stories.

What do they know of coaching who only technique know? When Paddy Upton was appointed the mental conditioning coach of the Indian team, he became by default its physical conditioning and strategic leadership coach too. No one was quite sure what that meant, and Upton made up his job description as he went along. It served Indian cricket well. Upton and national coach Gary Kirsten set themselves (and India) a target: winning the 2011 World Cup. The year after they took charge, India became the No.1 Test team in the world. Upton's focus was on "building extraordinary team cultures in high performance environments", he says in his **The Barefoot Coach**.

The Indian cricket team is notoriously difficult to coach. If Kirsten was a success, some of the credit should go to Upton. When Kirsten first asked Sachin Tendulkar what kind of a coach he wanted, the batsman replied: "I want you to be my friend."

"Managing the ego," writes Upton "was one of the most important factors in nurturing the growth and performance of the Indian team." *The Barefoot Coach* is as much about how Upton changed Indian cricket as vice versa. The cast of characters, besides the cricketers, includes Albert Einstein, the philosopher Karl Popper, Malcolm Gladwell, the historian Theodore White, Bob Dylan, Paulo Coelho and more.

I once asked the legendary Tiger Pataudi if he always got the team he wanted. "I got my eleven; the reserves were sometimes so-and-so's cousin or that other one's nephew," he said. So, even in the 1960s, the squad was a mixture of merit and compromise. The proportions have steadily changed since. "Seventy years after Independence, we could well argue that cricket is one of the few largely meritocratic activities in the country," says Rajdeep Sardesai in **Democracy's XI**. It is an important transformation.

As a compilation of the tales of popular players from similar backgrounds, it suffers from familiarity. The stories are well known, the statistics even more so. Sardesai has got around this to some extent by dipping into his bag of interviews, both formal and informal. As he says, "There is a democratic fervour that makes cricket the ultimate authentic Indian dream … this book is a journey to discover and relive that great Indian story through the prism of cricket and … of cricketers who in their unique way represent the universal and pluralistic appeal of the sport."

There is an essential decency about Alan Wilkins that makes him the popular broadcaster he is; but it works against him as an author. If his autobiography, **Easier Said Than Done** is any guide, he keeps his secrets well. Four decades in cricket, first as player and then as broadcaster, make him privy to stories and impressions involving some of the greatest players over many generations. Yet, he is not telling. For the book, like the man, is all good intentions, humour and humility.

As a left-arm medium-pacer, Wilkins was, in his own words, "a journeyman county cricketer", playing for Glamorgan and then Gloucestershire, and good enough to claim 243 wickets (best, 8 for 57) before a shoulder injury ended that phase of his career. "My broadcasting career began in 1984," writes Wilkins, "when I was sent to cover the Transvaal Ladies Bowls Union Annual championships." Wilkins is generous in his praise for co-commentators, honest about playing in South Africa in the apartheid days, and grateful for how listeners in India and around the world have taken him to their hearts. With Vijay Amritraj, he forms one of the finest combinations in sports commentary anywhere, playing Watson to Amritraj's Holmes with grace and manifest enjoyment. These are qualities that have stood out in Wilkins' career — the apparent lack of ego, the professionalism and the ability to communicate his pleasure to an audience sitting in homes or bars.

Cricket, one would imagine, is best deconstructed by someone who has played at the highest level, or a psychoanalyst or perhaps a philosopher. So what happens when someone who is all three writes a book? Or two? The change in our publication schedule has meant two gems from Mike Brearley arrived in this period. **On Form** and **On Cricket**. The former is the more complex, and thus the more fascinating; it was the earlier book too.

MIKE BREARLEY
ON FORM

"Cricket helped me to be psychologically more aware," says Brearley, this unique personality in his unique book. The warning comes early, however: "There is no simple narrative logic to this book." *On Form* is a guided tour through the realms of psychoanalysis as it bears upon cricket. But unlike on a guided tour, you are left to your own devices — you take a path or ignore it, you meander, you spend time in certain areas, you may even lose your way, for the wonderful thing is, not all these paths actually lead to a destination.

Losing our way, says Brearley, is an opportunity for serendipity, and ends the book with the delightful instruction: Get lost!

Perhaps guided tour is a false analogy. Brearley seems to be wilfully avoiding any attempt at joining the dots, leaving it to the reader to do so. It is impossible to know whether your final pattern agrees with his for you may have joined the dots differently.

Brearley read classics and moral sciences at Cambridge, was briefly a lecturer in philosophy before (following his retirement from cricket) becoming a practising therapist. So when he evokes Wittgenstein or Descartes or Hume, Huizinga, or the Hungarian psychologist Mihaly Csikszentmihalyi (who wrote about 'flow', synonymous with 'zone'), Sartre's *mauvaise fois* (bad faith) is definitely not involved.

On Form is a quasi-autobiography. Forty years ago, when Brearley wrote his first book, co-author Dudley Doust commented on his temperament that made him look at ideas from different angles. Brearley's autobiography should be called On the Other Hand, Doust suggested. Brearley sees both sides of that too.

On Cricket is a collection of Brearley's writings on the game, written with authority but with no compulsion to drill everything into our heads. The combination of gentleness and authority is rare, as is the open-endedness that comes from a temperament trained in taking on board the other man's point of view.

The essays tell us as much about one of the greatest captains and thinkers to have played the game, as about the issues and personalities in cricket. There is a section devoted to Indian batsmanship with essays on Ranji, Pataudi, Tendulkar and Kohli. The section on his heroes discusses Viv Richards, Bishan Bedi, Dennis Lillee, Michael Holding and Tom Cartwright. Brearley wears his learning lightly, and this is a book about a captain and a cricketer revealing his passion for the sport.

That India took nearly two decades to win their first Test match puts the pace of recent changes in perspective. **Eleven Gods and a Billion Indians** by Boria Majumdar swings between the past and present, juxtaposing a chapter on how Indian sepoys appropriated an English game in the 19th century with the miracle of Kolkata 2001, and "challenging the Chappell shenanigans". It is a format that makes for an unevenness both in style and content, but allows us occasionally to glimpse at history repeating itself, especially where officialdom versus players is concerned.

The book's strength lies in detailing recent well-known stories, but the weakness is the lack of any fresh insights into them. What you know is what you get; what you want is the story behind the story.

I started reading **The Dhoni Touch** by Bharat Sundaresan with much anticipation because the author is one of our brightest young writers on the game. It begins unlike any other book, with the story of the "hair friends", the subject and the author who both wore their hair long at one time. Well-written, if journalistically, with the requisite interviews and personal touches, the question the reader asks himself at the end of it is: Did I learn anything new about the Indian captain? The answer, sadly, is in the negative. Dhoni emerges as Captain Cool, a loyal friend, a lover of bikes and the Indian army, and a man who notices things on the field that others don't. The dots may be different, but they join to form the same picture as before.

Cricket is possibly the only sport where

commentators and writers (particularly of a certain vintage) are as well known and venerated as some of the players. In his prime, Neville Cardus was as popular as the men he wrote about; later John Arlott of the Hampshire burr and neat turn of phrase was probably even better known. Then there was Jim Swanton, with his pronouncements from on high, described variously as pompous, snobbish and stentorian. Arlott and Swanton were seen, respectively, as the poet laureate of the game and the Lord Protector of English Cricket.

The two "voices of cricket" have been brought together in a delightful book by historian David Kynaston and journalist Stephen Fay. **Arlott, Swanton and the Soul of English Cricket** is not so much biography as social and cultural history. It gently unpeels a class-based society turning into a more egalitarian one, the influence of the media in national affairs, and the role of cricket in all this. In doing so the authors have expanded the range of the cricket book, telling the story through the eyes of two characters who could be dismissed as being peripheral to its unfolding or, as shown here, central to it. This is the triumph of the book — to make it all sound so inevitable.

Swanton was son of a stockbroker and middle class, Arlott son of a working-class council employee. Neither went to university. Arlott married thrice, Swanton married at 51. Swanton was a Conservative and worked for the *Daily Telegraph*; Arlott, a Liberal, appeared in *The Guardian*. Two men, from different backgrounds, with different approaches to broadcasting and writing, with different emphases in their work spoke in one voice on the big issues of the day: racism, apartheid, one-day cricket, the Kerry Packer's revolution. The underlying theme was: cricket is important, not just as a sport but as a representation of something bigger.

Additional reviews by Tanya Aldred

In **Pushing the Boundaries**, a preposterous cricketing tale of shagging and boozing through the 1980s, Derek Pringle embarks on a jolly romp through the decade of big hair and seismic societal change, in which cricket slowly moved from a sport for frisky dilettantes to something requiring Cromwellian discipline. Picked for England while a student at Cambridge, Pringle caught the eye of the press because of his earring and erroneous rumours that he was squiring two of the chief selector's daughters.

His selection didn't go down so well with die-hard cricket fans, but luckily our hero has a thick skin. He yomps across the years, discovering with delight the aphrodisiac that comes when you pull on an England shirt, and achieving an insight into the mind of a professional sportsman, with his "ability to compartmentalise one's feelings so they don't bleed into each other".

Moeen Ali's autobiography, **Moeen**, is co-written by Mihir Bose. Ali is a captivating character, whose good nature, modesty and joie de vivre hide a steely interior: remember he wore a 'Save Gaza' wristband during a Test.

This book gives us a better understanding of why English cricket's most popular beard is the player he is, and what makes him tick. It is no surprise that Ali came to the sport from a different pipeline — but the sheer soap opera of his background is revealing. His paternal grandparents, Shafayat and Betty, met in Birmingham in the late 1940s. Shafayat had come over from Kashmir to find work in a factory. Betty was a widow — her first husband was killed in the war — with two small children. They broke all conventions, and Betty converted to Islam. Shafayat then decided their children should have an Islamic education, so Ali's father, Munir, was packed off to Kashmir aged two, staying until he was ten. Betty spent long periods in Dadyal, learning Urdu and living like a local. The marriage eventually broke up, and the children returned to England. Munir and his twin brother Shabir married sisters, and the two families raised a cricketing dynasty — Moeen, brother Kadeer, cousin Kabir — by an esoteric mixture of superstition, sacrifice, dedication and improbable triumph.

If some of the later chapters slip towards formulaic match reports, the book is very good on Moeen's upbringing in Sparkhill, an inner-city area prone to the usual bedfellows of drugs, crime and violence. Cricket, he believes, saved him from the miserable fate that befell some of his friends.

Simon Wilde's **England: The Biography 1877–2018**, at 614 pages is a tome and a half, and Wilde admits that the sheer quantity of evidence he trawled through was sometimes overwhelming.

It's a great yarn, though, a potted history of English (men's) cricket, with all the idiosyncrasies of an imperial game trying to live in the modern world but always falling at least one step behind. Run generally by double-breasted ex-public schoolboys, English cricket, imbued with a superiority complex, gets a frog in its throat at almost every turn. It struggles with the end of the amateur-professional divide; is preoccupied by attracting the right sort; is far too closely entangled with apartheid South Africa; and does not understand that players might actually like to be financially secure. There are many be-fuddling episodes. As Wilde points out, those at the top — men who were perfectly capable stockbrokers or captains of industry — found themselves in some kind of high-church tangle when having to manage the English game.

The Test is a first novel by Nathan Leamon, who for nine years was an analyst for the England team. Cricket is peculiarly unsuited to fiction — perhaps such a complex game ends up sucking the lifeblood out of authors as they strive for description — but Leamon pitches it just right. He deftly avoids the clichés of green and pleasant land, or plucky but hopeless ama-teurs, and uses his expertise to bring both technical and emotional insight.

Last summer James Taylor was appointed a full-time selector by Ed Smith and was regularly spotted around county grounds. It might have slipped peo-ple's minds as to why, in April 2016, he finished playing cricket at the tender age of 26. The opening lines of **Cut Short** soon act as an aide-memoire: "By rights, I shouldn't be writing this book. I should have been found dead at the bottom of a flight of stairs. Or in the passenger seat of a car. Or on a cold wooden bench in a distant dressing-room far from friends and family."

From there, Taylor — and his ghost, John Woodhouse — narrate a fast-paced tale of what happens when the future is ripped from under your feet. Taylor was a talented sportsman and we learn about his journey from brash teen through the Lions to becoming a near-fixture in the England team the winter before he had to retire because of a rare heart disease.

Sandpapergate. The story of the day is tackled in their different ways by Gideon Haigh and Geoff Lemon.

Crossing the Line, a small book written in a hurry, plays to all Haigh's strengths. Subtitled "How Australian cricket lost its way", it is an unsparing

examination of the minutiae of authority, full of intelligent analysis and trademark fearlessness. The rationale behind the book was noble: "Nobody goes to bed honest and wakes up a cheat." Suspicious of Cricket Australia's cultural review, Haigh undertakes his own, interviewing 50 unnamed people whose views he re-spects. The first unattributable quote de-scribes CA as "bullies and sycophants". Their reputation does not improve from there.

It's a super book. As Haigh, an expert on governance, turns on his Dictaphone and traipses through the labyrinth, he wonders whether the big cricket he watches has become "less precious, less special, less representative". The players, he concludes, are the fall guys.

Lemon's **Steve Smith's Men** is a different animal, more emotional, more soulful. From a pulsating introductory chapter to an almost wistful epilogue, Lemon retraces the steps that led to the pants-down denouement at Cape Town. The book, he says, casts no moral judgment, but I envisage him scratching his poetic curls as he plots the long line in the sand – the crazy scheduling, the CA-sanctioned whipping-up of David Warner, the long-time fetishising of nastiness.

Lemon was physically present through pretty much the whole mess, and if his on-the-spot reporting has a hint of swagger, his writing is touched by a golden pen and an eye for detail. There is empathy, there is sympathy and there is despair. The chapters on the individual players work best, titled simply David, Steven, Cameron, Timothy [Paine, the new captain]. The four men were linked by nothing more, nothing less, than a Baggy Green.

Smith, the ultimate illustration of C L R James's what-do-they-know line, is "impressively dull" — a cricket geek, desperate to be good, handed the leadership without showing any aptitude, inheriting a team shorn of senior men, and unable to put a leash on Warner. Warner himself is a hero-villain, a useful idiot willing to do the team's dirty work, and a young man lacking guidance, one who was driven to madness by the vilification of his adored wife, Candice. She was tormented and, devastatingly, at the end of the whole sorry saga, when the game was up, when Warner was sent home, had a miscarriage. "The abstract figure people thought they were attacking turned out to be a real human, flesh and blood, tough and fragile," writes Lemon. "In no world, under no justification, should she ever have been forced into the middle of this mess."

Tanya Aldred is a freelance writer and editor.

OBITUARIES

ABED, SULAIMAN, died on January 19, 2018, aged 74. The youngest of five sporting brothers from Cape Town, 'Dik' Abed led the Netherlands in the 1982 ICC Trophy. He followed Basil D'Oliveira in forging a professional career in England, since he was barred from first-class cricket in South Africa by the colour of his skin. Abed jumped at the chance to sign for the Lancashire club Enfield in 1967, even though he had to pay his own way there. Unlike D'Oliveira, Abed never made the leap to county or Test cricket, despite playing a few second-team games (and scoring a century for Surrey in his first). Some suggested the powers that be at Lord's had discouraged counties from signing him, to avoid a repeat of the D'Oliveira affair.

ACHREKAR, RAMAKANT VITHALRAO, died in Mumbai on January 2, 2019, after a long illness. He was 86.

It is doubtful if any coach has featured in a movie and had a book written about him. Achrekar earned that distinction largely because he was the first coach of the schoolboy Sachin Tendulkar. Sachin's older brother Ajit took him to Achrekar's famed coaching camp at Shivaji Park in 1984 to keep the mischievous 11-year-old out of trouble. Tendulkar had never before played with a cricket ball and was the smallest at the camp. But Achrekar claimed he was a natural and he did not have to change much in his technique. He paid extra attention to his star pupil and, to ensure he got to bat as much as possible, would ferry him from ground to ground on his scooter so that he

Ramakant Achrekar, with his most famous student after Sachin Tendulkar won the Bharat Ratna. — *Wisden Archives/ Getty Images/ AFP*

could play in three to four games a day. "He would hide behind trees to see our games, and then point out the errors later. We would have fun, but it was guarded," Tendulkar once said of his mentor.

Achrekar was coach at Shardashram Vidyamandir and on his advice and persuaded by Ajit, Sachin's parents decided to switch his school as they too were by now were convinced of his potential. The then world record partnership in the Lord Harris Shield between Tendulkar and Vinod Kambli happened under Achrekar's watch in February 1988.

Apart from these two, the other men from Achrekar's stable to play for India included opener Ramnath Parkar, Praveen Amre, Lalchand Rajput, Chandrakant Pandit, Balwinder Sandhu, Sameer Dighe, Ajit Agarkar, Sanjay Bangar and Ramesh Powar, veritable India XI.

Not unusually for an accomplished coach, Achrekar did not have a distinguished career. In fact he played a solitary first-class match and that was for his employers State Bank of India in the Moin-ud-Dowlah Gold Cup in Hyderabad in 1963-64.

Achrekar was given the Dronacharya award for coaches in 1992 and the Padma Shri in 2010. He is survived by three daughters, one of whom is a cricket coach. His wife Suvarnalata, two infant sons and two daughters predeceased him.

AHMED, ZUBAIR MOHMAD died on August 14, 2017, after being hit on the head twice during a game in Mardan, in northern Pakistan. He was 18. After being struck near the ear, Zubair was hit again on the side of the neck and died on the way to hospital. His coach confirmed he had been wearing a helmet. Among the other players in the festival match to celebrate Pakistan's Independence Day was Fakhar Zaman, who two months previously had hit a century in the Champions Trophy final at The Oval.

AIZAZUDDIN, FAQIR SYED, who died on May 8, 2017, aged 81, played three unofficial Tests for Pakistan in 1963-64 against the Commonwealth XI, scoring 72 at Karachi and an undefeated 62 at Dacca. He had started his first-class career while studying economics at Cambridge, but in five matches in 1957 never passed 18. He had more luck when he returned to Fenner's in 1963 with the Pakistan Eaglets (a precursor of today's A team), hitting 187 — which remained his highest score — against the university, captained by Mike Brearley. Aizazuddin was chosen for the 1967 tour of England, despite having played little recent domestic cricket, but did not make the Test side.

ALLOM, ANTHONY THOMAS CARRICK, who died on September 26, 2017, aged 78, was thought to be the tallest English county cricketer: 6ft 10in, according to *Wisden* 1958. A fast bowler, Allom played five first-class matches, taking six wickets in the third, for MCC against Cambridge University at Lord's in 1960. Not long after, he made what turned out to be his only Championship appearance, for Surrey. Warwickshire's openers Norman Horner and Billy Ibadulla put on 377 at The Oval without being separated, still a county record. His father, Maurice — a mere 6ft 6in — played five Tests for England.

AMROLIWALA, HOSHANG DADIBA, died on December 29, 2017, aged 86. A consistent scorer for Bombay, Hoshie Amroliwala hit 139 against Bengal in the Ranji Trophy final in March 1959, after entering at 80 for 5. Bombay went on to win the first of what became 15 successive Ranji titles. Amroliwala had also made 84 not out in the semi-final against Services, sharing a partnership of 144 with the 17-year-old Ajit Wadekar. He was considered for the tour of England that followed, but missed out, possibly because Bombay already had several representatives in the side. In March 1960, in the inaugural Irani Trophy match, between the Ranji champions and the Rest of India, Amroliwala dismissed five Test players with his leg-breaks on the way to 6 for 44, then made 76 not out. He scored another century against Maharashtra later that year, but never did win a Test cap. "Hoshie was one of the finest batsmen at that time," said the former Indian captain Nari Contractor, a fellow Parsi. "He never played in the air, and was fantastic with the square cut and pull."

ANAND, K N, who died on July 21, 2018, aged 66, was a sportswriter for *The Hindu* newspaper and India's *Sportstar* magazine. Although his main sport was athletics, he also wrote widely on cricket, and was a regular contributor to the old Indian Cricket annual.

BAILEY, JACK ARTHUR, died on July 12, 2018, aged 88. MCC's bicentenary in 1987 should have been a grand celebration. Instead, a civil war was being fought in the corridors of the Lord's Pavilion. When the smoke cleared, Jack Bailey was the chief casualty. He had been one of the club's leading administrators for 20 years, and secretary since 1974. But his refusal to give way in negotiations with the TCCB (now the ECB) cost him his job. The disputes between MCC and the TCCB ranged from the staging of major matches to who should meet the Queen when she visited Lord's.

He was born in Brixton, the son of a policeman, and read geography at University College, Oxford. Imposingly tall, he bowled lively fast-medium, making good use of his height. On his debut for Essex in August 1953, he took seven second-innings wickets against Nottinghamshire at Southend.

He moved into teaching, then a business career. In 1967, he became assistant secretary at Lord's, with responsibility for marketing and publicity. Bailey negotiated improved television deals with the BBC, and was involved in the creation of the John Player League and the Benson and Hedges Cup.

But he was not always a moderniser: players at Lord's had to practise in whites and admission to the playing area was strictly controlled. The rules brought him into conflict with Dennis Lillee when some of the 1981 Australians turned up without permission during the Eton-Harrow match. Lillee broke another of Bailey's regulations by walking back from the Nursery Ground around the edge of the boundary, waving to the crowd. When Bailey remonstrated, Lillee threw orange juice over him.

BAKER, ANTHONY FRANK, died on October 13, 2017, aged 77. Tony Baker was the man charged with the epic task of moving Hampshire from their ramshackle historic home at Northlands Road to the spanking new Rose Bowl in 2001. That Hampshire completed the transition smoothly was down to Baker's calm efficiency and logistical skills. "Over the two decades that I knew him, I don't recall him ever raising his voice," said Hampshire chairman Rod Bransgrove.

Baker was an outstanding club cricketer in the Southampton area. He opened the batting and bowling for Old Tauntonians in the 1960s and '70s, and in a local cup final in 1972 took all ten.

BANERJEE, TAPAN JYOTI, who died on May 29, 2017, aged 73, was a seamer who played 17 matches for Bengal and one for East Zone over 17 years from his debut in December 1965. He took 15 wickets in his first two games, and in 1966-67 claimed 6 for 58 against Assam at Jorhat. Banerjee later coached the Bengal women's team to the national title. "He was the only coach who told us: 'Eat sweets, it won't harm you,'" remembered India's leading wicket-taker Jhulan Goswami. "But he was strict on the field and had a clear knowledge of the game."

BARRETT, ARTHUR GEORGE, who died on March 6, 2018, aged 73, was a tidy Jamaican leg-spinner whose opportunities were limited by Lance Gibbs, often the only slow bowler chosen as West Indies concentrated on pace. But Barrett was hard to ignore when Jamaica won the Shell Shield for the first time in 1968-69: he took 6 for 18 against a powerful Barbados batting line-up at Bridgetown. Club-mates rated his stylish batting so highly they nicknamed him 'Trumper', but Barrett managed only one first-class century, against the Combined Islands in St Lucia in March 1970, to go with ten wickets in the match. Told he was the first to manage such a double in regional cricket in the West Indies, Barrett joked that "obviously Garry Sobers never played regionally".

He made his Test debut against India under Sobers early in 1971, but won just five more caps, spread over three series. Barrett's best first-class figures were 7 for 90, for Jamaica against a strong International Cavaliers XI at Sabina Park in February 1970, when his victims included Colin Cowdrey, Ted Dexter and Mushtaq Mohammad.

BHALEKAR, RAJENDRA BALAKRISHNA, who died on April 14, 2018, following a second by-pass surgery was 66. 'Raju' was a middle-order batsman who captained Maharashtra and had a highest first-class score

The class prefect

KARUNYA KESHAV

The girls that formed the first Indian women's teams in the 1970s were just that: girls. High school students, teenagers of just around 14, single-minded, having a bit of fun with cricket between classes and exams. In this high-spirited environment, the slightly older Sreerupa Bose was the steadying influence.

When her SSC exams were just a month or so away, Shubhangi Kulkarni, the leg-spinner, had to be at an India camp in Kolkata. Sreerupa cleared her room of distractions and insisted that the younger girl study there.

Her Bengal girls — Sreerupa was captain of that team — would run to her after matches and practice in the Kolkata maidans to ask her for money to eat *paani puri* and *jhaal mudi*. "She would tell us that if we played well, she would give us money," laughs Lopamudra Bhattacharjee, former India pacer and selector.

If from its serendipitous start, organised women's cricket in India has survived, the maturity and presence of someone like Sreerupa can't be discounted. Strong, protective, encouraging, firm, no-nonsense, she was a natural leader. Lopamudra speaks of a commanding presence: "Everyone would listen to her and we were all very disciplined."

The records won't show her as captain of the Indian side, but she did take the helm in their third match ever as 'team India', playing what is now considered an unofficial Test against the visiting Australian Under-25 side. That series, India's first ever, had more than a hint of parochialism in their captaincy selections, with Pune girl Ujwala Nikam skipper in the first and localite Sreerupa at the coin toss for the third game in Kolkata. But few would question the Bengal player's leadership credentials. Her side were the undisputed domestic champions for seven straight years, and the consensus is that it was because of her cricketing brain and the talent at her disposal.

In fact, she led the first team from India to beat an international side: in that same Australia series, East Zone, full of players from the domestic champion side, got the better of an (admittedly tiring) Australian side in the last match of their tour.

A bowling all-rounder, Sreerupa's international career was short. Just two ODIs against New Zealand in 1985, for seven runs and no wickets.

Technically, she wasn't strong. Yet, like her contemporaries Shantha Rangaswamy, Diana Eduljee and Shubhangi Kulkarni, she has been a constant in the background of Indian cricket. She represented the Indian women's cricket association in meetings of the erstwhile International Women's Cricket Council — often travelling abroad at her own expense. She was coach in three World Cups: 1993, 1997 and 2000, and went on to be selector as well. India's most successful multi-nation tournament to this date, the 1995 quadrangular in New Zealand, came with her as coach.

Yet, her personality meant she often became the bad cop, and banked on the managers to play good cop. Players refer to her as "strong", some steer clear of the euphemism to call her "strict". Shantha described her to *Sportstar* as a "class monitor". In that quadrangular, for example, controversy erupted when it was widely reported that she slapped captain Purnima Rau; according to Purnima, it was because she preferred company rather than the single room she was entitled to and put in a request. A couple of years later back home against England, with the Jamshedpur Test on the line and Neetu David having taken a world record 8 for 53, the Purnima-Sreerupa equation further soured. The coach had reportedly left the ground early to catch a flight, and the captain, known for her aggressive style, took the call of going for the win — only to lose by two runs, the narrowest margin in all women's Tests. Right after that, Purnima was sacked.

In her time, Sreerupa was an all-rounder, even outside the cricket field. Working at Eastern Railway, she had also played basketball and hockey, and tried golf after her retirement. She was also a pioneer in cricket broadcasting, doing commentary for All India Radio, and went on to teach at the University of Calcutta's department of journalism. Hers is a family deeply involved in sport: she was joint director at SAI Kolkata, husband Paresh Nath Mukherjee is the former Bengal Olympic Association president and daughter Amrita a tennis player.

She was in Derby as a spectator when Mithali Raj scored a century against New Zealand to take India to the 2017 World Cup semi-final. That would be the last association of any kind with the Indian team.

Raju Bhalekar

of 207 not out — made against Saurashtra in Pune in 1981-82. In all, he scored 3877 runs with seven centuries and also claimed 35 wickets with off-spin in his 74 first-class matches. His bowling was useful to break partnerships: he took 4 for 60 against eventual Ranji champions Bombay in 1979-80.

The diminutive Bhalekar came close to Test selection in 1976-77: chosen for West Zone against Tony Greig's England tourists, he made the most of being dropped twice by top-scoring with 66, but fell away later in the season.

BHANDARI, PANAMBUR NARASIMHA, died on November 17, 2017, aged 83. 'Bab' Bhandari made 102 on first-class debut, for Bihar against Assam in Jamshedpur in 1959-60. He also played for Karnataka, but never improved on that, and played only six more matches, the last for East Zone in the Duleep Trophy in October 1961.

BHATIA, PREM, who died on March 13, 2018, aged 78 after a prolonged illness will be remembered best for being a 12th man who batted in both innings of a first-class match. In the inaugural Irani Cup match in 1960, Bhatia turned out for Rest of India against Bombay and made 22 and 50. He was the 12th man but batted at the insistence of national selector Lala Amarnath who wanted to watch him play. Bhatia, who as player, selector and administrator served Delhi, said later he had been "delighted with the opportunity".

According to former Delhi and Services batsman Bharat Awasthi, Bhatia was "a daring cricketer and an extremely gifted batsman. He was an under-achiever." Bhatia once made an emergency appearance for North Zone in the Deodhar Trophy against South Zone when he was 45. Kapil Dev, Mohinder Amarnath, Yashpal Sharma, Manoj Prabhakar and Chetan Sharma could not reach the venue in time, and Bhatia, the manager of the team was forced to include himself in the playing XI. South skipper Krishnamachari Srikkanth sportingly offered to field in place of Bhatia, but a local cricketer was called up. In all, Bhatia played 56 matches for 2548 runs and including six centuries. His highest score was 151 for Delhi against Southern Punjab in 1962-63, which was his best season — 532 runs at 53 — but India had no Tests, and his chance disappeared. Bhatia had started as a handy off-spinner and took 3 for 69 for North Zone against the 1960-61 Pakistan tourists, including Mushtaq Mohammad for a duck.

BHAVANARAYANAN, M G, who died on August 29, 2018, aged 90, was a defensive batsman and handy medium-pacer who played eight first-class matches for Tamil Nadu with a highest score of 71 in the Gopalan Trophy against Sri Lanka in 1952-53.

BINNS, ALFRED PHILLIP, died on December 29, 2017, aged 88. The Jamaican Allie Binns was one of several wicketkeepers tried by West Indies in the 1950s, after Clyde Walcott gave up the gloves to spare his back for batting. Binns was noted for his quick hands, which brought several stumpings, and won his first cap against India in 1952-53, not long after hitting a career-best 157 against British Guiana at Georgetown. He conceded no byes as India amassed more than 700 in the match at Port-of-Spain, but missed four chances on a nervy first day, earning catcalls from a Trinidadian crowd who wanted their own man, Ralph Legall, in the side instead. Binns failed twice with the bat, and was replaced by Legall. Two years later, an aggressive 151 against an Australian attack containing Lindwall, Miller, Davidson and Benaud — in a sixth-wicket partnership of 277 with Collie Smith after Jamaica had been 81 for 5 — earned Binns a Test recall, but again he did little with the bat. In all, he made four first-class centuries, but his highest score in five Tests was 27. He eventually moved to the United States and became a teacher.

BLAND, KENNETH COLIN, died on April 14, 2018, nine days after his 80th birthday. The South African Test player elevated fielding into compelling theatre. Nicknamed 'the Golden Eagle', Bland swooped on the ball as if it were prey; his throws usually zeroed in on the stumps. "He took our fielding to another dimension," said Peter Pollock. Bland stood 6ft 1in, a strong, athletic figure — he was offered a rugby scholarship as a boy — and a graceful mover who covered the ground in swift strides. He was quiet and undemonstrative, but his impact was profound. "He led by example, and the whole team wanted to become better fielders," said Pollock. "We realised that runs saved could make a big difference."

At Lord's in 1965, England were threatening a match-winning lead when Ken Barrington, on 91, set off for a single towards midwicket. Bland pounced from in front of the square-leg umpire, picked up the ball one-handed, swivelled, and hit the stumps at the bowler's end. In *The Observer*, Alan Ross called it "staggering". Two days later, his run-out of Jim Parks was even better. Fred Titmus tickled a ball off his pads, and Parks called him for a single, but Titmus — spotting that Bland was in pursuit — sent him back. Parks attempted to put his body between the wickets and the ball, but Bland hit them anyway.

Bland's reputation had been burnished at Canterbury in 1965 in the tour match against Kent that followed the Lord's Test. With a wet outfield delaying the start, a big crowd in the ground and the BBC having no cricket to show, Colin Cowdrey persuaded a reluctant Bland to give a fielding exhibition. Picking up balls on the run, he hit the stumps 12 times out of 15. "They spoiled me by giving me three stumps to aim at," he said. "I always practise with one." Bland recalled: "The best part was at the end, when the cameraman wanted a close-up of the wicket exploding. They gave six balls to Graeme Pollock. He stood about three yards away and missed all six."

BOSE, GOPAL KRISHNA, died of a cardiac arrest in Birmingham on April 26, 2018, aged 71. He was visiting his son Arijit. Bose was an opening batsman, seen at one time as a long-term partner of Sunil Gavaskar in the 1970s. But he didn't get to play a Test — although he did open the batting with Gavaskar and put on 194 in an unofficial Test against Sri Lanka. Bose also bowled off-breaks: he had 72 wickets. His only ODI was in England, which was India's second ever, where he made 13. His highest first-class score of 170 came in an Irani Trophy match against Mumbai (for the Rest) in 1973-74. Bose, who later became coach and selector for Bengal — for whom he scored 3757 runs — was coach of the Virat Kohli-led Under-19 team which won the World Cup in 2008.

"Lost a very dear person today. Luckily he was with his family in Birmingham. We will miss him," tweeted Sourav Ganguly.

BOSE, SREERUPA, who died on November 30, 2017, aged 66, opened the bowling in two ODIs for India Women against New Zealand in 1984-85, without taking a wicket. She captained Bengal for many years, and coached the Indian team at the 1993, 1997 and 2000 World Cups. She also commentated on sport for Doordarshan and All India Radio. *(See page 902)*

CONGDON, BEVAN ERNEST, died on February 10, 2018, the day before his 80th birthday. When skipper Graham Dowling suffered career-ending back trouble during New Zealand's tour of the West Indies in 1971-72, Congdon took over for the Third Test. He had just scored 166 not out at Port of Spain, the highest score of a modest career that until then had produced only one other century in 33 Tests. But in 17 as captain, he made four more, including 176 and 175 in successive innings in England in 1973. His bowling was even more transformed: previously a fill-in with just 18 wickets, he became an important third or fourth seamer, and picked up a further 33 while captain. New Zealand first beat Australia under his captaincy. He was also the first ODI captain to score a century when he made 101 against England in Wellington in 1975.

When Walter Hadlee, Richard's father, picked an all-time New Zealand XI for his 1993 autobiography, he wasn't sure whom to put at No.3. "Glenn Turner would be my preferred choice," he mused. "But if the opposition had bowlers of real pace, I would replace him with Bevan Congdon — one of the best players of fast bowling, as he positioned himself well on the back foot and into line with the ball, whereas Turner tended to slash outside off stump."

CUMBERBATCH, CLYDE ELLIOT, who died on December 29, 2017, aged 81, was a tall 6ft 6in umpire from Trinidad who stood in 63 first-class matches, 12 of them Tests, as well as 26 ODIs. His first Test, England's visit to Port-of-Spain in 1980-81, had an unusual start: it was delayed for four hours after the pitch had been damaged by locals upset at the omission of Trinidad wicketkeeper Deryck Murray. Cumberbatch was well respected in the Caribbean, although he might have ended one famous career almost before it started, by no-balling Curtly Ambrose for throwing when the Leeward Islands visited Trinidad in January 1988. After retiring, Cumberbatch headed the training committee for West Indian umpires for 12 years.

Clyde Cumberbatch went on to be a respected umpire in the West Indies.

CURRAN, KEVIN PATRICK, who died on August 23, 2017, aged 88, was the father of the late Zimbabwe all-rounder Kevin, and grandfather of the Surrey brothers Sam and Tom. Kevin senior had six first-class matches for Rhodesia, never surpassing the unbeaten 52 he made on debut against Western Province in 1947-48. He also played for a South African XI against the Australian tourists in Salisbury (now Harare) in November 1949.

DE GRANDHOMME, LAURENCE LEONARD, who died on December 13, 2017, aged 61, was an off-spinner and handy batsman who played several representative matches for Zimbabwe in pre-Test days, and toured England with them in 1985. In the first match of the trip, against Oxford University, his 32 not out was dwarfed by the 19-year-old Graeme Hick's 230. Zimbabwe had no domestic first-class cricket at the time, so de Grandhomme's senior opportunities were limited to visits from touring teams.

In September 1985, he captained Zimbabwe B against a strong Young Australia side, which included Steve Waugh. Three years later he played the last of his 16 first-class games, taking three wickets against Sri Lanka B, but bagging a pair.

His son, Colin, played for Zimbabwe A, before moving to New Zealand and making his Test debut for them in November 2016; he scored a maiden Test century against West Indies at Wellington little more than a week before his father's death.

DHARMALINGAM, P K, who died in Chennai on June 2, 2019, aged 84 was best known as a coach. He played 29 first class matches for Tamil Nadu and Services, making 1132 runs with a highest of 162 and claimed 44 wickets with his leg-spin. He was an outstanding fielder, besides. He coached the

Tamil Nadu women's team. W V Raman, coach of the Indian women's team, said of Dharmalingam, "He played a key role in the early part of my career. He always wanted players to be sharp while fielding because he realised that unlike batting and bowling, form is irrelevant to fielding." R Ashwin tweeted that Dharmalingam was a man who "spent his entire life for the sport. His 'Cricket Kanavugal' (Cricket Dreams) programme on local TV will always be remembered by the kids from the 1990s."

When, as a teenager, Dharmalingam spent a lot of time on the cricket field, his mother asked him if the game was going to feed him. He was fond of saying decades later that the game did feed him, after all. His father, worried about his lack of interest in academics, insisted he join the Indian Air Force as a teenager. Soon he was playing for the Services Ranji team alongside Test players Hemu Adhikari, Bal Dani, A K Sengupta and C V Gadkari.

While still in his 20s, Dharmalingam qualified as a coach from the National Institute of Sports, Patiala. Back in Chennai following a transfer to that city, he quit the IAF and joined the new league side, India Cements. His career with Tamil Nadu, he said, came to an end with a reverse sweep, a shot that displeased the selectors so much that he never played again.

DHAROD, RAMJI PREMJI, who died on March 27, 2017, aged 77, was a well-known swing bowler in club cricket in Bombay. He never played first-class cricket, but made a mark during the first Test played at the Wankhede Stadium, against West Indies in January 1975. Crowd trouble flared after a spectator intent on congratulating Clive Lloyd on his double-century was manhandled by police, but Dharod and a friend jumped over the fence from the members' enclosure, risking arrest themselves, and successfully persuaded the protesters not to damage the pitch. Play was able to resume next morning. Karsan Ghavri, who opened the bowling for India in that match, attended Dharod's funeral.

DOGGART, GEORGE HUBERT GRAHAM, died on February 16, 2018, aged 92. Hubert Doggart was not the only England batsman bewildered by Sonny Ramadhin and Alf Valentine in the summer of 1950. In four innings, they each took his wicket twice, but his potential was such that, after scores of 29, 22 and 25 (plus a duck), he might have expected further opportunities. At the end of the season, however, he began a career in teaching, turning his back on top-level cricket — although he later captained Sussex in 1954.

But Doggart was not lost to the game. He became a tireless supporter of schools cricket, firing the enthusiasm and nurturing the talent of scores of youngsters — Tiger Pataudi was a protégé — and was later the president of MCC. Yet the weight and style of his early run-scoring made it tempting to wonder how good he might have become.

DOGGART, SIMON JONATHON GRAHAM, who died on July 23, 2017, aged 56, followed his father Hubert in representing Cambridge University. An off-spinner who batted left-handed, he made 35 first-class appearances and played in the Varsity Match four times. His highest score and best figures both came against Nottinghamshire at Fenner's in 1983: 70, and 3 for 3. He also played ten times for Combined Universities in the Benson and Hedges Cup, and a handful of Second XI games for his father's old county, but went into teaching, becoming headmaster of Caldicott School in Berkshire. He retired two months before his death.

DOTIWALA, DARA NADIRSHAH, who died on January 30, 2019, aged 85, spent his last 33 years loyally defending Vikram Raju, his fellow-umpire in the famous second tied Test between Australia and India in Chennai, 1986. It was Raju's trigger finger that ruled last man Maninder Singh lbw to Greg Matthews on the penultimate ball of the match, a decision hotly disputed to this day by the batsman and non-striker Ravi Shastri. Dotiwala at square leg always maintained he heard nothing, although he did admit in 2016 he was lucky not to be umpiring at the bowler's end in that final over. A no-nonsense type, he threatened to send Australian captain Allan Border off the field for alleged time wasting on that dramatic last day. He also had a run-in with Viv Richards in the Delhi Test in 1983-84.

Dotiwala stood in a total of six Tests and eight ODI; he gave Mohsin Khan out lbw off the first ball bowled in a Test ground (Gandhi Stadium, Jalandhar, 1982-83). After retirement, he dedicated his life to teaching umpiring.

DUTTA, BISWANATH, who died on September 24, 2018, aged 92 was a president of the BCCI and acknowledged as successor Jagmohan Dalmiya's mentor. Dutta took over as president in 1989 after six years as vice-president. In 1977, he put Dalmiya on the road to cricket administration by making him treasurer of the Cricket Association of Bengal.

Ganguly called Dutta a "master administrator" and recalled seeking his blessings before making his debut for India Under-19 in 1989-90. "It will be a void which will be very, very difficult to fill," he said. The CAB named a gallery at the Eden Gardens after Dutta. He was also involved in soccer administration in Bengal and in different capacities in the Indian Football Association.

FELSINGER, HERBERT CLEMEN, who died on April 29, 2018, aged 83 was one of the umpires for Sri Lanka's inaugural Test, against England in Colombo in February 1982. He stood in five further Tests and 11 ODIs. He had been a good club batsman, sharing an opening partnership of 351 with Makkin Salih for Moors in the Sara Trophy in 1952-53; soon after, he toured India with a Ceylon team. His brother, Alane, was also a first-class umpire, who stood in one Test; they officiated together in a representative match against the West Indian tourists in 1978-79.

FRANCIS, GEORGE, who died on April 11, 2019, aged 57 wanted to become a priest. Instead he became a sports photographer. His began with *Indian Express* in Chennai where he got hooked on motorsports after his first visit to the Sholavaram motor track in 1984, the year he launched his photo agency, *Scorp News*. He also covered cricket matches including the tied Test match between India and Australia at Chepauk in 1986 and contributed photos to cricket books.

GAUTAM, SHUBAM, died on June 19, 2017 after collapsing on a bus taking his side to a cricket tournament in Bangalore. He was 22, and had been playing for the Hubli Cricket Academy. Gautam reportedly fell off his seat during the journey and was declared dead on arrival at hospital. Mourners at his funeral protested that he had been murdered, but initial police enquiries drew a blank.

GERA, AMAN LAJPAT, who died of cancer on June 26, 2018, aged 49, was an off-spinner who played nine Ranji Trophy matches for Uttar Pradesh, taking 5 for 133 against Haryana in Faridabad in 1996-97.

GHAI, SHARAD, who died on May 20, 2017, aged 64, was closely involved with the Kenyan Cricket Association (later Cricket Kenya) from 1996 to 2005, latterly as chairman. He was credited with modernising it, especially in marketing. When one reporter joked that he must have made a million dollars from an ICC tournament in Nairobi in October 2000, Ghai shot back: "No, I didn't. I made 1.6 million." He was hailed as a hero when Kenya reached the semi-finals of the 2003 World Cup, but that high point preceded a rapid decline; starved of resources and players, they have hardly won an important match since, and lost ODI status in 2014. By then Ghai was long gone, sacked by the government amid allegations of financial misconduct on a grand scale. In 2006, he was cleared of stealing $3.3m from the old board, but was still frozen out by the new.

GHODGE, RAJESH DAMODAR, who died on January 13, 2019, in Margao, Goa, two days before his 44th birthday, played two Ranji Trophy and eight List A matches for Goa as an opening batsman, from 1997-98 to 2004-05. His highest score of 63 came in the Ranji Trophy one-day match against Karnataka in December 1998. It was his lone half-century.

GREAVES, WILLIAM, died on November 28, 2017, aged 79. Yorkshireman Bill Greaves was a journalist who spent 20 years with the *Daily Mail*, writing entertainingly on travel and general subjects. In retirement he co-founded the Capital Kids Cricket charity, after discovering that in 1990 only 20 of London's 800 state schools were playing cricket. His "Greaves's Guide" to the etiquette of ordering a round of drinks hangs behind the bar in many a pub.

GUPTE, MAHENDRANATH YESHWANT, died on May 7, 2017, aged 86. He had a long career as an umpire in India, standing in 26 first-class matches from 1970-71, including one Test, against England in Madras in 1984-85. He had little to do while Graeme Fowler and Mike Gatting were amassing double-centuries in a total of 652. His son, Vineet, also became an umpire, and stood in two ODIs in 1999.

JADEJA, MANOHARSINHJI PRADYUMANSINHJI, who died on September 27, 2018, aged 82, played 14 times for Saurashtra under his princely name of the Yuvraj of Rajkot, usually as captain. No mere figurehead, he scored 144 in 1957-58 against a Gujarat side containing four present or future Test players, after making 59 on debut against them two years earlier. He succeeded his father — who had captained Kathiawar in the 1948-49 Ranji Trophy match they conceded when Bhausaheb Nimbalkar reached 443 not out for Maharashtra — as the 15th Thakore Saheb of Rajkot in 1973.

The Yuvraj of Rajkot was no mere figurehead.

He was active in local politics, and in 2010 secured the return from a German museum of the 'Star of India', a saffron-yellow Rolls-Royce Phantom originally built for his grandfather in 1934.

JADEJA, MULABHA V, who died on June 12, 2018, aged 87, played 31 Ranji Trophy matches, mainly for Saurashtra. Usually an opener, he made two centuries: 102 against Gujarat in Rajkot in 1955-56, and 110 as Saurashtra followed on against Mumbai two seasons later. His son, Bimal Jadeja, also played for Saurashtra.

JICHKAR, AMOL MANOHAR, hanged himself in Nagpur on April 25, 2017, while depressed about financial problems. He was 38. An off-spinner, Jichkar played six first-class and eight List A matches for Vidarbha, with a best of 4 for 45 — including Test batsman Mohammad Kaif — in what turned out to be his last game, a one-dayer against Uttar Pradesh in Udaipur in December 2001.

KALIA, SUMIT, drowned on July 8, 2018, aged 30, in the Gobind Sagar Lake in Himachal Pradesh. Kalia, who had performed with some success for Punjab's age-group teams before taking up coaching, made two appearances for the state's T20 side. A slow left-armer, he also played in the Indian Cricket League (the short-lived rival to the IPL), taking 4 for 20 — all Pakistan Test players — for Ahmedabad Rockets against Lahore Badshahs in March 2008.

Sharmeen Khan was a pioneer of women's cricket in Pakistan.

KHAN, SHARMEEN, who died of pneumonia on December 12, 2018, aged 46, was one of the pioneers of women's cricket in Pakistan. She and her sister, Shaiza, decided to establish a national side after they watched the 1993 Women's World Cup final at Lord's — and did so, in the face of indifference and occasional opposition from the Pakistan authorities. Sharmeen herself played in Pakistan's first two Tests, against Sri Lanka and Ireland. Fittingly, she bowled their first delivery and soon took their first wicket. She also appeared in 26 ODIs, including the 1997-98 World Cup in India, and was a playing member of MCC.

KRISHNAMURTHY, DR SUBBARAO, who died on December 7, 2017, aged 79, was a wicketkeeper-batsman who sometimes captained Mysore (now Karnataka). His highest score of 95 came in his third match, opening against Andhra in Bangalore in November 1959. He was later chairman of Karnataka's selectors.

LAVER, JACK FRANCIS LEE, died on October 3, 2017, seven months after his 100th birthday. Born in Victoria, he moved to Tasmania in 1940, but spent the next four years as a military policeman. He represented Tasmania and its combined teams in 13 matches between 1946-47 and 1951-52, bowling quickish off-spinners and occasionally wielding a pugnacious bat. Laver made his presence felt twice against MCC touring teams. In 1946-47 he took 5 for 34, including Denis Compton, Bill Edrich and Norman Yardley. Four years later, batting at No. 9, he made 59 of the 72 scored while he was in.

LAWTON, JAMES, who died on September 27, 2018, aged 75, was one of British journalism's most prolific sports columnists. Jim Lawton's versatility extended to long stints as chief sportswriter of the *Daily Express* and *The Independent*. In Antigua in 1990, Viv Richards, who should have been leading his team on to the field, stomped instead up to the press box, where he subjected the mild-mannered and cherubic Lawton to a bizarre harangue complete with veiled threats. The casus belli was a press conference the previous day where Lawton had asked about a V-sign to the crowd, which was followed by the *Express*'s front-page headline "Captain Viv blows his top" — which was true when written, and became even truer when the page arrived by fax just before play began that morning. Richards made peace two tours later: the incident had been a PR disaster for him, since Lawton was much liked and admired by his colleagues.

LEWIS, DESMOND MICHAEL, who died on March 25, 2018, aged 72,

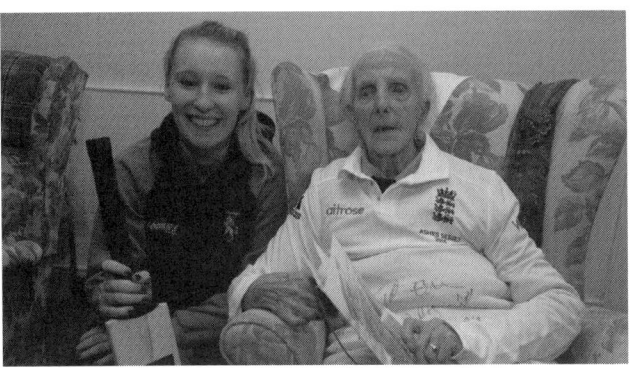

Megan Lowe's 100th birthday was marked with a card from the Queen and a signed England shirt.

was a wicketkeeper who had a rapid rise to Test cricket, but faded equally quickly. In only his second home match for Jamaica, he made what remained a career-best 96 after opening against the 1970-71 Indian tourists, and was chosen to replace Mike Findlay for the Third Test in Georgetown. Lewis started with an unbeaten 81 after being dropped early at slip: he survived for three and a half hours and shared an unlikely ninth-wicket partnership of 84 with Lance Gibbs. In the Fourth Test, he made 88 after being promoted to open, then 72 in the Fifth, to finish with 259 runs at 86 — which turned out to be his final average. Findlay, a smoother gloveman, was preferred when New Zealand toured the following year. "It was easily one of the worst selection blunders in West Indies cricket," wrote Lewis's friend and club-mate Karl Goodison. "But Desmond did not allow the disappointment to consume him, as he said his father told him there was enough bitterness in the world."

LOWE, DOROTHY MEGAN, died on May 16, 2017, aged 101. Medium-pacer Megan Lowe played in all four of England's Tests in Australasia in 1948-49, taking 3 for 34 — the top three in the order — in the drawn Second Test in Melbourne. She had taken time off from her job as a teacher (she later became a headmistress) to make the long tour. Aged only 14, Lowe had collected 6 for 39 for a Women's Cricket Association XI against Torquay and South Devon in 1929. Her 100th birthday in 2015 was marked with a card from the Queen, and a signed England shirt.

LUTHRA, SURESH, who died aged 74 on February 12, 2019, was a left-arm medium-pacer who played for Delhi and North Zone. In the 1970s, when spin ruled Indian cricket, left-arm pace bowler Luthra struck terror in the hearts of Indian batsmen in domestic cricket with his speed and intimidation. But despite his 262 wickets in 67 first-class matches (and three List A matches) with a best of 9 for 70 for Delhi v Services in 1976-77 (and one century), he was never in serious contention for a place in the national side largely due to doubts over the legality of his bowling action. Nor was he ever exposed to any visiting teams despite a career stretching from 1965-66 to 1980-81, during which he represented Northern Punjab, Delhi and Punjab in the Ranji Trophy. It would be ten years into his career before he was called for chucking. That happened in the Ranji Trophy quarterfinal between Delhi and Bihar at Feroz Shah Kotla where Piloo Reporter called him four times from square leg, forcing Luthra to turn to spin. Reporter claimed many cricketers thanked him for taking the tough call. Post retirement he was coach, selector, manager and match referee.

MITRA, SHYAM SUNDAR, who died on June 27, 2019, aged 82, captained Bengal in the Ranji Trophy and finished with an average of 50.13 over 59 matches with seven centuries and 17 fifties and a highest of 155. He also bowled occasional medium-pace with a best of 4 for 16. Supporters wondered why he never donned national colours. The answer it appears is mired in inter-club politics of Kolkata cricket, which harmed the careers of many talented cricketers in a period where East was the forgotten zone of Indian cricket. In just his second match in March 1959, he was on the losing side of the Ranji Trophy final against Mumbai. It was against the formidable Mumbai that he scored two heroic centuries, first in the semi-final in 1967-68 and then again in the semi-final on his home turf in 1970-71. Bengal lost both on first innings. 'Chuni' Goswami, who succeeded him as Bengal captain, bemoaned the fact the Mitra never played Test cricket. He was conferred the Lifetime Achievement Award by the Cricket Association of Bengal in 2009.

MURRAY, JOHN THOMAS, who died aged 83 on July 24, 2018, was one of the game's finest wicketkeepers. His 1527 first-class dismissals is second on the all-time list. Murray played 21 times for England during the 1960s. He made his only Test hundred against West Indies at The Oval in 1966, batting at No.9. A stylist with the bat and gloves, he played more than 650 times for Middlesex, scoring 17,519 runs during a 24-year career.

Cricket writer John Thicknesse said Murray was "one of cricket's greatest stylists" and "with palms uppermost before each ball, his gloves traced flowing semi-circles, one the mirror image of the other". He noted that Murray specialised in "elegant 30s" rather than more substantial innings. While his technique was good and he was by no stretch a poor batsman, it was his batting that prevented him from making more of an impact on the international stage.

NARAYANAN, PERUNGULAM SUNDARESAN, who died on May 18, 2017, aged 75, played one first-class match for Madras (later Tamil Nadu)

Seymour Nurse bowed out on a high. — *Getty Images*

in 1969-70 against Andhra, bowling one over and not batting. A consistent scorer at lower levels, he was part of a famous cricket family: cousins V Sivaramakrishnan and V Ramnarayan both played first-class cricket. He was later the publisher of *Sruti*, a Chennai cultural magazine, while his brother P N Sundaresan edited the *Indian Cricket* annual and also contributed to *Wisden*.

NURSE, SEYMOUR MACDONALD, who died on May 5, 2019, aged 85, was a stylish middle-order batsman who played 29 Tests in a career spanning less than 10 years. He scored 70 and 11 on debut against MCC at Kingston, Jamaica, in February 1960. But it was his final innings at Lancaster Park, Christchurch, nine years later that has remained in the record books even after 50 years. Nurse had a disappointing tour of Australia and had announced at the start of the New Zealand series that followed that it would be his last due to family commitments. With just one half-century in the previous eight innings, he finally came into his own in the Fifth Test in Sydney with 137 in the second innings. But it was too late for West Indies, who lost the Test by a massive 382 runs and the series 1–3. Nurse was the star of the victory in the First Test at Eden Park, Auckland, with 95 and 168. Then with the series locked 1–1, he recorded his highest first-class score with 258 in West Indies' only innings in the final Test. It remains the highest score by a batsman in his final Test innings.   Captain Garry Sobers tried, but could not persuade Nurse to retract his decision. He ended with the excellent average of 47.60.

An acclaimed coach, he was born in the quaintly named Jack-My-Nanny Gap, Black Rock, St Michael in Barbados and also represented the island in football.

OAKMAN, ALAN STANLEY MYLES, who died on September 6, 2018, aged 88, was at home in Hastings one July evening in 1956 when a policeman popped by with an urgent message from England's chairman of selectors. Gubby Allen had enlisted the Sussex constabulary after discovering Oakman was not on the phone. Tom Graveney was injured, and Oakman was needed at Old Trafford for the Fourth Ashes Test. He gathered his kit and drove north to take his place in cricket history. Stationed in the leg trap, he had a close-up view as Jim Laker collected 19 for 90, the greatest figures in first-class history. He took five catches and, thanks to the television and newsreel commentaries, became forever linked with Laker's achievement. "When Jim and I met up afterwards, he would always say: 'Are you still living off those five catches?'"

They were just as well: Oakman had been given only eight overs in Australia's second innings and made ten from No.7. His second Test was his last — there were no more visits from the Hastings police.

But Oakman was not the sort to dwell on his thwarted career. As an opening batsman and prolific off-spinner, he was a significant figure at Sussex: ninth on their all-time list of appearances, 11th for runs, 17th for wickets and second for catches by a non-wicketkeeper. After leaving Hove, he coached Warwickshire, winning the Championship in 1972. The next quip was never far away: Keith Cook, then Warwickshire's membership secretary, said Oakman could make you laugh while proof-reading the fixture list.

OSLEAR, DONALD OSMUND, who died on May 10, 2018, aged 89, had a short but eventful career as an international umpire. His five Tests included two in Botham's Ashes series in 1981, while the 1983 World Cup match between England and Pakistan — one of his eight ODIs — had him wrestling a streaker.

But it was a match in 1992 in which he was not in the middle that earned Oslear lasting fame — and two appearances in court. At the tail-end of a rancorous summer, England's ODI against Pakistan at Lord's had been extended by rain into a second day. The umpires, John Hampshire and Ken Palmer, believed Pakistan's bowlers had tampered with the ball. At lunch, they showed it to Oslear, the third umpire, and match referee Deryck Murray. The ball was changed. Pakistan won a thrilling victory, but the ICC announced no action would be taken. Oslear's typically thorough report was quietly shelved.

The issue of how Wasim Akram and Waqar Younis achieved prodigious reverse swing had been rumbling for weeks. In the *Daily Mirror*, Allan Lamb, in his final season as an England batsman, fuelled the flames by accusing them of roughing up one side of the ball, and suggested that Sarfraz Nawaz, his former Northamptonshire team-mate, had invented the method. Sarfraz sued Lamb for libel, and in 1993 the case was heard. In court, Oslear said: "In my opinion it is not possible to scour the ball like that by legal means."

The case was dropped, but the story would not go away. Three years later, Oslear was back in court when Lamb and Botham sued Imran Khan for libel, after he said they were ill-educated and had made racially motivated remarks about him. Oslear duelled with the ferocious libel lawyer George Carman, correcting him for calling him a referee, and pointing out that cricket had laws not rules.

By then, Oslear's career was over. He had been forced to retire at the end of the 1993 season, blaming the bad publicity from the ball-tampering row. But the TCCB insisted he had been told months earlier that he would be retiring around his 65th birthday.

PAL, RAJINDER, who died on May 9, 2018, aged 80, was a tireless Indian seamer who had a long first-class career, mainly for Delhi and North Zone. On often unresponsive pitches, he took 337 wickets at 21, including 8 for 27 for Southern Punjab against Jammu and Kashmir in Srinagar in 1966-67. Three years earlier he won his only Test cap, against England in Mumbai, apparently at the request of the captain, Tiger Pataudi. The experiment was not a success: he bowled 13 overs without a wicket, and never played again, partly because he later fell out with Pataudi.

Rajinder, who represented Haryana towards the end of his career, was credited there with broadening Kapil Dev's repertoire after taking up coaching. "He taught me inswing in three weeks," said Kapil.

His brother, Ravinder Pal, also played for Delhi. They opened the bowling in one match in 1964-65; then the following season, after Rajinder had moved to Southern Punjab, shared 15 wickets in the game on opposite sides.

PANDYA, HARESH, jumped from a bridge in his home town of Rajkot on November 11, 2017. He was 53, and had been troubled by health issues. An English teacher, Pandya was also passionate about cricket. He wrote long letters to many players and journalists, and eventually became a freelance journalist himself, contributing to many publications at home and abroad, once writing on Indian music for the *New York Times*. His correspondence with

Haresh Pandya was passionate about cricket.

Don Bradman formed the basis of a feature article in the 2017 *Wisden India Almanack*.

"I have known him since my Under-14 days," Cheteshwar Pujara — the India Test player was often the topic of Pandya's writing — recalled. "He always had a soft corner for players from Gujarat … The moment you spoke to him, you could make out the kind of energy he had."

PATNAIK, SIDHANTA, who succumbed to cancer on June 1, 2019, aged 34, had been a senior staff writer of *Wisden India Almanack* since its inception, and played an important role in its success. His passion for the less-publicised cricket at the junior levels and his deep understanding of women's cricket made him a walking encyclopaedia in these fields. His book, on women's cricket in India, *The Fire Burns Blue*, co-authored with colleague Karunya Keshav, is a seminal publication. It was released even as his cancer, which had been in remission, struck again. (*See page 922*)

PUNJABI, PAPAN RAMCHAND, died on February 25, 2018, aged 89. Ram Punjabi was an umpire from Hyderabad who officiated in 37 first-class matches in India, including seven Tests between 1978-79 and 1981-82, as well as two ODIs. Sunil Gavaskar scored 107 in Punjabi's first Test, and 172 in his last. But three Indians received what they thought were poor decisions in that game, as did England's captain Keith Fletcher — who was disciplined after gently knocking off the bails on being adjudged caught behind — and Punjabi was not called on again.

RAO, PRABHAKAR, who died on June 9, 2019, aged 84, was a Tamil Nadu and South Zone medium-pacer who captured 84 wickets in a ten-year career. His best of 7 for 28 came against Andhra at Chepauk in 1959-60. Rao held various posts in the Tamil Nadu Cricket Association, including secretary, vice-president and chairman of the state selectors. Tall, slim and invariably cheerful, he was nicknamed the 'White Horse' because of his light complexion. His two daughters represented the country in rowing in the Asian Games.

RAO, VITTAL M B, who died on December 8, 2017, aged 92, had the unenviable experience of keeping wicket for Mysore throughout Holkar's total of 912 for 8 in the Ranji Trophy semi-final in Indore in 1945-46. After 214.5 overs in almost ten hours, during which six batsmen, including the 50-year-old C K Nayudu, made centuries, Vittal Rao went straight back out to open, but was soon dismissed for 14. In the follow-on, he retired hurt (or possibly exhausted) before he had scored. This was the third of his four first-class appearances; he later played for Mysore Gymkhana.

RYNEVELD, VAN CLIVE, who died January 29, 2018, aged 89, captained South Africa in cricket, played rugby for England, was a Rhodes Scholar and one of the founding members of the Progressive political party and also served a term in parliament. His work as a lawyer included providing assistance to players — the most notable one being Basil D'Oliveira — with their contracts.

A leg-spin-bowling all-rounder, van Ryneveld was part of South Africa's famous Test win in England in 1951. It was his debut match. In all, he played 19 Tests between 1951 and 1958, captaining South Africa in eight of them, and finished with 724 runs and 17 wickets. He had a more successful first-class career, playing 101 games, making 4803 runs and taking 206 wickets.

As one of the 12 United Party MPs who quit the organisation in 1959 and started the Progressive Party, van Ryneveld helped demonstrate that there was a tangible anti-apartheid community among white South Africans, even if H F Verwoerd's National Party was at the time an unstoppable political force.

SATHE, CHANDRA KANT, who died on August 3, 2017, aged 69, had a long career as an umpire in India. He stood in 49 first-class matches over 21 years from 1982, and in five ODIs, the first of them during England's 1992-93 tour.

SHUKLA, RAKESH CHANDRA, who died on June 29, 2019, aged 71, managed to stay above the fray of the mud pit of cricket politics in Delhi. By the time he made his Test debut in Chennai against Sri Lanka in 1982, he was 34 years old and it turned out to be his lone Test. A leg-break bowler and more than useful batsman, he failed to take a wicket in the first innings but in the second dismissed the rampaging Roy Dias (97) and Duleep Mendis (105).

He had his moment of glory in the Ranji Trophy final at the Feroz Shah Kotla in 1981-82. Karnataka had amassed a mammoth 705 in their first innings and were all set to win on first-innings lead with Delhi at 589 for 8 when young Rajesh Peter (67 not out) joined Shukla (69 not out) at the crease with only last man Maninder Singh to follow. The pair held their nerve amidst mounting tension to add an unbroken 118 runs to take Delhi home.

Shukla, built like a wrestler, had an older brother Anand who also bowled and batted in the same style. Rakesh played in six finals for Delhi, being on the winning side four times. He represented Delhi and Bengal, but the bulk of his 121 matches came for Delhi and North Zone. He was also a coach, selector and commentator. His former captain Bishan Bedi described him as a "no-fuss cricketer who was extremely committed with both bat and ball".

Jasdev Singh receiving the Padma Bhushan from President Pratibha Patil in 2008.
— *Getty Images/ Hindustan Times*

SINGH, JASDEV, who died on September 25, 2018, aged 87, was a commentator and regarded as the voice of Indian sports on Doordarshan. During the late 1970s and early '80s, Jasdev Singh, Ravi Chaturvedi and Sushil Doshi, were household names for sports lovers. "It is with deep sadness that I note the demise of Jasdev Singh, one of our finest commentators. A veteran of All India Radio and Doordarshan, he covered nine Olympics, six Asian Games and made numerous Independence Day and Republic Day broadcasts," said Minister of State for Sports Rajyavardhan Singh Rathore. Former International Olympic Council chief Juan Antonio Samaranch honoured Jasdev with the 'Olympic Order' at the Seoul edition in 1988, for his role in spreading the Olympic movement.

SINGH, MILKHA AMRITSAR GOVINDSINGH, who died on November 10, 2017, aged 75, belonged to the first family of cricket in Tamil Nadu, with three generations having played first-class cricket. Father Ram Singh was hero of the inaugural Ranji Trophy match (he took 11 wickets), his brother Kripal made a century on Test debut, while Kripal's son Arjan made a triple-century in the Ranji Trophy. Another brother and two nephews also played for Tamil Nadu. Brothers Milkha and Kripal played together against England in Bombay in 1961-62.

The turbaned Milkha Singh was a consistent performer for Madras and South Zone throughout the 1960s, scoring five centuries — the highest a 151 against North Zone in Madras in 1961-62, making him the first centurion in the Duleep Trophy tournament.

An aggressive left-hander, he had made his Test debut the previous season, just days after turning 18, but struggled at the top level: his best score in four appearances for India was 35, against Pakistan in Delhi in 1960-61. "I bowled to a lot of world-class left-handers, including Garry Sobers, but Milkha was up there," said the Test leg-spinner V V Kumar, a former teammate. "He could play any shot against any type of bowling."

SINHA, AFZALUR REHMAN, who died on August 8, 2018, aged 68, was the chairman of the Bangladesh Premier League, and a director of the national board. He had been a freedom fighter in the war of independence from Pakistan in 1971, forged a successful business career and joined the Bangladesh Cricket Board in 1998.

SRIDHAR, MARUTI VENKAT, died of a heart attack on October 30, 2017, aged 51. A month earlier, he resigned as the BCCI's general manager of cricket operations as he had failed to inform the board he was also involved with several cricket clubs in his native Hyderabad. Until then, 'Doc' Sridhar had seemed a born administrator, having gained plaudits for his calm assurance as media manager during India's fractious tour of Australia in 2007-08, which came close to being called off when Harbhajan Singh was accused of racially abusing Andrew Symonds. He was also tournament director of the World Twenty20 in India in 2016.

Sridhar had been a stylish and highly effective batsman for Hyderabad, especially good on turning pitches. He scored 21 first-class centuries, including a 366 against Andhra at Secunderabad in 1993-94, the third-highest individual innings in the Ranji Trophy, as Hyderabad ran up the largest total, 944 for 6. It was also the highest score by a medical practitioner, beating W G Grace's 344 in 1876. The next man to score a triple for Hyderabad was V V S Laxman, who said: "He was an elder brother to me, who taught me the art of batting long. The entire cricket fraternity will miss him."

STRAUSS, RUTH (nee McDonald), who died on December 29, 2018, aged 46, was the wife of the former England captain Andrew Strauss. He called a halt to a successful spell as England's director of cricket to help nurse her through the final stages of her illness, a rare form of lung cancer which can afflict non-smokers. She was born in Ballarat and met Strauss when he was playing club cricket in Australia; they married in 2003 and had two sons. Even before her husband became Test captain, she was an important part of the backroom set-up. "It is hard to think any woman has done more for the England men's team behind the scenes, given her ability to tune into everyone's wavelength, which translated into making every new player's wife or partner feel integrated," wrote the former *Wisden* editor Scyld Berry, who came to know the family well while assisting Strauss with his book about England's 2009 Ashes victory.

A champion for good

If Sidhanta Patnaik were the one writing this obituary, he'd have opened with warm anecdotes from a childhood friend, a teacher who sparked a fondness for cricket during the 1992 World Cup, the uncle who took him to Barabati stadium, a young reporter he made feel welcome at the press box … interviewing at least a dozen people for a thousand words. But as most cricket writers who work with Patnaik soon realise, we are not 'SidhPat' and it's hard work keeping up.

As a writer, Patnaik was prolific and emotive. As a reporter, he was

dogged and a trove of stats and abstruse facts. As a storyteller, he heroed the underdogs and the diamonds in the rough. His interest was in the grass roots, the dreams, the sweat, the sacrifices that came before the funky hairstyles, tattoos and nationwide adulation. Having understood early that his sister was the better sportsperson, women's cricket was a pet project and he produced seminal work on it.

Cricket wasn't just a passion, but an obsession — and soon, the best medicine. The sport gave him purpose even as he battled cancer, twice. Late in 2018, when the doctors gave him two days, he

pressed them for ten: he was determined to wrap up his work for the Almanack. From his hospital bed, he shot out 1300 words on Hanuma Vihari, India's Test debutant.

Defying expectation, Patnaik recovered enough to see three new Test caps, launched his book *The Fire Burns Blue* (on Indian women's cricket), and conceptualised the country's first magazine on women's cricket. He planned his next book (on the Ranji Trophy) and took his daughter Anantrika to her first match at Bengaluru's Chinnaswamy stadium. As ever, he was building a foundation.   *KK*

SUBRAMANYAM, PETER, who died on May 4, aged 81, was a London-based representative of *The Hindu*. He was a regular in the Lord's press box for more than 30 years from the early 1970s. He played one first-class match, alongside several future Test players, for Indian Universities against the Pakistan tourists in Pune in 1960-61, and dismissed Hanif Mohammad (for 222) with his leg-break bowling.

THAKRE, BHARAT BAPURAO, who died of lung cancer on June 19, 2017, aged 53, was a seamer who took 36 wickets in 16 matches for Vidarbha. He claimed 5 for 44 on debut, against Rajasthan in Jodhpur in 1985-86, and improved his career-best to 7 for 129 against Uttar Pradesh in 1990-91. He was a state selector from 2003 until his death.

VENKATANARAYANA, AMRUTHUR VENKATSHAIYER, who died on October 21, 2017, aged 73 was a left-arm medium-pacer who represented Karnataka in three Ranji Trophy games in the 1960s and '70s. He finished with eight first-class wickets.

VIJAYAKUMAR, SESHADHRI VIJALAPURA, who died on May 31, 2019, aged 73, opened the batting for Karnataka in the Ranji Trophy and for South Zone in the Duleep, and often opened the bowling too. He was an attacking batsman who made his debut alongside Gundappa Viswanath against Andhra in 1967-68. He played a significant role in Karnataka winning the national championship for the first time in 1973-74, claiming 4 for 9 — his best figures — in the final against Rajasthan, including the wicket of skipper Hanumant Singh. He also scored 66. In a quarterfinal against Rajasthan two seasons earlier he had scores of 94 and 94 as Karnataka won. His 2891 first class runs in 57 matches included a highest of 158; in all he claimed 46 wickets. "His passing is a loss to Karnataka cricket," said Viswanath. "As an attacking opener, he was a handsome driver of the ball."

WADEKAR, AJIT LAXMAN, who died on India's Independence Day (August 15), aged 77, led the country to successive series wins in the West Indies and England in 1970-71 and made it a hat-trick with a win at home against England. A stylish left-handed batsman who had to wait for nearly a decade to play for India after making his first-class debut, his international record was disappointing — 37 Tests, one century — but his impact was profound. He was India's first ODI captain. He was that rare creature, a left-hander at No.3 in the years when India's openers were often mere guest artistes sent out to smile at the fast bowlers and put them in good humour. Wadekar oversaw Indian cricket's transition from an also-ran to a world power. He wore that achievement lightly, responding with a lopsided grin when anyone spoke about it. The surface softness hid a certain determination and awareness. That sometimes made opponents take him lightly; they usually paid for it. Later he became a successful coach of the national side. *(See Ayaz Memon's tribute, page 65)*

WATERS, ROBIN HENRY CLOUGH, who died on December 9, 2017, three days after his 80th birthday, was a wicketkeeper-batsman who became a well-known figure as player and coach in Ireland, without fulfilling the potential he had shown for Oxford University. He also played a role in a key moment in Indian cricket: at Hove in 1961 he was at the wheel of the car involved in the accident in which Tiger Pataudi suffered the serious eye injury that hampered his career.

Waters was born in Kolkata. At Oxford in the summer of 1961, he was the regular wicketkeeper. In July, having already been selected for the Varsity Match, he was unbeaten overnight on the first day of the game against Sussex, when he took Pataudi out in his Mini Minor for a meal. As they approached the statue of Queen Victoria on Grand Avenue on their return to the team hotel, they were hit by a car which emerged from a side road. Waters appeared more badly hurt — "pretty badly mangled," he said — but Pataudi's injury was worse: a shard of glass had damaged his right eye. Years later, on a visit to Ireland with a touring Indian team, Pataudi made it clear he had never held Waters responsible.

WAPAKHABULO, YONA NAMAWA, who died of a heart attack on August 6, 2018, aged 46, was said to be the first Ugandan cricketer to score a double-century — 212 for Kampala's Wanderers club in a league match in 1992 — and was also a handy pace bowler. He was a big hitter who, one team-mate recalled, "was responsible for a surge in repair expenses for some of the nearby buildings". His father had been a government minister, and Speaker of the Ugandan parliament. The president attended the funeral.

WASIM, AMER, who died of tuberculosis on September 26, 2018, aged 57, was a slow left-armer who took 242 wickets in an 18-year career for various domestic teams in Pakistan. His best return was 7 for 169, for Railways against the Pakistan National Shipping Corporation in Multan in 1995-96. In October 2000, by now captaining Sialkot, he took 8 for 68 against Okara in the Quaid-e-Azam Trophy — but this was a second-division match without first-class status. The Test player Shoaib Malik, born in Sialkot, was one of several local players mentored by Wasim.

WEIR, ROBERT SCOTT, died on October 4, 2018, aged 65. Tall and talented, and usually sporting a luxuriant moustache cultivated during his days as an RAF helicopter pilot, Scott Weir played 26 matches for Scotland, four first-class, from 1975. He hit 61 and 102 not out in a two-day game against MCC at Lord's in 1982. Weir captained Clydesdale to three Scottish Cup wins, and the league title in 1995. Team-mates fondly recalled his answer to criticism of their late arrival for one Sunday friendly: "Look, pal, this game starts whenever we arrive — and finishes whenever we've won."

WETTIMUNY, MITHRA DE SILVA, died on January 20, 2019, aged 67, following kidney failure. He was the middle brother of three, all of whom opened the batting for Sri Lanka. Sunil and Sidath were the others. He played two Tests and one ODI in 1983. While Sidath scored Sri Lanka's first Test century, Sunil, who played in two World Cups in the 1970s, was the pilot who flew the Sri Lankan team back home from Lahore with the World Cup in 1996. Mithra and Sidath became the third pair of brothers to open in a Test after the Grace brothers E M and W G and Pakistan's Hanif and Sadiq Mohammad.

Mithra came to prominence as captain of the successful Ceylon Schools team that toured India in 1969-70, and included future Test captains Bandula Warnapura and Duleep Mendis. Mithra's first-class career comprised nine matches in four countries in 127 days. "He played two Tests with me in New Zealand," recalled younger brother Sidath, "He was an accountant and then went to Hong Kong."

YARDLEY, BRUCE, who died on March 27, 2019, aged 71, held aloft the flag of spin bowling in an era of testosterone-driven speed merchants. Making his Test debut against India in the Fifth Test in Adelaide in 1977-78, after the age of 30, when the ranks of the national side had been severely depleted by Kerry Packer and his WSC, the tall, gangling off-spinner bowled Australia to victory by 47 runs to secure the rubber 3–2. Yardley, who went wicketless in the first innings, accounted for Chauhan, Mohinder Amarnath, Vengsarkar and Gaekwad to halt India's improbable victory march to 493.

Nicknamed Roo for his bounding run up to the wicket, the off-spinner had made his first-class debut in 1966-67 and was originally a medium-pacer. In the Second Test at Bridgetown in March 1978, he swung merrily against the mighty West Indies pace battery to record his highest Test score of 74. The 50 was reached in 29 balls, which remained an Australian record for 38 years. All but ten of those runs came from boundaries.

Yardley toured India in 1979-80 even as peace was being brokered in Australian cricket. Though he had his foot broken by Kapil Dev in Kanpur, he wrote in his autobiography *Roo's Book*, "I fell in love with India the moment I touched down." He became an Australian cult figure in the 1981-82 home season when he captured 38 wickets in six Tests against Pakistan and West Indies. A brilliant fielder at gully, he was voted the International Cricketer of the Year. Sunil Gavaskar confessed Yardley was the bowler who troubled him most. As coach of the Sri Lanka national team from 1996 to 1999, Yardley mentored the great Muttiah Muralitharan and, in contrast to most of his countrymen, was a strong advocate of his style of bowling.

CHRONICLES

It was first-class, after all

Vilas Godbole, 76, discovered he was a first-class cricketer 53 years late, when he learned he was an answer in a quiz on Facebook. He also found out this entitled him to a Rs 20,000 monthly pension. Godbole played a single match for Bombay against Ceylon in January 1965 without realising it had first-class status: in his only innings, he hit a six off his first ball, before being out for 15. He has started receiving the pension, but not the 12 years' unpaid arrears he believes he is owed.

Unfortunate six

1 0 0 0 0 0 0 0 0 0 – Not a code or a random number but these are the scores of Mali Women batters who were bowled out for a record total of just six runs against Rwanda women who chased down the target in just four balls in Match two of the Kwibuka Women's T20 tournament at the Gahanga International Cricket Stadium, Rwanda. Five of those six runs came in the form of extras — a couple of byes, couple of leg byes and a wide. It was only thanks to the opener Mariam Samake that they got a run off the bat, on the board in an innings which lasted all of nine overs. The previous record for the lowest score in a women's T20I was held by China who were chasing UAE's score of 203 but were bundled out for just 14 during the Women's T20 Smash in Bangkok, back in January.

Mohammed double

Shehzar Mohammad, grandson of the great Hanif, became the sixth member of his family to score a first-class double-century when he made 265 for Karachi Whites against Multan in a Quaid-e-Azam Trophy match at Multan. Shehzar, 26, followed Hanif, his own father Shoaib, his great-uncles Mushtaq and Sadiq, and Sadiq's son Imran.

Another drive, but no runs

A major security breach at the Air Force Sports Complex in Palam allowed a man, who identified himself as Girish Sharma, to drive his car onto the field of play and into the pitch during the Delhi-Uttar

Pradesh Ranji game at Palam 'A' ground in New Delhi. The man claimed he didn't see any security and was merely lost, despite what looked like deliberate swerves to drive over the pitch twice, completely ignoring attempts from players and umpires to stop him. A number of international players like Gautam Gambhir, Suresh Raina, Ishant Sharma and Rishabh Pant were in action. "Very disturbing," tweeted Raina. The match referee deemed the pitch "playable" after examining potential damage.

Burnt toast stops play

Your team is batting. Victory is in sight, with an entire day to spare. And it seems like you won't be needed at the crease. Nathan Lyon was in paradise at Allan Border Field in Brisbane. At least until he decided to make himself a piece of toast. A few minutes later, an alarm sounded, play was stopped, fire engines arrived and a sheepish confession had to be made. "(The toast) popped up first and I wasn't happy so I put it back down and I got carried away watching the cricket," Lyon said dryly. "There's a first for everything." In this case, it was burnt toast stopping play in the match between New South Wales and Queensland in Australia's Sheffield Shield.

1045 runs, but no record

If it had been an official match, Tanishq Gavate's knock of 1045 would have been a world record in schools cricket. Unfortunately for the 13-year-old, his mammoth innings came in the Under-14 Navi Mumbai Shield invitational cricket tournament. Tanishq represented Yashwantrao Chavan XI, a team made up of players from the academy run by his coach. He played 515 balls and hit 149 boundaries and 67 sixes.

Impressive six

Left-arm spinner Sarfaraz Ashraf took six for nought in seven balls in a Karnataka state T20 tournament in Bangalore.

All in the ninth

Aled Carey, 29, took six wickets in an over for Golden Point against East Ballarat in Victoria. Carey, unable to take a wicket in his first eight overs, fared dramatically better in the ninth.

Training session?

Ranji Trophy cricketer Harmeet Singh caused chaos by driving his car on to the platform of a Mumbai suburban railway station during the morning rush hour. No one was hurt, but Harmeet was charged with endangering the safety of passengers. He claimed to have taken a wrong turning. Early reports suggested the player involved was the better-known Harpreet Singh, who had been hoping to attract bids in the IPL auction that morning. By the time a correction was issued, it was too late (though Harpreet did get a chance as a replacement for Royal Challengers Bangalore).

Eat and run

Winners of an annual tournament in Jawhar, Maharashtra, were given edible prizes instead of the customary money. The winning team were awarded a goat, the runners-up five cockerels, and every boundary-hitter a boiled egg. "In the past we have experienced allegations of rigging and fights over prize money. This time, all willingly shared their prizes," said local coach Umesh Tamore.

Covering more than stumps

A disgruntled team protested to the Bangladesh Cricket Board that electronic scorecards had been manipulated to hide the true number of lbws. Kathal Bagan Green Crescent were relegated after losing to North Bengal Cricket Academy. Screenshots showed that at various times the number of lbws given had been six, five and four. Kathal Bagan claimed the actual number was seven, implying there had been a cover-up to hide unjust decisions.

92 ways to protest

Lalmatia bowler Sujon Mahmud conceded 92 runs in the opening over of an innings in the Dhaka League Second Division. He gave away 65 in wides (from 13 deliveries) and 15 from three no-balls, before opponents Axiom secured a ten-wicket win. Lalmatia were protesting against decisions taken by the umpires when they were all out for 88. Their secretary Adnan Rahman Dipon said the problems began at the toss: "My captain was not allowed to see the coin. We were sent to bat first and, as expected, the umpires' decisions came against us."

In a similar incident, Tasnim Hasan of Fear Fighters conceded 69 off seven legitimate balls. The Bangladesh board were unimpressed by the grievances: they banned both bowlers for ten years for "tarnishing the image of Bangladesh cricket"; several club officials were banned for five years, and the teams were suspended from the league indefinitely.

Cricket ball making an extinct skill

Research into traditional crafts, sponsored by the Radcliffe Trust, lists cricket-ball making as one of four skills now extinct in Britain — along with gold-beating and the manufacture of lacrosse sticks, and of sieves and riddles. Today, no one makes hand-stitched cricket balls in the UK, says the Radcliffe Red List. "In some cases, the raw materials are sent from the UK to the Indian subcontinent for fabrication, and the balls are then finished in the UK." Cricket- bat making is listed as "endangered", but not "critically endangered".

Cricket a la Brexit

After being invited to the England v South Africa Test at Lord's, French ambassador Sylvie Bermann thought it was like the Brexit negotiations in Brussels. "Both can be a slow, precise and technical game," she said. "And it can be quite difficult for the uninitiated to understand what is happening. After days of play and exchanges, the match can end in a draw — with each side claiming they've won."

Six in six

Luke Robinson, 13, took six wickets in an over, all bowled, in an Under-13 match for Philadelphia CC, County Durham, against Langley Park. "Time stood still, and I thought, 'Is this really happening?'" said the umpire at the bowler's end, Stephen Robinson, who also happened to be the bowler's father. Luke's mother, Helen, was scoring. The opposition were dismissed for 18, and Philadelphia won by 58 runs.

Arthritic 40

Needing 35 off the final over, Dorchester-on-Thames scored 40 to win their Oxfordshire Cricket Association match against Swinbrook. Steve McComb, who says he prefers to hit boundaries due to an arthritic ankle, hit 66044666 off Mihai Cucos — there were two no-balls.

A moving story

An Indian family have sought refuge in Dubai after falling out with their neighbours in a middle-class residential complex in Mumbai: their son, who was playing cricket in a car park, damaged a windscreen wiper. "We couldn't face the harassment and torture any more," said Anil D'Souza, father of 13-year-old Aryan. "We cannot stay in a place where people are jealous and violent, and do not like children."

Court stops play

Judges stopped play after 13 overs of the Under-23 match between Jammu & Kashmir and Goa in Srinagar. The regional high court issued an order halting the game after Hashim Saleem, a J&K player who had been dropped from the squad, lodged a petition claiming one of the selectors had unjustly picked his own son instead. The match was rescheduled after the court modified the order.

Tiger Moth birthday

Winter Eileen Ash (nee Whelan), the last survivor of the first women's Test played in England, in 1937, marked her 106th birthday on October 30 by taking a flight in a Tiger Moth over the Norfolk coast. The plane was a mere 76-year-old.

The Perfect 10

Akash Choudhary, a 15-year-old left-arm seamer, had figures of 4–4–0–10 in a Twenty20 match for Disha Cricket Academy against Pearl Academy in Jaipur. Choudhary took two wickets in each of his first three overs and four in the last, including a hat-trick. "All luck," he said.

Flintoff shows another facet

Former England captain Andrew Flintoff opened to polite but mixed reviews when *Fat Friends: The Musical*, an adaptation of a TV show about slimming, began its run at the Leeds Grand Theatre prior to a national tour. Lancastrian Flintoff played nice-but-dim Kevin, fiancé of a bride desperate to fit into her wedding dress, in a story set in the un-Lancastrian suburb of Headingley. Flintoff "proves he can do more than play cricket", said the *Yorkshire Post*. He captured Kevin well and won plenty of laughs, according to the *Huddersfield Daily Examiner*, "but sadly his vocals just weren't up to the task". *The Press*, from York, praised his "warm-toned" singing, but said his movement was "not exactly comfortable".

A bit of a batsman scores 490

On his 20th birthday, Shane Dadswell scored 490 off 151 balls, playing for North-West University in Potchefstroom against Potch Dorp CC. He hit 57 sixes and 27 fours, while the team made 677 for 3 off 50 overs, and won by 387 runs. The previous week Dadswell had scored 126 off 38. He said he was "a bit of an attacking batsman".

A wide doubles the score

The Nagaland Women's Under-19s were bowled out for two by Kerala. Their only runs — a single and a wide — came during the six-over opening partnership. Head coach Hokaito Zhimoni said that Nagaland had been forced to advertise for players and had hardly any time to practise. "Now the girls have got a sense of where they stand and where they need to improve," he said.

Wheat, mustard or T20?

Farmers near Delhi are turning their land into cricket grounds, staging Twenty20 matches for amateur players and charging far more than they ever earned growing wheat or mustard. Some villages now boast several mini- stadiums, complete with canteens and floodlights. With lights, grounds can stage up to five games a day for the city's growing middle classes.

On another field

Former England goalkeeper Joe Hart, 31, decided not to watch England play Sweden and turned out instead for Shrewsbury CC for the first time in 13 years. Hart was omitted from the World Cup squad, despite having played in nine of the ten qualifying matches. Against Knowle & Dorridge in the Birmingham Premier League, he scored six and took a catch.

New partnership

South Africa women's captain Dane van Niekerk and fast-bowling all-rounder Marizanne Kapp became the second set of current international team-mates to get married after New Zealand's Amy Satterthwaite and Lea Tahuhu last year. (Lynsey Askew of England married Alex Blackwell of Australia in 2015.)

TEST MATCHES

BATTING

Highest individual innings

Score	Player	For/Against	Venue	Season
400*	Brian Lara	WI v Eng	St John's	2003-04
380	Matthew Hayden	Aus v Zim	Perth	2003-04
375	Brian Lara	WI v Eng	St John's	1993-94

Triple-hundred and hundred in a Test

1st Inn	2nd Inn	Player	For/Against	Venue	Season
333	123	Graham Gooch	Eng v Ind	Lord's	1990
319	105	Kumar Sangakkara	Ban v SL	Chittagong	2013-14

Highest aggregates

Player	Team	M	I	NO	R	HS	Avg	100s/50s
Sachin Tendulkar	Ind	200	329	33	15921	248*	53.78	51/68
Ricky Ponting	Aus	168	287	29	13378	257	51.85	41/62
Jacques Kallis	SA/ICC	166	280	40	13289	224	55.37	45/58

Fastest 50s (balls)

Balls	Player	For/Against	Venue	Season
21	Misbah-ul-Haq	Pak v Aus	Abu Dhabi	2014-15
23	David Warner	Aus v Pak	Sydney	2016-17
24	Jacques Kallis	SA v Zim	Cape Town	2004-05

Fastest 100s (balls)

Balls	Player	For/Against	Venue	Season
54	Brendon McCullum	NZ v AUS	Christchurch	2015/16
56	Viv Richards	WI v Eng	St John's	1985-86
56	Misbah-ul-Haq	Pak v Aus	Abu Dhabi	2014-15

Fastest 200s (balls)

Balls	Player	For/Against	Venue	Season
153	Nathan Astle	NZ v Eng	Christchurch	2001-02
163	Ben Stokes	Eng v SA	Cape Town	2015-16
168	Virender Sehwag	Ind v SL	Mumbai	2009-10

Fastest 300s (balls)

Balls	Player	For/Against	Venue	Season
278	Virender Sehwag	Ind v SA	Chennai	2007-08
362	Mathew Hayden	Aus v Zim	Perth	2003-04
364	Virender Sehwag	Ind v Pak	Multan	2003-04

Most runs in one over

Runs	Batsman	Details	Bowler	For/Against	Venue	Season
28	Brian Lara	(466444)	Robin Peterson	WI v SA	Johannesburg	2003-04
28	George Bailey	(462466)	James Anderson	Aus v Eng	Perth	2013-14
27	Shahid Afridi	(666621)	Harbhajan Singh	Pak v Ind	Lahore	2005-06

Slowest hundreds (balls)

Balls	Player	For/Against	Venue	Season
419	Mudassar Nazar	Pak v Eng	Lahore	1977-78
397	Sanjay Manjrekar	Ind v Zim	Harare	1992-93
396	Clive Radley	Eng v NZ	Auckland	1977-78

Highest partnerships for each wicket

Wicket	Runs	Batsmen	For/Against	Venue	Season
1st	415	Neil McKenzie (226) & Graeme Smith (232)	SA v Ban	Chittagong	2007-08
2nd	576	Sanath Jayasuriya (340) & Roshan Mahanama (225)	SL v Ind	Colombo (RPS)	1997
3rd	624	Kumar Sangakkara (287) & Mahela Jayawardene (374)	SL v SA	Colombo (SSC)	2006
4th	449	Adam Voges (269*) & Shaun Marsh (182)	Aus v WI	Hobart	2015-16
5th	405	Sydney Barnes (234) & Don Bradman (234)	Aus v Eng	Sydney	1946-47
6th	399	Ben Stokes (258) & Jonathan Bairstow (150*)	Eng v SA	Cape Town	2015-16
7th	347	Denis Atkinson (219) & Clairmonte Depeiaza (122)	WI v Aus	Bridgetown	1954-55
8th	332	Jonathan Trott (184) & Stuart Broad (169)	Eng v Pak	Lord's	2010
9th	195	Mark Boucher (78) & Pat Symcox (108)	SA v Pak	Johannesburg	1997-98
10th	198	Joe Root (154*) & James Anderson (81)	Eng v Ind	Nottingham	2014

BOWLING

Most wickets

Player	Team	W	Balls	R	BBI	BBM	Avg	5wI	10wM
Muttiah Muralitharan	SL/ICC	800	44,039	18,180	9-51	16-220	22.72	67	22
Shane Warne	Aus	708	40,705	17,995	8-71	12-128	25.41	37	10
Anil Kumble	Ind	619	40,850	18,355	10-74	14-149	29.65	35	8

Most wickets in an innings

Figures	Player	For/Against	Venue	Season
10-53	Jim Laker	Eng v Aus	Manchester	1956
10-74	Anil Kumble	Ind v Pak	Delhi	1998-99
9-28	George Lohmann	Eng v SA	Johannesburg	1895-96

Most wickets in a Test

Match Figures	Innings Figures	Player	For/Against	Venue	Season
19-90	(9-37, 10-53)	Jim Laker	Eng v Aus	Manchester	1956
17-159	(8-56, 9-103)	Sydney Barnes	Eng v SA	Johannesburg	1913-14
16-136	(8-61, 8-75)	Narendra Hirwani	Ind v WI	Chennai	1987-88

Most wickets in a series

Player	M	W	R	BBI	BBM	For/Against	Season
Sydney Barnes	4	49	536	9/103	17/159	Eng v SA	1913-14
Jim Laker	5	46	442	10/53	19/90	Eng v Aus	1956
Clarrie Grimmett	5	44	642	7/40	13/173	Aus v SA	1935-36

ALL-ROUND

Century and ten wickets in a Test

Player	Batting	Bowling	For/Against	Venue	Season
Ian Botham	114	6-58 7-48	Eng v Ind	Mumbai	1979-80
Imran Khan	117	6-98 5-82	Pak v Ind	Faisalabad	1982-83
Shakib Al Hasan	137	5-80 5-44	Ban v Zim	Khulna	2014-15

3000 runs and 300 wickets

Player	Team	M	R	Bat Avg	W	Bowl Avg
Kapil Dev	Ind	131	5248	31.05	434	29.64
Ian Botham	Eng	102	5200	33.54	383	28.40
Daniel Vettori	NZ/ICC	113	4531	30.00	362	34.36
Imran Khan	Pak	88	3807	37.69	362	22.81
Shaun Pollock	SA	108	3781	32.31	421	23.11
Shane Warne	Aus	145	3154	17.32	708	25.41
Richard Hadlee	NZ	86	3124	27.16	431	22.29
Chaminda Vaas	SL	111	3089	24.32	355	29.58
Stuart Broad	Eng	126	3064	19.27	437	29.05

WICKETKEEPING

Most dismissals in an innings

Dismissal	Ct.	St.	Player	For/Against	Venue	Season
7	7	0	Wasim Bari	Pak v NZ	Auckland	1978-79
7	7	0	Bob Taylor	Eng v Ind	Mumbai	1979-80
7	7	0	Ian Smith	NZ v SL	Hamilton	1990-91
7	7	0	Ridley Jacobs	WI v Aus	Melbourne	2000-01

Most dismissals in a Test

Dismissal	Ct.	St.	Player	For/Against	Venue	Season
11	11	0	Jack Russell	Eng v SA	Johannesburg	1995-96
11	11	0	AB de Villiers	SA v Pak	Johannesburg	2012-13
11	11	0	Rishabh Pant	Ind v Aus	Adelaide	2018-19

Most dismissals in a series

Player	M	Inn	Dismissal	Ct.	St.	Dism./Inn	For/Against	Season
Brad Haddin	5	10	29	29	0	2.900	Aus v Eng	2013-14
Rod Marsh	5	10	28	28	0	2.800	Aus v Eng	1982-83
Jack Russell	5	7	27	25	2	3.857	Eng v SA	1995-96
Ian Healy	6	12	27	25	2	2.250	Aus v Eng	1997

Most dismissals in a career

Dismissals	Player	Team	M	Ct.	St.
555	Mark Boucher	South Africa/ICC	147	532	23
416	Adam Gilchrist	Australia	96	379	37
395	Ian Healy	Australia	119	366	29

FIELDING

Most catches in a Test

Ct.	Player	For/Against	Venue	Season
8	Ajinkya Rahane	Ind v SL	Galle	2015

Most catches in a career

Ct.	M	Player	Team
210	164	Rahul Dravid	India/ICC
205	149	Mahela Jayawardene	Sri Lanka
200	166	Jacques Kallis	South Africa/ICC

TEAM RECORDS

Highest innings totals

Score	For/Against	Venue	Season
952-6d	SL v Ind	Colombo (RPS)	1997
903-7d	Eng v Aus	The Oval	1938
849	Eng v WI	Kingston	1929-30

Lowest innings total

Score	For/Against	Venue	Season
26	NZ v Eng	Auckland	1954-55
30	SA v Eng	Port Elizabeth	1895-96
30	SA v Eng	Birmingham	1924

Lowest aggregates in a completed Test

Runs	Teams	Venue	Season
234	Aus v SA	Melbourne	1931-32
291	Eng v Aus	Lord's	1888
295	NZ v Aus	Wellington	1945-46

Tied Tests

Teams and Score	Venue	Season
Aus (505 & 232) v WI (453 & 284)	Brisbane	1960-61
Ind (397 & 347) v Aus (574-7d & 170-5d)	Chennai	1986-87

PLAYERS
Most capped players

Matches	Player	For
200	Sachin Tendulkar	Ind
168	Ricky Ponting	Aus
168	Steve Waugh	Aus

Youngest Test players

Age	Player	For/Against	Venue	Season
14 y 227 d	Hasan Raza	Pak v Zim	Faisalabad	1996-97
15 y 124 d	Mushtaq Mohammad	Pak v WI	Lahore	1958-59
15 y 128 d	Mohammad Sharif	Ban v Zim	Bulawayo	2000-01

Oldest players on debut

Age	Player	For/Against	Venue	Season
49 y 119 d	James Southerton	Eng v Aus	Melbourne	1876-77
47 y 284 d	Miran Bakhsh	Pak v Ind	Lahore	1954-55
46 y 253 d	Don Blackie	Aus v Eng	Sydney	1928-29

Oldest Test players

Age	Player	For/Against	Venue	Season
52 y 165 d	Wilfred Rhodes	Eng v WI	Kingston	1929-30
50 y 327 d	Bert Ironmonger	Aus v Eng	Sydney	1932-33
50 y 320 d	WG Grace	Eng v Aus	Nottingham	1899

Most consecutive Test appearances

Matches	Player	Team	Duration	
159	Alastair Cook	Eng	May 2006	September 2018
153	Allan Border	Aus	March 1979	March 1994
107	Mark Waugh	Aus	June 1993	October 2002

Most Tests as captain

Matches	Won	Player	Team
109	53	Graeme Smith	SA/ICC
93	32	Allan Border	Aus
80	28	Stephen Fleming	NZ

UMPIRES

Most Tests

Tests	Umpire	Country	Duration	
128	Steve Bucknor	WI	1988-89	2008-09
125	Aleem Dar	Pak	2003-04	2018-19
108	Rudi Koertzen	SA	1992-93	2010

ONE-DAY INTERNATIONALS

BATTING

Highest aggregates

Player	Team	R	M	Inn	NO	HS	Avg	100s/50s
Sachin Tendulkar	Ind	18,426	463	452	41	200*	44.83	49/96
Kumar Sangakkara	SL/Asia/ICC	14,234	404	380	41	169	41.98	25/93
Ricky Ponting	Aus/ICC	13,704	375	365	39	164	42.03	30/82

Highest individual innings

Score	Player	For/Against	Venue	Season
264	Rohit Sharma	Ind v SL	Kolkata	2014-15
237*	Martin Guptill	NZ v WI	Wellington	2014-15
219	Virender Sehwag	Ind v WI	Indore	2011-12

Fastest 50s

Balls	Player	For/Against	Venue	Season
16	AB de Villiers	SA v WI	Johannesburg	2014-15
17	Sanath Jayasuriya	SL v Pak	Singapore	1995-96
17	Kusal Perera	SL v Pak	Pallekele	2015
17	Martin Guptill	NZ v SL	Christchurch	2015-16

Fastest 100s

Balls	Player	For/Against	Venue	Season
31	AB de Villiers	SA v WI	Johannesburg	2014-15
36	Corey Anderson	NZ v WI	Queenstown	2013-14
37	Shahid Afridi	Pak v SL	Nairobi	1996-97

Highest partnerships for each wicket

Wicket	Runs	Batsmen	For/Against	Venue	Season
1st	365	John Campbell & Shai Hope	WI v Ire	Dublin	2019
2nd	372	Chris Gayle & Marlon Samuels	WI v Zim	Canberra	2014-15
3rd	258	Darren Bravo & Denesh Ramdin	WI v Ban	Basseterre	2014
4th	275*	Mohammad Azharuddin & Ajay Jadeja	Ind v Zim	Cuttack	1997-98
5th	256*	David Miller & JP Duminy	SA v Zim	Hamilton	2014-15
6th	267*	Grant Elliott & Luke Ronchi	NZ v SL	Dunedin	2014-15
7th	177	Jos Buttler & Adil Rashid	Eng v NZ	Harare	2015
8th	138*	Justin Kemp & Andrew Hall	SA v Ind	Cape Town	2006-07
9th	132	Angelo Mathews & Lasith Malinga	SL v Aus	Melbourne	2010-11
10th	106*	Vivian Richards & Michael Holding	WI v Eng	Manchester	1984

BOWLING

Most wickets

Player	Team	W	Balls	R	BB	Avg	5w
Muttiah Muralitharan	SL/ICC/Asia	534	18,811	12,326	7-30	23.08	10
Wasim Akram	Pak	502	18,186	11,812	5-15	23.52	6
Waqar Younis	Pak	416	12,698	9,919	7-36	23.84	13

Best bowling analysis

Figures	Player	For/Against	Venue	Season
8-19	Chaminda Vaas	SL v Zim	Colombo (SSC)	2001-02
7-12	Shahid Afridi	Pak v WI	Providence	2013
7-15	Glenn McGrath	Aus v Nam	Potchefstroom	2002-03

WICKETKEEPING

Most dismissals in career

Dismissals	Player	Team	Matches	Ct.	St.
482	Kumar Sangakkara	SL/Asia/ICC	404	384	98
472	Adam Gilchrist	Aus/ICC	287	417	55
444	MS Dhoni	Ind/Asia	350	321	123

FIELDING

Most catches in an innings

5	Jonty Rhodes	SA v WI	Mumbai	1993-94

Most catches in a career

Ct.	Matches	Player	Team
218	448	Mahela Jayawardene	SL/Asia
160	375	Ricky Ponting	Australia/ICC
156	334	Mohammad Azharuddin	Ind

TEAM

Highest totals

Score	Overs	For/Against	Venue	Season
481-6	50	Eng v Aus	Nottingham	2018
444-3	50	Eng v Pak	Nottingham	2016
443-9	50	SL v Net	Amstelveen	2006

Highest totals batting second

Score	Overs	For/Against	Venue	Season
438-9	49.5	SA v Aus	Johannesburg	2005-06
411-8	50	SL v Ind	Rajkot	2009-10
389	48	WI v Eng	St George's	2018-19

Highest match aggregates

Runs	Wickets	Overs	Teams	Venue	Season
872	13	99.5	SA v Aus	Johannesburg	2005-06
825	15	100	Ind v SL	Rajkot	2009-10
807	16	98	WI v Eng	St George's	2018-19

Lowest totals

Score	Overs	For/Against	Venue	Season
35	18	Zim v SL	Harare	2004
36	18.4	Can v SL	Paarl	2002-03
38	15.4	Zim v SL	Colombo (SSC)	2001-02

PLAYER

Most matches as captain

Matches	Won	Player	Team
230	165	Ricky Ponting	Aus/ICC

| 218 | 98 | Stephen Fleming | NZ |
| 200 | 110 | MS Dhoni | Ind |

Most capped cricketers

Matches	Player	Team
463	Sachin Tendulkar	Ind
448	Mahela Jayawardene	SL/Asia
445	Sanath Jayasuriya	SL/Asia

TWENTY20 INTERNATIONALS

BATTING

Highest aggregates

Player	Team	Runs	M	Inn	NO	HS	Avg	100s/50s
Rohit Sharma	Ind	2331	94	86	14	118	32.37	4/16
Martin Guptill	NZ	2272	76	74	7	105	33.91	2/14
Virat Kohli	Ind	2263	67	62	17	90*	50.28	0/20

Highest individual innings

Runs	Player	For/Against	Venue	Season
172	Aaron Finch	Aus v Zim	Harare	2018
162*	Hazratullah Zazai	Afg v Ire	Dehradun	2018-19
156	Aaron Finch	Aus v Eng	Southampton	2013

Highest partnerships for each wicket

Wicket	Runs	Batsmen	For/Against	Venue	Season
1st	236	Hazratullah Zazai & Usman Ghani	Afg v Ire	Dehradun	2018-19
2nd	166	Mahela Jayawardene & Kumar Sangakkara	SL v WI	Bridgetown	2010
3rd	152	Alex Hales & Eoin Morgan	Eng v SL	Chittagong	2013-14
4th	161	David Warner & Glenn Maxwell	Aus v SA	Johannesburg	2015-16
5th	119*	Shoaib Malik & Misbah-ul-Haq	Pak v Aus	Johannesburg	2007-08
6th	101*	Cameron White & Michael Hussey	Aus v SL	Bridgetown	2010
7th	91	Paul Collingwood & Michael Yardy	Eng v WI	The Oval	2007
8th	80	Preston Mommsen & Safyaan Sharif	Sco v Net	Edinburgh	2015
9th	66	Dwayne Bravo & Jerome Taylor	WI v Pak	Dubai	2016-17
10th	38	Mohammad Adnan & Usman Ali	Saudi Arabia v Qatar	Al Amerat	2018-19

BOWLING

Most wickets

Player	Team	W	Balls	R	BB	Avg	4w
Shahid Afridi	Pak	98	2,168	2,396	4-11	24.44	3
Lasith Malinga	SL	97	1,571	1,911	5-31	19.70	1
Shakib Al Hasan	Ban	88	1,571	1,775	5-20	20.17	3

Best bowling analysis

Figures	Player	For/Against	Venue	Season
6-8	Ajantha Mendis	SL v Zim	Hambantota	2012-13
6-16	Ajantha Mendis	SL v Aus	Pallekele	2011
6-25	Yuzvendra Chahal	Ind v Eng	Bengaluru	2016-17

WICKETKEEPING

Most dismissals in an innings

Dismissals	Ct.	St.	Player	For/Against	Venue	Season
5	3	2	Mohammad Shahzad	Afg v Oman	Abu Dhabi	2015-16
5	5	0	MS Dhoni	Ind v Eng	Bristol	2018

Most dismissals in a career

Dismissals	Player	Team	Matches	Ct	St
91	MS Dhoni	Ind	98	57	34
60	Kamran Akmal	Pak	53	28	32
58	Denesh Ramdin	WI	68	38	20

FIELDING

Most catches in career

Ct.	Matches*	Player	Team
50	111	Shoaib Malik	Pak, ICC
48	69	David Miller	SA, World XI
44	52	AB de Villiers	SA
44	88	Ross Taylor	NZ

* Matches as a fielder

TEAM

Highest team totals

Score	Overs	For/Against	Venue	Season
278-3	20	Afg v Ire	Dehradun	2018-19
263-3	20	Aus v SL	Pallekele	2016
260-5	20	Ind v SL	Indore	2017-18
260-6	20	SL v Ken	Johannesburg	2007-08

Lowest team totals

Score	Overs	For/Against	Venue	Season
39	10.3	Ned v SL	Chittagong	2013-14
45	11.5	WI v Eng	Basseterre	2018-19
46	12.1	Botswana v Namibia	Kampala	2019

FIRST-CLASS

BATTING

Highest aggregates

Player	Runs	M	Inns	NO	HS	Avg	100s/50s
Jack Hobbs	61,760	834	1325	107	316*	50.70	199/273
Frank Woolley	58,959	978	1,530	84	305*	40.77	145/295
Patsy Hendren	57,611	833	1,300	166	301*	50.80	170/272

Highest individual innings

Score	Player	For/Against	Venue	Season
501*	Brian Lara	Warwickshire v Durham	Birmingham	1994
499	Hanif Mohammad	Karachi v Bahawalpur	Karachi	1958-59
452*	Don Bradman	New South Wales v Queensland	Sydney	1929-30

Highest career averages (qualification 10,000 runs)

Player	M	Inn	NO	R	HS	Avg	100s/50s
Don Bradman	234	338	43	28,067	452*	95.14	117/69
Vijay Merchant	150	234	46	13,470	359*	71.64	45/52
Ajay Sharma	129	166	16	10,120	259*	67.46	38/36

Highest partnerships for each wicket

Wicket	Runs	Batsmen	For/Against	Venue	Season
1st	561	Waheed Mirza (324) & Mansoor Akhtar (224*)	Karachi Whites v Quetta	Karachi	1976-77
2nd	580	Rafatullah Mohmand (302*) & Aamer Sajjad (289)	Water and Power Development Authority v Sui Southern Gas Corporation	Sheikhupura	2009-10
3rd	624	Kumar Sangakkara (287) & Mahela Jayawardene (374)	Sri Lanka v South Africa	Colombo (SSC)	2006
4th	577	Vijay Hazare (288) & Gul Mahomed (319)	Baroda v Holkar	Vadodara	1946-47
5th	520*	Cheteshwar Pujara (302*) & Ravindra Jadeja (232*)	Saurashtra v Orissa	Rajkot	2008-09
6th	487*	George Headley (344*) & Charles Passailaigue (261*)	Jamaica v Lord Tennyson's XI	Kingston	1931-32
7th	460	Bhupinder Singh jun. (297) & Pankaj Dharmani (202*)	Punjab v Delhi	Delhi	1994-95
8th	433	Arthur Sims (184*) & Victor Trumper (293)	Australians v Canterbury	Christchurch	1913-14
9th	283	Arnold Warren (123) & John Chapman (165)	Derbyshire v Warwickshire	Blackwell	1910
10th	307	Alan Kippax (260*) & Hal Hooker (62)	New South Wales v Victoria	Melbourne	1928-29

BOWLING

Most wickets in career

Player	W	B	R	BBI	Avg	5wI	10wM
Wilfred Rhodes	4,204	185,742	70,322	9-24	16.72	287	68
Tich Freeman	3,776	154,658	69,577	10-53	18.42	386	140
Charlie Parker	3,278	157,059	63,817	10-79	19.46	277	91

Most wickets in an innings

Figures	Player	For/Against	Venue	Season
10-10	Hedley Verity	Yorkshire v Nottinghamshire	Leeds	1932
10-18	George Geary	Leicestershire v Glamorgan	Pontypridd	1929
10-20	Premangsu Chatterjee	Bengal v Assam	Jorhat	1956-57

There have been 81 instances of bowlers taking all ten wickets in an innings, plus a further three in 12-a-side matches.

Most wickets in a match

Match Figures	Innings Figures	Player	For/Against	Venue	Season
19-90	(9-37, 10-53)	Jim Laker	Eng v Aus	Manchester	1956
17-48	(10-30, 7-18)	Colin Blythe	Northamptonshire v Kent	Northampton	1907
17-50	(8-13, 9-37)	Charlie Turner	Australians v England XI	Hastings	1888

WICKETKEEPING

Most dismissals in an innings

Dismissals	Ct.	St.	Player	For/Against	Venue	Season
9	8	1	Tahir Rashid	Habib Bank Limited v Pakistan Automobiles Corporation	Gujranwala	1992-93
9	7	2	Wayne James	Matabeleland v Mashonaland Country Districts	Bulawayo	1995-96

Most dismissals in a match

Dismissals	Ct.	St.	Player	For/Against	Venue	Season
14	11	3	Ibrahim Khaleel	Hyderabad v Assam	Guwahati	2011-12
13	11	2	Wayne James	Matabeleland v Mashonaland Country Districts	Bulawayo	1995-96

Most dismissals in career

Dismissal	Player	Matches	Ct.	St.
1649	Bob Taylor	639	1,473	176
1,518	John Murray	635	1268	259
1,495	Bert Strudwick	674	1237	258

FIELDING

Most catches in an innings

Ct.	Player	For/Against	Venue	Season
7	Micky Stewart	Surrey v Northamptonshire	Northampton	1957
7	Tony Brown	Gloucestershire v Nottinghamshire	Nottingham	1966
7	Rikki Clarke	Warwickshire v Lancashire	Liverpool	2011

Most catches in a match

Ct.	Player	For/Against	Venue	Season
10	Wally Hammond	Gloucestershire v Surrey	Cheltenham	1928
9	Rikki Clarke	Warwickshire v Lancashire	Liverpool	2011

Most catches in career

Ct.	Matches	Player
1,018	979	Frank Woolley
887	879	WG Grace
831	654	Tony Lock

The record for WG Grace excludes 1 catch as wicketkeeper but includes 7 catches in 48 matches in which it is not known whether he kept wicket.

TEAM

Highest innings totals

Score	For/Against	Venue	Season
1,107	Victoria v New South Wales	Melbourne	1926-27
1,059	Victoria v Tasmania	Melbourne	1922-23
952-6d	Sri Lanka v India	Colombo (RPS)	1997

Lowest innings totals

Total	For/Against	Venue	Season
12	Oxford University v Marylebone Cricket Club	Oxford	1877
12	Northamptonshire v Gloucestershire	Gloucester	1907
13	Auckland v Canterbury	Auckland	1877-78
13	Nottinghamshire v Yorkshire	Nottingham	1901

RANJI TROPHY

BATTING

Highest aggregates

Player	R	M	Inn	NO	HS	Avg	100s/50s
Wasim Jaffer	11,775	149	229	25	314*	57.72	40/46
Amol Muzumdar	9,202	136	200	21	260	51.40	28/45
Devendra Bundela	9,201	145	232	29	188	45.32	24/50

Highest individual Innings

Runs	Player	For/Against	Venue	Season
443*	Bhausaheb Nimbalkar	Maharashtra v Kathiawar	Pune	1948-49
377	Sanjay Manjrekar	Bombay v Hyderabad	Mumbai	1990-91
366	MV Sridhar	Hyderabad v Andhra	Secunderabad	1993-94

Most centuries

100s	Player
40	Wasim Jaffer
31	Ajay Sharma
28	Hrishikesh Kanitkar
28	Amol Muzumdar

Highest partnerships for each wicket

Wicket	Runs	Players	For/Against	Venue	Season
1st	464	Ravi Sehgal & Raman Lamba	Delhi v Himachal Pradesh	Delhi	1994-95
2nd	475	Zahir Alam & Lalchand Rajput	Assam v Tripura	Guwahati	1991-92
3rd	594*	Swapnil Gugale & Ankit Bawne	Maharashtra v Delhi	Mumbai	2016-17
4th	577	Vijay Hazare & Gul Mahomed	Baroda v Holkar	Vadodara	1946-47
5th	520*	Cheteshwar Pujara & Ravindra Jadeja	Saurashtra v Orissa	Rajkot	2008-09
6th	417	Wriddhiman Saha & Laxmi Ratan Shukla	Bengal v Assam	Kolkata	2010-11
7th	460	Bhupinder Singh, jun. & Pankaj Dharmani	Punjab v Delhi	Delhi	1994-95
8th	392	Amit Mishra & Jayant Yadav	Haryana v Karnataka	Hubli	2012-13
9th	249*	Amkit Srivastava & Kapil Seth	Madhya Pradesh v Vidarbha	Indore	2000-01
10th	233	Ajay Sharma & Maninder Singh	Delhi v Bombay	Mumbai	1991-92

BOWLING

Most wickets in career

Bowler	W	B	R	BBI	Avg	5wI	10wI
Rajinder Goel	637	31,945	11,010	8-55	17.28	53	17
S Venkataraghavan	530	26,775	9,658	7-42	18.22	45	11
Sunil Joshi	479	28,884	11,139	7-29	23.25	27	5

Most wickets in an innings

Figures	Player	For/Against	Venue	Season
10-20	Premangsu Chatterjee	Bengal v Assam	Jorhat	1956-57
10-78	Pradeep Sunderam	Rajasthan v Vidarbha	Jodhpur	1985-86
9-23	Ankeet Chavan	Mumbai v Punjab	Mumbai	2012-13

Most wickets in a match

Match Figures	Innings Figures	Player	For/Against	Venue	Season
16-99	(8-58, 8-41)	Anil Kumble	Karnataka v Kerala	Thalassery	1994-95
16-154	(10-78, 6-76)	Pradeep Sunderam	Rajasthan v Vidarbha	Jodhpur	1985-86
16-154	(8-96, 8-54)	Jalaj Saxena	Madhya Pradesh v Railways	Gwalior	2015-16

WICKETKEEPING

Most dismissals in a match

Dismissals	Ct.	St.	Player	For/Against	Venue	Season
14	11	3	Ibrahim Khaleel	Hyderabad v Assam	Guwahati	2011-12
11	10	1	Samarjit Nath	Assam v Tripura	Guwahati	2001-02
11	9	2	Manvinder Bisla	Himachal Pradesh v Saurashtra	Dharmasala	2004-05

Most dismissals in career

Dismissals	Player	Matches	Ct.	St.
351	Naman Ojha	105	312	39
335	Vinayak Samant	94	298	37
313	Mahesh Rawat	99	277	36

FIELDING

Most catches in a match

Catches	Player	For/Against	Venue	Season
7	Shaukat Dukanwala	Baroda v Saurashtra	Bhavnagar	1981-82
7	Pradeep Khanna	Bihar v Assam	Jamshedpur	1987-88
7	K. Bhaskar Pillai	Delhi v Services	Delhi	1990-91
7	S. Abbas Ali	Madhya Pradesh v Orissa	Cuttack	1996-97
7	Sunil Oasis	Kerala v Andhra	Kozhikode	1999-00
7	Balachandra Akhil	Karnataka v Andhra	Anantapur	2006-07

Most catches in career

Catches	Matches	Player
197	149	Wasim Jaffer
128	136	Amol Muzumdar
127	125	Sanjay Bangar

TEAM

Highest team total

Score	For/Against	Venue	Season
944-6d	Hyderabad v Andhra	Secunderabad	1993-94
912-8d	Holkar v Mysore	Indore	1945-46
912-6d	Tamil Nadu v Goa	Panaji	1988-89

Lowest team total

Score	For/Against	Venue	Season
21	Hyderabad v Rajasthan	Jaipur	2010-11
22	Southern Punjab v Northern India	Amritsar	1934-35
23	Sind v Southern Punjab	Patiala	1938-39
23	Jammu and Kashmir v Delhi	Srinagar	1960-61
23	Jammu and Kashmir v Haryana	Rai	1977-78

Most-capped cricketers

Matches	Player	Teams
149	Wasim Jaffer	Mumbai, Vidarbha
145	Devendra Bundela	Madhya Pradesh
136	Amol Muzumdar	Mumbai, Assam, Andhra

All records are updated till July 15, 2019.

M - Matches, **T** – Tests, **I** – Innings, **NO** – Not Out, **R** - Runs, **HS** – Highest Score, **Avg** – Average, **W** – Wickets, **BBI** – Best Bowling in an Innings, **BBM** – Best Bowling in a Match, **5wI** –Five wickets in an innings, **10wM** – 10 wickets in a match, **SR** – Strike Rate, **Econ** – Economy Rate, **Ct.** – Catches, **St.** – Stumpings, **Dism./Inn** – Dismissal/Innings, **BB** – Best Bowling.

INDIA WOMEN

TESTS

Span	Matches	Won	Drawn	Lost
1976-2014	36	5	25	6

Against	Span	Matches	Won	Drawn	Lost
Australia	1977-2006	9	0	5	4
England	1986-2014	13	2	10	1
New Zealand	1977-2013	6	0	6	0
South Africa	2002-2014	2	2	0	0
West Indies	1976-1976	6	1	4	1

Highest total: 467 against England (Taunton, August 2002)
Lowest total: 65 against West Indies (Jammu, November 1976)
Largest victory (wickets): By ten wickets against South Africa (Paarl, March 2002)
Largest victory (innings): By an innings and 34 runs against South Africa (Mysore, November 2014)

Most runs: Sandhya Agarwal – 1110 in 13 matches
Highest individual score: Mithali Raj – 214 against England (Taunton, August 2002)
Most hundreds: Sandhya Agarwal – 4
Most runs in a series: Shanta Rangaswamy – 381 against West Indies (1976-77)

Most wickets: Diana Edulji – 63 in 20 matches
Best bowling (innings): Neetu David – 8-53 against England (Jamshedpur, November 1995)
Best bowling (match): Jhulan Goswami – 10-78 against England (Taunton, August 2006)
Most five-wicket hauls (innings): Shubhangi Kulkarni – 5
Most wickets in a series: Shubhangi Kulkarni – 23 against West Indies (1976-77)

Most dismissals (wicketkeeper): Anju Jain – 23 in 8 matches
Most dismissals (innings): Fowzieh Khalili – 5 against Australia (Perth, January 1977) and Anju Jain – 5 against England (Shenley, July 1999)
Most dismissals (match): Anju Jain – 7 against England (Shenley, July 1999)
Most dismissals in a series: Nilima Jogalekar – 10 against Australia (1983-84)
Most catches (fielder): Sudha Shah – 21 in 21 matches
Most catches in a series: Sudha Shah – 9 against West Indies (1976-77)

Highest partnership: 275 by Thirush Kamini and Poonam Raut for 2nd wicket against South Africa (Mysore, November 2014)

Most-capped player: Sudha Shah – 21
Most matches as captain: Shanta Rangaswamy – 12
Most successful captain: Mithali Raj – 3 wins in 6 matches

List of players (82): Sandhya Mazumdar, Shobha Pandit, Sudha Shah, **Shanta Rangaswamy**,

Shubhangi Kulkarni, Susan Itticheria, Sharmilla Chakraborty, Fowzieh Khalili, Ujwala Nikam, **Diana Edulji**, Behroze Edulji, Runa Basu, Jyotsna Patel, Rajeshwari Dholakia, Uthpala Chakraborty, Gargi Banerji, Vrinda Bhagat, Shashi Gupta, **Nilima Jogalekar**, Anjali Pendharker, Sujata Sridhar, **Sandhya Agarwal**, Arundhati Ghosh, Rita Dey, Sandra Braganza, Mithu Mukherjee, Lopamudra Bhattacharj, Rajani Venugopal, Neeta Kadam, Minoti Desai, V Kalpana, Rekha Punekar, Manimala Singhal, **Pramila Bhatt**, Seema Desai, Sangita Dabir, Neetu David, Laya Francis, Anju Jain, Chanderkanta Aheer, Renu Margrate, Rishijae Mudgel, **Purnima Rau**, Arati Vaidya, **Anjum Chopra**, Shyama Shaw, Kalyani Dhokarikar, Hemlata Kala, Deepa Marathe, Rupanjali Shastri, Jhulan Goswami, Bindeshwari Goyal, Arundhati Kirkire, **Mamatha Maben, Mithali Raj**, Amrita Shinde, Jaya Sharma, Sunita Singh, Sulakshana Naik, Sunetra Paranjpe, Nooshin Al Khadeer, Amita Sharma, Rumeli Dhar, Karuna Jain, Sravanthi Naidu, Asha Rawat, Monica Sumra, Devika Palshikar, Nidhi Buley, Preeti Dimri, Reema Malhotra, Ekta Bisht, Thirush Kamini, Harmanpreet Kaur, Smriti Mandhana, N Niranjana, Shikha Pandey, Poonam Raut, Shubhlakshmi Sharma, Rajeshwari Gayakwad, Poonam Yadav, Sushma Verma.

ODIs

Span	Matches	Won	Lost	Tied	No result
1978-2019	266	146	115	1	4

Against	Span	Matches	Won	Lost	Tied	No result
Australia	1978-2018	46	9	37	0	0
Bangladesh	2013-2017	4	4	0	0	0
Denmark	1993-1993	1	1	0	0	0
England	1978-2019	69	30	37	0	2
International XI	1982-1982	3	3	0	0	0
Ireland	1993-2017	12	12	0	0	0
Netherlands	1993-2000	3	3	0	0	0
New Zealand	1978-2019	48	19	28	1	0
Pakistan	2005-2017	10	10	0	0	0
South Africa	1997-2018	19	11	7	0	1
Sri Lanka	2000-2018	29	26	2	0	1
West Indies	1993-2017	22	18	4	0	0

Highest total: 358/2 against Ireland (Potchefstroom, May 2017)
Lowest total: 26 against New Zealand (St Saviour, July 2002)
Largest victory: By 249 runs against Ireland (Potchefstroom, May 2017)

Most runs: Mithali Raj – 6720 in 203 matches
Highest individual score: Deepti Sharma – 188 against Ireland (Potchefstroom, May 2017)
Most hundreds: Mithali Raj – 7

Most wickets: Jhulan Goswami – 218 in 177 matches
Best bowling: Mamatha Maben – 6-10 against Sri Lanka (Kandy, April 2004)
Most five-wicket hauls: Ekta Bisht, Neetu David & Jhulan Goswami – 2

Most dismissals (wicketkeeper): Anju Jain – 81 in 65 matches
Most dismissals (innings): V Kalpana – 6 against Denmark (Slough, July 1993)
Most catches (fielder): Jhulan Goswami – 63 in 177 matches

Highest partnership: 320 by Deepti Sharma and Punam Raut for first wicket against Ireland (Potchefstroom, May 2017)

Most-capped player: Mithali Raj – 203
Most matches as captain: Mithali Raj – 126
Most successful captain: Mithali Raj – 77 wins in 126 matches

List of players (126): Gargi Banerji, Runa Basu, Lopamudra Bhattacharj, Sharmilla Chakraborty, **Diana Edulji**, Nilima Jogalekar, Fowzieh Khalili, Sandhya Mazumdar, Shobha Pandit, Kalpan Paropkari, Anjali Sharma, Susan Itticheria, **Shubhangi Kulkarni**, Ujwala Nikam, Sudha Shah, Rajeshwari Dholakia, Vrinda Bhagat, Anjali Pendharker, **Shanta Rangaswamy**, Sujata Sridhar, Rita Dey, Arundhati Ghosh, Shashi Gupta, Rekha Godbole, Sandra Braganza, Sandhya Agarwal, Sirupa Bose, Manimala Singhal, Rita Patel, Neeta Kadam, Rajani Venugopal, Minoti Desai, Rekha Punekar, V Kalpana, **Pramila Bhatt**, Laya Francis, **Anju Jain**, **Chanderkanta Aheer**, **Mamatha Maben**, **Purnima Rau**, Sangita Dabir, **Anjum Chopra**, Neetu David, Smitha Harikrishna, Renu Margrate, Rishijae Mudgel, Arati Vaidya, Kalyani Dhokarikar, Manju Nadgoda, Shyama Shaw, Lissy Samuel, Purnima Choudhary, Deepa Marathe, Reshma Gandhi, Hemlata Kala, **Mithali Raj**, Rupanjali Shastri, Sunita Singh, Arundhati Kirkire, Kavita Roy, **Jhulan Goswami**, Jaya Sharma, Nooshin Al Khadeer, Amrita Shinde, Bindeshwari Goyal, Sulakshana Naik, Sunetra Paranjpe, Amita Sharma, **Rumeli Dhar**, Reema Malhotra, Babita Mandlik, Mamatha Kanojia, Beas Sarkar, Diana David, Karuna Jain, Varsha Raffel, Monica Sumra, Asha Rawat, Sravanthi Naidu, Devika Palshikar, Preeti Dimri, Nidhi Buley, Thirush Kamini, Rajeshwari Goyal, Seema Pujare, Priyanka Roy, Gouher Sultana, Anagha Deshpande, Snehal Pradhan, N Niranjana, **Harmanpreet Kaur**, Poonam Raut, Soniya Dabir, Samantha Lobatto, Neha Tanwar, Veda Krishnamurthy, Ekta Bisht, Shilpa Gupta, Archana Das, Madhuri Mehta, Shubhlakshmi Sharma, Mona Meshram, Rasanara Parwin, Ritu Dhrub, Swagatika Rath, Smriti Mandhana, Poonam Yadav, V Sneha Deepthi, Rajeshwari Gayakwad, Sneh Rana, VR Vanitha, Shikha Pandey, Sushma Verma, Deepti Sharma, RV Kalpana, Preeti Bose, Devika Vaidya, Sukanya Parida, Soni Yadav, Mansi Joshi, Nuzhat Parween, Pooja Vastrakar, Jemimah Rodrigues, Taniya Bhatia, Dayalan Hemalatha, Harleen Deol.

T20Is

Span	Matches	Won	Lost	Tied	No result
2006-2019	104	53	49	0	2

Against	Span	Matches	Won	Lost	Tied	No result
Australia	2008-2018	15	4	11	0	0
Bangladesh	2013-2018	11	9	2	0	0
England	2006-2018	17	3	14	0	0
Ireland	2018-2018	1	1	0	0	0
Malaysia	2018-2018	1	1	0	0	0
New Zealand	2009-2015	11	3	8	0	0

Pakistan	2009-2018	11	9	2	0	0
South Africa	2014-2018	6	4	1	0	1
Sri Lanka	2009-2016	17	13	3	0	0
Thailand	2018-2018	1	1	0	0	0
West Indies	2011-2016	13	5	8	0	0

Highest total: 198/4 against England (Mumbai, March 2018)
Lowest total: 62 against Australia (Billericay, June 2011)
Largest victory: By 142 runs against Malaysia (Kuala Lumpur, June 2018)

Most runs: Mithali Raj – 2364 in 89 matches
Highest individual score: Harmanpreet Kaur – 103 against New Zealand (Providence, November 2018)
Most fifty-plus scores: Mithali Raj – 17

Most wickets: Poonam Yadav – 74 in 54 matches
Best bowling: Jhulan Goswami – 5-11 against Australia (Visakhapatnam, March 2012)
Most five-wicket hauls: Jhulan Goswami & Priyanka Roy – 1

Most dismissals (wicketkeeper): Taniya Bhatia – 38 in 31 matches
Most dismissals (innings): Sulkashana Naik (twice), Karuna Jain, Sushma Verma – 4
Most catches (fielder): Harmanpreet Kaur – 38 in 96 matches

Highest partnership: 134 by Jemimah Rodrigues and Harmanpreet Kaur for the fourth wicket against New Zealand (Providence, November 2018)

Most-capped player: Harmanpreet Kaur – 96
Most matches as captain: Harmanpreet Kaur – 41
Most successful captain: Harmanpreet Kaur – 25 wins in 41 matches

List of players (63): Anjum Chopra, Rumeli Dhar, **Jhulan Goswami**, Hemlata Kala, Reema Malhotra, Sulakshana Naik, **Mithali Raj**, Amita Sharma, Noor Al Khadeer, Preeti Dimri, Monica Sumra, Thirush Kamini, Jaya Sharma, Gouher Sultana, Seema Pujare, **Harmanpreet Kaur**, Latika Kumari, Priyanka Roy, Poonam Raut, Soniya Dabir, Babita Mandlik, Diana David, Samantha Lobatto, Ekta Bisht, Anagha Deshpande, Veda Krishnamurthy, Snehal Pradhan, Neha Tanwar, Archana Das, Mamatha Kanojia, Shubhlakshmi Sharma, Madhuri Mehta, Mona Meshram, N Niranjana, Anuja Patil, Rasanara Parwin, Ritu Dhrub, V Sneha Deepthi, Swagatika Rath, Smriti Mandhana, Poonam Yadav, Sushma Verma, Rajeshwari Gayakwad, VR Vanitha, Sneh Rana, Karuna Jain, Sravanthi Naidu, Shikha Pandey, Devika Vaidya, Deepti Sharma, Nuzhat Parween, Preeti Bose, Meghana S, Mansi Joshi, Taniya Bhatia, Jemimah Rodrigues, Pooja Vastraka, Radha Yadav, Arundhati Reddy, Dayalan Hemalatha, Priya Punia, Harleen Deol, Bharati Fulmali.

Records as on July 15, 2019

Wisden India Honours Board

Year	Hall of Fame	Cricketers of The Year	Book of The Year	Beyond the Boundary
2013	MAK Pataudi Kapil Dev Sunil Gavaskar	Rahul Dravid Virat Kohli Umesh Yadav Saeed Ajmal Kumar Sangakkara Shakib Al Hasan	Out of the Blue by Aakash Chopra	
2014	CK Nayudu Anil Kumble	MS Dhoni Ravindra Jadeja Cheteshwar Pujara Misbah-ul-Haq Rangana Herath Mushfiqur Rahim	On Warne by Gideon Haigh	
2015	Vijay Hazare Bishan Singh Bedi	Ajinkya Rahane Mithali Raj Rishi Dhawan Umar Akmal Angelo Mathews Mominul Haque	Wounded Tiger: A History of Cricket in Pakistan by Peter Oborne	
2016	Vijay Merchant BS Chandrasekhar	R Ashwin R Vinay Kumar Younis Khan Dhammika Prasad Mashrafe Mortaza Joe Root	The Unquiet Ones: A History of Pakistan Cricket by Osman Samiuddin	Mukul Mudgal
2017	Vinoo Mankad Sourav Ganguly	Virat Kohli Shreyas Iyer Yasir Shah Kusal Mendis Mustafizur Rahman David Warner	Stroke of Genius: Victor Trumper and the Shot that Changed Cricket by Gideon Haigh	Rajendra Mal Lodha
2018	Erapalli Prasanna Shantha Rangaswamy	K L Rahul Priyank Panchal Deepti Sharma Hasan Ali Tamim Iqbal Ben Stokes	Feeling is the Thing That Happens in 1000th of a Second by Christian Ryan	Clare Connor
2019 & 2020	Lala Amarnath Gundappa Viswanath	Jasprit Bumrah Smriti Mandhana Mayank Agarwal Fakhar Zaman Dimuth Karunaratne Rashid Khan	Cricket Country: The Untold History of the First All India Team by Prashant Kidambi	Imran Khan